BENCHMARK SERIES

MICROSOFT® WORD 2013

LEVELS 1 & 2

NITA RUTKOSKY
Pierce College Puyallup
Puyallup, Washington

AUDREY ROGGENKAMP
Pierce College Puyallup
Puyallup, Washington

IAN RUTKOSKY
Pierce College Puyallup
Puyallup, Washington

PARADIGM
EDUCATION SOLUTIONS
St. Paul

Director of Editorial	Christine Hurney
Director of Production	Timothy W. Larson
Production Editor	Sarah Kearin
Copy Editor	Communicáto, Ltd.; Nan Brooks, Abshier House
Cover Designer	Leslie Anderson
Text Designers	Leslie Anderson, Jaana Bykonich
Desktop Production	Jaana Bykonich, Julie Johnston, Valerie King, Timothy W. Larson, Jack Ross, Sara Schmidt Boldon
Proofreader	Katherine Lee
Indexer	Terry Casey
VP & Director of Digital Projects	Chuck Bratton
Digital Projects Manager	Tom Modl

Acknowledgements: The authors, editors, and publisher thank the following instructors for their helpful suggestions during the planning and development of the books in the Benchmark Office 2013 Series: Olugbemiga Adekunle, Blue Ridge Community College, Harrisonburg, VA; Letty Barnes, Lake WA Institute of Technology, Kirkland, WA; Erika Nadas, Wilbur Wright College, Chicago, IL; Carolyn Walker, Greenville Technical College, Greenville, SC; Carla Anderson, National College, Lynchburg, VA; Judy A. McLaney, Lurleen B. Wallace Community College, Opp, AL; Sue Canter, Guilford Technical Community College, Jamestown, NC; Reuel Sample, National College, Knoxville, TN; Regina Young, Wiregrass Georgia Technical College, Valdosta, GA; William Roxbury, National College, Stow, OH; Charles Adams, II, Danville Community College, Danville, VA; Karen Spray, Northeast Community College, Norfolk, NE; Deborah Miller, Augusta Technical College, Augusta, GA; Wanda Stuparits, Lanier Technical College, Cumming, GA; Gale Wilson, Brookhaven College, Farmers Branch, TX; Jocelyn S. Pinkard, Arlington Career Institute, Grand Prairie, TX; Ann Blackman, Parkland College, Champaign, IL; Fathia Williams, Fletcher Technical Community College, Houma, LA; Leslie Martin, Gaston College, Dallas, NC; Tom Rose, Kellogg Community College, Battle Creek, MI; Casey Thompson, Wiregrass Georgia Technical College, Douglas, GA; Larry Bush, University of Cincinnati, Clermont College, Amelia, OH; Tim Ellis, Schoolcraft College, Liconia, MI; Miles Cannon, Lanier Technical College, Oakwood, GA; Irvin LaFleur, Lanier Technical College, Cumming, GA; Patricia Partyka, Schoolcraft College, Prudenville, MI.

The authors and publishing team also thanks the following individuals for their contributions to this project: checking the accuracy of the instruction and exercises—Brienna McWade, Traci Post, and Janet Blum, Fanshawe College, London, Ontario; creating annotated model answers and developing lesson plans—Ann Mills, Ivy Tech Community College, Evansville, Indiana; developing rubrics—Marjory Wooten, Laneir Techncial College, Cumming, Georgia.

ISBN 978-0-76385-343-3 (Text)
ISBN 978-0-76385-386-0 (Text + CD)
ISBN 978-0-76385-365-5 (eBook)

875 Montreal Way
St. Paul, MN 55102
Email: educate@emcp.com
Website: www.emcp.com

Printed in the United States of America

23 22 21 20 19 18 17 16 15 14 3 4 5 6 7 8 9 10 11 12

Contents

Microsoft Word 2013 Level 2

Preface

Benchmark Series Microsoft Word 2013 is designed for students who want to learn how to use this powerful word processing program to create professional-looking documents for workplace, school, and personal communication needs. No prior knowledge of word processing is required. After successfully completing a course using this textbook, students will be able to

- Create and edit memos, letters, fliers, announcements, and reports of varying complexity
- Apply appropriate formatting elements and styles to a range of document types
- Add graphics and other visual elements to enhance written communication
- Plan, research, write, revise, and publish documents to meet specific information needs
- Given a workplace scenario requiring a written solution, assess the communication purpose and then prepare the materials that achieve the goal efficiently and effectively

In addition to mastering Word skills, students will learn the essential features and functions of computer hardware, the Windows 8 operating system, and Internet Explorer 10. Upon completing the text, they can expect to be proficient in using Word to organize, analyze, and present information.

Well-designed textbook pedagogy is important, but students learn technology skills from practice and problem solving. Technology provides opportunities for interactive learning as well as excellent ways to quickly and accurately assess student performance. To this end, this textbook is supported with SNAP, Paradigm Publishing's web-based training and assessment learning management system. Details about SNAP as well as additional student courseware and instructor resources can be found on page xiv.

Achieving Proficiency in Word 2013

Since its inception several Office versions ago, the Benchmark Series has served as a standard of excellence in software instruction. Elements of the book function individually and collectively to create an inviting, comprehensive learning environment that produces successful computer users. The following visual tour highlights the text's features.

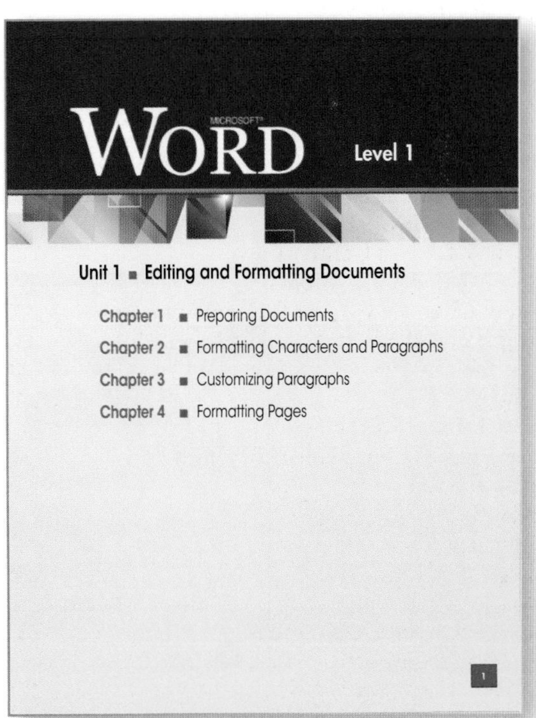

UNIT OPENERS display the unit's four chapter titles. Each level has two units, which conclude with a comprehensive unit performance assessment.

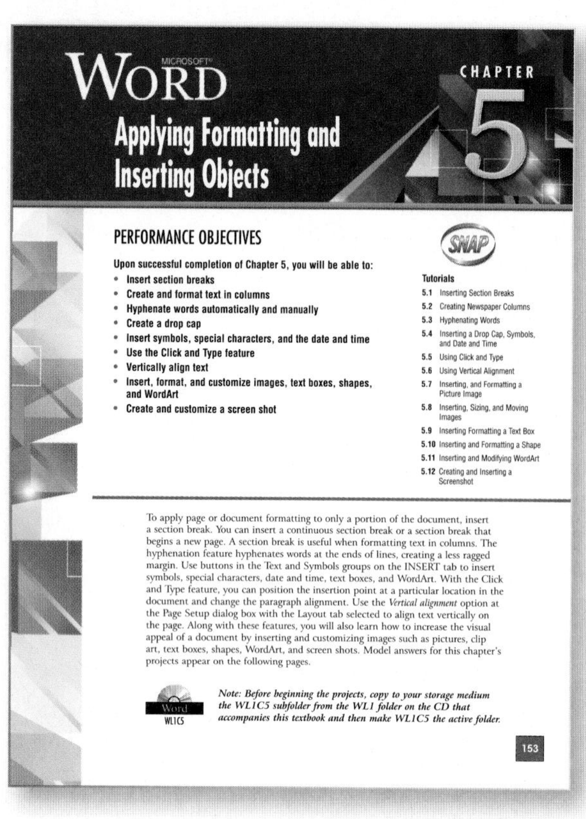

CHAPTER OPENERS present the performance objectives and an overview of the skills taught.

SNAP interactive tutorials are available to support chapter-specific skills at snap2013.emcp.com.

DATA FILES are provided for each chapter. A prominent note reminds students to copy the appropriate chapter data folder and make it active.

PROJECT APPROACH: Builds Skill Mastery within Realistic Context

MODEL ANSWERS provide a preview of the finished chapter projects and allow students to confirm they have created the materials accurately.

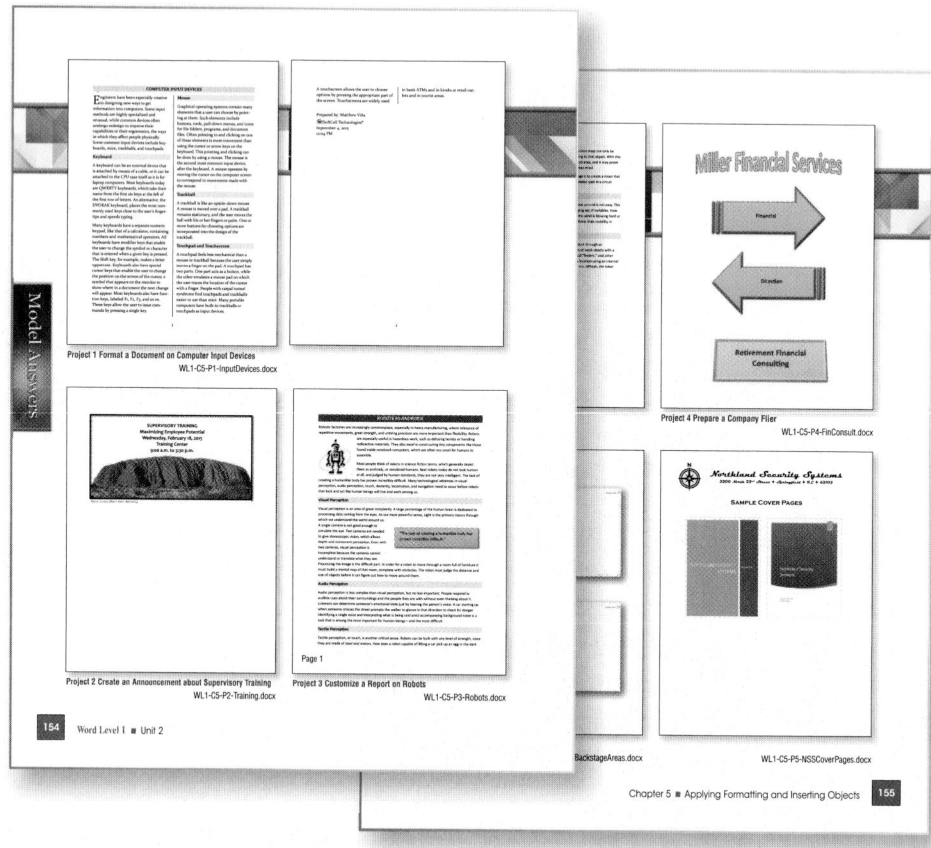

Project 1 Format a Document on Computer Input Devices — 8 Parts

You will format into columns text in a document on computer input devices, improve the readability of the document by hyphenating long words, and improve the visual appeal by inserting a drop cap.

Inserting a Section Break

Quick Steps

Insert a Section Break
1. Click PAGE LAYOUT tab.
2. Click Breaks button.
3. Click section break type in drop-down list.

Breaks

HINT If you delete a section break, the text that follows the section break takes on the formatting of the text preceding the break.

You can change the layout and formatting of specific portions of a document by inserting section breaks. For example, you can insert section breaks and then change margins for the text between the section breaks. If you want to format specific text in a document into columns, insert a section break.

Insert a section break in a document by clicking the PAGE LAYOUT tab, clicking the Breaks button in the Page Setup group, and then clicking the desired option in the *Section Breaks* section of the drop-down list. You can insert a section break that begins a new page or a continuous section break that does not begin a new page. A ***continuous section break*** separates the document into sections but does not insert a page break. Click one of the other three options in the *Section Breaks* section of the Breaks drop-down list if you want to insert a section break that begins a new page.

A section break inserted in a document is not visible in Print Layout view. Change to Draft view or click the Show/Hide ¶ button on the HOME tab to turn on the display of nonprinting characters and a section break displays in the document as a double row of dots with the words *Section Break* in the middle. Depending on the type of section break you insert, text follows *Section Break*. For example, if you insert a continuous section break, the words *Section Break (Continuous)* display in the middle of the row of dots. To delete a section break, change to Draft view, click on any character in the *Section Break (Continuous)* text, and then press the Delete key. (This moves the insertion point to the beginning of the section break.) Another option is to click the Show/Hide ¶ button to turn on the display of nonprinting characters, click on any character in the *Section Break (Continuous)* text, and then press the Delete key.

Project 1a Inserting a Continuous Section Break — Part 1 of 8

1. Open **InputDevices.docx** and then save it with Save As and name it **WL1-C5-P1-InputDevices**.
2. Insert a continuous section break by completing the following steps:
   a. Move the insertion point to the beginning of the *Keyboard* heading.
   b. Click the PAGE LAYOUT tab.
   c. Click the Breaks button in the Page Setup group and then click *Continuous* in the *Section Breaks* section of the drop-down list.
3. Click the HOME tab, click the Show/Hide ¶ button in the Paragraph group, and then notice the section break that displays at the end of the first paragraph of text.
4. Click the Show/Hide ¶ button to turn off the display of nonprinting characters.

MULTIPART PROJECTS provide a framework for the instruction and practice on software features. A project overview identifies tasks to accomplish and key features to use in completing the work.

STEP-BY-STEP INSTRUCTIONS guide students to the desired outcome for each project part. Screen captures illustrate what the student's screen should look like at key points.

Between project parts, the text presents instruction on the features and skills necessary to accomplish the next section of the project.

HINTS provide useful tips on how to use features efficiently and effectively.

Typically, a file remains open throughout all parts of the project. Students save their work incrementally.

Removing Column Formatting

To remove column formatting using the Columns button, position the insertion point in the section containing columns, click the PAGE LAYOUT tab, click the Columns button, and then click *One* at the drop-down list. You can also remove column formatting at the Columns dialog box by selecting the *One* option in the *Presets* section.

Inserting a Column Break

When formatting text into columns, Word automatically breaks the columns to fit the page. At times, column breaks may appear in an undesirable location. You can insert a column break by positioning the insertion point where you want the column to end, clicking the PAGE LAYOUT tab, clicking the Breaks button, and then clicking *Column* at the drop-down list.

HINT You can also insert a column break with the keyboard shortcut Ctrl + Shift + Enter.

Project 1c Formatting Columns at the Columns Dialog Box — Part 3 of 8

1. With **WL1-C5-P1-InputDevices.docx** open, delete the section break by completing the following steps:
   a. Click the VIEW tab and then click the Draft button in the Views group.
   b. Click on any character in the *Section Break (Continuous)* text and then press the Delete key.
   c. Click the Print Layout button in the Views group on the VIEW tab.
2. Remove column formatting by clicking the PAGE LAYOUT tab, clicking the Columns button in the Page Setup group, and then clicking *One* at the drop-down list.
3. Format text in columns by completing the following steps:
   a. Position the insertion point at the beginning of the first paragraph of text in the document.
   b. Click the Columns button in the Page Setup group and then click *More Columns* at the drop-down list.
   c. At the Columns dialog box, click *Two* in the *Presets* section.
   d. Click the down-pointing arrow at the right of the *Spacing* measurement box until *0.3"* displays.
   e. Click the *Line between* check box to insert a check mark.
   f. Click the down-pointing arrow at the right side of the *Apply to* option box and then click *This point forward* at the drop-down list.
   g. Click OK to close the dialog box.

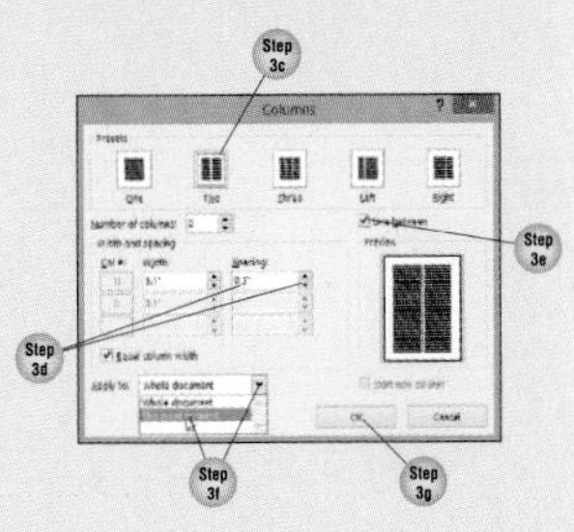

MAGENTA TEXT identifies material to type.

At the end of the project, students save, print, and then close the file.

QUICK STEPS provide feature summaries for reference and review.

f. Click the Keep Changes button in the Close group on the BACKGROUND REMOVAL tab. (The picture should now display with the sky removed.)

19. Insert a caption by completing the following steps:
    a. Right-click the picture. (This displays the shortcut menu.)
    b. Click the *Insert Caption* option at the shortcut menu.
    c. At the Caption dialog box with the insertion point positioned in the *Caption* text box after the *Figure 1* text, press the spacebar and then type Uluru (Ayers Rock, Australia).
    d. Click OK. (The caption displays below and at the left side of the picture.)
20. Save, print, and then close **WL1-C5-P2-Training.docx**.

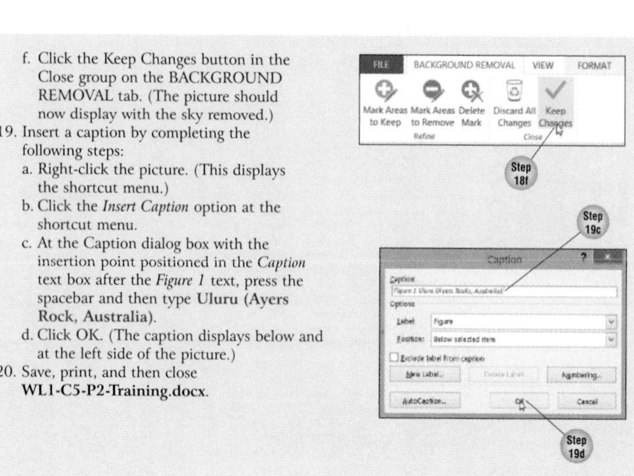

Project 3 Customize a Report on Robots **2 Parts**

You will open a report on robots and then add visual appeal to the report by inserting and formatting an image from Office.com and a built-in text box.

Inserting an Image from Office.com

Microsoft Office includes a gallery of media images you can insert in a document, such as clip art images and photographs. To insert an image in a Word document, click the INSERT tab and then click the Online Pictures button in the Illustrations group. This displays the Insert Pictures window, as shown in Figure 5.7.

At the Insert Pictures window, click in the search text box to the right of *Office.com Clip Art*, type the search term or topic, and then press Enter. Images that match your search term or topic display in the window. To insert an image, click the desired image and then click the Insert button or double-click the image. This downloads the image from the Office.com website to your document.

When you insert an image in the document, the image is selected and the PICTURE TOOLS FORMAT tab is active. Use buttons on this tab to customize an image just as you learned to customize a picture.

Quick Steps

Insert an Image from Office.com
1. Click INSERT tab.
2. Click Online Pictures button.
3. Type search word or topic.
4. Press Enter.
5. Double-click desired image.

Online Pictures

Chapter 5 ■ Applying Formatting and Inserting Objects 173

CHAPTER REVIEW ACTIVITIES: A Hierarchy of Learning Assessments

Chapter Summary

- Group Word documents logically into folders. Create a new folder at the Open or Save As dialog box.
- You can select one or several documents at the Open dialog box. Copy, move, rename, delete, or open a document or selected documents.
- Use the *Cut*, *Copy*, and *Paste* options from the Organize button drop-down list or the Open dialog box shortcut menu to move or copy a document from one folder to another. (If you are using your SkyDrive, go to www.skydrive.com, log in to your account, and then use the skydrive.com toolbar to move or copy a document or folder to another location.)
- Delete documents and/or folders with the *Delete* option from the Organize button drop-down list or shortcut menu.
- Click the *Change File Type* option at the Export backstage area and options display for saving the document in a different file format. You can also save documents in a different file format with the *Save as type* option box at the Save As dialog box.
- Move among the open documents by clicking the buttons on the Taskbar representing the various documents, or by clicking the VIEW tab, clicking the Switch Windows button in the Window group, and then clicking the desired document name.
- View a portion of all open documents by clicking the Arrange All button in the W
- Use the Minimize, Restore, and Maximiz corner of the window to reduce or increa
- Divide a window into two panes by click the Split button in the Window group. T of the same document at one time.
- View the contents of two open documen tab and then clicking the View Side by S
- Open a new window containing the same and then clicking the New Window butt
- Insert a document into the open docume clicking the Object button arrow, and th down list. At the Insert File dialog box, d
- Preview a document at the Print backsta document with the Next Page and the Pr the preview page. Use the Zoom slider b of the preview page.
- Use options at the Print backstage area t the page orientation, size, and margins; s print on one page; indicate the number c the pages; and specify the printer.
- With Word's envelope feature, you can c Envelopes and Labels dialog box with th

CHAPTER SUMMARY captures the purpose and execution of key features.

- If you open the Envelopes and Labels dialog box in a document containing a name and address (with each line ending with a press of the Enter key), that information is automatically inserted in the *Delivery address* text box in the dialog box.
- Use Word's labels feature to print text on mailing labels, file labels, disc labels, or other types of labels.
- Available templates display in the New backstage area. Double-click a template to open a document based on the template. Search for templates online by typing in the search text or category in the search text box and then pressing Enter.

Commands Review

FEATURE	RIBBON TAB, GROUP/OPTION	BUTTON, OPTION	KEYBOARD SHORTCUT
arrange documents	VIEW, Window		
Envelopes and Labels dialog box with Envelopes tab selected	MAILINGS, Create		
Envelopes and Labels dialog box with Labels tab selected	MAILINGS, Create		
Export backstage area	FILE, *Export*		
Insert File dialog box	INSERT, Text	*Text from File*	
maximize document			
minimize document			
New backstage area	FILE, *Ne*		
new window	VIEW, W		
Open dialog box	FILE, *Op*		
Print backstage area	FILE, *Pr*		
restore document			
Save As dialog box	FILE, *Sa*		
split window	VIEW, W		
switch windows	VIEW, W		
synchronous scrolling	VIEW, W		
view documents side by side	VIEW, W		

230 **Word Level 1** ■ Unit 2

COMMANDS REVIEW summarizes visually the major features and alternative methods of access.

Concepts Check Test Your Knowledge SNAP

Completion: In the space provided at the right, indicate the correct term, command, or number.

1. Create a new folder with this button at the Open dialog box or the Save As dialog box. ________
2. At the Open dialog box, the current folder path displays in this. ________
3. Using the mouse, select nonadjacent documents at the Open dialog box by holding down this key while clicking the desired documents. ________
4. Documents deleted from the computer's hard drive are automatically sent here. ________
5. The letters *PDF* stand for this. ________
6. Saving a document in this format strips out all formatting. ________
7. Click this button in the Window group on the VIEW tab to arrange all open documents so a portion of each document displays. ________
8. Click this button and the active document fills the editing window. ________
9. Click this button to reduce the active document to a button on the Taskbar. ________
10. To display documents side by side, click this button in the Window group on the VIEW tab. ________
11. Display the Insert File dialog box by clicking the Object button arrow on the INSERT tab and then clicking this option. ________
12. Type this in the *Pages* text box at the Print backstage area to print pages 3 through 6 of the open document. ________
13. Type this in the *Pages* text box at the Print backstage area to print pages 4 and 9 of the open document. ________
14. The Envelopes button is located in the Create group on this tab. ________
15. Download a template at this backstage area. ________

Chapter 6 ■ Maintaining Documents 231

CONCEPTS CHECK questions assess knowledge recall. Students enrolled in SNAP can complete the Concepts Check online. SNAP automatically scores student work.

Skills Check Assess Your Performance

Assessment

1 APPLY CHARACTER FORMATTING TO A LEASE AGREEMENT DOCUMENT  Grade It

1. Open **LeaseAgrmnt.docx**.
2. Save the document with Save As and name it **WL1-C2-A1-LeaseAgrmnt**.
3. Press Ctrl + End to move the insertion point to the end of the document and then type the text shown in Figure 2.8. Bold, italicize, and underline text as shown.
4. Select the entire document and then change the font to 12-point Candara.
5. Select and then b
6. Select and then it
7. Select the title *LE* Corbel and the fo formatting.)
8. Select the heading caps formatting. (
9. Use Format Painte for the remaining *Premises*, *Alteration*
10. Save, print, and t

Figure 2.8 Assessment 1

Inspection of Premises

Lessor shall have the right at al exhibit the Premises and to dis any time within forty-five days

Assessment

2 APPLY STYLES, A STYLE TECHNOLOGY DOCUME

1. Open **NetworkH**
2. Save the documen
3. Apply the Headin
4. Apply the Headin *Repeaters*, *Routers*,
5. Apply the Lines (
6. Apply the Savon
7. Apply the Green
8. Apply the Georgi
9. Apply the Open p
10. Highlight in yello
11. Save, print, and t

SKILLS CHECK exercises ask students to create a variety of documents using multiple features without how-to directions. Versions of the activities marked with a SNAP Grade It icon are available for automatic scoring in SNAP.

Visual Benchmark Demonstrate Your Proficiency

1 CREATE A FLIER

1. Create the flier shown in Figure 5.10 with the following specifications:
   - Create the title *Pugs on Parade!* as WordArt using the Fill - Black, Text 1, Shadow option. Change the width to 6.5 inches, apply the Can Up transform effect, and change the text fill color to Dark Red.
   - Create the shape containing the text *Admission is free!* using the Explosion 1 shape in the Stars and Banners section of the Shapes button drop-down list.
   - Insert the **Pug.jpg** picture (use the Pictures button on the INSERT tab) located in the WL1C5 folder on your storage medium. Change the text wrapping for the picture to Behind Text and size and position the picture as shown in the figure.
   - Create the line above the last line of text as a top border. Change the color to Dark Red and the width to 3 points.
   - Make any other changes so your document appears similar to Figure 5.10.
2. Save the document and name it **WL1-C5-VB1-PugFlier**.
3. Print and then close the document.

Figure 5.10 Visual Benchmark 1

Pugs on Parade!

Come join us for the fifth annual "Pugs on Parade" party, Saturday, July 18, at Mercer Way Park from 1:00 to 3:30 p.m.

VISUAL BENCHMARK assessments test students' problem-solving skills and mastery of program features.

Case Study Apply Your Skills

Part 1

You are the office manager for a real estate company, Macadam Realty, and have been asked by the senior sales associate, Lucy Hendricks, to organize contract forms into a specific folder. Create a new folder named *RealEstate* and then copy into the folder documents that begin with the letters "RE." Ms. Hendricks has also asked you to prepare mailing labels for Macadam Realty. Include on the labels the name, Macadam Realty, and the address, 100 Third Street, Suite 210, Denver, CO 80803. Use a decorative font for the name and address and make the *M* in *Macadam* and the *R* in *Realty* larger and more pronounced than surrounding text. Save the completed document and name it **WL1-C6-CS-RELabels**. Print and then close the document.

Part 2

One of your responsibilities is to format contract forms. Open the document named **REConAgrmnt.docx** and then save it and name it **WL1-C6-CS-REConAgrmnt**. The sales associate has asked you to insert signature information at the end of the document, and so you decide to insert at the end of the document the file named **RESig.docx**. With **WL1-C6-CS-REConAgrmnt.docx** still open, open **REBuildAgrmnt.docx**. Format the **WL1-C6-CS-REConAgrmnt.docx** document so it is formatted in a manner similar to the **REBuildAgrmnt.docx** document. Consider the following when specifying formatting: fonts, font sizes, and paragraph shading. Save, print, and then close **WL1-C6-CS-REConAgrmnt.docx**. Close **REBuildAgrmnt.docx**.

Part 3

As part of the organization of contracts, Ms. Hendricks has asked you to insert document properties for the **REBuildAgrmnt.docx** and **WL1-C6-CS-REConAgrmnt.docx** documents. Use the Help feature to learn how to insert document properties. With the information you learn from the Help feature, open each of the two documents separately, display the Info backstage area, click the Show All Properties hyperlink (you may need to scroll down the backstage area to display this hyperlink), and then insert document properties in the following fields (you determine the information to type): *Title*, *Subject*, *Categories*, and *Company*. Print the document properties for each document. (Change the first gallery in the *Settings* category in the Print backstage area to *Document Info*.) Save each document with the original name and close the documents.

Help

Part 4

A client of the real estate company, Anna Hurley, is considering purchasing several rental properties and has asked for information on how to locate real estate rental forms. Using the Internet, locate at least three websites that offer real estate rental forms. Write a letter to Anna Hurley at 2300 South 22nd Street, Denver, CO 80205. In the letter, list the websites you found and include information on which site you thought offered the most resources. Also include in the letter that Macadam Realty is very interested in helping her locate and purchase rental properties. Save the document and name it **WL1-C6-CS-RELtr**. Create an envelope for the letter and add it to the letter document. Save, print, and then close **WL1-C6-CS-RELtr.docx**. (You may need to manually feed the envelope in the printer.)

238 Word Level 1 ■ Unit 2

CASE STUDY requires analyzing a workplace scenario and then planning and executing multipart projects.

Students search the Web and/or use the program's Help feature to locate additional information required to complete the Case Study.

UNIT PERFORMANCE ASSESSMENT: Cross-Disciplinary, Comprehensive Evaluation

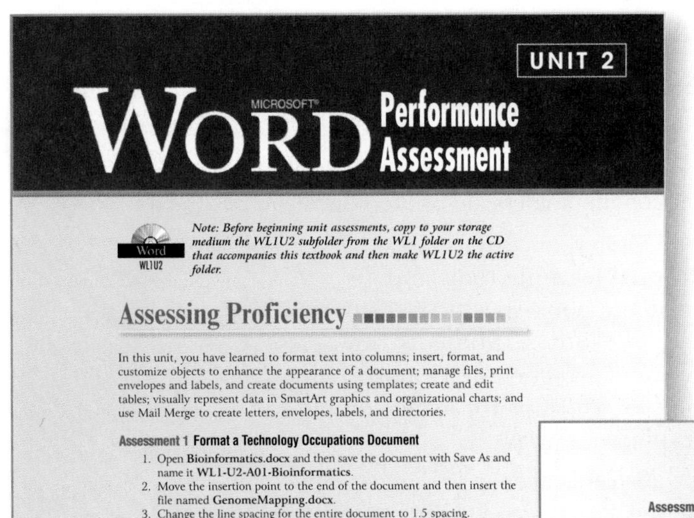

UNIT 2

MICROSOFT® WORD Performance Assessment

Note: Before beginning unit assessments, copy to your storage medium the WL1U2 subfolder from the WL1 folder on the CD that accompanies this textbook and then make WL1U2 the active folder.

Assessing Proficiency

In this unit, you have learned to format text into columns; insert, format, and customize objects to enhance the appearance of a document; manage files, print envelopes and labels, and create documents using templates; create and edit tables; visually represent data in SmartArt graphics and organizational charts; and use Mail Merge to create letters, envelopes, labels, and directories.

Assessment 1 Format a Technology Occupations Document

1. Open **Bioinformatics.docx** and then save the document with Save As and name it **WL1-U2-A01-Bioinformatics**.
2. Move the insertion point to the end of the document and then insert the file named **GenomeMapping.docx**.
3. Change the line spacing for the entire document to 1.5 spacing.
4. Insert a continuous section break at the beginning of the first paragraph of text (the paragraph that begins *Bioinformatics is the mixed application*).
5. Format the text below the section break into two columns.
6. Balance the columns on the second page.
7. Press Ctrl + Home to move the insertion point to the beginning of the document, insert the Motion Quote text box, and then type "**Understanding our DNA is similar to understanding a number that is billions of digits long.**" in the text box. Select the text in the text box, change the font size to 12 points, change the width of the text box to 2.6 inches, and then position the text box in the middle of the page with square text wrapping.
8. Create a drop cap with the first letter of the first word *Bioinformatics* that begins the first paragraph of text. Make the drop cap two lines in height.
9. Manually hyphenate words in the document.
10. Insert page numbering at the bottom of the page using the Thin Line page numbering option.
11. Save, print, and then close **WL1-U2-A01-Bioinformatics.docx**.

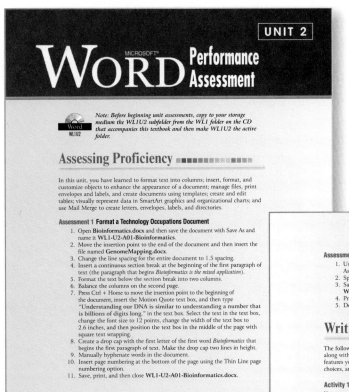

ASSESSING PROFICIENCY checks mastery of features.

WRITING ACTIVITIES involve applying program skills in a communication context.

Assessment 12 Merge and Print Envelopes

1. Use the Mail Merge feature to prepare envelopes for the letters created in Assessment 11.
2. Specify **WL1-U2-A11-DS.mdb** as the data source document.
3. Save the merged envelopes document and name the document **WL1-U2-A12-Envs**.
4. Print and then close **WL1-U2-A12-Envs.docx**.
5. Do not save the envelope main document.

Writing Activities

The following activities give you the opportunity to practice your writing skills along with demonstrating an understanding of some of the important Word features you have mastered in this unit. Use correct grammar, appropriate word choices, and clear sentence construction.

Activity 1 Compose a Letter to Volunteers

You are an employee of the city of Greenwater and are responsible for coordinating volunteers for the city's Safe Night program. Compose a letter to the volunteers listed in Figure U2.9 and include the following information in the letter:

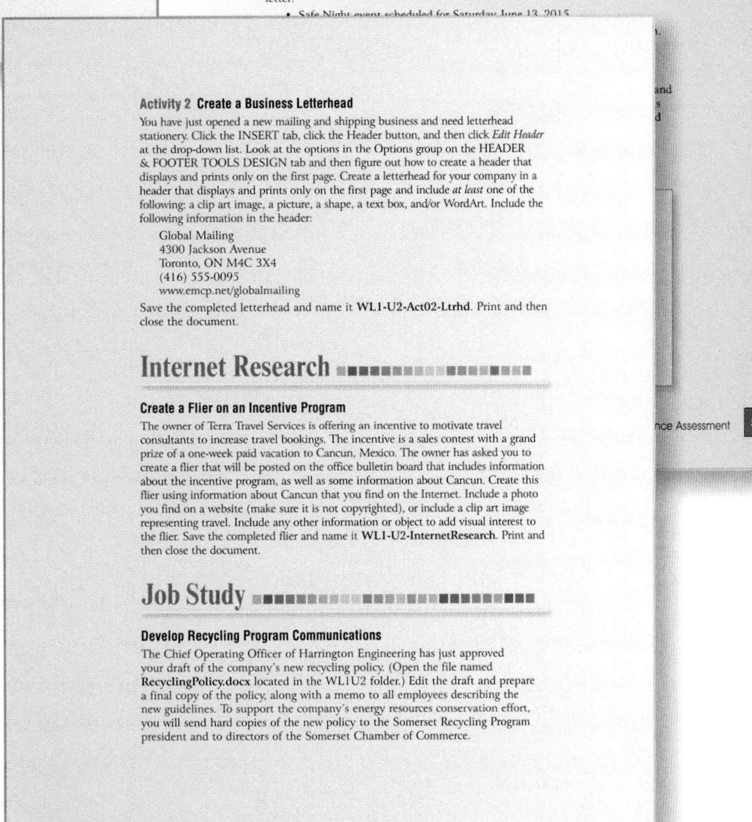

Activity 2 Create a Business Letterhead

You have just opened a new mailing and shipping business and need letterhead stationery. Click the INSERT tab, click the Header button, and then click *Edit Header* at the drop-down list. Look at the options in the Options group on the HEADER & FOOTER TOOLS DESIGN tab and then figure out how to create a header that displays and prints only on the first page. Create a letterhead for your company in a header that displays and prints only on the first page and include *at least* one of the following: a clip art image, a picture, a shape, a text box, and/or WordArt. Include the following information in the header:

Global Mailing
4300 Jackson Avenue
Toronto, ON M4C 3X4
(416) 555-0095
www.emcp.net/globalmailing

Save the completed letterhead and name it **WL1-U2-Act02-Ltrhd**. Print and then close the document.

Internet Research

Create a Flier on an Incentive Program

The owner of Terra Travel Services is offering an incentive to motivate travel consultants to increase travel bookings. The incentive is a sales contest with a grand prize of a one-week paid vacation to Cancun, Mexico. The owner has asked you to create a flier that will be posted on the office bulletin board that includes information about the incentive program, as well as some information about Cancun. Create this flier using information about Cancun that you find on the Internet. Include a photo you find on a website (make sure it is not copyrighted), or include a clip art image representing travel. Include any other information or object to add visual interest to the flier. Save the completed flier and name it **WL1-U2-InternetResearch**. Print and then close the document.

Job Study

Develop Recycling Program Communications

The Chief Operating Officer of Harrington Engineering has just approved your draft of the company's new recycling policy. (Open the file named **RecyclingPolicy.docx** located in the WL1U2 folder.) Edit the draft and prepare a final copy of the policy, along with a memo to all employees describing the new guidelines. To support the company's energy resources conservation effort, you will send hard copies of the new policy to the Somerset Recycling Program president and to directors of the Somerset Chamber of Commerce.

334 Word Level 1 ■ Unit 2 Performance Assessment

INTERNET RESEARCH project reinforces research and word processing skills.

JOB STUDY at the end of Unit 2 presents a capstone assessment requiring critical thinking and problem solving.

Student Courseware

Student Resources CD Each Benchmark Series textbook is packaged with a Student Resources CD containing the data files required for completing the projects and assessments. A CD icon and folder name displayed on the opening page of chapters reminds students to copy a folder of files from the CD to the desired storage medium before beginning the project exercises. Directions for copying folders are printed on the inside back cover.

Internet Resource Center Additional learning tools and reference materials are available at the book-specific website at www.paradigmcollege.net/BenchmarkWord13. Students can access the same files that are on the Student Resources CD along with study tools, study quizzes, web links, and tips for using computers effectively in academic and workplace settings.

SNAP Training and Assessment Available at snap2013.emcp.com, SNAP is a web-based program offering an interactive venue for learning Microsoft Office 2013, Windows 8, and Internet Explorer 10. Along with a web-based learning management system, SNAP provides multimedia tutorials, performance skill items, Concepts Check matching activities, Grade It Skills Check Assessment activities, comprehensive performance evaluations, a concepts test bank, an online grade book, and a set of course planning tools. A CD of tutorials teaching the basics of Office, Windows, and Internet Explorer is also available if instructors wish to assign additional SNAP tutorial work without using the web-based SNAP program.

eBook For students who prefer studying with an eBook, the texts in the Benchmark Series are available in an electronic form. The web-based, password-protected eBooks feature dynamic navigation tools, including bookmarking, a linked table of contents, and the ability to jump to a specific page. The eBook format also supports helpful study tools, such as highlighting and note taking.

Instructor Resources

Instructor's Guide and Disc Instructor support for the Benchmark Series includes an *Instructor's Guide* and Instructor Resources Disc package. This resource includes course planning resources, such as Lesson Blueprints, teaching hints, and sample course syllabi; presentation resources, such as PowerPoint slide shows with lecture notes; and assessment resources, including an overview of available assessment venues, live model answers for chapter projects, and live and annotated PDF model answers for end-of-chapter exercises. Contents of the *Instructor's Guide* and Instructor Resources Disc package are also available on the password-protected section of the Internet Resource Center for this title at www.paradigmcollege.net/BenchmarkWord13.

Computerized Test Generator Instructors can use the ExamView® Assessment Suite and test banks of multiple-choice items to create customized web-based or print tests.

Blackboard Cartridge This set of files allows instructors to create a personalized Blackboard website for their course and provides course content, tests, and the mechanisms for establishing communication via e-discussions and online group conferences. Available content includes a syllabus, test banks, PowerPoint presentations, and supplementary course materials. Upon request, the files can be available within 24–48 hours. Hosting the site is the responsibility of the educational institution.

System Requirements

This text is designed for the student to complete projects and assessments on a computer running a standard installation of Microsoft Office Professional Plus 2013 and the Microsoft Windows 8 operating system. To effectively run this suite and operating system, your computer should be outfitted with the following:

- 1 gigahertz (GHz) processor or higher; 1 gigabyte (GB) of RAM (32 bit) or 2 GB of RAM (64 bit)
- 3 GB of available hard-disk space
- .NET version 3.5, 4.0, or 4.5
- DirectX 10 graphics card
- Minimum 1024 × 576 resolution (or 1366 × 768 to use Windows Snap feature)
- Computer mouse, multi-touch device, or other compatible pointing device

Office 2013 will also operate on computers running the Windows 7 operating system.

Screen captures in this book were created using a screen resolution display setting of 1600 × 900. Refer to the *Customizing Settings* section of *Getting Started in Office 2013* following this preface for instructions on changing your monitor's resolution. Figure G.9 on page 10 shows the Microsoft Office Word ribbon at three resolutions for comparison purposes. Choose the resolution that best matches your computer; however, be aware that using a resolution other than 1600 × 900 means that your screens may not match the illustrations in this book.

About the Authors

Nita Rutkosky began teaching business education courses at Pierce College Puyallup, Washington, in 1978. Since then she has taught a variety of software applications to students in postsecondary Information Technology certificate and degree programs. In addition to *Benchmark Office 2013,* she has co-authored *Marquee Series: Microsoft Office 2013, 2010, 2007,* and *2003; Signature Series: Microsoft Word 2013, 2010, 2007,* and *2003; Using Computers in the Medical Office: Microsoft Word, Excel, and PowerPoint 2010, 2007* and *2003*; and *Computer and Internet Essentials: Preparing for IC³*. She has also authored textbooks on keyboarding, WordPerfect, desktop publishing, and voice recognition for Paradigm Publishing, Inc.

Audrey Roggenkamp has been teaching courses in the Business Information Technology department at Pierce College Puyallup since 2005. Her courses have included keyboarding, skill building, and Microsoft Office programs. In addition to this title, she has co-authored *Marquee Series: Microsoft Office 2013, 2010,* and *2007; Signature Series: Microsoft Word 2013, 2010,* and *2007; Using Computers in the Medical Office: Microsoft Word, Excel, and PowerPoint 2010, 2007,* and *2003*; and *Computer and Internet Essentials: Preparing for IC³* for Paradigm Publishing, Inc.

Ian Rutkosky teaches Business Technology courses at Pierce College Puyallup, Washington. In addition to this title, he has coauthored *Computer and Internet Essentials: Preparing for IC³, Marquee Series: Microsoft Office 2013*, and *Using Computers in the Medical Office: Microsoft Word, Excel, and PowerPoint 2010*. He is also a co-author and consultant for Paradigm's SNAP training and assessment software.

Getting Started in Office 2013

In this textbook, you will learn to operate several computer programs that combine to make the Microsoft Office 2013 application suite. The programs you will learn are known as ***software***, and they contain instructions that tell the computer what to do. Some of the application programs in the suite include Word, a word processing program; Excel, a spreadsheet program; Access, a database program; and PowerPoint, a presentation program.

Identifying Computer Hardware

The computer equipment you will use to operate the Microsoft Office suite is referred to as ***hardware***. You will need access to a computer system that includes a CPU, monitor, keyboard, printer, drives, and mouse. If you are not sure what equipment you will be operating, check with your instructor. The computer system shown in Figure G.1 consists of six components. Each component is discussed separately in the material that follows.

Figure G.1 Computer System

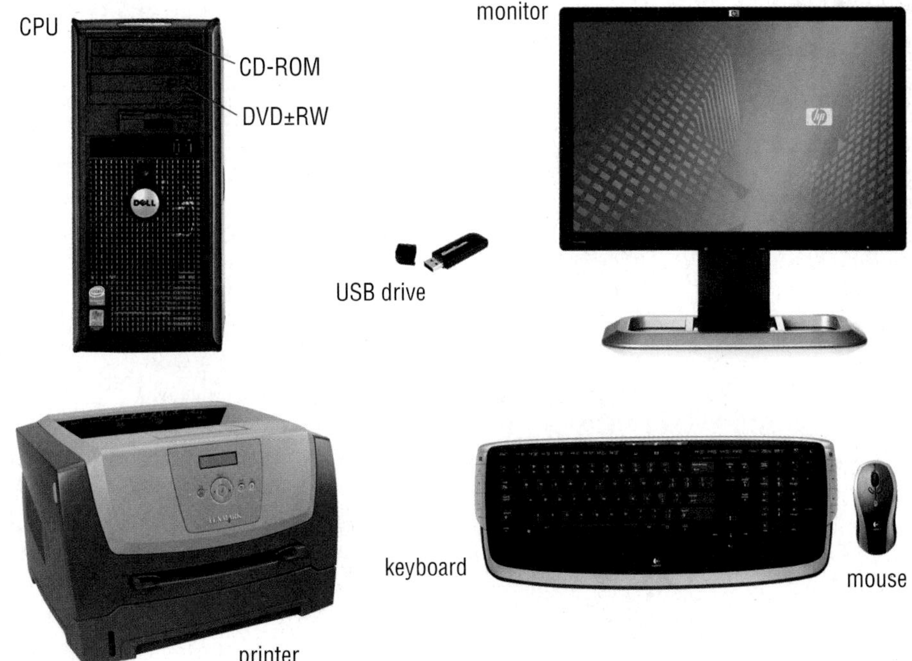

CPU

The ***central processing unit (CPU)*** is the brain of the computer and is where all processing occurs. Silicon chips, which contain miniaturized circuitry, are placed on boards that are plugged into slots within the CPU. Whenever an instruction is given to the computer, it is processed through the circuitry in the CPU.

Monitor

A computer ***monitor*** looks like a television screen. It displays the information in a program and the text you input using the keyboard. The quality of display for monitors varies depending on the type of monitor and the level of resolution. Monitors can also vary in size—generally from 13 inches to 26 inches or larger.

Keyboard

The ***keyboard*** is used to input information into the computer. The number and location of the keys on a keyboard can vary. In addition to letters, numbers, and symbols, most computer keyboards contain function keys, arrow keys, and a numeric keypad. Figure G.2 shows an enhanced keyboard.

The 12 keys at the top of the keyboard, labeled with the letter F followed by a number, are called ***function keys***. Use these keys to perform functions within each of the Office programs. To the right of the regular keys is a group of ***special*** or ***dedicated keys***. These keys are labeled with specific functions that will be performed when you press the key. Below the special keys are arrow keys. Use these keys to move the insertion point in the document screen.

Some keyboards include mode indicator lights. When you select certain modes, a light appears on the keyboard. For example, if you press the Caps Lock key, which disables the lowercase alphabet, a light appears next to Caps Lock. Similarly, pressing the Num Lock key will disable the special functions on the numeric keypad, which is located at the right side of the keyboard.

Figure G.2 Keyboard

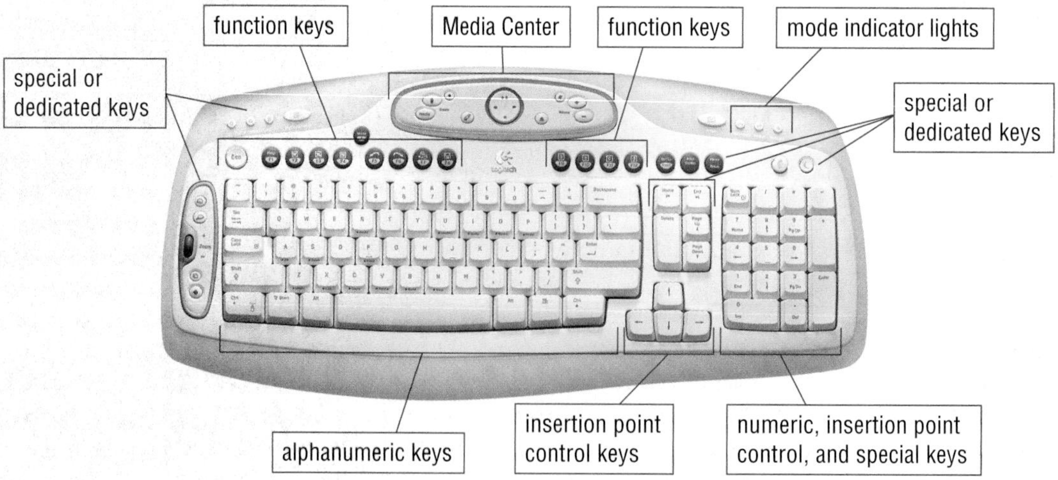

Drives and Ports

Depending on the computer system you are using, Microsoft Office 2013 is installed on a hard drive or as part of a network system. Either way, you will need to have a CD or DVD drive to complete the projects and assessments in this book. If you plan to use a USB drive as your storage medium, you will also need a USB port. You will insert the CD that accompanies this textbook into the CD or DVD drive and then copy folders from the disc to your storage medium. You will also save documents you create to folders on your storage medium.

Printer

An electronic version of a file is known as a ***soft copy***. If you want to create a ***hard copy*** of a file, you need to print it. To print documents you will need to access a printer, which will probably be either a laser printer or an ink-jet printer. A ***laser printer*** uses a laser beam combined with heat and pressure to print documents, while an ***ink-jet printer*** prints a document by spraying a fine mist of ink on the page.

Mouse or Touchpad

Most functions and commands in the Microsoft Office suite are designed to be performed using a mouse or a similar pointing device. A ***mouse*** is an input device that sits on a flat surface next to the computer. You can operate a mouse with your left or right hand. Moving the mouse on the flat surface causes a corresponding pointer to move on the screen, and clicking the left or right mouse buttons allows you to select various objects and commands. Figure G.1 contains an image of a mouse.

If you are working on a laptop computer, you may use a touchpad instead of a mouse. A ***touchpad*** allows you to move the mouse pointer by moving your finger across a surface at the base of the keyboard. You click by using your thumb to press the button located at the bottom of the touchpad.

Using the Mouse

The programs in the Microsoft Office suite can be operated with the keyboard and a mouse. The mouse generally has two buttons on top, which you press to execute specific functions and commands. A mouse may also contain a wheel, which can be used to scroll in a window or as a third button. To use the mouse, rest it on a flat surface or a mouse pad. Put your hand over it with your palm resting on top of the mouse, your wrist resting on the table surface, and your index finger resting on the left mouse button. As you move your hand, and thus the mouse, a corresponding pointer moves on the screen.

When using the mouse, you should understand four terms — point, click, double-click, and drag. When operating the mouse, you may need to point to a specific command, button, or icon. To ***point*** means to position the mouse pointer on the desired item. With the mouse pointer positioned on the desired item, you may need to click a button on the mouse to select the item. To ***click*** means to quickly tap a button on the mouse once. To complete two steps at one time, such as choosing and then executing a function, double-click the mouse button. To ***double-click*** means to tap the left mouse button twice in quick succession. The term ***drag*** means to press and hold the left mouse button, move the mouse pointer to a specific location, and then release the button.

Using the Mouse Pointer

The mouse pointer will look different depending on where you have positioned it and what function you are performing. The following are some of the ways the mouse pointer can appear when you are working in the Office suite:

- The mouse pointer appears as an I-beam (called the ***I-beam pointer***) when you are inserting text in a file. The I-beam pointer can be used to move the insertion point or to select text.
- The mouse pointer appears as an arrow pointing up and to the left (called the ***arrow pointer***) when it is moved to the Title bar, Quick Access toolbar, ribbon, or an option in a dialog box, among other locations.
- The mouse pointer becomes a double-headed arrow (either pointing left and right, pointing up and down, or pointing diagonally) when you perform certain functions such as changing the size of an object.
- In certain situations, such as when you move an object or image, the mouse pointer displays with a four-headed arrow attached. The four-headed arrow means that you can move the object left, right, up, or down.
- When a request is being processed or when a program is being loaded, the mouse pointer may appear as a moving circle. The moving circle means "please wait." When the process is completed, the circle is replaced with a normal arrow pointer.
- When the mouse pointer displays as a hand with a pointing index finger, it indicates that more information is available about an item. The mouse pointer also displays as a hand with a pointing index finger when you hover the mouse over a hyperlink.

Choosing Commands

Once a program is open, you can use several methods in the program to choose commands. A ***command*** is an instruction that tells the program to do something. You can choose a command using the mouse or the keyboard. When a program such as Word or PowerPoint is open, the ribbon contains buttons and options for completing tasks, as well as tabs you can click to display additional buttons and options. To choose a button on the Quick Access toolbar or on the ribbon, position the tip of the mouse arrow pointer on the button and then click the left mouse button.

The Office suite provides ***accelerator keys*** you can press to use a command in a program. Press the Alt key on the keyboard to display KeyTips that identify the accelerator key you can press to execute a command. For example, if you press the Alt key in a Word document with the HOME tab active, KeyTips display as shown in Figure G.3. Continue pressing accelerator keys until you execute the desired command. For example, to begin spell checking a document, press the Alt key, press the R key on the keyboard to display the REVIEW tab, and then press the letter S on the keyboard.

Figure G.3 Word HOME Tab KeyTips

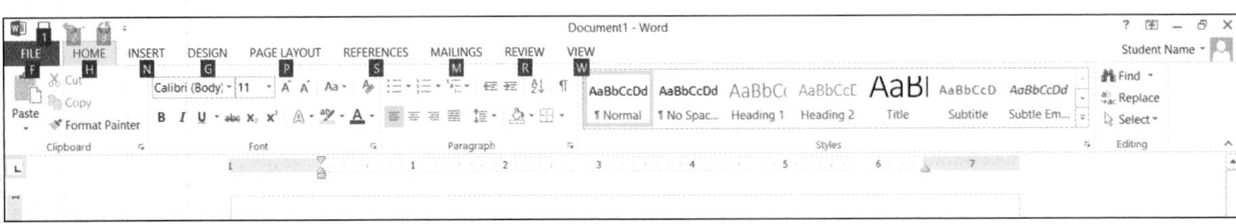

Choosing Commands from Drop-Down Lists

To choose a command from a drop-down list with the mouse, position the mouse pointer on the desired option and then click the left mouse button. To make a selection from a drop-down list with the keyboard, type the underlined letter in the desired option.

Some options at a drop-down list may appear in gray (dimmed), indicating that the option is currently unavailable. If an option at a drop-down list displays preceded by a check mark, it means the option is currently active. If an option at a drop-down list displays followed by an ellipsis (...), clicking that option will display a dialog box.

Choosing Options from a Dialog Box

A ***dialog box*** contains options for applying formatting or otherwise modifying a file or data within a file. Some dialog boxes display with tabs along the top that provide additional options. For example, the Font dialog box shown in Figure G.4 contains two tabs — the Font tab and the Advanced tab. The tab that displays in the front is the active tab. To make a tab active using the mouse, position the arrow pointer on the desired tab and then click the left mouse button. If you are using the keyboard, press Ctrl + Tab or press Alt + the underlined letter on the desired tab.

Figure G.4 Word Font Dialog Box

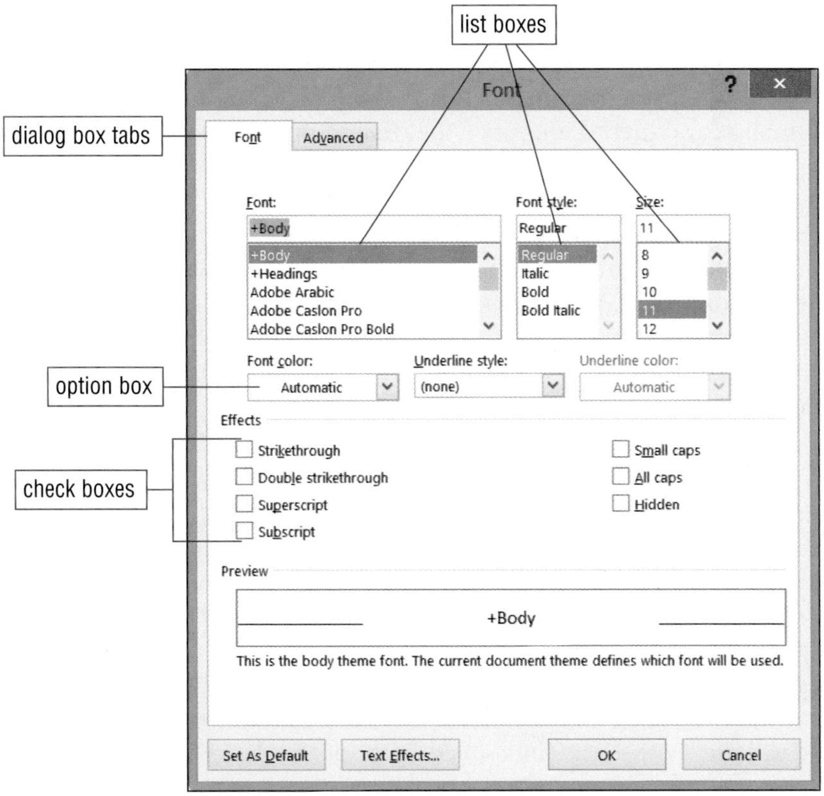

To choose options from a dialog box with the mouse, position the arrow pointer on the desired option and then click the left mouse button. If you are using the keyboard, press the Tab key to move the insertion point forward from option to option. Press Shift + Tab to move the insertion point backward from option to option. You can also hold down the Alt key and then press the underlined letter of the desired option. When an option is selected, it displays with a blue background or surrounded by a dashed box called a ***marquee***. A dialog box contains one or more of the following elements: list boxes, option boxes, check boxes, text boxes, option buttons, measurement boxes, and command buttons.

List Boxes and Option Boxes

The fonts below the *Font* option in the Font dialog box in Figure G.4 are contained in a ***list box***. To make a selection from a list box with the mouse, move the arrow pointer to the desired option and then click the left mouse button.

Some list boxes may contain a scroll bar. This scroll bar will display at the right side of the list box (a vertical scroll bar) or at the bottom of the list box (a horizontal scroll bar). Use a vertical scroll bar or a horizontal scroll bar to move through the list if the list is longer (or wider) than the box. To move down a list using a vertical scroll bar, position the arrow pointer on the down-pointing arrow and hold down the left mouse button. To scroll up through the list, position the arrow pointer on the up-pointing arrow and hold down the left mouse button. You can also move the arrow pointer above the scroll box and click the left mouse button to scroll up the list or move the arrow pointer below the scroll box and click the left mouse button to move down the list. To navigate a list with a horizontal scroll bar, click the left-pointing arrow to scroll to the left of the list or click the right-pointing arrow to scroll to the right of the list.

To use the keyboard to make a selection from a list box, move the insertion point into the box by holding down the Alt key and pressing the underlined letter of the desired option. Press the Up and/or Down Arrow keys on the keyboard to move through the list, and press Enter once the desired option is selected.

In some dialog boxes where there is not enough room for a list box, lists of options are contained in a drop-down list box called an ***option box***. Option boxes display with a down-pointing arrow. For example, in Figure G.4, the font color options are contained in an option box. To display the different color options, click the down-pointing arrow at the right of the *Font color* option box. If you are using the keyboard, press Alt + C.

Check Boxes

Some dialog boxes contain options preceded by a box. A check mark may or may not appear in the box. The Word Font dialog box shown in Figure G.4 displays a variety of check boxes within the *Effects* section. If a check mark appears in the box, the option is active (turned on). If the check box does not contain a check mark, the option is inactive (turned off). Any number of check boxes can be active. For example, in the Word Font dialog box, you can insert a check mark in several of the boxes in the *Effects* section to activate the options.

To make a check box active or inactive with the mouse, position the tip of the arrow pointer in the check box and then click the left mouse button. If you are using the keyboard, press Alt + the underlined letter of the desired option.

Text Boxes

Some options in a dialog box require you to enter text. For example, the boxes below the *Find what* and *Replace with* options at the Excel Find and Replace dialog box shown in Figure G.5 are text boxes. In a text box, you type text or edit existing text. Edit text in a text box in the same manner as normal text. Use the Left and Right Arrow keys on the keyboard to move the insertion point without deleting text and use the Delete key or Backspace key to delete text.

Option Buttons

The Word Insert Table dialog box shown in Figure G.6 contains options in the *AutoFit behavior* section preceded by ***option buttons***. Only one option button can be selected at any time. When an option button is selected, a blue or black circle displays in the button. To select an option button with the mouse, position the tip of the arrow pointer inside the option button or on the option and then click the left mouse button. To make a selection with the keyboard, hold down the Alt key and then press the underlined letter of the desired option.

Measurement Boxes

Some options in a dialog box contain measurements or amounts you can increase or decrease. These options are generally located in a ***measurement box***. For example, the Word Insert Table dialog box shown in Figure G.6 contains the *Number of columns* and *Number of rows* measurement boxes. To increase a number in a measurement box, position the tip of the arrow pointer on the up-pointing arrow at the right of the desired option and then click the left mouse button. To decrease the number, click the down-pointing arrow. If you are using the keyboard, press and hold down Alt + the underlined letter of the desired option and then press the Up Arrow key to increase the number or the Down Arrow key to decrease the number.

Command Buttons

The buttons at the bottom of the Excel Find and Replace dialog box shown in Figure G.5 are called ***command buttons***. Use a command button to execute or cancel a command. Some command buttons display with an ellipsis (...), which means another dialog box will open if you click that button. To choose a command button with the mouse, position the arrow pointer on the desired button and then click the left mouse button. To choose a command button with the keyboard, press the Tab key until the desired command button is surrounded by a marquee and then press the Enter key.

Figure G.5 Excel Find and Replace Dialog Box

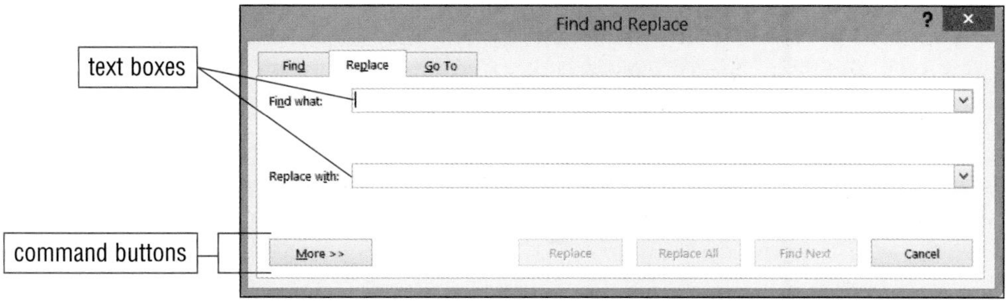

Choosing Commands with Keyboard Shortcuts

Applications in the Office suite offer a variety of keyboard shortcuts you can use to execute specific commands. Keyboard shortcuts generally require two or more keys. For example, the keyboard shortcut to display the Open dialog box in an application is Ctrl + F12. To use this keyboard shortcut, hold down the Ctrl key, press the F12 function on the keyboard, and then release the Ctrl key. For a list of keyboard shortcuts, refer to the Help files.

Choosing Commands with Shortcut Menus

The software programs in the Office suite include shortcut menus that contain commands related to different items. To display a shortcut menu, position the mouse pointer over the item for which you want to view more options, and then click the right mouse button or press Shift + F10. The shortcut menu will appear wherever the insertion point is positioned. For example, if the insertion point is positioned in a paragraph of text in a Word document, clicking the right mouse button or pressing Shift + F10 will cause the shortcut menu shown in Figure G.7 to display in the document screen (along with the Mini toolbar).

To select an option from a shortcut menu with the mouse, click the desired option. If you are using the keyboard, press the Up or Down Arrow key until the desired option is selected and then press the Enter key. To close a shortcut menu without choosing an option, click anywhere outside the shortcut menu or press the Esc key.

Figure G.6 Word Insert Table Dialog Box

Insert Table
Table size
Number of columns: 5
Number of rows: 2
AutoFit behavior
Fixed column width: Auto
AutoFit to contents
AutoFit to window
Remember dimensions for new tables
OK
Cancel
option buttons

Figure G.7 Word Shortcut Menu

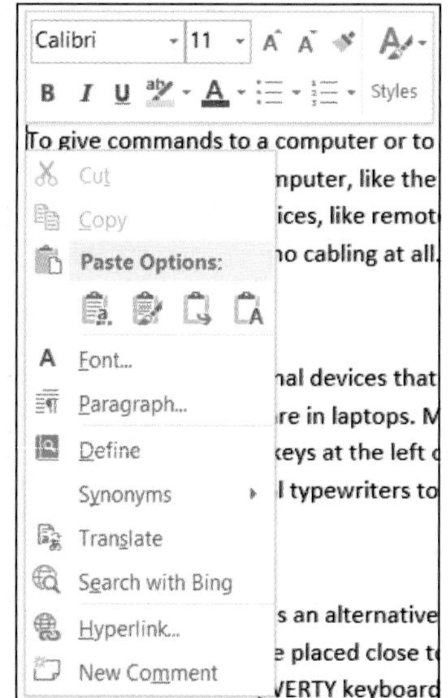

Working with Multiple Programs

As you learn the various programs in the Microsoft Office suite, you will notice many similarities between them. For example, the steps to save, close, and print are virtually the same whether you are working in Word, Excel, or PowerPoint. This consistency between programs greatly enhances a user's ability to transfer knowledge learned in one program to another within the suite. Another benefit to using Microsoft Office is the ability to have more than one program open at the same time and to integrate content from one program with another. For example, you can open Word and create a document, open Excel and create a spreadsheet, and then copy the Excel spreadsheet into Word.

When you open a program, a button containing an icon representing the program displays on the Taskbar. If you open another program, a button containing an icon representing that program displays to the right of the first program button on the Taskbar. Figure G.8 on the next page, shows the Taskbar with Word, Excel, Access, and PowerPoint open. To move from one program to another, click the Taskbar button representing the desired program.

Figure G.8 Taskbar with Word, Excel, Access, and PowerPoint Open

Customizing Settings

Before beginning computer projects in this textbook, you may need to customize your monitor's settings and turn on the display of file extensions. Projects in the chapters in this textbook assume that the monitor display is set at 1600 x 900 pixels and that the display of file extensions is turned on.

Before you begin learning the applications in the Microsoft Office 2013 suite, take a moment to check the display settings on the computer you are using. Your monitor's display settings are important because the ribbon in the Microsoft Office suite adjusts to the screen resolution setting of your computer monitor. A computer monitor set at a high resolution will have the ability to show more buttons in the ribbon than will a monitor set to a low resolution. The illustrations in this textbook were created with a screen resolution display set at 1600 × 900 pixels. In Figure G.9 on the next page, the Word ribbon is shown three ways: at a lower screen resolution (1366 × 768 pixels), at the screen resolution featured throughout this textbook, and at a higher screen resolution (1920 × 1080 pixels). Note the variances in the ribbon in all three examples. If possible, set your display to 1600 × 900 pixels to match the illustrations you will see in this textbook.

Figure G.9 Monitor Resolution

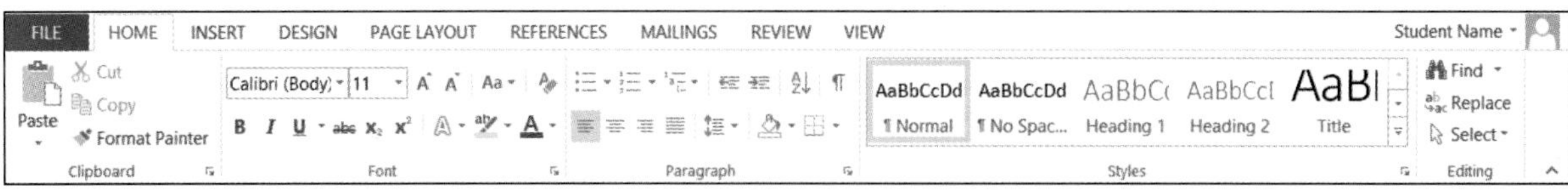

1366 × 768 screen resolution

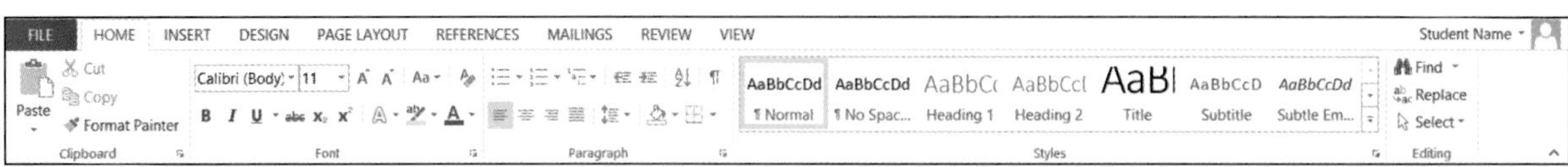

1600 × 900 screen resolution

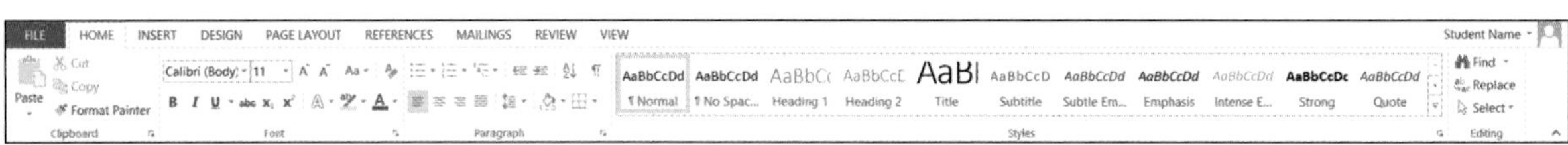

1920 × 1080 screen resolution

Project 1 Setting Monitor Display to 1600 by 900

1. At the Windows desktop, right-click a blank area of the screen.
2. At the shortcut menu, click the *Screen resolution* option.
3. At the Screen Resolution window, click the *Resolution* option box. (This displays a slider bar. Your slider bar may display differently than what you see in the image at the right.)
4. Drag the button on the slider bar until *1600 × 900* displays to the right of the slider bar.
5. Click in the Screen Resolution window to remove the slider bar.
6. Click the Apply button.
7. Click the Keep Changes button.
8. Click the OK button.

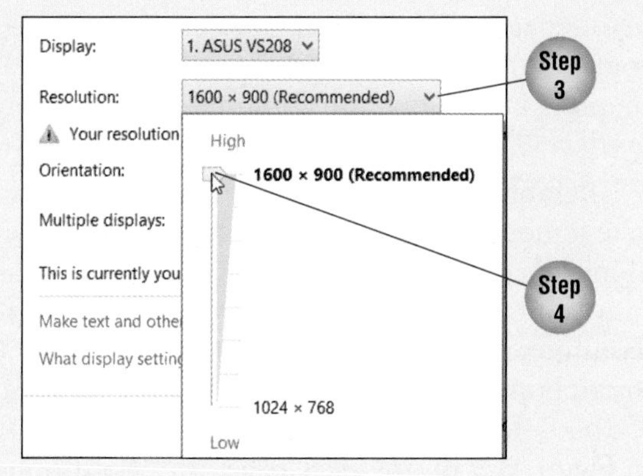

Project 2 Displaying File Extensions

1. At the Windows desktop, position the mouse pointer in the lower left corner of the Taskbar until the Start screen thumbnail displays and then click the right mouse button.
2. At the pop-up list, click the *File Explorer* option.
3. At the Computer window, click the View tab on the ribbon and then click the *File name extensions* check box in the Show/hide group to insert a check mark.
4. Close the Computer window.

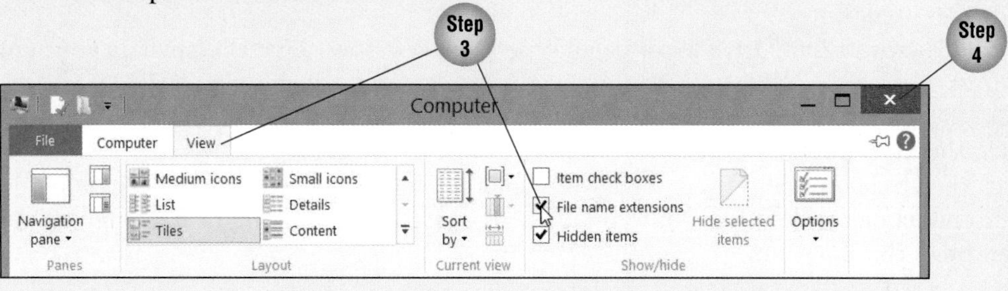

Completing Computer Projects

Some projects in this textbook require that you open an existing file. Project files are saved on the Student Resources CD in individual chapter folders. Before beginning a chapter, copy the necessary folder from the CD to your storage medium (such as a USB flash drive or your OneDrive) using the Computer window. To maximize storage capacity, delete previous chapter folders before copying a new chapter folder onto your storage medium.

Project 3 Copying a Folder from the Student Resources CD to a USB Flash Drive

1. Insert the CD that accompanies this textbook into your computer's CD/DVD drive.
2. Insert your USB flash drive into an available USB port.
3. At the Windows Start screen, click the Desktop tile.
4. Open File Explorer by clicking the File Explorer button on the Taskbar.
5. Click *Computer* in the Navigation pane at the left side of the File Explorer window.
6. Double-click the CD/DVD drive that displays with the name *BM13StudentResources* preceded by the drive letter.
7. Double-click ***StudentDataFiles*** in the Content pane.
8. Double-click the desired program folder name (and level number, if appropriate) in the Content pane.
9. Click once on the desired chapter (or unit performance assessment) folder name to select it.
10. Click the Home tab and then click the Copy button in the Clipboard group.
11. Click your USB flash drive that displays in the Navigation pane at the left side of the window.
12. Click the Home tab and then click the Paste button in the Clipboard group.
13. Close the File Explorer window by clicking the Close button located in the upper right corner of the window.

Project 4 Copying a Folder from the Student Resources CD to your OneDrive Account

Note: OneDrive is updated periodically, so the steps to create folders and upload files may vary from the steps below.

1. Insert the CD that accompanies this textbook into your computer's CD/DVD drive.
2. At the Windows Start screen, click the Desktop tile.
3. Open Internet Explorer by clicking the Internet Explorer button on the Taskbar.
4. At the Internet Explorer home page, click in the Address bar, type **www.onedrive.com**, and then press Enter.
5. At the Microsoft OneDrive login page, type your Windows Live ID (such as your email address).
6. Press the Tab key, type your password, and then press Enter.
7. Click the Documents tile in your OneDrive.
8. Click the Create option on the OneDrive menu bar and then click *Folder* at the drop-down list.
9. Type the name of the folder that you want to copy from the Student Resources CD and then press the Enter key.
10. Click the folder tile you created in the previous step.
11. Click the Upload option on the menu bar.
12. Click the CD/DVD drive that displays in the Navigation pane at the left side of the Choose File to Upload dialog box.
13. Open the chapter folder on the CD that contains the required student data files.
14. Select all of the files in the folder by pressing Ctrl + A and then click the Open button.

Project 5 Deleting a Folder

Note: Check with your instructor before deleting a folder.

1. Insert your storage medium (such as a USB flash drive) into your computer's USB port.
2. At the Windows desktop, open File Explorer by right-clicking the Start screen thumbnail and then clicking *File Explorer* at the shortcut menu.
3. Double-click the drive letter for your storage medium (the drive containing your USB flash drive, such as *Removable Disk (F:)*).
4. Click the chapter folder in the Content pane.
5. Click the Home tab and then click the Delete button in the Organize group.
6. At the message asking if you want to delete the folder, click the Yes button.
7. Close the Computer window by clicking the Close button located in the upper right corner of the window.

Using Windows 8

A computer requires an operating system to provide necessary instructions on a multitude of processes including loading programs, managing data, directing the flow of information to peripheral equipment, and displaying information. Windows 8 is an operating system that provides functions of this type (along with much more) in a graphical environment. Windows is referred to as a ***graphical user interface*** (GUI—pronounced *gooey*) that provides a visual display of information with features such as icons (pictures) and buttons. In this introduction, you will learn these basic features of Windows 8:

- Use the Start screen to launch programs
- Use desktop icons and the Taskbar to launch programs and open files or folders
- Organize and manage data, including copying, moving, creating, and deleting files and folders; and create a shortcut
- Explore the Control Panel and personalize the desktop
- Use the Windows Help and Support features
- Use search tools
- Customize monitor settings

Before using the software programs in the Microsoft Office suite, you will need to start the Windows 8 operating system. To do this, turn on the computer. Depending on your computer equipment configuration, you may also need to turn on the monitor and printer. If you are using a computer that is part of a network system or if your computer is set up for multiple users, a screen will display showing the user accounts defined for your computer system. At this screen, click your user account name; if necessary, type your password; and then press the Enter key. The Windows 8 operating system will start and, after a few moments, the Windows 8 Start screen will display as shown in Figure W.1. (Your Windows 8 Start screen may vary from what you see in Figure W.1.)

Exploring the Start Screen and Desktop

When Windows is loaded, the Windows 8 Start screen displays. This screen contains tiles that open various applications. Open an application by clicking an application's tile or display the Windows 8 desktop by clicking the Desktop tile. Click the Desktop tile and the screen displays as shown in Figure W.2. Think of the desktop in Windows as the top of a desk in an office. A businessperson places necessary tools—such as pencils, pens, paper, files, calculator—on the desktop to perform functions. Like the tools that are located on a desk, the Windows 8 desktop contains tools for operating the computer. These tools are logically grouped and placed in dialog boxes or panels that you can display using icons on the desktop. The desktop contains a variety of features for using your computer and applications installed on the computer.

Figure W.1 Windows 8 Start Screen

Figure W.2 Windows 8 Desktop

Recycle Bin icon

Position the mouse pointer here to access the Start screen.

Taskbar

Using Icons

Icons are visual symbols that represent programs, files, or folders. Figure W.2 identifies the Recycle Bin icon on the Windows desktop. The Windows desktop on your computer may contain additional icons. Applications that have been installed on your computer may be represented by an icon on the desktop. Icons that represent files or folders may also display on your desktop. Double-click an icon and the application, file, or folder it represents opens on the desktop.

Using the Taskbar

The bar that displays at the bottom of the desktop (see Figure W.2) is called the ***Taskbar***. The Taskbar, shown in Figure W.3, contains the Start screen area (a spot where you point to access the Start screen), pinned items, a section that displays task buttons representing active tasks, the notification area, and the Show desktop button.

Position the mouse pointer in the lower left corner of the Taskbar to display the Start screen thumbnail. When the Start screen thumbnail displays, click the left mouse button to access the Windows 8 Start screen, shown in Figure W.1. (Your Start screen may look different.) You can also display the Start screen by pressing the Windows key on your keyboard or by pressing Ctrl + Esc. The left side of the Start menu contains tiles you can click to access the most frequently used applications. The name of the active user (the person who is currently logged on) displays in the upper right corner of the Start screen.

To open an application from the Start screen, drag the arrow pointer to the desired tile (referred to as ***pointing***) and then click the left mouse button. When a program is open, a task button representing the program appears on the Taskbar. If multiple programs are open, each program will appear as a task button on the Taskbar (a few specialized tools may not).

Figure W.3 Windows 8 Taskbar

Manipulating Windows

When you open a program, a defined work area known as a ***window*** displays on the screen. A Title bar displays at the top of the window and contains buttons at the right side for minimizing, maximizing, and restoring the size of the window, as well as for closing it. You can open more than one window at a time and the open windows can be cascaded or stacked. Windows 8 contains a Snap feature that causes a window to "stick" to the edge of the screen when the window is moved to the left or right side of the screen. Move a window to the top of the screen and the window is automatically maximized. If you drag down a maximized window, the window is automatically restored down (returned to its previous smaller size).

In addition to moving and sizing a window, you can change the display of all open windows. To do this, position the mouse pointer on the Taskbar and then click the right mouse button. At the pop-up menu that displays, you can choose to cascade all open windows, stack all open windows, or display all open windows side by side.

Project 1 Opening Programs, Switching between Programs, and Manipulating Windows

1. Open Windows 8. (To do this, turn on the computer and, if necessary, turn on the monitor and/or printer. If you are using a computer that is part of a network system or if your computer is set up for multiple users, you may need to click your user account name, type your password, and then press the Enter key. Check with your instructor to determine if you need to complete any additional steps.)
2. When the Windows 8 Start screen displays, open Microsoft Word by positioning the mouse pointer on the *Word 2013* tile and then clicking the left mouse button. (You may need to scroll to the right to display the Word 2013 tile.)
3. When the Microsoft Word program is open, notice that a task button representing Word displays on the Taskbar.
4. Open Microsoft Excel by completing the following steps:
   a. Position the arrow pointer in the lower left corner of the Taskbar until the Start screen thumbnail displays and then click the left mouse button.
   b. At the Start screen, position the mouse pointer on the *Excel 2013* tile and then click the left mouse button.
5. When the Microsoft Excel program is open, notice that a task button representing Excel displays on the Taskbar to the right of the task button representing Word.
6. Switch to the Word program by clicking the Word task button on the Taskbar.
7. Switch to the Excel program by clicking the Excel task button on the Taskbar.
8. Restore down the Excel window by clicking the Restore Down button that displays immediately left of the Close button in the upper right corner of the screen. (This reduces the Excel window so it displays along the bottom half of the screen.)
9. Restore down the Word window by clicking the Restore Down button located immediately left of the Close button in the upper right corner of the screen.

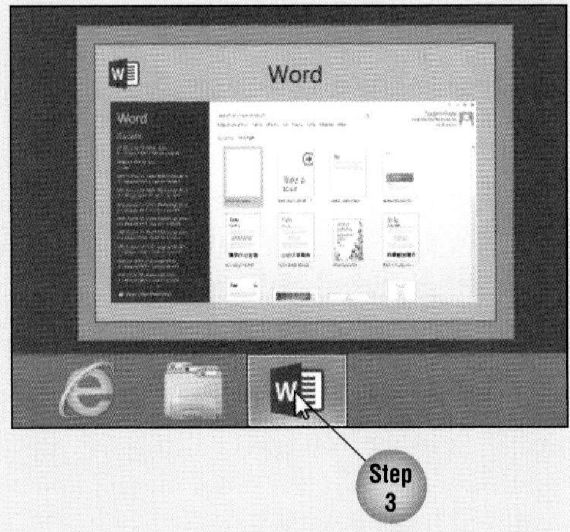

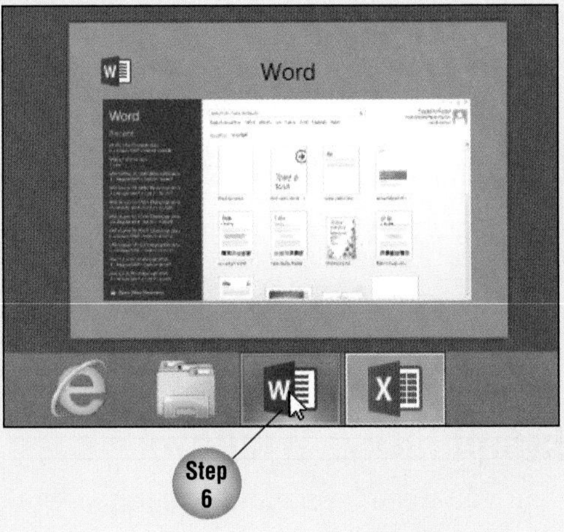

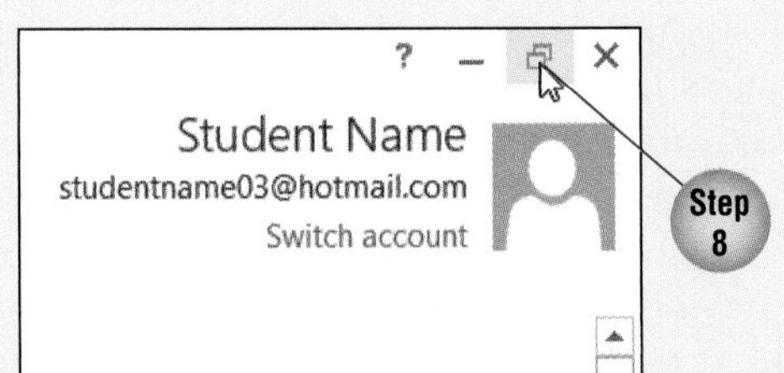

10. Position the mouse pointer at the top of the Word window screen, hold down the left mouse button, drag to the left side of the screen until an outline of the window displays in the left half of the screen, and then release the mouse button. (This "sticks" the window to the left side of the screen.)
11. Position the mouse pointer at the top of the Excel window screen, hold down the left mouse button, drag to the right until an outline of the window displays in the right half of the screen, and then release the mouse button.
12. Minimize the Excel window by clicking the Minimize button that displays in the upper right corner of the Excel window screen.

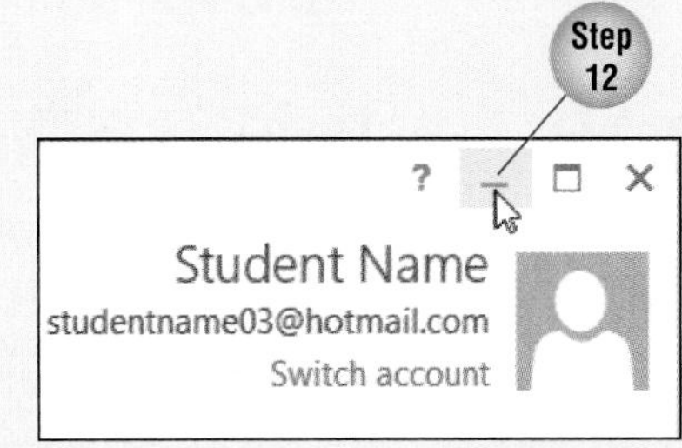

13. Hover your mouse over the Excel button on the Taskbar and then click the Excel window thumbnail that displays. (This displays the Excel window at the right side of the screen.)
14. Cascade the Word and Excel windows by positioning the arrow pointer in an empty area of the Taskbar, clicking the right mouse button, and then clicking *Cascade windows* at the shortcut menu.

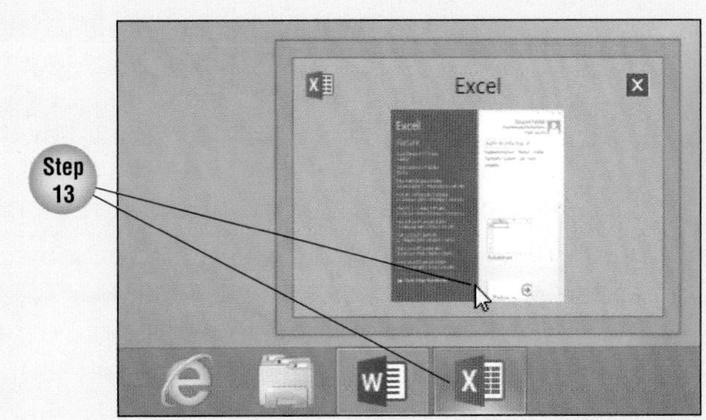

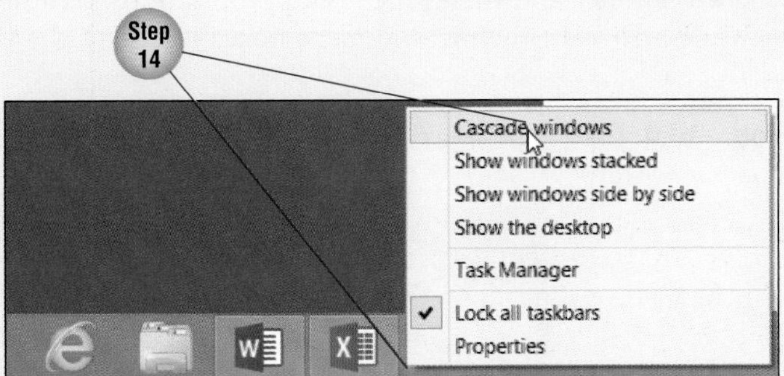

15. After viewing the windows cascaded, display them stacked by right-clicking an empty area of the Taskbar and then clicking *Show windows stacked* at the shortcut menu.
16. Display the desktop by right-clicking an empty area of the Taskbar and then clicking *Show the desktop* at the shortcut menu.
17. Display the windows stacked by right-clicking an empty area of the Taskbar and then clicking *Show open windows* at the shortcut menu.
18. Position the mouse pointer at the top of the Word window screen, hold down the left mouse button, drag the window to the top of the screen, and then release the mouse button. This maximizes the Word window so it fills the screen.
19. Close the Word window by clicking the Close button located in the upper right corner of the window.
20. At the Excel window, click the Maximize button located immediately left of the Close button in the upper right corner of the Excel window.
21. Close the Excel window by clicking the Close button located in the upper right corner of the window.

Using the Pinned Area

The icons that display immediately right of the Start screen area represent ***pinned applications***. Clicking an icon opens the application associated with the icon. Click the first icon to open the Internet Explorer web browser and click the second icon to open a File Explorer window containing Libraries.

Exploring the Notification Area

The notification area is located at the right side of the Taskbar and contains icons that show the status of certain system functions such as a network connection or battery power. The notification area contains icons for managing certain programs and Windows 8 features, as well as the system clock and date. Click the time or date in the notification area and a window displays with a clock and a calendar of the current month. Click the Change date and time settings hyperlink that displays at the bottom of the window and the Date and Time dialog box displays. To change the date and/or time, click the Change date and time button and the Date and Time Settings dialog box displays, similar to the dialog box shown in Figure W.4. (If a dialog box displays telling you that Windows needs your permission to continue, click the Continue button.)

Change the month and year by clicking the left-pointing or right-pointing arrow at the top of the calendar. Click the left-pointing arrow to display the previous month(s) and click the right-pointing arrow to display the next month(s).

To change the day, click the desired day in the monthly calendar that displays in the dialog box. To change the time, double-click either the hour, minute, or seconds number and then type the appropriate time or use the up- and down-pointing arrows in the measurement boxes to adjust the time.

Figure W.4 Date and Time Settings Dialog Box

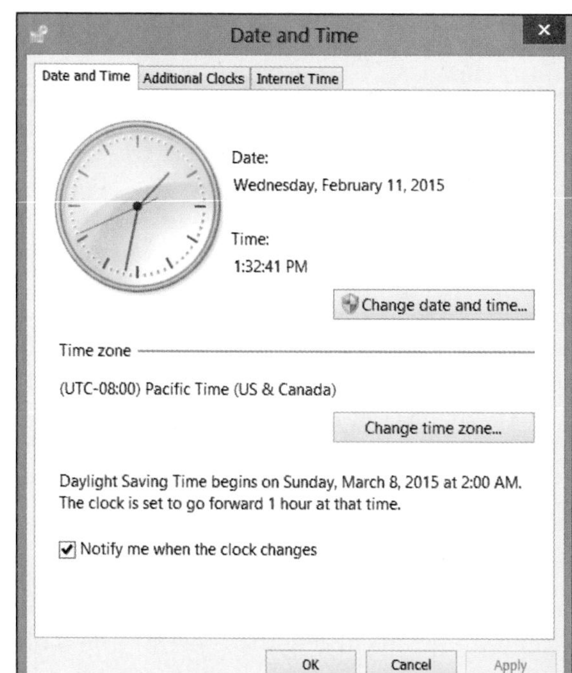

Some applications, when installed, will add an icon to the notification area of the Taskbar. To determine the name of an icon, position the mouse pointer on the icon and, after approximately one second, its label will display. If more icons have been inserted in the notification area than can be viewed at one time, an up-pointing arrow button displays at the left side of the notification area. Click this up-pointing arrow to display the remaining icons.

Setting Taskbar Properties

Customize the Taskbar with options at the Taskbar shortcut menu. Display this menu by right-clicking in an empty portion of the Taskbar. The Taskbar shortcut menu contains options for turning on or off the display of specific toolbars, specifying the display of multiple windows, displaying the Start Task Manager dialog box, locking or unlocking the Taskbar, and displaying the Taskbar Properties dialog box.

With options in the Taskbar Properties dialog box, shown in Figure W.5, you can change settings for the Taskbar. Display this dialog box by right-clicking an empty area on the Taskbar and then clicking *Properties* at the shortcut menu.

Each Taskbar property is controlled by a check box or an option box. If a property's check box contains a check mark, that property is active. Click the check box to remove the check mark and make the option inactive. If an option is inactive, clicking the check box will insert a check mark and turn on the option (make it active). A property option box displays the name of the currently active option. Click the option box to select a different option from the drop-down list.

Figure W.5 Taskbar Properties Dialog Box

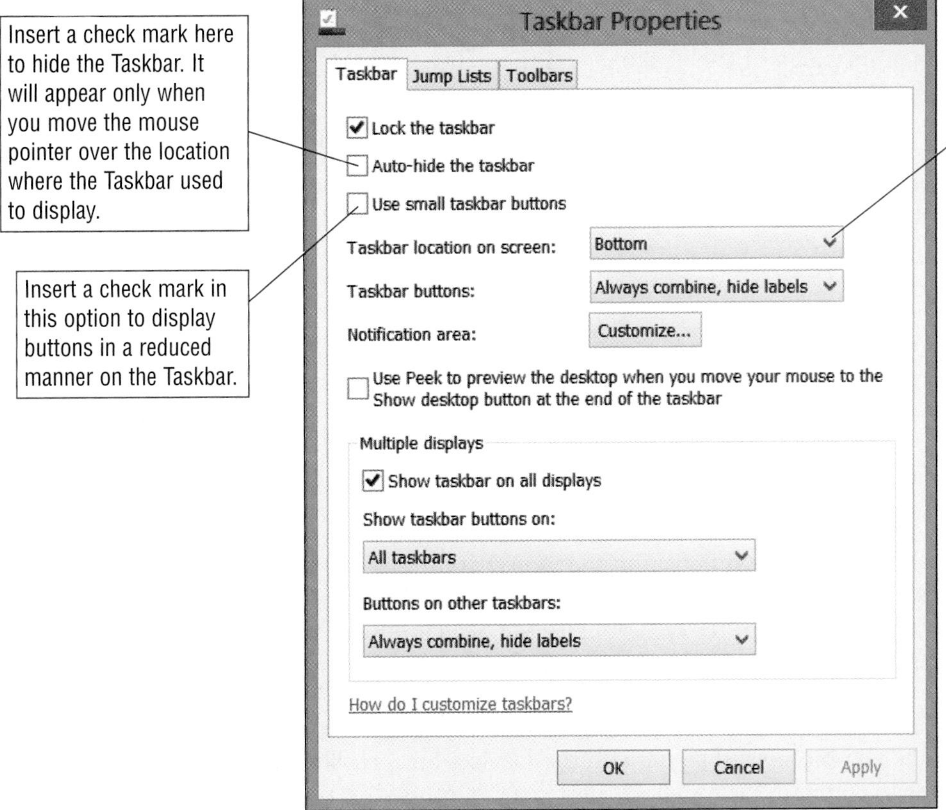

Project 2 Changing Taskbar Properties

1. Make sure the Windows 8 desktop displays.
2. Change the Taskbar properties by completing the following steps:
   a. Position the arrow pointer in an empty area of the Taskbar and then click the right mouse button.
   b. At the shortcut menu that displays, click *Properties*.
   c. At the Taskbar Properties dialog box, click the *Auto-hide the taskbar* check box to insert a check mark.
   d. Click the *Use small taskbar buttons* check box to insert a check mark.
   e. Click the option box (contains the word *Bottom*) that displays at the right side of the *Taskbar location on screen:* option and then click *Right* at the drop-down list.
   f. Click OK to close the dialog box.

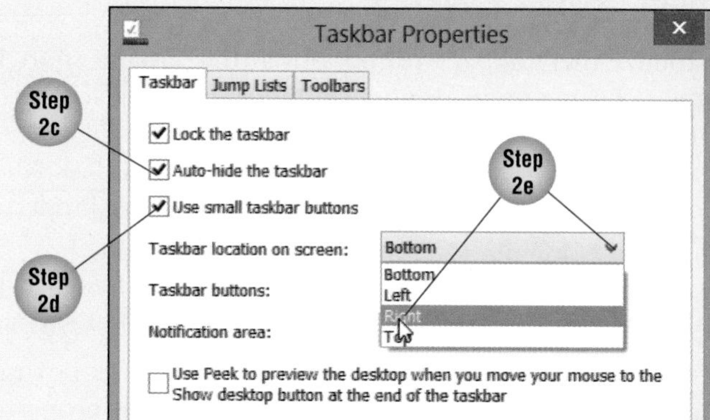

3. Since the *Auto-hide the taskbar* check box contains a check mark, the Taskbar does not display. Display the Taskbar by moving the mouse pointer to the right side of the screen. Notice that the buttons on the Taskbar are smaller than they were before.
4. Return to the default Taskbar properties by completing the following steps:
   a. Move the mouse pointer to the right side of the screen to display the Taskbar.
   b. Right-click an empty area of the Taskbar and then click *Properties* at the shortcut menu.
   c. Click the *Auto-hide the taskbar* check box to remove the check mark.
   d. Click the *Use small taskbar buttons* check box to remove the check mark.
   e. Click the *Taskbar location on screen* option box (displays with the word *Right*) and then click *Bottom* at the drop-down list.
   f. Click OK to close the dialog box.

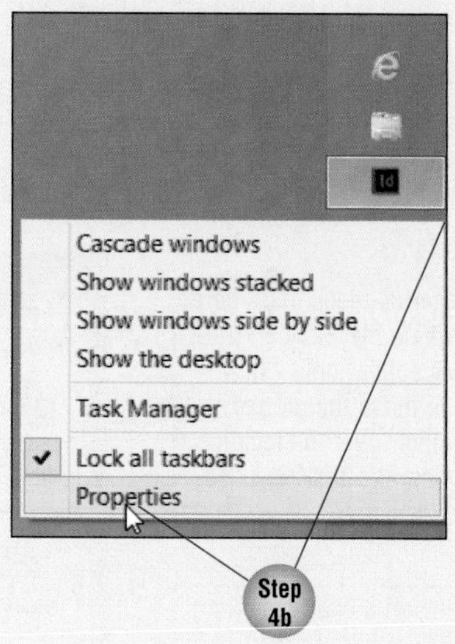

Using the Charm Bar

Windows 8 contains a new feature called the ***Charm bar***. The Charm bar is a bar that displays when you position the mouse pointer in the upper or lower right corner of the screen. Use the buttons on the Charm bar, shown in Figure W.6, to access certain features or tools. Use the Search button to search the computer for applications, files, folders and settings. With the Share button, you can share information with others via email or social networks. Clicking the Start button displays the Windows 8 Start screen. Access settings for various devices such as printers, monitors, and so on with the Devices button. The Settings button gives you access to common computer settings and is also used to power down the computer.

Figure W.6 Charm Bar

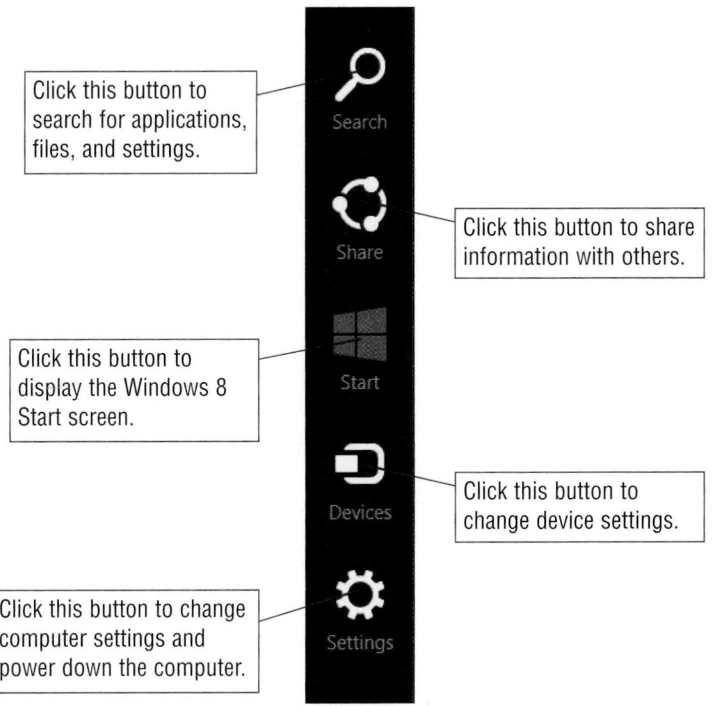

Click this button to search for applications, files, and settings.
Search
Share
Click this button to share information with others.
Click this button to display the Windows 8 Start screen.
Start
Devices
Click this button to change device settings.
Click this button to change computer settings and power down the computer.
Settings

Powering Down the Computer

If you want to shut down Windows, first close any open programs and then display the Charm bar. Click the Settings button on the Charm bar, click the Power tile, and then click the *Shut down* option. The Power tile also contains options for restarting the computer or putting the computer to sleep. Restarting the computer may be useful when installing new applications or if Windows 8 stops working properly. In sleep mode, Windows saves files and information about applications and then powers down the computer to a low-power state. To "wake up" the computer, press the computer's power button.

In a multi-user environment, you can sign out of or lock your account so that no one can tamper with your work. To access these features, display the Windows 8 Start screen and then click your user account tile in the upper right corner. This displays a shortcut menu with three options. The *Lock* option locks the computer, which means that it is still powered on but requires a user password in order to access any applications or files that were previously opened. (To unlock the computer, click the icon on the login screen representing your account, type your password, and then press Enter.) Use the *Sign out* option to sign out of your user account while still keeping the computer turned on so that others may log on to it. Click the *Change account picture* option if you want to change the picture associated with your user account.

Managing Files and Folders

As you begin working with programs in Windows 8, you will create files in which data (information) is saved. A file might be a Word document, an Excel workbook, an Access database, or a PowerPoint presentation. As you begin creating files, consider creating folders in which to store these files. Complete file management tasks such as creating a folder or moving a file at the Computer window. To display the Computer window, shown in Figure W.7, position your mouse pointer in the lower left corner of the screen to display the Start screen thumbnail, click the right mouse button, and then click *File Explorer* at the shortcut menu. The various components of the Computer window are identified in Figure W.7.

In the Content pane of the Computer window, icons display representing each hard disk drive and removable storage medium (such as a CD, DVD, or USB device) connected to your computer. Next to each storage device icon, Windows displays the amount of storage space available as well as a bar with the amount of used space shaded with color. This visual cue allows you to see at a glance the amount of space available relative to the capacity of the device. Double-click a device icon in the Content pane to change the display to show the contents stored on the device. Display contents from another device or folder using the Navigation pane or the Address bar on the Computer window.

Figure W.7 Computer Window

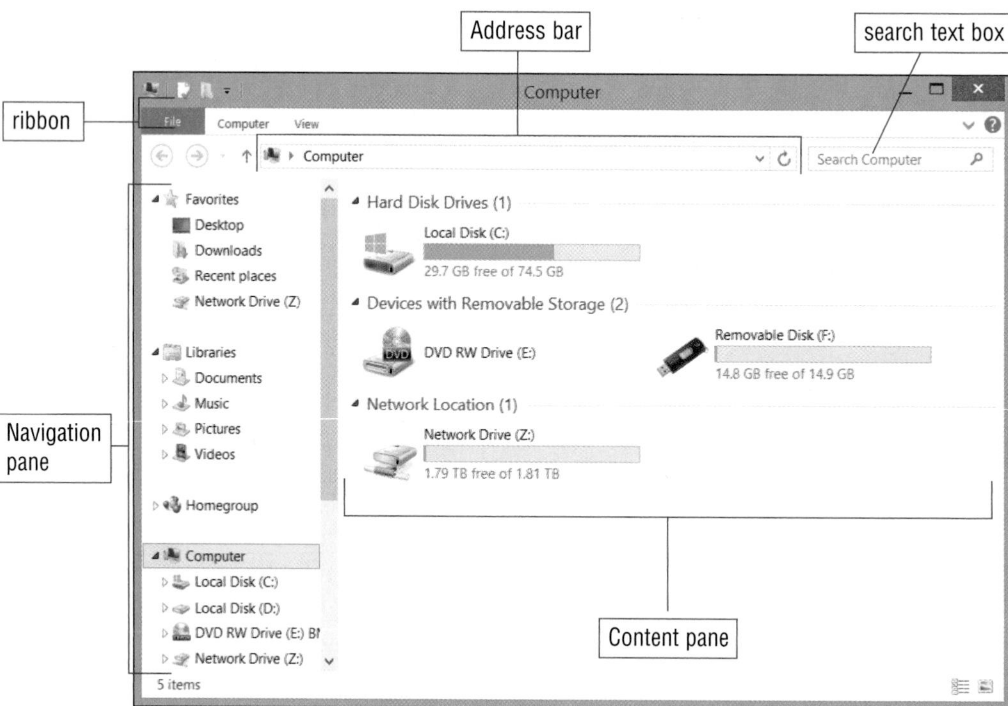

Copying, Moving, and Deleting Files and Folders

File and folder management activities include copying and moving files and folders from one folder or drive to another, as well as deleting files and folders. The Computer window offers a variety of methods for performing these actions. This section will provide you with steps for copying, moving, and deleting files and folders using options from the Home tab (shown in Figure W.8) and the shortcut menu (shown in Figure W.9).

To copy a file to another folder or drive, first display the file in the Content pane. If the file is located in the Documents folder, click the *Documents* folder in the *Libraries* section of the Navigation pane and then, in the Content pane, click the name of the file you want to copy. Click the Home tab on the ribbon and then click the Copy button in the Clipboard group. Use the Navigation pane to navigate to the location where you want to paste the file. Click the Home tab and then click the Paste button in the Clipboard group. Complete similar steps to copy and paste a folder to another location.

If the desired file is located on a storage medium such as a CD, DVD, or USB device, double-click the device in the section of the Content pane labeled *Devices with Removable Storage*. (Each removable device is assigned an alphabetic drive letter by Windows, usually starting at E or F and continuing through the alphabet depending on the number of removable devices that are currently in use.) After double-clicking the storage medium in the Content pane, navigate to the desired folder and then click the file to select it. Click the Home tab on the ribbon and then click the Copy button in the Clipboard group. Navigate to the desired folder, click the Home tab, and then click the Paste button in the Clipboard group.

To move a file, click the desired file in the Content pane, click the Home tab on the ribbon, and then click the Cut button in the Clipboard group. Navigate to the desired location, click the Home tab, and then click the Paste button in the Clipboard group.

To delete a file or folder, click the file or folder in the Content pane in the Computer window. Click the Home tab and then click the Delete button in the Organize group. At the message asking if you want to move the file or folder to the Recycle Bin, click the Yes button.

Figure W.8 File Explorer Home tab

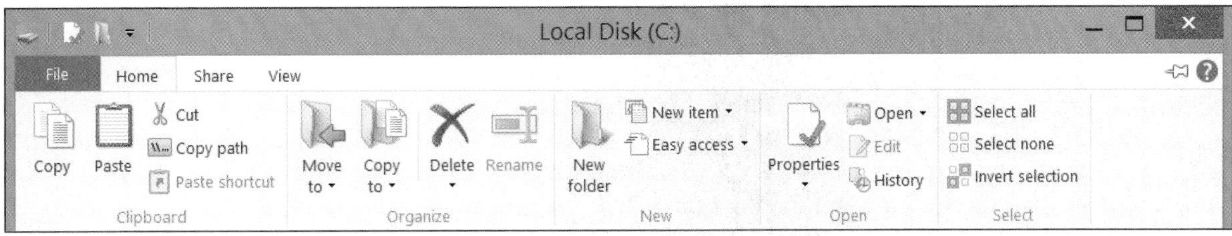

Figure W.9 Shortcut Menu

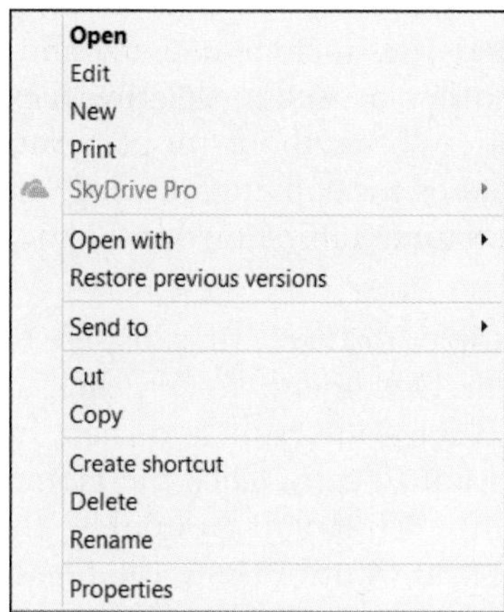

Project 3 Copying a File and Folder and Deleting a File

1. Insert the CD that accompanies this textbook into the appropriate drive.
2. Insert your storage medium (such as a USB flash drive) into the appropriate drive.
3. At the Windows 8 desktop, position the mouse pointer in the lower left corner of the Taskbar to display the Start screen thumbnail, click the right mouse button, and then click *File Explorer* at the shortcut menu.
4. Copy a file from the CD that accompanies this textbook to the drive containing your storage medium by completing the following steps:
   a. In the Content pane, double-click the drive into which you inserted the CD that accompanies this textbook.
   b. Double-click the *StudentDataFiles* folder in the Content pane.
   c. Double-click the *Windows8* folder in the Content pane.
   d. Click ***WordDocument01.docx*** in the Content pane.
   e. Click the Home tab and then click *Copy* in the Clipboard group.

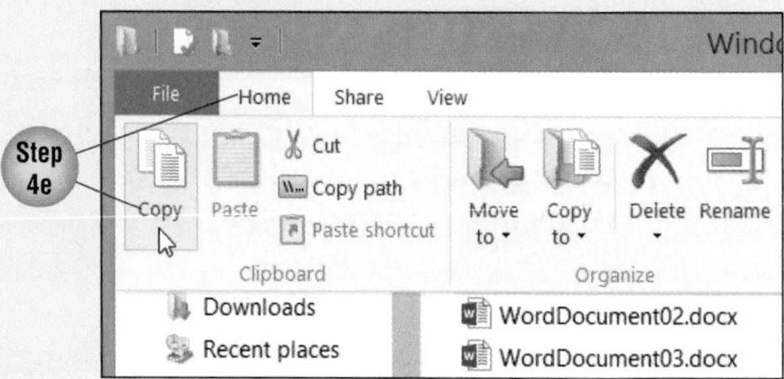
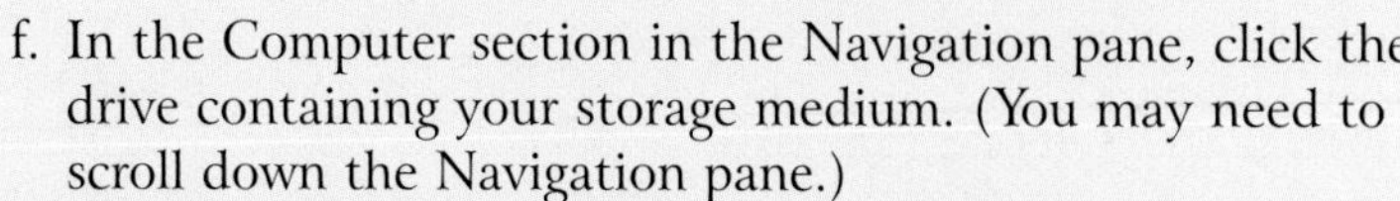

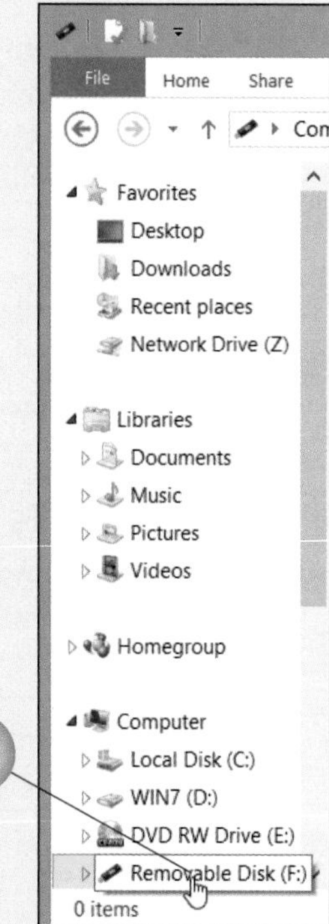

   f. In the Computer section in the Navigation pane, click the drive containing your storage medium. (You may need to scroll down the Navigation pane.)
   g. Click the Home tab and then click the Paste button in the Clipboard group.
5. Delete ***WordDocument01.docx*** from your storage medium by completing the following steps:
   a. Make sure the contents of your storage medium display in the Content pane in the Computer window.

b. Click ***WordDocument01.docx*** in the Content pane to select it.
c. Click the Home tab and then click the Delete button in the Organize group.
d. At the message asking if you want to permanently delete the file, click the Yes button.

6. Copy the Windows8 folder from the CD to your storage medium by completing the following steps:
   a. With the Computer window open, click the drive in the *Computer* section in the Navigation pane that contains the CD that accompanies this book.
   b. Double-click *StudentDataFiles* in the Content pane.
   c. Click the *Windows8* folder in the Content pane.
   d. Click the Home tab and then click the Copy button in the Clipboard group.
   e. In the *Computer* section in the Navigation pane, click the drive containing your storage medium.
   f. Click the Home tab and then click the Paste button in the Clipboard group.
7. Close the Computer window by clicking the Close button located in the upper right corner of the window.

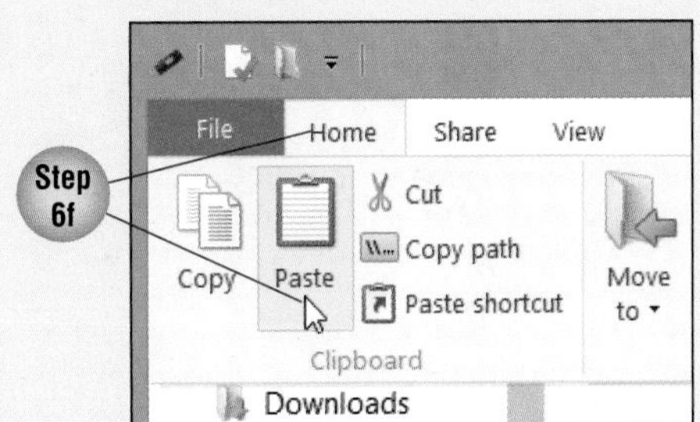

In addition to options on the Home tab, you can use options in a shortcut menu to copy, move, and delete files or folders. To use a shortcut menu, select the desired file(s) or folder(s), position the mouse pointer on the selected item, and then click the right mouse button. At the shortcut menu that displays, click the desired option, such as *Copy*, *Cut*, or *Delete*.

Selecting Files and Folders

You can move, copy, or delete more than one file or folder at the same time. Before moving, copying, or deleting files or folders, select the desired files or folders. To make selecting easier, consider displaying the files in the Content pane in a list or detailed list format. To change the display, click the View tab on the ribbon and then click *List* or *Details* in the Layout group.

To select adjacent files or folders, click the first file or folder, hold down the Shift key, and then click the last file or folder. To select nonadjacent files or folders, click the first file or folder, hold down the Ctrl key, and then click the other files or folders you wish to select.

Project 4 Copying and Deleting Files

1. At the Windows 8 desktop, position the mouse pointer in the lower left corner of the Taskbar to display the Start screen thumbnail, click the right mouse button, and then click *File Explorer* at the shortcut menu.
2. Copy files from the CD that accompanies this textbook to the drive containing your storage medium by completing the following steps:
   a. Make sure the CD that accompanies this textbook and your storage medium are inserted in the appropriate drives.
   b. Double-click the CD drive in the Content pane in the Computer window.

c. Double-click the *StudentDataFiles* folder in the Content pane.
d. Double-click the *Windows8* folder in the Content pane.
e. Change the display to List by clicking the View tab and then clicking *List* in the Layout group list box.

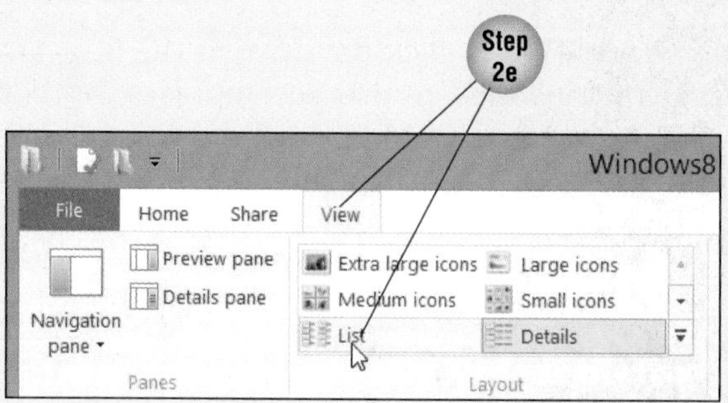

f. Click ***WordDocument01.docx*** in the Content pane.
g. Hold down the Shift key, click ***WordDocument05.docx***, and then release the Shift key. (This selects five documents.)

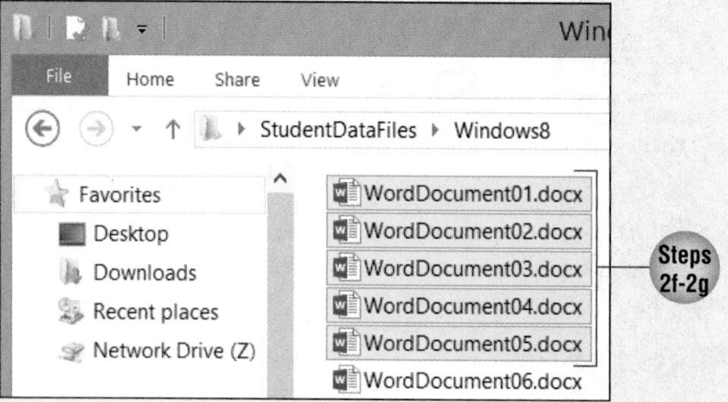

h. Click the Home tab and then click the Copy button in the Clipboard group.
i. In the *Computer* section of the Navigation pane, click the drive containing your storage medium.
j. Click the Home tab and then click the Paste button in the Clipboard group.

3. Delete the files you just copied to your storage medium by completing the following steps:
   a. Change the display by clicking the View tab and then clicking *List* in the Layout group.
   b. Click ***WordDocument01.docx*** in the Content pane.
   c. Hold down the Shift key, click ***WordDocument05.docx***, and then release the Shift key.
   d. Position the mouse pointer on any selected file, click the right mouse button, and then click *Delete* at the shortcut menu.
   e. At the message asking if you are sure you want to permanently delete the files, click Yes.
4. Close the Computer window by clicking the Close button located in the upper right corner of the window.

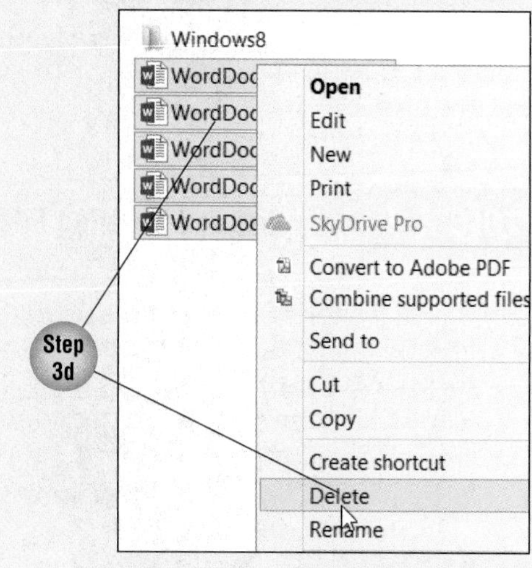

Manipulating and Creating Folders

As you begin working with and creating multiple files, consider creating folders in which you can logically group and store the files. To create a folder, display the Computer window and then display the drive or folder where you want to create the folder in the Content pane. To create the new folder, click the New folder button in the New group on the Home tab; click the New folder button on the Quick Access toolbar; or click in a blank area in the Content pane, click the right mouse button, point to *New* in the shortcut menu, and then click *Folder* at the side menu. Any of the three methods inserts a folder icon in the Content pane and names the folder *New folder*. Type the desired name for the new folder and then press Enter.

Project 5 Creating a New Folder

1. At the Windows 8 desktop, open the Computer window.
2. Create a new folder by completing the following steps:
   a. In the Content pane, double-click the drive that contains your storage medium.
   b. Double-click the *Windows8* folder in the Content pane. (This opens the folder.)
   c. Click the View tab and then click *List* in the Layout group.
   d. Click the Home tab and then click the New folder button in the New group.
   e. Type **SpellCheckFiles** and then press Enter. (This changes the name from *New folder* to *SpellCheckFiles*.)

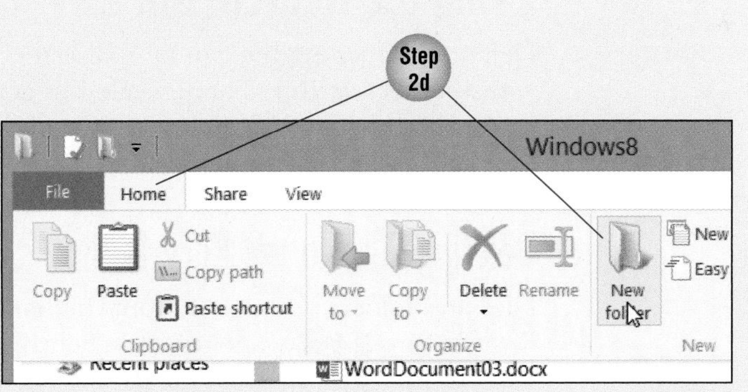

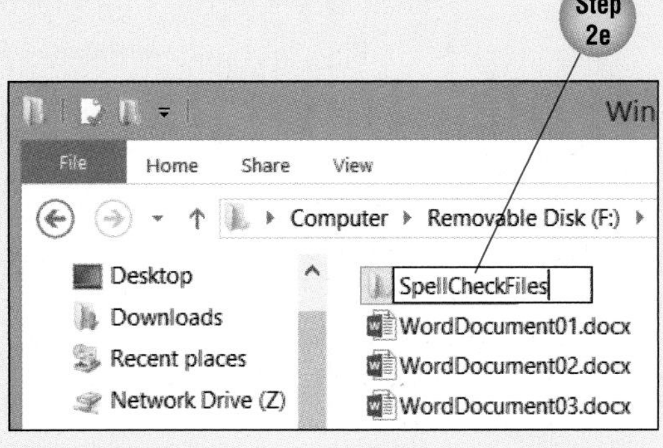

3. Copy **WordSpellCheck01.docx**, **WordSpellCheck02.docx**, and **WordSpellCheck03.docx** into the SpellCheckFiles folder you just created by completing the following steps:
   a. Click the View tab and then click *List* in the Layout group. (Skip this step if *List* is already selected.)
   b. Click ***WordSpellCheck01.docx*** in the Content pane.
   c. Hold down the Shift key, click ***WordSpellCheck03.docx***, and then release the Shift key. (This selects three documents.)
   d. Click the Home tab and then click the Copy button in the Clipboard group.
   e. Double-click the *SpellCheckFiles* folder in the Content pane.
   f. Click the Home tab and then click the Paste button in the Clipboard group.

4. Delete the SpellCheckFiles folder and its contents by completing the following steps:
   a. Click the Back button (contains a left-pointing arrow) located at the left side of the Address bar.
   b. With the SpellCheckFiles folder selected in the Content pane, click the Home tab and then click the Delete button in the Organize group.
   c. At the message asking you to confirm the deletion, click Yes.
5. Close the window by clicking the Close button located in the upper right corner of the window.

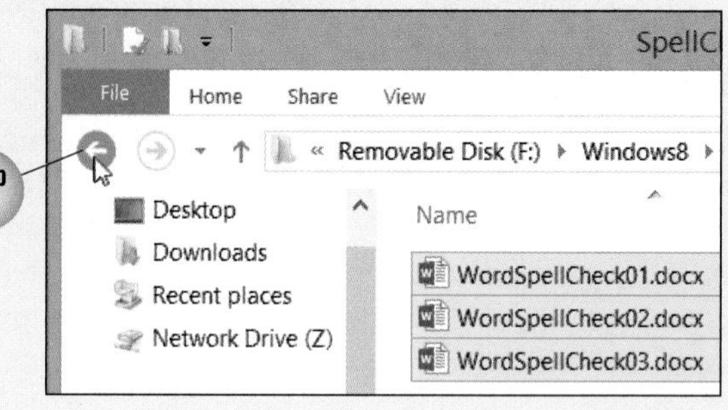

Using the Recycle Bin

Deleting the wrong file can be a disaster, but Windows 8 helps protect your work with the ***Recycle Bin***. The Recycle Bin acts just like an office wastepaper basket; you can "throw away" (delete) unwanted files, but you can also "reach in" to the Recycle Bin and take out (restore) a file if you threw it away by accident.

Deleting Files to the Recycle Bin

Files and folders you delete from the hard drive are sent automatically to the Recycle Bin. If you want to permanently delete files or folders from the hard drive without first sending them to the Recycle Bin, select the desired file(s) or folder(s), right-click one of the selected files or folders, hold down the Shift key, and then click *Delete* at the shortcut menu.

Files and folders deleted from a USB flash drive or disc are deleted permanently. (Recovery programs are available, however, that will help you recover deleted files or folders. If you accidentally delete a file or folder from a USB flash drive or disc, do not do anything more with the USB flash drive or disc until you can run a recovery program.)

You can delete files in the manner described earlier in this section and you can also delete a file by dragging the file icon to the Recycle Bin. To do this, click the desired file in the Content pane in the Computer window, drag the file icon to the Recycle Bin icon on the desktop until the text *Move to Recycle Bin* displays, and then release the mouse button.

Restoring Files from the Recycle Bin

To restore a file from the Recycle Bin, double-click the Recycle Bin icon on the desktop. This opens the Recycle Bin window, shown in Figure W.10. (The contents of the Recycle Bin will vary.) To restore a file, click the file you want restored, click the Recycle Bin Tools Manage tab and then click the Restore the selected items button in the Restore group. This removes the file from the Recycle Bin and returns it to its original location. You can also restore a file by positioning the mouse pointer on the file, clicking the right mouse button, and then clicking *Restore* at the shortcut menu.

Figure W.10 Recycle Bin Window

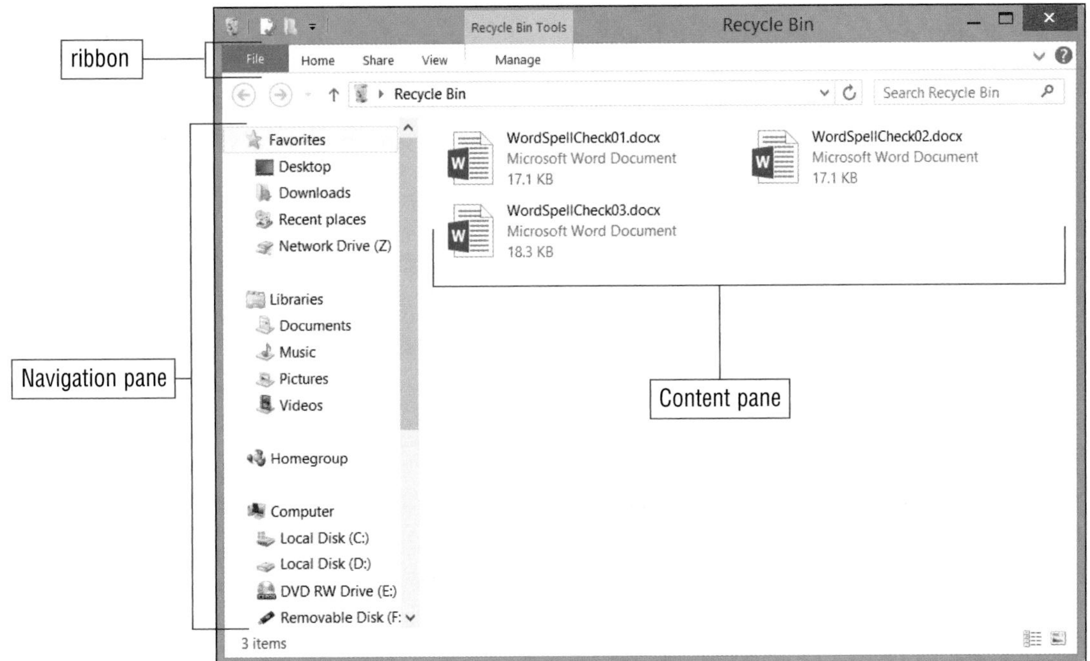

Project 6 Deleting Files to and Restoring Files from the Recycle Bin

Before beginning this project, check with your instructor to determine if you can copy files to the hard drive.

1. At the Windows 8 desktop, open the Computer window.
2. Copy files from your storage medium to the Documents folder on your hard drive by completing the following steps:
   a. In the Content pane, double-click the drive containing your storage medium.
   b. Double-click the *Windows8* folder in the Content pane.
   c. Click the View tab and then click *List* in the Layout group. (Skip this step if *List* is already selected.)
   d. Click ***WordSpellCheck01.docx*** in the Content pane.
   e. Hold down the Shift key, click ***WordSpellCheck03.docx***, and then release the Shift key.
   f. Click the Home tab and then click the Copy button in the Clipboard group.
   g. Click the *Documents* folder in the *Libraries* section of the Navigation pane.
   h. Click the Home tab and then click the Paste button in the Clipboard group.

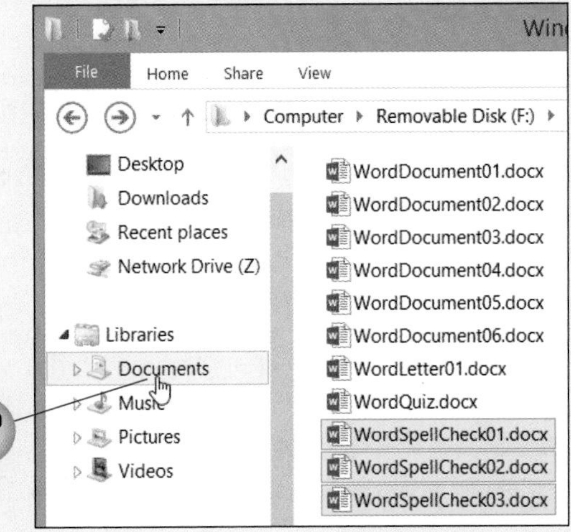

3. With **WordSpellCheck01.docx** through **WordSpellCheck03.docx** selected in the Content pane, click the Home tab and then click the Delete button in the Organize group to delete the files to the Recycle Bin.
4. Close the Computer window.
5. At the Windows 8 desktop, display the contents of the Recycle Bin by double-clicking the Recycle Bin icon.
6. Restore the files you just deleted by completing the following steps:
   a. Select **WordSpellCheck01.docx** through **WordSpellCheck03.docx** in the Recycle Bin Content pane. (If these files are not visible, you will need to scroll down the list of files in the Content pane.)
   b. Click the Recycle Bin Tools Manage tab and then click the Restore the selected items button in the Restore group.

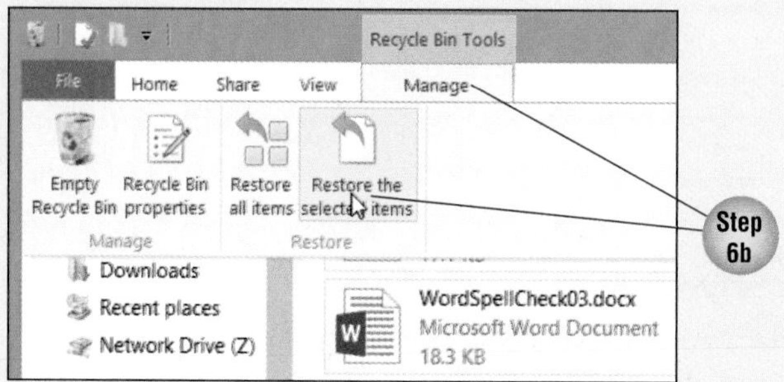

7. Close the Recycle Bin by clicking the Close button located in the upper right corner of the window.
8. Display the Computer window.
9. Click the *Documents* folder in the *Libraries* section of the Navigation pane.
10. Delete the files you restored.
11. Close the Computer window.

Emptying the Recycle Bin

Just like a wastepaper basket, the Recycle Bin can get full. To empty the Recycle Bin, position the arrow pointer on the Recycle Bin icon on the desktop and then click the right mouse button. At the shortcut menu that displays, click the *Empty Recycle Bin* option. At the message asking if you want to permanently delete the items, click Yes. You can also empty the Recycle Bin by displaying the Recycle Bin window and then clicking the Empty Recycle Bin button in the Manage group on the Recycle Bin Tools Manage tab. At the message asking if you want to permanently delete the items, click Yes. To delete a specific file from the Recycle Bin window, click the desired file in the Recycle Bin window, click the Home tab, and then click the Delete button in the Organize group. At the message asking if you want to permanently delete the file, click Yes. When you empty the Recycle Bin, the files cannot be recovered by the Recycle Bin or by Windows 8. If you have to recover a file, you will need to use a file recovery program.

Project 7 Emptying the Recycle Bin

Note: Before beginning this project, check with your instructor to determine if you can delete files/folders from the Recycle Bin.

1. At the Windows 8 desktop, double-click the Recycle Bin icon.
2. At the Recycle Bin window, empty the contents by clicking the Empty Recycle Bin button in the Manage group on the Recycle Bin Tools Manage tab.
3. At the message asking you if you want to permanently delete the items, click Yes.
4. Close the Recycle Bin by clicking the Close button located in the upper right corner of the window.

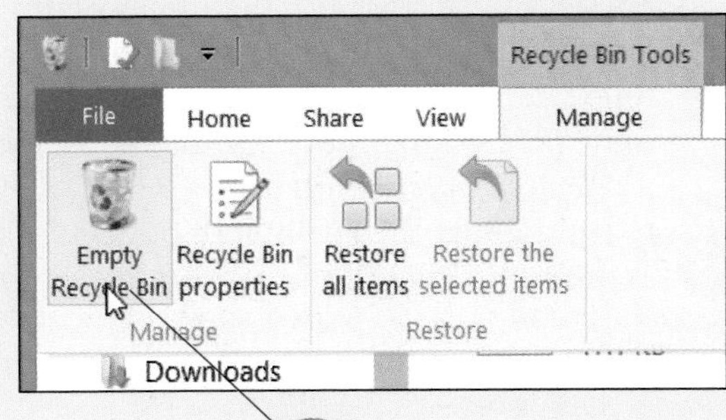

Creating a Shortcut

If you use a file or application on a consistent basis, consider creating a shortcut to the file or application. A ***shortcut*** is a specialized icon that points the operating system to an actual file, folder, or application. If you create a shortcut to a Word document, the shortcut icon is not the actual document but a very small file that contains the path to the document. Double-click the shortcut icon and Windows 8 opens the document in Word.

One method for creating a shortcut is to display the Computer window and then make active the drive or folder where the file is located. Right-click the desired file, point to *Send to*, and then click *Desktop (create shortcut)*. You can easily delete a shortcut icon from the desktop by dragging the shortcut icon to the Recycle Bin icon. This deletes the shortcut icon but does not delete the file to which the shortcut pointed.

Project 8 Creating a Shortcut

1. At the Windows 8 desktop, display the Computer window.
2. Double-click the drive containing your storage medium.
3. Double-click the *Windows8* folder in the Content pane.
4. Change the display of files to a list by clicking the View tab and then clicking *List* in the Layout group. (Skip this step if *List* is already selected.)
5. Create a shortcut to the file named **WordQuiz.docx** by right-clicking ***WordQuiz.docx***, pointing to *Send to*, and then clicking *Desktop (create shortcut)*.
6. Close the Computer window.

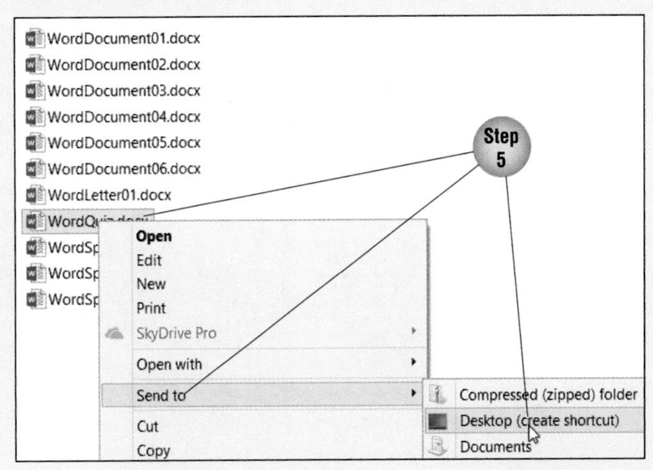

7. Open Word and **WordQuiz.docx** by double-clicking the *WordQuiz.docx* shortcut icon on the desktop.
8. After viewing the file in Word, close Word by clicking the Close button that displays in the upper right corner of the window.
9. Delete the *WordQuiz.docx* shortcut icon by completing the following steps:
   a. At the desktop, position the mouse pointer on the *WordQuiz.docx* shortcut icon.
   b. Hold down the left mouse button, drag the icon on top of the Recycle Bin icon, and then release the mouse button.

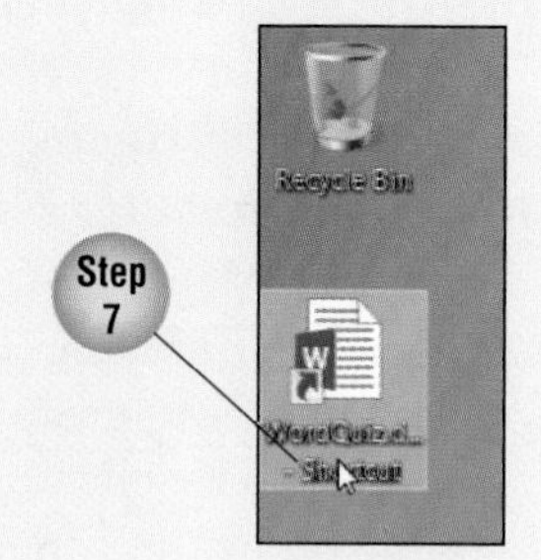

Exploring the Control Panel

The Control Panel, shown in Figure W.11, contains a variety of icons for customizing the appearance and functionality of your computer as well as accessing and changing system settings. Display the Control Panel by right-clicking the Start screen thumbnail and then clicking *Control Panel* at the shortcut menu. The Control Panel organizes settings into categories to make them easier to find. Click a category icon and the Control Panel displays lower-level categories and tasks within each of them.

Hover your mouse over a category icon in the Control Panel and a ScreenTip displays with an explanation of what options are available. For example, if you hover the mouse over the Appearance and Personalization icon, a ScreenTip displays with information about the tasks available in the category, such as changing the appearance of desktop items, applying a theme or screen saver to your computer, or customizing the Taskbar.

If you click a category icon in the Control Panel, the Control Panel displays all of the available subcategories and tasks in the category. Also, the categories display in text form at the left side of the Control Panel. For example, if you click the Appearance and Personalization icon, the Control Panel displays as shown in Figure W.12. Notice how the Control Panel categories display at the left side of the Control Panel and options for changing the appearance and personalizing your computer display in the middle of the Control Panel.

By default, the Control Panel displays categories of tasks in what is called *Category* view. You can change this view to display large or small icons. To change the view, click the down-pointing arrow that displays at the right side of the text *View by* that displays in the upper right corner of the Control Panel, and then click the desired view at the drop-down list (see Figure W.11).

Figure W.11 The Control Panel

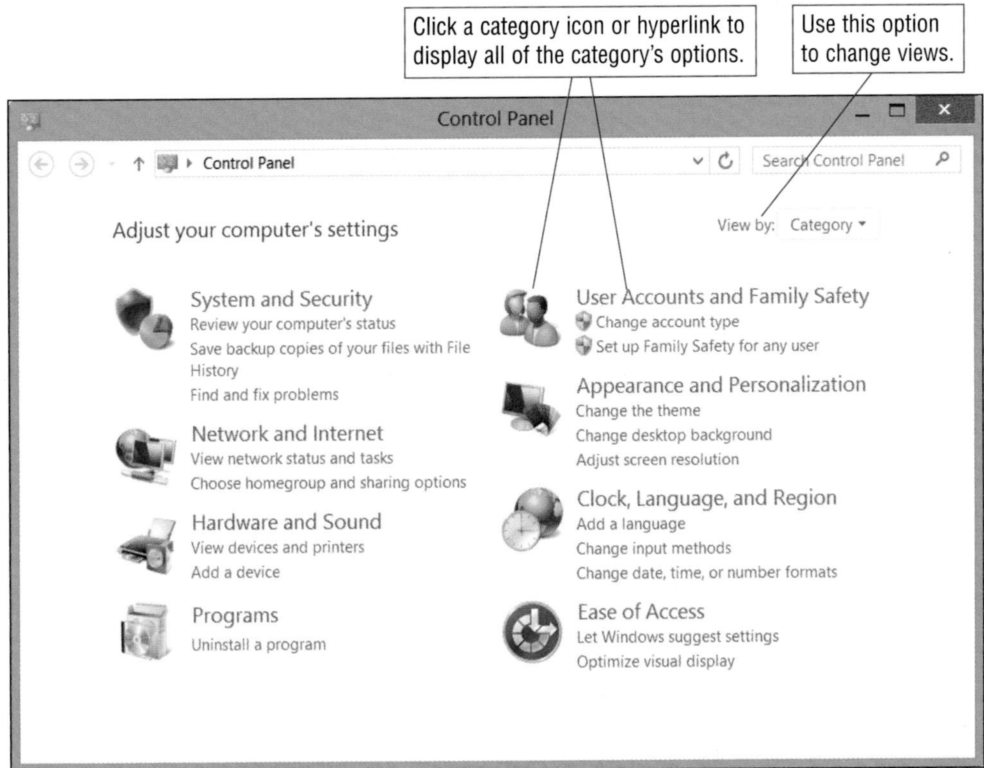

Figure W.12 Appearance and Personalization Window

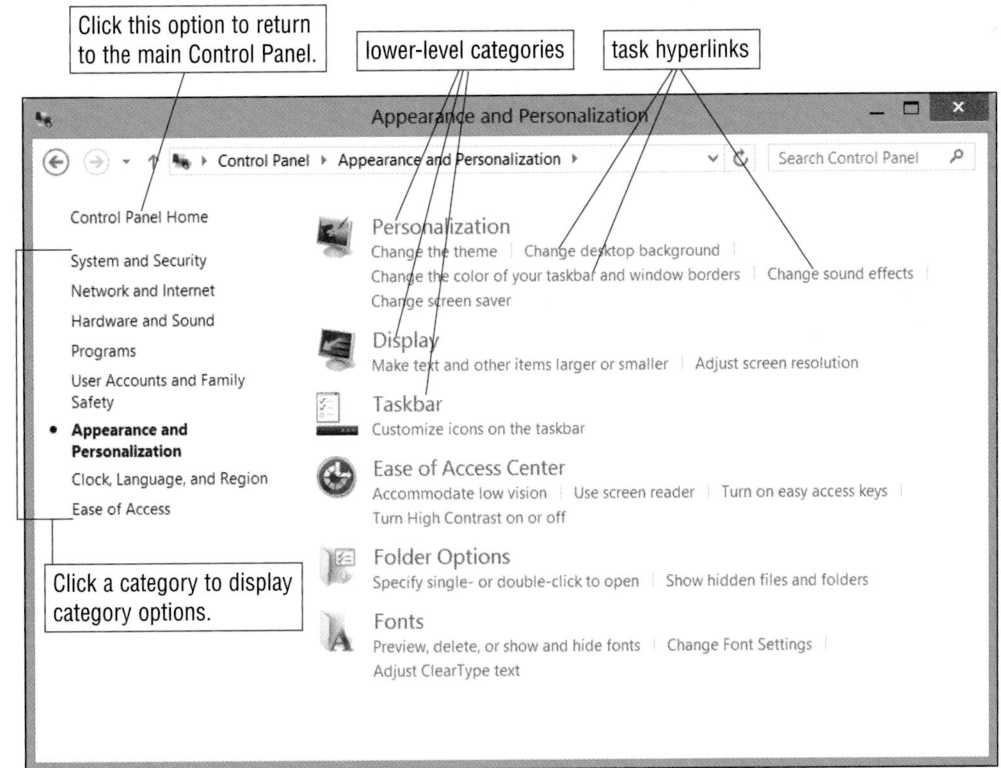

Project 9 Changing the Desktop Theme

1. At the Windows 8 desktop, right-click the Start screen thumbnail and then click *Control Panel* at the shortcut menu.
2. At the Control Panel, click the Appearance and Personalization icon.

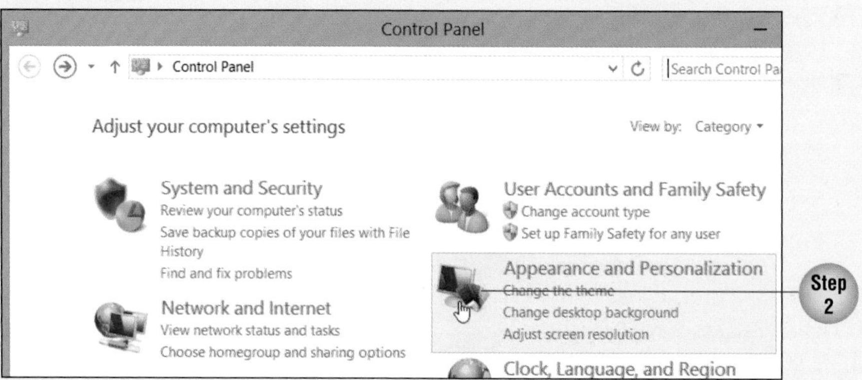

3. Click the Change the theme hyperlink that displays below *Personalization* in the panel at the right in the Control Panel.
4. At the window that displays with options for changing visuals and sounds on your computer, click *Earth* in the *Windows Default Themes* section.
5. Click the Desktop Background hyperlink that displays in the lower left corner of the panel.
6. Click the button that displays below the text *Change picture every* and then click *10 Seconds* at the drop-down list. (This tells Windows to change the picture on your desktop every 10 seconds.)
7. Click the Save changes button that displays in the lower right corner of the Control Panel.
8. Click the Close button located in the upper right corner to close the Control Panel.
9. Look at the picture that displays as the desktop background. Wait for 10 seconds and then look at the second picture that displays.
10. Right-click the Start screen thumbnail and then click *Control Panel* at the shortcut menu.
11. At the Control Panel, click the Appearance and Personalization icon.
12. Click the Change the theme hyperlink that displays below *Personalization* in the panel at the right.
13. At the window that displays with options for changing visuals and sounds on your computer, click *Windows* in the *Windows Default Themes* section. (This is the default theme.)
14. Click the Close button located in the upper right corner of the Control Panel.

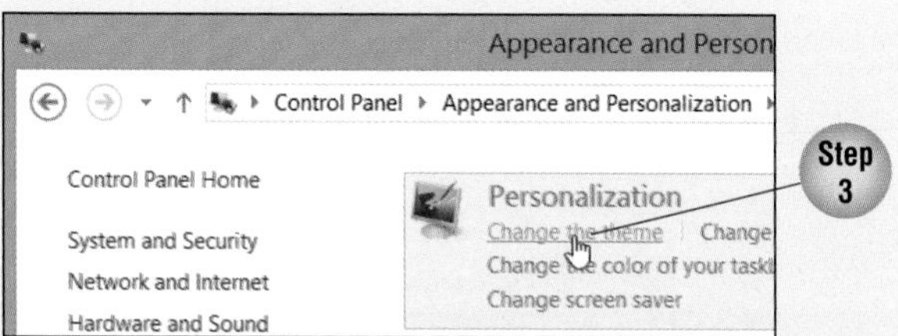

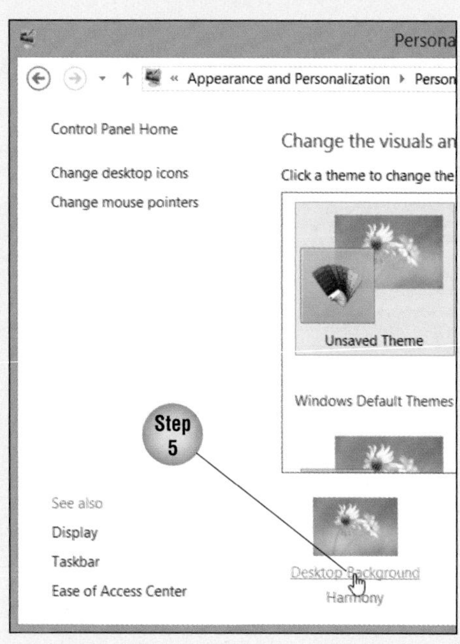

Searching in the Control Panel

The Control Panel contains a large number of options for customizing the appearance and functionality of your computer. If you want to customize a feature and are not sure where the options for the feature are located, search for the feature. To do this, display the Control Panel and then type the name of the desired feature. By default, the insertion point is positioned in the *Search Control Panel* text box. When you type the feature name in the text box, options related to the feature display in the Control Panel.

Project 10 Customizing the Mouse

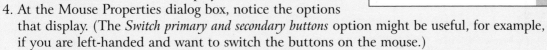

1. Right-click the Start screen thumbnail and then click *Control Panel*.
2. At the Control Panel, type **mouse**. (The insertion point is automatically located in the *Search Control Panel* text box when you open the Control Panel. When you type *mouse*, features for customizing the mouse display in the Control Panel.)
3. Click the Mouse icon that displays in the Control Panel.
4. At the Mouse Properties dialog box, notice the options that display. (The *Switch primary and secondary buttons* option might be useful, for example, if you are left-handed and want to switch the buttons on the mouse.)

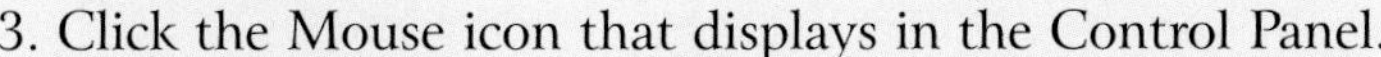

5. Click the Cancel button to close the dialog box.
6. At the Control Panel, click the Change the mouse pointer display or speed hyperlink.

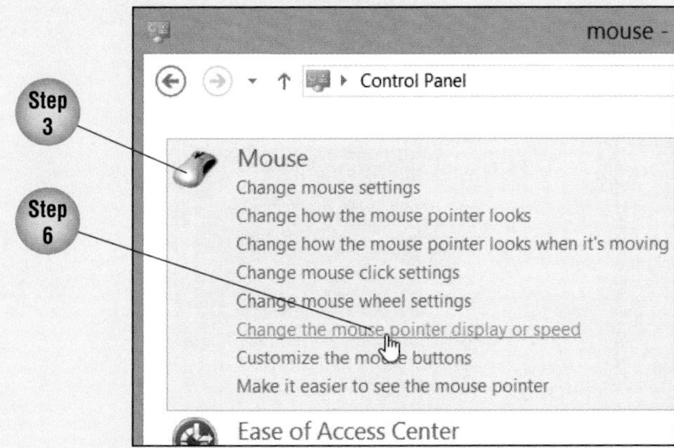

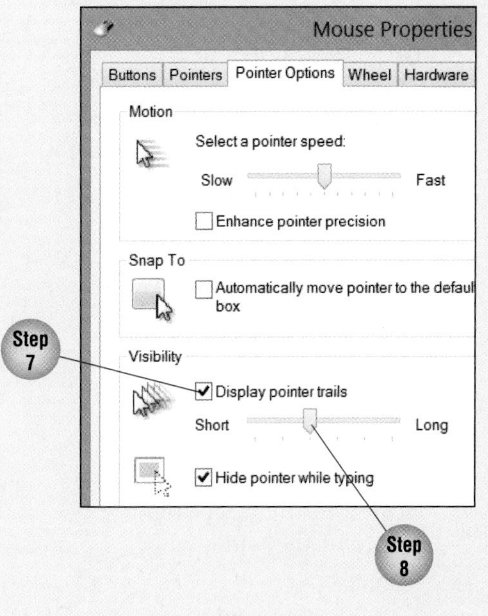

7. At the Mouse Properties dialog box with the Pointer Options tab selected, click the *Display pointer trails* check box in the *Visibility* section to insert a check mark.
8. Drag the button on the slider bar (located below the *Display pointer trails* check box) approximately to the middle of the bar.
9. Click OK to close the dialog box.
10. Close the Control Panel.
11. Move the mouse pointer around the screen to see the pointer trails.

Displaying Personalize Options with a Shortcut Command

In addition to the Control Panel, display customization options with a command from a shortcut menu. Display a shortcut menu by positioning the mouse pointer in the desired position and then clicking the right mouse button. For example, display a shortcut menu with options for customizing the desktop by positioning the mouse pointer in an empty area of the desktop and then clicking the right mouse button. At the shortcut menu that displays, click the desired shortcut command.

Project 11 Customizing with a Shortcut Command

1. At the Windows 8 desktop, position the mouse pointer in an empty area on the desktop, click the right mouse button, and then click *Personalize* at the shortcut menu.
2. At the Control Panel Appearance and Personalization window that displays, click the Change mouse pointers hyperlink that displays at the left side of the window.
3. At the Mouse Properties dialog box, click the Pointer Options tab.
4. Click in the *Display pointer trails* check box to remove the check mark.
5. Click OK to close the dialog box.
6. At the Control Panel Appearance and Personalization window, click the Screen Saver hyperlink that displays in the lower right corner of the window.
7. At the Screen Saver Settings dialog box, click the option button below the *Screen saver* option and then click *Ribbons* at the drop-down list.
8. Check the number in the *Wait* measurement box. If a number other than *1* displays, click the down-pointing arrow at the right side of the measurement box until *1* displays. (This tells Windows to display the screen saver after one minute of inactivity.)
9. Click OK to close the dialog box.
10. Close the Control Panel by clicking the Close button located in the upper right corner of the window.

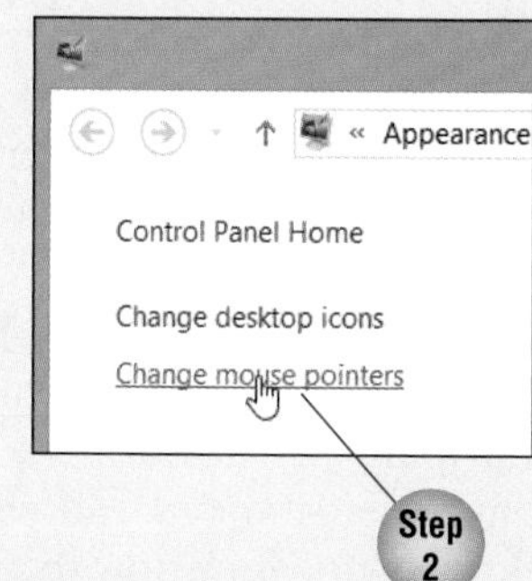

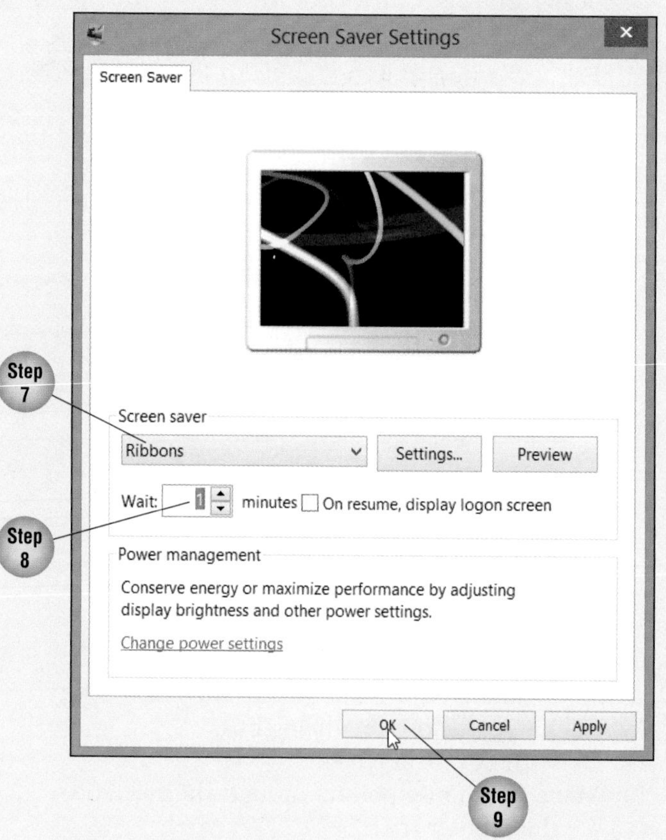

11. Do not touch the mouse or keyboard and wait over one minute for the screen saver to display. After watching the screen saver, move the mouse. (This redisplays the desktop.)
12. Right-click in an empty area of the desktop and then click *Personalize* at the shortcut menu.
13. At the Control Panel Appearance and Personalization window, click the Screen Saver hyperlink.
14. At the Screen Saver Settings dialog box, click the option button below the *Screen saver* option and then click *(None)* at the drop-down list.
15. Click OK to close the dialog box.
16. Close the Control Panel Appearance and Personalization window.

Exploring Windows Help and Support

Windows 8 includes an on-screen reference guide providing information, explanations, and interactive help on learning Windows features. Get help at the Windows Help and Support window, shown in Figure W.13. Display this window by clicking the Start screen thumbnail to display the Windows 8 Start screen. Right-click a blank area of the Start screen, click the All apps button, and then click the *Help and Support* tile in the Windows System group. Use options in the Windows Help and Support window to search for help on a specific feature; display the opening Windows Help and Support window; print the current information; and display information on getting started with Windows 8, setting up a network, and protecting your computer.

Figure W.13 Windows Help and Support Window

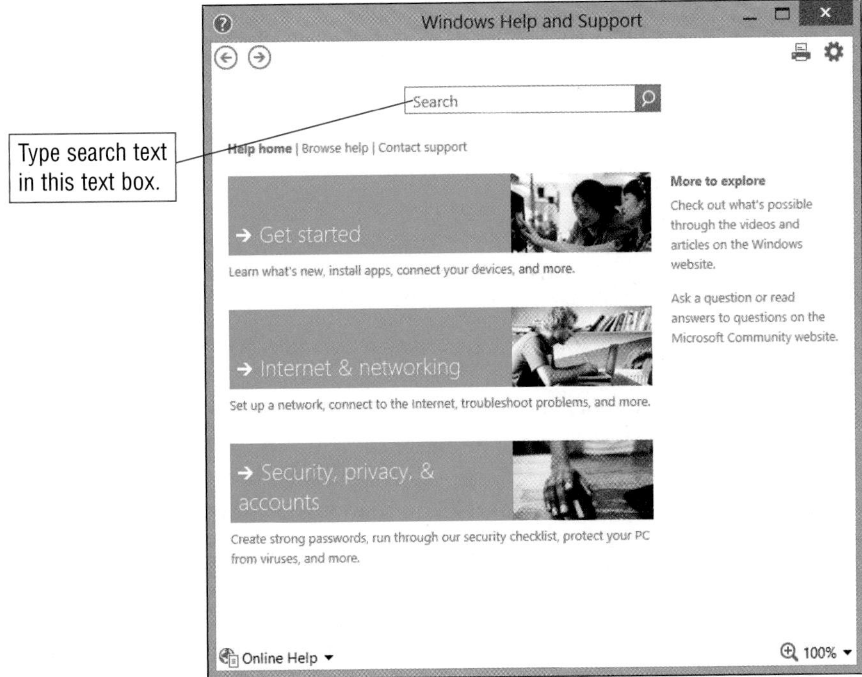

Project 12 Getting Help

1. Display the Windows 8 Help and Support window by following these steps:
   a. At the Windows 8 desktop, position the mouse pointer in the lower left corner of the screen and then click the Start screen thumbnail.
   b. Position the mouse in a blank area of the Windows 8 Start screen and then click the right mouse button.
   c. Click the All apps button that appears in the lower right corner of the Start screen and then scroll to the right of the Start screen.
   d. Click the *Help and Support* tile located in the *Windows System* category.
2. At the Windows Help and Support window, click the Get started hyperlink.
3. Click a hyperlink that interests you, read the information, and then click the Back button. (The Back button is located in the upper left corner of the window.)
4. Click another hyperlink that interests you and then read the information.
5. Click the Help home hyperlink that displays below the search text box. (This returns you to the opening Windows Help and Support window.)
6. Click in the search text box, type **delete files**, and then press Enter.
7. Click the How to work with files and folders hyperlink that displays in the window.
8. Read the information that displays about working with files or folders and then click the Print button located in the upper right corner of the Windows Help and Support window.
9. At the Print dialog box, click the Print button.
10. Click the Close button to close the Windows Help and Support window.

Using Search Tools

The Charm bar contains a search tool you can use to quickly find an application or file on your computer. To use the search tool, display the Charm bar, click the Search button and then type in the search text box the first few characters of the application or file for which you are searching. As you type characters in the text box, a list displays with application names or file names that begin with the characters. As you continue typing characters, the search tool refines the list.

You can also search for programs or files with the search text box in the Computer window. The search text box displays in the upper right corner of the Computer window at the right side of the Address bar. If you want to search a specific folder, make that folder active in the Content pane and then type the search text in the text box.

When conducting a search, you can use the asterisk (*) as a wildcard character in place of any letters, numbers, or symbols within a file name. For example, in the following project you will search for file names containing *check* by typing ***check** in the search text box. The asterisk indicates that the file name can start with any letter but it must contain the letters *check* somewhere in the file name.

Project 13 Searching for Programs and Files

1. At the Windows 8 desktop, display the Charm bar and then click the Search button.
2. With the insertion point positioned in the search text box, type **paint**. (Notice as you type the letters that Windows displays applications that begin with the same letters you are typing or that are associated with the same letters in a keyword. Notice that the Paint program displays below the heading *Apps* at the top of the list. Depending on the contents stored in the computer you are using, additional items may display below Paint.)

3. Click *Paint* that displays below the *Apps* heading.
4. Close the Paint window.
5. Right-click the Start screen thumbnail and then click *File Explorer*.
6. At the Computer window, double-click the icon representing your storage medium.
7. Double-click the *Windows8* folder.
8. Click in the search text box located at the right of the Address bar and then type **document**. (As you begin typing the letters, Windows filters the list of files in the Content pane to those that contain the letters you type. Notice that the Address bar displays *Search Results in Windows8* to indicate that the files that display matching your criteria are limited to the current folder.)

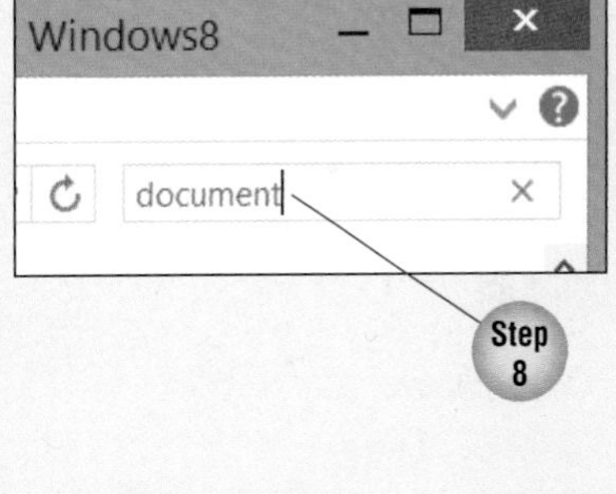

9. Select the text *document* that displays in the search text box and then type ***check**. (Notice that the Content pane displays file names containing the letters *check* no matter how the file name begins.)
10. Double-click ***WordSpellCheck02.docx*** to open the document in Word.
11. Close the document and then close Word by clicking the Close button located in the upper right corner of the window.
12. Close the Computer window.

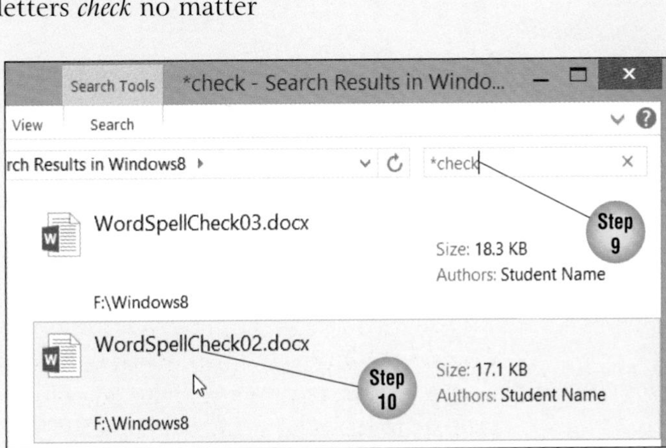

Browsing the Internet Using Internet Explorer 10

Microsoft Internet Explorer 10 is a web browser with options and features for displaying sites as well as navigating and searching for information on the Internet. The ***Internet*** is a network of computers connected around the world. Users access the Internet for several purposes: to communicate using instant messaging and/or email, to subscribe to newsgroups, to transfer files, to socialize with other users around the globe on social websites, and to access virtually any kind of information imaginable.

Using the Internet, people can find a phenomenal amount of information for private or public use. To use the Internet, three things are generally required: an ***Internet Service Provider (ISP)***, software to browse the Web (called a ***web browser***), and a ***search engine***. In this section, you will learn how to:

- Navigate the Internet using URLs and hyperlinks
- Use search engines to locate information
- Download web pages and images

You will use the Microsoft Internet Explorer web browser to locate information on the Internet. A ***Uniform Resource Locator***, referred to as a ***URL***, identifies a location on the Internet. The steps for browsing the Internet vary but generally include opening Internet Explorer, typing the URL for the desired site, navigating the various pages of the site, navigating to other sites using links, and then closing Internet Explorer.

To launch Internet Explorer 10, click the Internet Explorer icon on the Taskbar at the Windows desktop. Figure IE.1 identifies the elements of the Internet Explorer 10 window. The web page that displays in your Internet Explorer window may vary from what you see in Figure IE.1.

If you know the URL for a desired website, click in the Address bar, type the URL, and then press Enter. The website's home page displays in a tab within the Internet Explorer window. The format of a URL is *http://server-name.path*. The first part of the URL, *http*, stands for HyperText Transfer Protocol, which is the protocol or language used to transfer data within the World Wide Web. The colon and slashes separate the protocol from the server name. The server name is the second component of the URL. For example, in the URL http://www.microsoft.com, the server name is *microsoft*. The last part of the URL specifies the domain to which the server belongs. For example, *.com* refers to "commercial" and establishes that the URL is a commercial company. Examples of other domains include *.edu* for "educational," *.gov* for "government," and *.mil* for "military."

Internet Explorer 10 has been streamlined to provide users with more browsing space and reduced clutter. By default, Microsoft has turned off many features in Internet Explorer 10 such as the Menu bar, Command bar, and Status bar. You can turn these features on by right-clicking the empty space above the Address bar and to the right of the new tab button (see Figure IE.1) and then clicking the desired option at the drop-down list that displays. For example, if you want to turn on the Menu bar (the bar that contains File, Edit, and so on), right-click the empty space above the Address bar and then click *Menu bar* at the drop-down list. (This inserts a check mark next to *Menu bar*.)

Figure IE.1 Internet Explorer Window

Project 1 Browsing the Internet Using URLs

1. Make sure you are connected to the Internet through an Internet Service Provider and that the Windows 8 desktop displays. (Check with your instructor to determine if you need to complete steps for accessing the Internet such as typing a user name and password to log on.)
2. Launch Microsoft Internet Explorer by clicking the Internet Explorer icon located at the left side of the Windows Taskbar, which is located at the bottom of the Windows desktop.
3. Turn on the Command bar by right-clicking the empty space above the Address bar or to the right of the new tab button (see Figure IE.1) and then clicking *Command bar* at the drop-down list.
4. At the Internet Explorer window, explore the website for Yosemite National Park by completing the following steps:
   a. Click in the Address bar, type www.nps.gov/yose, and then press Enter.
   b. Scroll down the home page for Yosemite National Park by clicking the down-pointing arrow on the vertical scroll bar located at the right side of the Internet Explorer window.

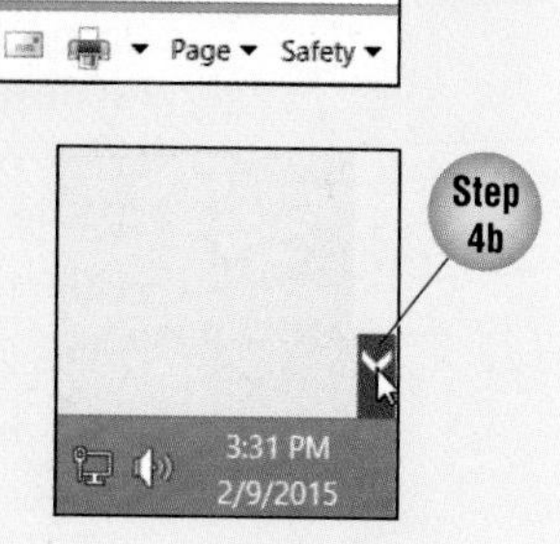

c. Print the home page by clicking the Print button located on the Command bar. (Note that some websites have a printer-friendly button you can click to print the page.)

5. Explore the website for Glacier National Park by completing the following steps:
   a. Click in the Address bar, type **www.nps.gov/glac**, and then press Enter.
   b. Print the home page by clicking the Print button located on the Command bar.
6. Close Internet Explorer by clicking the Close button (contains an X) located in the upper right corner of the Internet Explorer window.

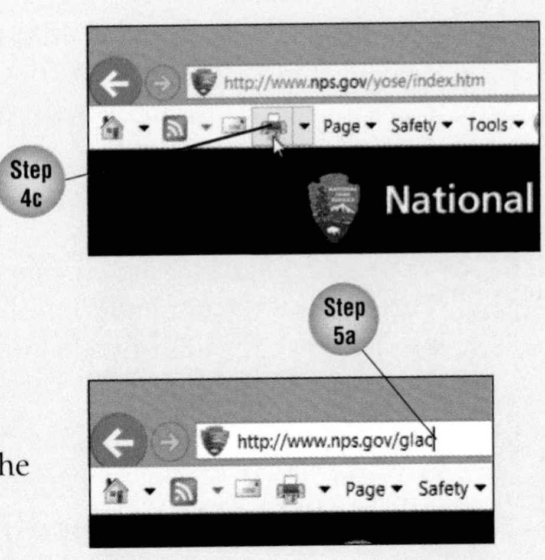

Navigating Using Hyperlinks

Most web pages contain ***hyperlinks*** that you click to connect to another page within the website or to another site on the Internet. Hyperlinks may display in a web page as underlined text in a specific color or as images or icons. To use a hyperlink, position the mouse pointer on the desired hyperlink until the mouse pointer turns into a hand and then click the left mouse button. Use hyperlinks to navigate within and between sites on the Internet. The Internet Explorer window contains a Back button (see Figure IE.1) that, when clicked, takes you to the previous web page viewed. If you click the Back button and then want to return to the previous page, click the Forward button. You can continue clicking the Back button to back your way out of several linked pages in reverse order since Internet Explorer maintains a history of the websites you visit.

Project 2 Navigating Using Hyperlinks

1. Make sure you are connected to the Internet and then click the Internet Explorer icon on the Windows Taskbar.
2. At the Internet Explorer window, display the White House web page and navigate in the page by completing the following steps:
   a. Click in the Address bar, type **whitehouse.gov**, and then press Enter.
   b. At the White House home page, position the mouse pointer on a hyperlink that interests you until the pointer turns into a hand and then click the left mouse button.
   c. At the linked web page, click the Back button. (This returns you to the White House home page.)
   d. At the White House home page, click the Forward button to return to the previous web page viewed.
   e. Print the web page by clicking the Print button on the Command bar.

3. Display the website for Amazon.com and navigate in the site by completing the following steps:
   a. Click in the Address bar, type **www.amazon.com**, and then press Enter.
   b. At the Amazon.com home page, click a hyperlink related to books.
   c. When a book web page displays, click the Print button on the Command bar.

4. Close Internet Explorer by clicking the Close button (contains an X) located in the upper right corner of the Internet Explorer window.

Searching for Specific Sites

If you do not know the URL for a specific site or you want to find information on the Internet but do not know what site to visit, complete a search with a search engine. A ***search engine*** is software created to search quickly and easily for desired information. A variety of search engines are available on the Internet, each offering the opportunity to search for specific information. One method for searching for information is to click in the Address bar, type a keyword or phrase related to your search, and then press Enter. Another method for completing a search is to visit the website for a search engine and use options at the site.

Bing is Microsoft's online search portal and is the default search engine used by Internet Explorer. Bing organizes search results by topic category and provides related search suggestions.

Project 3 Searching for Information by Topic

1. Start Internet Explorer.
2. At the Internet Explorer window, search for sites on bluegrass music by completing the following steps:
   a. Click in the Address bar.
   b. Type **bluegrass music** and then press Enter.
   c. When a list of sites displays in the Bing results window, click a site that interests you.
   d. When the page displays, click the Print button. 
3. Use the Yahoo! search engine to find sites on bluegrass music by completing the following steps:
   a. Click in the Address bar, type **www.yahoo.com**, and then press Enter.
   b. At the Yahoo! website, with the insertion point positioned in the search text box, type **bluegrass music** and then press Enter. (Notice that the sites displayed vary from sites displayed in the earlier search.)

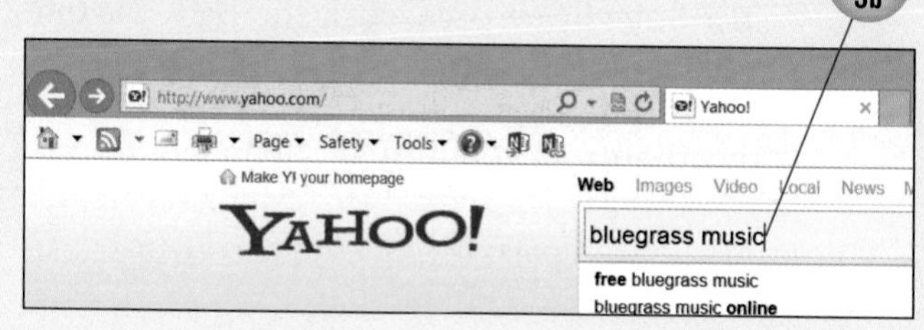

c. Click hyperlinks until a website displays that interests you.
d. Print the page.

4. Use the Google search engine to find sites on jazz music by completing the following steps:
   a. Click in the Address bar, type www.google.com, and then press Enter.
   b. At the Google website, with the insertion point positioned in the search text box, type jazz music and then press Enter.
   c. Click a site that interests you.
   d. Print the page.
5. Close Internet Explorer.

Using a Metasearch Engine

Bing, Yahoo!, and Google are search engines that search the Web for content and display search results. In addition to individual search engines, you can use a metasearch engine, such as Dogpile, that sends your search text to other search engines and then compiles the results in one list. With a metasearch engine, you type the search text once and then access results from a wider group of search engines. The Dogpile metasearch engine provides search results from Google, Yahoo!, and Yandex.

Project 4 Searching with a Metasearch Search Engine

1. Start Internet Explorer.
2. Click in the Address bar.
3. Type www.dogpile.com and then press Enter.
4. At the Dogpile website, type jazz music in the search text box and then press Enter.
5. Click a hyperlink that interests you.
6. Close the Internet Explorer window. If a message displays asking if you want to close all tabs, click the Close all tabs button.

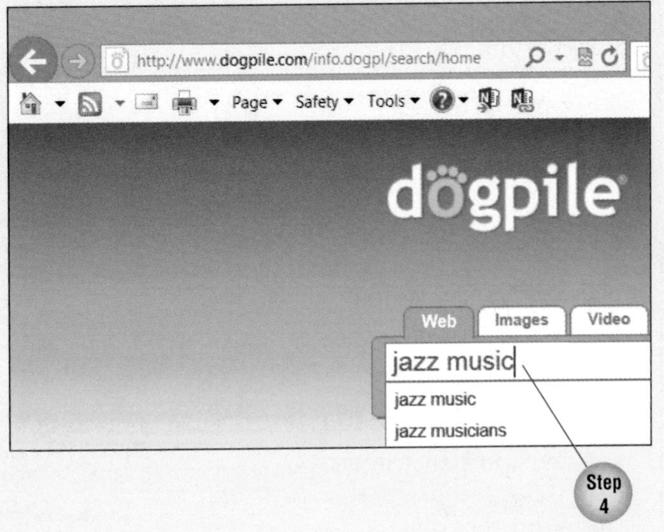

Completing Advanced Searches for Specific Sites

The Internet contains an enormous amount of information. Depending on what you are searching for on the Internet and the search engine you use, some searches can result in several thousand "hits" (sites). Wading through a large number of sites can be very time-consuming and counterproductive. Narrowing a search to very specific criteria can greatly reduce the number of hits for a search. To narrow a search, use the advanced search options offered by the search engine.

Project 5 Narrowing a Search

1. Start Internet Explorer.
2. Search for sites on skydiving in Oregon by completing the following steps:
   a. Click in the Address bar, type **www.yahoo.com**, and then press Enter.
   b. At the Yahoo! home page, click the Search button next to the search text box.
   c. Click the More hyperlink located above the search text box and then click *Advanced Search* at the drop-down list.
   d. At the Advanced Web Search page, click in the search text box next to *all of these words*.
   e. Type **skydiving Oregon tandem static line**. (This limits the search to web pages containing all of the words typed in the search text box.)
   f. Click the Yahoo! Search button.
   g. When the list of websites displays, click a hyperlink that interests you.
   h. Click the Back button until the Yahoo! Advanced Web Search page displays.
   i. Click in the *the exact phrase* text box and then type **skydiving in Oregon**.
   j. Click the *Only .com domains* option in the *Site/Domain* section.
   k. Click the Yahoo! Search button.
   l. When the list of websites displays, click a hyperlink that interests you.
   m. Print the page.
3. Close Internet Explorer.

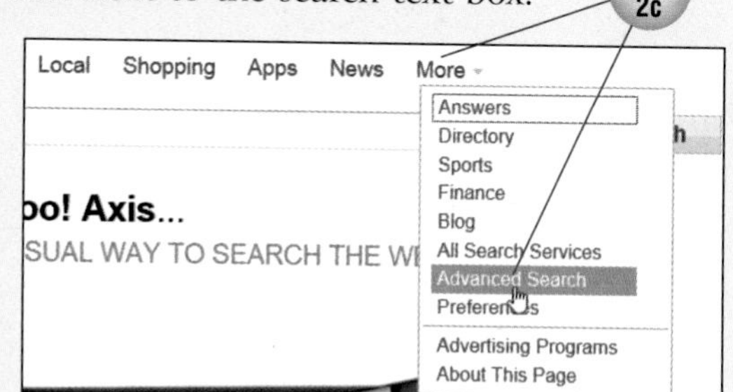

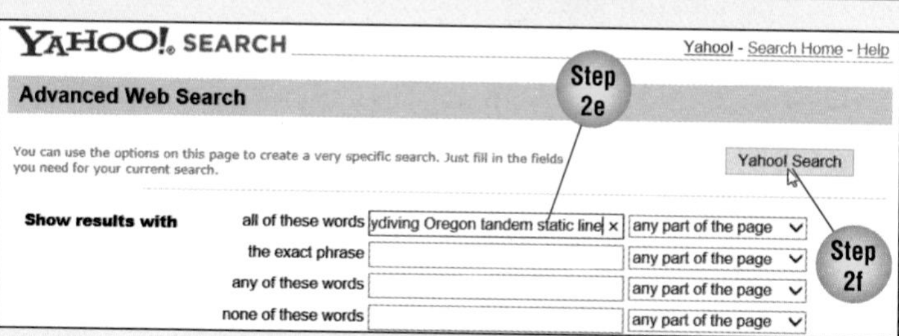

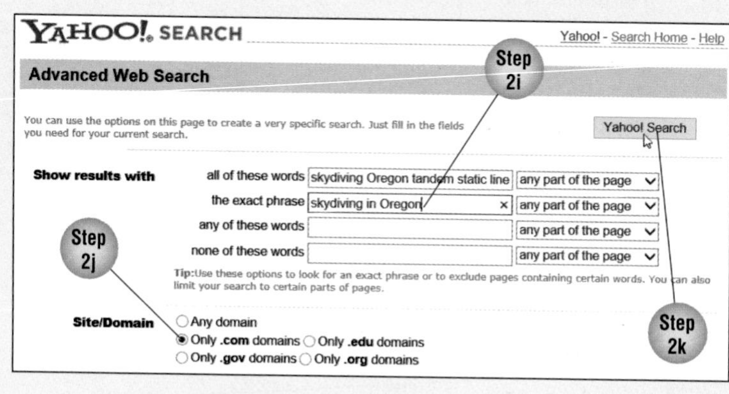

Downloading Images, Text, and Web Pages from the Internet

The image(s) and/or text that display when you open a web page, as well as the web page itself, can be saved as a separate file. This separate file can be viewed, printed, or inserted in another file. The information you want to save in a separate file is downloaded from the Internet by Internet Explorer and saved in a folder of your choosing with the name you specify. Copyright laws protect much of the information on the Internet. Before using information downloaded from the Internet, check the site for restrictions. If you do use information, make sure you properly cite the source.

Project 6 Downloading Images and Web Pages

1. Start Internet Explorer.
2. Download a web page and image from Banff National Park by completing the following steps:
   a. Search for websites related to Banff National Park.
   b. From the list of sites that displays, choose a site that contains information about Banff National Park and at least one image of the park.
   c. Make sure the Command bar is turned on. (If the Command bar is turned off, turn it on by right-clicking the empty space above the Address bar or to the right of the new tab button and then clicking *Command bar* at the drop-down list.)

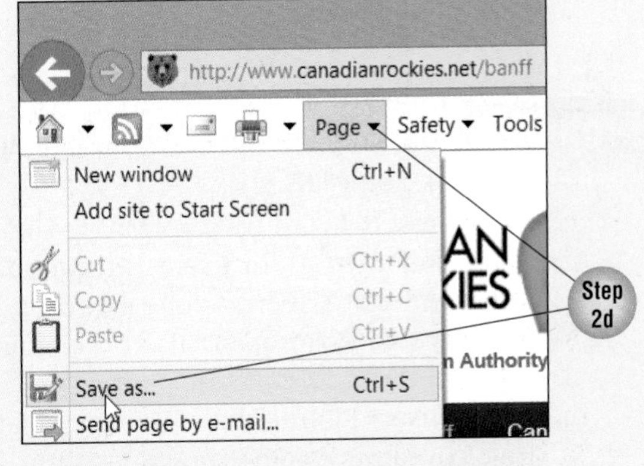

   d. Save the web page as a separate file by clicking the Page button on the Command bar and then clicking *Save as* at the drop-down list.
   e. At the Save Webpage dialog box, type **BanffWebPage**.
   f. Click the down-pointing arrow for the *Save as type* option and then click *Web Archive, single file (*.mht)*.
   g. Navigate to the drive containing your storage medium and then click the Save button.

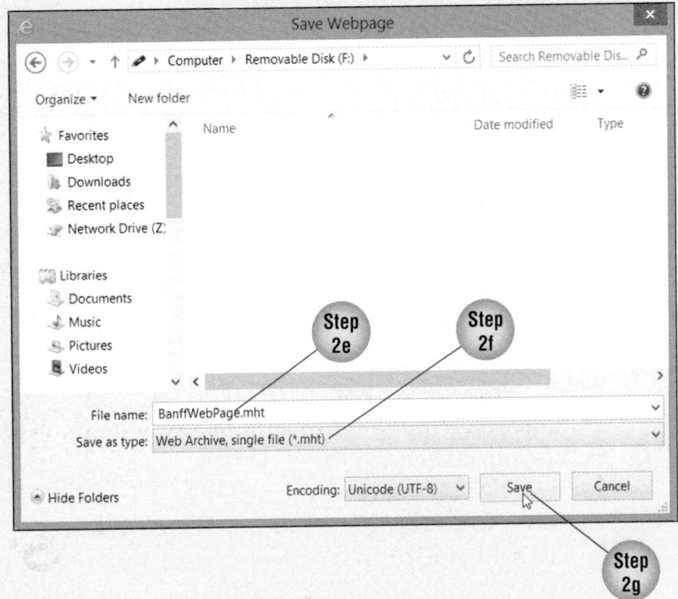

3. Save an image file by completing the following steps:
   a. Right-click an image that displays at the website.
   b. At the shortcut menu that displays, click *Save picture as*.

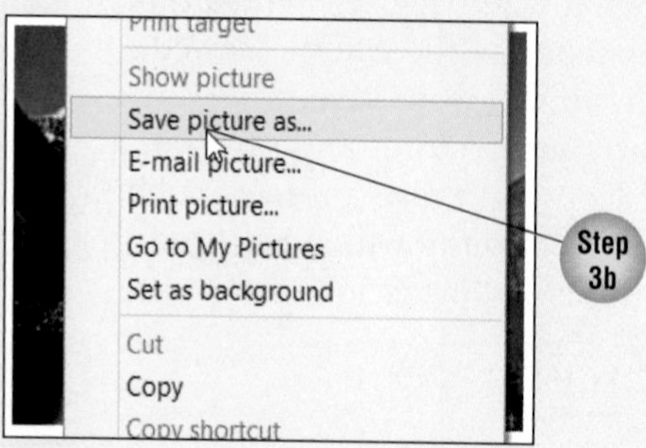

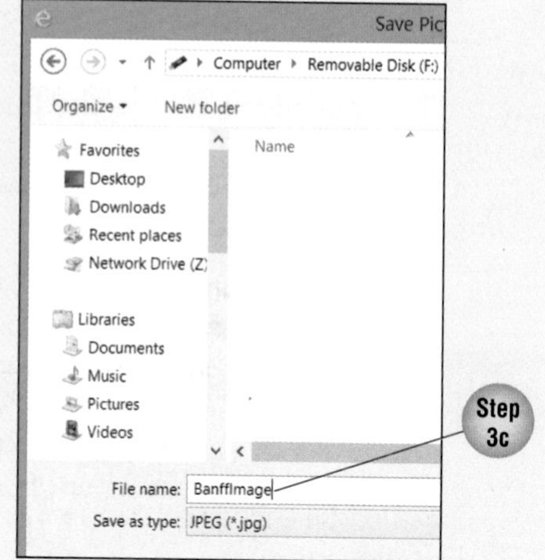

   c. At the Save Picture dialog box, type **BanffImage** in the *File name* text box.
   d. Navigate to the drive containing your storage medium and then click the Save button.
4. Close Internet Explorer.

Project 7 Opening the Saved Web Page and Image in a Word Document

1. Open Microsoft Word by positioning the mouse pointer in the lower left corner of the Taskbar, clicking the Start screen thumbnail, and then clicking the *Word 2013* tile in the Windows 8 Start screen. At the Word opening screen, click the *Blank document* template.
2. With Microsoft Word open, insert the image in a document by completing the following steps:
   a. Click the INSERT tab and then click the Pictures button in the Illustrations group.
   b. At the Insert Picture dialog box, navigate to the drive containing your storage medium and then double-click ***BanffImage.jpg***.

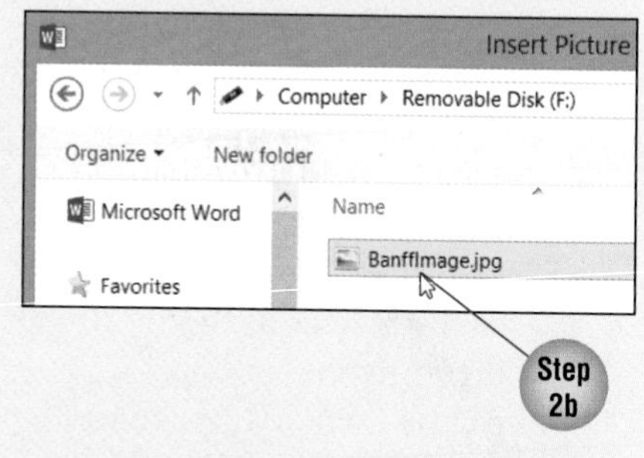

   c. When the image displays in the Word document, print the document by pressing Ctrl + P and then clicking the Print button.
   d. Close the document by clicking the FILE tab and then clicking the *Close* option. At the message asking if you want to save the changes, click the Don't Save button.
3. Open the **BanffWebPage.mht** file by completing the following steps:
   a. Click the FILE tab and then click the *Open* option.
   b. Double-click the *Computer* option.
   c. At the Open dialog box, navigate to the drive containing your storage medium and then double-click ***BanffWebPage.mht***.

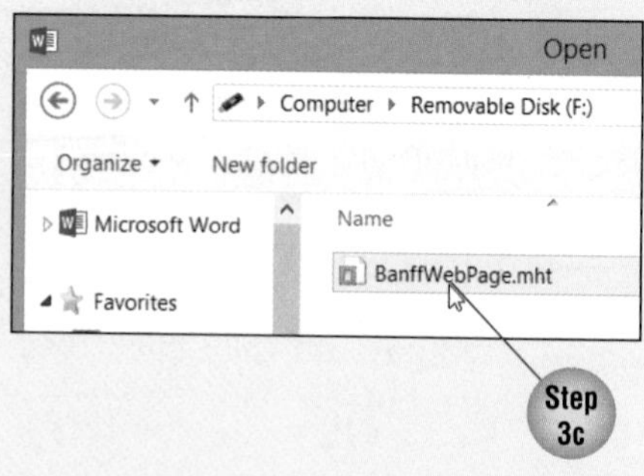

   d. Preview the web page(s) by pressing Ctrl + P. At the Print backstage area, preview the page shown at the right side of the backstage area.
4. Close Word by clicking the Close button (contains an X) that displays in the upper right corner of the screen.

MICROSOFT®

WORD Level 1

Unit 1 ■ Editing and Formatting Documents

MICROSOFT®

WORD

CHAPTER 1

Preparing Documents

PERFORMANCE OBJECTIVES

Upon successful completion of Chapter 1, you will be able to:

- **Open Microsoft Word**
- **Create, save, name, print, open, and close a Word document**
- **Close Word**
- **Edit a document**
- **Move the insertion point within a document**
- **Scroll within a document**
- **Select text in a document**
- **Use the Undo and Redo buttons**
- **Check spelling and grammar in a document**
- **Use the Help feature**

Tutorials

1.1 Creating, Saving, and Printing a Document

1.2 Opening a Document

1.3 Pinning Documents and Folders to the Recent Lists

1.4 Editing a Document

1.5 Checking the Spelling and Grammar in a Document

1.6 Using the Word Help Feature

In this chapter, you will learn to create, save, name, print, open, close, and edit a Word document as well as complete a spelling and grammar check. You will also learn about the Help feature, which is an on-screen reference manual providing information on features and commands for each program in the Office suite. Before continuing, make sure you read the *Getting Started* section presented at the beginning of this book. This section contains information about computer hardware and software, using the mouse, executing commands, and exploring Help files. Model answers for this chapter's projects appear on the following page.

WL1C1

Note: Before beginning the projects, copy to your OneDrive or storage medium (such as a USB drive) the WL1C1 subfolder from the WL1 folder on the CD that accompanies this textbook. Steps on how to copy a folder are presented on the inside of the back cover of this textbook. Do this every time you start a chapter's projects.

The traditional chronological resume lists your work experience in reverse-chronological order (starting with your current or most recent position). The functional style deemphasizes the "where" and "when" of your career and instead groups similar experiences, talents, and qualifications regardless of when they occurred.

Like the chronological resume, the hybrid resume includes specifics about where you worked, when you worked there, and what your job titles were. Like a functional resume, a hybrid resume emphasizes your most relevant qualifications in an expanded summary section, in several "career highlights" bullet points at the top of your resume, or in project summaries.

Created:
Thursday, December 8, 2015
Note: The two paragraphs will become the 2nd and 3rd paragraphs in the 5th section.

Project 1 Prepare a Word Document

WL1-C1-P1-Resume.docx

The majority of new jobs being created in the United States today involve daily work with computers. Computer-related careers include technical support jobs, sales and training, programming and applications development, network and database administration, and computer engineering.

A technician is an entry-level worker who installs and maintains hardware and/or software. Technical sales and technical training jobs emphasize interpersonal skills as much as they do technical skills. Programming is one of the most difficult and highly skilled jobs in the industry. Programmers create new software, such as Microsoft Windows or computer games, and often have college degrees. Software engineers are programmers trained to create software in teams with other programmers. Application developers are similar to programmers, but they use existing software such as a database to create applications for business solutions. Application development jobs include database administration, network administration, and systems analysis. Database and network administration involves overseeing and maintaining databases and networks, respectively. Systems analysts design information systems or evaluate and improve existing ones.

Project 2 Save and Edit a Word Document

WL1-C1-P2-CompCareers.docx

COMPUTER KEYBOARDS

To enter commands into a computer or to enter data into it, a user needs an input device. An input device can be built into the computer, like the keyboard in a laptop, or it can be connected to the computer by a cable. Some input devices, like remote keyboards, send directions to the computer by means of an infrared signal.

Keyboards can be external devices that are attached by a cable, or they can be attached to the CPU case itself as they are in laptops. Most keyboards today are QWERTY keyboards, which take their name from the first six keys at the left of the first row of letters. The QWERTY design was invented in the early days of mechanical typewriters to slow down typists and thus keep keys from jamming.

The DVORAK keyboard is an alternative to the QWERTY keyboard. On the DVORAK keyboard, the most commonly used keys are placed close to the user's fingertips and this increases typing speed. You can install software on a QWERTY keyboard that emulates a DVORAK keyboard. The ability to emulate other keyboards is convenient especially when working with foreign languages.

Project 4 Insert and Delete Text

WL1-C1-P4-CompKeyboards.docx

ON THE HORIZON

The march of computer technology continues to change the nature of our jobs and workplaces. Considering the global economic and technology scene, some major changes in occupations involve changes in communications media, work locations, and communications tools.

Communications Media

One key to being successful in our modern, technological world is spotting trends early and adjusting one's career direction accordingly. For example, 80 percent of daily newspaper readers are over 50 years old. Young reader are not as interested in the printed word, and each year the industry suffers from a shrinking number of subscriptions. The young are still reading, but they are reading online media sites rather than the printed page. Websites make excellent dynamic newspapers, as they can be changed at will, they require no printing or distribution costs, and they do not require the newspaper delivery person to go door to door asking for payment. This switch to the new media is causing many jobs to change. The number of printing and lithography jobs is shrinking, but web developers and graphic artists are in demand.

Industry-morphing trends are sweeping away many traditional approaches to the marketing and distribution of products. Increasingly, music and movies are being downloaded versus being bought on a disc. Fewer movies are being rented, while more people are watching them on-demand through their cable systems. Once a successful approach is discovered, every type of media that can be digitized rather than produced and distributed in physical form will come under increasing pressure to modernize in order to match the competition. Individuals managing career paths need to be aware of these trends and avoid becoming part of a downsizing effort.

Telecommuting

Telecommuting, sometimes called telework, involves working via computer from home or while traveling rather than going to the office on a daily basis. Approximately 25 million Americans telecommute at least one day per week. Telework plans have been especially successful for commissioned salespeople, who are often more productive when away from the office environment.

Project 5 Complete a Spelling and Grammar Check

WL1-C1-P5-TechOccTrends.docx

Project 1 Prepare a Word Document — 2 Parts

You will create a short document containing information on resumes and then save, print, and close the document.

Opening Microsoft Word

Microsoft Office 2013 contains a word processing program named Word that you can use to create, save, edit, and print documents. The steps to open Word may vary depending on your system setup. Generally, to open Word, you click the Word 2013 tile at the Windows Start screen. At the Word 2013 opening screen, click the *Blank document* template.

Quick Steps

Open Word and Open a Blank Document

1. Click the Word 2013 tile at the Windows Start screen.
2. Click the *Blank document* template.

Creating, Saving, Printing, and Closing a Document

When you click the Blank document template, a blank document displays on the screen, as shown in Figure 1.1. The features of the document screen are described in Table 1.1.

To avoid opening the same program twice, use the Taskbar to see which programs are open.

At a blank document, type information to create a document. A document is any information you choose — for instance, a letter, report, term paper, table, and so on. Some things to consider when typing text are:

- **Word wrap:** As you type text to create a document, you do not need to press the Enter key at the end of each line because Word wraps text to the next line. A word is wrapped to the next line if it begins before the right margin and continues past the right margin. The only times you need to press Enter are to end a paragraph, create a blank line, or end a short line.
- **AutoCorrect:** Word contains a feature that automatically corrects certain words as you type them. For example, if you type the word *adn* instead of *and*, Word automatically corrects it when you press the spacebar after the word. AutoCorrect will also superscript the letters that follow an ordinal number (a number indicating a position in a series). For example, if you type *2nd* and then press the spacebar or Enter key, Word will convert this ordinal number to 2nd.
- **Automatic spelling checker:** By default, Word will automatically insert a red wavy line below words that are not contained in the Spelling dictionary or automatically corrected by AutoCorrect. This may include misspelled words, proper names, some terminology, and some foreign words. If you type a word not recognized by the Spelling dictionary, leave it as written if the word is correct. However, if the word is incorrect, you have two choices — you can delete the word and then type it correctly, or you can position the I-beam pointer on the word, click the *right* mouse button, and then click the correct spelling in the pop-up list.
- **Automatic grammar checker:** Word includes an automatic grammar checker. If the grammar checker detects a sentence containing a grammatical error, a blue wavy line is inserted below the error in the sentence. You can leave the sentence as written or position the mouse I-beam pointer on the error, click the *right* mouse button, and a pop-up list will display with possible corrections.
- **Spacing punctuation:** Typically, Word uses Calibri as the default typeface, which is a proportional typeface. (You will learn more about typefaces in Chapter 2.) When typing text in a proportional typeface, space once (rather than twice) after

A book icon displays in the Status bar. A check mark on the book indicates no spelling errors detected in the document by the spell checker, while an X on the book indicates errors. Double-click the book icon to move to the next error. If the book icon is not visible, right-click the Status bar and then click the *Spelling and Grammar Check* option at the pop-up list.

Figure 1.1 Blank Document

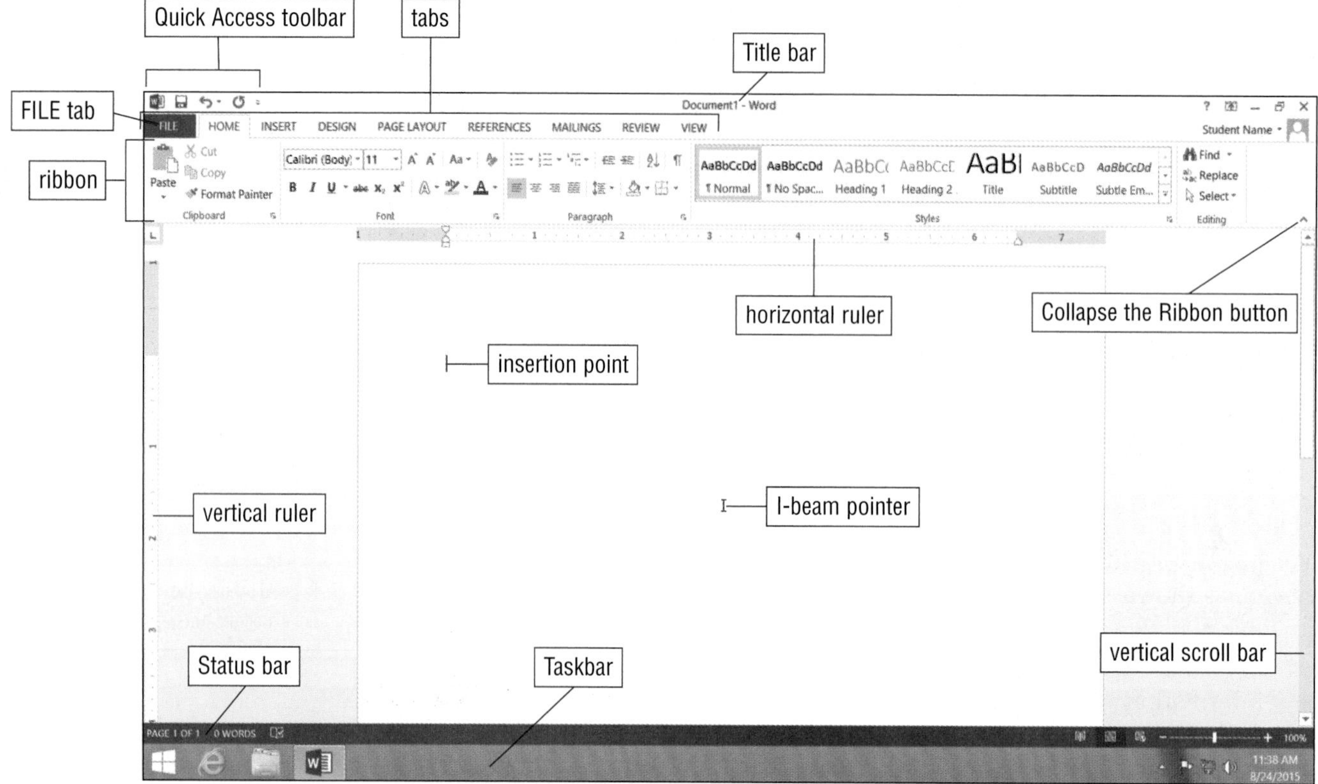

Table 1.1 Microsoft Word Screen Features

Feature	***Description***
Collapse the Ribbon button	when clicked, removes the ribbon from the screen
FILE tab	when clicked, displays backstage area that contains options for working with and managing documents
horizontal ruler	used to set margins, indents, and tabs
I-beam pointer	used to move the insertion point or to select text
insertion point	indicates location of next character entered at the keyboard
Quick Access toolbar	contains buttons for commonly used commands
ribbon	area containing the tabs with options and buttons divided into groups
Status bar	displays number of pages and words, view buttons, and Zoom slider bar
tabs	contain commands and features organized into groups
Taskbar	contains icons for launching programs, buttons for active tasks, and a notification area
Title bar	displays document name followed by program name
vertical ruler	used to set top and bottom margins
vertical scroll bar	used to view various parts of the document beyond the screen

end-of-sentence punctuation such as a period, question mark, or exclamation point, and after a colon. Proportional typeface is set closer together, and extra white space at the end of a sentence or after a colon is not needed.

- **Option buttons:** As you insert and edit text in a document, you may notice an option button popping up in your text. The name and appearance of this option button varies depending on the action. If a word you type is corrected by AutoCorrect, if you create an automatic list, or if autoformatting is applied to text, the AutoCorrect Options button appears. Click this button to undo the specific automatic action. If you paste text in a document, the Paste Options button appears near the text. Click this button to display the Paste Options gallery with buttons for controlling how the pasted text is formatted.
- **AutoComplete:** Microsoft Word and other Office applications include an AutoComplete feature that inserts an entire item when you type a few identifying characters. For example, type the letters *Mond* and *Monday* displays in a ScreenTip above the letters. Press the Enter key or press F3 and Word inserts *Monday* in the document.

Using the New Line Command

A Word document is based on a template that applies default formatting. Some basic formatting includes 1.08 line spacing and 8 points of spacing after a paragraph. Each time you press the Enter key, a new paragraph begins and 8 points of spacing is inserted after the paragraph. If you want to move the insertion point down to the next line without including the additional 8 points of spacing, use the New Line command, Shift + Enter.

Project 1a Creating a Document — Part 1 of 2

1. Open Word by clicking the Word 2013 tile at the Windows Start screen. At the Word opening screen, click the *Blank document* template. (These steps may vary. Check with your instructor for specific instructions.)
2. At a blank document, type the information shown in Figure 1.2 with the following specifications:
   a. Correct any errors highlighted by the spell checker or grammar checker as they occur.
   b. Press the spacebar once after end-of-sentence punctuation.
   c. After typing *Created:* press Shift + Enter to move the insertion point to the next line without adding 8 points of additional spacing.
   d. To insert the word *Thursday* located towards the end of the document, type Thur and then press F3. (This is an example of the AutoComplete feature.)
   e. To insert the word *December*, type Dece and then press the Enter key. (This is another example of the AutoComplete feature.)
   f. Press Shift + Enter after typing *December 8, 2015*.
   g. When typing the last line (the line containing the ordinal numbers), type the ordinal number text and AutoCorrect will automatically convert the letters in the ordinal numbers to superscript.
3. When you are finished typing the text, press the Enter key once.

Figure 1.2 Project 1a

The traditional chronological resume lists your work experience in reverse-chronological order (starting with your current or most recent position). The functional style deemphasizes the "where" and "when" of your career and instead groups similar experiences, talents, and qualifications regardless of when they occurred.

Like the chronological resume, the hybrid resume includes specifics about where you worked, when you worked there, and what your job titles were. Like a functional resume, a hybrid resume emphasizes your most relevant qualifications in an expanded summary section, in several "career highlights" bullet points at the top of your resume, or in project summaries.

Created:
Thursday, December 8, 2015
Note: The two paragraphs will become the 2nd and 3rd paragraphs in the 5th section.

Quick Steps

Save a Document
1. Click Save button on Quick Access toolbar.
2. Click desired location.
3. Click Browse button.
4. Type document name in *File name* text box.
5. Press Enter or click Save button.

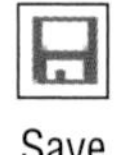
Save

HINT

Save a document approximately every 15 minutes or when interrupted.

Saving a Document

Save a document if you want to use it in the future. You can use a variety of methods to save a document, such as clicking the Save button on the Quick Access toolbar, clicking the FILE tab and then clicking the *Save* option or *Save As* option, or using the keyboard shortcut Ctrl + S. When you choose one of these options, the Save As backstage area displays, as shown in Figure 1.3. At this backstage area, click the desired location. For example, click the *OneDrive* option preceded by your name if you are saving to your OneDrive or click the *Computer* option if you are saving to your computer. After specifying the place, click the Browse button and the Save As dialog box displays, as shown in Figure 1.4. If you are saving to your computer, you can double-click the *Computer* option to display the Save As dialog box. At this dialog box, type the name of the document in the *File name* text box and then press Enter or click the Save button. You can go directly to the Save As dialog box without displaying the Save As backstage area by pressing the F12 function key.

Figure 1.3 Save As Backstage Area

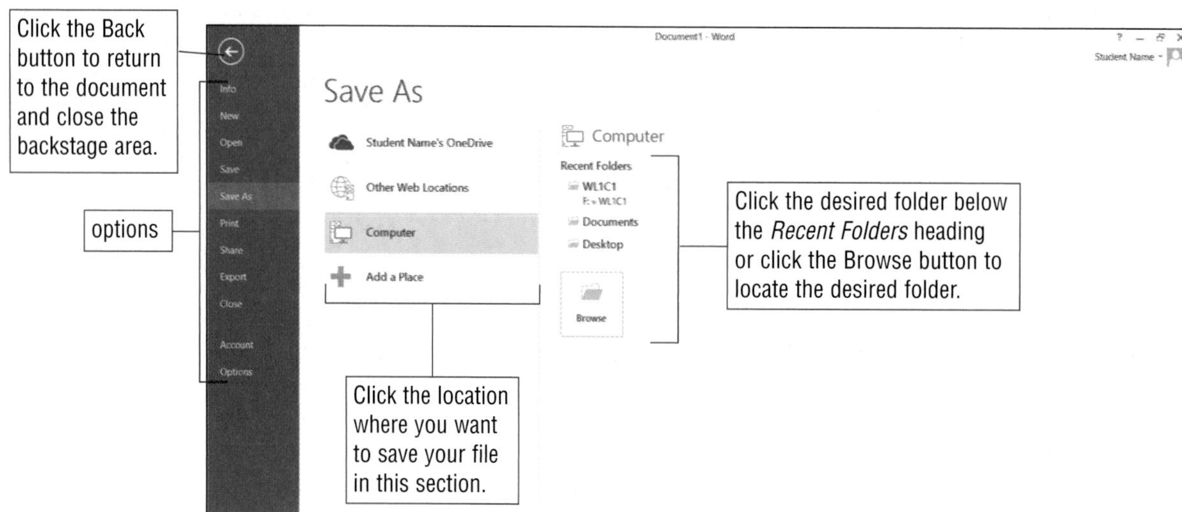
Click the Back button to return to the document and close the backstage area.
options
Save As
Info
New
Open
Save
Save As
Print
Share
Export
Close
Account
Options
Student Name's OneDrive
Other Web Locations
Computer
Add a Place
Computer
Recent Folders
WL1C1
Documents
Desktop
Browse
Click the desired folder below the *Recent Folders* heading or click the Browse button to locate the desired folder.
Click the location where you want to save your file in this section.

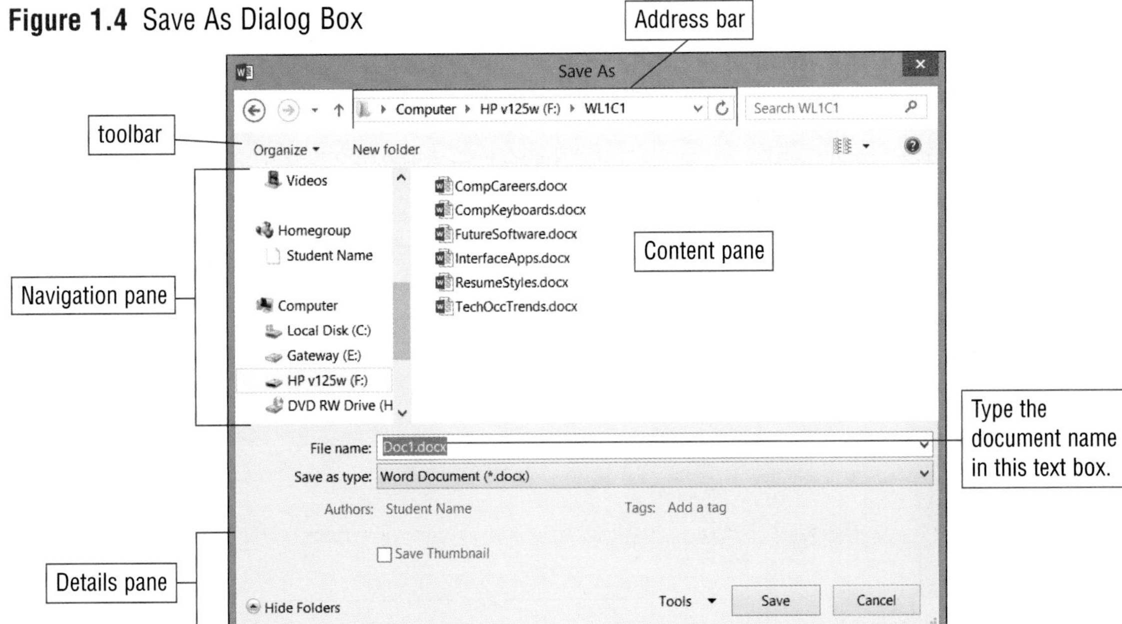

Figure 1.4 Save As Dialog Box

Naming a Document

Document names created in Word and other applications in the Office suite can be up to 255 characters in length, including the drive letter and any folder names, and may include spaces. File names cannot include any of the following characters:

forward slash (/)	asterisk (*)	colon (:)
backslash (\)	question mark (?)	semicolon (;)
greater than sign (>)	quotation marks (" ")	pipe symbol (|)
less than sign (<)		

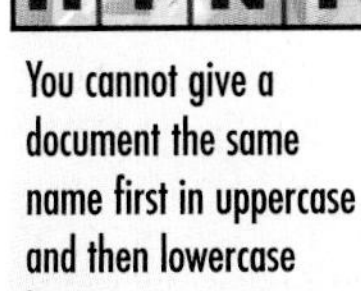

HINT

You cannot give a document the same name first in uppercase and then lowercase letters.

Printing a Document

Click the FILE tab and the backstage area displays. The buttons and options at the backstage area change depending on the option selected at the left side of the backstage area. If you want to remove the backstage area without completing an action, click the Back button located in the upper left corner of the backstage area or press the Esc key on your keyboard.

Quick Steps

Print a Document

Click Quick Print button on Quick Access toolbar.

OR

1. Click FILE tab.
2. Click *Print* option.
3. Click Print button.

Many of the files you create will need to be printed. A printing of a document on paper is referred to as ***hard copy***, and a document displayed on the screen is referred to as ***soft copy***. Print a document with options at the Print backstage area, shown in Figure 1.5. To display this backstage area, click the FILE tab and then click the *Print* option. You can also display the Print backstage area using the keyboard shortcut Ctrl + P.

Click the Print button located toward the upper left side of the backstage area to send the document to the printer and specify the number of copies you want printed with the *Copies* option. Below the Print button are two categories—*Printer* and *Settings*. Use the gallery in the *Printer* category to specify the desired printer. The *Settings* category contains a number of galleries, each with options for specifying how you want your document printed, including whether you want the pages collated when printed; the orientation, page size, and margins of your document; and how many pages of your document you want to print on a sheet of paper.

Figure 1.5 Print Backstage Area

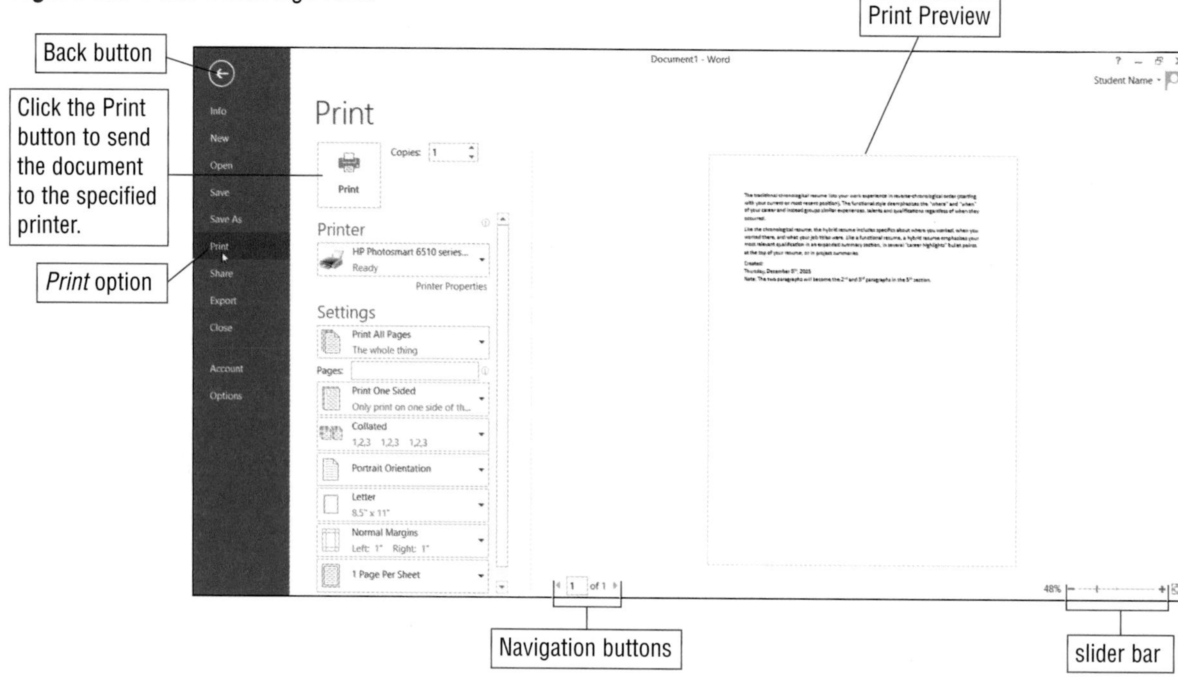

Quick Print

Another method for printing a document is to insert the Quick Print button on the Quick Access toolbar and then click the button. This sends the document directly to the printer without displaying the Print backstage area. To insert the button on the Quick Access toolbar, click the Customize Quick Access Toolbar button that displays at the right side of the toolbar and then click *Quick Print* at the drop-down list. To remove the Quick Print button from the Quick Access toolbar, right-click the button and then click the *Remove from Quick Access Toolbar* option that displays in the drop-down list.

Closing a Document

Quick Steps

Close a Document
1. Click FILE tab.
2. Click *Close* option.

OR

Press Ctrl + F4.

When you save a document, it is saved on your OneDrive or other storage medium and remains in the document screen. To remove the document from the screen, click the FILE tab and then click the *Close* option or use the keyboard shortcut Ctrl + F4. When you close a document, the document is removed and a blank screen displays. At this screen, you can open a previously saved document, create a new document, or close Word.

Project 1b Saving, Printing, and Closing a Document — Part 2 of 2

1. Save the document you created for Project 1a and name it **WL1-C1-P1-Resume** (*WL1-* for Word Level 1, *C1-* for Chapter 1, *P1-* for Project 1, and *Resume* because the document is about resumes) by completing the following steps:
   a. Click the Save button on the Quick Access toolbar.
   b. At the Save As backstage area, click the *OneDrive* option preceded by your name if you are saving to your OneDrive, or click the *Computer* option if you are saving to your computer or USB flash drive.
   c. Click the Browse button.

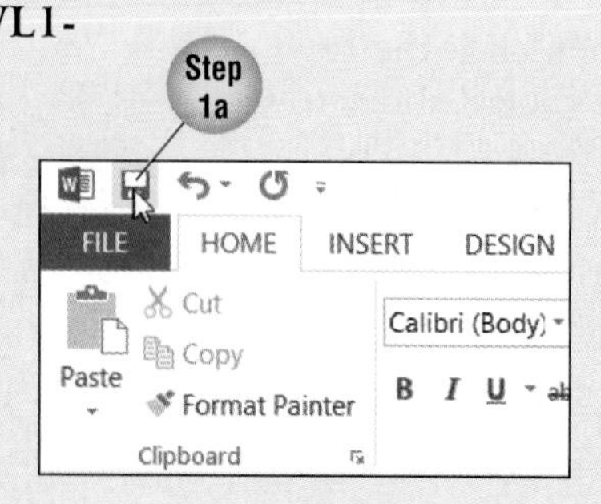

d. At the Save As dialog box, if necessary, navigate to the WL1C1 folder.

e. Click in the *File name* text box (this selects any text in the box), type **WL1-C1-P1-Resume**, and then press Enter.

2. Print the document by clicking the FILE tab, clicking the *Print* option, and then clicking the Print button at the Print backstage area.

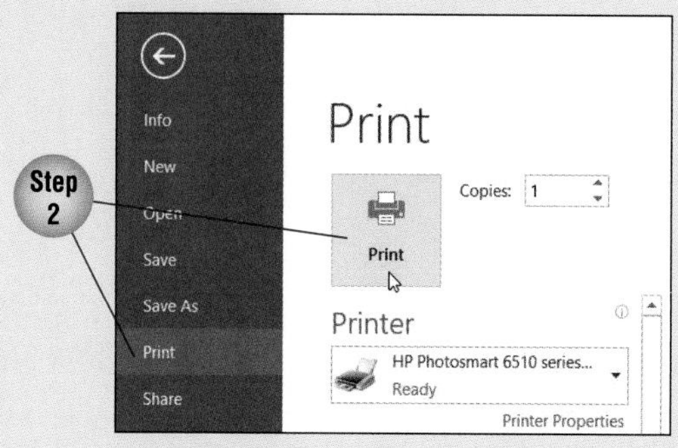

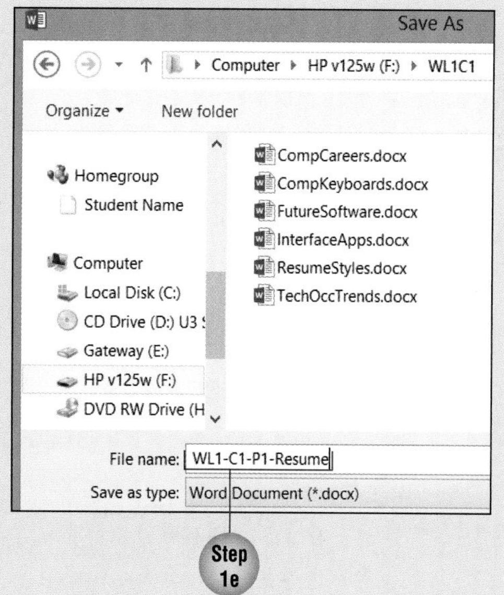

3. Close the document by clicking the FILE tab and then clicking the *Close* option.

Project 2 Save and Edit a Word Document — 2 Parts

You will open a document located in the WL1C1 folder on your storage medium, add text to the document, and then save the document with a new name.

Creating a New Document

When you close a document, a blank screen displays. If you want to create a new document, display a blank document. To do this, click the FILE tab, click the *New* option, and then click the Blank document template. You can also open a new document using the keyboard shortcut, Ctrl + N, or by inserting a New button on the Quick Access toolbar. To insert the button, click the Customize Quick Access Toolbar button that displays at the right side of the toolbar and then click *New* at the drop-down list.

Quick Steps

Create a New Document
1. Click FILE tab.
2. Click *New* option.
3. Click Blank document template.

Opening a Document

After you save and close a document, you can open it at the Open dialog box, shown in Figure 1.6. To display this dialog box, click the FILE tab and then click the *Open* option. This displays the Open backstage area. You can also display the Open backstage area with the keyboard shortcut Ctrl + O, by inserting an Open button on the Quick Access toolbar, or by clicking the Open Other Documents hyperlink that displays in the lower left corner of the Word 2013 opening screen. At the Open backstage area, click the desired location (such as your OneDrive or *Computer*) and then click the Browse button. (If you are opening a document from your computer or USB flash drive, you can double-click the *Computer* option.) When you click the Browse button (or double-click the *Computer* option) the

Quick Steps

Open a Document
1. Click FILE tab.
2. Click *Open* option.
3. Click desired location.
4. Click Browse button.
5. Double-click document name.

Open dialog box displays. You can go directly to the Open dialog box without displaying the Open backstage area by pressing Ctrl + F12. At the Open dialog box, open a document by double-clicking the document name in the Content pane.

If a document is open, Word will display the folder name where the document is located below the *Current Folder* heading in the Open backstage area with your OneDrive or the *Computer* option selected. Click this folder name to display the folder contents. In addition to the current folder, the Open backstage area also displays a list of the most recently accessed folders below the *Recent Folders* heading. Open a folder by clicking the folder name.

Opening a Document from the Recent Documents List

At the Open backstage area with Recent Documents selected, the Recent Documents list displays the names of the most recently opened documents. By default, Word displays 25 of the most recently opened documents. To open a document from the Recent Documents list, scroll down the list and then click the desired document. The Word 2013 opening screen also displays a list of the most recently opened documents. Click a document name in the Recent list at the opening screen to open the document.

Pinning a Document to the Recent Documents List

If you want a document to remain in the Recent Documents list at the Open backstage area, "pin" the document to the list. To pin a document, position the mouse pointer over the desired document name and then click the small left-pointing stick pin that displays at the right side of the document name. This changes it to a down-pointing stick pin. The next time you display the Open backstage area, the document you "pinned" displays at the top of the Recent

Figure 1.6 Open Dialog Box

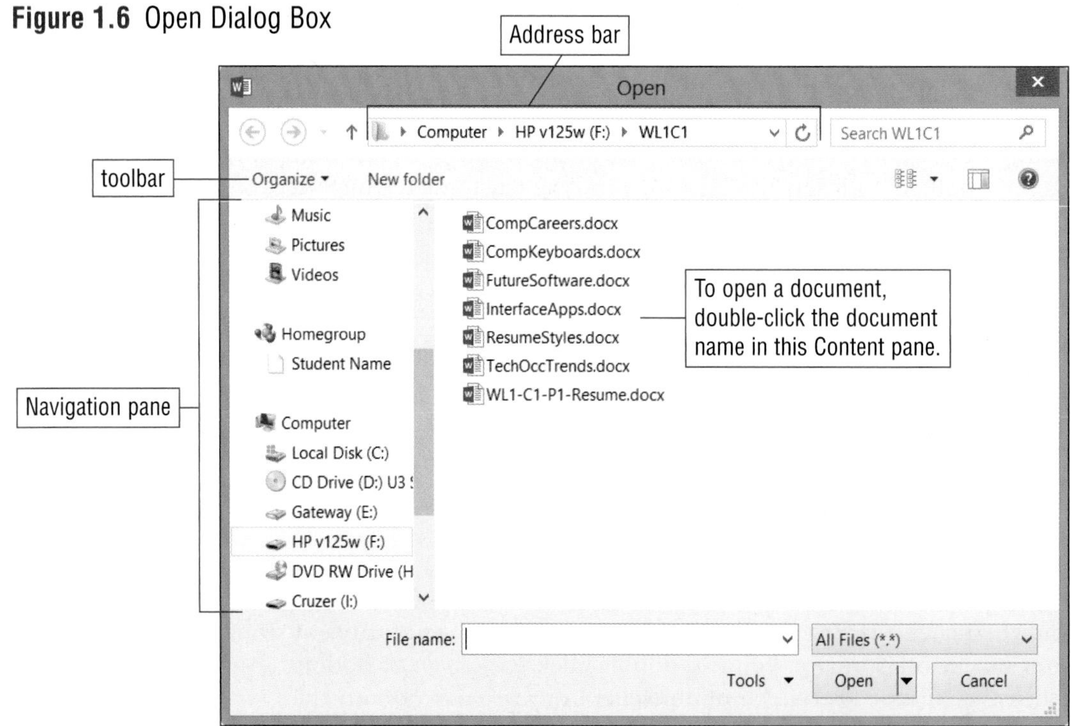

Documents list. You can also pin a document to the Recent list at the Word 2013 opening screen. When you pin a document, it displays at the top of the Recent list as well as the Recent Documents list at the Open backstage area. To "unpin" a document from the Recent or Recent Documents list, click the pin to change it from a down-pointing pin to a left-pointing pin. You can pin more than one document to a list. Another method for pinning and unpinning documents is to use the shortcut menu. Right-click a document name and then click *Pin to list* or *Unpin from list*.

In addition to pinning documents to a list, you can pin a folder to the Recent Folders list. Pin a folder in the same manner as pinning a document. If you access a particular folder on a regular basis, consider pinning it to the list.

Project 2a Opening and Pinning/Unpinning a Document — Part 1 of 2

1. Open **CompCareers.docx** by completing the following steps:
   a. Click the FILE tab and then click the *Open* option.
   b. At the Open backstage area, click the desired location. (For example, click your OneDrive if you are using your OneDrive account, or click the *Computer* option if you are opening a document from your computer's hard drive or a USB flash drive.)
   c. Click the WL1C1 folder that displays below the *Recent Folders* heading. (If the folder name does not display, click the Browse button and then navigate to the WL1C1 folder.)
   d. At the Open dialog box, double-click *CompCareers.docx* in the Content pane.

Open
Computer ▸ HP v125w (F:) ▸ WL1C1
Organize ▾ New folder
Music
Pictures
Videos
Homegroup
Student Name
CompCareers.docx
CompKeyboards.docx
FutureSoftware.docx
InterfaceApps.docx
ResumeStyles.docx
TechOccTrends.docx
WL1-C1-P1-Resume.docx
Step 1d

2. Close **CompCareers.docx**.
3. Open **FutureSoftware.docx** by completing steps similar to those in Step 1.
4. Close **FutureSoftware.docx**.
5. Pin **CompCareers.docx** to the list of recent documents by completing the following steps:
   a. Click the FILE tab and then, if necessary, click the *Open* option.
   b. Hover the mouse over **CompCareers.docx** in the Recent Documents list and then click the left-pointing stick pin that displays at the right side of the document. (This moves the document to the top of the list and changes the left-pointing stick pin to a down-pointing stick pin.)

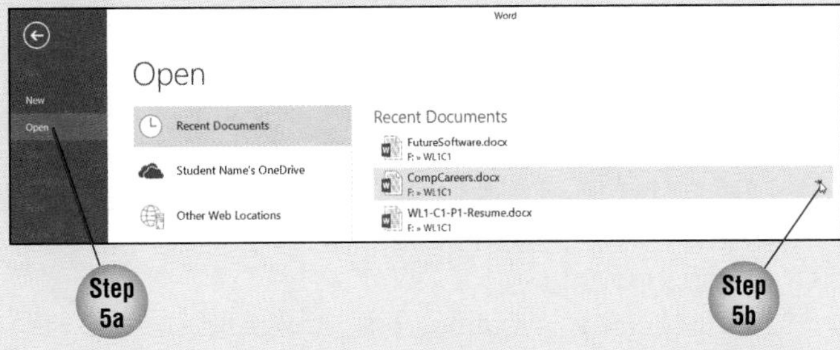

6. Click *CompCareers.docx* at the top of the Recent Documents list to open the document.
7. With the insertion point positioned at the beginning of the document, type the text shown in Figure 1.7.
8. Unpin **CompCareers.docx** from the Recent Documents list by completing the following steps:
   a. Click the FILE tab and then click the *Open* option.
   b. Click the down-pointing stick pin that displays at the right of **CompCareers.docx** in the Recent Documents list. (This changes the pin from a down-pointing stick pin to a left-pointing stick pin.)
   c. Click the Back button to return to the document.

Figure 1.7 Project 2a

> The majority of new jobs being created in the United States today involve daily work with computers. Computer-related careers include technical support jobs, sales and training, programming and applications development, network and database administration, and computer engineering.

Quick Steps

Save a Document with Save As
1. Click FILE tab.
2. Click *Save As* option.
3. At Save As backstage area, click desired location.
4. Click Browse button.
5. At Save As dialog box, navigate to desired folder.
6. Type document name in *File name* text box.
7. Press Enter.

Close Word
Click Close button.
OR
Press Alt + F4.

Saving a Document with Save As

If you open a previously saved document and want to give it a new name, use the *Save As* option at the backstage area rather than the *Save* option. Click the FILE tab and then click the *Save As* option. At the Save As backstage area, click the desired location and then click the Browse button or click the desired folder below the *Current Folder* or *Recent Folders* headings. At the Save As dialog box, type the new name for the document in the *File name* text box and then press Enter.

Closing Word

When you are finished working with Word and have saved all necessary information, close Word by clicking the Close button located in the upper right corner of the screen. You can also close Word with the keyboard shortcut Alt + F4.

Project 2b Saving a Document with Save As

Part 2 of 2

1. With **CompCareers.docx** open, save the document with a new name by completing the following steps:
   a. Click the FILE tab and then click the *Save As* option.
   b. At the Save As backstage area, click the *WL1C1* folder below the *Current Folder* heading or the *Recent Folders* heading. (If the folder does not display, double-click your OneDrive or the *Computer* option and then navigate to the WL1C1 folder.)
   c. At the Save As dialog box, press the Home key on your keyboard to move the insertion point to the beginning of the file name and then type **WL1-C1-P2-**. (Pressing the Home key saves you from having to type the entire document name.)
   d. Press the Enter key.

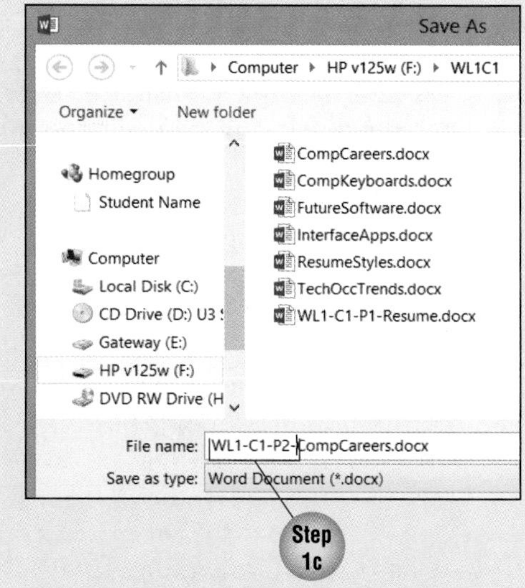

2. Print the document by clicking the FILE tab, clicking the *Print* option, and then clicking the Print button at the Print backstage area. (If your Quick Access toolbar contains the Quick Print button, you can click the button to send the document directly to the printer.)
3. Close the document by pressing Ctrl + F4.

Project 3 Scroll and Browse in a Document — 2 Parts

You will open a previously created document, save it with a new name, and then use scrolling and browsing techniques to move the insertion point to specific locations in the document.

Editing a Document

When editing a document, you may decide to insert or delete text. To edit a document, use the mouse, the keyboard, or a combination of the two to move the insertion point to a specific location in the document. To move the insertion point using the mouse, position the I-beam pointer where you want to place the insertion point and then click the left mouse button.

You can also scroll in a document, which changes the text display but does not move the insertion point. Use the mouse with the ***vertical scroll bar*** located at the right side of the screen to scroll through text in a document. Click the up scroll arrow at the top of the vertical scroll bar to scroll up through the document, and click the down scroll arrow to scroll down through the document. The scroll bar contains a scroll box that indicates the location of the text in the document screen in relation to the remainder of the document. To scroll up one screen at a time, position the arrow pointer above the scroll box (but below the up scroll arrow) and then click the left mouse button. Position the arrow pointer below the scroll box and click the left button to scroll down a screen. If you hold down the left mouse button, the action becomes continuous. You can also position the arrow pointer on the scroll box, hold down the left mouse button, and then drag the scroll box along the scroll bar to reposition text in the document screen. As you drag the scroll box along the vertical scroll bar in a longer document, page numbers display in a box at the right side of the document screen.

Project 3a Scrolling in a Document — Part 1 of 2

1. Open **InterfaceApps.docx** (from the WL1C1 folder you copied to your storage medium).
2. Save the document with Save As and name it **WL1-C1-P3-InterfaceApps**.
3. Position the I-beam pointer at the beginning of the first paragraph and then click the left mouse button.
4. Click the down scroll arrow on the vertical scroll bar several times. (This scrolls down lines of text in the document.) With the mouse pointer on the down scroll arrow, hold down the left mouse button and keep it down until the end of the document displays.
5. Position the mouse pointer on the up scroll arrow and hold down the left mouse button until the beginning of the document displays.
6. Position the mouse pointer below the scroll box and then click the left mouse button. Continue clicking the mouse button (with the mouse pointer positioned below the scroll box) until the end of the document displays.
7. Position the mouse pointer on the scroll box in the vertical scroll bar. Hold down the left mouse button, drag the scroll box to the top of the vertical scroll bar, and then release the mouse button. (Notice that the document page numbers display in a box at the right side of the document screen.)
8. Click in the title at the beginning of the document. (This moves the insertion point to the location of the mouse pointer.)

Moving the Insertion Point to a Specific Line or Page

Word includes a Go To feature you can use to move the insertion point to a specific location in a document such as a line or page. To use the feature, click the Find button arrow located in the Editing group on the HOME tab and then click *Go To* at the drop-down list. At the Find and Replace dialog box with the Go To tab selected, move the insertion point to a specific page by typing the page number in the *Enter page number* text box and then pressing Enter. Move to a specific line by clicking the *Line* option in the *Go to what* list box, typing the line number in the *Enter line number* text box and then pressing Enter. Click the Close button to close the dialog box.

Moving the Insertion Point with the Keyboard

To move the insertion point with the keyboard, use the arrow keys located to the right of the regular keyboard or use the arrow keys on the numeric keypad. If you use these keys, make sure Num Lock is off. Use the arrow keys together with other keys to move the insertion point to various locations in the document, as shown in Table 1.2.

When moving the insertion point, Word considers a word to be any series of characters between spaces. A paragraph is any text that is followed by a stroke of the Enter key. A page is text that is separated by a soft or hard page break.

Table 1.2 Insertion Point Movement Commands

To move insertion point	*Press*
one character left	Left Arrow
one character right	Right Arrow
one line up	Up Arrow
one line down	Down Arrow
one word left	Ctrl + Left Arrow
one word right	Ctrl + Right Arrow
to end of line	End
to beginning of line	Home
to beginning of current paragraph	Ctrl + Up Arrow
to beginning of next paragraph	Ctrl + Down Arrow
up one screen	Page Up
down one screen	Page Down
to top of previous page	Ctrl + Page Up
to top of next page	Ctrl + Page Down
to beginning of document	Ctrl + Home
to end of document	Ctrl + End

Resuming Reading or Editing in a Document

If you open a previously saved document, you can move the insertion point to where the insertion point was last located when the document was closed by pressing Shift + F5.

When you work in a multiple-page document and then close the document, Word remembers the page where the insertion point was last positioned. When you reopen the document, Word displays a "Welcome back!" message at the right side of the screen near the vertical scroll bar. The message tells you that you can pick up where you left off and identifies the page where your insertion point was last located. Click the message and the insertion point is positioned at the top of that page.

Project 3b **Moving the Insertion Point in a Document** **Part 2 of 2**

1. With **WL1-C1-P3-InterfaceApps.docx** open, move the insertion point to line 15 and then to page 3 by completing the following steps:
   a. Click the Find button arrow located in the Editing group on the HOME tab and then click *Go To* at the drop-down list.
   b. At the Find and Replace dialog box with the Go To tab selected, click *Line* in the *Go to what* list box.
   c. Type 15 in the *Enter line number* text box and then press Enter.
   d. Click *Page* in the *Go to what* list box.
   e. Click in the *Enter page number* text box, type 3, and then press Enter.
   f. Click the Close button to close the Find and Replace dialog box. 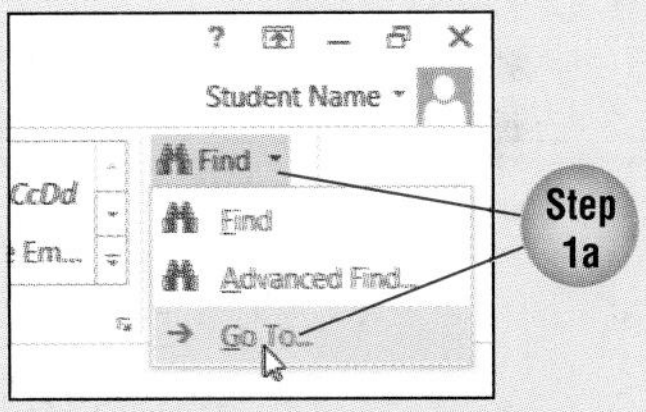 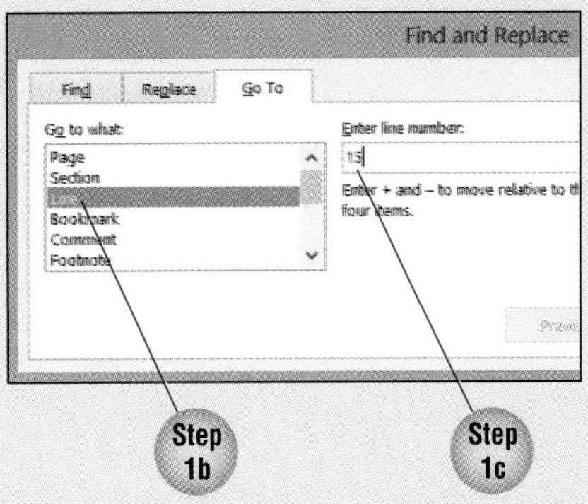
2. Close the document.
3. Open the document by clicking the FILE tab, clicking the *Open* option (if necessary), and then double-clicking the document name ***WL1-C1-P3-InterfaceApps.docx*** that displays at the top of the Recent Documents list.
4. Move the mouse pointer to the right side of the screen to display the "Welcome back!" message. Hover the mouse over the message and then click the left mouse button. (This positions the insertion point at the top of the third page—the page where the insertion point was positioned when you closed the document.) 
5. Press Ctrl + Home to move the insertion point to the beginning of the document.
6. Practice using the keyboard commands shown in Table 1.2 to move the insertion point within the document.
7. Close **WL1-C1-P3-InterfaceApps.docx**.

Project 4 Insert and Delete Text — 2 Parts

You will open a previously created document, save it with a new name, and then make editing changes to the document. The editing changes include selecting, inserting, and deleting text.

Inserting and Deleting Text

Editing a document may include inserting and/or deleting text. To insert text in a document, position the insertion point in the desired location and then type the text. Existing characters move to the right as you type the text. A number of options are available for deleting text. Some deletion commands are shown in Table 1.3.

Selecting Text

Use the mouse and/or keyboard to select a specific amount of text. Once you have selected the text, you can delete it or perform other Word functions on it. When text is selected, it displays with a gray background, as shown in Figure 1.8, and the Mini toolbar displays. The Mini toolbar contains buttons for common tasks. (You will learn more about the Mini toolbar in Chapter 2.)

Table 1.3 Deletion Commands

To delete	*Press*
character right of insertion point	Delete key
character left of insertion point	Backspace key
text from insertion point to beginning of word	Ctrl + Backspace
text from insertion point to end of word	Ctrl + Delete

Figure 1.8 Selected Text and Mini Toolbar

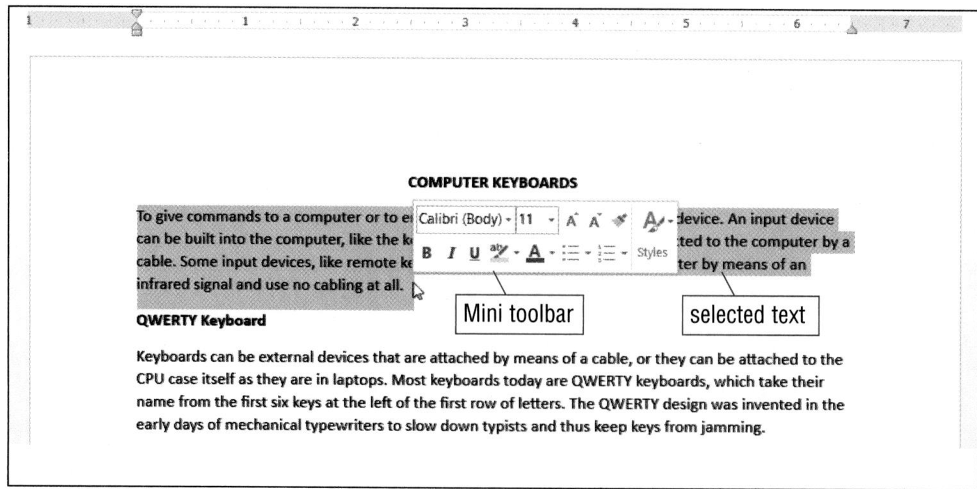

Selecting Text with the Mouse

Use the mouse to select a word, line, sentence, paragraph, or the entire document. Table 1.4 indicates the steps to follow to select various amounts of text. To select a specific amount of text, such as a line or a paragraph, click in the selection bar. The selection bar is the space located toward the left side of the document screen between the left edge of the page and the text. When the mouse pointer is positioned in the selection bar, the pointer turns into an arrow pointing up and to the right (instead of to the left).

To select an amount of text other than a word, sentence, or paragraph, position the I-beam pointer on the first character of the text to be selected, hold down the left mouse button, drag the I-beam pointer to the last character of the text to be selected, and then release the mouse button. You can also select all text between the current insertion point and the I-beam pointer. To do this, position the insertion point where you want the selection to begin, hold down the Shift key, click the I-beam pointer at the end of the selection, and then release the Shift key. To cancel a selection using the mouse, click anywhere in the document screen outside the selected text.

Select text vertically in a document by holding down the Alt key while dragging with the mouse. This is especially useful when selecting a group of text, such as text set in columns.

Selecting Text with the Keyboard

To select a specific amount of text using the keyboard, turn on the Selection mode by pressing the F8 function key. With the Selection mode activated, use the arrow keys to select the desired text. If you want to cancel the selection, press the Esc key and then press any arrow key. You can customize the Status bar to display text indicating that the Selection mode is activated. To do this, right-click any blank location on the Status bar and then click *Selection Mode* at the pop-up list. When you press F8 to turn on the Selection mode, the words *EXTEND SELECTION* display on the Status bar. You can also select text with the commands shown in Table 1.5.

If text is selected, any character you type replaces the selected text.

Table 1.4 Selecting Text with the Mouse

To select	*Complete these steps using the mouse*
a word	Double-click the word.
a line of text	Click in the selection bar to the left of the line.
multiple lines of text	Drag in the selection bar to the left of the lines.
a sentence	Hold down the Ctrl key and then click anywhere in the sentence.
a paragraph	Double-click in the selection bar next to the paragraph, or triple-click anywhere in the paragraph.
multiple paragraphs	Drag in the selection bar.
an entire document	Triple-click in the selection bar.

Table 1.5 Selecting Text with the Keyboard

To select	*Press*
one character to right	Shift + Right Arrow
one character to left	Shift + Left Arrow
to end of word	Ctrl + Shift + Right Arrow
to beginning of word	Ctrl + Shift + Left Arrow
to end of line	Shift + End
to beginning of line	Shift + Home
one line up	Shift + Up Arrow
one line down	Shift + Down Arrow
to beginning of paragraph	Ctrl + Shift + Up Arrow
to end of paragraph	Ctrl + Shift + Down Arrow
one screen up	Shift + Page Up
one screen down	Shift + Page Down
to end of document	Ctrl + Shift + End
to beginning of document	Ctrl + Shift + Home
entire document	Ctrl + A or click Select button in Editing group and then click *Select All*

Project 4a Editing a Document

Part 1 of 2

1. Open **CompKeyboards.docx**. (This document is located in the WL1C1 folder you copied to your storage medium.)
2. Save the document with Save As and name it **WL1-C1-P4-CompKeyboards**.
3. Change the word *give* in the first sentence of the first paragraph to *enter*.
4. Change the second *to* in the first sentence to *into*.
5. Delete the words *means of* in the first sentence in the *QWERTY Keyboard* section.

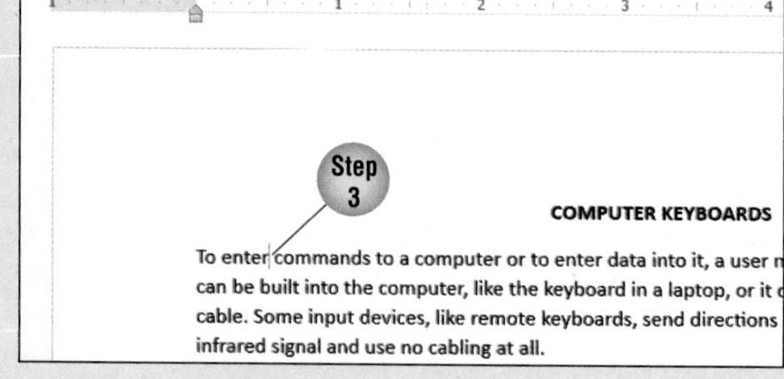

6. Select the words *and use no cabling at all* and the period that follows located at the end of the last sentence in the first paragraph, and then press the Delete key.
7. Insert a period immediately following the word *signal*.

8. Delete the heading line containing the text *QWERTY Keyboard* using the Selection mode by completing the following steps:
    a. Position the insertion point immediately before the *Q* in *QWERTY*.
    b. Press F8 to turn on the Selection mode.
    c. Press the Down Arrow key.
    d. Press the Delete key.
9. Complete steps similar to those in Step 8 to delete the heading line containing the text *DVORAK Keyboard*.
10. Begin a new paragraph with the sentence that reads *Keyboards have different physical appearances* by completing the following steps:
    a. Position the insertion point immediately left of the *K* in *Keyboards* (the first word of the fifth sentence in the last paragraph).
    b. Press the Enter key.
11. Save **WL1-C1-P4-CompKeyboards.docx**.

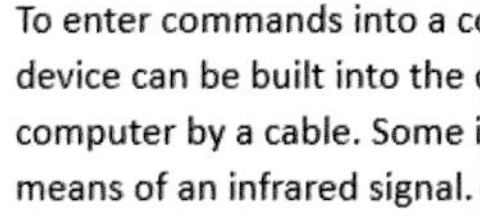

To enter commands into a c
device can be built into the
computer by a cable. Some i
means of an infrared signal.

QWERTY Keyboard

Keyboards can be external d
itself as they are in laptops.
the first six keys at the left o
of mechanical typewriters t

To enter commands into a computer or
device can be built into the computer, l
computer by a cable. Some input devic
means of an infrared signal.

Keyboards can be external devices that
itself as they are in laptops. Most keyb
the first six keys at the left of the first r
of mechanical typewriters to slow dow

The DVORAK keyboard is an alternative
commonly used keys are placed close t
install software on a QWERTY keyboard
keyboards is convenient especially whe

Keyboards have different physical appe
that of a calculator, containing number
"broken" into two pieces to reduce stra
change the symbol or character entere

Steps
10a-10b

Using the Undo and Redo Buttons

If you make a mistake and delete text that you did not intend to, or if you change your mind after deleting text and want to retrieve it, you can use the Undo or Redo buttons on the Quick Access toolbar. For example, if you type text and then click the Undo button, the text will be removed. You can undo text or commands. For example, if you add formatting such as bolding to text and then click the Undo button, the bolding is removed.

Undo

Redo

If you use the Undo button and then decide you do not want to reverse the original action, click the Redo button. For example, if you select and underline text and then decide to remove underlining, click the Undo button. If you then decide you want the underlining back on, click the Redo button. Many Word actions can be undone or redone. Some actions, however, such as printing and saving, cannot be undone or redone.

You cannot undo a save.

Word maintains actions in temporary memory. If you want to undo an action performed earlier, click the Undo button arrow. This causes a drop-down list to display. To make a selection from this drop-down list, click the desired action and the action, along with any actions listed above it in the drop-down list, is undone.

Project 4b Undoing and Redoing Deletions

Part 2 of 2

1. With **WL1-C1-P4-CompKeyboards.docx** open, delete the last sentence in the last paragraph using the mouse by completing the following steps:
   a. Hover the I-beam pointer anywhere over the sentence that begins *All keyboards have modifier keys*.
   b. Hold down the Ctrl key and then click the left mouse button.

> install software on a QWERTY keyboard that emulates a DVORAK keyboard. The ability to emulate other keyboards is convenient especially when working with foreign languages.
>
> Keyboards have different physical appearances. Many keyboards have a separate numeric keypad, like that of a calculator, containing numbers and mathematical operators. Some keyboards are sloped and "broken" into two pieces to reduce strain. All keyboards have modifier keys that enable the user to change the symbol or character entered when a given key is pressed.

   c. Press the Delete key.
2. Delete the last paragraph by completing the following steps:
   a. Position the I-beam pointer anywhere in the last paragraph (the paragraph that begins *Keyboards have different physical appearances*).
   b. Triple-click the left mouse button.
   c. Press the Delete key.
3. Undo the deletion by clicking the Undo button on the Quick Access toolbar.

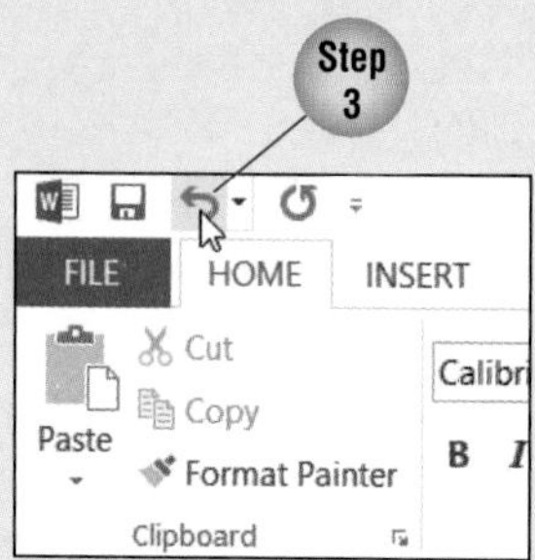

4. Redo the deletion by clicking the Redo button on the Quick Access toolbar.
5. Select the first sentence in the second paragraph and then delete it.
6. Select the first paragraph in the document and then delete it.
7. Undo the two deletions by completing the following steps:
   a. Click the Undo button arrow.
   b. Click the second *Clear* listed in the drop-down list. (This will redisplay the first sentence in the second paragraph as well as display the first paragraph. The sentence will be selected.)
8. Click outside the sentence to deselect it.
9. Save, print, and then close **WL1-C1-P4-CompKeyboards.docx**.

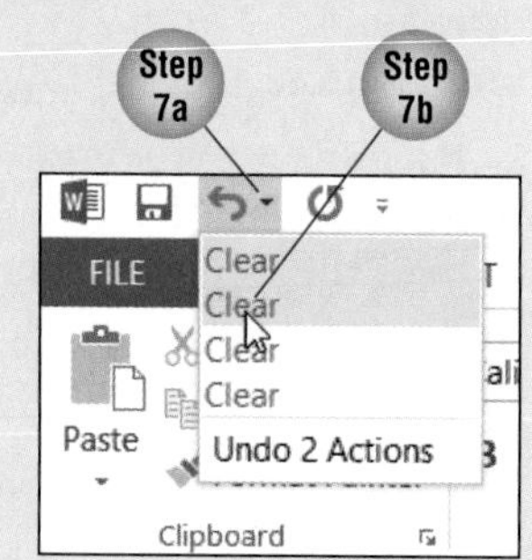

Project 5 Complete a Spelling and Grammar Check

1 Part

You will open a previously created document, save it with a new name, and then check the spelling and grammar in the document.

Checking the Spelling and Grammar in a Document

Two tools for creating thoughtful and well-written documents include a spelling checker and a grammar checker. The spelling checker finds misspelled words and offers replacement words. It also finds duplicate words and irregular capitalizations. When you spell check a document, the spelling checker compares the words in your document with the words in its dictionary. If the spelling checker finds a match, it passes over the word. If a match is not found for the word, the spelling checker will stop, select the word, and offer possible corrections.

The grammar checker will search a document for errors in grammar, punctuation, and word usage. If the grammar checker finds an error, it stops and offers possible corrections. The spelling checker and the grammar checker can help you create a well-written document but do not eliminate the need for proofreading.

To complete a spelling and grammar check, click the REVIEW tab and then click the Spelling & Grammar button in the Proofing group. You can also begin spelling and grammar checking by pressing the keyboard shortcut, F7. If Word detects a possible spelling error, the text containing the error is selected and the Spelling task pane displays. The Spelling task pane contains a list box with possible correction(s) along with buttons you can click to either change or ignore the spelling error, as described in Table 1.6. A definition of the selected word in the list box may display toward the bottom of the Spelling task pane if you have a dictionary installed.

If Word detects a gammar error, the word(s) or sentence is selected and possible corrections display in the Grammar task pane list box. Depending on the error selected, some or all of the buttons described in Table 1.6 may display in the Grammar task pane and a description of the grammar rule with suggestions may display toward the bottom of the task pane. With the buttons that display, you can choose to ignore or change the grammar error.

When checking the spelling and grammar in a document, you can temporarily leave the Spelling task pane or Grammar task pane by clicking in the document. To resume the spelling and grammar check, click the Resume button in the Spelling task pane or Grammar task pane.

Quick Steps

Check Spelling and Grammar

1. Click REVIEW tab.
2. Click Spelling & Grammar button.
3. Change or ignore errors.
4. Click OK.

Spelling & Grammar

Complete a spelling and grammar check on a portion of a document by selecting the text first and then clicking the Spelling & Grammar button.

Table 1.6 Spelling Task Pane and Grammar Task Pane Buttons

Button	Function
Ignore	During spell checking, skips that occurrence of the word; in grammar checking, leaves currently selected text as written.
Ignore All	During spell checking, skips that occurrence of the word and all other occurrences of the word in the document.
Add	Adds the selected word to the spelling check dictionary.
Delete	Deletes the currently selected word(s).
Change	Replaces the selected word with a word in the task pane list box.
Change All	Replaces the selected word and all other occurrences of it with a word in the task pane list box.

Project 5 Checking the Spelling and Grammar in a Document

Part 1 of 1

1. Open **TechOccTrends.docx**.
2. Save the document with Save As and name it **WL1-C1-P5-TechOccTrends**.
3. Click the REVIEW tab.
4. Click the Spelling & Grammar button in the Proofing group.
5. The spelling checker selects the word *tecnology* and displays the Spelling task pane. The proper spelling is selected in the Spelling task pane list box, so click the Change button (or Change All button).

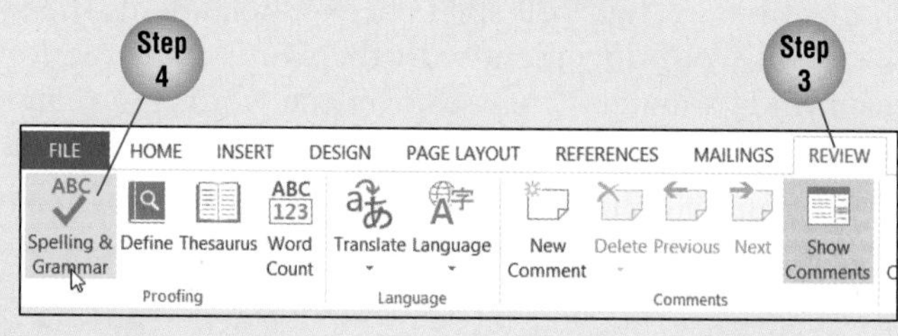

6. The grammar checker selects the sentence containing the word *job's* and displays the Grammar task pane with *jobs* selected in the list box. The grammar checker also displays toward the bottom of the Grammar task pane information about plurals or possessives. Read the information and then click the Change button.

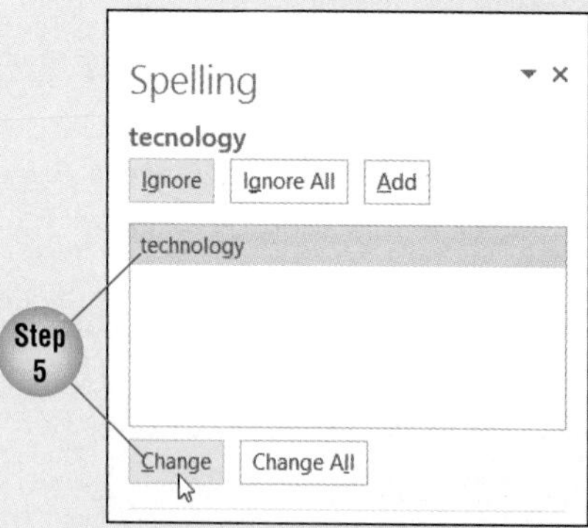

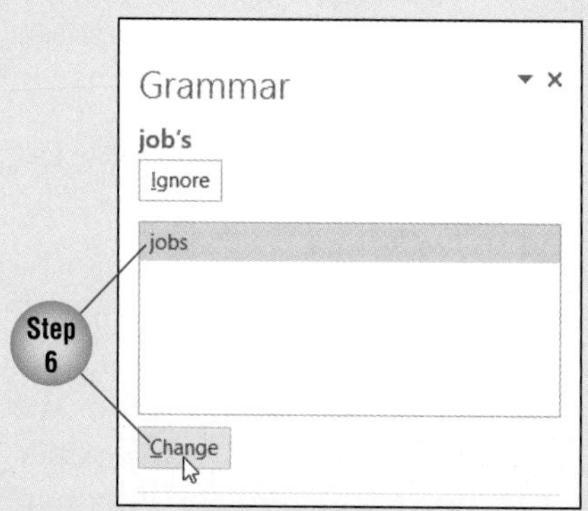

7. The grammar checker selects the word *too* in the document and displays the Grammar task pane, with *to* selected in the list box. If definitions of *to* and *too* display toward the bottom of the task pane, read the information. Click the Change button.
8. The grammar checker selects the sentence containing the words *downloaded* and *versus*, which contain two spaces between the words. The Grammar task pane displays in the list box the two words with only one space between. Read the information about spaces between words that displays toward the bottom of the Grammar task pane and then click the Change button.
9. The spelling checker selects the word *sucessful* and offers *successful* in the Spelling task pane list box. Since this word is misspelled in another location in the document, click the Change All button.
10. The spelling checker selects the word *are*, which is used twice in a row. Click the Delete button in the Spelling task pane to delete the second *are*.
11. When the message displays telling you that the spelling and grammar check is complete, click the OK button.
12. Save, print, and then close **WL1-C1-P5-TechOccTrends.docx**.

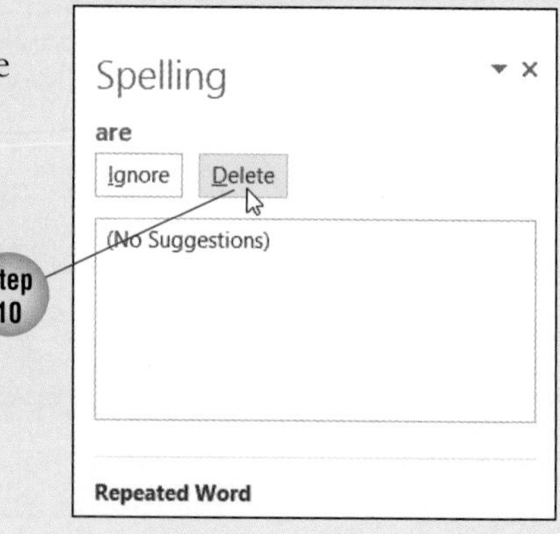

Project 6 Use the Help Feature 2 Parts

You will use the Help feature to learn more about printing and opening documents.

Using Help

Quick Steps

Use Help Feature

1. Click Microsoft Word Help button.
2. Type search text in search text box.
3. Press Enter.
4. Click desired topic.

Word's Help feature is an on-screen reference manual containing information about Word features and commands. Word's Help feature is similar to the Help features in Excel, PowerPoint, and Access. Get help by clicking the Microsoft Word Help button located in the upper right corner of the screen (a question mark) or by pressing the keyboard shortcut, F1. This displays the Word Help window, as shown in Figure 1.9. In this window, type a topic, feature, or question in the search text box and then press Enter. Topics related to the search text display in the Word Help window. Click a topic that interests you. If the topic window contains a Show All hyperlink in the upper right corner, click this hyperlink and the information expands to show all help information related to the topic. When you click the Show All hyperlink, it becomes the Hide All hyperlink.

The Word Help window contains five buttons that display to the left of the search text box. Use the Back and Forward buttons to navigate in the window. Click the Home button to return to the Word Help window opening screen. If you want to print information on a topic or feature, click the Print button and then click the Print button at the Print dialog box. You can make the text in the Word Help window larger by clicking the Use Large Text button. In addition to these five buttons, the Word Help window contains a Keep Help on Top button located near the upper right corner of the window. Click this button and the Word Help window remains on the screen even when you work in a document. Click the button again to remove the window from the screen.

Figure 1.9 Word Help Window

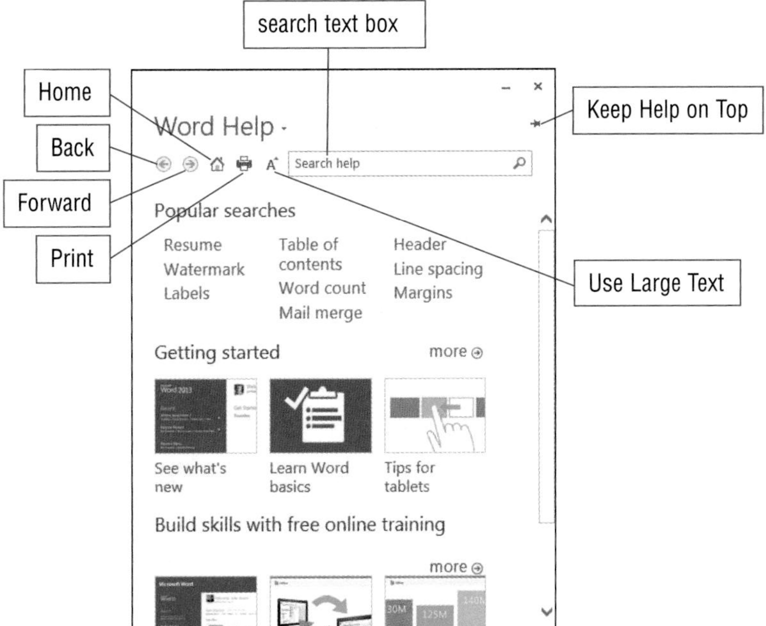

Getting Help from a ScreenTip

If you hover your mouse over some buttons, the ScreenTip that displays may include a Help icon and the Tell me more hyperlinked text. Click Tell me more, and the Word Help window opens with information about the button feature. You can also press F1 to display the Word Help window with information about the button feature.

Project 6a **Using the Help Feature** **Part 1 of 2**

1. At a blank document, click the Microsoft Word Help button located in the upper right corner of the screen.
2. At the Word Help window, click in the search text box and then type **print**.
3. Press the Enter key.
4. When the list of topics displays, click the Print and preview documents hyperlinked topic.

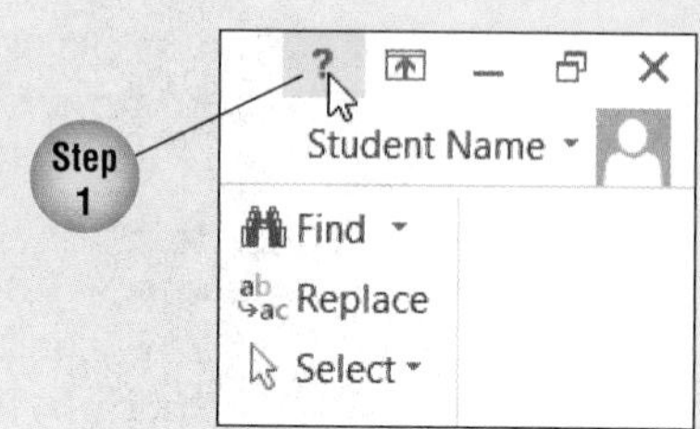

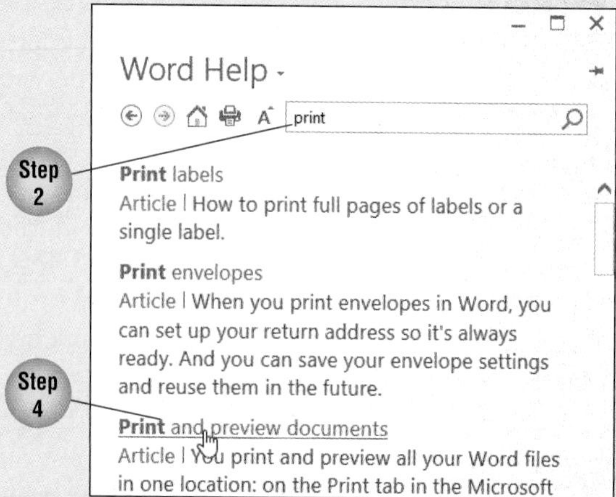

5. Scroll down the Word Help window and read the information about printing and previewing documents.
6. Click the Print button in the Word Help window. This displays the Print dialog box. If you want to print the topic, click the Print button; otherwise, click the Cancel button to close the dialog box.

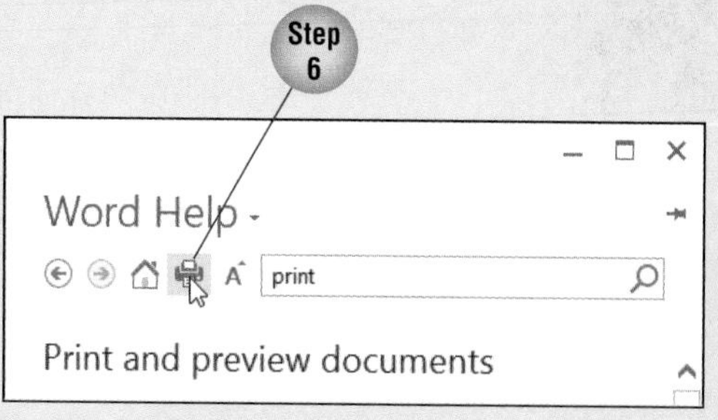

7. At the Word Help window, click the Use Large Text button to increase the size of the text in the window.
8. Click the Use Large Text button again to return the text to the normal size.
9. Click the Back button to return to the previous window.

10. Click the Forward button to redisplay the article on printing and previewing a document.
11. Click the Home button to return to the original Word Help window screen.
12. Click the Close button to close the Word Help window.
13. Hover your mouse over the Format Painter button in the Clipboard group on the HOME tab.
14. Click the Tell me more hyperlinked text, which displays at the bottom of the ScreenTip.
15. Read the information in the Word Help window about the Format Painter feature.
16. Click the Close button to close the Word Help window.

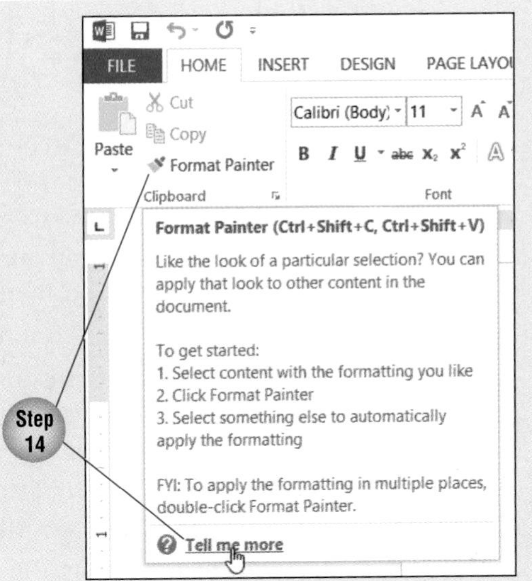

Getting Help in a Dialog Box

Some dialog boxes contain a help button you can click to display specific information about the dialog box. Open a dialog box and then click the help button and information about the dialog box displays in the Word Help window. After reading and/or printing the information, close the Word Help window and then close the dialog box by clicking the Close button located in the upper right corner.

Project 6b Getting Help in a Dialog Box

Part 2 of 2

1. At a blank document, click the Paragraph group dialog box launcher that displays in the lower right corner of the Pararaph group on the HOME tab.
2. Click the Help button that displays in the upper right corner of the Paragraph dialog box.
3. Read the information that displays in the Word Help window.
4. Close the Word Help window and then close the Paragraph dialog box.
5. Click the FILE tab and then click the *Open* option.
6. At the Open backstage area, double-click the *Computer* option.
7. At the Open dialog box, click the Get help button, which displays toward the upper right corner of the dialog box.
8. At the Windows Help and Support window, read the information that displays about opening a file or folder, and then click the Close button located in the upper right corner of the window.
9. Close the Open dialog box.
10. At the Open backstage area, press the Esc key on your keyboard.
11. Close the blank document without saving changes.

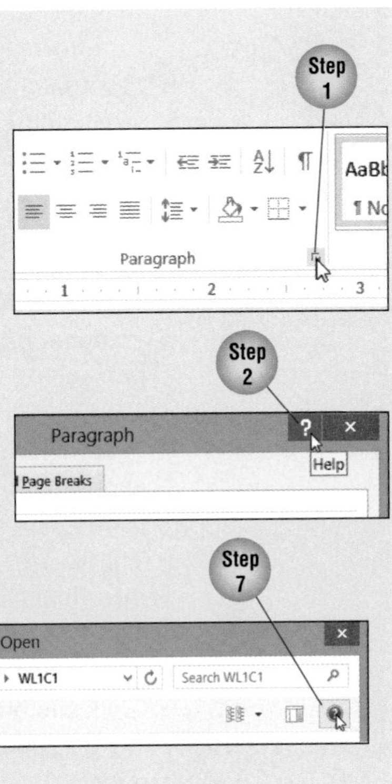

Chapter Summary

- Refer to Figure 1.1 and Table 1.1 for an example and a list of key Word screen features.
- The Quick Access toolbar contains buttons for commonly used commands.
- Click the FILE tab and the backstage area displays, containing options for working with and managing documents.
- The ribbon area contains tabs with options and buttons divided into groups.
- The insertion point displays as a blinking vertical line and indicates the position of the next character to be entered in the document.
- Document names can contain a maximum of 255 characters, including the drive letter and folder names, and may include spaces.
- The insertion point can be moved throughout the document without interfering with text by using the mouse, the keyboard, or the mouse combined with the keyboard.
- The scroll box on the vertical scroll bar indicates the location of the text in the document in relation to the remainder of the document.
- You can move the insertion point by character, word, screen, or page and from the first to the last character in a document. Refer to Table 1.2 for keyboard insertion point movement commands.
- Delete text by character, word, line, several lines, or partial page using specific keys or by selecting text using the mouse or the keyboard. Refer to Table 1.3 for deletion commands.
- You can select a specific amount of text using the mouse or the keyboard. Refer to Table 1.4 for information on selecting with the mouse, and refer to Table 1.5 for information on selecting with the keyboard.
- Use the Undo button on the Quick Access toolbar if you change your mind after typing, deleting, or formatting text and want to undo the action. Use the Redo button to redo something that had been undone with the Undo button.
- The spelling checker matches the words in your document with the words in its dictionary. If a match is not found, the word is selected and possible corrections are suggested in the Spelling task pane. The grammar checker searches a document for errors in grammar, style, punctuation, and word usage. When a grammar error is detected, possible corrections display in the Grammar task pane along with information about the grammar rule or error. Refer to Table 1.6 for Spelling task pane and Grammar task pane buttons.
- Word's Help feature is an on-screen reference manual containing information about Word features and commands. Click the Microsoft Word Help button or press F1 to display the Word Help window.
- The Word Help window contains five buttons to the left of the search text box, including the Back, Forward, Home, Print, and Use Large Text buttons.
- The Word Help window contains a Keep Help on Top button you can click to keep the Word Help window on the screen even when working in a document. Click the button again to remove the window from the screen.

- If you hover your mouse over some buttons, the ScreenTip that displays may include a Help icon and the Tell me more hyperlinked text. Click this hyperlinked text to display the Word Help window with information about the button feature.
- Some dialog boxes contain a help button you can click to display information specific to the dialog box.

Commands Review

FEATURE	RIBBON TAB, GROUP/OPTION	BUTTON, OPTION	KEYBOARD SHORTCUT
close document	FILE, *Close*		Ctrl + F4
close Word			Alt + F4
Find and Replace dialog box with Go To tab selected	HOME, Editing	, *Go To*	Ctrl + G
new blank document	FILE, *New*	*Blank document*	Ctrl + N
Open backstage area	FILE, *Open*		Ctrl + O
Print backstage area	FILE, *Print*		Ctrl + P
redo an action			Ctrl + Y
save	FILE, *Save*		Ctrl + S
Save As backstage area	FILE, *Save As*		F12
select document	HOME, Editing	, *Select All*	Ctrl + A
spelling and grammar checker	REVIEW, Proofing		F7
undo an action			Ctrl + Z
Word Help			F1

Concepts Check Test Your Knowledge 

Completion: In the space provided at the right, indicate the correct term, symbol, or command.

1. This toolbar contains the Save button. ____________________
2. Click this tab to display the backstage area. ____________________
3. This is the area located toward the top of the screen that contains tabs with options and buttons divided into groups. ____________________
4. This bar, located toward the bottom of the screen, displays the numbers of pages and words, view buttons, and the Zoom slider bar. ____________________
5. This tab is active by default. ____________________
6. This feature automatically corrects certain words as you type them. ____________________
7. This feature inserts an entire item when you type a few identifying characters and then press Enter or F3. ____________________
8. This is the keyboard shortcut to display the Print backstage area. ____________________
9. This is the keyboard shortcut to close a document. ____________________
10. This is the keyboard shortcut to display a new blank document. ____________________
11. Use this keyboard shortcut to move the insertion point to the beginning of the previous page. ____________________
12. Use this keyboard shortcut to move the insertion point to the end of the document. ____________________
13. Press this key on the keyboard to delete the character left of the insertion point. ____________________
14. Using the mouse, do this to select one word. ____________________
15. To select various amounts of text using the mouse, click in this bar. ____________________
16. Click this tab to display the Spelling & Grammar button in the Proofing group. ____________________
17. This is the keyboard shortcut to display the Word Help window. ____________________

Skills Check Assess Your Performance

Assessment 1

TYPE AND EDIT A DOCUMENT ON WRITING RESUMES

1. Open Word and then type the text in Figure 1.10. Correct any errors highlighted by the spelling checker, and space once after end-of-sentence punctuation.
2. Make the following changes to the document:
   a. Delete the first occurrence of the word *currently* in the first sentence of the first paragraph.
   b. Select the word *important* in the first sentence in the first paragraph and then type **essential**.
   c. Type **and hard-hitting** between the words *concise* and *written* located in the second sentence of the second paragraph.
   d. Delete the words *over and over,* (including the comma) located in the third sentence in the second paragraph.
   e. Select and then delete the second sentence of the third paragraph (the sentence that begins *So do not take*).
   f. Join the second and third paragraphs.
   g. Delete the name *Marie Solberg* and then type your first and last names.
3. Save the document and name it **WL1-C1-A1-WriteResume**.
4. Print and then close **WL1-C1-A1-WriteResume.docx**.

Figure 1.10 Assessment 1

Writing a Resume

For every job seeker, including those currently employed and those currently not working, a powerful resume is an important component of the job search. In fact, conducting a job search without a resume is virtually impossible. A resume is your calling card that briefly communicates the skills, qualifications, experience, and value you bring to the prospective employer. It is the document that will open doors and generate interviews.

Your resume is a sales document, and you are the product. You must identify the features of that product, and then communicate them in a concise written presentation. Remind yourself over and over, as you work your way through the resume process, that you are writing marketing literature designed to market yourself.

Your resume can have tremendous power and a phenomenal impact on your job search. So do not take it lightly. You should devote the time, energy, and resources that are essential to developing a resume that is well written, visually attractive, and effective in communicating who you are and how you want to be perceived.

Created by Marie Solberg
Monday, October 5, 2015
Note: Please insert this information between the 2nd and 3rd sections.

Assessment 2

CHECK THE SPELLING AND GRAMMAR OF A RESUME STYLES DOCUMENT

1. Open **ResumeStyles.docx**.
2. Save the document with Save As and name it **WL1-C1-A2-ResumeStyles**.
3. Complete a spelling and grammar check on the document and correct the selected errors.
4. Type the sentence **Different approaches work for different people.** between the first and second sentences in the first paragraph of text below the title *RESUME STYLES*.
5. Move the insertion point to the end of the document, type your first and last names, press Shift + Enter, and then type the current date.
6. Save, print, and then close **WL1-C1-A2-ResumeStyles.docx**.

Assessment 3

CREATE A DOCUMENT DESCRIBING KEYBOARD SHORTCUTS

1. Click the Microsoft Word Help button, type **keyboard shortcuts**, and then press Enter.
2. At the Word Help window, click the Keyboard shortcuts for Microsoft Word hyperlink.
3. At the keyboard shortcut window, click the Show All hyperlink.
4. Read through the information in the Word Help window.
5. Create a document describing four keyboard shortcuts.
6. Save the document and name it **WL1-C1-A3-KeyboardShortcuts**.
7. Print and then close **WL1-C1-A3-KeyboardShortcuts.docx**.

Visual Benchmark Demonstrate Your Proficiency

CREATE A LETTER

1. At a blank document, press the Enter key three times and then type the personal business letter shown in Figure 1.11 on the next page. Follow the directions in red.
2. Save the completed letter and name it **WL1-C1-VB-CoverLtr**.
3. Print and then close the document.

Figure 1.11 Visual Benchmark

(press Enter three times)

4520 South Park Street *(press Shift + Enter)*
Newark, NJ 07122 *(press Shift + Enter)*
Current Date *(press Enter two times)*

Mrs. Sylvia Hammond *(press Shift + Enter)*
Sales Director, Eastern Division *(press Shift + Enter)*
Grand Style Products *(press Shift + Enter)*
1205 Sixth Street *(press Shift + Enter)*
Newark, NJ 07102 *(press Enter)*

Dear Mrs. Hammond: *(press Enter)*

Thank you for agreeing to meet with me next Wednesday. Based on our initial conversation, it seems that my ability to sell solutions rather than products is a good fit for your needs as you seek to expand your visibility in the region. *(press Enter)*

As noted in the enclosed resume, I have led an under-performing product division to generating 33 percent of total revenue (up from 5 percent) at our location, and delivering, from a single location, 25 percent of total sales for our 20-site company. Having completed this turnaround over the last 5 years, I'm eager for new challenges where my proven skills in sales, marketing, and program/event planning can contribute to a company's bottom line. *(press Enter)*

I have been thinking about the challenges you described in building your presence at the retail level, and I have some good ideas to share at our meeting. I am excited about the future of Grand Style Products and eager to contribute to your growth. *(press Enter)*

Sincerely, *(press Enter two times)*

Student Name *(press Enter)*

Enclosure

Case Study Apply Your Skills

Part 1

You are the assistant to Paul Brewster, the training coordinator at a medium-sized service-oriented business. You have been asked by Mr. Brewster to prepare a document for Microsoft Word users within the company explaining the steps employees need to take to save an open company contract document to a folder named *Contracts* that is located in the *Documents* main folder. Save the document and name it **WL1-C1-CS-Saving**. Print and then close the document.

Part 2

Help

Mr. Brewster would like a document containing a brief summary of some basic Word commands for use in Microsoft Word training classes. He has asked you to prepare a document containing the following information:

- A brief explanation of how to move the insertion point to a specific page
- Keyboard shortcuts to move the insertion point to the beginning and end of a text line and beginning and end of a document
- Commands to delete text from the insertion point to the beginning of a word and from the insertion point to the end of a word
- Steps to select a word and a paragraph using the mouse
- A keyboard shortcut to select the entire document

Save the document and name it **WL1-C1-CS-WordCommands**. Print and then close the document.

Part 3

WWW

According to Mr. Brewster, the company is considering updating the Resources Department computers to Microsoft Office 2013. He has asked you to use the Internet to go to the Microsoft home page at www.microsoft.com and then use the search feature to find information on the system requirements for Office Professional Plus 2013. When you find the information, type a document that contains the Office Professional Plus 2013 system requirements for the computer and processor, memory, hard disk space, and operating system. Save the document and name it **WL1-C1-CS-SystemReq**. Print and then close the document.

MICROSOFT® WORD

Formatting Characters and Paragraphs

PERFORMANCE OBJECTIVES

Upon successful completion of Chapter 2, you will be able to:

- **Change the font and font effects**
- **Format selected text with buttons on the Mini toolbar**
- **Apply styles from style sets**
- **Apply themes**
- **Change the alignment of text in paragraphs**
- **Indent text in paragraphs**
- **Increase and decrease spacing before and after paragraphs**
- **Repeat the last action**
- **Automate formatting with Format Painter**
- **Change line spacing in a document**
- **Reveal and compare formatting**

Tutorials

2.1 Modifying the Font Using the Font Group
2.2 Formatting with the Mini Toolbar
2.3 Highlighting Text
2.4 Applying Formatting Using the Font Dialog Box
2.5 Applying Styles, Style Sets, and Themes
2.6 Aligning Text in Paragraphs
2.7 Changing Text Indentation
2.8 Using the Format Painter
2.9 Setting Line and Paragraph Spacing
2.10 Revealing and Comparing Formatting

The appearance of a document in the document screen and when printed is called the ***format***. A Word document is based on a template that applies default formatting. Some of the default formats include 11-point Calibri font, line spacing of 1.08, 8 points of spacing after each paragraph, and left-aligned text. In this chapter, you will learn about changing the typeface, type size, and typestyle as well as applying font effects such as bold and italics. The Paragraph group on the HOME tab includes buttons for applying formatting to paragraphs of text. In Word, a paragraph is any amount of text followed by a press of the Enter key. In this chapter, you will learn to format paragraphs by changing text alignment, indenting text, applying formatting with Format Painter, and changing line spacing. Model answers for this chapter's projects appear on the following pages.

Note: Before beginning the projects, copy to your storage medium the WL1C2 subfolder from the WL1 folder on the CD that accompanies this textbook and then make WL1C2 the active folder.

GLOSSARY OF TERMS

A

Access time: The time a storage device spends locating a particular file.
Aggregation software: E-commerce software application that combines online activities to provide *one-stop shopping* for consumers.
Analog signals: Signals composed of continuous waves transmitted at a certain frequency range over a medium, such as a telephone line.

B

Backup: A second copy kept of valuable data.
Bandwidth: The number of *bits* that can be transferred per second over a given medium or network.
Beta-testing: One of the last steps in software development that involves allowing outside people to use the software to see if it works as designed.

C

Chinese abacus: Pebbles strung on a rod inside a frame. Pebbles in the upper part of an abacus correspond to 5×10^0, or 5, for the first column; 5×10^1, or 50, for the second column; 5×10^2, or 500, for the third column; and so on.
Chip: A thin wafer of *silicon* containing electronic circuitry that performs various functions, such as mathematical calculations, storage, or controlling computer devises.
Cluster: A group of two or more sectors on a dish, which is the smallest unit of storage space used to store data.
Coding: A term used by programmers to refer to the act of writing source code.
Crackers: A term coined by computer hackers for those who intentionally enter ~~(or hack)~~ computer systems to damage them.

Created by Susan Ashby
Wednesday, February 18, 2015

Project 1 Apply Character Formatting

WL1-C2-P1-CompTerms.docx

COMMERCIAL LIFE CYCLE

The software life cycle is the term used to describe the phases involved in the process of creating, testing, and releasing new commercial software products. This cycle is similar to the process used in developing information systems, except that in this case the cycle focuses on the creation and release of a software program, not the development of a customized information system. The commercial software life cycle is repeated every time a new version of a program is needed. The phases in the software life cycle include the following: proposal and planning, design, implementation, testing, and public release.

Proposal and Planning

In the proposal and planning phase of a new software product, software developers will describe the proposed software program and what it is supposed to accomplish. In the case of existing software, the proposal and planning stage can be used to describe any new features and improvements. Older software programs are often revised to take advantage of new hardware or software developments and to add new functions or features.

Design

Developers are ready to begin the design process once the decision has been made to create or upgrade a software program. This step produces specifications documenting the details of the software to be written by programmers. Developers use problem-solving steps to determine the appropriate specifications.

Implementation

The implementation phase of the software life cycle is usually the most difficult. Development teams often spend late nights and weekends writing code and making it work. If the planning and design efforts have been successful, this phase should go well, but unanticipated problems inevitably crop up and have to be solved. The end result of the implementation phase is the production of a prototype called an alpha product, which is used by the development team for testing purposes. The alpha product can be revised to incorporate any improvements suggested by team members.

Testing

A quality assurance (QA) team usually develops a testing harness, which is a scripted set of tests that a program must undergo before being considered ready for public release. These tests might cover events such as very large input loads, maximum number of users, running on several different platforms, and simulated power outages. Once testing is finished, a beta version of the software program is created for testing outside of the development group, often by a select group of knowledgeable consumers. Any suggestions they make can be used to improve the product before it is released to the general public. Once the beta version is finalized, the user manual can be written or updated. At this point, the software developers would send the master CDs to duplicators for mass production.

Public Release and Support

When the product is deemed ready for widespread use, it is declared "gold" and released to the public. The software life cycle now goes back to the beginning phases as software developers think of new ways to improve the product.

Project 2 Apply Styles and Themes

WL1-C2-P2-SoftwareCycle.docx

PROPERTY PROTECTION ISSUES

The ability to link computers through the Internet offers many advantages. With linked computers, we can quickly and easily communicate with other users around the world, sharing files and other data with a few simple keystrokes. The convenience provided by linking computers through the Internet also has some drawbacks. Computer viruses can travel around the world in seconds, damaging programs and files. Hackers can enter into systems without authorization and steal or alter data. In addition, the wealth of information on the Web and the increased ease with which it can be copied have made plagiarizing easy. Plagiarism is using others' ideas and creations (their intellectual property) without permission.

All of these ethical issues revolve around property rights, the right of someone to protect and control the things he or she owns. A solid legal framework ensuring the protection of personal property exists, but computers have created many new issues that challenge conventional interpretations of these laws.

Intellectual Property

Intellectual property includes just about anything that can be created by the agency of the human mind. To encourage innovation and improvement and thus benefit society as a whole, our legal system grants patents to those who invent new and better ways of doing things. A patent awards ownership of an idea or invention to its creator for a fixed number of years. This allows the inventor the right to charge others for the use of the invention. To encourage and protect artistic and literary endeavors, authors and artists are awarded copyrights to the material they create, allowing them the right to control the use of their works and charge others for their use. Patent and copyright violation is punishable by law, and prosecutions and convictions are frequent. The legal framework protecting intellectual property has come under constant challenge as technology has moved forward.

With the Internet, accessing and copying written works that may be protected is easy. Today, authors are increasingly dismayed to find copies of their works appearing on the Internet without their permission. The same problem occurs with graphic and artistic images on the Internet, such as photographs and artwork. Once placed on the Web, they can be copied and reused numerous times. Unauthorized copying of items appearing on websites is difficult and sometimes even technically impossible to prevent.

Page 1

Fair Use

Situations exist in which using work written by others is permissible. Using another person's material without permission is allowed as long as the use is acknowledged, is used for noncommercial purposes, and involves only the use of limited excerpts of protected material, such as no more than 300 words of prose and one line of poetry. Such a right is called fair use and is dealt with under the U.S. Copyright Act, Section 107. Here, in part, is what the Fair Use law states:

> [A] copyrighted work, including such use by reproduction in copies of phonorecords or by any other means specified by that section, for purposes such as criticism, comment, news reporting, teaching (including multiple copies for classroom use), scholarship, or research, is not an infringement of copyright.

Even under the Fair Use provision, describing the source of the material is important. Plagiarism may be punished by law, and in many educational institutions it can result in suspension or even expulsion.

Intellectual Property Protection

The problem faced by intellectual property owners in the digital age is twofold. First, new technology has presented new difficulties in interpreting previous understandings dealing with the protection of intellectual property, such as difficulties applying the Fair Use provision to Internet material. Second, the new technical capabilities brought about by digital technologies have greatly increased the ease with which intellectual property can be appropriated and used without authorization, making policing and protecting intellectual property very difficult. Intellectual property owners have formed new organizations to ensure the protection of their property.

REFERENCES

Fuller, Floyd and Brian Larson. (2013) *Computers: Understanding Technology* (pp. 659-661). St. Paul, MN: Paradigm Publishing.

Myerson, Jean A. (2011) *Intellectual Properties* (pp. 123-126). New Orleans, LA: Robicheaux Publishing House.

Patterson, Margaret and Montgomery Littleton. (2014) *Issues of Plagiarism*. Chicago, IL: Lansing and Edelman Publishers.

Page 2

Project 3 Apply Paragraph Formatting and Use Format Painter

WL1-C2-P3-IntelProp.docx

Talbot, Lenora J. and Marcella S. Angleton. (2013) *Internet Considerations*. Portland, OR: Pacific Blue Publishing Group.

Prepared by Clarissa Markham
Edited by Joshua Streeter

Page 3

Solving Problems

In groups or individually, brainstorm possible solutions to the issues presented.

- Computers currently offer both *visual* and *audio* communications. Under development are devices and technologies that will allow users to smell various types of products while looking at them in the computer screen. What are some new applications of this technology for the food industry? Can you think of other industries that could use this capability?
- Picture yourself working in the Information Technology department of a mid-sized company. Your responsibilities include evaluating employees' computer system needs and recommending equipment purchases. Recently, the company president hired a new employee and you must evaluate her computer system needs. Considering that you have a budget of $5,500 for equipping the new employee with the computer system (or systems), research possible configurations and prepare a report outlining your recommendations, including costs. Assume that for her office she needs a complete system, including a system unit, monitor, printer, speakers, keyboard, and mouse.

Project 4 Format Computer Issues Document
WL1-C2-P4-CompIssues.docx

Project 1 Apply Character Formatting — 4 Parts

You will open a document containing a glossary of terms, add additional text, and then format the document by applying character formatting.

Changing Fonts

The Font group shown in Figure 2.1 contains a number of buttons for applying character formatting to text in a document. The top row contains buttons for changing the font and font size as well as buttons for increasing and decreasing the size of the font, changing the text case, and clearing formatting. You can remove character formatting (as well as paragraph formatting) applied to text by clicking the Clear All Formatting button in the Font group. Remove only character formatting from selected text by pressing the keyboard shortcut, Ctrl + spacebar. The bottom row contains buttons for applying typestyles such as bold, italic, and underline and for applying text effects, highlighting, and color.

Change the default font by selecting the desired font at the Font dialog box and then clicking the Set As Default button.

A Word document is based on a template that formats text in 11-point Calibri. You may want to change this default to some other font for such reasons as changing the mood of the document, enhancing the visual appeal, and increasing the readability of the text. A font consists of three elements: typeface, type size, and typestyle.

A typeface is a set of characters with a common design and shape and can be decorative or plain and either monospaced or proportional. Word refers to a typeface as a ***font***. A monospaced typeface allots the same amount of horizontal space for

Figure 2.1 Font Group Buttons

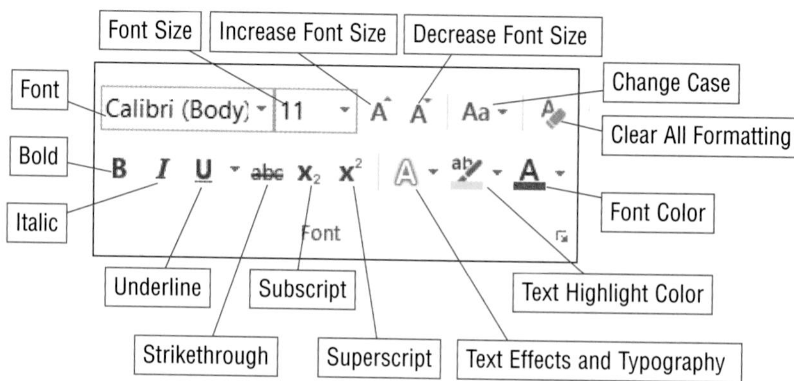

each character, while a proportional typeface allots a varying amount of space for each character. Proportional typefaces are divided into two main categories: ***serif*** and ***sans serif***. A serif is a small line at the end of a character stroke. Consider using a serif typeface for text-intensive documents because the serifs help move the reader's eyes across the page. Use a sans serif typeface for headings, headlines, and advertisements. Some of the popular typefaces are shown in Table 2.1.

Use a serif typeface for text-intensive documents.

Type is generally set in proportional size. The size of proportional type is measured vertically in units called ***points***. A point is approximately 1/72 of an inch—the higher the point size, the larger the characters. Within a typeface, characters may have varying styles. Type styles are divided into four main categories: regular, bold, italic, and bold italic.

Use the Font button arrow in the Font group to change the font. When you select text and then click the Font button arrow, a drop-down gallery of font options displays. Hover your mouse pointer over a font option and the selected text in the document displays with the font applied. You can continue hovering your mouse pointer over different font options to see how the selected text displays in each specified font. The Font button arrow drop-down gallery is an example of the ***live preview*** feature, which allows you to see how the font formatting affects your text without having to return to the document. The live preview feature is also available when you click the Font Size button arrow to change the font size.

Press Ctrl +] to increase font size by one point and press Ctrl + [to decrease font size by one point.

Table 2.1 Categories of Typefaces

Serif Typefaces	*Sans Serif Typefaces*	*Monospaced Typefaces*
Cambria	Calibri	Consolas
Constantia	Candara	Courier New
Times New Roman	Corbel	Lucida Console
Bookman Old Style	Arial	MS Gothic

Project 1a Changing the Font and Font Size

Part 1 of 4

1. Open **CompTerms.docx**.
2. Save the document with Save As and name it **WL1-C2-P1-CompTerms**.
3. Change the typeface to Cambria by completing the following steps:
   a. Select the entire document by pressing Ctrl + A. (You can also select all text in the document by clicking the Select button in the Editing group and then clicking *Select All* at the drop-down list.)
   b. Click the Font button arrow, scroll down the Font drop-down gallery until *Cambria* displays, and then hover the mouse pointer over *Cambria*. This displays a live preview of the text set in Cambria.
   c. Click the mouse button on *Cambria*.

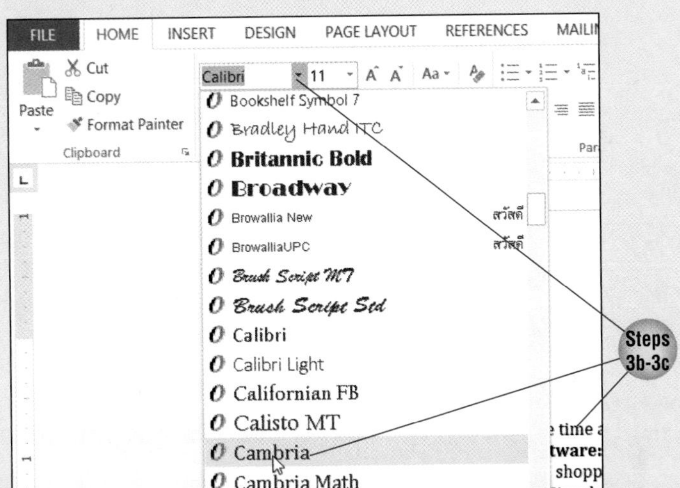

4. Change the type size to 14 points by completing the following steps:
   a. With the text in the document still selected, click the Font Size button arrow.
   b. At the drop-down gallery that displays, hover the mouse pointer on *14* and look at the live preview of the text with 14 points applied.
   c. Click the left mouse button on *14*.
5. At the document screen, deselect the text by clicking anywhere in the document.
6. Change the type size and typeface by completing the following steps:
   a. Press Ctrl + A to select the entire document.
   b. Click three times on the Decrease Font Size button in the Font group. (This decreases the size to 10 points.)
   c. Click twice on the Increase Font Size button. (This increases the size of the font to 12 points.)

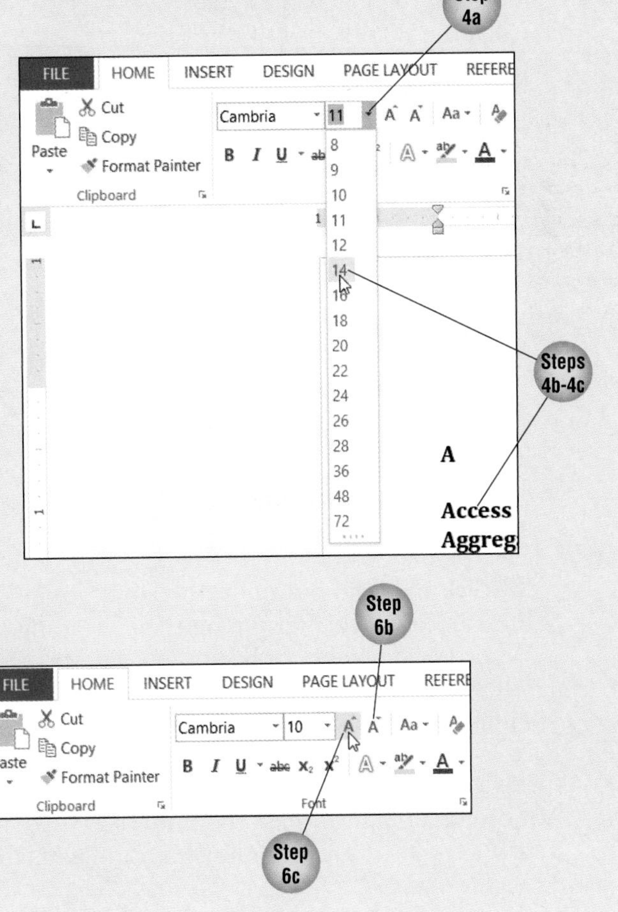

d. Click the Font button arrow, scroll down the drop-down gallery, and then click *Constantia*. (The most recently used fonts display at the beginning of the gallery, followed by a listing of all fonts.)

7. Save **WL1-C2-P1-CompTerms.docx**.

Choosing a Typestyle

Bold

Italic

Underline

Apply a particular typestyle to text with the Bold, Italic, or Underline buttons in the bottom row in the Font group. You can apply more than one style to text. For example, you can bold and italicize the same text or apply all three styles to the same text. Click the Underline button arrow and a drop-down gallery displays with underlining options such as a double line, dashed line, and thicker underline. Click the *Underline Color* option at the Underline button drop-down gallery and a side menu displays with color options.

Project 1b Applying Character Formatting to Text as You Type — Part 2 of 4

1. With **WL1-C2-P1-CompTerms.docx** open, press Ctrl + Home to move the insertion point to the beginning of the document.
2. Type a heading for the document by completing the following steps:
   a. Click the Bold button in the Font group. (This turns on bold.)
   b. Click the Underline button in the Font group. (This turns on underline.)
   c. Type Glossary of Terms. 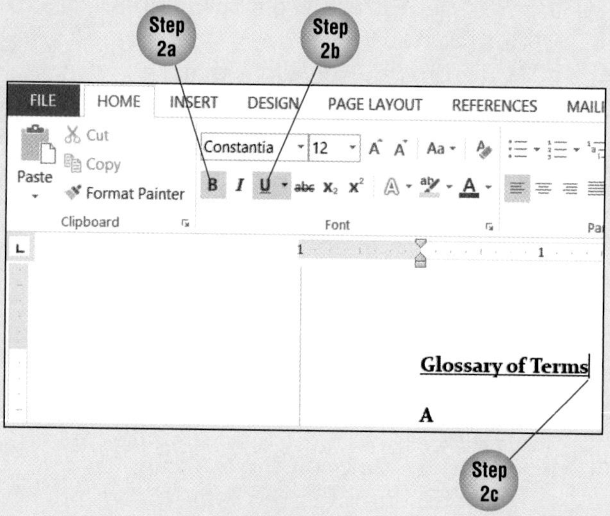
3. Press Ctrl + End to move the insertion point to the end of the document.
4. Type the text shown in Figure 2.2 with the following specifications:
   a. While typing, make the appropriate text bold as shown in the figure by completing the following steps:
      1) Click the Bold button in the Font group. (This turns on bold.)
      2) Type the text.
      3) Click the Bold button in the Font group. (This turns off bold.)
   b. Press Enter twice after typing the *C* heading.
   c. While typing, italicize the appropriate text as shown in the figure by completing the following steps:
      1) Click the Italic button in the Font group.
      2) Type the text.
      3) Click the Italic button in the Font group.
5. After typing the text, press the Enter key twice and then press Ctrl + Home to move the insertion point to the beginning of the document.

6. Change the underlining below the title by completing the following steps:
   a. Select the title *Glossary of Terms*.
   b. Click the Underline button arrow and then click the third underline option from the top of the drop-down gallery.
   c. Click the Underline button arrow, point to the *Underline Color* option, and then click the *Red* color (second color option) in the *Standard Colors* section.

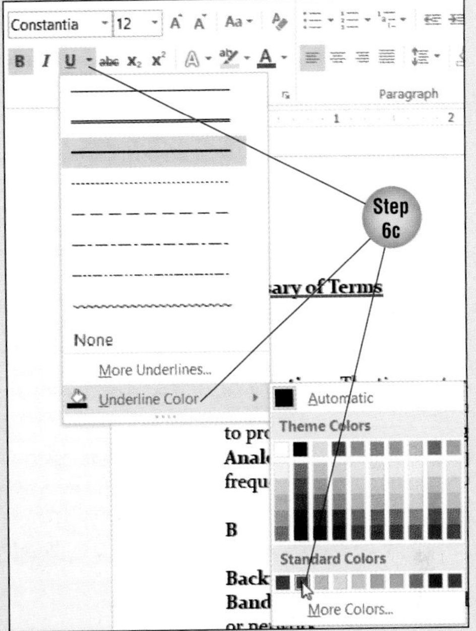

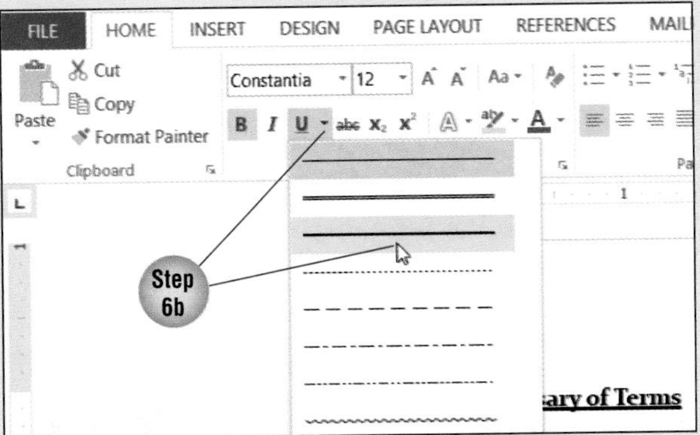

7. With the title still selected, change the font size to 14 points.
8. Save **WL1-C2-P1-CompTerms.docx**.

Figure 2.2 Project 1b

> **C**
>
> **Chip:** A thin wafer of *silicon* containing electronic circuitry that performs various functions, such as mathematical calculations, storage, or controlling computer devices.
> **Cluster:** A group of two or more *sectors* on a disk, which is the smallest unit of storage space used to store data.
> **Coding:** A term used by programmers to refer to the act of writing source code.
> **Crackers:** A term coined by computer hackers for those who intentionally enter (or hack) computer systems to damage them.

Choosing a Font Effect

Apply font effects with some of the buttons in the top and bottom rows in the Font group, or clear all formatting from selected text with the Clear All Formatting button. Change the case of text with the Change Case button drop-down list. Click the Change Case button in the top row in the Font group and a drop-down list displays with the options *Sentence case*, *lowercase*, *UPPERCASE*, *Capitalize Each Word*, and *tOGGLE cASE*. You can also change the case of selected text with the keyboard shortcut Shift + F3. Each time you press Shift + F3, the selected text displays in the next case option in the list.

Clear All Formatting

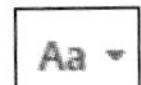

Change Case

Strikethrough

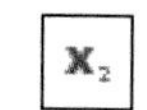
Subscript

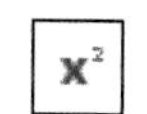
Superscript

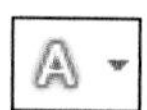
Text Effects and Typography

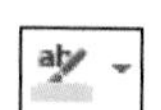
Text Highlight Color

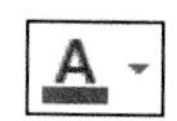
Font Color

The bottom row in the Font group contains buttons for applying font effects. Use the Strikethrough button to draw a line through selected text. This has a practical application in some legal documents in which deleted text must be retained in the document. Use the Subscript button to create text that is lowered slightly below the line, as in the chemical formula H_2O. Use the Superscript button to create text that is raised slightly above the text line, as in the mathematical equation four to the third power (written as 4^3). Click the Text Effects and Typography button in the bottom row and a drop-down gallery displays with effect options. Use the Text Highlight Color button to highlight specific text in a document and use the Font Color button to change the color of text.

Using Keyboard Shortcuts

Several of the buttons in the Font group have keyboard shortcuts. For example, you can press Ctrl + B to turn on/off bold or press Ctrl + I to turn on/off italics. Position the mouse pointer on a button and an enhanced ScreenTip displays with the name of the button; the keyboard shortcut, if any; a description of the action performed by the button; and sometimes, access to the Word Help window. Table 2.2 identifies the keyboard shortcuts available for buttons in the Font group.

Formatting with the Mini Toolbar

When you select text, the Mini toolbar displays above the selected text. Click a button on the Mini toolbar to apply formatting to the selected text. When you move the mouse pointer away from the Mini toolbar, it disappears.

Table 2.2 Font Group Button Keyboard Shortcuts

Font Group Button	Keyboard Shortcut
Font	Ctrl + Shift + F
Font Size	Ctrl + Shift + P
Increase Font Size	Ctrl + Shift + >
Decrease Font Size	Ctrl + Shift + <
Bold	Ctrl + B
Italic	Ctrl + I
Underline	Ctrl + U
Subscript	Ctrl + =
Superscript	Ctrl + Shift + +
Change Case	Shift + F3

Project 1c **Applying Font Effects** **Part 3 of 4**

1. With **WL1-C2-P1-CompTerms.docx** open, move the insertion point to the beginning of the term *Chip*, press the Enter key, and then press the Up Arrow key. Type the text shown in Figure 2.3. Create each superscript number by clicking the Superscript button, typing the number, and then clicking the Superscript button.
2. Change the case of text and remove underlining from the title by completing the following steps:
   a. Select the title *Glossary of Terms*.
   b. Remove all formatting from the title by clicking the Clear All Formatting button in the Font group.
   c. Click the Change Case button in the Font group and then click *UPPERCASE* at the drop-down list.
   d. Click the Text Effects and Typography button in the Font group and then click the *Gradient Fill - Blue, Accent 1, Reflection* option (second column, second row) at the drop-down gallery.
   e. Change the font size to 14.
3. Strike through text by completing the following steps:
   a. Select the words and parentheses *(or hack)* in the *Crackers* definition.
   b. Click the Strikethrough button in the Font group.

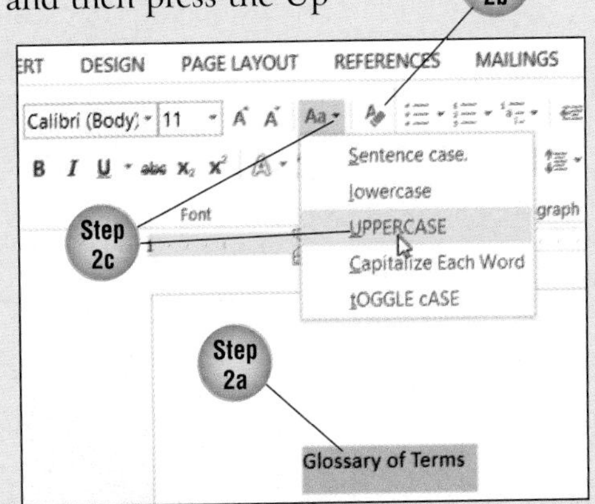

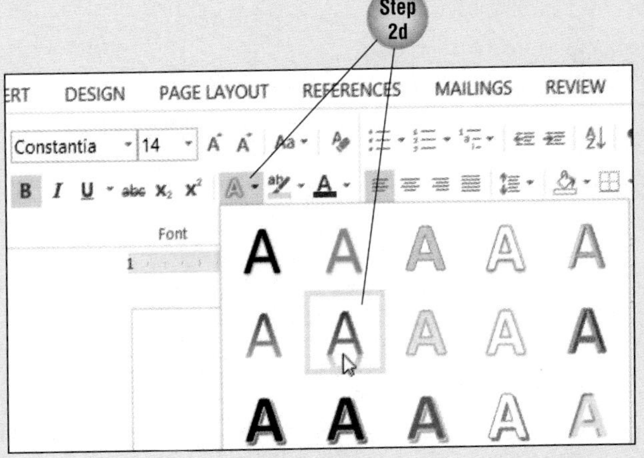

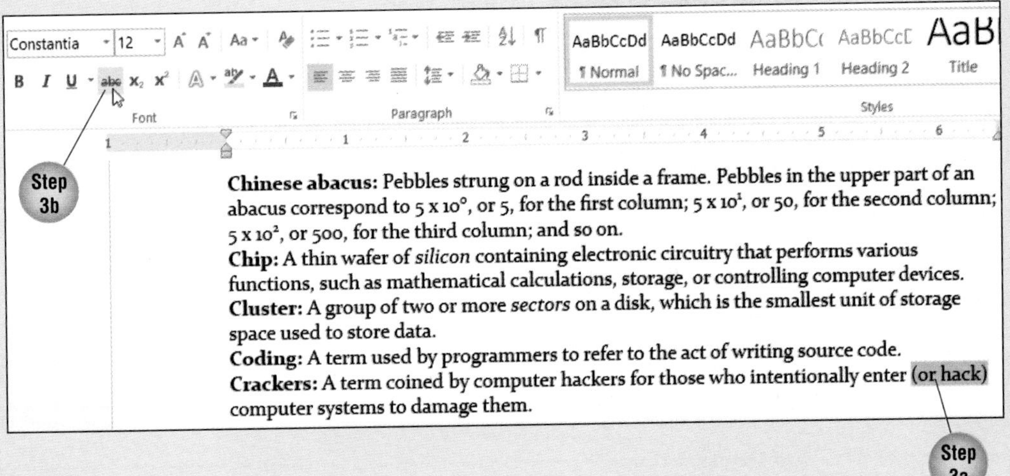

Constantia 12
AaBbCcDd ¶ Normal
AaBbCcDd ¶ No Spac...
AaBbCc Heading 1
AaBbCcC Heading 2
AaB Title
Font
Paragraph
Styles
Step 3b
Chinese abacus: Pebbles strung on a rod inside a frame. Pebbles in the upper part of an abacus correspond to 5 x 10°, or 5, for the first column; 5 x 10¹, or 50, for the second column; 5 x 10², or 500, for the third column; and so on.
Chip: A thin wafer of silicon containing electronic circuitry that performs various functions, such as mathematical calculations, storage, or controlling computer devices.
Cluster: A group of two or more sectors on a disk, which is the smallest unit of storage space used to store data.
Coding: A term used by programmers to refer to the act of writing source code.
Crackers: A term coined by computer hackers for those who intentionally enter (or hack) computer systems to damage them.
Step 3a

4. Change the font color by completing the following steps:
   a. Press Ctrl + A to select the entire document.
   b. Click the Font Color button arrow.
   c. Click the *Dark Red* color (first color option in the *Standard Colors* section) at the drop-down gallery.
   d. Click in the document to deselect text.
5. Highlight text in the document by completing the following steps:
   a. Click the Text Highlight Color button arrow in the Font group and then click the *Yellow* color (first column, first row) at the drop-down palette. (This causes the mouse pointer to display as an I-beam pointer with a highlighter pen attached.)
   b. Select the term *Beta-testing* and the definition that follows.
   c. Click the Text Highlight Color button arrow and then click the *Turquoise* color (third column, first row).
   d. Select the term *Cluster* and the definition that follows.
   e. Click the Text Highlight Color button arrow and then click the *Yellow* color at the drop-down gallery.
   f. Click the Text Highlight Color button to turn off highlighting.
6. Apply italic formatting using the Mini toolbar by completing the following steps:
   a. Select the text *one-stop shopping* located in the definition for the term *Aggregation software*. (When you select the text, the Mini toolbar displays.)
   b. Click the Italic button on the Mini toolbar.
   c. Select the word *bits* located in the definition for the term *Bandwidth* and then click the Italic button on the Mini toolbar.
7. Save **WL1-C2-P1-CompTerms.docx**.

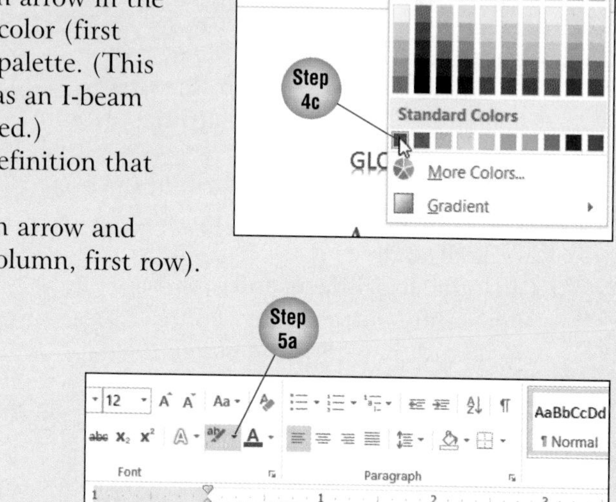

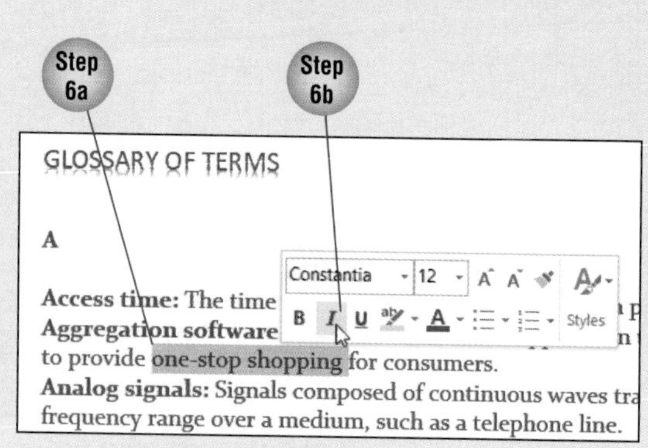

Figure 2.3 Project 1c

> **Chinese abacus:** Pebbles strung on a rod inside a frame. Pebbles in the upper part of an abacus correspond to 5×10^0, or 5, for the first column; 5×10^1, or 50, for the second column; 5×10^2, or 500, for the third column; and so on.

Figure 2.4 Font Dialog Box

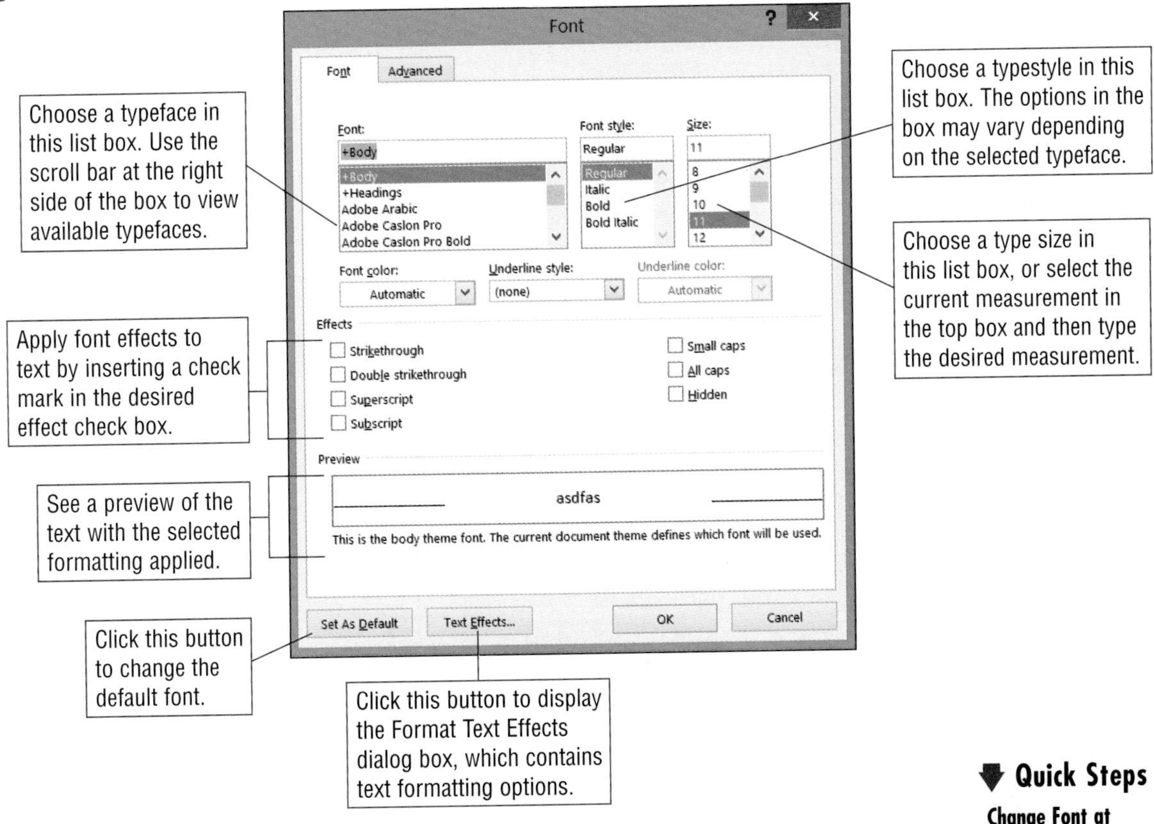

Font
Font
Advanced
Font:
+Body
+Headings
Adobe Arabic
Adobe Caslon Pro
Adobe Caslon Pro Bold
Font style:
Regular
Italic
Bold
Bold Italic
Size:
11
8
9
10
12
Font color:
Automatic
Underline style:
(none)
Underline color:
Automatic
Effects
Strikethrough
Double strikethrough
Superscript
Subscript
Small caps
All caps
Hidden
Preview
asdfas
This is the body theme font. The current document theme defines which font will be used.
Set As Default
Text Effects...
OK
Cancel
Choose a typeface in this list box. Use the scroll bar at the right side of the box to view available typefaces.
Apply font effects to text by inserting a check mark in the desired effect check box.
See a preview of the text with the selected formatting applied.
Click this button to change the default font.
Click this button to display the Format Text Effects dialog box, which contains text formatting options.
Choose a typestyle in this list box. The options in the box may vary depending on the selected typeface.
Choose a type size in this list box, or select the current measurement in the top box and then type the desired measurement.

Quick Steps

Change Font at Font Dialog Box
1. Select text if necessary.
2. Click Font group dialog box launcher.
3. Choose desired options at dialog box.
4. Click OK.

Changing Fonts at the Font Dialog Box

In addition to buttons in the Font group, you can use options at the Font dialog box shown in Figure 2.4 to change the typeface, type size, and typestyle of text as well as apply font effects. Display the Font dialog box by clicking the Font group dialog box launcher. The dialog box launcher is a small square containing a diagonal-pointing arrow that displays in the lower right corner of the Font group.

Project 1d **Changing the Font at the Font Dialog Box** **Part 4 of 4**

1. With **WL1-C2-P1-CompTerms.docx** open, press Ctrl + End to move the insertion point to the end of the document. (Make sure the insertion point is positioned a double space below the last line of text.)
2. Type **Created by Susan Ashby** and then press the Enter key.
3. Type **Wednesday, February 18, 2015**.
4. Change the font to 13-point Candara and the color to dark blue for the entire document by completing the following steps:
   a. Press Ctrl + A to select the entire document.
   b. Click the Font group dialog box launcher.

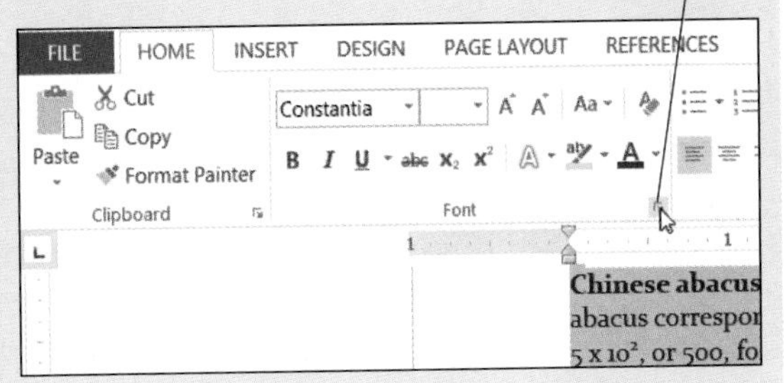

Step 4b
FILE
HOME
INSERT
DESIGN
PAGE LAYOUT
REFERENCES
Cut
Copy
Paste
Format Painter
Clipboard
Constantia
Font
Chinese abacus
abacus correspo
5 x 10², or 500, fo

c. At the Font dialog box, click the up-pointing arrow at the right side of the *Font* list box to scroll down the list box and then click *Candara*.
d. Click in the *Size* text box, select the current number, and then type 13.
e. Click the down-pointing arrow at the right side of the *Font color* option box and then click the *Dark Blue* color in the *Standard Colors* section at the drop-down color palette.
f. Click OK to close the dialog box.

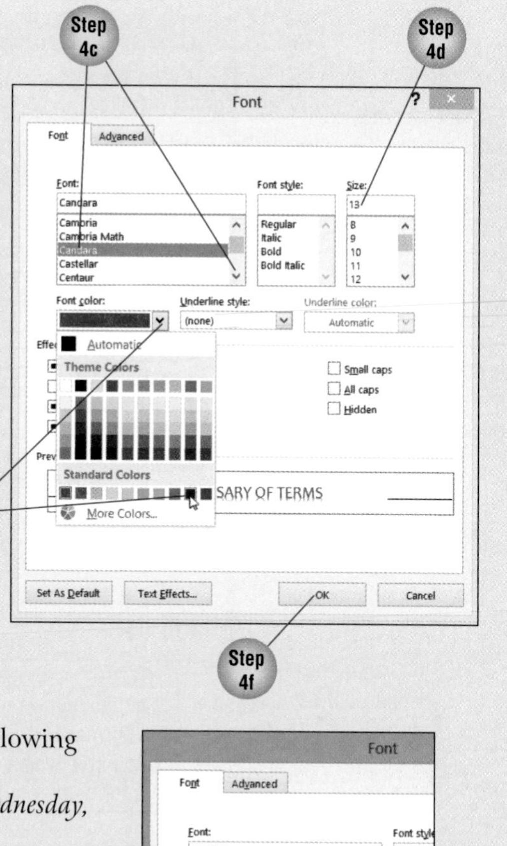

5. Double underline text by completing the following steps:
    a. Select *Wednesday, February 18, 2015*.
    b. Click the Font group dialog box launcher.
    c. At the Font dialog box, click the down-pointing arrow at the right side of the *Underline style* option box and then click the double-line option at the drop-down list.
    d. Click OK to close the dialog box.

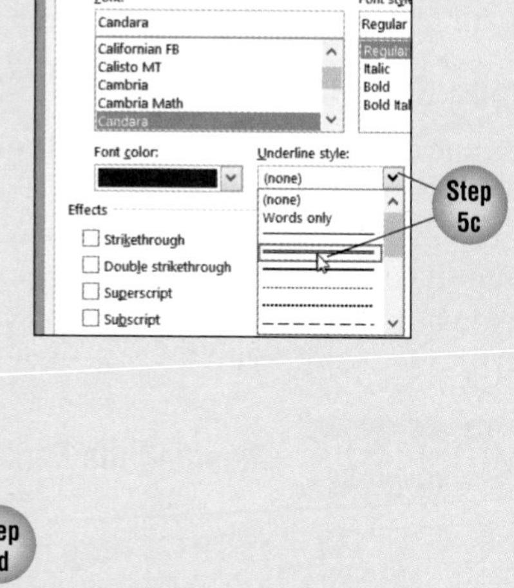

6. Change text to small caps by completing the following steps:
    a. Select the text *Created by Susan Ashby* and *Wednesday, February 18, 2015*.
    b. Display the Font dialog box.
    c. Click the *Small caps* option in the *Effects* section. (This inserts a check mark in the check box.)
    d. Click OK to close the dialog box.

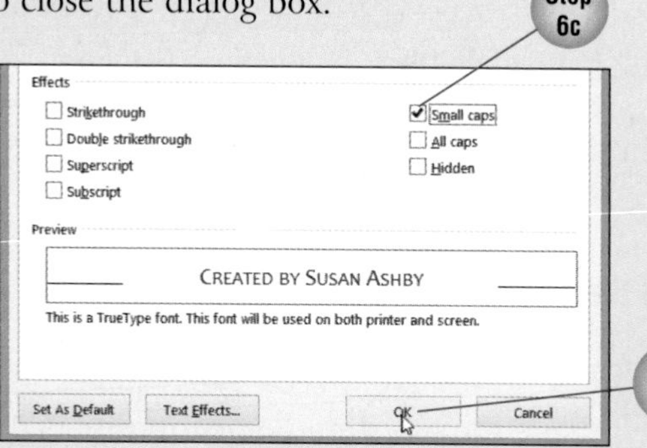

7. Save, print, and then close **WL1-C2-P1-CompTerms.docx**.

Project 2 Apply Styles and Themes — 3 Parts

You will open a document containing information on the life cycle of software, apply styles to text, and then change the style set. You will also apply a theme and then change the theme colors and fonts.

Applying Styles from a Style Set

A Word document contains a number of predesigned formats grouped into style sets. Several thumbnails of the styles in the default style set display in the Styles group on the HOME tab. Display additional styles by clicking the More button that displays at the right side of the style thumbnails. This displays a drop-down gallery of style choices. To apply a style, position the insertion point in the text or paragraph of text to which you want the style applied, click the More button at the right side of the style thumbnails in the Styles group, and then click the desired style at the drop-down gallery.

If you apply a heading style (such as Heading 1, Heading 2, and so on) to text, you can collapse and expand text below the heading(s). Hover your mouse over text with a heading style applied and a collapse triangle (solid, right- and down-pointing triangle) displays to the left of the heading. Click this collapse triangle and any text below the heading is collapsed (hidden). Redisplay the text below a heading by hovering the mouse over the heading text until an expand triangle displays (hollow, right-pointing triangle) and then click the expand triangle. This expands (redisplays) the text below the heading.

Quick Steps

Apply a Style
1. Position insertion point in desired text or paragraph of text.
2. Click More button in Styles group.
3. Click desired style.

Change Style Set
1. Click DESIGN tab.
2. Click desired style set thumbnail.

More

Removing Default Formatting

A Word document contains some default formatting, including 8 points of spacing after paragraphs and line spacing of 1.08. (You will learn more about these formatting options later in this chapter.) You can remove this default formatting, as well as any character formatting applied to text in your document by applying the No Spacing style to your text. This style is located in the Styles group.

Changing the Style Set

Word contains a number of style sets containing styles you can use to apply formatting to a document. To change to a different style set, click the DESIGN tab and then click the desired style set thumbnail in the Document Formatting group.

Project 2a **Applying Styles and Changing the Style Set** **Part 1 of 3**

1. Open **SoftwareCycle.docx**.
2. Save the document with Save As and name it **WL1-C2-P2-SoftwareCycle**.
3. Position the insertion point on any character in the title *COMMERCIAL LIFE CYCLE* and then click the *Heading 1* style thumbnail that displays in the Styles group.

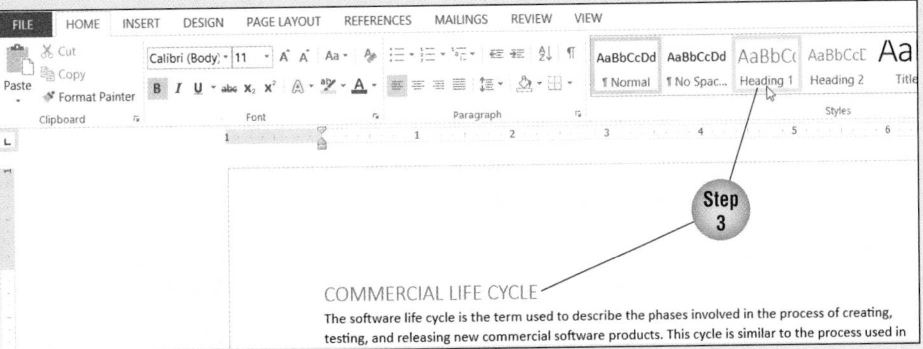

4. Position the insertion point on any character in the heading *Proposal and Planning* and then click the *Heading 2* style thumbnail that displays in the Styles group.
5. Position the insertion point on any character in the heading *Design* and then click the *Heading 2* style thumbnail in the Styles group.

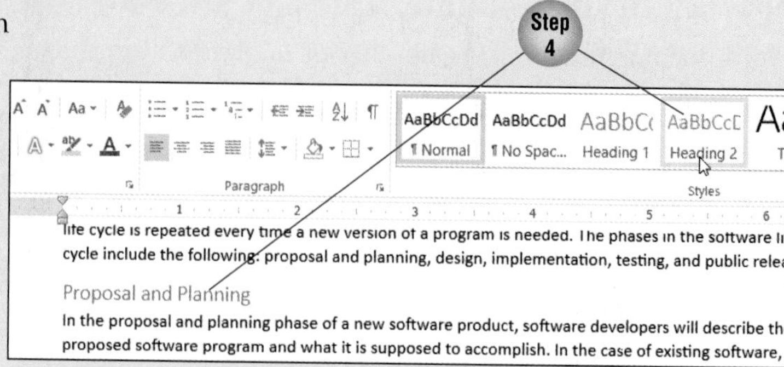
Step 4
Paragraph
Styles
AaBbCcDd
¶ Normal
AaBbCcDd
¶ No Spac...
AaBbC(
Heading 1
AaBbCcI
Heading 2
life cycle is repeated every time a new version of a program is needed. The phases in the software li
cycle include the following: proposal and planning, design, implementation, testing, and public relea
Proposal and Planning
In the proposal and planning phase of a new software product, software developers will describe th
proposed software program and what it is supposed to accomplish. In the case of existing software,

6. Apply the Heading 2 style to the remaining headings (*Implementation*, *Testing*, and *Public Release and Support*).
7. Collapse and expand text below the heading with the Heading 1 style applied by completing the following steps:
   a. Hover the mouse over the heading *COMMERCIAL LIFE CYCLE* until a collapse triangle displays at the left side of the heading and then click the triangle. (This collapses all of the text below the heading.)
   b. Hover the mouse over the heading *COMMERCIAL LIFE CYCLE* until an expand triangle displays at the left side of the heading and then click the triangle. (This redisplays the text in the document.)

Step 7a
COMMERCIAL LIFE CYCLE
The software life cycle is the term used to
testing, and releasing new commercial so
developing information systems, except t

8. Click the DESIGN tab.
9. Click the *Casual* style set thumbnail in the Document Formatting group. (Notice how the Heading 1 and Heading 2 formatting changes.)
10. Save and then print **WL1-C2-P2-SoftwareCycle.docx**.

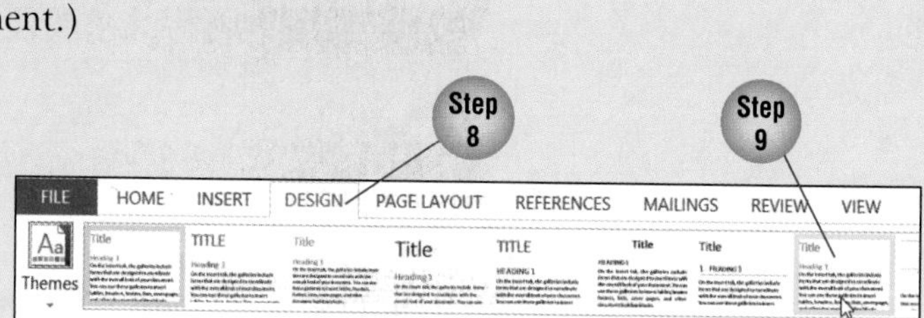
Step 8
Step 9
FILE
HOME
INSERT
DESIGN
PAGE LAYOUT
REFERENCES
MAILINGS
REVIEW
VIEW
Themes
Title
TITLE
Document Formatting

Applying a Theme

Quick Steps

Apply a Theme
1. Click DESIGN tab.
2. Click Themes button.
3. Click desired theme.

Themes

Word provides a number of themes for formatting text in your document. A theme is a set of formatting choices that include a color theme (a set of colors), a font theme (a set of heading and body text fonts), and an effects theme (a set of lines and fill effects). To apply a theme, click the DESIGN tab and then click the Themes button in the Document Formatting group. At the drop-down gallery that displays, click the desired theme. Hover the mouse pointer over a theme and the live preview feature will display your document with the theme formatting applied. With the live preview feature, you can see how the theme formatting affects your document before you make your final choice. Applying a theme is an easy way to give your document a professional look.

Project 2b Applying a Theme to Text in a Document

Part 2 of 3

1. With **WL1-C2-P2-SoftwareCycle.docx** open, click the DESIGN tab and then click the Themes button in the Document Formatting group.
2. At the drop-down gallery, hover your mouse pointer over several different themes and notice how the text formatting changes in your document.
3. Click the *Organic* theme.
4. Save and then print **WL1-C2-P2-SoftwareCycle.docx**.

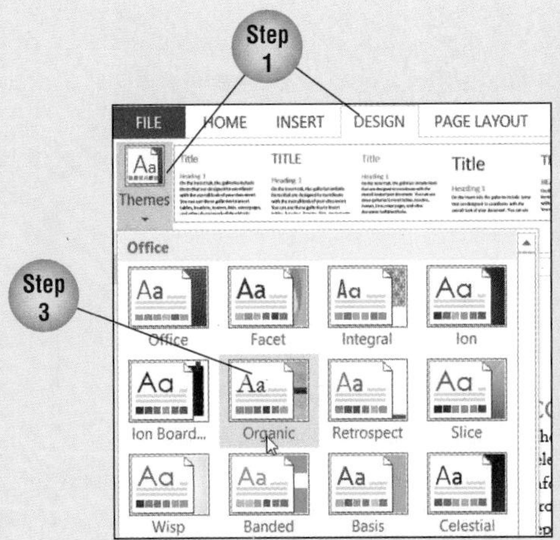

Customizing Style Sets and Themes

Customize the color applied by a style or theme with the Colors button in the Document Formatting group. Click the Colors button and a drop-down gallery displays with named color schemes. Customize the fonts applied to text in a document with the Fonts button in the Document Formatting group. Click this button and a drop-down gallery displays with font choices. Each font group in the drop-down gallery contains two choices. The first choice in the group is the font that is applied to headings, and the second choice is the font that is applied to body text in the document. If you are formatting a document containing graphics with lines and fills, you can apply a specific theme effect with options at the Effects button drop-down gallery.

The buttons in the Document Formatting group display a visual representation of the current theme. If you change the theme colors, the small color squares in the Themes button and the Colors button reflect the change. Change the theme fonts and the *As* on the Themes button as well as the uppercase *A* on the Fonts button reflect the change. If you change the theme effects, the circle in the Effects button reflects the change.

The Paragraph Spacing button in the Document Formatting group on the DESIGN tab contains predesigned paragraph spacing options. To change paragraph spacing, click the Paragraph Spacing button and then click the desired option at the drop-down gallery. You can hover your mouse over an option at the drop-down gallery and, after a moment, a ScreenTip displays with information about the formatting applied by the option. For example, if you hover the mouse over the *Compact* option at the side menu, a ScreenTip displays telling you that the Compact option will change the spacing before paragraphs to 0 points, the spacing after paragraphs to 4 points, and the line spacing to single spacing.

Quick Steps

Change Theme Color
1. Click DESIGN tab.
2. Click Colors button.
3. Click desired theme color option.

Change Theme Fonts
1. Click DESIGN tab.
2. Click Fonts button.
3. Click desired theme fonts option.

Change Paragraph Spacing
1. Click DESIGN tab.
2. Click Paragraph Spacing button.
3. Click desired paragraph spacing option.

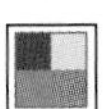
Theme Colors

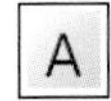
Theme Fonts

Theme Effects

Paragraph Spacing

Project 2c Customizing a Theme

Part 3 of 3

1. With **WL1-C2-P2-SoftwareCycle.docx** open, click the Colors button in the Document Formatting group and then click *Red Orange* at the drop-down gallery. (Notice how the colors in the title and headings change.)
2. Click the Fonts button arrow and then click the *Corbel* option. (Notice how the document text font changes.)
3. Click the Paragraph Spacing button and then, one at a time, hover the mouse over each of the paragraph spacing options, beginning with *Compact*. For each option, read the ScreenTip that explains the paragraph spacing applied by the option.
4. Click the *Double* option.
5. Scroll through the document and notice the paragraph spacing.
6. Change the paragraph spacing by clicking the Paragraph Spacing button and then clicking *Compact*.
7. Save, print, and then close **WL1-C2-P2-SoftwareCycle.docx**.

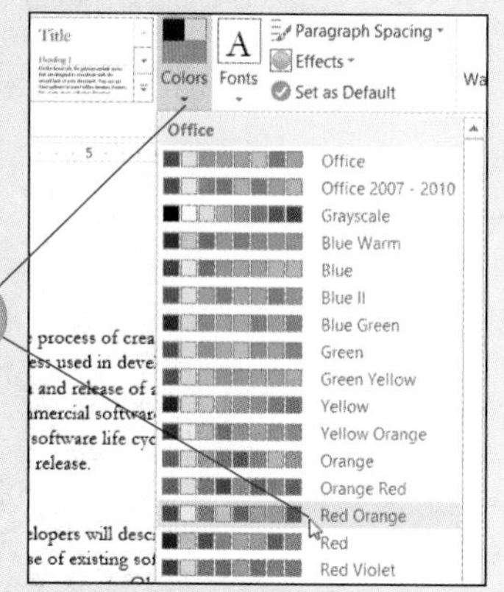

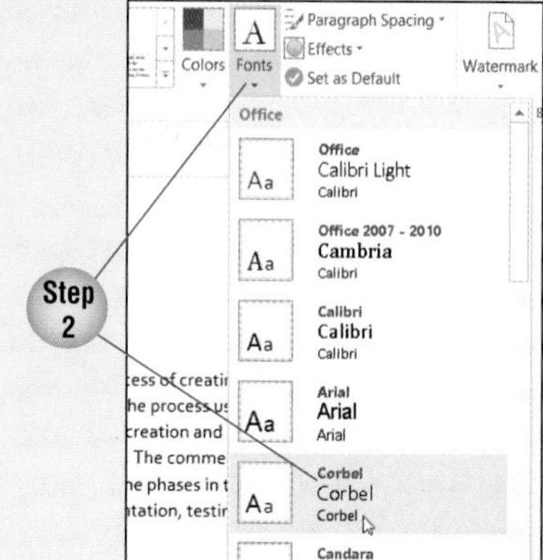

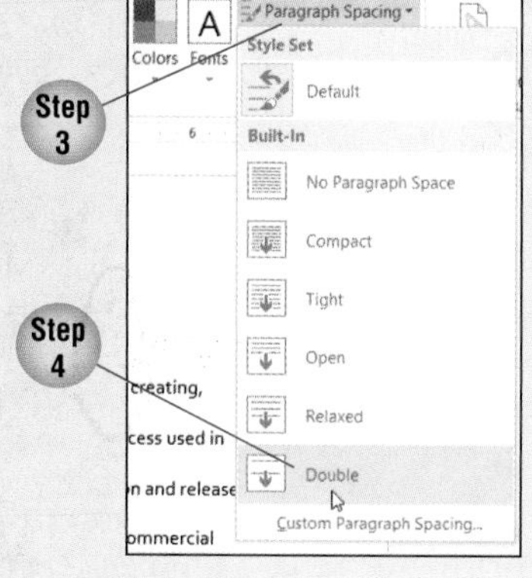

Project 3 Apply Paragraph Formatting and Use Format Painter

6 Parts

You will open a report on intellectual property and fair use issues and then format the report by changing the alignment of text in paragraphs, applying spacing before and after paragraphs of text, and repeating the last formatting action.

Changing Paragraph Alignment

By default, paragraphs in a Word document are aligned at the left margin and ragged at the right margin. Change this default alignment with buttons in the Paragraph group on the HOME tab or with keyboard shortcuts, as shown in Table 2.3. You can change the alignment of text in paragraphs before you type the text, or you can change the alignment of existing text.

Table 2.3 Paragraph Alignment Buttons and Keyboard Shortcuts

To align text	*Paragraph Group Button*	*Keyboard Shortcut*
At the left margin		Ctrl + L
Between margins		Ctrl + E
At the right margin		Ctrl + R
At the left and right margins		Ctrl + J

Changing Paragraph Alignment as You Type

If you change the alignment before typing text, the alignment formatting is inserted in the paragraph mark. As you type text and press Enter, the paragraph formatting is continued. For example, if you click the Center button in the Paragraph group, type text for the first paragraph, and then press the Enter key, the center alignment formatting is still active and the insertion point displays centered between the left and right margins. To display the paragraph symbols in a document, click the Show/Hide ¶ button in the Paragraph group. With the Show/Hide ¶ button active (displays with a light blue background), nonprinting formatting symbols display, such as the paragraph symbol ¶ indicating a press of the Enter key or a dot indicating a press of the spacebar.

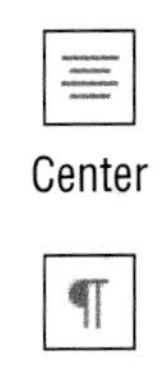

Center

Show/Hide ¶

Changing Paragraph Alignment of Existing Text

To change the alignment of existing text in a paragraph, position the insertion point anywhere within the paragraph. You do not need to select the entire paragraph. To change the alignment of several adjacent paragraphs in a document, select a portion of the first paragraph through a portion of the last paragraph. You do not need to select all of the text in the paragraphs.

To return paragraph alignment to the default (left-aligned), click the Align Left button in the Paragraph group. You can also return all paragraph formatting to the default with the keyboard shortcut Ctrl + Q. This keyboard shortcut removes paragraph formatting from selected text. If you want to remove all formatting from selected text, including character and paragraph formatting, click the Clear All Formatting button in the Font group.

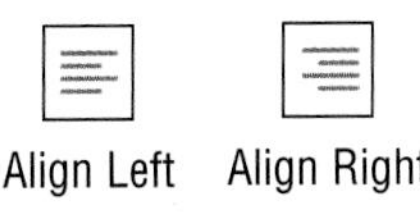

Align Left Align Right

Align text to help the reader follow the message of a document and to make the layout look appealing.

Changing Paragraph Alignment **Part 1 of 6**

1. Open **IntelProp.docx**. (Some of the default formatting in this document has been changed.)
2. Save the document with Save As and name it **WL1-C2-P3-IntelProp**.
3. Click the Show/Hide ¶ button in the Paragraph group on the HOME tab to turn on the display of nonprinting characters.

Step 3

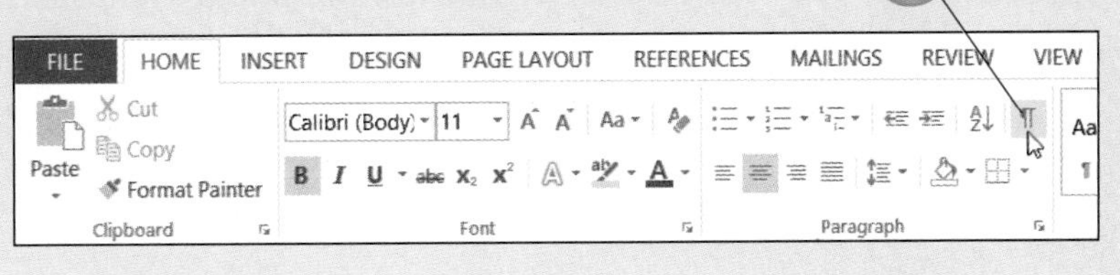

4. With the insertion point positioned immediately left of the paragraph symbol at the beginning of the document, press the Delete key to delete the blank paragraph.
5. Press Ctrl + A to select the entire document and then change the paragraph alignment to justified alignment by clicking the Justify button in the Paragraph group on the HOME tab.
6. Press Ctrl + End to move the insertion point to the end of the document.
7. Press the Enter key once.
8. Press Ctrl + E to move the insertion point to the middle of the page.
9. Type **Prepared by Clarissa Markham**.
10. Press Shift + Enter and then type **Edited by Joshua Streeter**.

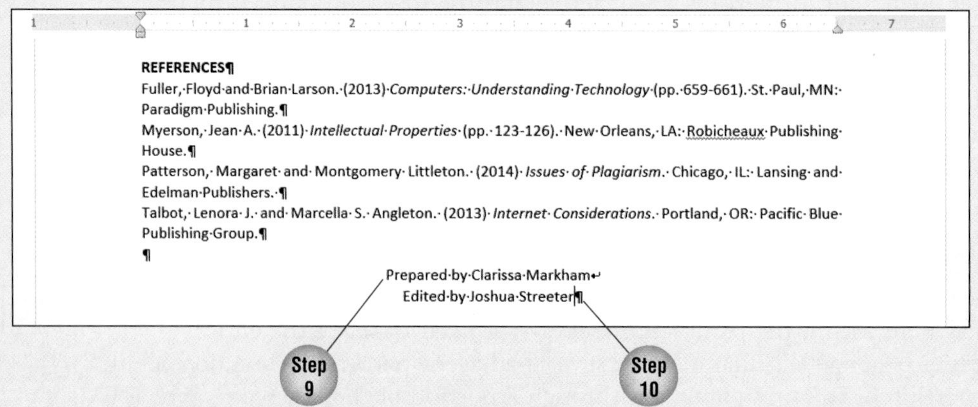

11. Click the Show/Hide ¶ button in the Paragraph group on the HOME tab to turn off the display of nonprinting characters.
12. Save **WL1-C2-P3-IntelProp.docx**.

Quick Steps

Change Paragraph Alignment

Click desired alignment button in Paragraph group on HOME tab.

OR

1. Click Paragraph group dialog box launcher.
2. Click *Alignment* option box arrow.
3. Click desired alignment.
4. Click OK.

Changing Alignment at the Paragraph Dialog Box

Along with buttons in the Paragraph group and keyboard shortcuts, you can also change paragraph alignment with the *Alignment* option box at the Paragraph dialog box shown in Figure 2.5. Display this dialog box by clicking the Paragraph group dialog box launcher. At the Paragraph dialog box, click the down-pointing arrow at the right side of the *Alignment* option box. At the drop-down list that displays, click the desired alignment option and then click OK to close the dialog box.

Figure 2.5 Paragraph Dialog Box with Alignment Options

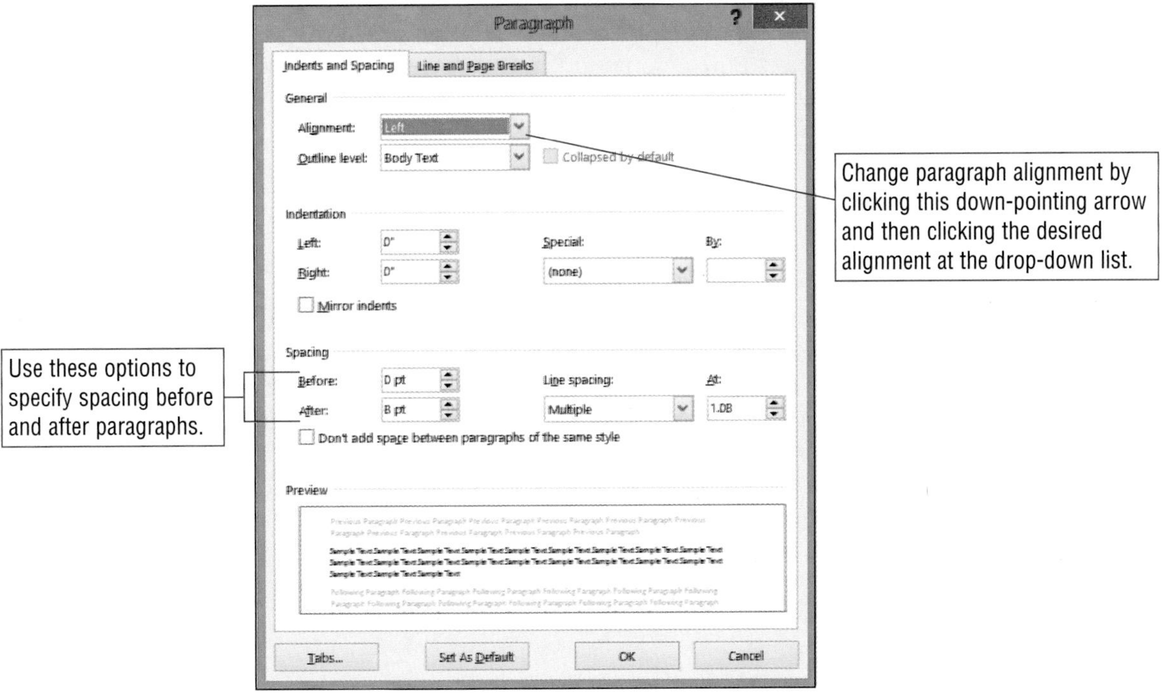

Project 3b Changing Paragraph Alignment at the Paragraph Dialog Box

Part 2 of 6

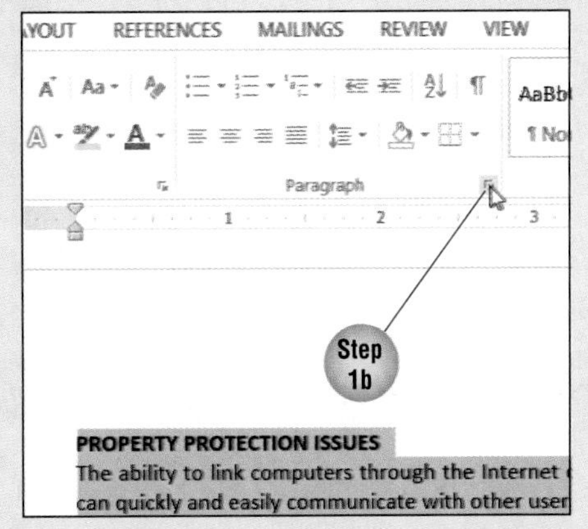

1. With **WL1-C2-P3-IntelProp.docx** open, change paragraph alignment by completing the following steps:
   a. Select the entire document.
   b. Click the Paragraph group dialog box launcher.
   c. At the Paragraph dialog box with the Indents and Spacing tab selected, click the down-pointing arrow at the right of the *Alignment* option box and then click *Left*.
   d. Click OK to close the dialog box.
   e. Deselect the text.
2. Change paragraph alignment by completing the following steps:
   a. Press Ctrl + End to move the insertion point to the end of the document.
   b. Position the insertion point on any character in the text *Prepared by Clarissa Markham.*
   c. Click the Paragraph group dialog box launcher.
   d. At the Paragraph dialog box with the Indents and Spacing tab selected, click the down-pointing arrow at the right of the *Alignment* option box and then click *Right.*

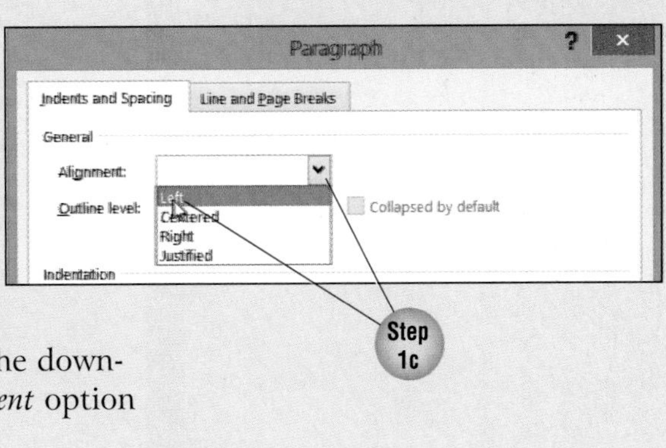

e. Click OK to close the dialog box. (The line of text containing the name *Clarissa Markham* and the line of text containing the name *Joshua Streeter* are both aligned at the right since you used the New Line command, Shift + Enter, to separate the lines of text without creating a new paragraph.)
3. Save and then print **WL1-C2-P3-IntelProp.docx**.

Quick Steps

Indent Text in Paragraph

Drag indent marker(s) on horizontal ruler.

OR

Press keyboard shortcut keys.

OR

1. Click Paragraph group dialog box launcher.
2. Insert measurement in *Left*, *Right*, and/or *By* text box.
3. Click OK.

Indenting Text in Paragraphs

By now you are familiar with the word wrap feature of Word, which ends lines and wraps the insertion point to the next line. To indent text from the left margin, the right margin, or both, use the indent buttons in the Paragraph group, on the PAGE LAYOUT tab, keyboard shortcuts, options from the Paragraph dialog box, markers on the horizontal ruler, or use the Alignment button that displays above the vertical ruler. Figure 2.6 identifies indent markers on the horizontal ruler and the Alignment button. Refer to Table 2.4 for methods for indenting text in a document. If the horizontal ruler is not visible, display the ruler by clicking the VIEW tab and then clicking the *Ruler* check box in the Show group to insert a check mark.

Figure 2.6 Horizontal Ruler and Indent Markers

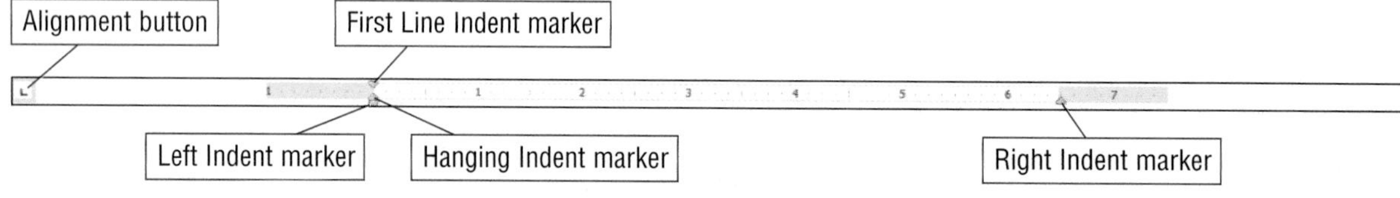

Table 2.4 Methods for Indenting Text

Indent	*Methods for Indenting*
First line of paragraph	• Press the Tab key. • Display the Paragraph dialog box, click the down-pointing arrow to the right of the *Special* list box, click *First line*, and then click OK. • Drag the First Line Indent marker on the horizontal ruler. • Click the Alignment button located left of the horizontal ruler and above the vertical ruler until the First Line Indent button displays, and then click the horizontal ruler at the desired location.

continues

Table 2.4 Methods for Indenting Text—*Continued*

Indent	*Methods for Indenting*
Text from left margin	• Click the Increase Indent button in the Paragraph group on the HOME tab to increase the indent or click the Decrease Indent button to decrease the indent. • Insert a measurement in the *Indent Left* measurement box in the Paragraph group on the PAGE LAYOUT tab. • Press Ctrl + M to increase the indent or press Ctrl + Shift + M to decrease the indent. • Display the Paragraph dialog box, type the desired indent measurement in the *Left* measurement box, and then click OK. • Drag the Left Indent marker on the horizontal ruler.
Text from right margin	• Insert a measurement in the *Indent Right* measurement box in the Paragraph group on the PAGE LAYOUT tab. • Display the Paragraph dialog box, type the desired indent measurement in the *Right* measurement box, and then click OK. • Drag the Right Indent marker on the horizontal ruler.
All lines of text except the first (called a hanging indent)	• Press Ctrl + T. (Press Ctrl + Shift + T to remove hanging indent.) • Display the Paragraph dialog box, click the down-pointing arrow to the right of the *Special* list box, click *Hanging*, and then click OK. • Click the Alignment button located left of the horizontal ruler and above the vertical ruler until the Hanging Indent button displays and then click the horizontal ruler at the desired location.
Text from both left and right margins	• Display the Paragraph dialog box, type the desired indent measurement in the *Left* measurement box, type the desired measurement in the *Right* measurement box, and then click OK. • Insert a measurement in the *Indent Right* and *Indent Left* measurement boxes in the Paragraph group on the PAGE LAYOUT tab. • Drag the Left Indent marker on the horizontal ruler; then drag the Right Indent marker on the horizontal ruler.

Project 3c Indenting Paragraphs

Part 3 of 6

1. With **WL1-C2-P3-IntelProp.docx** open, indent the first line of text in paragraphs by completing the following steps:
   a. Select the first two paragraphs of text in the document (the text after the title *PROPERTY PROTECTION ISSUES* and before the heading *Intellectual Property*.
   b. Make sure the horizontal ruler displays. (If it does not display, click the VIEW tab and then click the *Ruler* check box in the Show group to insert a check mark.)
   c. Position the mouse pointer on the First Line Indent marker on the horizontal ruler, hold down the left mouse button, drag the marker to the 0.5-inch mark, and then release the mouse button.

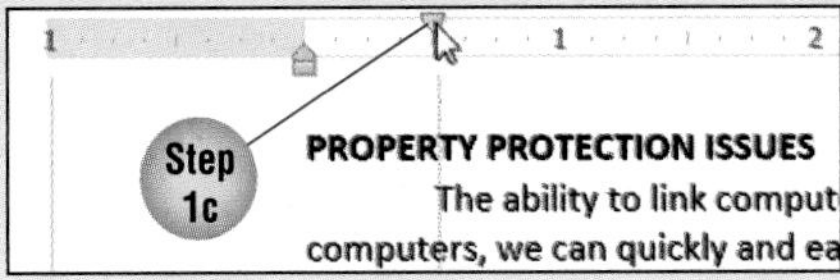

d. Select the paragraphs of text in the *Intellectual Property* section, and then drag the First Line Indent marker on the horizontal ruler to the 0.5-inch mark.

e. Select the paragraphs of text in the *Fair Use* section, click the Alignment button located at the left side of the horizontal ruler until the First Line Indent button displays, and then click the horizontal ruler at the 0.5-inch mark.

f. Position the insertion point on any character in the paragraph of text below the *Intellectual Property Protection* heading, make sure the First Line Indent button displays in the Alignment button, and then click at the 0.5-inch mark on the horizontal ruler.

2. Since the text in the second paragraph in the *Fair Use* section is a quote, indent the text from the left and right margins by completing the following steps:

a. Position the insertion point anywhere within the second paragraph in the *Fair Use* section (the paragraph that begins *[A] copyrighted work, including such*).

b. Click the Paragraph group dialog box launcher.

c. At the Paragraph dialog box, with the Indents and Spacing tab selected, select the current measurement in the *Left* measurement box and then type 0.5.

d. Select the current measurement in the *Right* measurement box and then type 0.5.

e. Click the down-pointing arrow at the right side of the *Special* list box and then click *(none)* at the drop-down list.

f. Click OK or press Enter.

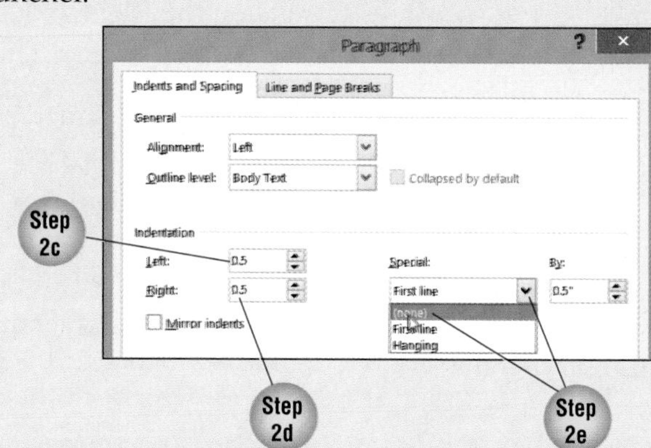

3. Create a hanging indent for the first paragraph in the *REFERENCES* section by positioning the insertion point anywhere in the first paragraph below *REFERENCES* and then pressing Ctrl + T.

4. Create a hanging indent for the second paragraph in the *REFERENCES* section by completing the following steps:

a. Position the insertion point anywhere in the second paragraph in the *REFERENCES* section.

b. Click the Alignment button located to the left of the horizontal ruler and above the vertical ruler until the Hanging Indent button displays.

c. Click the 0.5-inch mark on the horizontal ruler.

5. Create a hanging indent for the third and fourth paragraphs by completing the following steps:
   a. Select a portion of the third and fourth paragraphs.
   b. Click the Paragraph group dialog box launcher.
   c. At the Paragraph dialog box with the Indents and Spacing tab selected, click the down-pointing arrow at the right side of the *Special* list box and then click *Hanging* at the drop-down list.
   d. Click OK or press Enter.
6. Save **WL1-C2-P3-IntelProp.docx**.

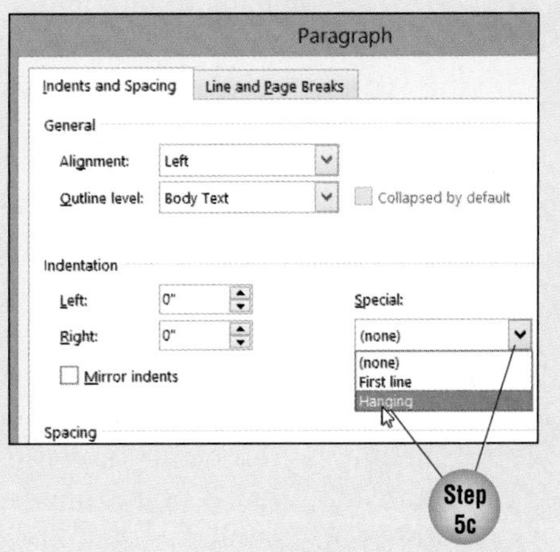

Spacing Before and After Paragraphs

By default, Word applies 8 points of additional spacing after a paragraph. You can remove this spacing, increase or decrease the spacing, and insert spacing above the paragraph. To change spacing before or after a paragraph, use the *Spacing Before* and *Spacing After* measurement boxes located in the Paragraph group on the PAGE LAYOUT tab or the *Before* and *After* options at the Paragraph dialog box with the Indents and Spacing tab selected. You can also add spacing before and after paragraphs at the Line and Paragraph Spacing button drop-down list.

HINT

Line spacing determines the amount of vertical space between lines, while paragraph spacing determines the amount of space above or below paragraphs of text.

Spacing before or after a paragraph is part of the paragraph and will be moved, copied, or deleted with the paragraph. If a paragraph, such as a heading, contains spacing before it and the paragraph falls at the top of a page, Word ignores the spacing.

Spacing before or after paragraphs is added in points, and a vertical inch contains approximately 72 points. To add spacing before or after a paragraph, click the PAGE LAYOUT tab, select the current measurement in the *Spacing Before* or the *Spacing After* measurement box, and then type the desired number of points. You can also click the up- or down-pointing arrows at the right side of the *Spacing Before* and *Spacing After* measurement boxes to increase or decrease the amount of spacing.

Repeating the Last Action

If you apply formatting to text and then want to apply the same formatting to other text in the document, consider using the Repeat command. To use this command, apply the desired formatting, move the insertion point to the next location where you want the formatting applied, and then press the F4 function key or press Ctrl + Y. The Repeat command will repeat only the last command you executed.

Quick Steps

Repeat Last Action
Press F4.
OR
Press Ctrl + Y.

Project 3d Spacing Before and After Paragraphs and Repeating Last Action Part 4 of 6

1. With **WL1-C2-P3-IntelProp.docx** open, add 6 points of spacing before and after each paragraph in the document by completing the following steps:
   a. Select the entire document.
   b. Click the PAGE LAYOUT tab.
   c. Click the up-pointing arrow at the right side of the *Spacing Before* measurement box in the Paragraph group (this inserts *6 pt* in the box).
   d. Click the up-pointing arrow at the right side of the *Spacing After* measurement box in the Paragraph group (this inserts *6 pt* in the box).
2. Add an additional 6 points of spacing above the headings by completing the following steps:
   a. Position the insertion point on any character in the heading *Intellectual Property* and then click the up-pointing arrow at the right side of the *Spacing Before* measurement box (this changes the measurement to *12 pt*).
   b. Position the insertion point on any character in the heading *Fair Use* and then press F4. (F4 is the Repeat command.)
   c. Position the insertion point on any character in the heading *Intellectual Property Protection* and then press F4.
   d. Position the insertion point on any character in the heading *REFERENCES* and then press Ctrl + Y. (Ctrl + Y is also the Repeat command.)
3. Save **WL1-C2-P3-IntelProp.docx**.

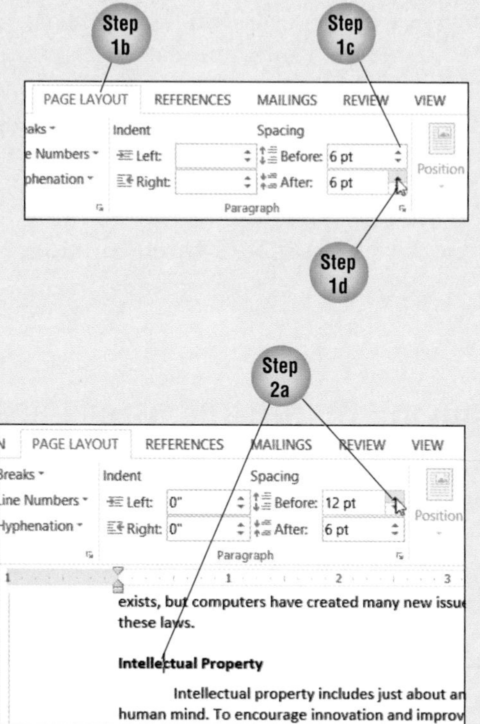

Formatting with Format Painter

Quick Steps

Format with Format Painter

1. Format text.
2. Double-click Format Painter button.
3. Select text.
4. Click Format Painter button.

Format Painter

The Clipboard group on the HOME tab contains a button for copying formatting and displays in the Clipboard group as a paintbrush. To use this button, called Format Painter, position the insertion point on a character containing the desired formatting, click the Format Painter button, and then select text to which you want the formatting applied. When you click the Format Painter button, the mouse I-beam pointer displays with a paintbrush attached. If you want to apply the formatting a single time, click the Format Painter button once. If you want to apply the formatting in more than one location in the document, double-click the Format Painter button and then select text to which you want formatting applied. When you are finished, click the Format Painter button to turn it off. You can also turn off Format Painter by pressing the Esc key.

Project 3e Formatting Headings with Format Painter

Part 5 of 6

1. With **WL1-C2-P3-IntelProp.docx** open, click the HOME tab.
2. Select the entire document and then change the font to 12-point Cambria.
3. Select the title *PROPERTY PROTECTION ISSUES*, click the Center button in the Paragraph group, and then change the font to 16-point Candara bold.
4. Apply 16-point Candara bold formatting to the *REFERENCES* heading by completing the following steps:
   a. Click any character in the title *PROPERTY PROTECTION ISSUES*.
   b. Click the Format Painter button in the Clipboard group.

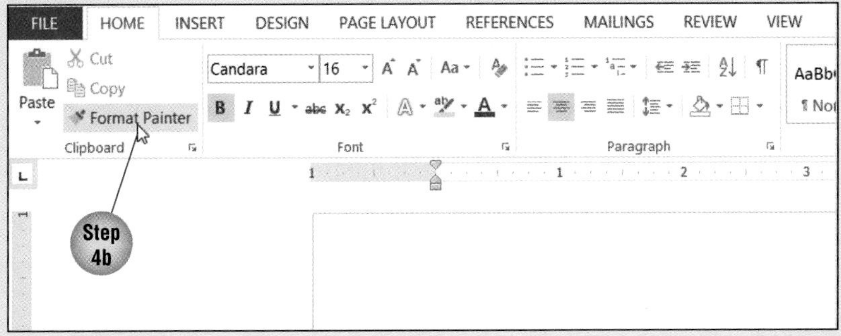

   c. Press Ctrl + End to move the insertion point to the end of the document and then click any character in the heading *REFERENCES*. (This applies the 16-point Candara bold formatting and centers the text.)
5. With the insertion point positioned on any character in the heading *REFERENCES*, add an additional 6 points of spacing before the heading (for a total of 12 points before the heading).
6. Select the heading *Intellectual Property* and then change the font to 14-point Candara bold.
7. Use the Format Painter button and apply 14-point Candara bold formatting to the other headings by completing the following steps:
   a. Position the insertion point on any character in the heading *Intellectual Property*.
   b. Double-click the Format Painter button in the Clipboard group.
   c. Using the mouse, select the heading *Fair Use*.
   d. Using the mouse, select the heading *Intellectual Property Protection*.
   e. Click the Format Painter button in the Clipboard group. (This turns off the feature.)
   f. Deselect the heading.
8. Save **WL1-C2-P3-IntelProp.docx**.

Changing Line Spacing

Quick Steps

Change Line Spacing

1. Click Line and Paragraph Spacing button in Paragraph group.
2. Click desired option at drop-down list.

OR

Press shortcut command keys.

OR

1. Click Paragraph group dialog box launcher.
2. Click *Line Spacing* option box arrow.
3. Click desired line spacing option.
4. Click OK.

OR

1. Click Paragraph group dialog box launcher.
2. Type line measurement in *At* measurement box.
3. Click OK.

Line and Paragraph Spacing

The default line spacing for a document is 1.08. (The line spacing for the **IntelProp.docx** document, which you opened at the beginning of Project 3, had been changed to single.) In certain situations, Word automatically adjusts the line spacing. For example, if you insert a large character or object, such as a graphic, Word increases the line spacing of that specific line. But you also may sometimes decide to change the line spacing for a section or for the entire document.

Change line spacing using the Line and Paragraph Spacing button in the Paragraph group on the HOME tab, with keyboard shortcuts, or with options from the Paragraph dialog box. Table 2.5 displays the keyboard shortcuts to change line spacing.

You can also change line spacing at the Paragraph dialog box with the *Line spacing* option or the *At* measurement box. If you click the down-pointing arrow at the right side of the *Line spacing* option, a drop-down list displays with a variety of spacing options. For example, to change the line spacing to double spacing, click *Double* at the drop-down list. You can type a specific line spacing measurement in the *At* measurement box. For example, to change the line spacing to 1.75, type *1.75* in the *At* measurement box.

Table 2.5 Line Spacing Keyboard Shortcuts

Press	*To change line spacing to*
Ctrl + 1	single spacing
Ctrl + 2	double spacing
Ctrl + 5	1.5 line spacing

Project 3f **Changing Line Spacing** **Part 6 of 6**

1. With **WL1-C2-P3-IntelProp.docx** open, change the line spacing for all paragraphs to double spacing by completing the following steps:
   a. Select the entire document.
   b. Click the Line and Paragraph Spacing button located in the Paragraph group on the HOME tab.
   c. Click *2.0* at the drop-down list.
2. With the entire document still selected, press Ctrl + 5. (This changes the line spacing to 1.5 line spacing.)

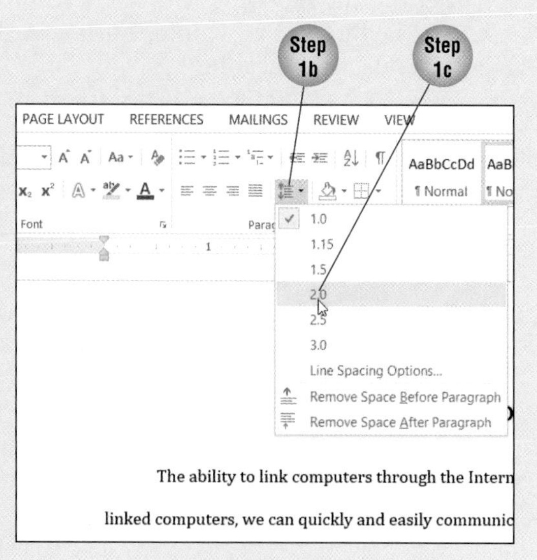

3. Change the line spacing to 1.3 using the Paragraph dialog box by completing the following steps:
   a. With the entire document still selected, click the Paragraph group dialog box launcher.
   b. At the Paragraph dialog box, make sure the Indents and Spacing tab is selected, click inside the *At* measurement box, and then type **1.3**. (This measurement box is located to the right of the *Line spacing* option box.)
   c. Click OK or press Enter.
   d. Deselect the text.
4. Save, print, and then close **WL1-C2-P3-IntelProp.docx**.

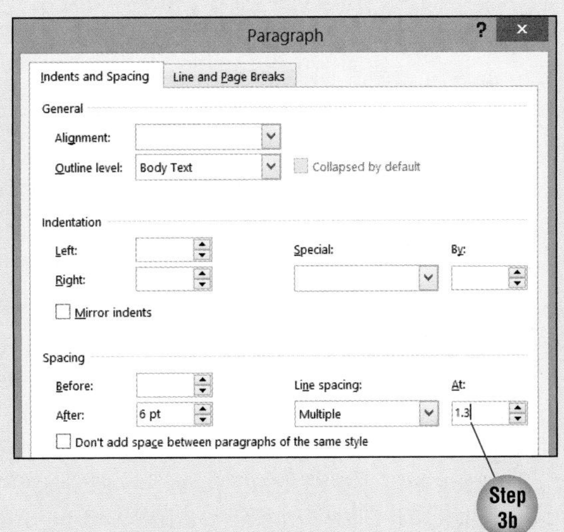

Step 3b

Project 4 Format Computer Issues Document — 2 Parts

You will open a document containing two computer-related problems to solve, reveal the formatting, compare the formatting, and make formatting changes.

Revealing and Comparing Formatting

Display formatting applied to specific text in a document at the Reveal Formatting task pane, as shown in Figure 2.7. The Reveal Formatting task pane displays font, paragraph, and section formatting applied to text where the insertion point is

Figure 2.7 Reveal Formatting Task Pane

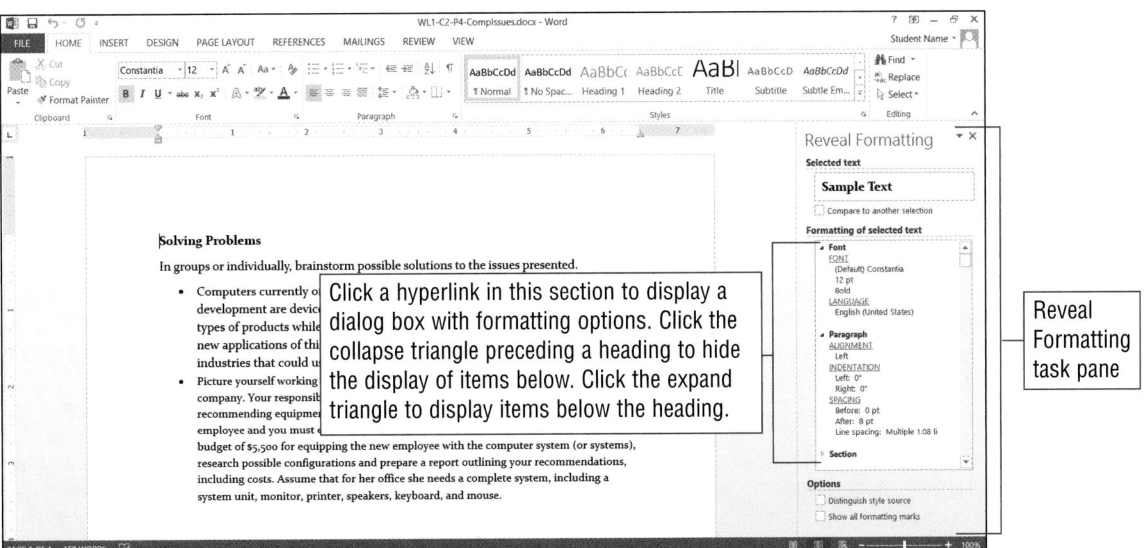

Click a hyperlink in this section to display a dialog box with formatting options. Click the collapse triangle preceding a heading to hide the display of items below. Click the expand triangle to display items below the heading.
Reveal Formatting task pane

positioned or to selected text. Display the Reveal Formatting task pane with the keyboard shortcut Shift + F1. Generally, a collapse triangle (a solid, right-and-down-pointing triangle) precedes *Font* and *Paragraph*, and an expand triangle (a hollow, right-pointing triangle) precedes *Section* in the *Formatting of selected text* list box in the Reveal Formatting task pane. Click the collapse triangle to hide any items below a heading, and click the expand triangle to reveal items. Some of the items below headings in the *Formatting of selected text* list box are hyperlinks. Click a hyperlink and a dialog box displays with the specific option.

Project 4a Revealing Formatting

Part 1 of 2

1. Open **CompIssues.docx**.
2. Save the document with Save As and name it **WL1-C2-P4-CompIssues**.
3. Press Shift + F1 to display the Reveal Formatting task pane.
4. Click anywhere in the heading *Solving Problems* and then notice the formatting information that displays in the Reveal Formatting task pane.
5. Click in the bulleted paragraph and notice the formatting information that displays in the Reveal Formatting task pane.

Quick Steps

Compare Formatting
1. Press Shift + F1 to display Reveal Formatting task pane.
2. Click or select text.
3. Click *Compare to another selection* check box.
4. Click or select text.

Along with displaying formatting applied to text, you can use the Reveal Formatting task pane to compare formatting of two text selections to determine what formatting is different. To compare formatting, select the first instance of formatting to be compared, click the *Compare to another selection* check box, and then select the second instance of formatting to compare. Any differences between the two selections display in the *Formatting differences* list box.

Project 4b Comparing Formatting

Part 2 of 2

1. With **WL1-C2-P4-CompIssues.docx** open, make sure the Reveal Formatting task pane displays. If it does not, turn it on by pressing Shift + F1.
2. Select the first bulleted paragraph (the paragraph that begins *Computers currently offer both*).
3. Click the *Compare to another selection* check box to insert a check mark.
4. Select the second bulleted paragraph (the paragraph that begins *Picture yourself working in the*).
5. Determine the formatting differences by reading the information in the *Formatting differences* list box. (The list box displays *12 pt -> 11 pt* below the FONT hyperlink, indicating that the difference is point size.)
6. Format the second bulleted paragraph so it is set in 12-point size.

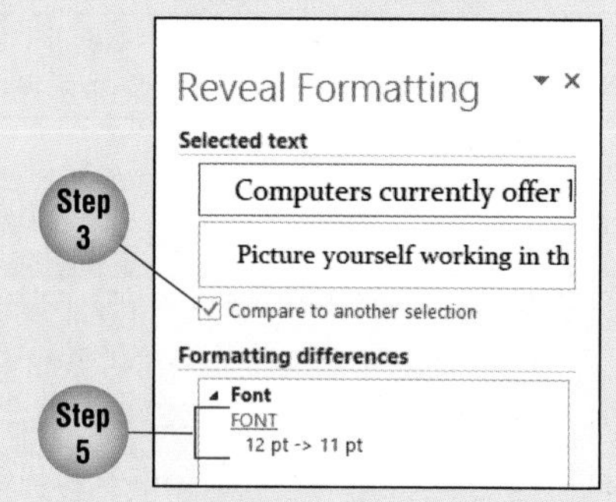

7. Click the *Compare to another selection* check box to remove the check mark.
8. Select the word *visual,* which displays in the first sentence in the first bulleted paragraph.
9. Click the *Compare to another selection* check box to insert a check mark.
10. Select the word *audio,* which displays in the first sentence of the first bulleted paragraph.
11. Determine the formatting differences by reading the information in the *Formatting differences* list box.
12. Format the word *audio* so it matches the formatting of the word *visual.*
13. Click the *Compare to another selection* check box to remove the check mark.
14. Close the Reveal Formatting task pane by clicking the Close button (contains an X), which displays in the upper right corner of the task pane.
15. Save, print, and then close **WL1-C2-P4-CompIssues.docx**.

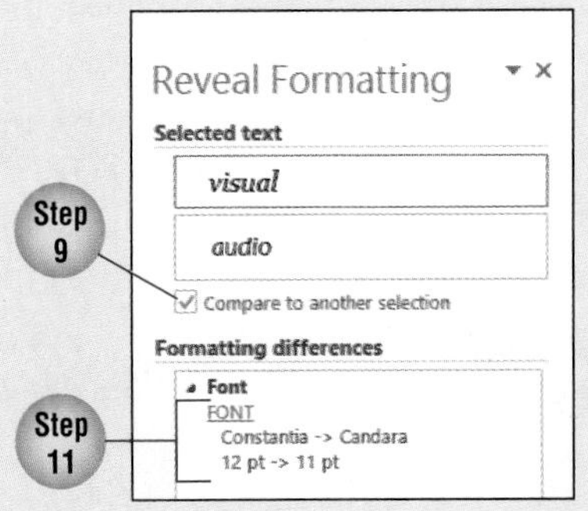

Chapter Summary

- A font consists of three parts: typeface, type size, and typestyle.
- A typeface (font) is a set of characters with a common design and shape. Typefaces are either monospaced, allotting the same amount of horizontal space for each character, or proportional, allotting a varying amount of space for each character. Proportional typefaces are divided into two main categories: serif and sans serif.
- Type size is measured in point size; the higher the point size, the larger the characters.
- A typestyle is a variation of style within a certain typeface, such as bold, italic, and underline. You can apply typestyle formatting with some of the buttons in the Font group.
- With some of the buttons in the Font group, you can apply font effects such as superscript, subscript, and strikethrough.
- The Mini toolbar automatically displays above selected text. Use buttons on this toolbar to apply formatting to selected text.
- With options at the Font dialog box, you can change the font, font size, and font style and apply specific effects. Display this dialog box by clicking the Font group dialog box launcher.
- A Word document contains a number of predesigned formats grouped into style sets. Change to a different style set by clicking the DESIGN tab and then clicking the desired style set thumbnail in the Document Formatting group.
- Apply a theme and change theme colors, fonts, and effects with buttons in the Document Formatting group on the DESIGN tab.
- Click the Paragraph Spacing button in the Document Formatting group on the DESIGN tab to apply a predesigned paragraph spacing option to text in a document.

- By default, paragraphs in a Word document are aligned at the left margin and ragged at the right margin. Change this default alignment with buttons in the Paragraph group, at the Paragraph dialog box, or with keyboard shortcuts.
- To turn on or off the display of nonprinting characters such as paragraph marks, click the Show/Hide ¶ button in the Paragraph group on the HOME tab.
- Indent text in paragraphs with indent buttons in the Paragraph group on the HOME tab, buttons in the Paragraph group on the PAGE LAYOUT tab, keyboard shortcuts, options from the Paragraph dialog box, markers on the horizontal ruler, or use the Alignment button above the vertical ruler.
- Increase and/or decrease spacing before and after paragraphs using the *Spacing Before* and *Spacing After* measurement boxes in the Paragraph group on the PAGE LAYOUT tab or using the *Before* and/or *After* options at the Paragraph dialog box.
- Use the Format Painter button in the Clipboard group on the HOME tab to copy formatting already applied to text to different locations in the document.
- Change line spacing with the Line and Paragraph Spacing button in the Paragraph group on the HOME tab, keyboard shortcuts, or options from the Paragraph dialog box.
- Display the Reveal Formatting task pane to display formatting applied to text. Use the *Compare to another selection* option in the task pane to compare formatting of two text selections to determine what formatting is different.

Commands Review

FEATURE	RIBBON TAB, GROUP	BUTTON	KEYBOARD SHORTCUT
bold text	HOME, Font	B	Ctrl + B
center-align text	HOME, Paragraph		Ctrl + E
change case of text	HOME, Font	Aa	Shift + F3
clear all formatting	HOME, Font		
clear character formatting			Ctrl + spacebar
clear paragraph formatting			Ctrl + Q
decrease font size	HOME, Font	A	Ctrl + Shift + <
display nonprinting characters	HOME, Paragraph	¶	Ctrl + Shift + *
font	HOME, Font	Calibri (Body)	
font color	HOME, Font	A	
Font dialog box	HOME, Font		Ctrl + Shift + F

FEATURE	RIBBON TAB, GROUP	BUTTON	KEYBOARD SHORTCUT
Format Painter	HOME, Clipboard		Ctrl + Shift + C Ctrl + Shift + V
highlight text	HOME, Font		
increase font size	HOME, Font		Ctrl + Shift + >
italicize text	HOME, Font		Ctrl + I
justify text	HOME, Paragraph		Ctrl + J
left-align text	HOME, Paragraph		Ctrl + L
line spacing	HOME, Paragraph		Ctrl + 1 (single) Ctrl + 2 (double) Ctrl + 5 (1.5)
Paragraph dialog box	HOME, Paragraph		
paragraph spacing	DESIGN, Document Formatting		
repeat last action			F4 or Ctrl + Y
Reveal Formatting task pane			Shift + F1
right-align text	HOME, Paragraph		Ctrl + R
spacing after paragraph	PAGE LAYOUT, Paragraph	After: 0 pt	
spacing before paragraph	PAGE LAYOUT, Paragraph	Before: 0 pt	
strikethrough text	HOME, Font		
subscript text	HOME, Font		Ctrl + =
superscript text	HOME, Font		Ctrl + Shift + +
text effects and typography	HOME, Font		
theme colors	DESIGN, Document Formatting		
theme effects	DESIGN, Document Formatting		
theme tonts	DESIGN, Document Formatting		
themes	DESIGN, Document Formatting		
underline text	HOME, Font		Ctrl + U

Concepts Check Test Your Knowledge 

Completion: In the space provided at the right, indicate the correct term, symbol, or command.

1. The Bold button is located in this group on the HOME tab. ____________
2. Click this button in the Font group to remove all formatting from selected text. ____________
3. Proportional typefaces are divided into two main categories: serif and this. ____________
4. This is the keyboard shortcut to italicize selected text. ____________
5. This term refers to text that is raised slightly above the regular text line. ____________
6. This automatically displays above selected text. ____________
7. Click this to display the Font dialog box. ____________
8. Change style sets with options in this group on the DESIGN tab. ____________
9. Apply a theme and change theme colors, fonts, and effects with buttons in the Document Formatting group on this tab. ____________
10. This is the default paragraph alignment. ____________
11. Click this button in the Paragraph group on the HOME tab to turn on the display of nonprinting characters. ____________
12. Return all paragraph formatting to normal with this keyboard shortcut. ____________
13. Click this button in the Paragraph group on the HOME tab to align text at the right margin. ____________
14. In this type of indent, the first line of text remains at the left margin and the remaining lines of text align at the first tab. ____________
15. Repeat the last action by pressing F4 or using this keyboard shortcut. ____________
16. Use this button in the Clipboard group on the HOME tab to copy formatting already applied to text to different locations in the document. ____________
17. Change line spacing to 1.5 with this keyboard shortcut. ____________
18. Press these keys to display the Reveal Formatting task pane. ____________

Skills Check Assess Your Performance

Assessment 1

APPLY CHARACTER FORMATTING TO A LEASE AGREEMENT DOCUMENT

1. Open **LeaseAgrmnt.docx**.
2. Save the document with Save As and name it **WL1-C2-A1-LeaseAgrmnt**.
3. Press Ctrl + End to move the insertion point to the end of the document and then type the text shown in Figure 2.8. Bold, italicize, and underline text as shown.
4. Select the entire document and then change the font to 12-point Candara.
5. Select and then bold *THIS LEASE AGREEMENT* located in the first paragraph.
6. Select and then italicize *12 o'clock midnight* in the *Term* section.
7. Select the title *LEASE AGREEMENT* and then change the font to 16-point Corbel and the font color to Dark Blue. (Make sure the title retains the bold formatting.)
8. Select the heading *Term*, change the font to 14-point Corbel, and apply small caps formatting. (Make sure the heading retains the bold formatting.)
9. Use Format Painter to change the formatting to small caps in 14-point Corbel for the remaining headings (*Rent*, *Damage Deposit*, *Use of Premises*, *Condition of Premises*, *Alterations and Improvements*, *Damage to Premises*, and *Inspection of Premises*).
10. Save, print, and then close **WL1-C2-A1-LeaseAgrmnt.docx**.

Figure 2.8 Assessment 1

Inspection of Premises

Lessor shall have the right at all reasonable times during the term of this Agreement to exhibit the Premises and to display the usual *for rent* or *vacancy* signs on the Premises at any time within <u>forty-five</u> days before the expiration of this Lease.

Assessment 2

APPLY STYLES, A STYLE SET, AND A THEME TO A HARDWARE TECHNOLOGY DOCUMENT

1. Open **NetworkHardware.docx**.
2. Save the document with Save As and name it **WL1-C2-A2-NetworkHardware**.
3. Apply the Heading 1 style to the title *Network Hardware*.
4. Apply the Heading 2 style to the headings in the document (*Hubs*, *Switches*, *Repeaters*, *Routers*, *Gateways*, *Bridges*, and *Network Interface Cards*).
5. Apply the Lines (Stylish) style set.
6. Apply the Savon theme.
7. Apply the Green theme colors.
8. Apply the Georgia theme fonts.
9. Apply the Open paragraph spacing.
10. Highlight in yellow the second sentence in the *Hubs* section.
11. Save, print, and then close **WL1-C2-A2-NetworkHardware.docx**.

Assessment

3 APPLY CHARACTER AND PARAGRAPH FORMATTING TO AN EMPLOYEE PRIVACY DOCUMENT

1. Open **WorkplacePrivacy.docx**.
2. Save the document with Save As and name it **WL1-C2-A3-WorkplacePrivacy**.
3. Move the insertion point to the beginning of the document and then type WORKPLACE PRIVACY.
4. Select the text from the beginning of the first paragraph to the end of the document (make sure you select the blank line at the end of the document) and then make the following changes:
   a. Change the line spacing to 1.5 lines.
   b. Change the spacing after paragraphs to 0 points.
   c. Indent the first line of each paragraph 0.5 inch.
   d. Change the paragraph alignment to justified alignment.
5. Move the insertion point to the end of the document and, if necessary, drag the First Line Indent marker on the horizontal ruler back to 0 inch. Type the text shown in Figure 2.9. (Create a hanging indent, as shown in Figure 2.9.)
6. Select the entire document and then change the font to Constantia.
7. Select the title *WORKPLACE PRIVACY*, center the title, change the font to 14-point Calibri bold, and then apply the Fill - Orange, Accent 2, Outline - Accent 2 text effect (third column, first row in the Text Effects and Typography button drop-down gallery).
8. Use the Format Painter to apply the same formatting to the title *BIBLIOGRAPHY* that you applied to the title *WORKPLACE PRIVACY*.
9. Save, print, and then close **WL1-C2-A3-WorkplacePrivacy.docx**.

Figure 2.9 Assessment 3

BIBLIOGRAPHY

Amaral, H. G. (2014). *Privacy in the workplace,* 2nd edition (pp. 103-112). Denver, CO: Goodwin Publishing Group.

Visual Benchmark Demonstrate Your Proficiency

CREATE AN ACTIVE LISTENING REPORT

1. At a blank document, press the Enter key twice and then type the document shown in Figure 2.10. Set the body text in 12-point Cambria, set the title in 16-point Candara bold, set the headings in 14-point Candara bold, change the paragraph spacing after the headings to 6 points, change the font color to dark blue for the entire document, and then apply additional formatting so the document appears as shown in the figure.
2. Save the document and name it **WL1-C2-VB-ActiveListen**.
3. Print and then close the document.

Figure 2.10 Visual Benchmark

ACTIVE LISTENING SKILLS

Speaking and listening is a two-way activity. When the audience pays attention, the speaker gains confidence, knowing that his or her message is being received and appreciated. At the same time, alert listeners obtain information, hear an amusing or interesting story, and otherwise benefit from the speaker's presentation.

Become an Active Listener

Active listeners pay attention to the speaker and to what is being said. They are respectful of the speaker and eager to be informed or entertained. In contrast, *passive listeners* "tune out" the presentation and may even display rudeness by not paying attention to the speaker, here are ways in which you can become an active listener:

<u>Listen with a purpose</u>: Stay focused on what the speaker is saying and you will gain useful information to hear a suspenseful story narrated well. Try to avoid letting your attention wander.

<u>Be courteous</u>: Consider that the speaker spent time preparing for the presentation and thus deserves your respect.

<u>Take brief notes</u>: If the speaker is providing information, take brief notes on the main ideas. Doing so will help you understand and remember what is being said. If you have questions or would like to hear more about a particular point, ask the speaker for clarification after the presentation.

Practice Active Listening Skills in Conversation

Most people have had the experience in being in a one-way conversation in which one person does all the talking and the others just listen. In fact, this is not a conversation, which is by definition an exchange of information and ideas. In a true conversation, everyone has a chance to be heard. Do not monopolize conversation. Give the other person or persons an opportunity to talk. Pay attention when others are speaking and show your interest in what is being said by making eye contact and asking questions. Avoid interrupting since this shows your disinterest an also suggests that what you have to say is more important.

Case Study Apply Your Skills

Part 1

You work for the local chamber of commerce and are responsible for assisting the office manager, Teresa Alexander. Ms. Alexander would like to maintain consistency in articles submitted for publication in the monthly chamber newsletter. She wants you to explore various decorative and plain fonts. She would like you to choose two handwriting fonts, two decorative fonts, and two plain fonts and then prepare a document containing an illustration of each of these fonts. Save the document and name it **WL1-C2-CS-Fonts**. Print and then close the document.

Part 2

Ms. Alexander has asked you to write a short article for the upcoming chamber newsletter. In the article, she would like you to describe an upcoming event at your school, a local college or university, or your local community. Effectively use at least two of the fonts you wrote about in the document you prepared for Case Study Part 1. Save the document and name it **WL1-C2-CS-Article**. Print and then close the document.

Part 3

Help

Ms. Alexander will be posting the Chamber of Commerce newsletter to the chamber's website and would like you to research how to save a Word document as a web page. Use the Help feature to research how to save a document as a web page—specifically, a filtered web page. With the information you find, create a Word document describing the steps for saving a document as a filtered web page. Save the document and name it **WL1-C2-CS-WebPage**. Print and then close the document. Open the **WL1-C2-CS-Article.docx** document you created in Case Study Part 2 and then save the document as a filtered web page.

MICROSOFT® WORD

CHAPTER 3

Customizing Paragraphs

PERFORMANCE OBJECTIVES

Upon successful completion of Chapter 3, you will be able to:

- **Apply numbering and bulleting formatting to text**
- **Insert paragraph borders and shading**
- **Apply custom borders and shading**
- **Sort paragraph text**
- **Set, clear, and move tabs on the horizontal ruler and at the Tabs dialog box**
- **Cut, copy, and paste text in a document**
- **Copy and paste text between documents**

Tutorials

3.1 Creating Bulleted and Numbered Lists

3.2 Adding a Border and Shading to Selected Text

3.3 Sorting Text in Paragraphs

3.4 Setting Tabs Using the Horizontal Ruler

3.5 Setting Tabs at the Tabs Dialog Box

3.6 Cutting, Copying, and Pasting Text

3.7 Using the Clipboard Task Pane

As you learned in Chapter 2, Word contains a variety of options for formatting text in paragraphs. In this chapter you will learn how to insert numbers and bullets in a document, how to apply borders and shading to paragraphs of text in a document, how to sort paragraphs of text, and how to manipulate tabs on the horizontal ruler and at the Tabs dialog box. Editing some documents might include selecting and then deleting, moving, or copying text. You can perform this type of editing with buttons in the Clipboard group on the HOME tab or with keyboard shortcuts. Model answers for this chapter's projects appear on the following pages.

Note: Before beginning the projects, copy to your storage medium the WL1C3 subfolder from the WL1 folder on the CD that accompanies this textbook and then make WL1C3 the active folder.

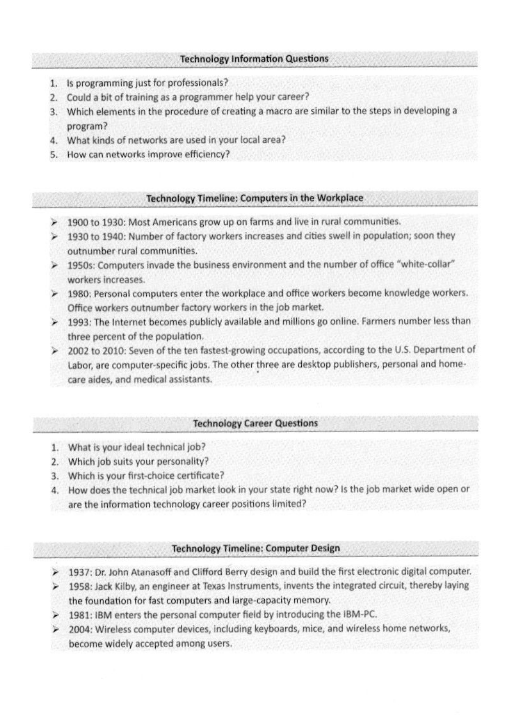

Technology Information Questions

1. Is programming just for professionals?
2. Could a bit of training as a programmer help your career?
3. Which elements in the procedure of creating a macro are similar to the steps in developing a program?
4. What kinds of networks are used in your local area?
5. How can networks improve efficiency?

Technology Timeline: Computers in the Workplace

- 1900 to 1930: Most Americans grow up on farms and live in rural communities.
- 1930 to 1940: Number of factory workers increases and cities swell in population; soon they outnumber rural communities.
- 1950s: Computers invade the business environment and the number of office "white-collar" workers increases.
- 1980: Personal computers enter the workplace and office workers become knowledge workers. Office workers outnumber factory workers in the job market.
- 1993: The Internet becomes publicly available and millions go online. Farmers number less than three percent of the population.
- 2002 to 2010: Seven of the ten fastest-growing occupations, according to the U.S. Department of Labor, are computer-specific jobs. The other three are desktop publishers, personal and home-care aides, and medical assistants.

Technology Career Questions

1. What is your ideal technical job?
2. Which job suits your personality?
3. Which is your first-choice certificate?
4. How does the technical job market look in your state right now? Is the job market wide open or are the information technology career positions limited?

Technology Timeline: Computer Design

- 1937: Dr. John Atanasoff and Clifford Berry design and build the first electronic digital computer.
- 1958: Jack Kilby, an engineer at Texas Instruments, invents the integrated circuit, thereby laying the foundation for fast computers and large-capacity memory.
- 1981: IBM enters the personal computer field by introducing the IBM-PC.
- 2004: Wireless computer devices, including keyboards, mice, and wireless home networks, become widely accepted among users.

Project 1 Format a Document on Computer Technology
WL1-C3-P1-TechInfo.docx

Online Shopping

Online shopping, also called electronic shopping or e-shopping, is defined as using a computer, modem, browser, and the Internet to locate, examine, purchase, and pay for products. Many businesses encourage consumers to shop online because it saves employee time, thus reducing staff needs and saving money for the company. For example, some major airlines offer special discounts to travelers who purchase their tickets over the Internet, and most are eliminating paper tickets altogether.

Advantages of Online Shopping

For the consumer, online shopping offers several distinct advantages over traditional shopping methods. Some of these conveniences include:

- Convenience. With e-shopping, you can browse merchandise and make purchases whenever you want from the privacy and comfort of your home or office.
- Ease of comparison shopping. E-shopping allows you to quickly find comparable items at similar stores and locate those venues with the best quality and lowest prices.
- Greater selection. Because they are not restricted by available shelf space, online stores can offer you an almost unlimited number of products.
- More product information. At many online stores, you can find detailed information about a wide variety of products, an advantage often unavailable in traditional stores.

Online Shopping Venues

Just as consumers can visit a variety of bricks-and-mortar retail outlets, such as stores and shopping malls, Internet shoppers can browse several types of online shopping venues, including online stores, superstores, and shopping malls.

Online Shopping Safety Tips

The number one concern about shopping online is security. The truth is, shopping online is safe and secure if you know what to look for. Following these guidelines can help you avoid trouble.

1. Only buy at secure sites.
2. Never provide your social security number.
3. Look for sites that follow privacy rules from a privacy watchdog such as TRUSTe.
4. Find out the privacy policy of shopping sites before you buy.
5. Keep current on the latest Internet scams.
6. Answer only the minimum questions when filling out forms.

REFERENCES

Claussen, Morgan. "Online Shopping Tips," *Technology Bytes*, October 2, 2014.
Fairmont, Gerald. "Securing Your Privacy," emcpnews.com, August 5, 2014.
Weyman, Jennifer. "Safe Online Shopping," *Computing Standards*, September 10, 2014.

Project 2 Customize a Document on Online Shopping
WL1-C3-P2-OnlineShop.docx

Model Answers

WORKSHOPS

Title	Price	Date
Quality Management	$240	Friday, February 6
Staff Development	229	Friday, February 20
Streamlining Production	175	Monday, March 2
Managing Records	150	Tuesday, March 17
Customer Service Training	150	Thursday, March 19
Sales Techniques	125	Tuesday, April 14

TRAINING DATES

January 6	February 3
January 15	February 12
January 20	February 17
January 22	February 24

TABLE OF CONTENTS

Computers and Creativity 1
Graphics Software 8
Page Layout Software 14
Multimedia Software 21
Educational and Reference Software 34
Programming Software 43

Project 3 Prepare a Document on Workshops and Training Dates WL1-C3-P3-Tabs.docx

Online Shopping Safety Tips

The number one concern about shopping online is security. The truth is, shopping online is safe and secure if you know what to look for. Following these guidelines should help you avoid trouble.

Find out the privacy policy of shopping sites before you buy. Ask what information they gather, how that information will be used, and whether they share that information.

Only buy at secure sites. Secure sites use encryption to scramble your credit card information so that no one except the site can read it. When you enter a secure site, you'll get a pop-up notice in your browser, and then an icon of a closed lock will appear at the bottom of the browser.

Keep current with the latest Internet scams. The U.S. Consumer Gateway reports on Internet scams and tells you what actions the Federal Trade Commission has taken against Internet scammers. The Internet Fraud Watch, run by the National Consumers League, is a great source as well.

Never provide your social security number. A legitimate site will not ask you for your social security number.

Look for sites that follow privacy rules from a privacy watchdog such as TRUSTe. TRUSTe (www.truste.org) is a nonprofit group that serves as a watchdog for Internet privacy. It allows sites to post an online seal if the site adheres to TRUSTe's Internet privacy policies.

Answer only the minimum questions when filling out forms. Many sites put an asterisk next to the questions that must be answered, so only answer those.

Project 4 Move and Copy Text in a Document on Online Shopping Tips WL1-C3-P4-ShoppingTips.docx

TECHNICAL SUPPORT TEAM
Staff Meeting
Wednesday, March 18, 2015
3:00 to 4:30 p.m., Room 20

TECHNICAL SUPPORT TEAM
Staff Meeting
Wednesday, March 18, 2015
3:00 to 4:30 p.m., Room 20

TECHNICAL SUPPORT TEAM
Staff Meeting
Wednesday, March 18, 2015
3:00 to 4:30 p.m., Room 20

TECHNICAL SUPPORT TEAM
Staff Meeting
Wednesday, March 18, 2015
3:00 to 4:30 p.m., Room 20

TECHNICAL SUPPORT TEAM
Staff Meeting
Wednesday, March 18, 2015
3:00 to 4:30 p.m., Room 20

TECHNICAL SUPPORT TEAM
Staff Meeting
Wednesday, March 18, 2015
3:00 to 4:30 p.m., Room 20

Project 5 Copy Text in a Staff Meeting Announcement
WL1-C3-P5-StaffMtg.docx

CONTRACT NEGOTIATION ITEMS

1. The Employer agrees that, during the term of this Agreement, it shall not cause or initiate any lockout of Employees.
2. During the term of this Agreement, the **LWU**, its members, and its representatives agree not to engage in, authorize, sanction, or support any strike, slowdown, or other acts of curtailment or work stoppage.
3. Employees transferring to another location at their own request due to bidding or exercise of seniority shall be provided with space-available transportation with no service charge for self and family.
4. Each employee requested by **RM** to be away from regular base on duty shall receive expenses.
5. An employee shall report to his/her **RM** supervisor that he/she is ill and unable to work at least two (2) hours prior to the start of his/her shift, if at all possible.
6. If **RM**, at any time, grants additional sick leave or assistance to any employee, the **LWU** will deem this a precedence requiring additional sick leave or assistance in any other case.

Project 6 Create a Contract Negotiations Document
WL1-C3-P6-NegotiateItems.docx

Project 1 Format a Document on Computer Technology — 5 Parts

You will open a document containing information on computer technology, type numbered text in the document, and apply numbering and bullet formatting to paragraphs in the document.

Applying Numbering and Bullets

Automatically number paragraphs or insert bullets before paragraphs using buttons in the Paragraph group on the HOME tab. Use the Bullets button to insert bullets before specific paragraphs and use the Numbering button to insert numbers.

Bullets

Numbering

Applying Numbering to Paragraphs

If you type *1.* and then press the spacebar, Word indents the number approximately 0.25 inch from the left margin and then hang indents the text in the paragraph approximately 0.5 inch from the left margin. Additionally, when you press Enter to end the first item, *2.* is inserted 0.25 inch from the left margin at the beginning of the next paragraph. Continue typing items, and Word inserts the next number in the list. To turn off numbering, press the Enter key twice or click the Numbering button in the Paragraph group. (You can also remove paragraph formatting from a paragraph, including automatic numbering, with the keyboard shortcut Ctrl + Q. Remove all formatting including character and paragraph formatting from selected text by clicking the Clear All Formatting button in the Font group on the HOME tab.)

Quick Steps

Type Numbered Paragraphs
1. Type **1**.
2. Press spacebar.
3. Type text.
4. Press Enter.

Define new numbering by clicking the Numbering button arrow and then clicking *Define New Number Format.*

If you press the Enter key twice between numbered paragraphs, the automatic number is removed. To turn it back on, type the next number in the list (and the period) followed by a space. Word will automatically indent the number and hang indent the text.

When the AutoFormat feature inserts numbering and indents text, the AutoCorrect Options button displays. Click this button and a drop-down list displays with options for undoing and/or stopping the automatic numbering. An AutoCorrect Options button also displays when AutoFormat inserts automatic bulleting in a document. If you want to insert a line break without inserting a bullet or number, you do not need to turn off the automatic numbering/bulleting and then turn it back on again. Instead, simply press Shift + Enter to insert the line break.

Project 1a **Typing Numbered Paragraphs** **Part 1 of 5**

1. Open **TechInfo.docx**.
2. Save the document with Save As and name it **WL1-C3-P1-TechInfo**.
3. Press Ctrl + End to move the insertion point to the end of the document and then type the text shown in Figure 3.1. Bold and center the title *Technology Career Questions*. When typing the numbered paragraphs, complete the following steps:
   a. Type 1. and then press the spacebar.
   b. Type the paragraph of text and then press the Enter key. (This moves the insertion point down to the next line, inserts *2.* indented 0.25 inch from the left margin, and also indents the first paragraph of text approximately 0.5 inch from the left margin. Also, the AutoCorrect Options button displays. Use this button if you want to undo or stop automatic numbering.)
   c. Continue typing the remaining text. (Remember, you do not need to type the paragraph number and period—these are automatically inserted. The last numbered item will wrap differently on your screen than shown in Figure 3.1.)
   d. After typing the last question, press the Enter key twice. (This turns off paragraph numbering.)
4. Save **WL1-C3-P1-TechInfo.docx**.

Figure 3.1 Project 1a

Technology Career Questions

1. What is your ideal technical job?
2. Which job suits your personality?
3. Which is your first-choice certificate?
4. How does the technical job market look in your state right now? Is the job market wide open or are the information technology career positions limited?

If you do not want automatic numbering in a document, turn off the feature at the AutoCorrect dialog box with the AutoFormat As You Type tab selected, as shown in Figure 3.2. To display this dialog box, click the FILE tab and then click *Options*. At the Word Options dialog box, click the *Proofing* option located in the left panel and then click the AutoCorrect Options button that displays in the *AutoCorrect options* section of the dialog box. At the AutoCorrect dialog box, click

Figure 3.2 AutoCorrect Dialog Box with AutoFormat As You Type Tab Selected

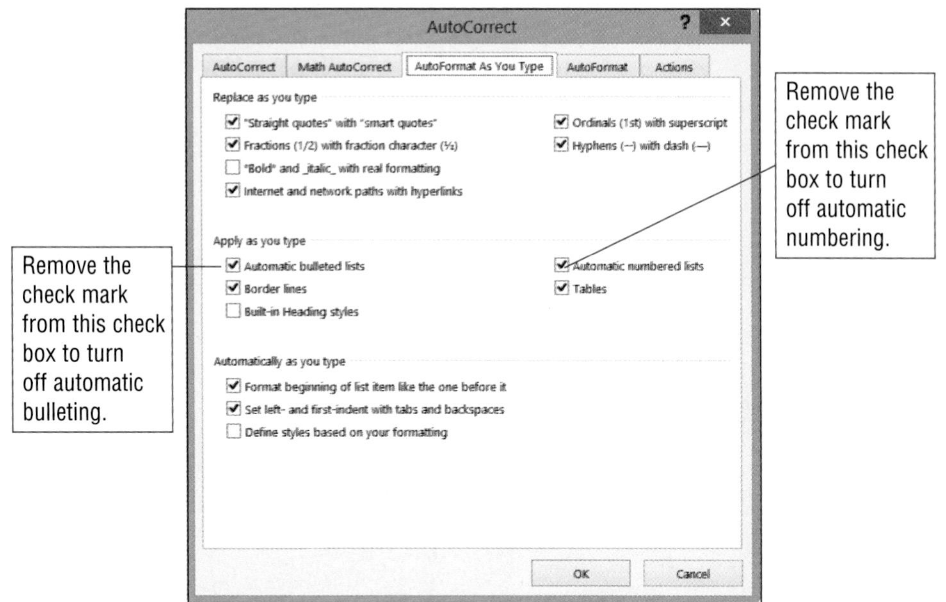

the AutoFormat As You Type tab and then click the *Automatic numbered lists* check box to remove the check mark. Click OK to close the AutoCorrect dialog box and then click OK to close the Word Options dialog box.

You can also automate the creation of numbered paragraphs with the Numbering button in the Paragraph group on the HOME tab. To use this button, type the text (do not type the number) for each paragraph to be numbered, select the paragraphs to be numbered, and then click the Numbering button in the Paragraph group. You can insert or delete numbered paragraphs in a document.

Quick Steps

Create Numbered Paragraphs
1. Select text.
2. Click Numbering button.

Project 1b Inserting Paragraph Numbering — Part 2 of 5

1. With **WL1-C3-P1-TechInfo.docx** open, apply numbers to paragraphs by completing the following steps:
   a. Select the five paragraphs of text in the *Technology Information Questions* section.
   b. Click the Numbering button in the Paragraph group on the HOME tab.

2. Add text between paragraphs 4 and 5 in the *Technology Information Questions* section by completing the following steps:
   a. Position the insertion point immediately to the right of the question mark at the end of the fourth paragraph.
   b. Press Enter.
   c. Type **What kinds of networks are used in your local area?**

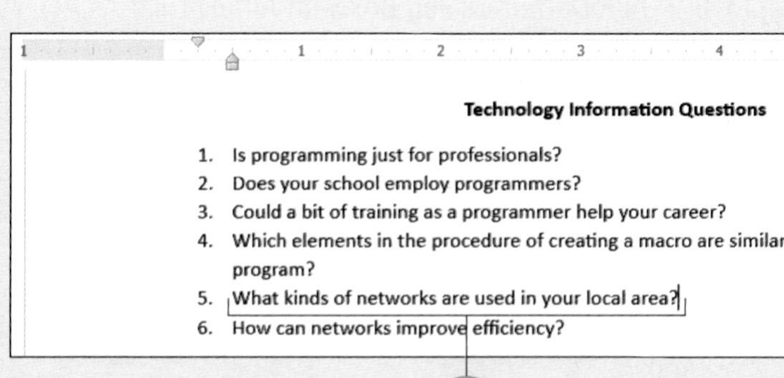

Technology Information Questions
1. Is programming just for professionals?
2. Does your school employ programmers?
3. Could a bit of training as a programmer help your career?
4. Which elements in the procedure of creating a macro are similar
program?
5. What kinds of networks are used in your local area?
6. How can networks improve efficiency?

3. Delete the second question (paragraph) in the *Technology Information Questions* section by completing the following steps:
   a. Select the text of the second paragraph. (You will not be able to select the number.)
   b. Press the Delete key.
4. Save **WL1-C3-P1-TechInfo.docx**.

Applying Bullets to Paragraphs

Quick Steps

Type Bulleted Paragraphs
1. Type *, >, or - symbol.
2. Press spacebar.
3. Type text.
4. Press Enter.

Create Bulleted Paragraphs
1. Select text.
2. Click Bullets button.

In addition to automatically numbering paragraphs, Word's AutoFormat feature will create bulleted paragraphs. Bulleted lists with hanging indents are automatically created when a paragraph begins with the symbol *, >, or -. Type one of the symbols and then press the spacebar, and the AutoFormat feature inserts a bullet approximately 0.25 inch from the left margin and indents the text following the bullet another 0.25 inch. You can turn off the automatic bulleting feature at the AutoCorrect dialog box with the AutoFormat As You Type tab selected. You can demote or promote bulleted text by pressing the Tab key to demote text or pressing Shift + Tab to promote bulleted text. Word uses different bullets for demoted text.

You can also create bulleted paragraphs with the Bullets button in the Paragraph group on the HOME tab. To create bulleted paragraphs using the Bullets button, type the text of the paragraphs (do not type the bullets), select the paragraphs, and then click the Bullets button in the Paragraph group.

Project 1c Typing and Inserting Bulleted Text — Part 3 of 5

1. With **WL1-C3-P1-TechInfo.docx** open, press Ctrl + End to move the insertion point to the end of the document and then press the Enter key once.
2. Type **Technology Timeline: Computer Design** in bold and centered, as shown in Figure 3.3, and then press the Enter key.
3. Turn off bold and change to left alignment.
4. Type a greater-than symbol (>), press the spacebar, type the text of the first bulleted paragraph in Figure 3.3, and then press the Enter key.
5. Press the Tab key (this demotes the bullet to a hollow circle) and then type the bulleted text.
6. Press the Enter key (this displays another hollow circle bullet), type the bulleted text, and then press the Enter key.
7. Press Shift + Tab (this promotes the bullet to an arrow), type the bulleted text, and then press the Enter key twice (this turns off bullets).

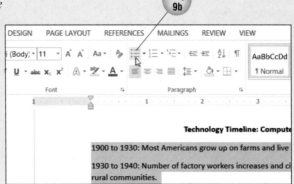

8. Promote bulleted text by positioning the insertion point at the beginning of the text *1958: Jack Kilby, an engineer* and then pressing Shift + Tab. Promote the other hollow circle bullet to an arrow. (The four paragraphs of text should be preceded by arrow bullets.)
9. Format the paragraphs of text in the *Technology Timeline: Computers in the Workplace* section as a bulleted list by completing the following steps:
   a. Select the paragraphs of text in the *Technology Timeline: Computers in the Workplace* section.
   b. Click the Bullets button in the Paragraph group. (Word will insert the same arrow bullets that you inserted in Step 2. Word keeps the same bullet formatting until you choose a different bullet style.)
10. Save and then print **WL1-C3-P1-TechInfo.docx**.

Figure 3.3 Project 1c

Technology Timeline: Computer Design

- ➢ 1937: Dr. John Atanasoff and Clifford Berry design and build the first electronic digital computer.
  - o 1958: Jack Kilby, an engineer at Texas Instruments, invents the integrated circuit, thereby laying the foundation for fast computers and large-capacity memory.
  - o 1981: IBM enters the personal computer field by introducing the IBM-PC.
- ➢ 2004: Wireless computer devices, including keyboards, mice, and wireless home networks, become widely accepted among users.

Inserting Paragraph Borders and Shading

Every paragraph you create in Word contains an invisible frame. You can apply a border to the frame around the paragraph. You can apply a border to specific sides of the paragraph or to all sides, customize the type of border lines, and add shading and fill to the border. Add borders and shading to paragraphs in a document using the Borders and Shading buttons in the Paragraph group on the HOME tab or options from the Borders and Shading dialog box.

Inserting Paragraph Borders

Quick Steps

Apply Border
1. Select text.
2. Click Borders button.

Borders

When a border is added to a paragraph of text, the border expands and contracts as text is inserted or deleted from the paragraph. You can create a border around a single paragraph or a border around selected paragraphs. One method for creating a border is to use options from the Borders button in the Paragraph group. Click the Borders button arrow and a drop-down list displays. At the drop-down list, click the option that will insert the desired border. For example, to insert a border at the bottom of the paragraph, click the *Bottom Border* option. Clicking an option will add the border to the paragraph where the insertion point is located. To add a border to more than one paragraph, select the paragraphs first and then click the desired option.

Project 1d Adding Borders to Paragraphs of Text

Part 4 of 5

1. With **WL1-C3-P1-TechInfo.docx** open, insert an outside border to specific text by completing the following steps:
   a. Select text from the title *Technology Information Questions* through the five numbered paragraphs of text.
   b. In the Paragraph group, click the Borders button arrow.
   c. Click the *Outside Borders* option at the drop-down list.
2. Select text from the title *Technology Timeline: Computers in the Workplace* through the six bulleted paragraphs of text and then click the Borders button in the Paragraph group. (The button will apply the border option that was previously selected.)
3. Select text from the title *Technology Career Questions* through the four numbered paragraphs of text below and then click the Borders button in the Paragraph group.
4. Select text from the beginning of the title *Technology Timeline: Computer Design* through the four bulleted paragraphs of text below and then click the Borders button in the Paragraph group.
5. Save and then print **WL1-C3-P1-TechInfo.docx**.

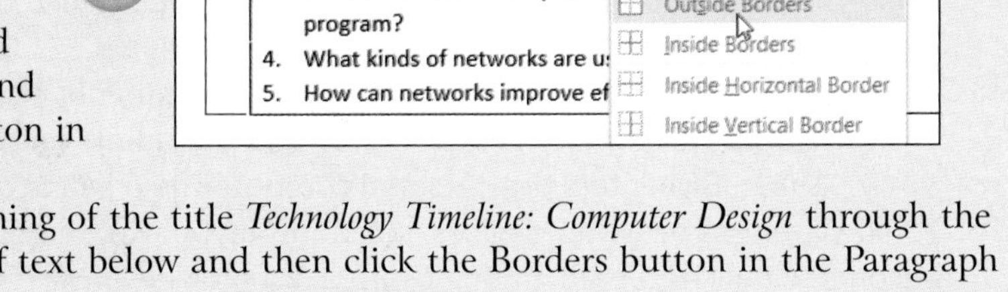

Adding Paragraph Shading

Quick Steps
Apply Shading
1. Select text.
2. Click Shading button.

Shading

Add shading to text in a document with the Shading button in the Paragraph group. Select text you want to shade and then click the Shading button. This applies a background color behind the text.

Click the Shading button arrow and a drop-down gallery displays. Paragraph shading colors display in themes in the drop-down gallery. Use one of the theme colors or click one of the standard colors that displays at the bottom of the gallery. Click the *More Colors* option, and the Colors dialog box displays. At the Colors dialog box with the Standard tab selected, click the desired color or click the Custom tab and then specify a custom color.

Project 1e Applying Shading to Paragraphs

Part 5 of 5

1. With **WL1-C3-P1-TechInfo.docx** open, apply paragraph shading and change border lines by completing the following steps:
   a. Position the insertion point on any character in the title *Technology Information Questions*.
   b. Click the Borders button arrow and then click *No Border* at the drop-down list.
   c. Click the Borders button arrow and then click *Bottom Border* at the drop-down list.
   d. Click the Shading button arrow and then click the *Gold, Accent 4, Lighter 60%* option (eighth column, third row).

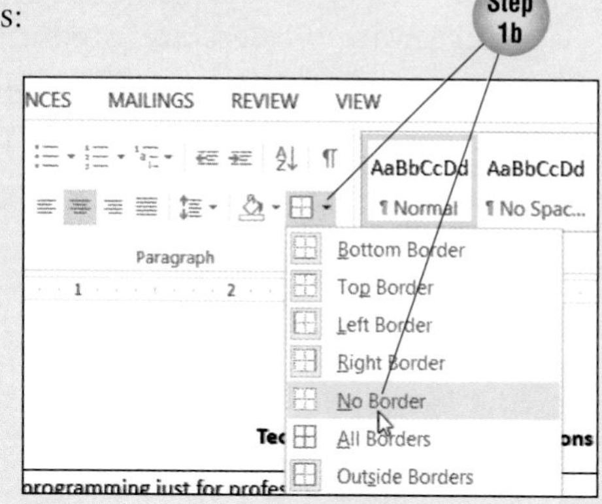

2. Apply the same formatting to the other titles by completing the following steps:
   a. With the insertion point positioned on any character in the title *Technology Information Questions*, double-click the Format Painter button in the Clipboard group.
   b. Select the title *Technology Timeline: Computers in the Workplace*.
   c. Select the title *Technology Career Questions*.
   d. Select the title *Technology Timeline: Computer Design*.
   e. Click the Format Painter button in the Clipboard group.

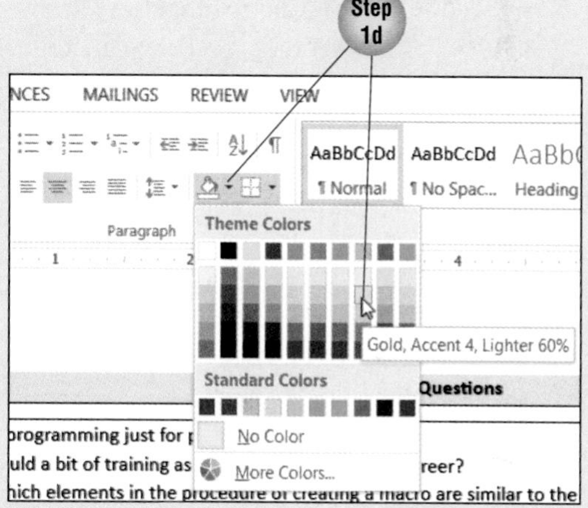

3. Remove the paragraph border and apply shading to paragraphs by completing the following steps:
   a. Select the numbered paragraphs of text below the *Technology Information Questions* title.
   b. Click the Borders button arrow and then click *No Border* at the drop-down list.
   c. Click the Shading button arrow and then click the *Gold, Accent 4, Lighter 80%* option (eighth column, second row).

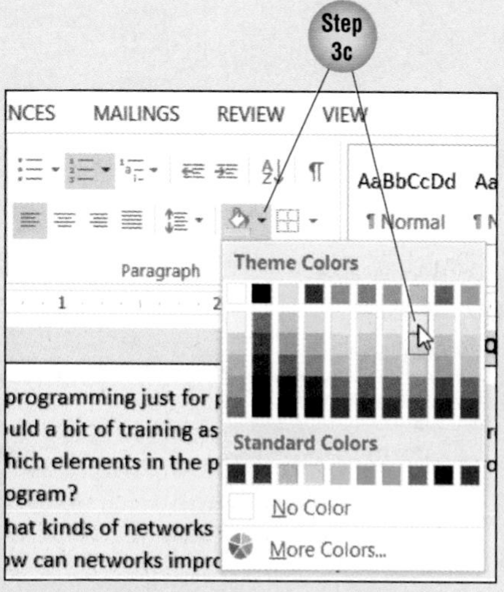

4. Select the bulleted paragraphs of text below the *Technology Timeline: Computers in the Workplace* title, click the Borders button, and then click the Shading button. (Clicking the Borders button will apply the previous border option, which was *No Border*. Clicking the Shading button will apply the previous shading option, which was *Gold, Accent 4, Lighter 80%*.)
5. Select the numbered paragraphs of text below the *Technology Career Questions* title, click the Borders button, and then click the Shading button.
6. Select the numbered paragraphs of text below the *Technology Timeline: Computer Design* title, click the Borders button, and then click the Shading button.
7. Save, print, and then close **WL1-C3-P1-TechInfo.docx**.

Project 2 Customize a Document on Online Shopping — 2 Parts

You will open a document containing information on online shopping, apply and customize borders and shading, and then sort text in the document.

Customizing Borders and Shading

If you want to further customize paragraph borders and shading, use options at the Borders and Shading dialog box. Display this dialog box by clicking the Borders button arrow and then clicking *Borders and Shading* at the drop-down list. Click the Borders tab and options display for customizing the border; click the Shading tab and shading options display.

As you learned in a previous section, you can add borders to a paragraph with the Borders button in the Paragraph group. If you want to further customize borders, use options at the Borders and Shading dialog box with the Borders tab selected, as shown in Figure 3.4. At the Borders and Shading dialog box, specify the desired border setting, style, color, and width. Click the Shading tab and the dialog box displays with shading options.

Figure 3.4 Borders and Shading Dialog Box with the Borders Tab Selected

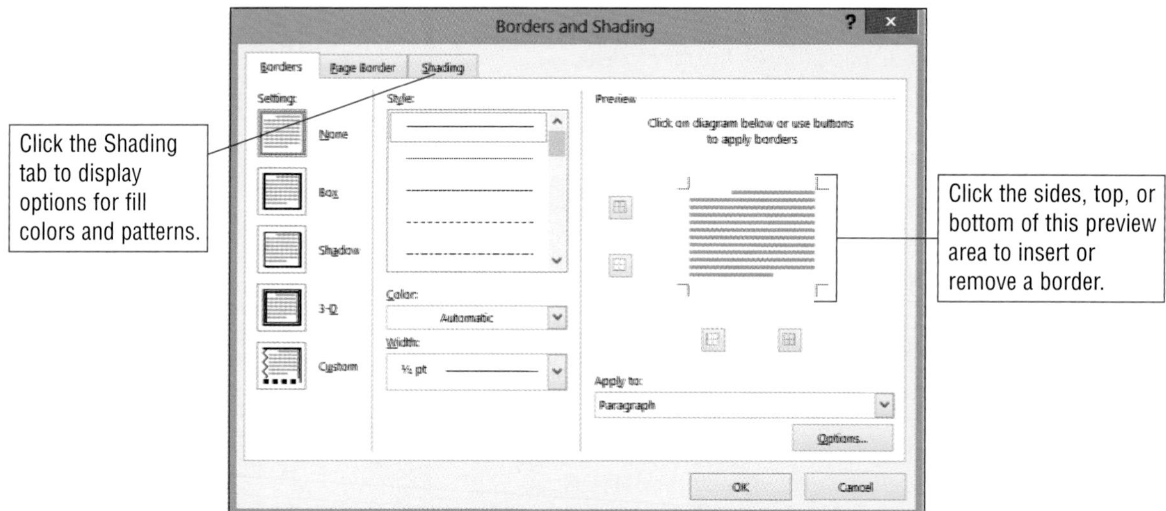

Project 2a Adding a Customized Border and Shading to a Document — Part 1 of 2

1. Open **OnlineShop.docx**.
2. Save the document with Save As and name it **WL1-C3-P2-OnlineShop**.
3. Make the following changes to the document:
   a. Insert 12 points of space before and 6 points of space after the headings *Online Shopping*, *Advantages of Online Shopping*, *Online Shopping Venues*, *Online Shopping Safety Tips*, and *REFERENCES*. (Do this with the *Spacing Before* and *Spacing After* measurement boxes on the PAGE LAYOUT tab.)
   b. Center the *REFERENCES* title.

4. Insert a custom border and add shading to a heading by completing the following steps:
   a. Move the insertion point to any character in the heading *Online Shopping*.
   b. Click the Borders button arrow and then click *Borders and Shading* at the drop-down list.
   c. At the Borders and Shading dialog box with the Borders tab selected, click the down-pointing arrow at the right side of the *Color* option box and then click the *Dark Blue* color in the *Standard Colors* section.
   d. Click the down-pointing arrow at the right of the *Width* option box and then click *1 pt* at the drop-down list.

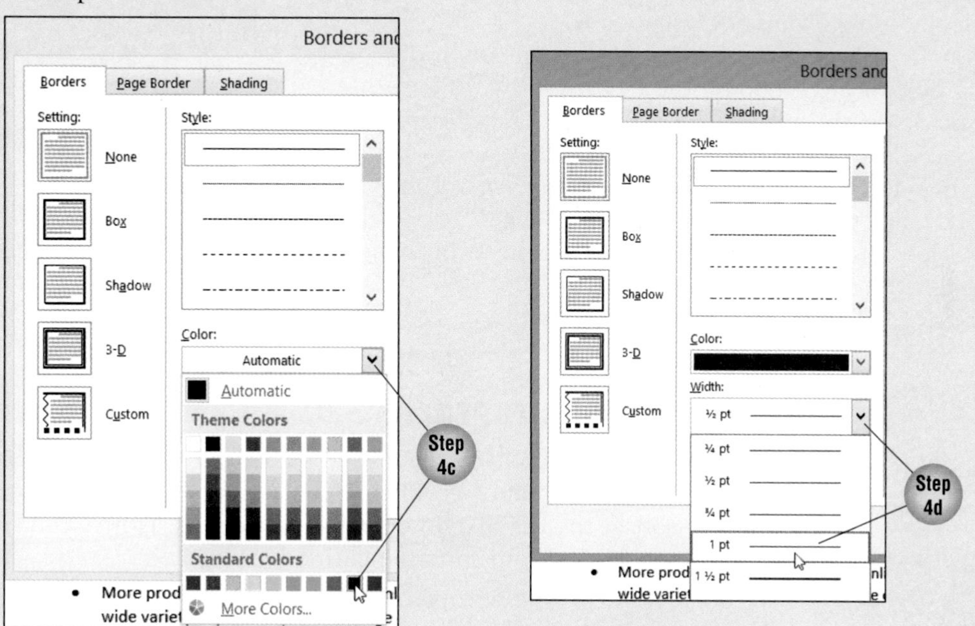

   e. Click the top border of the box in the *Preview* section of the dialog box.
   f. Scroll down the *Style* list box and then click the first thick/thin line.
   g. If necessary, click the down-pointing arrow at the right side of the *Color* option box and then click the *Dark Blue* color in the *Standard Colors* section.
   h. Click the bottom border of the box in the *Preview* section of the dialog box.

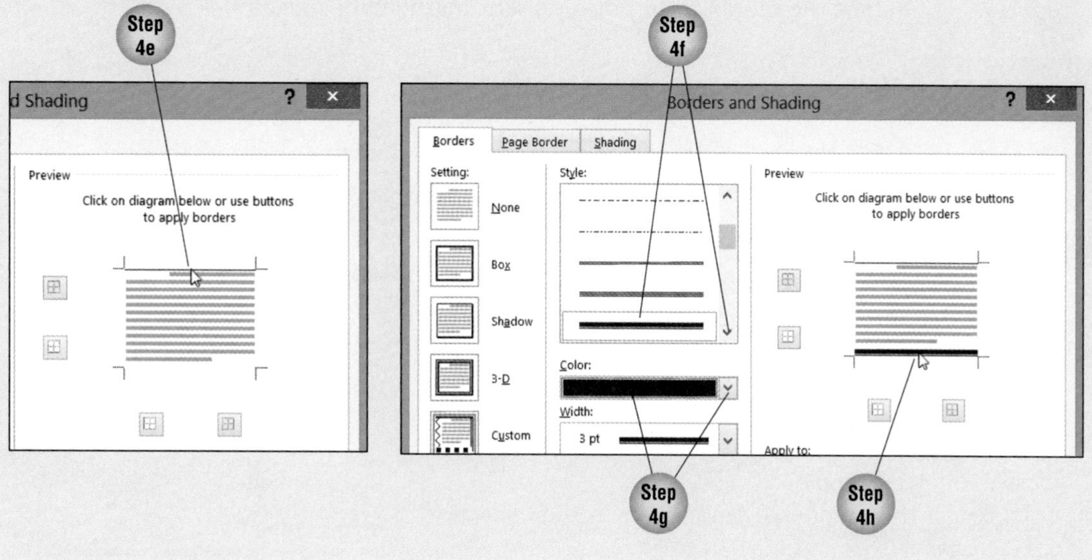

i. Click the Shading tab.
j. Click the down-pointing arrow at the right side of the *Fill* option box and then click *Green, Accent 6, Lighter 60%* (last column, third row).
k. Click OK to close the dialog box.

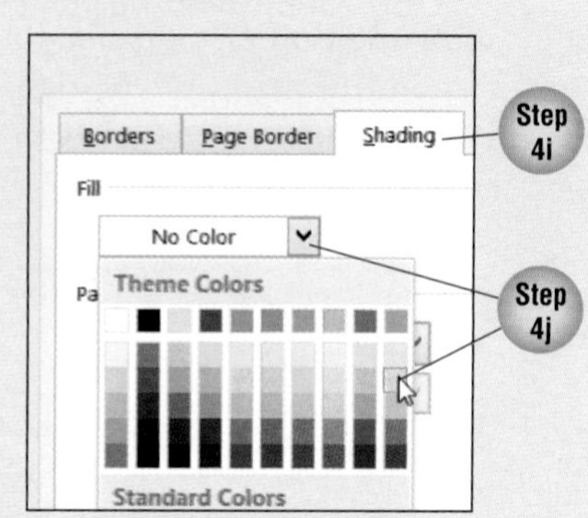

5. Use Format Painter to apply the same border and shading formatting to the remaining headings by completing the following steps:
   a. Position the insertion point on any character in the heading *Online Shopping*.
   b. Double-click the Format Painter button in the Clipboard group on the HOME tab.
   c. Select the heading *Advantages of Online Shopping*.
   d. Select the heading *Online Shopping Venues*.
   e. Select the heading *Online Shopping Safety Tips*.
   f. Click the Format Painter button once.
6. Move the insertion point to any character in the heading *Online Shopping* and then remove the 12 points of spacing above.
7. Save **WL1-C3-P2-OnlineShop.docx**.

Sorting Text in Paragraphs

Quick Steps

Sort Paragraphs of Text
1. Click Sort button.
2. Make any needed changes at Sort Text dialog box.
3. Click OK.

Sort

You can sort text arranged in paragraphs alphabetically by the first character. The first character can be a number, symbol (such as $ or #), or letter. Type paragraphs you want to sort at the left margin or indented to a tab. Unless you select specific paragraphs for sorting, Word sorts the entire document.

To sort text in paragraphs, open the document. If the document contains text you do not want sorted, select the specific paragraphs you do want sorted. Click the Sort button in the Paragraph group and the Sort Text dialog box displays. At this dialog box, click OK. The *Type* option at the Sort Text dialog box will display *Text*, *Number*, or *Date* depending on the text selected. Word will attempt to determine the data type and choose one of the three options. For example, if you select numbers with a mathematical value, Word will assign them the *Number* type. However, if you select a numbered list, Word assigns them the *Text* type since the numbers do not represent mathematical values.

Project 2b Sorting Paragraphs Alphabetically — Part 2 of 2

1. With **WL1-C3-P2-OnlineShop.docx** open, sort the bulleted text alphabetically by completing the following steps:
   a. Select the bulleted paragraphs in the *Advantages of Online Shopping* section.
   b. Click the Sort button in the Paragraph group.
   c. At the Sort Text dialog box, make sure *Paragraphs* displays in the *Sort by* option box and the *Ascending* option is selected.
   d. Click OK.

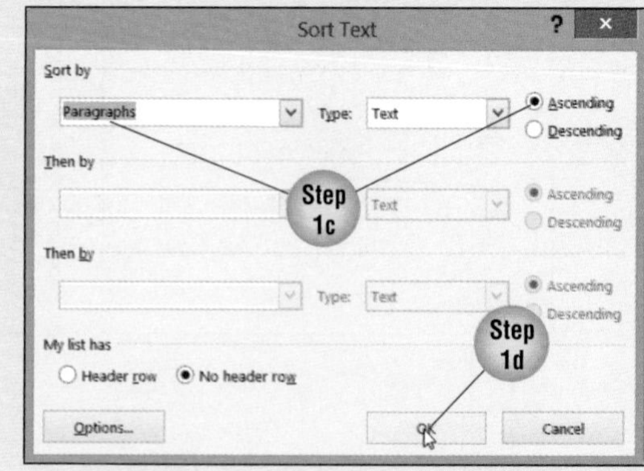

2. Sort the numbered paragraphs by completing the following steps:
   a. Select the numbered paragraphs in the *Online Shopping Safety Tips* section.

b. Click the Sort button in the Paragraph group.
c. Click OK at the Sort Text dialog box.

3. Sort alphabetically the three paragraphs of text below the *REFERENCES* title by completing the following steps:
   a. Select the paragraphs of text below the *REFERENCES* title.
   b. Click the Sort button in the Paragraph group.
   c. Click the down-pointing arrow at the right side of the *Type* option box and then click *Text* at the drop-down list.
   d. Click OK.
4. Save, print, and then close **WL1-C3-P2-OnlineShop.docx**.

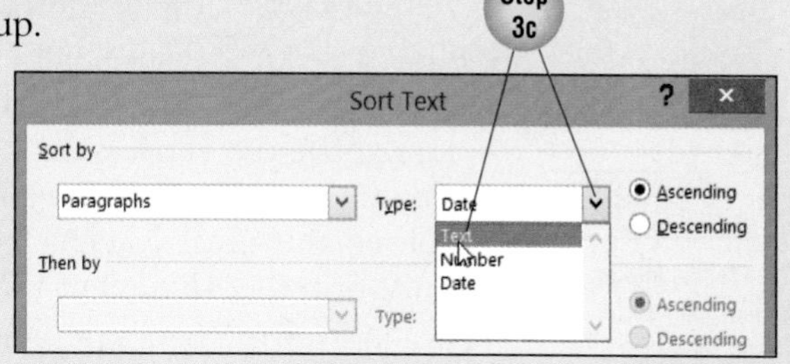

Project 3 Prepare a Document on Workshops and Training Dates — 4 Parts

You will set and move tabs on the horizontal ruler and at the Tabs dialog box and type tabbed text about workshops, training dates, and a table of contents.

Manipulating Tabs

When you work with a document, Word offers a variety of default settings, such as margins and line spacing. One of these defaults is a left tab set every 0.5 inch. In some situations, these default tabs are appropriate; in others, you may want to create your own. Two methods exist for setting tabs. Tabs can be set on the horizontal ruler or at the Tabs dialog box.

Manipulating Tabs on the Horizontal Ruler

Use the horizontal ruler to set, move, and delete tabs. If the ruler is not visible, click the VIEW tab and then click the *Ruler* check box in the Show group. By default, tabs are set every 0.5 inch on the horizontal ruler. With a left tab, text aligns at the left edge of the tab. The other types of tabs that can be set on the horizontal ruler are center, right, decimal, and bar. Use the Alignment button that displays above the vertical ruler to specify tabs. Each time you click the Alignment button, a different tab or paragraph alignment symbol displays. Table 3.1 shows the tab alignment buttons and what type of tab each will set.

Table 3.1 Tab Alignment Buttons

Tab Alignment Button	Type of Tab	Tab Alignment Button	Type of Tab
∟	left	⊥:	decimal
⊥	center	|	bar
┘	right		

Setting Tabs

Quick Steps

Set Tabs on Horizontal Ruler

1. Click Alignment button above vertical ruler.
2. Click desired location on horizontal ruler.

When setting tabs on the horizontal ruler, a dotted guideline displays to help align tabs.

Position the insertion point in any paragraph of text, and tabs for the paragraph appear on the horizontal ruler.

To set a left tab on the horizontal ruler, make sure the left alignment symbol (see Table 3.1) displays in the Alignment button. Position the arrow pointer on the tick mark (the marks on the ruler) where you want the tab symbol to appear and then click the left mouse button. When you set a tab on the horizontal ruler, any default tabs to the left are automatically deleted by Word. Set a center, right, decimal, or bar tab on the horizontal ruler in a similar manner.

Before setting a tab on the horizontal ruler, click the Alignment button that displays above the vertical ruler until the appropriate tab symbol displays and then set the tab. If you change the tab symbol in the Alignment button, the symbol remains until you change it again or you close Word. If you close and then reopen Word, the Alignment button displays with the left tab symbol.

If you want to set a tab at a specific measurement on the horizontal ruler, hold down the Alt key, position the arrow pointer at the desired position, and then hold down the left mouse button. This displays two measurements in the white portion in the horizontal ruler. The first measurement displays the location of the arrow pointer on the ruler in relation to the left margin. The second measurement is the distance from the location of the arrow pointer on the ruler to the right margin. With the left mouse button held down, position the tab symbol at the desired location and then release the mouse button and the Alt key.

If you change tab settings and then create columns of text using the New Line command, Shift + Enter, the tab formatting is stored in the paragraph mark at the end of the columns. If you want to make changes to the tab settings for text in the columns, position the insertion point anywhere within the columns (all of the text in the columns does not have to be selected) and then make the changes.

Project 3a **Setting Left, Center, and Right Tabs on the Horizintal Ruler** **Part 1 of 4**

1. At a new blank document, type **WORKSHOPS** centered and bolded as shown in Figure 3.5.
2. Press the Enter key. In the new paragraph, return the paragraph alignment back to left alignment and then turn off bold formatting.
3. Set a left tab at the 0.5-inch mark, a center tab at the 3.25-inch mark, and a right tab at the 6-inch mark by completing the following steps:
   a. Click the Show/Hide ¶ button in the Paragraph group on the HOME tab to turn on the display of nonprinting characters.
   b. Make sure the horizontal ruler is displayed. (If not, click the VIEW tab and then click the *Ruler* check box in the Show group.)
   c. Make sure the left tab symbol displays in the Alignment button located above the vertical ruler.
   d. Position the arrow pointer on the 0.5-inch mark on the horizontal ruler and then click the left mouse button.

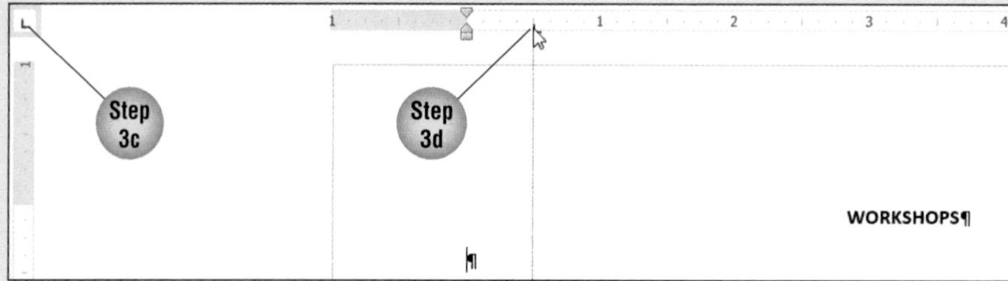

e. Position the arrow pointer on the Alignment button above the vertical ruler and then click the left mouse button until the center tab symbol displays (see Table 3.1).

f. Position the arrow pointer below the 3.25-inch mark on the horizontal ruler. Hold down the Alt key and then the left mouse button. Make sure the first measurement on the horizontal ruler displays as *3.25"* and then release the mouse button and the Alt key.

g. Position the arrow pointer on the Alignment button above the vertical ruler and then click the left mouse button until the right tab symbol displays (see Table 3.1).

h. Position the arrow pointer below the 6-inch mark on the horizontal ruler. Hold down the Alt key and then the left mouse button. Make sure the first measurement on the horizontal ruler displays as *6"* and then release the mouse button and the Alt key.

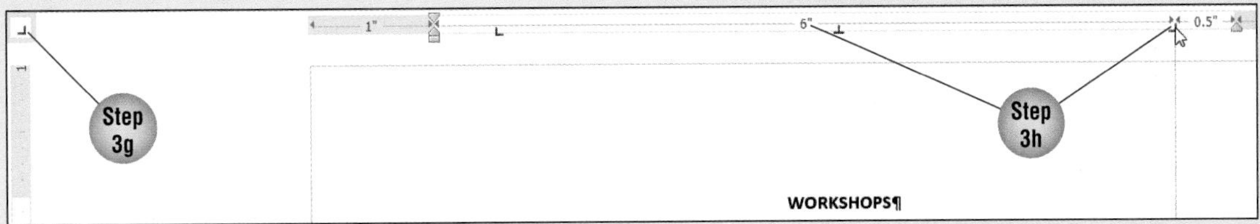

4. Type the text in columns, as shown in Figure 3.5. Press the Tab key before typing each column entry and press Shift + Enter after typing the text in the third column.
5. After typing the last column entry, press the Enter key twice.
6. Press Ctrl + Q to remove paragraph formatting (tab settings).
7. Click the Show/Hide ¶ button to turn off the display of nonprinting characters.
8. Save the document and name it **WL1-C3-P3-Tabs**.

Figure 3.5 Project 3a

WORKSHOPS

Title	**Price**	**Date**
Quality Management	$240	Friday, February 6
Staff Development	229	Friday, February 20
Streamlining Production	175	Monday, March 2
Managing Records	150	Tuesday, March 17
Customer Service Training	150	Thursday, March 19
Sales Techniques	125	Tuesday, April 14

Moving Tabs and Deleting Tabs

After a tab has been set on the horizontal ruler, it can be moved to a new location. To move a tab, position the arrow pointer on the tab symbol on the ruler, hold down the left mouse button, drag the symbol to the new location on the ruler, and then release the mouse button. To delete a tab from the ruler, position the arrow pointer on the tab symbol you want deleted, hold down the left mouse button, drag the symbol down into the document, and then release the mouse button.

Project 3b **Moving Tabs** **Part 2 of 4**

1. With **WL1-C3-P3-Tabs.docx** open, position the insertion point on any character in the first entry in the tabbed text.
2. Position the arrow pointer on the left tab symbol at the 0.5-inch mark on the horizontal ruler, hold down the left mouse button, drag the left tab symbol to the 1-inch mark on the ruler, and then release the mouse button. ***Hint: Use the Alt key to help you precisely position the tab symbol.***

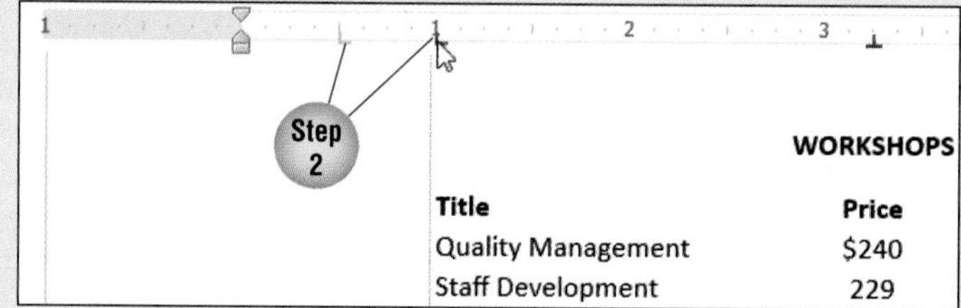

3. Position the arrow pointer on the right tab symbol at the 6-inch mark on the horizontal ruler, hold down the left mouse button, drag the right tab symbol to the 5.5-inch mark on the ruler, and then release the mouse button. ***Hint: Use the Alt key to help you precisely position the tab symbol.***
4. Save **WL1-C3-P3-Tabs.docx**.

Manipulating Tabs at the Tabs Dialog Box

Use the Tabs dialog box, shown in Figure 3.6, to set tabs at specific measurements. You can also use the Tabs dialog box to set tabs with preceding leaders and clear one tab or all tabs. To display the Tabs dialog box, click the Paragraph group dialog box launcher. At the Paragraph dialog box, click the Tabs button located in the bottom left corner of the dialog box.

Figure 3.6 Tabs Dialog Box

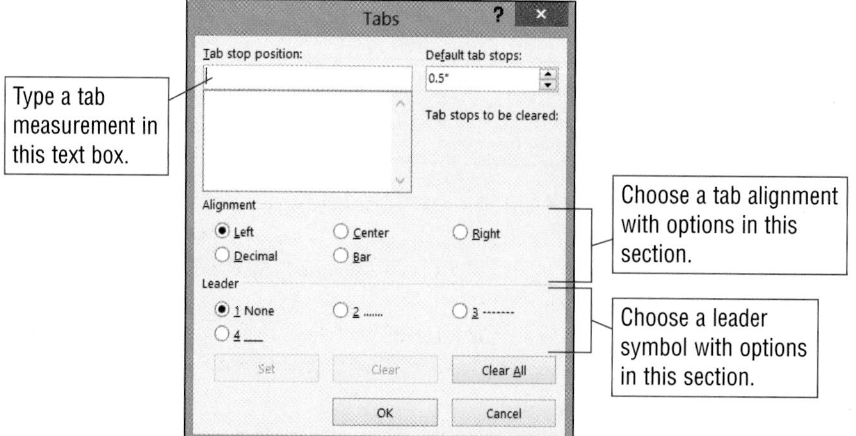

Clearing Tabs and Setting Tabs

At the Tabs dialog box, you can clear an individual tab or all tabs. To clear all tabs, click the Clear All button. To clear an individual tab, specify the tab position, and then click the Clear button.

At the Tabs dialog box, you can set a left, right, center, or decimal tab as well as a bar tab. (For an example of a bar tab, refer to Figure 3.7.) You can also set a left, right, center, or decimal tab with preceding leaders. To change the type of tab at the Tabs dialog box, display the dialog box and then click the desired tab in the *Alignment* section. Type the desired measurement for the tab in the *Tab stop position* text box.

Quick Steps

Set Tabs at Tabs Dialog Box

1. Click Paragraph group dialog box launcher.
2. Click Tabs button.
3. Specify tab positions, alignments, and leader options.
4. Click OK.

Project 3c **Setting Left Tabs and a Bar Tab at the Tabs Dialog Box** **Part 3 of 4**

1. With **WL1-C3-P3-Tabs.docx** open, press Ctrl + End to move the insertion point to the end of the document.
2. Type the title **TRAINING DATES** bolded and centered as shown in Figure 3.7, press the Enter key, return the paragraph alignment back to left, and then turn off bold formatting.
3. Display the Tabs dialog box and then set left tabs and a bar tab by completing the following steps:
   a. Click the Paragraph group dialog box launcher.
   b. At the Paragraph dialog box, click the Tabs button located in the lower left corner of the dialog box.
   c. Make sure *Left* is selected in the *Alignment* section of the dialog box.
   d. Type 1.75 in the *Tab stop position* text box.
   e. Click the Set button.
   f. Type 4 in the *Tab stop position* text box and then click the Set button.
   g. Type 3.25 in the *Tab stop position* text box, click *Bar* in the *Alignment* section, and then click the Set button.
   h. Click OK to close the Tabs dialog box.
4. Type the text in columns, as shown in Figure 3.7. Press the Tab key before typing each column entry and press Shift + Enter to end each line.

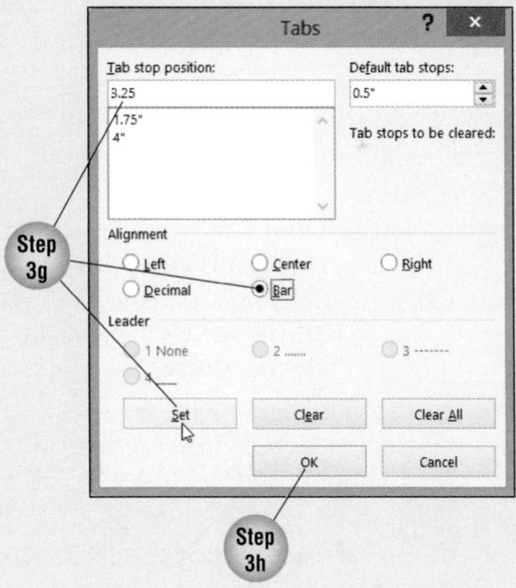

5. After typing *February 24*, complete the following steps:
   a. Press the Enter key.
   b. Clear tabs by displaying the Tabs dialog box, clicking the Clear All button, and then clicking OK.
   c. Press the Enter key.
6. Remove the 8 points of spacing after the last entry in the text by completing the following steps:
   a. Position the insertion point on any character in the *January 22* entry.
   b. Click the PAGE LAYOUT tab.
   c. Click twice on the down-pointing arrow at the right side of the *Spacing After* measurement box. (This changes the measurement to *0 pt.*)
7. Save **WL1-C3-P3-Tabs.docx**.

Figure 3.7 Project 3c

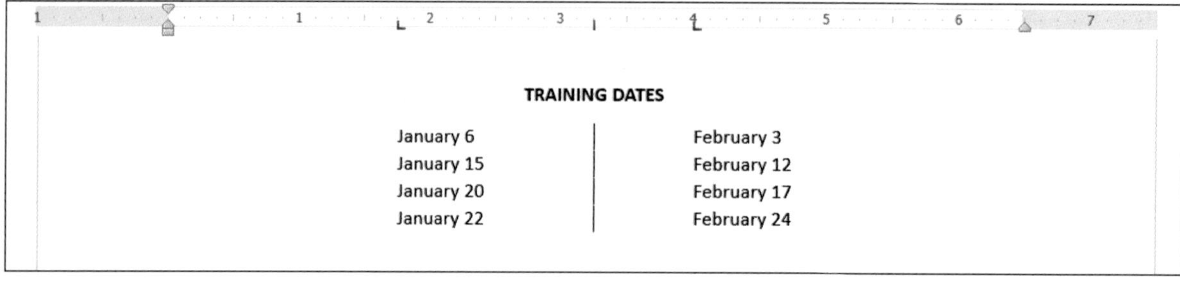

TRAINING DATES
January 6
January 15
January 20
January 22
February 3
February 12
February 17
February 24

Setting Leader Tabs

Four types of tabs (left, right, center, and decimal) can be set with leaders. Leaders are useful in a table of contents or other material where you want to direct the reader's eyes across the page. Figure 3.8 shows an example of leaders. Leaders can be periods (.), hyphens (-), or underlines (_). To add leaders to a tab, click the type of leader desired in the *Leader* section of the Tabs dialog box.

Project 3d Setting a Left Tab and a Right Tab with Dot Leaders

Part 4 of 4

1. With **WL1-C3-P3-Tabs.docx** open, press Ctrl + End to move the insertion point to the end of the document.
2. Type the title TABLE OF CONTENTS bolded and centered, as shown in Figure 3.8.
3. Press the Enter key and then return the paragraph alignment back to left and turn off bold formatting.
4. Set a left tab and a right tab with dot leaders by completing the following steps:
   a. Click the Paragraph group dialog box launcher.
   b. Click the Tabs button located in the lower left corner of the Paragraph dialog box.
   c. At the Tabs dialog box, make sure *Left* is selected in the *Alignment* section of the dialog box.
   d. With the insertion point positioned in the *Tab stop position* text box, type 1 and then click the Set button.
   e. Type 5.5 in the *Tab stop position* text box.
   f. Click *Right* in the *Alignment* section of the dialog box.
   g. Click *2 ......* in the *Leader* section of the dialog box and then click the Set button.
   h. Click OK to close the dialog box.

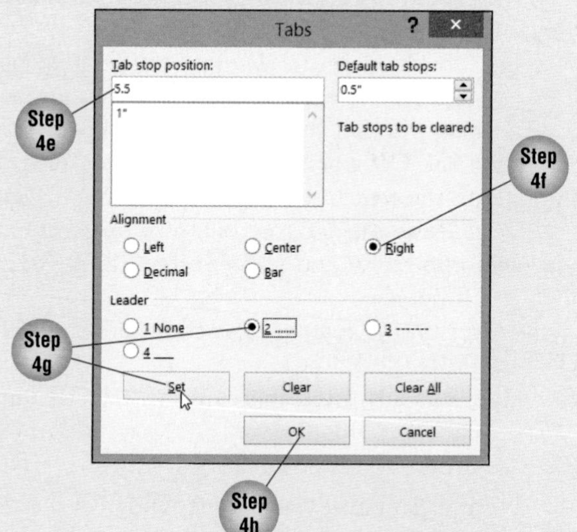

5. Type the text in columns, as shown in Figure 3.8. Press the Tab key before typing each column entry and press Shift + Enter to end each line.
6. Save, print, and then close **WL1-C3-P3-Tabs.docx**.

Figure 3.8 Project 3d

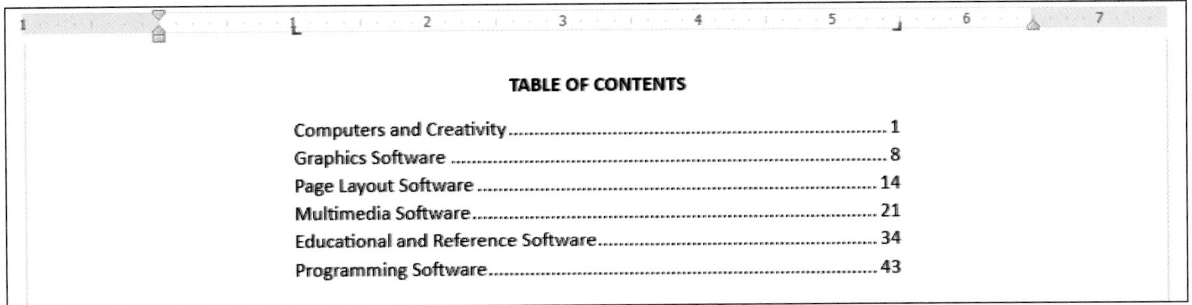

TABLE OF CONTENTS

Computers and Creativity..1
Graphics Software..8
Page Layout Software..14
Multimedia Software..21
Educational and Reference Software..34
Programming Software..43

Project 4 Move and Copy Text in a Document on Online Shopping Tips

2 Parts

You will open a document containing information on online shopping safety tips and then cut, copy, and paste text in the document.

Cutting, Copying, and Pasting Text

When editing a document, you may need to delete specific text, move text to a different location in the document, and/or copy text to various locations in the document. You can complete these activities using buttons in the Clipboard group on the HOME tab.

Deleting Selected Text

Word offers different methods for deleting text from a document. To delete a single character, you can use either the Delete key or the Backspace key. To delete more than a single character, select the text and then press the Delete key on the keyboard or click the Cut button in the Clipboard group. If you press the Delete key, the text is deleted permanently. (You can restore deleted text with the Undo button on the Quick Access toolbar.) The Cut button in the Clipboard group will remove the selected text from the document and insert it in Word's ***Clipboard***, which is a temporary area of memory. The Clipboard holds text while it is being moved or copied to a new location in the document or to a different document.

The Clipboard contents are deleted when the computer is turned off. Text you want to save permanently should be saved as a separate document.

Cutting and Pasting Text

To move text to a different location in the document, select the text, click the Cut button in the Clipboard group, position the insertion point at the location where you want the text inserted, and then click the Paste button in the Clipboard group.

You can also move selected text with a shortcut menu. To do this, select the text and then position the insertion point inside the selected text until it turns into an arrow pointer. Click the right mouse button and then click *Cut* at the shortcut menu. Position the insertion point where you want the text inserted, click the right mouse button, and then click *Paste* at the shortcut menu. Keyboard shortcuts are also available for cutting and pasting text. Use Ctrl + X to cut text and Ctrl + V to paste text.

Quick Steps

Move Selected Text

1. Select text.
2. Click Cut button.
3. Move to desired location.
4. Click Paste button.

Cut

Paste

When selected text is cut from a document and inserted in the Clipboard, it stays in the Clipboard until other text is inserted in the Clipboard. For this reason, you can paste text from the Clipboard more than just once. For example, if you cut text to the Clipboard, you can paste this text in different locations within the document or other documents as many times as desired.

Quick Steps

Move Text with the Mouse

1. Select text.
2. Position mouse pointer in selected text.
3. Hold down left mouse button and drag to desired location.
4. Release left mouse button.

Moving Text by Dragging with the Mouse

You can also use the mouse to move text. To do this, select text to be moved and then position the I-beam pointer inside the selected text until it turns into an arrow pointer. Hold down the left mouse button, drag the arrow pointer (displays with a gray box attached) to the location where you want the selected text inserted, and then release the button. If you drag and then drop selected text in the wrong location, immediately click the Undo button.

Project 4a **Moving and Dragging Selected Text** **Part 1 of 2**

1. Open **ShoppingTips.docx**.
2. Save the document with Save As and name it **WL1-C3-P4-ShoppingTips**.
3. Move a paragraph by completing the following steps:
   a. Select the paragraph that begins with *Only buy at secure sites,* including the blank line below the paragraph.
   b. Click the Cut button in the Clipboard group on the HOME tab.
   c. Position the insertion point at the beginning of the paragraph that begins with *Look for sites that follow.*
   d. Click the Paste button in the Clipboard group. (If the first and second paragraphs are not separated by a blank line, press the Enter key once.)
4. Following steps similar to those in Step 3, move the paragraph that begins with *Never provide your social* so it is positioned before the paragraph that begins *Look for sites that follow privacy* and after the paragraph that begins *Only buy at secure.*
5. Use the mouse to select the paragraph that begins with *Keep current with the latest Internet,* including one blank line below the paragraph.
6. Move the I-beam pointer inside the selected text until it becomes an arrow pointer.
7. Hold down the left mouse button and drag the arrow pointer (displays with a small gray box attached) so that the insertion point, which displays as a black vertical bar, is positioned at the beginning of the paragraph that begins with *Never provide your social.* Release the mouse button.
8. Deselect the text.
9. Save **WL1-C3-P4-ShoppingTips.docx**.

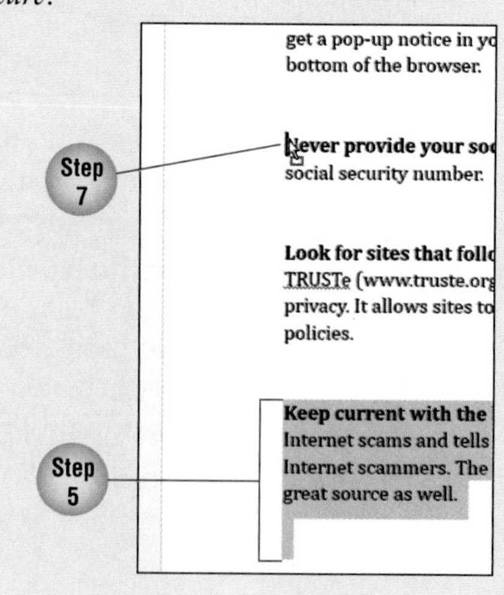

Using the Paste Options Button

When selected text is pasted, the Paste Options button displays in the lower right corner of the text. Click this button (or press the Ctrl key on the keyboard) and the *Paste Options* gallery displays, as shown in Figure 3.9. Use options from this gallery to specify how you want information pasted in the document. Hover the mouse over a button in the gallery and the live preview displays the text in the document as it will appear when pasted.

Paste Options

By default, pasted text retains the formatting of the selected text. You can choose to match the formatting of the pasted text with the formatting where the text is pasted or paste only the text without retaining formatting. To determine the function of a button in the *Paste Options* gallery, hover the mouse over a button and a ScreenTip displays with an explanation of the button function as well as the keyboard shortcut. For example, hover the mouse pointer over the first button from the left in the *Paste Options* gallery and the ScreenTip displays with the information *Keep Source Formatting (K)*. Click this button or press K on the keyboard, and the pasted text keeps its original formatting.

Figure 3.9 Paste Options Button Drop-down List

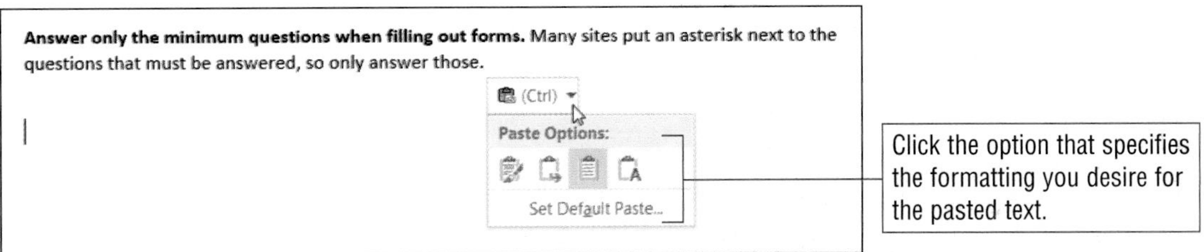

Click the option that specifies the formatting you desire for the pasted text.

Project 4b **Using the Paste Options Button** **Part 2 of 2**

1. With **WL1-C3-P4-ShoppingTips.docx** open, open **Tip.docx**.
2. Select the paragraph of text in the document, including the blank line below the paragraph, and then click the Copy button in the Clipboard group.
3. Close **Tip.docx**.
4. Move the insertion point to the end of **WL1-C3-P4-ShoppingTips.docx**.
5. Click the Paste button in the Clipboard group.
6. Click the Paste Options button that displays at the end of the paragraph and then click the second button in the *Paste Options* gallery (Merge Formatting (M) button). (This changes the font so it matches the formatting of the other paragraphs in the document.)

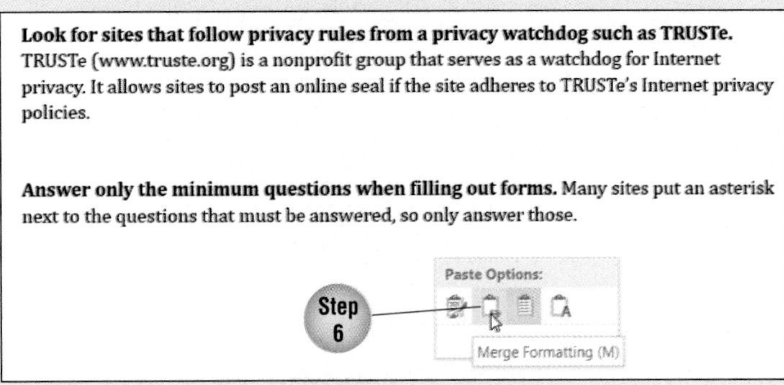

7. Save, print, and then close **WL1-C3-P4-ShoppingTips.docx**.

Project 5 Copy Text in a Staff Meeting Announcement 1 Part

You will copy and paste text in a document announcing a staff meeting for the Technical Support Team.

Copying and Pasting Text

Quick Steps

Copy Selected Text
1. Select text.
2. Click Copy button.
3. Move to desired location.
4. Click Paste button.

Copy

Copying selected text can be useful in documents that contain repeated information. Use copy and paste to insert duplicate portions of text in a document instead of retyping them. After you have selected text, copy the text to a different location with the Copy and Paste buttons in the Clipboard group on the HOME tab or using the mouse. You can also use the keyboard shortcut Ctrl + C to copy text.

To use the mouse to copy text, select the text and then position the I-beam pointer inside the selected text until it becomes an arrow pointer. Hold down the left mouse button and hold down the Ctrl key. Drag the arrow pointer (displays with a small gray box and a box containing a plus symbol) and a black vertical bar moves with the pointer. Position the black bar in the desired location, release the mouse button, and then the Ctrl key.

Project 5 Copying Text Part 1 of 1

1. Open **StaffMtg.docx**.
2. Save the document with Save As and name it **WL1-C3-P5-StaffMtg**.
3. Copy the text in the document to the end of the document by completing the following steps:
   a. Select all of the text in the document and include one blank line below the text. ***Hint: Click the Show/Hide ¶ button to turn on the display of nonprinting characters. When you select the text, select one of the paragraph markers below the text.***
   b. Click the Copy button in the Clipboard group.
   c. Move the insertion point to the end of the document.
   d. Click the Paste button in the Clipboard group.
4. Paste the text again at the end of the document. To do this, position the insertion point at the end of the document and then click the Paste button in the Clipboard group. (This inserts a copy of the text from the Clipboard.)
5. Select all of the text in the document using the mouse and include one blank line below the text. (Consider turning on the display of nonprinting characters.)
6. Move the I-beam pointer inside the selected text until it becomes an arrow pointer.
7. Hold down the Ctrl key and then the left mouse button. Drag the arrow pointer (displays with a box with a plus symbol inside) so the vertical black bar is positioned at the end of the document, release the mouse button, and then release the Ctrl key.

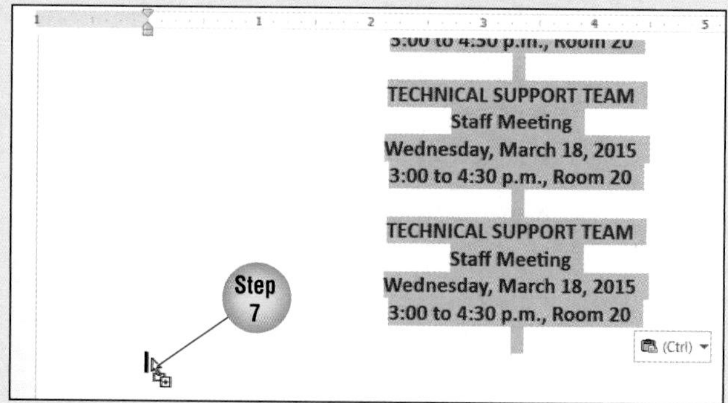

8. Deselect the text.
9. Make sure all text fits on one page. If not, consider deleting any extra blank lines.
10. Save, print, and then close **WL1-C3-P5-StaffMtg.docx**.

Project 6 Create a Contract Negotiations Document — 1 Part

You will use the Clipboard to copy and paste paragraphs to and from separate documents to create a contract negotiations document.

Using the Clipboard

Use the Clipboard to collect and paste multiple items. You can collect up to 24 different items and then paste them in various locations. To display the Clipboard task pane, click the Clipboard task pane launcher located in the lower right corner of the Clipboard group. The Clipboard task pane displays at the left side of the screen in a manner similar to what you see in Figure 3.10.

Select text or an object you want to copy and then click the Copy button in the Clipboard group. Continue selecting text or items and clicking the Copy button. To insert an item, position the insertion point in the desired location and then click the option in the Clipboard task pane representing the item. Click the Paste All button to paste all of the items in the Clipboard into the document. If the copied item is text, the first 50 characters display in the list box on the Clipboard task pane. When all desired items are inserted, click the Clear All button to remove any remaining items.

Quick Steps

Use the Clipboard

1. Click Clipboard task pane launcher.
2. Select and copy desired text.
3. Move to desired location.
4. Click desired option in Clipboard task pane.

You can copy items to the Clipboard from various Office applications and then paste them into any Office file.

Figure 3.10 Clipboard Task Pane

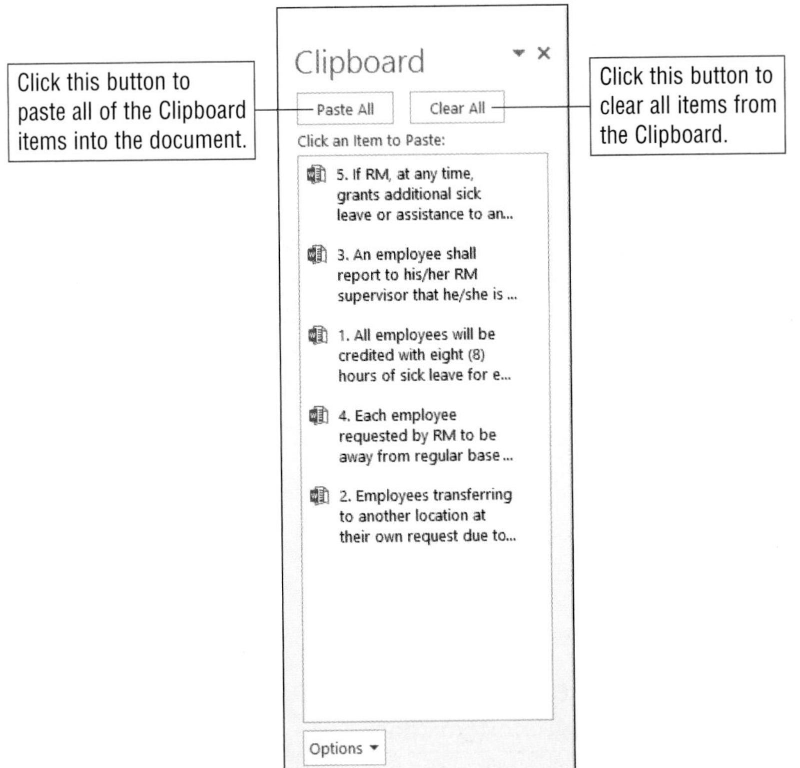

Project 6 Collecting and Pasting Paragraphs of Text

Part 1 of 1

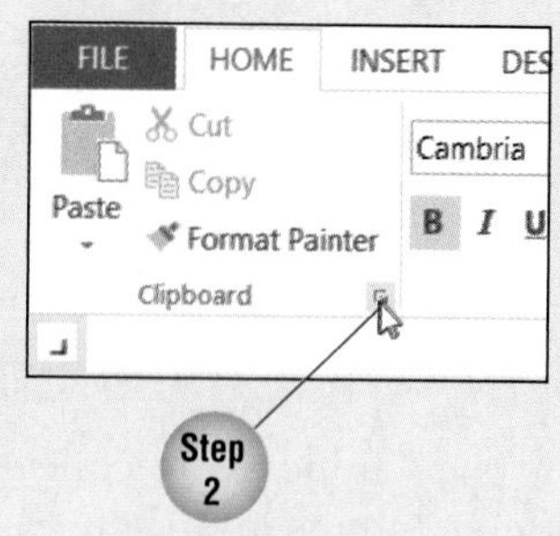

1. Open **ContractItems.docx**.
2. Turn on the display of the Clipboard task pane by clicking the Clipboard task pane launcher located in the bottom right corner of the Clipboard group. (If the Clipboard task pane list box contains any text, click the Clear All button located toward the top of the task pane.)
3. Select paragraph 1 in the document (the 1. is not selected) and then click the Copy button in the Clipboard group.
4. Select paragraph 3 in the document (the 3. is not selected) and then click the Copy button in the Clipboard group.
5. Close **ContractItems.docx**.
6. Paste the paragraphs by completing the following steps:
   a. Press Ctrl + N to display a new blank document. (If the Clipboard task pane does not display, click the Clipboard task pane launcher.)
   b. Type **CONTRACT NEGOTIATION ITEMS** centered and bolded.
   c. Press the Enter key, turn off bold formatting, and return the paragraph alignment back to left alignment.
   d. Click the Paste All button in the Clipboard task pane to paste both paragraphs in the document.
   e. Click the Clear All button in the Clipboard task pane.
7. Open **UnionContract.docx**.
8. Select and then copy each of the following paragraphs:
   a. Paragraph 2 in the *Transfers and Moving Expenses* section.
   b. Paragraph 4 in the *Transfers and Moving Expenses* section.
   c. Paragraph 1 in the *Sick Leave* section.
   d. Paragraph 3 in the *Sick Leave* section.
   e. Paragraph 5 in the *Sick Leave* section.
9. Close **UnionContract.docx**.
10. Make sure the insertion point is positioned at the end of the document and then paste the paragraphs by completing the following steps:
    a. Click the button in the Clipboard task pane representing paragraph 2. (When the paragraph is inserted in the document, the paragraph number changes to 3.)
    b. Click the button in the Clipboard task pane representing paragraph 4.
    c. Click the button in the Clipboard task pane representing paragraph 3.
    d. Click the button in the Clipboard task pane representing paragraph 5.
11. Click the Clear All button located toward the top of the Clipboard task pane.
12. Close the Clipboard task pane.
13. Save the document and name it **WL1-C3-P6-NegotiateItems**.
14. Print and then close **WL1-C3-P6-NegotiateItems.docx**.

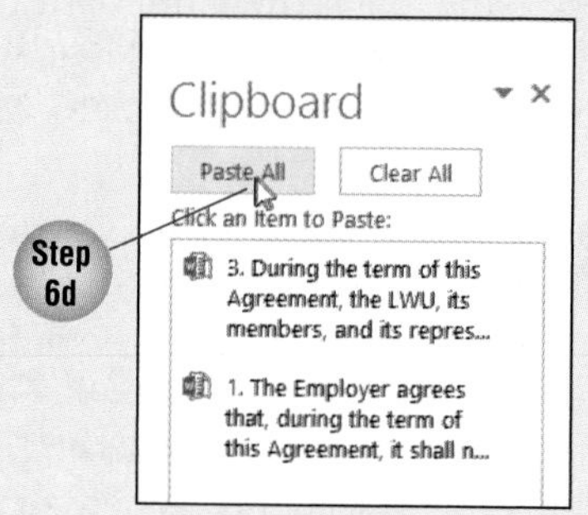

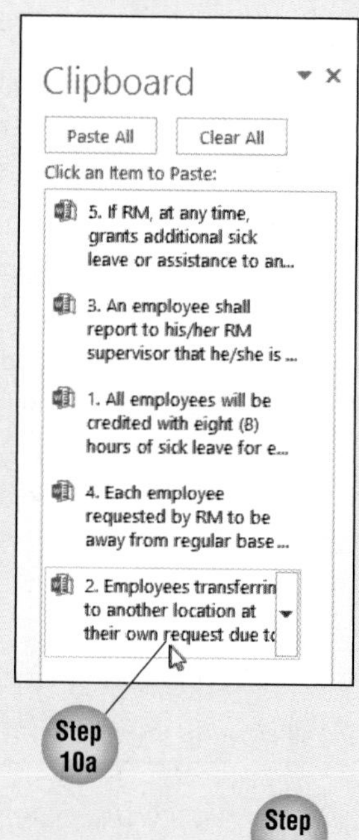

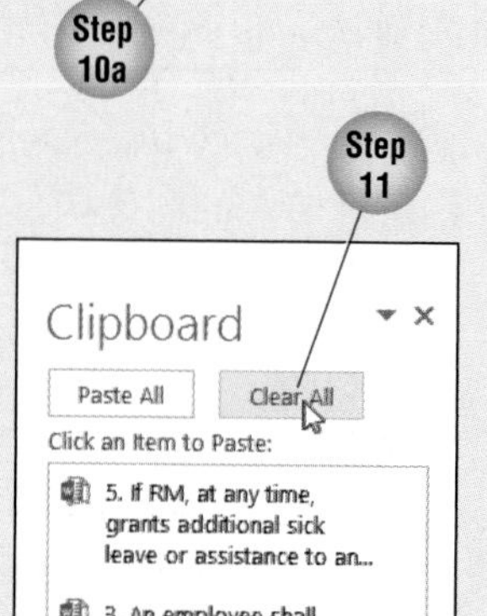

Chapter Summary

- Number paragraphs with the Numbering button in the Paragraph group on the HOME tab and insert bullets before paragraphs with the Bullets button.
- Remove all paragraph formatting from a paragraph by pressing the keyboard shortcut Ctrl + Q, and remove all character and paragraph formatting by clicking the Clear All Formatting button in the Font group.
- The AutoCorrect Options button displays when the AutoFormat feature inserts numbers. Click this button to display options for undoing and/or stopping automatic numbering.
- Bulleted lists with hanging indents are automatically created when a paragraph begins with *, >, or -. The type of bullet inserted depends on the type of character entered.
- You can turn off automatic numbering and bullets at the AutoCorrect dialog box with the AutoFormat As You Type tab selected.
- A paragraph created in Word contains an invisible frame, and you can insert a border around this frame. Click the Borders button arrow to display a drop-down list of border choices.
- Apply shading to text by clicking the Shading button arrow and then clicking the desired color at the drop-down gallery.
- Use options at the Borders and Shading dialog box with the Borders tab selected to add a customized border to a paragraph or selected paragraphs, and use options with Shading tab selected to add shading or a pattern to a paragraph or selected paragraphs.
- With the Sort button in the Paragraph group on the HOME tab, you can sort text arranged in paragraphs alphabetically by the first character, which can be a number, symbol, or letter.
- By default, tabs are set every 0.5 inch. These settings can be changed on the horizontal ruler or at the Tabs dialog box.
- Use the Alignment button that displays above the vertical ruler to select a left, right, center, decimal, or bar tab. When you set a tab on the horizontal ruler, any default tabs to the left are automatically deleted.
- After a tab has been set on the horizontal ruler, it can be moved or deleted using the mouse pointer.
- At the Tabs dialog box, you can set any of the five types of tabs at a specific measurement. You can also set tabs with preceding leaders and clear one tab or all tabs. Preceding leaders can be periods, hyphens, or underlines.
- Cut, copy, and paste text using buttons in the Clipboard group on the HOME tab or with keyboard shortcuts.
- When selected text is pasted, the Paste Options button displays in the lower right corner of the text. Click the button, and the *Paste Options* gallery displays with buttons for specifying how you want information pasted in the document.
- With the Clipboard, you can collect up to 24 items and then paste them in various locations in a document.

Commands Review

FEATURE	RIBBON TAB, GROUP	BUTTON, OPTION	KEYBOARD SHORTCUT
borders	HOME, Paragraph		
Borders and Shading dialog box	HOME, Paragraph	, *Borders and Shading*	
bullets	HOME, Paragraph		
clear all formatting	HOME, Font		
clear paragraph formatting			Ctrl + Q
Clipboard task pane	HOME, Clipboard		
copy text	HOME, Clipboard		Ctrl + C
cut text	HOME, Clipboard		Ctrl + X
New Line command			Shift + Enter
numbering	HOME, Paragraph		
Paragraph dialog box	HOME, Paragraph		
paste text	HOME, Clipboard		Ctrl + V
shading	HOME, Paragraph		
Sort Text dialog box	HOME, Paragraph		
Tabs dialog box	HOME, Paragraph	, Tabs	

Concepts Check

Test Your Knowledge

Completion: In the space provided at the right, indicate the correct term, symbol, or command.

1. The Numbering button is located in this group on the HOME tab. ____________
2. Automate the creation of bulleted paragraphs with this button on the HOME tab. ____________
3. This button displays when the AutoFormat feature inserts numbers. ____________
4. You can turn off automatic numbering and bullets at the AutoCorrect dialog box with this tab selected. ____________

5. Bulleted lists with hanging indents are automatically created when you begin a paragraph with the asterisk symbol (*), the hyphen (-), or this symbol. ____________

6. The Borders button is located in this group on the HOME tab. ____________

7. Use options at this dialog box to add a customized border to a paragraph or selected paragraphs. ____________

8. Sort text arranged in paragraphs alphabetically by the first character, can be a number, symbol, or this. ____________

9. By default, tabs are set apart from one another by this measurement. ____________

10. This is the default tab type. ____________

11. When setting tabs on the horizontal ruler, choose the tab type with this button. ____________

12. Tabs can be set on the horizontal ruler or here. ____________

13. This group on the HOME tab contains the Cut, Copy, and Paste buttons. ____________

14. To copy selected text with the mouse, hold down this key while dragging selected text. ____________

15. With this task pane, you can collect up to 24 items and then paste the items in various locations in the document. ____________

Skills Check Assess Your Performance

Assessment

1 APPLY PARAGRAPH FORMATTING TO A COMPUTER ETHICS DOCUMENT

1. Open **CompEthics.docx**.
2. Save the document with Save As and name it **WL1-C3-A1-CompEthics**.
3. Move the insertion point to the end of the document and then type the text shown in Figure 3.11. Apply bullet formatting as shown in the figure.
4. Select the paragraphs of text in the *Computer Ethics* section and then apply numbering formatting.
5. Select the paragraphs of text in the *Technology Timeline* section and then apply bullet formatting.
6. Insert the following paragraph of text between paragraphs 2 and 3 in the *Computer Ethics* section: **Find sources relating to the latest federal and/or state legislation on privacy protection.**
7. Apply the Heading 1 style to the three headings in the document.
8. Apply the Shaded style set.
9. Apply the Slice theme.

10. Apply Light Turquoise, Background 2, Lighter 80% paragraph shading (third column, second row) to the numbered paragraphs in the *Computer Ethics* section and the bulleted paragraphs in the *Technology Timeline* and *ACLU Fair Electronic Monitoring Policy* sections.
11. Save, print, and then close **WL1-C3-A1-CompEthics.docx**.

Figure 3.11 Assessment 1

ACLU Fair Electronic Monitoring Policy

- Notice to employees of the company's electronic monitoring practices
- Use of a signal to let an employee know he or she is being monitored
- Employee access to all personal data collected through monitoring
- No monitoring of areas designed for the health or comfort of employees
- The right to dispute and delete inaccurate data
- A ban on the collection of data unrelated to work performance
- Restrictions on the disclosure of personal data to others without the employee's consent

Assessment 2

TYPE TABBED TEXT AND APPLY FORMATTING TO A COMPUTER SOFTWARE DOCUMENT

1. Open **ProdSoftware.docx**.
2. Save the document with Save As and name it **WL1-C3-A2-ProdSoftware**.
3. Move the insertion point to the end of the document and then set left tabs at the 0.75-inch, 2.75-inch, and 4.5-inch marks on the horizontal ruler. Type the text in Figure 3.12 and type the tabbed text at the tabs you set. Use the New Line command after typing each line of text in columns (except the last line).
4. Apply the Heading 1 style to the three headings in the document (*Productivity Software*, *Personal-Use Software*, and *Software Training Schedule*).
5. Apply the Retrospect theme.
6. Select the productivity software categories in the *Productivity Software* section (from *Word processing* through *Computer-aided design*) and then sort the text alphabetically.
7. With the text still selected, apply bullet formatting.
8. Select the personal-use software categories in the *Personal-Use Software* section (from *Personal finance software* through *Games and entertainment software*) and then sort the text alphabetically.
9. With the text still selected, apply bullet formatting.
10. Apply to the heading *Productivity Software* a single-line top border and Olive Green, Text 2, Lighter 80% paragraph shading (fourth column, second row).
11. Apply the same single-line top border and the same olive green shading to the other two headings (*Personal-Use Software* and *Software Training Schedule*).
12. With the insertion point positioned on the first line of tabbed text, move the tab symbols on the horizontal ruler as follows:
    a. Move the tab at the 0.75-inch mark to the 1-inch mark.
    b. Move the tab at the 4.5-inch mark to the 4-inch mark.
13. Save, print, and then close **WL1-C3-A2-ProdSoftware.docx**.

Figure 3.12 Assessment 2

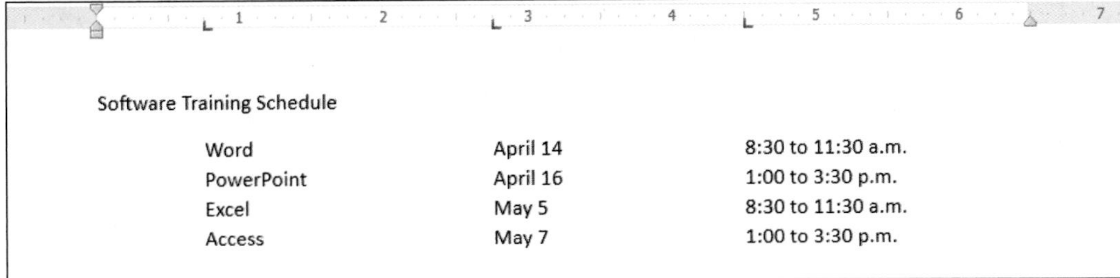

Software Training Schedule		
Word	April 14	8:30 to 11:30 a.m.
PowerPoint	April 16	1:00 to 3:30 p.m.
Excel	May 5	8:30 to 11:30 a.m.
Access	May 7	1:00 to 3:30 p.m.

Assessment 3

TYPE AND FORMAT A TABLE OF CONTENTS DOCUMENT

1. At a new blank document, type the document shown in Figure 3.13 with the following specifications:
   a. Change the font to 11-point Cambria.
   b. Bold and center the title as shown.
   c. Before typing the text in columns, display the Tabs dialog box. Set two left tabs at the 1-inch mark and the 1.5-inch mark and a right tab with dot leaders at the 5.5-inch mark.
   d. Press Enter to end each line of text.
2. Save the document and name it **WL1-C3-A3-TofC**.
3. Print **WL1-C3-A3-TofC.docx**.
4. Select the text in columns and then move the tab symbols on the horizontal ruler as follows. (Because you pressed Enter instead of Shift + Enter at the end of each line of text, you need to select all the text in the columns before moving the tabs.)
   a. Delete the left tab symbol that displays at the 1.5-inch mark.
   b. Set a new left tab at the 0.5-inch mark.
   c. Move the right tab at the 5.5-inch mark to the 6-inch mark.
5. Insert single-line top and bottom borders to the title *TABLE OF CONTENTS*.
6. Apply Orange, Accent 2, Lighter 80% paragraph shading to the title *TABLE OF CONTENTS*.
7. Save, print, and then close **WL1-C3-A3-TofC.docx**.

Figure 3.13 Assessment 3

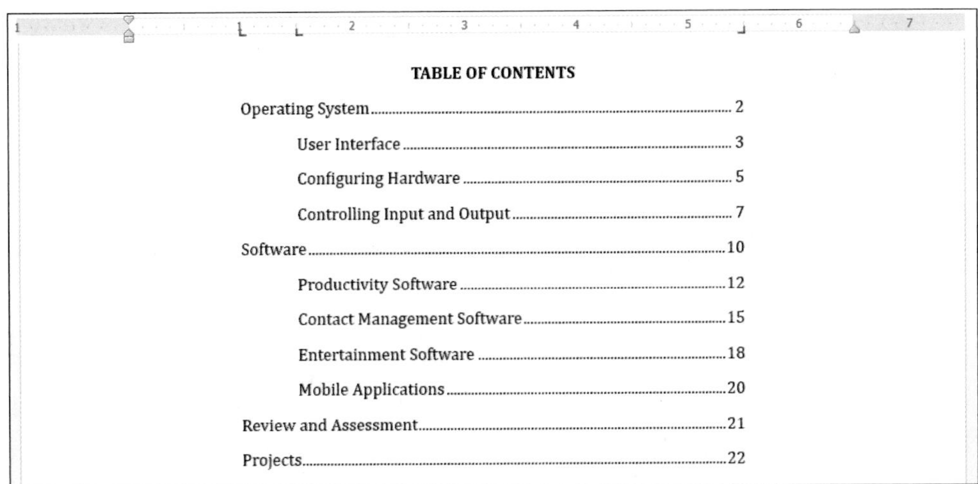

TABLE OF CONTENTS

Operating System..2
User Interface..3
Configuring Hardware..5
Controlling Input and Output..7
Software..10
Productivity Software..12
Contact Management Software..15
Entertainment Software..18
Mobile Applications..20
Review and Assessment..21
Projects..22

Assessment

4 FORMAT A BUILDING CONSTRUCTION AGREEMENT DOCUMENT

1. Open **ConstructAgrmnt.docx**.
2. Save the document with Save As and name it **WL1-C3-A4-ConstructAgrmnt**.
3. Select and then delete the paragraph (including the blank line below the paragraph) that begins *Supervision of Work*.
4. Select and then delete the paragraph (including the blank line below the paragraph) that begins *Builder's Right to Terminate Contract*.
5. Move the paragraph (including the blank line below the paragraph) that begins *Financing Arrangements* above the paragraph that begins *Start of Construction*.
6. Open **AgrmntItems.docx**.
7. Turn on the display of the Clipboard task pane and then clear all the contents, if necessary.
8. Select and then copy the first paragraph.
9. Select and then copy the second paragraph.
10. Select and then copy the third paragraph.
11. Close **AgrmntItems.docx**.
12. With **WL1-C3-A4-ConstructAgrmnt.docx** open, turn on the display of the Clipboard and then paste the *Supervision* paragraph *above* the *Changes and Alterations* paragraph and then merge the formatting. (Make sure you position the insertion point *above* the paragraph before you paste the text.)
13. Paste the *Pay Review* paragraph *above* the *Possession of Residence* paragraph and then merge the formatting.
14. Clear all items from the Clipboard and then close the Clipboard task pane.
15. Check the spacing between paragraphs. Insert or delete blank lines to maintain consistent spacing.
16. Save, print, and then close **WL1-C3-A4-ConstructAgrmnt.docx**.

Assessment

5 HYPHENATE WORDS IN A REPORT

1. In some Word documents, especially documents with left and right margins wider than 1 inch, the right margin may appear quite ragged. If the paragraph alignment is changed to justified alignment, the right margin will appear even, but there will be extra space added throughout the line. In these situations, hyphenating long words that fall at the ends of text lines provides the document with a more balanced look. Use Word's Help feature to learn how to automatically hyphenate words in a document.
2. Open **InterfaceApps.docx**.
3. Save the document with Save As and name it **WL1-C3-A5-InterfaceApps**.
4. Automatically hyphenate words in the document, limiting the number of consecutive hyphens to 2. ***Hint: Specify the number of consecutive hyphens at the Hyphenation dialog box.***

Visual Benchmark Demonstrate Your Proficiency

CREATE A RESUME

1. At a blank document, click the *No Spacing* style and then type the resume document shown in Figure 3.14 on the next page. Apply character and paragraph formatting as shown in the figure. Insert 6 points of spacing after the headings *PROFESSIONAL EXPERIENCE, EDUCATION, TECHNOLOGY SKILLS,* and *REFERENCES*. Change the font size of the name, *DEVON CHAMBERS*, to 16 points.
2. Save the document and name it **WL1-C3-VB-Resume.**
3. Print and then close the document.

Case Study Apply Your Skills

Part 1

You are the assistant to Gina Coletti, manager of La Dolce Vita, an Italian restaurant. She has been working on updating and formatting the lunch menu. She has asked you to complete the menu by opening the **Menu.docx** document (located in the WL1C3 folder), determining how the appetizer section is formatted, and then applying the same formatting to the *Soups and Salads*; *Sandwiches, Calzones and Burgers*; and *Individual Pizzas* sections. Save the document and name it **WL1-C3-CS-Menu**. Print and then close the document.

Part 2

Ms. Coletti has reviewed the completed menu and is pleased with it, but she wants to add a page border around the entire page to increase visual interest. Open **WL1-C3-CS-Menu.docx** and then save the document and name it **WL1-C3-CS-MenuPgBorder**. Display the Borders and Shading dialog box with the Page Border tab selected and then experiment with the options available. Apply an appropriate page border to the menu. (Consider applying an art page border.) Save, print, and then close **WL1-C3-CS-MenuPgBorder.docx**.

Part 3

Each week, the restaurant offers daily specials. Ms. Coletti has asked you to open and format the text in the **MenuSpecials.docx** document. She has asked you to format the specials menu in a similar manner as the main menu but to make some changes so it is unique from the main menu. Apply the same page border to the specials menu document that you applied to the main menu document. Save the document and name it **WL1-C3-CS-MenuSpecials**. Print and then close the document.

Part 4

You have been asked by the head chef to research a new recipe for an Italian dish. Using the Internet, find a recipe that interests you and then prepare a Word document containing the recipe and ingredients. Use bullets before each ingredient and use numbering for each step in the recipe preparation. Save the document and name it **WL1-C3-CS-Recipe**. Print and then close the document.

Figure 3.14 Visual Benchmark

DEVON CHAMBERS

344 North Anderson Road * Oklahoma City, OK 73177 * (404) 555-3228

PROFILE

Business manager with successful track record at entrepreneurial start-up and strong project management skills. Keen ability to motivate and supervise employees, a strong hands-on experience with customer service, marketing, and operations. Highly organized and motivated professional looking to leverage strengths in leadership and organizational skills in a project coordinator role.

PROFESSIONAL EXPERIENCE

Midwest Deli, Oklahoma City, OK .... 07/13 to present
Assistant Manager

- Coordinated the opening of a new business, which included budgeting start-up costs, establishing relationships with vendors, ordering supplies, purchasing and installing equipment, and marketing the business to the community
- Manage business personnel, which includes recruitment, interviewing, hiring, training, motivating staff, and conflict resolution
- Manage daily business operations through customer satisfaction, quality control, employee scheduling, process improvement, and maintaining product inventory

Marin Associates, Shawnee, OK.. 06/11 to 06/13
Projects Coordinator

- Developed and maintained a secure office network and installed and repaired computers
- Provided support for hardware and software issues
- Directed agency projects such as equipment purchases, office reorganization, and building maintenance and repair

Moore Insurance Agency, Shawnee, OK.. 04/09 to 04/11
Administrative Assistant

- Prepared documents and forms for staff and clients
- Organized and maintained paper and electronic files and scheduled meetings and appointments
- Disseminated information using the telephone, mail services, websites, and email

EDUCATION

Associate of Arts, Business 2013
Oklahoma City Community College

TECHNOLOGY SKILLS

- Proficient in Microsoft Word, Excel, and PowerPoint
- Knowledgeable in current and previous versions of the Windows operating system
- Experience with networking, firewalls, and security systems

REFERENCES

Professional and personal references available upon request.

MICROSOFT®

WORD

Formatting Pages

PERFORMANCE OBJECTIVES

Upon successful completion of Chapter 4, you will be able to:

- **Change document views**
- **Navigate in a document with the Navigation pane**
- **Change margins, page orientation, and paper size in a document**
- **Format pages at the Page Setup dialog box**
- **Insert a page break, blank page, and cover page**
- **Insert page numbering**
- **Insert and edit predesigned headers and footers**
- **Insert a watermark, page color, and page border**
- **Find and replace text and formatting**

Tutorials

4.1 Changing Document Views
4.2 Navigating Using the Navigation Pane
4.3 Changing Margins, Page Orientation, and Paper Size
4.4 Inserting a Blank Page and a Cover Page
4.5 Inserting Page Numbers and Page Breaks
4.6 Creating Headers and Footers
4.7 Modifying Headers and Footers
4.8 Inserting a Watermark, Page Color, and Page Border
4.9 Finding and Replacing Text
4.10 Finding and Replacing Formatting

A document generally displays in Print Layout view. You can change this default view with buttons in the view area on the Status bar or with options on the VIEW tab. Use the Navigation pane to navigate in a document. A Word document, by default, contains 1-inch top, bottom, left, and right margins. You can change these default margins with the Margins button in the Page Setup group on the PAGE LAYOUT tab or with options at the Page Setup dialog box. You can insert a variety of features in a Word document, including a page break, blank page, and cover page as well as page numbers, headers, footers, a watermark, page color, and page border. Use options at the Find and Replace dialog box to search for specific text or formatting and replace with other text or formatting. Model answers for this chapter's projects appear on the following pages.

Note: Before beginning the projects, copy to your storage medium the WL1C4 subfolder from the WL1 folder on the CD that accompanies this textbook and then make WL1C4 thae active folder.

NETIQUETTE GUIDELINES

Distance conveys a degree of anonymity, and as a result, many people feel less inhibited in online situations than in their everyday lives. This lessening of inhibitions sometimes leads people to drop their normal standards of decorum when communicating online. In response, good cybercitizens have developed, over the years, an informal set of guidelines for online behavior called ***netiquette.*** Netiquette can be summarized by three simple precepts: Remember that there is a human being on the other end of your communication, treat that human being with respect, and do not transmit any message that you wouldn't be willing to communicate face to face. Some specific guidelines include:

- Be careful what you write about others. Assume that anyone about whom you are writing will read your comments or receive them by some circuitous route.
- Be truthful. Do not pretend to be someone or something that you are not.
- Be brief. Receiving and reading messages costs time and money.
- Use titles that accurately and concisely describe the contents of email and other postings.
- Consider your audience, and use language that is appropriate. Excessive use of jargon in a nontechnical chat room, for example, can be bad manners, and remember that children sometimes join chat rooms.
- Avoid offensive language, especially comments that might be construed as racist or sexist.
- Remember that the law still applies in cyberspace. Do not commit illegal acts online, such as libeling or slandering others, and do not joke about committing illegal acts.
- Be careful with humor and sarcasm. One person's humorous comment can be another person's boorish or degrading remark.
- Do not post a message more than once.
- Generally speaking, avoid putting words into full capitals. Online, all-caps is considered SHOUTING.
- If you are following up a previous message or posting, summarize that message or posting.
- Do not post irrelevant messages, referred to in hacker's jargon as spam.
- Do not post messages whose sole purpose is to sucker others into an irrelevant or unimportant discussion. Such messages are known as trolls.
- Read existing follow-up postings and don't repeat what has already been said.
- Respect other people's intellectual property. Don't post, display, or otherwise provide access to materials belonging to others, and cite references as appropriate.
- Temper online expressions of hostility; in hacker's jargon, avoid excessive flaming of others.
- Never send online chain letters.
- Some email programs allow one to place a signature containing text and graphics at the end of a mailing. Remember that elaborate materials take up valuable transmission time, and do not overdo these signatures.
- Limit the length of typed lines to less than 78 characters, and avoid unusual formatting.
- Identify any financial interests related to an email message or posting. If you are selling something, make that fact clear.
- Do not send email to people who might have no interest in it. In particular, avoid automatically copying email to large numbers of people.
- Online messages can be quite informal, but try, nevertheless, to express yourself using proper spelling, capitalization, grammar, usage, and punctuation.
- Avoid chastising others for their online typos. To err is human. To forgive is good cybercitizenship.

Project 2 Format a Document on Online Etiquette Guidelines
WL1-C4-P2-Netiquette.docx

2015

Computer Devices

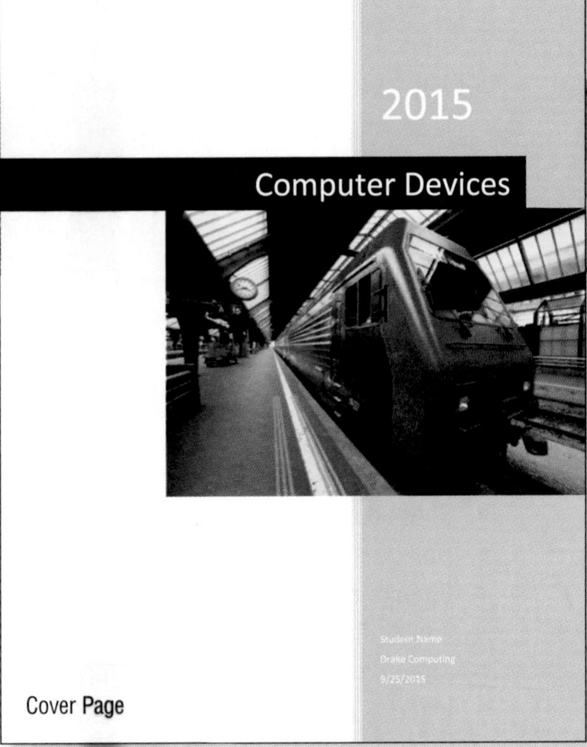

Student Name
Drake Computing
9/25/2015

Cover Page

Project 3 Customize a Report on Computer Input and Output Devices
WL1-C4-P3-CompDevices.docx

COMPUTER INPUT DEVICES

Engineers have been especially creative in designing new ways to get information into computers. Some input methods are highly specialized and unusual, while common devices often undergo redesign to improve their capabilities or their ergonomics, the ways in which they affect people physically. Some common input devices include keyboards, mice, trackballs, and touchpads.

Keyboard

A keyboard can be an external device that is attached by means of a cable, or it can be attached to the CPU case itself as it is for laptop computers. Most keyboards today are QWERTY keyboards, which take their name from the first six keys at the left of the first row of letters. An alternative, the DVORAK keyboard, places the most commonly used keys close to the user's fingertips and speeds typing.

Many keyboards have a separate numeric keypad, like that of a calculator, containing numbers and mathematical operators. All keyboards have modifier keys that enable the user to change the symbol or character that is entered when a given key is pressed. The Shift key, for example, makes a letter uppercase. Keyboards also have special cursor keys that enable the user to change the position on the screen of the cursor, a symbol that appears on the monitor to show where in a document the next change will appear. Most keyboards also have function keys, labeled F1, F2, F3, and so on. These keys allow the user to issue commands by pressing a single key.

1 | Page

Page 1

Mouse

Graphical operating systems contain many elements that a user can choose by pointing at them. Such elements include buttons, tools, pull-down menus, and icons for file folders, programs, and document files. Often pointing to and clicking on one of these elements is more convenient than using the cursor or arrow keys on the keyboard. This pointing and clicking can be done by using a mouse. The mouse is the second most common input device, after the keyboard. A mouse operates by moving the cursor on the computer screen to correspond to movements made with the mouse.

Trackball

A trackball is like an upside-down mouse. A mouse is moved over a pad. A trackball remains stationary, and the user moves the ball with his or her fingers or palm. One or more buttons for choosing options are incorporated into the design of the trackball.

Touchpad and Touchscreen

A touchpad feels less mechanical than a mouse or trackball because the user simply moves a finger on the pad. A touchpad has two parts. One part acts as a button, while the other emulates a mouse pad on which the user traces the location of the cursor with a finger. People with carpal tunnel syndrome find touchpads and trackballs easier to use than mice. Many portable computers have built-in trackballs or touchpads as input devices.

A touchscreen allows the user to choose options by pressing the appropriate part of the screen. Touchscreens are widely used in bank ATMs and in kiosks at retail outlets and in tourist areas.

2 | Page

Page 2

COMPUTER OUTPUT DEVICES

To get information into a computer, a person uses an input device. To get information out, a person uses an output device. Some common output devices include monitors, printers, and speakers.

Monitor

A monitor, or screen, is the most common output device used with a personal computer. A monitor creates a visual display and is either built into the CPU case or attached as an external device by means of a cable. Sometimes the cable is connected to a circuit board called a video card placed into an expansion slot in the CPU.

The most common monitors use either a thin film transistor (TFT) active matrix liquid crystal display (LCD) or a plasma display. Plasma displays have a very true level of color reproduction compared with LCDs. Emerging display technologies include surface-conduction electron-emitter displays (SED) and organic light emitting diodes (OLED).

Printer

After monitors, printers are the most important output devices. The print quality produced by these devices is measured in dpi, or dots per inch. As with screen resolution, the greater the number of dots per inch, the better the quality. The earliest printers for personal computers were dot matrix printers that used perforated computer paper. These impact printers worked something like typewriters, transferring the image of a character by using pins to strike a ribbon.

A laser printer uses a laser beam to create points of electrical charge on a cylindrical drum. Toner, composed of particles of ink with a negative electrical charge, sticks to the charged points on the positively charged drum. As the page moves past the drum, heat and pressure fuse the toner to the page.

Inkjet printers generally provide at least 300 dpi resolution, although high-resolution inkjets are available. Quieter than dot matrix printers, these also use a print head that moves across the page. Instead of striking the page, the small cartridge sprays a fine mist of ink when an electrical charge moves through the print cartridge. An inkjet printer can use color cartridges and so provides affordable color printing suitable for home and small office use.

3 | Page

Page 3

The Writing Process

THE WRITING PROCESS

An effective letter or memo does not simply appear on your paper or computer screen. Instead, it begins to take shape when you think carefully about the situation in which you must write, when you define your purpose for writing. It continues to develop as you consider your reader, the information you must communicate, and the way in which you plan to present that information. Finally, a document that communicates clearly is the result of good writing and good rewriting; you can usually improve anything you have written. This document represents a process for approaching any writing task.

Define Purpose

Knowing your purpose for writing is the foundation of any written project. Before you begin writing your memo, letter, or other document, ask yourself the following questions:

- What am I trying to accomplish?
- What is my purpose for writing?
- To request information or products?
- To respond to a question or request?
- To persuade someone?
- To direct someone?

Identify Reader

As you define your purpose, you will need to develop a good picture of the person who will be reading your document. Ask yourself:

- Who is my reader?
- What do I know about my reader that will help determine the best approach?
- Is the audience one person or a group?
- Is my reader a coworker, a subordinate, a superior, or a customer?
- How is the reader likely to feel about my message?

Select and Organize Information

Once you have defined your purpose and identified your reader, decide what information you will include. Ask yourself questions such as:

- What does my reader want or need to know?
- What information must I include?
- What information will help my reader respond positively?
- What information should I not include?

STUDENT NAME 1

Page 1

Project 4 Add Elements to a Report on the Writing Process

WL1-C4-P4-WritingProcess.docx

The Writing Process

To answer these questions, you may find it helpful to spend a few minutes listing all the information you *could* include in your document. You may also find it helpful to write a rough draft of your document. Write the draft quickly, including any information that comes to you. Once you have it all on paper, you can work with it, deciding what to include and what to leave out.

Write First Draft

Once you are ready to write, do not allow yourself to stare at a blank sheet of paper (or the computer screen) for more than a few seconds. A first effort is rarely a final draft, even for the best writers; therefore, write something to get started. Let your purpose, reader, and organizational plan guide you, but do not let them stifle you. Keep going even if you occasionally lose your focus. Once you have a full draft, you can add or delete information, reorganize, and edit sentences.

Write Strong Paragraphs

Most of your written business communication will be too complex to be conveyed in a single sentence. Memos, letters, and even simple informal messages often (though not always) require that you state a general idea and follow with more information about that idea: support for the idea, reasons, examples, explanation, further discussion, and so on. If you include one main idea in each paragraph, you can move your reader through complicated information idea by idea—paragraph by paragraph—until you believe your reader can draw a logical conclusion.

Occasionally, a good paragraph is a single sentence. More often, a good paragraph is a group of sentences that focus on one main idea. This focus on a single idea is called *unity*. Good paragraphs also help the reader understand relationships between ideas (from paragraph to paragraph) and between ideas and their supporting details. This clarity of relationships is called *coherence*. Both unity and coherence improve when a paragraph begins with a sentence that states or implies the main idea.

Use Active Voice

Use the active voice most of the time. Active-voice sentences use fewer words and are more direct than passive-voice sentences. Although the active voice is more direct and efficient, the passive voice is useful at times. Use passive voice when:

- Your writing is so formal or impersonal that you must avoid names and pronouns, as in formal reports
- Active-voice options sound awkward or forced
- You want to improve sentence variety
- You wish to deemphasize the subject of the sentence

STUDENT NAME 2

Page 2

The Writing Process

Edit and Proofread

Editing ar
informati
to the rea

STUDEN

Page 3

The Writing Process

REFERENCES

Branson, Jeannette. *Writing Efficiently and Effectively*. Cincinnati: Davidson & Appleby Publishing Services, 2014.

Gilleland, Maureen. "Business Writing." http://www.emcpnews.net. Accessed August 15, 2015.

Lehnard, Arthur, and Taylor, Patricia. *The Writing Reference Manual*. St. Paul: Moreland House Publishing, 2014.

STUDENT NAME 4

Page 4

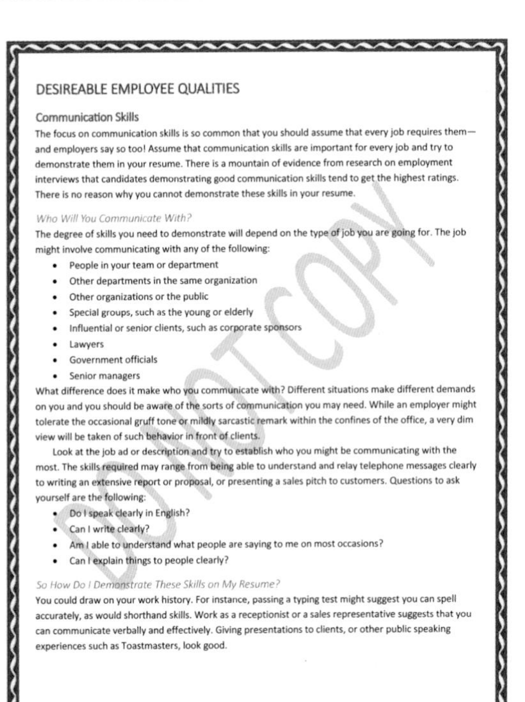

DESIREABLE EMPLOYEE QUALITIES

Communication Skills

The focus on communication skills is so common that you should assume that every job requires them—and employers say so too! Assume that communication skills are important for every job and try to demonstrate them in your resume. There is a mountain of evidence from research on employment interviews that candidates demonstrating good communication skills tend to get the highest ratings. There is no reason why you cannot demonstrate these skills in your resume.

Who Will You Communicate With?

The degree of skills you need to demonstrate will depend on the type of job you are going for. The job might involve communicating with any of the following:

- People in your team or department
- Other departments in the same organization
- Other organizations or the public
- Special groups, such as the young or elderly
- Influential or senior clients, such as corporate sponsors
- Lawyers
- Government officials
- Senior managers

What difference does it make who you communicate with? Different situations make different demands on you and you should be aware of the sorts of communication you may need. While an employer might tolerate the occasional gruff tone or mildly sarcastic remark within the confines of the office, a very dim view will be taken of such behavior in front of clients.

Look at the job ad or description and try to establish who you might be communicating with the most. The skills required may range from being able to understand and relay telephone messages clearly to writing an extensive report or proposal, or presenting a sales pitch to customers. Questions to ask yourself are the following:

- Do I speak clearly in English?
- Can I write clearly?
- Am I able to understand what people are saying to me on most occasions?
- Can I explain things to people clearly?

So How Do I Demonstrate These Skills on My Resume?

You could draw on your work history. For instance, passing a typing test might suggest you can spell accurately, as would shorthand skills. Work as a receptionist or a sales representative suggests that you can communicate verbally and effectively. Giving presentations to clients, or other public speaking experiences such as Toastmasters, look good.

Page 1

Team Skills

What this means is that you are happy and effective working in groups with other people. You are happy to work together, share information, and help out team members when they are struggling. You tend to like people, and are reasonably well liked. It sometimes seems that "team player" is added to just about every job ad without any real reason. As a general rule, it is code for saying "Do you get along with other people, or are you selfish and unpleasant?" Some people think the expression "team player" refers to membership in sporting teams. Generally, this is not the case, and it is better to use examples of your team skills drawn from work experience. Of course, if you cannot think of any convincing examples from work, then you might consider using some limited examples from your hobbies.

Attention to Detail

Many jobs request this skill. Just because this quality is not included in an advertisement, do not assume it is not important. Making silly mistakes in some jobs, such as an accounting clerk position where large sums of money may be involved, can lead to very expensive outcomes! In a study we conducted, where we deliberately included spelling mistakes on some resumes but not on others, we found that even one error reduced the chance of the candidate being interviewed by between 30 and 45 percent. Think about it—just a minor effort can reduce your chances of being interviewed by almost half!

Energy, Dynamism, Enthusiasm, Drive, and Initiative

Nobody wants to employ somebody who slumps in their seat, seems to take forever to carry out the most trivial tasks, and sighs deeply every time they are asked to do something. The organization looking for qualities such as energy and enthusiasm is looking for someone who is alert, gets on with their work quickly and without unnecessary complaint, and (within reason) will find solutions to problems rather than find problems with solutions.

Ability to Handle Pressure

Pressure varies from job to job, but the request for this ability is an indication that things might get very busy from time to time—for example, work in a fire department or with the police force, where lapses of concentration or failures of nerve have potentially fatal outcomes. What the employer wants to see is evidence that you will respond to the challenge and perhaps work faster or longer hours on occasion to meet deadlines or reduce the backlog. What they are saying is they do not expect you to lose your temper or take sick leave at the first sign of pressure. Pressure in some jobs will be immediate, such as a long line of irritated customers. Or it could be long-term stress, such as the pressure to build all the stadiums for the Olympic Games on time!

Leadership

Leadership is one of those qualities that tends to get thrown into a job ad without much justification. For a start, nobody can agree on what makes a good leader. However, if you can demonstrate that you have managed a team of people successfully—either by length of time in the position (this says that if you were not a good leader, you would have been moved on quickly) or by tasks achieved by a group under your management—this may be the sort of thing the employer is looking for. Equally, being elected to a chairperson's role or similar job would suggest that you inspire the confidence of others.

Page 2

Project 5 Format a Report on Employee Qualities

WL1-C4-P5-EmpQualities.docx

RENT AGREEMENT

THIS RENT AGREEMENT (hereinafter referred to as the "Agreement") is made and entered into this ____ day of ________________, 2015, by and between Tracy Hartford and Michael Iwami.

Term

Tracy Hartford rents to Michael Iwami and Michael Iwami rents from Tracy Hartford the described premises together with any and all appurtenances thereto, for a term of _____ year(s), such term beginning on __________________, and ending at 12 o'clock midnight on ____________________.

Rent

The total rent for the term hereof is the sum of _________________ DOLLARS ($_________) payable on the ______ day of each month of the term. All such payments shall be made to Tracy Hartford at Tracy Hartford's address on or before the due date and without demand.

Damage Deposit

Upon the due execution of this Agreement, Michael Iwami shall deposit with Tracy Hartford the sum of ______________ DOLLARS ($_________), receipt of which is hereby acknowledged by Tracy Hartford, as security for any damage caused to the Premises during the renting term hereof. Such deposit shall be returned to Michael Iwami, without interest, and minus any set off for damages to the Premises, upon the termination of this renting Agreement.

Use of Premises

The Premises shall be used and occupied by Michael Iwami and Michael Iwami's immediately family, exclusively, as a private single-family dwelling, and no part of the Premises shall be used at any time during the term of this Agreement by Michael Iwami for the purpose of carrying on any business, profession, or trade of any kind, or for any purpose other than as a private single-family dwelling. Michael Iwami shall not allow any other person, other than Michael Iwami's immediate family or transient relatives and friends who are guests of Michael Iwami, to use or occupy the Premises without first obtaining Tracy Hartford's written consent to such use.

Condition of Premises

Michael Iwami stipulates, represents, and warrants that Michael Iwami has examined the Premises, and that they are at the time of this Agreement in good order and repair and in a safe, clean, and tenantable condition.

Alterations and Improvements

Michael Iwami shall make no alterations to the buildings or improvements on the Premises without the prior written consent of Tracy Hartford. Any and all alterations, changes, and/or improvements built, constructed, or placed on the Premises by Michael Iwami shall, unminus otherwise provided by written agreement between Tracy Hartford and Michael Iwami, be and become the property of Tracy Hartford and remain on the Premises at the expiration or earlier termination of this Agreement.

Page 1

Damage to Premises

In the event the Premises are destroyed or rendered wholly unlivable, by fire, storm, earthquake, or other casualty not caused by the negligence of Michael Iwami, this Agreement shall terminate from such time except for the purpose of enforcing rights that may have then accrued hereunder.

Page 2

Project 6 Format a Lease Agreement

WL1-C4-P6-LeaseAgrmnt.docx

Project 1 Navigate in a Report on Navigating and Searching the Web — 2 Parts

You will open a document containing information on navigating and searching the web, change document views, navigate in the document using the Navigation pane, and show and hide white space at the tops and bottoms of pages.

Changing the View

By default, a Word document displays in Print Layout view. This view displays the document on the screen as it will appear when printed. Other views are available, such as Draft and Read Mode. Change views with buttons in the view area on the Status bar or with options on the VIEW tab. The buttons in the view area on the Status bar are identified in Figure 4.1. Along with the View buttons, the Status bar also contains a Zoom slider bar, as shown in Figure 4.1. Drag the button on the Zoom slider bar to increase or decrease the size of the display, or click the Zoom Out button to decrease the size and click the Zoom In button to increase the size.

Click the 100% that displays at the right side of the Zoom slider bar to display the Zoom dialog box.

Zoom Out Zoom In

Displaying a Document in Draft View

Change to Draft view and the document displays in a format for efficient editing and formatting. At this view, margins and other features such as headers and footers do not display on the screen. Change to Draft view by clicking the VIEW tab and then clicking the Draft button in the Views group.

Draft

Displaying a Document in Read Mode View

The Read Mode view displays a document in a format for easy viewing and reading. Change to Read Mode view by clicking the Read Mode button in the view area on the Status bar or by clicking the VIEW tab and then clicking the Read Mode button in the Views group. Navigate in Read Mode view using the keys on the keyboard, as shown in Table 4.1. Or, navigate with the mouse by clicking at the right side of the screen or clicking the Next button (right-pointing triangle in a circle) to display the next pages or clicking at the left side of the screen or clicking the Previous button (left-pointing triangle in a circle) to display the previous pages.

Read Mode

The FILE, TOOLS, and VIEW tabs display in the upper left corner of the screen in Read Mode view. Click the FILE tab to display the backstage area. Click the TOOLS tab and a drop-down list displays with options for finding specific text in the document and searching for information on the Internet using the Bing search engine. Click the VIEW tab and options display for customizing what you see in Read Mode view. You can display the Navigation pane to navigate to specific locations

Figure 4.1 View Buttons and Zoom Slider Bar

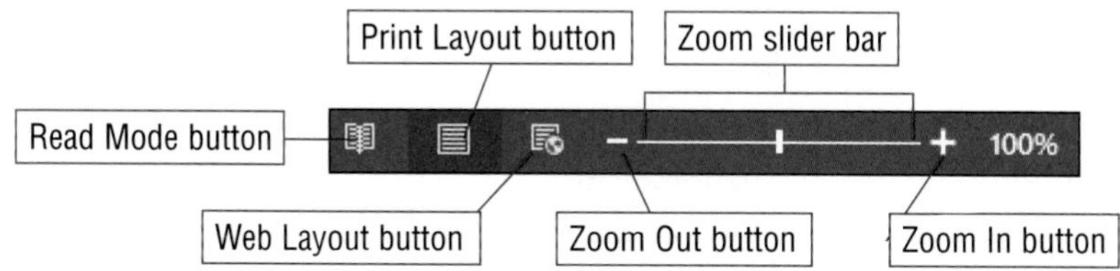

Table 4.1 Keyboard Commands in Read Mode View

Press this key	*To complete this action*
Page Down key, Right Arrow key, or spacebar	Display next two pages
Page Up key, Left Arrow key, or Backspace key	Display previous two pages
Home	Display first page in document
End	Display last page in document
Esc	Return to previous view

in the document, show comments inserted in the document, change the width of the columns or change to a page layout, and change the page colors in Read Mode view.

If your document contains an object such as a table, SmartArt graphic, image, or shape, you can zoom in on the object in Read Mode view. To do this, double-click the object. When you double-click an object, a button containing a magnifying glass with a plus symbol inside displays just outside the upper right corner of the object. Click this button to zoom in even more on the object. Click the button again and the object returns to the original zoom size. Click once outside the object to return it to its original size.

To close Read Mode view and return to the previous view, press the Esc key on your keyboard or click the VIEW tab and then click *Edit Document* at the drop-down list.

Changing Ribbon Display Options

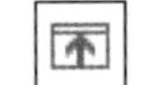

Ribbon Display Options

If you want to view more of your document, use the Ribbon Display Options button that displays in the upper right corner of the screen to the right of the Microsoft Word Help button. Click the Ribbon Display Options button and a drop-down list displays with three options—*Auto-hide Ribbon*, *Show Tabs*, and *Show Tabs and Commands*. The default is Show Tabs and Commands, which displays the Quick Access toolbar, the ribbon, and the Status bar on the screen. Click the first option, *Auto-hide Ribbon*, and the Quick Access toolbar, ribbon, and Status bar are hidden, allowing you to see more of your document. To temporarily redisplay these features, click at the top of the screen. Turn these features back on by clicking the Ribbon Display Options button and then clicking the *Show Tabs and Commands* option. Click the *Show Tabs* option at the drop-down list and the tabs display on the ribbon while the buttons and commands remain hidden.

Navigating Using the Navigation Pane

Quick Steps

Display Navigation Pane

1. Click VIEW tab.
2. Click *Navigation Pane* check box.

Word includes a number of features for navigating in a document. Along with the navigation features you have already learned, you can also navigate using the Navigation pane shown in Figure 4.2. When you click the *Navigation Pane* check box in the Show group on the VIEW tab, the Navigation pane displays at the left side of the screen and includes a search text box and a pane with three tabs. Click the HEADINGS tab to display in the pane titles and headings with styles applied. Click a title or heading in the pane to move the insertion point to that title or heading.

Figure 4.2 Navigation Pane

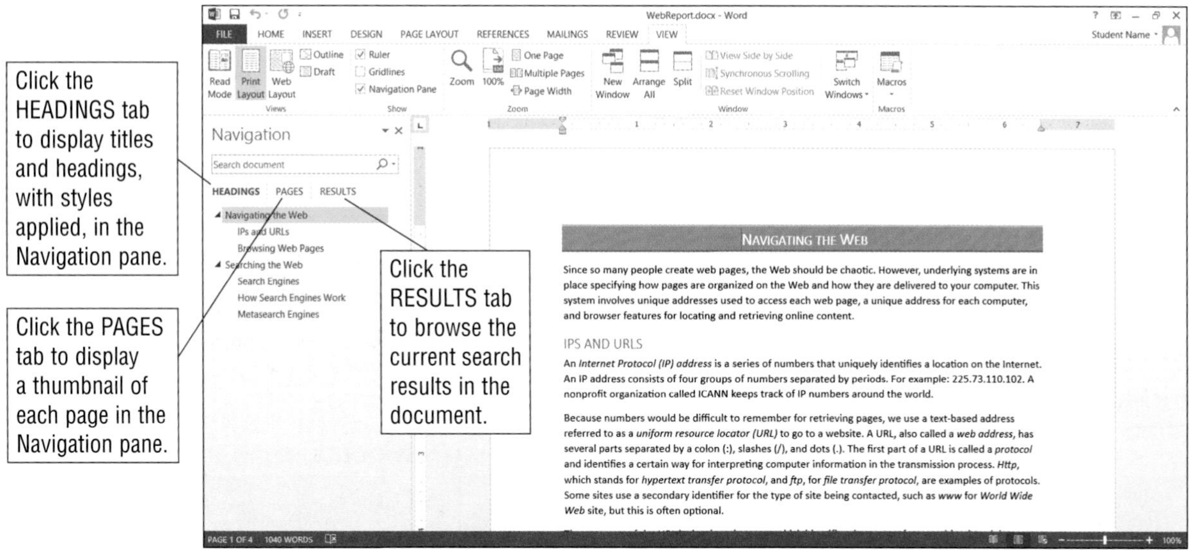

Click the PAGES tab to display a thumbnail of each page in the pane. Click a thumbnail to move the insertion point to the specific page. Click the RESULTS tab to browse the current search results in the document. Close the Navigation pane by clicking the *Navigation Pane* check box in the Show group on the VIEW tab or by clicking the Close button located in the upper right corner of the pane.

Project 1a Changing Views and Navigating in a Document — Part 1 of 2

1. Open **WebReport.docx**.
2. Click the VIEW tab and then click the Draft button in the Views group.
3. Click three times on the Zoom Out button that displays to the left of the Zoom slider bar. (This changes the percentage displays and *70%* displays at the right side of the Zoom In button.)
4. Using the mouse, drag the Zoom slider bar button to the middle until *100%* displays at the right side of the Zoom In button.
5. Click the Print Layout button located in the view area on the Status bar.
6. Click the Read Mode button located in the view area on the Status bar.
7. Increase the display of the table located at the right side of the screen by double-clicking the table. (If the table is not visible, click the right-pointing arrow located at the right side of the screen to view the next page.)
8. Click the button (contains a magnifying glass with a plus symbol) that displays outside the upper right corner of the table. (This increases the zoom.)

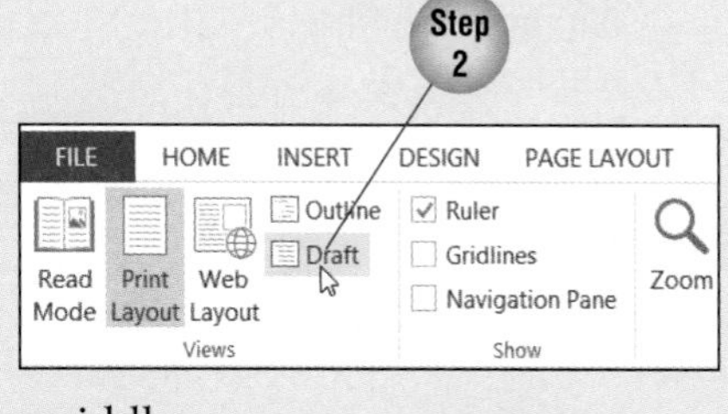

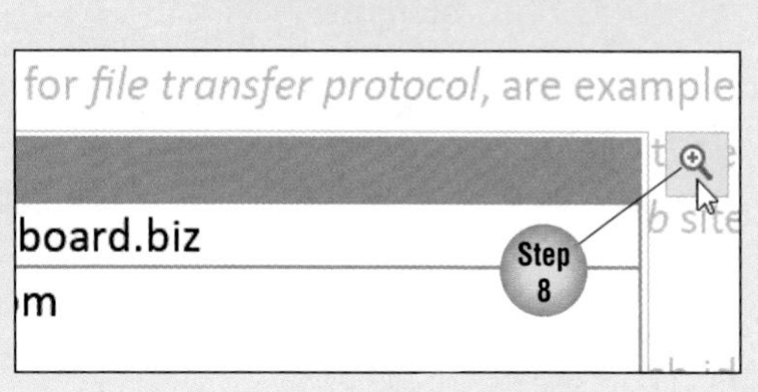

9. Click outside the table to return the table to the original size.
10. Practice navigating in Read Mode view using the actions shown in Table 4.1 (except the last option).
11. Press the Esc key to return to the Print Layout view.
12. Click the Ribbon Display Options button that displays in the upper right corner of the screen to the right of the Microsoft Word Help button and then click *Auto-hide Ribbon* at the drop-down list.
13. Press Ctrl + End to display the last page in the document and then press the Page Up key until the beginning of the document displays.
14. Click at the top of the screen to temporarily redisplay the Quick Access toolbar, ribbon, and Status bar.
15. Click the Ribbon Display Options button and then click *Show Tabs* at the drop-down list.
16. Click the Ribbon Display Options button and then click *Show Tabs and Commands* at the drop-down list.
17. Click the *Navigation Pane* check box in the Show group on the VIEW tab to insert a check mark.
18. Click the *Navigating the Web* heading that displays in the Navigation pane.
19. Click the *Searching the Web* heading that displays in the Navigation pane.
20. Click the PAGES tab in the Navigation pane to display the page thumbnails in the pane.
21. Click the number 4 thumbnail in the Navigation pane.
22. Scroll up the pane and then click the number 1 thumbnail.
23. Close the Navigation pane by clicking the Close button located in the upper right corner of the Navigation pane.

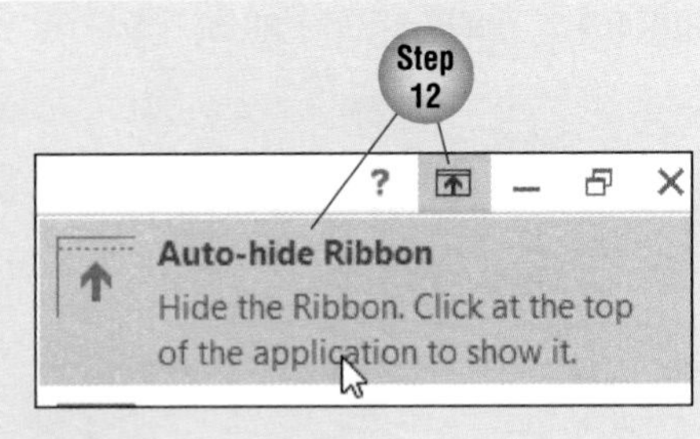

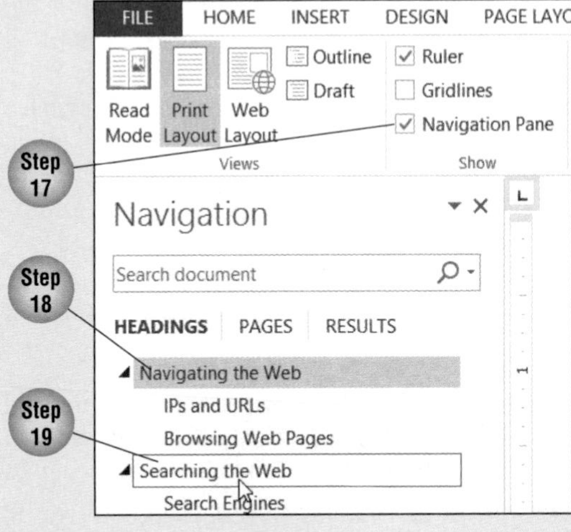

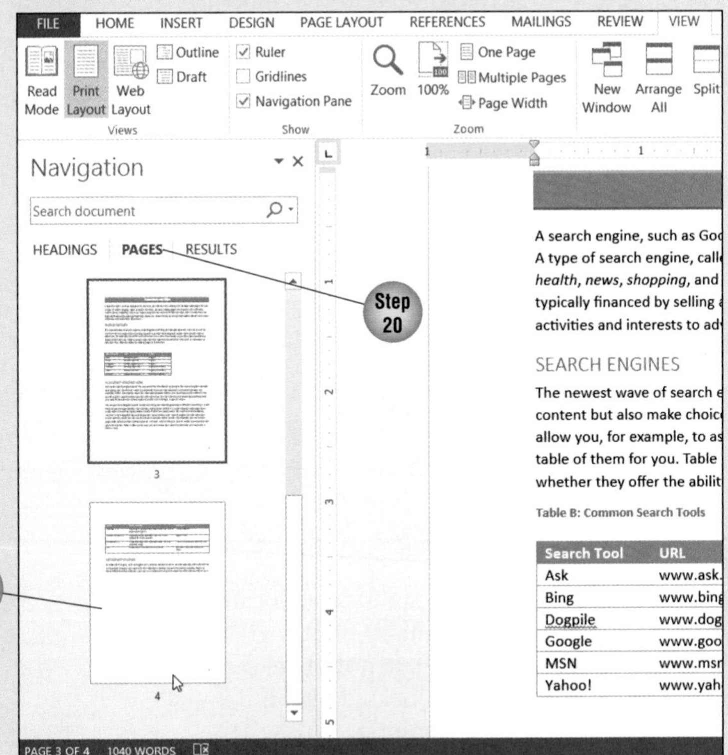

Hiding/Showing White Space in Print Layout View

In Print Layout view, a page displays as it will appear when printed including the white space at the top and bottom of the page representing the document's margins. To save space on the screen in Print Layout view, you can remove the white space by positioning the mouse pointer at the top edge or bottom edge of a page or between pages until the pointer displays as the Hide White Space icon and then double-clicking the left mouse button. To redisplay the white space, position the mouse pointer on the thin, gray line separating pages until the pointer turns into the Show White Space icon and then double-click the left mouse button.

Quick Steps

Hide/Show White Space
1. Position mouse pointer at top of page until pointer displays as Hide White Space icon or Show White Space icon.
2. Double-click left mouse button.

Hide White Space

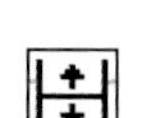

Show White Space

Project 1b Hiding/Showing White Space — Part 2 of 2

1. With **WebReport.docx** open, make sure the document displays in Print Layout view.
2. Press Ctrl + Home to move the insertion point to the beginning of the document.
3. Hide the white spaces at the tops and bottoms of pages by positioning the mouse pointer at the top edge of the page until the pointer turns into the Hide White Space icon and then double-clicking the left mouse button.

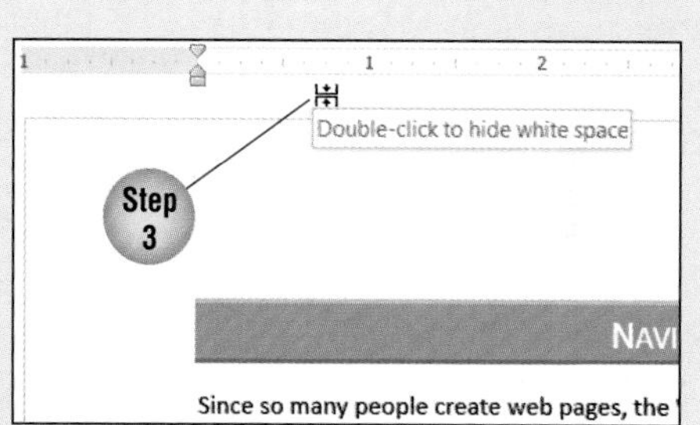

4. Scroll through the document and notice the display of pages.
5. Redisplay the white spaces at the tops and bottoms of pages by positioning the mouse pointer on any thin, gray line separating pages until the pointer turns into the Show White Space icon and then double-clicking the left mouse button.

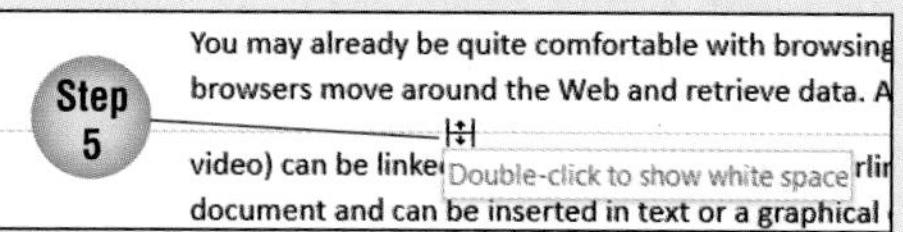

6. Close **WebReport.docx**.

Project 2 Format a Document on Online Etiquette Guidelines — 2 Parts

You will open a document containing information on guidelines for online etiquette and then change the margins, page orientation, and page size.

Changing Page Setup

The Page Setup group on the PAGE LAYOUT tab contains a number of options for affecting pages in a document. With options in the Page Setup group, you can perform such actions as changing margins, orientation, and page size and inserting page breaks. The Pages group on the INSERT tab contains three buttons for inserting a cover page, blank page, and page break.

Changing Margins

Quick Steps

Change Margins
1. Click PAGE LAYOUT tab.
2. Click Margins button.
3. Click desired margin option.

Change Page Orientation
1. Click PAGE LAYOUT tab.
2. Click Orientation button.
3. Click desired orientation.

Change Page Size
1. Click PAGE LAYOUT tab.
2. Click Size button.
3. Click desired size option.

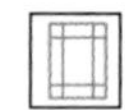

Margins

Orientation

Size

Change page margins with options at the Margins button drop-down list, as shown in Figure 4.3. To display this list, click the PAGE LAYOUT tab and then click the Margins button in the Page Setup group. To change the margins, click one of the preset margins that display in the drop-down list. Be aware that most printers have a required margin (between ¼ and ⅜ inch) because printers cannot print to the edge of the page.

Changing Page Orientation

Click the Orientation button in the Page Setup group on the PAGE LAYOUT tab, and two options display—*Portrait* and *Landscape*. At the portrait orientation, which is the default, the page is 11 inches tall and 8.5 inches wide. At the landscape orientation, the page is 8.5 inches tall and 11 inches wide. Change the page orientation and the page margins automatically change.

Changing Page Size

By default, Word uses a page size of 8.5 inches wide and 11 inches tall. Change this default setting with options at the Size button drop-down list. Display this drop-down list by clicking the Size button in the Page Setup group on the PAGE LAYOUT tab.

Figure 4.3 Margins Drop-down List

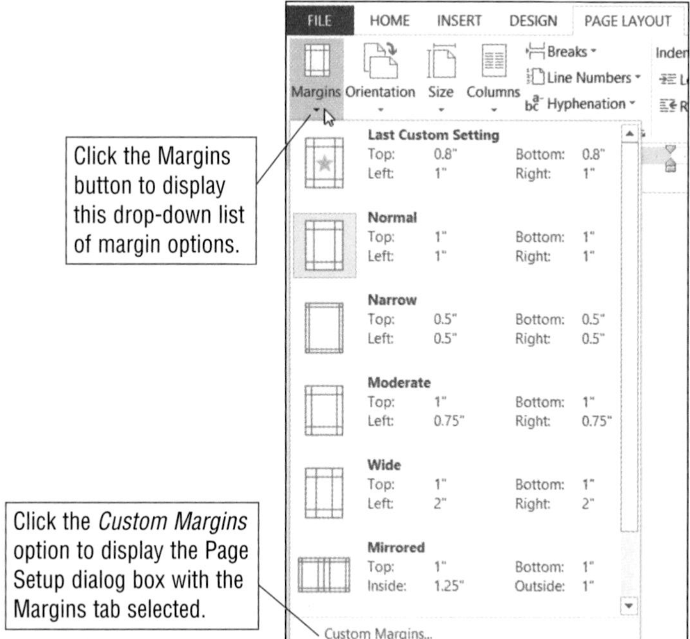

Project 2a Changing Margins, Page Orientation, and Size — Part 1 of 2

1. Open **Netiquette.docx**.
2. Save the document with Save As and name it **WL1-C4-P2-Netiquette**.
3. Click the PAGE LAYOUT tab.
4. Click the Margins button in the Page Setup group and then click the *Narrow* option.
5. Click the Orientation button in the Page Setup group.
6. Click *Landscape* at the drop-down list.

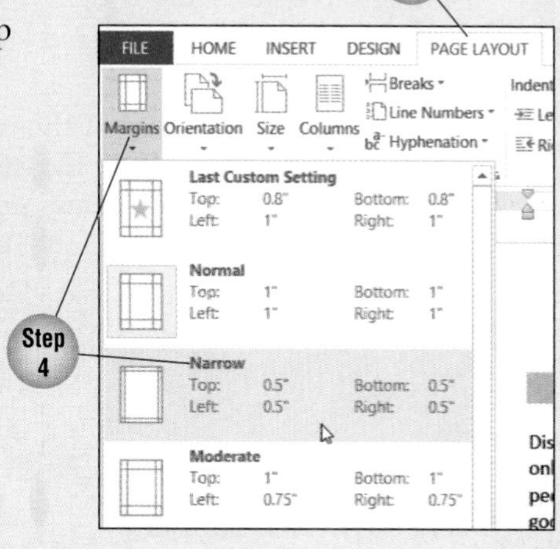

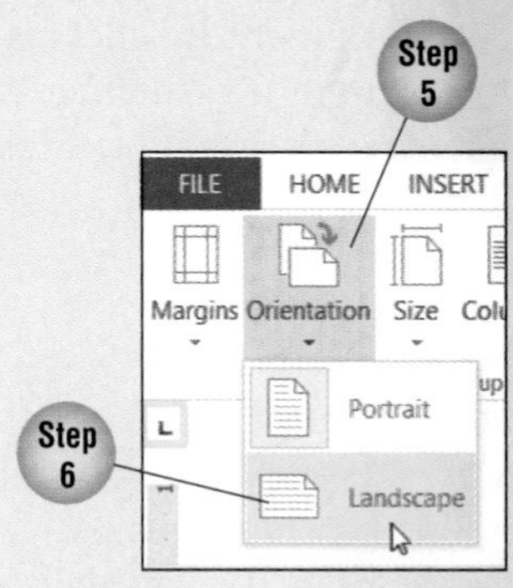

7. Scroll through the document and notice how the text displays on the page in landscape orientation.
8. Click the Orientation button in the Page Setup group and then click *Portrait* at the drop-down list. (This changes the orientation back to the default.)
9. Click the Size button in the Page Setup group.
10. Click the *Executive* option (displays with *7.25" × 10.5"* below *Executive*). If this option is not available, choose an option with a similar size.

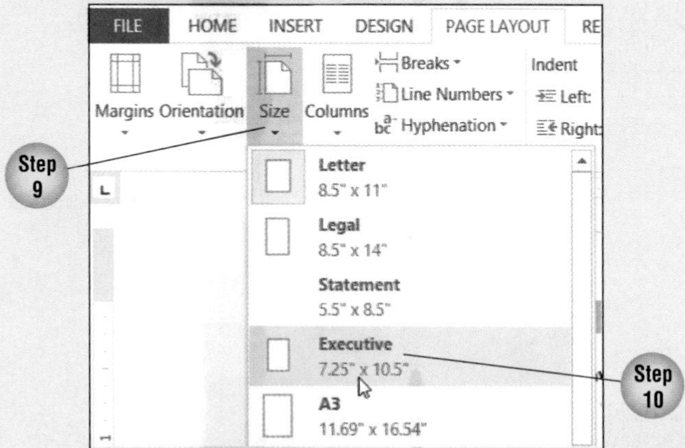

11. Scroll through the document and notice how the text displays on the page.
12. Click the Size button and then click *Legal* (displays with *8.5" × 14"* below *Legal*).
13. Scroll through the document and notice how the text displays on the page.
14. Click the Size button and then click *Letter* (displays with *8.5" × 11"* below *Letter*). (This returns the size back to the default.)
15. Save **WL1-C4-P2-Netiquette.docx**.

Changing Margins at the Page Setup Dialog Box

Quick Steps

Change Margins at the Page Setup Dialog Box
1. Click PAGE LAYOUT tab.
2. Click Page Setup group dialog box launcher.
3. Specify desired margins.
4. Click OK.

Change Page Size at the Page Setup Dialog Box
1. Click PAGE LAYOUT tab.
2. Click Size button.
3. Click *More Paper Sizes* at drop-down list.
4. Specify desired size.
5. Click OK.

The Margins button in the Page Setup group provides you with a number of preset margins. If these margins do not fit your needs, you can set specific margins at the Page Setup dialog box with the Margins tab selected, as shown in Figure 4.4. Display this dialog box by clicking the Page Setup group dialog box launcher or by clicking the Margins button and then clicking *Custom Margins* at the bottom of the drop-down list.

To change one of the margins, select the current measurement in the *Top*, *Bottom*, *Left*, or *Right* measurement box, and then type the new measurement. You can also increase a measurement by clicking the up-pointing arrow at the right side of the measurement box. Decrease a measurement by clicking the down-pointing arrow. As you make changes to the margin measurements at the Page Setup dialog box, the sample page in the *Preview* section illustrates the effects of the changes.

Changing Paper Size at the Page Setup Dialog Box

The Size button drop-down list contains a number of preset page sizes. If these sizes do not fit your needs, specify a page size at the Page Setup dialog box with the Paper tab selected. Display this dialog box by clicking the Size button in the Page Setup group and then clicking *More Paper Sizes* that displays at the bottom of the drop-down list.

Figure 4.4 Page Setup Dialog Box with Margins Tab Selected

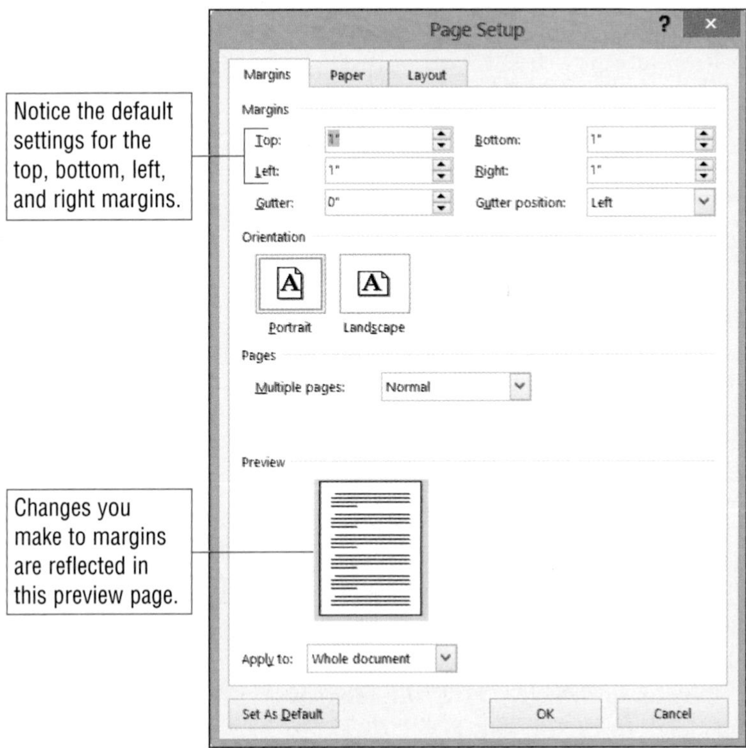

Project 2b Changing Margins at the Page Setup Dialog Box — Part 2 of 2

1. With **WL1-C4-P2-Netiquette.docx** open, make sure the PAGE LAYOUT tab is selected.
2. Click the Page Setup group dialog box launcher.
3. At the Page Setup dialog box with the Margins tab selected, click the up-pointing arrow at the right side of the *Top* measurement box until *0.7"* displays.
4. Click the up-pointing arrow at the right side of the *Bottom* measurement box until *0.7"* displays.
5. Select the current measurement in the *Left* measurement box and then type **0.75**.
6. Select the current measurement in the *Right* measurement box and then type **0.75**.
7. Click OK to close the dialog box.
8. Click the Size button in the Page Setup group and then click *More Paper Sizes* at the drop-down list.
9. At the Page Setup dialog box with the Paper tab selected, click the down-pointing arrow at the right side of the *Paper size* option box and then click *Legal* at the drop-down list.
10. Click OK to close the dialog box.
11. Scroll through the document and notice how the text displays on the page.
12. Click the Size button in the Page Setup group and then click *Letter* at the drop-down list.
13. Save, print, and then close **WL1-C4-P2-Netiquette.docx**.

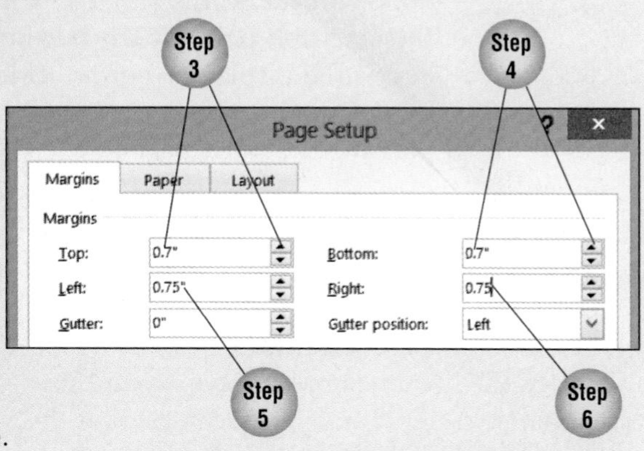

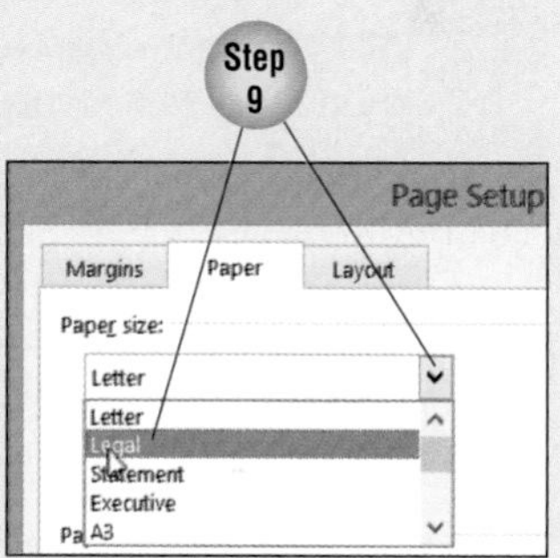

Project 3 Customize a Report on Computer Input and Output Devices — 3 Parts

You will open a document containing information on computer input and output devices and then insert page breaks, a blank page, a cover page, and page numbering.

Inserting a Page Break

With the default top and bottom margins of 1 inch, approximately 9 inches of text print on the page. At approximately the 10-inch mark, Word automatically inserts a page break. You can insert your own page break in a document with the keyboard shortcut Ctrl + Enter or with the Page Break button in the Pages group on the INSERT tab.

A page break inserted by Word is considered a ***soft page break***, and a page break inserted by you is considered a ***hard page break***. Soft page breaks automatically adjust if you add or delete text from a document. Hard page breaks do not adjust and are therefore less flexible than soft page breaks.

Quick Steps

Insert a Page Break
1. Click INSERT tab.
2. Click Page Break button.

OR

Press Ctrl + Enter.

Page Break

If you add or delete text from a document with a hard page break, check the break to determine whether it is still in a desirable location. Display a hard page break along with other nonprinting characters by clicking the Show/Hide ¶ button in the Paragraph group on the HOME tab. A hard page break displays as a row of dots with the words *Page Break* in the center. To delete a hard page break, position the insertion point at the beginning of the page break and then press the Delete key. If the display of nonprinting characters is turned off, delete a hard page break by positioning the insertion point immediately below the page break and then pressing the Backspace key.

Project 3a **Inserting Page Breaks** Parts 1 of 3

1. Open **CompDevices.docx**.
2. Save the document with Save As and name it **WL1-C4-P3-CompDevices**.
3. Change the top margin by completing the following steps:
   a. Click the PAGE LAYOUT tab.
   b. Click the Page Setup group dialog box launcher.
   c. At the Page Setup dialog box, click the Margins tab and then type 1.5 in the *Top* measurement box.
   d. Click OK to close the dialog box.

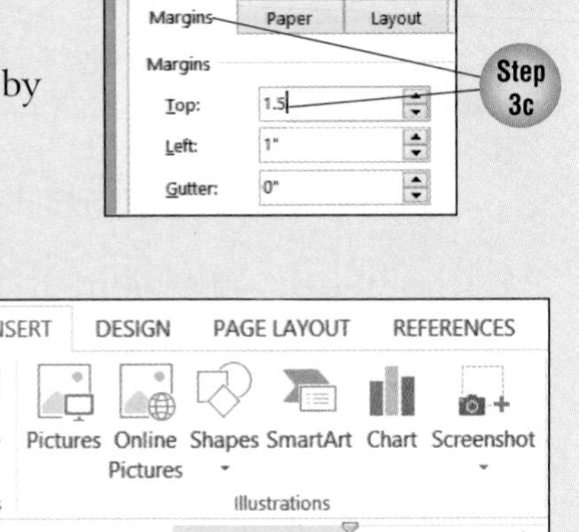

4. Insert a page break at the beginning of the heading *Mouse* by completing the following steps:
   a. Position the insertion point at the beginning of the heading *Mouse* (located toward the bottom of page 1).
   b. Click the INSERT tab and then click the Page Break button in the Pages group.
5. Move the insertion point to the beginning of the title *COMPUTER OUTPUT DEVICES* (located on the second page) and then insert a page break by pressing Ctrl + Enter.
6. Move the insertion point to the beginning of the heading *Printer* and then press Ctrl + Enter to insert a page break.
7. Delete a page break by completing the following steps:
   a. Click the HOME tab.
   b. Click the Show/Hide ¶ button in the Paragraph group.
   c. Scroll up to display the bottom of the third page, position the insertion point at the beginning of the page break (displays with the words *Page Break*), and then press the Delete key.
   d. Press the Delete key again to remove the blank line.
   e. Turn off the display of nonprinting characters by clicking the Show/Hide ¶ button in the Paragraph group on the HOME tab.
8. Save **WL1-C4-P3-CompDevices.docx**.

Inserting a Blank Page

Click the Blank Page button in the Pages group on the INSERT tab to insert a blank page at the position of the insertion point. This might be useful in a document where you want to insert a blank page for an illustration, graphic, or figure.

Inserting a Cover Page

If you are preparing a document for distribution to others or you want to simply improve the visual appeal of your document, consider inserting a cover page. With the Cover Page button in the Pages group on the INSERT tab, you can insert a predesigned and formatted cover page and then type personalized text in specific locations on the page. Click the Cover Page button and a drop-down list displays. The drop-down list provides a visual representation of the cover page. Scroll through the list and then click the desired cover page.

A predesigned cover page contains location placeholders where you enter specific information. For example, a cover page might contain the placeholder *[Document title]*. Click anywhere in the placeholder text and the placeholder text is selected. With the placeholder text selected, type the desired text. Delete a placeholder by clicking anywhere in the placeholder text, clicking the placeholder tab, and then pressing the Delete key.

Quick Steps

Insert Blank Page
1. Click INSERT tab.
2. Click Blank Page button.

Insert Cover Page
1. Click INSERT tab.
2. Click Cover Page button.
3. Click desired cover page at drop-down list.

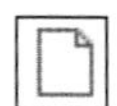
Blank Page

Cover Page

A cover page provides a polished and professional look to a document.

Project 3b **Inserting a Blank Page and a Cover Page** **Part 2 of 3**

1. With **WL1-C4-P3-CompDevices.docx** open, create a blank page by completing the following steps:
   a. Move the insertion point to the beginning of the heading *Touchpad and Touchscreen* located on the second page.
   b. Click the INSERT tab.
   c. Click the Blank Page button in the Pages group.

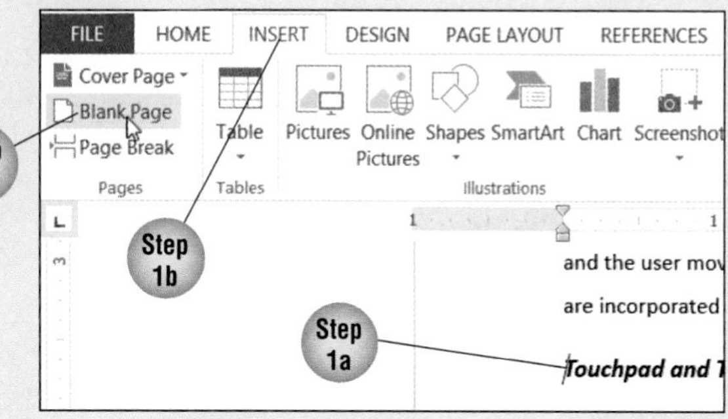

2. Insert a cover page by completing the following steps:
   a. Press Ctrl + Home to move the insertion point to the beginning of the document.
   b. Click the Cover Page button in the Pages group.
   c. At the drop-down list, scroll down and then click the *Motion* cover page.

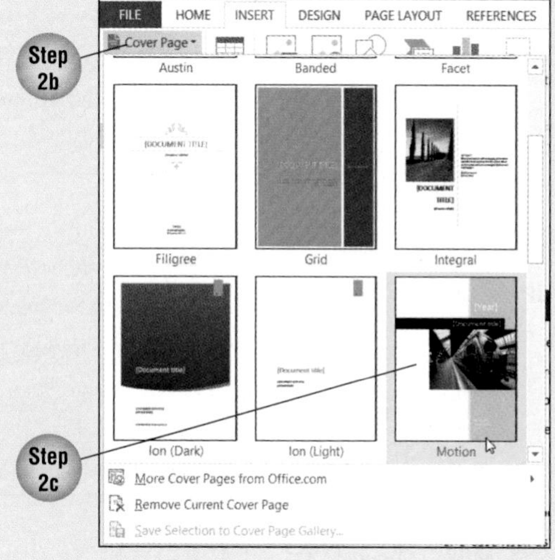

d. Click anywhere in the placeholder text *[Document title]* and then type **Computer Devices**.

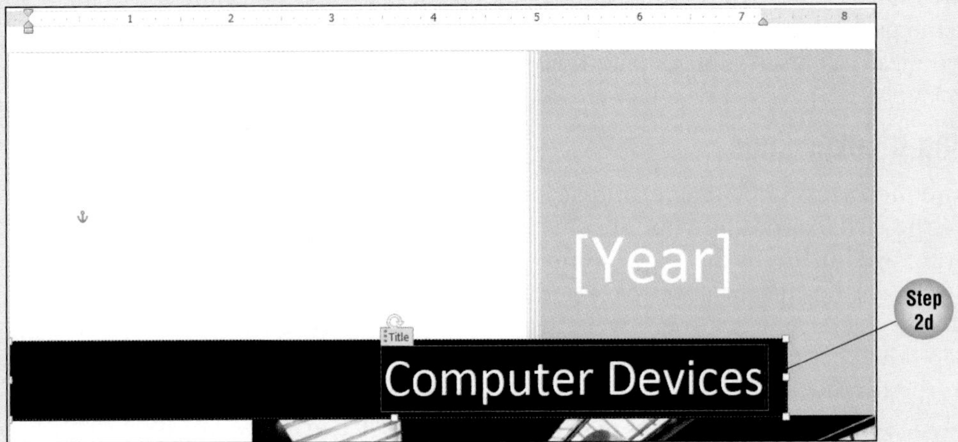

e. Click the placeholder text *[Year]*. Click the down-pointing arrow that displays at the right side of the placeholder and then click the Today button that displays at the bottom of the drop-down calendar.

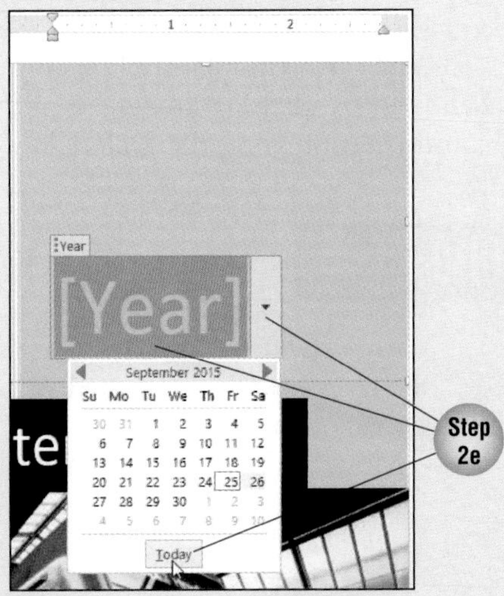

f. Click anywhere in the placeholder text *[Company name]* and then type **Drake Computing**. (If a name displays in the placeholder, select the name and then type **Drake Computing**.)

g. Select the name that displays above the company name and then type your first and last names. If, instead of a name, the *[Author name]* placeholder displays above the company name, click anywhere in the placeholder text and then type your first and last names.

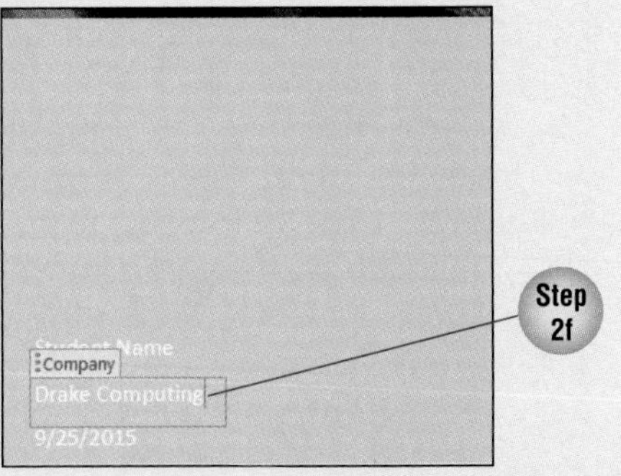

3. Remove the blank page you inserted in Step 1 by completing the following steps:
   a. Move the insertion point immediately right of the period that ends the last sentence in the paragraph of text in the *Trackball* heading (located toward the bottom of page 3).
   b. Press the Delete key on the keyboard approximately six times until the heading *Touchpad and Touchscreen* displays on page 3.

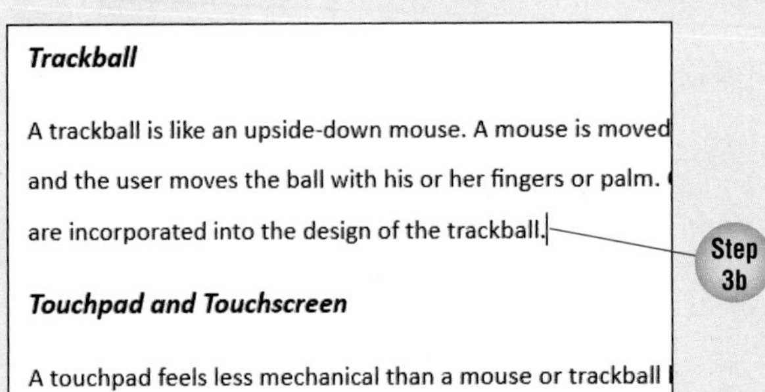

Trackball
A trackball is like an upside-down mouse. A mouse is moved
and the user moves the ball with his or her fingers or palm.
are incorporated into the design of the trackball.
Touchpad and Touchscreen
A touchpad feels less mechanical than a mouse or trackball
Step 3b

4. Save **WL1-C4-P3-CompDevices.docx**.

Inserting Predesigned Page Numbering

Word, by default, does not print page numbers on pages. If you want to insert page numbering in a document, use the Page Number button in the Header & Footer group on the INSERT tab. When you click the Page Number button, a drop-down list displays with options for specifying the page number location. Point to an option at this list and a drop-down list displays of predesigned page number formats. Scroll through the options in the drop-down list and then click the desired option.

If you want to change the format of page numbering in a document, double-click the page number, select the page number text, and then apply the desired formatting. Remove page numbering from a document by clicking the Page Number button and then clicking *Remove Page Numbers* at the drop-down list.

Quick Steps

Insert Page Numbering

1. Click INSERT tab.
2. Click Page Number button.
3. Click desired option at drop-down list.

Page Number

Project 3c **Inserting Predesigned Page Numbering** **Part 3 of 3**

1. With **WL1-C4-P3-CompDevices.docx** open, insert page numbering by completing the following steps:
   a. Move the insertion point so it is positioned on any character in the title *COMPUTER INPUT DEVICES*.
   b. Click the INSERT tab.
   c. Click the Page Number button in the Header & Footer group and then point to *Top of Page*.
   d. Scroll through the drop-down list and then click the *Brackets 2* option.

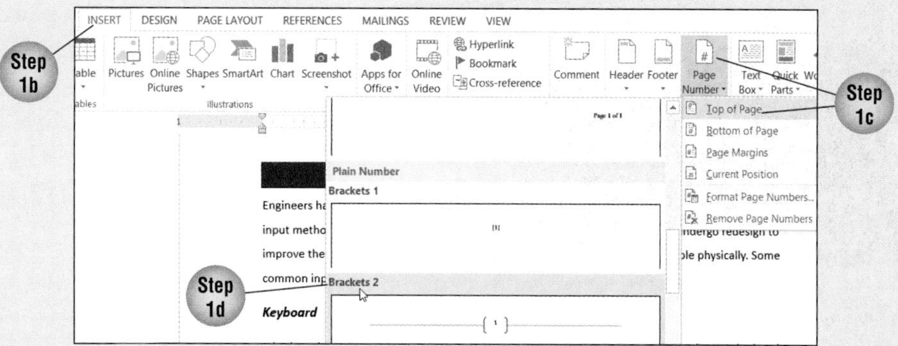

2. Double-click in the document text. (This makes the document text active and dims the page number.)
3. Scroll through the document and notice the page numbering that displays at the top of each page except the cover page. (The cover page and text are divided by a page break. Word does not include the cover page when numbering pages.)
4. Remove the page numbering by clicking the INSERT tab, clicking the Page Number button, and then clicking *Remove Page Numbers* at the drop-down list.
5. Click the Page Number button, point to *Bottom of Page*, scroll down the drop-down list, and then click the *Accent Bar 2* option.
6. Double-click in the document to make it active.
7. Save, print, and then close **WL1-C4-P3-CompDevices.docx**.

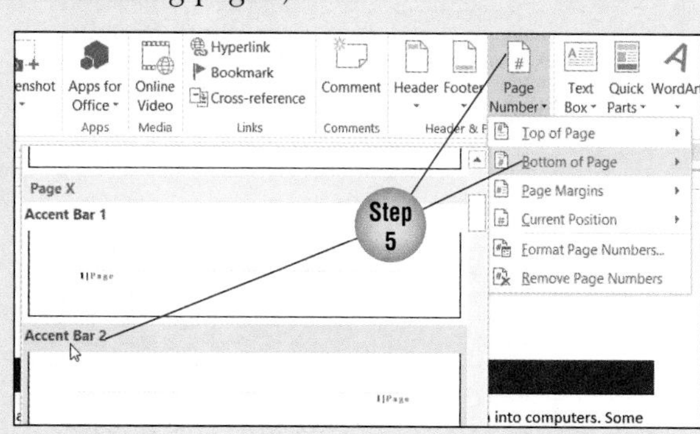

Project 4 Add Elements to a Report on the Writing Process — 3 Parts

You will open a document containing information on the process of writing effectively, insert a predesigned header and footer in the document, remove a header, and format and delete header and footer elements.

Inserting Predesigned Headers and Footers

Quick Steps

Insert Predesigned Header
1. Click INSERT tab.
2. Click Header button.
3. Click desired option at drop-down list.
4. Type text in specific placeholders in header.

Header

Text that appears in the top margin of a page is called a ***header*** and text that appears in the bottom margin of a page is referred to as a ***footer***. Headers and footers are common in manuscripts, textbooks, reports, and other publications. Insert a predesigned header in a document by clicking the INSERT tab and then clicking the Header button in the Header & Footer group. This displays the Header button drop-down list. At this list, click the desired predesigned header option and the header is inserted in the document. Headers and footers are visible in Print Layout view but not Draft view.

A predesigned header or footer may contain location placeholders for entering specific information. For example, a header might contain the placeholder *[Document title]*. Click anywhere in the placeholder text and all of the placeholder text is selected. With the placeholder text selected, type the desired text. Delete a placeholder by clicking anywhere in the placeholder text, clicking the placeholder tab, and then pressing the Delete key.

To return to your document after inserting a header or footer, double-click in the document. You can also return to the document by clicking the Close Header and Footer button on the HEADER & FOOTER TOOLS DESIGN tab.

Project 4a Inserting a Predesigned Header in a Document — Part 1 of 3

1. Open **WritingProcess.docx**.
2. Save the document with Save As and name it **WL1-C4-P4-WritingProcess**.
3. Move the insertion point to the end of the document.
4. Move the insertion point to the beginning of the *REFERENCES* heading and then insert a page break by clicking the INSERT tab and then clicking the Page Break button in the Pages group.

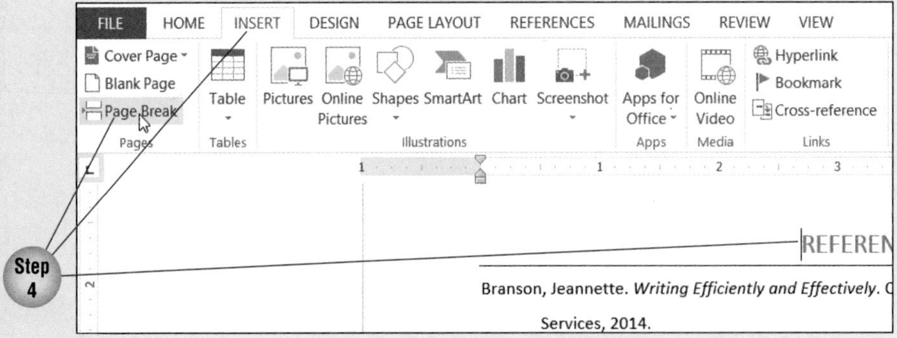

5. Press Ctrl + Home to move the insertion point to the beginning of the document and then insert a header by completing the following steps:
   a. If necessary, click the INSERT tab.
   b. Click the Header button in the Header & Footer group.
   c. Scroll to the bottom of the drop-down list that displays and then click the *Sideline* option.

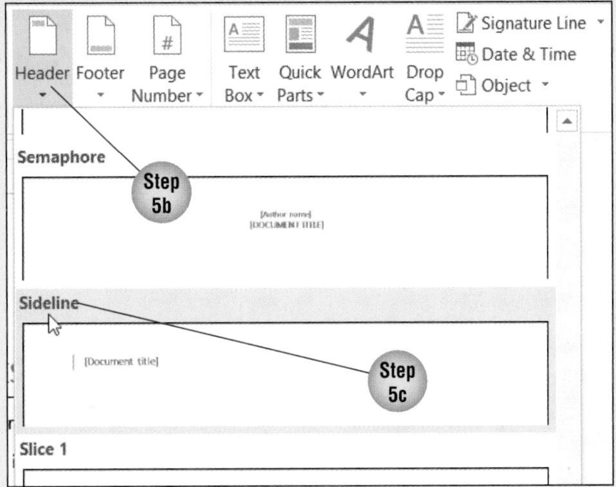

   d. Click anywhere in the placeholder text *[Document title]* and then type **The Writing Process**.
   e. Double-click in the document text. (This makes the document text active and dims the header.)

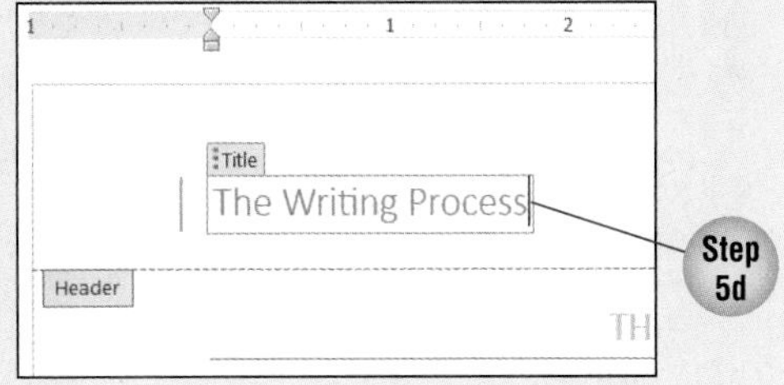

6. Scroll through the document to see how the header will print.
7. Save and then print **WL1-C4-P4-WritingProcess.docx**.

Insert a predesigned footer in the same manner as inserting a header. Click the Footer button in the Header & Footer group on the INSERT tab and a drop-down list displays similar to the Header button drop-down list. Click the desired footer and the predesigned footer formatting is applied to the document.

Quick Steps

Insert Predesigned Footer

1. Click INSERT tab.
2. Click Footer button.
3. Click desired option at drop-down list.
4. Type text in specific placeholders in footer.

Footer

Removing a Header or Footer

Remove a header from a document by clicking the INSERT tab and then clicking the Header button in the Header & Footer group. At the drop-down list that displays, click the *Remove Header* option. Complete similar steps to remove a footer.

Project 4b Removing a Header and Inserting a Predesigned Footer Part 2 of 3

1. With **WL1-C4-P4-WritingProcess.docx** open, press Ctrl + Home to move the insertion point to the beginning of the document.
2. Remove the header by clicking the INSERT tab, clicking the Header button in the Header & Footer group, and then clicking the *Remove Header* option at the drop-down menu.
3. Insert a footer in the document by completing the following steps:
   a. Click the Footer button in the Header & Footer group.
   b. Scroll down the drop-down list and then click *Ion (Light)*.

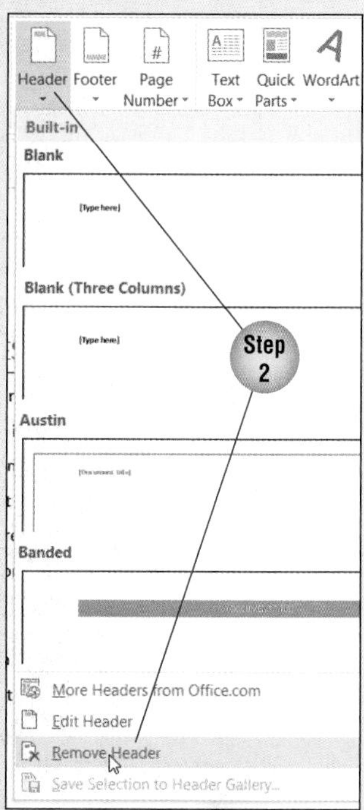

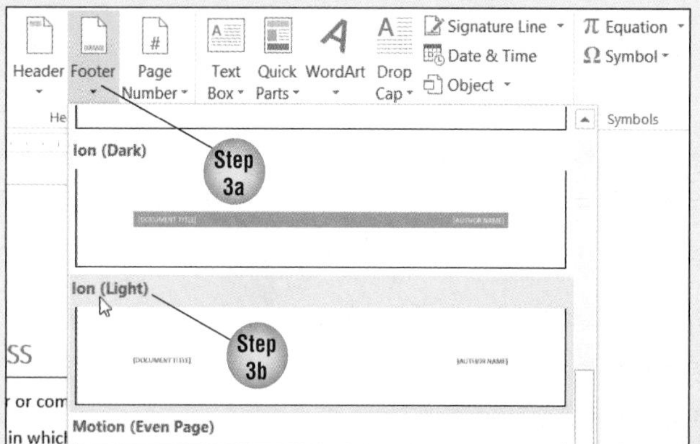

   c. Notice that Word inserted the document title at the left side of the footer (Word remembered the document title you entered in the header) and your name at the right side of the footer. If the document title does not display, click anywhere in the placeholder *[DOCUMENT TITLE]* and then type **THE WRITING PROCESS**, and if your name does not display, click anywhere in the placeholder *[AUTHOR NAME]* and then type your first and last names.
   d. Click the Close Header and Footer button on the HEADER & FOOTER TOOLS DESIGN tab to close the Footer pane and return to the document.
4. Scroll through the document to see how the footer will print.
5. Save and then print **WL1-C4-P4-WritingProcess.docx**.

Editing a Predesigned Header or Footer

Predesigned headers and footers contain elements such as page numbers and a title. You can change the formatting of the element by clicking the desired element and then applying the desired formatting. You can also select and then delete an item.

Project 4c Formatting and Deleting Header and Footer Elements Part 3 of 3

1. With **WL1-C4-P4-WritingProcess.docx** open, remove the footer by clicking the INSERT tab, clicking the Footer button, and then clicking *Remove Footer* at the drop-down list.

2. Insert and then format a header by completing the following steps:
   a. Click the Header button in the Header & Footer group on the INSERT tab, scroll down the drop-down list, and then click *Grid*. (This header inserts the document title as well as a date placeholder.)
   b. Delete the Date placeholder by clicking anywhere in the *[Date]* placeholder text, clicking the placeholder tab, and then pressing the Delete key.
   c. Double-click in the document text.

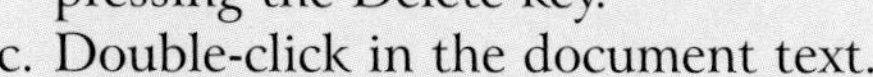

3. Insert and then format a footer by completing the following steps:
   a. Click the INSERT tab.
   b. Click the Footer button, scroll down the drop-down list, and then click *Retrospect*.
   c. Select the name that displays in the Author tab located at the left side of the footer and then type your first and last names.
   d. Select your name and the page number, turn on bold formatting, and then change the font size to 10 points.
   e. Double-click in the document text.
4. Scroll through the document to see how the header and footer will print.
5. Save, print, and then close **WL1-C4-P4-WritingProcess.docx**.

Project 5 Format a Report on Desirable Employee Qualities 2 Parts

You will open a document containing information on desirable employee qualities and then insert a watermark, change page background color, and insert a page border.

Formatting the Page Background

The Page Background group on the DESIGN tab contains three buttons for customizing a page background. Click the Watermark button and choose a predesigned watermark from a drop-down list. If a document is going to be viewed on-screen or on the Web, consider adding a page color. In Chapter 3, you learned how to apply borders and shading to text at the Borders and Shading dialog box. This dialog box also contains options for inserting a page border.

Inserting a Watermark

A ***watermark*** is a lightened image that displays behind text in a document. Use a watermark to add visual appeal to a document or to identify a document as a draft, sample, or confidential document. Word provides a number of predesigned watermarks you can insert in a document. Display these watermarks by clicking the Watermark button in the Page Background group on the DESIGN tab. Scroll through the list of watermarks and then click the desired option.

Quick Steps

Insert a Watermark
1. Click DESIGN tab.
2. Click Watermark button.
3. Click desired option at drop-down list.

Change the Page Color
1. Click DESIGN tab.
2. Click Page Color button.
3. Click desired option at color palette.

Watermark

Changing Page Color

Page Color

Use the Page Color button in the Page Background group to apply background color to a document. This background color is intended for viewing a document on-screen or on the Web. The color is visible on the screen but does not print. Insert a page color by clicking the Page Color button and then clicking the desired color at the color palette.

Project 5a Inserting a Watermark and Changing Page Color — Part 1 of 2

1. Open **EmpQualities.docx** and then save the document with Save As and name it **WL1-C4-P5-EmpQualities**.
2. Insert a watermark by completing the following steps:
   a. With the insertion point positioned at the beginning of the document, click the DESIGN tab.
   b. Click the Watermark button in the Page Background group.
   c. At the drop-down list, click the *CONFIDENTIAL 1* option.
3. Scroll through the document and notice how the watermark displays behind the text.
4. Remove the watermark and insert a different one by completing the following steps:
   a. Click the Watermark button in the Page Background group and then click *Remove Watermark* at the drop-down list.
   b. Click the Watermark button and then click the *DO NOT COPY 1* option at the drop-down list.
5. Scroll through the document and notice how the watermark displays.
6. Move the insertion point to the beginning of the document.
7. Click the Page Color button in the Page Background group and then click *Tan, Background 2* (third column, first row) at the color palette.

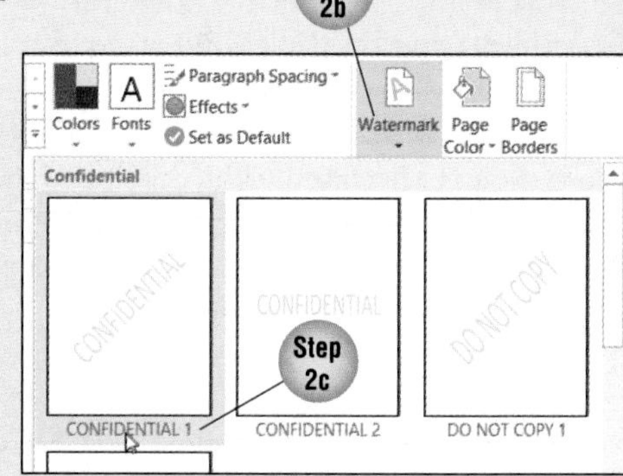

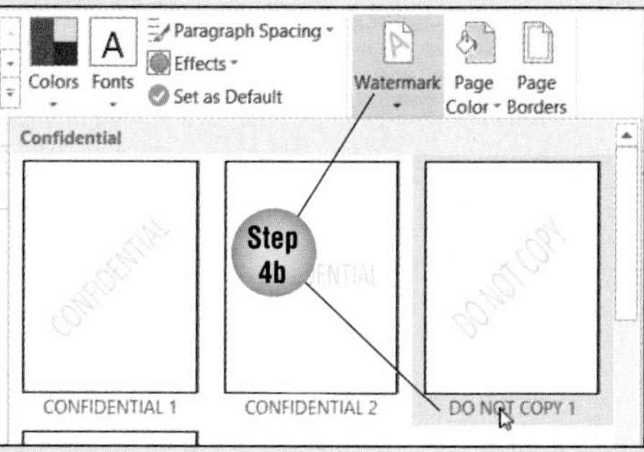

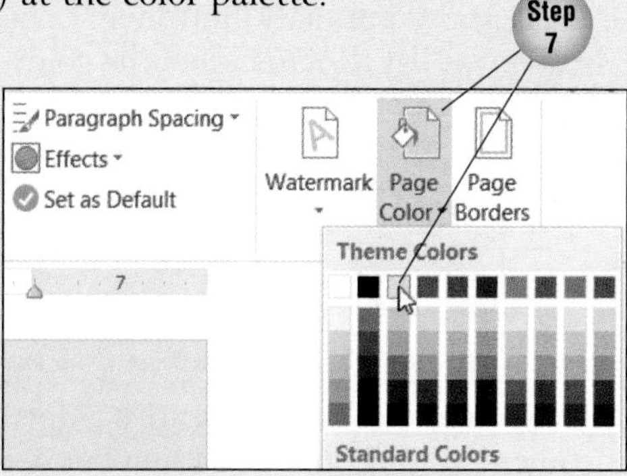

8. Save **WL1-C4-P5-EmpQualities.docx**.

Inserting a Page Border

To improve the visual appeal of a document, consider inserting a page border. When you insert a page border in a multiple-page document, the border prints on each page. To insert a page border, click the Page Borders button in the Page Background group on the DESIGN tab. This displays the Borders and Shading dialog box with the Page Border tab selected, as shown in Figure 4.5. At this dialog box, specify the border style, color, and width.

The dialog box contains an option for inserting a page border containing an image. To display the images available, click the down-pointing arrow at the right side of the *Art* option box. Scroll down the drop-down list and then click the desired image.

Quick Steps

Insert Page Border
1. Click DESIGN tab.
2. Click Page Borders button.
3. Specify desired options at dialog box.

Page Borders

Changing Page Border Options

By default, a page border displays and prints 24 points from the top, left, right, and bottom edges of the page. Some printers, particularly inkjet printers, have a nonprinting area around the outside edges of the page that can interfere with the printing of a border. Before printing a document with a page border, click the FILE tab and then click the *Print* option. Look at the preview of the page at the right side of the Print backstage area and determine whether the entire border is visible. If a portion of the border is not visible in the preview page (generally at the bottom and right sides of the page), consider changing measurements at the Border and Shading Options dialog box shown in Figure 4.6. You can also change measurements at the Border and Shading Options dialog box to control the location of the page border on the page.

Display the Border and Shading Options dialog box by clicking the DESIGN tab and then clicking the Page Borders button. At the Borders and Shading dialog box with the Page Border tab selected, click the Options button that displays in the lower right corner of the dialog box. The options at the Border and Shading Options dialog box change depending on whether you click the Options button at the Borders and Shading dialog box with the Borders tab selected or the Page Border tab selected.

Figure 4.5 Borders and Shading Dialog Box with Page Border Tab Selected

Click this down-pointing arrow to scroll through a list of page border styles.

Click this down-pointing arrow to display a list of width points.

Click this down-pointing arrow to display a list of art border images.

Preview the page border in this section.

Click this down-pointing arrow to display a palette of page border colors.

Click this button to display the Border and Shading Options dialog box.

Figure 4.6 Border and Shading Options Dialog Box

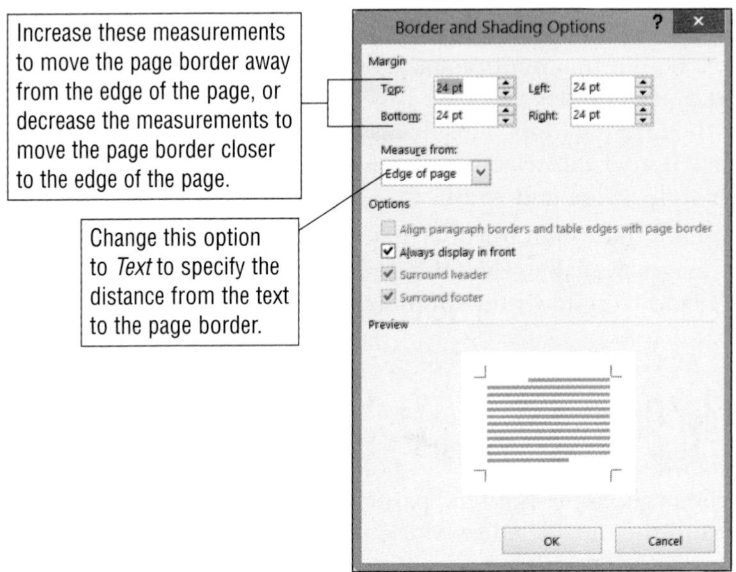

If your printer contains a nonprinting area and the entire page border will not print, consider increasing the spacing from the page border to the edge of the page. Do this with the *Top*, *Left*, *Bottom*, and/or *Right* measurement boxes. The *Measure from* option box has a default setting of *Edge of page*. You can change this option to *Text*, which changes the top and bottom measurements to *1 pt* and the left and right measurements to *4 pt* and moves the page border into the page. Use the measurement boxes to specify the distance you want the page border displayed and printed from the text in the document.

Project 5b Inserting a Page Border

Part 2 of 2

1. With **WL1-C4-P5-EmpQualities.docx** open, remove the page color by clicking the Page Color button in the Page Background group on the DESIGN tab and then clicking *No Color* at the color palette.
2. Insert a page border by completing the following steps:
   a. Click the Page Borders button in the Page Background group on the DESIGN tab.
   b. Click the *Box* option in the *Setting* section.
   c. Scroll down the list of line styles in the *Style* list box until the last line style displays and then click the third line from the end.
   d. Click the down-pointing arrow at the right of the *Color* option box and then click *Dark Red, Accent 2* (sixth column, first row) at the color palette.
   e. Click OK to close the dialog box.

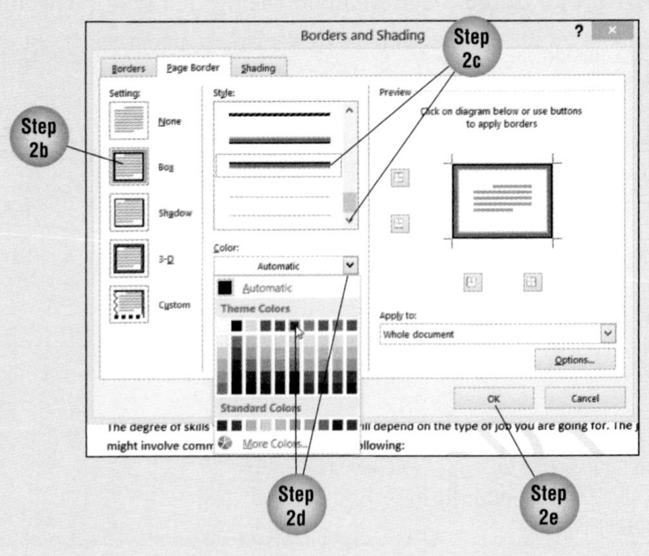

3. Increase the spacing from the page border to the edges of the page by completing the following steps:
   a. Click the Page Borders button in the Page Background group on the DESIGN tab.
   b. At the Borders and Shading dialog box with the Page Border tab selected, click the Options button located in the lower right corner.
   c. At the Border and Shading Options dialog box, click the up-pointing arrow at the right side of the *Top* measurement box until *31 pt* displays. (This is the maximum measurement allowed.)
   d. Increase the measurement for the *Left, Bottom,* and *Right* measurement boxes to *31 pt*.
   e. Click OK to close the Border and Shading Options dialog box.
   f. Click OK to close the Borders and Shading dialog box.

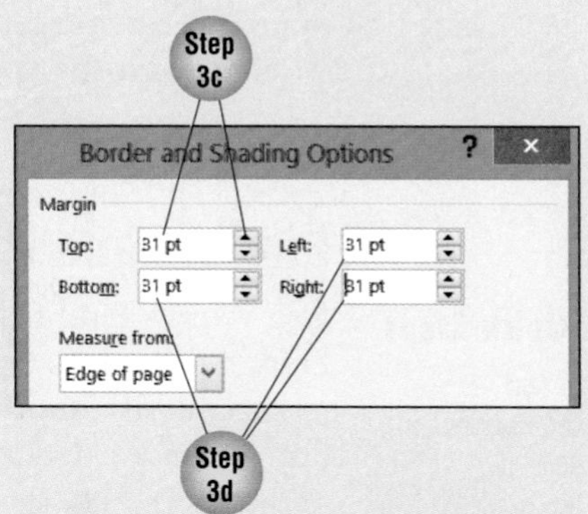

4. Save **WL1-C4-P5-EmpQualities.docx** and then print only page 1.
5. Insert an image page border and change the page border spacing options by completing the following steps:
   a. Click the Page Borders button in the Page Background group on the DESIGN tab.
   b. Click the down-pointing arrow at the right side of the *Art* option box and then click the border image shown at the right (located approximately one-third of the way down the drop-down list).
   c. Click the Options button located in the lower right corner of the Borders and Shading dialog box.
   d. At the Border and Shading Options dialog box, click the down-pointing arrow at the right of the *Measure from* option box and then click *Text* at the drop-down list.
   e. Click the up-pointing arrow at the right of the *Top* measurement box until *10 pt* displays.
   f. Increase the measurement for the *Bottom* measurement to *10 pt* and the measurements in the *Left* and *Right* measurement boxes to *14 pt*.
   g. Click the *Surround header* check box to remove the check mark.
   h. Click the *Surround footer* check box to remove the check mark.
   i. Click OK to close the Border and Shading Options dialog box.
   j. Click OK to close the Borders and Shading dialog box.

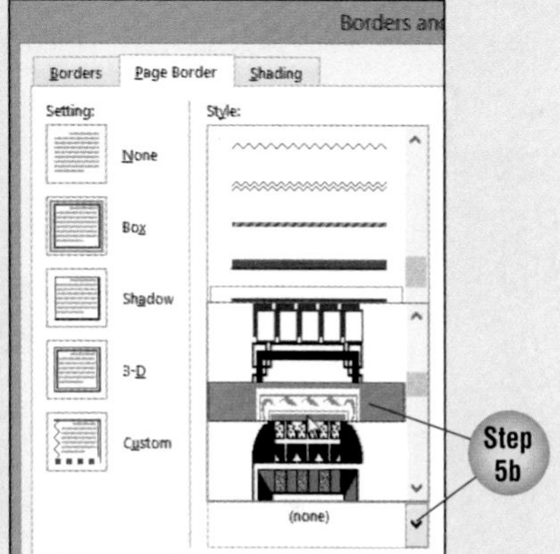

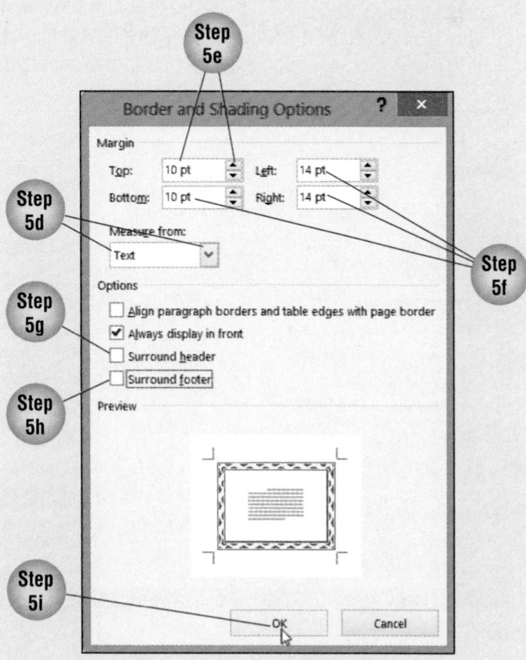

6. Save, print, and then close **WL1-C4-P5-EmpQualities.docx**.

Project 6	**Format a Lease Agreement**	**4 Parts**

You will open a lease agreement, search for specific text and replace it with other text, and then search for specific formatting and replace it with other formatting.

Finding and Replacing Text and Formatting

Quick Steps

Find Text
1. Click Find button on HOME tab.
2. Type search text.
3. Click Next Search Result button.

Find

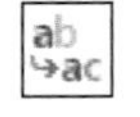
Replace

Use Word's Find feature to search for a specific character or format. With the Find and Replace feature, you can search for a specific character or format and replace it with another character or format. The Find button and the Replace button are located in the Editing group on the HOME tab.

Click the Find button in the Editing group on the HOME tab (or press the keyboard shortcut Ctrl + F) and the Navigation pane displays at the left side of the screen with the RESULTS tab selected. With this tab selected, type search text in the search text box, and any occurrence of the text in the document is highlighted. A fragment of the text surrounding the search text also displays in a thumbnail in the Navigation pane. For example, search for *Lessee* in the **WL1-C4-P6-LeaseAgrmnt.docx** document and the screen displays as shown in Figure 4.7. Notice that any occurrence of *Lessee* displays highlighted in yellow in the document and the Navigation pane displays thumbnails of text surrounding the occurrences of *Lessee*.

Figure 4.7 Navigation Pane Showing Search Results

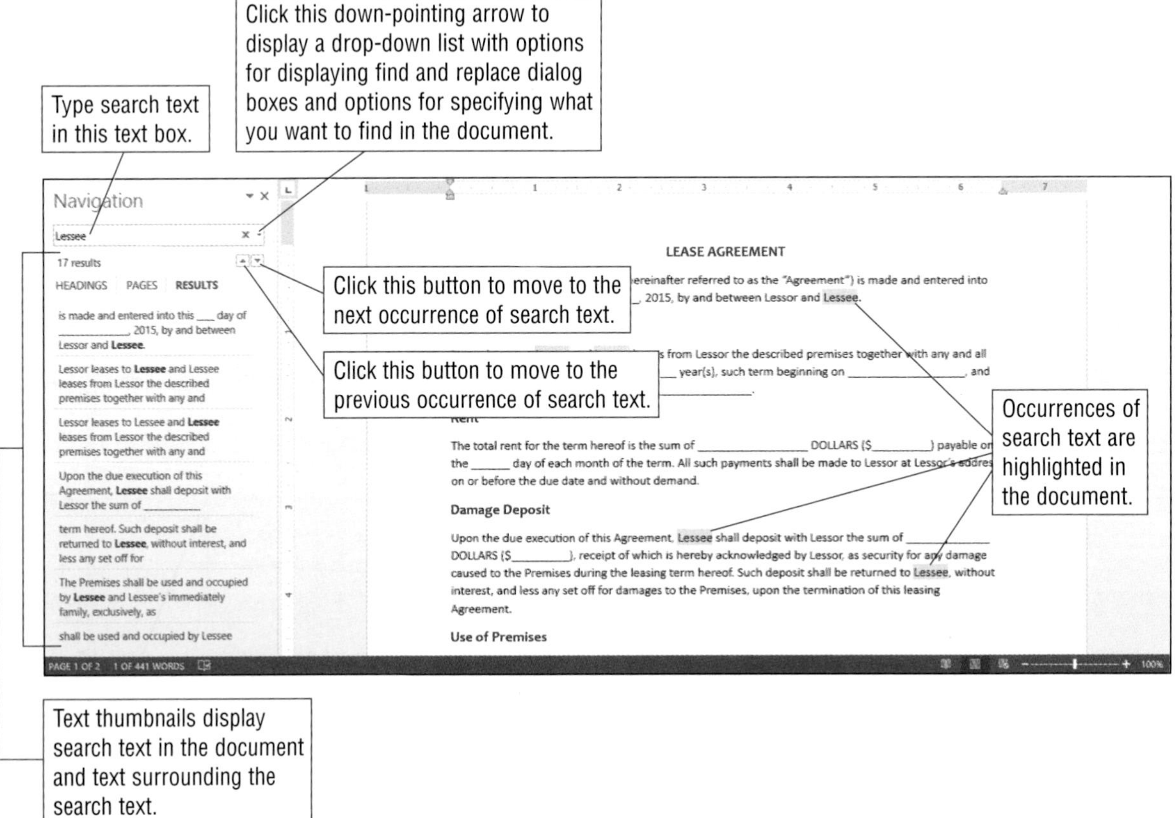

Click a text thumbnail in the Navigation pane and the occurrence of the search text is selected in the document. If you hover your mouse over a text thumbnail in the Navigation pane, the page number location displays in a small box near the mouse pointer. You can also move to the next occurrence of the search text by clicking the Next button (contains a down-pointing triangle) that displays below and to the right of the search text box. Click the Previous button (contains an up-pointing triangle) to move to the previous occurrence of the search text.

Click the down-pointing arrow at the right side of the search text box and a drop-down list displays. It shows options for displaying dialog boxes, such as the Find Options dialog box and the Find and Replace dialog box, and also options for specifying what you want to find in the document, such as figures, tables, and equations.

You can also highlight search text in a document with options at the Find and Replace dialog box with the Find tab selected. Display this dialog box by clicking the Find button arrow in the Editing group on the HOME tab and then clicking *Advanced Find* at the drop-down list. Another method for displaying the Find and Replace dialog box is to click the down-pointing arrow at the right side of the search text box in the Navigation pane and then click the *Advanced Find* option at the drop-down list. To highlight found text, type the search text in the *Find what* text box, click the Reading Highlight button, and then click *Highlight All* at the drop-down list. All occurrences of the text in the document are highlighted. To remove highlighting, click the Reading Highlight button and then click *Clear Highlighting* at the drop-down list.

Project 6a Finding and Highlighting Text — Part 1 of 4

1. Open **LeaseAgrmnt.docx** and then save the document with Save As and name it **WL1-C4-P6-LeaseAgrmnt**.
2. Find all occurrences of *lease* by completing the following steps:
   a. Click the Find button in the Editing group on the HOME tab.
   b. Click the RESULTS heading in the Navigation pane.
   c. Type lease in the search text box in the Navigation pane.
   d. After a moment, all occurrences of *lease* in the document are highlighted and text thumbnails display in the Navigation pane. Click a couple of the text thumbnails in the Navigation pane to select the text in the document.
   e. Click the Previous button (contains an up-pointing triangle) to select the previous occurrence of *lease* in the document.

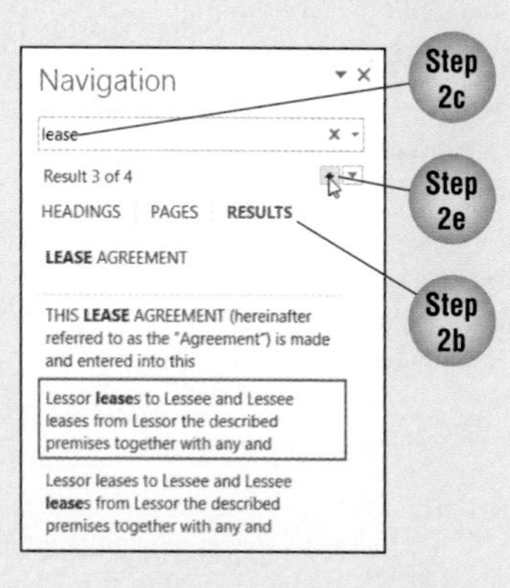

3. Use the Find and Replace dialog box with the Find tab selected to highlight all occurrences of *Premises* in the document by completing the following steps:
   a. Click in the document and press Ctrl + Home to move the insertion point to the beginning of the document.
   b. Click the down-pointing arrow at the right side of the search text box in the Navigation pane and then click *Advanced Find* at the drop-down list.

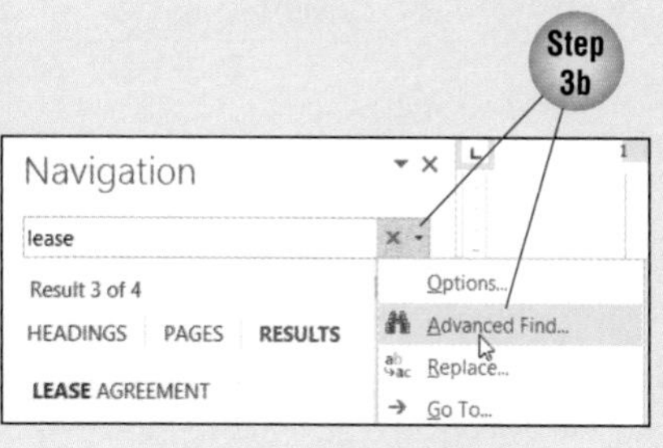

c. At the Find and Replace dialog box with the Find tab selected (and *lease* selected in the *Find what* text box), type **Premises**.
d. Click the Reading Highlight button and then click *Highlight All* at the drop-down list.
e. Click in the document to make it active and then scroll through the document and notice the occurrences of highlighted text.
f. Click in the dialog box to make it active.
g. Click the Reading Highlight button and then click *Clear Highlighting* at the drop-down list.
h. Click the Close button to close the Find and Replace dialog box.

4. Close the Navigation pane by clicking the Close button that displays in the upper right corner of the pane.

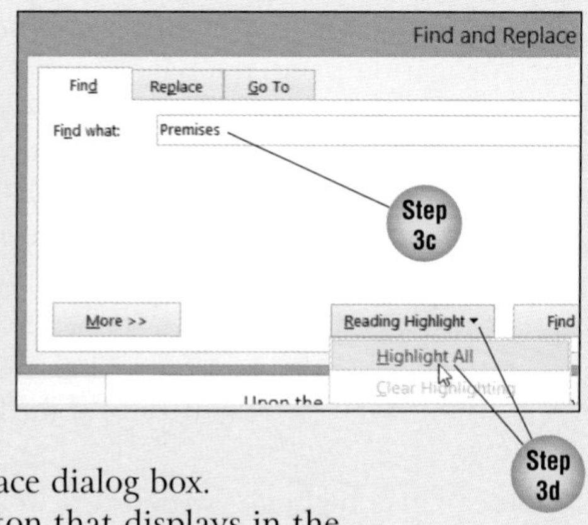

Finding and Replacing Text

Quick Steps

Find and Replace Text

1. Click Replace button on HOME tab.
2. Type search text.
3. Press Tab key.
4. Type replace text.
5. Click Replace or Replace All button.

If the Find and Replace dialog box is in the way of specific text, drag the dialog box to a different location.

To find and replace text, click the Replace button in the Editing group on the HOME tab or use the keyboard shortcut Ctrl + H. This displays the Find and Replace dialog box with the Replace tab selected, as shown in Figure 4.8. Type the text you want to find in the *Find what* text box, press the Tab key, and then type the replacement text in the Replace with text box.

The Find and Replace dialog box contains several command buttons. Click the Find Next button to tell Word to find the next occurrence of the text. Click the Replace button to replace the text and find the next occurrence. If you know that you want all occurrences of the text in the *Find what* text box replaced with the text in the *Replace with* text box, click the Replace All button. This replaces every occurrence from the location of the insertion point to the beginning or end of the document (depending on the search direction).

Figure 4.8 Find and Replace Dialog Box with the Replace Tab Selected

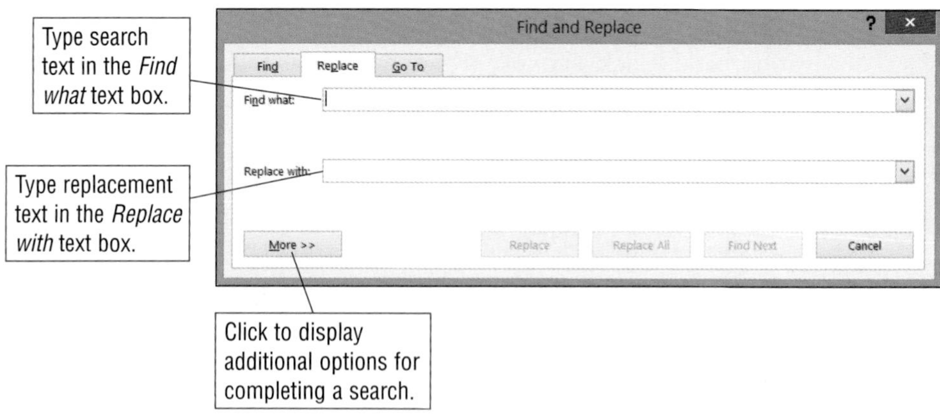

Project 6b **Finding and Replacing Text** **Part 2 of 4**

1. With **WL1-C4-P6-LeaseAgrmnt.docx** open, make sure the insertion point is positioned at the beginning of the document.
2. Find all occurrences of *Lessor* and replace with *Tracy Hartford* by completing the following steps:
   a. Click the Replace button in the Editing group on the HOME tab.
   b. At the Find and Replace dialog box with the Replace tab selected, type Lessor in the *Find what* text box.
   c. Press the Tab key to move the insertion point to the *Replace with* text box.
   d. Type Tracy Hartford.
   e. Click the Replace All button.
   f. At the message telling you that 11 replacements were made, click OK. (Do not close the Find and Replace dialog box.)
3. With the Find and Replace dialog box still open, complete steps similar to those in Step 2 to find all occurrences of *Lessee* and replace with *Michael Iwami.*
4. Click the Close button to close the Find and Replace dialog box.
5. Save **WL1-C4-P6-LeaseAgrmnt.docx**.

Choosing Check Box Options

The Find and Replace dialog box contains a variety of check boxes with options for completing a search. To display these options, click the More button located at the bottom left side of the dialog box. This causes the Find and Replace dialog box to expand, as shown in Figure 4.9. Each option and what will occur if it is selected

Figure 4.9 Expanded Find and Replace Dialog Box

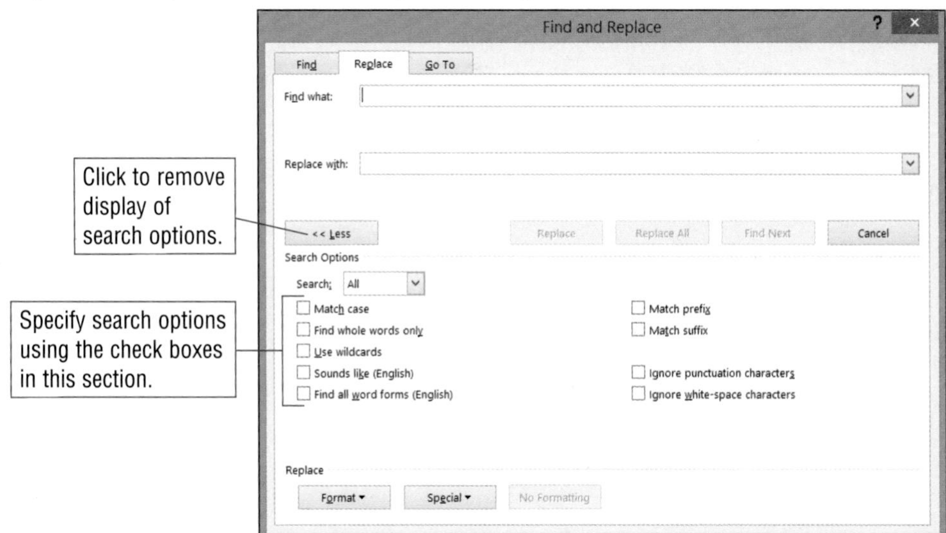

is described in Table 4.2. To remove the display of options, click the Less button. (The Less button was previously the More button.) Note that if you make a mistake when replacing text, close the Find and Replace dialog box and then click the Undo button on the Quick Access toolbar.

Table 4.2 Options at the Expanded Find and Replace Dialog Box

Choose this option	*To*
Match case	Exactly match the case of the search text. For example, if you search for *Book* and select the *Match case* option, Word will stop at *Book* but not *book* or *BOOK*.
Find whole words only	Find a whole word, not a part of a word. For example, if you search for *her* and did not select *Find whole words only*, Word will stop at *there*, *here*, *hers*, etc.
Use wildcards	Search for wildcards, special characters, or special search operators.
Sounds like	Match words that sound alike but are spelled differently, such as *know* and *no*.
Find all word forms	Find all forms of the word entered in the *Find what* text box. For example, if you enter *hold*, Word will stop at *held* and *holding*.
Match prefix	Find only those words that begin with the letters in the *Find what* text box. For example, if you enter *per*, Word will stop at words such as *perform* and *perfect* but skip words such as *super* and *hyperlink*.
Match suffix	Find only those words that end with the letters in the *Find what* text box. For example, if you enter *ly*, Word will stop at words such as *accurately* and *quietly* but skip words such as *catalyst* and *lyre*.
Ignore punctuation characters	Ignore punctuation within characters. For example, if you enter *US* in the *Find what* text box, Word will stop at *U.S.*
Ignore white-space characters	Ignore spaces between letters. For example, if you enter *F B I* in the *Find what* text box, Word will stop at *FBI*.

Project 6c Finding and Replacing Word Forms and Suffixes — Part 3 of 4

1. With **WL1-C4-P6-LeaseAgrmnt.docx** open, make sure the insertion point is positioned at the beginning of the document.
2. Find all word forms of the word *lease* and replace with *rent* by completing the following steps:
   a. Click the Replace button in the Editing group on the HOME tab.
   b. At the Find and Replace dialog box with the Replace tab selected, type **lease** in the *Find what* text box.

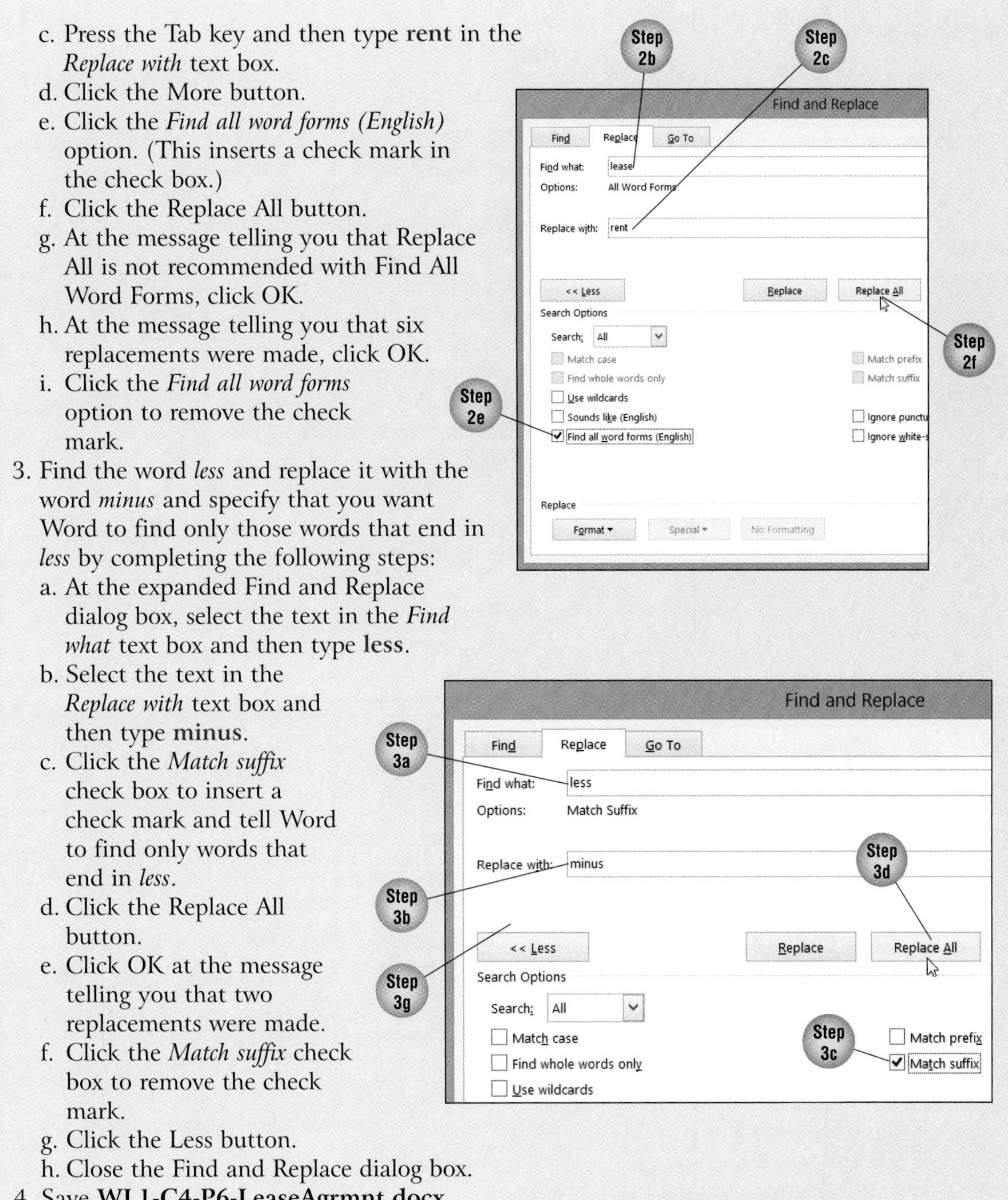

c. Press the Tab key and then type **rent** in the *Replace with* text box.
d. Click the More button.
e. Click the *Find all word forms (English)* option. (This inserts a check mark in the check box.)
f. Click the Replace All button.
g. At the message telling you that Replace All is not recommended with Find All Word Forms, click OK.
h. At the message telling you that six replacements were made, click OK.
i. Click the *Find all word forms* option to remove the check mark.

3. Find the word *less* and replace it with the word *minus* and specify that you want Word to find only those words that end in *less* by completing the following steps:
   a. At the expanded Find and Replace dialog box, select the text in the *Find what* text box and then type **less**.
   b. Select the text in the *Replace with* text box and then type **minus**.
   c. Click the *Match suffix* check box to insert a check mark and tell Word to find only words that end in *less*.
   d. Click the Replace All button.
   e. Click OK at the message telling you that two replacements were made.
   f. Click the *Match suffix* check box to remove the check mark.
   g. Click the Less button.
   h. Close the Find and Replace dialog box.
4. Save **WL1-C4-P6-LeaseAgrmnt.docx**.

Finding and Replacing Formatting

With options at the Find and Replace dialog box with the Replace tab selected, you can search for characters containing specific formatting and replace them with other characters or formatting. To specify formatting in the Find and Replace dialog box, click the More button and then click the Format button that displays toward the bottom of the dialog box. At the pop-up list that displays, identify the type of formatting you want to find.

Project 6d Finding and Replacing Fonts

Part 4 of 4

1. With **WL1-C4-P6-LeaseAgrmnt.docx** open, make sure the insertion point displays at the beginning of the document.
2. Find text set in 12-point Candara bold Dark Red and replace it with text set in 14-point Calibri bold Dark Blue by completing the following steps:
   a. Click the Replace button in the Editing group.
   b. At the Find and Replace dialog box, press the Delete key. (This deletes any text that displays in the *Find what* text box.)
   c. Click the More button. (If a check mark displays in any of the check boxes, click the option to remove the check mark.)
   d. With the insertion point positioned in the *Find what* text box, click the Format button located toward the bottom of the dialog box and then click *Font* at the pop-up list.
   e. At the Find Font dialog box, choose the *Candara* font and change the font style to *Bold*, the size to *12*, and the font color to *Dark Red* (first color option in the *Standard Colors* section).

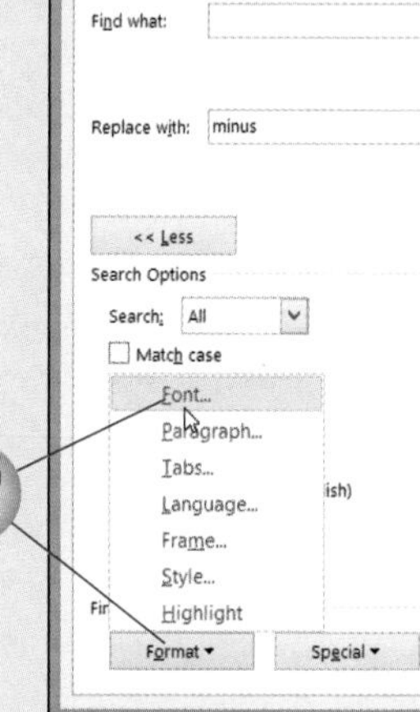

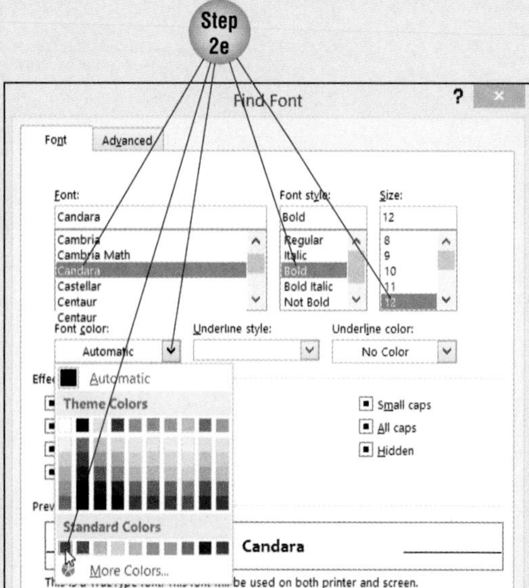

   f. Click OK to close the Find Font dialog box.
   g. At the Find and Replace dialog box, click inside the *Replace with* text box and then delete any text that displays.
   h. Click the Format button located toward the bottom of the dialog box and then click *Font* at the pop-up list.
   i. At the Replace Font dialog box, choose the *Calibri* font and change the font style to *Bold*, the size to *14*, and the font color to *Dark Blue* (second color option from the right in the *Standard Colors* section).

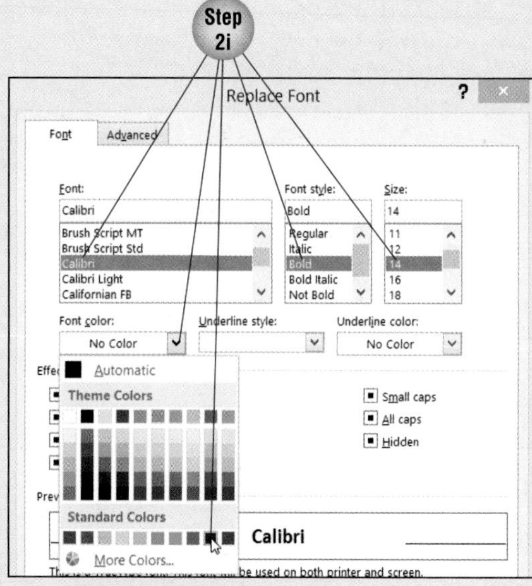

   j. Click OK to close the Replace Font dialog box.
   k. At the Find and Replace dialog box, click the Replace All button.
   l. Click OK at the message telling you that eight replacements were made.

m. Click in the *Find what* text box and then click the No Formatting button.
n. Click in the *Replace with* text box and then click the No Formatting button.
o. Click the Less button.
p. Close the Find and Replace dialog box.
3. Save, print, and then close **WL1-C4-P6-LeaseAgrmnt.docx**.

Chapter Summary

- Change the document view with buttons in the view area on the Status bar or with options in the Views group on the VIEW tab.
- Print Layout is the default view, but the view can be changed to other views, such as Draft view and Read Mode view.
- The Draft view displays the document in a format for efficient editing and formatting.
- Use the Zoom slider bar to change the percentage of the display.
- The Read Mode view displays a document in a format for easy viewing and reading.
- Use options at the Ribbon Display Options button drop-down list to specify whether you want the Quick Access toolbar, ribbon, and Status bar visible or hidden.
- Navigate in a document using the Navigation pane. Display the pane by inserting a check mark in the *Navigation Pane* check box in the Show group on the VIEW tab.
- By default, a Word document contains 1-inch top, bottom, left, and right margins. Change margins with preset margin settings at the Margins button drop-down list or with options at the Page Setup dialog box with the Margins tab selected.
- The default page orientation is portrait, which can be changed to landscape with the Orientation button in the Page Setup group on the PAGE LAYOUT tab.
- The default page size is 8.5 inches by 11 inches, which can be changed with options at the Size button drop-down list or options at the Page Setup dialog box with the Paper tab selected.
- The page break that Word inserts automatically is a soft page break. A page break that you insert is a hard page break. Insert a hard page break with the Page Break button in the Pages group on the INSERT tab or by pressing Ctrl + Enter.
- Insert a predesigned and formatted cover page by clicking the Cover Page button in the Pages group on the INSERT tab and then clicking the desired option at the drop-down list.
- Insert predesigned and formatted page numbering by clicking the Page Number button in the Header & Footer group on the INSERT tab, specifying the desired location of page numbers, and then clicking the desired page numbering option.
- Insert predesigned headers and footers in a document with the Header button and the Footer button in the Header & Footer group on the INSERT tab.
- A watermark is a lightened image that displays behind text in a document. Use the Watermark button in the Page Background group on the DESIGN tab to insert a watermark.

- Insert page color in a document with the Page Color button in the Page Background group on the DESIGN tab. Page color is designed for viewing a document on-screen and does not print.
- Click the Page Borders button in the Page Background group on the DESIGN tab and the Borders and Shading dialog box with the Page Border tab selected displays. Use options at this dialog box to insert a page border or an image page border in a document.
- Use the Find feature to search for specific characters or formatting. Use the Find and Replace feature to search for specific characters or formatting and replace with other characters or formatting.
- At the Find and Replace dialog box, click the Find Next button to find the next occurrence of the characters and/or formatting. Click the Replace button to replace the characters or formatting and find the next occurrence, or click the Replace All button to replace all occurrences of the characters or formatting.
- Click the More button at the Find and Replace dialog box to display additional options for completing a search.

Commands Review

FEATURE	RIBBON TAB, GROUP	BUTTON, OPTION	KEYBOARD SHORTCUT
blank page	INSERT, Pages		
Borders and Shading dialog box with Page Border tab selected	DESIGN, Page Background		
Border and Shading Options dialog box	DESIGN, Page Background	, *Options*	
cover page	INSERT, Pages		
Draft view	VIEW, Views		
Find and Replace dialog box with Find tab selected	HOME, Editing	, *Advanced Find*	
Find and Replace dialog box with Replace tab selected	HOME, Editing		Ctrl + H
footer	INSERT, Header & Footer		
header	INSERT, Header & Footer		
margins	PAGE LAYOUT, Page Setup		
Navigation pane	VIEW, Show	*Navigation Pane*	Ctrl + F
orientation	PAGE LAYOUT, Page Setup		
page break	INSERT, Pages		Ctrl + Enter
page color	DESIGN, Page Background		

FEATURE	RIBBON TAB, GROUP	BUTTON, OPTION	KEYBOARD SHORTCUT
page numbering	INSERT, Header & Footer		
Page Setup dialog box with Margins tab selected	PAGE LAYOUT, Page Setup	, *Custom Margins* OR	
Page Setup dialog box with Paper tab selected	PAGE LAYOUT, Page Setup	, *More Paper Sizes*	
page size	PAGE LAYOUT, Page Setup		
Print Layout view	VIEW, Views		
Read Mode view	VIEW, Views		
ribbon display options			
watermark	DESIGN, Page Background		

Concepts Check Test Your Knowledge

Completion: In the space provided at the right, indicate the correct term, symbol, or command.

1. This is the default measurement for the top, bottom, left, and right margins. ________________
2. This view displays a document in a format for efficient editing and formatting. ________________
3. This view displays a document in a format for easy viewing and reading. ________________
4. The *Navigation Pane* check box is located in this group on the VIEW tab. ________________
5. To remove white space, double-click this icon. ________________
6. This is the default page orientation. ________________
7. Set specific margins at this dialog box with the Margins tab selected. ________________
8. Press these keys on the keyboard to insert a page break. ________________
9. The Cover Page button is located in the Pages group on this tab. ________________
10. Text that appears at the top of every page is called this. ________________
11. A lightened image that displays behind text in a document is called this. ________________
12. Change the position of the page border from the edge of the page with options at this dialog box. ________________

13. The Page Borders button displays in this group on the DESIGN tab. ____________

14. If you want to replace every occurrence of what you are searching for in a document, click this button at the Find and Replace dialog box. ____________

15. Click this option at the Find and Replace dialog box if you are searching for a word and all of its forms. ____________

Skills Check Assess Your Performance

Assessment 1

FORMAT A COVER LETTER DOCUMENT AND CREATE A COVER PAGE

1. Open **CoverLetter.docx** and then save the document with Save As and name it **WL1-C4-A1-CoverLetter**.
2. Change the left and right margins to 1.25 inches.
3. Move the insertion point to the beginning of the heading *Writing Cover Letters to People You Know* and then insert a blank page.
4. Insert a page break at the beginning of the heading *Writing Cover Letters to People You Don't Know*.
5. Move the insertion point to the beginning of the document and then insert the Filigree cover page.
6. Insert the following text in the specified fields:
   a. Type **job search strategies** in the *[DOCUMENT TITLE]* placeholder.
   b. Type **Writing a Cover Letter** in the *[Document subtitle]* placeholder.
   c. Type **february 3, 2015** in the *[DATE]* placeholder.
   d. Type **career finders** in the *[COMPANY NAME]* placeholder.
   e. Delete the *[Company address]* placeholder.
7. Move the insertion point to any character in the title *WRITING A COVER LETTER* and then insert the Brackets 1 page numbering at the bottom of the page. (The page numbering will not appear on the cover page.)
8. Make the document active, turn on the display of nonprinting characters, move the insertion point to the blank line above the page break below the first paragraph of text in the document, and then press the Delete key six times. (This deletes the page break on the first page and the page break creating a blank page 2 as well as extra hard returns.) Turn off the display of nonprinting characters.
9. Save, print, and then close **WL1-C4-A1-CoverLetter.docx**.

Assessment 2

FORMAT AN INTELLECTUAL PROPERTY REPORT AND INSERT HEADERS AND FOOTERS

1. Open **PropProtect.docx** and then save the document with Save As and name it **WL1-C4-A2-PropProtect**.
2. Insert a page break at the beginning of the *REFERENCES* title (located on the second page).
3. Change the top margin to 1.5 inches.

4. Change the page orientation to landscape orientation.
5. Move the insertion point to the beginning of the document and then insert the Retrospect footer. Select the name that displays at the left side of the footer and then type your first and last names.
6. Save the document and then print only page 1 of the document.
7. Change the orientation back to portrait orientation.
8. Apply the Moderate page margins.
9. Remove the footer.
10. Insert the Ion (Dark) header.
11. Insert the Ion (Dark) footer. Type **property protection issues** as the title and make sure your first and last names display at the right side of the footer.
12. Select the footer text (document name and your name), turn on bold, and then change the font size to 8 points.
13. Insert the DRAFT 1 watermark in the document.
14. Apply the Green, Accent 3, Lighter 80% page color (seventh column, second row).
15. Save and then print **WL1-C4-A2-PropProtect.docx**.
16. With the document still open, change the paper size to legal (8.5 inches by 14 inches).
17. Save the document with Save As and name it **WL1-C4-A2-PropProtect-Legal**.
18. Check with your instructor to determine if you can print legal-sized documents. If so, print page 1 of the document.
19. Save and then close **WL1-C4-A2-PropProtect-Legal.docx**.

Assessment 3

FORMAT A REAL ESTATE AGREEMENT

1. Open **REAgrmnt.docx** and then save the document with Save As and name it **WL1-C4-A3-REAgrmnt**.
2. Find all occurrences of *BUYER* (matching the case) and replace with *James Berman*.
3. Find all occurrences of *SELLER* (matching the case) and replace with *Mona Trammell*.
4. Find all word forms of the word *buy* and replace with *purchase*.
5. Search for 14-point Tahoma bold formatting in Dark Red and replace with 12-point Constantia bold formatting in Black, Text 1.
6. Insert Plain Number 2 page numbers at the bottom center of the page.
7. Insert a page border with the following specifications:
   - Choose the first double-line border in the *Style* list box.
   - Change the color of the page border to *Dark Red* (located in the *Standard Colors* section).
   - Change the width of the page border to *1½ pt*.
8. Display the Border and Shading Options dialog box and then change the top, left, bottom, and right measurements to *30 pt*. ***Hint: Display the Border and Shading Options dialog box by clicking the Options button at the Borders and Shading dialog box with the Page Border tab selected.***
9. Save, print, and then close **WL1-C4-A3-REAgrmnt.docx**.

Visual Benchmark Demonstrate Your Proficiency

FORMAT A RESUME STYLES REPORT

1. Open **Resumes.docx** and then save it with Save As and name it **WL1-C4-VB-Resumes**.
2. Format the document so it appears as shown in Figure 4.10 on page 141 with the following specifications:
   - Change the top margin to 1.5 inches.
   - Apply the Heading 1 style to the title and the Heading 2 style to the headings.
   - Apply the Lines (Simple) style set.
   - Apply the Savon theme.
   - Apply the Blue Green theme colors.
   - Insert the Austin cover page and insert text in the placeholders and delete placeholders as shown in the figure. (If a name displays in the Author placeholder, delete the current name, and then type your first and last names.)
   - Insert the Ion (Dark) header and the Ion (Dark) footer.
3. Save, print, and then close **WL1-C4-VB-Resumes.docx**.

Case Study Apply Your Skills

Part 1

You work for Citizens for Consumer Safety, a nonprofit organization providing information on household safety. Your supervisor, Melinda Johansson, has asked you to attractively format a document on smoke detectors. She will be using the document as an informational handout during a presentation on smoke detectors. Open **SmokeDetectors.docx** and then save the document with Save As and name it **WL1-C4-CS1-SmokeDetectors**. Apply appropriate styles to the title and headings and apply a theme. Ms. Johansson has asked you to change the page orientation to landscape and to change the left and right margins to 1.5 inches. She wants the extra space at the left and right margins so audience members can write notes in the margins. Use the Help feature or experiment with the options in the HEADER & FOOTER TOOLS DESIGN tab and figure out how to number pages on every page but the first page. Insert page numbering in the document that prints at the top right side of every page except the first page. Save, print, and then close **WL1-C4-CS1-SmokeDetectors.docx**.

Figure 4.10 Visual Benchmark

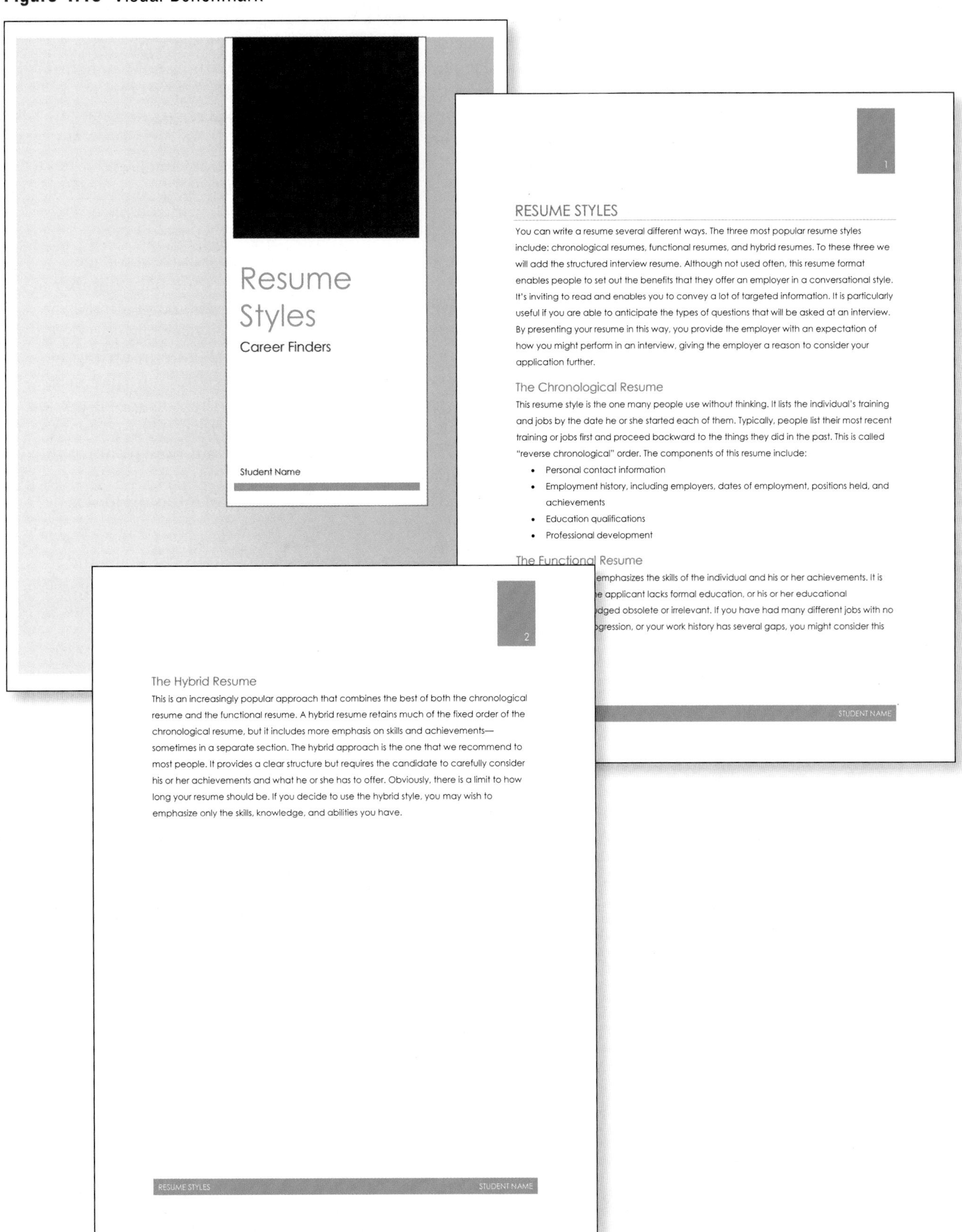

Resume
Styles
Career Finders
Student Name
1
RESUME STYLES
You can write a resume several different ways. The three most popular resume styles include: chronological resumes, functional resumes, and hybrid resumes. To these three we will add the structured interview resume. Although not used often, this resume format enables people to set out the benefits that they offer an employer in a conversational style. It's inviting to read and enables you to convey a lot of targeted information. It is particularly useful if you are able to anticipate the types of questions that will be asked at an interview. By presenting your resume in this way, you provide the employer with an expectation of how you might perform in an interview, giving the employer a reason to consider your application further.
The Chronological Resume
This resume style is the one many people use without thinking. It lists the individual's training and jobs by the date he or she started each of them. Typically, people list their most recent training or jobs first and proceed backward to the things they did in the past. This is called "reverse chronological" order. The components of this resume include:
Personal contact information
Employment history, including employers, dates of employment, positions held, and achievements
Education qualifications
Professional development
The Functional Resume
emphasizes the skills of the individual and his or her achievements. It is
e applicant lacks formal education, or his or her educational
dged obsolete or irrelevant. If you have had many different jobs with no
gression, or your work history has several gaps, you might consider this
STUDENT NAME
2
The Hybrid Resume
This is an increasingly popular approach that combines the best of both the chronological resume and the functional resume. A hybrid resume retains much of the fixed order of the chronological resume, but it includes more emphasis on skills and achievements—sometimes in a separate section. The hybrid approach is the one that we recommend to most people. It provides a clear structure but requires the candidate to carefully consider his or her achievements and what he or she has to offer. Obviously, there is a limit to how long your resume should be. If you decide to use the hybrid style, you may wish to emphasize only the skills, knowledge, and abilities you have.
RESUME STYLES
STUDENT NAME

Part 2

Help

After reviewing the formatted document on smoke detectors, Ms. Johansson has decided that she wants the document to print in the default orientation (portrait) and would like to see different theme and style choices. She also noticed that the term "smoke alarm" should be replaced with "smoke detector." She has asked you to open and then format the original document. Open **SmokeDetectors.docx** and then save the document with Save As and name it **WL1-C4-CS2-SmokeDetectors**. Apply styles to the title and headings and apply a theme to the document (other than the one you chose for Part 1). Search for all occurrences of *smoke alarm* and replace with *smoke detector*. Insert a cover page of your choosing and insert the appropriate information in the page. Use the Help feature or experiment with the options in the HEADER & FOOTER TOOLS DESIGN tab and figure out how to insert odd-page and even-page footers in a document. Insert an odd-page footer that prints the page number at the right margin and insert an even-page footer that prints the page number at the left margin. You do not want the footer to print on the cover page, so make sure you position the insertion point below the cover page before inserting the footers. After inserting the footers in the document, you decide that they need to be moved down the page to create more space between the last line of text on a page and the footer. Use the Help feature or experiment with the options in the HEADER & FOOTER TOOLS DESIGN tab to figure out how to move the footers down and then edit each footer so it displays 0.3 inch from the bottom of the page. Save, print, and then close **WL1-C4-CS2-SmokeDetectors.docx**.

Part 3

Ms. Johansson has asked you to prepare a document on infant car seats and car seat safety. She wants this informational car seat safety document available for distribution at a local community center. Use the Internet to find websites that provide information on child and infant car seats and car seat safety. Write a report on the information you find that includes at least the following information:

- Description of the types of car seats (such as rear-facing, convertible, forward-facing, built-in, and booster)
- Safety rules and guidelines
- Installation information
- Specific child and infant seat models
- Sites on the Internet that sell car seats
- Price ranges
- Internet sites providing safety information

Format the report using styles and a theme and include a cover page and headers and/or footers. Save the completed document and name it **WL1-C4-CS-CarSeats**. Print and then close the document.

MICROSOFT® WORD Performance Assessment

Word
WL1U1

Note: Before beginning unit assessments, copy to your storage medium the WL1U1 subfolder from the WL1 folder on the CD that accompanies this textbook and then make WL1U1 the active folder.

Assessing Proficiency

In this unit, you have learned to create, edit, save, and print Word documents. You have also learned to format characters, paragraphs, and pages.

Assessment 1 Format a Document on Website Design

1. Open **Website.docx** and then save the document with Save As and name it **WL1-U1-A1-Website**.
2. Complete a spelling and grammar check.
3. Select from the paragraph that begins *Make your home page work for you.* through the end of the document and then apply bullet formatting.
4. Select and then bold the first sentence of each bulleted paragraph.
5. Apply a single-line bottom border to the document title and apply Gold, Accent 4, Lighter 80% paragraph shading to the title.
6. Save and then print **WL1-U1-A1-Website.docx**.
7. Change the top, left, and right margins to 1.5 inches.
8. Select the bulleted paragraphs, change the paragraph alignment to justified alignment, and then apply numbering formatting.
9. Select the entire document and then change the font to 12-point Cambria.
10. Insert the text shown in Figure U1.1 after paragraph number 2. (The number 3. should be inserted preceding the text you type.)
11. Save, print, and then close **WL1-U1-A1-Website.docx**.

Figure U1.1 Assessment 1

> **Avoid a cluttered look.** In design, less is more. Strive for a clean look to your pages, using ample margins and white space.

Assessment 2 Format Accumulated Returns Document

1. Open **ReturnChart.docx** and then save the document with Save As and name it **WL1-U1-A2-ReturnChart**.
2. Select the entire document and then make the following changes:
   a. Apply the No Spacing style.
   b. Change the line spacing to 1.5.
   c. Change the font to 12-point Cambria.
   d. Apply 6 points of spacing after paragraphs.
3. Select the title *TOTAL RETURN CHARTS*, change the font to 14-point Corbel bold, change the alignment to centered, and apply Blue-Gray, Text 2, Lighter 80% paragraph shading.
4. Bold the following text that appears at the beginning of the second through the fifth paragraphs:

   Average annual total return: *Annual total return:*
   Accumulation units: *Accumulative rates:*
5. Select the paragraphs of text in the body of the document (all paragraphs except the title) and then change the paragraph alignment to justified alignment.
6. Select the paragraphs that begin with the bolded words, sort the paragraphs in ascending order, and then indent the text 0.5 inch from the left margin.
7. Insert a watermark that prints *DRAFT* diagonally across the page.
8. Save, print, and then close **WL1-U1-A2-ReturnChart.docx**.

Assessment 3 Format Computer Ethics Report

1. Open **FutureEthics.docx** and then save the document with Save As and name it **WL1-U1-A3-FutureEthics.docx**.
2. Apply the Heading 1 style to the titles *FUTURE OF COMPUTER ETHICS* and *REFERENCES*.
3. Apply the Heading 2 style to the headings in the document.
4. Apply the Shaded style set.
5. Apply the Open paragraph spacing.
6. Apply the Parallax theme and then change the theme fonts to Garamond.
7. Center the two titles (*FUTURE OF COMPUTER ETHICS* and *REFERENCES*).
8. Add 6 points of paragraph spacing after each heading with the Heading 1 and Heading 2 styles applied in the document.
9. Hang indent the paragraphs of text below the *REFERENCES* title.
10. Insert page numbering that prints at the bottom center of each page.
11. Save, print, and then close **WL1-U1-A3-FutureEthics.docx**.

Assessment 4 Set Tabs and Type Income by Division Text in Columns

1. At a new blank document, type the text shown in Figure U1.2 with the following specifications:
   a. Bold and center the title as shown.
   b. You determine the tab settings for the text in columns.
   c. Select the entire document and then change the font to 12-point Arial.
2. Save the document and name it **WL1-U1-A4-Income**.
3. Print and then close **WL1-U1-A4-Income.docx**.

Figure U1.2 Assessment 4

INCOME BY DIVISION

	2013	2014	2015
Public Relations	$14,375	$16,340	$16,200
Database Services	9,205	15,055	13,725
Graphic Design	18,400	21,790	19,600
Technical Support	5,780	7,325	9,600

Assessment 5 Set Tabs and Type Table of Contents Text

1. At a blank document, type the text shown in Figure U1.3 with the following specifications:
   a. Bold and center the title as shown.
   b. You determine the tab settings for the text in columns.
   c. Select the entire document, change the font to 12-point Cambria, and then change the line spacing to 1.5.
2. Save the document and name it **WL1-U1-A5-TofC**.
3. Print and then close **WL1-U1-A5-TofC.docx**.

Figure U1.3 Assessment 5

TABLE OF CONTENTS

Online Shopping. 2

Online Services. 4

Peer-to-Peer Online Transactions. 5

Transaction Payment Methods. 8

Transaction Security and Encryption 11

Establishing a Website. 14

Assessment 6 Format Union Agreement Contract

1. Open **LaborContract.docx** and then save the document with Save As and name it **WL1-U1-A6-LaborContract**.
2. Find all occurrences of *REINBERG MANUFACTURING* and replace with *MILLWOOD ENTERPRISES*.
3. Find all occurrences of *RM* and replace with *ME*.
4. Find all occurrences of *LABOR WORKERS' UNION* and replace with *SERVICE EMPLOYEES' UNION*.
5. Find all occurrences of *LWU* and replace with *SEU*.
6. Select the entire document and then change the font to 12-point Cambria and the line spacing to double spacing.

7. Select the numbered paragraphs in the *Transfers and Moving Expenses* section and change to bulleted paragraphs.
8. Select the numbered paragraphs in the *Sick Leave* section and change them to bulleted paragraphs.
9. Change the page orientation to landscape and the top margin to 1.5 inches.
10. Save and then print **WL1-U1-A6-LaborContract.docx**.
11. Change the page orientation to portrait and the left margin (previously the top margin) back to 1 inch.
12. Insert the Wisp cover page (may display as *Whisp*) and insert the current date in the Date placeholder, the title *Union Agreement* as the document title and *Millwood Enterprises* as the document subtitle. Select the Author placeholder (or the name that displays) located toward the bottom of the document and then type your first and last names. Delete the Company Name placeholder.
13. Move the insertion point to the page after the cover page, insert the Ion Dark footer, and then make sure *UNION AGREEMENT* displays in the Title placeholder and your name displays in the Author placeholder. If not, type UNION AGREEMENT in the Title placeholder and your first and last names in the Author placeholder.
14. Save, print, and then close **WL1-U1-A6-LaborContract.docx**.

Assessment 7 Copy and Paste Text in Health Plan Document

1. Open **KeyLifePlan.docx** and then save the document with Save As and name it **WL1-U1-A7-KeyLifePlan**.
2. Open **PlanOptions.docx** and then turn on the display of the Clipboard task pane. Make sure the Clipboard is empty.
3. Select the heading *Plan Highlights* and the six paragraphs of text below the heading and then copy the selected text to the Clipboard.
4. Select the heading *Plan Options* and the two paragraphs of text below the heading and then copy the selected text to the Clipboard.
5. Select the heading *Quality Assessment* and the six paragraphs of text below the heading and then copy the selected text to the Clipboard.
6. Close **PlanOptions.docx**.
7. With **WL1-U1-A7-KeyLifePlan.docx** open, display the Clipboard task pane.
8. Move the insertion point to the beginning of the *Provider Network* heading, paste the *Plan Options* item from the Clipboard, and merge the formatting.
9. With the insertion point positioned at the beginning of the *Provider Network* heading, paste *Plan Highlights* from the Clipboard and merge the formatting.
10. Move the insertion point to the beginning of the *Plan Options* heading, paste the *Quality Assessment* item from the Clipboard, and merge the formatting.
11. Clear the Clipboard and then close it.
12. Apply the Heading 1 style to the title, *KEY LIFE HEALTH PLAN*.
13. Apply the Heading 2 style to the four headings in the document.
14. Change the top margin to 1.5 inches.
15. Apply the Lines (Simple) style set.
16. Apply the Compact paragraph spacing.
17. Apply the Red Orange theme colors.
18. Insert a double-line, Dark Red page border.
19. Insert the Slice 1 header.
20. Insert the Slice footer and type your first and last names in the Author placeholder.
21. Insert a page break at the beginning of the heading *Plan Highlights*.
22. Save, print, and then close **WL1-U1-A7-KeyLifePlan.docx**.

Assessment 8 Create and Format a Resume

1. Apply the No spacing style to a blank document and then create the resume shown in Figure U1.4. Change the font to Candara and apply the character, paragraph, border, shading, and bullet formatting as shown in the figure.
2. Save the completed document and name it **WL1-U1-A8-Resume**.
3. Print and then close **WL1-U1-A8-Resume.docx**.

Figure U1.4 Assessment 8

KIERNAN O'MALLEY

1533 Baylor Street East, Auburn, WA 98020 (253) 555-3912

NETWORK ADMINISTRATION PROFESSIONAL

Pursuing **Cisco Certified Network Associate (CCNA)** and **Network+** credentials

Proficient in Microsoft Office applications in Windows environment

EDUCATION

Information Systems (IS), Western Washington University, Bellingham, WA...................... 2012
Medical Specialist, Seattle University, Seattle, WA .... 2010 to 2012
Medical Terminology, Green River Community College, Auburn, WA................................. 2009

APPLIED RESEARCH PROJECTS

Completed **Applied Research Projects (ARPs)**, in conjunction with IS degree requirements, covering all aspects of design and management of organizational technical resources, as follows:

- **Organizational Culture and Leadership** (2015): Evaluated the organizational culture of Bellevue Surgery Center's endoscopy unit and operating room (OR) in order to ensure that the mission and vision statements were being appropriately applied at the staff level.
- **Human Resources (HR) Management** (2015): Established a comprehensive orientation package for the Bellevue Surgery Center's clinical staff.
- **Strategic Management and Planning** (2014): Conducted internal/external environmental assessments in order to identify an approach for Bellevue Surgery Center to expand its OR facilities.
- **Financial Accounting** (2014): Created a quarterly operating budget for the Bellevue Surgery Center and implemented an expenditure tracking system.
- **Database Management Systems** (2013): Created an inventory-control system that optimizes inventory maintenance in a cost-effective manner.
- **Statistics and Research Analysis** (2013): Generated graphics to illustrate the Valley Hospital's assisted-reproduction success rate.
- **Management Support System** (2012): Identified solutions to resolve inventory-control vulnerabilities at minimal cost for Valley Hospital.

PROFESSIONAL EXPERIENCE

CERTIFIED SURGICAL TECHNOLOGIST

Bellevue Surgery Center, Bellevue, WA...2013 to present
Valley Hospital, Renton, WA ....2011 to 2013
Kenmore Ambulatory Surgery Center, Kenmore, WA ....2009 to 2011
South Sound Medical Center, Auburn, WA...2008 to 2009

Writing Activities

The following activities give you the opportunity to practice your writing skills along with demonstrating an understanding of some of the important Word features you have mastered in this unit. Use correct grammar, appropriate word choices, and clear sentence constructions. Follow the steps in Figure U1.5 to improve your writing skills.

Activity 1 Write Steps on Using KeyTips

Use Word's Help feature to learn about KeyTips. To do this, open the Word Help window, type **keytips**, and then press Enter. Click the Keyboard shortcuts for Microsoft Word article hyperlink. Click the Show All hyperlink and then scroll down the article to the *Navigating the ribbon* heading. Read the information about accessing any command with a few keystrokes. (Read only the information in the *Navigating the ribbon* section.)

At a blank document, write a paragraph summarizing the information you read in the Word Help article. After writing the paragraph, write steps on how to use KeyTips to accomplish the following tasks:

- Turn on bold formatting.
- Display the Font dialog box.
- Print the open document.

Save the completed document and name it **WL1-U1-Act1-KeyTips**. Print and then close **WL1-U1-Act1-KeyTips.docx**.

Activity 2 Write Information on Customizing Grammar Style Options

Use Word's Help feature to learn about grammar and style options. (You can also experiment with the *Writing Style* and *Settings* options at the Word Options dialog box with Proofing selected. Display this dialog box by clicking the FILE tab, clicking *Options*, and then clicking *Proofing* in the left panel of the Word Options dialog box.) Learn how to choose which grammar errors to detect and which style errors to detect. Also learn how to set rules for grammar and style. Once you have determined this information, create a document describing at least two grammar errors and at least two style errors you can choose for detection. Also include in this document the steps required to have Word check the grammar and style rather than just the grammar in a document. Save the completed document and name it **WL1-U1-Act2-CustomSpell**. Print and then close **WL1-U1-Act2-CustomSpell.docx**.

Figure U1.5 The Writing Process

The Writing Process

Plan Gather ideas, select which information to include, and choose the order in which to present the information.

Checkpoints
- What is the purpose?
- What information does the reader need in order to reach your intended conclusion?

Write Following the information plan and keeping the reader in mind, draft the document using clear, direct sentences that say what you mean.

Checkpoints
- What are the subpoints for each main thought?
- How can you connect paragraphs so the reader moves smoothly from one idea to the next?

Revise Improve what is written by changing, deleting, rearranging, or adding words, sentences, and paragraphs.

Checkpoints
- Is the meaning clear?
- Do the ideas follow a logical order?
- Have you included any unnecessary information?
- Have you built your sentences around strong nouns and verbs?

Edit Check spelling, sentence construction, word use, punctuation, and capitalization.

Checkpoints
- Can you spot any redundancies or clichés?
- Can you reduce any phrases to an effective word (for example, change *the fact that* to *because*)?
- Have you used commas only where there is a strong reason for doing so?
- Did you proofread the document for errors that your spelling checker cannot identify?

Publish Prepare a final copy that could be reproduced and shared with others.

Checkpoints
- Which design elements, such as boldface or different fonts, would help highlight important ideas or sections?
- Would charts or other graphics help clarify meaning?

Internet Research

Research Business Desktop Computer Systems

You hold a part-time job at the local Chamber of Commerce, where you assist the office manager, Ryan Woods. Mr. Woods will be purchasing new desktop computers for the office staff. He has asked you to research on the Internet and identify at least three PCs that can be purchased directly over the Internet, and he requests that you put your research and recommendations in writing. Mr. Woods is looking for solid, reliable, economical, and powerful desktop computers with good warranties and service plans. He has given you a budget of $800 per unit.

Search the Internet for three desktop PC computer systems from three different manufacturers. Consider price, specifications (processor speed, amount of RAM, hard drive space, and monitor type and size), performance, warranties, and service plans when making your choice of systems. Print your research findings and include them with your report. (For helpful information on shopping for a computer, read the articles "Buying and Installing a PC" and "Purchasing a Computer," posted in the Course Resources section of this book's Internet Resource Center, either at www.paradigmcollege.net/BenchmarkOffice13 or www.paradigmcollege.net/BenchmarkWord13.)

Using Word, write a brief report in which you summarize the capabilities and qualities of each of the three computer systems you recommend. Include a final paragraph detailing which system you suggest for purchase and why. If possible, incorporate user opinions and/or reviews about this system to support your decision. At the end of your report, include a table comparing the computer systems. Format your report using the concepts and techniques you learned in Unit 1. Save the report and name it **WL1-U1-InternetResearch**. Print and then close the file.

MICROSOFT®

WORD Level 1

Unit 2 ■ Enhancing and Customizing Documents

MICROSOFT®

WORD

Applying Formatting and Inserting Objects

PERFORMANCE OBJECTIVES

Upon successful completion of Chapter 5, you will be able to:

- **Insert section breaks**
- **Create and format text in columns**
- **Hyphenate words automatically and manually**
- **Create a drop cap**
- **Insert symbols, special characters, and the date and time**
- **Use the Click and Type feature**
- **Vertically align text**
- **Insert, format, and customize images, text boxes, shapes, and WordArt**
- **Create and customize a screen shot**

Tutorials

5.1 Inserting Section Breaks
5.2 Creating Newspaper Columns
5.3 Hyphenating Words
5.4 Inserting a Drop Cap, Symbols, and Date and Time
5.5 Using Click and Type
5.6 Using Horizontal Alignment
5.7 Inserting and Formatting an Image
5.8 Inserting, Sizing, and Moving an Image from Office.com
5.9 Inserting and Formatting a Text Box
5.10 Inserting and Formatting a Shape
5.11 Inserting and Modifying WordArt
5.12 Creating and Inserting a Screenshot

To apply page or document formatting to only a portion of the document, insert a section break. You can insert a continuous section break or a section break that begins a new page. A section break is useful when formatting text in columns. The hyphenation feature hyphenates words at the ends of lines, creating a less ragged margin. Use buttons in the Text and Symbols groups on the INSERT tab to insert symbols, special characters, date and time, text boxes, and WordArt. With the Click and Type feature, you can position the insertion point at a particular location in the document and change the paragraph alignment. Use the *Vertical alignment* option at the Page Setup dialog box with the Layout tab selected to align text vertically on the page. Along with these features, you will also learn how to increase the visual appeal of a document by inserting and customizing images such as pictures, clip art, text boxes, shapes, WordArt, and screen shots. Model answers for this chapter's projects appear on the following pages.

Note: Before beginning the projects, copy to your storage medium the WL1C5 subfolder from the WL1 folder on the CD that accompanies this textbook and then make WL1C5 the active folder.

Model Answers

COMPUTER INPUT DEVICES

Engineers have been especially creative in designing new ways to get information into computers. Some input methods are highly specialized and unusual, while common devices often undergo redesign to improve their capabilities or their ergonomics, the ways in which they affect people physically. Some common input devices include keyboards, mice, trackballs, and touchpads.

Keyboard

A keyboard can be an external device that is attached by means of a cable, or it can be attached to the CPU case itself as it is for laptop computers. Most keyboards today are QWERTY keyboards, which take their name from the first six keys at the left of the first row of letters. An alternative, the DVORAK keyboard, places the most commonly used keys close to the user's fingertips and speeds typing.

Many keyboards have a separate numeric keypad, like that of a calculator, containing numbers and mathematical operators. All keyboards have modifier keys that enable the user to change the symbol or character that is entered when a given key is pressed. The Shift key, for example, makes a letter uppercase. Keyboards also have special cursor keys that enable the user to change the position on the screen of the cursor, a symbol that appears on the monitor to show where in a document the next change will appear. Most keyboards also have function keys, labeled F1, F2, F3, and so on. These keys allow the user to issue commands by pressing a single key.

Mouse

Graphical operating systems contain many elements that a user can choose by pointing at them. Such elements include buttons, tools, pull-down menus, and icons for file folders, programs, and document files. Often pointing to and clicking on one of these elements is more convenient than using the cursor or arrow keys on the keyboard. This pointing and clicking can be done by using a mouse. The mouse is the second most common input device, after the keyboard. A mouse operates by moving the cursor on the computer screen to correspond to movements made with the mouse.

Trackball

A trackball is like an upside-down mouse. A mouse is moved over a pad. A trackball remains stationary, and the user moves the ball with his or her fingers or palm. One or more buttons for choosing options are incorporated into the design of the trackball.

Touchpad and Touchscreen

A touchpad feels less mechanical than a mouse or trackball because the user simply moves a finger on the pad. A touchpad has two parts. One part acts as a button, while the other emulates a mouse pad on which the user traces the location of the cursor with a finger. People with carpal tunnel syndrome find touchpads and trackballs easier to use than mice. Many portable computers have built-in trackballs or touchpads as input devices.

1

A touchscreen allows the user to choose options by pressing the appropriate part of the screen. Touchscreens are widely used in bank ATMs and in kiosks at retail outlets and in tourist areas.

Prepared by: Matthew Viña
SoftCell Technologies®
September 4, 2015
12:04 PM

2

Project 1 Format a Document on Computer Input Devices
WL1-C5-P1-InputDevices.docx

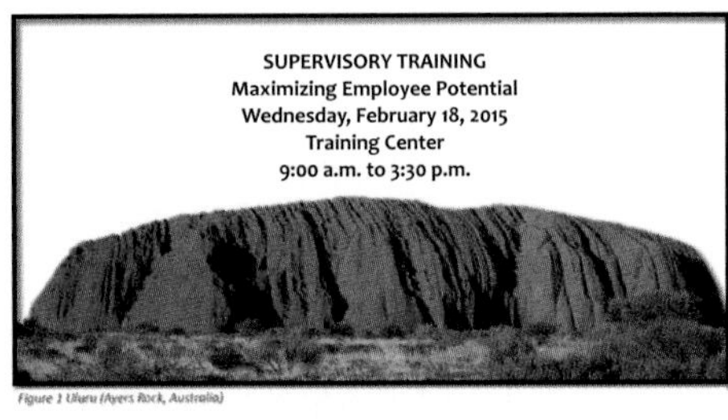

SUPERVISORY TRAINING
Maximizing Employee Potential
Wednesday, February 18, 2015
Training Center
9:00 a.m. to 3:30 p.m.

Figure 1 Uluru (Ayers Rock, Australia)

Project 2 Create an Announcement about Supervisory Training
WL1-C5-P2-Training.docx

ROBOTS AS ANDROIDS

Robotic factories are increasingly commonplace, especially in heavy manufacturing, where tolerance of repetitive movements, great strength, and untiring precision are more important than flexibility. Robots are especially useful in hazardous work, such as defusing bombs or handling radioactive materials. They also excel in constructing tiny components like those found inside notebook computers, which are often too small for humans to assemble.

Most people think of robots in science fiction terms, which generally depict them as androids, or simulated humans. Real robots today do not look human at all, and judged by human standards, they are not very intelligent. The task of creating a humanlike body has proven incredibly difficult. Many technological advances in visual perception, audio perception, touch, dexterity, locomotion, and navigation need to occur before robots that look and act like human beings will live and work among us.

Visual Perception

Visual perception is an area of great complexity. A large percentage of the human brain is dedicated to processing data coming from the eyes. As our most powerful sense, sight is the primary means through which we understand the world around us.

A single camera is not good enough to simulate the eye. Two cameras are needed to give stereoscopic vision, which allows depth and movement perception. Even with two cameras, visual perception is incomplete because the cameras cannot understand or translate what they see.

"The task of creating a humanlike body has proven incredibly difficult."

Processing the image is the difficult part. In order for a robot to move through a room full of furniture it must build a mental map of that room, complete with obstacles. The robot must judge the distance and size of objects before it can figure out how to move around them.

Audio Perception

Audio perception is less complex than visual perception, but no less important. People respond to audible cues about their surroundings and the people they are with without even thinking about it. Listeners can determine someone's emotional state just by hearing the person's voice. A car starting up when someone crosses the street prompts the walker to glance in that direction to check for danger. Identifying a single voice and interpreting what is being said amid accompanying background noise is a task that is among the most important for human beings—and the most difficult.

Tactile Perception

Tactile perception, or touch, is another critical sense. Robots can be built with any level of strength, since they are made of steel and motors. How does a robot capable of lifting a car pick up an egg in the dark

Page 1

Project 3 Customize a Report on Robots
WL1-C5-P3-Robots.docx

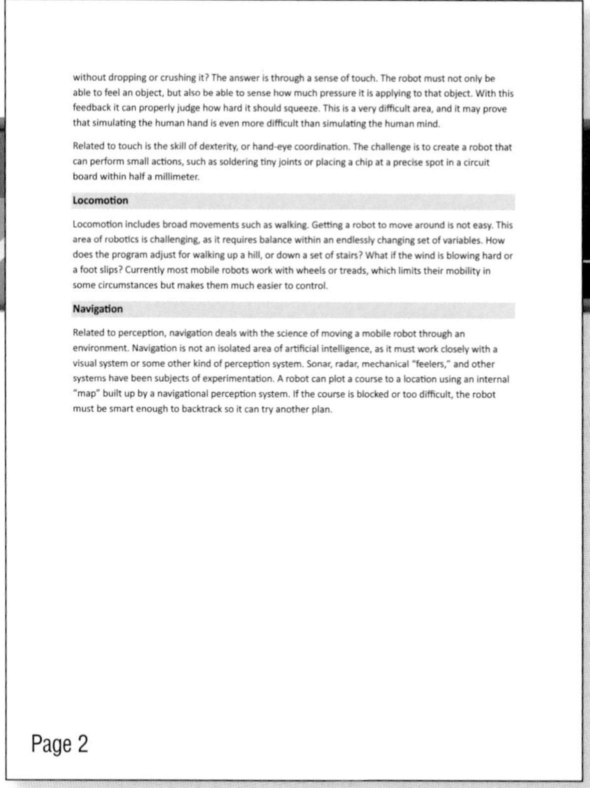

without dropping or crushing it? The answer is through a sense of touch. The robot must not only be able to feel an object, but also be able to sense how much pressure it is applying to that object. With this feedback it can properly judge how hard it should squeeze. This is a very difficult area, and it may prove that simulating the human hand is even more difficult than simulating the human mind.

Related to touch is the skill of dexterity, or hand-eye coordination. The challenge is to create a robot that can perform small actions, such as soldering tiny joints or placing a chip at a precise spot in a circuit board within half a millimeter.

Locomotion

Locomotion includes broad movements such as walking. Getting a robot to move around is not easy. This area of robotics is challenging, as it requires balance within an endlessly changing set of variables. How does the program adjust for walking up a hill, or down a set of stairs? What if the wind is blowing hard or a foot slips? Currently most mobile robots work with wheels or treads, which limits their mobility in some circumstances but makes them much easier to control.

Navigation

Related to perception, navigation deals with the science of moving a mobile robot through an environment. Navigation is not an isolated area of artificial intelligence, as it must work closely with a visual system or some other kind of perception system. Sonar, radar, mechanical "feelers," and other systems have been subjects of experimentation. A robot can plot a course to a location using an internal "map" built up by a navigational perception system. If the course is blocked or too difficult, the robot must be smart enough to backtrack so it can try another plan.

Page 2

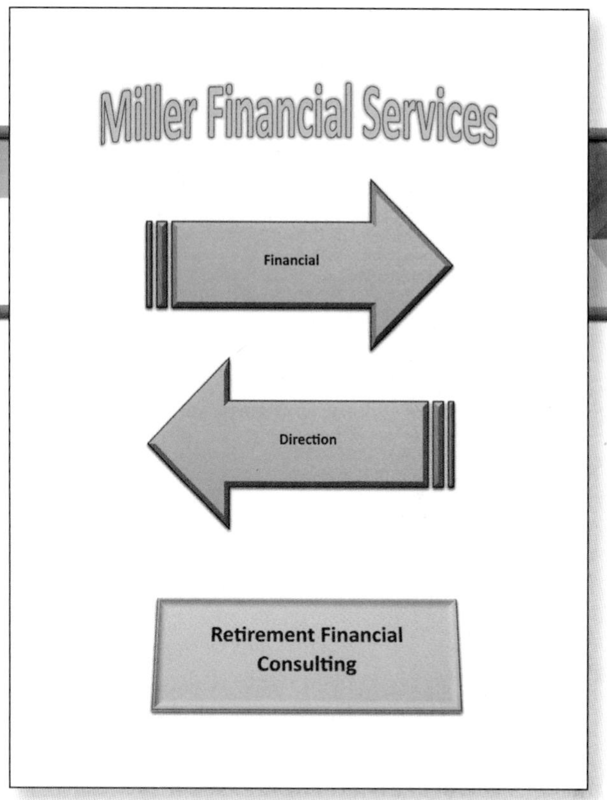

Project 4 Prepare a Company Flier

WL1-C5-P4-FinConsult.docx

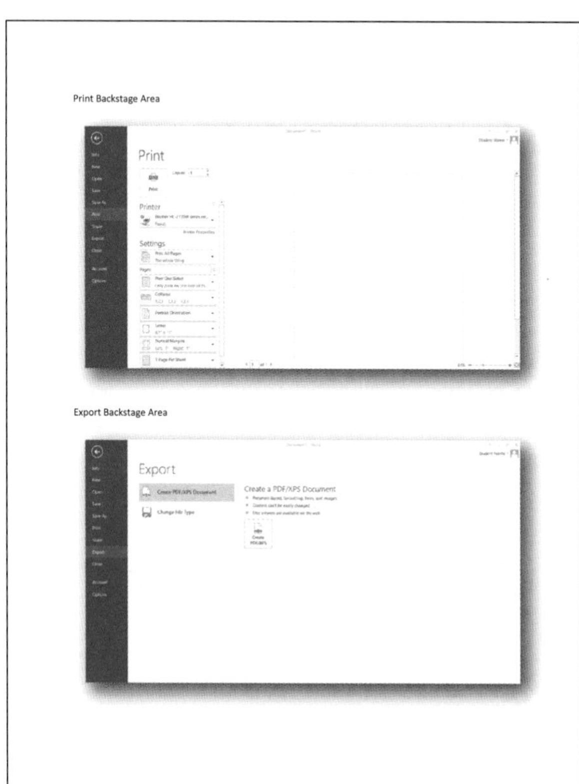

Print Backstage Area

Print

Export Backstage Area

Export

Create a PDF/XPS Document

Project 5 Create and Format Screenshots

WL1-C5-P5-BackstageAreas.docx

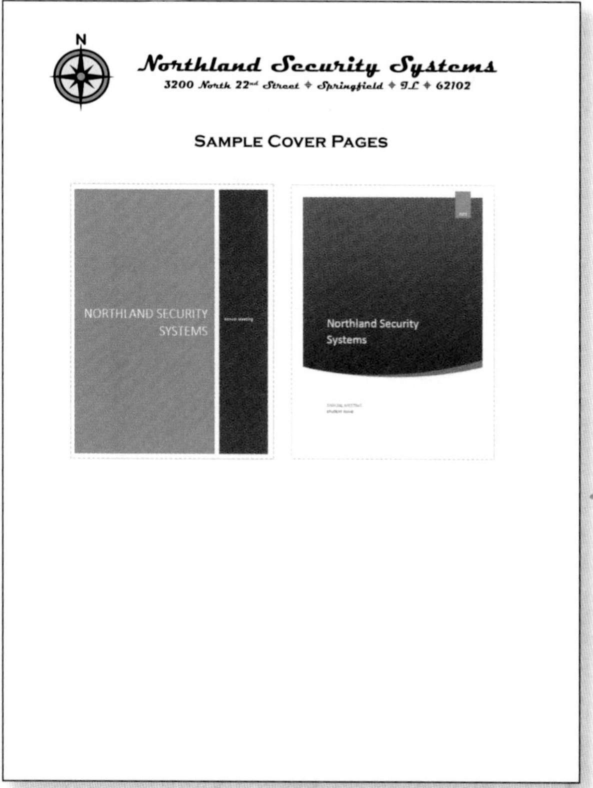

Northland Security Systems

3200 North 22nd Street ✦ Springfield ✦ IL ✦ 62102

SAMPLE COVER PAGES

NORTHLAND SECURITY SYSTEMS

Northland Security Systems

WL1-C5-P5-NSSCoverPages.docx

Project 1 Format a Document on Computer Input Devices — 8 Parts

You will format into columns text in a document on computer input devices, improve the readability of the document by hyphenating long words, and improve the visual appeal by inserting a drop cap.

Inserting a Section Break

Quick Steps

Insert a Section Break
1. Click PAGE LAYOUT tab.
2. Click Breaks button.
3. Click section break type in drop-down list.

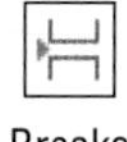

Breaks

HINT

If you delete a section break, the text that follows the section break takes on the formatting of the text preceding the break.

You can change the layout and formatting of specific portions of a document by inserting section breaks. For example, you can insert section breaks and then change margins for the text between the section breaks. If you want to format specific text in a document into columns, insert a section break.

Insert a section break in a document by clicking the PAGE LAYOUT tab, clicking the Breaks button in the Page Setup group, and then clicking the desired option in the *Section Breaks* section of the drop-down list. You can insert a section break that begins a new page or a continuous section break that does not begin a new page. A ***continuous section break*** separates the document into sections but does not insert a page break. Click one of the other three options in the *Section Breaks* section of the Breaks drop-down list if you want to insert a section break that begins a new page.

A section break inserted in a document is not visible in Print Layout view. Change to Draft view or click the Show/Hide ¶ button on the HOME tab to turn on the display of nonprinting characters and a section break displays in the document as a double row of dots with the words *Section Break* in the middle. Depending on the type of section break you insert, text follows *Section Break*. For example, if you insert a continuous section break, the words *Section Break (Continuous)* display in the middle of the row of dots. To delete a section break, change to Draft view, click on any character in the *Section Break (Continuous)* text, and then press the Delete key. (This moves the insertion point to the beginning of the section break.) Another option is to click the Show/Hide ¶ button to turn on the display of nonprinting characters, click on any character in the *Section Break (Continuous)* text, and then press the Delete key.

Project 1a Inserting a Continuous Section Break — Part 1 of 8

1. Open **InputDevices.docx** and then save it with Save As and name it **WL1-C5-P1-InputDevices**.
2. Insert a continuous section break by completing the following steps:
   a. Move the insertion point to the beginning of the *Keyboard* heading.
   b. Click the PAGE LAYOUT tab.
   c. Click the Breaks button in the Page Setup group and then click *Continuous* in the *Section Breaks* section of the drop-down list.
3. Click the HOME tab, click the Show/Hide ¶ button in the Paragraph group, and then notice the section break that displays at the end of the first paragraph of text.
4. Click the Show/Hide ¶ button to turn off the display of nonprinting characters.

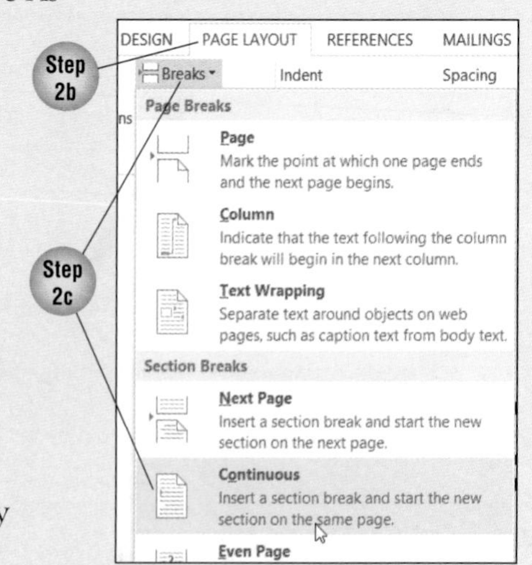

5. With the insertion point positioned at the beginning of the *Keyboard* heading, change the left and right margins to 1.5 inches. (The margin changes affect only the text after the continuous section break.)
6. Save and then print **WL1-C5-P1-InputDevices.docx**.

Creating Columns

Quick Steps

Create Columns
1. Click PAGE LAYOUT tab.
2. Click Columns button.
3. Click desired number of columns.

Columns

When preparing a document containing text, an important point to consider is the readability of the document. Readability refers to the ease with which a person can read and understand groups of words. The line length of text in a document can enhance or detract from the readability of text. If the line length is too long, the reader may lose his or her place on the line and have a difficult time moving to the next line below. To improve the readability of documents such as newsletters or reports, you may want to set the text in columns. One common type of column is newspaper, which is typically used for text in newspapers, newsletters, and magazines. ***Newspaper columns*** contain text in vertical columns.

Create newspaper columns with the Columns button in the Page Setup group on the PAGE LAYOUT tab or with options at the Columns dialog box. The Columns button creates columns of equal width. Use the Columns dialog box to create columns with varying widths. A document can include as many columns as room available on the page. Word determines how many columns can be included on the page based on the page width, the margin widths, and the size and spacing of the columns. Columns must be at least 0.5 inch in width. Changes in columns affect the entire document or the section of the document in which the insertion point is positioned.

Project 1b **Formatting Text into Columns** **Part 2 of 8**

1. With **WL1-C5-P1-InputDevices.docx** open, make sure the insertion point is positioned below the section break and then change the left and right margins back to 1 inch.
2. Delete the section break by completing the following steps:
   a. Click the Show/Hide ¶ button in the Paragraph group on the HOME tab to turn on the display of nonprinting characters.
   b. Click any character in the *Section Break (Continuous)* text located at the end of the first paragraph in the document.

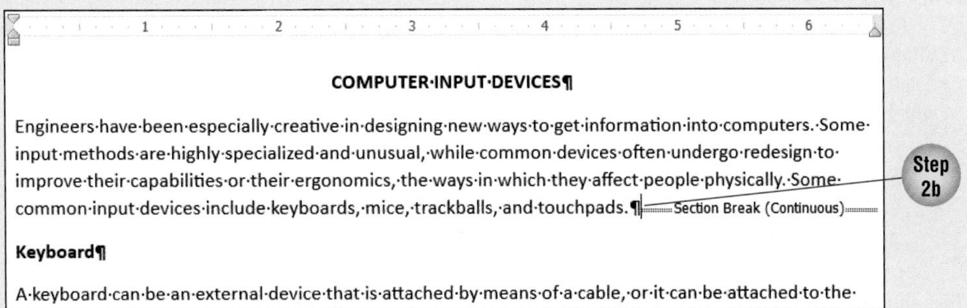

   c. Press the Delete key.
   d. Click the Show/Hide ¶ button to turn off the display of nonprinting characters.

3. Move the insertion point to the beginning of the first paragraph of text in the document and then insert a continuous section break.
4. Format the text into columns by completing the following steps:
   a. Make sure the insertion point is positioned below the section break.
   b. If necessary, click the PAGE LAYOUT tab.
   c. Click the Columns button in the Page Setup group.
   d. Click *Two* at the drop-down list.
5. Save **WL1-C5-P1-InputDevices.docx**.

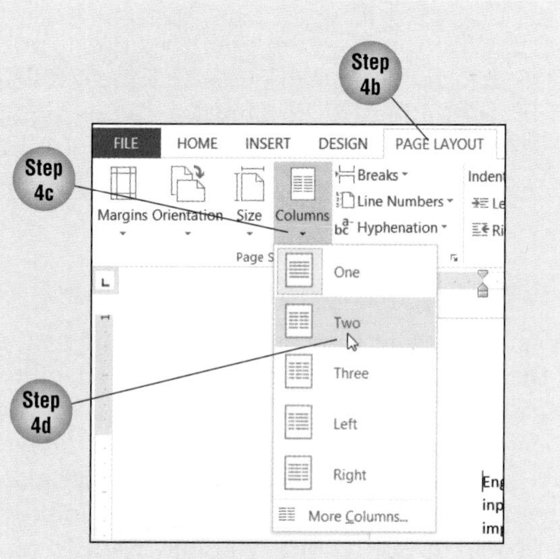

Creating Columns with the Columns Dialog Box

Quick Steps

Create Columns with the Columns Dialog Box
1. Click PAGE LAYOUT tab.
2. Click Columns button.
3. Click *More Columns* at the drop-down list.
4. Specify column options.
5. Click OK.

Use the Columns dialog box to create newspaper columns that are equal or unequal in width. To display the Columns dialog box, shown in Figure 5.1, click the Columns button in the Page Setup group on the PAGE LAYOUT tab and then click *More Columns* at the drop-down list.

With options at the Columns dialog box, specify the style and number of columns, enter your own column measurements, create unequal columns, and insert a line between columns. By default, column formatting is applied to the whole document. With the *Apply to* option box at the bottom of the Columns dialog box, you can change this from *Whole document* to *This point forward*. With the *This point forward* option, a section break is inserted and the column formatting is applied to text from the location of the insertion point to the end of the document or until other column formatting is encountered. The *Preview* section of the dialog box displays an example of how the columns will appear in the document.

Figure 5.1 Columns Dialog Box

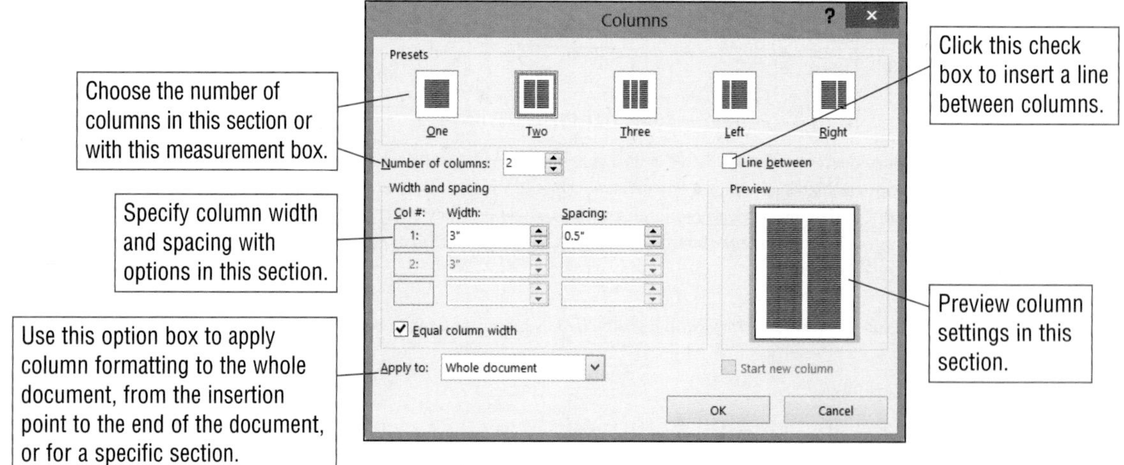

Removing Column Formatting

To remove column formatting using the Columns button, position the insertion point in the section containing columns, click the PAGE LAYOUT tab, click the Columns button, and then click *One* at the drop-down list. You can also remove column formatting at the Columns dialog box by selecting the *One* option in the *Presets* section.

Inserting a Column Break

When formatting text into columns, Word automatically breaks the columns to fit the page. At times, column breaks may appear in an undesirable location. You can insert a column break by positioning the insertion point where you want the column to end, clicking the PAGE LAYOUT tab, clicking the Breaks button, and then clicking *Column* at the drop-down list.

You can also insert a column break with the keyboard shortcut Ctrl + Shift + Enter.

Project 1c **Formatting Columns at the Columns Dialog Box** **Part 3 of 8**

1. With **WL1-C5-P1-InputDevices.docx** open, delete the section break by completing the following steps:
   a. Click the VIEW tab and then click the Draft button in the Views group.
   b. Click on any character in the *Section Break (Continuous)* text and then press the Delete key.
   c. Click the Print Layout button in the Views group on the VIEW tab.
2. Remove column formatting by clicking the PAGE LAYOUT tab, clicking the Columns button in the Page Setup group, and then clicking *One* at the drop-down list.
3. Format text in columns by completing the following steps:
   a. Position the insertion point at the beginning of the first paragraph of text in the document.
   b. Click the Columns button in the Page Setup group and then click *More Columns* at the drop-down list.
   c. At the Columns dialog box, click *Two* in the *Presets* section.
   d. Click the down-pointing arrow at the right of the *Spacing* measurement box until *0.3"* displays.
   e. Click the *Line between* check box to insert a check mark.
   f. Click the down-pointing arrow at the right side of the *Apply to* option box and then click *This point forward* at the drop-down list.
   g. Click OK to close the dialog box.

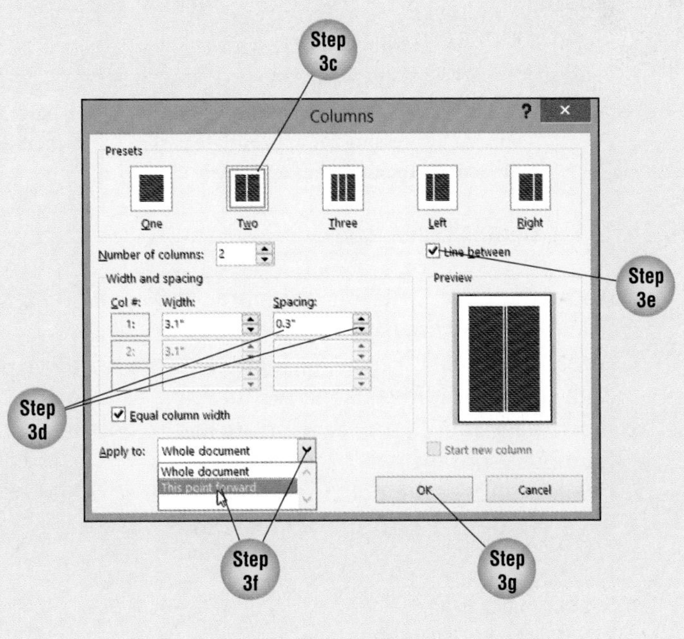

4. Insert a column break by completing the following steps:
   a. Position the insertion point at the beginning of the *Mouse* heading.
   b. Click the Breaks button in the Page Setup group and then click *Column* at the drop-down list.
5. Save and then print **WL1-C5-P1-InputDevices.docx**.

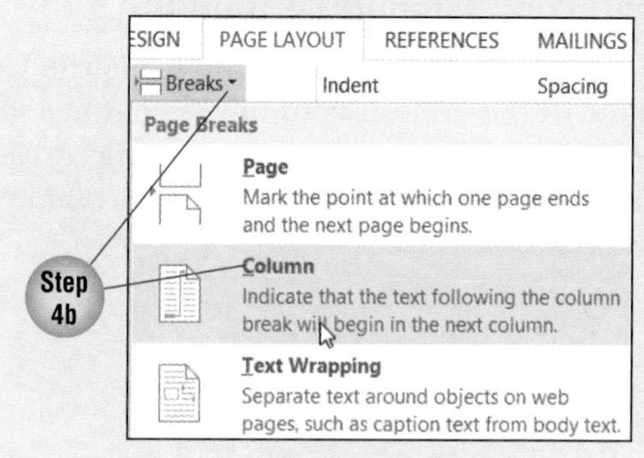

Balancing Columns on a Page

In a document containing text formatted into columns, Word automatically lines up (balances) the last line of text at the bottom of each column, except the last page. Text in the first column of the last page may flow to the end of the page, while the text in the second column may end far short of the end of the page. You can balance columns by inserting a continuous section break at the end of the text.

Project 1d Formatting and Balancing Columns of Text Part 4 of 8

1. With **WL1-C5-P1-InputDevices.docx** open, delete the column break by positioning the insertion point at the beginning of the *Mouse* heading and then pressing the Backspace key.
2. Select the entire document and then change the font to 12-point Constantia.
3. Move the insertion point to the end of the document and then balance the columns by clicking the PAGE LAYOUT tab, clicking the Breaks button, and then clicking *Continuous* at the drop-down list.

A touchscreen allows the user to choose options by pressing the appropriate part of the screen. Touchscreens are widely used in bank ATMs and in kiosks at retail outlets and in tourist areas.

Step 3

4. Apply the Green, Accent 6, Lighter 60% paragraph shading (last column, third row) to the title *COMPUTER INPUT DEVICES*.
5. Apply the Green, Accent 6, Lighter 80% paragraph shading (last column, second row) to each of the headings in the document.
6. Insert page numbering that prints at the bottom center of each page using the Plain Number 2 option.
7. Double-click in the document to make it active.
8. Save **WL1-C5-P1-InputDevices.docx**.

Hyphenating Words

In some Word documents, especially those with left and right margins wider than 1 inch or those with text set in columns, the right margin may appear quite ragged. To improve the display of text lines by making line lengths more uniform, consider hyphenating long words that fall at the ends of lines. When using the hyphenation feature, you can tell Word to hyphenate words automatically in a document or you can manually insert hyphens.

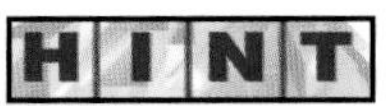

Avoid dividing words at the ends of more than two consecutive lines.

Automatically Hyphenating Words

To automatically hyphenate words in a document, click the PAGE LAYOUT tab, click the Hyphenation button in the Page Setup group, and then click *Automatic* at the drop-down list. Scroll through the document and check to see if hyphens display in appropriate locations within the words. If after hyphenating words in a document you want to remove all hyphens, immediately click the Undo button on the Quick Access toolbar.

Quick Steps

Turn on Automatic Hyphenation

1. Click PAGE LAYOUT tab.
2. Click Hyphenation button.
3. Click *Automatic* at drop-down list.

Apply Manual Hyphenation

1. Click PAGE LAYOUT tab.
2. Click Hyphenation button.
3. Click *Manual* at drop-down list.
4. Click Yes or No to hyphenate indicated words.
5. When complete, click OK.

Hyphenation

Manually Hyphenating Words

If you want to control where a hyphen appears in a word during hyphenation, choose manual hyphenation. To do this, click the PAGE LAYOUT tab, click the Hyphenation button in the Page Setup group, and then click *Manual* at the drop-down list. This displays the Manual Hyphenation dialog box, as shown in Figure 5.2. (The word in the *Hyphenate at* text box will vary.) At this dialog box, click Yes to hyphenate the word as indicated in the *Hyphenate at* text box, click No if you do not want the word hyphenated, or click Cancel to cancel hyphenation. You can also reposition the hyphen in the *Hyphenate at* text box. Word displays the word with syllable breaks indicated by hyphens. The position where the word will be hyphenated displays as a blinking black bar. If you want to hyphenate at a different location in the word, position the blinking black bar where you want the hyphen and then click Yes. Continue clicking Yes or No at the Manual Hyphenation dialog box.

Be careful with words ending in *-ed*. Several two-syllable words can be divided before that final syllable—for example, *noted*. However, one-syllable words ending in *-ed* should not be divided. An example is *served*. Watch for this type of occurrence and click No to cancel the hyphenation. At the hyphenation complete message, click OK.

Figure 5.2 Manual Hyphenation Dialog Box

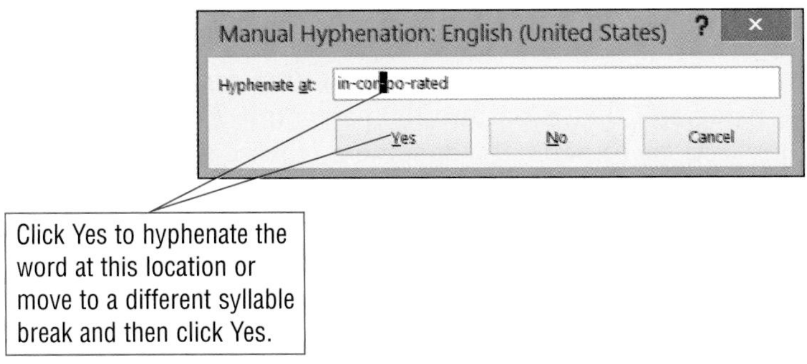
Manual Hyphenation: English (United States)
Hyphenate at: in-cor-po-rated
Yes
No
Cancel
Click Yes to hyphenate the word at this location or move to a different syllable break and then click Yes.

If you want to remove all hyphens in a document, immediately click the Undo button on the Quick Access toolbar. To delete a few but not all of the optional hyphens inserted during hyphenation, use the Find and Replace dialog box. To do this, display the Find and Replace dialog box with the Replace tab selected, insert an optional hyphen symbol in the *Find what* text box (to do this, click the More button, click the Special button, and then click *Optional Hyphen* at the pop-up list), and make sure the *Replace with* text box is empty. Complete the find and replace, clicking the Replace button to replace the hyphen with nothing or clicking the Find Next button to leave the hyphen in the document.

Project 1e **Automatically and Manually Hyphenating Words** **Part 5 of 8**

1. With **WL1-C5-P1-InputDevices.docx** open, hyphenate words automatically by completing the following steps:
   a. Press Ctrl + Home.
   b. Click the PAGE LAYOUT tab.
   c. Click the Hyphenation button in the Page Setup group and then click *Automatic* at the drop-down list.
2. Scroll through the document and notice the hyphenation.
3. Click the Undo button to remove the hyphens.
4. Manually hyphenate words by completing the following steps:
   a. Click the Hyphenation button in the Page Setup group and then click *Manual* at the drop-down list.
   b. At the Manual Hyphenation dialog box, make one of the following choices:
      - Click Yes to hyphenate the word as indicated in the *Hyphenate at* text box.
      - Move the hyphen in the word to a more desirable location and then click Yes.
      - Click No if you do not want the word hyphenated.
   c. Continue clicking Yes or No at the Manual Hyphenation dialog box.
   d. At the hyphenation complete message, click OK.
5. Save **WL1-C5-P1-InputDevices.docx**.

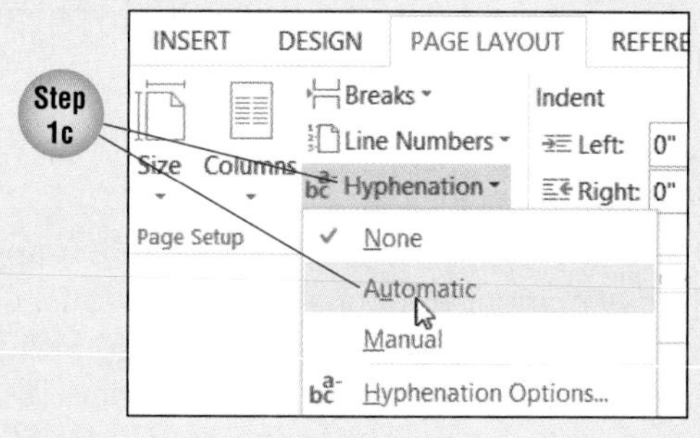

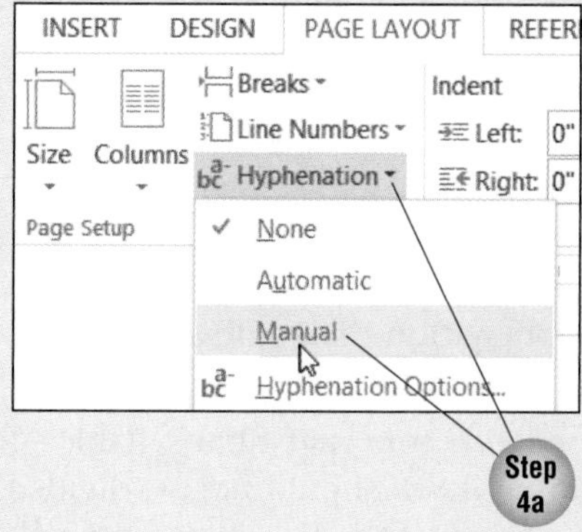

Quick Steps

Create a Drop Cap
1. Click INSERT tab.
2. Click Drop Cap button.
3. Click desired type in drop-down list.

Drop Cap

Creating a Drop Cap

Use a drop cap to enhance the appearance of text. A ***drop cap*** is the first letter of the first word of a paragraph that is set into the paragraph. Drop caps identify the beginnings of major sections or parts of a document. Create a drop cap with the Drop Cap button in the Text group on the INSERT tab. You can choose to set the drop cap in the paragraph or in the margin. At the Drop Cap dialog box, specify a font, the numbers of lines you want the letter to drop, and the distance you want the letter positioned from the text of the paragraph. Add a drop cap at the first word by selecting the word and then clicking the Drop Cap button.

Project 1f Inserting Drop Caps

Part 6 of 8

1. With **WL1-C5-P1-InputDevices.docx** open, create a drop cap by completing the following steps:
   a. Position the insertion point on the first word of the first paragraph of text (*Engineers*).
   b. Click the INSERT tab.
   c. Click the Drop Cap button in the Text group.
   d. Click *In margin* at the drop-down gallery.

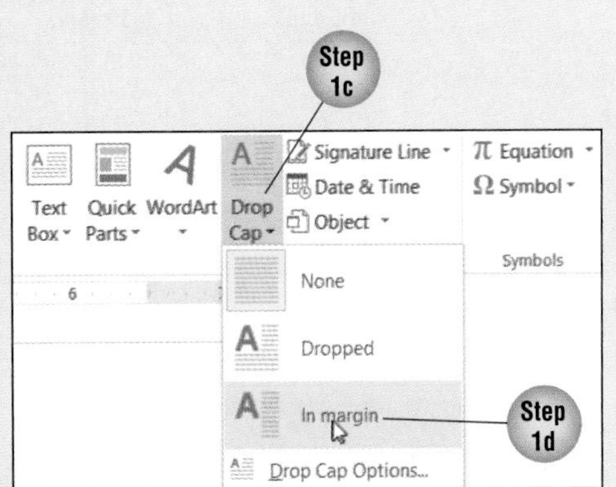

2. Looking at the drop cap, you decide that you do not like it in the margin and want it to be a little smaller. To change the drop cap, complete the following steps:
   a. With the E in the word *Engineers* selected, click the Drop Cap button in the Text group and then click *None* at the drop-down gallery.
   b. Click the Drop Cap button and then click *Drop Cap Options* at the drop-down gallery.
   c. At the Drop Cap dialog box, click *Dropped* in the *Position* section.
   d. Click the down-pointing arrow at the right side of the *Font* option box, scroll down the drop-down list, and then click *Cambria*.
   e. Click the down arrow at the right side of the *Lines to drop* measurement box to change the number to *2*.
   f. Click OK to close the dialog box.
   g. Click outside the drop cap to deselect it.
3. Save **WL1-C5-P1-InputDevices.docx**.

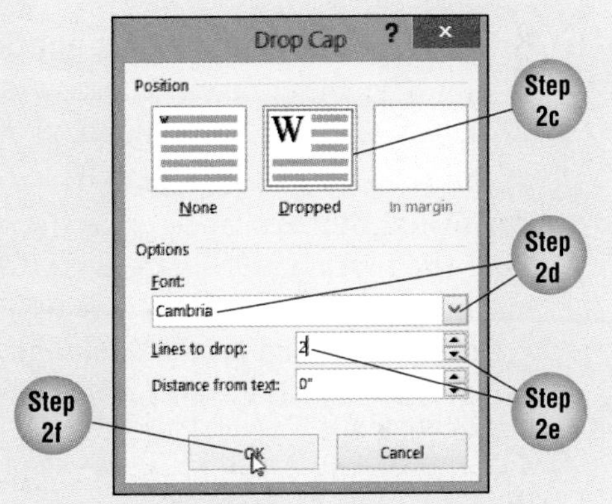

Inserting Symbols and Special Characters

Use the Symbol button on the INSERT tab to insert special symbols in a document. Click the Symbol button in the Symbols group on the INSERT tab and a drop-down list displays with the most recently inserted symbols along with a *More Symbols* option. Click one of the symbols that displays in the list to insert it in the document or click the *More Symbols* option to display the Symbol dialog box, as shown in Figure 5.3. At the Symbol dialog box, double-click the desired symbol and then click Close or click the desired symbol, click the Insert button, and then click Close.

At the Symbol dialog box with the Symbols tab selected, you can change the font with the *Font* option box. When you change the font, different symbols display in the dialog box. Click the Special Characters tab at the Symbol dialog box, and a list of special characters displays along with keyboard shortcuts to create these characters.

Quick Steps

Insert a Symbol
1. Click INSERT tab.
2. Click Symbol button.
3. Click desired symbol in drop-down list.

OR

1. Click INSERT tab.
2. Click Symbol button.
3. Click *More Symbols*.
4. Double-click desired symbol.
5. Click Close.

Symbol

Figure 5.3 Symbol Dialog Box with Symbols Tab Selected

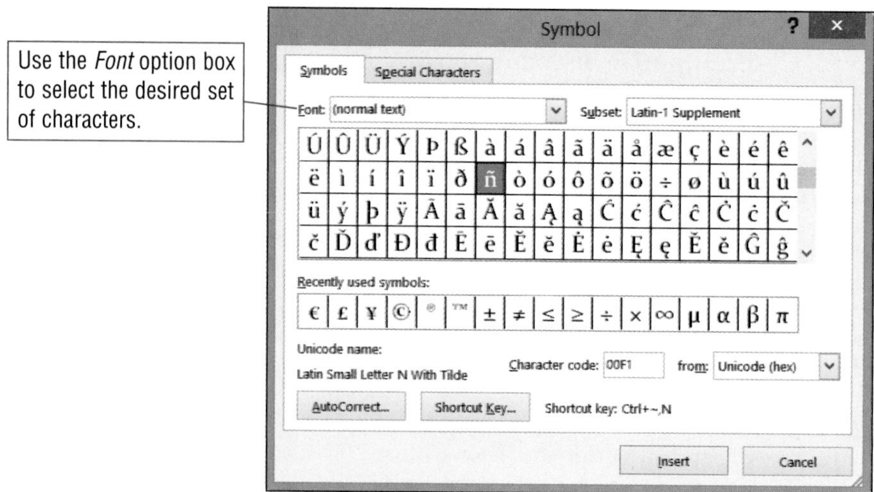

Project 1g Inserting Symbols and Special Characters

Part 7 of 8

1. With **WL1-C5-P1-InputDevices.docx** open, press Ctrl + End to move the insertion point to the end of the document.
2. Press the Enter key once, type **Prepared by:**, and then press the spacebar once.
3. Type the first name **Matthew** and then press the spacebar once.
4. Insert the last name *Viña* by completing the following steps:
   a. Type **Vi**.
   b. Click the Symbol button in the Symbols group on the INSERT tab.
   c. Click *More Symbols* at the drop-down list.
   d. At the Symbol dialog box, make sure the *Font* option box displays *(normal text)* and then double-click the ñ symbol (located in approximately the tenth through twelfth row).
   e. Click the Close button.
   f. Type **a**.

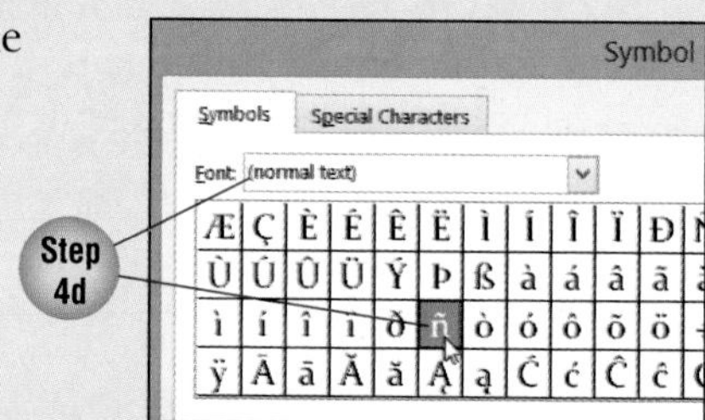

5. Press Shift + Enter.
6. Insert the keyboard symbol (⌨) by completing the following steps:
   a. Click the Symbol button and then click *More Symbols*.
   b. At the Symbol dialog box, click the down-pointing arrow at the right side of the *Font* option box and then click *Wingdings* at the drop-down list. (You will need to scroll down the list to display this option.)
   c. Double-click ⌨ (located approximately in the second row).
   d. Click the Close button.
7. Type **SoftCell Technologies**.

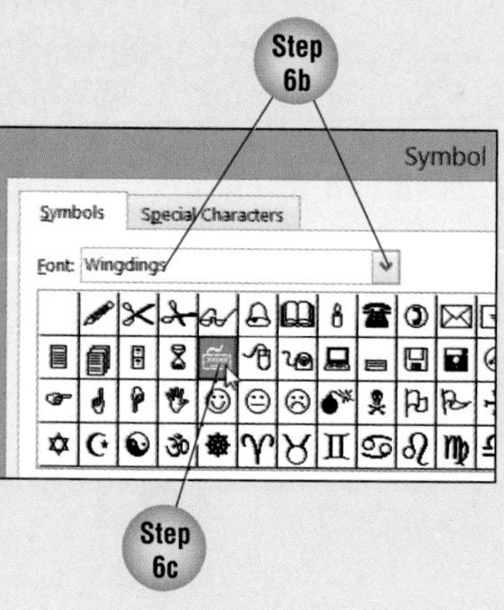

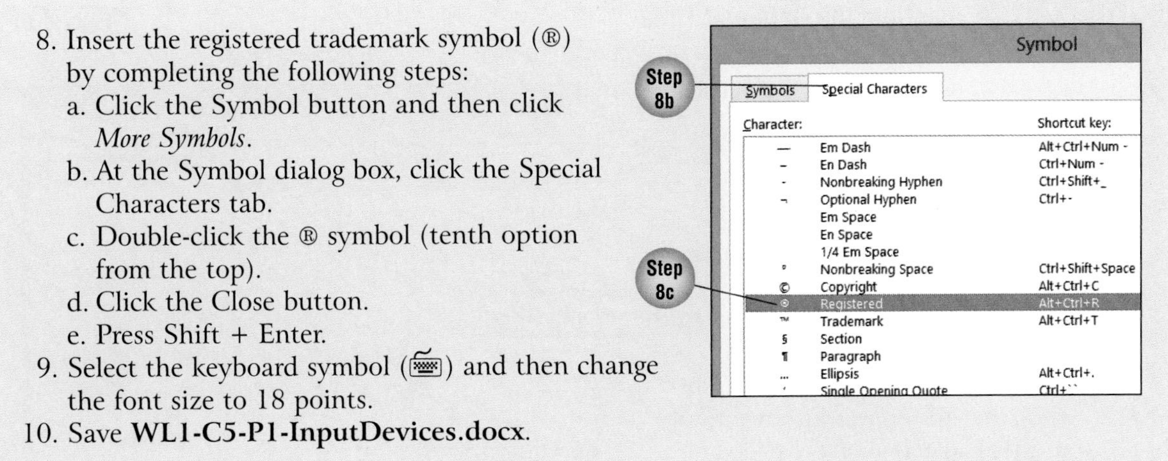

8. Insert the registered trademark symbol (®) by completing the following steps:
   a. Click the Symbol button and then click *More Symbols*.
   b. At the Symbol dialog box, click the Special Characters tab.
   c. Double-click the ® symbol (tenth option from the top).
   d. Click the Close button.
   e. Press Shift + Enter.
9. Select the keyboard symbol (⌨) and then change the font size to 18 points.
10. Save **WL1-C5-P1-InputDevices.docx**.

Inserting the Date and Time

Use the Date & Time button in the Text group on the INSERT tab to insert the current date and time in a document. Click this button and the Date and Time dialog box displays, as shown in Figure 5.4. (Your date will vary from what you see in the figure.) At the Date and Time dialog box, click the desired date and/or time format in the *Available formats* list box.

If the *Update automatically* check box does not contain a check mark, the date and/or time are inserted in the document as normal text that you can edit in the normal manner. You can also insert the date and/or time as a field. The advantage to inserting the date or time as a field is that the date and time are updated when you reopen the document. You can also update the date and time in the document with the Update Field keyboard shortcut, F9. Insert a check mark in the *Update automatically* check box to insert the date and/or time as a field. You can also insert the date as a field using the keyboard shortcut Alt + Shift + D, and insert the time as a field with the keyboard shortcut Alt + Shift + T.

Quick Steps

Insert the Date and Time
1. Click INSERT tab.
2. Click Date & Time button.
3. Click desired option in list box.
4. Click OK.

Date & Time

Figure 5.4 Date and Time Dialog Box

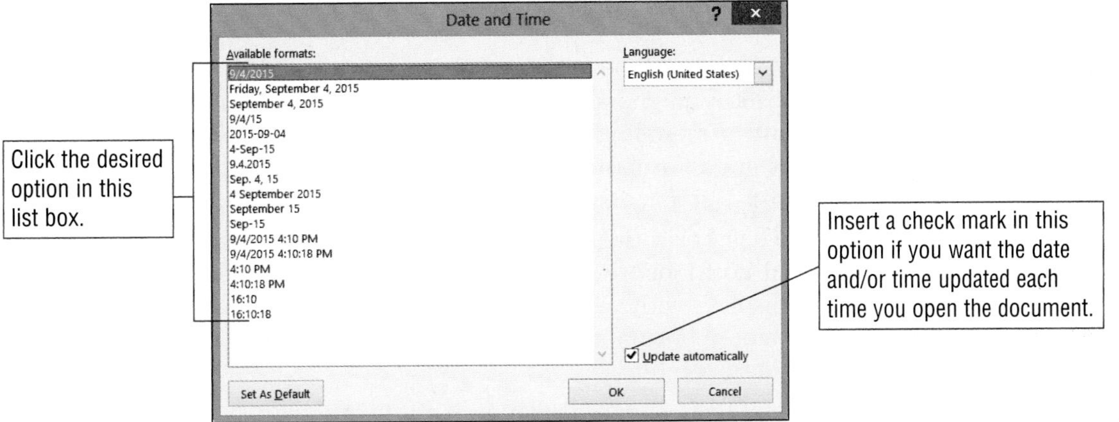

Project 1h Inserting the Date and Time

Part 8 of 8

1. With **WL1-C5-P1-InputDevices.docx** open, press Ctrl + End and make sure the insertion point is positioned below the company name.
2. Insert the current date by completing the following steps:
   a. Click the Date & Time button in the Text group on the INSERT tab.
   b. At the Date and Time dialog box, click the third option from the top in the *Available formats* list box. (Your date and times will vary from what you see in the image at the right.)
   c. Click in the *Update automatically* check box to insert a check mark.
   d. Click OK to close the dialog box.

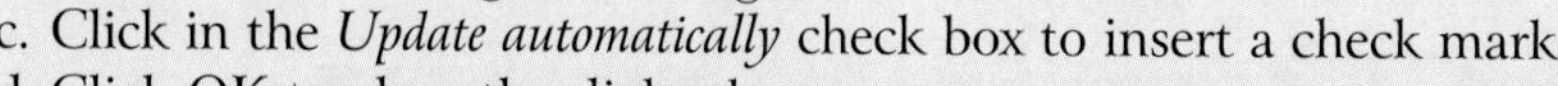

3. Press Shift + Enter.

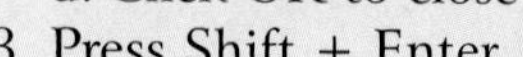

4. Insert the current time by pressing Alt + Shift + T.
5. Save **WL1-C5-P1-InputDevices.docx**.
6. Update the time by clicking the time and then pressing F9.
7. Save, print, and then close **WL1-C5-P1-InputDevices.docx**.

Project 2 Create an Announcement about Supervisory Training

3 Parts

You will create an announcement about upcoming supervisory training and use the Click and Type feature to center and right align text. You will vertically center the text on the page and insert and format a picture to add visual appeal to the announcement.

Using the Click and Type Feature

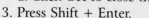

Quick Steps

Use Click and Type
1. Hover mouse at left margin, between left and right margins, or at right margin.
2. Double-click left mouse button.

Word contains a Click and Type feature you can use to position the insertion point at a specific location and alignment in the document. This feature allows you to position one or more lines of text as you type, rather than typing the text and then selecting and reformatting the text, which requires multiple steps.

To use the Click and Type feature, make sure the document displays in Print Layout view and then hover the mouse pointer at the location where you want the insertion point positioned. As you move the mouse pointer, you will notice that the pointer displays with varying horizontal lines representing the alignment. Double-click the mouse button and the insertion point is positioned at the location of the mouse pointer.

If the horizontal lines do not display next to the mouse pointer when you double-click the mouse button, a left tab is set at the position of the insertion point. If you want to change the alignment and not set a tab, make sure the horizontal lines display near the mouse pointer before double-clicking the mouse.

Project 2a **Using Click and Type** **Part 1 of 3**

1. At a blank document, create the centered text shown in Figure 5.5 by completing the following steps:
   a. Position the I-beam pointer between the left and right margins at about the 3.25-inch mark on the horizontal ruler and the top of the vertical ruler.
   b. When the center alignment lines display below the I-beam pointer, double-click the left mouse button.

   c. Type the centered text shown in Figure 5.5. Press Shift + Enter to end each text line.
2. Change to right alignment by completing the following steps:
   a. Position the I-beam pointer near the right margin at approximately the 1-inch mark on the vertical ruler until the right alignment lines display at the left side of the I-beam pointer.
   b. Double-click the left mouse button.
   c. Type the right-aligned text shown in Figure 5.5. Press Shift + Enter to end the text line.
3. Select the centered text and then change the font to 14-point Candara bold and the line spacing to double spacing.
4. Select the right-aligned text, change the font to 10-point Candara bold, and then deselect the text.
5. Save the document and name it **WL1-C5-P2-Training**.

Figure 5.5 Project 2a

SUPERVISORY TRAINING
Maximizing Employee Potential
Wednesday, February 18, 2015
Training Center
9:00 a.m. to 3:30 p.m.

Sponsored by
Cell Systems

Vertically Aligning Text

Text in a Word document is aligned at the top of the page by default. You can change this alignment with the *Vertical alignment* option box at the Page Setup dialog box with the Layout tab selected, as shown in Figure 5.6. Display this dialog box by clicking the PAGE LAYOUT tab, clicking the Page Setup group dialog box launcher, and then clicking the Layout tab at the Page Setup dialog box.

Figure 5.6 Page Setup Dialog Box with Layout Tab Selected

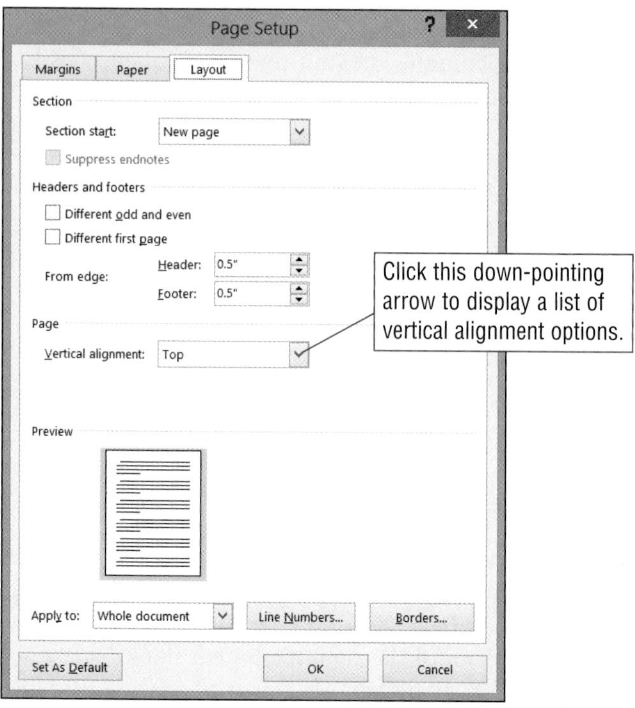

Quick Steps

Vertically Align Text

1. Click PAGE LAYOUT tab.
2. Click Page Setup group dialog box launcher.
3. Click Layout tab.
4. Click *Vertical alignment* option box.
5. Click desired alignment.
6. Click OK.

The *Vertical alignment* option box in the Page Setup dialog box contains four choices: *Top*, *Center*, *Justified*, and *Bottom*. The default setting is *Top*, which aligns text at the top of the page. Choose *Center* if you want text centered vertically on the page. The *Justified* option will align text between the top and the bottom margins. The *Center* option positions text in the middle of the page vertically, while the *Justified* option adds space between paragraphs of text (not within) to fill the page from the top to bottom margins. If you center or justify text, the text does not display centered or justified on the screen in the Draft view, but it does display centered or justified in the Print Layout view. Choose the *Bottom* option to align text in the document vertically along the bottom of the page.

Project 2b Vertically Centering Text

Part 2 of 3

1. With **WL1-C5-P2-Training.docx** open, click the PAGE LAYOUT tab and then click the Page Setup group dialog box launcher.
2. At the Page Setup dialog box, click the Layout tab.
3. Click the down-pointing arrow at the right side of the *Vertical alignment* option box and then click *Center* at the drop-down list.
4. Click OK to close the dialog box.
5. Save and then print **WL1-C5-P2-Training.docx**.

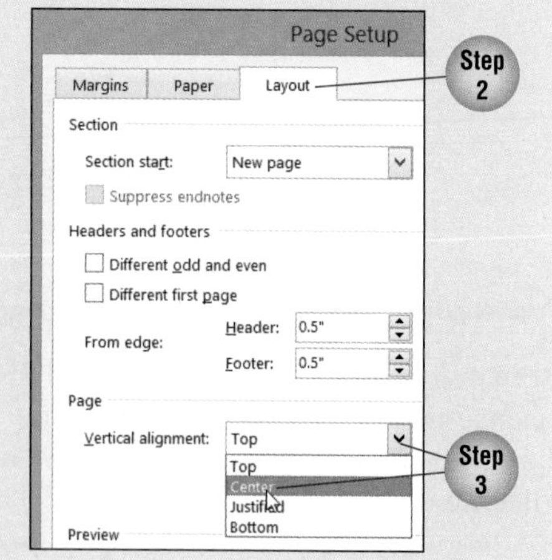

Inserting an Image

You can insert an image such as a picture or clip art in a Word document with buttons in the Illustrations group on the INSERT tab. Click the Pictures button to display the Insert Picture dialog box, where you can specify the desired picture file, or click the Online Pictures button and search online for images such as pictures and clip art. When you insert an image in a document, the PICTURE TOOLS FORMAT tab displays. Use options on this tab to customize and format the image.

Customizing and Formatting an Image

Use options in the Adjust group on the PICTURE TOOLS FORMAT tab to remove unwanted portions of the image, correct the brightness and contrast, change the image color, apply artistic effects, compress the size of the image file, change to a different image, and reset the image back to the original formatting. Use buttons in the Picture Styles group to apply a predesigned style to the image, change the image border, and apply other effects to the image. With options in the Arrange group, you can position the image on the page, specify how text will wrap around it, align the image with other elements in the document, and rotate the image. Use the Crop button in the Size group to remove any unnecessary parts of the image and specify the image size with the *Shape Height* and *Shape Width* measurement boxes.

Crop

In addition to the PICTURE TOOLS FORMAT tab, you can customize and format an image with options at the shortcut menu. Display this menu by right-clicking the image. With options at the shortcut menu, you can change the picture, insert a caption, choose text wrapping, size and position the image, and display the Format Picture task pane.

When you insert a picture or image in a document, the default text wrapping style is *Top and Bottom*. At this wrapping style, text wraps above and below the image. Change text wrapping with the Position and Wrap Text buttons on the PICTURE TOOLS FORMAT tab and with options from the Layout Options button side menu. The Layout Options button displays just outside the upper right corner of a selected image. Click this button to display a side menu with wrapping options and click the *See more* hyperlink that displays at the bottom of the side menu to display the Layout dialog box containing additional options for positioning the image on the page. Close the Layout Options button side menu by clicking the button or clicking the Close button located in the upper right corner of the side menu.

Position

Wrap Text

Layout Options

Sizing an Image

Change the size of an image with the *Shape Height* and *Shape Width* measurement boxes in the Size group on the PICTURE TOOLS FORMAT tab or with the sizing handles that display around the selected image. To change size with a sizing handle, position the mouse pointer on a sizing handle until the pointer turns into a double-headed arrow and then hold down the left mouse button. Drag the sizing handle in or out to decrease or increase the size of the image and then release the mouse button. Use the middle sizing handles at the left or right side of the image to make the image wider or thinner. Use the middle sizing handles at the top or bottom of the image to make the image taller or shorter. Use the sizing handles at the corners of the image to change both the width and height at the same time.

Resize a selected object horizontally, vertically, or diagonally from the center outward by holding down the Ctrl key and then dragging a sizing handle.

Moving an Image

Move an image to a specific location on the page with options at the Position button drop-down gallery in the Arrange group on the PICTURE TOOLS FORMAT tab. When you choose an option from this gallery, the image is moved to the specified location on the page and square text wrapping is applied to the image.

You can also move the image by dragging it to the desired location. Before dragging an image, however, you must first choose how the text will wrap around it by clicking the Wrap Text button in the Arrange group and then clicking the desired wrapping style at the drop-down list. After choosing a wrapping style, move the image by positioning the mouse pointer on the image border until the arrow pointer turns into a four-headed arrow. Hold down the left mouse button, drag the image to the desired position, and then release the mouse button. As you move an image to the top, left, right, or bottom margins or to the center of the document, green alignment guides display. Use these guides to help you position an image on the page. You can also turn on gridlines to help you precisely position an image. Do this by clicking the Align button in the Arrange group on the PICTURE TOOLS FORMAT tab and then clicking *View Gridlines.*

Rotate the image by positioning the mouse pointer on the round rotation handle (circular arrow) that displays above the image until the pointer displays with a black circular arrow attached. Hold down the left mouse button, drag in the desired direction, and then release the mouse button.

Quick Steps

Insert a Picture
1. Click INSERT tab.
2. Click Pictures button.
3. Double-click desired picture in Insert Picture dialog box.

Pictures

Inserting a Picture

To insert a picture in a document, click the INSERT tab and then click the Pictures button in the Illustrations group. At the Insert Picture dialog box, navigate to the folder containing the desired picture and then double-click the picture. Use buttons on the PICTURE TOOLS FORMAT tab to format and customize the picture.

Project 2c **Inserting and Customizing a Picture** **Part 3 of 3**

1. With **WL1-C5-P2-Training.docx** open, return the vertical alignment back to top alignment by completing the following steps:
   a. Click the PAGE LAYOUT tab.
   b. Click the Page Setup group dialog box launcher.
   c. At the Page Setup dialog box, make sure the Layout tab is selected.
   d. Click the down-pointing arrow at the right side of the *Vertical alignment* option box and then click *Top* at the drop-down list.
   e. Click OK to close the dialog box.
2. Select and then delete the text *Sponsored by* and the text *Cell Systems.*
3. Select the remaining text and change the line spacing to single spacing.
4. Move the insertion point to the beginning of the document, press the Enter key, and then move the insertion back to the beginning of the document.
5. Insert a picture by completing the following steps:
   a. Click the INSERT tab and then click the Pictures button in the Illustrations group.
   b. At the Insert Picture dialog box, navigate to your WL1C5 folder.
   c. Double-click *Uluru.jpg* in the Content pane.

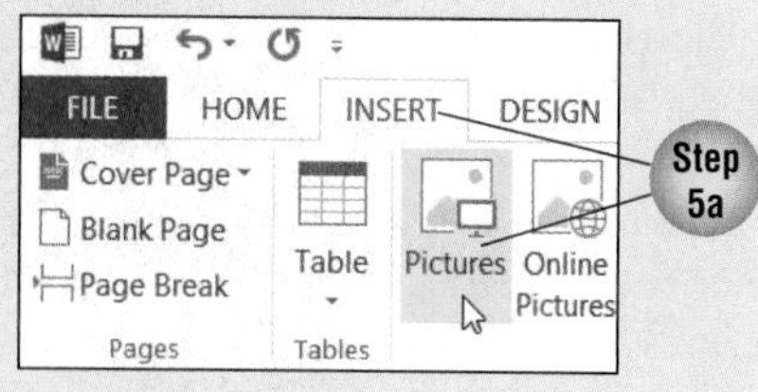

6. Crop the picture by completing the following steps:
   a. Click the Crop button in the Size group on the PICTURE TOOLS FORMAT tab.
   b. Position the mouse pointer on the bottom middle crop handle (displays as a short black line) until the pointer turns into the crop tool (displays as a small black T).
   c. Hold down the left mouse button, drag up to just below the rock as shown at the right, and then release the mouse button.
   d. Click the Crop button in the Size group to turn off the feature.

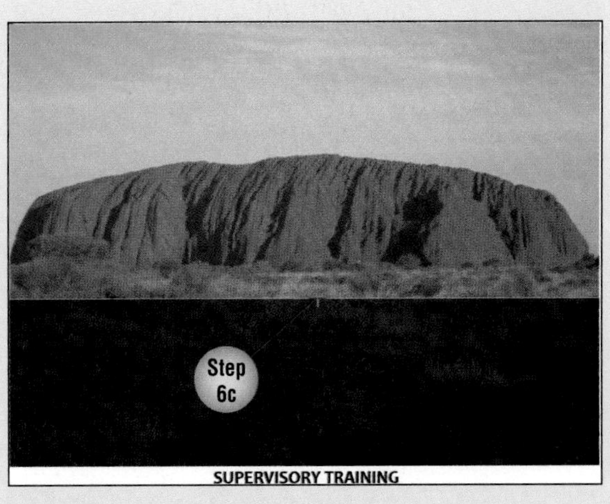

7. Change the size of the picture by clicking in the *Shape Height* measurement box in the Size group, typing 3.1, and then pressing Enter.
8. Move the picture behind the text by clicking the Layout Options button that displays outside the upper right corner of the picture and then clicking the *Behind Text* option at the side menu (second column, second row in the *With Text Wrapping* section). Close the side menu by clicking the Close button located in the upper right corner of the side menu.

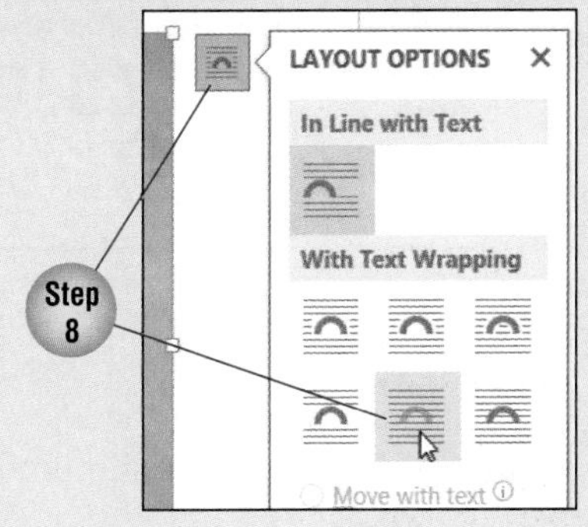

9. Rotate the image by clicking the Rotate Objects button in the Arrange group and then clicking *Flip Horizontal* at the drop-down list.

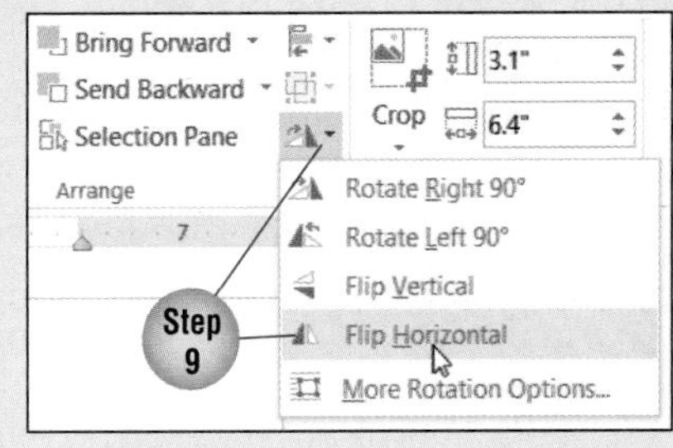

10. Change the picture color by clicking the Color button in the Adjust group and then clicking *Saturation: 300%* (sixth option in the *Color Saturation* section.)

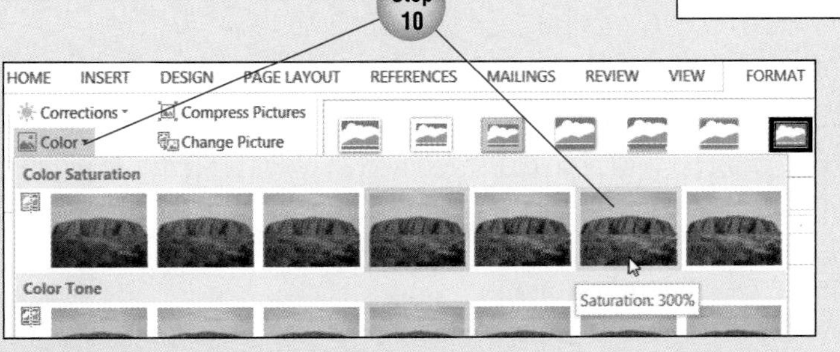

11. After looking at the coloring, you decide to return to the original color by clicking the Undo button on the Quick Access toolbar.
12. Sharpen the picture by clicking the Corrections button in the Adjust group and then clicking the *Sharpen: 25%* option (fourth option in the *Sharpen/Soften* section).

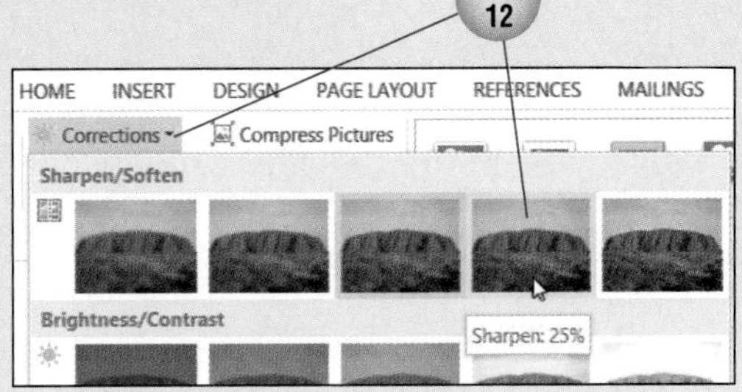

13. Change the contrast of the picture by clicking the Corrections button in the Adjust group and then clicking the *Brightness: 0% (Normal) Contrast: +40%* option (third option in the bottom row in the *Brightness/Contrast* section).
14. Apply a picture style by clicking the More button at the right side of the thumbnails in the Picture Styles group and then clicking the *Simple Frame, Black* option (second column, second row).

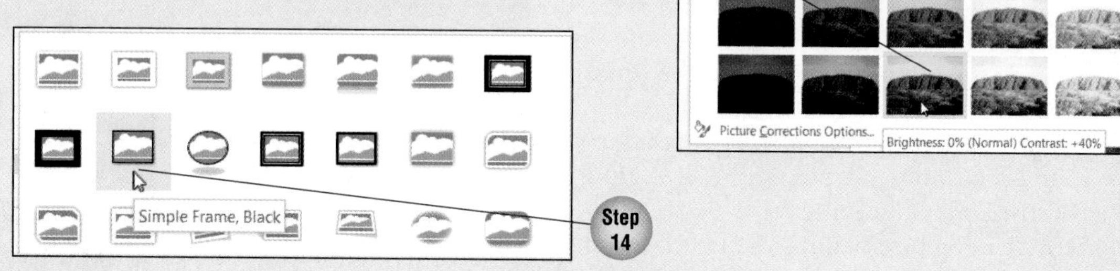

15. Compress the picture by completing the following steps:
    a. Click the Compress Pictures button in the Adjust group.
    b. At the Compress Pictures dialog box, make sure a check mark displays in both options in the *Compression options* section and then click OK.
16. Position the mouse pointer on the border of the selected picture until the pointer displays with a four-headed arrow attached. Hold down the left mouse button, drag the picture up and slightly to the left until you see green alignment guides at the top margin and the center of the page, and then release the mouse button.
17. Save and then print **WL1-C5-P2-Training.docx**.
18. With the picture selected, remove the background by completing the following steps:
    a. Click the Remove Background button in the Adjust group on the PICTURE TOOLS FORMAT tab.
    b. Using the left middle sizing handle, drag the left border to the left border line of the image.
    c. Drag the right middle sizing handle to the right border line of the image.
    d. Drag the bottom middle sizing handle to the very bottom border of the image, which displays as a dashed line.
    e. Drag the top middle sizing handle down to just above the top of the rock.

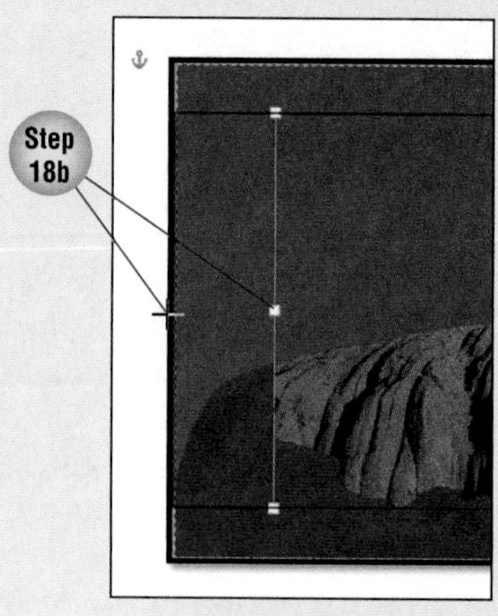

f. Click the Keep Changes button in the Close group on the BACKGROUND REMOVAL tab. (The picture should now display with the sky removed.)
19. Insert a caption by completing the following steps:
    a. Right-click the picture. (This displays the shortcut menu.)
    b. Click the *Insert Caption* option at the shortcut menu.
    c. At the Caption dialog box with the insertion point positioned in the *Caption* text box after the *Figure 1* text, press the spacebar and then type **Uluru (Ayers Rock, Australia)**.
    d. Click OK. (The caption displays below and at the left side of the picture.)
20. Save, print, and then close **WL1-C5-P2-Training.docx**.

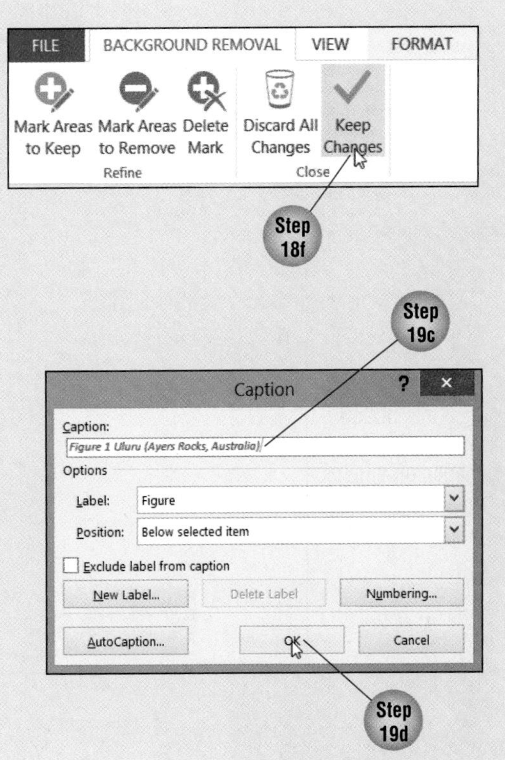

Project 3 Customize a Report on Robots — 2 Parts

You will open a report on robots and then add visual appeal to the report by inserting and formatting an image from Office.com and a built-in text box.

Inserting an Image from Office.com

Microsoft Office includes a gallery of media images you can insert in a document, such as clip art images and photographs. To insert an image in a Word document, click the INSERT tab and then click the Online Pictures button in the Illustrations group. This displays the Insert Pictures window, as shown in Figure 5.7.

At the Insert Pictures window, click in the search text box to the right of *Office.com Clip Art*, type the search term or topic, and then press Enter. Images that match your search term or topic display in the window. To insert an image, click the desired image and then click the Insert button or double-click the image. This downloads the image from the Office.com website to your document.

When you insert an image in the document, the image is selected and the PICTURE TOOLS FORMAT tab is active. Use buttons on this tab to customize an image just as you learned to customize a picture.

Quick Steps

Insert an Image from Office.com
1. Click INSERT tab.
2. Click Online Pictures button.
3. Type search word or topic.
4. Press Enter.
5. Double-click desired image.

Online Pictures

Figure 5.7 Insert Pictures Window

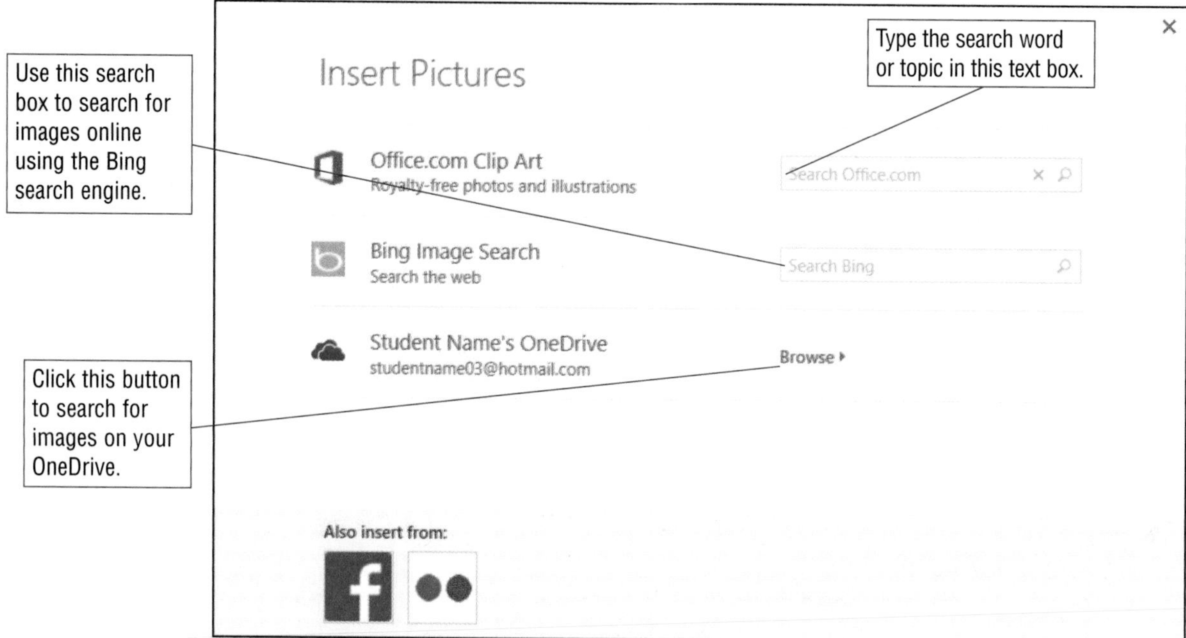

Project 3a Inserting an Image

Part 1 of 2

1. Open **Robots.docx** and then save the document with Save As and name it **WL1-C5-P3-Robots**.
2. Insert a clip art image of a robot by completing the following steps:
   a. Move the insertion point so it is positioned at the beginning of the first paragraph of text (the sentence that begins *Robotic factories are increasingly*).
   b. Click the INSERT tab.
   c. Click the Online Pictures button in the Illustrations group.
   d. At the Insert Pictures window, type robot antenna and then press Enter.
   e. Double-click the robot image shown at the right.

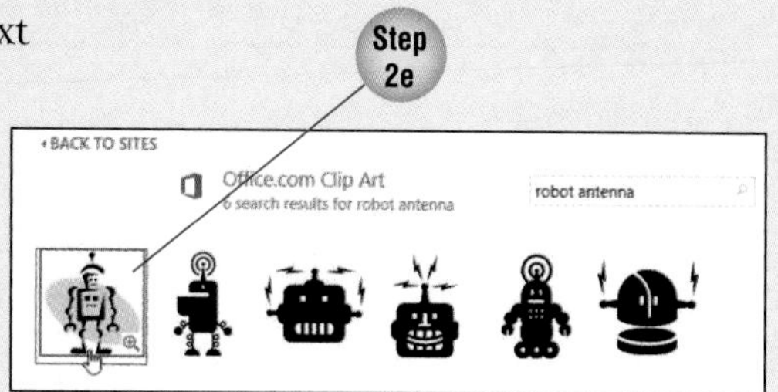

3. Format the clip art image by completing the following steps:
   a. Click the *Drop Shadow Rectangle* option in the Pictures Styles group (fourth option).
   b. Click the Color button in the Adjust group and then click the *Blue, Accent color 1 Dark* option (second column, second row).
   c. Click in the *Shape Height* measurement box in the Size group, type 3, and then press Enter.

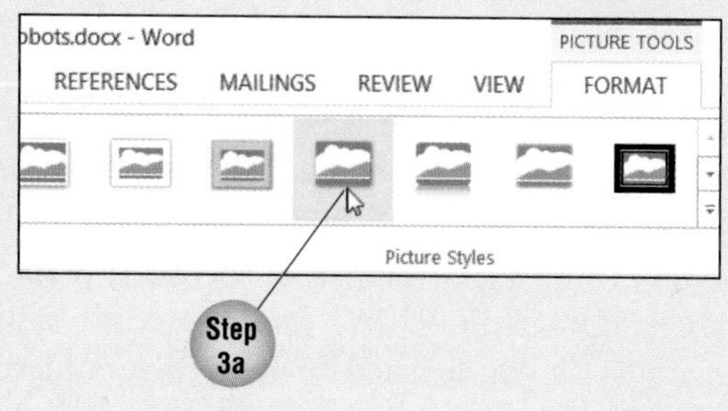

4. Reset the image and the image size by clicking the Reset Picture button arrow in the Adjust group and then clicking the *Reset Picture & Size* option at the drop-down list.
5. Make transparent the green oval behind the robot by completing the following steps:
   a. Click the Color button in the Adjust group.
   b. Click the *Set Transparent Color* option that displays toward the bottom of the drop-down list. (The mouse pointer turns into a dropper tool.)
   c. Position the dropper tool on the green color in the image and then click the left mouse button.
6. Decrease the size of the image by clicking in the *Shape Height* measurement box in the Size group, typing 1.3, and then pressing Enter.
7. Change the text wrapping by clicking the Wrap Text button in the Arrange group and then clicking *Square* at the drop-down list.

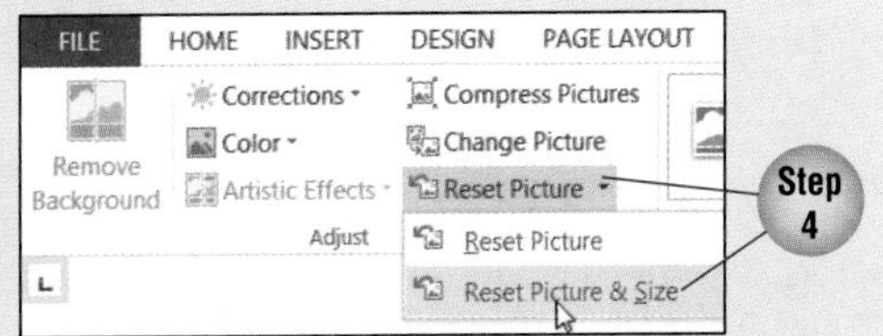

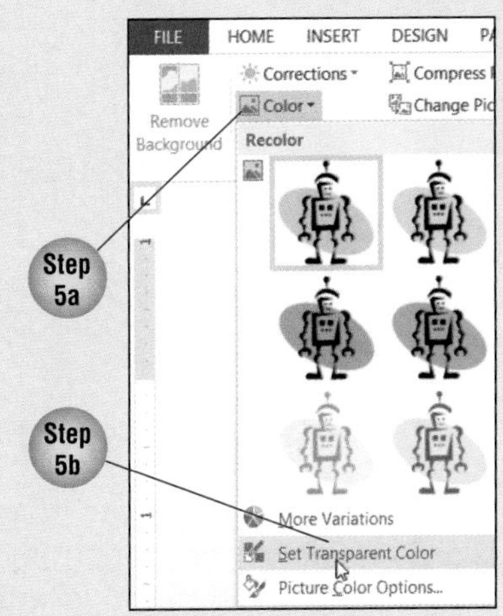

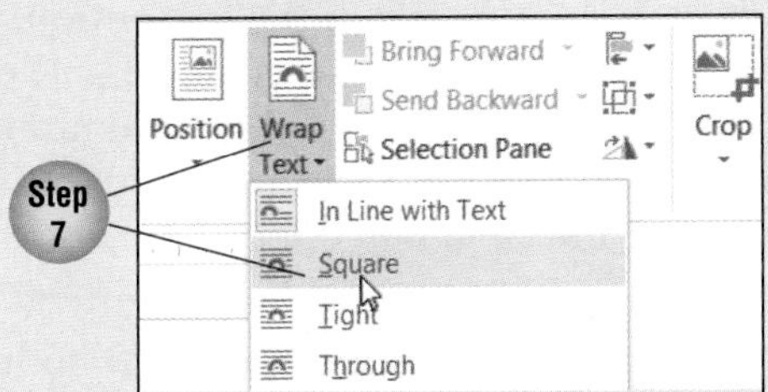

8. Rotate the image by clicking the Rotate Objects button in the Arrange group and then clicking *Flip Horizontal* at the drop-down list.
9. Click the Corrections button in the Adjust group and then click the *Brightness: -40% Contrast: 0% (Normal)* option (first column, third row).
10. Click the Picture Effects button in the Picture Styles group, point to *Shadow*, and then click the *Offset Diagonal Bottom Left* option (third column, first row in the *Outer* section).

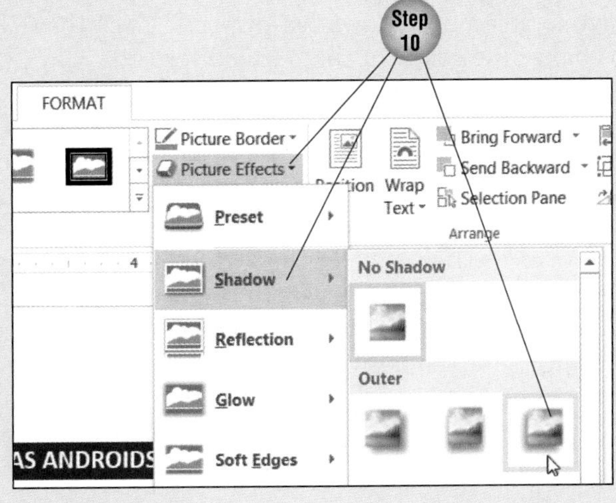

11. Position the mouse pointer on the border of the selected picture until the pointer turns into a four-headed arrow and then drag the picture so it is positioned as shown at the right. (Use the green alignment guide to position the image at the left margin.)
12. Click outside the clip art image to deselect it.
13. Save **WL1-C5-P3-Robots.docx**.

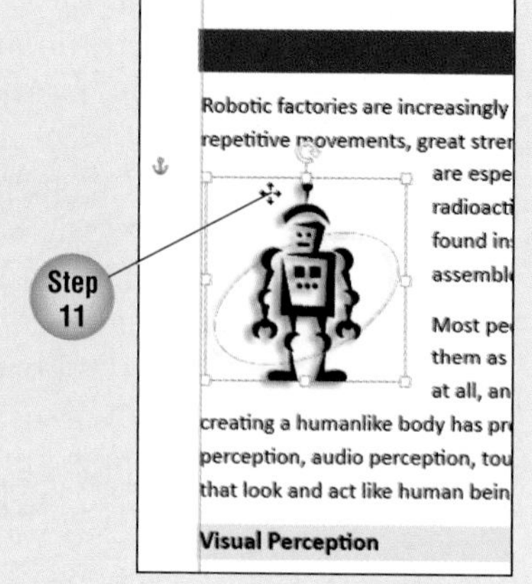

Inserting and Customizing a Pull Quote Text Box

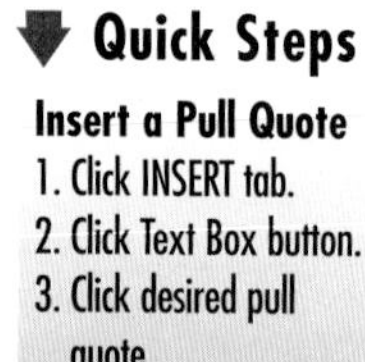

Quick Steps

Insert a Pull Quote
1. Click INSERT tab.
2. Click Text Box button.
3. Click desired pull quote.

Text Box

Use a pull quote in a document such as an article to attract attention. A ***pull quote*** is a quote from an article that is "pulled out" and enlarged and positioned in an attractive location on the page. Some advantages of pull quotes are that they reinforce important concepts, summarize your message, and break up text blocks to make them easier to read. If you use multiple pull quotes in a document, keep them in order to ensure clear comprehension for readers.

You can insert a pull quote in a document with a predesigned built-in text box. Display the available pull quote built-in text boxes by clicking the INSERT tab and then clicking the Text Box button in the Text group. Click the desired pull quote from the drop-down list that displays and the built-in text box is inserted in the document. Type the quote inside the text box and then format the text and/or customize the text box. Use buttons on the DRAWING TOOLS FORMAT tab to format and customize the built-in text box.

Use options in the Insert Shapes group on the DRAWING TOOLS FORMAT tab to insert a shape in the document. Click the Edit Shape button in the Insert Shapes group and a drop-down list displays. Click the *Change Shape* option if you want to change the shape of the selected text box. Click the *Edit Points* option and small black squares display at points around the text box. Use the mouse on these points to increase or decrease specific points of the text box. Apply predesigned styles to a text box with options in the Shape Styles group. You can also change the shape fill, outline, and effects. Change the formatting of the text in the text box with options in the WordArt Styles group. Click the More button that displays at the right side of the WordArt style options and then click the desired style at the drop-down gallery. You can further customize text with the Text Fill, Text Outline, and Text Effects buttons in the Text group. Use options in the Arrange group to position the text box on the page, specify text wrapping in relation to the text box, align the text box with other objects in the document, and rotate the text box. Specify the text box size with the *Shape Height* and *Shape Width* measurement boxes in the Size group.

Project 3b Inserting a Built-in Text Box

Part 2 of 2

1. With **WL1-C5-P3-Robots.docx** open, click the INSERT tab.
2. Click the Text Box button in the Text group.
3. Scroll down the drop-down list and then click the *Ion Quote (Dark)* option.
4. Type the following text in the text box: **"The task of creating a humanlike body has proven incredibly difficult."**
5. Delete the line and the source placeholder in the text box by pressing the F8 function key (this turns on the Selection Mode), pressing Ctrl + End (this selects text from the location of the insertion point to the end of the text box), and then pressing the Delete key.

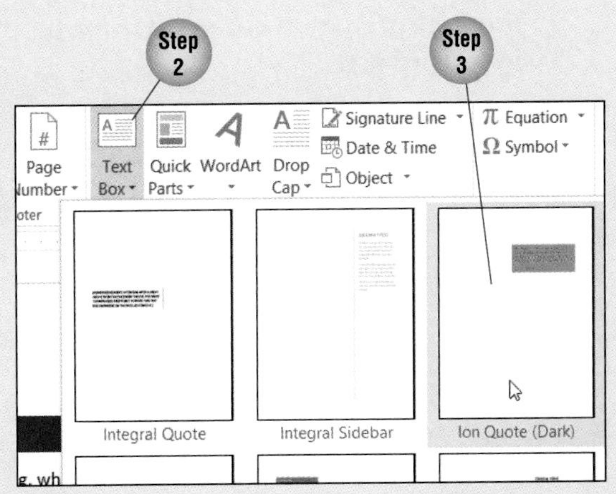

6. With the DRAWING TOOLS FORMAT tab active, click the More button at the right side of the style options in the Shape Styles group and then click the *Subtle Effect - Blue, Accent 5* option (sixth column, fourth row).
7. Click the Shape Effects button in the Shape Styles group, point to *Shadow*, and then click the *Offset Diagonal Bottom Right* option (first column, first row in the *Outer* section).

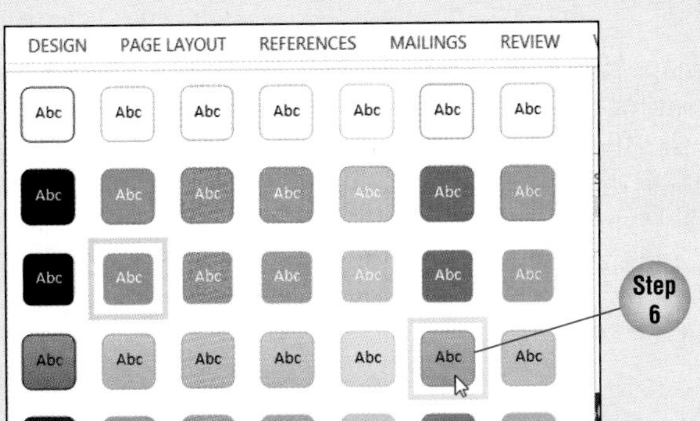

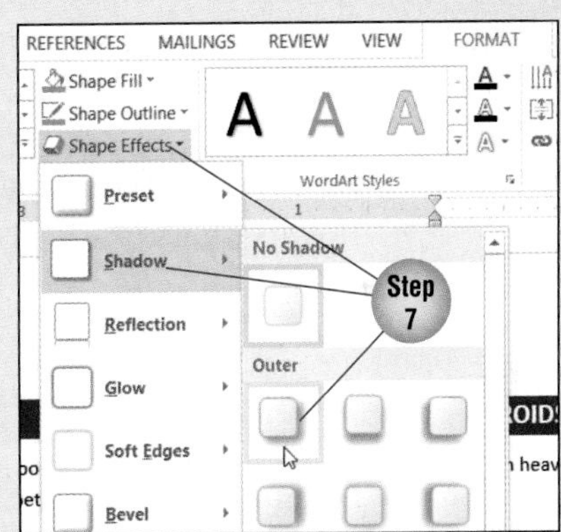

8. Position the mouse pointer on the border of the selected text box until the pointer turns into a four-headed arrow and then drag the text box so it is positioned as shown below.

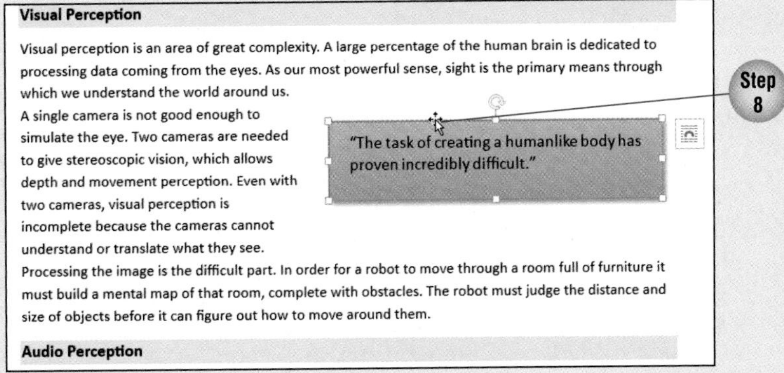

9. Save, print, and then close **WL1-C5-P3-Robots.docx**.

Project 4 Prepare a Company Flier

3 Parts

You will prepare a company flier by inserting and customizing shapes, text boxes, and WordArt.

Quick Steps

Draw a Shape
1. Click INSERT tab.
2. Click Shapes button.
3. Click desired shape at drop-down list.
4. Click in document or drag in document screen to create shape.

Shapes

To draw a square, choose the Rectangle shape and then hold down the Shift key while drawing the shape. To draw a circle, choose the Oval shape and then hold down the Shift key while drawing the shape.

Drawing Shapes

Use the Shapes button on the INSERT tab to draw shapes in a document, including lines, basic shapes, block arrows, flow chart shapes, stars and banners, and callouts. Click a shape and the mouse pointer displays as crosshairs (plus sign). Position the crosshairs in the document where you want the shape to display and then click the left mouse button. You can also hold down the left mouse button, drag to create the shape, and then release the mouse button. The shape is inserted in the document and the DRAWING TOOLS FORMAT tab is active.

If you choose a shape in the *Lines* section of the drop-down list, the shape you draw is considered a ***line drawing***. If you choose an option in the other sections of the drop-down list, the shape you draw is considered an ***enclosed object***. When drawing an enclosed object, you can maintain the proportions of the shape by holding down the Shift key while dragging with the mouse to create the shape.

Copying Shapes

To copy a shape, select the shape and then click the Copy button in the Clipboard group on the HOME tab. Position the insertion point at the location you want the copied shape and then click the Paste button. You can also copy a selected shape by holding down the Ctrl key while dragging a copy of the shape to the desired location.

Project 4a Drawing Arrow Shapes

Part 1 of 3

1. At a blank document, press the Enter key twice and then draw an arrow shape by completing the following steps:
   a. Click the INSERT tab.
   b. Click the Shapes button in the Illustrations group and then click the *Striped Right Arrow* shape in the *Block Arrows* section.
   c. Position the mouse pointer (displays as crosshairs) immediately right of the insertion point and then click the left mouse button. (This inserts the arrow shape in the document.)
2. Format the arrow by completing the following steps:
   a. Click in the *Shape Height* measurement box in the Size group, type 2.4, and then press Enter.
   b. Click in the *Shape Width* measurement box in the Size group, type 4.5, and then press Enter.

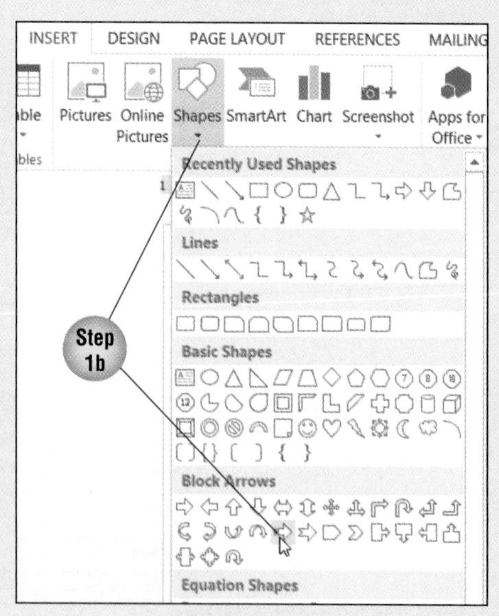

c. Horizontally align the arrow by clicking the Align button in the Arrange group and then clicking *Distribute Horizontally* at the drop-down list.

d. Click the More button at the right side of the options in the Shape Styles group and then click the *Intense Effect - Green, Accent 6* option (last option at the drop-down gallery).

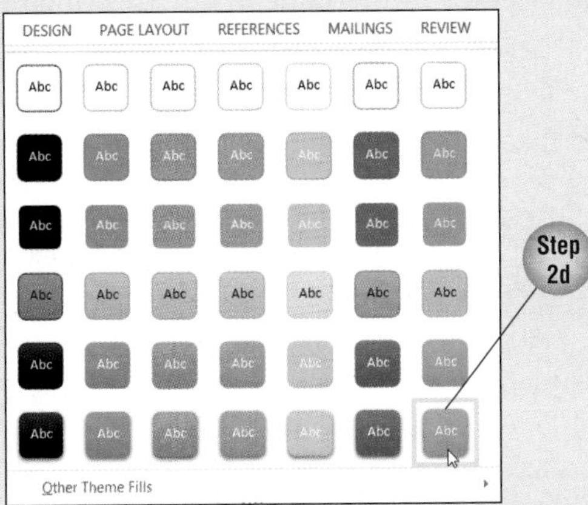

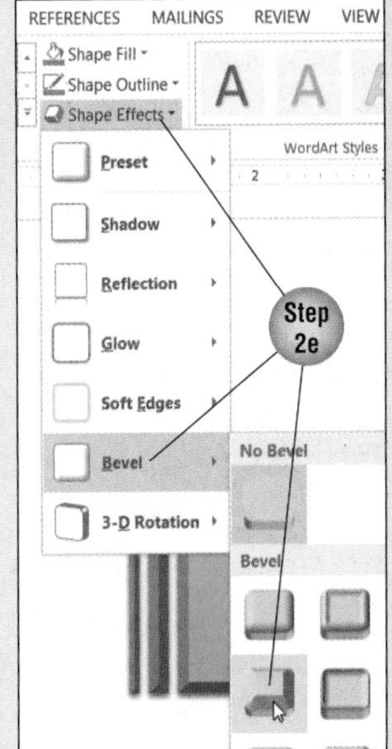

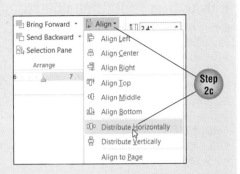

e. Click the Shape Effects button in the Shape Styles group, point to *Bevel*, and then click the *Angle* option (first column, second row in the *Bevel* section).

f. Click the Shape Outline button arrow in the Shape Styles group and then click the *Dark Blue* color (ninth option in the *Standard Colors* section).

3. Copy the arrow by completing the following steps:
   a. With the mouse pointer positioned in the arrow (mouse pointer displays with a four-headed arrow attached), hold down the Ctrl key and the left mouse button.
   b. Drag down until the copied arrow displays just below the top arrow, release the mouse button, and then release the Ctrl key.
   c. Copy the arrow again by holding down the Ctrl key and the left mouse button and then dragging the copied arrow just below the second arrow.
4. Flip the middle arrow by completing the following steps:
   a. Click the middle arrow to select it.
   b. Click the Rotate button in the Arrange group on the DRAWING TOOLS FORMAT tab and then click *Flip Horizontal* at the drop-down gallery.
5. Insert the text *Financial* in the top arrow by completing the following steps:
   a. Click the top arrow to select it.
   b. Type **Financial**.
   c. Select *Financial*.
   d. Click the HOME tab.
   e. Change the font size to 16 points, turn on bold formatting, and then apply the Dark Blue font color (ninth option in the *Standard Colors* section).
6. Complete steps similar to those in Step 5 to insert the word *Direction* in the middle arrow.
7. Complete steps similar to those in Step 5 to insert the word *Retirement* in the bottom arrow.
8. Save the document and name it **WL1-C5-P4-FinConsult**.
9. Print the document.

Quick Steps

Draw a Text Box

1. Click INSERT tab.
2. Click Text Box button in Text group.
3. Click *Draw Text Box.*
4. Click in document or drag in document to create box.

Drawing and Formatting a Text Box

You can use the built-in text boxes provided by Word, or you can draw your own text box. To draw a text box, click the INSERT tab, click the Text Box button in the Text group, and then click *Draw Text Box* at the drop-down list. The mouse pointer displays as crosshairs. Click in the document to insert the text box or position the crosshairs in the document and then drag to create the text box. When a text box is selected, the DRAWING TOOLS FORMAT tab is active. Use buttons on this tab to format text boxes in the same manner as when formatting built-in text boxes.

Project 4b Inserting and Formatting a Text Box

Part 2 of 3

1. With **WL1-C5-P4-FinConsult.docx** open, delete the bottom arrow by completing the following steps:
   a. Click the bottom arrow. (This displays a border around the arrow.)
   b. Position the mouse pointer on the border (displays with four-headed arrow attached) and then click the left mouse button. (This changes the dashed border to a solid border.)
   c. Press the Delete key.
2. Insert, size, and format a text box by completing the following steps:
   a. Click the INSERT tab.
   b. Click the Text Box button in the Text group and then click *Draw Text Box* at the drop-down list.
   c. Click in the document at about the 1-inch mark on the horizontal ruler and about 1 inch below the bottom arrow. (This inserts a text box in the document.)
   d. Click in the *Shape Height* measurement box in the Size group and then type 1.7.
   e. Click in the *Shape Width* measurement box, type 4.5, and then press Enter.
   f. Click the More button at the right side of the options in the Shape Styles group and then click the *Intense Effect - Green, Accent 6* option (last option at the drop-down gallery).
   g. Click the Shape Effects button in the Shape Styles group, point to *Bevel*, and then click the *Soft Round* option at the side menu (second column, second row in the *Bevel* section).

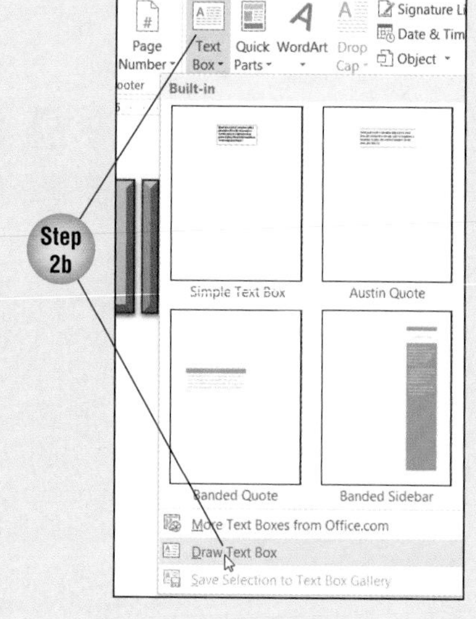

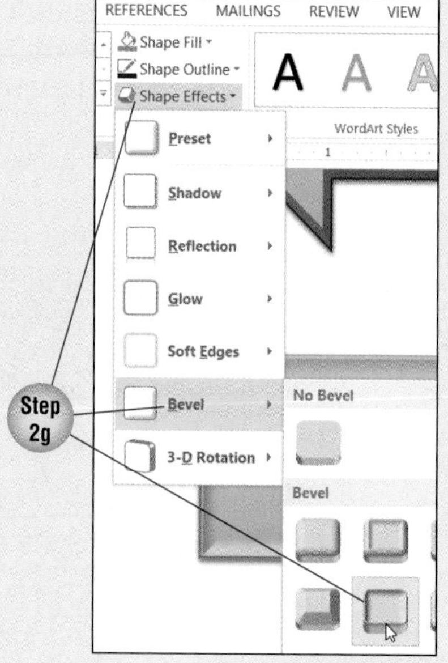

h. Click the Shape Effects button in the Shape Styles group, point to *3-D Rotation*, and then click the *Perspective Above* option (first column, second row in the *Perspective* section).

3. Insert and format text in the text box by completing the following steps:
   a. Press the Enter key twice. (The insertion point should be positioned in the text box.)
   b. Click the HOME tab.
   c. Change the font size to 24 points, turn on bold formatting, and change the font color to *Dark Blue*.
   d. Click the Center button in the Paragraph group.
   e. Type **Retirement Financial Consulting**. (Your text box should appear as shown below.)

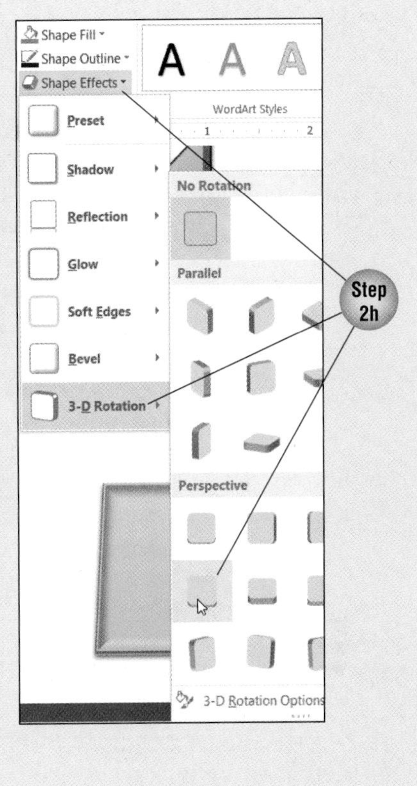

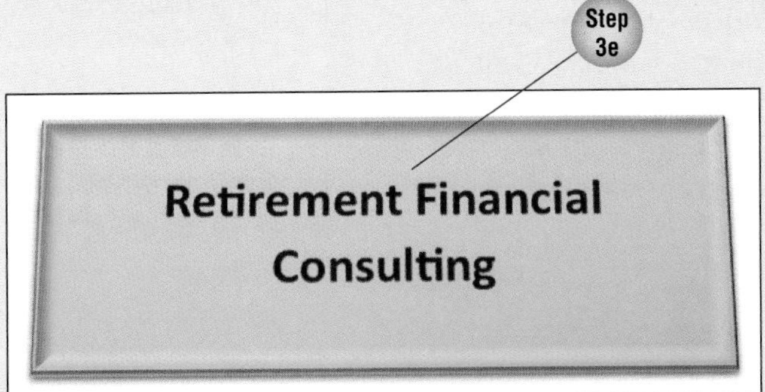

4. Save **WL1-C5-P4-FinConsult.docx**.

Creating and Modifying WordArt Text

With the WordArt feature, you can distort or modify text to conform to a variety of shapes. This is useful for creating company logos, letterheads, flier titles, or headings. To insert WordArt in a document, click the INSERT tab and then click the WordArt button in the Text group. At the drop-down list that displays, click the desired option and a WordArt text box is inserted in the document containing the words *Your text here* and the DRAWING TOOLS FORMAT tab is active. Type the desired WordArt text and then format the WordArt with options on the DRAWING TOOLS FORMAT tab. You can also type text in a document, select the text, and then choose a WordArt option at the WordArt button drop-down list.

Quick Steps

Create WordArt Text
1. Click INSERT tab.
2. Click WordArt button.
3. Click desired WordArt option at drop-down list.
4. Type WordArt text.

WordArt

Project 4c **Inserting and Modifying WordArt** **Part 3 of 3**

1. With **WL1-C5-P4-FinConsult.docx** open, press Ctrl + Home to move the insertion point to the beginning of the document.
2. Insert WordArt text by completing the following steps:
   a. Type **Miller Financial Services** and then select *Miller Financial Services*.

b. Click the INSERT tab.

c. Click the WordArt button in the Text group and then click the *Fill - Orange, Accent 2, Outline - Accent 2* option (third column, first row).

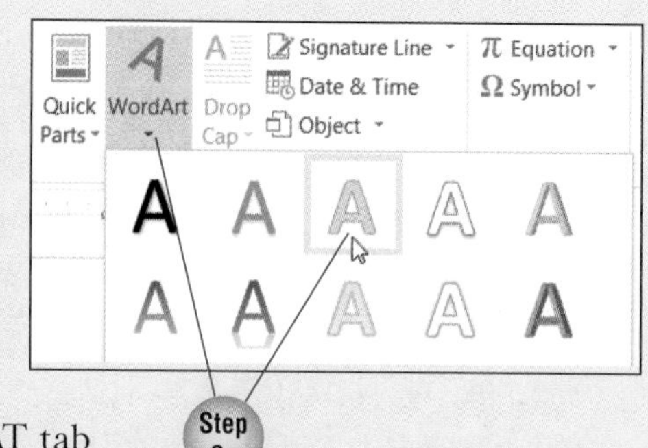

3. Format the WordArt text by completing the following steps:

   a. Make sure the WordArt text border displays as a solid line.

   b. Click the Text Fill button arrow in the WordArt Styles group on the DRAWING TOOLS FORMAT tab and then click the *Light Green* option (fifth option in the *Standard Colors* section).

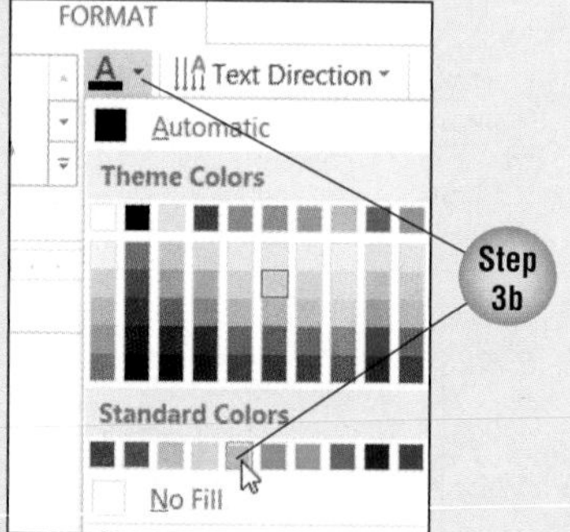

   c. Click the Text Outline button arrow in the WordArt Styles group and then click the *Green, Accent 6, Darker 50%* option (last option in *Theme Colors* section).

   d. Click the Text Effects button in the WordArt Styles group, point to *Glow*, and then click the *Blue, 5 pt glow, Accent color 1* option (first option in the *Glow Variations* section).

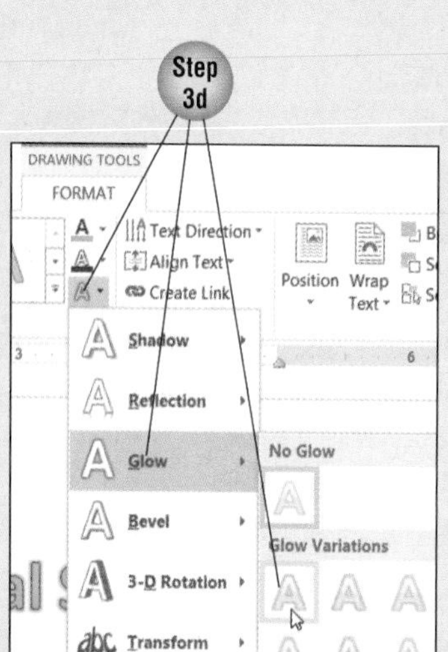

   e. Click in the *Shape Height* measurement box in the Size group and then type **1**.

   f. Click in the *Shape Width* measurement box in the Size group, type **6**, and then press Enter.

   g. Click the Text Effects button in the WordArt Styles group, point to *Transform*, and then click the *Can Up* option (third column, fourth row in the *Warp* section).

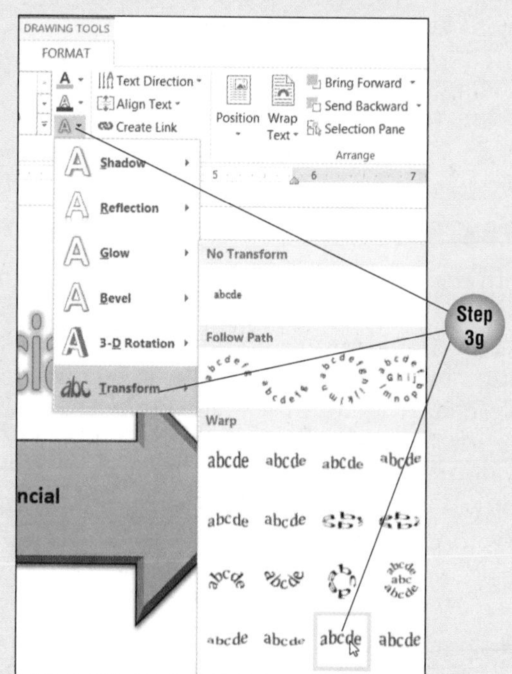

h. Click the Position button in the Arrange group and then click the *Position in Top Center with Square Text Wrapping* option (second column, first row in the *With Text Wrapping* section).
4. Check to make sure that the WordArt, the two arrows, and the text box all fit on one page. If they do not, consider moving and/or sizing the arrows or text box to ensure that they fit on one page.
5. Save, print, and then close **WL1-C5-P4-FinConsult.docx**.

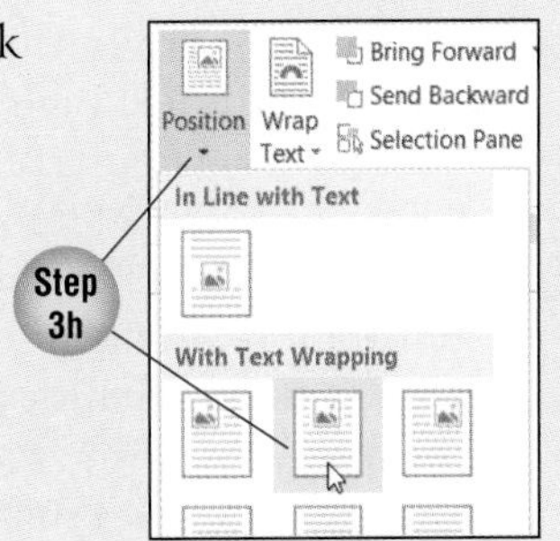

Project 5 Create and Format Screenshots — 2 Parts

You will create screenshots of the Print and Export backstage areas, screen clippings of cover pages, and a sample cover page document.

Creating and Inserting a Screenshot

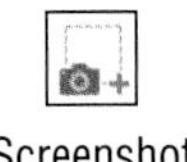

Screenshot

The Illustrations group on the INSERT tab contains a Screenshot button, which you can use to capture the contents of a screen as an image or capture a portion of a screen. If you want to capture the entire screen, open a new document, click the INSERT tab, click the Screenshot button in the Illustrations group, and then click the desired screen thumbnail at the drop-down list. The currently active document does not display as a thumbnail at the drop-down list—only any other documents or files that you have open. When you click the desired thumbnail, the screenshot is inserted as an image in the open document, the image is selected, and the PICTURE TOOLS FORMAT tab is active. Use buttons on this tab to customize the screenshot image.

Project 5a Inserting and Formatting Screenshots — Part 1 of 2

1. Press Ctrl + N to open a blank document.
2. Press Ctrl + N to open a second blank document, type **Print Backstage Area** at the left margin, and then press the Enter key.
3. Save the document and name it **WL1-C5-P5-BackstageAreas**.
4. Point to the Word button on the Taskbar and then click the thumbnail representing the blank document.
5. Display the Print backstage area by clicking the FILE tab and then clicking the *Print* option.

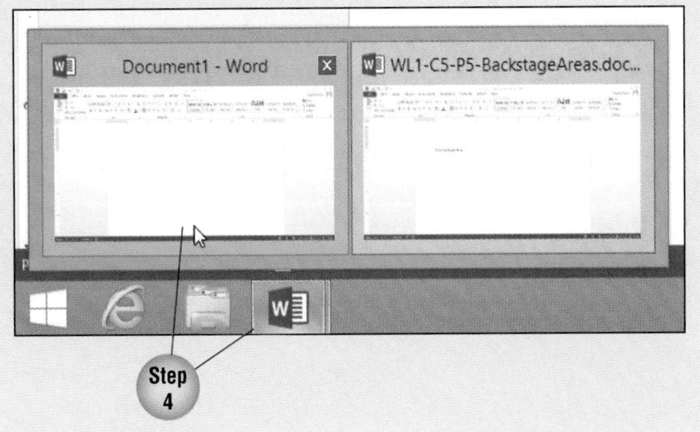

6. Point to the Word buttons on the Taskbar and then click the thumbnail representing **WL1-C5-P5-BackstageAreas.docx**.
7. Insert and format a screenshot of the Print backstage area by completing the following steps:
   a. Click the INSERT tab.
   b. Click the Screenshot button in the Illustrations group and then click the thumbnail that displays in the drop-down list. (This inserts a screenshot of the Print backstage area in the document.)

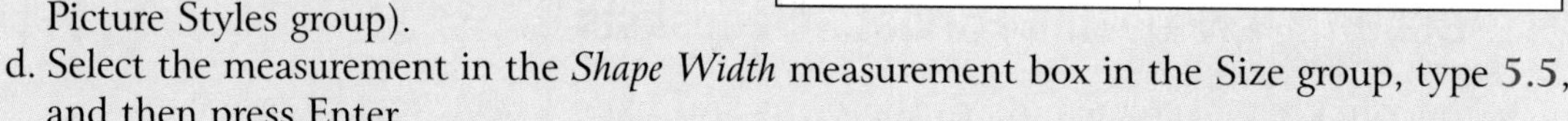

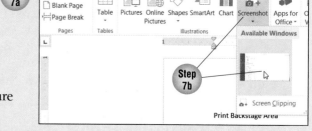

   c. With the screenshot image selected, click the *Drop Shadow Rectangle* picture style option (fourth option in the Picture Styles group).
   d. Select the measurement in the *Shape Width* measurement box in the Size group, type 5.5, and then press Enter.
8. Press Ctrl + End and then press the Enter key. (The insertion point should be positioned below the screenshot image.)
9. Type Export Backstage Area at the left margin and then press the Enter key.
10. Point to the Word buttons on the Taskbar and then click the thumbnail representing the blank document.
11. At the backstage area, click the *Export* option. (This displays the Export backstage area.)
12. Point to the Word buttons on the Taskbar and then click the thumbnail representing **WL1-C5-P5-BackstageAreas.docx**.
13. Insert and format a screenshot of the Export backstage area by completing steps similar to those in Step 7.
14. Press Ctrl + Home to move the insertion point to the beginning of the document.
15. Save, print, and then close **WL1-C5-P5-BackstageAreas.docx**.
16. At the Export backstage area, press the Esc key to redisplay the blank document.
17. Close the blank document.

In addition to making a screenshot of an entire screen, you can make a screenshot of a specific portion of the screen by clicking the *Screen Clipping* option at the Screenshot button drop-down list. When you click this option, the other open document, file, or Windows Start screen or desktop displays in a dimmed manner and the mouse pointer displays as a crosshair. Using the mouse, draw a border around the specific area of the screen you want to capture. The specific area you identified is inserted in the other document as an image, the image is selected, and the PICTURE TOOLS FORMAT tab is active. If you have only one document or file open when you click the Screenshot button, clicking the *Screen Clipping* option will cause the Windows Start screen or desktop to display.

Project 5b Creating and Formatting a Screen Clipping

Part 2 of 2

1. Open **NSSLtrhd.docx** and save it with Save As with the new name **WL1-C5-P5-NSSCoverPages**.
2. Type the text **Sample Cover Pages** and then press the Enter key twice.
3. Select the text you just typed, change the font to 18-point Copperplate Gothic Bold, and then center the text.
4. Press Ctrl + End to move the insertion point below the text.
5. Open the document named **NSSCoverPg01.docx** and then change the zoom to 40% by clicking six times on the Zoom Out button located at the left side of the Zoom slider bar on the Status bar.
6. Point to the Word buttons on the Taskbar and then click the thumbnail representing **WL1-C5-P5-NSSCoverPages.docx**.
7. Create and format a screenshot screen clipping by completing the following steps:
    a. Click the INSERT tab.
    b. Click the Screenshot button in the Illustrations group and then click *Screen Clipping*.
    c. When **NSSCoverPg01.docx** displays in a dimmed manner, position the mouse crosshairs in the upper left corner of the cover page, hold down the left mouse button, drag down to the lower right corner of the cover page, and then release the mouse button. (See image at the right.)
    d. With the cover page screenshot image inserted in **WL1-C5-P5-NSSCoverPages.docx**, make sure the image is selected (sizing handles display around the cover page image).
    e. Click the Wrap Text button in the Arrange group on the PICTURE TOOLS FORMAT tab and then click *Square* at the drop-down gallery.
    f. Select the current measurement in the *Shape Width* measurement box in the Size group, type 3, and then press Enter.

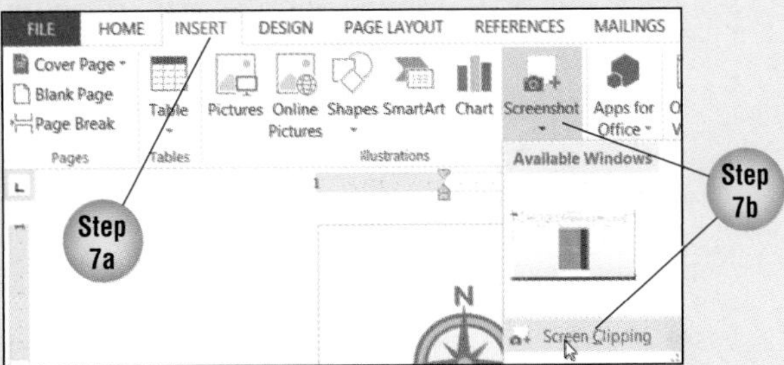

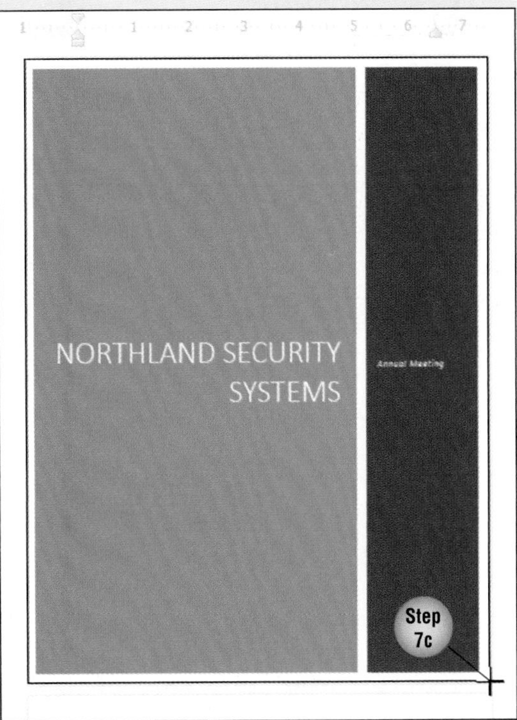

8. Point to the Word buttons on the Taskbar and then click the thumbnail representing **NSSCoverPg01.docx**.
9. Close **NSSCoverPg01.docx**.
10. Open **NSSCoverPg02.docx** and then, if neccessary, change the zoom to 40%.
11. Point to the Word buttons on the Taskbar and then click the thumbnail representing **WL1-C5-P5-NSSCoverPages.docx**.
12. Create and format a screenshot by completing steps similar to those in Step 7.
13. Position the two cover page screenshot images so they are side by side in the document.
14. Save, print, and then close **WL1-C5-P5-NSSCoverPages.docx**.
15. Close **NSSCoverPg02.docx**.

Chapter Summary

- Insert a section break in a document to apply formatting to a portion of a document. You can insert a continuous section break or a section break that begins a new page. Turn on the display of nonprinting characters or change to Draft view to see section breaks, since they are not visible in Print Layout view.
- Set text in columns to improve the readability of documents such as newsletters and reports. Format text in columns using the Columns button in the Page Setup group on the PAGE LAYOUT tab or with options at the Columns dialog box.
- Remove column formatting with the Columns button on the PAGE LAYOUT tab or at the Columns dialog box. Balance column text on the last page of a document by inserting a continuous section break at the end of the text.
- Improve the display of text lines by hyphenating long words that fall at the ends of lines. You can automatically or manually hyphenate words in a document.
- To enhance the appearance of text, use drop caps to identify the beginnings of major sections or paragraphs. Create drop caps with the Drop Cap button in the Text group on the INSERT tab.
- Insert symbols with options at the Symbol dialog box with the Symbols tab selected, and insert special characters with options at the Symbol dialog box with the Special Characters tab selected.
- Click the Date & Time button in the Text group on the INSERT tab to display the Date and Time dialog box. Insert the date or time with options at this dialog box or with keyboard shortcuts. If the date or time is inserted as a field, update the field with the Update Field key, F9.
- Use the Click and Type feature to center, right-align, and left-align text.
- Vertically align text in a document with the *Vertical alignment* option at the Page Setup dialog box with the Layout tab selected.
- Insert an image such as a picture or clip art with buttons in the Illustrations group on the INSERT tab.
- Customize and format an image with options and buttons on the PICTURE TOOLS FORMAT tab. Size an image with the *Shape Height* and *Shape Width* measurement boxes in the Size group or with the sizing handles that display around the selected image.
- Move an image with options from the Position button drop-down gallery located on the PICTURE TOOLS FORMAT tab or by choosing a text wrapping style and then moving the image by dragging it with the mouse.
- To insert a picture, click the INSERT tab, click the Pictures button, navigate to the desired folder at the Insert Picture dialog box, and then double-click the picture.
- To insert an image from Office.com, click the INSERT tab and then click the Online Pictures button. At the Insert Pictures window, type the search text or topic and then press Enter. Double-click the desired image.
- Insert a pull quote in a document with a built-in text box by clicking the INSERT tab, clicking the Text Box button, and then clicking the desired built-in text box at the drop-down list.

- Draw shapes in a document by clicking the Shapes button in the Illustrations group on the INSERT tab, clicking the desired shape at the drop-down list, and then clicking or dragging in the document to draw the shape. Customize a shape with options on the DRAWING TOOLS FORMAT tab. Copy a shape by holding down the Ctrl key while dragging the selected shape.
- Draw a text box by clicking the Text Box button in the Text group on the INSERT tab, clicking *Draw Text Box* at the drop-down list, and then clicking or dragging in the document. Customize a text box with buttons on the DRAWING TOOLS FORMAT tab.
- Use WordArt to distort or modify text to conform to a variety of shapes. Customize WordArt with options on the DRAWING TOOLS FORMAT tab.
- Use the Screenshot button in the Illustrations group on the INSERT tab to capture the contents of a screen or capture a portion of a screen. Use buttons on the PICTURE TOOLS FORMAT tab to customize a screenshot image.

Commands Review

FEATURE	RIBBON TAB, GROUP	BUTTON, OPTION	KEYBOARD SHORTCUT
columns	PAGE LAYOUT, Page Setup		
Columns dialog box	PAGE LAYOUT, Page Setup	, *More Columns*	
continuous section break	PAGE LAYOUT, Page Setup	, *Continuous*	
Date and Time dialog box	INSERT, Text		
drop cap	INSERT, Text		
hyphenate words automatically	PAGE LAYOUT, Page Setup	, *Automatic*	
insert date			Alt + Shift + D
Insert Picture dialog box	INSERT, Illustrations		
Insert Pictures window	INSERT, Illustrations		
insert time			Alt + Shift + T
Manual Hyphenation dialog box	PAGE LAYOUT, Page Setup	, *Manual*	
Page Setup dialog box	PAGE LAYOUT, Page Setup		
pull quote (built-in text box)	INSERT, Text		
screenshot	INSERT, Illustrations		
shapes	INSERT, Illustrations		

FEATURE	RIBBON TAB, GROUP	BUTTON, OPTION	KEYBOARD SHORTCUT
Symbol dialog box	INSERT, Symbols	Ω, *More Symbols*	
text box	INSERT, Text		
update field			F9
WordArt	INSERT, Text		

Concepts Check

Test Your Knowledge

Completion: In the space provided at the right, indicate the correct term, symbol, or command.

1. View a section break by turning on the display of nonprinting characters or using this view. ____________
2. Format text into columns with the Columns button located in this group on the PAGE LAYOUT tab. ____________
3. Balance column text on the last page of a document by inserting this type of break at the end of the text. ____________
4. The first letter of the first word of a paragraph that is set into a paragraph is called this. ____________
5. The Symbol button is located on this tab. ____________
6. This is the keyboard shortcut to insert the current date. ____________
7. Use this feature to position the insertion point at a specific location and alignment in a document. ____________
8. Vertically align text with the *Vertical alignment* option at the Page Setup dialog box with this tab selected. ____________
9. Insert an image in a document with buttons in this group on the INSERT tab. ____________
10. Customize and format an image with options and buttons on this tab. ____________
11. Size an image with the sizing handles that display around the selected image or with these measurement boxes on the PICTURE TOOLS FORMAT tab. ____________
12. Click the Picture button on the INSERT tab and this dialog box displays. ____________
13. Click the Online Pictures button on the INSERT tab and this window displays. ____________
14. This is the term for a quote that is enlarged and positioned in an attractive location on the page. ____________

15. The Shapes button is located on this tab. ____________

16. To copy a selected shape, hold down this key while dragging the shape. ____________

17. Use this feature to distort or modify text to conform to a variety of shapes. ____________

18. To capture a portion of a screen, click the Screenshot button in the Illustrations group on the INSERT tab and then click this option at the drop-down list. ____________

Skills Check Assess Your Performance

Assessment 1

ADD VISUAL APPEAL TO A REPORT ON INTELLECTUAL PROPERTY

1. Open **ProtectIssues.docx** and then save the document with Save As and name it **WL1-C5-A1-ProtectIssues**.
2. Format the text from the first paragraph of text below the title to the end of the document into two columns with 0.4 inch between columns.
3. Move the insertion point to the end of the document and then insert a continuous section break to balance the columns on the second page.
4. Press Ctrl + Home to move the insertion point to the beginning of the document.
5. Display the Insert Pictures window (click the Online Pictures button on the INSERT tab), type **computer privacy magnifying glass** in the search text box, and then press Enter. Insert the clip art image with a man in a blue hat. (If this clip art image is not available, choose another related to *computer* and *privacy*.)
6. Make the following customizations to the clip art image:
   a. Change the height to 1 inch.
   b. Change the color of the clip art image to *Blue, Accent color 1 Light*.
   c. Correct the contrast to *Brightness: 0% (Normal) Contrast: +20%*.
   d. Change the position of the clip art image to *Position in Middle Left with Square Text Wrapping*.
   e. Use the Rotate Objects button in the Arrange group and flip the clip art image horizontally.
7. Move the insertion point to the beginning of the paragraph immediately below the *Intellectual Property Protection* heading (located on the second page). Insert the Austin Quote built-in text box and then make the following customizations:
   a. Type the following text in the text box: "**Plagiarism may be punished by law, and in many educational institutions it can result in suspension or even expulsion.**"
   b. Select the text and then change the font size to 11 points.
   c. Change the width of the text box to 2.8 inches.
   d. Change the position of the text box to *Position in Top Center with Square Text Wrapping*.

8. Press Ctrl + End to move the insertion point to the end of the document. (The insertion point will be positioned below the continuous section break you inserted on the second page to balance the columns of text.)
9. Change back to one column.
10. Press the Enter key twice and then insert a shape near the insertion point using the Plaque shape (located in the second row in the *Basic Shapes* section) and make the following customizations:
    a. Change the shape height to 1.4 inches and the shape width to 3.9 inches.
    b. Use the Align button in the Arrange group and distribute the shape horizontally.
    c. Apply the Subtle Effect - Blue Accent 1 shape style (second column, fourth row).
    d. Type the text **Felicité Compagnie** inside the shape. Insert the é symbol at the Symbol dialog box with the *(normal text)* font selected.
    e. Insert the current date below *Felicité Compagnie* and insert the current time below the date.
    f. Select the text in the shape, change the font size to 14 points, and apply bold formatting.
11. Manually hyphenate the document. (Do not hyphenate headings or proper names.)
12. Create a drop cap with the first letter of the word *The* that begins the first paragraph of text below the title.
13. Save, print, and then close **WL1-C5-A1-ProtectIssues.docx**.

Assessment 2

CREATE A SALES MEETING ANNOUNCEMENT

1. At a blank document, press the Enter key twice, and then create WordArt with the following specifications:
    a. Choose the *Fill - Black, Text 1, Outline - Background 1, Hard Shadow - Background 1* WordArt style option and then type **Inlet Corporation** in the WordArt text box.
    b. Change the width of the WordArt text box to 6.5 inches.
    c. Use the Transform option from the Text Effects button in the WordArt Styles group to apply the Chevron Up text effect.
2. Press Ctrl + End and then press the Enter key three times. Change the font to 18-point Candara, turn on bold formatting, change to center alignment, and then type the following text:

    National Sales Meeting

    Northwest Division

    Ocean View Resort

    August 19 through August 21, 2015
3. Insert the picture named **Ocean.jpg** and then make the following changes to the picture:
    a. Change the width of the picture to 6.5 inches.
    b. Apply the Brightness: +40% Contrast: -40% correction.
    c. Apply the Compound Frame, Black picture style.
    d. Change the position of the picture to *Position in Top Center with Square Text Wrapping*.
    e. Change text wrapping to *Behind Text*.
4. Save the announcement document and name it **WL1-C5-A2-SalesMtg**.
5. Print and then close **WL1-C5-A2-SalesMtg.docx**.

Assessment 3

CREATE AN ANNOUNCEMENT

1. Open **FirstAidCourse.docx** and then save the document with Save As and name it **WL1-C5-A3-FirstAidCourse**.
2. Format the announcement shown in Figure 5.8. Insert the caduceus clip art image as shown in the figure with the following specifications:
   a. Use the word *caduceus* at the Insert Pictures window to search online for the clip art image.
   b. Change the text wrapping to *Tight*.
   c. Change the clip art image color to *Blue, Accent color 1 Light*.
   d. Correct the brightness and contrast to *Brightness: -20% Contrast: +40%*.
   e. Size and move the clip art image as shown in the figure.
3. Apply paragraph shading, insert the page border, and add leaders to the tabs as shown in Figure 5.8.
4. Save, print, and then close **WL1-C5-A3-FirstAidCourse.docx**. (If some of the page border does not print, consider increasing the measurements at the Border and Shading Options dialog box.)

Figure 5.8 Assessment 3

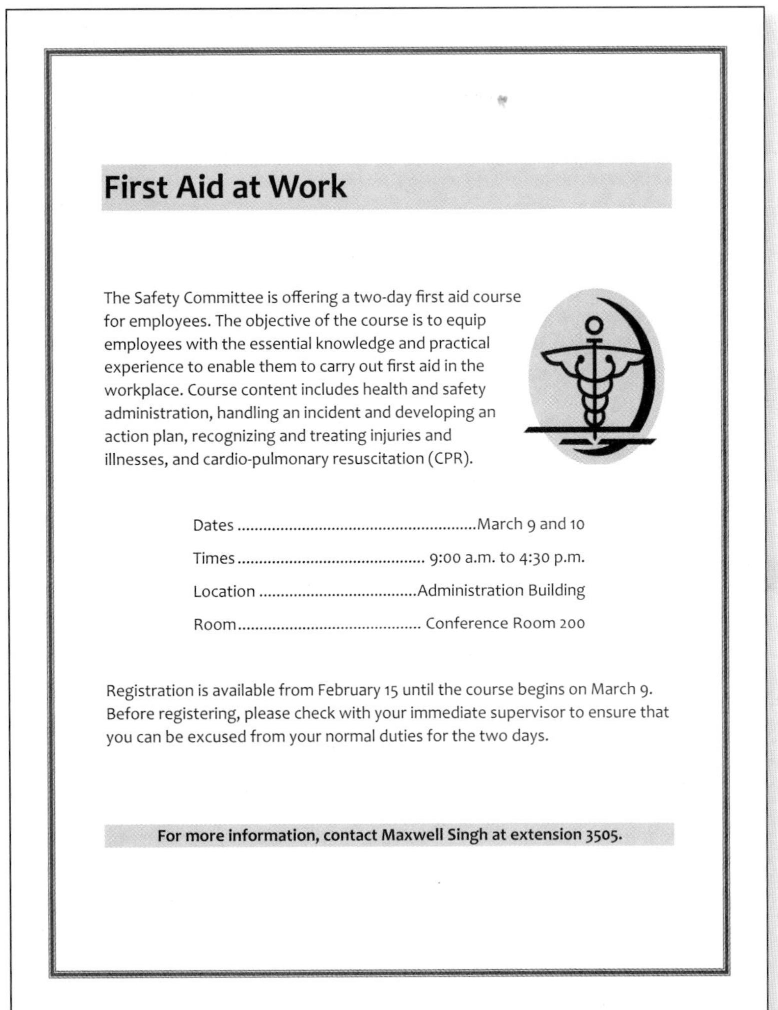

Assessment

4 INSERT SCREENSHOTS IN A MEMO

1. Open **FirstAidMemo.docx** and then save it with Save As and name it **WL1-C5-A4-FirstAidMemo**.
2. Insert screenshots so your document appears as shown in Figure 5.9. Use the **FirstAidAnnounce.docx** document located in your WL1C5 folder to create the first screenshot, and use the document **WL1-C5-A3-FirstAidCourse.docx** you created in Assessment 3 for the second screenshot. ***Hint: Decrease the size of the document so the entire document is visible on the screen.***
3. Move the insertion point below the screenshot images and then insert the text as shown in the figure. Insert your initials in place of the *XX*.
4. Save, print, and close **WL1-C5-A4-FirstAidMemo.docx**.

Figure 5.9 Assessment 4

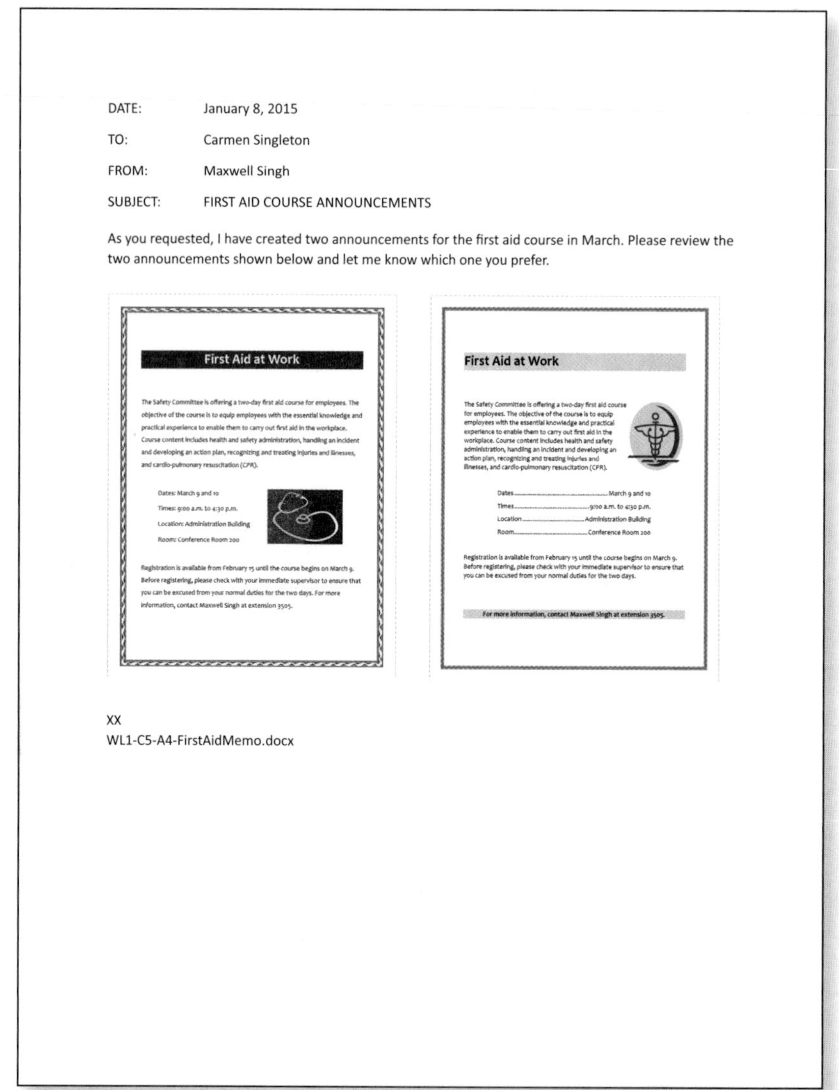

DATE: January 8, 2015

TO: Carmen Singleton

FROM: Maxwell Singh

SUBJECT: FIRST AID COURSE ANNOUNCEMENTS

As you requested, I have created two announcements for the first aid course in March. Please review the two announcements shown below and let me know which one you prefer.

First Aid at Work

First Aid at Work

XX
WL1-C5-A4-FirstAidMemo.docx

Visual Benchmark Demonstrate Your Proficiency

1 CREATE A FLIER

1. Create the flier shown in Figure 5.10 with the following specifications:
   - Create the title *Pugs on Parade!* as WordArt using the *Fill - Black, Text 1, Shadow* option. Change the width to 6.5 inches, apply the Can Up transform effect, and change the text fill color to *Dark Red*.
   - Create the shape containing the text *Admission is free!* using the Explosion 1 shape in the Stars and Banners section of the Shapes button drop-down list.
   - Insert the **Pug.jpg** picture (use the Pictures button on the INSERT tab) located in the WL1C5 folder on your storage medium. Change the text wrapping for the picture to *Behind Text* and size and position the picture as shown in the figure.
   - Create the line above the last line of text as a top border. Change the color to *Dark Red* and the width to 3 points.
   - Make any other changes so your document appears similar to Figure 5.10.
2. Save the document and name it **WL1-C5-VB1-PugFlier**.
3. Print and then close the document.

Figure 5.10 Visual Benchmark 1

2 FORMAT A REPORT

1. Open **Resume.docx** and then save it with Save As and name it **WL1-C5-VB2-Resume**.
2. Format the report so it appears as shown in Figure 5.11 with the following specifications:
   a. Insert the WordArt text *Résumé Writing* with the following specifications:
      - Use the Fill - *Black, Text 1, Outline - Background 1, Hard Shadow - Background 1* option (first column, third row).
      - Type the text **Résumé Writing** and insert the é symbol using the Insert Symbol dialog box.
      - Change the position to *Position in Top Center with Square Text Wrapping*.
      - Change the width of the WordArt to 5.5 inches.
      - Apply the Can Up transform text effect.

   b. Format the report into two columns beginning with the first paragraph of text below the title and balance the columns on the second page.
   c. Insert the pull quote with the following specifications:
      - Use the Motion Quote built in text box.
      - Type the text shown in the pull quote in Figure 5.11. (Use the Insert Symbol dialog box to insert the two é symbols in the word résumé.)
      - Select the text and then change the font size to 11 points.
      - Change the width of the text box to 2.3 inches.
      - Position the pull quote as shown in Figure 5.11.

   d. Insert the cake clip art image with the following specifications:
      - Search for the cake image using the words *cakes, desserts, dining, food* in the Insert Pictures window. Insert the cake image shown in the figure. (The original image colors are brown and black.) If this image is not available, choose a similar image of a cake.
      - Change the image color to *Black and White: 50%*.
      - Change the width to 0.9 inches.
      - Change the text wrapping to *Tight*.
      - Position the cake image as shown in Figure 5.11.

   e. Insert page numbering at the bottom center of each page with the *Thick Line* option.
3. Save, print, and then close **WL1-C5-VB2-Resume.docx**.

Figure 5.11 Visual Benchmark 2

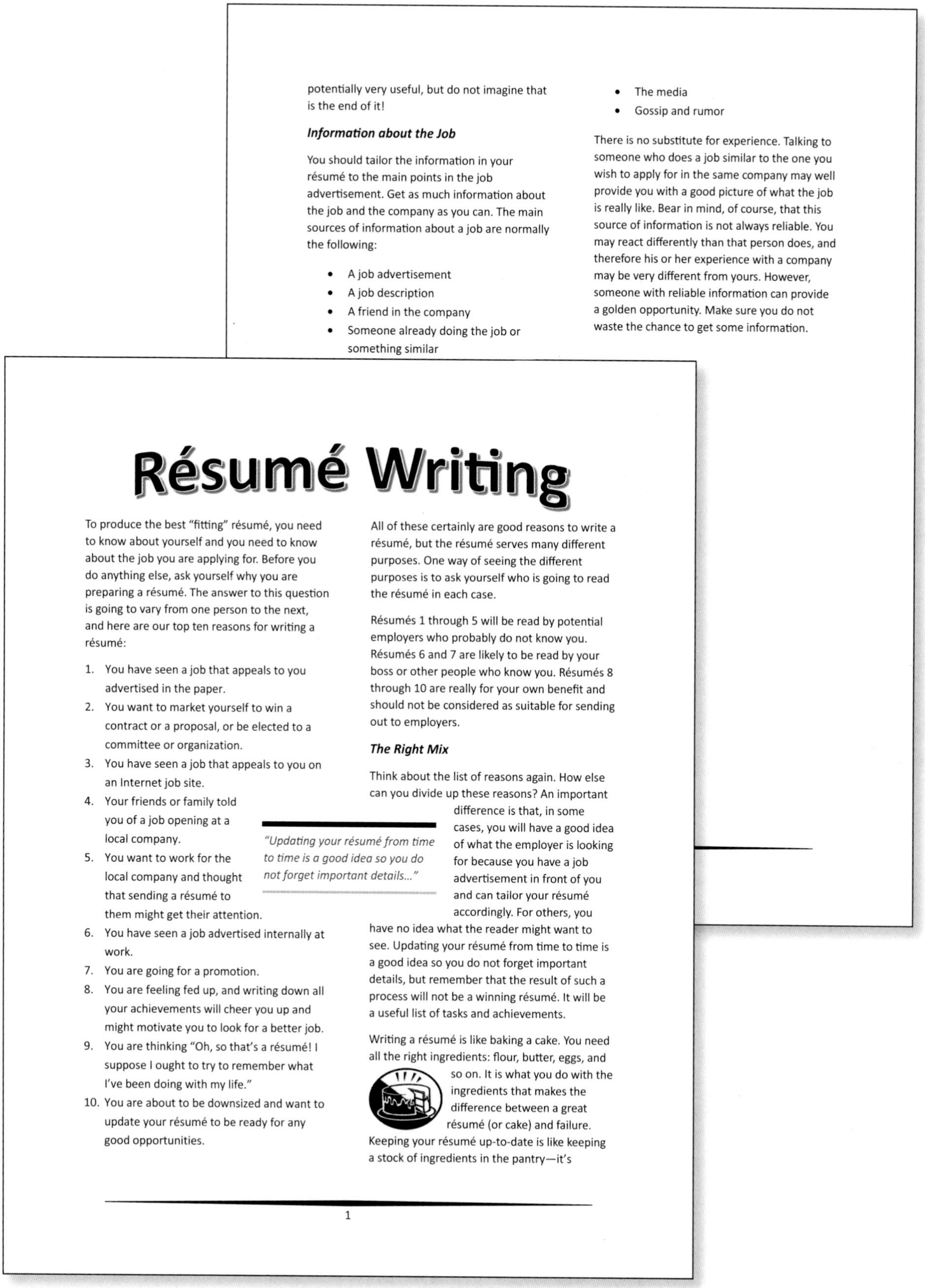

potentially very useful, but do not imagine that is the end of it!

Information about the Job

You should tailor the information in your résumé to the main points in the job advertisement. Get as much information about the job and the company as you can. The main sources of information about a job are normally the following:

- A job advertisement
- A job description
- A friend in the company
- Someone already doing the job or something similar
- The media
- Gossip and rumor

There is no substitute for experience. Talking to someone who does a job similar to the one you wish to apply for in the same company may well provide you with a good picture of what the job is really like. Bear in mind, of course, that this source of information is not always reliable. You may react differently than that person does, and therefore his or her experience with a company may be very different from yours. However, someone with reliable information can provide a golden opportunity. Make sure you do not waste the chance to get some information.

Résumé Writing

To produce the best "fitting" résumé, you need to know about yourself and you need to know about the job you are applying for. Before you do anything else, ask yourself why you are preparing a résumé. The answer to this question is going to vary from one person to the next, and here are our top ten reasons for writing a résumé:

1. You have seen a job that appeals to you advertised in the paper.
2. You want to market yourself to win a contract or a proposal, or be elected to a committee or organization.
3. You have seen a job that appeals to you on an Internet job site.
4. Your friends or family told you of a job opening at a local company.
5. You want to work for the local company and thought that sending a résumé to them might get their attention.
6. You have seen a job advertised internally at work.
7. You are going for a promotion.
8. You are feeling fed up, and writing down all your achievements will cheer you up and might motivate you to look for a better job.
9. You are thinking "Oh, so that's a résumé! I suppose I ought to try to remember what I've been doing with my life."
10. You are about to be downsized and want to update your résumé to be ready for any good opportunities.

All of these certainly are good reasons to write a résumé, but the résumé serves many different purposes. One way of seeing the different purposes is to ask yourself who is going to read the résumé in each case.

Résumés 1 through 5 will be read by potential employers who probably do not know you. Résumés 6 and 7 are likely to be read by your boss or other people who know you. Résumés 8 through 10 are really for your own benefit and should not be considered as suitable for sending out to employers.

The Right Mix

Think about the list of reasons again. How else can you divide up these reasons? An important difference is that, in some cases, you will have a good idea of what the employer is looking for because you have a job advertisement in front of you and can tailor your résumé accordingly. For others, you have no idea what the reader might want to see. Updating your résumé from time to time is a good idea so you do not forget important details, but remember that the result of such a process will not be a winning résumé. It will be a useful list of tasks and achievements.

"Updating your résumé from time to time is a good idea so you do not forget important details..."

Writing a résumé is like baking a cake. You need all the right ingredients: flour, butter, eggs, and so on. It is what you do with the ingredients that makes the difference between a great résumé (or cake) and failure. Keeping your résumé up-to-date is like keeping a stock of ingredients in the pantry—it's

1

Case Study Apply Your Skills

Part 1

You work for Honoré Financial Services and have been asked by the office manager, Jason Monroe, to prepare an information newsletter. Mr. Monroe has asked you to open the document named **Budget.docx** and then format it into columns. You are to determine the number of columns and any additional enhancements to the columns. He also wants you to proofread the document and correct any spelling and grammatical errors. Save the completed newsletter, naming it **WL1-C5-CS-Budget**, and then print the newsletter. When Mr. Monroe reviews the newsletter, he decides that it needs additional visual appeal. He wants you to insert visual elements in the newsletter, such as WordArt, clip art, a built-in text box, and/or a drop cap. Save **WL1-C5-CS-Budget.docx** and then print and close the document.

Part 2

Honoré Financial Services will be offering a free workshop titled Planning for Financial Success. Mr. Monroe has asked you to prepare an announcement containing information on the workshop. You determine what to include in the announcement such as the date, time, location, and so forth. Enhance the announcement by inserting a picture or clip art and by applying formatting such as font, paragraph alignment, and borders. Save the completed document and name it **WL1-C5-CS-Announce**. Print and then close the document.

Part 3

Honoré Financial Services has adopted a new slogan, and Mr. Monroe has asked you to create a shape with the new slogan inside. Experiment with the shadow and 3-D shape effects available on the DRAWING TOOLS FORMAT tab and then create a shape and enhance the shape with shadow and/or 3-D effects. Insert the new Honoré Financial Services slogan "Retirement Planning Made Easy" in the shape. Include any additional enhancements to improve the visual appeal of the shape and slogan. Save the completed document and name it **WL1-C5-CS-Slogan**. Print and then close the document.

Part 4

Mr. Monroe has asked you to prepare a document containing information on teaching children how to budget. Use the Internet to find websites and articles that provide information on how to teach children to budget their money. Write a synopsis of the information you find and include at least four suggestions on how to teach children to manage their money. Format the text in the document into newspaper columns. Add additional enhancements to improve the appearance of the document. Save the completed document and name it **WL1-C5-CS-ChildBudget**. Print and then close the document.

MICROSOFT®
WORD

Maintaining Documents

PERFORMANCE OBJECTIVES

Upon successful completion of Chapter 6, you will be able to:

- **Create and rename a folder**
- **Select, delete, copy, move, rename, and print documents**
- **Save documents in different file formats**
- **Open, close, arrange, split, maximize, minimize, and restore documents**
- **Insert a file into an open document**
- **Print specific pages and sections in a document**
- **Print multiple copies of a document**
- **Print envelopes and labels**
- **Create a document using a Word template**

Tutorials

6.1 Managing Folders
6.2 Managing Documents
6.3 Saving a Document in a Different Format
6.4 Working with Windows
6.5 Inserting a File
6.6 Previewing and Printing Documents
6.7 Creating and Printing Envelopes
6.8 Preparing Mailing Labels
6.9 Creating a Document Using a Word Template

Almost every company that conducts business maintains a filing system. The system may consist of documents, folders, and cabinets, or it may be a computerized filing system where information is stored on the computer's hard drive or other storage medium. Whatever type of filing system a business uses, daily maintenance of files is important to its operation. In this chapter, you will learn to maintain files (documents) in Word, performing such activities as creating additional folders and copying, moving, and renaming documents. You will also learn how to create and print documents, envelopes, and labels and create a document using a Word template. Model answers for this chapter's projects appear on the following pages.

Note: Before beginning the projects, copy to your storage medium the WL1C6 subfolder from the WL1 folder on the CD that accompanies this textbook and then make WL1C6 the active folder.

Model Answers

APARTMENT LEASE AGREEMENT
This Apartment Lease Agreement (hereinafter referred to as the "Agreement") is made and entered into this 30th day of September, 2015, by and between Monica Spellman, Lessor, and Jack Lowell, Lessee.
Term
Lessor leases to Lessee the described premises together with any and all appurtenances thereto, for a term of 1 year, such term beginning on October 1, 2015, and ending at 12 o'clock midnight on September 30, 2016.
Rent
The total rent for the term hereof is the sum of one thousand five hundred dollars ($1,500) payable on the 5th day of each month of the term. All such payments shall be made to Lessor on or before the due date and without demand.
Damage Deposit
Upon the due execution of this Agreement, Lessee shall deposit with Lessor the sum of seven hundred dollars ($700), receipt of which is hereby acknowledged by Lessor, as security for any damage caused to the Premises during the term hereof. Such deposit shall be returned to Lessee, without interest, and less any set off for damages to the Premises upon the termination of this Agreement.
Use of Premises
The Premises shall be used and occupied by Lessee and Lessee's immediate family, exclusively, as a private single family dwelling, and no part of the Premises shall be used at any time during the term of this Agreement by Lessee for the purpose of carrying on any business, profession, or trade of any kind, or for any purpose other than as a private single family dwelling. Lessee shall not allow any other person, other than Lessee's immediate family or transient relatives and friends who are guests, to use or occupy the Premises without first obtaining written consent to such use.

Project 1 Manage Documents

WL1-C6-P1-AptLease-PlainTxt.txt

APARTMENT LEASE AGREEMENT

This Apartment Lease Agreement (hereinafter referred to as the "Agreement") is made and entered into this 30th day of September, 2015, by and between Monica Spellman, Lessor, and Jack Lowell, Lessee.

Term

Lessor leases to Lessee the described premises together with any and all appurtenances thereto, for a term of 1 year, such term beginning on October 1, 2015, and ending at 12 o'clock midnight on September 30, 2016.

Rent

The total rent for the term hereof is the sum of one thousand five hundred dollars ($1,500) payable on the 5th day of each month of the term. All such payments shall be made to Lessor on or before the due date and without demand.

Damage Deposit

Upon the due execution of this Agreement, Lessee shall deposit with Lessor the sum of seven hundred dollars ($700), receipt of which is hereby acknowledged by Lessor, as security for any damage caused to the Premises during the term hereof. Such deposit shall be returned to Lessee, without interest, and less any set off for damages to the Premises upon the termination of this Agreement.

Use of Premises

The Premises shall be used and occupied by Lessee and Lessee's immediate family, exclusively, as a private single family dwelling, and no part of the Premises shall be used at any time during the term of this Agreement by Lessee for the purpose of carrying on any business, profession, or trade of any kind, or for any purpose other than as a private single family dwelling. Lessee shall not allow any other person, other than Lessee's immediate family or transient relatives and friends who are guests, to use or occupy the Premises without first obtaining written consent to such use.

WL1-C6-P1-AptLease-RichTxt.rtf

N

Northland Security Systems

NORTHLAND SECURITY SYSTEMS MISSION

Northland Security Systems is a full-service computer information security management and consulting firm offering a comprehensive range of services to help businesses protect electronic data.

SECURITY SERVICES

Northland Security Systems is dedicated to helping business, private and public, protect vital company data through on-site consultation, product installation and training, and 24-hour telephone support services. We show you how computer systems can be compromised and steps you can take to protect your company's computer system.

SECURITY SOFTWARE

We offer a range of security management software to protect your business against viruses, spyware, adware, intrusion, spam, and policy abuse.

Security Management Software

Security Software Training

On-site Consultation

24-Hour Telephone Support

WL1-C6-P1-NSS.pdf

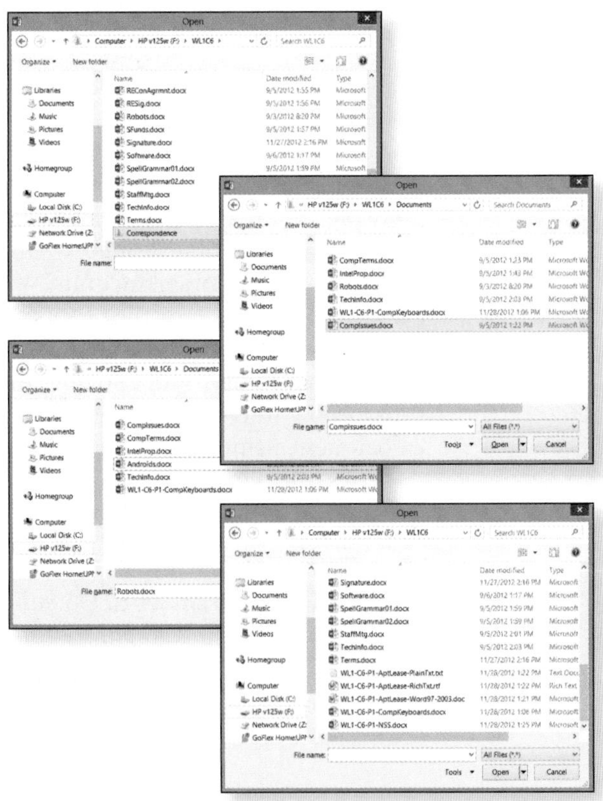

Open dialog box in Part a, Part d, Part e, and Part h

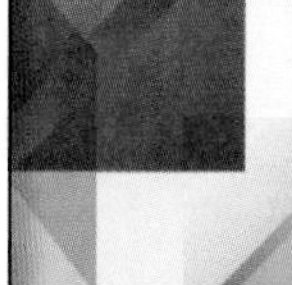

SECTION 1: GRAPHICS AND MULTIMEDIA SOFTWARE

Graphics and multimedia software allows both professional and home users to work with graphics, video, and audio. A variety of application software is focused in this area including painting and drawing software, image-editing software, video and audio editing software, and computer-aided design (CAD) software.

Painting and Drawing Software

Painting and drawing programs are available for both professional and home users. The more expensive professional versions typically include more features and greater capabilities than do the less expensive personal versions. Both painting programs and drawing programs provide an intuitive interface through which users can draw pictures, make sketches, create various shapes, and edit images. Programs typically include a variety of templates that simplify painting or drawing procedures.

Image-Editing Software

The market demand for image-editing programs has increased concurrently with the popularity of digital cameras. An image-editing program allows a user to touch up, modify, and enhance image quality. Once edited, images can be stored in a variety of forms and inserted into other files, such as letters, advertisements, and electronic scrapbooks.

Video and Audio Editing Software

As digital video cameras and other portable technologies have become more common, users have desired the ability to create and modify recorded video and audio clips using video and audio editing software. To create digital video or audio files, home users can often use basic video and audio editing software contained within their computer's operating system. Some users prefer the additional features of an application software package.

Computer-aided Design Software

Computer-aided design software is a sophisticated kind of drawing software, providing tools that enable professionals to create architectural, engineering, product, and scientific designs. Engineers can use the software to design buildings or bridges, and scientists can create graphical designs of plant, animal, and chemical structures. Some software programs display designs in three-dimensional form so they can be viewed from various angles. Once a design has been created, changes can be easily made until it is finalized.

SECTION 2: PERSONAL-USE SOFTWARE

When browsing computer stores, shoppers are likely to see numerous software applications designed for use in the household. Among the many products available are applications for writing letters, making out wills, designing a new home, landscaping a lawn, preparing and filing tax returns, and managing finances. Software suites are also available for home and personal use, although sometimes the suites available for home use do not contain all the features in business versions.

Page 1

ing bills, balancing checkbooks, keeping track of income and
other financial activities. The software also enables users to
me personal finance software provides online services available on
s to go online to learn the status of their investments and insurance
transactions, including accessing and printing bank statements

alyzing federal and state tax status, as well as to prepare and
de tips for preparing tax documents that can help identify
ome programs include actual state and federal tax forms for
orms provide instructions for downloading them from the
s can be printed for mailing or filing electronically. Because federal
rms, users will probably need to obtain the software version for

and prepare a variety of legal documents, including wills and
documents, such as the forms required for real estate purchases or
ded in most packages are standard templates for various legal
them.

ught about an increase in the availability of educational and
r learning and reference tools. Examples of educational and
aries, and tutorials.

ctionary at one time or another. An encyclopedia is a
ed articles on a broad range of subjects. Before computers,
They are now available electronically and many new PCs include a

ning an alphabetical listing of words, with definitions that provide
xamples include *Webster's Dictionary* and *Webster's New World*

es, such as multi-language dictionaries, contain words
translation. Many dictionaries are available on CD.

torials. A tutorial is a form of instruction in which
ess. Tutorials are available for almost any subject,
rocessor, or write a letter. Once an electronic tutorial is
yed on the screen. Many tutorials include graphics to

Project 2 Manage Multiple Documents

WL1-C6-P2-CompSoftware.docx

WENDY STEINBERG
4532 S 52 ST
BOSTON MA 21002-2334

GREGORY LINCOLN
4455 SIXTH AVE
BOSTON MA 21100-4409

Project 3 Create and Print Envelopes

WL1-C6-P3-Env.docx

DAVID LOWRY 12033 S 152 ST HOUSTON TX 77340	MARCELLA SANTOS 394 APPLE BLOSSOM FRIENDSWOOD TX 77533	KEVIN DORSEY 26302 PRAIRIE DR HOUSTON TX 77316
AL AND DONNA SASAKI 1392 PIONEER DR BAYTOWN TX 77903	JACKIE RHYNER 29039 107 AVE E HOUSTON TX 77302	MARK AND TINA ELLIS 607 FORD AVE HOUSTON TX 77307

Project 4 Create Mailing Labels

WL1-C6-P4-Labels.docx

Mr. and Mrs. Matthew Adair 12201 North 21st Street Jennings, LA 70563	Mr. and Mrs. Matthew Adair 12201 North 21st Street Jennings, LA 70563	Mr. and Mrs. Matthew Adair 12201 North 21st Street Jennings, LA 70563
Mr. and Mrs. Matthew Adair 12201 North 21st Street Jennings, LA 70563	Mr. and Mrs. Matthew Adair 12201 North 21st Street Jennings, LA 70563	Mr. and Mrs. Matthew Adair 12201 North 21st Street Jennings, LA 70563
Mr. and Mrs. Matthew Adair 12201 North 21st Street Jennings, LA 70563	Mr. and Mrs. Matthew Adair 12201 North 21st Street Jennings, LA 70563	Mr. and Mrs. Matthew Adair 12201 North 21st Street Jennings, LA 70563
Mr. and Mrs. Matthew Adair 12201 North 21st Street Jennings, LA 70563	Mr. and Mrs. Matthew Adair 12201 North 21st Street Jennings, LA 70563	Mr. and Mrs. Matthew Adair 12201 North 21st Street Jennings, LA 70563
Mr. and Mrs. Matthew Adair 12201 North 21st Street Jennings, LA 70563	Mr. and Mrs. Matthew Adair 12201 North 21st Street Jennings, LA 70563	Mr. and Mrs. Matthew Adair 12201 North 21st Street Jennings, LA 70563
Mr. and Mrs. Matthew Adair 12201 North 21st Street Jennings, LA 70563	Mr. and Mrs. Matthew Adair 12201 North 21st Street Jennings, LA 70563	Mr. and Mrs. Matthew Adair 12201 North 21st Street Jennings, LA 70563
Mr. and Mrs. Matthew Adair 12201 North 21st Street Jennings, LA 70563	Mr. and Mrs. Matthew Adair 12201 North 21st Street Jennings, LA 70563	Mr. and Mrs. Matthew Adair 12201 North 21st Street Jennings, LA 70563
Mr. and Mrs. Matthew Adair 12201 North 21st Street Jennings, LA 70563	Mr. and Mrs. Matthew Adair 12201 North 21st Street Jennings, LA 70563	Mr. and Mrs. Matthew Adair 12201 North 21st Street Jennings, LA 70563
Mr. and Mrs. Matthew Adair 12201 North 21st Street Jennings, LA 70563	Mr. and Mrs. Matthew Adair 12201 North 21st Street Jennings, LA 70563	Mr. and Mrs. Matthew Adair 12201 North 21st Street Jennings, LA 70563
Mr. and Mrs. Matthew Adair 12201 North 21st Street Jennings, LA 70563	Mr. and Mrs. Matthew Adair 12201 North 21st Street Jennings, LA 70563	Mr. and Mrs. Matthew Adair 12201 North 21st Street Jennings, LA 70563

WL1-C6-P4-LAProg.docx

Model Answers

BG Consulting 3205 Central Avenue Portland, OR 99304	BG Consulting 3205 Central Avenue Portland, OR 99304	BG Consulting 3205 Central Avenue Portland, OR 99304
BG Consulting 3205 Central Avenue Portland, OR 99304	BG Consulting 3205 Central Avenue Portland, OR 99304	BG Consulting 3205 Central Avenue Portland, OR 99304
BG Consulting 3205 Central Avenue Portland, OR 99304	BG Consulting 3205 Central Avenue Portland, OR 99304	BG Consulting 3205 Central Avenue Portland, OR 99304
BG Consulting 3205 Central Avenue Portland, OR 99304	BG Consulting 3205 Central Avenue Portland, OR 99304	BG Consulting 3205 Central Avenue Portland, OR 99304
BG Consulting 3205 Central Avenue Portland, OR 99304	BG Consulting 3205 Central Avenue Portland, OR 99304	BG Consulting 3205 Central Avenue Portland, OR 99304
BG Consulting 3205 Central Avenue Portland, OR 99304	BG Consulting 3205 Central Avenue Portland, OR 99304	BG Consulting 3205 Central Avenue Portland, OR 99304
BG Consulting 3205 Central Avenue Portland, OR 99304	BG Consulting 3205 Central Avenue Portland, OR 99304	BG Consulting 3205 Central Avenue Portland, OR 99304
BG Consulting 3205 Central Avenue Portland, OR 99304	BG Consulting 3205 Central Avenue Portland, OR 99304	BG Consulting 3205 Central Avenue Portland, OR 99304
BG Consulting 3205 Central Avenue Portland, OR 99304	BG Consulting 3205 Central Avenue Portland, OR 99304	BG Consulting 3205 Central Avenue Portland, OR 99304
BG Consulting 3205 Central Avenue Portland, OR 99304	BG Consulting 3205 Central Avenue Portland, OR 99304	BG Consulting 3205 Central Avenue Portland, OR 99304

WL1-C6-P4-BGCLabels.pdf

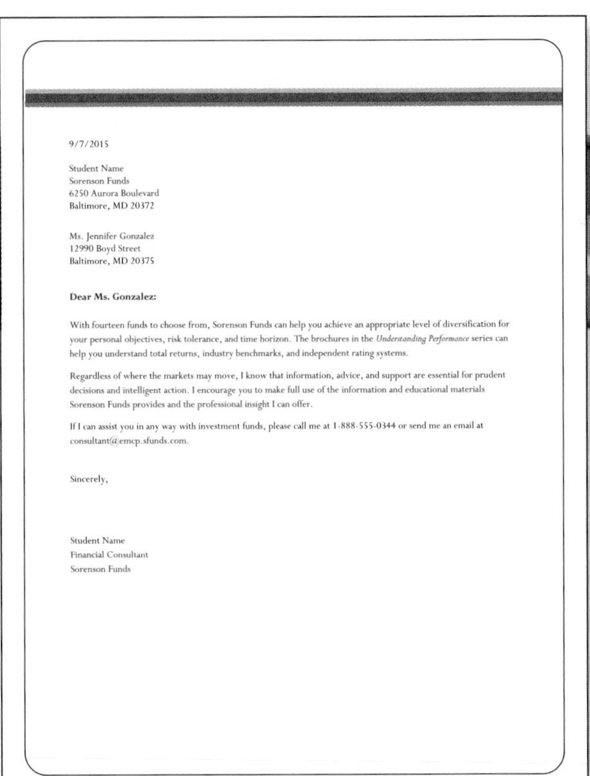

9/7/2015

Student Name
Sorenson Funds
6250 Aurora Boulevard
Baltimore, MD 20372

Ms. Jennifer Gonzalez
12990 Boyd Street
Baltimore, MD 20375

Dear Ms. Gonzalez:

With fourteen funds to choose from, Sorenson Funds can help you achieve an appropriate level of diversification for your personal objectives, risk tolerance, and time horizon. The brochures in the *Understanding Performance* series can help you understand total returns, industry benchmarks, and independent rating systems.

Regardless of where the markets may move, I know that information, advice, and support are essential for prudent decisions and intelligent action. I encourage you to make full use of the information and educational materials Sorenson Funds provides and the professional insight I can offer.

If I can assist you in any way with investment funds, please call me at 1-888-555-0344 or send me an email at consultant@emcp.sfunds.com.

Sincerely,

Student Name
Financial Consultant
Sorenson Funds

Project 5 Use a Template to Create a Business Letter

WL1-C6-P5-SFunds.docx

Project 1 Manage Documents — 8 Parts

You will perform a variety of file management tasks, including creating and renaming a folder; selecting and then deleting, copying, cutting, pasting, and renaming documents; deleting a folder; and opening, printing, and closing a document.

Maintaining Documents

Many file (document) management tasks can be completed at the Open dialog box (and some at the Save As dialog box). These tasks can include copying, moving, printing, and renaming documents; opening multiple documents; and creating a new folder and renaming a folder.

Directions and projects in this chapter assume that you are managing documents and folders on a USB flash drive or your computer's hard drive. If you are using your OneDrive, some of the document and folder management tasks may vary.

Using Print Screen

Keyboards contain a Print Screen key that will capture the contents of the screen into a file. That file can then be inserted in a Word document. Press the Print Screen key to capture the entire screen as an image or press Alt + Print Screen to capture only a dialog box or window that is open on the screen. The Print Screen feature is useful for file management in that you can print folder contents to help you keep track of documents and folders. To use the Print Screen key, display the desired information on the screen and then press the Print Screen key on your keyboard (generally located in the top row) or press Alt + Print Screen to capture a dialog box or window on the screen. When you press the Print Screen key or Alt + Print Screen, nothing seems to happen, but in fact, the screen image is captured in a file that is inserted in the Clipboard. To insert this file in a document, display a blank document and then click the Paste button in the Clipboard group on the HOME tab. You can also paste the file by right-clicking in a blank location in a document screen and then clicking the *Paste* option at the shortcut menu.

Creating a Folder

Word documents, like paper documents, should be grouped logically and placed in ***folders***. The main folder on a storage medium is called the ***root folder*** and you can create additional folders within the root folder. At the Open or Save As dialog box, documents display in the Content pane preceded by a document icon and folders display preceded by a folder icon. Create a new folder by clicking the New folder button located on the dialog box toolbar. This inserts a folder in the Content pane that contains the text *New folder*. Type a name for the folder (the name you type replaces *New folder*) and then press Enter. A folder name can contain a maximum of 255 characters. Numbers, spaces, and symbols can be used in the folder name, except those symbols explained in the *Naming a Document* section in Chapter 1.

To make the new folder active, double-click the folder name in the Open dialog box Content pane. The current folder path displays in the Address bar and includes the current folder as well as any previous folders. If the folder is located in an external storage device, the drive letter and name may display in the path. A right-pointing triangle displays to the right of each folder name in the Address bar. Click this right-pointing triangle and a drop-down list displays containing the names of any subfolders within the folder.

Quick Steps

Create a Folder

1. Display Open dialog box.
2. Click New folder button.
3. Type folder name.
4. Press Enter.

New folder

HINT

Display the Open dialog box with the keyboard shortcut Ctrl + F12.

Project 1a Creating a Folder — Part 1 of 8

1. Open a blank document and then press Ctrl + F12 to display the Open dialog box.
2. In the *Computer* list in the Navigation pane, click the drive containing your storage medium. (You may need to scroll down the list to display the drive.)
3. Double-click the *WL1C6* folder in the Content pane.
4. Click the New folder button on the dialog box toolbar.
5. Type **Correspondence** and then press Enter.
6. Capture the Open dialog box as an image file and insert the file in a document by completing the following steps:
   a. With the Open dialog box displayed, hold down the Alt key and then press the Print Screen key on your keyboard (generally located in the top row of your keyboard).
   b. Close the Open dialog box.

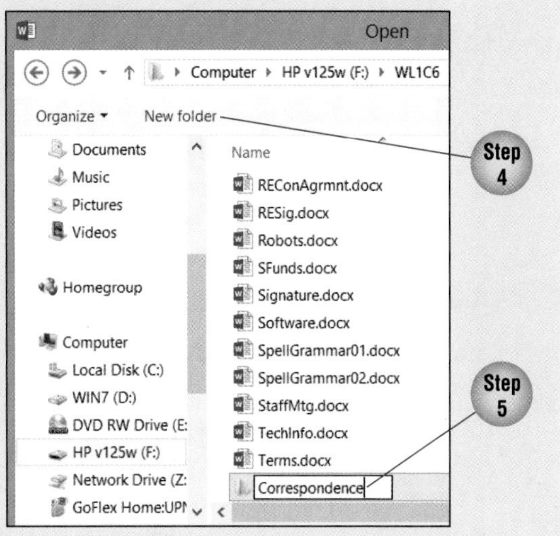

c. At the blank document, click the Paste button in the Clipboard group on the HOME tab. (If a blank document does not display on your screen, press Ctrl + N to open a blank document.)
d. With the print screen file inserted in the document, print the document by clicking the FILE tab, clicking the *Print* option, and then clicking the Print button at the Print backstage area.
7. Close the document without saving it.
8. Display the Open dialog box and make WL1C6 the active folder.

Renaming a Folder

Quick Steps

Rename a Folder
1. Display Open dialog box.
2. Right-click folder.
3. Click *Rename*.
4. Type new name.
5. Press Enter.

Organize ▾

Organize

As you organize your files and folders, you may decide to rename a folder. Rename a folder using the Organize button on the toolbar in the Open or Save As dialog box or using a shortcut menu. To rename a folder using the Organize button, display the Open or Save As dialog box, click the folder you want to rename, click the Organize button located on the toolbar in the dialog box, and then click *Rename* at the drop-down list. This selects the folder name and inserts a border around the name. Type the new name for the folder and then press Enter. To rename a folder using a shortcut menu, display the Open dialog box, right-click the folder name in the Content pane, and then click *Rename* at the shortcut menu. Type a new name for the folder and then press Enter.

Project 1b **Renaming a Folder** **Part 2 of 8**

1. With the Open dialog box open, right-click the *Correspondence* folder name in the Content pane.
2. Click *Rename* at the shortcut menu.
3. Type Documents and then press Enter.

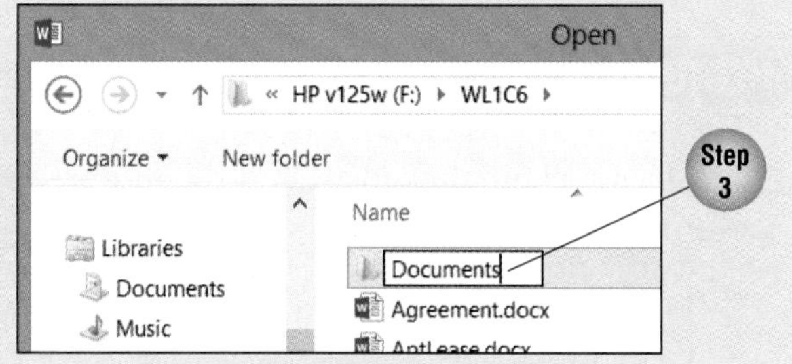

Selecting Documents

You can complete document management tasks on one document or selected documents. To select one document, display the Open dialog box and then click the desired document. To select several adjacent documents (documents that display next to each other), click the first document, hold down the Shift key, and then click the last document. To select documents that are not adjacent, click the first document, hold down the Ctrl key, click any other desired documents, and then release the Ctrl key.

Deleting Documents

At some point, you may want to delete documents from your storage medium or any other drive or folder in which you may be working. To delete a document, display the Open or Save As dialog box, select the document, click the Organize button on the toolbar, and then click *Delete* at the drop-down list. If you are deleting a document from an external drive such as a USB flash drive, click the Yes button at the message that displays asking you to confirm the deletion. This message does not display if you are deleting a document from the computer's hard drive. To delete a document using a shortcut menu, right-click the document name in the Content pane and then click *Delete* at the shortcut menu. If a confirmation message displays, click Yes.

Documents deleted from the hard drive are automatically sent to the Recycle Bin. If you accidentally send a document to the Recycle Bin, it can be easily restored. To free space on the drive, empty the Recycle Bin on a periodic basis. Restoring a document from or emptying the contents of the Recycle Bin is completed at the Windows desktop (not in Word). To display the Recycle Bin, minimize the Word window, display the Windows desktop, and then double-click the *Recycle Bin* icon located on the Windows desktop. At the Recycle Bin, you can restore a file and empty the Recycle Bin.

Quick Steps

Delete a Folder or Document
1. Display Open dialog box.
2. Click folder or document name.
3. Click Organize button.
4. Click *Delete* at drop-down list.
5. Click Yes.

Remember to empty the Recycle Bin on a regular basis.

Project 1c **Selecting and Deleting Documents** **Part 3 of 8**

1. Open **FutureHardware.docx** and then save the document with Save As and name it **WL1-C6-P1-FutureHardware**.
2. Close **WL1-C6-P1-FutureHardware.docx**.
3. Delete **WL1-C6-P1-FutureHardware.docx** by completing the following steps:
   a. Display the Open dialog box.
   b. Click ***WL1-C6-P1-FutureHardware.docx*** to select it.
   c. Click the Organize button on the toolbar and then click *Delete* at the drop-down list.
   d. At the question asking if you want to delete **WL1-C6-P1-FutureHardware.docx**, click Yes. (This question will not display if you are deleting the file from your computer's hard drive.)

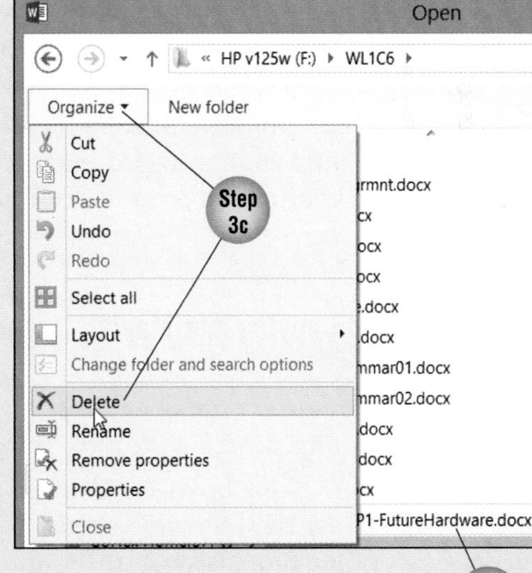

4. Delete selected documents by completing the following steps:
   a. At the Open dialog box, click ***CompCareers.docx***.
   b. Hold down the Shift key and then click ***CompEthics.docx***.
   c. Position the mouse pointer on a selected document and then click the right mouse button.
   d. At the shortcut menu that displays, click *Delete*.
   e. At the question asking if you want to delete the items, click Yes.
5. Open **CompKeyboards.docx** and then save the document with Save As and name it **WL1-C6-P1-CompKeyboards**.
6. Save a copy of the **WL1-C6-P1-CompKeyboards.docx** document in the Documents folder by completing the following steps.
   a. With **WL1-C6-P1-CompKeyboards.docx** open, press F12 to display the Save As dialog box.

b. At the Save As dialog box, double-click the *Documents* folder located at the beginning of the Content pane. (Folders are listed before documents.)
c. Click the Save button located in the lower right corner of the dialog box.
7. Close **WL1-C6-P1-CompKeyboards.docx**.
8. Press Ctrl + F12 to display the Open dialog box and then click *WL1C6* in the Address bar.

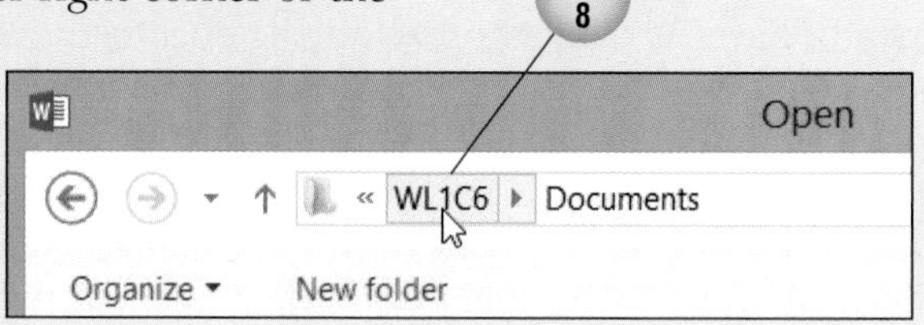

Quick Steps

Copy a Document
1. Display Open dialog box.
2. Right-click document name.
3. Click *Copy*.
4. Navigate to desired folder.
5. Right-click blank area in Content pane.
6. Click *Paste*.

Move Document
1. Display Open dialog box.
2. Right-click document name.
3. Click *Cut*.
4. Navigate to desired folder.
5. Right-click blank area in Content pane.
6. Click *Paste*.

Copying and Moving Documents

You can copy a document to another folder without opening the document first. To do this, use the *Copy* and *Paste* options from the Organize button drop-down list or the shortcut menu at the Open dialog box or the Save As dialog box. You can copy a document or selected documents into the same folder. When you do this, Word inserts a hyphen followed by the word *Copy* to the document name. You can copy one document or selected documents into the same folder.

Remove a document from one folder and insert it in another folder using the *Cut* and *Paste* options from the Organize button drop-down list or the shortcut menu at the Open dialog box. To do this with the Organize button, display the Open dialog box, select the desired document, click the Organize button, and then click *Cut* at the drop-down list. Navigate to the desired folder, click the Organize button, and then click *Paste* at the drop-down list. To do this with the shortcut menu, display the Open dialog box, position the arrow pointer on the document to be removed (cut), click the right mouse button, and then click *Cut* at the shortcut menu. Navigate to the desired folder, position the arrow pointer in a blank area in the Content pane, click the right mouse button, and then click *Paste* at the shortcut menu.

To move or copy files or folders on your OneDrive, go to onedrive.com, make sure you are logged in to your account, and then use the OneDrive.com toolbar to copy and/or move a document or folder to another location.

Project 1d **Copying and Moving Documents** **Part 4 of 8**

Note: If you are using your OneDrive, the steps for copying and moving files will vary from the steps in this project. Check with your instructor.

1. At the Open dialog box with WL1C6 the active folder, copy a document to another folder by completing the following steps:
   a. Click ***CompTerms.docx*** in the Content pane, click the Organize button, and then click *Copy* at the drop-down list.
   b. Navigate to the Documents folder by double-clicking *Documents* at the beginning of the Content pane.
   c. Click the Organize button and then click *Paste* at the drop-down list.
2. Change back to the WL1C6 folder by clicking *WL1C6* in the Address bar.
3. Copy several documents to the Documents folder by completing the following steps:
   a. Click once on ***IntelProp.docx***. (This selects the document.)

b. Hold down the Ctrl key, click ***Robots.docx***, click ***TechInfo.docx***, and then release the Ctrl key. (You may need to scroll down the Content pane to display the three documents and then select the documents.)
c. Position the arrow pointer on one of the selected documents, click the right mouse button, and then click *Copy* at the shortcut menu.
d. Double-click the *Documents* folder.
e. Position the arrow pointer in any blank area in the Content pane, click the right mouse button, and then click *Paste* at the shortcut menu.

4. Click *WL1C6* in the Address bar.
5. Move **CompIssues.docx** to the Documents folder by completing the following steps:
   a. Position the arrow pointer on ***CompIssues.docx***, click the right mouse button, and then click *Cut* at the shortcut menu.
   b. Double-click *Documents* to make it the active folder.
   c. Position the arrow pointer in any blank area in the Content pane, click the right mouse button, and then click *Paste* at the shortcut menu.
6. Capture the Open dialog box as an image file and insert the file in a document by completing the following steps:
   a. With the Open dialog box displayed, press Alt + Print Screen.
   b. Close the Open dialog box.
   c. At a blank document, click the Paste button in the Clipboard group on the HOME tab. (If a blank document does not display on your screen, press Ctrl + N to open a blank document.)
   d. With the print screen file inserted in the document, print the document by clicking the FILE tab, clicking the *Print* option, and then clicking the Print button at the Print backstage area.
7. Close the document without saving it.
8. Display the Open dialog box and make WL1C6 the active folder.

Renaming Documents

At the Open dialog box, use the *Rename* option from the Organize button drop-down list to give a document a different name. The *Rename* option changes the name of the document and keeps it in the same folder. To use Rename, display the Open dialog box, click once on the document to be renamed, click the Organize button, and then click *Rename* at the drop-down list. This causes a black border to surround the document name and the name to be selected. Type the desired name and then press Enter. You can also rename a document by right-clicking the document name at the Open dialog box and then clicking *Rename* at the shortcut menu. Type the desired name for the document and then press the Enter key.

Quick Steps

Rename a Document
1. Display Open dialog box.
2. Click document name.
3. Click Organize button and then *Rename*.
4. Type new name.
5. Press Enter.

Open a recently opened document by clicking the FILE tab, clicking the *Open* option, and then clicking the document in the Recent Documents list.

Deleting a Folder

As you learned earlier in this chapter, you can delete a document or several selected documents. Delete a folder and all its contents in the same manner as you would delete a document.

Opening Multiple Documents

To open more than one document, select the documents in the Open dialog box, and then click the Open button. You can also open multiple documents by positioning the arrow pointer on one of the selected documents, clicking the right mouse button, and then clicking *Open* at the shortcut menu.

Project 1e Renaming and Opening Documents and Deleting a Folder Part 5 of 8

1. Rename a document located in the Documents folder by completing the following steps:
   a. At the Open dialog box with the WL1C6 folder open, double-click the *Documents* folder to make it active.
   b. Click once on ***Robots.docx*** to select it.
   c. Click the Organize button.
   d. Click *Rename* at the drop-down list.
   e. Type **Androids** and then press the Enter key.

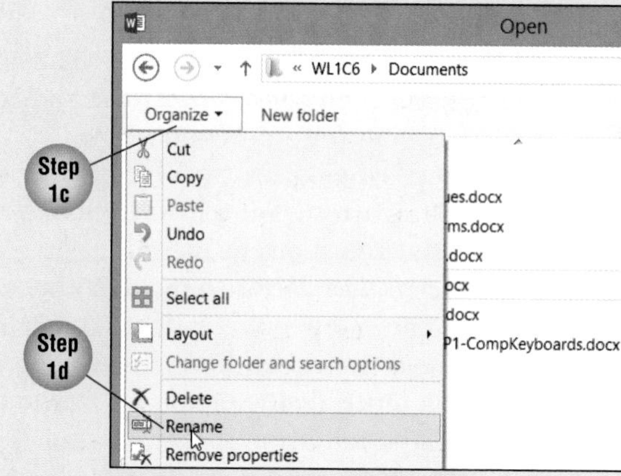

2. Capture the Open dialog box as an image file and insert the file in a document by completing the following steps:
   a. Press Alt + Print Screen.
   b. Close the Open dialog box.
   c. At a blank document, click the Paste button in the Clipboard group on the HOME tab. (If a blank document does not display on your screen, press Ctrl + N to open a blank document.)
   d. With the print screen file inserted in the document, print the document.
3. Close the document without saving it.
4. Display the Open dialog box and make WL1C6 the active folder.
5. At the Open dialog box, click the *Documents* folder to select it.
6. Click the Organize button and then click *Delete* at the drop-down list.
7. If a message displays asking if you want to remove the folder and its contents, click Yes.
8. Select ***CompKeyboards.docx***, ***CompSoftware.docx***, and ***CompTerms.docx***.
9. Click the Open button located toward the lower right corner of the dialog box.
10. Close the open documents.

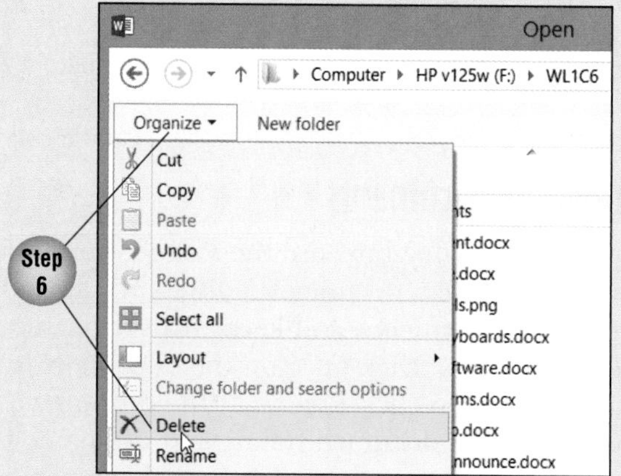

Saving a Document in a Different Format

When you save a document, the document is saved automatically as a Word document with the .docx file extension. If you need to share a document with someone who is using a different word processing program or a different version of Word, you may want to save the document in another format. At the Export backstage area, click the *Change File Type* option and the backstage area displays as shown in Figure 6.1.

With options in the *Document File Types* section below the *Change File Type* heading, you can choose to save a Word document with the default file format, save the document in a previous version of Word, save the document in the OpenDocument Text format, or save the document as a template. The OpenDocument Text format is an XML-based file format for displaying, storing, and editing files such as word processing, spreadsheet, and presentation files. OpenDocument Text format is free from any licensing, royalty payments, or other restrictions, and since technology changes at a rapid pace, saving a document in the OpenDocument Text format ensures that the information in the file can be accessed, retrieved, and used now and in the future.

Additional file types are available in the *Other File Types* section. If you need to send your document to another user who does not have access to Microsoft Word, consider saving the document in plain text or rich text file format. Use the *Plain Text (*.txt)* option to save the document with all formatting stripped, which is good for universal file exchange. Use the *Rich Text Format (*.rtf)* option to save the document with most of the character formatting applied to text in the document, such as bold, italic, underline, bullets, and fonts as well as some paragraph formatting. Before the widespread use of Adobe's portable document format (PDF), rich text format was the most portable file format used to exchange files. With the *Single File Web Page (*.mht, *.mhtml)* option, you can save your document as a single-page web document. Click the *Save as Another File Type* option and the Save As dialog box displays. Click the *Save as type* option box and a drop-down list displays with a variety of available file type options.

Quick Steps

Save a Document in a Different Format

1. Click FILE tab.
2. Click *Export* option.
3. Click *Change File Type* option.
4. Click desired format in *Document File Types* or *Other File Types* section.
5. Click Save As button.

Figure 6.1 Export Backstage Area with *Change File Type* Option Selected

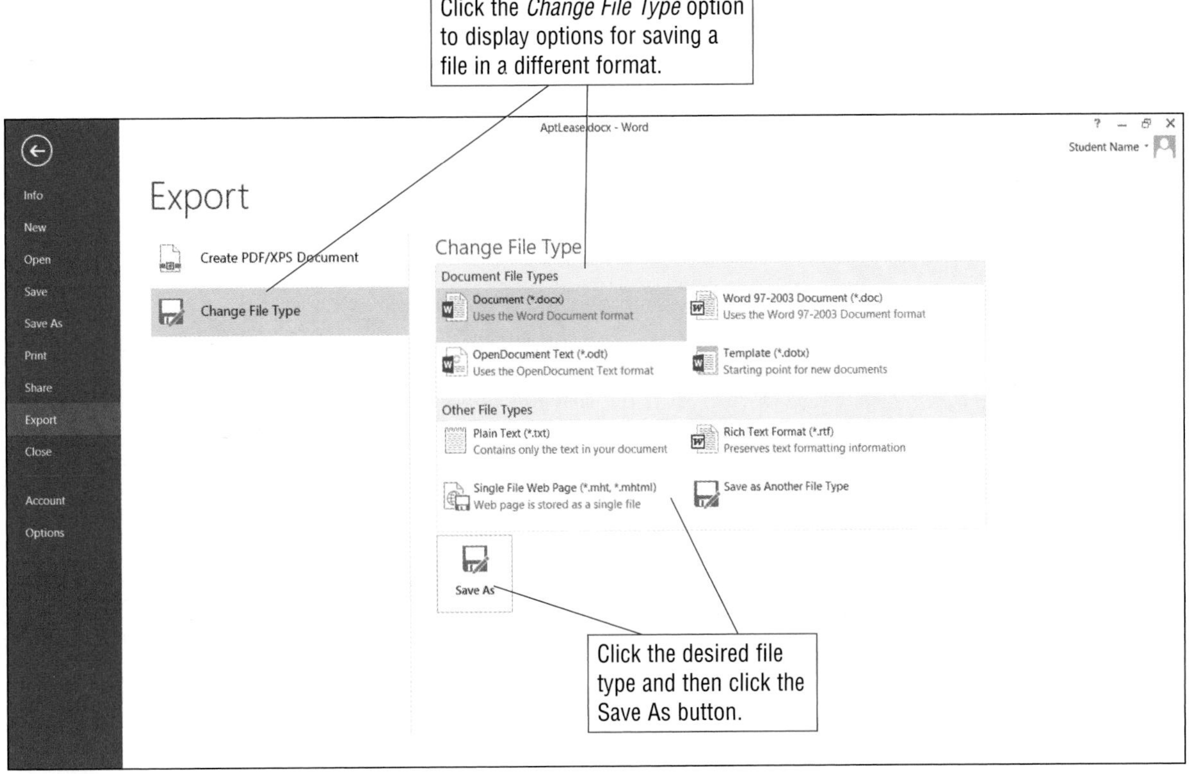

Project 1f Saving a Document in Different File Formats Part 6 of 8

1. Open **AptLease.docx** and then save the document in Word 97-2003 format by completing the following steps:
   a. Click the FILE tab and then click the *Export* option.
   b. At the Export backstage area, click the *Change File Type* option.
   c. Click the *Word 97-2003 Document (*.doc)* option in the *Document File Types* section and then click the Save As button.

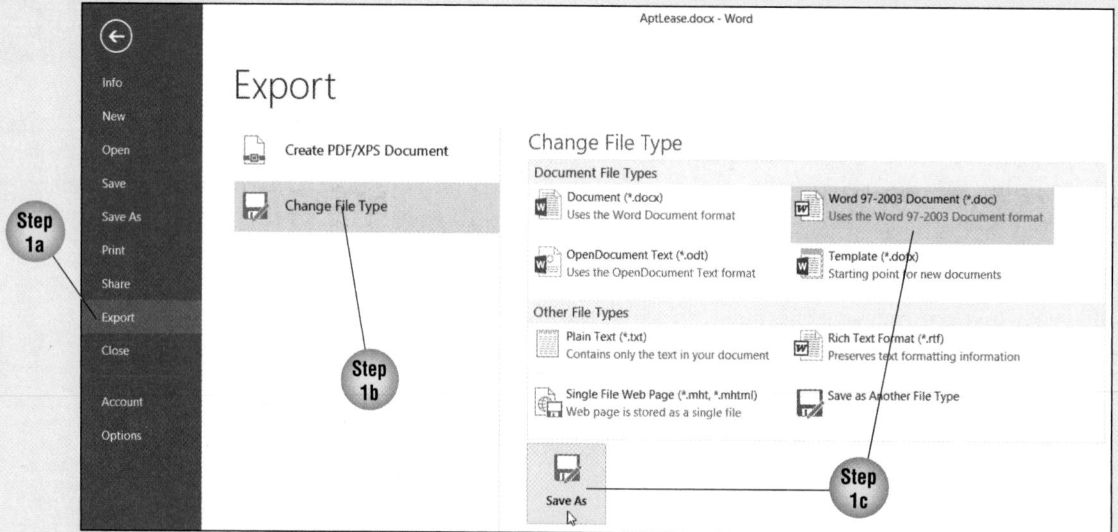

   d. At the Save As dialog box with the *Save as type* option changed to *Word 97-2003 Document (*.doc)*, type **WL1-C6-P1-AptLease-Word97-2003** in the *File name* text box and then press Enter.
2. At the document, notice the title bar displays the words *[Compatibility Mode]* after the document name.
3. Click the DESIGN tab and notice the Themes, Colors, and Fonts buttons are dimmed. (This is because the themes features were not available in Word 97 through 2003.)
4. Close **WL1-C6-P1-AptLease-Word97-2003.doc**.
5. Open **AptLease.docx**
6. Save the document in plain text format by completing the following steps:
   a. Click the FILE tab and then click the *Export* option.
   b. At the Export backstage area, click the *Change File Type* option.
   c. Click the *Plain Text (*.txt)* option in the *Other File Types* section and then click the Save As button.
   d. At the Save As dialog box, type **WL1-C6-P1-AptLease-PlainTxt** and then press Enter.
   e. At the File Conversion dialog box, click OK.
7. Close **WL1-C6-P1-AptLease-PlainTxt.txt**.
8. Display the Open dialog box and, if necessary, display all files. To do this, click the file type button at the right side of the *File name* text box and then click *All Files (*.*)* at the drop-down list.
9. Double-click ***WL1-C6-P1-AptLease-PlainTxt.txt***. (If a File Conversion dialog box displays, click OK. Notice that the character and paragraph formatting has been removed from the document.)
10. Close **WL1-C6-P1-AptLease-PlainTxt.txt**.

In addition to options in the Export backstage area with the *Change File Type* option selected, you can save a document in a different format using the *Save as type* option box at the Save As dialog box. Click the *Save as type* option box, and a drop-down list displays containing all available file formats for saving a document. Click the desired format and then click the Save button.

Quick Steps

Save a Document in a Different Format at the Save As Dialog Box

1. Display Save As dialog box.
2. Type document name.
3. Click *Save as type* option box.
4. Click desired format.
5. Click Save button.

Project 1g **Saving a Document in a Different Format at the Save As Dialog Box** **Part 7 of 8**

1. Open **AptLease.docx**.
2. Save the document in rich text format by completing the following steps:
   a. Press F12 to display the Save As dialog box.
   b. At the Save As dialog box, type **WL1-C6-P1-AptLease-RichTxt** in the *File name* text box.
   c. Click in the *Save as type* option box.
   d. Click *Rich Text Format (*.rtf)* at the drop-down list.
   e. Click the Save button.
3. Close the document.
4. Display the Open dialog box and, if necessary, display all files.
5. Double-click ***WL1-C6-P1-AptLease-RichTxt.rtf***. (Notice that the formatting was retained in the document.)
6. Close the document.

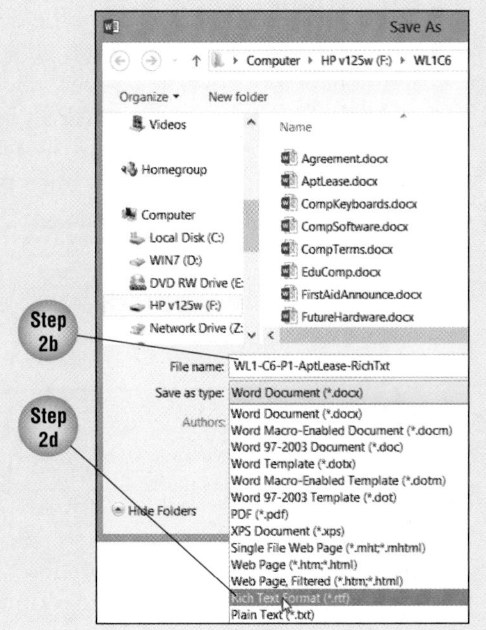

Saving in PDF/XPS Format

A Word document can be saved in the PDF or XPS file format. PDF stands for *portable document format* and is a file format that preserves fonts, formatting, and images in a printer-friendly version that looks the same on most computers. A person who receives a Word file saved in PDF format does not need to have the Word application on his or her computer to open, read, and print the file. Exchanging PDF files is a popular method for collaborating with others, since this file type has cross-platform compatibility, allowing users to open PDF files on a Windows-based personal computer, Macintosh computer, tablet, and smartphone. The XML paper specification (XPS) format is a fixed-layout format with all formatting preserved (similar to PDF) that was developed by Microsoft.

Quick Steps

Save a Document in PDF/XPS Format

1. Click FILE tab.
2. Click *Export* option.
3. Click Create PDF/XPS button.
4. At Publish as PDF or XPS dialog box, specify PDF or XPS format.
5. Click Publish button.

To save a document in PDF or XPS format, click the FILE tab, click the *Export* option, and then click the Create PDF/XPS button. This displays the Publish as PDF or XPS dialog box with the *PDF (*.pdf)* option selected in the *Save as type* option box.

If you want to save the document in XPS format, click the *Save as type* option box and then click *XPS Document (*.xps)* at the drop-down list. At the Save As dialog box, type a name in the *File name* text box and then click the Publish button.

A PDF file will open in Adobe Reader, Internet Explorer, Microsoft Word, and Windows Reader. An XPS file will open in Internet Explorer, Windows Reader, and XPS Viewer. One method for opening a PDF or XPS file is to open File Explorer, navigate to the folder containing the file, right-click on the file, and then point to *Open with*. This displays a side menu with the programs you can choose from to open the file. You can open a PDF file in Word and make edits to the file, but you cannot open an XPS file in Word.

Project 1h Saving a Document in PDF Format and Editing a PDF File in Word — Part 8 of 8

1. Open **NSS.docx** and then save the document in PDF format by completing the following steps:
   a. Click the FILE tab and then click the *Export* option.
   b. At the Export backstage area, click the Create PDF/XPS button.
   c. At the Publish as PDF or XPS dialog box, make sure *PDF (*.pdf)* is selected in the *Save as type* option box and that the *Open file after publishing* check box contains a check mark and then click the Publish button.

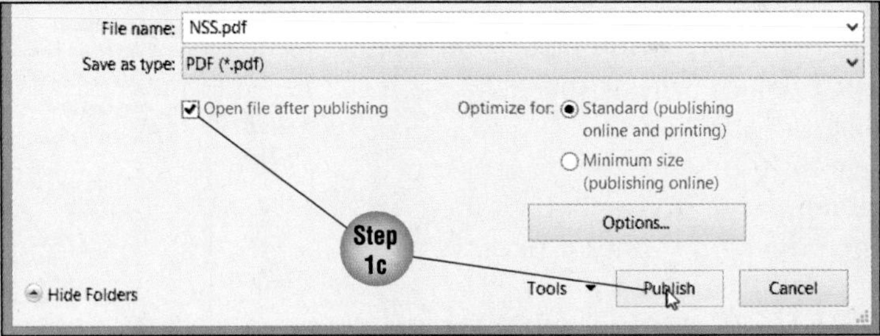

2. Scroll through the document in Adobe Reader and then click the Close button in the upper right corner of the window to close Adobe Reader. (If Adobe Reader is not installed on your computer, the file will open in Windows Reader. Close the Windows Reader window by positioning the mouse pointer at the top of the window [mouse turns into a hand], holding down the left mouse button, dragging down to the bottom of the screen, and then releasing the mouse button. At the Windows Start screen, click the Desktop icon.)
3. Close **NSS.docx**.
4. Open the **NSS.pdf** file in Windows Reader by completing the following steps:
   a. Click the File Explorer button on the Taskbar.
   b. At the Libraries dialog box, navigate to the WL1C6 folder on your storage medium.
   c. Right-click the **NSS.pdf** file in the Content pane, point to *Open with* at the shortcut menu, and then click *Reader* at the side menu.

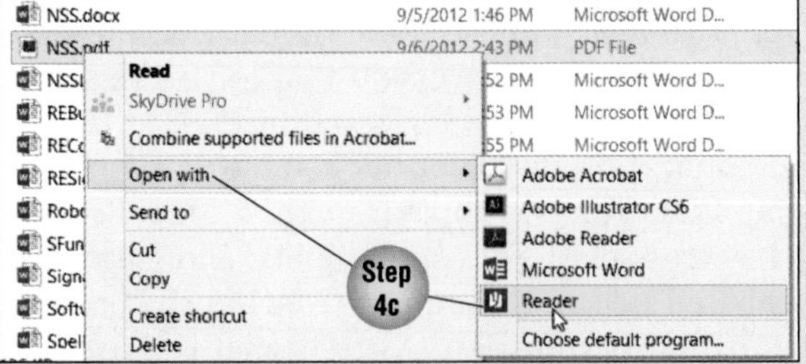

   d. After looking at the file in Windows Reader, close the window by positioning the mouse pointer at the top of the window (mouse turns into a hand), holding down the left mouse button, dragging down to the bottom of the screen, and then releasing the mouse button.

e. At the Windows Start screen, click the Desktop icon. (This step may vary.)
f. Close the WL1C6 window.
5. In Word, open the **NSS.pdf** file you saved to your WL1C6 folder. At the message that displays telling you that Word will convert the file to an editable Word document, click the OK button.
6. Notice that the formatting of the text is slightly different than the original formatting and that the graphic was moved to the second page. Edit the file by completing the following steps:
a. Click the DESIGN tab and then click the *Lines (Distinctive)* style set.
b. Delete the text "We are" in the text below the first heading and replace it with **Northland Security Systems is.**
7. Save the file with Save As and name it **WL1-C6-P1-NSS**. (The file will save in the *.docx* file format.)
8. Print and then close **WL1-C6-P1-NSS.docx**.
9. Display the Open dialog box, capture the Open dialog box as an image file, and then close the Open dialog box. Press Ctrl + N to open a blank document, paste the image file in the document, print the document, and then close the document without saving it.

Project 2 Manage Multiple Documents — 7 Parts

You will work with windows by arranging, maximizing, restoring, and minimizing windows; move selected text between split windows; compare formatting of documents side by side; print specific text, pages, and multiple copies; and create and modify document properties.

Working with Windows

In Word, you can open multiple documents and move the insertion point between the documents. You can also move and copy information between documents or compare the contents of documents. The maximum number of documents that you can have open at one time depends on the memory of your computer system and the amount of data in each document. When you open a new window, it displays on top of any previously opened window(s). Once you have multiple windows open, you can resize the windows to see all or a portion of each on the screen.

When a document is open, a Word button displays on the Taskbar. Hover the mouse over this button and a thumbnail of the document displays above the button. If you have more than one document open, another Word button displays behind the first button in a cascaded manner with only a portion of the button displaying at the right side of the first button. If you have multiple documents open, hovering the mouse over the Word buttons on the Taskbar will cause thumbnails of all of the documents to display above the buttons. To change to the desired document, click the thumbnail that represents the document.

Press Ctrl + F6 to switch between open documents.

Press Ctrl + W or Ctrl + F4 to close the active document window.

Another method for determining what documents are open is to click the VIEW tab and then click the Switch Windows button in the Window group. The document name that displays in the list with the check mark in front of it is the ***active document***. The active document contains the insertion point. To make one of the other documents active, click the document name. If you are using the keyboard, type the number shown in front of the desired document.

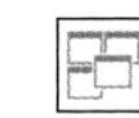
Switch Windows

Arranging Windows

Quick Steps

Arrange Windows
1. Open documents.
2. Click VIEW tab.
3. Click Arrange All button.

Arrange All

If you have several documents open, you can arrange them so a portion of each document displays. The portions that display are the title (if present) and the opening paragraph of each document. To arrange a group of open documents, click the VIEW tab and then click the Arrange All button in the Window group.

Maximizing, Restoring, and Minimizing Documents

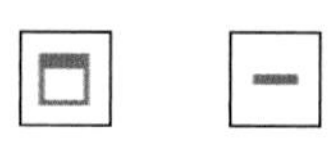

Maximize Minimize

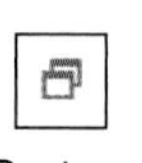

Restore

Use the Maximize and Minimize buttons located in the upper right corner of the active document to change the size of the window. The two buttons are located to the left of the Close button. (The Close button is located in the upper right corner of the screen and contains an X.)

If you arrange all open documents and then click the Maximize button in the active document, the active document expands to fill the document screen. In addition, the Maximize button changes to the Restore button. To return the active document back to its size before it was maximized, click the Restore button. If you click the Minimize button in the active document, the document is reduced and a button displays on the Taskbar representing the document. To maximize a document that has been minimized, click the button on the Taskbar representing the document.

Project 2a **Arranging, Maximizing, Restoring, and Minimizing Windows** **Part 1 of 7**

Note: If you are using Word on a network system that contains a virus checker, you may not be able to open multiple documents at once. Continue by opening each document individually.

1. Open the following documents: **AptLease.docx**, **CompSoftware.docx**, **IntelProp.docx**, and **NSS.docx**.
2. Arrange the windows by clicking the VIEW tab and then clicking the Arrange All button in the Window group.
3. Make **AptLease.docx** the active document by clicking the Switch Windows button in the Window group on the VIEW tab of the document at the top of your screen, and then clicking ***AptLease.docx*** at the drop-down list.
4. Close **AptLease.docx**.
5. Make **IntelProp.docx** active and then close it.
6. Make **CompSoftware.docx** active and minimize it by clicking the Minimize button in the upper right corner of the active window.
7. Maximize **NSS.docx** by clicking the Maximize button (located immediately left of the Close button).
8. Close **NSS.docx**.
9. Restore **CompSoftware.docx** by clicking the button on the Taskbar representing the document.
10. Maximize **CompSoftware.docx**.

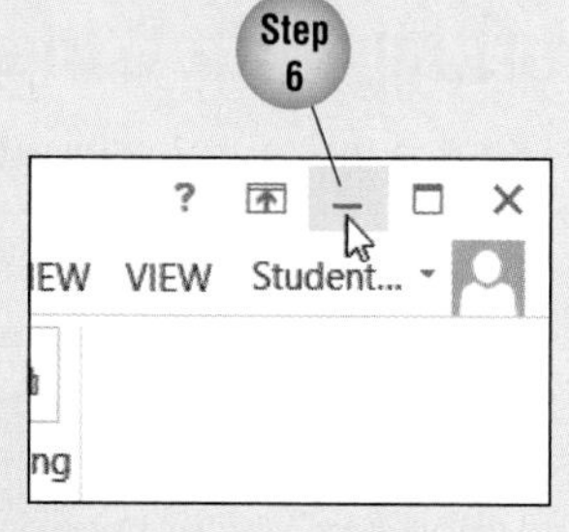

Splitting a Window

You can divide a window into two ***panes***, which is helpful if you want to view different parts of the same document at one time. You may want to display an outline for a report in one pane, for example, and the portion of the report that you are editing in the other. The original window is split into two panes that extend horizontally across the screen.

Split a window by clicking the VIEW tab and then clicking the Split button in the Window group. This splits the window in two with a split bar and another horizontal ruler. You can change the location of the split bar by positioning the mouse pointer on the split bar until it displays as an up-and-down-pointing arrow with two small lines in the middle, holding down the left mouse button, dragging to the desired position, and then releasing the mouse button.

Quick Steps

Split a Window
1. Open document.
2. Click VIEW tab.
3. Click Split button.

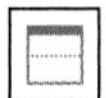

Split

When a window is split, the insertion point is positioned in the bottom pane. To move the insertion point to the other pane with the mouse, position the I-beam pointer in the other pane, and then click the left mouse button. To remove the split bar from the document, click the VIEW tab and then click the Remove Split button in the Window group. You can also double-click the split bar or drag the split bar to the top or bottom of the screen.

Project 2b **Moving Selected Text between Split Windows** **Part 2 of 7**

1. With **CompSoftware.docx** open, save the document with Save As and name it **WL1-C6-P2-CompSoftware**.
2. Click the VIEW tab and then click the Split button in the Window group.
3. Move the first section below the second section by completing the following steps:
   a. Click in the top pane and then click the HOME tab.
   b. Select the *SECTION 1: PERSONAL-USE SOFTWARE* section from the title to right above *SECTION 2: GRAPHICS AND MULTIMEDIA SOFTWARE.*
   c. Click the Cut button in the Clipboard group in the HOME tab.
   d. Click in the bottom pane and then move the insertion point to the end of the document.
   e. Click the Paste button in the Clipboard group on the HOME tab.
   f. Change the number in the two titles to *SECTION 1: GRAPHICS AND MULTIMEDIA SOFTWARE* and *SECTION 2: PERSONAL-USE SOFTWARE.*
4. Remove the split from the window by clicking the VIEW tab and then clicking the Remove Split button in the Window group.
5. Press Ctrl + Home to move the insertion point to the beginning of the document.

Viewing Documents Side by Side

If you want to compare the contents of two documents, open both documents, click the VIEW tab, and then click the View Side by Side button in the Window group. Both documents are arranged in the screen side by side, as shown in Figure 6.2. By default, synchronous scrolling is active. With this feature active, scrolling in one document causes the same scrolling to occur in the other document. This feature is useful in situations where you want to compare text, formatting, or other features between documents. If you want to scroll in one document and not the other, click the Synchronous Scrolling button in the Window group to turn it off.

Quick Steps

View Side by Side
1. Open two documents.
2. Click VIEW tab.
3. Click View Side by Side button.

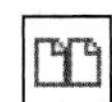

View Side by Side

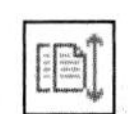

Synchronous Scrolling

Figure 6.2 Viewing Documents Side by Side

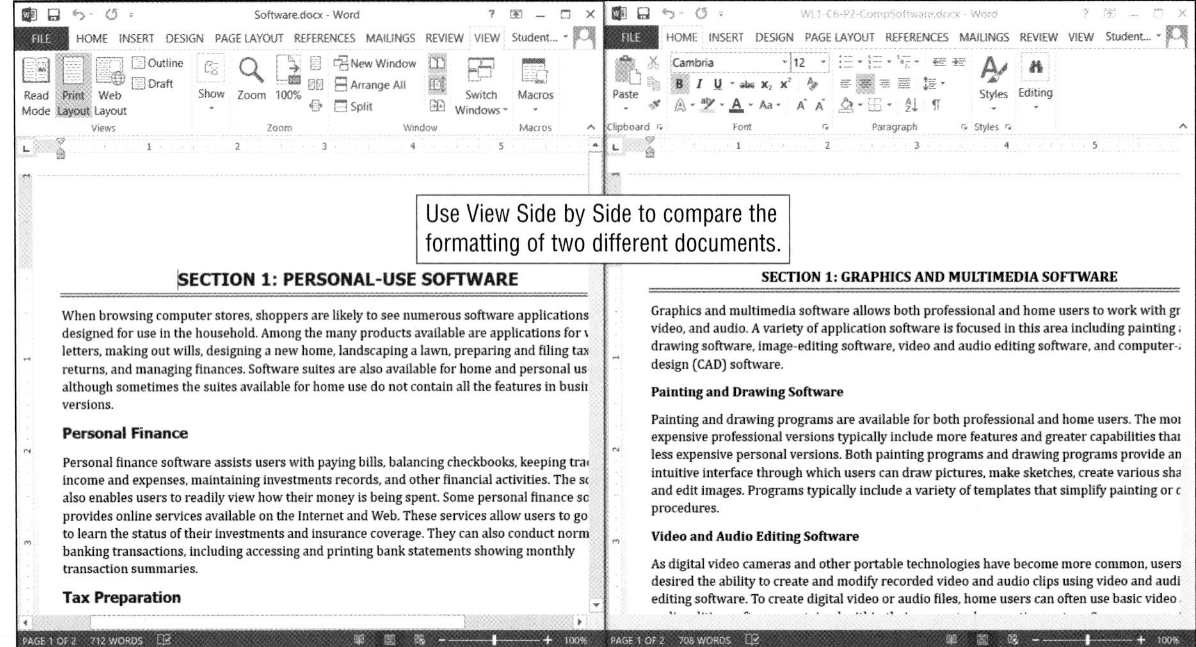
Use View Side by Side to compare the formatting of two different documents.
SECTION 1: PERSONAL-USE SOFTWARE
SECTION 1: GRAPHICS AND MULTIMEDIA SOFTWARE

Project 2c Viewing Documents Side by Side

Part 3 of 7

1. With **WL1-C6-P2-CompSoftware.docx** open, open **Software.docx**.
2. Click the VIEW tab and then click the View Side by Side button in the Window group.
3. Scroll through both documents simultaneously. Notice the difference between the two documents. (The titles and headings are set in different fonts and colors.) Select and then format the title and headings in **WL1-C6-P2-CompSoftware.docx** so they match the formatting in **Software.docx**. ***Hint: Use the Format Painter to copy the formats.***

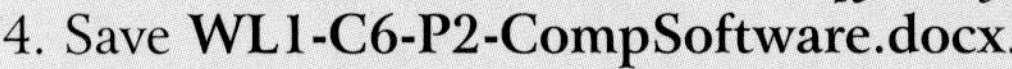

4. Save **WL1-C6-P2-CompSoftware.docx**.
5. Turn off synchronous scrolling by clicking the Synchronous Scrolling button in the Window group on the VIEW tab.
6. Scroll through the document and notice that the other document does not scroll.
7. Make **Software.docx** the active document and then close it.

Step 2

VIEW

Arrange All | Split | View Side by Side | Synchronous Scrolling | Reset Window Position | Switch Windows | Window

Quick Steps

Open a New Window

1. Open document.
2. Click VIEW tab.
3. Click New Window button.

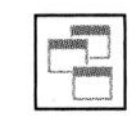

New Window

Opening a New Window

In addition to splitting a document to view two locations of the same document, you can open a new window containing the same document. When you open a new window, the document name in the Title bar displays followed by *:2*. The document name in the original window displays followed by *:1*. Any change you make to the document in one window is reflected in the document in the other window. If you want to view both documents on the screen, click the Arrange All button to arrange them horizontally or click the View Side by Side button to arrange them vertically.

Project 2d Opening a New Window

Part 4 of 7

1. With **WL1-C6-P2-CompSoftware.docx** open, open a new window by clicking the New Window button in the Window group on the VIEW tab. (Notice the document name in the Title bar displays followed by *:2*.)
2. Click the VIEW tab and then click the View Side by Side button in the Window group.
3. Click the Synchronous Scrolling button to turn off synchronous scrolling.
4. With the **WL1-C6-P2-CompSoftware.docx:2** window active, look at the first paragraph of text and notice the order in which the software is listed in the last sentence (painting and drawing software, image-editing software, video and audio editing software, and computer-aided design [CAD] software).
5. Click in the **WL1-C6-P2-CompSoftware.docx:1** window and then cut and paste the headings and text so the software displays in the order listed in the paragraph.
6. Click the Save button on the Quick Access toolbar.
7. Close the second version of the document by hovering the mouse pointer over the Word buttons on the Taskbar and then clicking the Close button in the upper right corner of the **WL1-C6-P2-CompSoftware.docx:2** thumbnail (the thumbnail that displays above the Word button on the Taskbar).

Inserting a File

If you want to insert the contents of one document into another, use the Object button in the Text group on the INSERT tab. Click the Object button arrow and then click *Text from File* and the Insert File dialog box displays. This dialog box contains similar features as the Open dialog box. Navigate to the desired folder and then double-click the document you want to insert in the open document.

Quick Steps

Insert a File
1. Click INSERT tab.
2. Click Object button arrow.
3. Click *Text from File*.
4. Navigate to folder.
5. Double-click document.

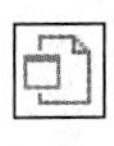

Object

Project 2e Inserting a File

Part 5 of 7

1. With **WL1-C6-P2-CompSoftware.docx** open, move the insertion point to the end of the document.
2. Insert a file into the open document by completing the following steps:
   a. Click the INSERT tab.
   b. Click the Object button arrow in the Text group.
   c. Click *Text from File* at the drop-down list.
   d. At the Insert File dialog box, navigate to the WL1C6 folder and then double-click *EduComp.docx*.
3. Save **WL1-C6-P2-CompSoftware.docx**.

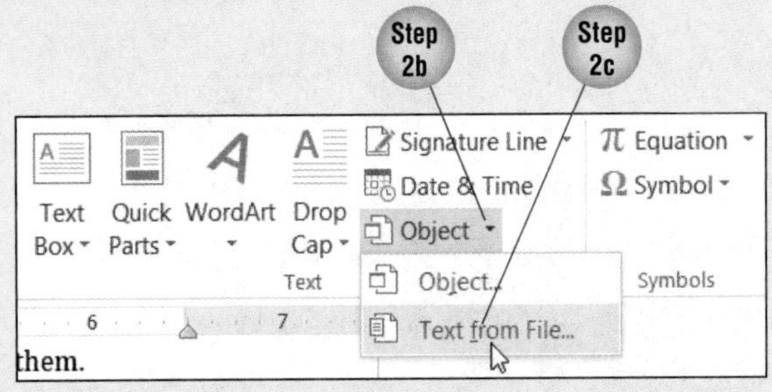

Printing and Previewing a Document

Display the Print backstage area with the keyboard shortcut Ctrl + P.

Use options at the Print backstage area, shown in Figure 6.3, to specify what you want to print and also preview the pages before printing. To display the Print backstage area, click the FILE tab and then click the *Print* option.

Previewing Pages in a Document

Zoom to Page

When you display the Print backstage area, a preview of the page where the insertion point is positioned displays at the right side (see Figure 6.3). Click the Next Page button (right-pointing triangle), located below and to the left of the page, to view the next page in the document, and click the Previous Page button (left-pointing triangle) to display the previous page in the document. Use the Zoom slider bar to increase/decrease the size of the page, and click the Zoom to Page button to fit the page in the viewing area in the Print backstage area.

Figure 6.3 Print Backstage Area

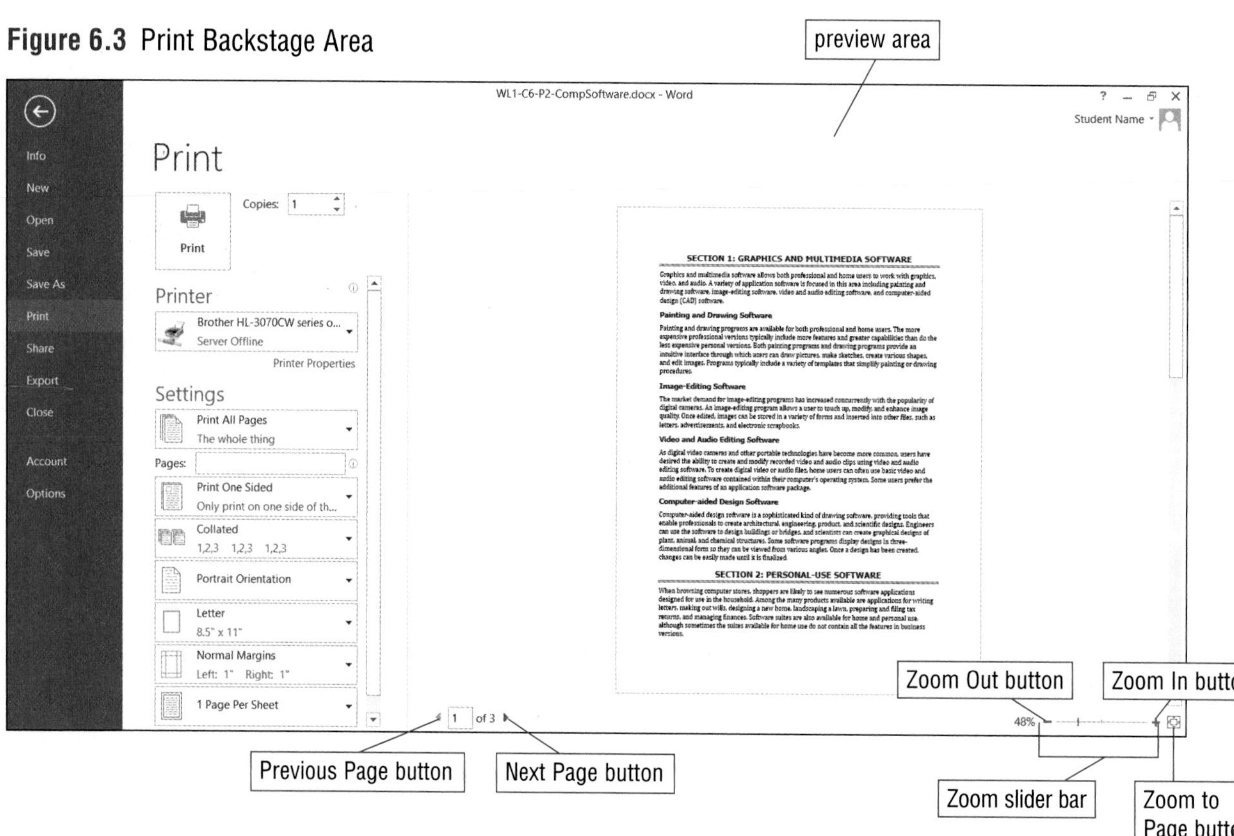

1. With **WL1-C6-P2-CompSoftware.docx** open, press Ctrl + Home to move the insertion point to the beginning of the document.
2. Preview the document by clicking the FILE tab and then clicking the *Print* option.
3. At the Print backstage area, click the Next Page button located below and to the left of the preview page. (This displays page 2 in the preview area.)
4. Click twice on the Zoom In button (plus symbol) that displays at the right side of the Zoom slider bar. (This increases the size of the preview page.)
5. Click the Zoom Out button (minus symbol) that displays at the left side of the Zoom slider bar until two pages of the document display in the preview area.
6. Change the zoom at the Zoom dialog box by completing the following steps:
   a. Click the percentage number that displays at the left side of the Zoom slider bar.
   b. At the Zoom dialog box, click the *Many pages* option in the *Zoom to* section.
   c. Click OK to close the dialog box. (Notice that all pages in the document display as thumbnails in the preview area.)
7. Click the Zoom to Page button that displays at the right side of the Zoom slider bar. (This returns the page to the default size.)
8. Click the Back button to return to the document.

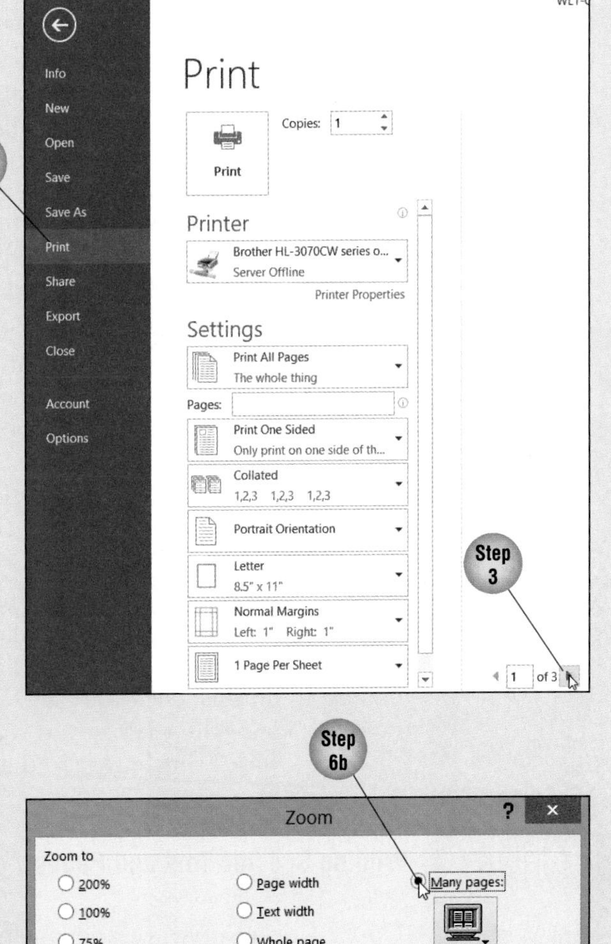

Printing Pages in a Document

If you want control over what prints in a document, use options at the Print backstage area. Click the first gallery in the *Settings* category and a drop-down list displays with options for printing all pages in the document, selected text, the current page, or a custom range of pages in the document. If you want to select and then print a portion of the document, choose the *Print Selection* option. With this option, only the text that you have selected in the current document prints. (This option is dimmed unless text is selected in the document.) Click the *Print Current Page* option to print only the page on which the insertion point is located.

HINT
Save a document before printing it.

With the *Custom Print* option, you can identify a specific page, multiple pages, or a range of pages to print. If you want specific pages printed, use a comma (,) to indicate *and* and use a hyphen (-) to indicate *through*. For example, to print pages 2 and 5, you would type **2,5** in the *Pages* text box. To print pages 6 through 10, you would type **6-10**.

With the other galleries available in the *Settings* category of the Print backstage area, you can specify whether you want to print on one or both sides of the page, change the page orientation (portrait or landscape), specify how you want the pages collated, choose a paper size, and specify margins of a document. The last gallery contains options for printing 1, 2, 4, 6, 8, or 16 pages of a multiple-page document on one sheet of paper. This gallery also contains the *Scale to Paper Size* option. Click this option and then use the side menu to choose the paper size to which you want to scale the document.

If you want to print more than one copy of a document, use the *Copies* text box located to the right of the Print button. If you print several copies of a document that has multiple pages, Word collates the pages as they print. For example, if you print two copies of a three-page document, pages 1, 2, and 3 print, and then the pages print a second time. Printing collated pages is helpful for assembly but takes more printing time. To reduce printing time, you can tell Word *not* to print collated pages. To do this, click the *Collated* gallery in the *Settings* category and then click *Uncollated*.

If you want to send a document directly to the printer without displaying the Print backstage area, consider adding the Quick Print button to the Quick Access toolbar. To do this, click the Customize Quick Access Toolbar button located at the right side of the toolbar and then click *Quick Print* at the drop-down gallery. Click the Quick Print button and all pages of the active document print.

Project 2g Printing Specific Text and Pages — Part 7 of 7

1. With **WL1-C6-P2-CompSoftware.docx** open, print selected text by completing the following steps:
   a. Select the heading *Painting and Drawing Software* and the paragraph of text that follows it.
   b. Click the FILE tab and then click the *Print* option.
   c. At the Print backstage area, click the first gallery in the *Settings* category and then click *Print Selection* at the drop-down list.
   d. Click the Print button.

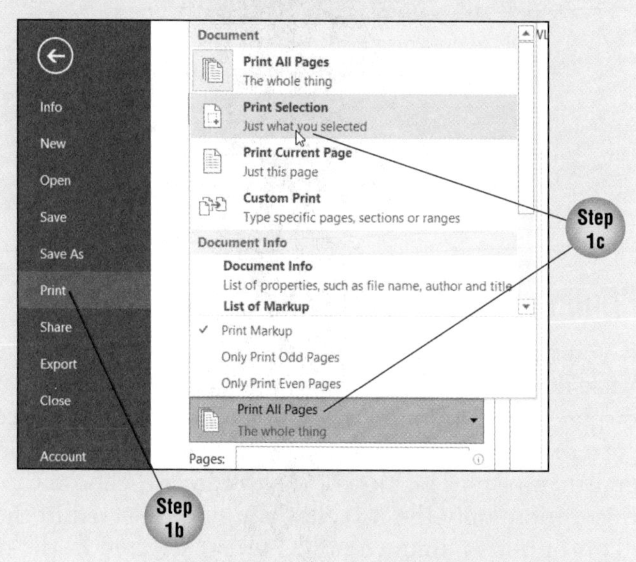

2. Change the margins and page orientation and then print only the first page by completing the following steps:
   a. Press Ctrl + Home to move the insertion point to the beginning of the document.

b. Click the FILE tab and then click the *Print* option.
c. At the Print backstage area, click the fourth gallery (displays with *Portrait Orientation)* in the *Settings* category and then click *Landscape Orientation* at the drop-down list.
d. Click the sixth gallery (displays with *Normal Margins*) in the *Settings* category and then click *Narrow* at the drop-down list.
e. Click the first gallery (displays with *Print All Pages*) in the *Settings* category and then click *Print Current Page* at the drop-down list.
f. Click the Print button. (The first page of the document prints in landscape orientation with 0.5-inch margins.)

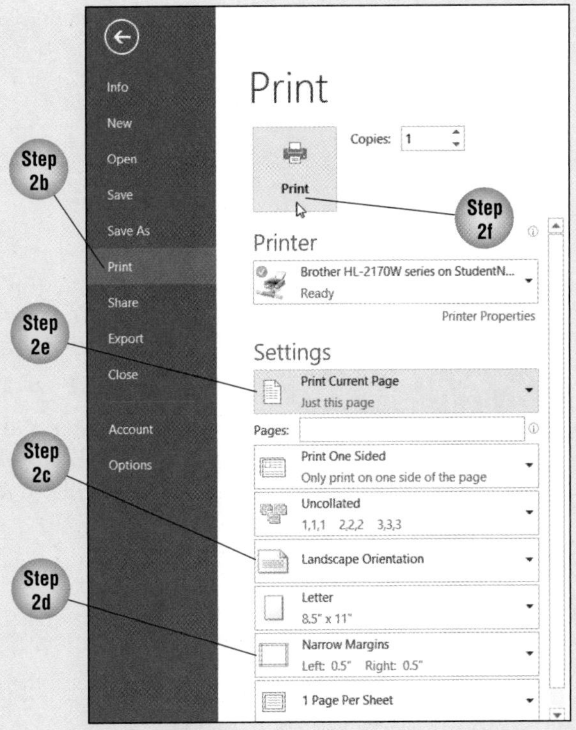

3. Print all of the pages as thumbnails on one page by completing the following steps:
   a. Click the FILE tab and then click the *Print* option.
   b. At the Print backstage area, click the bottom gallery (displays with *1 Page Per Sheet*) in the *Settings* category and then click *4 Pages Per Sheet* at the drop-down list.
   c. Click the first gallery (displays with *Print Current Page*) in the *Settings* category and then click *Print All Pages* at the drop-down list.
   d. Click the Print button.
4. Select the entire document, change the line spacing to 1.5, and then deselect the text.
5. Print two copies of specific pages by completing the following steps:
   a. Click the FILE tab and then click the *Print* option.

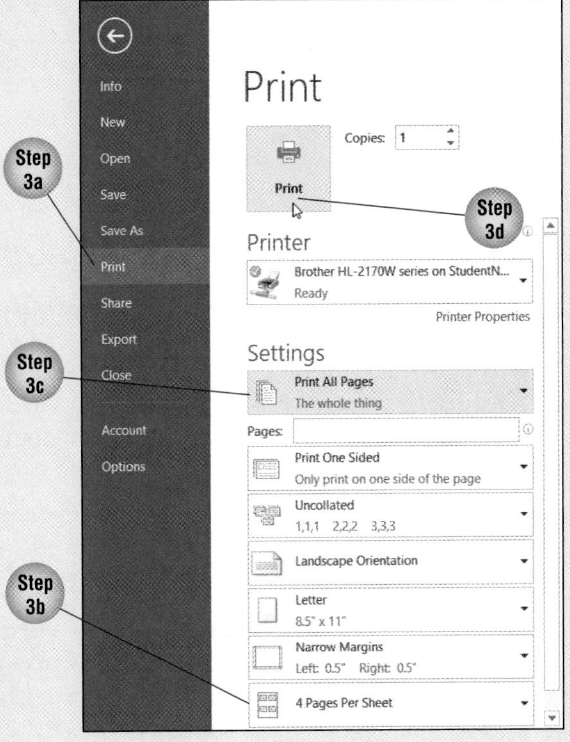

b. Click the fourth gallery (displays with *(Landscape Orientation)* in the *Settings* category and then click *Portrait Orientation* in the drop-down list.
c. Click in the *Pages* text box located below the first gallery in the *Settings* category and then type 1,3.
d. Click the up-pointing arrow at the right side of the *Copies* text box (located to the right of the Print button) to display *2*.
e. Click the third gallery (displays with *Collated*) in the *Settings* category and then click *Uncollated* at the drop-down list.
f. Click the bottom gallery (displays with *4 Pages Per Sheet*) in the *Settings* category and then click *1 Page Per Sheet* at the drop-down list.
g. Click the Print button. (The first page of the document will print twice and then the third page will print twice.)

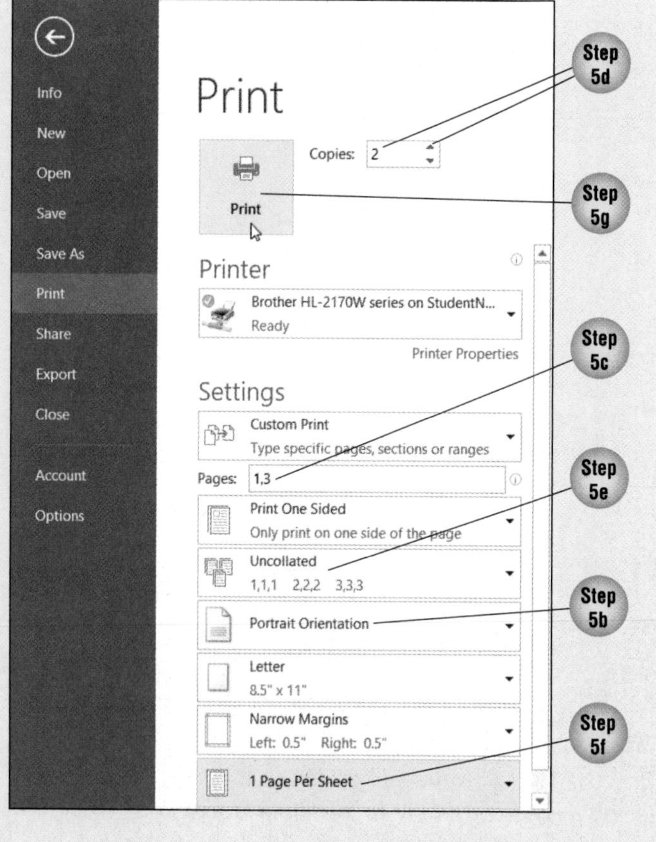

6. Save and then close **WL1-C6-P2-CompSoftware.docx**.

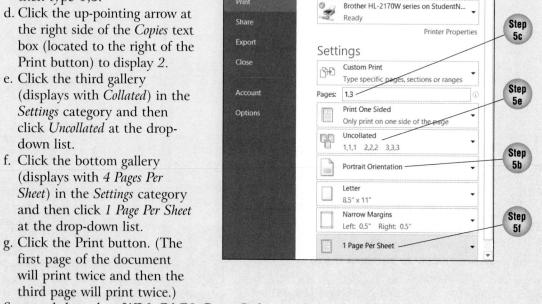

Project 3 Create and Print Envelopes — 2 Parts

You will create an envelope document and type the return address and delivery address using envelope addressing guidelines issued by the United States Postal Service. You will also open a letter document and then create an envelope using the inside address.

Creating and Printing Envelopes

Envelopes

Word automates the creation of envelopes with options at the Envelopes and Labels dialog box with the Envelopes tab selected, as shown in Figure 6.4. Display this dialog box by clicking the MAILINGS tab and then clicking the Envelopes button in the Create group. At the dialog box, type the delivery address in the *Delivery address* text box and the return address in the *Return address* text box. Send the envelope directly to the printer by clicking the Print button or insert the envelope in the current document by clicking the Add to Document button.

Figure 6.4 Envelopes and Labels Dialog Box with Envelopes Tab Selected

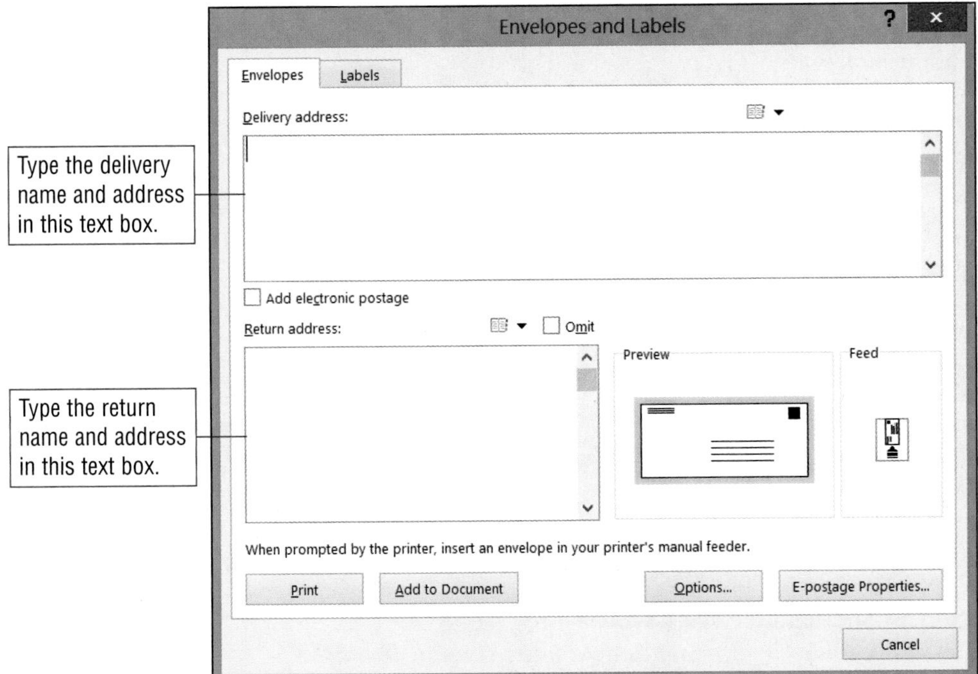

If you enter a return address before printing the envelope, Word will display the question *Do you want to save the new return address as the default return address?* At this question, click Yes if you want the current return address available for future envelopes or click No if you do not want the current return address used as the default. If a default return address displays in the *Return address* section of the dialog box, you can tell Word to omit the return address when printing the envelope. To do this, click the *Omit* check box to insert a check mark.

Quick Steps

Create an Envelope
1. Click MAILINGS tab.
2. Click Envelopes button.
3. Type delivery address.
4. Click in *Return address* text box.
5. Type return address.
6. Click Add to Document button or Print button.

The Envelopes and Labels dialog box contains a *Preview* sample box and a *Feed* sample box. The *Preview* sample box shows how the envelope will appear when printed and the *Feed* sample box shows how the envelope should be inserted into the printer.

When addressing envelopes, consider following general guidelines issued by the United States Postal Service (USPS). The USPS guidelines suggest using all capital letters with no commas or periods for return and delivery addresses. Figure 6.5 shows envelope addresses that follow the USPS guidelines. Use abbreviations for street suffixes (such as *ST* for *Street* and *AVE* for *Avenue*). For a complete list of address abbreviations, visit the www.emcp.net/usps site and then search for *Official USPS Abbreviations*.

Project 3a Printing an Envelope

Part 1 of 2

1. At a blank document, create an envelope that prints the delivery address and return address shown in Figure 6.5. Begin by clicking the MAILINGS tab.
2. Click the Envelopes button in the Create group.

3. At the Envelopes and Labels dialog box with the Envelopes tab selected, type the delivery address shown in Figure 6.5 (the one containing the name *GREGORY LINCOLN*). (Press the Enter key to end each line in the name and address.)
4. Click in the *Return address* text box. (If any text displays in the *Return address* text box, select and then delete it.)
5. Type the return address shown in Figure 6.5 (the one containing the name *WENDY STEINBERG*). (Press the Enter key to end each line in the name and address.)
6. Click the Add to Document button.
7. At the message *Do you want to save the new return address as the default return address?*, click No.
8. Save the document and name it **WL1-C6-P3-Env**.
9. Print and then close **WL1-C6-P3-Env.docx**. ***Note: Manual feed of the envelope may be required. Please check with your instructor.***

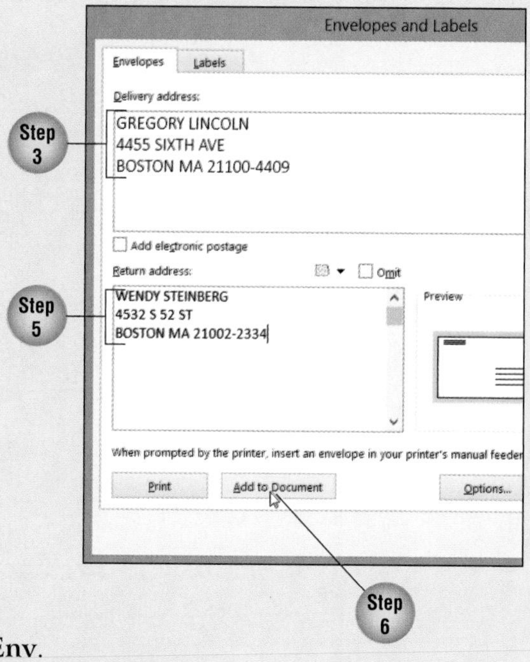

Envelopes and Labels

Envelopes | Labels

Delivery address:

GREGORY LINCOLN
4455 SIXTH AVE
BOSTON MA 21100-4409

Step 3

Add electronic postage

Return address: Omit

WENDY STEINBERG
4532 S 52 ST
BOSTON MA 21002-2334

Step 5

Preview

When prompted by the printer, insert an envelope in your printer's manual feeder

Print | Add to Document | Options...

Step 6

Figure 6.5 Project 3a

WENDY STEINBERG
4532 S 52 ST
BOSTON MA 21002-2334

GREGORY LINCOLN
4455 SIXTH AVE
BOSTON MA 21100-4409

If you open the Envelopes and Labels dialog box in a document containing a name and address (the name and address lines must end with a press of the Enter key and not Shift + Enter), the name and address are automatically inserted in the *Delivery address* text box in the dialog box. To do this, open a document containing a name and address and then click the Envelopes button to display the Envelopes and Labels dialog box. The name and address are inserted in the *Delivery address* text box as they appear in the letter and may not conform to the USPS guidelines. The USPS guidelines for addressing envelopes are only suggestions, not requirements.

Project 3b Creating an Envelope in an Existing Document Part 2 of 2

1. Open **LAProg.docx**.
2. Click the MAILINGS tab.
3. Click the Envelopes button in the Create group.
4. At the Envelopes and Labels dialog box (with the Envelopes tab selected), make sure the delivery address displays properly in the *Delivery address* text box.
5. If any text displays in the *Return address* text box, insert a check mark in the *Omit* check box (located to the right of the *Return address* option). (This tells Word not to print the return address on the envelope.)
6. Click the Print button.
7. Close **LAProg.docx** without saving changes.

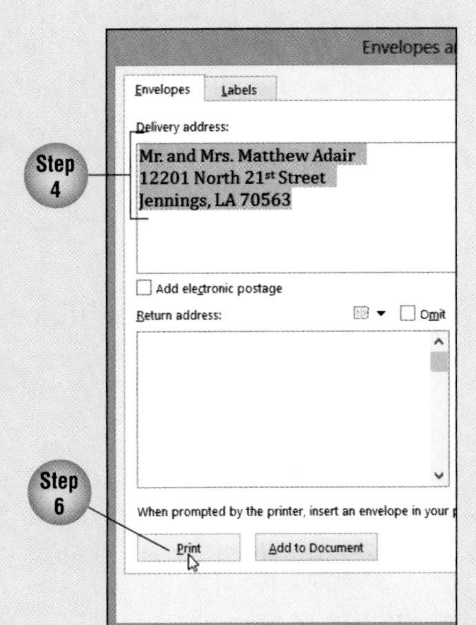

Project 4 Create Mailing Labels 2 Parts

You will create mailing labels containing names and addresses and then create mailing labels containing the inside address of a letter.

Creating and Printing Labels

Use Word's labels feature to print text on mailing labels, file labels, disc labels, or other types of labels. Word includes a variety of predefined formats for labels that can be purchased at any office supply store. With the Labels feature, you can create a sheet of mailing labels with the same name and address or image or enter a different name and address on each label.

To create a sheet of mailing labels, click the Labels button in the Create group on the MAILINGS tab. At the Envelopes and Labels dialog box with the Labels tab selected, as shown in Figure 6.6, type the desired address in the *Address* text box if you want to create a sheet of labels with the same name and address. If you want to create a sheet of labels with different names and addresses in each label, leave the *Address* text box empty. Click the New Document button to insert the mailing label in a new document or click the Print button to send the mailing label directly to the printer.

Quick Steps

Create Labels

1. Click MAILINGS tab.
2. Click Labels button.
3. Type desired address(es).
4. Click New Document button or Print button.

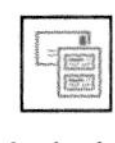

Labels

If you are creating labels with different names and addresses, the insertion point is positioned in the first label form when you click the New Document button. Type the name and address in the label and then press the Tab key once or twice (depending on the label) to move the insertion point to the next label. Pressing Shift + Tab will move the insertion point to the preceding label.

Changing Label Options

Click the Options button at the Envelopes and Labels dialog box with the Labels tab selected and the Label Options dialog box displays as shown in Figure 6.7. At the Label Options dialog box, choose the type of printer, the desired label product, and the product number. This dialog box also displays information about the selected label, such as type, height, width, and paper size. When you select a label, Word automatically determines label margins. If you want to customize these default settings, click the Details button at the Label Options dialog box.

Figure 6.6 Envelopes and Labels Dialog Box with Labels Tab Selected

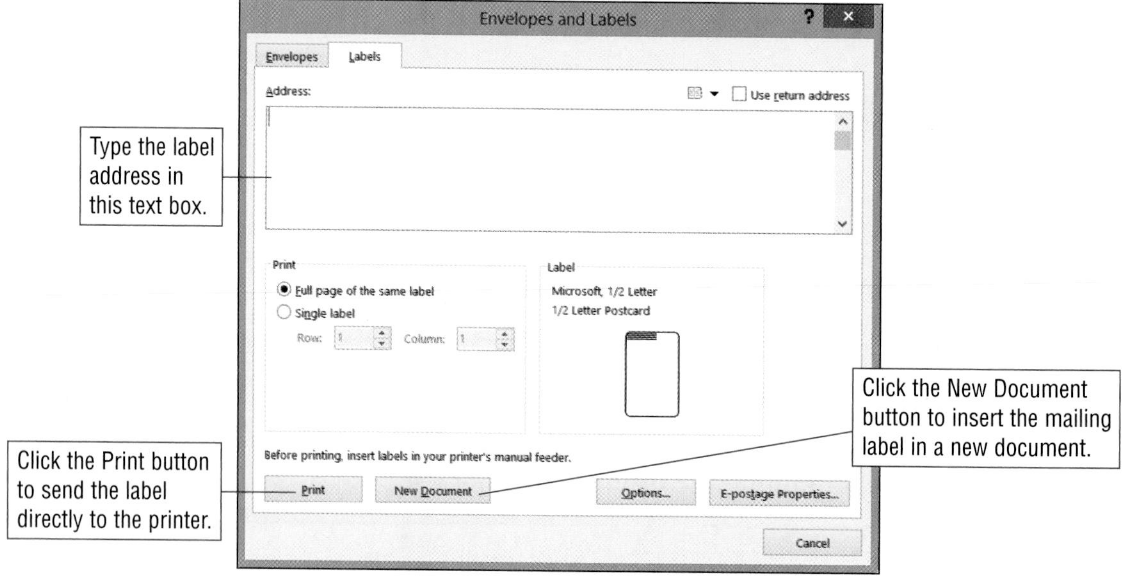

Figure 6.7 Label Options Dialog Box

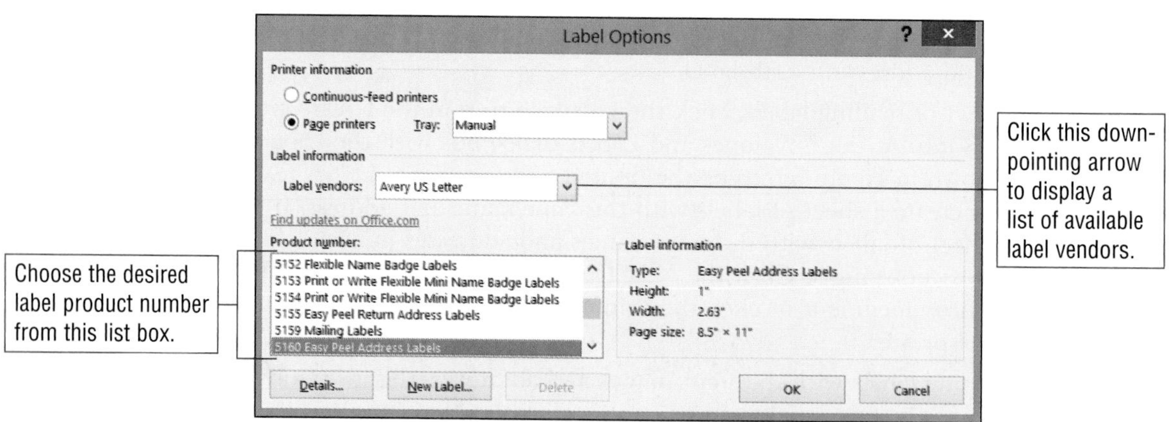

Project 4a Creating Mailing Labels Part 1 of 2

1. At a blank document, click the MAILINGS tab.
2. Click the Labels button in the Create group.
3. At the Envelopes and Labels dialog box with the Labels tab selected, click the Options button.
4. At the Label Options dialog box, click the down-pointing arrow at the right side of the *Label vendors* option box and then click *Avery US Letter* at the drop-down list.
5. Scroll down the *Product number* list box and then click *5160 Easy Peel Address Labels*.
6. Click OK or press Enter.
7. At the Envelopes and Labels dialog box, click the New Document button.
8. At the document screen, type the first name and address shown in Figure 6.8 in the first label.
9. Press the Tab key twice to move the insertion point to the next label and then type the second name and address shown in Figure 6.8.
10. Continue in this manner until all names and addresses in Figure 6.8 have been typed.
11. Save the document and name it **WL1-C6-P4-Labels**.
12. Print and then close **WL1-C6-P4-Labels.docx**.
13. Open **LAProg.docx** and create mailing labels with the delivery address. Begin by clicking the MAILINGS tab.
14. Click the Labels button in the Create group.
15. At the Envelopes and Labels dialog box with the Labels tab selected, make sure the delivery address displays properly in the *Address* text box.
16. Make sure *Avery US Letter, 5160 Easy Peel Address Labels* displays in the *Label* section; if not, refer to Steps 3 through 6 to select the label type.
17. Click the New Document button.
18. Save the mailing label document and name it **WL1-C6-P4-LAProg.docx**.
19. Print and then close **WL1-C6-P4-LAProg.docx**.
20. Close **LAProg.docx**.

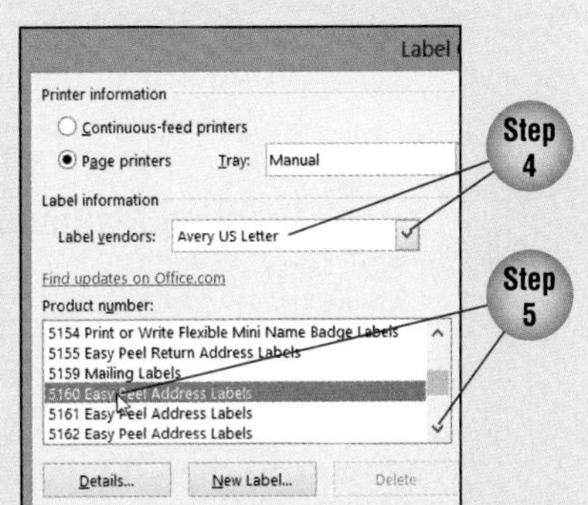

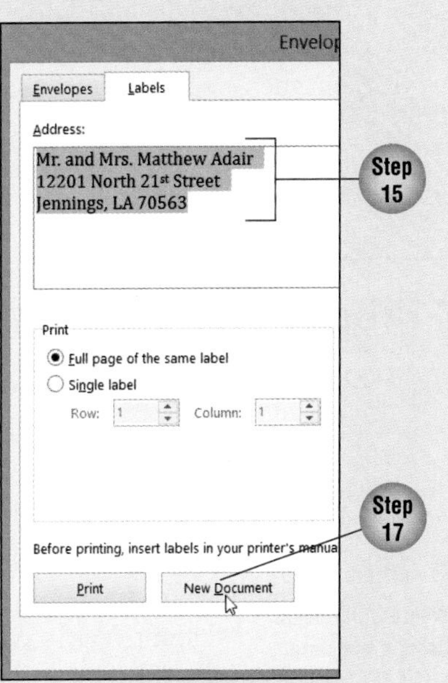

Figure 6.8 Project 4a

DAVID LOWRY
12033 S 152 ST
HOUSTON TX 77340

MARCELLA SANTOS
394 APPLE BLOSSOM
FRIENDSWOOD TX 77533

KEVIN DORSEY
26302 PRAIRIE DR
HOUSTON TX 77316

AL AND DONNA SASAKI
1392 PIONEER DR
BAYTOWN TX 77903

JACKIE RHYNER
29039 107 AVE E
HOUSTON TX 77302

MARK AND TINA ELLIS
607 FORD AVE
HOUSTON TX 77307

Creating Mailings Labels with an Image

Labels can be created with a graphic image. For example, you may want to create mailing labels with a company's logo and address or create labels with a company's slogan. Create labels with a graphic image by inserting the image in a blank document, clicking the MAILINGS tab and then clicking the Labels button. At the Envelopes and Labels dialog box, make sure the desired label vendor and product number are selected, and then click the New Document button.

Project 4b **Creating Mailing Labels with an Image** **Part 2 of 2**

1. At a blank document, insert a graphic image by completing the following steps:
   a. Click the INSERT tab and then click the Pictures button.
   b. At the Insert Picture dialog box, make sure the WL1C6 folder on your storage medium is active and then double-click ***BGCLabels.png***.
2. With the image selected in the document, click the MAILINGS tab and then click the Labels button.
3. At the Envelopes and Labels dialog box, make sure *Avery US Letter, 5160 Easy Peel Address Labels* displays in the *Label* section and then click the New Document button.
4. Save the document and name it **WL1-C6-P4-BGCLabels**.
5. Print and then close **WL1-C6-P4-BGCLabels.docx**.
6. Close the document containing the image without saving changes.

Project 5 **Use a Template to Create a Business Letter** **1 Part**

You will use a letter template provided by Word to create a business letter.

Creating a Document Using a Template

Quick Steps

Create a Document Using a Template
1. Click FILE tab.
2. Click *New* option.
3. Click desired template.

OR
1. Click FILE tab.
2. Click *New* option.
3. Click in search text box.
4. Type search text.
5. Press Enter.
6. Double-click desired template.

Word includes a number of template documents formatted for specific uses. Each Word document is based on a template document with the Normal template the default. With Word templates, you can easily create a variety of documents with special formatting, such as letters, calendars, and awards. Display templates by clicking the FILE tab and then clicking the *New* option. This displays the New backstage area, as shown in Figure 6.9. Open one of the templates that displays in the New backstage area by clicking the desired template. This opens a document based on the template, not the template file.

In addition to the templates that display at the New backstage area, you can download templates from the Office.com website. To do this, click in the search text box, type the search text or category, and then press Enter. Templates that match the search text or category display in the New backstage area. Click the desired template once and then click the Create button, or double-click the desired template. This downloads the template from the Office.com website and opens a document based on the template. Locations for personalized text may display in placeholders in the document. Click in the placeholder or select placeholder text and then type the personalized text.

Figure 6.9 New Backstage Area

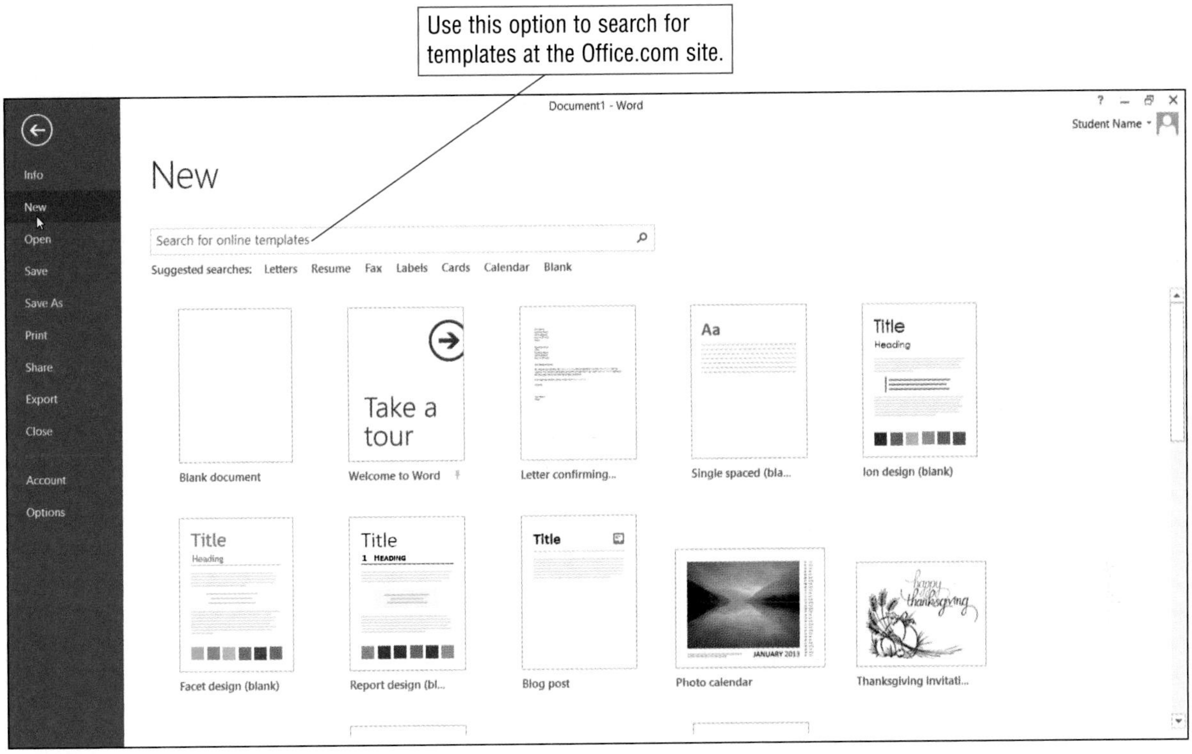
Use this option to search for templates at the Office.com site.
Document1 - Word
Student Name
Info
New
Open
Save
Save As
Print
Share
Export
Close
Account
Options
New
Search for online templates
Suggested searches: Letters Resume Fax Labels Cards Calendar Blank
Take a tour
Aa
Title
Heading
Blank document
Welcome to Word
Letter confirming...
Single spaced (bla...
Ion design (blank)
Title
Title
Title
Facet design (blank)
Report design (bl...
Blog post
Photo calendar
Thanksgiving invitati...

If you use a template on a regular basis, consider pinning the template to the New backstage area. To do this, search for the desired template, hover your mouse over the template, and then click the gray, left-pointing stick pin (Pin to list) that displays to the right of the template name. To unpin a template, click the down-pointing stick pin (Unpin from list).

Project 5 Creating a Letter Using a Template

Part 1 of 1

1. Click the FILE tab and then click the *New* option.
2. At the New backstage area, click in the search text box, type letter, and then press Enter.
3. When templates display that match *letter*, notice the Category list box that displays at the right side of the New backstage area.
4. Click the *Business* option in the Category list box. (This displays only business letter templates.)

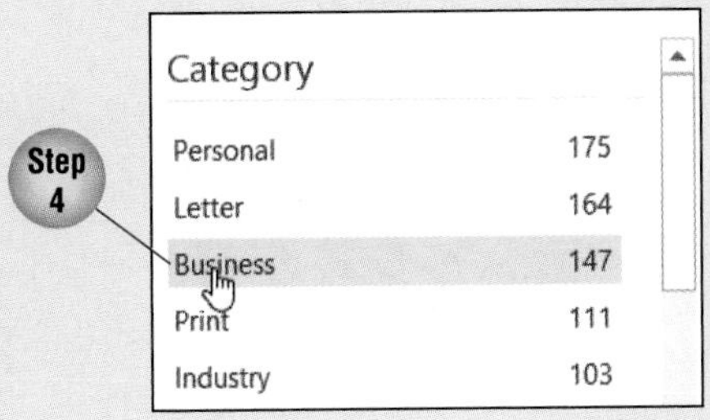
Step 4
Category
Personal 175
Letter 164
Business 147
Print 111
Industry 103

5. Scroll down the template list and then double-click the *Letter (Equity theme)* template.

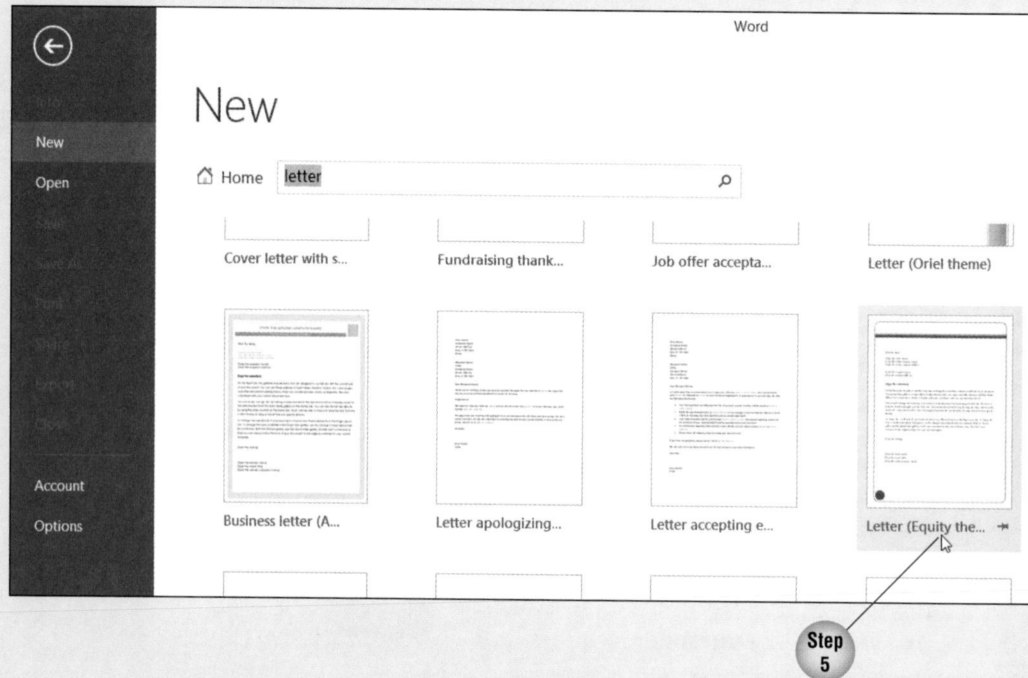

6. When the letter document displays on the screen, click the placeholder text *[Pick the date]*, click the down-pointing arrow at the right side of the placeholder, and then click the Today button located at the bottom of the calendar.
7. Click in the name that displays below the date, select the name, and then type your first and last names.
8. Click the placeholder text *[Type the sender company name]* and then type **Sorenson Funds**.
9. Click the placeholder text *[Type the sender company address]*, type **6250 Aurora Boulevard**, press the Enter key, and then type **Baltimore, MD 20372**.
10. Click the placeholder text *[Type the recipient name]* and then type **Ms. Jennifer Gonzalez**.
11. Click the placeholder text *[Type the recipient address]*, type **12990 Boyd Street**, press the Enter key, and then type **Baltimore, MD 20375**.
12. Click the placeholder text *[Type the salutation]* and then type **Dear Ms. Gonzalez:**.
13. Insert a file in the document by completing the following steps:
    a. Click anywhere in the three paragraphs of text in the body of the letter and then click the Delete key.
    b. Click the INSERT tab.
    c. Click the Object button arrow in the Text group and then click *Text from File* at the drop-down list.
    d. At the Insert File dialog box, navigate to the WL1C6 folder on your storage medium and then double-click ***SFunds.docx***.
    e. Press the Backspace key once to delete a blank line.
14. Click the placeholder text *[Type the closing]* and then type **Sincerely,**.
15. If your name does not display above the placeholder text *[Type the sender title]*, select the name and then type your first and last names.
16. Click the placeholder text *[Type the sender title]* and then type **Financial Consultant**.
17. Save the document and name it **WL1-C6-P5-SFunds**.
18. Print and then close **WL1-C6-P5-SFunds.docx**.

Chapter Summary

- Group Word documents logically into folders. Create a new folder at the Open or Save As dialog box.
- You can select one or several documents at the Open dialog box. Copy, move, rename, delete, or open a document or selected documents.
- Use the *Cut*, *Copy*, and *Paste* options from the Organize button drop-down list or the Open dialog box shortcut menu to move or copy a document from one folder to another. (If you are using your OneDrive, go to www.onedrive.com, log in to your account, and then use the onedrive.com toolbar to move or copy a document or folder to another location.)
- Delete documents and/or folders with the *Delete* option from the Organize button drop-down list or shortcut menu.
- Click the *Change File Type* option at the Export backstage area and options display for saving the document in a different file format. You can also save documents in a different file format with the *Save as type* option box at the Save As dialog box.
- Move among the open documents by clicking the buttons on the Taskbar representing the various documents, or by clicking the VIEW tab, clicking the Switch Windows button in the Window group, and then clicking the desired document name.
- View a portion of all open documents by clicking the VIEW tab and then clicking the Arrange All button in the Window group.
- Use the Minimize, Restore, and Maximize buttons located in the upper right corner of the window to reduce or increase the size of the active window.
- Divide a window into two panes by clicking the VIEW tab and then clicking the Split button in the Window group. This enables you to view different parts of the same document at one time.
- View the contents of two open documents side by side by clicking the VIEW tab and then clicking the View Side by Side button in the Window group.
- Open a new window containing the same document by clicking the VIEW tab and then clicking the New Window button in the Window group.
- Insert a document into the open document by clicking the INSERT tab, clicking the Object button arrow, and then clicking *Text from File* at the drop-down list. At the Insert File dialog box, double-click the desired document.
- Preview a document at the Print backstage area. Scroll through the pages in the document with the Next Page and the Previous Page buttons that display below the preview page. Use the Zoom slider bar to increase/decrease the display size of the preview page.
- Use options at the Print backstage area to customize the print job by changing the page orientation, size, and margins; specify how many pages you want to print on one page; indicate the number of copies and whether or not to collate the pages; and specify the printer.
- With Word's envelope feature, you can create and print an envelope at the Envelopes and Labels dialog box with the Envelopes tab selected.

- If you open the Envelopes and Labels dialog box in a document containing a name and address (with each line ending with a press of the Enter key), that information is automatically inserted in the *Delivery address* text box in the dialog box.
- Use Word's labels feature to print text on mailing labels, file labels, disc labels, or other types of labels.
- Available templates display in the New backstage area. Double-click a template to open a document based on the template. Search for templates online by typing in the search text or category in the search text box and then pressing Enter.

Commands Review

FEATURE	RIBBON TAB, GROUP/OPTION	BUTTON, OPTION	KEYBOARD SHORTCUT
arrange documents	VIEW, Window		
Envelopes and Labels dialog box with Envelopes tab selected	MAILINGS, Create		
Envelopes and Labels dialog box with Labels tab selected	MAILINGS, Create		
Export backstage area	FILE, *Export*		
Insert File dialog box	INSERT, Text	, *Text from File*	
maximize document			Ctrl + F10
minimize document			
New backstage area	FILE, *New*		
new window	VIEW, Window		
Open dialog box	FILE, *Open*	Double-click *Computer*	Ctrl + F12
Print backstage area	FILE, *Print*		Ctrl + P
restore document			
Save As dialog box	FILE, *Save As*	Double-click *Computer*	F12
split window	VIEW, Window		Alt + Ctrl + S
switch windows	VIEW, Window		
synchronous scrolling	VIEW, Window		
view documents side by side	VIEW, Window		

Concepts Check Test Your Knowledge 

Completion: In the space provided at the right, indicate the correct term, command, or number.

1. Create a new folder with this button at the Open dialog box or the Save As dialog box. ____________
2. At the Open dialog box, the current folder path displays in this. ____________
3. Using the mouse, select nonadjacent documents at the Open dialog box by holding down this key while clicking the desired documents. ____________
4. Documents deleted from the computer's hard drive are automatically sent here. ____________
5. The letters *PDF* stand for this. ____________
6. Saving a document in this format strips out all formatting. ____________
7. Click this button in the Window group on the VIEW tab to arrange all open documents so a portion of each document displays. ____________
8. Click this button and the active document fills the editing window. ____________
9. Click this button to reduce the active document to a button on the Taskbar. ____________
10. To display documents side by side, click this button in the Window group on the VIEW tab. ____________
11. Display the Insert File dialog box by clicking the Object button arrow on the INSERT tab and then clicking this option. ____________
12. Type this in the *Pages* text box at the Print backstage area to print pages 3 through 6 of the open document. ____________
13. Type this in the *Pages* text box at the Print backstage area to print pages 4 and 9 of the open document. ____________
14. The Envelopes button is located in the Create group on this tab. ____________
15. Download a template at this backstage area. ____________

Skills Check Assess Your Performance

Assessment 1

MANAGE DOCUMENTS

Note: If you are using your OneDrive, please check with your instructor before completing this assessment.

1. Display the Open dialog box with WL1C6 on your storage medium the active folder and then create a new folder named *CheckingTools*.
2. Copy (be sure to copy and not cut) all documents that begin with *SpellGrammar* into the CheckingTools folder.
3. With the CheckingTools folder as the active folder, rename **SpellGrammar01.docx** to ***Technology.docx***.
4. Rename **SpellGrammar02.docx** to ***Software.docx***.
5. Capture the Open dialog box as an image file by completing the following steps:
   a. With the Open dialog box displayed, press Alt + Print Screen.
   b. Close the Open dialog box.
   c. If necessary, press Ctrl + N to display a blank document and then click the Paste button.
   d. Print the document.
   e. Close the document without saving it.
6. Display the Open dialog box and make WL1C6 on your storage medium the active folder.
7. Delete the CheckingTools folder and all documents contained within it.
8. Open **StaffMtg.docx**, **Agreement.docx**, and **Robots.docx**.
9. Make **Agreement.docx** the active document.
10. Make **StaffMtg.docx** the active document.
11. Arrange all of the windows.
12. Make **Robots.docx** the active document and then minimize it.
13. Minimize the remaining documents.
14. Restore **StaffMtg.docx**.
15. Restore **Agreement.docx**.
16. Restore **Robots.docx**.
17. Maximize and then close **StaffMtg.docx** and then maximize and close **Robots.docx**.
18. Maximize **Agreement.docx** and then save the document and name it **WL1-C6-A1-Agreement**.
19. Open **AptLease.docx**.
20. View the **WL1-C6-A1-Agreement.docx** document and **AptLease.docx** document side by side.
21. Scroll through both documents simultaneously and notice the formatting differences between the title, headings, and font in the two documents. Change the font and apply shading to only the title and headings in **WL1-C6-A1-Agreement.docx** to match the font and shading of the title and headings in **AptLease.docx**.
22. Make **AptLease.docx** active and then close it.
23. Save **WL1-C6-A1-Agreement.docx**.
24. Move the insertion point to the end of the document and then insert the document named **Terms.docx**.

25. Apply formatting to the inserted text so it matches the formatting of the text in the **WL1-C6-A1-Agreement.docx** document.
26. Move the insertion point to the end of the document and then insert the document named **Signature.docx**.
27. Save, print, and then close **WL1-C6-A1-Agreement.docx**.

Assessment 2

CREATE AN ENVELOPE

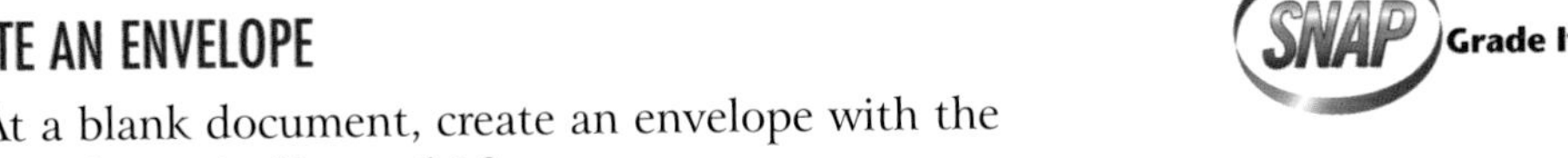

1. At a blank document, create an envelope with the text shown in Figure 6.10.
2. Save the envelope document and name it **WL1-C6-A2-Env**.
3. Print and then close **WL1-C6-A2-Env.docx**.

Figure 6.10 Assessment 2

DR ROSEANNE HOLT
21330 CEDAR DR
LOGAN UT 84598

GENE MIETZNER
4559 CORRIN AVE
SMITHFIELD UT 84521

Assessment 3

CREATE MAILING LABELS

SNAP Grade It

1. Create mailing labels with the names and addresses shown in Figure 6.11. Use a label option of your choosing. (You may need to check with your instructor before choosing an option.) When entering street numbers such as 147TH, Word will convert the th to superscript letters when you press the spacebar after typing *147TH*. To remove the superscript formatting, immediately click the Undo button on the Quick Access toolbar.

Figure 6.11 Assessment 3

SUSAN LUTOVSKY 1402 MELLINGER DR FAIRHOPE OH 43209	JIM AND PAT KEIL 413 JACKSON ST AVONDALE OH 43887	IRENE HAGEN 12930 147TH AVE E CANTON OH 43296
VINCE KILEY 14005 288TH S CANTON OH 43287	LEONARD KRUEGER 13290 N 120TH CANTON OH 43291	HELGA GUNDSTROM PO BOX 3112 AVONDALE OH 43887

2. Save the document and name it **WL1-C6-A3-Labels**.
3. Print and then close **WL1-C6-A3-Labels.docx**.
4. At the blank document screen, close the document without saving changes.

Assessment 4

PREPARE A FAX

1. At the New backstage area, search for *fax*, download the Fax (Equity theme) template and then insert the following information in the specified fields:
   To: **Frank Gallagher**
   From: (your first and last names)
   Fax: **(206) 555-9010**
   Pages: **3**
   Phone: **(206) 555-9005**
   Date: (insert current date)
   Re: **Consultation Agreement**
   CC: **Jolene Yin**
   Insert an X in the *For Review* check box.
   Comments: **Please review the Consultation Agreement and advise me of any legal issues.**
2. Save the fax document and name it **WL1-C6-A4-Fax**.
3. Print and then close the document.

Assessment 5

SAVE A DOCUMENT AS A WEB PAGE

1. Experiment with the *Save as type* option box at the Save As dialog box and figure out how to save a document as a single-file web page.
2. Open **NSS.docx**, display the Save As dialog box, and then change the *Save as type* option to a single-file web page. Click the Change Title button that displays in the Save As dialog box. At the Enter Text dialog box, type **Northland Security Systems** in the *Page title* text box and then close the dialog box by clicking the OK button. Click the Save button in the Save As dialog box.
3. Close the **NSS.mht** file.
4. Open your web browser and then open the **NSS.mht** file.
5. Close your web browser.

Assessment

6 CREATE PERSONAL MAILING LABELS

1. At a blank document, type your name and address and then apply formatting to enhance the appearance of the text. (You determine the font, font size, and font color.)
2. Create labels with your name and address. (You determine the label vendor and product number.)
3. Save the label document and name it **WL1-C6-A6-PersonalLabels**.
4. Print and then close the document.

Assessment 7

DOWNLOAD AND COMPLETE A STUDENT AWARD CERTIFICATE

1. Display the New backstage area and then search for and download a student of the month award certificate template. (Type **certificate for student of the month** in the search text box and then download the Basic certificate for student of the month template. If this template is not available, choose another student of the month award template.)
2. Insert the appropriate information in the award template placeholders, identifying yourself as the recipient of the student of the month award.
3. Save the completed award and name the document **WL1-C6-A7-Award**.
4. Print and then close the document.

Visual Benchmark Demonstrate Your Proficiency

1 CREATE CUSTOM LABELS

1. You can create a sheet of labels with the same information in each label by typing the information in the *Address* text box at the Envelopes and Labels dialog box, or you can type the desired information, select it, and then create the label. Using this technique, create the sheet of labels shown in Figure 6.12 with the following specifications:
   - Open **NSSLabels.docx**.
   - Set the text in 12-point Magneto.
   - Select the entire document and then create the labels by displaying the Envelopes and Labels dialog box with the Labels tab selected. Use the Avery US Letter label vendor and the 5161 product number, and then click the New Document button.
2. Save the label document and name it **WL1-C6-VB-NSSLabels**.
3. Print and then close the document.
4. Close **NSSLabels.docx** without saving it.

2 CREATE AN INVITATION

1. At the New backstage area, search for *movie awards party invitation* and then download the template document shown in Figure 6.13. (The template does not include the background image of the movie reel.)
2. Bold the text below the *hooray for hollywood!* heading.
3. Insert the movie reel clip art image (using the Online Pictures button) with the following specifications:
   - Size the image so it appears as shown in the figure and change the position of the image so it is positioned at the bottom center of the page.
   - Move the image behind the text.
4. Make any other changes so your document is similar to what you see in Figure 6.13.
5. Save the invitation and name it **WL1-C6-VB-MovieInvite**.
6. Save the invitation document in PDF format with the same name.
7. Open the **WL1-C6-VB-MovieInvite.pdf** file in Adobe Reader, print the file, and then close Adobe Reader. If Adobe Reader is not available, open the file in Internet Explorer, print the file, and then close Internet Explorer.

Figure 6.12 Visual Benchmark 1

Northland Security Systems
3200 North 22nd Street
Springfield, IL 62102

Northland Security Systems
3200 North 22nd Street
Springfield, IL 62102

Northland Security Systems
3200 North 22nd Street
Springfield, IL 62102

Northland Security Systems
3200 North 22nd Street
Springfield, IL 62102

Northland Security Systems
3200 North 22nd Street
Springfield, IL 62102

Northland Security Systems
3200 North 22nd Street
Springfield, IL 62102

Northland Security Systems
3200 North 22nd Street
Springfield, IL 62102

Northland Security Systems
3200 North 22nd Street
Springfield, IL 62102

Northland Security Systems
3200 North 22nd Street
Springfield, IL 62102

Northland Security Systems
3200 North 22nd Street
Springfield, IL 62102

Northland Security Systems
3200 North 22nd Street
Springfield, IL 62102

Northland Security Systems
3200 North 22nd Street
Springfield, IL 62102

Northland Security Systems
3200 North 22nd Street
Springfield, IL 62102

Northland Security Systems
3200 North 22nd Street
Springfield, IL 62102

Northland Security Systems
3200 North 22nd Street
Springfield, IL 62102

Northland Security Systems
3200 North 22nd Street
Springfield, IL 62102

Northland Security Systems
3200 North 22nd Street
Springfield, IL 62102

Northland Security Systems
3200 North 22nd Street
Springfield, IL 62102

Northland Security Systems
3200 North 22nd Street
Springfield, IL 62102

Northland Security Systems
3200 North 22nd Street
Springfield, IL 62102

Figure 6.13 Visual Benchmark 2

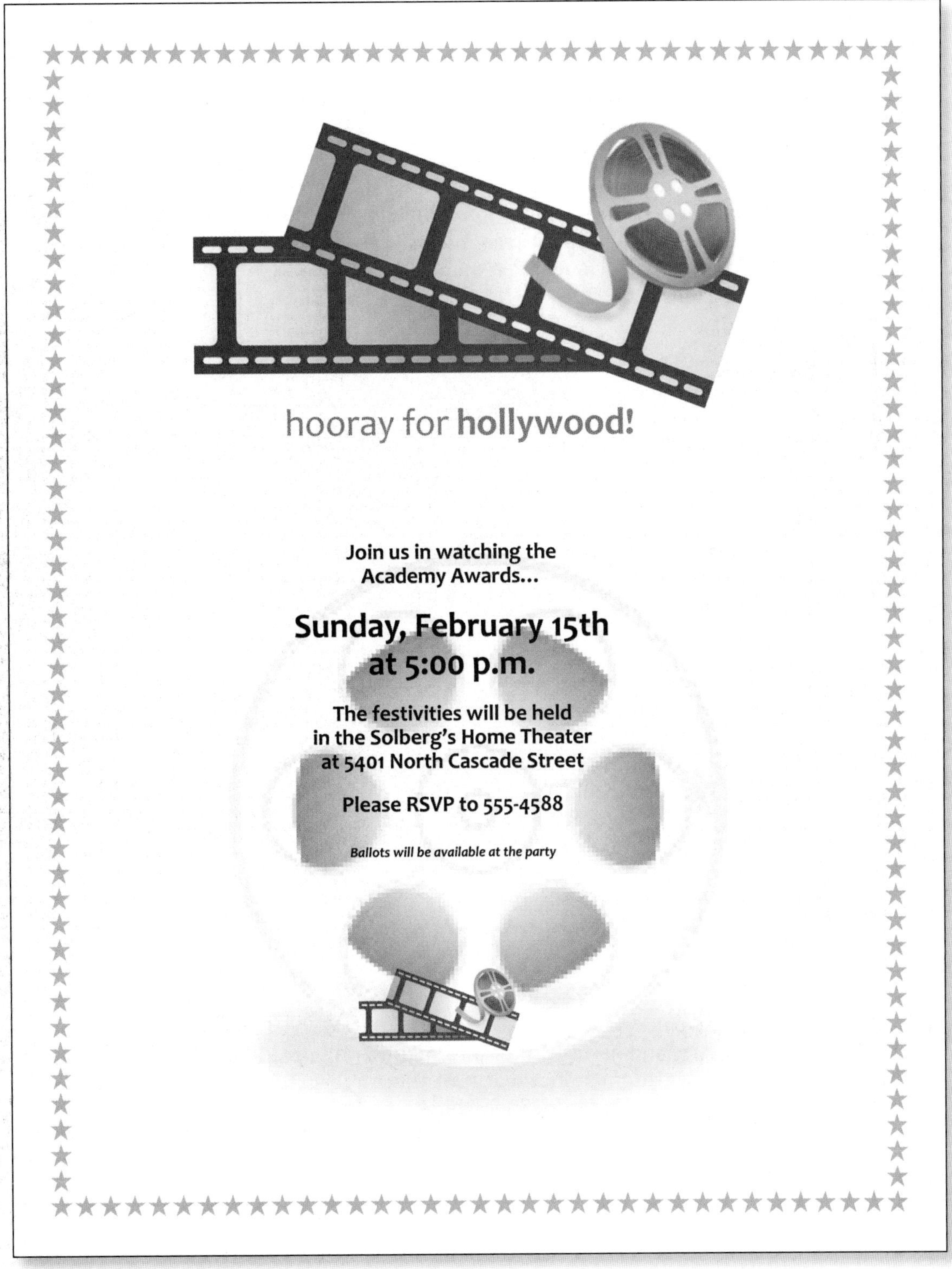

hooray for **hollywood!**
Join us in watching the
Academy Awards...
Sunday, February 15th
at 5:00 p.m.
The festivities will be held
in the Solberg's Home Theater
at 5401 North Cascade Street
Please RSVP to 555-4588
Ballots will be available at the party

Case Study Apply Your Skills

Part 1

You are the office manager for a real estate company, Macadam Realty, and have been asked by the senior sales associate, Lucy Hendricks, to organize contract forms into a specific folder. Create a new folder named *RealEstate* and then copy into the folder documents that begin with the letters "RE." Ms. Hendricks has also asked you to prepare mailing labels for Macadam Realty. Include on the labels the name, Macadam Realty, and the address, 100 Third Street, Suite 210, Denver, CO 80803. Use a decorative font for the name and address and make the *M* in *Macadam* and the *R* in *Realty* larger and more pronounced than surrounding text. Save the completed document and name it **WL1-C6-CS-RELabels**. Print and then close the document.

Part 2

One of your responsibilities is to format contract forms. Open the document named **REConAgrmnt.docx** and then save it and name it **WL1-C6-CS-REConAgrmnt**. The sales associate has asked you to insert signature information at the end of the document, and so you decide to insert at the end of the document the file named **RESig.docx**. With **WL1-C6-CS-REConAgrmnt.docx** still open, open **REBuildAgrmnt.docx**. Format the **WL1-C6-CS-REConAgrmnt.docx** document so it is formatted in a manner similar to the **REBuildAgrmnt.docx** document. Consider the following when specifying formatting: fonts, font sizes, and paragraph shading. Save, print, and then close **WL1-C6-CS-REConAgrmnt.docx**. Close **REBuildAgrmnt.docx**.

Part 3

Help

As part of the organization of contracts, Ms. Hendricks has asked you to insert document properties for the **REBuildAgrmnt.docx** and **WL1-C6-CS-REConAgrmnt.docx** documents. Use the Help feature to learn how to insert document properties. With the information you learn from the Help feature, open each of the two documents separately, display the Info backstage area, click the Show All Properties hyperlink (you may need to scroll down the backstage area to display this hyperlink), and then insert document properties in the following fields (you determine the information to type): *Title*, *Subject*, *Categories*, and *Company*. Print the document properties for each document. (Change the first gallery in the *Settings* category in the Print backstage area to *Document Info*.) Save each document with the original name and close the documents.

Part 4

A client of the real estate company, Anna Hurley, is considering purchasing several rental properties and has asked for information on how to locate real estate rental forms. Using the Internet, locate at least three websites that offer real estate rental forms. Write a letter to Anna Hurley at 2300 South 22nd Street, Denver, CO 80205. In the letter, list the websites you found and include information on which site you thought offered the most resources. Also include in the letter that Macadam Realty is very interested in helping her locate and purchase rental properties. Save the document and name it **WL1-C6-CS-RELtr**. Create an envelope for the letter and add it to the letter document. Save, print, and then close **WL1-C6-CS-RELtr.docx**. (You may need to manually feed the envelope in the printer.)

MICROSOFT®
WORD

CHAPTER 7

Creating Tables and SmartArt

PERFORMANCE OBJECTIVES

Upon successful completion of Chapter 7, you will be able to:

- **Create, format, and modify a table**
- **Sort text in a table**
- **Perform calculations on data in a table**
- **Create, format, and modify a SmartArt graphic**

Tutorials

7.1 Creating Tables

7.2 Changing the Table Design

7.3 Changing the Table Layout

7.4 Merging and Splitting Cells and Tables

7.5 Changing Column Width and Height and Cell Margins

7.6 Inserting a Quick Table

7.7 Converting Text to a Table and a Table to Text

7.8 Drawing a Table

7.9 Sorting Text in a Table and Performing Calculations

7.10 Creating SmartArt

7.11 Arranging and Moving SmartArt

Some Word data can be organized in a table, which is a combination of columns and rows. Use the Tables feature to insert data in columns and rows. This data can consist of text, values, and formulas. In this chapter, you will learn how to create and format a table and insert and format data in the table. Word also includes a SmartArt feature that provides a number of predesigned graphics. In this chapter, you will learn how to use these graphics to create diagrams and organizational charts. Model answers for this chapter's projects appear on the following pages.

Note: Before beginning the projects, copy to your storage medium the WL1C7 subfolder from the WL1 folder on the CD that accompanies this textbook and then make WL1C7 the active folder.

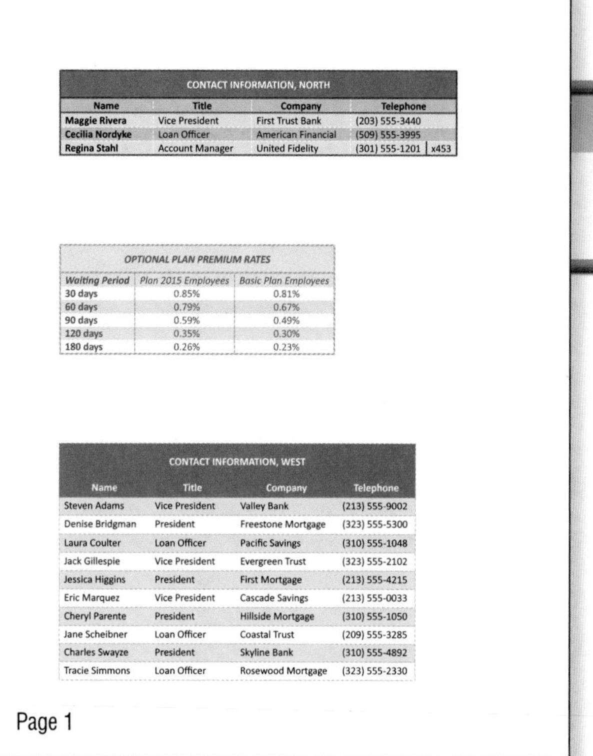

CONTACT INFORMATION, NORTH				
Name	**Title**	**Company**	**Telephone**	
Maggie Rivera	Vice President	First Trust Bank	(203) 555-3440	
Cecilia Nordyke	Loan Officer	American Financial	(509) 555-3995	
Regina Stahl	Account Manager	United Fidelity	(301) 555-1201	x453

OPTIONAL PLAN PREMIUM RATES		
Waiting Period	*Plan 2015 Employees*	*Basic Plan Employees*
30 days	0.85%	0.81%
60 days	0.79%	0.67%
90 days	0.59%	0.49%
120 days	0.35%	0.30%
180 days	0.26%	0.23%

CONTACT INFORMATION, WEST			
Name	Title	Company	Telephone
Steven Adams	Vice President	Valley Bank	(213) 555-9002
Denise Bridgman	President	Freestone Mortgage	(323) 555-5300
Laura Coulter	Loan Officer	Pacific Savings	(310) 555-1048
Jack Gillespie	Vice President	Evergreen Trust	(323) 555-2102
Jessica Higgins	President	First Mortgage	(213) 555-4215
Eric Marquez	Vice President	Cascade Savings	(213) 555-0033
Cheryl Parente	President	Hillside Mortgage	(310) 555-1050
Jane Scheibner	Loan Officer	Coastal Trust	(209) 555-3285
Charles Swayze	President	Skyline Bank	(310) 555-4892
Tracie Simmons	Loan Officer	Rosewood Mortgage	(323) 555-2330

Page 1

CONTACT INFORMATION, WEST			
Name	Title	Company	Telephone
Carole Wagner	President	Main Street Bank	(310) 555-5394
Dawn Wingstrand	Vice President	Lakeland Savings	(323) 555-2348
Cora Yates	Loan Officer	Douglas Mortgage	(213) 555-6588
Robert Ziebell	President	Central Trust	(310) 555-3444

SEPTEMBER

SUN	MON	TUE	WED	THU	FRI	SAT
		1	2	3	4	5
6	7	8	9	10	11	12
13	14	15	16	17	18	19
20	21	22	23	24	25	26
27	28	29	30			

Page 2

Project 1 Create and Format Tables with Company Information

WL1-C7-P1-Tables.docx

	Name	Department
Tri-State Products	Charles Hartman	Technical Support
	Erin Dodd-Trent	Public Relations
	Grace Murakami	Research and Development
	Elizabeth Gentry	Technical Support
	William Thatcher	Technical Support
	Stewart Zimmerman	Research and Development

TRI-STATE PRODUCTS		
Name	**Employee #**	**Department**
Whitaker, Christine	1432-323-09	Financial Services
Higgins, Dennis	1230-933-21	Public Relations
Coffey, Richard	1321-843-22	Research and Development
Porter, Robbie	1122-361-38	Public Relations
Buchanan, Lillian	1432-857-87	Research and Development
Kensington, Jacob	1112-473-31	Human Resources

TRI-STATE PRODUCTS	
Title	**Name**
President	Martin Sherwood
Vice President	Gina Lopez
Vice President	Sydney Fox
Manager	Stephen Powell
Manager	Linda Wu

Tri-State Products		
Washington Division	**Oregon Division**	**California Division**

Project 2 Create and Format Tables with Employee Information

WL1-C7-P2-TSPTables.docx

TRI-STATE PRODUCTS
Sales Division

Salesperson	**Sales, 2014**	**Sales, 2015**
Guthrie, Jonathon	$623,214	$635,099
Novak, Diana	$543,241	$651,438
Byers, Darren	$490,655	$500,210
Kurkova, Martina	$490,310	$476,005
Whittier, Michelle	$395,630	$376,522
Sogura, Jeffrey	$375,630	$399,120
Lagasa, Brianna	$294,653	$300,211
Total	$3,213,333	$3,338,605
Average	$459,048	$476,944
Top Sales	$623,214	$651,438

Region	**First Qtr.**	**Second Qtr.**	**Third Qtr.**	**Fourth Qtr.**	**Total**
Northwest	$125,430	$157,090	$139,239	$120,340	$542,099
Southwest	$133,450	$143,103	$153,780	$142,498	$572,831
Northeast	$275,340	$299,342	$278,098	$266,593	$1,119,373
Southeast	$211,349	$222,330	$201,849	$239,432	$874,960
Total	$745,569	$821,865	$772,966	$768,863	$3,109,263
Average	$186,392	$205,466	$193,242	$192,216	$777,316

Project 3 Sort and Calculate Sales Data

WL1-C7-P3-TSPSalesTables.docx

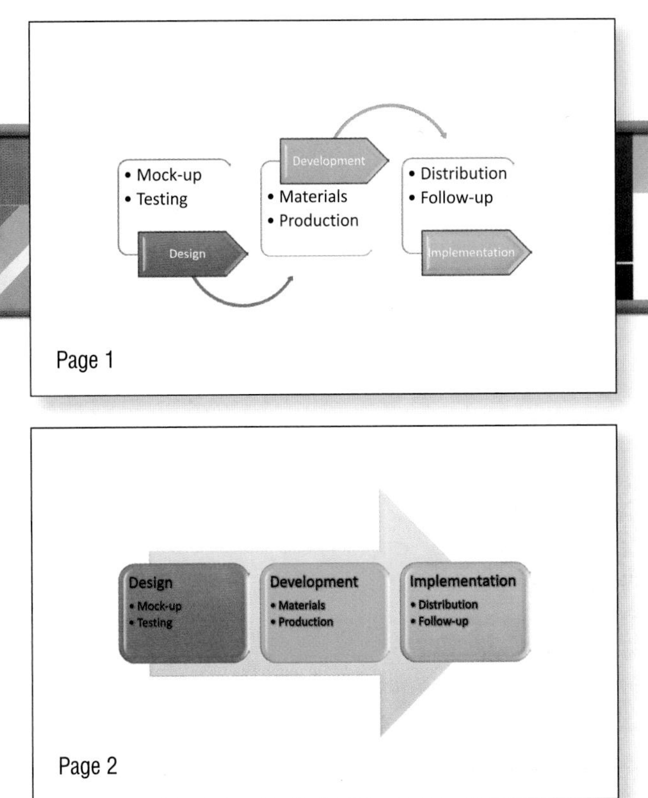

Project 4 Prepare and Format a SmartArt Graphic
WL1-C7-P4-SAGraphics.docx

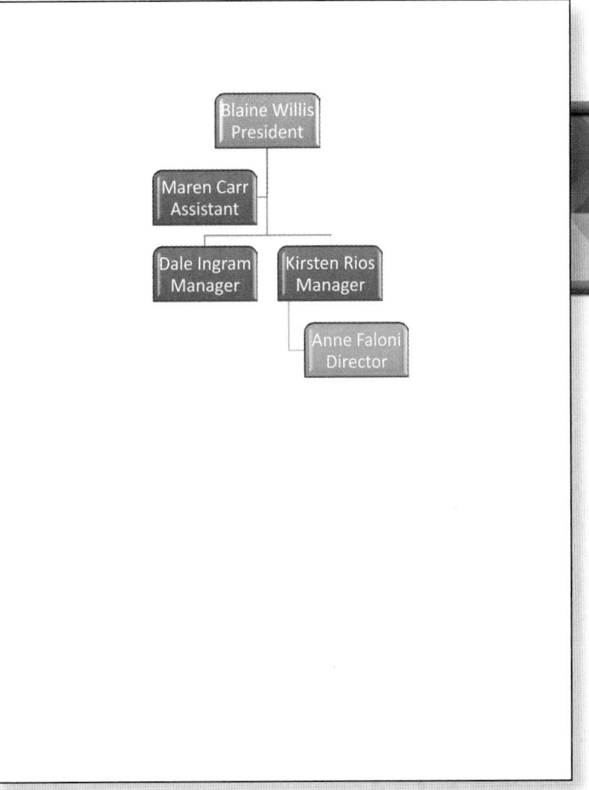

Project 5 Prepare and Format a Company Organizational Chart
WL1-C7-P5-OrgChart.docx

Project 1 Create and Format Tables with Company Information — 9 Parts

You will create one table containing contact information and another containing information on plans offered by the company. You will then change the design and layout of each table.

Creating a Table

Use the Tables feature to create boxes of information called ***cells***. A cell is the intersection between a row and a column. A cell can contain text, characters, numbers, data, graphics, or formulas. Create a table by clicking the INSERT tab, clicking the Table button, dragging down and to the right in the drop-down grid until the correct number of rows and columns displays, and then clicking the mouse button. You can also create a table with options at the Insert Table dialog box. Display this dialog box by clicking the Table button in the Tables group on the INSERT tab and then clicking *Insert Table* at the drop-down list.

Figure 7.1 shows an example of a table with three columns and four rows. Various parts of the table are identified in Figure 7.1, such as the gridlines, move table column marker, end-of-cell marker, end-of-row marker, table move handle, and resize handle. In a table, nonprinting characters identify the ends of cells and the ends of rows. To view these characters, click the Show/Hide ¶ button in the

Quick Steps

Create a Table
1. Click INSERT tab.
2. Click Table button.
3. Drag to create desired number of columns and rows.
4. Click mouse button.

OR
1. Click INSERT tab.
2. Click Table button.
3. Click *Insert Table.*
4. Specify number of columns and rows.
5. Click OK.

Figure 7.1 Table with Nonprinting Characters Displayed

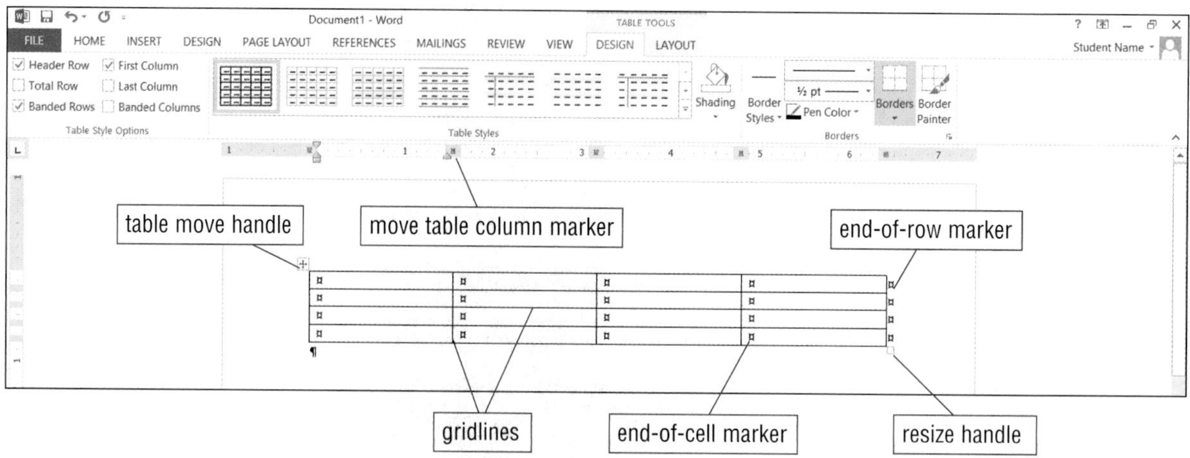

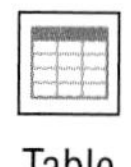
Table

You can create a table within a table, creating a *nested* table.

Paragraph group on the HOME tab. The end-of-cell marker displays inside each cell and the end-of-row marker displays at the end of a row of cells. These markers are identified in Figure 7.1.

When you create a table, the insertion point is located in the cell in the upper left corner of the table. Cells in a table contain a cell designation. Columns in a table are lettered from left to right, beginning with *A*. Rows in a table are numbered from top to bottom beginning with *1*. The cell in the upper left corner of the table is cell A1. The cell to the right of A1 is B1, the cell to the right of B1 is C1, and so on.

When the insertion point is positioned in a cell in the table, move table column markers display on the horizontal ruler. These markers represent the end of a column and are useful in changing the widths of columns. Figure 7.1 identifies a move table column marker.

Entering Text in Cells

HINT

Pressing the Tab key in a table moves the insertion point to the next cell. Pressing Ctrl + Tab moves the insertion point to the next tab within a cell.

With the insertion point positioned in a cell, type or edit text. Move the insertion point to another cell with the mouse by clicking in the desired cell. If you are using the keyboard, press the Tab key to move the insertion point to the next cell or press Shift + Tab to move the insertion point to the previous cell.

If the text you type does not fit on one line, it wraps to the next line within the same cell, or if you press Enter within a cell, the insertion point is moved to the next line within the same cell. The cell vertically lengthens to accommodate the text, and all cells in that row also lengthen. Pressing the Tab key in a table causes the insertion point to move to the next cell in the table. If you want to move the insertion point to a tab within a cell, press Ctrl + Tab. If the insertion point is located in the last cell of the table and you press the Tab key, Word adds another row to the table. Insert a page break within a table by pressing Ctrl + Enter. The page break is inserted between rows, not within a row.

Moving the Insertion Point within a Table

To use the mouse to move the insertion point to a different cell within the table, click in the desired cell. To use the keyboard to move the insertion point to a different cell within the table, refer to the information shown in Table 7.1.

Table 7.1 Insertion Point Movement within a Table Using the Keyboard

To move the insertion point	*Press these keys*
to next cell	Tab
to preceding cell	Shift + Tab
forward one character	Right Arrow key
backward one character	Left Arrow key
to previous row	Up Arrow key
to next row	Down Arrow key
to first cell in row	Alt + Home
to last cell in row	Alt + End
to top cell in column	Alt + Page Up
to bottom cell in column	Alt + Page Down

Project 1a Creating a Table

Part 1 of 9

1. At a blank document, turn on bold and then type the title CONTACT INFORMATION, as shown in Figure 7.2.
2. Turn off bold and then press the Enter key.
3. Create the table shown in Figure 7.2. To do this, click the INSERT tab, click the Table button in the Tables group, drag down and to the right in the drop-down grid until the number above the grid displays as *3x5*, and then click the mouse button.
4. Type the text in the cells as indicated in Figure 7.2. Press the Tab key to move to the next cell or press Shift + Tab to move to the preceding cell. (If you accidentally press the Enter key within a cell, immediately press the Backspace key. Do not press Tab after typing the text in the last cell. If you do, another row is inserted in the table. If this happens, immediately click the Undo button on the Quick Access toolbar.)
5. Save the table and name it **WL1-C7-P1-Tables**.

Figure 7.2 Project 1a

CONTACT INFORMATION

Maggie Rivera	First Trust Bank	(203) 555-3440
Les Cromwell	Madison Trust	(602) 555-4900
Cecilia Nordyke	American Financial	(509) 555-3995
Regina Stahl	United Fidelity	(301) 555-1201
Justin White	Key One Savings	(360) 555-8963

Using the Insert Table Dialog Box

You can also create a table with options at the Insert Table dialog box shown in Figure 7.3. To display this dialog box, click the INSERT tab, click the Table button in the Tables group, and then click *Insert Table*. At the Insert Table dialog box, enter the desired number of columns and rows and then click OK.

Figure 7.3 Insert Table Dialog Box

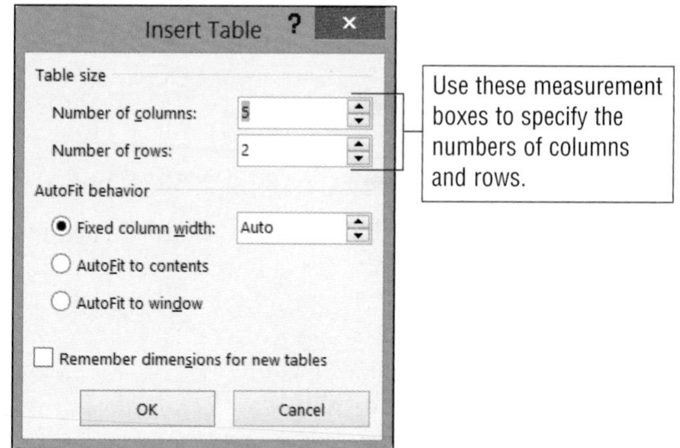

Project 1b **Creating a Table with the Insert Table Dialog Box** **Part 2 of 9**

1. With **WL1-C7-P1-Tables.docx** open, press Ctrl + End to move the insertion point below the table.
2. Press the Enter key twice.
3. Turn on bold and then type the title **OPTIONAL PLAN PREMIUM RATES**, as shown in Figure 7.4.
4. Turn off bold and then press the Enter key.
5. Click the INSERT tab, click the Table button in the Tables group, and then click *Insert Table* at the drop-down list.
6. At the Insert Table dialog box, type 3 in the *Number of columns* measurement box. (The insertion point is automatically positioned in this text box.)
7. Press the Tab key (this moves the insertion point to the *Number of rows* measurement box) and then type 5.
8. Click OK.
9. Type the text in the cells as indicated in Figure 7.4. Press the Tab key to move to the next cell or press Shift + Tab to move to the preceding cell. To indent the text in cells B2 through B5 and cells C2 through C5, press Ctrl + Tab to move the insertion point to a tab within a cell and then type the text.
10. Save **WL1-C7-P1-Tables.docx**.

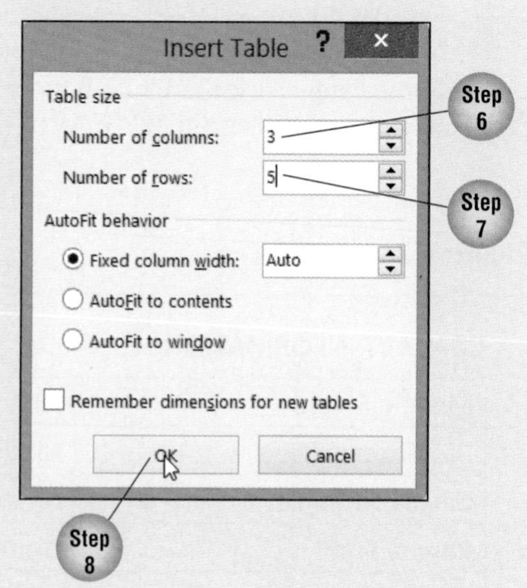

Figure 7.4 Project 1b

OPTIONAL PLAN PREMIUM RATES

Waiting Period	Basic Plan Employees	Plan 2015 Employees
60 days	0.67%	0.79%
90 days	0.49%	0.59%
120 days	0.30%	0.35%
180 days	0.23%	0.26%

Changing the Table Design

When you create a table, the TABLE TOOLS DESIGN tab is active. This tab contains a number of options for enhancing the appearance of the table, as shown in Figure 7.5. With options in the Table Styles group, apply a predesigned style that applies color and border lines to a table as well as shading to cells. Maintain further control over the predesigned style formatting applied to columns and rows with options in the Table Style Options group. For example, if your table contains a total row, you would insert a check mark in the *Total Row* option.

With options in the Borders group, you can customize the borders of cells in a table. Click the Border Styles button to display a drop-down list of predesigned border lines. Use other buttons in the Borders group to change the line style, width, and color; add or remove borders; and apply the same border style formatting to other cells with the Border Painter button.

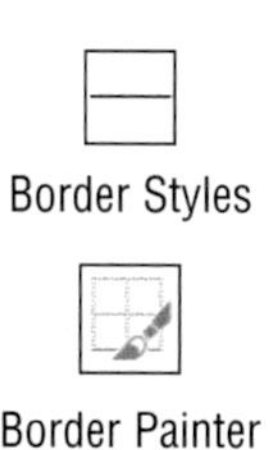

Figure 7.5 TABLE TOOLS DESIGN Tab

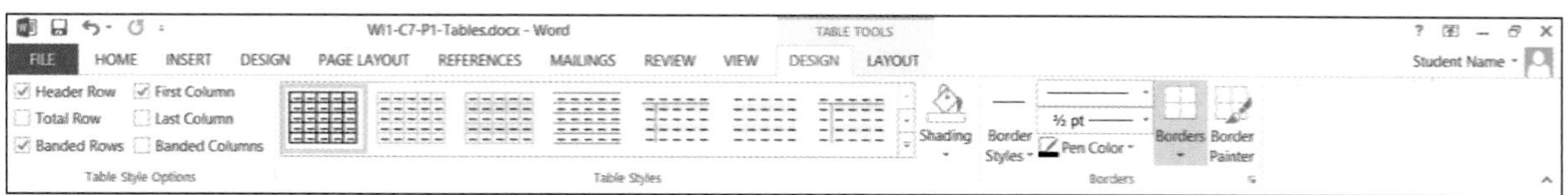

Project 1c **Applying Table Styles** **Part 3 of 9**

1. With **WL1-C7-P1-Tables.docx** open, click in any cell in the top table.
2. Apply a table style by completing the following steps:
   a. Make sure the TABLE TOOLS DESIGN tab is active.
   b. Click the More button at the right side of the table style thumbnails in the Table Styles group.
   c. Click the *Grid Table 5 Dark - Accent 5* style thumbnail (sixth column, fifth row in the *Grid Tables* section).

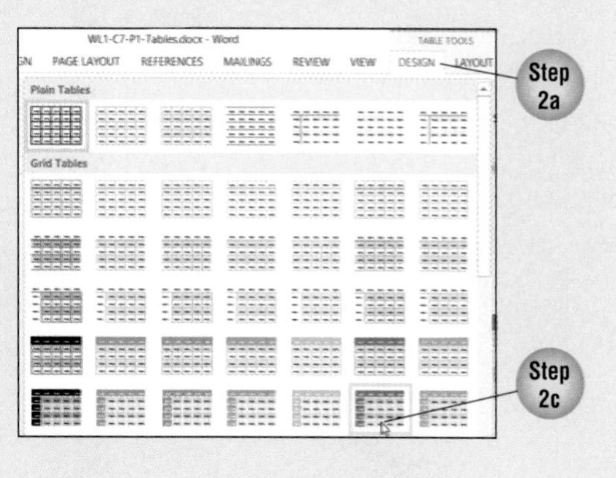

3. After looking at the table, you realize that the first row is not a header row and the first column should not be formatted differently than the other columns. To format the first row and first column in the same manner as the other rows and columns, click the *Header Row* check box and the *First Column* check box in the Table Style Options group to remove the check marks.
4. Click in any cell in the bottom table, apply the List Table 6 Colorful - Accent 5 table style (sixth column, sixth row in the *List Tables* section).
5. Add color borders to the top table by completing the following steps:
   a. Click in any cell in the top table.
   b. Click the Pen Color button arrow in the Borders group and then click the *Orange, Accent 2, Darker 50%* color (sixth column, bottom row in the *Theme Colors* section).
   c. Click the Line Weight button arrow in the Borders group and then click *1 ½ pt* at the drop-down list. (When you choose a line weight, the Border Painter button is automatically activated.)

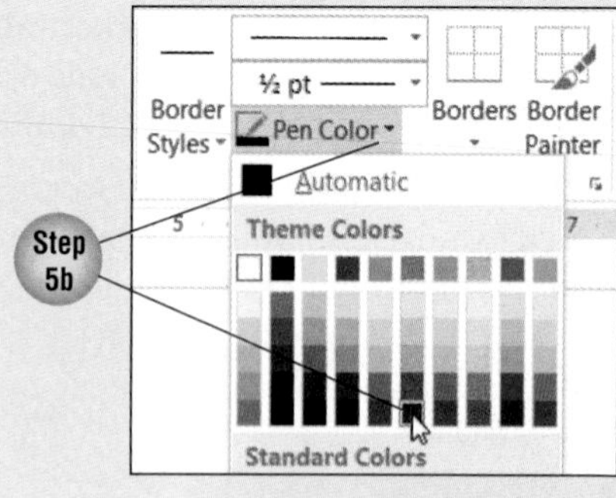

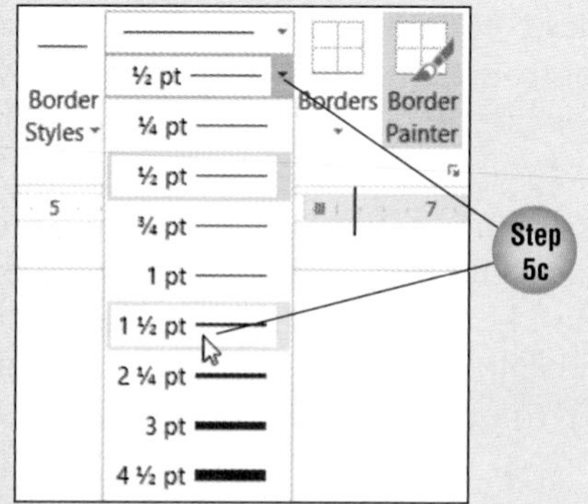

   d. Using the mouse (mouse pointer displays as a pen), drag along all four sides of the table. (As you drag with the mouse, a thick, brown border line is inserted. If you make a mistake or the line does not display as you intended, click the Undo button and then continue drawing along each side of the table.)
6. Click the Border Styles button arrow and then click the *Double solid lines, 1/2 pt, Accent 2* option (third column, third row in the *Theme Borders* section).
7. Drag along all four sides of the bottom table.

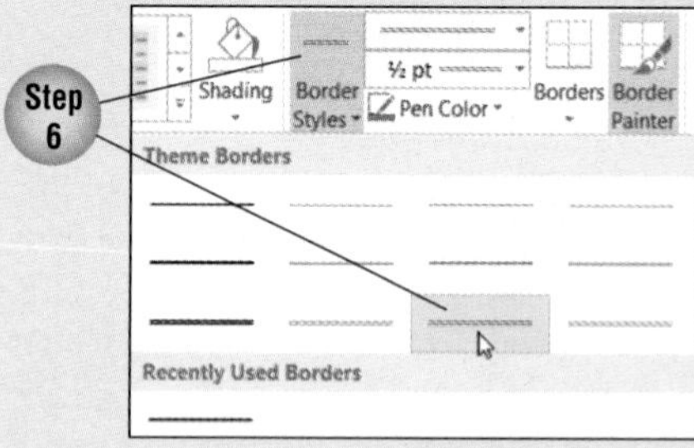

8. Click the Border Painter button to turn off the feature.
9. Save **WL1-C7-P1-Tables.docx**.

Selecting Cells

You can format data within a table in several ways. For example, you can change the alignment of text within cells or rows, select and then move or copy rows or columns, or add character formatting such as bold, italic, or underlining. To format specific cells, rows, or columns, you must first select them.

Selecting in a Table with the Mouse

Use the mouse pointer to select a cell, row, or column, or to select an entire table. Table 7.2 describes methods for selecting in a table with the mouse. The left edge of each cell, between the left column border and the end-of-cell marker or first character in the cell, is called the ***cell selection bar***. When you position the mouse pointer in the cell selection bar, it turns into a small, black arrow pointing up and to the right. Each row in a table contains a ***row selection bar***, which is the space just to the left of the left edge of the table. When you position the mouse pointer in the row selection bar, the mouse pointer turns into a white arrow pointing up and to the right.

Table 7.2 Selecting in a Table with the Mouse

To select this	*Do this*
cell	Position the mouse pointer in the cell selection bar at the left edge of the cell until it turns into a small, black arrow pointing up and to the right and then click the left mouse button.
row	Position the mouse pointer in the row selection bar at the left edge of the table until it turns into an arrow pointing up and to the right and then click the left mouse button.
column	Position the mouse pointer on the uppermost horizontal gridline of the table in the appropriate column until it turns into a small, black, down-pointing arrow and then click the left mouse button.
adjacent cells	Position the mouse pointer in the first cell to be selected, hold down the left mouse button, drag the mouse pointer to the last cell to be selected, and then release the mouse button.
all cells in a table	Click the table move handle or position the mouse pointer in the row selection bar for the first row at the left edge of the table until it turns into an arrow pointing up and to the right, hold down the left mouse button, drag down to select all rows in the table, and then release the left mouse button.
text within a cell	Position the mouse pointer at the beginning of the text and then hold down the left mouse button as you drag the mouse across the text. (When a cell is selected, the cell background color changes to gray. When text within cells is selected, only those lines containing text are selected.)

Selecting in a Table with the Keyboard

In addition to the mouse, you can also use the keyboard to select specific cells within a table. Table 7.3 displays the commands for selecting specific amounts of a table.

If you want to select only the text within a cell, rather than the entire cell, press F8 to turn on the Extend mode and then move the insertion point with an arrow key. When a cell is selected, the cell background color changes to gray. When text within a cell is selected, only those lines containing text are selected.

Table 7.3 Selecting in a Table with the Keyboard

To select	*Press*
next cell's contents	Tab
preceding cell's contents	Shift + Tab
entire table	Alt + 5 (on numeric keypad with Num Lock off)
adjacent cells	Hold down the Shift key and then press an arrow key repeatedly.
column	Position the insertion point in the top cell of the column, hold down the Shift key, and then press the down-pointing arrow key until the column is selected.

Project 1d **Selecting, Moving and Formatting Cells in a Table** **Part 4 of 9**

1. With **WL1-C7-P1-Tables.docx** open, move two rows in the top table by completing the following steps:
   a. Position the mouse pointer in the row selection bar at the left side of the row containing the name *Cecilia Nordyke*, hold down the left mouse button, and then drag down to select two rows (the *Cecilia Nordyke* row and the *Regina Stahl* row).

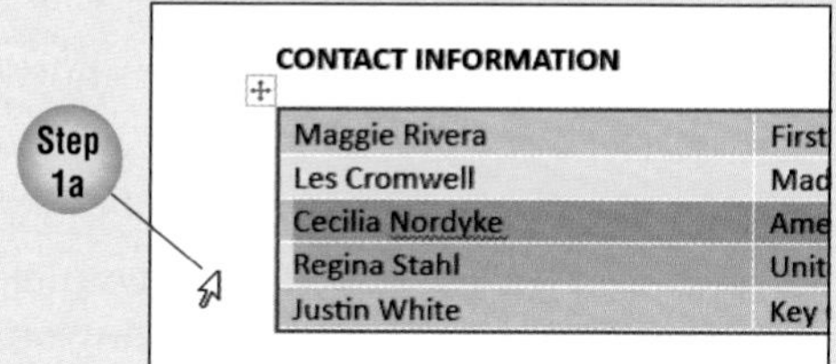

   b. Click the HOME tab and then click the Cut button in the Clipboard group.
   c. Move the insertion point so it is positioned at the beginning of the name *Les Cromwell* and then click the Paste button in the Clipboard group.
2. Move the third column in the bottom table by completing the following steps:
   a. Position the mouse pointer on the top border of the third column in the bottom table until the pointer turns into a short, black, down-pointing arrow and then click the left mouse button. (This selects the entire column.)
   b. Click the Cut button in the Clipboard group on the HOME tab.
   c. With the insertion point positioned at the beginning of the text *Basic Plan Employees*, click the Paste button in the Clipboard group. (Moving the column removed the right border.)
   d. Insert the right border by clicking the TABLE TOOLS DESIGN tab, clicking the Border Styles button arrow, and then clicking the *Double solid lines, 1/2 pt, Accent 2* option at the drop-down list (third column, third row in the *Theme Borders* section).

e. Drag along the right border of the bottom table.

f. Click the Border Painter button to turn off the feature.

3. Apply shading to a row by completing the following steps:
   a. Position the mouse pointer in the row selection bar at the left edge of the first row in the bottom table until the pointer turns into an arrow pointing up and to the right and then click the left mouse button. (This selects the entire first row of the bottom table.)
   b. Click the Shading button arrow in the Table Styles group and then click the *Orange, Accent 2, Lighter 80%* color option (sixth column, second row in the *Theme Colors* section).
4. Apply a border line to the right side of two columns by completing the following steps:
   a. Position the mouse pointer on the top border of the first column in the bottom table until the pointer turns into a short, black, down-pointing arrow and then click the left mouse button.
   b. Click the Line Style button arrow and then click the top line option (a single line).
   c. Click the Borders button arrow and then click *Right Border* at the drop-down list.
   d. Select the second column in the bottom table.
   e. Click the Borders button arrow and then click *Right Border* at the drop-down list.
5. Apply italic formatting to a column by completing the following steps:
   a. Click in the first cell of the first row in the top table.
   b. Hold down the Shift key and then press the Down Arrow key four times. (This should select all cells in the first column.)
   c. Press Ctrl + I.
6. Save **WL1-C7-P1-Tables.docx**.

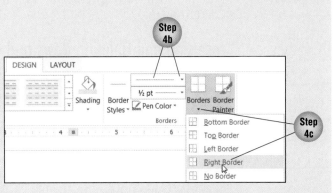

Changing Table Layout

Some table layout options are available at a shortcut menu that can be viewed by right-clicking a table.

To further customize a table, consider changing the table layout by inserting or deleting columns and rows and specifying cell alignments. Change table layout with options at the TABLE TOOLS LAYOUT tab shown in Figure 7.6. Use options and buttons on the tab to select specific cells, delete and insert rows and columns, merge and split cells, specify cell height and width, sort data in cells, and insert formulas.

Figure 7.6 TABLE TOOLS LAYOUT Tab

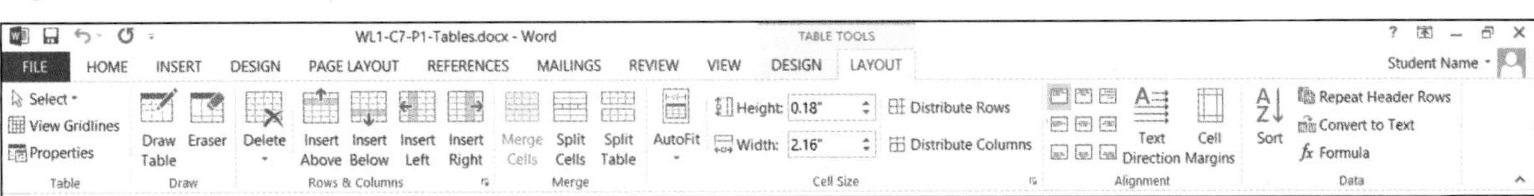

Selecting with the Select Button

Select

Along with selecting cells with the keyboard and mouse, you can also select specific cells with the Select button in the Table group on the TABLE TOOLS LAYOUT tab. To select with this button, position the insertion point in the desired cell, column, or row and then click the Select button. At the drop-down list that displays, specify what you want to select: the entire table or a column, row, or cell.

Viewing Gridlines

View Gridlines

When you create a table, cell borders are identified by horizontal and vertical thin, black gridlines. You can remove a cell border gridline but maintain the cell border. If you remove cell border gridlines or apply a table style that removes gridlines, nonprinting gridlines display as dashed lines. This helps you visually determine cell borders. You can turn on or off the display of these nonprinting, dashed gridlines with the View Gridlines button in the Table group on the TABLE TOOLS LAYOUT tab.

Inserting and Deleting Rows and Columns

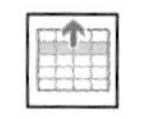

Insert Above

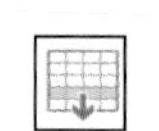

Insert Below

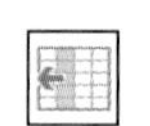

Insert Left

Insert Right

Delete

Insert a row or column and delete a row or column with buttons in the Rows & Columns group on the TABLE TOOLS LAYOUT tab. Click the button in the group that inserts the row or column in the desired location, such as above, below, to the left, or to the right. Add a row to the bottom of a table by positioning the insertion point in the last cell and then pressing the Tab key. To delete a table, row, or column, click the Delete button and then click the option identifying what you want to delete. If you make a mistake while formatting a table, immediately click the Undo button on the Quick Access toolbar.

You can also insert a row or column with insert icons. Display the insert row icon by positioning the mouse pointer just outside the left border of the table at the left of the desired row border. When the insert row icon displays (a plus symbol in a circle and a border line), click the icon and a row is inserted below the insert icon border line. To insert a column, position the mouse pointer above the column border line until the column icon displays and then click the icon. This inserts a new column immediately left of the insert column icon border line.

Project 1e **Selecting, Inserting, and Deleting Columns and Rows** **Part 5 of 9**

1. Make sure **WL1-C7-P1-Tables.docx** is open.
2. The table style applied to the bottom table removed row border gridlines. If you do not see dashed row border gridlines in the bottom table, turn on the display of these nonprinting gridlines by positioning your insertion point in the table, clicking the TABLE TOOLS LAYOUT tab, and then clicking the View Gridlines button in the Table group. (The button should display with a light blue background indicating it is active.)
3. Select a column and apply formatting by completing the following steps:
   a. Click in any cell in the first column in the top table.
   b. Click the Select button in the Table group and then click *Select Column* at the drop-down list.
   c. With the first column selected, press Ctrl + I to remove italics and then press Ctrl + B to apply bold formatting.

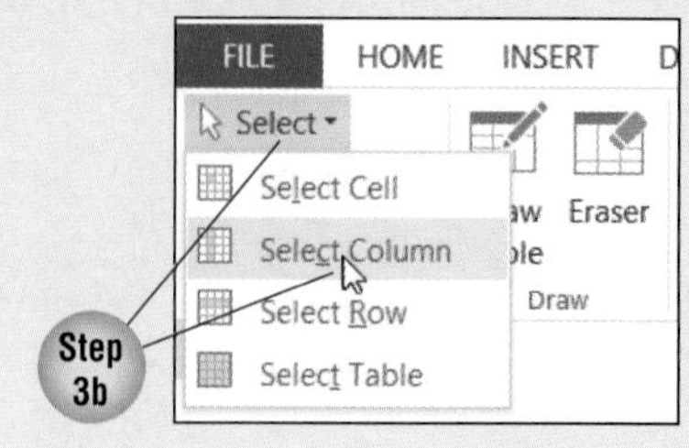

4. Select a row and apply formatting by completing the following steps:
   a. Click in any cell in the first row in the bottom table.
   b. Click the Select button in the Table group and then click *Select Row* at the drop-down list.
   c. With the first row selected in the bottom table, press Ctrl + I to apply italic formatting.
5. Insert a new row in the bottom table and type text in the new cells by completing the following steps:
   a. Click in the cell containing the text *60 days*.
   b. Click the Insert Above button in the Rows & Columns group.
   c. Type 30 days in the first cell of the new row. Press the Tab key, press Ctrl + Tab, and then type 0.85% in the second cell of the new row. Press the Tab key, press Ctrl + Tab, and then type 0.81% in the third cell of the new row:

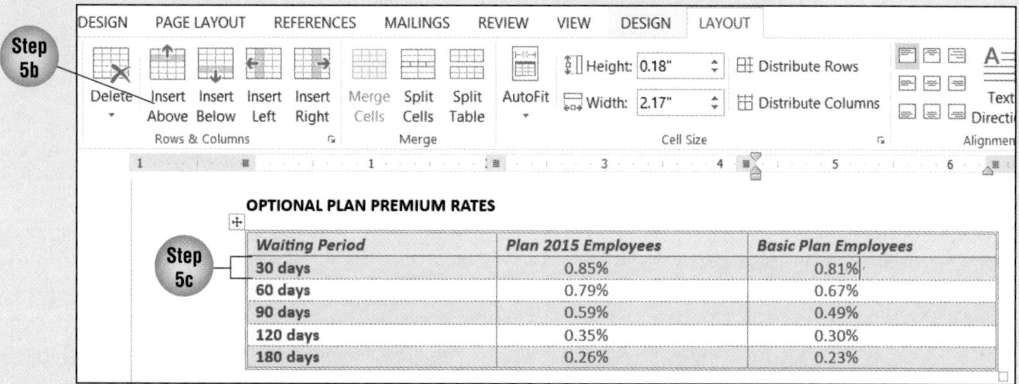

Waiting Period	*Plan 2015 Employees*	*Basic Plan Employees*
30 days	0.85%	0.81%
60 days	0.79%	0.67%
90 days	0.59%	0.49%
120 days	0.35%	0.30%
180 days	0.26%	0.23%

6. Insert two new rows in the top table by completing the following steps:
   a. Select the two rows of cells that begin with the names *Cecilia Nordyke* and *Regina Stahl*.
   b. Click the Insert Below button in the Rows & Columns group.
   c. Click in any cell of the top table to deselect the new rows.
7. Insert a new row in the top table by positioning the mouse pointer at the left side of the table next to the border line below *Regina Stahl* until the insert row icon displays and then click the icon.

Step 7

CONTACT INFORMATION

Maggie Rivera
Cecilia Nordyke
Regina Stahl
Les Cromwell
Justin White

8. Type the following text in the new cells:

Teresa Getty	Meridian Bank	(503) 555-9800
Michael Vazquez	New Horizon Bank	(702) 555-2435
Samantha Roth	Cascade Mutual	(206) 555-6788

CONTACT INFORMATION

Maggie Rivera	First Trust Bank	(203) 555-3440
Cecilia Nordyke	American Financial	(509) 555-3995
Regina Stahl	United Fidelity	(301) 555-1201
Teresa Getty	Meridian Bank	(503) 555-9800
Michael Vazquez	New Horizon Bank	(702) 555-2435
Samantha Roth	Cascade Mutual	(206) 555-6788
Les Cromwell	Madison Trust	(602) 555-4900
Justin White	Key One Savings	(360) 555-8963

Step 8

9. Delete a row by completing the following steps:
   a. Click in the cell containing the name *Les Cromwell*.
   b. Click the Delete button in the Rows & Columns group and then click *Delete Rows* at the drop-down list.

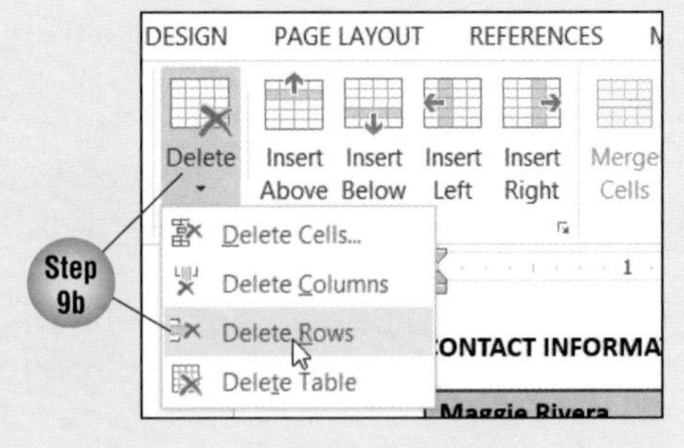

10. Insert a new column in the top table by completing the following steps:
    a. Position the mouse pointer immediately above the border line between the first and second columns in the top table until the insert column icon displays.
    b. Click the insert column icon.

Step 10b

CONTACT INFORMATION

Maggie Rivera	First Trust Bank
Cecilia Nordyke	American Financial

11. Type the following text in the new cells:
    B1 = Vice President
    B2 = Loan Officer
    B3 = Account Manager
    B4 = Branch Manager
    B5 = President
    B6 = Vice President
    B7 = Regional Manager
12. Save **WL1-C7-P1-Tables.docx**.

Step 11

CONTACT INFORMATION

Maggie Rivera	Vice President	First Tru
Cecilia Nordyke	Loan Officer	America
Regina Stahl	Account Manager	United F
Teresa Getty	Branch Manager	Meridiar
Michael Vazquez	President	New Hoi
Samantha Roth	Vice President	Cascade
Justin White	Regional Manager	Key One

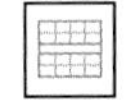
Merge Cells

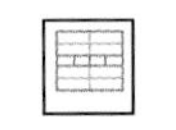
Split Cells

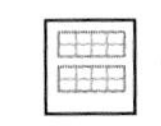
Split Table

Merging and Splitting Cells and Tables

Click the Merge Cells button in the Merge group on the TABLE TOOLS LAYOUT tab to merge selected cells and click the Split Cells button to split the currently active cell. When you click the Split Cells button, the Split Cells dialog box displays where you specify the number of columns or rows into which you want to split the active cell. If you want to split one table into two tables, position the insertion point in a cell in the row that you want to be the first row in the new table and then click the Split Table button.

Project 1f Merging and Splitting Cells and Splitting a Table — Part 6 of 9

1. With **WL1-C7-P1-Tables.docx** open, insert a new row and merge cells in the row by completing the following steps:
   a. Click in the cell containing the text *Waiting Period* (located in the bottom table).
   b. Click the Insert Above button in the Rows & Columns group on the TABLE TOOLS LAYOUT tab.

c. With all of the cells in the new row selected, click the Merge Cells button in the Merge group.
d. Type **OPTIONAL PLAN PREMIUM RATES** and then press Ctrl + E to center-align the text in the cell. (The text you type will be italicized.)

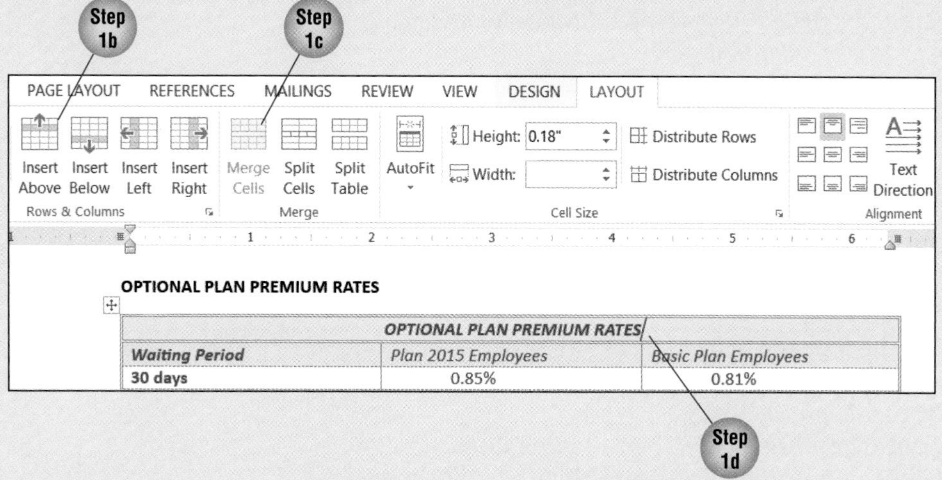

2. Select and then delete the text *OPTIONAL PLAN PREMIUM RATES* that displays above the bottom table.
3. Insert rows and text in the top table and merge cells by completing the following steps:
   a. Click in the cell containing the text *Maggie Rivera*.
   b. Click the TABLE TOOLS LAYOUT tab.
   c. Click the Insert Above button twice. (This inserts two rows at the top of the table.)
   d. With the cells in the top row selected, click the Merge Cells button in the Merge group.
   e. Type **CONTACT INFORMATION, NORTH** and then press Ctrl + E to change the paragraph alignment to center.
   f. Type the following text in the four cells in the new second row.

      Name **Title** **Company** **Telephone**

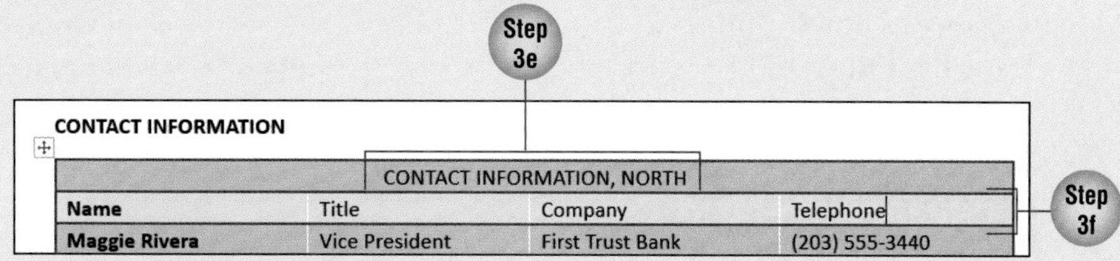

4. Apply heading formatting to the new top row by completing the following steps:
   a. Click the TABLE TOOLS DESIGN tab.
   b. Click the *Header Row* check box in the Table Style Options group.
5. Select and then delete the text *CONTACT INFORMATION* that displays above the top table.
6. Split a cell by completing the following steps:
   a. Click in the cell containing the telephone number *(301) 555-1201*.
   b. Click the TABLE TOOLS LAYOUT tab.
   c. Click the Split Cells button in the Merge group.
   d. At the Split Cells dialog box, click OK. (The telephone number will wrap to a new line. You will change this in the next project.)

e. Click in the new cell.

f. Type **x453** in the new cell. If AutoCorrect automatically capitalizes the *x*, hover the mouse pointer over the *X* until the AutoCorrect Options button displays. Click the AutoCorrect Options button and then click *Undo Automatic Capitalization* or click *Stop Auto-capitalizing First Letter of Table Cells*.

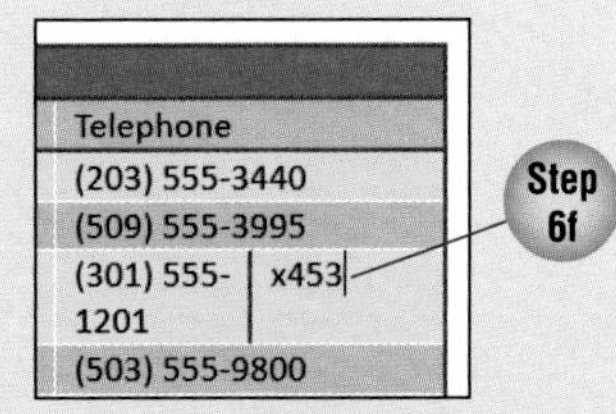

7. Split the cell containing the telephone number *(206) 555-6788* and then type **x2310** in the new cell. (If necessary, make the *x* lowercase.)
8. Split the top table into two tables by completing the following steps:
   a. Click in the cell containing the name *Teresa Getty*.
   b. Click the Split Table button in the Merge group.
   c. Click in the cell containing the name *Teresa Getty* (in the first row of the new table).
   d. Click the Insert Above button in the Rows and Columns group on the TABLE TOOLS LAYOUT tab.
   e. With the new row selected, click the Merge Cells button.
   f. Type **CONTACT INFORMATION, SOUTH** in the new row and then press Ctrl + E to center-align the text.
9. Save and then print **WL1-C7-P1-Tables.docx**.
10. Delete the middle table by completing the following steps:
    a. Click in any cell in the middle table.
    b. Click the TABLE TOOLS LAYOUT tab.
    c. Click the Delete button in the Rows & Columns group and then click *Delete Table* at the drop-down list.
11. Draw a dark orange border at the bottom of the top table by completing the following steps:
    a. Click in any cell in the top table and then click the TABLE TOOLS DESIGN tab.
    b. Click the Line Weight button arrow in the Borders group and then click *1 ½ pt* at the drop-down list. (This activates the Border Painter button.)
    c. Click the Pen Color button and then click the *Orange, Accent 2, Darker, 50%* option (sixth column, bottom row in the *Theme Colors* section).
    d. Using the mouse, drag along the bottom border of the top table.
    e. Click the Border Painter button to turn it off.
12. Save **WL1-C7-P1-Tables.docx**.

Customizing Cell Size

When you create a table, column width and row height are equal. You can customize the width of columns or height of rows with buttons in the Cell Size group on the TABLE TOOLS LAYOUT tab. Use the *Table Row Height* measurement box to increase or decrease the height of rows and use the *Table Column Width* measurement box to increase or decrease the width of columns. The Distribute Rows button will distribute equally the height of selected rows, and the Distribute Columns button will distribute equally the width of selected columns.

Distribute Rows

Distribute Columns

You can also change column width using the move table column markers on the horizontal ruler or by using the table gridlines. To change column width using the horizontal ruler, position the mouse pointer on a move table column marker until it turns into a left-and-right-pointing arrow, and then drag the marker to the desired position. Hold down the Shift key while dragging a table column marker and the horizontal ruler remains stationary while the table column marker moves.

Hold down the Alt key while dragging a table column marker and measurements display on the horizontal ruler. To change column width using gridlines, position the arrow pointer on the gridline separating columns until the insertion point turns into a left-and-right-pointing arrow with a vertical line in the middle and then drag the gridline to the desired position. If you want to see the column measurements on the horizontal ruler as you drag a gridline, hold down the Alt key.

Adjust row height in a manner similar to adjusting column width. You can drag the adjust table row marker on the vertical ruler or drag the gridline separating rows. Hold down the Alt key while dragging the adjust table row marker or the row gridline, and measurements display on the vertical ruler.

Use the AutoFit button in the Cell Size group to make the column widths in a table automatically fit the contents. To do this, position the insertion point in any cell in the table, click the AutoFit button in the Cell Size group, and then click *AutoFit Contents* at the drop-down list.

AutoFit

Project 1g Changing Column Width and Row Height — Part 7 of 9

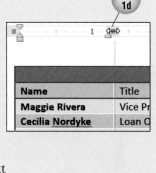

1. With **WL1-C7-P1-Tables.docx** open, change the width of the first column in the top table by completing the following steps:
   a. Click in the cell containing the name *Maggie Rivera*.
   b. Position the mouse pointer on the move table column marker that displays just right of the 1.5-inch mark on the horizontal ruler until the pointer turns into a left-and-right-pointing arrow.
   c. Hold down the Shift key and then the left mouse button.
   d. Drag the marker to the 1.25-inch mark, release the mouse button, and then release the Shift key.
2. Complete steps similar to those in Step 1 to drag the move table column marker that displays just right of the 3-inch mark on the horizontal ruler to the 2.75-inch mark. (Make sure the text *Account Manager* in the second column does not wrap to the next line. If it does, slightly increase the width of the column.)
3. Change the width of the third column in the top table by completing the following steps:
   a. Position the mouse pointer on the gridline separating the third and fourth columns until the pointer turns into a left-and-right-pointing arrow with a vertical double line in the middle.
   b. Hold down the Alt key and then the left mouse button, drag the gridline to the left until the measurement for the third column on the horizontal ruler displays as *1.31"*, and then release the Alt key and then the mouse button.

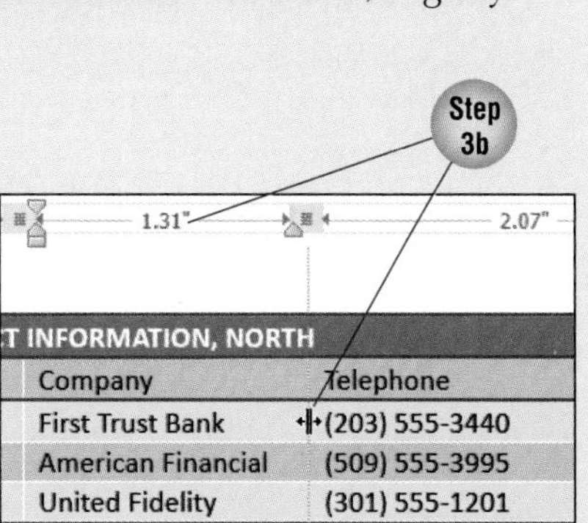

4. Position the mouse pointer on the gridline that separates the telephone number *(301) 555-1201* from the extension *x453* and then drag the gridline to the 5.25-inch mark on the horizontal ruler. (Make sure the phone number does not wrap down to the next line.)
5. Drag the right border of the top table to the 5.75-inch mark on the horizontal ruler.

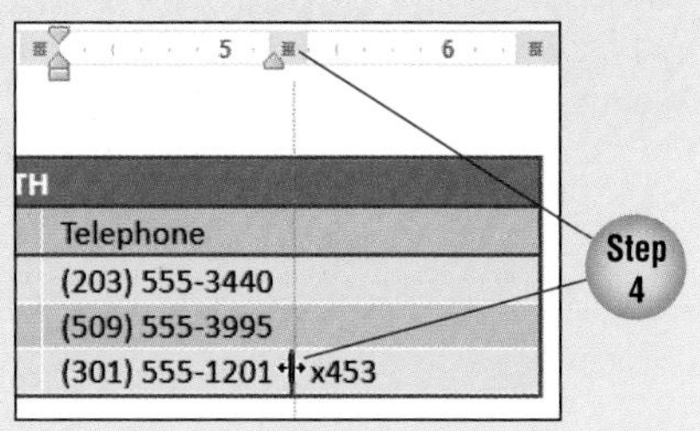

6. Automatically fit the columns in the bottom table by completing the following steps:
   a. Click in any cell in the bottom table.
   b. Click the AutoFit button in the Cell Size group on the TABLE TOOLS LAYOUT tab and then click *AutoFit Contents* at the drop-down list.

7. Increase the height of the first row in the bottom table by completing the following steps:
   a. Make sure the insertion point is located in one of the cells in the bottom table.
   b. Position the mouse pointer on the top adjust table row marker on the vertical ruler.
   c. Hold down the left mouse button and hold down the Alt key.
   d. Drag the adjust table row marker down until the first row measurement on the vertical ruler displays as *0.39"*, release the mouse button, and then release the Alt key.

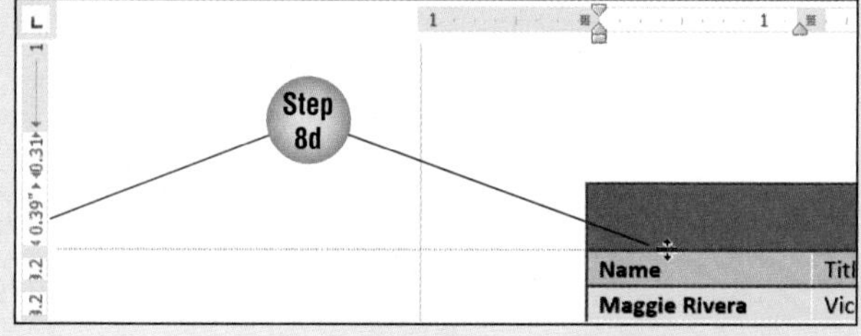

8. Increase the height of the first row in the top table by completing the following steps:
   a. Click in any cell in the top table.
   b. Position the arrow pointer on the gridline that displays at the bottom of the top row until the arrow pointer turns into an up-and-down-pointing arrow with a vertical double line in the middle.
   c. Hold down the left mouse button and then hold down the Alt key.
   d. Drag the gridline down until the first row measurement on the vertical ruler displays as *0.39"*, release the mouse button, and then release the Alt key.

9. Save **WL1-C7-P1-Tables.docx**.

Changing Cell Alignment

Quick Steps

Repeat a Header Row

1. Click in header row or select rows.
2. Click TABLE TOOLS LAYOUT tab.
3. Click Repeat Header Rows button.

Repeat Header Rows

The Alignment group on the TABLE TOOLS LAYOUT tab contains a number of buttons for specifying the horizontal and vertical alignment of text in cells. Each button contains a visual representation of the alignment, and you can also hover the mouse pointer over a button to determine the alignment.

Repeating a Header Row

If a table is divided between pages, consider adding the header row at the beginning of the table that continues on the next page. This helps the reader understand the data that displays in each column. To repeat a header row, click in the header row and then click the Repeat Header Rows button in the Data group on the TABLE TOOLS LAYOUT tab. If you want to repeat more than one header row, select the rows and then click the Repeat Header Rows button.

Project 1h Aligning Text in Cells and Repeating Header Rows

Part 8 of 9

1. With **WL1-C7-P1-Tables.docx** open, click in the top cell in the top table (the cell containing the title *CONTACT INFORMATION, NORTH*).
2. Click the Align Center button in the Alignment group on the TABLE TOOLS LAYOUT tab.
3. Format and align text in the second row in the top table by completing the following steps:
   a. Select the second row.
   b. Press Ctrl + B to turn off bold formatting for the entry in the first cell and then press Ctrl + B again to turn on bold formatting for all entries in the second row.
   c. Click the Align Top Center button in the Alignment group.
4. Click in the top cell in the bottom table and then click the Align Center button in the Alignment group.
5. Press Ctrl + End to move the insertion point to the end of the document, press the Enter key four times, and then insert a table into the current document by completing the following steps:
   a. Click the INSERT tab.
   b. Click the Object button arrow in the Text group and then click *Text from File* at the drop-down list.
   c. At the Insert File dialog box, navigate to the WL1C7 folder on your storage medium and then double-click ***ContactsWest.docx***.
6. Repeat the header row by completing the following steps:
   a. Select the first two rows in the table you just inserted.
   b. Click the TABLE TOOLS LAYOUT tab.
   c. Click the Repeat Header Rows button in the Data group.

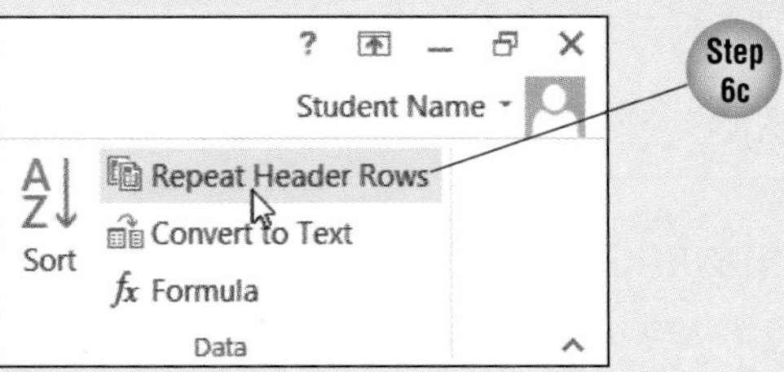

7. Save **WL1-C7-P1-Tables.docx**.

Inserting a Quick Table

Word includes a Quick Tables feature you can use to insert predesigned tables in a document. To insert a quick table, click the INSERT tab, click the Table button, point to *Quick Tables*, and then click the desired table at the side menu. A quick table has formatting applied, but you can further format the table with options at the TABLE TOOLS DESIGN tab and the TABLE TOOLS LAYOUT tab.

Quick Steps

Insert a Quick Table
1. Click INSERT tab.
2. Click Table button.
3. Point to *Quick Tables*.
4. Click desired table.

Project 1i Inserting a Quick Table

1. With **WL1-C7-P1-Tables.docx** open, press Ctrl + End to move the insertion point to the end of the document and then press the Enter key.
2. Insert a quick table by clicking the INSERT tab, clicking the Table button, pointing to *Quick Tables*, and then clicking the *Calendar 3* option at the side menu.

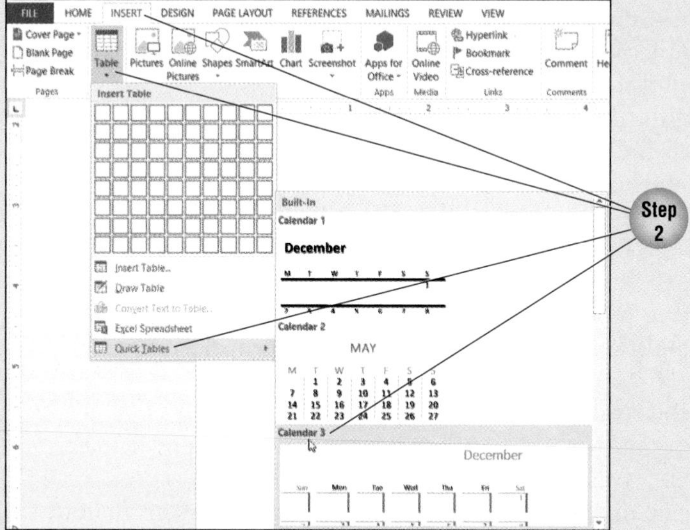

3. Edit text in each cell so the calendar reflects the current month. (If the bottom row is empty, select and then delete the row.)
4. Select the entire table by clicking the table move handle that displays outside the upper left corner of the table and then change the font to Copperplate Gothic Light.
5. Save, print, and then close **WL1-C7-P1-Tables.docx**.

Project 2 Create and Format Tables with Employee Information

5 Parts

You will create and format a table containing information on the names and departments of employees of Tri-State Products and also insert a table containing additional information on employees and then format the table.

Changing Cell Margin Measurements

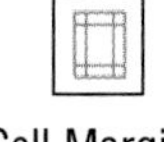
Cell Margins

By default, cells in a table contain specific margin settings. Top and bottom margins in a cell have a default measurement of 0 inch and left and right margins have a default setting of 0.08 inch. Change these default settings with options at the Table Options dialog box shown in Figure 7.7. Display this dialog box by clicking the Cell Margins button in the Alignment group on the TABLE TOOLS LAYOUT tab. Use the measurement boxes in the *Default cell margins* section to change the top, bottom, left, and/or right cell margin measurements.

Figure 7.7 Table Options Dialog Box

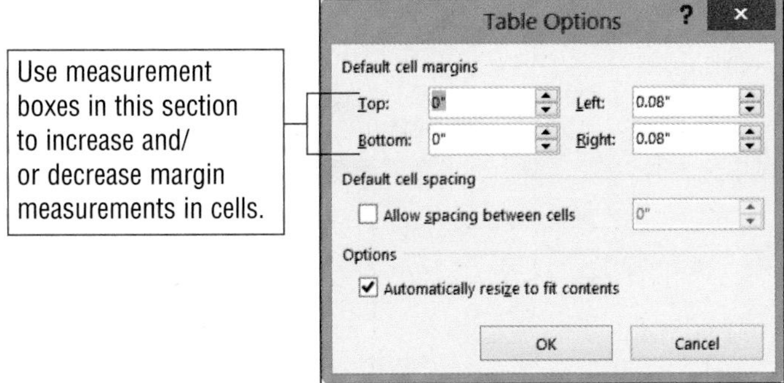

Changes to cell margins will affect all cells in a table. If you want to change the cell margin measurements for one cell or for selected cells, position the insertion point in the cell or select the desired cells and then click the Properties button in the Table group on the TABLE TOOLS LAYOUT tab. (You can also click the Cell Size group dialog box launcher.) At the Table Properties dialog box that displays, click the Cell tab and then the Options button that displays in the lower right corner of the dialog box. This displays the Cell Options dialog box shown in Figure 7.8.

Properties

Before setting the new cell margin measurements, remove the check mark from the *Same as the whole table* option. With the check mark removed from this option, the cell margin options become available. Specify the new cell margin measurements and then click OK to close the dialog box.

Figure 7.8 Cell Options Dialog Box

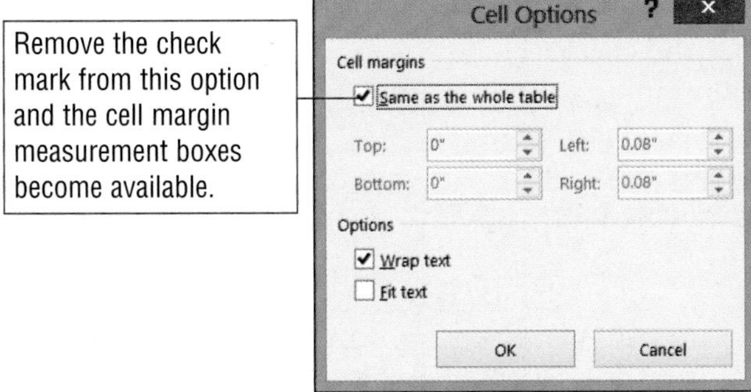

Project 2a Changing Cell Margin Measurements

Part 1 of 5

1. Open **TSPTables.docx** and then save the document with Save As and name it **WL1-C7-P2-TSPTables**.
2. Change the top and bottom margins for all cells in the table by completing the following steps:
   a. Position the insertion point in any cell in the table and then click the TABLE TOOLS LAYOUT tab.
   b. Click the Cell Margins button in the Alignment group.

c. At the Table Options dialog box, change the *Top* and *Bottom* measurements to 0.05 inch.
d. Click OK to close the Table Options dialog box.

3. Change the top and bottom cell margin measurements for the first row of cells by completing the following steps:
   a. Select the first row of cells (the cells containing *Name* and *Department*).
   b. Click the Properties button in the Table group.
   c. At the Table Properties dialog box, click the Cell tab.
   d. Click the Options button located in the lower right corner of the dialog box.
   e. At the Cell Options dialog box, remove the check mark from the *Same as the whole table* option.
   f. Change the *Top* and *Bottom* measurements to 0.1 inch.
   g. Click OK to close the Cell Options dialog box.
   h. Click OK to close the Table Properties dialog box.
4. Change the left cell margin measurement for specific cells by completing the following steps:
   a. Select all rows in the table *except* the top row.
   b. Click the Cell Size group dialog box launcher.
   c. At the Table Properties dialog box, make sure the Cell tab is active.
   d. Click the Options button.
   e. At the Cell Options dialog box, remove the check mark from the *Same as the whole table* option.
   f. Change the *Left* measurement to 0.3 inch.
   g. Click OK to close the Cell Options dialog box.
   h. Click OK to close the Table Properties dialog box.
5. Save **WL1-C7-P2-TSPTables.docx**.

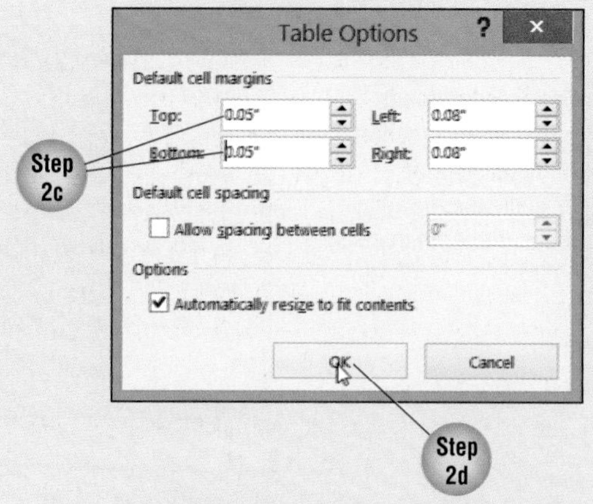

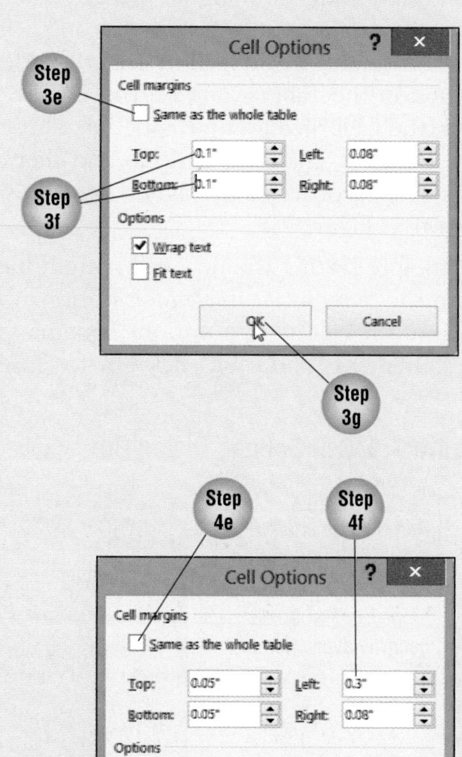

Changing Cell Direction

Text Direction

Change the direction of text in a cell using the Text Direction button in the Alignment group on the TABLE TOOLS LAYOUT tab. Each time you click the Text Direction button, the text rotates in the cell 90 degrees.

Changing Table Alignment and Dimensions

By default, a table aligns at the left margin. Change this alignment with options at the Table Properties dialog box with the Table tab selected, as shown in Figure 7.9. To change the alignment, click the desired alignment option in the *Alignment* section of the dialog box. Change table dimensions by clicking the *Preferred width* check box to insert a check mark. This makes the width measurement box active as well as the *Measure in* option box. Type a width measurement in the measurement box and specify whether the measurement type is inches or a percentage with the *Measurement in* option box.

Figure 7.9 Table Properties Dialog Box with Table Tab Selected

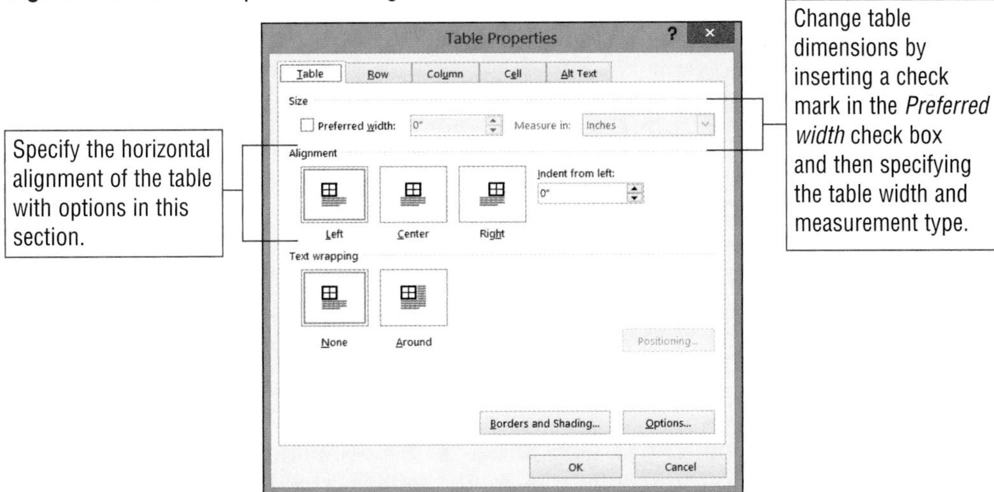

Project 2b **Changing Table Alignment and Dimensions** **Part 2 of 5**

1. With **WL1-C7-P2-TSPTables.docx** open, insert a new column and change text direction by completing the following steps:
   a. Click in any cell in the first column.
   b. Click the Insert Left button in the Rows & Columns group.
   c. With the cells in the new column selected, click the Merge Cells button in the Merge group.
   d. Type **Tri-State Products.**
   e. Click the Align Center button in the Alignment group.
   f. Click twice on the Text Direction button in the Alignment group.
   g. With *Tri-State Products* selected, click the HOME tab and then increase the font size to 16 points.

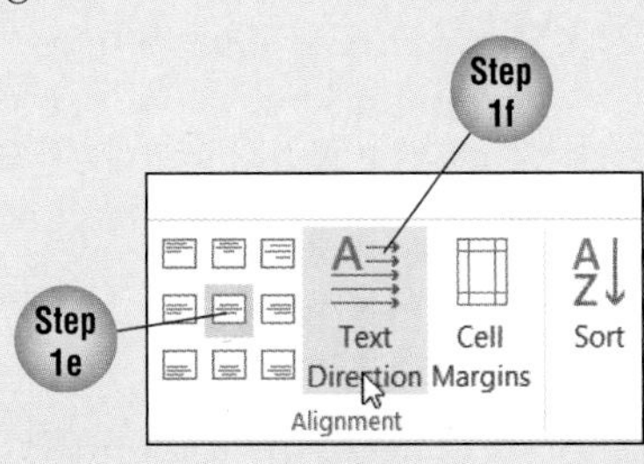

2. Automatically fit the contents by completing the following steps:
   a. Click in any cell in the table.
   b. Click the TABLE TOOLS LAYOUT tab.
   c. Click the AutoFit button in the Cell Size group and then click *AutoFit Contents* at the drop-down list.

3. Change the table dimension and alignment by completing the following steps:
   a. Click the Properties button in the Table group on the TABLE TOOLS LAYOUT tab.
   b. At the Table Properties dialog box, click the Table tab.
   c. Click the *Preferred width* check box.
   d. Select the measurement in the measurement box and then type 4.5.
   e. Click the *Center* option in the *Alignment* section.
   f. Click OK. 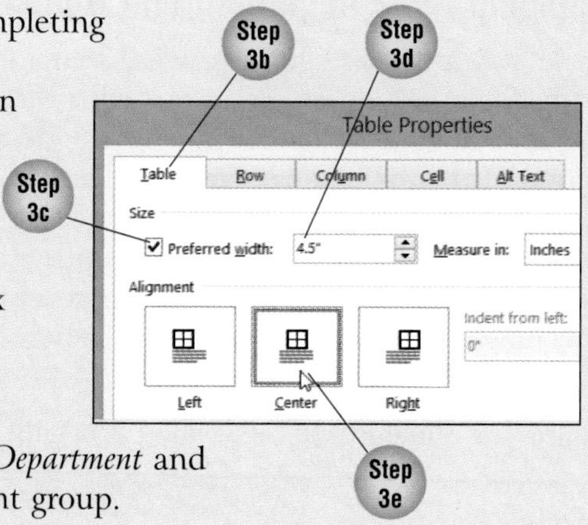
4. Select the two cells containing the text *Name* and *Department* and then click the Align Center button in the Alignment group.
5. Save **WL1-C7-P2-TSPTables.docx**.

Step 3b Step 3d Step 3c Step 3e

Table Properties
Table Row Column Cell Alt Text
Size
Preferred width: 4.5" Measure in: Inches
Alignment
Left Center Right
Indent from left: 0"

Changing Table Size with the Resize Handle

When you hover the mouse pointer over a table, a resize handle displays in the lower right corner of the table. The resize handle displays as a small, white square. Drag this resize handle to increase and/or decrease the size and proportion of the table.

Quick Steps

Move a Table
1. Position mouse pointer on table move handle until pointer displays with four-headed arrow attached.
2. Hold down left mouse button.
3. Drag table to desired position.
4. Release mouse button.

Moving a Table

Position the mouse pointer in a table and a table move handle displays in the upper left corner. Use this handle to move the table in the document. To move a table, position the mouse pointer on the table move handle until the pointer displays with a four-headed arrow attached, hold down the left mouse button, drag the table to the desired position, and then release the mouse button.

Project 2c **Resizing and Moving Tables** **Part 3 of 5**

1. With **WL1-C7-P2-TSPTables.docx** open, insert a table into the current document by completing the following steps:
   a. Press Ctrl + End to move the insertion point to the end of the document and then press the Enter key.
   b. Click the INSERT tab.
   c. Click the Object button arrow in the Text group and then click *Text from File* at the drop-down list.
   d. At the Insert File dialog box, navigate to the WL1C7 folder and then double-click ***TSPEmps.docx***.
2. Automatically fit the bottom table by completing the following steps:
   a. Click in any cell in the bottom table.
   b. Click the TABLE TOOLS LAYOUT tab.
   c. Click the AutoFit button in the Cell Size group and then click *AutoFit Contents* at the drop-down list.
3. Format the bottom table by completing the following steps:
   a. Click the TABLE TOOLS DESIGN tab.

b. Click the More button that displays at the right side of the styles thumbnails in the Table Styles group and then click the *List Table 4 - Accent 6* table style thumbnail (last column, fourth row in the *List Tables* section).

c. Click the *First Column* check box in the Table Style Options group to remove the check mark.

d. Select the first and second rows, click the TABLE TOOLS LAYOUT tab, and then click the Align Center button in the Alignment group.

e. Select the second row and then press Ctrl + B to turn on bold formatting.

Step 3b

4. Resize the bottom table by completing the following steps:

a. Position the mouse pointer on the resize handle located in the lower right corner of the bottom table.

b. Hold down the left mouse button, drag down and to the right until the width and height of the table increase approximately 1 inch, and then release the mouse button.

TRI-STATE PRODUCTS		
Name	**Employee #**	**Department**
Whitaker, Christine	1432-323-09	Financial Services
Higgins, Dennis	1230-933-21	Public Relations
Coffey, Richard	1321-843-22	Research and Development
Lee, Yong	1411-322-76	Human Resources
Fleishmann, Jim	1246-432-90	Public Relations
Schaffer, Mitchell	1388-340-44	Purchasing
Porter, Robbie	1122-361-38	Public Relations
Buchanan, Lillian	1432-857-87	Research and Development
Kensington, Jacob	1112-473-31	Human Resources

Steps 4a-4b

5. Move the bottom table by completing the following steps:

a. Move the mouse pointer over the bottom table and then position the mouse pointer on the table move handle until the pointer displays with a four-headed arrow attached.

b. Hold down the left mouse button, drag the table so it is positioned equally between the left and right margins, and then release the mouse button.

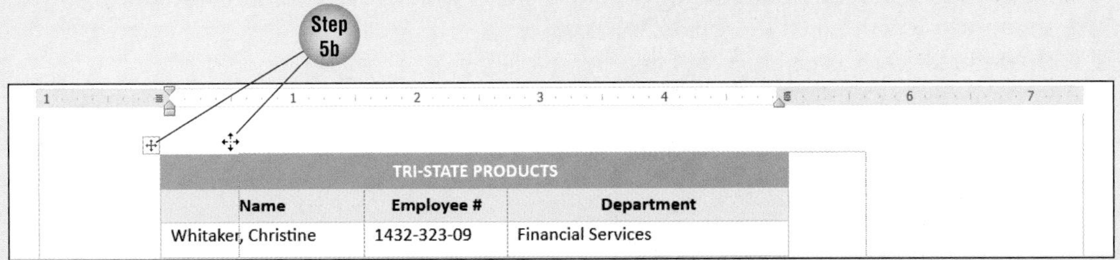

6. Select the cells in the column below the heading *Employee #* and then click the Align Top Center button in the Alignment group.

7. Save **WL1-C7-P2-TSPTables.docx**.

Quick Steps

Convert Text to a Table
1. Select text.
2. Click INSERT tab.
3. Click Table button.
4. Click *Convert Text to Table.*
5. Click OK.

Convert a Table to Text
1. Click TABLE TOOLS LAYOUT tab.
2. Click Convert to Text button.
3. Specify separator.
4. Click OK.

Convert to Text

Converting Text to a Table and a Table to Text

You can create a table and then enter text in the cells, or you can create the text and then convert it to a table. When typing the text, separate it with a separator character, such as a comma or tab. The separator character identifies where you want text divided into columns. To convert text, select the text, click the INSERT tab, click the Table button in the Tables group, and then click *Convert Text to Table* at the drop-down list.

You can convert a table to text by positioning the insertion point in any cell of the table, clicking the TABLE TOOLS LAYOUT tab, and then clicking the Convert to Text button in the Data group. At the Convert Table to Text dialog box, specify the desired separator and then click OK.

Project 2d Converting Text to a Table — Part 4 of 5

1. With **WL1-C7-P2-TSPTables.docx** open, press Ctrl + End to move the insertion point to the end of the document. (If the insertion point does not display below the second table, press the Enter key until the insertion point is below the second table.)
2. Insert the document named **TSPExecs.docx** into the current document.
3. Convert the text to a table by completing the following steps:
   a. Select the text you just inserted.
   b. Make sure the INSERT tab is active.
   c. Click the Table button in the Tables group and then click *Convert Text to Table* at the drop-down list.
   d. At the Convert Text to Table dialog box, type 2 in the *Number of columns* measurement box.
   e. Click the *AutoFit to contents* option in the *AutoFit behavior* section.
   f. Click the *Commas* option in the *Separate text at* section.
   g. Click OK.

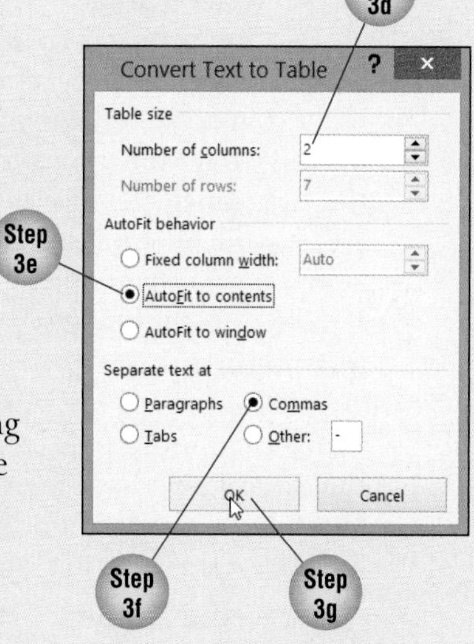

4. Select and merge the cells in the top row (the row containing the title *TRI-STATE PRODUCTS*) and then center-align the text in the merged cell.
5. Apply the List Table 4 - Accent 6 style (last column, fourth row in the *List Tables* section) and remove the check mark from the *First Column* check box in the Table Style Options group on the TABLE TOOLS DESIGN tab.
6. Drag the table so it is centered below the table above.
7. Apply the List Table 4 - Accent 6 style to the top table. Increase the width of the columns so the text *TRI-STATE PRODUCTS* is visible and the text in the second and third columns displays on one line.
8. Drag the table so it is centered above the middle table. Make sure the three tables fit on one page.
9. Click in the middle table and then convert the table to text by completing the following steps:
   a. Click the TABLE TOOLS LAYOUT tab and then click the Convert to Text button in the Data group.
   b. At the Convert Table to Text dialog box, click *Tabs* and then click OK.
10. Print **WL1-C7-P2-TSPTables.docx**.
11. Click the Undo button to return the text to a table.
12. Save **WL1-C7-P2-TSPTables.docx**.

Drawing a Table

In Project 1, you used options in the Borders group in the TABLE TOOLS DESIGN tab to draw borders around an existing table. You can also use these options to draw an entire table. To draw a table, click the INSERT tab, click the Table button in the Tables group, and then click *Draw Table* at the drop-down list; or, click the Draw Table button in the Draw group on the TABLE TOOLS LAYOUT tab. This turns the mouse pointer into a pen. Drag the pen pointer in the document to create the table. If you make a mistake while drawing a table, click the Eraser button in the Draw group on the TABLE TOOLS LAYOUT tab (which changes the mouse pointer to an eraser) and then drag over any border lines you want to erase. You can also click the Undo button to undo your most recent action.

Eraser

Project 2e Drawing and Formatting a Table — Part 5 of 5

1. With **WL1-C7-P2-TSPTables.docx** open, select and then delete three rows in the middle table from the row that begins with the name *Lee, Yong* through the row that begins with the name *Schaffer, Mitchell*.
2. Move the insertion point to the end of the document (outside of any table) and then press the Enter key.
3. Click the INSERT tab, click the Table button, and then click the *Draw Table* option at the drop-down list. (This turns the insertion point into a pen.)
4. Using the mouse, drag in the document (below the bottom table) to create the table shown at the right. If you make a mistake, click the Undo button. You can also click the Eraser button in the Draw group on the TABLE TOOLS LAYOUT tab and drag over a border line to erase it. Click the Draw Table button in the Draw group to turn the pen off.

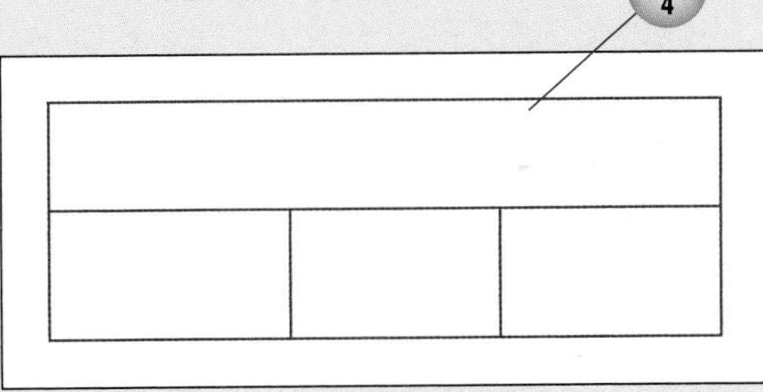

5. After drawing the table, type **Tri-State Products** in the top cell, **Washington Division** in the cell at the left, **Oregon Division** in the middle bottom cell, and **California Division** in the cell at the right.
6. Apply the Grid Table 4 - Accent 6 table style.
7. Select the table, change the font size to 12 points, turn on bold formatting, and then center-align the text in the cells.
8. Make any adjustments needed to border lines so text displays on one line in each cell.
9. Drag the table so it is centered and positioned below the bottom table.
10. Save, print, and then close **WL1-C7-P2-TSPTables.docx**.

Project 3 Sort and Calculate Sales Data — 2 Parts

You will sort data in tables on Tri-State Products sales and then insert formulas to calculate total sales, average sales, and top sales.

Sorting Text in a Table

Quick Steps

Sort Text in a Table

1. Select desired rows.
2. Click Sort button on TABLE TOOLS LAYOUT tab.
3. Specify column containing text to sort.
4. Click OK.

Sort

Use the Sort button in the Data group on the TABLE TOOLS LAYOUT tab to sort text in selected cells in a table in ascending or descending alphabetic or numeric order. To sort text, select the desired rows in the table and then click the Sort button in the Data group. At the Sort dialog box, specify the column containing the text on which you want to sort, and then click OK.

Project 3a **Sorting Text in a Table** **Part 1 of 2**

1. Open **TSPSalesTables.docx** and then save the document with Save As and name it **WL1-C7-P3-TSPSalesTables**.
2. Sort text in the top table by completing the following steps:
   a. Select all of the rows containing names (from *Novak, Diana* through *Sogura, Jeffrey*).
   b. Click the TABLE TOOLS LAYOUT tab.
   c. Click the Sort button in the Data group.
   d. At the Sort dialog box, click OK. (This sorts the last names in the first column in alphabetical order.)

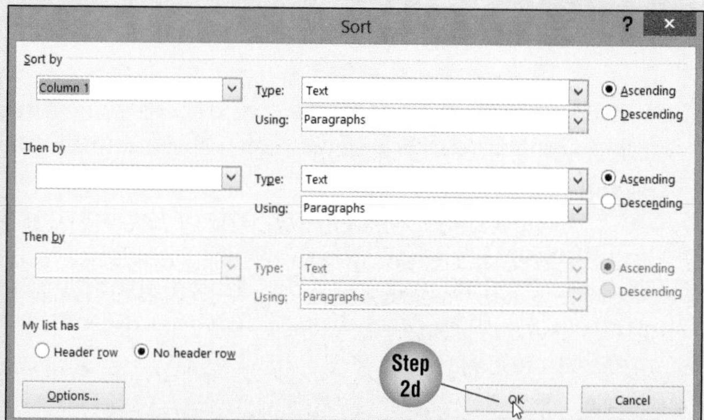

3. After looking at the table, you decide to sort by sales in 2014. To do this, complete the following steps:
   a. With the rows still selected, click the Sort button in the Data group.
   b. At the Sort dialog box, click the down-pointing arrow at the right side of the *Sort by* option box and then click *Column 2* at the drop-down list.
   c. Click the Descending option in the *Sort by* section.
   d. Click OK.
   e. Deselect the rows.
4. Save **WL1-C7-P3-TSPSalesTables.docx**.

Performing Calculations in a Table

Quick Steps

Insert a Formula in a Table

1. Click in cell.
2. Click TABLE TOOLS LAYOUT tab.
3. Click Formula button.
4. Type formula in Formula dialog box.
5. Click OK.

Formula

Use the Formula button in the Data group on the TABLE TOOLS LAYOUT tab to insert formulas that calculate data in a table. Numbers in cells in a table can be added, subtracted, multiplied, and divided. In addition, you can perform other calculations, such as determine averages, count items, and identify minimum and maximum values. You can calculate data in a Word table, but for complex calculations you should use an Excel worksheet.

To perform a calculation on data in a table, position the insertion point in the cell where you want the result of the calculation inserted and then click the Formula button in the Data group on the TABLE TOOLS LAYOUT tab. This displays the Formula dialog box, as shown in Figure 7.10. At this dialog box, accept the default formula that displays in the *Formula* text box or type the desired calculation, and then click OK.

Figure 7.10 Formula Dialog Box

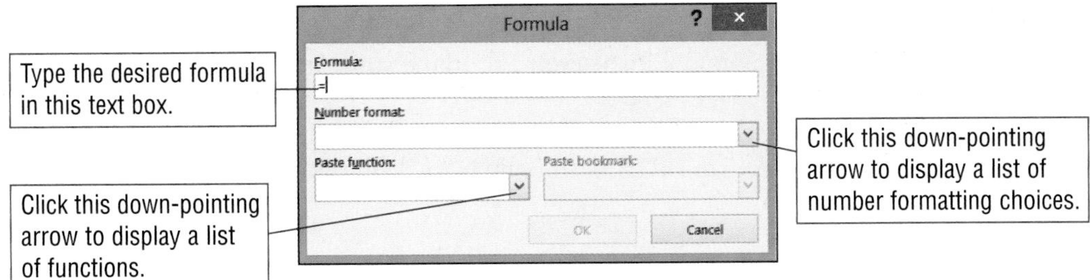

You can use four basic operators when writing a formula, including the plus sign (+) for addition, the minus sign (–) for subtraction, the asterisk (*) for multiplication, and the forward slash (/) for division. If a calculation contains two or more operators, Word calculates from left to right. If you want to change the order of calculation, use parentheses around the part of the calculation to be performed first.

In the default formula, the **SUM** part of the formula is called a ***function***. Word provides other functions you can use to write a formula. These functions are available in the *Paste function* option box in the Formula dialog box. For example, you can use the AVERAGE function to average numbers in cells.

Specify the numbering format with the *Number format* option box in the Formula dialog box. For example, if you are calculating money amounts, you can specify that the calculated numbers display with no numbers or two numbers following the decimal point.

If you make changes to the values in a formula, you need to update the result of the formula. To do this, right-click the formula result and then click *Update Field* at the shortcut menu. You can also select the formula result and then press the F9 function key, which is the Update Field keyboard shortcut. To update the results of all formulas in a table, select the entire table and then press the F9 function key.

Project 3b Inserting Formulas

Part 2 of 2

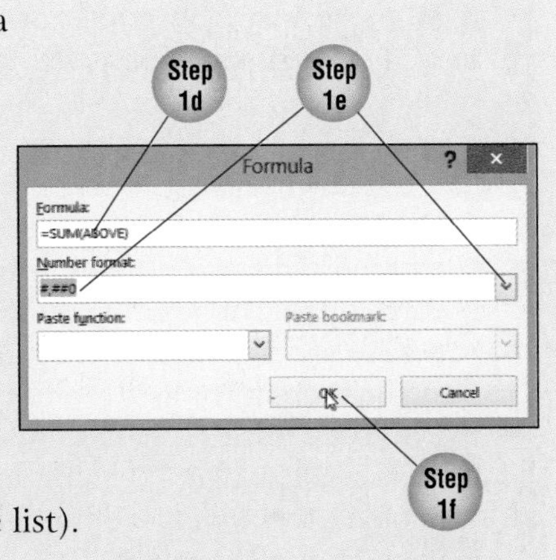

1. With **WL1-C7-P3-TSPSalesTables.docx** open, insert a formula by completing the following steps:
   a. Click in cell B9. (Cell B9 is the empty cell located immediately below the cell containing the amount *$294,653.*)
   b. Click the TABLE TOOLS LAYOUT tab.
   c. Click the Formula button in the Data group.
   d. At the Formula dialog box, make sure *=SUM(ABOVE)* displays in the *Formula* text box.
   e. Click the down-pointing arrow at the right side of the *Number format* option box and then click *#,##0* at the drop-down list (top option in the list).
   f. Click OK to close the Formula dialog box.
   g. At the table, type a dollar sign ($) before the number just inserted in cell B9.
2. Complete steps similar to those in Steps 1c through 1g to insert a formula in cell C9. (Cell C9 is the empty cell located immediately below the cell containing the amount *$300,211.*)

3. Complete steps similar to those in Steps 1c through 1g to insert in the bottom table formulas that calculate totals. Insert formulas in the cells in the *Total* row and *Total* column. When inserting formulas in cells F2 through F6, make sure the formula at the Formula dialog box displays as *=SUM(LEFT)*.
4. Insert a formula that calculates the average of amounts by completing the following steps:
   a. Click in cell B10 in the top table. (Cell B10 is the empty cell immediately right of the cell containing the word *Average*.)
   b. Click the Formula button in the Data group.
   c. At the Formula dialog box, delete the formula in the *Formula* text box *except* the equals sign.
   d. With the insertion point positioned immediately right of the equals sign, click the down-pointing arrow at the right side of the *Paste function* option box and then click *AVERAGE* at the drop-down list.
   e. With the insertion point positioned between the left and right parentheses, type **B2:B8**. (When typing cell designations in a formula, you can type either uppercase or lowercase letters.)
   f. Click the down-pointing arrow at the right side of the *Number format* option box and then click *#,##0* at the drop-down list (top option in the list).
   g. Click OK to close the Formula dialog box.
   h. Type a dollar sign ($) before the number just inserted in cell B10.

Step 4e
Formula
Formula:
=AVERAGE(B2:B8)
Number format:

5. Complete steps similar to those in Steps 4b through 4h to insert a formula in cell C10 in the top table that calculates the average of cells C2 through C8.
6. Complete steps similar to those in Steps 4b through 4h to insert a formula in cell B7 in the bottom table that calculates the average of cells B2 through B5. Complete similar steps to insert in cell C7 the average of cells C2 through C5; insert in cell D7 the average of cells D2 through D5; insert in cell E7 the average of cells E2 through E5; and insert in cell F7 the average of cells F2 through F5.
7. Insert a formula that calculates the maximum number by completing the following steps:
   a. Click in cell B11 in the top table. (Cell B11 is the empty cell immediately right of the cell containing the words *Top Sales*.)
   b. Click the Formula button in the Data group.
   c. At the Formula dialog box, delete the formula in the *Formula* text box *except* the equals sign.
   d. With the insertion point positioned immediately right of the equals sign, click the down-pointing arrow at the right side of the *Paste function* option box and then click *MAX* at the drop-down list. (You will need to scroll down the list to display the *MAX* option.)
   e. With the insertion point positioned between the left and right parentheses, type **B2:B8**.
   f. Click the down-pointing arrow at the right side of the *Number format* option box and then click *#,##0* at the drop-down list (top option in the list).
   g. Click OK to close the Formula dialog box.
   h. Type a dollar sign ($) before the number just inserted in cell B11.

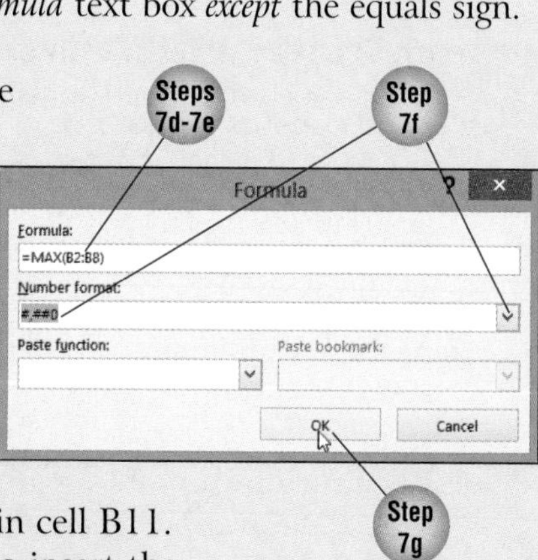

8. Complete steps similar to those in Steps 7b through 7h to insert the maximum number in cell C11.
9. Apply to each table the Grid Table 2 - Accent 6 table style and remove the check mark from the *First Column* option.
10. Drag the tables so they are centered and positioned below the title and subtitle.
11. Save, print, and then close **WL1-C7-P3-TSPSalesTables.docx**.

Project 4 Prepare and Format a SmartArt Graphic 2 Parts

You will prepare a SmartArt process graphic identifying steps in the production process and then apply formatting to enhance the graphic.

Creating SmartArt

With Word's SmartArt feature you can insert graphics such as diagrams and organizational charts in a document. SmartArt offers a variety of predesigned graphics that are available at the Choose a SmartArt Graphic dialog box, as shown in Figure 7.11. At this dialog box, by default, *All* is selected in the left panel and all available predesigned SmartArt graphics display in the middle panel.

Use SmartArt to communicate your message and ideas in a visual manner.

Inserting and Formatting a SmartArt Graphic

To insert a SmartArt graphic, click the INSERT tab and then click the SmartArt button in the Illustrations group to open the Choose a SmartArt Graphic dialog box. Predesigned SmartArt graphics display in the middle panel of the dialog box. Use the scroll bar at the right side of the middle panel to scroll down the list of choices. Click a graphic in the middle panel and its name displays in the right panel along with a description. SmartArt includes graphics for presenting a list of data; showing data processes, cycles, and relationships; and presenting data in a matrix or pyramid. Double-click a graphic in the middle panel of the dialog box and the graphic is inserted in the document.

When you double-click a graphic at the dialog box, the graphic is inserted in the document and a text pane displays at the left side of the graphic. Type text in the text pane or directly in the graphic. Apply formatting to a graphic with options at the SMARTART TOOLS DESIGN tab. This tab becomes active when the graphic is inserted in the document. With options and buttons on this tab, you add objects, change the graphic layout, apply a style to the graphic, and reset the graphic back to the original formatting.

Quick Steps

Insert a SmartArt Graphic

1. Click INSERT tab.
2. Click SmartArt button.
3. Double-click desired graphic.

SmartArt

Limit the number of shapes and the amount of text in your SmartArt graphic.

Figure 7.11 Choose a SmartArt Graphic Dialog Box

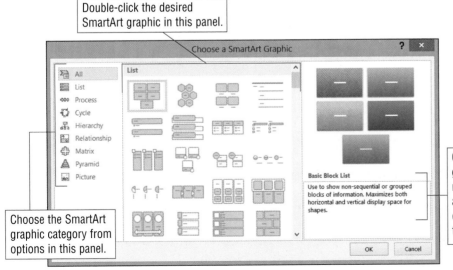

Double-click the desired SmartArt graphic in this panel.

Choose the SmartArt graphic category from options in this panel.

Click a SmartArt graphic in the middle panel and then read a description of the graphic here.

Apply formatting to a graphic with options on the SMARTART TOOLS FORMAT tab. Use options and buttons on this tab to change the size and shape of objects in the graphic; apply shape styles and WordArt styles; change the shape fill, outline, and effects; and arrange and size the graphic.

Project 4a Inserting and Formatting a SmartArt Graphic

Part 1 of 2

1. At a blank document, insert the SmartArt graphic shown in Figure 7.12 by completing the following steps:
   a. Click the INSERT tab.
   b. Click the SmartArt button in the Illustrations group.
   c. At the Choose a SmartArt Graphic dialog box, click *Process* in the left panel and then double-click the *Alternating Flow* graphic.
   d. If a *Type your text here* text pane does not display at the left side of the graphic, click the Text Pane button in the Create Graphic group to display the pane.
   e. With the insertion point positioned after the top bullet in the *Type your text here* text pane, type **Design**.
   f. Click *[Text]* that displays below *Design* and then type **Mock-up**.
   g. Continue clicking occurrences of *[Text]* and typing text so the text pane displays as shown at the right.
   h. Close the text pane by clicking the Close button (a gray X) that displays in the upper right corner of the pane. (You can also click the Text Pane button in the Create Graphic group.)
2. Change the graphic colors by clicking the Change Colors button in the SmartArt Styles group and then clicking the *Colorful Range - Accent Colors 5 to 6* option (last option in the *Colorful* section).

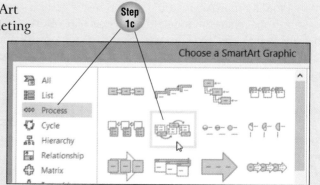

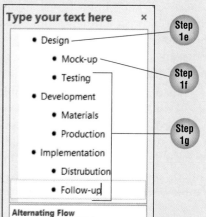

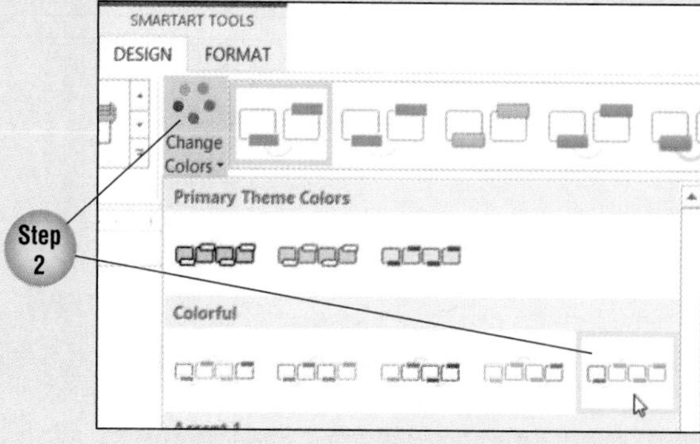

3. Apply a style by clicking the More button that displays at the right side of the option in the SmartArt Styles group and then clicking the *Inset* option (second column, first row in the *3-D* section).
4. Copy the graphic and then change the layout by completing the following steps:
   a. Click inside the SmartArt graphic border but outside any shapes.
   b. Click the HOME tab and then click the Copy button in the Clipboard group.
   c. Press Ctrl + End, press the Enter key once, and then press Ctrl + Enter to insert a page break.
   d. Click the Paste button in the Clipboard group.
   e. With the SmartArt graphic on the second page selected (the one you just pasted), click the SMARTART TOOLS DESIGN tab.
   f. Click the More button that displays at the right side of the options in the Layouts group and then click the *Continuous Block Process* layout.
   g. Click outside the graphic to deselect it.
5. Save the document and name it **WL1-C7-P4-SAGraphics**.

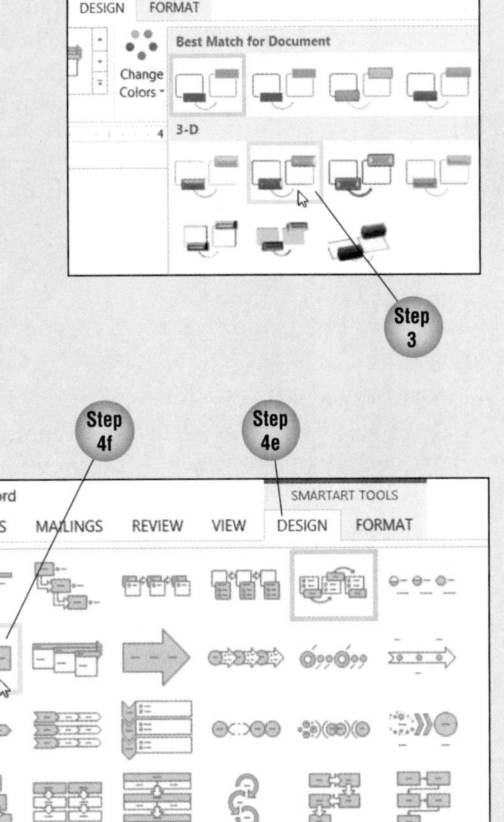

Figure 7.12 Project 4a

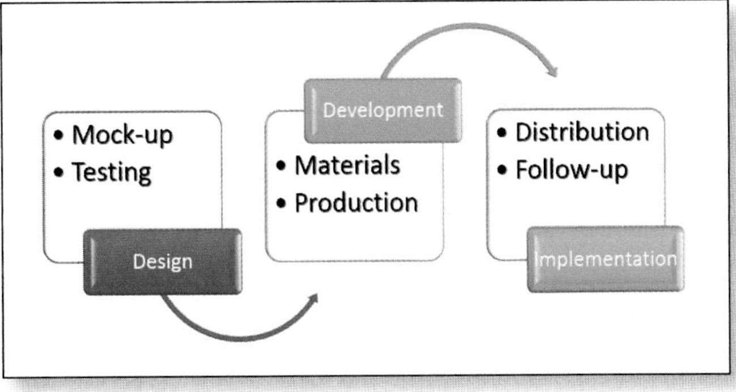

Arranging and Moving a SmartArt Graphic

Position a SmartArt graphic by clicking the Arrange button on the SMARTART TOOLS FORMAT tab, clicking the Position button, and then clicking the desired position option at the drop-down gallery. Along with positioning the SmartArt graphic, the options at the Position button drop-down gallery apply the Square text wrapping. You can also apply text wrapping by clicking the Arrange button, clicking the Wrap Text button, and then clicking the desired wrapping style at the drop-down

gallery or with options from the Layout Options button that displays outside the upper right corner of the selected SmartArt graphic. Move a SmartArt graphic by positioning the arrow pointer on the graphic border until the pointer displays with a four-headed arrow attached, holding down the left mouse button, and then dragging the graphic to the desired location. Nudge the SmartArt graphic or a shape or selected shapes in the graphic with the up, down, left, or right arrow keys on the keyboard.

Project 4b Formatting SmartArt Graphics — Part 2 of 2

1. With **WL1-C7-P4-SAGraphics.docx** open, format shapes by completing the following steps:
   a. Click the graphic on the first page to select it (a border surrounds the graphic).
   b. Click the SMARTART TOOLS FORMAT tab.
   c. In the graphic, click the rectangle shape containing the word *Design*.
   d. Hold down the Shift key and then click the shape containing the word *Development*.
   e. With the Shift key still down, click the shape containing the word *Implementation*. (All three shapes should now be selected.)
   f. Click the Change Shape button in the Shapes group.
   g. Click the *Pentagon* shape (seventh column, second row in the *Block Arrows* section).
   h. With the shapes still selected, click the Larger button in the Shapes group.
   i. With the shapes still selected, click the Shape Outline button arrow in the Shape Styles group and then click the *Dark Blue* option (ninth option in the *Standard Colors* section).
   j. Click inside the graphic border but outside any shape. (This deselects the shapes but keeps the graphic selected.)

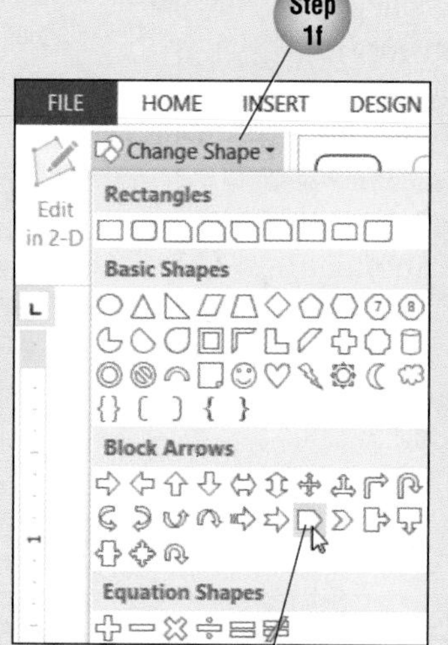

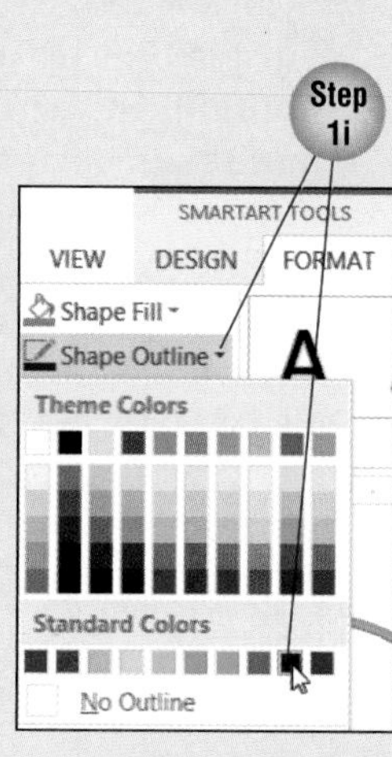

2. Change the size of the graphic by completing the following steps:
   a. Click the Size button located at the right side of the SMARTART TOOLS FORMAT tab.
   b. Click in the *Shape Height* measurement box, type 4, and then press Enter.
3. Position the graphic by completing the following steps:
   a. Click the Arrange button on the SMARTART TOOLS FORMAT tab and then click the Position button at the drop-down list.
   b. Click the *Position in Middle Center with Square Text Wrapping* option (second column, second row in the *With Text Wrapping* section).
   c. Click outside the graphic to deselect it.

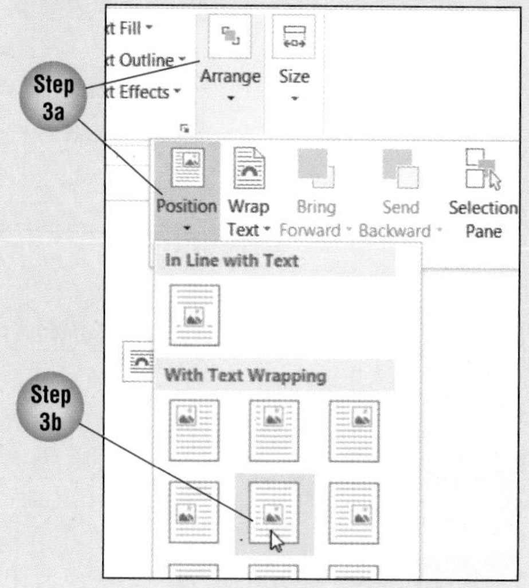

4. Format the bottom SmartArt graphic by completing the following steps:
   a. Press Ctrl + End to move to the end of the document and then click in the bottom SmartArt graphic to select it.
   b. Hold down the Shift key and then click each of the three shapes.
   c. Click the More button at the right side of the style options in the WordArt Styles group on the SMARTART TOOLS FORMAT tab.
   d. Click the *Fill - Black, Text 1, Shadow* option (first column, first row).
   e. Click the Text Outline button arrow in the WordArt Styles group and then click the *Dark Blue* option (ninth color in the *Standard Colors* section).
   f. Click the Text Effects button in the WordArt Styles group, point to *Glow* at the drop-down list, and then click the *Orange, 5 pt glow, Accent color 2* option (second column, first row in the *Glow Variations* section).
   g. Click inside the SmartArt graphic border but outside any shape.
5. Arrange the graphic by clicking the Arrange button, clicking the Position button, and then clicking the *Position in Middle Center with Square Text Wrapping* option (second column, second row in the *With Text Wrapping* section).
6. Click outside the graphic to deselect it.
7. Save, print, and then close **WL1-C7-P4-SAGraphics.docx**.

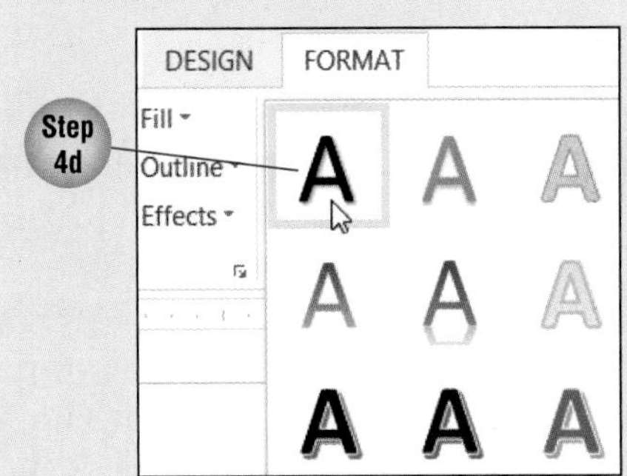

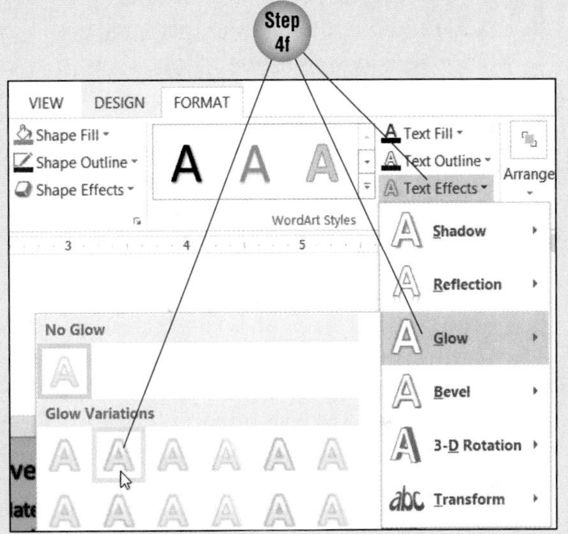

Project 5 Prepare and Format a Company Organizational Chart 1 Part

You will prepare an organizational chart for a company and then apply formatting to enhance the visual appeal of the chart.

Creating an Organizational Chart with SmartArt

If you need to visually illustrate hierarchical data, consider creating an organizational chart with a SmartArt option. To display organizational chart SmartArt options, click the INSERT tab and then click the SmartArt button in the Illustrations group. At the Choose a SmartArt Graphic dialog box, click *Hierarchy* in the left panel. Organizational chart options display in the middle panel of the dialog box. Double-click the desired organizational chart, and the chart is inserted in the document. Type text in a SmartArt graphic by selecting

Quick Steps

Insert an Organizational Chart
1. Click INSERT tab.
2. Click SmartArt button.
3. Click *Hierarchy*.
4. Double-click desired organizational chart.

the shape and then typing text in the shape, or type text in the *Type your text here* window that displays at the left side of the graphic. Format a SmartArt organizational chart with options and buttons on the SMARTART TOOLS DESIGN tab, the SMARTART TOOLS FORMAT tab, and the Layout Options button.

Project 5 Creating and Formatting a SmartArt Organizational Chart — Part 1 of 1

1. At a blank document, create the organizational chart shown in Figure 7.13. To begin, click the INSERT tab.
2. Click the SmartArt button in the Illustrations group.
3. At the Choose a SmartArt Graphic dialog box, click *Hierarchy* in the left panel of the dialog box and then double-click the *Organization Chart* option (first option in the middle panel).

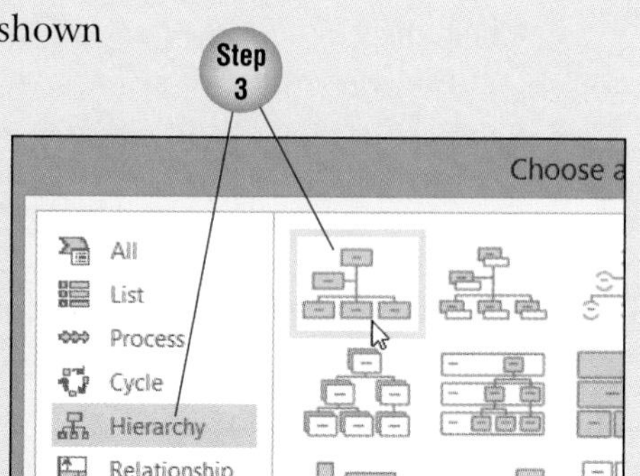

4. If a *Type your text here* pane displays at the left side of the organizational chart, close the pane by clicking the Text Pane button in the Create Graphic group.
5. Delete one of the boxes in the organizational chart by clicking the border of the box in the lower right corner to select it and then pressing the Delete key. (Make sure that the selection border that surrounds the box is a solid line and not a dashed line. If a dashed line displays, click the box border again. This should change it to a solid line.)

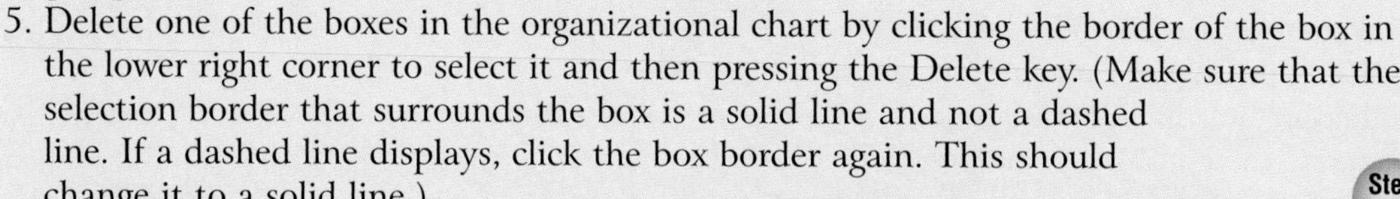

6. With the bottom right box selected, click the Add Shape button arrow in the Create Graphic group and then click the *Add Shape Below* option.
7. Click *[Text]* in the top box, type **Blaine Willis**, press Shift + Enter, and then type **President**. Click in each of the remaining boxes and type the text as shown in Figure 7.13. (Press Shift + Enter after typing the name.)
8. Click the More button located at the right side of the style options in the SmartArt Styles group and then click the *Inset* style (second column, first row in the *3-D* section).
9. Click the Change Colors button in the SmartArt Styles group and then click the *Colorful Range - Accent Colors 4 to 5* option (fourth column, first row in the *Colorful* section).
10. Click the SMARTART TOOLS FORMAT tab.
11. Click the text pane control (displays with a left-pointing arrow) that displays at the left side of the graphic border. (This displays the *Type your text here* window.)
12. Using the mouse, select all of the text that displays in the *Type your text here* window.

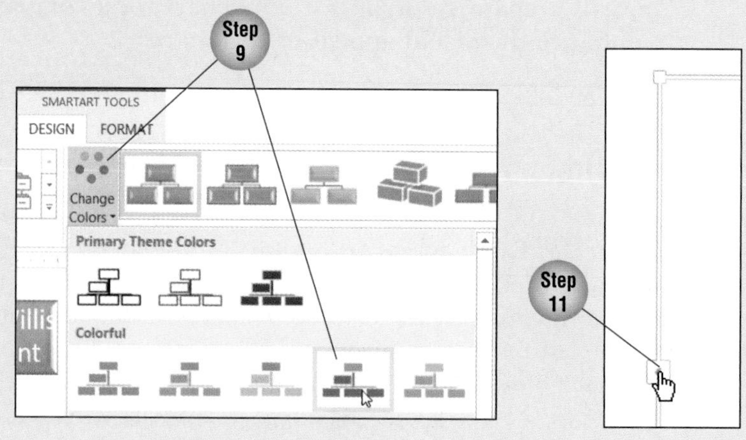

13. Click the Change Shape button in the Shapes group and then click the *Round Same Side Corner Rectangle* option (eighth option in the *Rectangles* section).
14. Click the Shape Outline button arrow in the Shape Styles group and then click the *Dark Blue* color (ninth option in the *Standard Colors* section).
15. Close the *Type your text here* window by clicking the Close button (gray X) located in the upper right corner of the window.
16. Click inside the organizational chart border but outside any shape.
17. Click the Size button located at the right side of the SMARTART TOOLS FORMAT tab, click in the *Shape Height* measurement box, and then type 4. Click in the *Shape Width* measurement box, type 6.5, and then press Enter.
18. Click outside the chart to deselect it.
19. Save the document and name it **WL1-C7-P5-OrgChart.**
20. Print and then close the document.

Figure 7.13 Project 5

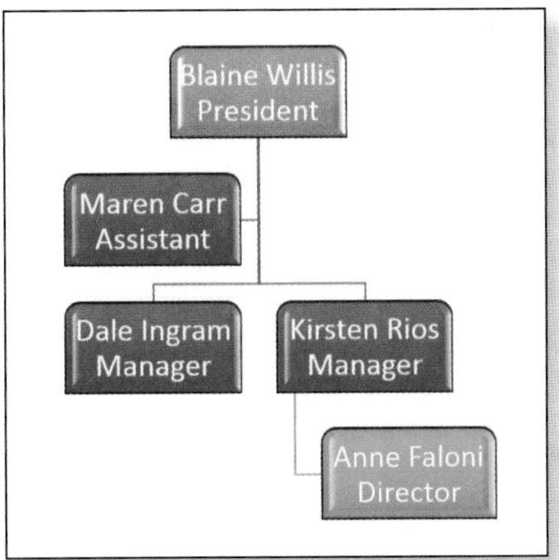

Chapter Summary

- Use the Tables feature to create columns and rows of information. Create a table with the Table button in the Tables group on the INSERT tab or with options at the Insert Table dialog box.
- A cell is the intersection between a row and a column. The lines that form the cells of the table are called gridlines.
- Move the insertion point to cells in a document using the mouse by clicking in the desired cell, or use the keyboard commands shown in Table 7.1.
- Change the table design with options and buttons on the TABLE TOOLS DESIGN tab.
- Refer to Table 7.2 for a list of mouse commands for selecting specific cells in a table and Table 7.3 for a list of keyboard commands for selecting specific cells in a table.
- Change the layout of a table with options and buttons on the TABLE TOOLS LAYOUT tab.

- Select a table, column, row, or cell using the Select button in the Table group on the TABLE TOOLS LAYOUT tab.
- Turn on and off the display of gridlines by clicking the TABLE TOOLS LAYOUT tab and then clicking the View Gridlines button in the Table group.
- Insert and delete columns and rows with buttons in the Rows & Columns group on the TABLE TOOLS LAYOUT tab.
- Merge selected cells with the Merge Cells button and split cells with the Split Cells button, both located in the Merge group on the TABLE TOOLS LAYOUT tab.
- Change column width and row height using the height and width measurement boxes in the Cell Size group on the TABLE TOOLS LAYOUT tab; by dragging move table column markers on the horizontal ruler, adjust table row markers on the vertical ruler, or gridlines in the table; or with the AutoFit button in the Cell Size group.
- Change alignment of text in cells with buttons in the Alignment group on the TABLE TOOLS LAYOUT tab.
- If a table spans two pages, you can insert a header row at the beginning of the rows that extend to the next page. To do this, click in the header row or select the desired header rows, and then click the Repeat Header Rows button in the Data group on the TABLE TOOLS LAYOUT tab.
- Quick Tables are predesigned tables you can insert in a document by clicking the INSERT tab, clicking the Table button, pointing to *Quick Tables*, and then clicking the desired table at the side menu.
- Change cell margins with options in the Table Options dialog box.
- Change text direction in a cell with the Text Direction button in the Alignment group.
- Change the table dimensions and alignment with options at the Table Properties dialog box with the Table tab selected.
- Use the resize handle to change the size of the table and the table move handle to move the table.
- Convert text to a table with the *Convert Text to Table* option at the Table button drop-down list. Convert a table to text with the Convert to Text button in the Data group on the TABLE TOOLS LAYOUT tab.
- Draw a table in a document by clicking the INSERT tab, clicking the Table button, and then clicking *Draw Table*. Using the mouse, drag in the document to create the table.
- Sort selected rows in a table with the Sort button in the Data group.
- Perform calculations on data in a table by clicking the Formula button in the Data group on the TABLE TOOLS LAYOUT tab and then specifying the formula and number format at the Formula dialog box.
- Use the SmartArt feature to insert predesigned graphics and organizational charts in a document. Click the SmartArt button on the INSERT tab to display the Choose a SmartArt Graphic dialog box.
- Format a SmartArt graphic with options and buttons on the SMARTART TOOLS DESIGN tab and the SMARTART TOOLS FORMAT tab.
- Choose a position or a text wrapping style for a SmartArt graphic with the Arrange button in the SMARTART TOOLS FORMAT tab or the Layout Options button that displays outside the upper right corner of the selected SmartArt graphic.

Commands Review

FEATURE	RIBBON TAB, GROUP	BUTTON	OPTION
AutoFit table contents	TABLE TOOLS LAYOUT, Cell Size		
cell alignment	TABLE TOOLS LAYOUT, Alignment		
Choose a SmartArt Graphic dialog box	INSERT, Illustrations		
convert table to text	TABLE TOOLS LAYOUT, Data		
convert text to table	INSERT, Tables		*Convert Text to Table*
delete column	TABLE TOOLS LAYOUT, Rows & Columns		*Delete Columns*
delete row	TABLE TOOLS LAYOUT, Rows & Columns		*Delete Rows*
delete table	TABLE TOOLS LAYOUT, Rows & Columns		*Delete Table*
draw table	INSERT, Tables		*Draw Table*
Formula dialog box	TABLE TOOLS LAYOUT, Data	*fx*	
insert column left	TABLE TOOLS LAYOUT, Rows & Columns		
insert column right	TABLE TOOLS LAYOUT, Rows & Columns		
insert row above	TABLE TOOLS LAYOUT, Rows & Columns		
insert row below	TABLE TOOLS LAYOUT, Rows & Columns		
Insert Table dialog box	INSERT, Tables		*Insert Table*
merge cells	TABLE TOOLS LAYOUT, Merge		
Quick Table	INSERT, Tables		*Quick Tables*
repeat header row	TABLE TOOLS LAYOUT, Data		
sort text in table	TABLE TOOLS LAYOUT, Data		
Split Cells dialog box	TABLE TOOLS LAYOUT, Merge		
table	INSERT, Tables		
Table Options dialog box	TABLE TOOLS LAYOUT, Alignment		
text direction	TABLE TOOLS LAYOUT, Alignment		
view gridlines	TABLE TOOLS LAYOUT, Table		

Concepts Check Test Your Knowledge 

Completion: In the space provided at the right, indicate the correct term, command, or number.

1. The Table button is located on this tab. ____________________
2. This is another name for the lines that form the cells of the table. ____________________
3. Use this keyboard shortcut to move the insertion point to the preceding cell in a table. ____________________
4. Use this keyboard shortcut to move the insertion point to a tab within a cell in a table. ____________________
5. This tab contains table styles you can apply to a table. ____________________
6. Click this button on the TABLE TOOLS LAYOUT tab to insert a column at the left side of the column containing the insertion point. ____________________
7. Insert and delete columns and rows with buttons in this group on the TABLE TOOLS LAYOUT tab. ____________________
8. One method for changing column width in a table is dragging this on the horizontal ruler. ____________________
9. Use this button in the Cell Size group to make the column widths in a table automatically fit the contents. ____________________
10. Change the table alignment at this dialog box with the Table tab selected. ____________________
11. Position the mouse pointer in a table and this displays in the lower right corner of the table. ____________________
12. Position the mouse pointer in a table and this displays in the upper left corner. ____________________
13. Display the Formula dialog box by clicking the Formula button in this group on the TABLE TOOLS LAYOUT tab. ____________________
14. A variety of predesigned graphics and organizational charts are available at this dialog box. ____________________
15. The SmartArt button is located on this tab. ____________________
16. If you need to visually illustrate hierarchical data, consider creating this with the SmartArt feature. ____________________

Skills Check Assess Your Performance

Assessment

1 CREATE, FORMAT, AND MODIFY A TRAINING SCHEDULE TABLE

1. At a blank document, create a table with four columns and five rows.
2. Type text in cells as shown in Figure 7.14.
3. Insert a new column at the right side of the table and then type the following text in the new cells:
   - Trainer
   - Marsden
   - Trujillo
   - Yong
   - Stein
4. Change the width of each column to the following measurements:
   - First column = 0.8 inch
   - Second column = 1.2 inches
   - Third column = 0.7 inch
   - Fourth column = 1.3 inches
   - Fifth column = 0.9 inch
5. Insert a new row above the first row and then with the new row selected, merge the cells. Type **APPLICATION TRAINING SCHEDULE** in the cell and then center the text.
6. Select the second row (contains the text *Section*, *Training*, *Days*, and so on) and then bold and center the text.
7. Display the TABLE TOOLS DESIGN tab, apply the Grid Table 4 table style (first column, fourth row in the *Grid Tables* section), and then remove the check mark from the *First Column* check box.
8. Horizontally center the table on the page. ***Hint: Do this at the Table Properties dialog box with the Table tab selected.***
9. Save the document and name it **WL1-C7-A1-SchTable**.
10. Print and then close **WL1-C7-A1-SchTable.docx**.

Figure 7.14 Assessment 1

Section	Training	Days	Time
WD100	Word Level 1	MWF	9:00-10:00 a.m.
WD110	Word Level 2	TTh	1:30-3:00 p.m.
EX100	Excel Level 1	MTW	3:00-4:00 p.m.
EX110	Excel Level 2	TTh	2:00-3:30 p.m.

Assessment 2

CREATE, FORMAT, AND MODIFY A PROPERTY REPLACEMENT COSTS TABLE

1. At a blank document, create a table with two columns and six rows.
2. Type the text in the cells in the table as shown in Figure 7.15. (Press the Enter key after typing the word *PROPERTY* in the first cell.)
3. Merge the cells in the top row and then center the text in the merged cell.
4. Right-align the cells containing the money amounts as well as the blank cell below the last amount (cells B2 through B6).
5. Click in the *Accounts receivable* cell and then insert a row below. Type **Equipment** in the new cell at the left, and type **$83,560** in the new cell at the right.
6. Select rows 2 through 6 and then sort the amounts in column 2 in descending order.
7. Insert a formula in cell B7 that sums the amounts in cells B2 through B6 and change the number format to *#,##0*. Insert a dollar sign before the amount in cell B7.
8. Automatically fit the contents of the cells.
9. Apply the Grid Table 4 - Accent 1 table style (second column, fourth row in the *Grid Tables* section) and remove the check mark from the *First Column* check box.
10. Click the Border Styles button arrow, click the *Double solid lines, 1/2 pt* option (first column, third row in the *Theme Borders* section), and then draw a border around all four sides of the table.
11. Save the document and name it **WL1-C7-A2-CostsTable**.
12. Print and then close **WL1-C7-A2-CostsTable.docx**.

Figure 7.15 Assessment 2

PROPERTY REPLACEMENT COSTS	
Accounts receivable	$95,460
Business personal property	$1,367,340
Legal liability	$75,415
Earnings and expenses	$945,235
Total	

Assessment 3

FORMAT A TABLE ON TRANSPORTATION SERVICES

1. Open **ServicesTable.docx** and then save the document with Save As and name it **WL1-C7-A3-ServicesTable**.
2. Insert a new column at the left and then merge the cells. Type Metro Area in the merged cell, press the Enter key, and then type Transportation Services.
3. Select the text in the first column, change the font size to 16 points, and then click the Text Direction button twice to rotate the text. ***Hint: The Text Direction button is located in the Alignment group on the TABLE TOOLS LAYOUT tab.***
4. Center-align (use the Align Center button) the text in the first column.
5. Change the width of the first column to 0.9 inch and the width of the third column to 1.1 inches.
6. Apply the Grid Table 5 Dark - Accent 5 table style (sixth column, fifth row in the *Grid Tables* section).
7. Horizontally center the table on the page.
8. Indent the text in the three cells below the cell containing the text *Valley Railroad,* as shown in Figure 7.16.
9. Apply italic and bold formatting to the four headings in the second column (*Langley City Transit*, *Valley Railroad*, *Mainline Bus*, and *Village Travel Card*).
10. Save, print, and then close **WL1-C7-A3-ServicesTable.docx**.

Figure 7.16 Assessment 3

Metro Area Transportation Services	Service	Telephone
	Langley City Transit	
	Subway and bus information	(507) 555-3049
	Service status hotline	(507) 555-4123
	Travel information	(507) 555-4993
	Valley Railroad	
	Railway information	(202) 555-2300
	Status hotline	(202) 555-2343
	Travel information	(202) 555-2132
	Mainline Bus	
	Bus routes	(507) 555-6530
	Emergency hotline	(507) 555-6798
	Travel information	(507) 555-7542
	Village Travel Card	
	Village office	(507) 555-1232
	Card inquiries	(507) 555-1930

Assessment

4 CREATE AND FORMAT A COMPANY SMARTART GRAPHIC

1. At a blank document, create the SmartArt graphic shown in Figure 7.17 with the following specifications:
   a. Use the Titled Matrix SmartArt graphic.
   b. Apply the Colorful - Accent Colors SmartArt style.
   c. Apply the Polished SmartArt style.
   d. With the middle shape selected, apply the Intense Effect - Green, Accent 6 shape style (located on the SMARTART TOOLS FORMAT tab).
   e. Type all of the text shown in Figure 7.17.
   f. Select only the SmartArt graphic (not a specific shape) and then apply the Fill - Black, Text 1, Outline - Background 1, Hard Shadow - Background 1 WordArt style (first column, third row) to the text.
   g. Change the height of the SmartArt graphic to 3.2 inches and the width to 5.3 inches.
   h. Change the position of the SmartArt graphic to *Position in Top Center with Square Text Wrapping*.
2. Save the document and name it **WL1-C7-A4-OCGraphic**.
3. Print and then close **WL1-C7-A4-OCGraphic.docx**.

Figure 7.17 Assessment 4

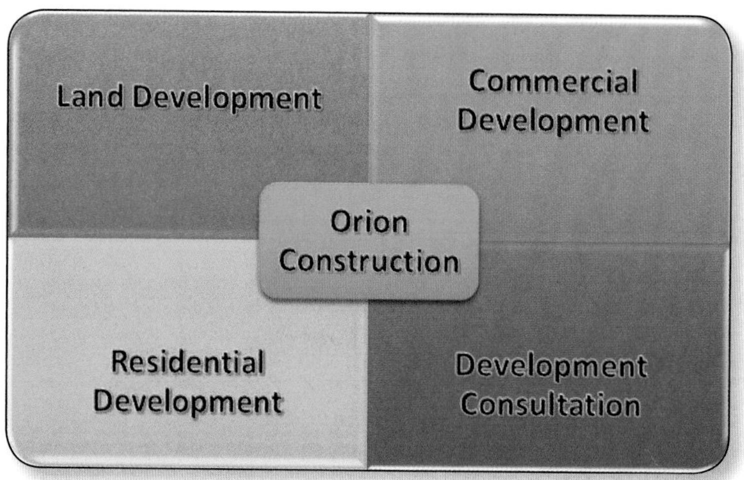

Assessment

5 CREATE AND FORMAT A COMPANY ORGANIZATIONAL CHART

1. At a blank document, create the organizational chart shown in Figure 7.18 with the following specifications:
   a. Use the Hierarchy SmartArt graphic.
   b. With the top text box selected, insert a shape above.
   c. Select the text box at the right in the third row and then add a shape below.
   d. Type the text shown in the organizational chart in Figure 7.18.
   e. Apply the Colorful Range - Accent Colors 3 to 4 SmartArt style.
   f. Increase the height to 4.5 inches and the width to 6.5 inches.
   g. Position the organizational chart in the middle of the page with square text wrapping.
2. Save the document and name it **WL1-C7-A5-OrgChart**.
3. Print and then close **WL1-C7-A5-OrgChart.docx**.

Figure 7.18 Assessment 5

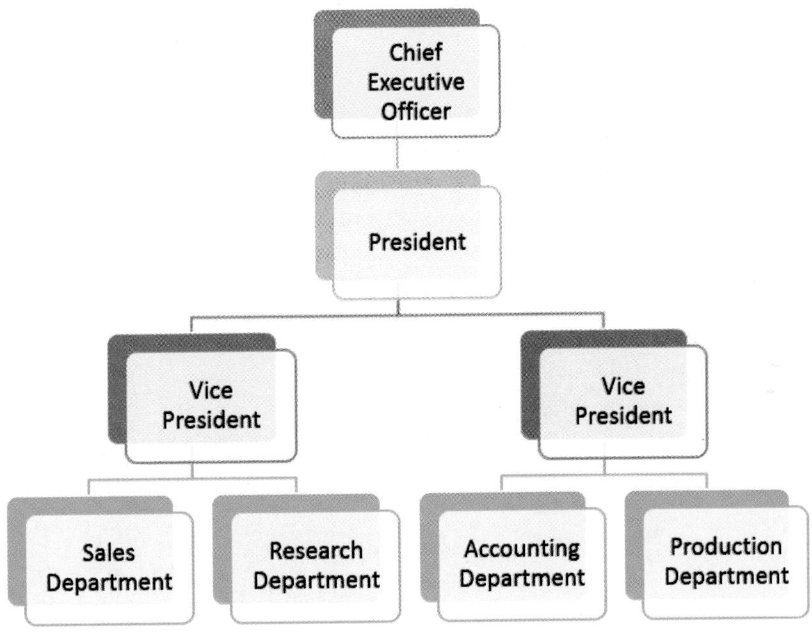

Assessment 6

INSERT FORMULAS IN A TABLE

1. In this chapter, you learned how to insert formulas in a table. Experiment with writing formulas (consider using the Help feature or other reference) and then open **FinAnalysis.docx**. Save the document with Save As and name it **WL1-C7-A6-FinAnalysis**.
2. Apply the Grid Table 4 - Accent 6 table style to the table and then apply other formatting so your table appears similar to the table in Figure 7.19.
3. Insert a formula in cell B13 that sums the amounts in cells B6 through B12. Type a dollar sign before the amount. Complete similar steps to insert formulas and dollar signs in cells C13, D13, and E13.
4. Insert a formula in cell B14 that subtracts the amount in B13 from the amount in B4. ***Hint: The formula should look like this:*** **=(B4-B13)**. Type a dollar sign before the amount. Complete similar steps to insert formulas and dollar signs in cells C14, D14, and E14.
5. Save, print, and then close **WL1-C7-A6-FinAnalysis.docx**.

Figure 7.19 Assessment 6

TRI-STATE PRODUCTS				
Financial Analysis				
	2012	**2013**	**2014**	**2015**
Revenue	$1,450,348	$1,538,239	$1,634,235	$1,523,455
Expenses				
Facilities	$250,220	$323,780	$312,485	$322,655
Materials	$93,235	$102,390	$87,340	$115,320
Payroll	$354,390	$374,280	$380,120	$365,120
Benefits	$32,340	$35,039	$37,345	$36,545
Marketing	$29,575	$28,350	$30,310	$31,800
Transportation	$4,492	$5,489	$5,129	$6,349
Miscellaneous	$4,075	$3,976	$4,788	$5,120
Total				
Net Revenue				

Visual Benchmark Demonstrate Your Proficiency

1 CREATE A COVER LETTER CONTAINING A TABLE

1. Click the FILE tab, click the *New* option, and then double-click the *Single spaced (blank)* template.
2. At the single-spaced blank document, type the letter shown in Figure 7.20. Create and format the table in the letter as shown in the figure. ***Hint: Apply the Grid Table 4 - Accent 1 table style.***
3. Save the completed document and name it **WL1-C7-VB1-CoverLtr**.
4. Print and then close **WL1-C7-VB1-CoverLtr.docx**.

Figure 7.20 Visual Benchmark 1

10234 Larkspur Drive
Cheyenne, WY 82002
July 15, 2015

Dr. Theresa Sullivan
Rocky Mountain News
100 Second Avenue
Cheyenne, WY 82001

Dear Dr. Sullivan:

Your advertised opening for a corporate communications staff writer describes interesting challenges. As you can see from the table below, my skills and experience are excellent matches for the position.

QUALIFICATIONS AND SKILLS	
Your Requirement	**My Experience, Skills, and Value Offered**
Two years of business writing experience	Four years of experience creating diverse business messages, from corporate communications to feature articles and radio broadcast material.
Ability to complete projects by deadline	Proven project coordination skills and tight deadline focus. My current role as producer of a daily three-hour talk-radio program requires planning, coordination, and execution of many detailed tasks, always in the face of inflexible deadlines.
Oral presentation skills	Unusually broad experience, including high-profile roles as an on-air radio presence and "the voice" for an on-hold telephone message company.
Relevant education (BA or BS)	BA in Mass Communications; one year post-graduate study in Multimedia Communications.

As you will note from the enclosed résumé, my experience encompasses corporate, print media, and multimedia environments. I offer a diverse and proven skill set that can help your company create and deliver its message to various audiences to build image, market presence, and revenue. I look forward to meeting with you to discuss the value I can offer your company.

Sincerely,

Marcus Tolliver

Enclosure: Résumé

2 CREATE AND FORMAT A SMARTART GRAPHIC

1. At a blank document, create the document shown in Figure 7.21. Create and format the SmartArt graphic as shown in the figure. ***Hint: Use the Step Up Process graphic***. Change the width of the SmartArt graphic to 6.5 inches.
2. Save the completed document and name it **WL1-C7-VB2-SalesGraphic**.
3. Print and then close **WL1-C7-VB2-SalesGraphic.docx**.

Figure 7.21 Visual Benchmark 2

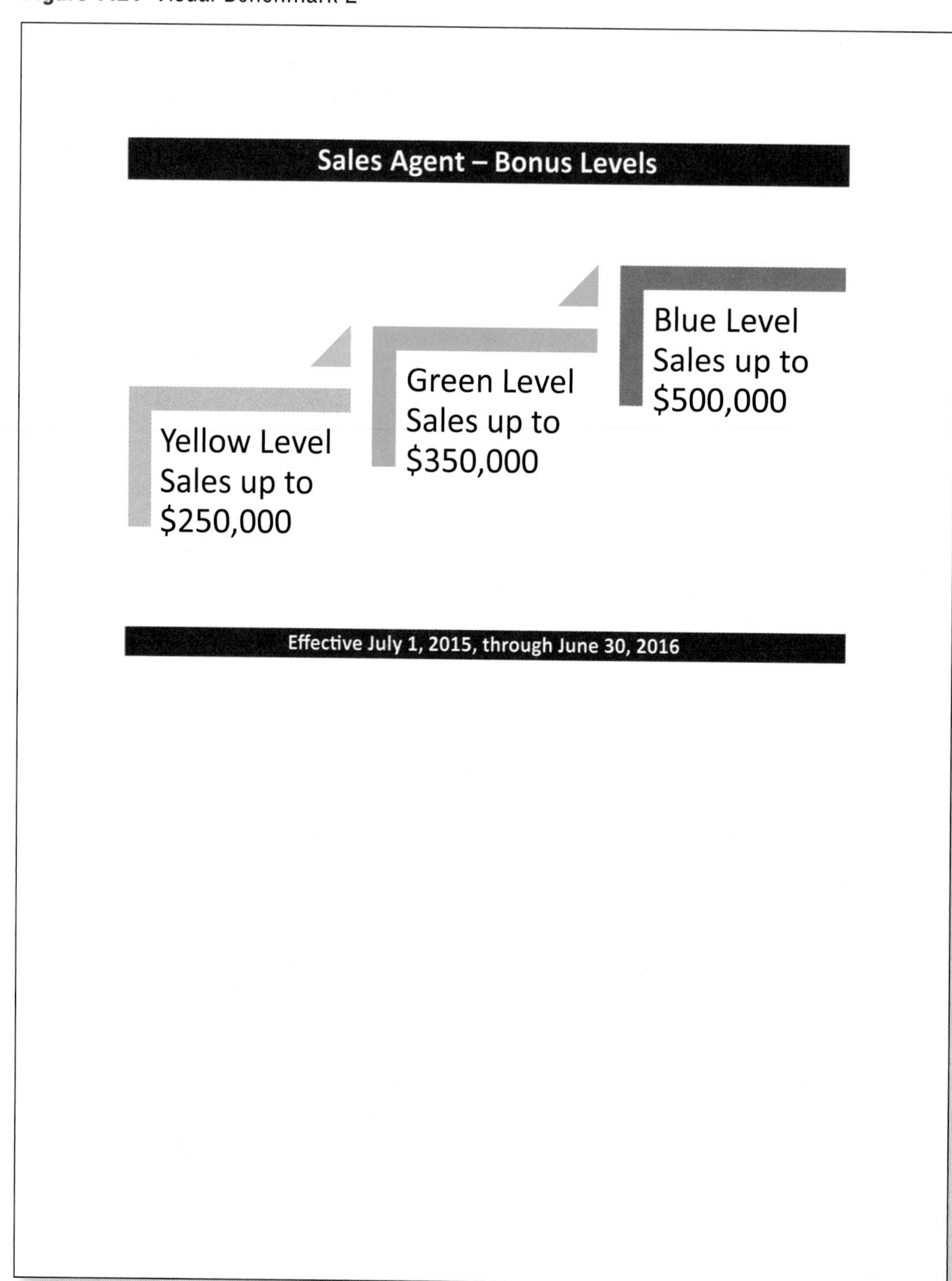

Case Study Apply Your Skills

Part 1

You have recently been hired as an accounting clerk for a landscaping business, Landmark Landscaping, which has two small offices in your city. The accounting clerk prior to you kept track of monthly sales using Word, and the manager would prefer that you continue using that application. Open the file named **LLMoSales.docx** and then save the document with Save As and name it **WL1-C7-CS-LLMoSales.** After reviewing the information, you decide that a table would be a better format for maintaining and displaying the data. Convert the data to a table and modify its appearance so that it is easy to read and understand. Insert a total row at the bottom of the table and then insert formulas to sum the totals in the columns containing amounts. Apply formatting to the table to enhance the appearance of the table. Determine a color theme for the table and then continue that same color theme when preparing other documents for Landmark Landscaping. Save, print, and then close the document.

Part 2

The president of Landmark Landscaping has asked you to prepare an organizational chart for the company that will become part of the company profile. Create a SmartArt organizational chart with the following company titles (in the order shown below):

President

Westside Manager

Landscape Architect

Landscape Director

Assistant

Eastside Manager

Landscape Architect

Landscape Director

Assistant

Format the organizational chart to enhance the appearance of the chart and apply colors that match the color scheme you chose for the company in Part 1. Save the document and name it **WL1-C7-CS-LLOrgChart**. Print and then close the document.

Part 3

As part of the company profile, the president of the company would like to include a graphic that represents the services offered by the company and use the graphic as a company marketing tool. Use SmartArt to create a graphic that contains the following services: Maintenance Contracts, Planting Services, Landscape Design, and Landscape Consultation. Format the SmartArt graphic to enhance the appearance of the graphic and apply colors that match the color scheme you chose for the company in Part 1. Save the document and name it **WL1-C7-CS-LLServices**. Print and then close the document.

Part 4

Help

The office manager has started a training document with information on using SmartArt. He has asked you to add information on keyboard shortcuts for working with shapes in a SmartArt graphic. Use the Help feature to learn about the keyboard shortcuts available for working with shapes and then create a table and insert the information in the table. Format the table to enhance the appearance of the table and apply colors that match the color scheme you chose for the company in Part 1. Save the document and name it **WL1-C7-CS-SAShortcuts**. Print and then close the document.

Part 5

One of the landscape architects has asked you to prepare a table containing information on trees that need to be ordered next month. She would also like to have you include the Latin names for the trees, since this information is important when ordering. Create a table that contains the common name of each tree, the Latin name, the number required, and the price per tree, as shown in Figure 7.22. Use the Internet (or any other resource available to you) to find the Latin name of each tree listed in Figure 7.22. Create a column in the table that multiplies the number of trees required by the price and include this formula for each tree. Format and enhance the table so it is attractive and easy to read. Save the document and name it **WL1-C7-CS-LLTrees**. Print and then close the document.

Figure 7.22 Case Study, Part 5

Douglas-fir, 15 required, $1.99 per tree
White Elm, 10 required, $2.49 per tree
Western Hemlock, 10 required, $1.89 per tree
Red Maple, 8 required, $6.99 per tree
Ponderosa Pine, 5 required, $2.69 per tree

MICROSOFT® WORD

Merging Documents

PERFORMANCE OBJECTIVES

Upon successful completion of Chapter 8, you will be able to:

- **Create a data source file**
- **Create a main document and merge with a data source file**
- **Create an envelope, labels, or directory main document and then merge with a data source file**
- **Create custom fields for a merge**
- **Edit main documents and data source files**
- **Input text during a merge**

Tutorials

8.1 Merging Documents
8.2 Creating a Data Source File
8.3 Creating a Main Document
8.4 Merging Envelopes and Labels
8.5 Merging a Directory
8.6 Editing a Data Source File
8.7 Inputting Text During a Merge
8.8 Using the Mail Merge Wizard

Word includes a Mail Merge feature you can use to create customized letters, envelopes, labels, directories, email messages, and faxes. The Mail Merge feature is useful for situations when you need to send the same letter to a number of people and create an envelope for each letter. Use Mail Merge to create a main document that contains a letter, envelope, or other data and then merge the main document with a data source. In this chapter, you will use Mail Merge to create letters, envelopes, labels, and directories. Model answers for this chapter's projects appear on the following pages.

Note: Before beginning the projects, copy to your storage medium the WL1C8 subfolder from the WL1 folder on the CD that accompanies this textbook and then make WL1C8 the active folder.

Model Answers

February 23, 2015

«AddressBlock»

«GreetingLine»

McCormack Funds is lowering its expense charges beginning May 1, 2015. The reduction in expense charges mean that more of your account investment performance in the «Fund» is returned to you, «Title» «Last_Name». The reductions are worth your attention because most of our competitors' fees have gone up.

Lowering expense charges is noteworthy because before the reduction, McCormack expense deductions were already among the lowest, far below most mutual funds and variable annuity accounts with similar objectives. At the same time, services for you, our client, will continue to expand. If you would like to discuss this change, please call us at (212) 555-2277. Your financial future is our main concern at McCormack.

Sincerely,

Jodie Langstrom
Director, Financial Services

XX
WL1-C8-P1-MFMD.docx

Project 1 Merge Letters to Customers

WL1-C8-P1-MFMD.docx

February 23, 2015

Mr. Kenneth Porter
7645 Tenth Street
Apt. 314
New York, NY 10192

Dear Mr. Porter:

McCormack Funds is lowering its expense charges beginning May 1, 2015. The reduction in expense charges mean that more of your account investment performance in the Mutual Investment Fund is returned to you, Mr. Porter. The reductions are worth your attention because most of our competitors' fees have gone up.

Lowering expense charges is noteworthy because before the reduction, McCormack expense deductions were already among the lowest, far below most mutual funds and variable annuity accounts with similar objectives. At the same time, services for you, our client, will continue to expand. If you would like to discuss this change, please call us at (212) 555-2277. Your financial future is our main concern at McCormack.

Sincerely,

Jodie Langstrom
Director, Financial Services

XX
WL1-C8-P1-MFMD.docx

Page 1

WL1-C8-P1-MFLtrs.docx

February 23, 2015

Ms. Carolyn Renquist
13255 Meridian Street
New York, NY 10435

Dear Ms. Renquist:

McCormack Funds is lowering its expense charges beginni
charges mean that more of your account investment perf
you, Ms. Renquist. The reductions are worth your attentio
gone up.

Lowering expense charges is noteworthy because before t
were already among the lowest, far below most mutual f
objectives. At the same time, services for you, our client,
discuss this change, please call us at (212) 555-2277. Your
McCormack.

Sincerely,

Jodie Langstrom
Director, Financial Services

XX
WL1-C8-P1-MFMD.docx

Page 2

February 23, 2015

Dr. Amil Ranna
433 South 17th
Apt. 17-D
New York, NY 10322

Dear Dr. Ranna:

McCormack Funds is lowering its expense charges beginni
charges mean that more of your account investment perf
you, Dr. Ranna. The reductions are worth your attention b
gone up.

Lowering expense charges is noteworthy because before t
were already among the lowest, far below most mutual f
objectives. At the same time, services for you, our client,
discuss this change, please call us at (212) 555-2277. Your
McCormack.

Sincerely,

Jodie Langstrom
Director, Financial Services

XX
WL1-C8-P1-MFMD.docx

Page 3

February 23, 2015

Mrs. Wanda Houston
566 North 22nd Avenue
New York, NY 10634

Dear Mrs. Houston:

McCormack Funds is lowering its expense charges beginning May 1, 2015. The reduction in expense charges mean that more of your account investment performance in the Quality Care Fund is returned to you, Mrs. Houston. The reductions are worth your attention because most of our competitors' fees have gone up.

Lowering expense charges is noteworthy because before the reduction, McCormack expense deductions were already among the lowest, far below most mutual funds and variable annuity accounts with similar objectives. At the same time, services for you, our client, will continue to expand. If you would like to discuss this change, please call us at (212) 555-2277. Your financial future is our main concern at McCormack.

Sincerely,

Jodie Langstrom
Director, Financial Services

XX
WL1-C8-P1-MFMD.docx

Page 4

Mr. Kenneth Porter
7645 Tenth Street
Apt. 314
New York, NY 10192

Ms. Carolyn Renquist
13255 Meridian Street
New York, NY 10435

Project 2 Merge Envelopes

WL1-C8-P2-MFEnvs.docx

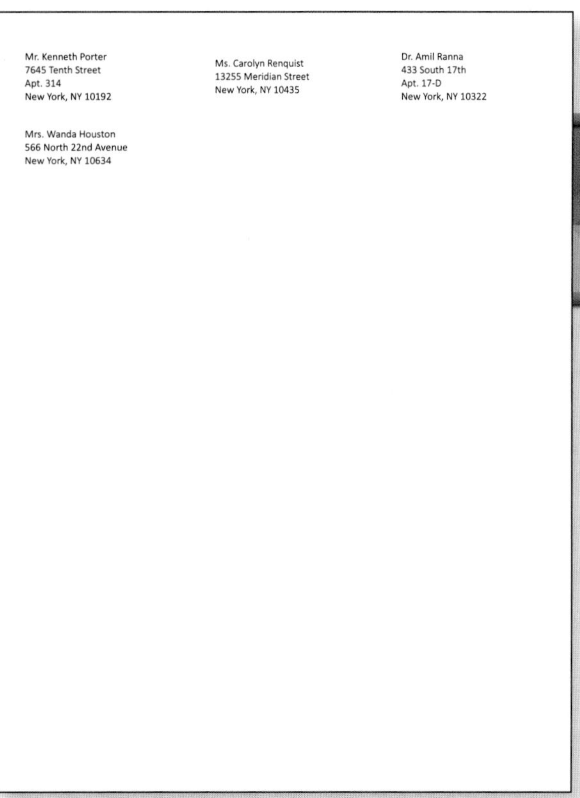

Mr. Kenneth Porter
7645 Tenth Street
Apt. 314
New York, NY 10192

Ms. Carolyn Renquist
13255 Meridian Street
New York, NY 10435

Dr. Amil Ranna
433 South 17th
Apt. 17-D
New York, NY 10322

Mrs. Wanda Houston
566 North 22nd Avenue
New York, NY 10634

Project 3 Merge Mailing Labels

WL1-C8-P3-MFLabels.docx

Last Name	First Name	Fund
Porter	Kenneth	Mutual Investment Fund
Renquist	Carolyn	Quality Care Fund
Ranna	Amil	Priority One Fund
Houston	Wanda	Quality Care Fund

Project 4 Merge a Directory

WL1-C8-P4-Directory.docx

Mr. Martin Saunders
231 South 41st Street
P.O. Box 3321
Baltimore, MD 20156

Ms. Amanda Perkins
9033 North Ridge Drive
Apt. #401
Baltimore, MD 20487

Ms. Anita Grenwald
580 Capital Lane
#1002-B
Baltimore, MD 20384

Mr. Steve Dutton
3490 East 145th
Apt. B
Baltimore, MD 20468

Mrs. Darlene Fernandez
12115 South 42nd
#20-G
Baltimore, MD 20376

Mrs. Kaycee Stahl
450 Washington Ave.
Baltimore, MD 20376

Project 5 Select Records and Merge Mailing Labels

WL1-C8-P5-SFLabels.docx

Name	Home Phone	Cell Phone
Saunders, Martin	410-555-3492	410-555-1249
Delaney, Antonia	410-555-2009	410-555-3492
Perkins, Amanda	410-555-5743	410-555-0695
Hogan, Gregory	410-555-3448	410-555-9488
Grenwald, Anita	410-555-6784	410-555-1200
Childers, Jillian	410-555-3833	410-555-7522
Bellamy, Rebecca	410-555-4755	410-555-8833
Benoit, Victoria	410-555-3482	410-555-9378
Fernandez, Darlene	410-555-7833	410-555-4261
Kaszycki, Brian	410-555-3842	410-555-9944
Stahl, Kaycee	410-555-2331	410-555-2321
Davis, Jennae	410-555-5774	410-555-9435

Project 6 Edit Records in a Data Source File

WL1-C8-P6-Directory.docx

Model Answers

February 23, 2015

Mr. Kenneth Porter
7645 Tenth Street
Apt. 314
New York, NY 10192

Dear Mr. Porter:

McCormack Funds is lowering its expense charges beginning May 1, 2015. The reduction in exp
charges mean that more of your account investment performance in the Mutual Investment Fu
returned to you, Mr. Porter. The reductions are worth your attention because most of our comp
fees have gone up.

Lowering expense charges is noteworthy because before the reduction, McCormack expense d
were already among the lowest, far below most mutual funds and variable annuity accounts w
objectives. At the same time, services for you, our client, will continue to expand. If you would
discuss this change, please call our service representative, Marilyn Smythe, at (646) 555-8944.

Sincerely,

Jodie Langstrom
Director, Financial Services

XX
WL1-C8-P1-MFMD.docx

Page 1

February 23, 2015

Ms. Carolyn Renquist
13255 Meridian Street
New York, NY 10435

Dear Ms. Renquist:

McCormack Funds is lowering its exp
charges mean that more of your acc
you, Ms. Renquist. The reductions ar
gone up.

Lowering expense charges is notewo
were already among the lowest, far b
objectives. At the same time, service
discuss this change, please call our se

Sincerely,

Jodie Langstrom
Director, Financial Services

XX
WL1-C8-P1-MFMD.docx

Page 2

February 23, 2015

Dr. Amil Ranna
433 South 17th
Apt. 17-D
New York, NY 10322

Dear Dr. Ranna:

McCormack Funds is lowering its exp
charges mean that more of your acc
you, Dr. Ranna. The reductions are w
gone up.

Lowering expense charges is notewo
were already among the lowest, far b
objectives. At the same time, service
discuss this change, please call our se

Sincerely,

Jodie Langstrom
Director, Financial Services

XX
WL1-C8-P1-MFMD.docx

Page 3

February 23, 2015

Mrs. Wanda Houston
566 North 22nd Avenue
New York, NY 10634

Dear Mrs. Houston:

McCormack Funds is lowering its expense charges beginning May 1, 2015. The reduction in expense charges mean that more of your account investment performance in the Quality Care Fund is returned to you, Mrs. Houston. The reductions are worth your attention because most of our competitors' fees have gone up.

Lowering expense charges is noteworthy because before the reduction, McCormack expense deductions were already among the lowest, far below most mutual funds and variable annuity accounts with similar objectives. At the same time, services for you, our client, will continue to expand. If you would like to discuss this change, please call our service representative, Thomas Rivers, at (646) 555-0793.

Sincerely,

Jodie Langstrom
Director, Financial Services

XX
WL1-C8-P1-MFMD.docx

Page 4

Project 7 Add Fill-in Fields to a Main Document

WL1-C8-P7-MFLtrs.docx

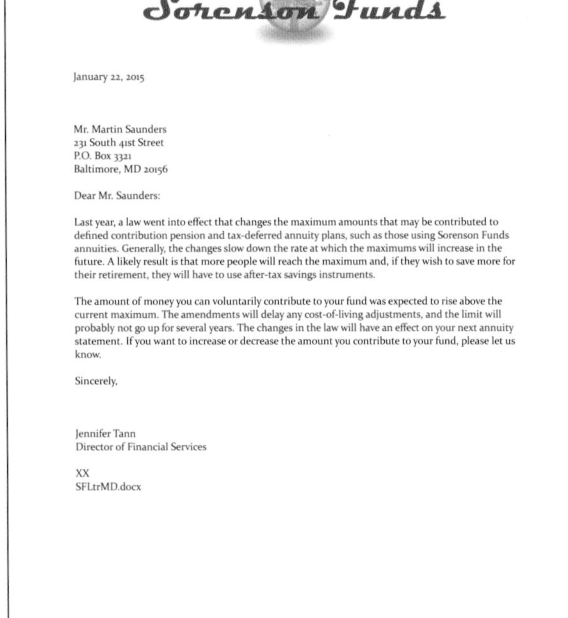

Sorenson Funds

January 22, 2015

Mr. Martin Saunders
231 South 41st Street
P.O. Box 3321
Baltimore, MD 20156

Dear Mr. Saunders:

Last year, a law went into effect that changes the maximum amounts that may be contributed to defined contribution pension and tax-deferred annuity plans, such as those using Sorenson Funds annuities. Generally, the changes slow down the rate at which the maximums will increase in the future. A likely result is that more people will reach the maximum and, if they wish to save more for their retirement, they will have to use after-tax savings instruments.

The amount of money you can voluntarily contribute to your fund was expected to rise above the current maximum. The amendments will delay any cost-of-living adjustments, and the limit will probably not go up for several years. The changes in the law will have an effect on your next annuity statement. If you want to increase or decrease the amount you contribute to your fund, please let us know.

Sincerely,

Jennifer Tann
Director of Financial Services

XX
SFLtrMD.docx

6250 Aurora Boulevard ✦ Baltimore, MD 20372 ✦ 1-888-555-0344

Page 1

Sorenson Funds

January 22, 2015

Mrs. Antonia Delaney
11220 East Madison
Rosedale, MD 21237

Dear Mrs. Delaney:

Last year, a law went into effect that changes the maximum amounts that may be contributed to defined contribution pension and tax-deferred annuity plans, such as those using Sorenson Funds annuities. Generally, the changes slow down the rate at which the maximums will increase in the future. A likely result is that more people will reach the maximum and, if they wish to save more for their retirement, they will have to use after-tax savings instruments.

The amount of money you can voluntarily contribute to your fund was expected to rise above the current maximum. The amendments will delay any cost-of-living adjustments, and the limit will probably not go up for several years. The changes in the law will have an effect on your next annuity statement. If you want to increase or decrease the amount you contribute to your fund, please let us know.

Sincerely,

Jennifer Tann
Director of Financial Services

XX
SFLtrMD.docx

6250 Aurora Boulevard ✦ Baltimore, MD 20372 ✦ 1-888-555-0344

Page 2

Project 8 Use Mail Merge Wizard

WL1-C8-P8-SFLtrs.docx

Project 1 Merge Letters to Customers — 3 Parts

You will create a data source file and a letter main document and then merge the main document with the records in the data source file.

Completing a Merge

Use buttons and options on the MAILINGS tab to complete a merge. A merge generally takes two files: the ***data source*** file and the ***main document***. The main document contains the standard text along with fields identifying where variable information is inserted during the merge. The data source file contains the variable information that will be inserted in the main document.

Start Mail Merge

Use the Start Mail Merge button on the MAILINGS tab to identify the type of main document you want to create and use the Select Recipients button to create a data source file or specify an existing data source file. You can also use the Mail Merge Wizard to guide you through the merge process.

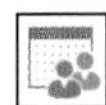

Select Recipients

Creating a Data Source File

Before creating a data source file, determine what type of correspondence you will be creating and the type of information you will need to insert in the correspondence. Word provides predetermined field names you can use when creating the data source file. Use these field names if they represent the data you are creating. Variable information in a data source file is saved as a ***record***. A record contains all of the information for one unit (for example, a person, family, customer, client, or business). A series of fields makes one record, and a series of records makes a data source file.

Quick Steps

Create a Data Source File

1. Click MAILINGS tab.
2. Click Select Recipients button.
3. Click *Type a New List* at drop-down list.
4. Type data in predesigned or custom fields.
5. Click OK.

Create a data source file by clicking the Select Recipients button in the Start Mail Merge group on the MAILINGS tab and then clicking *Type a New List* at the drop-down list. At the New Address List dialog box, shown in Figure 8.1, use the predesigned fields offered by Word or edit the fields by clicking the Customize Columns button. At the Customize Address List dialog box that displays, insert new fields or delete existing fields and then click OK. With the desired fields established,

Figure 8.1 New Address List Dialog Box

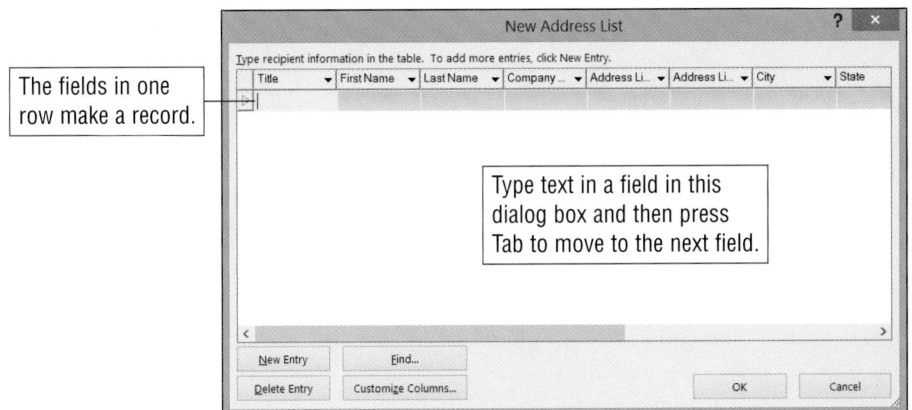

type the required data. Note that fields in the main document correspond to the column headings in the data source file. When all records have been entered, click OK. At the Save Address List dialog box, navigate to the desired folder, type a name for the data source file, and then click OK. Word saves a data source file as an Access database. You do not need Access on your computer to complete a merge with a data source file.

Project 1a Creating a Data Source File Part 1 of 3

1. At a blank document, click the MAILINGS tab.
2. Click the Start Mail Merge button in the Start Mail Merge group and then click *Letters* at the drop-down list.
3. Click the Select Recipients button in the Start Mail Merge group and then click *Type a New List* at the drop-down list.

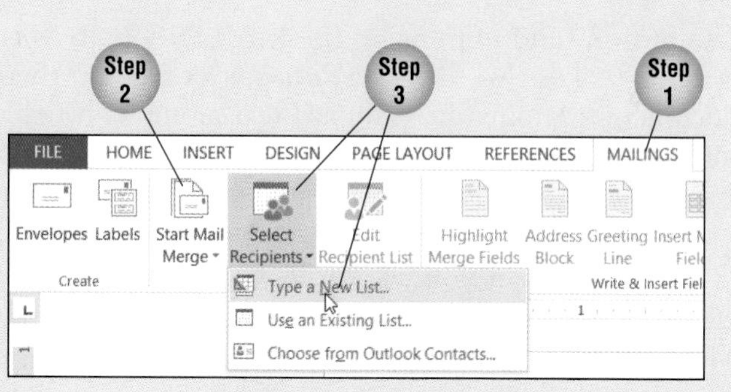

4. At the New Address List dialog box, Word provides a number of predesigned fields. Delete the fields you do not need by completing the following steps:
   a. Click the Customize Columns button.
   b. At the Customize Address List dialog box, click *Company Name* to select it and then click the Delete button.
   c. At the message that displays, click the Yes button.
   d. Complete steps similar to those in 4b and 4c to delete the following fields:
      Country or Region
      Home Phone
      Work Phone
      E-mail Address

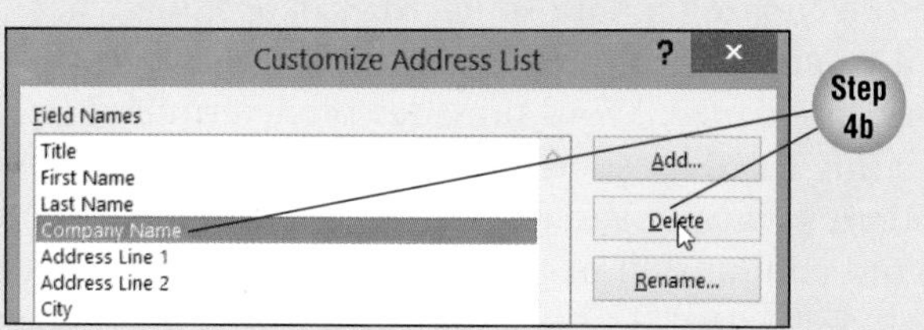

5. Insert a custom field by completing the following steps:
   a. At the Customize Address List dialog box, click the Add button.
   b. At the Add Field dialog box, type **Fund** and then click OK.
   c. Click the OK button to close the Customize Address List dialog box.

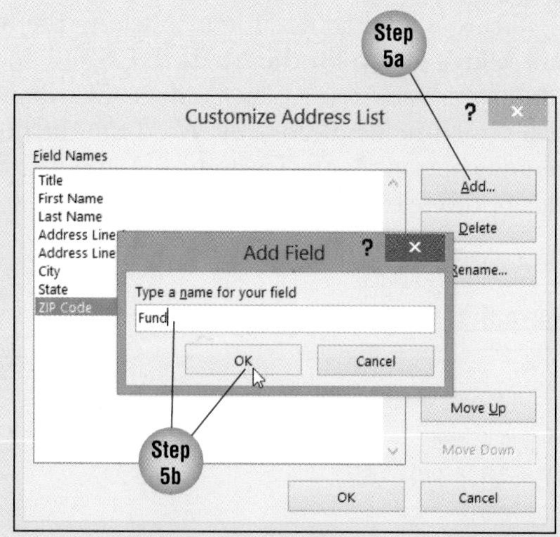

6. At the New Address List dialog box, enter the information for the first client shown in Figure 8.2 by completing the following steps:
   a. Type **Mr.** in the Title field and then press the Tab key. (This moves the insertion point to the *First Name* field. You can also press Shift + Tab to move to the previous field.)
   b. Type **Kenneth** and then press the Tab key.
   c. Type **Porter** and then press the Tab key.
   d. Type **7645 Tenth Street** and then press the Tab key.

e. Type **Apt. 314** and then press the Tab key.
f. Type **New York** and then press the Tab key.
g. Type **NY** and then press the Tab key.
h. Type **10192** and then press the Tab key.
i. Type **Mutual Investment Fund** and then press the Tab key. (This makes the Title field active in the next row.)
j. With the insertion point positioned in the Title field, complete steps similar to those in 6a through 6i to enter the information for the three other clients shown in Figure 8.2 (reading the records from left to right).

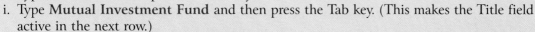

7. After entering all of the information for the last client in Figure 8.2 (Mrs. Wanda Houston), click the OK button located in the bottom right corner of the New Address List dialog box.
8. At the Save Address List dialog box, navigate to the WL1C8 folder on your storage medium, type **WL1-C8-P1-MFDS** in the *File name* text box, and then click the Save button.

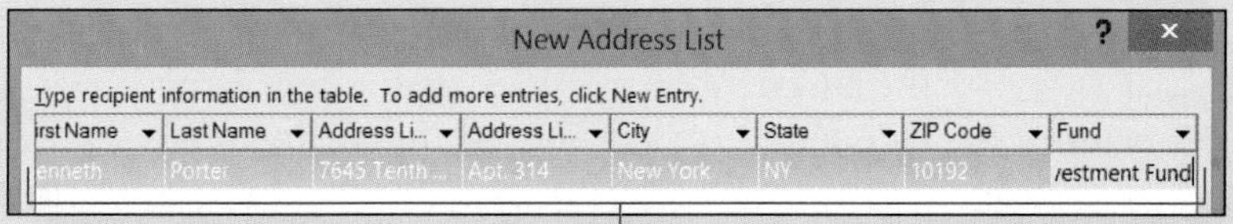

New Address List

Type recipient information in the table. To add more entries, click New Entry.

irst Name	Last Name	Address Li...	Address Li...	City	State	ZIP Code	Fund
enneth	Porter	7645 Tenth ...	Apt. 314	New York	NY	10192	vestment Fund

Steps 6a-6i

Figure 8.2 Project 1a

Title	= Mr.	Title	= Ms.
First Name	= Kenneth	First Name	= Carolyn
Last Name	= Porter	Last Name	= Renquist
Address Line 1	= 7645 Tenth Street	Address Line 1	= 13255 Meridian Street
Address Line 2	= Apt. 314	Address Line 2	= (leave this blank)
City	= New York	City	= New York
State	= NY	State	= NY
Zip Code	= 10192	Zip Code	= 10435
Fund	= Mutual Investment Fund	Fund	= Quality Care Fund
Title	= Dr.	Title	= Mrs.
First Name	= Amil	First Name	= Wanda
Last Name	= Ranna	Last Name	= Houston
Address Line 1	= 433 South 17th	Address Line 1	= 566 North 22nd Avenue
Address Line 2	= Apt. 17-D	Address Line 2	= (leave this blank)
City	= New York	City	= New York
State	= NY	State	= NY
Zip Code	= 10322	Zip Code	= 10634
Fund	= Priority One Fund	Fund	= Quality Care Fund

Creating a Main Document

When you begin a mail merge, you specify the type of main document you are creating. After creating and typing the records in the data source file, type the main document. Insert in the main document fields identifying where you want the variable information inserted when the document is merged with the data source file. Use buttons in the Write & Insert Fields group to insert fields and field blocks in the main document.

Quick Steps

Create a Main Document

1. Click MAILINGS tab.
2. Click Start Mail Merge button.
3. Click desired document type at drop-down list.
4. Type main document text and insert fields as needed.

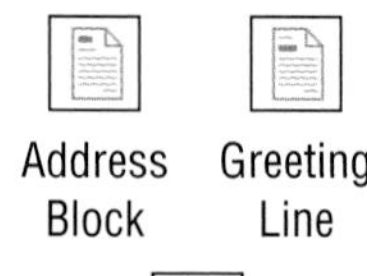

Address Block   Greeting Line

Insert Merge Field

Insert all of the fields required for the inside address of a letter with the Address Block button in the Write & Insert Fields group. Click this button and the Insert Address Block dialog box displays with a preview of how the fields will be inserted in the document to create the inside address; the dialog box also contains buttons and options for customizing the fields. Click OK and the «AddressBlock» field is inserted in the document. The «AddressBlock» field is an example of a composite field that groups a number of fields together (such as *Title*, *First Name*, *Last Name*, *Address Line 1*, and so on).

Click the Greeting Line button and the Insert Greeting Line dialog box displays with options for customizing how the fields are inserted in the document to create the greeting line. When you click OK at the dialog box, the «GreetingLine» composite field is inserted in the document.

If you want to insert an individual field from the data source file, click the Insert Merge Field button. This displays the Insert Merge Field dialog box with a list of fields from the data source file. Click the Insert Merge Field button arrow and a drop-down list displays containing the fields in the data source file.

A field or composite field is inserted in the main document surrounded by chevrons (« and »). The chevrons distinguish fields in the main document and do not display in the merged document. If you want merged data formatted, you can format the merge fields at the main document.

Project 1b Creating a Main Document Part 2 of 3

1. At the blank document, create the letter shown in Figure 8.3. Begin by clicking the *No Spacing* style thumbnail in the Styles group on the HOME tab.
2. Press the Enter key six times and then type **February 23, 2015**.
3. Press the Enter key four times and then insert the address composite field by completing the following steps:
   a. Click the MAILINGS tab and then click the Address Block button in the Write & Insert Fields group.
   b. At the Insert Address Block dialog box, click the OK button.
   c. Press the Enter key twice.
4. Insert the greeting line composite field by completing the following steps:
   a. Click the Greeting Line button in the Write & Insert Fields group.
   b. At the Insert Greeting Line dialog box, click the down-pointing arrow at the right of the option box containing the comma (the box to the right of the box containing *Mr. Randall*).
   c. At the drop-down list that displays, click the colon.
   d. Click OK to close the Insert Greeting Line dialog box.
   e. Press the Enter key twice.

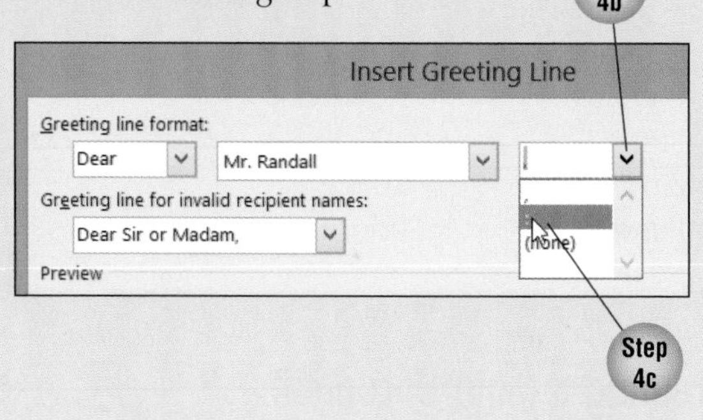

5. Type the letter shown in Figure 8.3 to the point where «Fund» displays and then insert the «Fund» field by clicking the Insert Merge Field button arrow and then clicking *Fund* at the drop-down list.
6. Type the letter to the point where the «Title» field displays and then insert the «Title» field by clicking the Insert Merge Field button arrow and then clicking *Title* at the drop-down list.
7. Press the spacebar and then insert the «Last_Name» field by clicking the Insert Merge Field button arrow and then clicking *Last_Name* at the drop-down list.
8. Type the remainder of the letter shown in Figure 8.3. (Insert your initials instead of *XX* at the end of the letter.)
9. Save the document and name it **WL1-C8-P1-MFMD**.

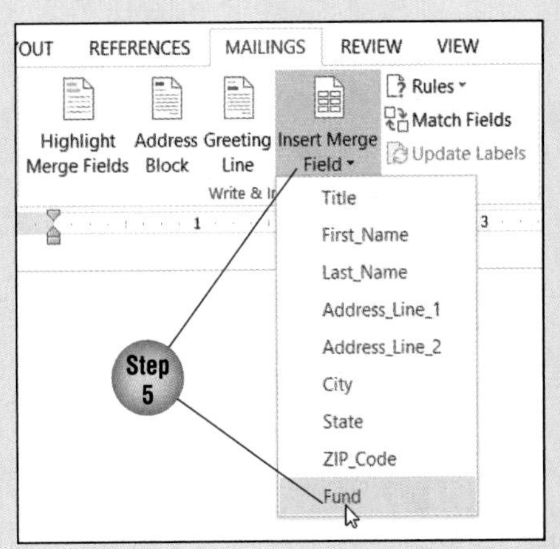

Figure 8.3 Project 1b

February 23, 2015

«AddressBlock»

«GreetingLine»

McCormack Funds is lowering its expense charges beginning May 1, 2015. The reductions in expense charges mean that more of your account investment performance in the «Fund» is returned to you, «Title» «Last_Name». The reductions are worth your attention because most of our competitors' fees have gone up.

Lowering expense charges is noteworthy because before the reduction, McCormack expense deductions were already among the lowest, far below most mutual funds and variable annuity accounts with similar objectives. At the same time, services for you, our client, will continue to expand. If you would like to discuss this change, please call us at (212) 555-2277. Your financial future is our main concern at McCormack.

Sincerely,

Jodie Langstrom
Director, Financial Services

XX
WL1-C8-P1-MFMD.docx

Previewing a Merge

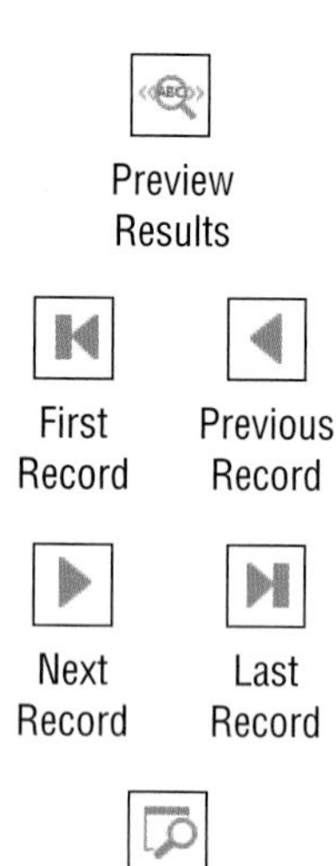

To view how the main document will appear when merged with the first record in the data source file, click the Preview Results button on the MAILINGS tab. You can view the main document merged with other records by using the navigation buttons in the Preview Results group. This group contains the First Record, Previous Record, Next Record, and Last Record buttons and the Go to Record text box. Click the button that will display the main document merged with the desired record. Viewing the merged document before printing is helpful to ensure that the merged data is correct. To use the Go to Record text box, click in the text box, type the number of the desired record, and then press Enter. Turn off the preview feature by clicking the Preview Results button.

The Preview Results group on the MAILINGS tab also includes a Find Recipient button. If you want to search for and preview merged documents with specific entries, click the Preview Results button and then click the Find Recipient button. At the Find Entry dialog box that displays, type the specific field entry for which you are searching in the *Find* text box and then click the Find Next button. Continue clicking the Find Next button until Word displays a message telling you that there are no more entries that contain the text you typed.

Checking for Errors

Check for Errors

Before merging documents, you can check for errors using the Check for Errors button in the Preview Results group on the MAILINGS tab. Click this button and the Checking and Reporting Errors dialog box, shown in Figure 8.4, displays containing three options. Click the first option, *Simulate the merge and report errors in a new document,* to tell Word to test the merge, not make any changes, and report errors in a new document. Choose the second option, *Complete the merge, pausing to report each error as it occurs,* and Word will merge the documents and display errors as they occur during the merge. Choose the third option, *Complete the merge without pausing. Report errors in a new document,* and Word will complete the merge without pausing and insert any errors in a new document.

Merging Documents

To complete the merge, click the Finish & Merge button in the Finish group on the MAILINGS tab. At the drop-down list that displays, you can choose to merge the records and create a new document, send the merged documents directly to the printer, or send the merged documents by email.

Figure 8.4 Checking and Reporting Errors Dialog Box

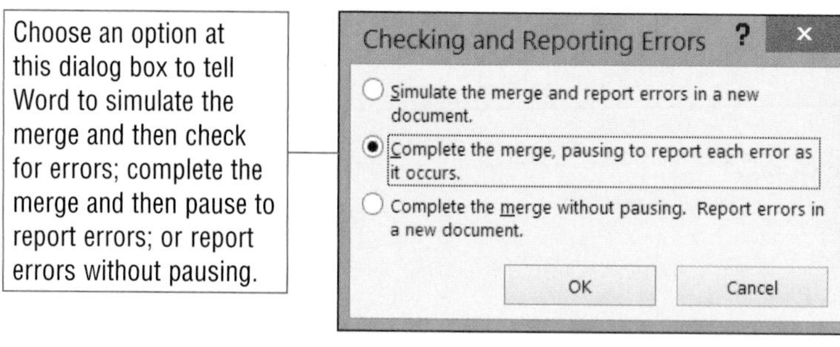

To merge the documents and create a new document with the merged records, click the Finish & Merge button and then click *Edit Individual Documents* at the drop-down list. At the Merge to New Document dialog box, make sure *All* is selected in the *Merge records* section and then click OK. This merges the records in the data source file with the main document and inserts the merged documents in a new document. You can also display the Merge to New Document dialog box by pressing Alt + Shift + N. Press Alt + Shift + M to display the Merge to Printer dialog box.

Identify specific records you want merged with options at the Merge to New Document dialog box. Display this dialog box by clicking the Finish & Merge button on the MAILINGS tab and then clicking the *Edit Individual Documents* option at the drop-down list. Click the *All* option in the Merge to New Document dialog box to merge all records in the data source and click the *Current record* option if you want to merge only the current record. If you want to merge specific adjacent records, click in the *From* text box, type the beginning record number, press the Tab key, and then type the ending record number in the *To* text box.

Quick Steps

Merge Documents

1. Click Finish & Merge button.
2. Click *Edit Individual Documents* at drop-down list.
3. Make sure *All* is selected in Merge to New Document dialog box.
4. Click OK.

Project 1c Merging the Main Document with the Data Source File

Part 3 of 3

1. With **WL1-C8-P1-MFMD.docx** open, preview the main document merged with the first record in the data source file by clicking the Preview Results button on the MAILINGS tab.
2. Click the Next Record button to view the main document merged with the second record in the data source file.
3. Click the Preview Results button to turn off the preview feature.
4. Automatically check for errors by completing the following steps:
   a. Click the Check for Errors button in the Preview Results group on the MAILINGS tab.
   b. At the Checking and Reporting Errors dialog box, click the first option, *Simulate the merge and report errors in a new document*.
   c. Click OK.
   d. If a new document displays with any errors, print the document and then close it without saving it. If a message displays telling you that no errors were found, click OK.
5. Click the Finish & Merge button in the Finish group and then click *Edit Individual Documents* at the drop-down list.
6. At the Merge to New Document dialog box, make sure *All* is selected and then click OK.
7. Save the merged letters and name the document **WL1-C8-P1-MFLtrs**.
8. Print **WL1-C8-P1-MFLtrs.docx**. (This document will print four letters.)
9. Close **WL1-C8-P1-MFLtrs.docx**.
10. Save and then close **WL1-C8-P1-MFMD.docx**.

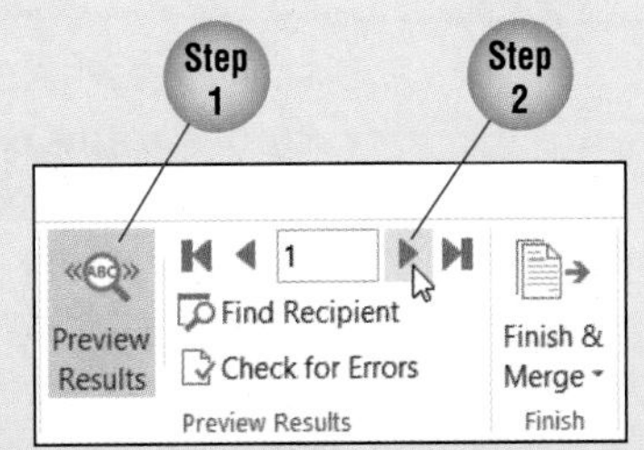

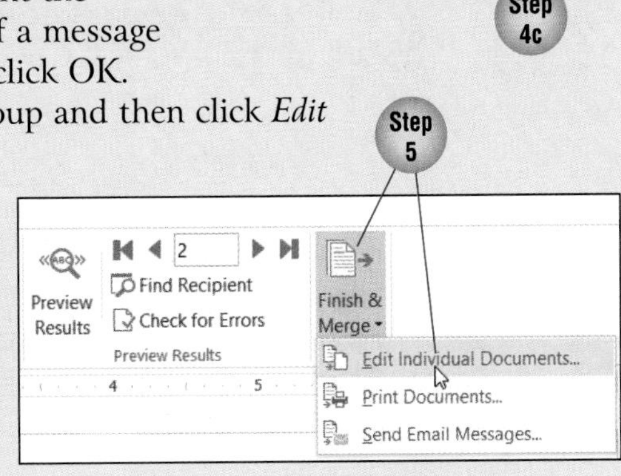

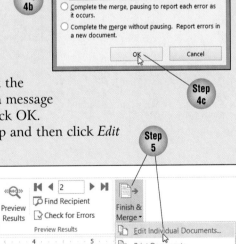

Project 2 Merge Envelopes — 1 Part

You will use Mail Merge to prepare envelopes with customer names and addresses.

Merging Envelopes

If you create a letter as a main document and then merge it with a data source file, more than likely you will need properly addressed envelopes in which to send the letters. To prepare an envelope main document that is merged with a data source file, click the MAILINGS tab, click the Start Mail Merge button, and then click *Envelopes* at the drop-down list. This displays the Envelope Options dialog box, as shown in Figure 8.5. At this dialog box, specify the desired envelope size, make any other changes, and then click OK.

The next step in the envelope merge process is to create the data source file or identify an existing data source file. To identify an existing data source file, click the Select Recipients button in the Start Mail Merge group and then click *Use an Existing List* at the drop-down list. At the Select Data Source dialog box, navigate to the folder containing the desired data source file and then double-click the file.

With the data source file attached to the envelope main document, the next step is to insert the appropriate fields. Click in the envelope in the approximate location the recipient's address will appear, and a box with a dashed gray border displays. Click the Address Block button in the Write & Insert Fields group and then click OK at the Insert Address Block dialog box.

Figure 8.5 Envelope Options Dialog Box

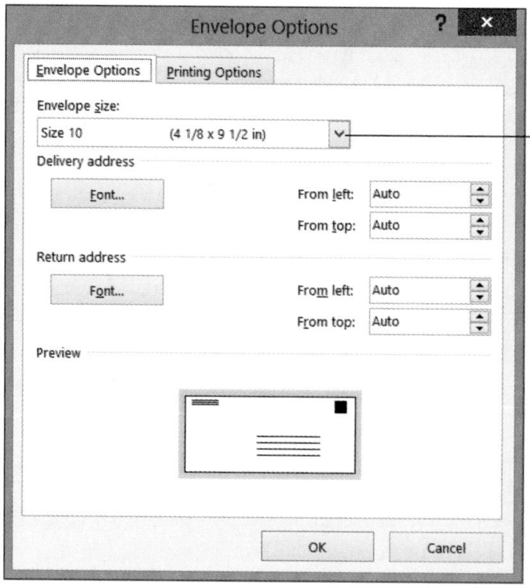

Click this down-pointing arrow to display a list of available envelope sizes.

Project 2 Merging Envelopes

1. At a blank document, click the MAILINGS tab.
2. Click the Start Mail Merge button in the Start Mail Merge group and then click *Envelopes* at the drop-down list.
3. At the Envelope Options dialog box, make sure the envelope size is Size 10 and then click OK.
4. Click the Select Recipients button in the Start Mail Merge group and then click *Use an Existing List* at the drop-down list.
5. At the Select Data Source dialog box, navigate to the WL1C8 folder on your storage medium and then double-click the data source file named ***WL1-C8-P1-MFDS.mdb***.
6. Click in the approximate location in the envelope document where the recipient's address will appear. (This causes a box with a dashed gray border to display. If you do not see this box, try clicking in a different location on the envelope.)

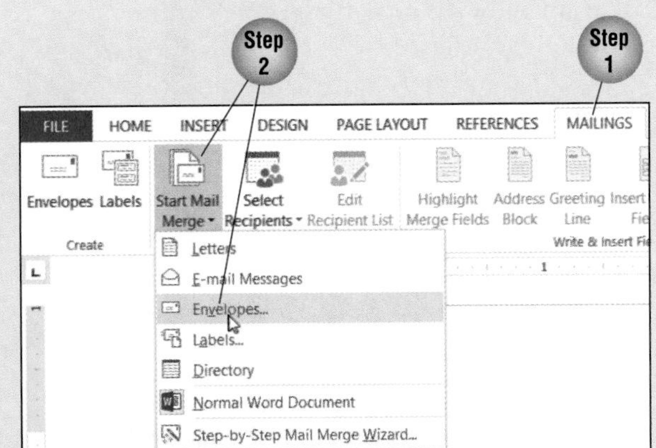

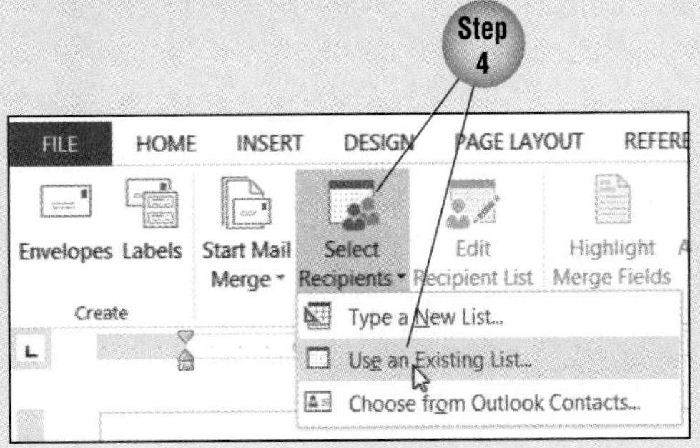

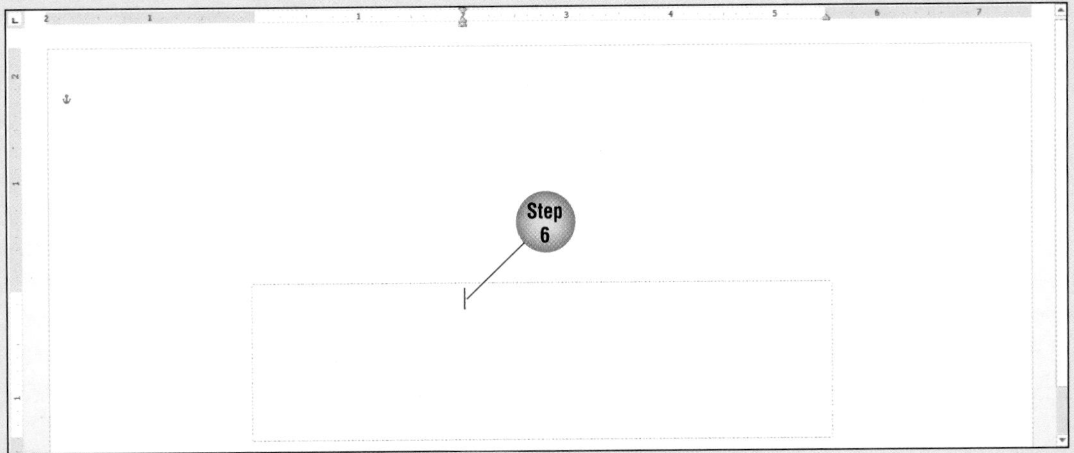

7. Click the Address Block button in the Write & Insert Fields group.
8. At the Insert Address Block dialog box, click the OK button.
9. Click the Preview Results button to see how the envelope appears merged with the first record in the data source file.
10. Click the Preview Results button to turn off the preview feature.
11. Click the Finish & Merge button in the Finish group and then click *Edit Individual Documents* at the drop-down list.

12. At the Merge to New Document dialog box, specify that you want only the first two records to merge by completing the following steps:
    a. Click in the *From* text box and then type **1**.
    b. Click in the *To* text box and then type **2**.
    c. Click OK. (This merges only the first two records and opens a document with two merged envelopes.)
13. Save the merged envelopes and name the document **WL1-C8-P2-MFEnvs**.
14. Print **WL1-C8-P2-MFEnvs.docx**. (This document will print two envelopes. Manual feeding of the envelopes may be required. Please check with your instructor.)
15. Close **WL1-C8-P2-MFEnvs.docx**.
16. Save the envelope main document and name it **WL1-C8-P2-EnvMD**.
17. Close **WL1-C8-P2-EnvMD.docx**.

Project 3 Merge Mailing Labels — 1 Part

You will use Mail Merge to prepare mailing labels with customer names and addresses.

Merging Labels

Create mailing labels for records in a data source file in much the same way that you create envelopes. Click the Start Mail Merge button and then click *Labels* at the drop-down list. This displays the Label Options dialog box, as shown in Figure 8.6. Make sure the desired label is selected and then click OK to close the dialog box. The next step is to create the data source file or identify an existing data source file. With the data source file attached to the label main document, insert the appropriate fields and then complete the merge.

Figure 8.6 Label Options Dialog Box

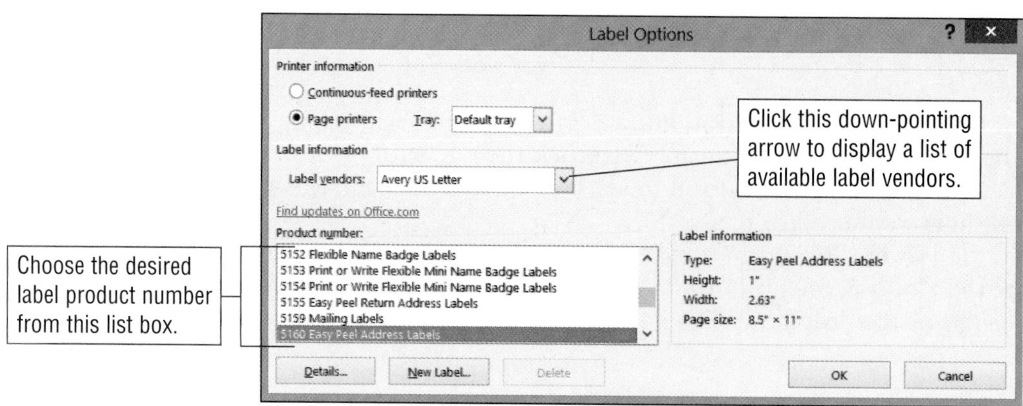

Project 3 Merging Mailing Labels

Part 1 of 1

1. At a blank document, change the document zoom to 100% and then click the MAILINGS tab
2. Click the Start Mail Merge button in the Start Mail Merge group and then click *Labels* at the drop-down list.
3. At the Label Options dialog box, complete the following steps:
   a. If necessary, click the down-pointing arrow at the right side of the *Label vendors* option box and then click *Avery US Letter* at the drop-down list. (If this product vendor is not available, choose a vendor name that offers labels that print on a full page.)
   b. Scroll in the *Product number* list box and then click *5160 Easy Peel Address Labels*. (If this option is not available, choose a label number that prints labels in two or three columns down a full page.)
   c. Click OK to close the dialog box.

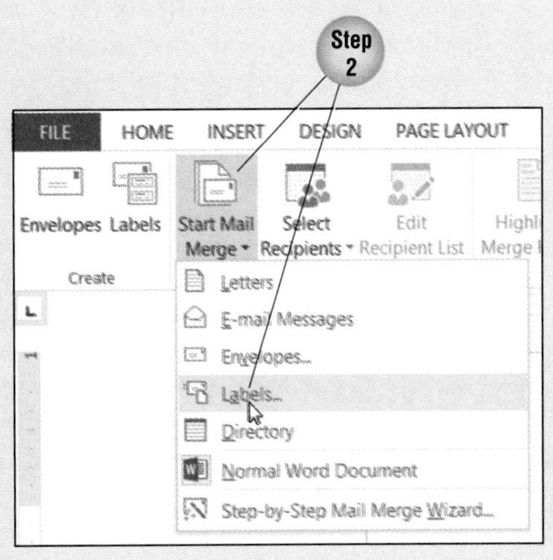

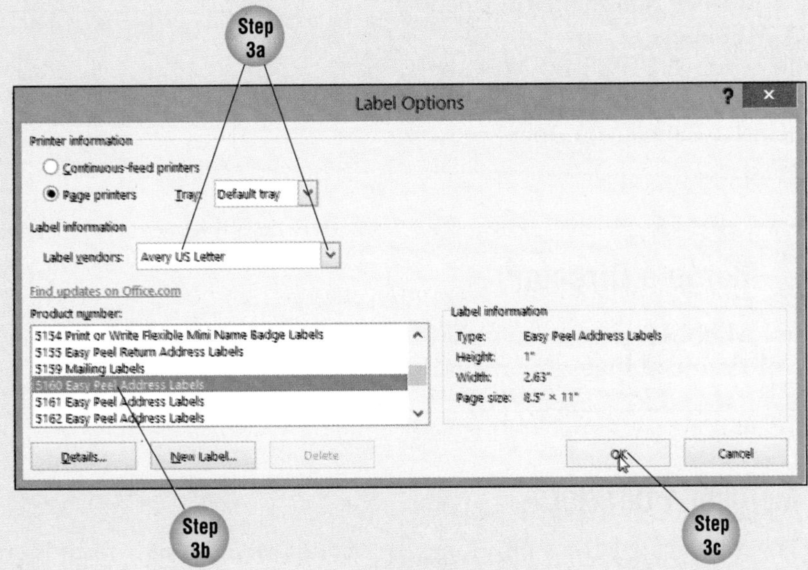

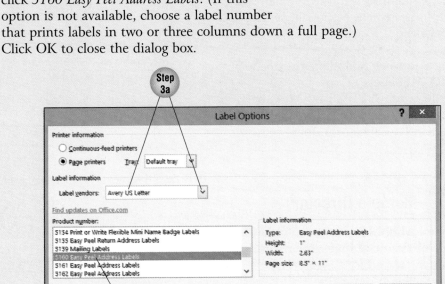

4. Click the Select Recipients button in the Start Mail Merge group and then click *Use an Existing List* at the drop-down list.
5. At the Select Data Source dialog box, navigate to the WL1C8 folder on your storage medium and then double-click the data source file named ***WL1-C8-P1-MFDS.mdb***.
6. At the labels document, click the Address Block button in the Write & Insert Fields group.
7. At the Insert Address Block dialog box, click the OK button. (This inserts «AddressBlock» in the first label. The other labels contain the «Next Record» field.)
8. Click the Update Labels button in the Write & Insert Fields group. (This adds the «AddressBlock» field after each «Next Record» field in the second and subsequent labels.)
9. Click the Preview Results button to see how the labels appear merged with the records in the data source file.
10. Click the Preview Results button to turn off the preview feature.

11. Click the Finish & Merge button in the Finish group and then click *Edit Individual Documents* at the drop-down list.
12. At the Merge to New Document dialog box, make sure *All* is selected, and then click OK.
13. Format the labels by completing the following steps:
    a. Click the TABLE TOOLS LAYOUT tab.
    b. Click the Select button in the Table group and then click *Select Table*.
    c. Click the Align Center Left button in the Alignment group.
    d. Click the HOME tab and then click the Paragraph group dialog box launcher.
    e. At the Paragraph dialog box, click the up-pointing arrow at the right of the *Before* measurement box to change the measurement to 0 points.
    f. Click the up-pointing arrow at the right of the *After* measurement box to change the measurement to 0 points.
    g. Click the up-pointing arrow at the right of the *Inside* measurement box to change the measurement to 0.3 inch.
    h. Click OK.
14. Save the merged labels and name the document **WL1-C8-P3-MFLabels.**
15. Print and then close **WL1-C8-P3-MFLabels.docx.**
16. Save the label main document and name it **WL1-C8-P3-LabelsMD.**
17. Close **WL1-C8-P3-LabelsMD.docx.**

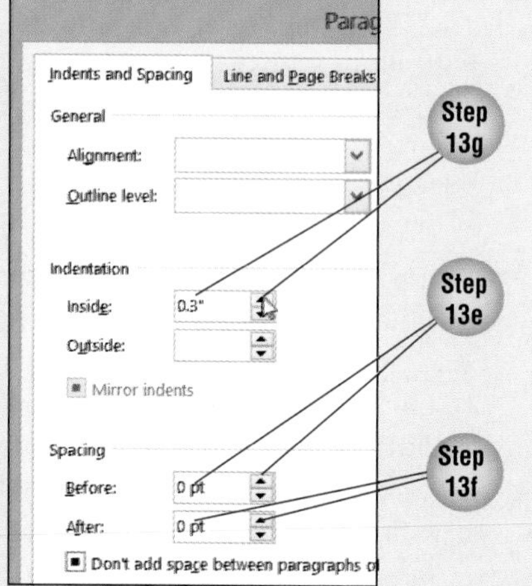

Project 4 Merge a Directory — 1 Part

You will use Mail Merge to prepare a directory list containing customer names and types of financial investment funds.

Merging a Directory

When merging letters, envelopes, or mailing labels, a new form is created for each record. For example, if the data source file merged with the letter contains eight records, eight letters are created. If the data source file merged with a mailing label contains twenty records, twenty labels are created. In some situations, you may want merged information to remain on the same page. This is useful, for example, when creating a list such as a directory or address list.

Begin creating a merged directory by clicking the Start Mail Merge button and then clicking *Directory* at the drop-down list. Create or identify an existing data source file and then insert the desired fields in the directory document. You may want to set tabs to insert text in columns.

Project 4 Merging a Directory

1. At a blank document, click the MAILINGS tab.
2. Click the Start Mail Merge button in the Start Mail Merge group and then click *Directory* at the drop-down list.
3. Click the Select Recipients button in the Start Mail Merge group and then click *Use an Existing List* at the drop-down list.
4. At the Select Data Source dialog box, navigate to the WL1C8 folder on your storage medium and then double-click the data source file named ***WL1-C8-P1-MFDS.mdb***.
5. At the document screen, set left tabs at the 1-inch mark, the 2.5-inch mark, and the 4-inch mark on the horizontal ruler and then press the Tab key. (This moves the insertion point to the tab set at the 1-inch mark.)

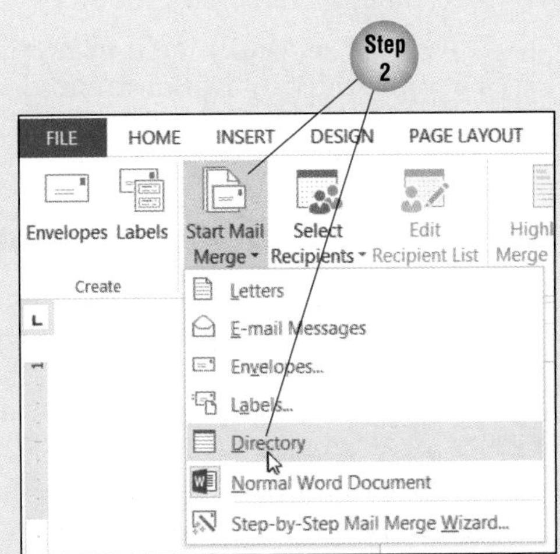

6. Click the Insert Merge Field button arrow and then click *Last_Name* at the drop-down list.
7. Press the Tab key to move the insertion point to the 2.5-inch mark.
8. Click the Insert Merge Field button arrow and then click *First_Name* at the drop-down list.
9. Press the Tab key to move the insertion point to the 4-inch mark.
10. Click the Insert Merge Field button arrow and then click *Fund* at the drop-down list.
11. Press the Enter key once.
12. Click the Finish & Merge button in the Finish group and then click *Edit Individual Documents* at the drop-down list.
13. At the Merge to New Document dialog box, make sure *All* is selected and then click OK. (This merges the fields in the document.)
14. Press Ctrl + Home, press the Enter key once, and then press the Up Arrow key once.
15. Press the Tab key, turn on bold, and then type **Last Name**.
16. Press the Tab key and then type **First Name**.
17. Press the Tab key and then type **Fund**.

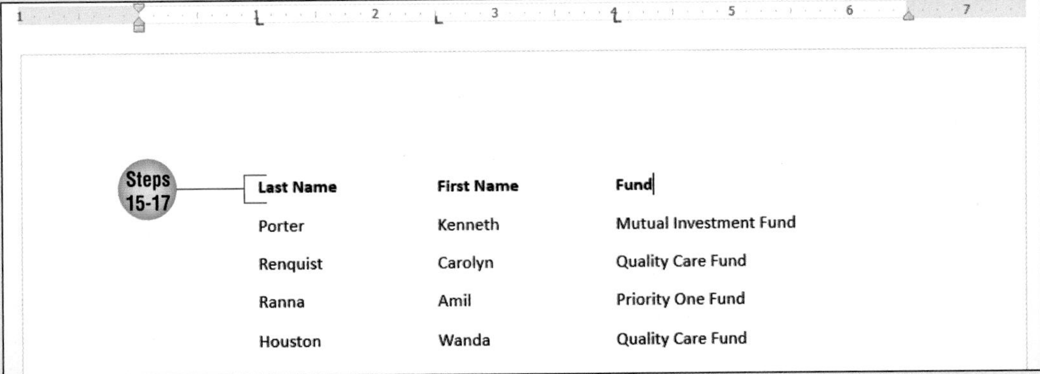

18. Save the directory document and name it **WL1-C8-P4-Directory**.
19. Print and then close the document.
20. Close the directory main document without saving it.

Project 5 Select Records and Merge Mailing Labels 1 Part

You will use Mail Merge to prepare mailing labels with names and addresses of customers living in Baltimore.

Editing a Data Source File

Quick Steps

Edit a Data Source File

1. Open main document.
2. Click MAILINGS tab.
3. Click Edit Recipient List button.
4. Make desired changes at Mail Merge Recipients dialog box.
5. Click OK.

Edit Recipient List

Edit a main document in the normal manner. Open the document, make the required changes, and then save the document. Since a data source is actually an Access database file, you cannot open it in the normal manner. Open a data source file for editing using the Edit Recipient List button in the Start Mail Merge group on the MAILINGS tab. When you click the Edit Recipient List button, the Mail Merge Recipients dialog box displays, as shown in Figure 8.7. Select or edit records at this dialog box.

Selecting Specific Records

Each record in the Mail Merge Recipients dialog box contains a check mark before the first field. If you want to select specific records, remove the check marks from those records you do not want included in a merge. This way, you can select and then merge only certain records in the data source file with the main document.

Figure 8.7 Mail Merge Recipients Dialog Box

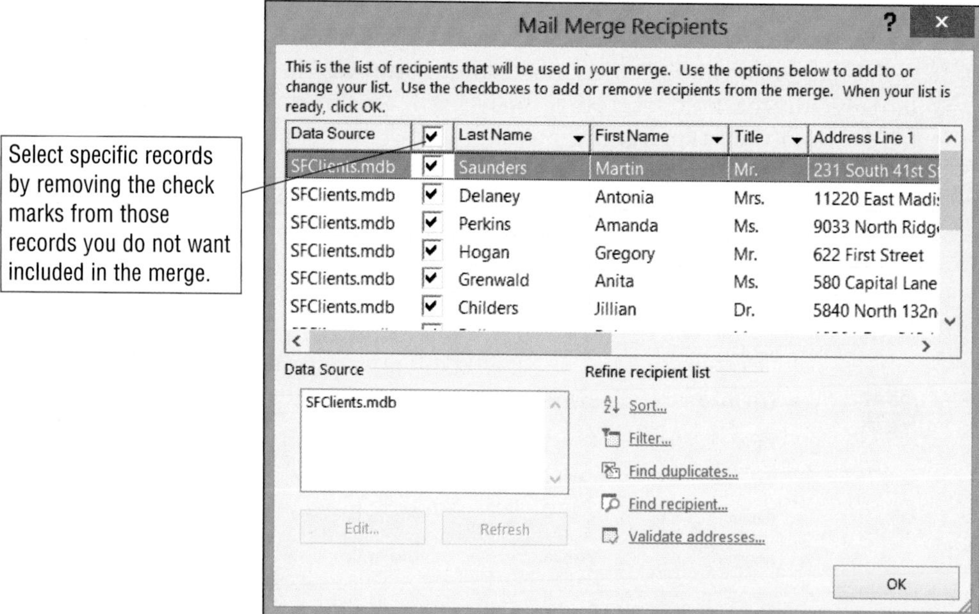

Project 5 Selecting Records and Merging Mailing Labels — Part 1 of 1

1. At a blank document, create mailing labels for customers living in Baltimore. Begin by clicking the MAILINGS tab.
2. Click the Start Mail Merge button in the Start Mail Merge group and then click *Labels* at the drop-down list.
3. At the Label Options dialog box, make sure *Avery US Letter* displays in the *Label vendors* option box and *5160 Easy Peel Address Labels* displays in the *Product number* list box. Click OK.
4. Click the Select Recipients button in the Start Mail Merge group and then click *Use an Existing List* at the drop-down list.
5. At the Select Data Source dialog box, navigate to the WL1C8 folder on your storage medium and then double-click the data source file named ***SFClients.mdb***.
6. Click the Edit Recipient List button in the Start Mail Merge group.
7. At the Mail Merge Recipients dialog box, complete the following steps:
   a. Click the check box located immediately left of the *Last Name* field column heading to remove the check mark. (This removes all of the check marks from the check boxes.)
   b. Click the check box immediately left of each of the following last names: *Saunders*, *Perkins*, *Grenwald*, *Dutton*, *Fernandez*, and *Stahl*. (These are the customers who live in Baltimore.)
   c. Click OK to close the dialog box.

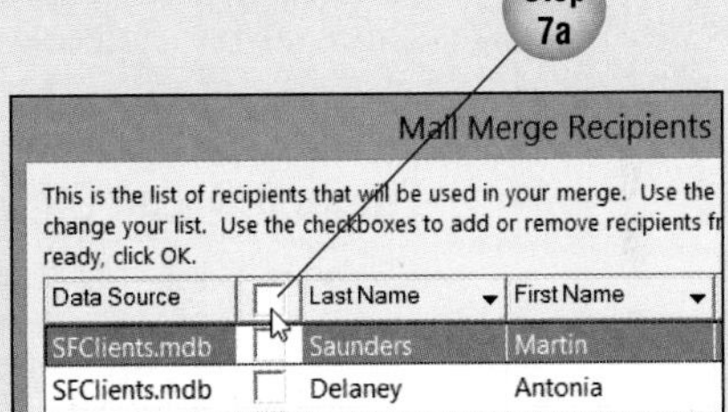

8. At the labels document, click the Address Block button in the Write & Insert Fields group.
9. At the Insert Address Block dialog box, click the OK button.
10. Click the Update Labels button in Write & Insert Fields group.
11. Click the Preview Results button and then click the Previous Record button to display each label. Make sure only labels for those customers living in Baltimore display.
12. Click the Preview Results button to turn off the preview feature.
13. Click the Finish & Merge button in the Finish group and then click *Edit Individual Documents* at the drop-down list.
14. At the Merge to New Document dialog box, make sure *All* is selected and then click OK.
15. Format the labels by completing the following steps:
   a. Click the TABLE TOOLS LAYOUT tab.
   b. Click the Select button in the Table group and then click *Select Table*.
   c. Click the Align Center Left button in the Alignment group.
   d. Click the HOME tab and then click the Paragraph group dialog box launcher.
   e. At the Paragraph dialog box, click the up-pointing arrow at the right of the *Before* measurement box to change the measurement to 0 points.
   f. Click the up-pointing arrow at the right of the *After* measurement box to change the measurement to 0 points.
   g. Click the up-pointing arrow at the right of the *Inside* measurement box to change the measurement to 0.3 inch.
   h. Click OK.
16. Save the merged labels and name the document **WL1-C8-P5-SFLabels**.
17. Print and then close **WL1-C8-P5-SFLabels.docx**.
18. Close the main labels document without saving it.

Project 6 Edit Records in a Data Source File — 1 Part

You will edit records in a data source file and then use Mail Merge to prepare a directory with the edited records that contains customer names, telephone numbers, and cell phone numbers.

Editing Records

A data source file may need editing on a periodic basis to add or delete customer names, update fields, insert new fields, or delete existing fields. To edit a data source file, click the Edit Recipient List button in the Start Mail Merge group. At the Mail Merge Recipients dialog box, click the data source file name in the *Data Source* list box and then click the Edit button that displays below the list box. This displays the Edit Data Source dialog box, as shown in Figure 8.8. At this dialog box, you can add a new entry, delete an entry, find a particular entry, and customize columns.

Figure 8.8 Edit Data Source Dialog Box

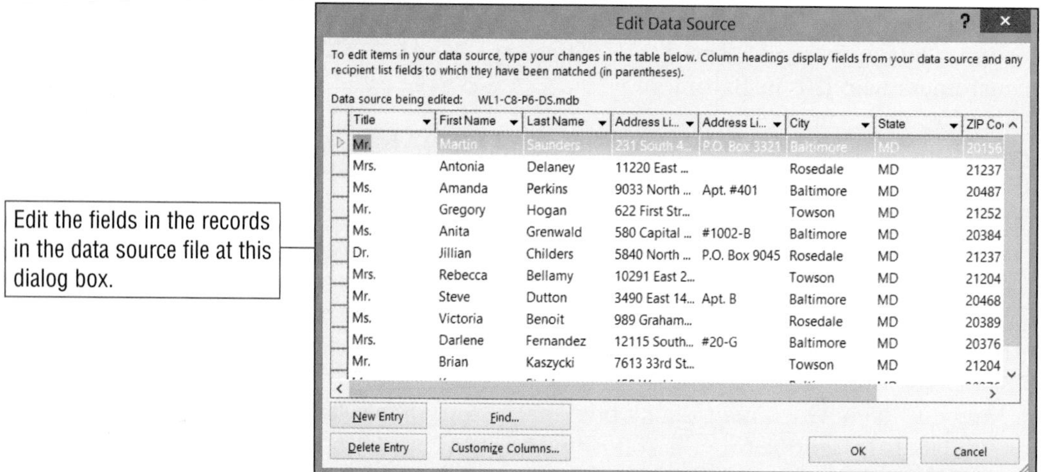

Project 6 Editing Records in a Data Source File — Part 1 of 1

1. Make a copy of the **SFClients.mdb** file by completing the following steps:
   a. Display the Open dialog box and make WL1C8 the active folder.
   b. If necessary, change the file type option to *All Files (*.*)*.
   c. Right-click on the ***SFClients.mdb*** file and then click *Copy* at the shortcut menu.
   d. Position the mouse pointer in a white portion of the Open dialog box Content pane (outside any file name), click the right mouse button, and then click *Paste* at the shortcut menu. (This inserts a copy of the file in the dialog box Content pane and names the file **SFClients - Copy.mdb**.)
   e. Right-click on the file name ***SFClients - Copy.mdb*** and then click *Rename* at the shortcut menu.

f. Type **WL1-C8-P6-DS** and then press Enter.
g. Close the Open dialog box.

2. At a blank document, click the MAILINGS tab.
3. Click the Select Recipients button and then click *Use an Existing List* from the drop-down list.
4. At the Select Data Source dialog box, navigate to the WL1C8 folder on your storage medium and then double-click the data source file named ***WL1-C8-P6-DS.mdb***.
5. Click the Edit Recipient List button in the Start Mail Merge group.
6. At the Mail Merge Recipients dialog box, click ***WL1-C8-P6-DS.mdb*** that displays in the *Data Source* list box and then click the Edit button.

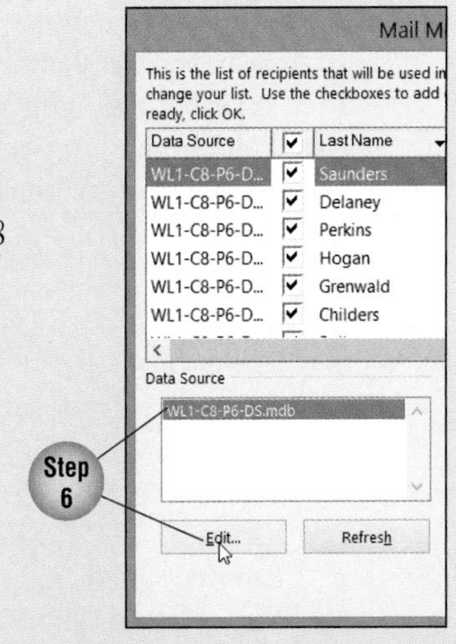

7. Delete the record for Steve Dutton by completing the following steps:
   a. Click the square that displays at the beginning of the row for *Mr. Steve Dutton*.
   b. Click the Delete Entry button.
   c. At the message asking if you want to delete the entry, click the Yes button.

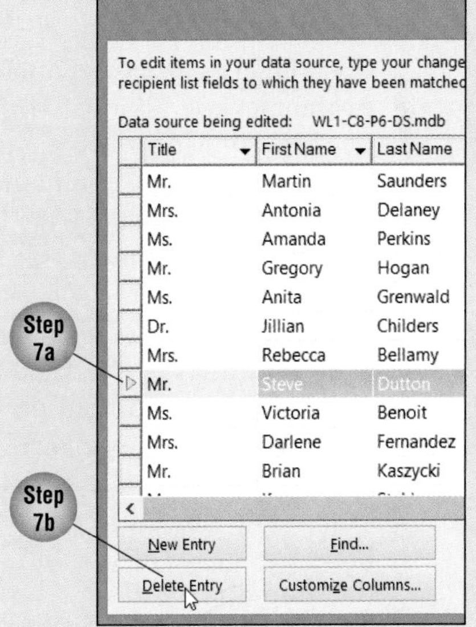

8. Insert a new record by completing the following steps:
   a. Click the New Entry button in the dialog box.
   b. Type the following text in the new record in the specified fields:

      Title: **Ms.**
      First Name: **Jennae**
      Last Name: **Davis**
      Address Line 1: **3120 South 21st**
      Address Line 2: (none)
      City: **Rosedale**
      State: **MD**
      ZIP Code: **20389**
      Home Phone: **410-555-5774**

9. Insert a new field and type text in the field by completing the following steps:
   a. At the Edit Data Source dialog box, click the Customize Columns button.
   b. At the message asking if you want to save the changes made to the data source file, click Yes.
   c. At the Customize Address List dialog box, click *ZIP Code* in the *Field Names* list box. (A new field is inserted below the selected field.)
   d. Click the Add button.
   e. At the Add Field dialog box, type **Cell Phone** and then click OK.

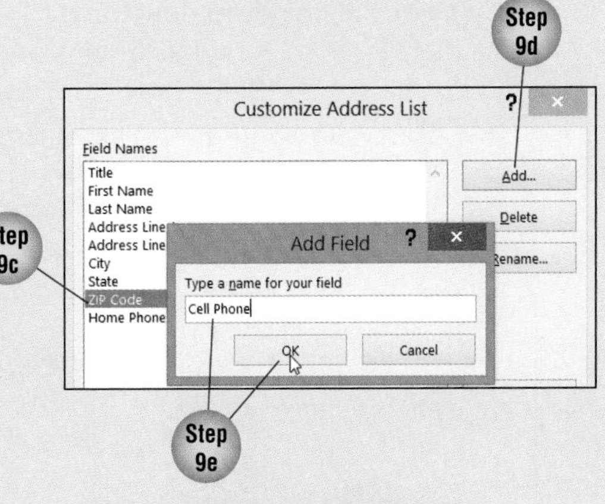

   f. You decide that you want the *Cell Phone* field to display after the *Home Phone* field. To move the *Cell Phone* field, make sure it is selected and then click the Move Down button.
   g. Click OK to close the Customize Address List dialog box.

h. At the Edit Data Source dialog box, scroll to the right to display the *Cell Phone* field (last field in the file) and then type the following cell phone numbers (after typing each cell phone number except the last number, press the Down Arrow key to make the next cell below active):

Record 1: 410-555-1249
Record 2: 410-555-3492
Record 3: 410-555-0695
Record 4: 410-555-9488
Record 5: 410-555-1200
Record 6: 410-555-7522
Record 7: 410-555-8833
Record 8: 410-555-9378
Record 9: 410-555-4261
Record 10: 410-555-9944
Record 11: 410-555-2321
Record 12: 410-555-9435

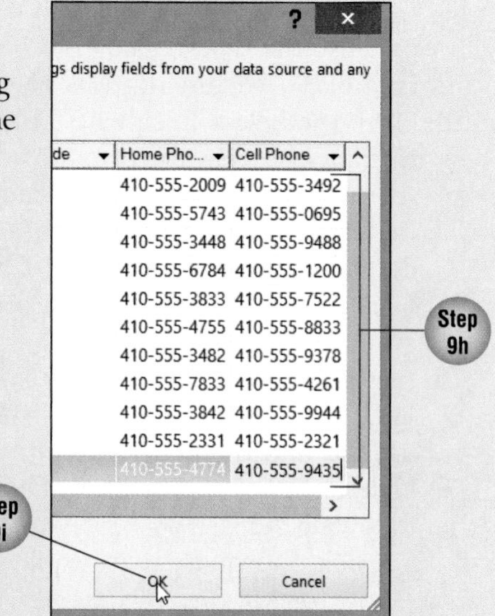

i. Click OK to close the Edit Data Source dialog box.
j. At the message asking if you want to update the recipient list and save changes, click Yes.
k. At the Mail Merge Recipients dialog box, click OK.

10. Create a directory by completing the following steps:
    a. Click the Start Mail Merge button and then click *Directory* at the drop-down list.
    b. At the blank document, set left tabs on the horizontal ruler at the 1-inch mark, the 3-inch mark, and the 4.5-inch mark.
    c. Press the Tab key. (This moves the insertion point to the first tab set at the 1-inch mark.)
    d. Click the Insert Merge Field button arrow and then click *Last_Name* at the drop-down list.
    e. Type a comma and then press the spacebar.
    f. Click the Insert Merge Field button arrow and then click *First_Name* at the drop-down list.
    g. Press the Tab key, click the Insert Merge Field button arrow, and then click *Home_Phone* at the drop-down list.
    h. Press the Tab key, click the Insert Merge Field button arrow, and then click *Cell_Phone* at the drop-down list.
    i. Press the Enter key once.
    j. Click the Finish & Merge button in the Finish group and then click *Edit Individual Documents* at the drop-down list.
    k. At the Merge to New Document dialog box, make sure *All* is selected and then click OK. (This merges the fields in the document.)
11. Press Ctrl + Home, press the Enter key once, and then press the Up Arrow key once.
12. Press the Tab key, turn on bold, and then type **Name**.
13. Press the Tab key and then type **Home Phone**.
14. Press the Tab key and then type **Cell Phone**.

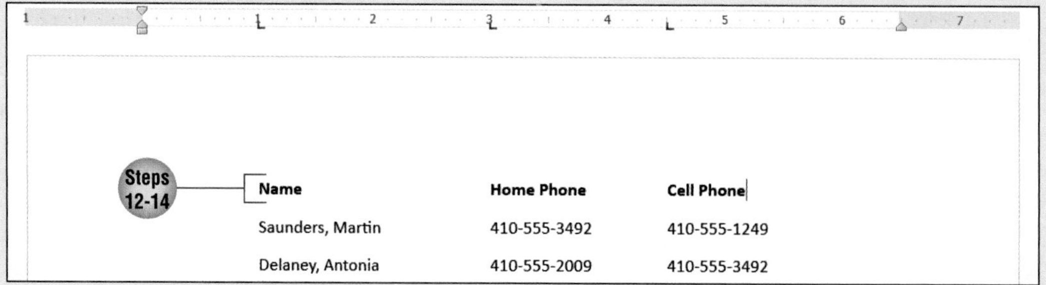

Steps 12-14
Name
Home Phone
Cell Phone
Saunders, Martin
410-555-3492
410-555-1249
Delaney, Antonia
410-555-2009
410-555-3492

15. Save the directory document and name it **WL1-C8-P6-Directory**.
16. Print and then close the document.
17. Close the directory main document without saving it.

Project 7 Add Fill-in Fields to a Main Document — 1 Part

You will edit a form letter and insert sales representative contact information during a merge.

Inputting Text during a Merge

Word's Merge feature contains a large number of merge fields you can insert in a main document. In this section, you will learn about the Fill-in field that is used for information input at the keyboard during a merge. For more information on the other merge fields, please refer to the on-screen help.

Quick Steps

Insert a Fill-in Field in a Main Document
1. Click MAILINGS tab.
2. Click Rules button.
3. Click *Fill-in* at drop-down list.
4. Type prompt text.
5. Click OK.
6. Type text to be inserted in document.
7. Click OK.

Rules

In some situations, you may not need to keep all variable information in a data source file. For example, variable information that changes on a regular basis might include a customer's monthly balance, a product price, and so on. Word lets you input variable information into a document during the merge using the keyboard. A Fill-in field is inserted in a main document by clicking the Rules button in the Write & Insert Fields group on the MAILINGS tab and then clicking *Fill-in* at the drop-down list. This displays the Insert Word Field: Fill-in dialog box, shown in Figure 8.9. At this dialog box, type a short message indicating what should be entered at the keyboard and then click OK. At the Microsoft Word dialog box with the message you entered displayed in the upper left corner, type the text you want to display in the document and then click OK. When the Fill-in field or fields are added, save the main document in the normal manner. A document can contain any number of Fill-in fields.

When you merge the main document with the data source file, the first record is merged with the main document and the Microsoft Word dialog box displays with the message you entered displayed in the upper left corner. Type the required information for the first record in the data source file and then click

Figure 8.9 Insert Word Field: Fill-in Dialog Box

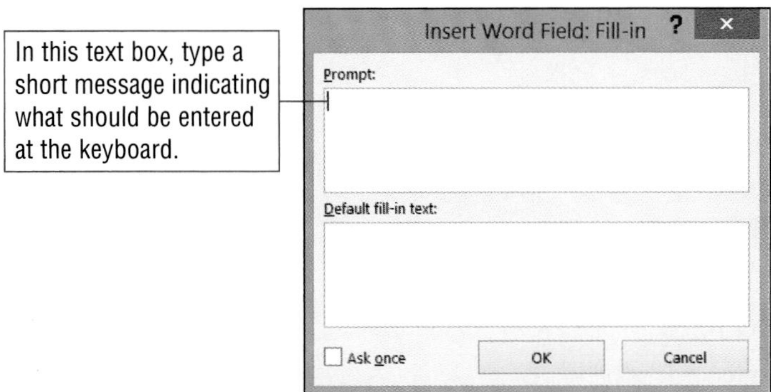
In this text box, type a short message indicating what should be entered at the keyboard.
Insert Word Field: Fill-in
Prompt:
Default fill-in text:
Ask once
OK
Cancel

the OK button. Word displays the dialog box again. Type the required information for the second record in the data source file and then click OK. Continue in this manner until the required information has been entered for each record in the data source file. Word then completes the merge.

Project 7 Adding Fill-in Fields to a Main Document **Part 1 of 1**

1. Open the document named **WL1-C8-P1-MFMD.docx**. (At the message asking if you want to continue, click Yes.) Save the document with Save As and name it **WL1-C8-P7-MFMD**.
2. Change the second paragraph in the body of the letter to the paragraph shown in Figure 8.10. Insert the first Fill-in field (representative's name) by completing the following steps:
   a. Click the MAILINGS tab.
   b. Click the Rules button in the Write & Insert Fields group and then click *Fill-in* at the drop-down list.
   c. At the Insert Word Field: Fill-in dialog box, type **Insert rep name** in the *Prompt* text box and then click OK.
   d. At the Microsoft Word dialog box with *Insert rep name* displayed in the upper left corner, type **(representative's name)** and then click OK.

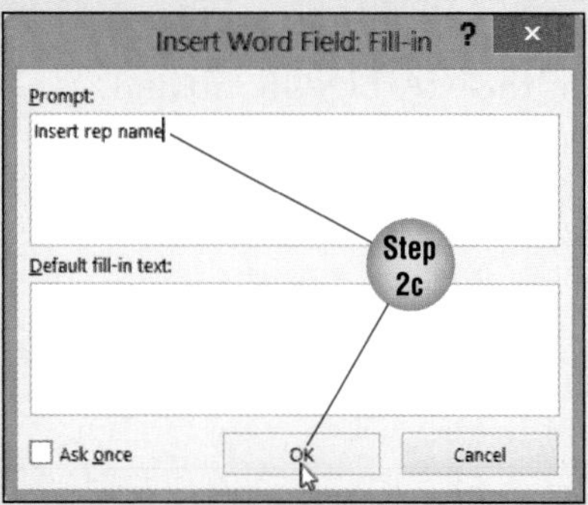

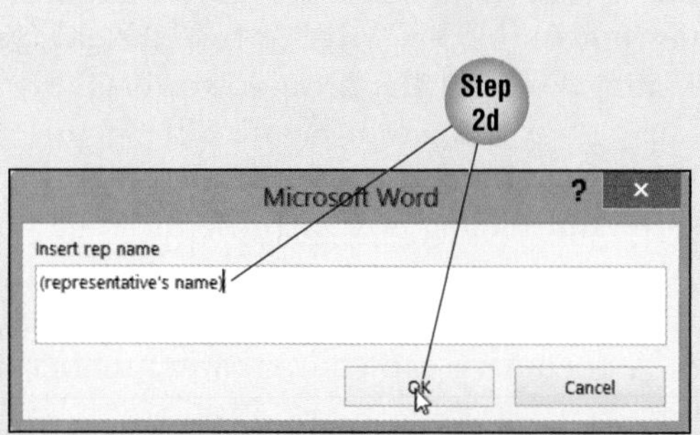

3. Complete steps similar to those in Step 2 to insert the second Fill-in field (phone number), except type **Insert phone number** in the *Prompt* text box at the Insert Word Field: Fill-in dialog box and type **(phone number)** at the Microsoft Word dialog box.
4. Save **WL1-C8-P7-MFMD.docx**.
5. Merge the main document with the data source file by completing the following steps:
   a. Click the Finish & Merge button and then click *Edit Individual Documents* at the drop-down list.
   b. At the Merge to New Document dialog box, make sure *All* is selected and then click OK.
   c. When Word merges the main document with the first record, a dialog box displays with the message *Insert rep name* and the text *(representative's name)* selected. At this dialog box, type **Marilyn Smythe** and then click OK.
   d. At the dialog box with the message *Insert phone number* and *(phone number)* selected, type **(646) 555-8944** and then click OK.

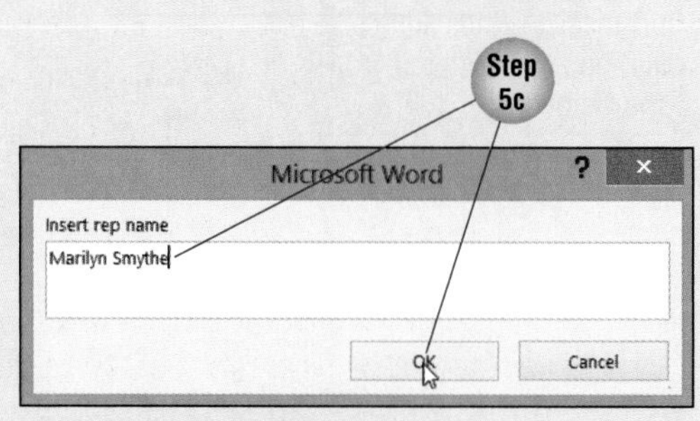

e. At the dialog box with the message *Insert rep name*, type **Anthony Mason** (over *Marilyn Smythe*) and then click OK.
f. At the dialog box with the message *Insert phone number*, type **(646) 555-8901** (over the previous number) and then click OK.
g. At the dialog box with the message *Insert rep name*, type **Faith Ostrom** (over *Anthony Mason*) and then click OK.
h. At the dialog box with the message *Insert phone number*, type **(646) 555-8967** (over the previous number) and then click OK.
i. At the dialog box with the message *Insert rep name*, type **Thomas Rivers** (over *Faith Ostrom*) and then click OK.
j. At the dialog box with the message *Insert phone number*, type **(646) 555-0793** (over the previous number) and then click OK.

6. Save the merged document and name it **WL1-C8-P7-MFLtrs**.
7. Print and then close **WL1-C8-P7-MFLtrs.docx**.
8. Save and then close **WL1-C8-P7-MFMD.docx**.

Figure 8.10 Project 7

Lowering expense charges is noteworthy because before the reduction, McCormack expense deductions were already among the lowest, far below most mutual funds and variable annuity accounts with similar objectives. At the same time, services for you, our client, will continue to expand. If you would like to discuss this change, please call our service representative, **(representative's name)**, at **(phone number)**.

Project 8 Use Mail Merge Wizard — 1 Part

You will use the Mail Merge wizard to merge a main document with a data source file and create letters to clients of Sorenson Funds.

Merging Using the Mail Merge Wizard

The Mail Merge feature includes a Mail Merge wizard that guides you through the merge process. To access the Wizard, click the MAILINGS tab, click the Start Mail Merge button, and then click the *Step-by-Step Mail Merge Wizard* option at the drop-down list. The first of six Mail Merge task panes displays at the right side of the screen. Completing the tasks at one task pane displays the next task pane. The options in each task pane may vary depending on the type of merge you are performing. Generally, you complete one of the following steps at each task pane:

- Step 1: Select the type of document you want to create such as a letter, email message, envelope, label, or directory.
- Step 2: Specify whether you want to use the current document to create the main document, start from a template, or start from an existing document.
- Step 3: Specify whether you are typing a new list, using an existing list, or selecting from an Outlook contacts list.

- Step 4: Use the items in this task pane to help you prepare the main document by performing tasks such as inserting fields.
- Step 5: Preview the merged documents.
- Step 6: Complete the merge.

Project 8 Preparing Form Letters Using the Mail Merge Wizard

Part 1 of 1

1. At a blank document, click the MAILINGS tab, click the Start Mail Merge button in the Start Mail Merge group, and then click *Step-by-Step Mail Merge Wizard* at the drop-down list.
2. At the first Mail Merge task pane, make sure *Letters* is selected in the *Select document type* section and then click the Next: Starting document hyperlink located toward the bottom of the task pane.
3. At the second Mail Merge task pane, click the *Start from existing document* option in the *Select starting document* section.
4. Click the Open button in the *Start from existing* section of the task pane.
5. At the Open dialog box, navigate to the WL1C8 folder on your storage medium and then double-click ***SFLtrMD.docx***.
6. Click the Next: Select recipients hyperlink located toward the bottom of the task pane.
7. At the third Mail Merge task pane, click the Browse hyperlink that displays in the *Use an existing list* section of the task pane.
8. At the Select Data Source dialog box, navigate to the WL1C8 folder on your storage medium and then double-click ***SFClients.mdb***.
9. At the Mail Merge Recipients dialog box, click OK.
10. Click the Next: Write your letter hyperlink that displays toward the bottom of the task pane.
11. At the fourth Mail Merge task pane, enter fields in the form letter by completing the following steps:
    a. Position the insertion point a double space above the first paragraph of text in the letter.
    b. Click the Address block hyperlink located in the *Write your letter* section of the task pane.
    c. At the Insert Address Block dialog box, click the OK button.
    d. Press the Enter key twice and then click the Greeting line hyperlink located in the *Write your letter* section of the task pane.
    e. At the Insert Greeting Line dialog box, click the down-pointing arrow at the right of the option box containing the comma (the box to the right of the box containing *Mr. Randall*).
    f. At the drop-down list that displays, click the colon.
    g. Click OK to close the Insert Greeting Line dialog box.

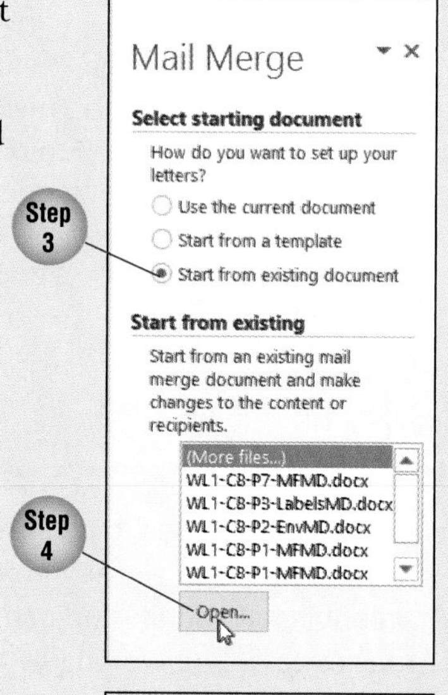

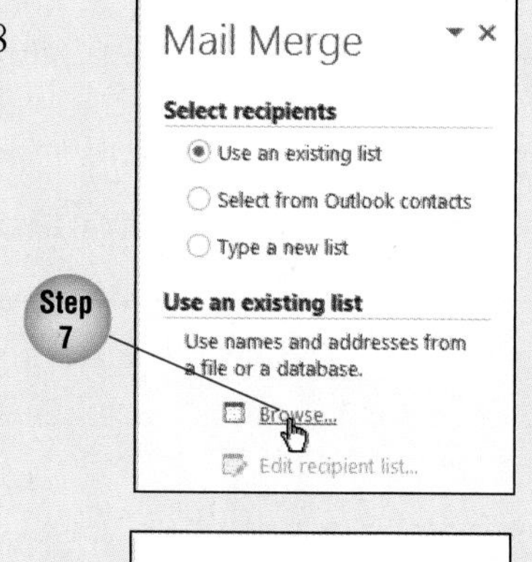

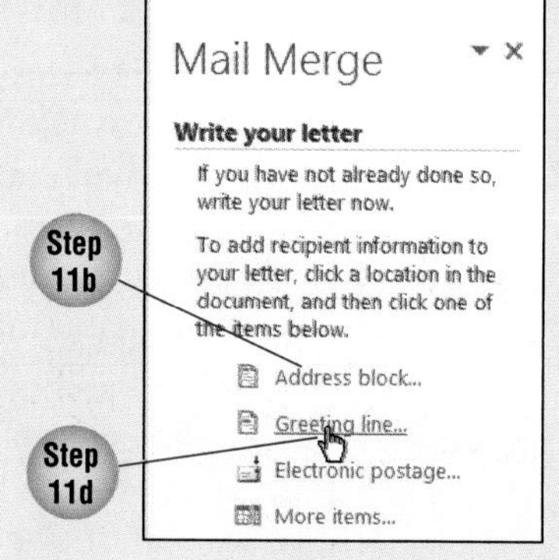

12. Click the Next: Preview your letters hyperlink located toward the bottom of the task pane.
13. At the fifth Mail Merge task pane, look over the letter that displays in the document window and make sure the information merged properly. If you want to see the letters for the other recipients, click the button in the Mail Merge task pane containing the right-pointing arrow.
14. Click the Preview Results button in the Preview Results group to turn off the preview feature.
15. Click the Next: Complete the merge hyperlink that displays toward the bottom of the task pane.
16. At the sixth Mail Merge task pane, click the Edit individual letters hyperlink that displays in the *Merge* section of the task pane.
17. At the Merge to New Document dialog box, make sure *All* is selected and then click the OK button.
18. Save the merged letters document with the name **WL1-C8-P8-SFLtrs**.
19. Print only the first two pages of **WL1-C8-P8-SFLtrs.docx**.
20. Close the document.
21. At the sixth Mail Merge task pane, close the letter main document without saving it.

Chapter Summary

- Use the Mail Merge feature to create documents such as letters, envelopes, labels, and directories with personalized information.
- Generally, a merge takes two documents—the data source file containing the variable information and the main document containing standard text—along with fields identifying where variable information is inserted during the merge process.
- Variable information in a data source file is saved as a record. A record contains all of the information for one unit. A series of fields makes a record, and a series of records makes a data source file.
- A data source file is saved as an Access database, but you do not need Access on your computer to complete a merge with a data source.
- Use predesigned fields when creating a data source file, or create your own custom field at the Customize Address List dialog box.
- Use the Address Block button in the Write & Insert Fields group on the MAILINGS tab to insert all of the fields required for the inside address of a letter. This inserts the «AddressBlock» field, which is considered a composite field because it groups a number of fields.
- Click the Greeting Line button in the Write & Insert Fields group on the MAILINGS tab to insert the «GreetingLine» composite field in the document.
- Click the Insert Merge Field button arrow in the Write & Insert Fields group on the MAILINGS tab to display a drop-down list of fields contained in the data source file.
- Click the Preview Results button on the MAILINGS tab to view the main document merged with the first record in the data source. Use the navigation buttons in the Preview Results group on the MAILINGS tab to display the main document merged with the desired record.

- Before merging documents, check for errors by clicking the Check for Errors button in the Preview Results group on the MAILINGS tab. This displays the Checking and Reporting Errors dialog box with three options for checking errors.
- Click the Finish & Merge button on the MAILINGS tab to complete the merge.
- Select specific records for merging by inserting or removing check marks from the desired records in the Mail Merge Recipients dialog box. Display this dialog box by clicking the Edit Recipient List button on the MAILINGS tab.
- Edit specific records in a data source file at the Edit Data Source dialog box. Display this dialog box by clicking the Edit Recipient List button on the MAILINGS tab, clicking the desired data source file name in the *Data Source* list box, and then clicking the Edit button.
- Use the Fill-in field in a main document to insert variable information at the keyboard during a merge.
- Word includes a Mail Merge wizard to guide you through the process of creating letters, envelopes, labels, directories, and email messages with personalized information.

Commands Review

FEATURE	RIBBON TAB, GROUP	BUTTON	OPTION
Address Block field	MAILINGS, Write & Insert Fields		
Checking and Reporting Errors dialog box	MAILINGS, Preview Results		
directory main document	MAILINGS, Start Mail Merge		*Directory*
envelopes main document	MAILINGS, Start Mail Merge		*Envelopes*
Fill-in merge field	MAILINGS, Write & Insert Fields		*Fill-in*
Greeting Line field	MAILINGS, Write & Insert Fields		
insert merge fields	MAILINGS, Write & Insert Fields		
labels main document	MAILINGS, Start Mail Merge		*Labels*
letter main document	MAILINGS, Start Mail Merge		*Letters*
Mail Merge Recipients dialog box	MAILINGS, Start Mail Merge		
Mail Merge wizard	MAILINGS, Start Mail Merge		*Step-by-Step Mail Merge Wizard*
New Address List dialog box	MAILINGS, Start Mail Merge		*Type a New List*
preview merge results	MAILINGS, Preview Results		

Concepts Check Test Your Knowledge

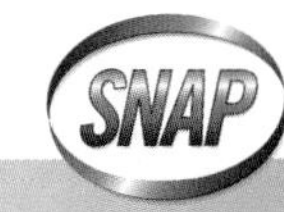

Completion: In the space provided at the right, indicate the correct term, command, or number.

1. A merge generally takes two files: a data source file and this. _______________
2. This term refers to all of the information for one unit in a data source file. _______________
3. Create a data source file by clicking this button on the MAILINGS tab and then clicking *Type a New List* at the drop-down list. _______________
4. A data source file is saved as this type of file. _______________
5. Create your own custom fields in a data source file with options at this dialog box. _______________
6. Use this button on the MAILINGS tab to insert all of the required fields for the inside address in a letter. _______________
7. The «GreetingLine» field is considered this type of field because it includes all of the fields required for the greeting line. _______________
8. Click this button on the MAILINGS tab to display the first record merged with the main document. _______________
9. Before merging a document, check for errors using this button in the Preview Results group on the MAILINGS tab. _______________
10. To complete a merge, click this button in the Finish group on the MAILINGS tab. _______________
11. When creating the envelope main document, click in the approximate location the recipient's address will appear and then click this button in the Write & Insert Fields group. _______________
12. Select specific records in a data source file by inserting or removing check marks from the records in this dialog box. _______________
13. Use this field to insert variable information at the keyboard during a merge. _______________
14. Click this option at the Start Mail Merge button drop-down list to begin the Mail Merge wizard. _______________

Skills Check Assess Your Performance

Assessment 1

CREATE A DATA SOURCE FILE

1. At a blank document, display the New Address List dialog box and then display the Customize Address List dialog box.
2. At the Customize Address List dialog box, delete the following fields: *Company Name*, *Country or Region*, *Work Phone*, and *E-mail Address* and then add a custom field named *Cell Phone*.
3. Close the Customize Address List box and then type the following information in the New Address List dialog box as the first record:
   Title: Mr.
   First Name: Tony
   Last Name: Benedetti
   Address Line 1: 1315 Cordova Road
   Address Line 2: Apt. 402
   City: Santa Fe
   State: NM
   ZIP Code: 87505
   Home Phone: (505) 555-0489
   Cell Phone: (505) 555-0551
4. Type the following information as the second record:
   Title: Ms.
   First Name: Theresa
   Last Name: Dusek
   Address Line 1: 12044 Ridgeway Drive
   Address Line 2: (leave blank)
   City: Santa Fe
   State: NM
   ZIP Code: 87504
   Home Phone: (505) 555-1120
   Cell Phone: (505) 555-6890
5. Type the following information as the third record:
   Title: Mrs.
   First Name: Mary
   Last Name: Arguello
   Address Line 1: 2554 Country Drive
   Address Line 2: #105
   City: Santa Fe
   State: NM
   ZIP Code: 87504
   Home Phone: (505) 555-7663
   Cell Phone: (505) 555-5472
6. Type the following information as the fourth record:
   Title: Mr.
   First Name: Preston
   Last Name: Miller
   Address Line 1: 120 Second Street
   Address Line 2: (leave blank)

City: Santa Fe
State: NM
ZIP Code: 87505
Home Phone: (505) 555-3551
Cell Phone: (505) 555-9630

7. Save the data source file and name it **WL1-C8-A1-CCDS**.
8. Close the blank document without saving changes.

Assessment 2

CREATE A MAIN DOCUMENT AND MERGE WITH A DATA SOURCE FILE

1. Open **CCVolunteerLtr.docx** and then save the document with Save As and name it **WL1-C8-A2-CCMD**.
2. Select **WL1-C8-A1-CCDS.mdb** you created in Assessment 1 as the data source file.
3. Move the insertion point to the beginning of the first paragraph of text in the body of the letter, insert the «AddressBlock» field, and then press Enter twice.
4. Insert the «GreetingLine» field specifying a colon rather than a comma as the greeting line format and then press Enter twice.
5. Move the insertion point one space to the right of the period that ends the second paragraph of text in the body of the letter and then type the following text inserting the «Title», «Last_Name», «Home_Phone», «Cell_Phone» fields where indicated:

   Currently, *«Title» «Last_Name»*, our records indicate your home telephone number is *«Home_Phone»* and your cell phone number is *«Cell_Phone»*. If this information is not accurate, please contact our office with the correct numbers.
6. Merge the main document with all records in the data source file.
7. Save the merged letters document as **WL1-C8-A2-CCLetters**.
8. Print and then close **WL1-C8-A2-CCLetters.docx**.
9. Save and then close **WL1-C8-A2-CCMD.docx**.

Assessment 3

CREATE AN ENVELOPE MAIN DOCUMENT AND MERGE WITH A DATA SOURCE FILE

1. Create an envelope main document using the Size 10 envelope size.
2. Select **WL1-C8-A1-CCDS.mdb** as the data source file.
3. Insert the «AddressBlock» field in the appropriate location in the envelope document.
4. Merge the envelope main document with all records in the data source file.
5. Save the merged envelopes document and name it **WL1-C8-A3-CCEnvs**.
6. Print and then close the envelopes document. (Check with your instructor before printing the envelopes.)
7. Close the envelope main document without saving it.

Assessment 4

CREATE A LABELS MAIN DOCUMENT AND MERGE WITH A DATA SOURCE FILE

1. Create a labels main document using the *Avery US Letter 5160 Easy Peel Address Labels* option.
2. Select **WL1-C8-A1-CCDS.mdb** as the data source file.
3. Insert the «AddressBlock» field.
4. Update the labels.
5. Merge the labels main document with all records in the data source file.
6. Select the entire document and then apply the No Spacing style.
7. Save the merged labels document and name it **WL1-C8-A4-CCLabels**.
8. Print and then close the labels document.
9. Close the labels main document without saving it.

Assessment 5

EDIT A DATA SOURCE FILE

1. Open **WL1-C8-A2-CCMD.docx**. (At the message asking if you want to continue, click Yes.) Save the main document with Save As and name it **WL1-C8-A5-CCMD**.
2. Edit the **WL1-C8-A1-CCDS.mdb** data source file by making the following changes:
   a. Change the address for Ms. Theresa Dusek from *12044 Ridgeway Drive* to *1390 Fourth Avenue*.
   b. Delete the record for Mrs. Mary Arguello.
   c. Insert a new record with the following information:
      Mr. Cesar Rivera
      3201 East Third Street
      Santa Fe, NM 87505
      Home Phone: (505) 555-6675
      Cell Phone: (505) 555-3528
3. At the main document, edit the third sentence of the second paragraph so it reads as follows (insert a Fill-in field for the *(number of hours)* shown in the sentence below):
   According to our volunteer roster, you have signed up to volunteer for *(number of hours)* **during the summer session.**
4. Merge the main document with the data source file and type the following text for each record:
   Record 1: **four hours a week**
   Record 2: **six hours a week**
   Record 3: **twelve hours a week**
   Record 4: **four hours a week**
5. Save the merged document and name it **WL1-C8-A5-CCLtrs**.
6. Print and then close **WL1-C8-A5-CCLtrs.docx**.
7. Save and then close **WL1-C8-A5-CCMD.docx**.

Visual Benchmark Demonstrate Your Proficiency

PREPARE AND MERGE LETTERS

1. Open **FPLtrhd.docx** and then save the document with Save As and name it **WL1-C8-VB-FPMD**.
2. Look at the information in Figure 8.13 and Figure 8.14 and then use Mail Merge to prepare four letters. (When creating the main document, as shown in Figure 8.14, insert the appropriate fields where you see the text *Title*; *First Name*; *Last Name*; *Street Address*; and *City, State ZIP*. Insert the appropriate fields where you see the text *Title* and *Last Name* in the first paragraph of text.) Create the data source file with the information in Figure 8.13 and then save the file and name it **WL1-C8-VB-FPDS**.
3. Merge the **WL1-C8-VB-FPMD.docx** main document with the **WL1-C8-VB-FPDS.mdb** data source file and then save the merged letters document and name it **WL1-C8-VB-FPLtrs**.
4. Print and then close **WL1-C8-VB-FPLtrs.docx**.
5. Save and then close **WL1-C8-VB-FPMD.docx**.

Figure 8.13 Visual Benchmark Data Source Records

Mr. and Mrs. Chris Gallagher
17034 234th Avenue
Newport, VT 05855

Ms. Heather Segarra
4103 Thompson Drive
Newport, VT 05855

Mr. Gene Goodrich
831 Cromwell Lane
Newport, VT 05855

Mrs. Sonya Kraus
15933 Ninth Street
Newport, VT 05855

Figure 8.14 Visual Benchmark Main Document

Frontline Photography Equipment and Supplies

Current Date

Title First Name Last Name
Street Address
City, State ZIP

Dear Title Last Name:

We have enjoyed being a part of the Newport community for the past two years. Our success in the community is directly related to you, Title Last Name, and all of our other loyal customers. Thank you for shopping at our store for all of your photography equipment and supply needs.

To show our appreciation for your loyalty and your business, we are enclosing a coupon for 20 percent off any item in our store, even our incredibly low-priced clearance items. Through the end of the month, all of our camera accessories are on sale. So, use your coupon and take advantage of additional savings on items such as camera lenses, tripods, cleaning supplies, and camera bags.

To accommodate our customers' schedules, we have increased our weekend hours. Our store will be open Saturdays until 7:00 p.m. and Sundays until 5:00 p.m. Come by and let our sales associates find just the right camera and camera accessories for you.

Sincerely,

Student Name

XX
WL1-C8-VB-FPMD.docx

Enclosure

559 Tenth Street, Suite A ◈ Newport, VT 05855 ◈ (802) 555-4411

Case Study Apply Your Skills

Part 1

You are the office manager for Freestyle Extreme, a sporting goods store that specializes in snowboarding and snow skiing equipment and supplies. The store has two branches: one on the east side of town and the other on the west side. One of your job responsibilities is to send letters to customers letting them know about sales, new equipment, and upcoming events. Next month, both stores are having a sale and all snowboard and snow skiing supplies will be 15 percent off the regular price. Create a data source file that contains the following customer information: first name, last name, address, city, state, ZIP code, and branch. Add six customers to the data source file. Indicate that three usually shop at the East branch and three usually shop at the West branch. Create a letter as a main document that includes information about the upcoming sale. The letter should contain at least two paragraphs, and in addition to the information on the sale, it might include information about the store, snowboarding, and/or snow skiing. Save the data source file with the name **WL1-C8-CS-FEDS**, save the main document with the name **WL1-C8-CS-FEMD**, and save the merged document with the name **WL1-C8-CS-FELtrs**. Create envelopes for the six merged letters, and name the merged envelope document **WL1-C8-CS-FEEnvs**. Do not save the envelope main document. Print the merged letters document and the merged envelopes document.

Part 2

A well-known extreme snowboarder will be visiting both branches of the store to meet with customers and sign autographs. Use the Help feature to learn how to insert an If...Then...Else... merge field in a document, and then create a letter that includes the name of the extreme snowboarder (you determine the name), the time (1:00 p.m. to 4:30 p.m.), and any additional information that might interest customers. Also include in the letter an If...Then...Else... merge field that will insert *Wednesday, September 23* if the customer's Branch is *East* and will insert *Thursday, September 24* if the Branch is *West*. Add visual appeal to the letter by inserting a picture, clip art image, WordArt, or any other feature that will attract readers' attention. Save the letter main document and name it **WL1-C8-CS-MD**. Merge the letter main document with the **WL1-C8-CS-FEDS.mdb** data source. Save the merged letters document and name it **WL1-C8-CS-AnnLtrs**. Print the merged letters document.

Part 3

The store owner wants to try selling short skis known as "snow blades" or "skiboards." He has asked you to research these skis and identify one type and model to sell only at the West branch of the store. If the model sells well, he will consider selling it at the East branch at a future time. Prepare a main document letter that describes the new snow blade or skiboard that the West branch is selling. Include information about pricing and tell customers that the new item is being offered at a 40 percent discount if purchased within the next week. Merge the letter main document with the **WL1-C8-CS-FEDS.mdb** data source file and include only those customers that shop at the West branch. Save the merged letters document and name it **WL1-C8-CS-SBLtrs**. Print the merged letters document. Save the letter main document and name it **WL1-C8-CS-SBMD**. Print and then close the main document.

MICROSOFT® WORD Performance Assessment

Note: Before beginning unit assessments, copy to your storage medium the WL1U2 subfolder from the WL1 folder on the CD that accompanies this textbook and then make WL1U2 the active folder.

Assessing Proficiency

In this unit, you have learned to format text into columns; insert, format, and customize objects to enhance the appearance of a document; manage files, print envelopes and labels, and create documents using templates; create and edit tables; visually represent data in SmartArt graphics and organizational charts; and use Mail Merge to create letters, envelopes, labels, and directories.

Assessment 1 Format a Bioinformatics Document

1. Open **Bioinformatics.docx** and then save the document with Save As and name it **WL1-U2-A01-Bioinformatics**.
2. Move the insertion point to the end of the document and then insert the file named **GenomeMapping.docx**.
3. Change the line spacing for the entire document to 1.5 spacing.
4. Insert a continuous section break at the beginning of the first paragraph of text (the paragraph that begins *Bioinformatics is the mixed application*).
5. Format the text below the section break into two columns.
6. Balance the columns on the second page.
7. Press Ctrl + Home to move the insertion point to the beginning of the document, insert the Motion Quote text box, and then type "Understanding our DNA is similar to understanding a number that is billions of digits long." in the text box. Select the text in the text box, change the font size to 12 points, change the width of the text box to 2.6 inches, and then position the text box in the middle of the page with square text wrapping.
8. Create a drop cap with the first letter of the first word *Bioinformatics* that begins the first paragraph of text. Make the drop cap two lines in height.
9. Manually hyphenate words in the document.
10. Insert page numbering at the bottom of the page using the Thin Line page numbering option.
11. Save, print, and then close **WL1-U2-A01-Bioinformatics.docx**.

Assessment 2 Create a Workshop Flier

1. Create the flier shown in Figure U2.1 with the following specifications:
   a. Create the WordArt with the following specifications:
      - Use the *Fill - White, Outline - Accent 1, Shadow* option (first row, fourth column) at the WordArt button drop-down gallery.
      - Increase the width to 6.5 inches and the height to 1 inch.
      - Apply the Deflate text effect transform shape.
      - Change the text fill color to *Green, Accent 6, Lighter 40%*.

   b. Type the text shown in the figure. Change the font to 22-point Calibri bold and center-align the text.

   c. Insert the clip art image shown in the figure (use the keyword *Paris* to find the clip art) and then change the wrapping style to *Square*. Position and size the image as shown in the figure.
2. Save the document and name it **WL1-U2-A02-TravelFlier**.
3. Print and then close **WL1-U2-A02-TravelFlier.docx**.

Figure U2.1 Assessment 2

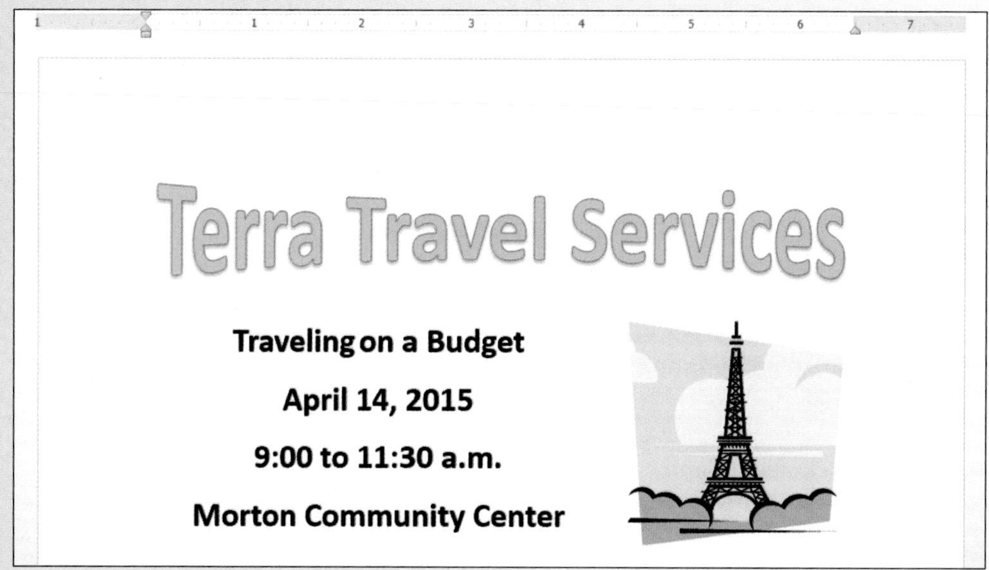

Assessment 3 Create a Staff Meeting Announcement

1. Create the announcement shown in Figure U2.2 with the following specifications:
   a. Use the Hexagon shape in the *Basic Shapes* section of the Shapes drop-down list to create the shape.
   b. Apply the Subtle Effect - Blue, Accent 1 shape style.
   c. Apply the Art Deco bevel shape effect.
   d. Type the letter A (this makes active many of the tab options), click the HOME tab, and then click the *No Spacing* style thumbnail in the Styles group.
   e. Type the remaining text in the shape as shown in the figure. Insert the ñ as a symbol (in the normal text font), and insert the clock as a symbol (in the Wingdings font). Set the text and clock symbol in larger font sizes.
2. Save the completed document and name it **WL1-U2-A03-MeetNotice**.
3. Print and then close **WL1-U2-A03-MeetNotice.docx**.

Figure U2.2 Assessment 3

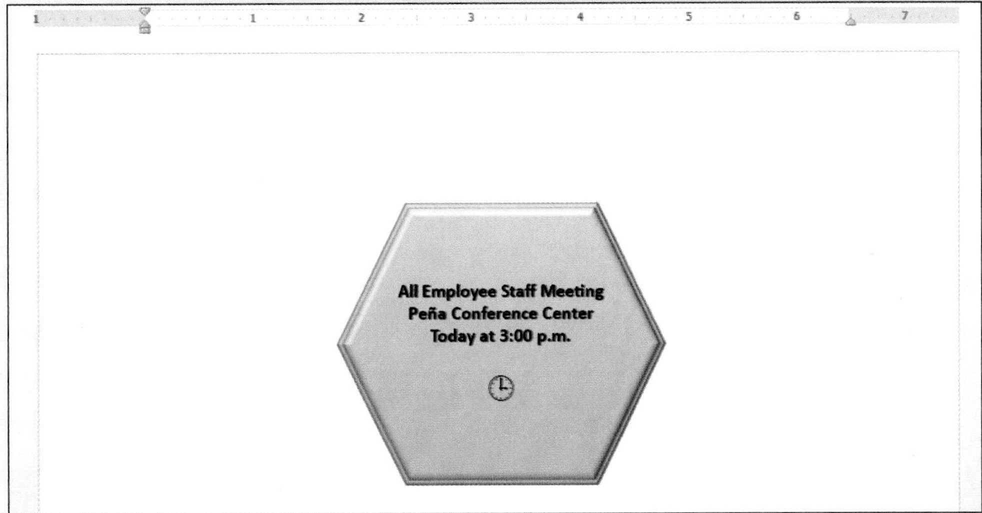

Assessment 4 Create a River Rafting Flier

1. At a blank document, insert the picture named **River.jpg**. (Insert the picture using the Picture button.)
2. Crop out a portion of the trees at the left and right and a portion of the hill at the top.
3. Correct the brightness and contrast to *Brightness: +20% Contrast: +40%*.
4. Specify that the picture should wrap behind text.
5. Type the text **River Rafting Adventures** on one line, **Salmon River, Idaho** on the next line, and **1-888-555-3322** on the third line.
6. Increase the size of the picture so it is easier to see and the size of the text so it is easier to read. Center the text and position it on the picture on top of the river so the text is readable.
7. Save the document and name it **WL1-U2-A04-RaftingFlier**.
8. Print and then close **WL1-U2-A04-RaftingFlier.docx**.

Assessment 5 Create an Envelope

1. At a blank document, create an envelope with the text shown in Figure U2.3.
2. Save the envelope document and name it **WL1-U2-A05-Env**.
3. Print and then close **WL1-U2-A05-Env.docx**.

Figure U2.3 Assessment 5

Mrs. Eileen Hebert
15205 East 42nd Street
Lake Charles, LA 71098

Mr. Earl Robicheaux
1436 North Sheldon Street
Jennings, LA 70542

Assessment 6 Create Mailing Labels

1. Create mailing labels with the name and address for Mrs. Eileen Hebert shown in Figure U2.3 using a label vendor and product of your choosing.
2. Save the document and name it **WL1-U2-A06-Labels**.
3. Print and then close **WL1-U2-A06-Labels.docx**.

Assessment 7 Create and Format a Table with Software Training Information

1. At a blank document, create the table shown in Figure U2.4. Format the table and the text (do not apply a table style) in a manner similar to what is shown in Figure U2.4.
2. Insert a formula in cell B8 that totals the numbers in cells B4 through B7.
3. Insert a formula in cell C8 that totals the numbers in cells C4 through C7.
4. Save the document and name it **WL1-U2-A07-TechTraining**.
5. Print and then close **WL1-U2-A07-TechTraining.docx**.

Figure U2.4 Assessment 7

TRI-STATE PRODUCTS		
Computer Technology Department Microsoft® Office 2013 Training		
Application	**# Enrolled**	**# Completed**
Access 2013	20	15
Excel 2013	62	56
PowerPoint 2013	40	33
Word 2013	80	72
Total		

Assessment 8 Create and Format a Table Containing Training Scores

1. Open **TrainingScores.docx** and then save the document with Save As and name it **WL1-U2-A08-TrainingScores**.
2. Insert formulas that calculate the averages in the appropriate row and column. (When writing the formulas, change the *Number format* option to *0*.)
3. Autofit the contents of the table.
4. Apply a table style of your choosing to the table.
5. Apply any other formatting to improve the appearance of the table.
6. Save, print, and then close **WL1-U2-A08-TrainingScores.docx**.

Assessment 9 Create an Organizational Chart

1. Use SmartArt to create an organizational chart for the text shown in Figure U2.5 (in the order displayed). Change the colors to *Colorful Range - Accent Colors 4 to 5* and apply the Metallic Scene SmartArt style.
2. Save the completed document and name it **WL1-U2-A09-OrgChart**.
3. Print and then close **WL1-U2-A09-OrgChart.docx**.

Figure U2.5 Assessment 9

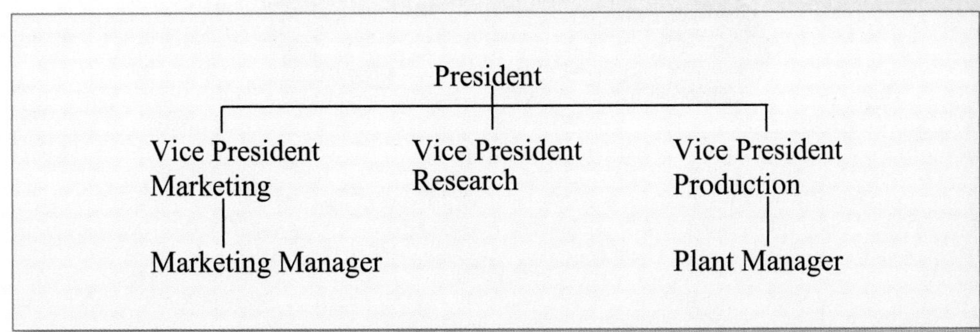

Assessment 10 Create a SmartArt Graphic

1. At a blank document, create the WordArt and SmartArt graphic shown in Figure U2.6 with the following specifications:
   a. Create the WordArt text using the *Fill - Blue, Accent 1, Outline - Background 1, Hard Shadow - Accent 1* option. Change the shape height to 1 inch and the shape width to 6 inches and then apply the Square transform text effect. Position the WordArt at the top center of the page with square text wrapping.
   b. Create the SmartArt graphic using the Vertical Picture Accent List graphic. Click the picture icon that displays in the top circle and then insert the picture named **Seagull.jpg** located in the WL1U2 folder. Insert the same picture in the other two circles. Type the text in each rectangle shape as shown in Figure U2.6. Change the colors to *Colorful Range - Accent Colors 5 to 6* and apply the Cartoon SmartArt style.
2. Save the document and name it **WL1-U2-A10-SPGraphic**.
3. Print and then close **WL1-U2-A10-SPGraphic.docx**.

Figure U2.6 Assessment 10

Assessment 11 Merge and Print Letters

1. Look at the information shown in Figure U2.7 and Figure U2.8. Use the Mail Merge feature to prepare six letters using the information shown in the figures. When creating the letter main document, open **SMLtrhd.docx** and then save the document with Save As and name it **WL1-U2-A11-MD**. Insert Fill-in fields in the main document in place of the *(coordinator name)* and *(telephone number)* text. Create the data source file with the text shown in Figure U2.7 and name the file **WL1-U2-A11-DS**.
2. Type the text in the main document as shown in Figure U2.8 and then merge the document with the **WL1-U2-A11-DS.mdb** data source file. When merging, enter the first name and telephone number shown below for the first three records and enter the second name and telephone number shown below for the last three records:

   Jeff Greenswald (813) 555-9886
   Grace Ramirez (813) 555-9807
3. Save the merged letters document and name it **WL1-U2-A11-Ltrs**. Print and then close the document.
4. Save and then close the main document.

Figure U2.7 Assessment 11

Mr. Antonio Mercado
3241 Court G
Tampa, FL 33623

Ms. Kristina Vukovich
1120 South Monroe
Tampa, FL 33655

Ms. Alexandria Remick
909 Wheeler South
Tampa, FL 33620

Mr. Minh Vu
9302 Lawndale Southwest
Tampa, FL 33623

Mr. Curtis Iverson
10139 93rd Court South
Tampa, FL 33654

Mrs. Holly Bernard
8904 Emerson Road
Tampa, FL 33620

Figure U2.8 Assessment 11

December 14, 2015

«AddressBlock»

«GreetingLine»

Sound Medical is switching hospital care in Tampa to St. Jude's Hospital beginning January 1, 2016. As mentioned in last month's letter, St. Jude's Hospital was selected because it meets our requirements for high-quality, customer-pleasing care that is also affordable and accessible. Our physicians look forward to caring for you in this new environment.

Over the past month, staff members at Sound Medical have been working to make this transition as smooth as possible. Surgeries planned after January 1 are being scheduled at St. Jude's Hospital. Mothers delivering babies any time after January 1 are receiving information about delivery room tours and prenatal classes available at St. Jude's. Your Sound Medical doctor will have privileges at St. Jude's and will continue to care for you if you need to be hospitalized.

You are a very important part of our patient family, «Title» «Last_Name», and we hope this information is helpful. If you have any additional questions or concerns, please call your Sound Medical health coordinator, (coordinator name), at (telephone number), between 8:00 a.m. and 4:30 p.m.

Sincerely,

Jody Tiemann
District Administrator

XX
WL1-U2-A11-MD.docx

Assessment 12 Merge and Print Envelopes

1. Use the Mail Merge feature to prepare envelopes for the letters created in Assessment 11.
2. Specify **WL1-U2-A11-DS.mdb** as the data source document.
3. Save the merged envelopes document and name the document **WL1-U2-A12-Envs**.
4. Print and then close **WL1-U2-A12-Envs.docx**.
5. Do not save the envelope main document.

Writing Activities

The following activities give you the opportunity to practice your writing skills along with demonstrating an understanding of some of the important Word features you have mastered in this unit. Use correct grammar, appropriate word choices, and clear sentence construction.

Activity 1 Compose a Letter to Volunteers

You are an employee of the city of Greenwater and are responsible for coordinating volunteers for the city's Safe Night program. Compose a letter to the volunteers listed in Figure U2.9 and include the following information in the letter:

- Safe Night event scheduled for Saturday, June 13, 2015.
- Volunteer orientation scheduled for Thursday, May 14, 2015, at 7:30 p.m. At the orientation, participants will learn about the types of volunteer positions available and the work schedule.

Include additional information in the letter, including a thank you to the volunteers. Use the Mail Merge feature to create a data source with the names and addresses shown in Figure U2.9 that is attached to the main document, which is the letter to the volunteers. Save the merged letters as **WL1-U2-Act01-Ltrs** and then print them.

Figure U2.9 Activity 1

Mrs. Laura Reston
376 Thompson Avenue
Greenwater, OR 99034

Ms. Cecilia Sykes
1430 Canyon Road
Greenwater, OR 99034

Mr. Ralph Emerson
1103 Highlands Avenue
Greenwater, OR 99034

Mr. Matthew Klein
7408 Ryan Road
Greenwater, OR 99034

Mr. Brian McDonald
8980 Union Street
Greenwater, OR 99034

Mrs. Nola Alverez
598 McBride Street
Greenwater, OR 99034

Activity 2 Create a Business Letterhead

You have just opened a new mailing and shipping business and need letterhead stationery. Click the INSERT tab, click the Header button, and then click *Edit Header* at the drop-down list. Look at the options in the Options group on the HEADER & FOOTER TOOLS DESIGN tab and then figure out how to create a header that displays and prints only on the first page. Create a letterhead for your company in a header that displays and prints only on the first page and include *at least* one of the following: a clip art image, a picture, a shape, a text box, and/or WordArt. Include the following information in the header:

Global Mailing
4300 Jackson Avenue
Toronto, ON M4C 3X4
(416) 555-0095
www.emcp.net/globalmailing

Save the completed letterhead and name it **WL1-U2-Act02-Ltrhd**. Print and then close the document.

Internet Research

Create a Flier on an Incentive Program

The owner of Terra Travel Services is offering an incentive to motivate travel consultants to increase travel bookings. The incentive is a sales contest with a grand prize of a one-week paid vacation to Cancun, Mexico. The owner has asked you to create a flier that will be posted on the office bulletin board that includes information about the incentive program, as well as some information about Cancun. Create this flier using information about Cancun that you find on the Internet. Include a photo you find on a website (make sure it is not copyrighted), or include a clip art image representing travel. Include any other information or object to add visual interest to the flier. Save the completed flier and name it **WL1-U2-InternetResearch**. Print and then close the document.

Job Study

Develop Recycling Program Communications

The Chief Operating Officer of Harrington Engineering has just approved your draft of the company's new recycling policy. (Open the file named **RecyclingPolicy.docx** located in the WL1U2 folder.) Edit the draft and prepare a final copy of the policy, along with a memo to all employees describing the new guidelines. To support the company's energy resources conservation effort, you will send hard copies of the new policy to the Somerset Recycling Program president and to directors of the Somerset Chamber of Commerce.

Using the concepts and techniques you learned in this unit, prepare the following documents:

- Format the recycling policy manual, including a cover page, appropriate headers and footers, and page numbers. Add at least one graphic where appropriate. Format the document using styles and a style set. Save the manual and name it **WL1-U2-JobStudyManual**. Print the manual.
- Download a memo template at the New backstage area and then create a memo from Susan Gerhardt, Chief Operating Officer of Harrington Engineering, to all employees that introduces the new recycling program. Copy the *Procedure* section of the recycling policy manual into the memo where appropriate. Include a table listing five employees who will act as Recycling Coordinators at Harrington Engineering (make up the names). Add columns for the employees' department names and telephone extensions. Save the memo and name it **WL1-U2-JobStudyMemo**. Print the memo.
- Write a letter to the president of the Somerset Recycling Program, William Elizondo, enclosing a copy of the recycling policy manual. Add a notation indicating that copies with enclosures were sent to all members of the Somerset Chamber of Commerce. Save the letter and name it **WL1-U2-JobStudyLetter**. Print the letter.
- Create mailing labels (see Figure U2.10). Save the labels and name the file **WL1-U2-JobStudyLabels**. Print the file.

Figure U2.10 Mailing Labels

William Elizondo, President
Somerset Recycling Program
700 West Brighton Road
Somerset, NJ 55123

Paul Schwartz
Somerset Chamber of Commerce
45 Wallace Road
Somerset, NJ 55123

Ashley Crighton
Somerset Chamber of Commerce
45 Wallace Road
Somerset, NJ 55123

Carol Davis
Somerset Chamber of Commerce
45 Wallace Road
Somerset, NJ 55123

Robert Knight
Somerset Chamber of Commerce
45 Wallace Road
Somerset, NJ 55123

A

B

C

D

E

F

G

H

I

K

L

M

N

O

P

Q

R

U

V

W

X

Z

MICROSOFT® WORD Level 2

Unit 1 ■ Formatting and Customizing Documents

Chapter 1 ■ Customizing Paragraphs and Pages

Chapter 2 ■ Proofing Documents

Chapter 3 ■ Automating and Customizing Formatting

Chapter 4 ■ Customizing Themes, Creating Macros, and Navigating in a Document

Customizing Paragraphs and Pages

PERFORMANCE OBJECTIVES

Upon successful completion of Chapter 1, you will be able to:

- **Apply custom numbering and bulleting formatting to text**
- **Define new bullets**
- **Insert and define multilevel list numbering**
- **Insert, format, and customize images and text boxes**
- **Insert headers and footers in documents**
- **Format, edit, and remove a header or footer**
- **Insert and print sections**
- **Control widows/orphans and keep text together on a page**
- **Insert and format charts**

Tutorials

1.1 Inserting Custom Numbers and Bullets
1.2 Inserting Multilevel Lists
1.3 Customizing and Formatting an Image
1.4 Applying Advanced Formatting to Images
1.5 Inserting and Formatting Text Boxes
1.6 Customizing Headers and Footers
1.7 Printing Sections of a Document
1.8 Keeping Text Together
1.9 Creating Charts
1.10 Formatting with Chart Buttons
1.11 Changing Chart Design and Formatting

Word contains a variety of options for formatting text in paragraphs and applying page formatting. In this chapter, you will learn how to insert custom numbers and bullets, define new numbering formats, define new picture and symbol bullets, apply multilevel numbering to text, and define a new multilevel list. You will also learn about inserting and editing headers and footers, printing specific sections of a document, controlling text flow on pages, and presenting text visually in a chart. Model answers for this chapter's projects appear on the following pages.

Note: Before beginning the projects, copy to your storage medium the WL2C1 subfolder from the WL2 folder on the CD that accompanies this textbook. Steps on how to copy a folder are presented on the inside of the back cover of this textbook. Do this every time you start a chapter's projects.

Model Answers

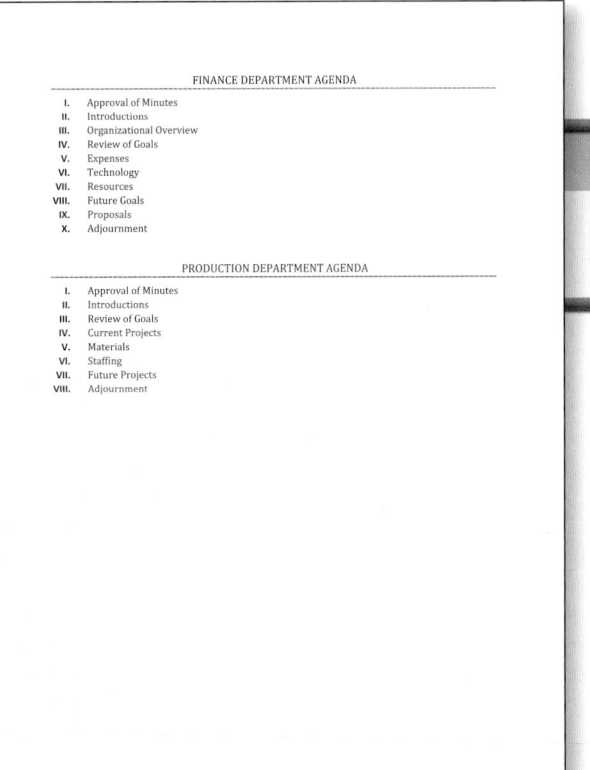

FINANCE DEPARTMENT AGENDA

I. Approval of Minutes
II. Introductions
III. Organizational Overview
IV. Review of Goals
V. Expenses
VI. Technology
VII. Resources
VIII. Future Goals
IX. Proposals
X. Adjournment

PRODUCTION DEPARTMENT AGENDA

I. Approval of Minutes
II. Introductions
III. Review of Goals
IV. Current Projects
V. Materials
VI. Staffing
VII. Future Projects
VIII. Adjournment

Project 1 Apply Number Formatting to an Agenda
WL2-C1-P1-FDAgenda.docx

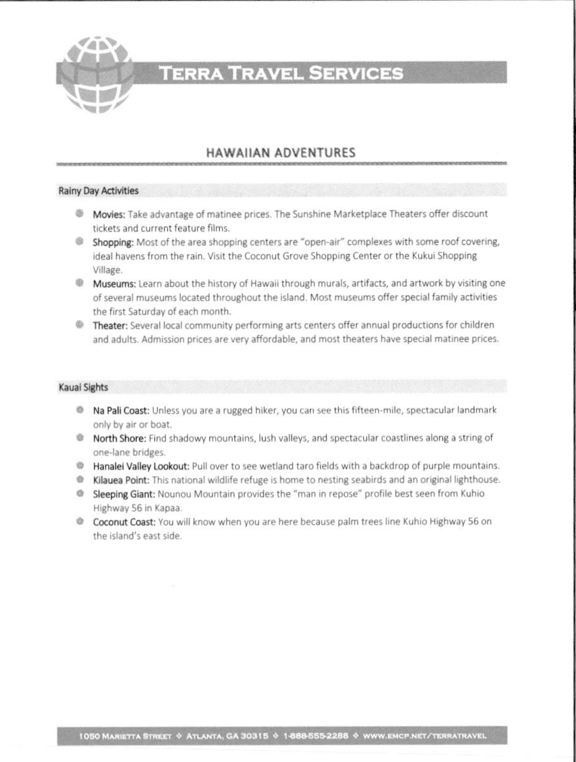

TERRA TRAVEL SERVICES

HAWAIIAN ADVENTURES

Rainy Day Activities

- **Movies:** Take advantage of matinee prices. The Sunshine Marketplace Theaters offer discount tickets and current feature films.
- **Shopping:** Most of the area shopping centers are "open-air" complexes with some roof covering, ideal havens from the rain. Visit the Coconut Grove Shopping Center or the Kukui Shopping Village.
- **Museums:** Learn about the history of Hawaii through murals, artifacts, and artwork by visiting one of several museums located throughout the island. Most museums offer special family activities the first Saturday of each month.
- **Theater:** Several local community performing arts centers offer annual productions for children and adults. Admission prices are very affordable, and most theaters have special matinee prices.

Kauai Sights

- **Na Pali Coast:** Unless you are a rugged hiker, you can see this fifteen-mile, spectacular landmark only by air or boat.
- **North Shore:** Find shadowy mountains, lush valleys, and spectacular coastlines along a string of one-lane bridges.
- **Hanalei Valley Lookout:** Pull over to see wetland taro fields with a backdrop of purple mountains.
- **Kilauea Point:** This national wildlife refuge is home to nesting seabirds and an original lighthouse.
- **Sleeping Giant:** Nounou Mountain provides the "man in repose" profile best seen from Kuhio Highway 56 in Kapaa.
- **Coconut Coast:** You will know when you are here because palm trees line Kuhio Highway 56 on the island's east side.

1050 MARIETTA STREET ✧ ATLANTA, GA 30315 ✧ 1-888-555-2288 ✧ WWW.EMCP.NET/TERRATRAVEL

Project 2 Apply Custom Bullets to a Technology Document
WL2-C1-P2-TTSHawaii.docx

PREPARING FOR A JOB SEARCH

A. Writing a Resume
  1. Resume Language
    a) Word Power
    b) Clichés
  2. Competency Statements
    a) Definition of Competency Statements
    b) Competency Statements on a Resume
    c) Writing a Competency Statement
B. Writing a Cover Letter
  1. Cover Letter Rules
  2. Cover Letter Examples
C. Electronic Resumes
  1. Getting Your Resume Online
    a) Creating an Electronic Resume
    b) Posting an Electronic Resume
  2. Internet Sites for Job Seekers
    a) Job Hunting Websites
    b) Search Terms

Project 3 Apply Multilevel List Numbering to a Job Search Document
WL2-C1-P3-JSList.docx

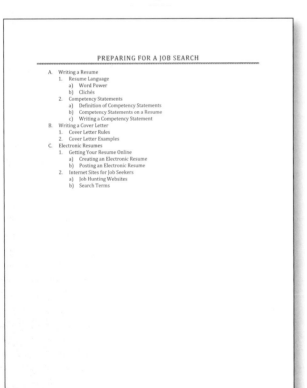

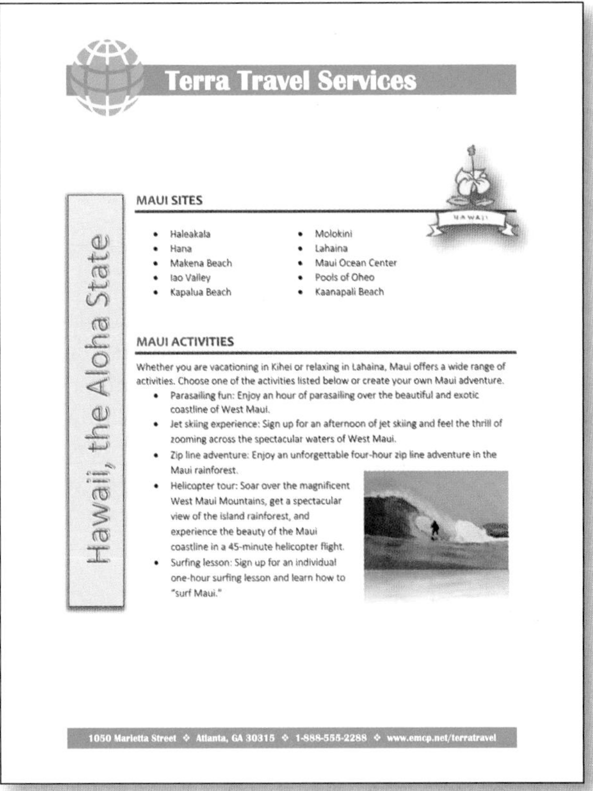

Terra Travel Services

Hawaii, the Aloha State

MAUI SITES

- Haleakala
- Hana
- Makena Beach
- Iao Valley
- Kapalua Beach
- Molokini
- Lahaina
- Maui Ocean Center
- Pools of Oheo
- Kaanapali Beach

MAUI ACTIVITIES

Whether you are vacationing in Kihei or relaxing in Lahaina, Maui offers a wide range of activities. Choose one of the activities listed below or create your own Maui adventure.

- Parasailing fun: Enjoy an hour of parasailing over the beautiful and exotic coastline of West Maui.
- Jet skiing experience: Sign up for an afternoon of jet skiing and feel the thrill of zooming across the spectacular waters of West Maui.
- Zip line adventure: Enjoy an unforgettable four-hour zip line adventure in the Maui rainforest.
- Helicopter tour: Soar over the magnificent West Maui Mountains, get a spectacular view of the island rainforest, and experience the beauty of the Maui coastline in a 45-minute helicopter flight.
- Surfing lesson: Sign up for an individual one-hour surfing lesson and learn how to "surf Maui."

1050 Marietta Street ✧ Atlanta, GA 30315 ✧ 1-888-555-2288 ✧ www.emcp.net/terratravel

Project 4 Insert Images and a Text Box in a Travel Document
WL2-C1-P4-TTSMaui.docx

Productivity Software

Productivity software includes software that people typically use to complete work, such as a word processor (working with words), spreadsheet (working with data, numbers, and calculations), database (organizing and retrieving data records), and presentation (creating slideshows with text and graphics) programs. Productivity software is often compiled into suites of applications, such as Microsoft Office, because many people use two or more of these products to get their work completed. Office suites often include a word processor, a spreadsheet application, presentation software, and database management software. Suites also allow users to integrate content from one program into another, such as including a spreadsheet chart in a report created with a word processor.

Word Processing Software

Word processor software certainly does "process" words, but today it does a great deal more. With a word processor you can create documents that include sophisticated formatting; change text fonts (styles applied to text); add special effects such as bold, italics, and underlining; add shadows, background colors, and other effects to text and objects; and include tables, photos, drawings, and links to online content. You can also use templates (predesigned documents with formatting and graphics already in place for you to fill in) to design web pages, newsletters, and more. A mail merge feature makes it easy to take a list of names and addresses and print personalized letters and envelopes or labels.

Section 1 Page 1

Spreadsheet Software

Spreadsheet software, such as Microsoft Excel, is an application where numbers rule. Using spreadsheet software you can perform calculations that range from simple (adding, averaging, and multiplying) to complex (estimating standard deviations based on a range of numbers, for example). In addition, spreadsheet software offers sophisticated charting and graphing capabilities. Formatting tools help you create polished looking documents such as budgets, invoices, schedules, attendance records, and purchase orders. With spreadsheet software, you can also keep track of data such as your holiday card list and sort that list or search for specific names or other data.

Database Software

Database software can manage large quantities of data. The software provides functions for organizing the data into related lists and retrieving useful information from these lists. For example, imagine that you are a salesperson who wants to create a list of customers. Of course you want to include the name, address, and company name for each person. However, you might also want each customer record to include the customer's birthday, spouse's name, and favorite hobby as well as a record of purchases in the past year. You can also set up fields to look up data such as city names based on a ZIP code, saving you time reentering data. Once that data is entered into a table you can view information in a spreadsheet-like list or as individual customer record forms. You can create queries that let you find specific data sets. For example, say you want to find every customer with a birthday in June who is interested in sports and has

Section 1 Page 2

Project 5 Insert Headers and Footers in a Computer Report

WL2-C1-P5-CompSoftware.docx

purchased at least $2,000 of products in the last year so you can invite them to a company sponsored sports event. With a database, you can generate a list of those records easily.

Presentation Software

Presentation software, such as Microsoft PowerPoint, uses the concept of individual slides that form a slideshow. Slides may contain bulleted lists of key concepts, graphics, tables, animations, hyperlinks to web pages, diagrams, and charts. A slideshow can support a presenter's comments during a talk, can run continuously on its own, or can be browsed by an individual online or on a computer. A presentation program can help users create attractive slides by allowing them to use background art from a template, placeholders for titles and bulleted lists, and graphics.

Section 1 Page 3

Graphics and Multimedia Software

With graphics software, you can create, edit, and format images such as pictures and photos. Use multimedia software to work with media such as animations, audio, and video.

Graphics Software

If you like working with drawings, photos, or other kinds of images, you may have used graphics software, which is software that allows you to create, edit, or manipulate images such as drawings and photos. Though most productivity software such as word processors and presentation software include graphics features, design professionals work with products that are much more feature-rich such as desktop publishing software, photo editing software, and screen capture software.

Desktop publishing software is used by design professionals to lay out pages for books, magazines, brochures, product packaging, and other print materials. Photo editing software is used by design professionals to enhance photo quality or apply special effects such as blurring elements or feathering the edges of a photo. With screen capture software you can capture an entire computer screen or only a portion of it, which is helpful for showing people how to use software features.

Section 2 Page 1

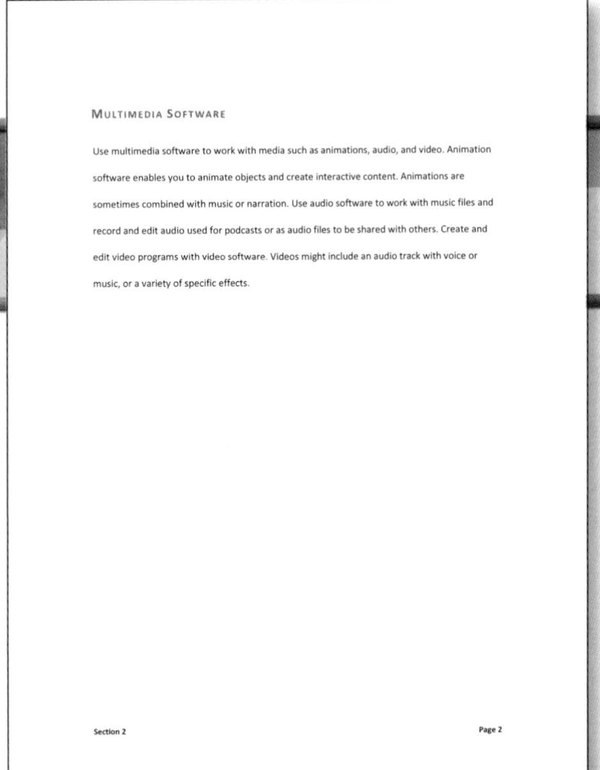

MULTIMEDIA SOFTWARE

Use multimedia software to work with media such as animations, audio, and video. Animation software enables you to animate objects and create interactive content. Animations are sometimes combined with music or narration. Use audio software to work with music files and record and edit audio used for podcasts or as audio files to be shared with others. Create and edit video programs with video software. Videos might include an audio track with voice or music, or a variety of specific effects.

Section 2 Page 2

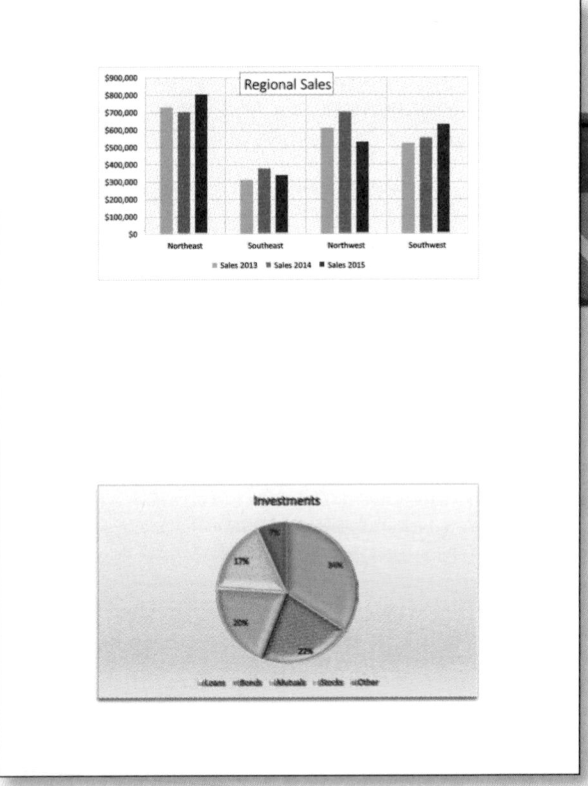

Project 6 Create and Format a Column Chart and Pie Chart
WL2-C1-P6-Charts.docx

Project 1 Apply Number Formatting to an Agenda — 2 Parts

You will open an agenda document, apply formatting that includes number formatting, and then define and apply custom numbering.

Inserting Custom Numbers and Bullets

You can automatically number paragraphs or insert bullets before paragraphs using buttons in the Paragraph group on the HOME tab. Use the Numbering button to insert numbers before specific paragraphs and use the Bullets button to insert bullets. If you want to insert custom numbering or bullets, click the button arrow and then choose from the drop-down gallery that displays.

Numbering

Bullets

Inserting Custom Numbers

If the automatic numbering or bullets feature is on, press Shift + Enter to insert a line break without inserting a bullet or number.

You can insert numbers as you type text or select text and then apply a numbering format. If you type *1.* and then press the spacebar, Word indents the number approximately 0.25 inch. When you type text and then press Enter, Word indents all of the lines in the paragraph 0.5 inch from the left margin (called a ***hanging indent***) and inserts the number 2 followed by a period 0.25 inch from the left margin at the beginning of the next paragraph. Continue typing items and Word adds successive numbers onto the list. To number existing paragraphs of text, select the paragraphs and then click the Numbering button in the Paragraph group on the HOME tab.

When you click the Numbering button in the Paragraph group, arabic numbers (1., 2., 3., etc.) are inserted in the document. You can change this default numbering by clicking the Numbering button arrow and then clicking the desired option at the Numbering drop-down gallery.

To change list levels, click the Numbering button arrow, point to the *Change List Level* option located toward the bottom of the drop-down gallery, and then click the desired list level at the side menu. You can set the numbering value with options at the Set Numbering Value dialog box. Display this dialog box by clicking the Numbering button arrow and then clicking the *Set Numbering Value* option at the bottom of the drop-down gallery.

Project 1a Inserting Custom Numbers

Part 1 of 2

1. Open **FDAgenda.docx** and then save the document and name it **WL2-C1-P1-FDAgenda**.
2. Restart the list numbering at 1 by completing the following steps:
   a. Select the numbered paragraphs.
   b. Click the Numbering button arrow in the Paragraph group on the HOME tab and then click *Set Numbering Value* at the drop-down gallery.
   c. At the Set Numbering Value dialog box, select the number in the *Set value to* measurement box, type 1, and then press the Enter key.

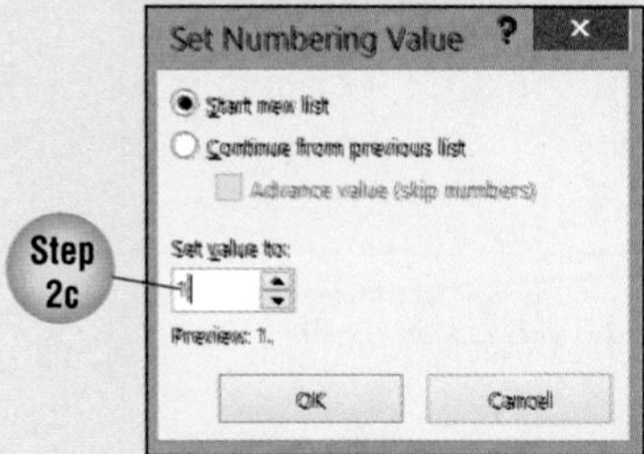

3. Change the paragraph numbers to letters by completing the following steps:
   a. With the numbered paragraphs selected, click the Numbering button arrow.
   b. At the Numbering drop-down gallery, click the option that uses capital letters. (The location of the option may vary.)

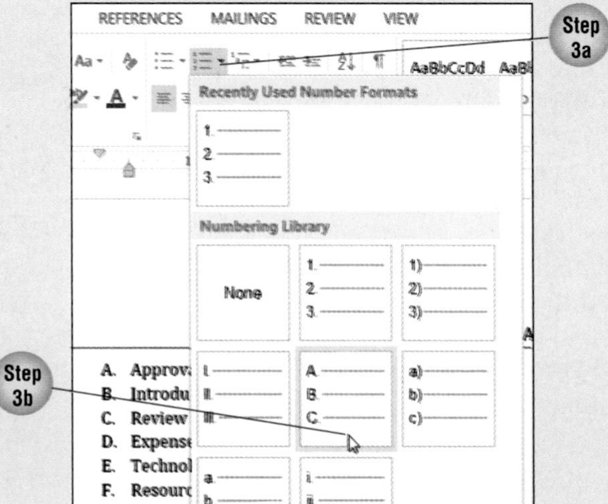

4. Add text to the agenda by positioning the insertion point immediately to the right of the text *Introductions*, pressing the Enter key, and then typing **Organizational Overview**.

5. Demote the lettered list by completing the following steps:
   a. Select the lettered paragraphs.
   b. Click the Numbering button arrow, point to the *Change List Level* option, and then click the *a.* option at the side menu (*Level 2*).
6. With the paragraphs still selected, promote the list by clicking the Decrease Indent button in the Paragraph group on the HOME tab. (The list changes back to capital letters.)
7. Move the insertion point to the end of the document and then type **The meeting will stop for lunch, which is catered and will be held in the main conference center from 12:15 to 1:30 p.m.**
8. Press the Enter key and then click the Numbering button.

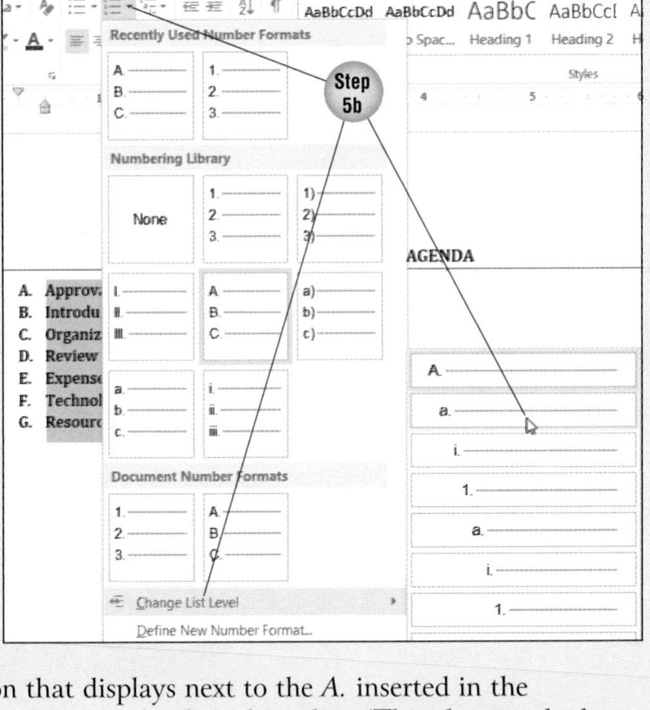

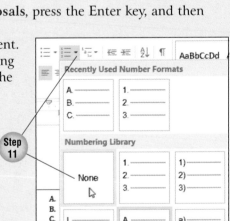

9. Click the AutoCorrect Options button that displays next to the *A.* inserted in the document and then click *Continue Numbering* at the drop-down list. (This changes the letter from *A.* to *H.*)

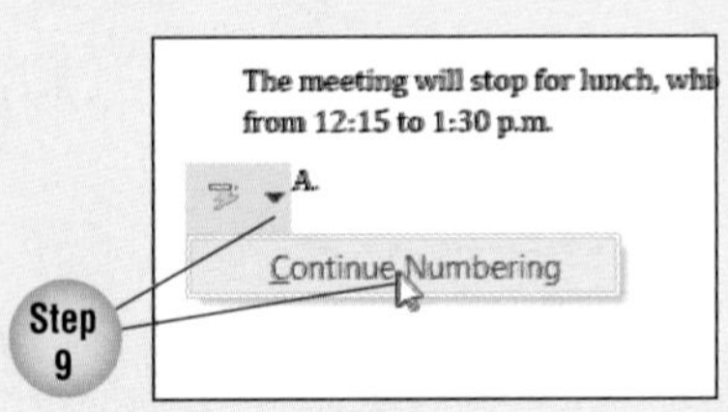

10. Type **Future Goals**, press the Enter key, type **Proposals**, press the Enter key, and then type **Adjournment**.
11. Press the Enter key and *K.* is inserted in the document. Turn off the list formatting by clicking the Numbering button arrow and then clicking the *None* option at the drop-down gallery.
12. Save and then print **WL2-C1-P1-FDAgenda.docx**.
13. Select and then delete the paragraph of text in the middle of the list (begins *The meeting will stop*). (All of the lettered items should be listed consecutively with the same spacing between them.)
14. Save **WL2-C1-P1-FDAgenda.docx**.

Defining Numbering Formatting

Along with default numbers and custom numbers, you can also define your own number format with options at the Define New Number Format dialog box, shown in Figure 1.1. Display this dialog box by clicking the Numbering button arrow and then clicking *Define New Number Format* at the drop-down gallery. Use options at the dialog box to specify the number style, font, and alignment. Preview the formatting in the *Preview* section.

Any number format that you create at the Define New Number Format dialog box is automatically included in the *Numbering Library* section of the Numbering button drop-down list. Remove a number format from the drop-down list by right-clicking the format and then clicking *Remove* at the shortcut menu.

Quick Steps

Define New Number Format

1. Click Numbering button arrow.
2. Click *Define New Number Format.*
3. Specify desired format.
4. Click OK.

Figure 1.1 Define New Number Format Dialog Box

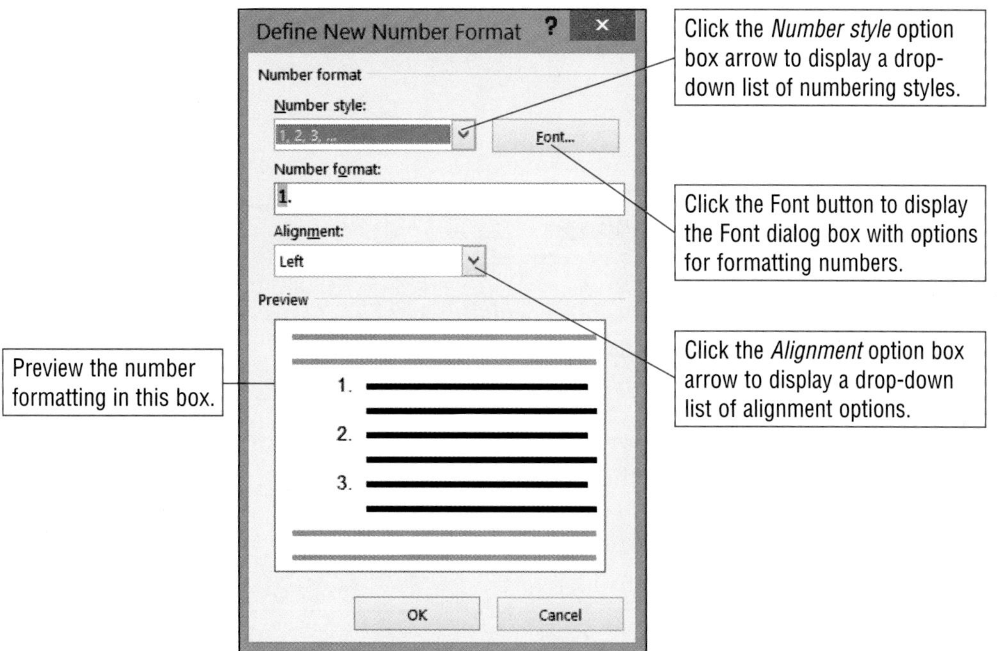

Project 1b **Defining a Numbering Format** **Part 2 of 2**

1. With **WL2-C1-P1-FDAgenda.docx** open, define a new number format by completing the following steps:
   a. With the insertion point positioned on any character in the numbered paragraphs, click the Numbering button arrow in the Paragraph group on the HOME tab.
   b. Click *Define New Number Format* at the drop-down list.
   c. At the Define New Number Format dialog box, click the down-pointing arrow at the right of the *Number style* option and then click the *I, II, III, …* option.
   d. Click the Font button that displays at the right side of the *Number style* list box.

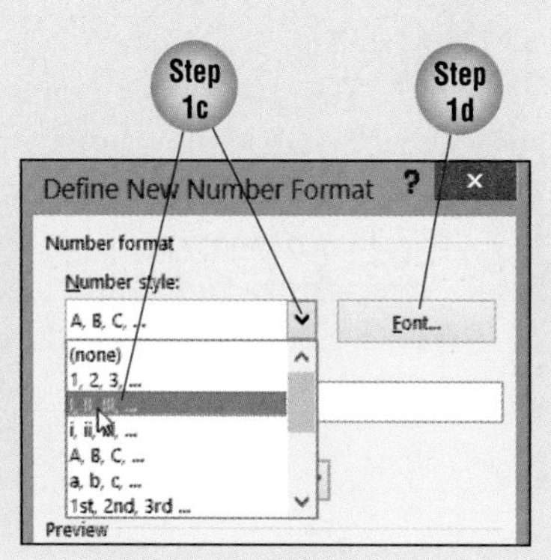

e. At the Font dialog box, scroll down the *Font* list box and then click *Calibri*.
f. Click *Bold* in the *Font style* list box.

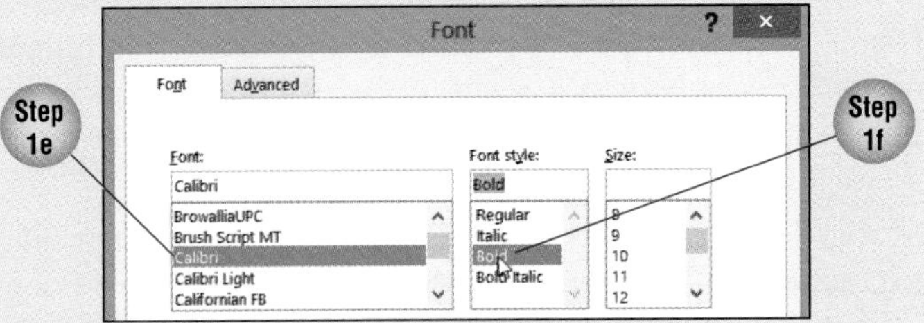

g. Click OK to close the Font dialog box.
h. Click the down-pointing arrow at the right of the *Alignment* option box and then click *Right* at the drop-down list.

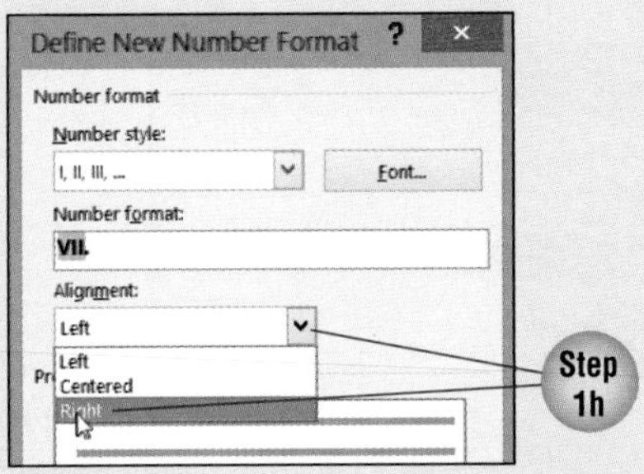

i. Click OK to close the Define New Number Format dialog box. (This applies the new formatting to the numbered paragraphs in the document.)

2. Insert a file into the current document by completing the following steps:
   a. Press Ctrl + End to move the insertion point to the end of the document and then press the Enter key.
   b. Click the INSERT tab.
   c. Click the Object button arrow in the Text group and then click *Text from File* at the drop-down list.
   d. At the Insert File dialog box, navigate to the WL2C1 folder and then double-click ***PDAgenda.docx***.

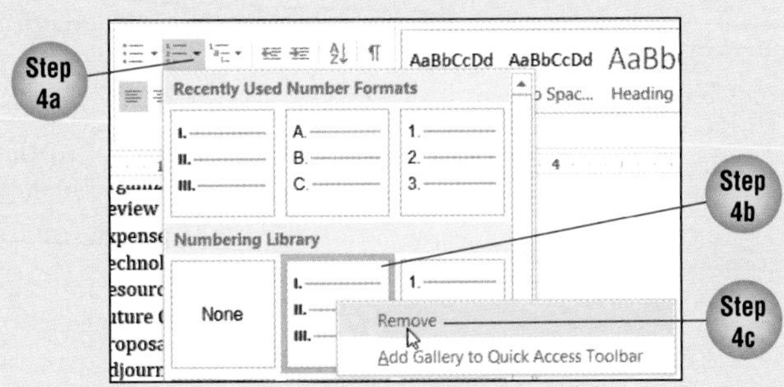

3. Select the text below the title *PRODUCTION DEPARTMENT AGENDA*, click the HOME tab, click the Numbering button arrow, and then click the roman numeral style that you created in Step 1.
4. Remove from the Numbering Library the number format you created by completing the following steps:
   a. Click the Numbering button arrow.
   b. In the *Numbering Library* section, right-click the roman numeral number format that you created.
   c. Click *Remove* at the shortcut menu.
5. Save, print, and then close **WL2-C1-P1-FDAgenda.docx**.

Project 2 Apply Custom Bullets to a Travel Document — 1 Part

You will open a travel document and then define and insert custom picture and symbol bullets.

Defining and Inserting Custom Bullets

When you click the Bullets button in the Paragraph group, a round bullet is inserted in the document. Insert custom bullets by clicking the Bullets button arrow and then clicking the desired bullet type at the drop-down gallery. This drop-down gallery displays the most recently used bullets along with an option for defining new bullets.

Click the *Define New Bullet* option and the Define New Bullet dialog box displays, as shown in Figure 1.2. From the options at the dialog box, you can choose a symbol or picture bullet, change the font size of the bullet, and specify the alignment of the bullet. When you choose a custom bullet, consider matching the theme or mood of the document to maintain a consistent look or creating a picture bullet to add visual interest.

A bullet that you create at the Define New Bullet dialog box is automatically included in the *Bullet Library* section of the Bullets button drop-down gallery. You can remove a bullet from the drop-down gallery by right-clicking the bullet and then clicking *Remove* at the shortcut menu.

As with a numbered list, you can change the level of a bulleted list. To do this, click the item or select the items you want to change, click the Bullets button arrow, and then point to *Change List Level*. At the side menu of bullet options that displays, click the desired bullet. If you want to insert a line break in the list while the automatic bullets feature is on without inserting a bullet, press Shift + Enter. (You can also insert a line break in a numbered list without inserting a number by pressing Shift + Enter.)

Quick Steps

Define a Custom Bullet

1. Click Bullets button arrow.
2. Click *Define New Bullet* at drop-down gallery.
3. Click Symbol button or Picture button.
4. Click desired symbol or picture.
5. Click OK.
6. Click OK.

Create a picture bullet to add visual interest to a document.

Figure 1.2 Define New Bullet Dialog Box

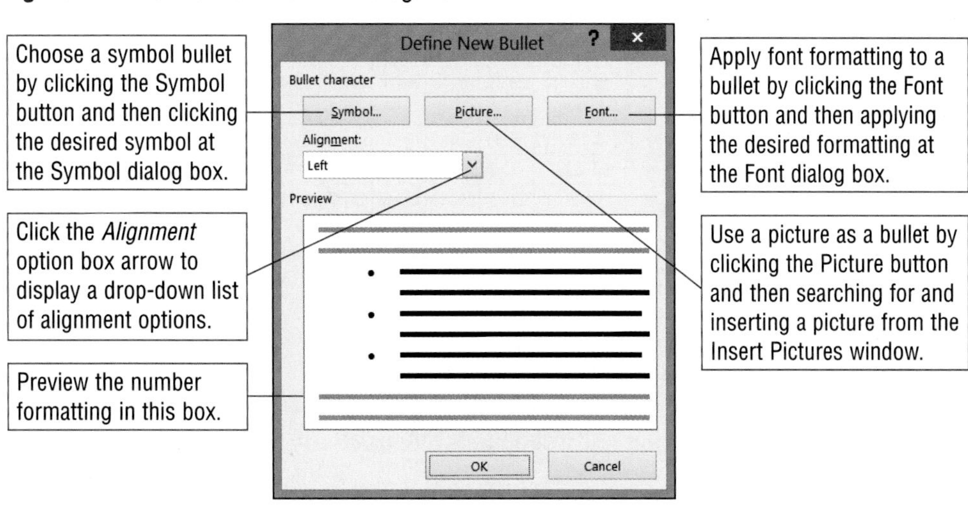
Choose a symbol bullet by clicking the Symbol button and then clicking the desired symbol at the Symbol dialog box.
Click the Alignment option box arrow to display a drop-down list of alignment options.
Preview the number formatting in this box.
Define New Bullet
Bullet character
Symbol...
Picture...
Font...
Alignment:
Left
Preview
OK
Cancel
Apply font formatting to a bullet by clicking the Font button and then applying the desired formatting at the Font dialog box.
Use a picture as a bullet by clicking the Picture button and then searching for and inserting a picture from the Insert Pictures window.

Project 2 Defining and Inserting Custom Bullets

Part 1 of 1

1. Open **TTSHawaii.docx** and then save the document and name it **WL2-C1-P2-TTSHawaii**.
2. Define and insert a picture bullet by completing the following steps:
   a. Select the four paragraphs of text below the heading *Rainy Day Activities*.
   b. Click the Bullets button arrow in the Paragraph group on the HOME tab and then click *Define New Bullet* at the drop-down gallery.
   c. At the Define New Bullet dialog box, click the Picture button.
   d. At the Insert Pictures window, click in the *Office.com Clip Art* text box, type **green flower**, and then press Enter.
   e. Double-click the green flower image shown at the right.
   f. Click OK to close the Define New Bullet dialog box. (The new bullet is applied to the selected paragraphs.)

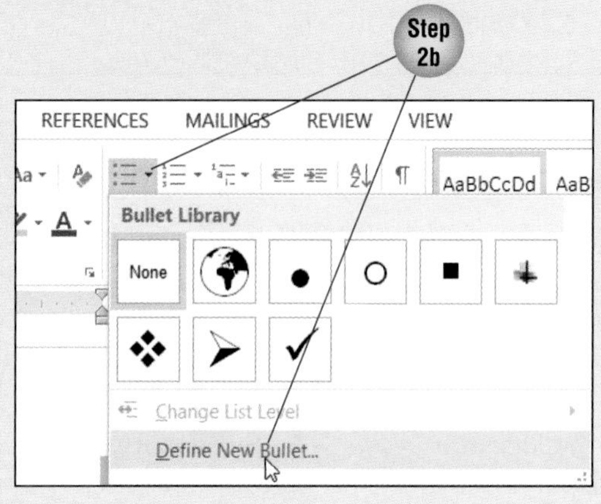

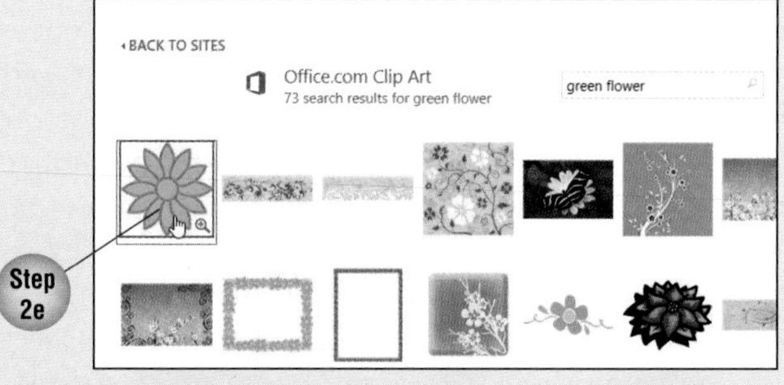

3. Define and insert a symbol bullet by completing the following steps:
   a. Select the six paragraphs below the heading *Kauai Sights*.
   b. Click the Bullets button arrow and then click *Define New Bullet* at the drop-down gallery.
   c. At the Define New Bullet dialog box, click the Symbol button.
   d. At the Symbol dialog box, click the down-pointing arrow at the right of the *Font* option, scroll down the drop-down list, and then click *Wingdings*.
   e. Click the flower symbol shown at the right.
   f. Click OK to close the Symbol dialog box.
   g. At the Define New Bullet dialog box, click the Font button.
   h. At the Font dialog box, click *11* in the *Size* list box.
   i. Click the down-pointing arrow at the right of the *Font color* option box and then click the *Green, Accent 5, Darker 25%* color option (ninth column, fifth row in the *Theme Colors* section).
   j. Click OK to close the Font dialog box and then click OK to close the Define New Bullet dialog box.

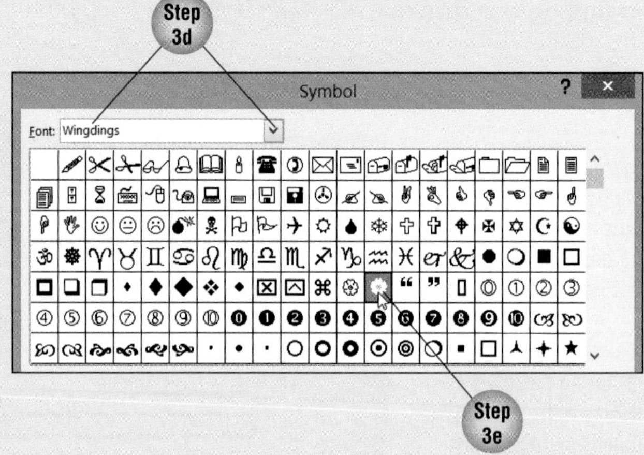

4. Remove the two bullets you defined from the *Bullet Library* section by completing the following steps:
   a. Click the Bullets button arrow.
   b. Right-click the green flower picture bullet in the *Bullet Library* section and then click *Remove* at the shortcut menu.
   c. Click the Bullets button arrow.
   d. Right-click the green symbol bullet in the *Bullet Library* section and then click *Remove* at the shortcut menu.
5. Save, print, and then close **WL2-C1-P2-TTSHawaii.docx**.

Project 3 Apply Multilevel List Numbering to a Job Search Document — 2 Parts

You will open a document containing a list of job search terms, apply multilevel list numbering to the text, and then define and apply a new multilevel list numbering style.

Inserting Multilevel List Numbering

Use the Multilevel List button in the Paragraph group on the HOME tab to specify the type of numbering for paragraphs of text at the left margin, first tab, second tab, and so on. To apply predesigned multilevel numbering to text in a document, click the Multilevel List button and then click the desired numbering style at the drop-down gallery.

Some options at the Multilevel List drop-down gallery display with *Heading 1*, *Heading 2*, and so on after the number. Click one of these options and Word inserts the numbering and applies the heading styles to the text.

Quick Steps
Insert Multilevel List Numbering
1. Click Multilevel List button.
2. Click desired style at drop-down gallery.

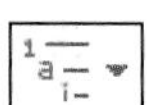
Multilevel List

Project 3a Inserting Multilevel List Numbering — Part 1 of 2

1. Open **JSList.docx** and then save the document and name it **WL2-C1-P3-JSList**.
2. Select the paragraphs of text below the title and then apply multilevel list numbers by completing the following steps:
   a. Click the Multilevel List button in the Paragraph group on the HOME tab.
   b. At the drop-down gallery, click the middle option in the top row of the *List Library* section.
   c. Deselect the text.
3. Save and then print **WL2-C1-P3-JSList.docx**.

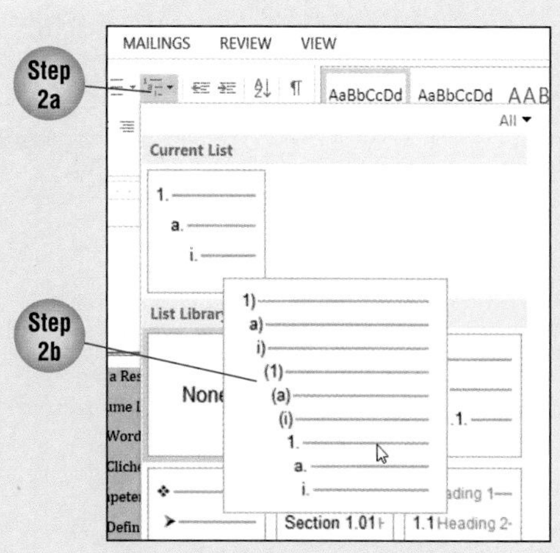

Defining a Multilevel List

Define a Multilevel List

1. Click Multilevel List button.
2. Click *Define New Multilevel List.*
3. Choose desired level, number format, and/or position.
4. Click OK.

HINT

When defining a multilevel list style, you can mix numbers and bullets in the same list.

The Multilevel List button drop-down gallery contains predesigned level numbering options. If the gallery does not contain the type of numbering you want, you can create your own. To do this, click the Multilevel List button and then click *Define New Multilevel List*. This displays the Define new Multilevel list dialog box, shown in Figure 1.3. At this dialog box, click a level in the *Click level to modify* list box and then specify the number format, style, position, and alignment.

Typing a Multilevel List

Select text and then apply a multilevel list or apply the list and then type the text. As you type text, press the Tab key to move to the next level or press Shift + Tab to move to the previous level.

Figure 1.3 Define New Multilevel List Dialog Box

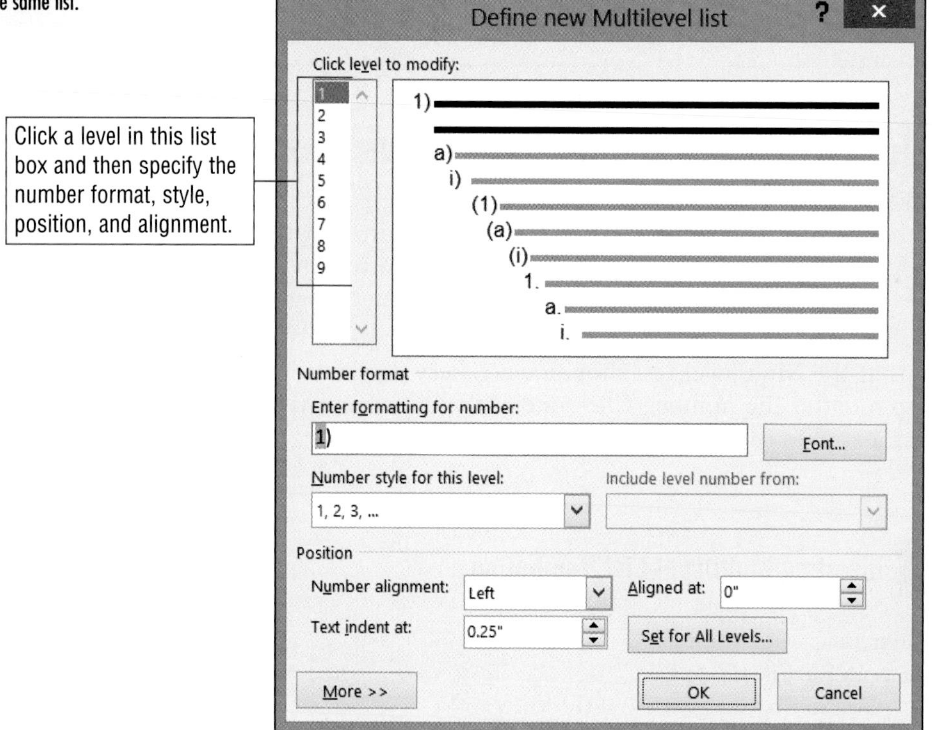

Project 3b Defining and Applying a New Multilevel List

Part 2 of 2

1. With **WL2-C1-P3-JSList.docx** open, select the paragraphs of text below the title.
2. Click the Multilevel List button in the Paragraph group on the HOME tab.
3. Click the *Define New Multilevel List* option at the drop-down gallery.
4. At the Define new Multilevel list dialog box, make sure *1* is selected in the *Click level to modify* list box.
5. Click the down-pointing arrow at the right side of the *Number style for this level* option box and then click *A, B, C, ...* at the drop-down list.
6. Click in the *Enter formatting for number* text box, delete any text that displays after *A*, and then type a period (.). (The entry in the text box should now display as *A.*)
7. Click the up-pointing arrow at the right side of the *Aligned at* measurement box until *0.3"* displays in the measurement box.
8. Click the up-pointing arrow at the right side of the *Text indent at* measurement box until *0.6"* displays in the measurement box.
9. Click *2* in the *Click level to modify* list box.
10. Click the down-pointing arrow at the right side of the *Number style for this level* option box and then click *1, 2, 3, ...* at the drop-down list.
11. Click in the *Enter formatting for number* text box, delete any text that displays after the *1*, and then type a period (.).
12. Click the up-pointing arrow at the right side of the *Aligned at* measurement box until *0.6"* displays in the measurement box.
13. Click the up-pointing arrow at the right side of the *Text indent at* measurement box until *0.9"* displays in the measurement box.

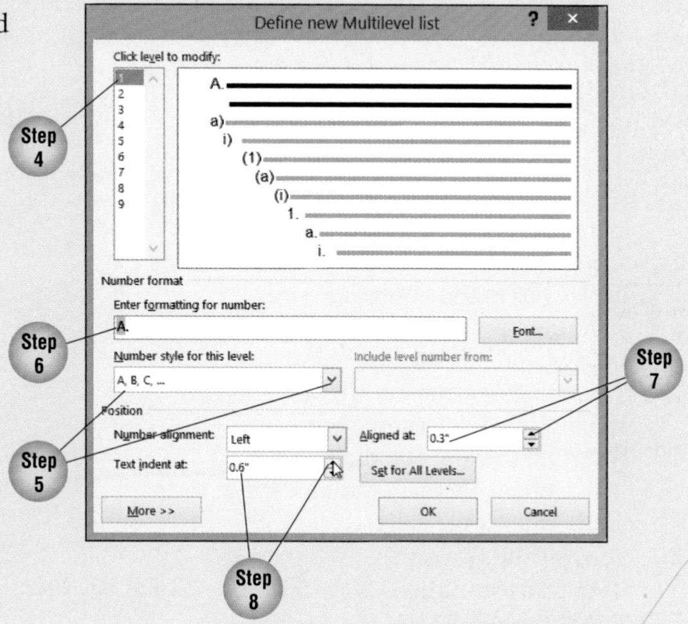

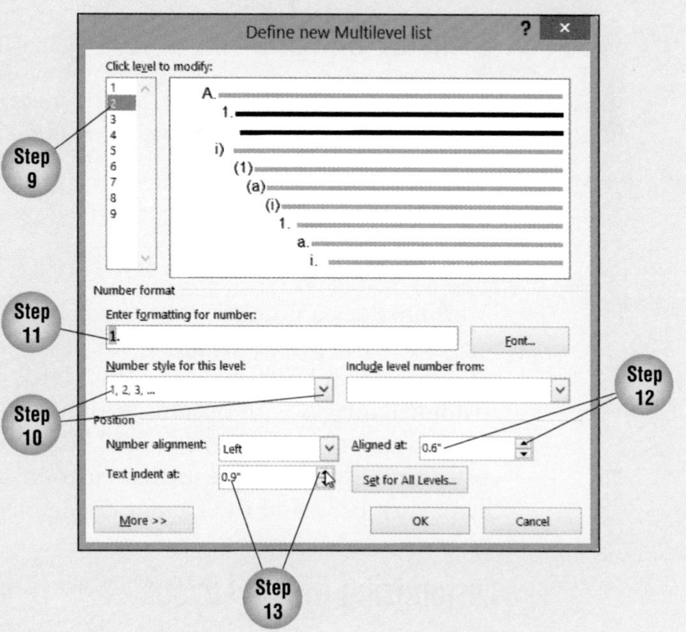

14. Click *3* in the *Click level to modify* list box.
15. Click the down-pointing arrow at the right side of the *Number style for this level* option box and then click *a, b, c, ...* at the drop-down list.
16. Make sure that *a)* displays in the *Enter formatting for number* text box. (If not, delete any text that displays after the *a* and then type a right parenthesis.)
17. Click the up-pointing arrow at the right side of the *Aligned at* measurement box until *0.9"* displays in the measurement box.
18. Click the up-pointing arrow at the right side of the *Text indent at* measurement box until *1.2"* displays in the measurement box.
19. Click OK to close the dialog box. (This applies the new multilevel list numbering to the selected text.)
20. Deselect the text.
21. Save, print, and then close **WL2-C1-P3-JSList.docx**.

Project 4 Insert Images and a Text Box in a Travel Document **3 Parts**

You will open a travel document on Maui, insert and customize a clip art image and photograph, and then insert and customize a text box.

Customizing Images and Text Boxes

Word provides a number of methods for formatting and customizing graphic images such as pictures, clip art images, and text boxes. Format pictures and clip art images with buttons on the PICTURE TOOLS FORMAT tab and further customize images with options at the Format Picture task pane and the Layout dialog box. Use buttons on the DRAWING TOOLS FORMAT tab to format and customize text boxes and further customize text boxes with options at the Format Shape task pane and the Layout dialog box.

Customizing Image Layout

Customize the layout of images with options at the Layout dialog box. Display the Layout dialog box by clicking the Size group dialog box launcher on the PICTURE TOOLS FORMAT tab. The Layout dialog box contains three tabs. Click the Position tab and the dialog box displays as shown in Figure 1.4.

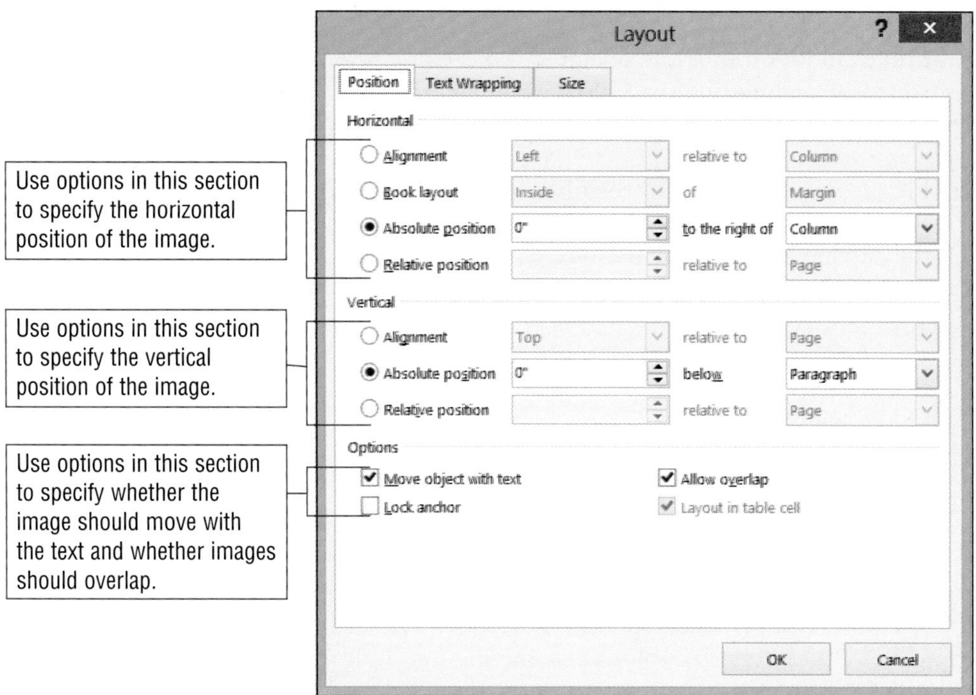

Figure 1.4 Layout Dialog Box with Position Tab Selected

Use options at the Layout dialog box with the Position tab selected to specify horizontal and vertical layout options. In the *Horizontal* section, choose the *Alignment* option to specify if you want the image horizontally left-, center-, or right-aligned relative to the margin, page, column, or character. Choose the *Book layout* option if you want to align the image with the inside or outside margins of the page. Use the *Absolute position* option to align the image horizontally with the specified amount of space between the left edge of the image and the left edge of the page, column, left margin, or character. In the *Vertical* section of the dialog box, use the *Alignment* option to align the image at the top, bottom, center, inside, or outside relative to the page, margin, or line. In the *Options* section, you can attach (anchor) the image to a paragraph so that the image and paragraph move together. Choose the *Move object with text* option if you want the image to move up or down on the page with the paragraph to which it is anchored. Keep the image anchored in the same place on the page by choosing the *Lock anchor* option. Choose the *Allow overlap* option if you want images with the same wrapping style to overlap.

Use options at the Layout dialog box with the Text Wrapping tab selected to specify the wrapping style for the image. You can also specify which sides of the image you want text to wrap around and the amount of space you want between the text and the top, bottom, left, and right edges of the image.

Click the Size tab at the Layout dialog box to display options for specifying the height and width of the image relative to the margin, page, top margin, bottom margin, inside margin, or outside margin. Use the *Rotation* option to rotate the image by degrees and use options in the *Scale* section to change the percentage of height and width scale. To reset the image size, click the Reset button in the lower right corner of the dialog box.

Project 4a Inserting and Customizing the Layout of a Clip Art Image

Part 1 of 3

1. Open **TTSMaui.docx** and then save the document and name it **WL2-C1-P4-TTSMaui**.
2. Insert a clip art image by completing the following steps:
   a. Click the INSERT tab and then click the Online Pictures button in the Illustrations group.
   b. At the Insert Pictures window, click in the *Office.com Clip Art* text box, type **banners, Hawaii**, and then press the Enter key.
   c. Double-click the clip art image in the list box, as shown below.

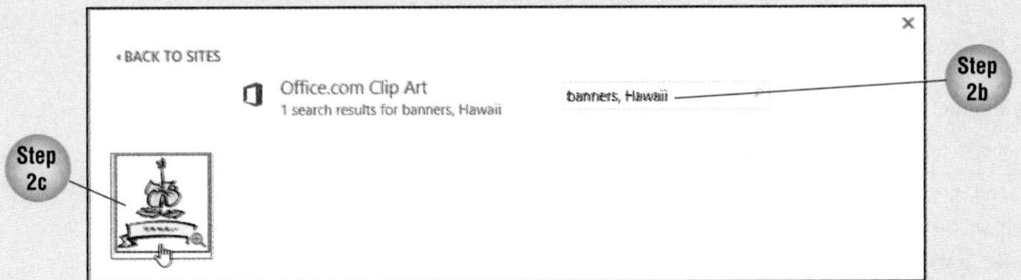

3. Select the current measurement in the *Shape Height* measurement box in the Size group on the PICTURE TOOLS FORMAT tab, type 1.5, and then press Enter.
4. Click the *Beveled Matte, White* style thumbnail in the Picture Styles group (second thumbnail from the left).

5. Click the Corrections button in the Adjust group and then click the *Brightness: –20% Contrast: +20%* option (second column, fourth row).
6. After looking at the image, you decide to reset it. Do this by clicking the Reset Picture button arrow in the Adjust group and then clicking *Reset Picture & Size* at the drop-down list.

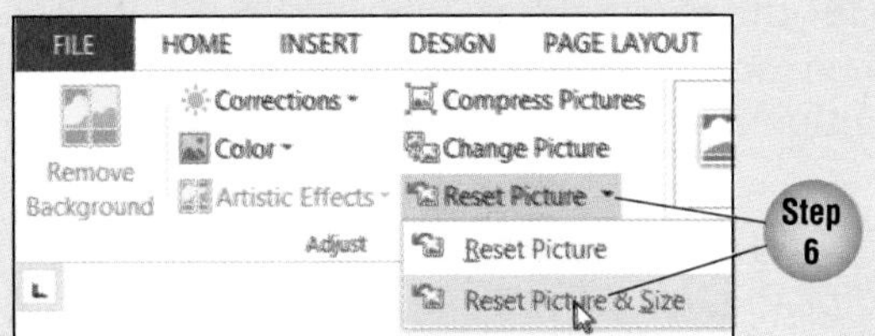

7. Select the current measurement in the *Shape Height* measurement box, type 1.3, and then press Enter.
8. Click the Wrap Text button in the Arrange group and then click *In Front of Text* at the drop-down list.

9. Position the clip art image precisely on the page by completing the following steps:
   a. With the image selected, click the Size group dialog box launcher.
   b. At the Layout dialog box, click the Position tab.
   c. Make sure the *Absolute position* option in the *Horizontal* section is selected.
   d. Press the Tab key twice and then type **6.2** in the *Absolute position* measurement box.
   e. Click the down-pointing arrow at the right of the *to the right of* option box and then click *Page* at the drop-down list.
   f. Click the *Absolute position* option in the *Vertical* section.

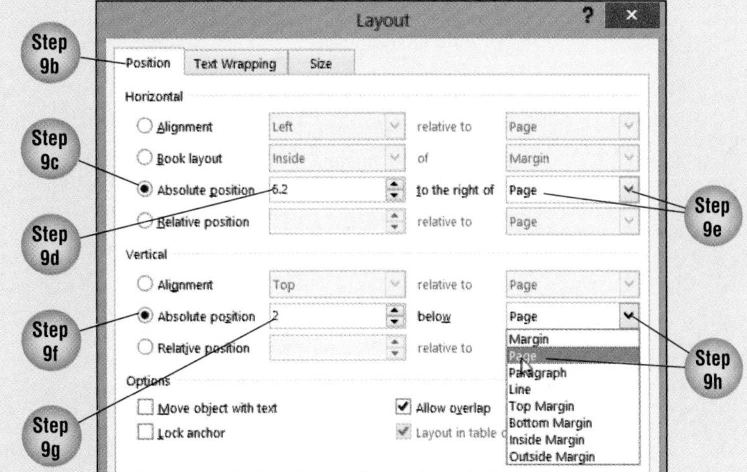

   g. Select the current measurement in the box to the right of the *Absolute position* option and then type 2.
   h. Click the down-pointing arrow at the right of the *below* option box and then click *Page* at the drop-down list.
   i. Click OK to close the Layout dialog box.
10. Click the *Drop Shadow Rectangle* style thumbnail in the Picture Styles group (fourth thumbnail from the left).
11. Click the Color button in the Adjust group and then click the *Blue, Accent color 1 Light* option (second column, third row).
12. Compress the clip art image by clicking the Compress Pictures button in the Adjust group and then clicking OK at the Compress Pictures dialog box.
13. Click outside the clip art image to deselect it.
14. Save **WL2-C1-P4-TSSMaui.docx**.

Applying Formatting at the Format Picture Task Pane

Options for formatting an image are available at the Format Picture task pane, shown in Figure 1.5 on the next page. Display this task pane box by clicking the Picture Styles group task pane launcher on the PICTURE TOOLS FORMAT tab.

The options in the Format Picture task pane vary depending on the icon selected. You may need to display (expand) the formatting options within the icons. For example, click *SHADOW* in the task pane with the Effects icon selected to display options for applying shadow effects to an image. Many of the options available at the Format Picture task pane are also available on the PICTURE TOOLS FORMAT tab. The task pane is a central location for formatting options and also includes some additional advanced formatting options.

Figure 1.5 Format Picture Task Pane

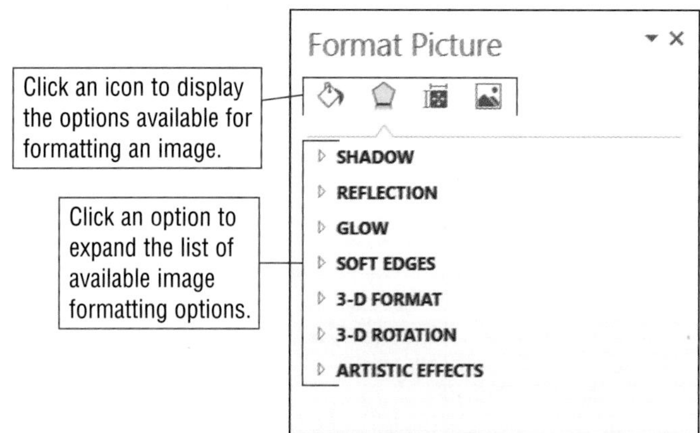

Applying Artistic Effects to Images

If you insert a picture or photograph into a document, the Artistic Effects button in the Adjust group on the PICTURE TOOLS FORMAT tab becomes active. Click this button and a drop-down gallery displays with effect options. Hover the mouse over an option in the drop-down gallery to see the effect applied to the selected picture or photograph. This button is not active when a clip art image is selected. You can also apply artistic effects at the Format Picture task pane with the Effects icon selected.

Project 4b **Inserting and Customizing a Photograph** **Part 2 of 3**

1. With **WL2-C1-P4-TTSMaui.docx** open, press Ctrl + End to move the insertion point to the end of the document and then insert a photograph by completing the following steps:
   a. Click the INSERT tab and then click the Online Pictures button in the Illustrations group.
   b. Type surfer riding wave in the *Office.com Clip Art* text box and then press the Enter key.
   c. Double-click the image in the list box, as shown below.

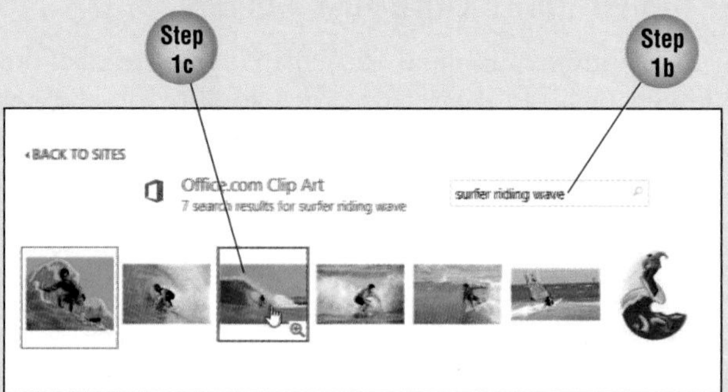

2. With the surfing photograph selected, click the Picture Effects button in the Picture Styles group, point to *Bevel*, and then click the *Circle* option (first option in the *Bevel* section).

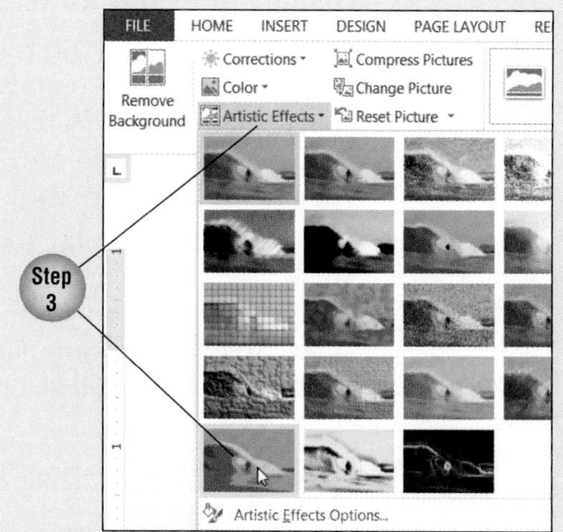

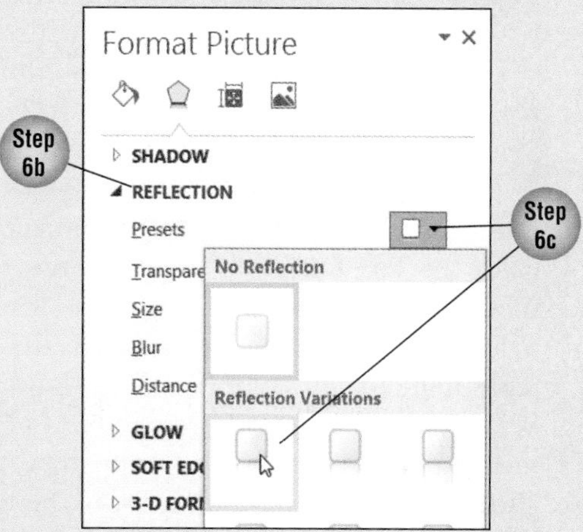

3. Click the Artistic Effects button in the Adjust group and then click the *Cutout* option (first column, bottom row).
4. After looking at the formatting, you decide to remove it from the image by clicking the Reset Picture button in the Adjust group.
5. Select the current measurement in the *Shape Height* measurement box, type **1.4**, and then press Enter.
6. Format the photograph by completing the following steps:
   a. Click the Picture Styles group task pane launcher.
   b. At the Format Picture task pane, click *REFLECTION* to expand the reflection options in the task pane.
   c. Click the Presets button and then click the *Tight Reflection, touching* option (first option in the *Reflection Variations* section).
   d. Click *ARTISTIC EFFECTS* in the task pane to expand the artistic effect options.
   e. Click the Artistic Effects button and then click the *Paint Brush* option (third column, second row).
   f. Close the task pane by clicking the Close button located in the upper right corner of the task pane.
7. Click the Wrap Text button in the Arrange group on the PICTURE TOOLS FORMAT tab and then click *Tight* at the drop-down list.
8. Position the photograph precisely on the page by completing the following steps:
   a. With the photograph selected, click the Position button in the Arrange group and then click *More Layout Options* at the bottom of the drop-down gallery.
   b. At the Layout dialog box with the Position tab selected, select the current measurement in the *Absolute position* measurement box in the *Horizontal* section and then type **5.3**.
   c. Click the down-pointing arrow to the right of the *to the right of* option box and then click *Page* at the drop-down list.
   d. Select the current measurement in the *Absolute position* measurement box in the *Vertical* section and then type **6.6**.
   e. Click the down-pointing arrow at the right of the *below* option box and then click *Page* at the drop-down list.
   f. Click OK to close the Layout dialog box.
9. Click outside the photograph to deselect it.
10. Save **WL2-C1-P4-TTSMaui.docx**.

Customizing Text Boxes

When you insert a text box in a document, the DRAWING TOOLS FORMAT tab is active. Use options on this tab to format and customize a text box. You can also format and customize a text box with options at the Format Shape task pane. Display the Format Shape task pane by clicking the Shape Styles group task pane launcher. The task pane displays with three icons: Fill & Line, Effects, and Layout & Properties.

You can also display the Format Shape task pane by clicking the WordArt Styles group task pane launcher. The Format Shape task pane displays with different icons than the Format Shape task pane that displays when you click the Shape Styles group task pane launcher. The task pane displays with three icons: Text Fill & Outline, Text Effects, and Layout & Properties.

Project 4c **Inserting and Customizing a Text Box** **Part 3 of 3**

1. With **WL2-C1-P4-TTSMaui.docx** open, insert a text box by completing the following steps:
   a. Click the INSERT tab, click the Text Box button in the Text group, and then click the *Draw Text Box* option at the drop-down list.
   b. Click above the heading *MAUI SITES* and then type **Hawaii, the Aloha State**.
2. Select the text box by clicking the border of the text box. (This changes the text box border from a dashed line to a solid line.)
3. Press Ctrl + E to center the text in the text box.
4. Click the Text Direction button in the Text group and then click *Rotate all text 270°* at the drop-down list.
5. Select the current measurement in the *Shape Height* measurement box, type 5.8, and then press Enter.
6. Select the current measurement in the *Shape Width* measurement box, type 0.8, and then press Enter.
7. Format the text box by completing the following steps:
   a. Click the Shape Styles group task pane launcher.
   b. At the Format Shape task pane with the Fill & Line icon selected, click *FILL* to expand the options.
   c. Click the Fill Color button (displays to the right of the *Color* option) and then click the *Blue, Accent 1, Lighter 80%* option (fifth column, second row).
   d. Click the Effects icon and then click *SHADOW* to expand the options.
   e. Click the Presets button and then click the *Offset Bottom* option (second column, first row in the *Outer* section).

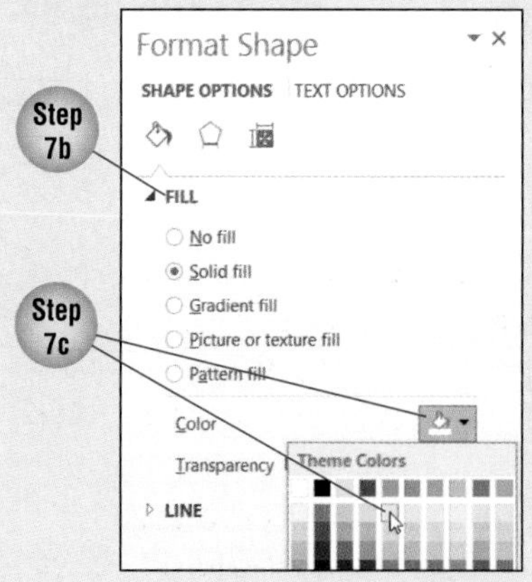

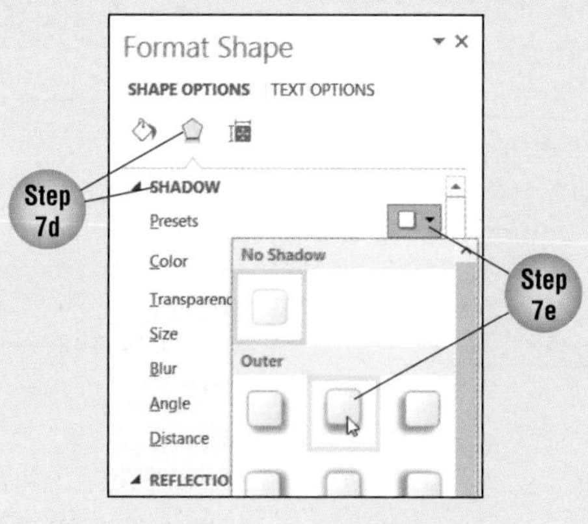

f. Scroll down the task pane and then click *GLOW* to display the glow options.
g. Click the Presets button in the *Glow* section and then click the *Blue, 5 pt glow, Accent color 1* option (first column, first row in the *Glow Variations* section).
h. Close the Format Shape task pane by clicking the Close button located in the upper right corner of the task pane.

8. Click the More button at the right side of the WordArt Styles thumbnails and then click the *Fill - Blue, Accent 1, Outline - Background 1, Hard Shadow - Accent 1* option (third column, third row).
9. Position the text box precisely on the page by completing the following steps:
   a. With the text box selected, click the Size group dialog box launcher.
   b. At the Layout dialog box, click the Position tab.
   c. Select the current measurement in the *Absolute position* measurement box in the *Horizontal* section and then type 1.
   d. Click the down-pointing arrow at the right of the *to the right of* option box and then click *Page* at the drop-down list.
   e. Select the current measurement in the *Absolute position* measurement box in the *Vertical* section and then type 2.7.
   f. Click the down-pointing arrow at the right of the *below* option box and then click *Page* at the drop-down list.
   g. Click OK to close the Layout dialog box.
10. Click the HOME tab, click the Font Size button arrow, and then click *36* at the drop-down list.
11. Click outside the text box to deselect it.
12. Save, print, and then close **WL2-C1-P4-TTSMaui.docx**.

Project 5 Insert Headers and Footers in a Computer Software Report — 7 Parts

You will open a report on productivity and graphics and multimedia software and then create and position headers and footers in the document. You will also create headers and footers for different pages in a document, divide a document into sections, and then create footers for specific sections.

Inserting Headers and Footers

One method for formatting a header or footer is to select the header or footer text and then use the options on the Mini toolbar.

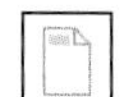
Header

Footer

Text that appears in the top margin of a page is called a ***header*** and text that appears in the bottom margin of a page is called a ***footer***. Headers and footers are commonly used in manuscripts, textbooks, reports, and other publications to display the page numbers and section or chapter titles. For example, see the footer at the bottom of this page.

You can insert a predesigned header by clicking the INSERT tab and then clicking the Header button. This displays a drop-down list of header choices. Click the predesigned header and the formatted header is inserted in the document. Complete similar steps to insert a predesigned footer.

Quick Steps

Insert an Element in a Header
1. Click INSERT tab.
2. Click Header button.
3. Click *Edit Header* at drop-down gallery.
4. Click desired element in insert group.

Insert an Element in a Footer
1. Click INSERT tab.
2. Click Footer button.
3. Click *Edit Footer* at drop-down gallery.
4. Click desired element in Insert group.

Date & Time

Picture

Online Pictures

If the predesigned headers and footers do not meet your needs, you can create your own. To create a header, click the INSERT tab, click the Header button in the Header & Footer group, and then click *Edit Header* at the drop-down list. This displays a Header pane in the document and also displays the HEADER & FOOTER TOOLS DESIGN tab, as shown in Figure 1.6. Use options on this tab to insert elements such as page numbers, pictures, and clip art; navigate to other headers or footers in the document; and position headers and footers on different pages in a document.

Inserting Elements in Headers and Footers

Use buttons in the Insert group on the HEADER & FOOTER TOOLS DESIGN tab to insert elements into the header or footer, such as the date and time, Quick Parts, pictures, and images. Click the Date & Time button and the Date and Time dialog box displays with options for inserting the current date and current time. Click the Pictures button and the Insert Picture dialog box displays. At this dialog box, navigate to the desired folder and double-click the picture file. Click the Online Pictures button and the Insert Pictures window displays, where you can search for and then insert an image into the header or footer.

Figure 1.6 HEADER & FOOTER TOOLS DESIGN Tab

Project 5a **Inserting Elements in a Header and Footer** **Part 1 of 7**

1. Open **CompSoftware.docx** and then save the document and name it **WL2-C1-P5-CompSoftware**.
2. Insert a header by completing the following steps:
   a. Click the INSERT tab.
   b. Click the Header button in the Header & Footer group.
   c. Click *Edit Header* at the drop-down list.
   d. With the insertion point positioned in the Header pane, click the Pictures button in the Insert group on the HEADER & FOOTER TOOLS DESIGN tab.

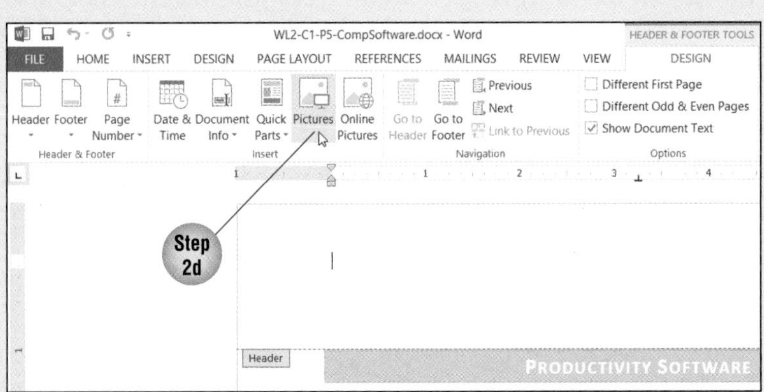

e. At the Insert Picture dialog box, navigate to the WL2C1 folder on your storage medium and then double-click ***Worldwide.jpg***.
f. With the image selected, click in the *Shape Height* measurement box, type 0.6, and then press Enter.
g. Click the Wrap Text button in the Arrange group and then click *Behind Text* at the drop-down list.
h. Drag the image up approximately one-third of an inch.
i. Click to the right of the image to deselect it.
j. Press the Tab key twice. (This moves the insertion point to the right margin.) 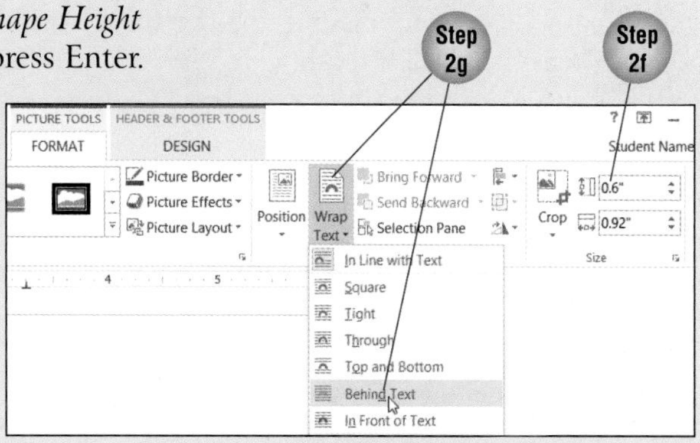
k. Click the HEADER & FOOTER TOOLS DESIGN tab and then click the Date & Time button in the Insert group.
l. At the Date and Time dialog box, click the twelfth option from the top (the option that displays the date in numbers and the time) and then click OK to close the dialog box.
m. Select the date and time text and then click the HOME tab. Click the Bold button in the Font group, click the Font Size button arrow, and then click *9* at the drop-down gallery.
n. Double-click in the document to make the document active and dim the header.

3. Save **WL2-C1-P5-CompSoftware.docx**.

Step 2g

Step 2f

PICTURE TOOLS HEADER & FOOTER TOOLS
FORMAT DESIGN
Picture Border
Picture Effects
Picture Layout
Position
Wrap Text
Bring Forward
Send Backward
Selection Pane
Crop
0.6"
0.92"
Size
Student Name
In Line with Text
Square
Tight
Through
Top and Bottom
Behind Text
In Front of Text

Positioning Headers and Footers

Word inserts a header 0.5 inch from the top of the page and a footer 0.5 inch from the bottom of the page. You can change these default positions with buttons in the Position group on the HEADER & FOOTER TOOLS DESIGN tab. Use the *Header from Top* and *Footer from Bottom* measurement boxes to adjust the position of the header and the footer, respectively, on the page.

By default, headers and footers contain two tab settings. A center tab is set at 3.25 inches and a right tab is set at 6.5 inches. If the document contains default left and right margin settings of 1 inch, the center tab set at 3.25 inches is the center of the document and the right tab set at 6.5 inches is at the right margin. If you make changes to the default margins, you may need to move the default center tab before inserting header or footer text at the center tab. You can also set and position tabs with the Insert Alignment Tab button in the Position group. Click this button and the Alignment Tab dialog box displays. Use options at this dialog box to change tab alignment and set tabs with leaders.

Project 5b **Positioning Headers and Footers** **Part 2 of 7**

1. With **WL2-C1-P5-CompSoftware.docx** open, change the margins by completing the following steps:
   a. Click the PAGE LAYOUT tab, click the Margins button in the Page Setup group, and then click the *Custom Margins* option that displays at the bottom of the drop-down list.
   b. At the Page Setup dialog box with the Margins tab selected, select the measurement in the *Left* measurement box and then type 1.25.

c. Select the measurement in the *Right* measurement box and then type **1.25**.
d. Click OK to close the dialog box.

2. Create a footer by completing the following steps:
   a. Click the INSERT tab.
   b. Click the Footer button in the Header & Footer group and then click *Edit Footer* at the drop-down list.
   c. With the insertion point positioned in the Footer pane, type your first and last names at the left margin.
   d. Press the Tab key. (This moves the insertion point to the center tab position.)
   e. Click the Page Number button in the Header & Footer group, point to *Current Position*, and then click *Accent Bar 2* at the drop-down list.
   f. Press the Tab key, click the Document Info button in the Insert group, and then click *File Name* at the drop-down list.

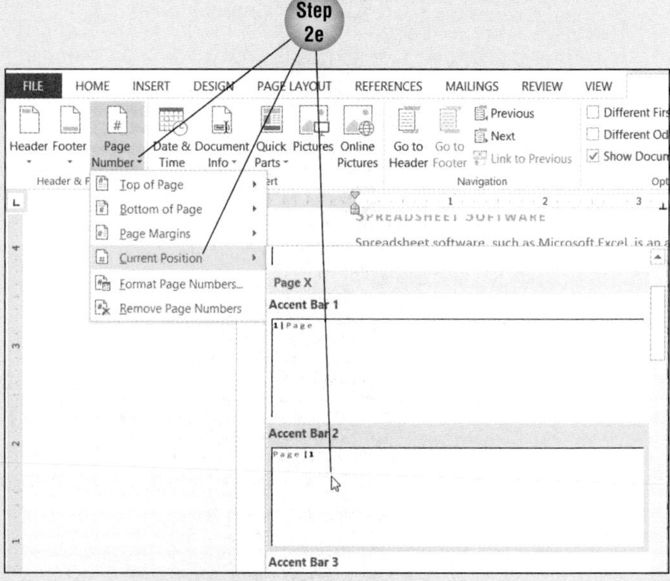

   g. You notice that the center tab and right tab are slightly off, because the left and right margins in the document are set at 1.25 inches instead of 1 inch. To align the tabs correctly, drag the center tab marker to the 3-inch mark on the horizontal ruler and drag the right tab marker to the 6-inch mark on the horizontal ruler.

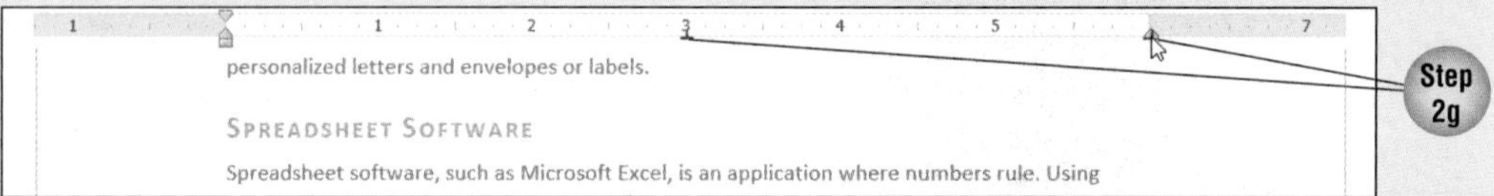

   h. Select all of the footer text and then change the font to 9-point Calibri bold.

3. Move the right tab in the header by completing the following steps:
   a. Click the HEADER & FOOTER TOOLS DESIGN tab.
   b. Click the Go to Header button in the Navigation group.
   c. Drag the right tab marker to the 6-inch mark on the horizontal ruler.

4. Change the position of the header and footer by completing the following steps:
   a. With the HEADER & FOOTER TOOLS DESIGN tab active, click the up-pointing arrow at the right side of the *Header from Top* measurement box until *0.8"* displays.
   b. Click in the *Footer from Bottom* measurement box, type **0.6**, and then press Enter.
   c. Click the Close Header and Footer button.

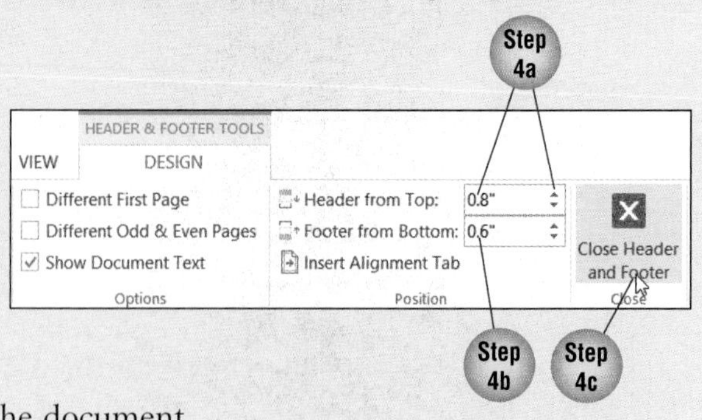

5. Save and then print the first two pages of the document.

Creating a Different First Page Header or Footer

When you insert a header or a footer in a document, Word will insert the header or footer on every page in the document by default. You can create different headers and footers within one document. For example, you can create a unique header or footer on the first page and insert a different header or footer on subsequent pages.

To create a different first page header, click the INSERT tab, click the Header button, and then click *Edit Header* at the drop-down list. Click the *Different First Page* check box to insert a check mark and the First Page Header pane displays with the insertion point inside. Insert elements or type text to create the first page header and then click the Next button in the Navigation group. This displays the Header pane with the insertion point positioned inside. Insert elements and/or type text to create the header. Complete similar steps to create a different first page footer.

In some situations, you may want the first page header or footer to be blank. This is particularly useful if a document contains a title page and you do not want the header or footer to print on this page.

Quick Steps

Create a Different First Page Header or Footer

1. Click INSERT tab.
2. Click Header or Footer button.
3. Click *Edit Header* or *Edit Footer* at drop-down list.
4. Click *Different First Page* check box.
5. Insert desired elements and/or text.
6. Click Next button.
7. Insert desired elements and/or text.

Project 5c **Creating a Header That Prints on All Pages Except the First Page** **Part 3 of 7**

1. With **WL2-C1-P5-CompSoftware.docx** open, press Ctrl + A to select the entire document and then press Ctrl + 2 to change the line spacing to 2.
2. Remove the header and footer by completing the following steps:
   a. Click the INSERT tab.
   b. Click the Header button in the Header & Footer group and then click *Remove Header* at the drop-down list.
   c. Click the Footer button in the Header & Footer group and then click *Remove Footer* at the drop-down list.
3. Press Ctrl + Home and then create a header that prints on all pages except the first page by completing the following steps:
   a. With the INSERT tab active, click the Header button in the Header & Footer group.
   b. Click *Edit Header* at the drop-down list.
   c. Click the *Different First Page* check box located in the Options group on the HEADER & FOOTER TOOLS DESIGN tab.
   d. With the insertion point positioned in the First Page Header pane, click the Next button in the Navigation group. (This tells Word that you want the first page header to be blank.)
   e. With the insertion point positioned in the Header pane, click the Page Number button in the Header & Footer group, point to *Top of Page*, and then click *Accent Bar 2* at the drop-down gallery.
   f. Click the Close Header and Footer button.
4. Scroll through the document and notice that the header appears on the second, third, fourth, and fifth pages.
5. Save and then print the first two pages of **WL2-C1-P5-CompSoftware.docx**.

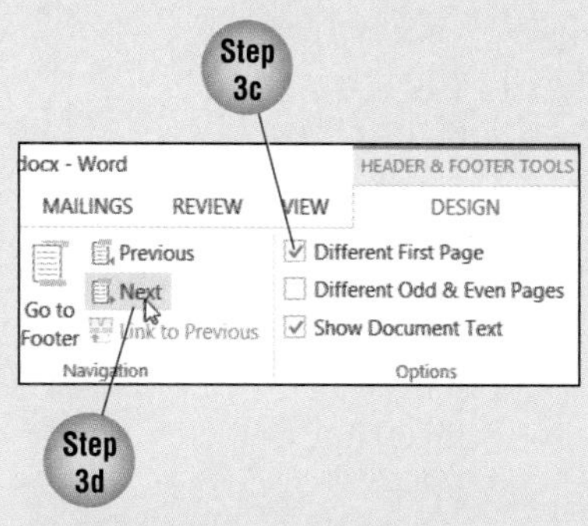

Quick Steps

Create Odd and Even Page Headers or Footers

1. Click INSERT tab.
2. Click Header or Footer button.
3. Click *Edit Header* or *Edit Footer* at drop-down gallery.
4. Click *Different Odd & Even Pages* check box.
5. Insert desired elements and/or text.

Creating Odd and Even Page Headers or Footers

If your document will be read in book form, consider inserting odd and even page headers or footers. When presenting pages in a document in book form with facing pages, the outside margin is the left side of the left page and the right side of the right page. Also, when a document has facing pages, the page at the right side is generally numbered with an odd number and the page at the left side is generally numbered with an even number.

You can create even and odd headers or footers to insert this type of page numbering. Use the *Different Odd & Even Pages* check box in the Options group on the HEADER & FOOTER TOOLS DESIGN tab to create odd and even headers and/or footers.

Project 5d **Creating Odd and Even Page Footers** **Part 4 of 7**

1. With **WL2-C1-P5-CompSoftware.docx** open, remove the header from the document by completing the following steps:
   a. Click the INSERT tab.
   b. Click the Header button in the Header & Footer group and then click *Edit Header* at the drop-down list.
   c. Click the *Different First Page* check box in the Options group on the HEADER & FOOTER TOOLS DESIGN tab to remove the check mark.
   d. Click the Header button in the Header & Footer group and then click *Remove Header* at the drop-down list. (This displays the insertion point in an empty Header pane.)
2. Create one footer that prints on odd pages and another that prints on even pages by completing the following steps:
   a. Click the Go to Footer button in the Navigation group on the HEADER & FOOTER TOOLS DESIGN tab.
   b. Click the *Different Odd & Even Pages* check box in the Options group. (This displays the Odd Page Footer pane with the insertion point inside.) 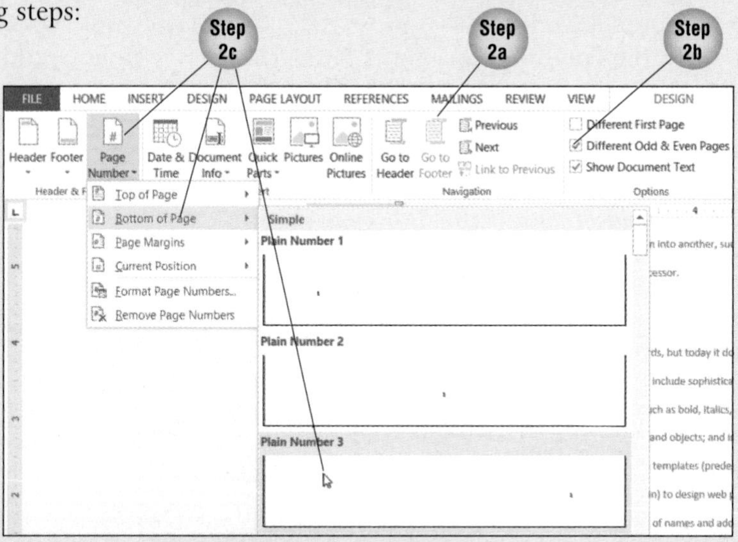
   c. Click the Page Number button in the Header & Footer group, point to *Bottom of Page*, and then click *Plain Number 3* at the drop-down list.
   d. Click the Next button in the Navigation group. (This displays the Even Page Footer pane with the insertion point inside.)

e. Click the Page Number button in the Header & Footer group, point to *Current Position*, and then click *Plain Number 1* at the drop-down list.
f. Click the Close Header and Footer button.
3. Scroll through the document and notice the page number at the right side of the odd page footer and the page number at the left side of the even page footer.
4. Save and then print the first two pages of **WL2-C1-P5-CompSoftware.docx**.

Creating Headers and Footers for Different Sections

You can divide a document into sections and then apply different formatting in each section. You can insert a section break that begins a new page or insert a continuous section break. You can also insert a section break that starts the new section on the next even-numbered page or a section break that starts the new section on the next odd-numbered page.

If you want different headers and/or footers for pages in a document, divide the document into sections. For example, if a document contains several chapters, you can create a section for each chapter and then create a different header and footer for each section. When dividing a document into sections by chapter, insert section breaks that also begin new pages.

When a header or footer is created for a specific section in a document, the header or footer can be created for all previous and next sections or just for next sections. If you want a header or footer to print on only those pages in a section and not the previous or next sections, you must deactivate the Link to Previous button. This tells Word not to print the header or footer on previous sections. Word will, however, print the header or footer on following sections. If you do not want the header or footer to print on following sections, create a blank header or footer at the next section. When creating a header or footer for a specific section in a document, preview the document to determine if the header or footer appears on the correct pages.

Quick Steps

Create Headers or Footers for Different Sections

1. Insert section break in desired location.
2. Click INSERT tab.
3. Click Header or Footer button.
4. Click *Edit Header* or *Edit Footer* at drop-down list.
5. Click Link to Previous button to deactivate.
6. Insert desired elements and/or text.
7. Click Next button.
8. Insert desired elements and/or text.

Link to Previous

Project 5e **Creating Footers for Different Sections** **Part 5 of 7**

1. With **WL2-C1-P5-CompSoftware.docx** open, remove the odd and even page footers by completing the following steps:
   a. Click the INSERT tab.
   b. Click the Footer button in the Header & Footer group and then click *Edit Footer* at the drop-down list.
   c. Click the *Different Odd & Even Pages* check box in the Options group on the HEADER & FOOTER TOOLS DESIGN tab to remove the check mark.
   d. Click the Footer button in the Header & Footer group and then click *Remove Footer* at the drop-down list.
   e. Click the Close Header and Footer button.
2. Remove the page break before the second title in the document by completing the following steps:
   a. Move the insertion point immediately right of the period that ends the paragraph in the *PRESENTATION SOFTWARE* section (located near the top of page 3).
   b. Press the Delete key twice. (The title *GRAPHICS AND MULTIMEDIA SOFTWARE* should now display below the paragraph on the third page.)

3. Insert an odd page section break by completing the following steps:
   a. Position the insertion point at the beginning of the title *GRAPHICS AND MULTIMEDIA SOFTWARE*.
   b. Click the PAGE LAYOUT tab, click the Breaks button in the Page Setup group, and then click *Odd Page* at the drop-down list. (The section break takes the place of the hard page break.)

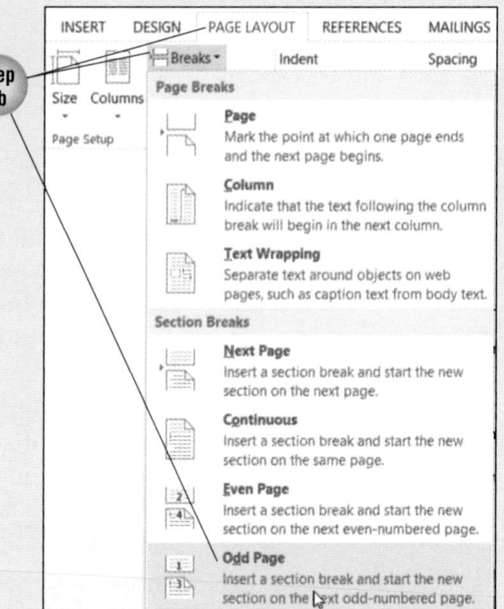

4. Create section titles and page numbering footers for the two sections by completing the following steps:
   a. Position the insertion point at the beginning of the document.
   b. Click the INSERT tab.
   c. Click the Footer button in the Header & Footer group and then click *Edit Footer* at the drop-down list.
   d. At the Footer - Section 1- pane, type **Section 1 Productivity Software** and then press the Tab key twice. (This moves the insertion point to the right margin.)
   e. Type **Page** and then press the spacebar.
   f. Click the Page Number button in the Header & Footer group, point to *Current Position*, and then click *Plain Number* at the side menu.
   g. Click the Next button in the Navigation group.
   h. Click the Link to Previous button to deactivate it. (This removes the message *Same as Previous* from the top right side of the footer pane.)

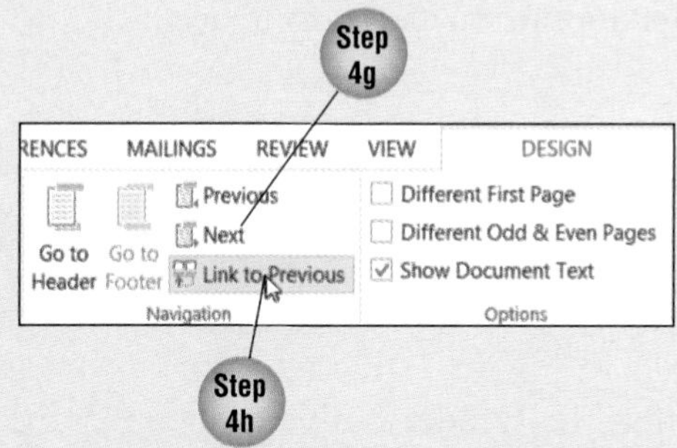

   i. Change the text *Section 1 Productivity Software* to *Section 2 Graphics and Multimedia Software* in the footer.
   j. Click the Close Header and Footer button.
5. Scroll through the document and notice the page numbering in the sections.
6. Save **WL2-C1-P5-CompSoftware.docx**.

Printing Sections

Print specific pages in a document by inserting page numbers in the *Pages* text box at the Print backstage area. When entering page numbers in this text box, use a hyphen to indicate a range of consecutive pages for printing or a comma to specify nonconsecutive pages.

If a document contains sections, use the *Pages* text box at the Print backstage area to specify the section and pages within the section that you want printed. For example, if a document is divided into three sections and you want to print only section two, type *s2* in the *Pages* text box. If a document contains six sections and you want to print sections three through five, type *s3-s5* in the *Pages* text box. You can also identify specific pages within or between sections for printing. For example, to print pages 2 through 5 of section 4, type *p2s4-p5s4*; to print from page 3 of section 1 through page 5 of section 4, type *p3s1-p5s4*; to print page 1 of section 3, page 4 of section 5, and page 6 of section 8, type *p1s3,p4s5,p6s8*.

Quick Steps

Print a Section

1. Click FILE tab.
2. Click *Print* option.
3. Click in *Pages* text box.
4. Type s followed by section number.
5. Click Print button.

If you insert section breaks in a document and then insert a header and footer with page numbering for each section, the page numbering is sequential throughout the document. The **WL2-C1-P5-CompSoftware.docx** document has a section break but the pages are numbered sequentially. If you want page numbering in a section to start with a new number, such as 1, use the *Start at* option at the Page Number Format dialog box. Display this dialog box by clicking the Page Number button in the Header & Footer group on the HEADER & FOOTER TOOLS DESIGN tab and then clicking the *Format Page Numbers* option at the drop-down list. At the Page Number Format dialog box, click the *Start at* option. This inserts *1* in the text box. You can leave this number or type a different page number in the text box.

Project 5f **Changing Section Numbering and Printing Section Pages** **Part 6 of 7**

1. With **WL2-C1-P5-CompSoftware.docx** open, change the starting page number to *1* for section 2 by completing the following steps:
   a. Click the INSERT tab, click the Footer button in the Header & Footer group, and then click *Edit Footer* at the drop-down list.
   b. At the *Footer - Section 1-* footer pane, click the Next button in the Navigation group on the HEADER & FOOTER TOOLS DESIGN tab.
   c. At the *Footer - Section 2-* footer pane, click the Page Number button in the Header & Footer group and then click the *Format Page Numbers* option at the drop-down list.
   d. At the Page Number Format dialog box, click the *Start at* option. (This inserts *1* in the text box.)
   e. Click OK to close the dialog box.
   f. Click the Close Header and Footer button.

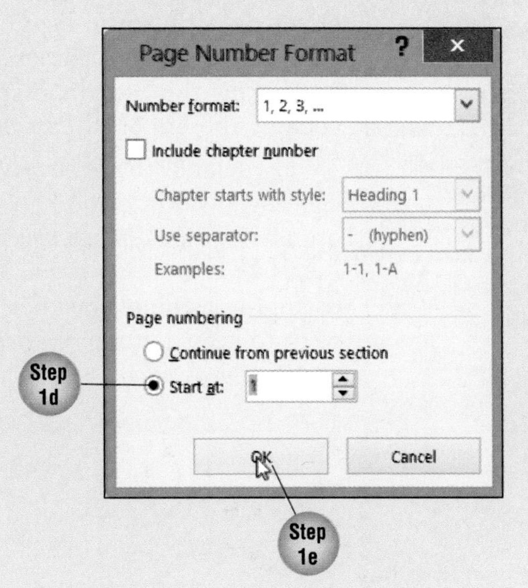

2. Print only page 1 of section 1 and page 1 of section 2 by completing the following steps:
   a. Click the FILE tab and then click the *Print* option.
   b. At the Print backstage area, click in the *Pages* text box in the *Settings* category and then type p1s1,p1s2.
   c. Click the Print button.
3. Save **WL2-C1-P5-CompSoftware.docx**.

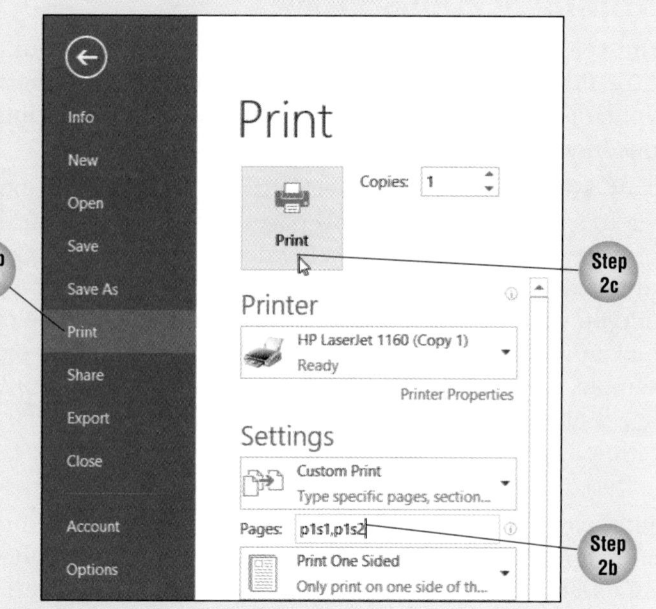

Keeping Text Together

Quick Steps

Keep Text Together
1. Click Paragraph group dialog box launcher.
2. Click Line and Page Breaks tab.
3. Click *Keep with next*, *Keep lines together*, and/or *Page break before*.
4. Click OK.

Text formatted with Keep with next formatting is identified with a ■ nonprinting character in the left margin.

In a multiple-page document, Word automatically inserts a soft page break, which is a page break that adjusts when you add or delete text from the document. A soft page break may occur in an undesirable location. For example, a soft page break may cause a heading to display at the bottom of a page while the text connected to the heading displays at the top of the next page. A soft page break may also create a ***widow*** or ***orphan***. A widow is the last line of text in a paragraph that appears at the top of a page and an orphan is the first line of text in a paragraph that appears at the bottom of a page.

Use options at the Paragraph dialog box with the Line and Page Breaks tab selected, as shown in Figure 1.7, to control widows and orphans and keep a paragraph, group of paragraphs, or group of lines together. Display this dialog box by clicking the Paragraph group dialog box launcher on the HOME tab and then clicking the Line and Page Breaks tab at the dialog box.

By default, the *Widow/Orphan control* option is active and Word tries to avoid creating a widow or orphan when inserting a soft page break. The other three options in the *Pagination* section of the dialog box are not active by default. Use the *Keep with next* option if you want to keep a line together with the next line. This is useful for keeping a heading together with the first line below the heading. If you want to keep a group of selected lines together, use the *Keep lines together* option. Use the *Page break before* option to tell Word to insert a page break before selected text.

Figure 1.7 Paragraph Dialog Box with Line and Page Breaks Tab Selected

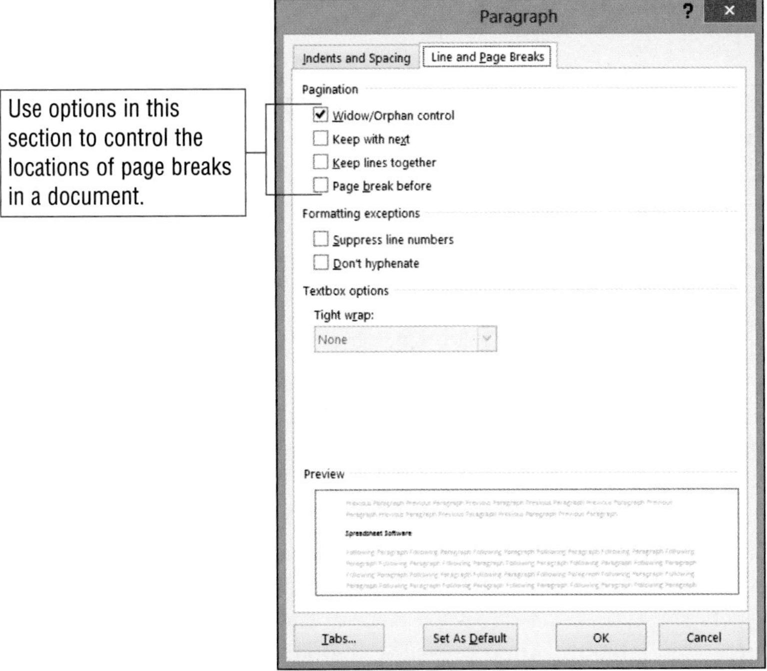

Project 5g Keeping Text Together

Part 7 of 7

1. With **WL2-C1-P5-CompSoftware.docx** open, scroll through the document and notice that the *Spreadsheet Software* heading displays at the bottom of page 1 and the paragraph that follows it displays at the top of page 2. Keep the heading together with the paragraph of text by completing the following steps:
   a. Position the insertion point on any character in the heading *Spreadsheet Software*.
   b. Make sure the HOME tab is active and then click the Paragraph group dialog box launcher.
   c. At the Paragraph dialog box, click the Line and Page Breaks tab.
   d. Click the *Keep with next* check box to insert a check mark.
   e. Click OK to close the dialog box.

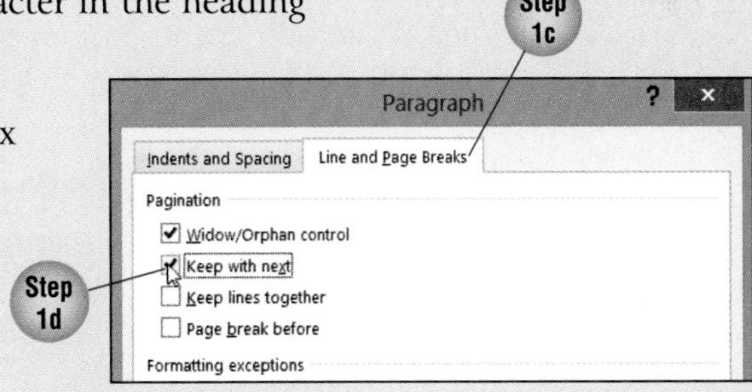

2. Scroll through the document and notice the heading *Multimedia Software* that displays near the end of the document. Insert a soft page break at the beginning of the heading by completing the following steps:
   a. Move the insertion point to the beginning of the *Multimedia Software* heading.
   b. Click the Paragraph group dialog box launcher.
   c. At the Paragraph dialog box with the Line and Page Breaks tab selected, click the *Page break before* check box to insert a check mark.
   d. Click OK to close the dialog box.
3. Save, print, and then close **WL2-C1-P5-CompSoftware.docx**.

Project 6 **Create and Format a Column Chart and Pie Chart** **5 Parts**

You will use the Chart feature to create and format a column chart and then create and format a pie chart.

Creating Charts

Quick Steps

Insert a Chart
1. Click INSERT tab.
2. Click Chart button.
3. Enter data in Excel worksheet.
4. Close Excel.

Chart

You can copy a chart from Excel to Word and embed it as static data or link it to the worksheet.

A ***chart*** is a visual presentation of data. In Word, you can create a variety of charts, including bar and column charts, pie charts, area charts, and many more. To create a chart, click the INSERT tab and then click the Chart button in the Illustrations group. This displays the Insert Chart dialog box, as shown in Figure 1.8. At this dialog box, choose the desired chart type in the list at the left side, click the chart style, and then click OK.

When you click OK, a sample chart is inserted in the document and Excel opens with sample data, as shown in Figure 1.9. Type the desired data in the Excel worksheet cells over the existing data. As you type data, the chart in the Word document reflects the typed data. To type data in the Excel worksheet, click in the desired cell, type the data, and then press the Tab key to make the next cell active, press Shift + Tab to make the previous cell active, or press Enter to make the cell below active.

The sample worksheet contains a data range of four columns and five rows and the cells in the data range display with a light fill color. Excel uses the data in the range to create the chart in the document. You are not limited to four columns and five rows. Simply type data in cells outside the data range and Excel will expand the data range and incorporate the new data in the chart. This occurs because the table AutoExpansion feature is on by default. If you type data in a cell outside the data range, an AutoCorrect Options button displays in the lower right corner of the cell when you move away from the cell. Use this button if you want to turn off AutoExpansion.

Figure 1.8 Insert Chart Dialog Box

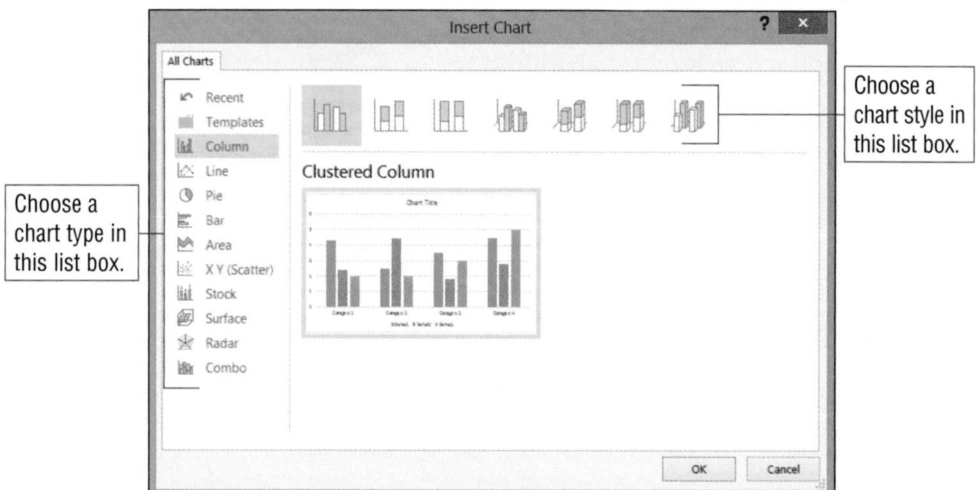

Figure 1.9 Sample Chart

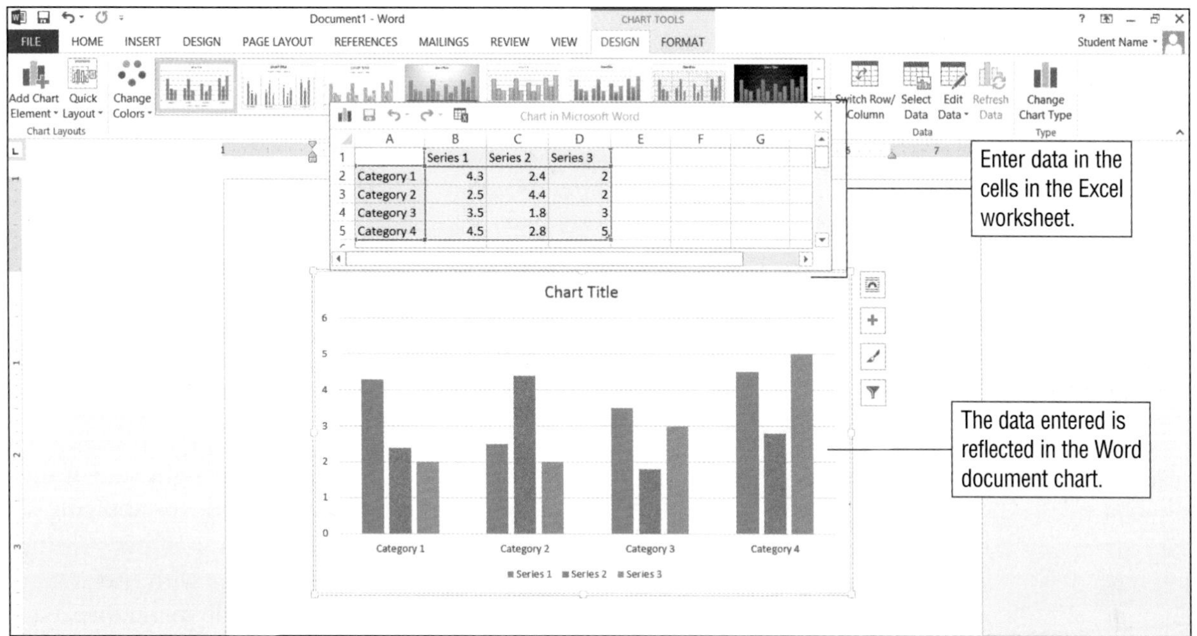
Enter data in the cells in the Excel worksheet.
The data entered is reflected in the Word document chart.
Chart Title

If you do not insert data in all four columns and five rows, decrease the size of the data range. To do this, position the mouse pointer on the small, square, blue icon that displays in the lower right corner of cell E5 until the pointer displays as a diagonally pointing two-headed arrow and then drag up to decrease the number of rows in the range and/or drag left to decrease the number of columns.

When you have entered all of the data in the worksheet, click the Close button that displays in the upper right corner of the screen. This closes the Excel window, expands the Word document window, and displays the chart in the document.

Project 6a Creating a Column Chart

Part 1 of 5

1. At a blank document, click the INSERT tab and then click the Chart button in the Illustrations group.
2. At the Insert Chart dialog box, click OK.
3. Type Sales 2013 in cell B1 in the Excel worksheet.
4. Press the Tab key and then type Sales 2014 in cell C1.
5. Press the Tab key and then type Sales 2015 in cell D1.
6. Press the Tab key. (This makes cell A2 active.)
7. Continue typing the remaining data in cells as indicated in Figure 1.10 on the next page. After typing the last entry, click in cell A1.
8. Click the Close button that displays in the upper right corner of the Excel window.
9. Save the document and name it **WL2-C1-P6-Charts**.

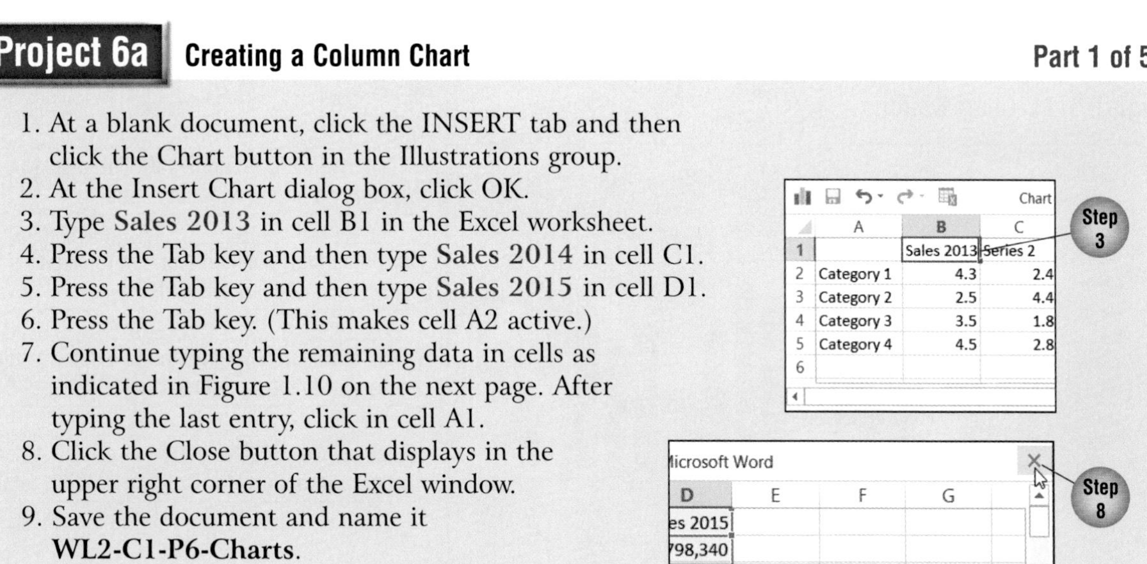
Step 3
Step 8

Figure 1.10 Project 6a

Chart in Microsoft Word

	A	B	C	D	E	F	G
1		Sales 2013	Sales 2014	Sales 2015			
2	Northeast	$729,300	$698,453	$798,340			
3	Southeast	$310,455	$278,250	$333,230			
4	Northwest	$610,340	$700,100	$525,425			
5	Southwest	$522,340	$500,278	$625,900			
6							
7							

Formatting with Chart Buttons

When you insert a chart in a document, four buttons display at the right side of the chart border, as shown in Figure 1.11. These buttons contain options for applying formatting to the entire chart.

Click the top button, Layout Options, and a side menu displays with text wrapping options. Click the next button, Chart Elements, and a side menu displays with chart elements, such as axis title, chart title, data labels, data table, gridlines, and a legend. Elements containing a check mark in the check box are included in the chart. Include other elements by inserting check marks in the check boxes for those elements you want in your chart.

Click the Chart Styles button that displays at the right side of the chart and a side menu gallery of styles displays. Scroll down the gallery and hover your mouse over an option and the style formatting is applied to your chart. Using this feature, you can scroll down the gallery and preview the style before you apply it to your chart. In addition to applying a chart style, you can use the Chart Styles button side menu gallery to change the chart colors. Click the Chart Styles button, click the COLOR tab that displays to the right of the STYLE tab, and then click the desired color option at the color palette that displays. Hover your mouse over a color option to view how the color change affects the elements in your chart.

Figure 1.11 Chart Buttons

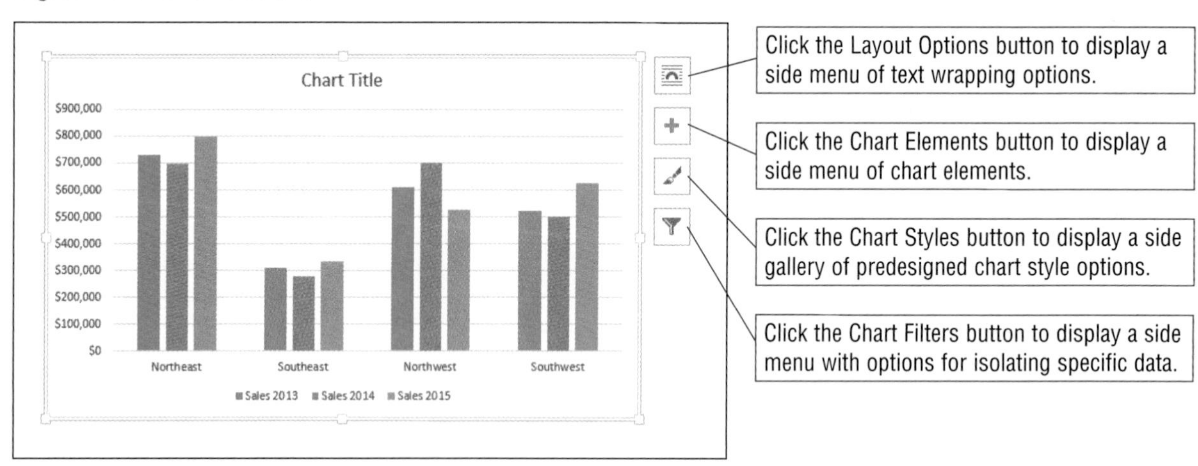
Chart Title
$900,000
$800,000
$700,000
$600,000
$500,000
$400,000
$300,000
$200,000
$100,000
$0
Northeast
Southeast
Northwest
Southwest
Sales 2013
Sales 2014
Sales 2015
Click the Layout Options button to display a side menu of text wrapping options.
Click the Chart Elements button to display a side menu of chart elements.
Click the Chart Styles button to display a side gallery of predesigned chart style options.
Click the Chart Filters button to display a side menu with options for isolating specific data.

Use the bottom button, Chart Filters, to isolate specific data in your chart. When you click the button, a side menu displays. Specify the series or categories you want to display in your chart. To do this, remove check marks from those elements that you do not want to appear in your chart. After removing the desired check marks, click the Apply button that displays toward the bottom of the side menu. Click the NAMES tab at the Chart Filters button side menu and options display for turning on/off the display of column and row names.

Use a pie chart if the data series you want to plot has seven categories or less and the categories represent parts of a whole.

Project 6b Formatting with Chart Buttons

Part 2 of 5

1. With **WL2-C1-P6-Charts.docx** open, make sure the chart is selected.
2. Click the Layout Options button that displays outside the upper right side of the chart and then click the *Square* option in the side menu (first option in the *With Text Wrapping* section).
3. Remove and add chart elements by completing the following steps:
   a. Click the Chart Elements button that displays below the Layout Options button outside the upper right side of the chart.
   b. At the side menu that displays, click the *Chart Title* check box to remove the check mark.
   c. Click the *Data Table* check box to insert a check mark.

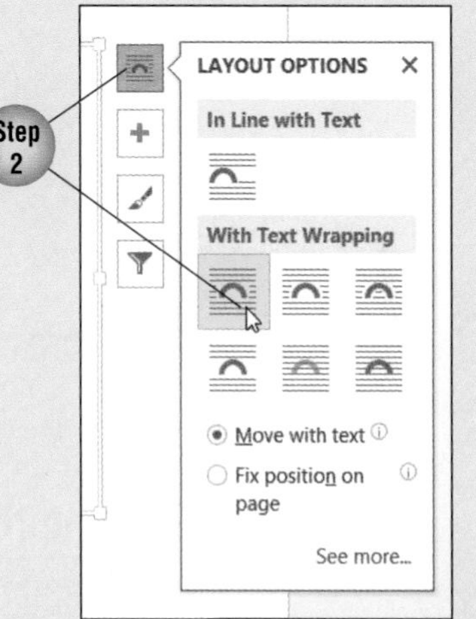

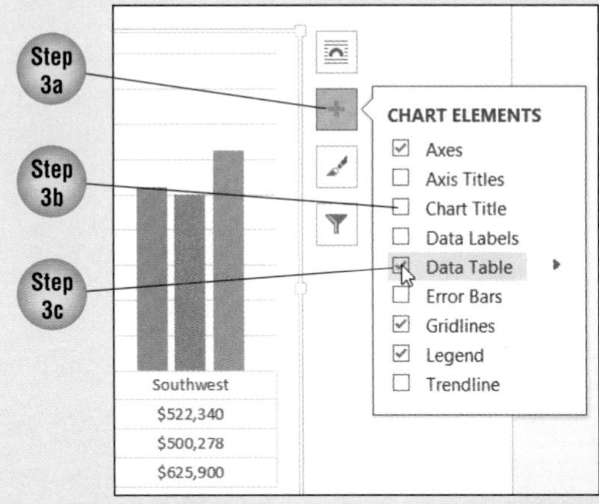

4. Apply a different chart style by completing the following steps:
   a. Click the Chart Styles button that displays below the Chart Elements button.
   b. At the side menu gallery, click the *Style 3* option (third option in the gallery).
   c. Click the COLOR tab at the top of the side menu and then click the *Color 4* option at the drop-down gallery (fourth row of color options in the *Colorful* section).
   d. Click the Chart Styles button to close the side menu.

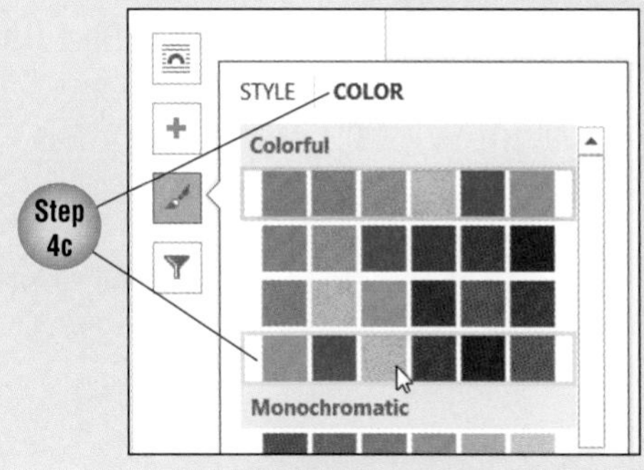

5. Display only Northeast and Southeast sales by completing the following steps:
   a. Click the Chart Filters button that displays below the Chart Styles button.
   b. Click the *Northwest* check box in the *CATEGORIES* section to remove the check mark.
   c. Click the *Southwest* check box in the *CATEGORIES* section to remove the check mark.
   d. Click the Apply button that displays near the bottom of the side menu.
   e. Click the Chart Filters button to close the side menu.
   f. After viewing only Northeast and Southeast sales, redisplay the other regions by clicking the Chart Filters button, clicking the *Northwest* and *Southwest* check boxes, and then clicking the Apply button.
   g. Click the Chart Filters button to close the side menu.
6. Save **WL2-C1-P6-Charts.docx**.

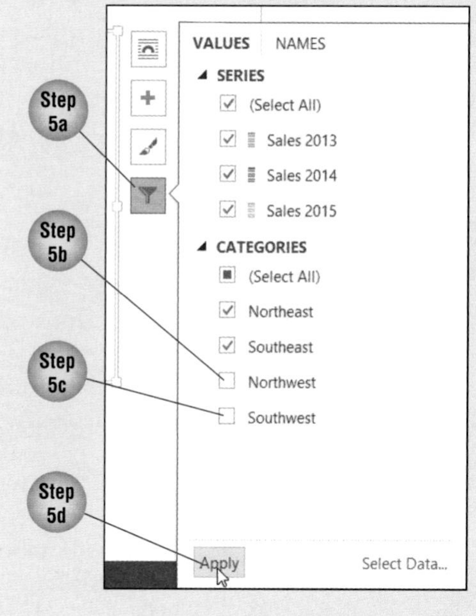

Changing the Chart Design

In addition to the buttons that display outside of the chart border, options on the CHART TOOLS DESIGN tab can be used to customize a chart, as shown in Figure 1.12. Use options on this tab to add a chart element, change the chart layout and colors, apply a chart style, select data and switch rows and columns, and change the chart type.

Figure 1.12 CHART TOOLS DESIGN Tab

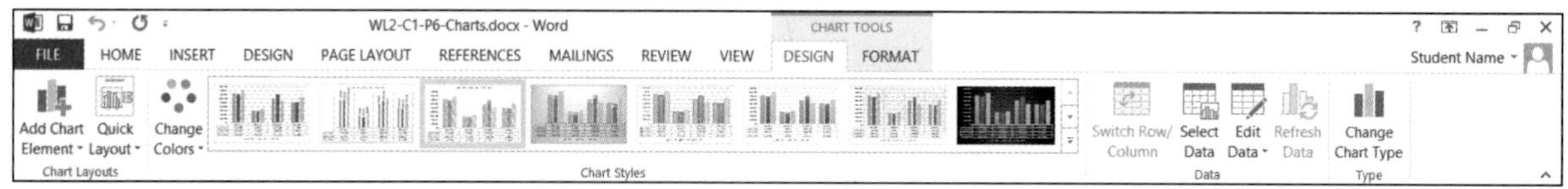

Project 6c **Changing the Chart Design** **Part 3 of 5**

1. With **WL2-C1-P6-Charts.docx** open, make sure that the chart is selected and the CHART TOOLS DESIGN tab is active.
2. Change to a different layout by clicking the Quick Layout button in the Chart Layouts group and then clicking the *Layout 3* option (third column, first row in the drop-down gallery).

3. Click the *Style 7* thumbnail that displays in the Chart Styles group (seventh thumbnail option from the left).
4. Click the Add Chart Element button in the Chart Layouts group, point to *Chart Title* at the drop-down list, and then click *Centered Overlay* at the side menu.

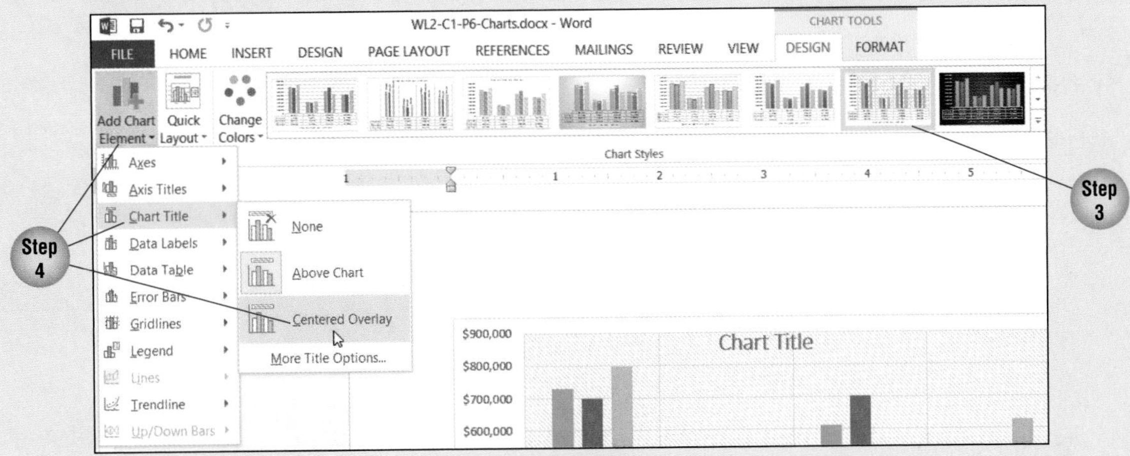

5. Select the words *Chart Title* and then type **Regional Sales**.
6. Click the chart border to deselect the chart title.
7. Edit the data by completing the following steps:
   a. Click the Edit Data button in the Data group.
   b. Click in cell C3.
   c. Type 375,250. (The text you type replaces the original amount of $278,250.)
   d. Click in cell C5, type 550,300, and then press the Tab key.
   e. Click the Close button that displays in the upper right corner of the Excel window.
8. Save **WL2-C1-P6-Charts.docx**.

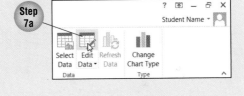

Formatting and Customizing a Chart and Chart Elements

Use buttons on the CHART TOOLS FORMAT tab, shown in Figure 1.13, to format and customize a chart and chart elements. To format or modify a specific element in a chart, select the element. Do this by clicking the element or by clicking the Chart Elements button in the Current Selection group and then clicking the element at the drop-down list. With other options on the CHART TOOLS FORMAT tab, apply a shape style and Word Art style and arrange and size the chart or chart element.

Figure 1.13 CHART TOOLS FORMAT Tab

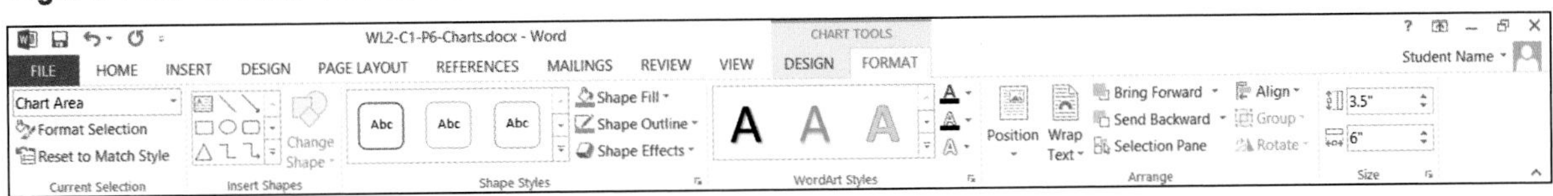

Project 6d Formatting a Chart and Chart Elements

Part 4 of 5

1. With **WL2-C1-P6-Charts.docx** open and the chart selected, click the CHART TOOLS FORMAT tab.
2. Apply a shape style to the chart title by completing the following steps:
   a. Click the Chart Elements button arrow in the Current Selection group.
   b. Click *Chart Title* at the drop-down list.
   c. Click the *Colored Outline - Blue, Accent 1* style option (second option in the Shape Styles group).
3. Change the color of the Sales 2015 series by completing the followings steps:
   a. Click the Chart Elements button arrow in the Current Selection group.
   b. Click *Series "Sales 2015"* at the drop-down list.
   c. Click the Shape Fill button arrow in the Shape Styles group.
   d. Click the *Dark Red* option (first color option in the *Standard Colors* section).

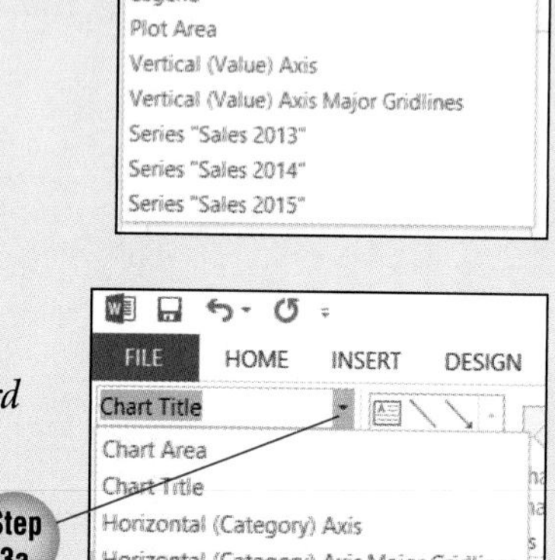

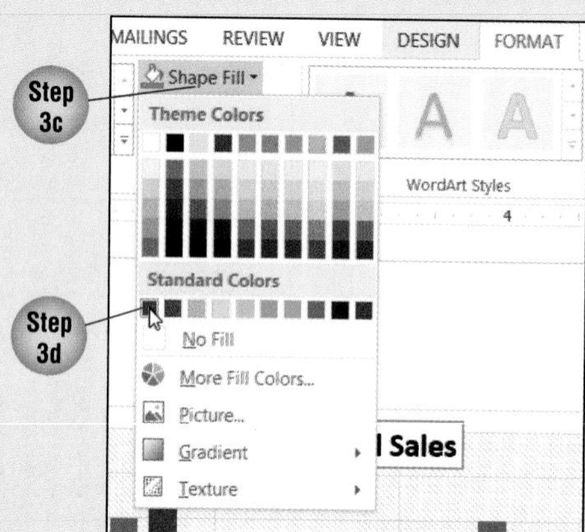

4. Apply a WordArt style to all of the text in the chart by completing the following steps:
   a. Click the Chart Elements button arrow.
   b. Click *Chart Area* at the drop-down list.
   c. Click the first WordArt style option in the WordArt Styles group (*Fill - Black, Text 1, Shadow*).
5. Change the size of the chart by completing the following steps:
   a. Click in the *Shape Height* measurement box and then type 3.
   b. Click in the *Shape Width* measurement box, type 5.5, and then press Enter.
6. With the chart selected (not a chart element), change the position of the chart by clicking the Position button in the Arrange group and then clicking the *Position in Top Center with Square Text Wrapping* option (second column, first row in the *With Text Wrapping* section).
7. Save and then print **WL2-C1-P6-Charts.docx**.

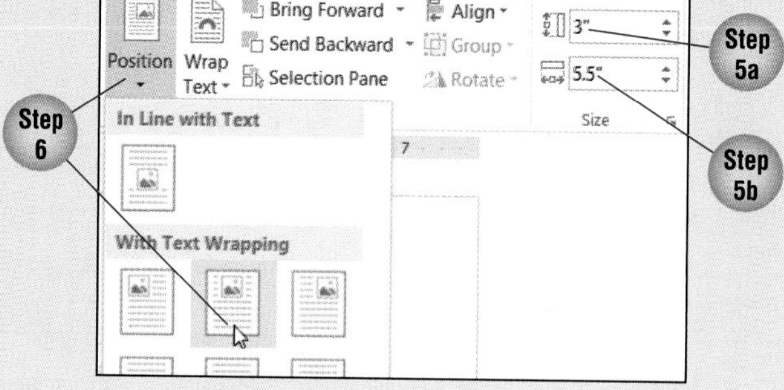

Formatting a Chart with Task Pane Options

Additional formatting options are available at various task panes. Display a task pane by clicking the Format Selection button in the Current Selection group on the CHART TOOLS FORMAT tab or a group task pane launcher. The Shape Styles and WordArt Styles groups on the CHART TOOLS FORMAT tab contain task pane launchers. The task pane that opens at the right side of the screen depends on the chart or chart element selected.

Project 6e Creating and Formatting a Pie Chart

Part 5 of 5

1. With **WL2-C1-P6-Charts.docx** open, press Ctrl + End (which deselects the chart) and then press the Enter key 12 times to move the insertion point below the chart.
2. Click the INSERT tab and then click the Chart button in the Illustrations group.
3. At the Insert Chart dialog box, click *Pie* in the left panel and then click OK.
4. Type the data in the Excel worksheet cells as shown in Figure 1.14 on the next page. After typing the last entry, click in cell A1.
5. Click the Close button located in the upper right corner of the Excel window.
6. Click in the title *Percentage* and then type **Investments**.
7. Add data labels to the pie chart by completing the following steps:
   a. Click the Add Chart Element button in the Chart Layouts group on the CHART TOOLS DESIGN tab.
   b. Point to *Data Labels* at the drop-down list and then click *Inside End* at the side menu.
8. Click on the chart border to select the chart (and not a chart element).
9. Click the CHART TOOLS FORMAT tab.
10. Apply formatting to the chart with options at the Format Chart Area task pane by completing the following steps:
   a. With the chart selected, click the Shape Styles group task pane launcher.
   b. At the Format Chart Area task pane with the Fill & Line icon selected, click *FILL*. (This expands the options below *FILL*.)
   c. Click the *Gradient fill* option.
   d. Click the Effects icon located near the top of the task pane.
   e. Click *SHADOW* to expand the shadow options.
   f. Click the Presets button.
   g. Click the *Offset Bottom* option (second column, first row in the *Outer* section).

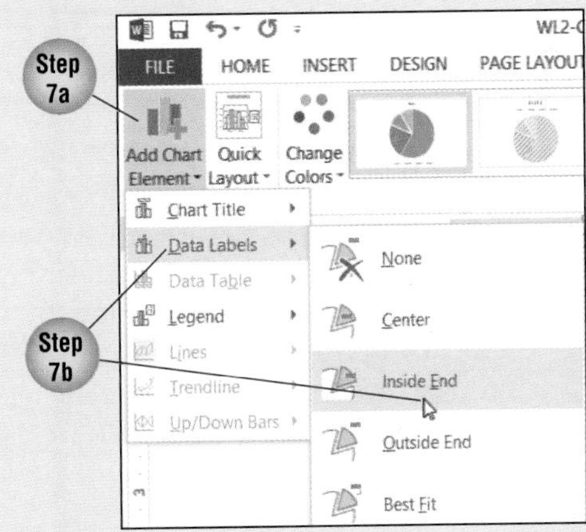

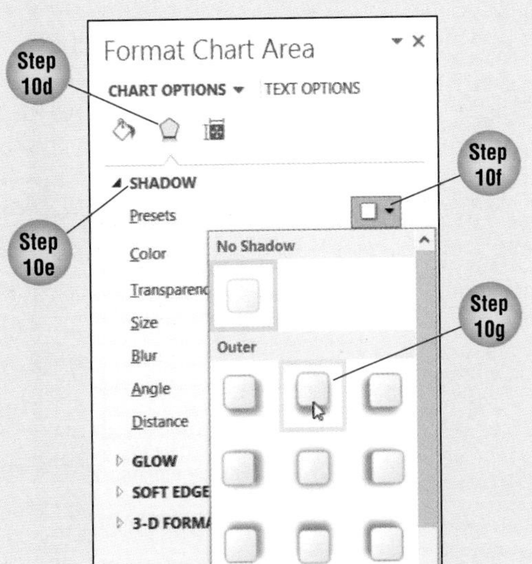

h. Click the TEXT OPTIONS tab that displays near the top of the task pane.
i. Click *TEXT OUTLINE* to expand the options.
j. Click the *Solid line* option.
k. Click the Color button and then click the *Blue, Accent 1, Darker 50%* option (fifth column, last row in the *Theme Colors* section).

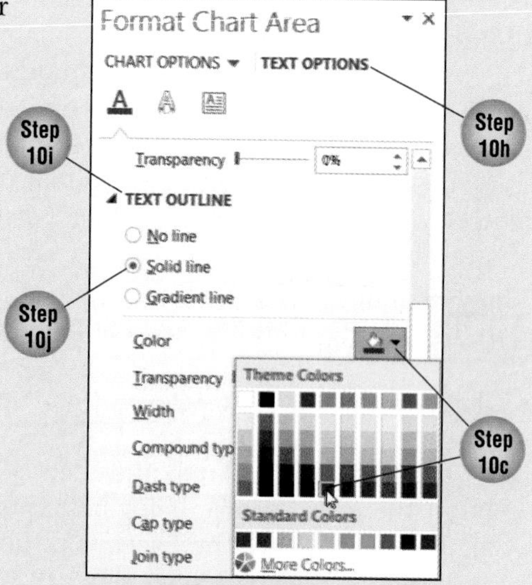

11. Format the pie by completing the following steps:
    a. Click in any piece of the pie. (This selects all of the pieces of the pie. Notice that the task pane name has changed to *Format Data Series*.)
    b. Click the Effects icon that displays near the top of the task pane.
    c. Click *3-D FORMAT* to expand the options.
    d. Click the Top bevel button.
    e. Click the *Soft Round* option at the drop-down gallery (second column, second row in the *Bevel* section).
    f. Close the task pane by clicking the Close button that displays in the upper right corner of the task pane.
12. Click the chart border to select the chart (and not a chart element).
13. Change the size of the chart by completing the following steps:
    a. Click in the *Shape Height* measurement box and then type 3.
    b. Click in the *Shape Width* measurement box, type 5.5, and then press Enter.
14. Change the position of the chart by clicking the Position button in the Arrange group and then clicking the *Position in Bottom Center with Square Text Wrapping* option (second column, third row in the *With Text Wrapping* section).
15. Save, print, and then close **WL2-C1-P6-Charts.docx**.

Figure 1.14 Project 6e

	A	B
1	Assets	Percentage
2	Loans	34%
3	Bonds	22%
4	Mutuals	20%
5	Stocks	17%
6	Other	7%
7		

Chapter Summary

- Use the Bullets button to insert bullets before specific paragraphs of text and use the Numbering button to insert numbers.
- Insert custom numbers by clicking the Numbering button arrow and then clicking the desired option at the drop-down gallery.
- Define your own numbering formatting with options at the Define New Number Format dialog box. Display this dialog box by clicking the Numbering button arrow and then clicking *Define New Number Format* at the drop-down gallery.
- Insert custom bullets by clicking the Bullets button arrow and then clicking the desired option at the drop-down gallery.
- Define your own custom bullet with options at the Define New Bullet dialog box. Display this dialog box by clicking the Bullets button arrow and then clicking *Define New Bullet* at the drop-down gallery.
- Apply numbering to multilevel paragraphs of text by clicking the Multilevel List button in the Paragraph group on the HOME tab.
- Define your own multilevel list numbering with options at the Define New Multilevel List dialog box. Display this dialog box by clicking the Multilevel List button and then clicking *Define New Multilevel List* at the drop-down gallery.
- When typing a multilevel list, press the Tab key to move to the next level and press the Shift + Tab key to move to the previous level.
- Customize the layout of images with options at the Layout dialog box. Display this dialog box by clicking the Size group dialog box launcher on the PICTURE TOOLS FORMAT tab.
- The Layout dialog box contains three tabs. Click the Position tab to specify the position of the image in the document, click the Text Wrapping tab to specify a wrapping style for the image, and click the Size tab to display options for specifying the height and width of the image.
- Format an image with options in the Format Picture task pane. Display this task pane by clicking the Picture Styles group task pane launcher.
- Apply artistic effects to a picture or photograph with the Artistic Effects button in the Adjust group on the PICTURE TOOLS FORMAT tab or with options at the Format Picture task pane with the Effects icon selected.
- Text that appears at the top of every page is called a *header*; text that appears at the bottom of every page is called a *footer*.
- Insert predesigned headers and footers in a document or create your own.
- To create a header, click the Header button in the Header & Footer group on the INSERT tab, and then click *Edit Header*. At the Header pane, insert the desired elements or text. Complete similar steps to create a footer.
- Use buttons in the Insert group on the HEADER & FOOTER TOOLS DESIGN tab to insert elements such as the date and time, Quick Parts, pictures, and images into a header or footer.
- Word inserts headers and footers 0.5 inch from the edge of the page. Reposition a header or footer with buttons in the Position group on the HEADER & FOOTER TOOLS DESIGN tab.

- You can create a unique header or footer on the first page; omit a header or footer on the first page; create different headers or footers for odd and even pages; or create different headers or footers for sections in a document. Use options in the Options group on the HEADER & FOOTER TOOLS DESIGN tab to specify the type of header or footer you want to create.
- Insert page numbers in a document in a header or footer or with options from the Page Number button, which is located in the Header & Footer group on the INSERT tab.
- Remove page numbers with the *Remove Page Numbers* option from the Page Number button drop-down list.
- If you want to remove the page number from the first page, edit the page number as a header or footer.
- Format page numbers with options at the Page Number Format dialog box.
- To print sections or specific pages within a section, use the *Pages* text box at the Print backstage area. When specifying sections and pages, use the letter *s* before a section number and the letter *p* before a page number.
- Word attempts to avoid creating widows and orphans when inserting soft page breaks. Turn on or off the widow/orphan control feature at the Paragraph dialog box with the Line and Page Breaks tab selected. This dialog box also contains options for keeping a paragraph, group of paragraphs, or group of lines together.
- To present data visually, create a chart with the Chart button on the INSERT tab. Choose the desired chart type at the Insert Chart dialog box. Enter chart data in an Excel worksheet.
- Four buttons display at the right side of a selected chart. Use the Layout Options button to apply a text wrapping option, the Chart Elements button to add or remove chart elements, the Chart Styles button to apply a predesigned chart style, and the Chart Filters button to isolate specific data in the chart.
- Modify a chart design with options and buttons on the CHART TOOLS DESIGN tab.
- Cells in the Excel worksheet used to create a chart are linked to the chart in the slide. To edit chart data, click the Edit Data button on the CHART TOOLS DESIGN tab and then make changes to the text in the Excel worksheet.
- Customize the format of a chart and chart elements with options and buttons on the CHART TOOLS FORMAT tab. You can select the chart or a specific element, apply a style to a shape, apply a WordArt style to text, and arrange and size the chart.
- Apply formatting to a chart with options in task panes. Display a task pane by clicking the Format Selection button on the CHART TOOLS FORMAT tab or a group task pane launcher. The options in the task pane vary depending on the chart or chart element selected.

Commands Review

FEATURE	RIBBON TAB, GROUP	BUTTON, OPTION
bullets	HOME, Paragraph	
create footer	INSERT, Header & Footer	, *Edit Footer*
create header	INSERT, Header & Footer	, *Edit Header*
Define New Bullet dialog box	HOME, Paragraph	, *Define New Bullet*
Define New Multilevel List dialog box	HOME, Paragraph	, *Define New Multilevel List*
Define New Number Format dialog box	HOME, Paragraph	, *Define New Number Format*
footer	INSERT, Header & Footer	
header	INSERT, Header & Footer	
Insert Chart dialog box	INSERT, Illustrations	
multilevel list	HOME, Paragraph	
numbering	HOME, Paragraph	
Paragraph dialog box	HOME, Paragraph	
text box	INSERT, Text	

Concepts Check

Test Your Knowledge

Completion: In the space provided at the right, indicate the correct term, symbol, or command.

1. Define your own numbering format with options at this dialog box. ____________________
2. A bullet that you create at the Define New Bullet dialog box is automatically included in this section in the Bullets button drop-down gallery. ____________________
3. Click this button to number paragraphs of text at the left margin, first tab, second tab, and so on. ____________________

4. When typing a multilevel list, press this combination of keys to move to the previous level. __________
5. Specify the horizontal and vertical layout of an image in the Layout dialog box with this tab selected. __________
6. Click this group task pane launcher on the PICTURE TOOLS FORMAT tab to display the Format Picture task pane. __________
7. To create your own header, click the INSERT tab, click the Header button in the Header & Footer group, and then click this option at the drop-down list. __________
8. By default, a header is positioned this distance from the top of the page. __________
9. By default, headers and footers contain two tab settings: a center tab and this type of tab. __________
10. When creating a header, clicking the *Different First Page* check box causes this pane to display. __________
11. Type this in the *Pages* text box at the Print backstage area to print section 5. __________
12. Type this in the *Pages* text box at the Print backstage area to print page 2 of section 4 and page 5 of section 8. __________
13. The *Keep lines together* option is available at the Paragraph dialog box with this tab selected. __________
14. When creating a chart, enter data in this. __________
15. The Edit Data button is located on this tab. __________
16. Use this button that displays at the right side of a selected chart to apply a text wrapping option. __________
17. Use this button that displays at the right side of a selected chart to isolate specific data in a chart. __________

Skills Check Assess Your Performance

Assessment 1 DEFINE AND APPLY CUSTOM BULLETS AND MULTILEVEL LISTS TO A TECHNOLOGY DOCUMENT

1. Open **TechTimeline.docx** and then save the document and name it **WL2-C1-A1-TechTimeline**.
2. Select the questions below the *TECHNOLOGY INFORMATION QUESTIONS* heading and then insert check mark (✓) bullets.
3. Define a cell phone symbol (📱)bullet in 14-point font size and then apply the symbol bullet to the seven paragraphs of text below the *TECHNOLOGY TIMELINE: PERSONAL COMMUNICATIONS TECHNOLOGY* heading. (You can find the cell phone symbol in the Webdings font [in approximately the ninth through eleventh rows].)
4. Select the paragraphs of text below the heading *INFORMATION SYSTEMS AND COMMERCE*, click the Multilevel List button, and then click the middle option in the top row of the *List Library* section.
5. Select the paragraphs of text below the heading *INTERNET* and then apply the same multilevel list numbering.
6. Save and then print page 3 of **WL2-C1-A1-TechTimeline.docx**.
7. Select the paragraphs of text below the heading *INFORMATION SYSTEMS AND COMMERCE* and then define a new multilevel list with the following specifications:
   a. Level 1 inserts arabic numbers (1, 2, 3), each followed by a period, and is aligned at 0 inch and indented at 0.25 inch.
   b. Level 2 inserts capital letters (A, B, C), each followed by a period, and is aligned at 0.25 inch and indented at 0.5 inch.
   c. Level 3 inserts arabic numbers (1, 2, 3), each followed by a right parenthesis, and is aligned at 0.5 inch and indented at 0.75 inch.
   d. Make sure the new multilevel list numbering is applied to the selected paragraphs.
8. Select the paragraphs of text below the heading *INTERNET* and then apply the new multilevel list numbering.
9. Insert a header that prints the page number at the right margin on all pages *except* the first page.
10. Insert the text *Cell phones* and *YouTube* in text boxes as shown in Figure 1.15 on the next page with the following specifications:
    a. Insert a text box below the arrow line located near the bottom of page 1 and then type **Cell phones** in the text box.
    b. Rotate the text in the text box 270 degrees.
    c. Remove the outline from the text box. ***Hint: Do this with the Shape Outline button in the Shape Styles group.***
    d. Change the text wrapping to *Behind Text*.
    e. Drag the text box so it is positioned as shown in Figure 1.15.
    f. Complete similar steps to create the text box with the text *YouTube* and position the text box as shown in Figure 1.15.

11. Move the insertion point to the right of the text *Electronic Commerce* (item 2) located on page 2 and then insert a photograph image as shown in Figure 1.16 with the following specifications:
    a. Display the Insert Pictures window, search for *credit card for shopping*, and then insert the image shown in Figure 1.16. (If this photograph image is not available, choose another one that shows a credit card.)
    b. Change the height of the image to 2 inches.
    c. Apply shadow and glow effects of your choosing to the image.
    d. Apply the Paint Strokes artistic effect.
    e. Apply Tight text wrapping.
    f. Precisely position the photograph on the second page with an absolute horizontal measurement of 4.5 inches from the right edge of the page and an absolute vertical measurement of 4 inches below the top of the page.
    g. Compress the photograph. (Use the Compress Pictures button in the Adjust group on the PICTURE TOOLS FORMAT tab.)
12. Save, print, and then close **WL2-C1-A1-TechTimeline.docx**.

Figure 1.15 Assessment 1, Step 10

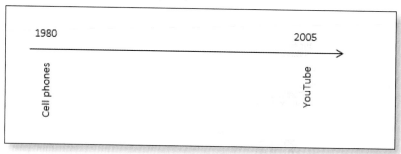

Figure 1.16 Assessment 1, Step 11

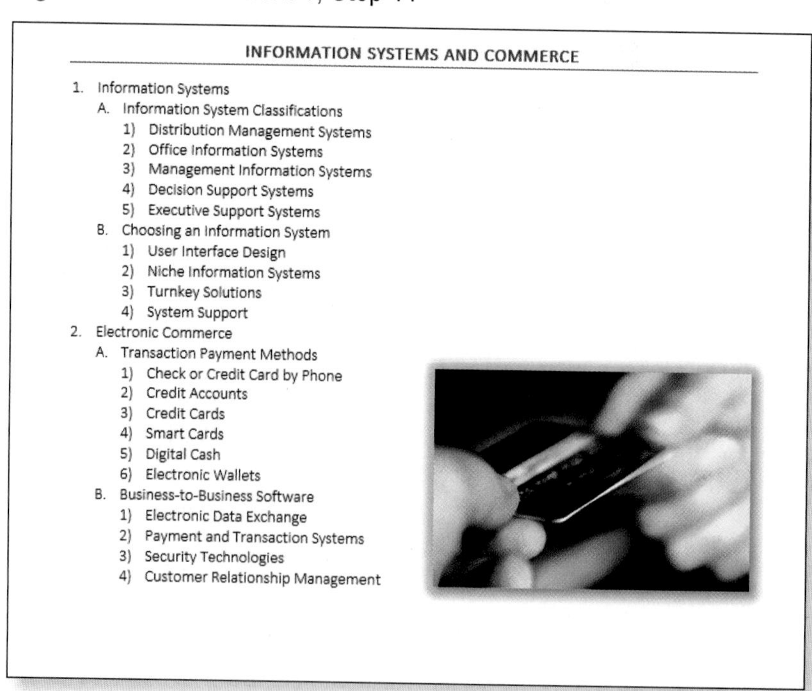

INFORMATION SYSTEMS AND COMMERCE

1. Information Systems
   A. Information System Classifications
      1) Distribution Management Systems
      2) Office Information Systems
      3) Management Information Systems
      4) Decision Support Systems
      5) Executive Support Systems
   B. Choosing an Information System
      1) User Interface Design
      2) Niche Information Systems
      3) Turnkey Solutions
      4) System Support
2. Electronic Commerce
   A. Transaction Payment Methods
      1) Check or Credit Card by Phone
      2) Credit Accounts
      3) Credit Cards
      4) Smart Cards
      5) Digital Cash
      6) Electronic Wallets
   B. Business-to-Business Software
      1) Electronic Data Exchange
      2) Payment and Transaction Systems
      3) Security Technologies
      4) Customer Relationship Management

Assessment 2

INSERT SPECIALIZED HEADERS AND FOOTERS IN A REPORT

1. Open **Robots.docx** and then save the document and name it **WL2-C1-A2-Robots**.
2. Make the following changes to the document:
   a. Apply the Heading 2 style to the title *ROBOTS AS ANDROIDS*.
   b. Apply the Heading 3 style to the headings *Visual Perception*, *Audio Perception*, *Tactile Perception*, *Locomotion*, and *Navigation*.
   c. Change the style set to *Lines (Distinctive)*.
   d. Change the paragraph spacing to *Relaxed*. (Use the Paragraph Spacing button in the Document Formatting group on the DESIGN tab.)
   e. Center the title *ROBOTS AS ANDROIDS*.
   f. Keep the heading *Navigation* together with the paragraph of text that follows it.
3. Create an odd page footer that includes the following:
   a. Insert the current date at the left margin. (Choose the date option that displays the month spelled out, such as *January 1, 2015*.)
   b. Insert a clip art image related to *robot* in the middle of the footer. Change the height of the robot image to approximately 0.7 inches and the text wrapping to *Behind Text*. Drag the robot image down so it is positioned below the footer pane border.
   c. At the right margin, type **Page**, press the spacebar, and then insert a page number at the current position.
4. Create an even page footer that includes the following:
   a. At the left margin, type **Page**, press the spacebar, and then insert a page number at the current position.
   b. Insert in the middle of the footer the same clip art image you inserted in the odd page footer.
   c. Insert the current date at the right margin in the same format you chose for the odd page footer.
5. Save, print, and then close **WL2-C1-A2-Robots.docx**.

Assessment 3

FORMAT A REPORT INTO SECTIONS AND THEN FORMAT AND PRINT THE SECTIONS

1. Open **CompViruses.docx** and then save the document and name it **WL2-C1-A3-CompViruses**.
2. Insert at the beginning of the title *CHAPTER 2: SECURITY RISKS* a section break that begins a new page.
3. Create a footer for the first section in the document that prints *Chapter 1* at the left margin, the page number in the middle, and your first and last names at the right margin.
4. Edit the footer for the second section so it prints *Chapter 2* instead of *Chapter 1*. ***Hint: Make sure you break the link.***
5. Print only section 2 pages.
6. Save and then close **WL2-C1-A3-CompViruses.docx**.

Assessment

4 CREATE AND FORMAT A COLUMN CHART AND PIE CHART

1. At a blank document, use the data in Figure 1.17 to create a column chart (using the default chart style at the Insert Chart dialog box) with the following specifications:
   a. Use the Chart Elements button located outside the upper right border of the chart to add a data table and remove the legend.
   b. Apply the Style 4 chart style.
   c. Change the chart title to *Units Sold First Quarter*.
   d. Apply the Fill - Black, Text 1, Shadow WordArt style (first style) to the chart area.
   e. Change the chart height to 4 inches.
   f. Change the position of the chart to *Position in Top Center with Square Text Wrapping*.
2. Move the insertion point to the end of the document, press the Enter key twice, and then create a pie chart (using the default chart style at the Insert Chart dialog box) with the data shown in Figure 1.18 and with the following specifications:
   a. Apply the Style 3 chart style.
   b. Move the data labels to the inside end.
   c. Change the chart title to *Expense Distribution*.
   d. Apply the Colored Outline - Orange, Accent 2 shape style to the title (third shape style).
   e. Change the chart height to 3 inches and the width to 5.5 inches.
   f. Change the position of the chart to *Position in Bottom Center with Square Text Wrapping*.
3. Save the document and name it **WL2-C1-A4-Charts**.
4. Print and then close **WL2-C1-A4-Charts.docx**.

Figure 1.17 Assessment 4, Data for Column Chart

Salesperson	January	February	March
Barnett	55	60	42
Carson	20	24	31
Fanning	15	30	13
Han	52	62	58
Mahoney	49	52	39

Figure 1.18 Assessment 4, Data for Pie Chart

Category	Percentage
Salaries	67%
Travel	15%
Equipment	11%
Supplies	7%

Assessment

5 INSERT A HORIZONTAL LINE IN A FOOTER

1. Word includes a horizontal line feature that you can use to insert a graphic line in a document or a header or footer. Look at the formatting options that are available at the Format Horizontal Line dialog box. At a blank document, display this dialog box by clicking the Borders button arrow in the Paragraph group on the HOME tab and then clicking *Horizontal Line* at the drop-down list. Click the horizontal line to select it, right-click the selected line, and then click *Format Horizontal Line* at the shortcut menu. When you are finished looking at the formatting options, click OK to close the dialog box.
2. Open **ShopOnline.docx** and then save the document and name it **WL2-C1-A5-ShopOnline**.
3. Keep the heading *ONLINE SHOPPING MALLS* together with the paragraph that follows it.
4. Create a footer and insert a 3-point horizontal line in Blue (eighth color option in the *Standard Colors* section).
5. Save, print, and then close **WL2-C1-A5-ShopOnline.docx**.

Visual Benchmark Demonstrate Your Proficiency

CREATE AND FORMAT AN INTERNATIONAL CORRESPONDENCE DOCUMENT

1. Open **IntlCorres.docx** and then save the document and name it **WL2-C1-VB-IntlCorres**.
2. Apply the following formatting so your document appears similar to the document shown in Figure 1.19 on the next page:
   - Change the top margin to 1.5 inches and the left and right margins to 1.25 inches.
   - Apply the Heading 1 style to the title and the Heading 2 style to the three headings. Change the style set to Shaded and change the theme colors to Green.
   - Use symbol bullets as shown in the figure. (Find the globe bullet in the Webdings font at the Symbol dialog box.)
   - Apply automatic numbering as shown in the figure and start numbering with 11 after the *CANADIAN CODES AND TERRITORIES* heading.
   - Apply any other formatting required to make your document look similar to the document in the figure.
3. Save, print, and then close **WL2-C1-VB-IntlCorres.docx**.

Figure 1.19 Visual Benchmark

INTERNATIONAL CORRESPONDENCE

With the increased number of firms conducting business worldwide, international written communication has assumed new importance. Follow these guidelines when corresponding internationally, especially with people for whom English is not the primary language:

- ✓ Use a direct writing style and clear, precise words.
- ✓ Avoid slang, jargon, and idioms.
- ✓ Develop an awareness of cultural differences that may interfere with the communication process.

INTERNATIONAL ADDRESSES

Use the company's letterhead or a business card as a guide for spelling and other information. Include the following when addressing international correspondence:

- Line 1: Addressee's Name, Title
- Line 2: Company Name
- Line 3: Street Address
- Line 4: City and Codes
- Line 5: COUNTRY NAME (capitalized)

CANADIAN CODES AND PROVINCES

1) ON – Ontario
2) QC – Quebec
3) NS – Nova Scotia
4) NB – New Brunswick
5) MB – Manitoba
6) BC – British Columbia
7) PE – Prince Edward Island
8) SK – Saskatchewan
9) AB – Alberta
10) NL – Newfoundland and Labrador

CANADIAN CODES AND TERRITORIES

11) NT – Northwest Territories
12) YT – Yukon
13) NU – Nunavut

Case Study Apply Your Skills

Part 1

You work in the Human Resources department at Oceanside Medical Services. Your supervisor, Michael Jennison, has given you a Word document containing employee handbook information and asked you to format the book. Open the **OMSHandbook.docx** document, save it and name it **WL2-C1-CS-OMSHandbook**, and then apply the following formatting:

- Apply heading styles to the titles and headings.
- Apply a style set of your choosing.
- Apply a theme that makes the handbook easy to read.
- Define a new symbol bullet and then apply it to all of the currently bulleted paragraphs.
- Insert a section break that begins a new page at the beginning of each section heading (beginning with *Section 1: General Information*).
- Insert a footer that prints the section name at the left margin (except the first page) and page number at the right margin. Insert the correct section name for each section footer.

Part 2

After reviewing the formatted handbook, you decide to apply additional formatting to improve its readability and appearance. With **WL2-C1-CS-OMSHandbook.docx** open, apply the following formatting:

- Select the lines of text on the first page beginning with *Section 1: General Information* through *Compensation Procedures* and then define and apply a new multilevel list number format that applies capital letters followed by periods to the first level and arabic numbers (1, 2, 3) followed by periods to the second level. You determine the indents.
- Insert a cover page of your choosing and insert the appropriate information in the placeholders.

Save, print, and then close **WL2-C1-CS-OMSHandbook.docx**.

Part 3

Help

An orientation for new employees is scheduled for Friday, October 15, 2015, from 9:00 a.m. until 3:30 p.m. Michael Jennison will conduct the orientation and has asked you to prepare a flier about it that can be placed on all bulletin boards in the clinic. Include in the flier the date and times as well as the location, which is Conference Room 100. Include as bullets additional information about what will be covered during the orientation. Use the information in the multilevel list in the **WL2-C1-CS-OMSHandbook.docx** document to produce six to eight bulleted points. Using the Help feature, learn how to insert a picture watermark and then insert the **Ocean.jpg** file as a watermark. Make sure the text in the flier is readable. Include any other additional features to improve the appearance of the flier. Save the completed flier document and name it **WL2-C1-CS-Flier**. Print and then close **WL2-C1-CS-Flier.docx**.

Part 4

During the orientation, Mr. Jennison will discuss vacation allowances with the new employees and he wants to present the information in a readable format. He has asked you to look at the information in **OMSVacAllowances.docx** and then insert the information in tables. Apply formatting to make the tables attractive and the information easily readable. Save the completed document and name it **WL2-C1-CS-OMSVacAllowances**. Save, print, and then close **WL2-C1-CS-OMSVacAllowances.docx**.

MICROSOFT® WORD

Proofing Documents

PERFORMANCE OBJECTIVES

Upon successful completion of Chapter 2, you will be able to:

- **Complete a spelling and grammar check on text in a document**
- **Display readability statistics**
- **Create a custom dictionary and change the default dictionary**
- **Display synonyms and antonyms for specific words using the thesaurus**
- **Display document word, paragraph, and character counts**
- **Use the translation features to translate words from English to other languages**

Tutorials

2.1 Checking the Spelling and Grammar in a Document
2.2 Customizing Spelling and Grammar Checking
2.3 Creating a Custom Dictionary
2.4 Displaying Word Count
2.5 Using the Thesaurus
2.6 Translating Text to and from Different Languages

Microsoft Word includes proofing tools to help you create well-written, error-free documents. These tools include a spelling checker, grammar checker, and thesaurus. Word includes options for translating words from English to other languages, as well as a Mini Translator that will translate specific words in a document. In this chapter, you will learn how to use these proofing tools and how to create a custom dictionary. Model answers for this chapter's projects appear on the following page.

WL2C2

Note: Before beginning the projects, copy to your storage medium the WL2C2 subfolder from the WL2 folder on the CD that accompanies this textbook and then make WL2C2 the active folder.

EARLY DISTRIBUTIONS

If you want to withdraw funds or begin income from any PLAN20, PLAN30, or PLAN40 before you reach age 59, you may have to pay an extra 10 percent "early distributions" tax on the taxable amount. However, you will not have to pay an early distribution tax on any part of a withdrawal if:

- the distribution is because you are disabled
- you separated from your job at or after age 55 and take your withdrawal after that (not applicable for PLAN20)
- you begin annuity income withdrawal after you leave your job (termination is not required for PLAN40), as long as your annuity income consists of a series of regular substantially equal payments (at least annually) over your lifetime or life expectancy
- you have medical expenses in excess of 8 percent of your adjusted gross income and the withdrawal is less than or equal to your expenses (not applicable for PLAN20)
- you are required to make a payment to someone besides yourself under a MIRA plan

Prepared by
Logan Haverson

Project 1 Check Spelling and Grammar in an Investment Plan Document WL2-C2-P1-PlanDists.docx

Nationwide Medical Databases

The medical community looks forward to the day when medical records change from manila folders full of dusty documents to a nationwide registry off electronic medical records available to medical personnel anywhere. With these new medical database systems, doctors located anywhere in the world could pull up charts immediately, with a few clicks of the mouse. Full color 3-D X-rays could be included in electronic patient records. People receiving care away from home would no longer have to worry that their doctor did not have all of their medical records.

At this point, some obstacles may obstruct the widespread use of this new technology. Medical systems tend to cost much more than other systems due to legalities and the need for complicated approval processes. Everyone involved must have medical training, raising costs even further. Data validation is critical, as lives may be lost if data is faulty. Privacy issues are another roadblock. Medical records are as private and closely guarded as financial ones. Should any doctor be able to see a record? Can patients access their own records? How would incapacitated patients grant permission?

Some medical providers are embracing such databases with a more limited scope, only sharing information about patients in the same HBO, for example. So far, no nationwide system exists, but such systems may appear within the next few years.

Project 2 Check the Grammar in a Medical Database Document Project 2b, WL2-C2-P2-MedData.docx

Online Banking in Brazil

Brazilian Rodrigo Abreu has not been inside a bank for several years, nor has he written a paper check for any regular expense. For about a decade, Mr. Abreu, a thirtyish technology executive, has made every kind of scheduled payment through the Internet arm of his Brazilian bank, Banco Itau. He pays his car insurance, buys stocks, and conducts e-commerce transactions through the bank's website. His mother, other family members, and all of his friends also do most of their business transactions online. Advanced Internet technology may not be generally associated with Brazil, where a vast majority of the population of 171.2 million has no online access. But when it comes to Internet banking, Brazil is the leader.

Brazil's economic problems in the early 1990s helped pressure major banks—Bradesco, Unibanco, and Banco Itau—to build advanced electronic payment systems that formed the backbone of the Internet services they offer today. At the time, the economy faced an almost daily inflationary rate of 3 percent. To battle the hyperinflation, banks built communications systems to clear checks and allow their customers to pay bills as soon as possible. That helped the customers avoid losing money during processing. "We were able to cash checks within 24 hours when the U.S. banks were still taking nearly a week," said Milton Monteiro, who is vice president and is in charge of Internet banking at Banco Itau. "We had to be very efficient."

By 1993, each major Brazilian bank had built a complex private network so that when a customer's paycheck came in it was cleared overnight and moved into an account that was hedged against inflation. Home banking was coming into fashion and people were already dialing directly into the banks' networks to move money and pay bills instantly. In the United States, meanwhile, manual check processing and human bank tellers were still the norm.

While many United States banks are catching up with the range of their online offerings, Bradesco, Banco Itau, and Unibanco still have a wider array of Internet services. Brazilians can complete nearly any type of financial transaction through the banks' websites. Banks offer e-commerce portals, advanced business-to-business services, brokerage services, direct deposit, and bill-paying, all integrated into their websites. In fact, under a bill-paying standard now used in Brazil, bank customers can simply type in the bar code number of any bill; the bank immediately knows its amount and pays it upon request.

Source: Lipschultz, David. *The New York Times.*

Project 3 Check the Spelling in an Online Banking Document WL2-C2-P3-BankBrazil.docx

Résumé Styles

The traditional chronological résumé lists your work experience in reverse-chronological order (starting with your current or most recent position). The functional style deemphasizes the "where" and "when" of your career and instead groups similar experience, talents, and qualifications, regardless of when they occurred. Today, however, most résumés follow neither a strictly chronological nor strictly functional format; rather, they are an effective mixture of the two styles usually known as a "combination" or "hybrid" format.

Estilos de currículum

El currículum cronológico tradicional muestra su experiencia de trabajo en orden cronológico inverso (comenzando con su posición actual o más reciente). El estilo funcional deemphasizes el "dónde" y "cuándo" de su carrera y en su lugar grupos similares experiencia, talentos y calificaciones, independientemente de cuando ocurrieron. Hoy, sin embargo, la mayoría currículos siguen ni un formato estrictamente cronológico ni estrictamente funcional; más bien, son una mezcla eficaz de los dos estilos generalmente conocido como una "combinación" o formato de "híbrido".

Project 4 Translate Text

WL2-C2-P4-ResumeStyles.docx

TRANSLATION
English to Spanish
English to French

Term	Spanish	French
Central	centrico	centre
Data	datos	donnees
Directory	directorio	repertoire
External	externo	exterieur

WL2-C2-P4-TranslateTerms.docx

Model Answers

Project 1 Check Spelling and Grammar in an Investment Plan Document — 1 Part

You will open an investment plan document and then complete a spelling and grammar check on the document.

Checking the Spelling and Grammar in a Document

Word provides proofing tools to help you create professional, polished documents. Two of these tools are the spelling checker and grammar checker.

The spelling checker works by finding misspelled words and offering replacement words. It also finds duplicate words and irregular capitalization. When you spell check a document, the spelling checker compares the words in your document with the words in its dictionary. If the spelling checker finds a match, it passes over the word. If the spelling checker does not find a match, it stops. The spelling checker stops when it discovers the following kinds of errors and unfamiliar words:

- a misspelled word (when the misspelling does not match another word in the dictionary)
- typographical errors (such as transposed letters)
- double word occurrences (such as *the the*)
- irregular capitalization
- some proper names
- jargon and some technical terms

The grammar checker searches a document for errors in grammar, punctuation, and word usage. Using the spelling checker and grammar checker can help you create well-written documents, but it does not replace the need for proofreading.

Begin a spelling and grammar check by clicking the REVIEW tab and then clicking the Spelling & Grammar button. (You can also press the keyboard shortcut F7.) If Word detects a possible spelling error, it selects the text containing the error and displays the Spelling task pane, similar to the one shown in Figure 2.1. Possible corrections for the word display in the Spelling task pane list box along with buttons you can click to change or ignore the spelling error, as described in Table 2.1. The Spelling task pane also displays a definition of the selected word in the task pane list box.

Quick Steps

Check Spelling and Grammar
1. Click REVIEW tab.
2. Click Spelling & Grammar button.
3. Change or ignore errors.
4. Click OK.

Spelling & Grammar

Complete a spelling and grammar check on a portion of a document by first selecting the text and then clicking the Spelling & Grammar button.

Figure 2.1 Spelling Task Pane with Error Selected

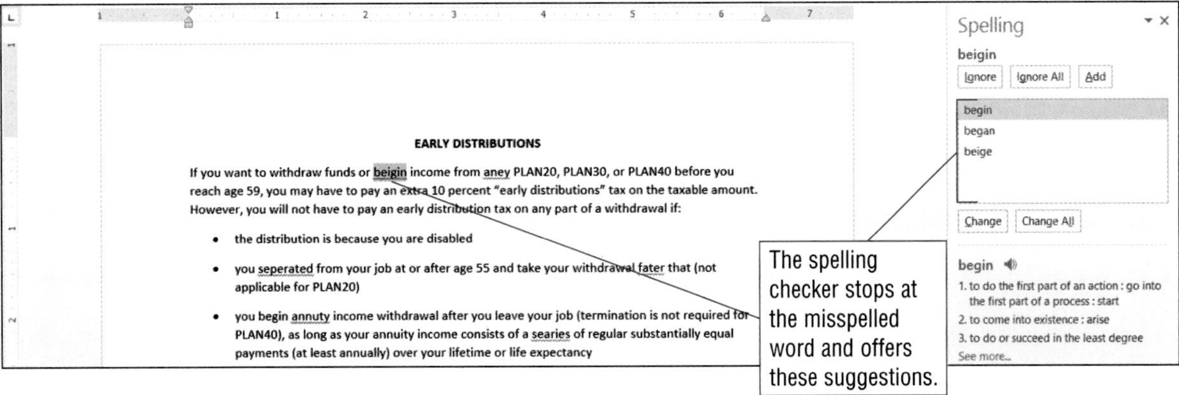

Table 2.1 Spelling Task Pane and Grammar Task Pane Buttons

Button	*Function*
Ignore	During spell checking, skips that occurrence of the word; in grammar checking, leaves currently selected text as written.
Ignore All	During spell checking, skips that occurrence of the word and all other occurrences of the word in the document.
Add	Adds the selected word to the main spelling check dictionary.
Delete	Deletes the currently selected word(s).
Change	Replaces the selected word with the selected word in the task pane list box.
Change All	Replaces the selected word and all other occurrences of it with the selected word in the task pane list box.

If Word detects a grammar error, it selects the word(s) or sentence containing the error and displays possible corrections in the Grammar task pane. Depending on the error selected, some of the buttons described in Table 2.1 may display in the Grammar task pane. A description of the grammar rule, with suggestions on how to correct an error, may display in the lower half of the Grammar task pane. Choose to ignore or change errors found by the grammar checker by clicking the Change, Change All, Ignore, or Ignore All buttons.

Editing During a Spelling and Grammar Check

When checking the spelling and grammar in a document, you can temporarily leave the Spelling or Grammar task pane, make corrections in the document, and then resume the spelling and grammar check. Click in the document oustide the task pane, make changes or edits, and then click the Resume button in the task pane.

Customizing Spell Checking

Quick Steps

Change Spell Checking Options
1. Click FILE tab.
2. Click *Options*.
3. Click *Proofing*.
4. Specify options.
5. Click OK.

Customize the spelling checker with options at the Word Options dialog box with the *Proofing* option selected, as shown in Figure 2.2. Display this dialog box by clicking the FILE tab and then clicking *Options*. At the Word Options dialog box, click *Proofing* in the left panel. Use options at this dialog box to customize spell checking by identifying what you want the spelling checker to review or ignore. You can also create or edit a custom dictionary for use in spell checking.

Figure 2.2 Word Options Dialog Box with *Proofing* Selected

Word Options

General
Display
Proofing
Save
Language
Advanced
Customize Ribbon
Quick Access Toolbar
Add-Ins
Trust Center

Change how Word corrects and formats your text.

AutoCorrect options

Change how Word corrects and formats text as you type: AutoCorrect Options...

When correcting spelling in Microsoft Office programs

Ignore words in UPPERCASE
Ignore words that contain numbers
Ignore Internet and file addresses
Flag repeated words
Enforce accented uppercase in French
Suggest from main dictionary only
Custom Dictionaries...
French modes: Traditional and new spellings
Spanish modes: Tuteo verb forms only

When correcting spelling and grammar in Word

Check spelling as you type
Mark grammar errors as you type
Frequently confused words
Check grammar with spelling
Show readability statistics
Writing Style: Grammar Only Settings...
Recheck Document

OK Cancel

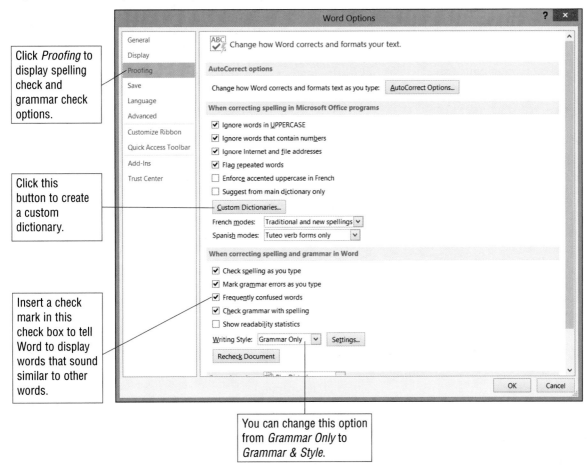

Click *Proofing* to display spelling check and grammar check options.

Click this button to create a custom dictionary.

Insert a check mark in this check box to tell Word to display words that sound similar to other words.

You can change this option from *Grammar Only* to *Grammar & Style*.

Project 1 Spell Checking a Document with Words in Uppercase and with Numbers — Part 1 of 1

1. Open **PlanDists.docx** and then save the document and name it **WL2-C2-P1-PlanDists**.
2. Review spell checking options by completing the following steps:
   a. Click the FILE tab.
   b. Click *Options*.
   c. At the Word Options dialog box, click the *Proofing* option in the left panel.
   d. Make sure that the *Ignore words in UPPERCASE* check box and the *Ignore words that contain numbers* check box each contain a check mark.
   e. Click OK to close the dialog box.

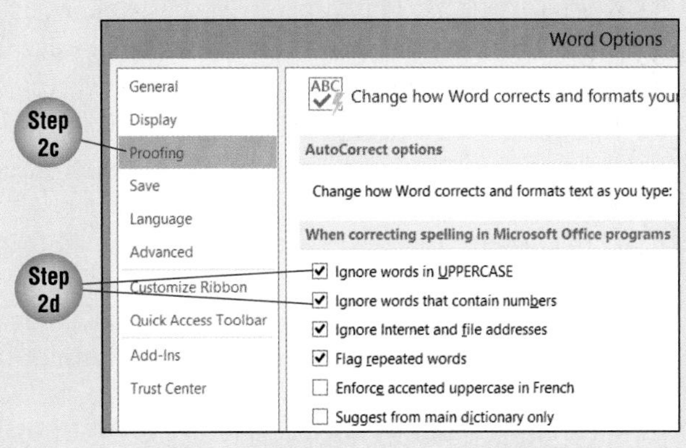

3. Complete a spelling check on the document by completing the following steps:
   a. Click the REVIEW tab.
   b. Click the Spelling & Grammar button in the Proofing group.
   c. The spelling checker selects the word *beigin* and displays the Spelling task pane. The proper spelling, *begin*, is selected in the Spelling task pane list box and a definition of *begin* displays below the list box. Click the Change button (or Change All button).

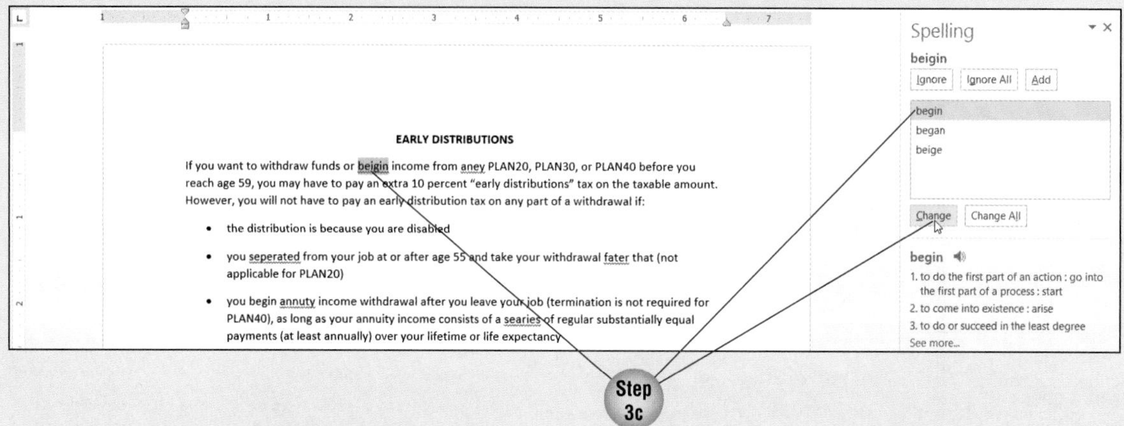

   d. The spelling checker selects the word *aney*. The proper spelling of the word is selected in the task pane list box, so click the Change button.
   e. The spelling checker selects *seperated*. The proper spelling is selected in the task pane list box, so click the Change button.
   f. The spelling checker selects *fater*. The proper spelling *after* is not selected in the task pane list box, but it is one of the words suggested. Click *after* in the task pane list box and then click the Change button.

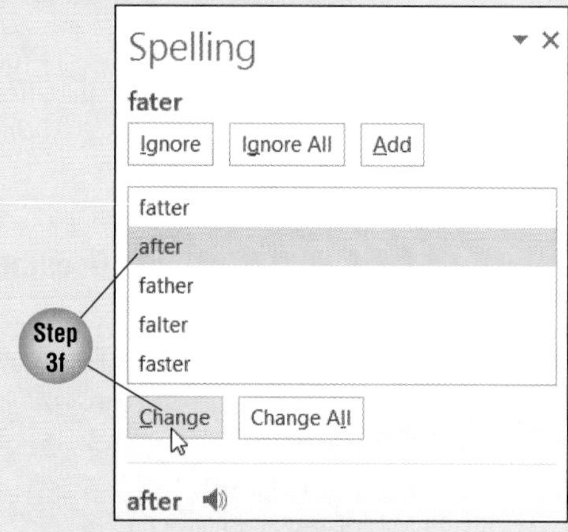

   g. The spelling checker selects *annuty*. The proper spelling is selected in the task pane list box, so click the Change button.
   h. The spelling checker selects *searies*. The proper spelling is selected in the task pane list box, so click the Change button.
   i. The spelling checker selects *to* (this is a double word occurrence). Click the Delete button to delete the second occurrence of *to*.

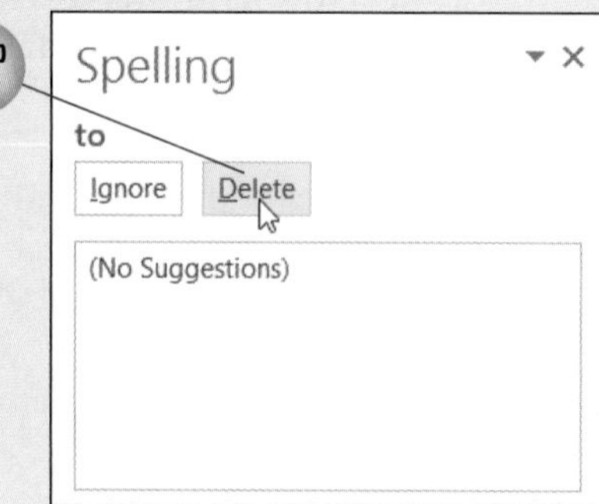

   j. The spelling checker selects *Haverson*. This is a proper name, so click the Ignore button.
   k. When the message displays telling you that the spelling and grammar check is complete, click the OK button.
4. Save, print, and then close **WL2-C2-P1-PlanDists.docx**.

Project 2 Check the Grammar in a Medical Database Document

3 Parts

You will check the grammar in a document, change grammar settings, and then check the grammar again. You will also display a word count for the document.

Checking the Grammar in a Document

When performing a spelling and grammar check, Word stops and highlights text that may contain grammatical errors and displays the Grammar task pane, similar to what is shown in Figure 2.3. Like the spelling checker, the grammar checker does not find every error in a document and may stop at correct sentences. Using the grammar checker can help you create well-written documents, but using it does not satisfy the need for proofreading.

If the grammar checker detects a possible grammatical error in the document, Word selects the sentence containing the possible error and inserts a possible correction in the Grammar task pane list box. The Grammar task pane may also display information on the grammar rule that may have been broken and offer possible methods for correcting the error. Choose to ignore or change errors found by the grammar checker by clicking the Change, Change All, Ignore, or Ignore All buttons.

Read grammar suggestions carefully. Some suggestions may not be valid and a problem identified by the grammar checker may not actually be an issue.

The Spelling task pane and the Grammar task pane include a pronunciation feature that will speak the word currently selected in the task pane list box. To hear the word pronounced, click the speaker icon located to the right of the word below the task pane list box. For this feature to work, you must turn on your computer speakers.

Figure 2.3 Grammar Task Pane with Grammar Error Selected

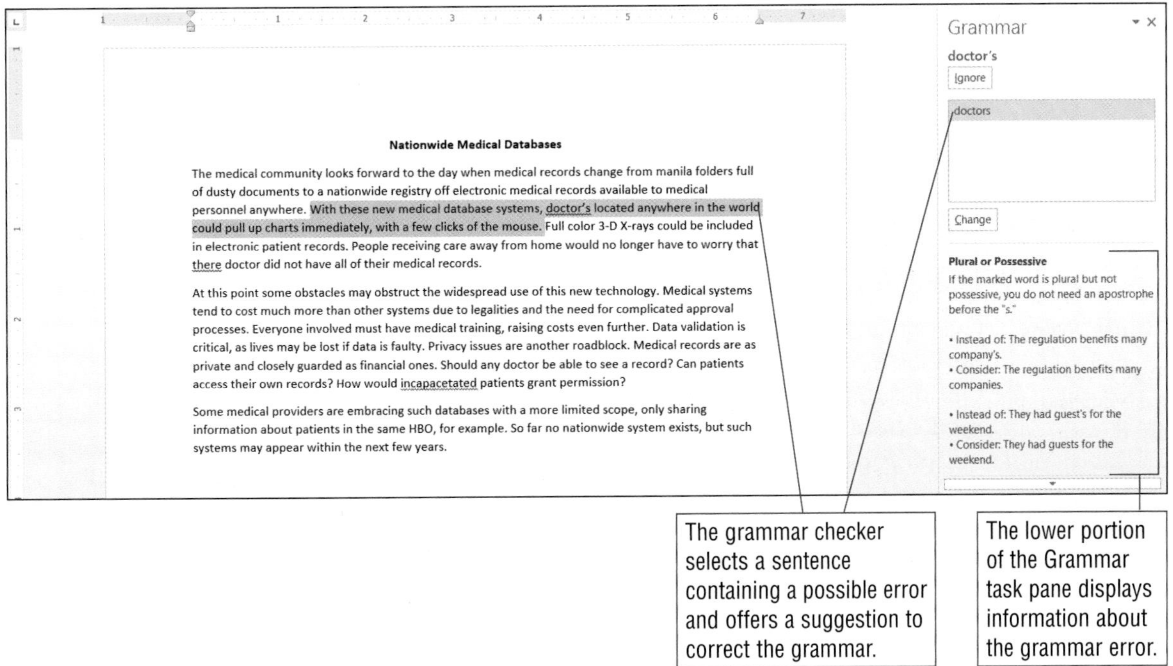

Nationwide Medical Databases
The medical community looks forward to the day when medical records change from manila folders full of dusty documents to a nationwide registry off electronic medical records available to medical personnel anywhere. With these new medical database systems, doctor's located anywhere in the world could pull up charts immediately, with a few clicks of the mouse. Full color 3-D X-rays could be included in electronic patient records. People receiving care away from home would no longer have to worry that there doctor did not have all of their medical records.
At this point some obstacles may obstruct the widespread use of this new technology. Medical systems tend to cost much more than other systems due to legalities and the need for complicated approval processes. Everyone involved must have medical training, raising costs even further. Data validation is critical, as lives may be lost if data is faulty. Privacy issues are another roadblock. Medical records are as private and closely guarded as financial ones. Should any doctor be able to see a record? Can patients access their own records? How would incapacetated patients grant permission?
Some medical providers are embracing such databases with a more limited scope, only sharing information about patients in the same HBO, for example. So far no nationwide system exists, but such systems may appear within the next few years.
Grammar
doctor's
Ignore
doctors
Change
Plural or Possessive
If the marked word is plural but not possessive, you do not need an apostrophe before the "s."
• Instead of: The regulation benefits many company's.
• Consider: The regulation benefits many companies.
• Instead of: They had guest's for the weekend.
• Consider: They had guests for the weekend.
The grammar checker selects a sentence containing a possible error and offers a suggestion to correct the grammar.
The lower portion of the Grammar task pane displays information about the grammar error.

Project 2a Checking Grammar in a Document

Part 1 of 3

1. Open **MedData.docx** and then save it and name it **WL2-C2-P2-MedData**.
2. Check the grammar in the document by completing the following steps:
   a. Click the REVIEW tab.
   b. Click the Spelling & Grammar button in the Proofing group.
   c. The grammar checker selects the sentence that begins *With these new medical database systems* and displays *doctors* in the list box.
   d. Read the information on plural or possessive that displays below the list box in the task pane.
   e. Click the Change button to change *doctor's* to *doctors*.
   f. The grammar checker selects *there* in the document and displays *their* in the list box.
   g. Read the definitions of *there* and *their* that display in the task pane and then click the Change button.
   h. The spelling checker selects the word *incapacetated* and displays the proper spelling in the task pane list box. Listen to the pronunciation of the word *incapacitated* by clicking the speaker icon that displays at the right of the word *incapacitated* located below the list box. (You must have your computer speakers turned on to hear the pronunciation.)
   i. With the proper spelling of *incapacitated* selected in the task pane list box, click the Change button.
   j. At the message telling you that the spelling and grammar check is complete, click OK.
3. Save **WL2-C2-P2-MedData.docx**.

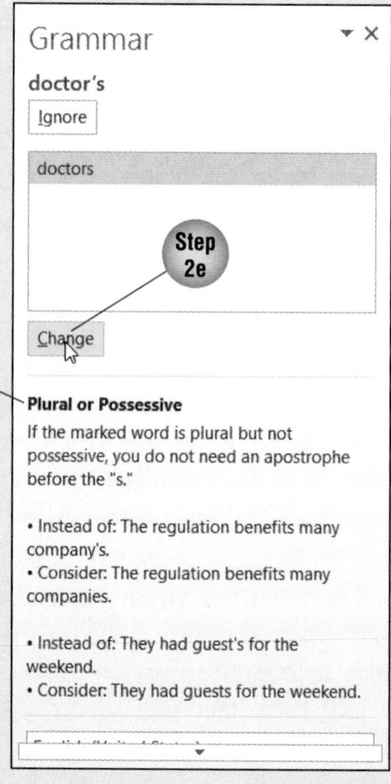

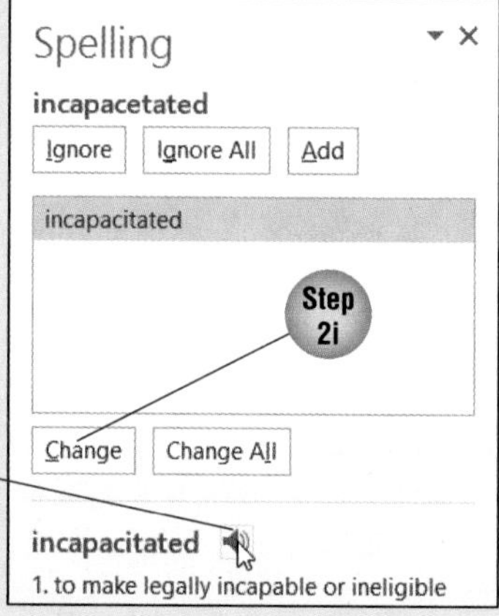

Changing Grammar Checking Options

Quick Steps

Change Grammar Checking Options
1. Click FILE tab.
2. Click *Options*.
3. Click *Proofing*.
4. Specify options.
5. Click OK.

Customize the type of grammar check that you perform on a document with options in the *When correcting spelling and grammar in Word* section of the Word Options dialog box with *Proofing* selected (see Figure 2.2). Remove the check marks from those options that you do not want active in a document.

By default, the grammar checker reviews only the grammar in a document. The *Writing Style* option at the Word Options dialog box with *Proofing* selected has a default setting of *Grammar Only*. You can change this default setting to *Grammar & Style*. To determine what style issues the grammar checker will select, click the Settings button to display the Grammar Settings dialog box with grammar and style options. Insert check marks for those options that you want active and remove the check marks from those options that you want inactive during a grammar check.

Project 2b Changing Grammar Checking Settings

Part 2 of 3

1. With **WL2-C2-P2-MedData.docx** open, change grammar checking settings by completing the following steps:
   a. Click the FILE tab.
   b. Click *Options*.
   c. At the Word Options dialog box, click the *Proofing* option in the left panel.
   d. Click the down-pointing arrow at the right side of the *Writing Style* option box and then click *Grammar & Style* at the drop-down list.
   e. Click the Recheck Document button.
   f. At the message that displays, click Yes.
   g. Click OK to close the Word Options dialog box.
2. Complete a grammar and style check on the document by completing the following steps:

When correcting spelling and grammar in Word
Check spelling as you type
Mark grammar errors as you type
Frequently confused words
Check grammar with spelling
Show readability statistics
Writing Style: Grammar Only
Settings...
Recheck Docu
Grammar & Style
Grammar Only
Step 1e
Step 1d

   a. Press Ctrl + Home to move the insertion point to the beginning of the document.
   b. Make sure the REVIEW tab is selected.
   c. Click the Spelling & Grammar button in the Proofing group.
   d. When the grammar checker selects the sentence that begins *At this point some obstacles may* and displays *point,* in the list box, click the Change button.

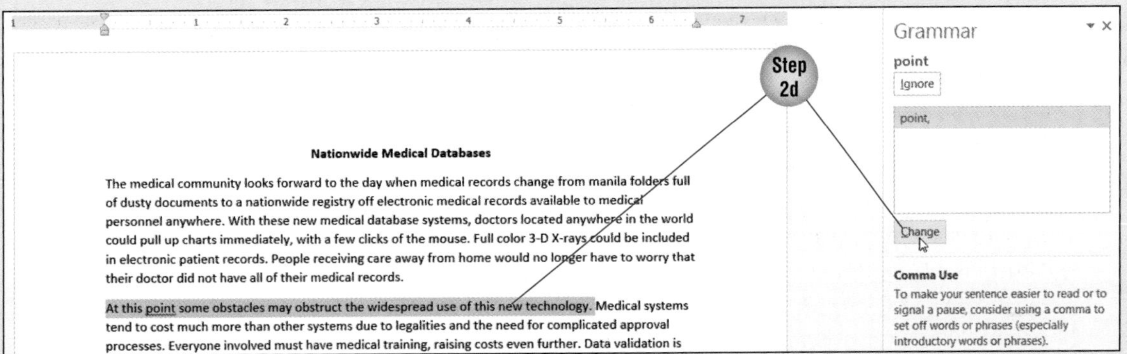

   e. When the grammar checker selects the sentence that begins *So far no nationwide system* and displays *far,* in the list box, click the Change button.
   f. At the message telling you that the spelling and grammar check is complete, click OK.
3. Save and then print **WL2-C2-P2-MedData.docx**.

Displaying Readability Statistics

When completing a spelling and grammar check, you can display readability statistics about the document. Figure 2.4 on the next page displays the readability statistics for **WL2-C2-P2-MedData.docx**. Statistics include word, character, paragraph, and sentence count; average number of sentences per paragraph, words per sentence, and characters per word; and readability information such as the percentage of passive sentences in the document, the Flesch Reading Ease score, and the Flesch-Kincaid grade-level rating. Control the display of readability statistics with the *Show readability statistics* check box in the Word Options dialog box with *Proofing* selected.

Quick Steps

Show Readability Statistics
1. Click FILE tab.
2. Click *Options*.
3. Click *Proofing*.
4. Click *Show readability statistics* check box.
5. Click OK.
6. Complete spelling and grammar check.

Figure 2.4 Readability Statistics Dialog Box

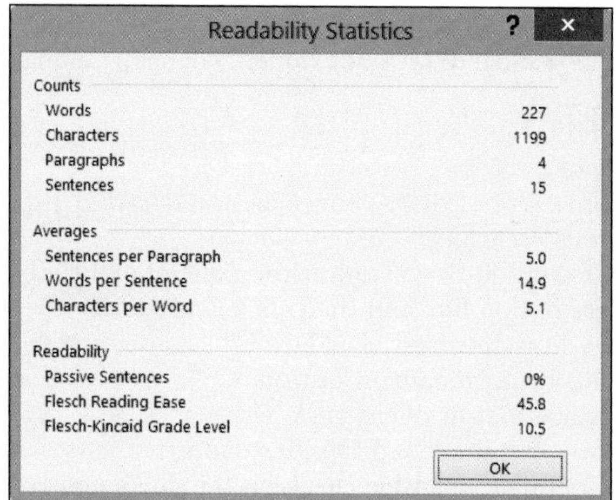

The Flesch Reading Ease score is based on the average number of syllables per word and the average number of words per sentence. The higher the score, the greater the number of people who will be able to understand the text in the document. Standard writing generally scores in the 60 to 70 range. The Flesch-Kincaid Grade Level score is based on the average number of syllables per word and the average number of words per sentence. The score indicates a grade level. Standard writing is generally scored at the seventh or eighth grade level.

Project 2c Displaying Readability Statistics — Part 3 of 3

1. With **WL2-C2-P2-MedData.docx** open, display readability statistics about the document by completing the following steps:
   a. Click the FILE tab and then click *Options*.
   b. At the Word Options dialog box, click *Proofing* in the left panel.
   c. Click the *Show readability statistics* check box to insert a check mark.
   d. Click OK to close the Word Options dialog box.
   e. At the document, make sure the REVIEW tab is selected and then click the Spelling & Grammar button.
   f. Look at the readability statistics that display in the Readability Statistics dialog box and then click OK to close the dialog box.

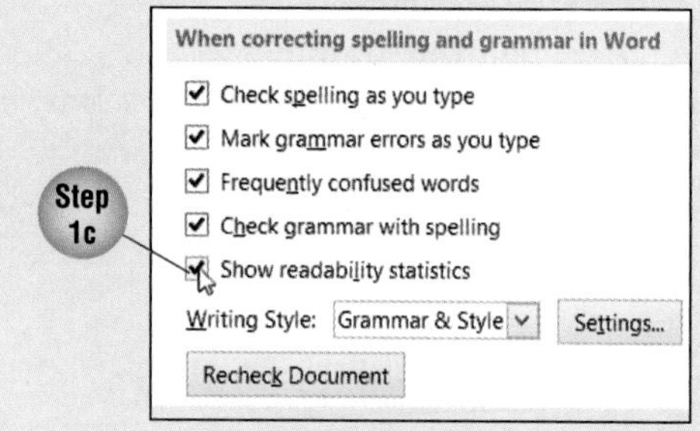

2. Change the grammar checking options back to the default by completing the following steps:
   a. Click the FILE tab and then click *Options*.
   b. At the Word Options dialog box, click *Proofing* in the left panel.
   c. Click the *Show readability statistics* check box to remove the check mark.
   d. Click the down-pointing arrow at the right side of the *Writing Style* option box and then click *Grammar Only* at the drop-down list.
   e. Click OK to close the Word Options dialog box.
3. Save and then close **WL2-C2-P2-MedData.docx**.

Project 3 Check the Spelling in an Online Banking Document 4 Parts

You will open a document, create a custom dictionary, add specific terms to the custom dictionary, and then complete a spelling check. You will also use a dictionary to define words in a document.

Creating a Custom Dictionary

When completing a spelling check on a document, Word uses the RoamingCustom.dic custom dictionary by default. You can add or remove words from this default dictionary. In a multiple-user environment, you might also consider adding your own custom dictionary and then selecting it as the default. This feature allows multiple users to create their own dictionaries to use when spell checking documents.

To create a custom dictionary, display the Word Options dialog box with *Proofing* selected and then click the Custom Dictionaries button. This displays the Custom Dictionaries dialog box, as shown in Figure 2.5. To create a new dictionary, click the New button. At the Create Custom Dictionary dialog box, type a name for the dictionary in the *File name* text box and then press Enter. The new dictionary name displays in the *Dictionary List* list box in the Custom Dictionaries dialog box. You can use more than one dictionary when spell checking a document. Insert a check mark in the check box next to any dictionary you want to use.

Quick Steps

Create a Custom Dictionary
1. Click FILE tab.
2. Click *Options*.
3. Click *Proofing*.
4. Click Custom Dictionaries button.
5. Click New button.
6. Type name for dictionary; press Enter.

When you change custom dictionary settings in one Microsoft Office program, the change affects all of the other programs in the suite.

Changing the Default Dictionary

At the Custom Dictionaries dialog box, the default dictionary displays in the *Dictionary List* list box followed by *(Default)*. Change this default by clicking the desired dictionary name in the list box and then clicking the Change Default button.

Removing a Dictionary

Remove a custom dictionary with the Remove button at the Custom Dictionaries dialog box. To do this, display the Custom Dictionaries dialog box, click the dictionary name in the *Dictionary List* list box, and then click the Remove button. You are not prompted to confirm the removal, so make sure you select the correct dictionary name before clicking the Remove button.

Quick Steps

Remove a Custom Dictionary
1. Click FILE tab.
2. Click *Options*.
3. Click *Proofing*.
4. Click Custom Dictionaries button.
5. Click custom dictionary name.
6. Click Remove.
7. Click OK.

Figure 2.5 Custom Dictionaries Dialog Box

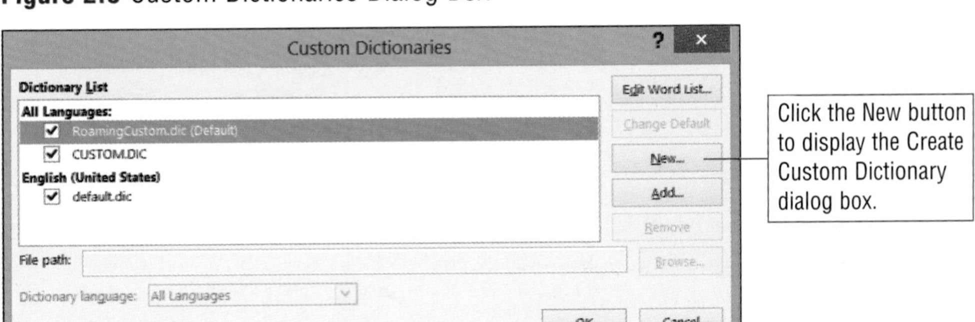

Project 3a Creating a Custom Dictionary and Changing the Default Dictionary Part 1 of 4

1. Open **BankBrazil.docx**, notice the wavy red lines indicating words not recognized by the spelling checker (words not in the custom dictionary), and then close the document.
2. Create a custom dictionary, add words to the dictionary, and then change the default dictionary by completing the following steps:
   a. Click the FILE tab and then click *Options*.
   b. At the Word Options dialog box, click *Proofing* in the left panel.
   c. Click the Custom Dictionaries button.
   d. At the Custom Dictionaries dialog box, click the New button.
   e. At the Create Custom Dictionary dialog box, type your first and last names (without a space between them) in the *File name* text box and then press Enter.
   f. At the Custom Dictionaries dialog box, add a word to your dictionary by completing the following steps:
      1) Click the name of your dictionary in the *Dictionary List* list box.
      2) Click the Edit Word List button.
      3) At the dialog box for your custom dictionary, type Abreu in the *Word(s)* text box.
      4) Click the Add button.

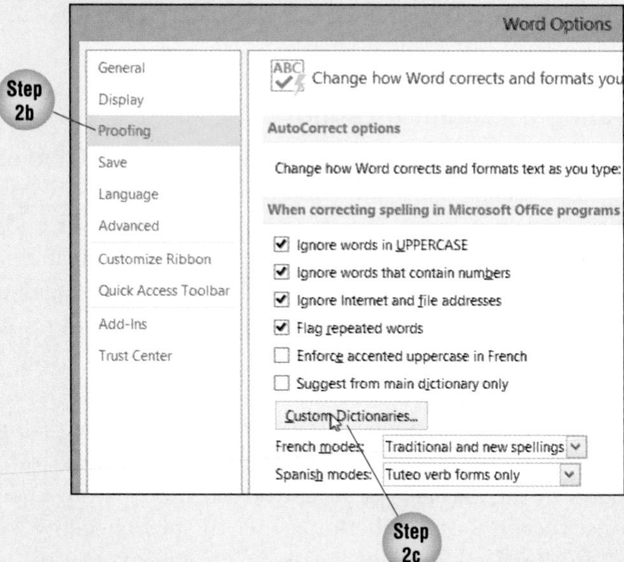

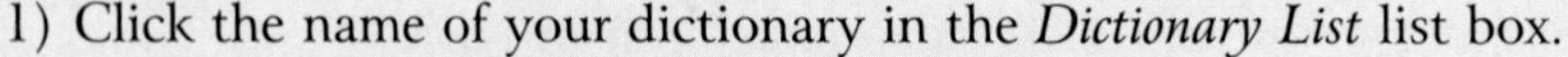

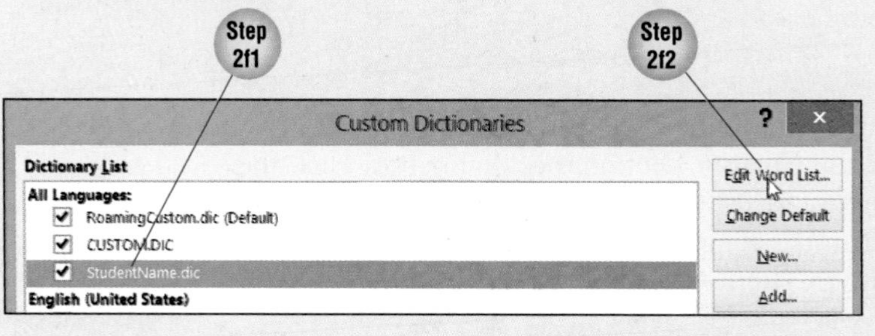

   g. Complete steps similar to those in Steps 2f3 and 2f4 to add the following words:
      Banco
      Itau
      Bradesco
      Unibanco
      Monteiro
      Lipschultz

h. When you have added all of the words, click the OK button to close the dialog box.
i. At the Custom Dictionaries dialog box with the name of your dictionary selected in the *Dictionary List* list box, click the Change Default button. (Notice that the word *(Default)* displays after your custom dictionary.)

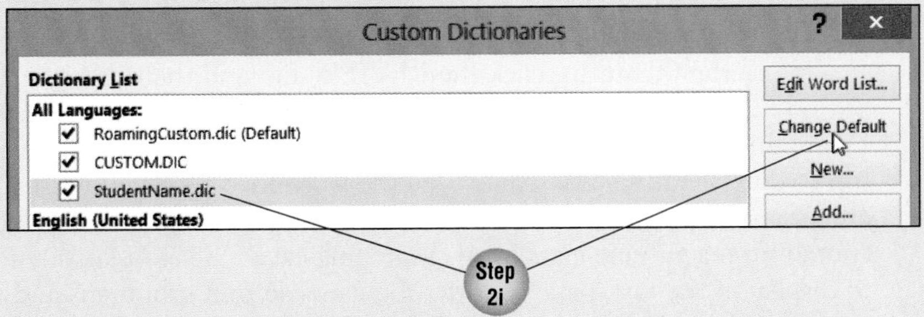

j. Click OK to close the Custom Dictionaries dialog box.
k. Click OK to close the Word Options dialog box.
3. Open **BankBrazil.docx** and then save the document and name it **WL2-C2-P3-BankBrazil**.
4. Complete a spelling and grammar check on your document and correct misspelled words. (The spelling checker will not stop at the words you added to your custom dictionary.)
5. Save and then print **WL2-C2-P3-BankBrazil.docx**.
6. Change the default dictionary and then remove your custom dictionary by completing the following steps:
   a. Click the FILE tab and then click *Options*.
   b. At the Word Options dialog box, click *Proofing* in the left panel.
   c. Click the Custom Dictionaries button.
   d. At the Custom Dictionaries dialog box, click *RoamingCustom.dic* in the *Dictionary List* list box.
   e. Click the Change Default button. (This changes the default back to the RoamingCustom.dic dictionary.)
   f. Click the name of your dictionary in the *Dictionary List* list box.
   g. Click the Remove button.
   h. Click OK to close the Custom Dictionaries dialog box.
   i. Click OK to close the Word Options dialog box.

Displaying Word Count

Word counts your words as you type and the Status bar displays the total number of words in your document. If you want to display more information—such as the number of pages, paragraphs, and lines—display the Word Count dialog box. Display the Word Count dialog box by clicking the word count section of the Status bar or by clicking the REVIEW tab and then clicking the Word Count button in the Proofing group.

Count words in a portion of the document, rather than the entire document, by selecting the portion of text and then displaying the Word Count dialog box. If you want to determine the total word count of several sections throughout a document, select the first section, hold down the Ctrl key, and then select the other sections.

Quick Steps

Display the Word Count Dialog Box
Click word count section of Status bar.
OR
1. Click REVIEW tab.
2. Click Word Count button.

Word Count

Using the Thesaurus

Word offers a Thesaurus feature for finding synonyms, antonyms, and related words for a particular word. ***Synonyms*** are words that have the same or nearly the same meaning. When you are using the thesaurus, Word may display ***antonyms*** for some words, which are words with opposite meanings. The thesaurus can help you to improve the clarity of business documents.

Quick Steps

Use the Thesaurus
1. Click REVIEW tab.
2. Click Thesaurus button.
3. Type word in search text box.
4. Press Enter.

Thesaurus

To use the thesaurus, click the REVIEW tab and then click the Thesaurus button in the Proofing group. (You can also use the keyboard shortcut Shift + F7.) Doing this displays the Thesaurus task pane. Click in the search box located near the top of the Thesaurus task pane, type the word for which you want to find synonyms and/or antonyms, and then press Enter or click the Start searching button (which contains a magnifying glass icon). Searching causes a list of synonyms and antonyms to display in the task pane list box. You can also find synonyms and antonyms for a word in a document by selecting the word and then displaying the Thesaurus task pane. Figure 2.6 shows the Thesaurus task pane with synonyms and antonyms for the word *normally* displayed.

Depending on the word you are looking up, the words in the Thesaurus task pane list box may display followed by *(n.)* for *noun*, *(adj.)* for *adjective* or *(adv.)* for *adverb*. Antonyms may display at the end of the list of related synonyms and are followed by *(Antonym)*. If a dictionary is installed on your computer, a definition of the selected word will display below the task pane list box.

The thesaurus provides synonyms for the selected word as well as a list of related synonyms. For example, in the task pane list box shown in Figure 2.6, the

Figure 2.6 Thesaurus Task Pane

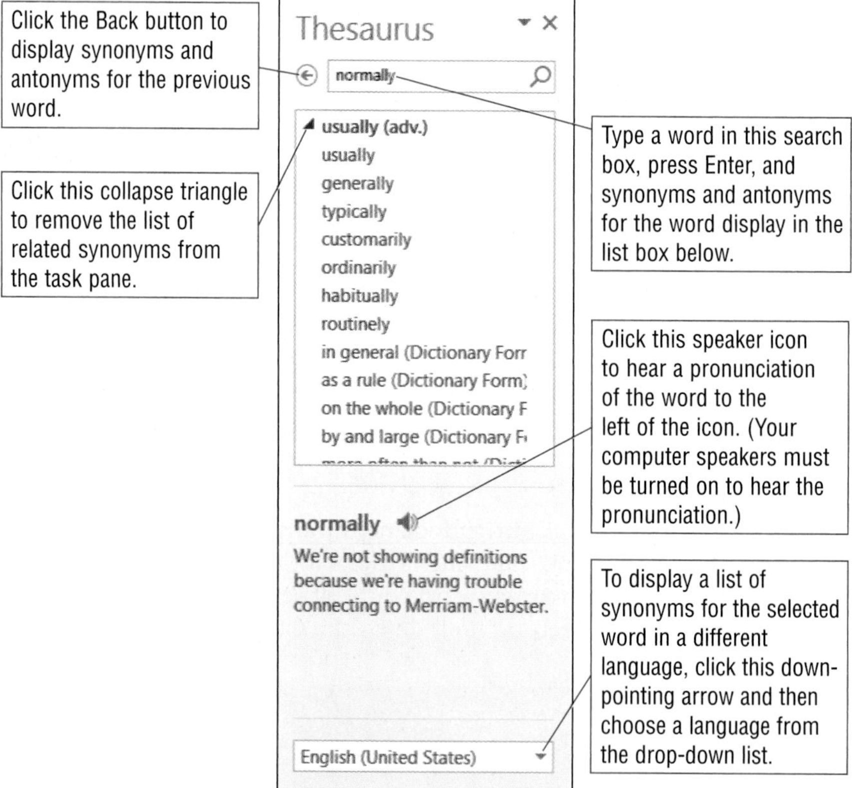

main synonym *usually* displays for *normally* and is preceded by a collapse triangle (a right-and-down-pointing triangle). The collapse triangle indicates that the list of related synonyms is displayed. When you click the collapse triangle, the list of related synonyms is removed from the task pane list box and the collapse triangle changes to an expand triangle (a right-pointing triangle). Click a word in the Thesaurus task pane list box to see synonyms for that word.

As you look up synonyms and antonyms for various words, you can display the list of synonyms and antonyms for the previous word by clicking the Back button (left-pointing arrow) located to the left of the search box. Click the down-pointing triangle located to the left of the Close button in the upper right corner of the task pane and a drop-down list displays with options for moving, sizing, and closing the task pane.

If you select a word in the document and then display the Thesaurus task pane, you can replace the selected word by hovering the mouse over the desired word in the task pane until a down-pointing arrow displays. Click the down-pointing arrow and then click *Insert* at the drop-down list.

The Thesaurus task pane, like the Spelling task pane and Grammar task pane, includes a pronunciation feature that will state the word currently selected in the Thesaurus task pane. To hear the word pronounced, click the speaker icon located to the right of the word below the task pane list box. (For this feature to work, your computer speakers must be turned on.)

The Thesaurus task pane also includes a language option for displaying synonyms of the selected word in a different language. To use this feature, click the down-pointing arrow at the right side of the option box located at the bottom of the task pane and then click the desired language at the drop-down list.

Project 3b Displaying the Word Count and Using the Thesaurus — Part 2 of 4

1. With **WL2-C2-P3-BankBrazil.docx** open, click the word count section of the Status bar.
2. After reading the statistics in the Word Count dialog box, click the Close button.
3. Display the Word Count dialog box by clicking the REVIEW tab and then clicking the Word Count button in the Proofing group.
4. Click the Close button to close the Word Count dialog box.
5. Use the thesaurus to change the word *normally* in the first paragraph to *generally* by completing the following steps:
   a. Select the word *normally* in the first paragraph (first word in the seventh line of text).
   b. Click the REVIEW tab, if necessary.
   c. Click the Thesaurus button in the Proofing group.
   d. At the Thesaurus task pane, hover the mouse pointer over the synonym *generally*, click the down-pointing arrow that displays at the right of the word, and then click *Insert* at the drop-down list.

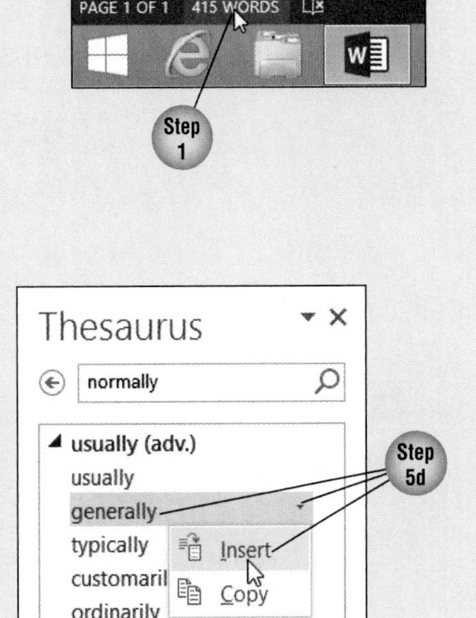

e. Click the word *generally* in the Thesaurus task pane.
f. If your computer speakers are turned on, listen to the pronunciation of the word *generally* by clicking the speaker icon next to the word located below the task pane list box.

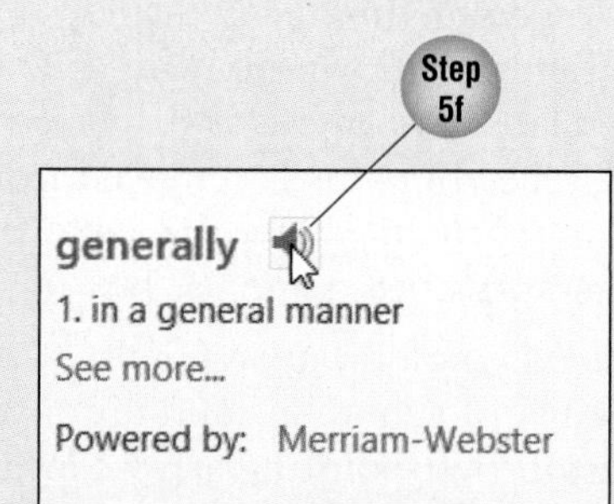

6. Follow similar steps to make the following changes using the thesaurus:
   a. Change *acquaintances* in the first paragraph to *friends*.
   b. Change *combat* in the second paragraph to *battle*.
7. Close the Thesaurus task pane by clicking the Close button located in the upper right corner of the task pane.
8. Save **WL2-C2-P3-BankBrazil.docx**.

Another method for displaying synonyms of a word is to use a shortcut menu. To do this, position the mouse pointer on the word and then click the right mouse button. At the shortcut menu that displays, point to *Synonyms* and then click the desired synonym at the side menu. Click the *Thesaurus* option at the bottom of the side menu to display synonyms and antonyms for the word in the Thesaurus task pane.

Project 3c **Replacing Synonyms Using a Shortcut Menu** **Part 3 of 4**

1. With **WL2-C2-P3-BankBrazil.docx** open, position the mouse pointer on the word *vogue* located in the second sentence of the third paragraph.
2. Click the right mouse button.
3. At the shortcut menu that displays, point to *Synonyms* and then click *fashion* at the side menu.
4. Save **WL2-C2-P3-BankBrazil.docx**.

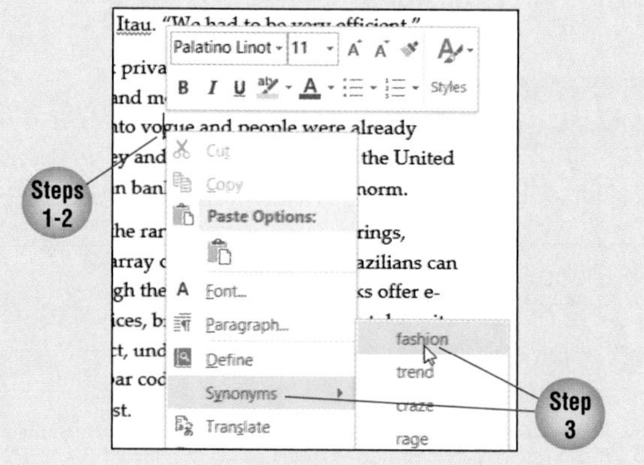

Defining Words

Define

If a dictionary is installed on your computer, the Thesaurus task pane displays a definition of the selected word. Another method for displaying the definition of a word is to click the Define button in the Proofing group on the REVIEW tab. A dictionary task pane opens at the right side of the screen with a definition of the word. If your computer does not have a dictionary installed, a list of dictionaries that you can download will display. Click the name of the dictionary that you want to use and then click *Download*.

Project 3d Using the Dictionary to Define Words — Part 4 of 4

Note: A dictionary must be installed on your computer to complete this project.

1. With **WL2-C2-P3-BankBrazil.docx** open, display definitions for words by completing the following steps:
   a. Select the word *e-commerce* that displays in the third sentence of the first paragraph.
   b. Make sure the REVIEW tab is active and then click the Define button in the Proofing group.
   c. Read the definition that displays in the dictionary task pane.

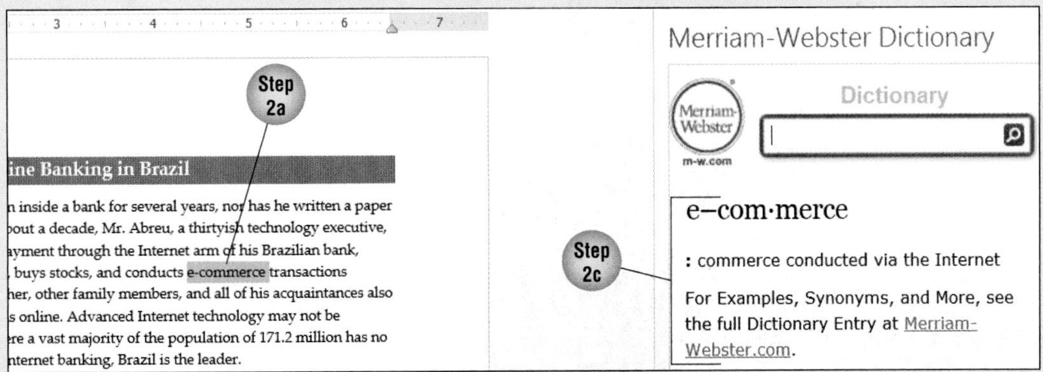

   d. Select the word *economy* that displays in the second sentence of the second paragraph.
   e. Read the definition that displays.
2. Close the dictionary task pane by clicking the Close button located in the upper right corner of the task pane.
3. Save, print, and then close **WL2-C2-P3-BankBrazil.com**.

Project 4 Translate Text — 1 Part

You will use the translation feature to translate text from English to Spanish and English to French.

Translating Text to and from Different Languages

Word provides features for translating text from one language into another. The Thesaurus task pane provides one method for translating words. The Translate button in the Language group on the REVIEW tab provides additional translation methods. Click the Translate button and a drop-down list displays with options for translating the entire document or selected text and for turning on the Mini Translator.

Click the first option, *Translate Document*, and Word sends your document for translation by Microsoft Translator. When you click the option, a message displays telling you that Word is about to send your document for translation in unencrypted HTML format and asking if you want to continue. To continue to the translator, click the Send button.

Click the second option, *Translate Selected Text*, and Microsoft Translator will translate the selected text in a document and insert the translation in the Research task pane. The Research task pane displays at the right side of the screen and includes options for translating text to and from different languages.

Quick Steps

Translate an Entire Document
1. Open document.
2. Click REVIEW tab.
3. Click Translate button.
4. Click *Translate Document* at drop-down list.
5. Click Send button.

Translate Selected Text
1. Select text.
2. Click REVIEW tab.
3. Click Translate button.
4. Click *Translate Selected Text*.

Translate

Quick Steps

Turn on Mini Translator
1. Click REVIEW tab.
2. Click Translate button.
3. Click *Mini Translator.*

HINT

Hold down the Alt key and then click anywhere in the document to display the Research task pane.

Click the third option, *Mini Translator*, to turn on this feature. With the Mini Translator turned on, point to a word or select a phrase in your document and the translation of the text displays in a box above the text. To turn off the Mini Translator, click the *Mini Translator* option at the Translate button drop-down list. When the Mini Translator is turned on, the icon positioned to the left of the *Mini Translator* option displays with a light blue background.

Use the fourth option in the Translate button drop-down list, *Choose Translation Language*, to specify the language from which you want to translate and the language to which you want to translate. When you click the option, the Translation Language Options dialog box displays, as shown in Figure 2.7. At this dialog box, specify the translation language and whether you want to translate the entire document or turn on the Mini Translator. You may need to specify languages in the *Translate from* and *Translate to* option boxes before using the Mini Translator.

Figure 2.7 Translation Language Options Dialog Box

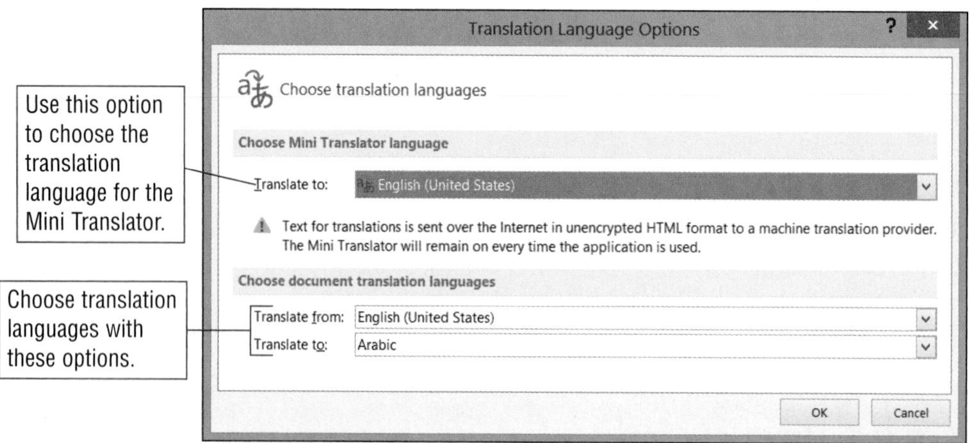

Project 4 Using the Translate Button

Part 1 of 1

Note: Check with your instructor before completing this exercise.

1. Open **ResumeStyles.docx** and then save the document and name it **WL2-C2-P4-ResumeStyles.**
2. Change the translation language to Spanish by completing the following steps:
   a. Click the REVIEW tab.
   b. Click the Translate button in the Language group and then click the *Choose Translation Language* option at the drop-down list.

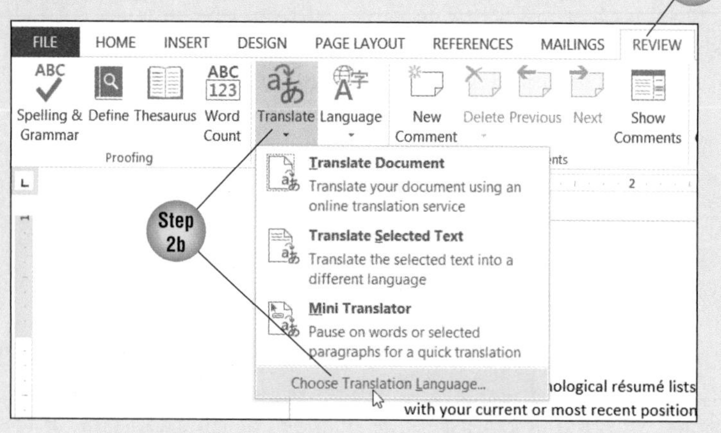

c. At the Translation Language Options dialog box, make sure that *English (United States)* displays in the *Translate from* option box.

d. Click the down-pointing arrow at the right of the *Translate to* option box in the *Choose document translation languages* section and then click *Spanish (Spain)* at the drop-down list. (Skip this step if *Spanish (Spain)* is already selected.)

e. Click OK to close the dialog box.

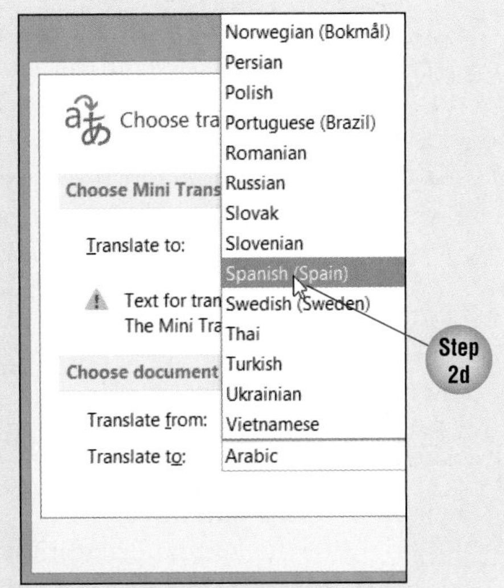

3. Translate the entire document to Spanish by completing the following steps:
   a. Click the Translate button and then click the *Translate Document [English (United States) to Spanish (Spain)]* option.
   b. At the message telling you that Word is about to send the document for translation over the Internet in unencrypted HTML format, click the Send button.
   c. In a few moments, the Microsoft Translator window will open. (If the window does not display, click the button representing the translator on the Status bar.)
   d. Select the translated text.
   e. Press Ctrl + C to copy the text.
   f. Close the Microsoft Translator window.
   g. At the **WL2-C2-P4-ResumeStyles.docx** document, press Ctrl + End to move the insertion point to the end of the document and then press Ctrl + V to insert the copied text.
4. Save, print, and then close **WL2-C2-P4-ResumeStyles.docx**.
5. Open **TranslateTerms.docx** and then save the document and name it **WL2-C2-P4-TranslateTerms**.
6. Translate the word *Central* into Spanish by completing the following steps:
   a. Click the REVIEW tab.
   b. Click the Translate button and then click the *Choose Translation Language* option at the drop-down list.
   c. At the Translation Language Options dialog box, click the down-pointing arrow at the right of the *Translate to* option box in the *Choose Mini Translator language* section and then click *Spanish (Spain)* at the drop-down list. (Skip this step if *Spanish (Spain)* is already selected.)

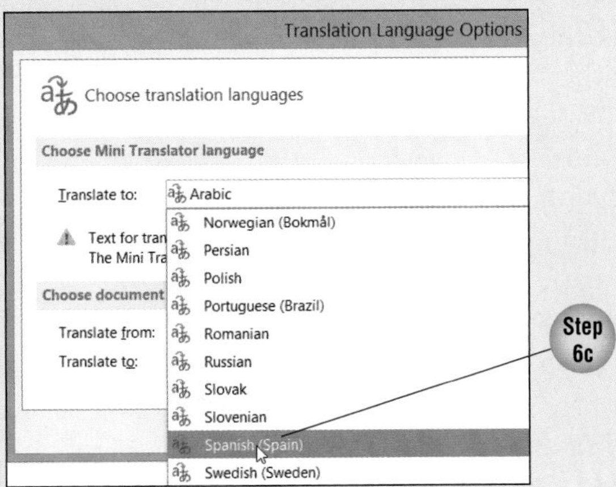

d. Click OK to close the dialog box.
e. Click the Translate button and then click *Mini Translator [Spanish (Spain)]* at the drop-down list. (This turns on the Mini Translator.)
f. Hover the mouse pointer over the word *Central* in the table. (The Mini Translator displays dimmed above the word.) Move the mouse pointer to the Mini Translator and then look at the translation that displays in the box above the word. Type one of the Spanish terms in the *Spanish* column.
g. Complete steps similar to those in Step 6f to display Spanish translations for the remaining terms. For each term, type the corresponding Spanish term in the appropriate location in the table. Type the terms without any accents or special symbols.

7. Use the Mini Translator to translate terms into French by completing the following steps:
   a. Click the Translate button and then click the *Choose Translation Language* option at the drop-down list.
   b. At the Translation Language Options dialog box, click the down-pointing arrow at the right of the *Translate to* option box in the *Choose Mini Translator Lanuguage* section, and then click *French (France)* at the drop-down list.
   c. Click OK to close the dialog box.
   d. With the Mini Translator turned on, hover the mouse pointer over the word *Central* in the table. (The Mini Translator displays dimmed above the word.)
   e. Move the mouse pointer to the Mini Translator and then choose one of the French terms and type it in the *French* column.
   f. Complete steps similar to those in Steps 7d and 7e to display French translations for the remaining terms. For each term, type the corresponding French term in the appropriate location in the table. Type the terms without any accents or special symbols.
8. Turn off the Mini Translator by clicking the Translate button and then clicking *Mini Translator [French (France)]* at the drop-down list.
9. Save, print, and then close **WL2-C2-P4-TranslateTerms.docx**.

Chapter Summary

- The spelling checker matches the words in your document with the words in its dictionary. If a match is not found, the word is selected and possible corrections are suggested.
- When checking the spelling and grammar in a document, you can temporarily leave the Spelling task pane or Grammar task pane, make corrections in the document, and then resume checking.
- Customize spell checking options at the Word Options dialog box with *Proofing* selected in the left panel.
- Use the grammar checker to search a document for correct grammar, style, punctuation, and word usage.
- Customize grammar checking with options in the *When correcting spelling and grammar in Word* section of the Word Options dialog box with *Proofing* selected.
- To display readability statistics for a document, insert a check mark in the *Show readability statistics* check box in the Word Options dialog box with *Proofing* selected and then complete a spelling and grammar check.

- Word uses the RoamingCustom.dic custom dictionary when spell checking a document. Add your own custom dictionary at the Custom Dictionaries dialog box. Display this dialog box by clicking the Custom Dictionaries button at the Word Options dialog box with *Proofing* selected.
- The Word Count dialog box displays the number of pages, words, characters, paragraphs, and lines in a document. Display this dialog box by clicking the word count section of the Status bar or clicking the Word Count button in the Proofing group on the REVIEW tab.
- Use the thesaurus to find synonyms and antonyms for words in your document. Display synonyms and antonyms at the Thesaurus task pane or by right-clicking a word and then pointing to *Synonyms* at the shortcut menu.
- Use the Translate button in the Language group on the REVIEW tab to translate a document, a selected section of text, or a word from one language to another.

Commands Review

FEATURE	RIBBON TAB, GROUP/OPTION	BUTTON, OPTION	KEYBOARD SHORTCUT
Mini Translator	REVIEW, Language	, *Mini Translator*	
spelling and grammar checker	REVIEW, Proofing		F7
Thesaurus task pane	REVIEW, Proofing		Shift + F7
translate selected text	REVIEW, Language	, *Translate Selected Text*	
translate text in document	REVIEW, Language	, *Translate Document*	
Translation Language Options dialog box	REVIEW, Language	, *Choose Translation Language*	
Word Count dialog box	REVIEW, Proofing		
Word Options dialog box	FILE, *Options*		

Concepts Check

Test Your Knowledge

Completion: In the space provided at the right, indicate the correct term, symbol, or command.

1. Click this tab to display the Proofing group. ____________________
2. Use this keyboard shortcut to begin checking the spelling and grammar in a document. ____________________

3. During a spelling check, click this button to skip the occurrence of the selected word and all other occurrences of the word in the document. ____________

4. Click this button in the Spelling task pane to replace the selected word with the selected word in the list box. ____________

5. To display the Word Options dialog box with spelling and grammar options, click the FILE tab, click *Options*, and then click this option in the left panel. ____________

6. This is the default setting for the *Writing Style* option at the Word Options dialog box with *Proofing* selected. ____________

7. When completing a spelling check on a document, Word uses this custom dictionary by default. ____________

8. This is the keyboard shortcut to display the Thesaurus task pane. ____________

9. When you click the Translate button and then click the *Translate Document* option, the text in the document is translated by this. ____________

10. Turn on this feature to point to a word or selected text and view a quick translation. ____________

Skills Check Assess Your Performance

Assessment 1

CHECK SPELLING IN A PUNCTUATION DOCUMENT

1. Open **QuoteMarks.docx** and then save the document and name it **WL2-C2-A1-QuoteMarks**.
2. Complete a spelling and grammar check on the document. (Make all of the suggested changes *except* ignore the suggestion to change *Another's* to *another's*.)
3. Apply the Heading 1 style to the title of the document and the Heading 2 style to the headings in the document (which currently display in bold).
4. Apply the Parallax theme.
5. Center the document title.
6. Save, print, and then close **WL2-C2-A1-QuoteMarks.docx**.

Assessment 2

CHECK SPELLING AND GRAMMAR AND PROOFREAD A LETTER

1. Open **AirMiles.docx** and then save the document and name it **WL2-C2-A2-AirMiles**.
2. Complete a spelling and grammar check on the document. (Proper names are spelled correctly.)
3. After completing the spelling and grammar check, proofread the letter and make necessary changes. (The letter contains mistakes that the spelling and grammar checker will not select.) Replace the *XX* near the end of the document with your initials.
4. Select the entire document and then change the font to 12-point Candara.
5. Save, print, and then close **WL2-C2-A2-AirMiles.docx**.

Assessment 3

CUSTOMIZE OPTIONS AND CHECK SPELLING AND GRAMMAR IN A DOCUMENT

1. Open **CyberScenario.docx** and then save the document and name it **WL2-C2-A3-CyberScenario**.
2. Display the Word Options dialog box with *Proofing* selected, change the *Writing Style* option to *Grammar & Style*, and then close the dialog box.
3. Complete a spelling and grammar check on the document.
4. Apply formatting to enhance the appearance of the document.
5. Display the Word Options dialog box with *Proofing* selected, change the *Writing Style* option to *Grammar Only*, and then close the dialog box.
6. Save, print, and then close **WL2-C2-A3-CyberScenario.docx**.

Assessment 4

TRANSLATE AND INSERT WORDS IN A TABLE

1. At a blank document, create a table and use the translation feature to find the Spanish and French translations for the following terms:
   abbreviation
   adjective
   adverb
   punctuation
   grammar
   hyphen
   paragraph
2. Type the English words in the first column of the table, the corresponding Spanish words in the second column, and the corresponding French words in the third column. (You do not need to include accents or special symbols.)
3. Apply formatting to enhance the appearance of the table.
4. Save the document and name it **WL2-C2-A4-Translations**.
5. Print and then close **WL2-C2-A4-Translations.docx**.

Visual Benchmark Demonstrate Your Proficiency

USE THE TRANSLATOR FEATURE

1. Open **CCDonations.docx** and then save it and name the document **WL2-C2-VB-CCDonations**.
2. Type the paragraph of text below the heading *English*: as shown in Figure 2.8 and then complete a spelling and grammar check of the text.
3. Select the paragraph of text below the heading *English:* and then translate the paragraph into Spanish and then into French. Copy the translated text into the document as shown in Figure 2.8. (Your translations may vary slightly from what is shown in Figure 2.8.)
4. Use the Curlz MT font for the headings at the beginning of each paragraph and for the quote that displays toward the bottom of the letter. Apply paragraph shading as shown in the figure.
5. Save, print, and then close **WL2-C2-VB-CCDonations.docx**.

Case Study Apply Your Skills

Part 1

You work in the executive offices at Nickell Industries and have been asked to develop a writing manual for employees. The company has not used a consistent theme when formatting documents, so you decide to choose a theme and use it when formatting all Nickell documents. Open **NIManual.docx** and then save the document and name it **WL2-C2-CS-NIManual**. Check the spelling and grammar in the document. Make the following changes to the document:

- Insert a section break at the beginning of the title *Editing and Proofreading*.
- Apply styles of your choosing to the titles and headings in the document.
- Apply the theme you have chosen for company documents.
- Insert headers and/or footers.
- Create a cover page.

Save the document.

Figure 2.8 Visual Benchmark

Support Your Local Community Center

English:
As you consider your donation contributions for the coming year, we ask that you consider supporting your community by supporting the Cordova Children's Community Center. The center is a nonprofit agency providing educational and recreational activities for children. Please stop by for a visit. Our dedicated staff will be available to discuss with you the services offered by the center, how your donation dollars are spent, and provide information on current and future activities and services.

Spanish:
Cuando usted considere sus contribuciones de donación para el próximo año, pedimos que usted considere apoyar su comunidad apoyando el Cordova comunidad centro infantil. El centro es una agencia sin fines de lucro actividades educativas y recreativas para los niños. Favor de pasar por una visita. Nuestro personal estará disponible para discutir con usted los servicios ofrecidos por el centro, cómo se gastan sus dólares de donación y proporcionar información sobre las actividades actuales y futuras y servicios.

French:
Lorsque vous envisagez vos contributions de don pour l'année prochaine, nous demandons que vous envisagez de soutenir votre communauté en soutenant le centre communautaire pour les enfants de Cordova. Le centre est un organisme à but non lucratif offrant des activités éducatives et récréatives pour les enfants. S'il vous plaît arrêter par pour une visite. Notre personnel dévoué sera disponible pour discuter avec vous des services offerts par le centre, comment vos dollars de dons sont dépensés et fournir des informations sur les services et les activités actuelles et futures.

"Children are our most valuable natural resources." ~ Herbert Hoover

770 Sunrise Terrace ◆ Santa Fe, NM 87509 ◆ 505-555-7700

Part 2

As you review the writing manual document, you decide to highlight the points for developing document sections. You decide that a vertical block list SmartArt graphic will present the ideas in an easy-to-read format and provide some visual interest to the manual. Insert a page break at the end of the **WL2-C2-CS-NIManual.docx** document, type the title *Developing a Document*, and insert the following in the appropriate shapes:

Beginning

- Introduce main idea.
- Get reader's attention.
- Establish positive tone.

Middle

- Provide detail for main idea.
- Lead reader to intended conclusion.

End

- State conclusion.
- State action you want reader to take.

Apply theme colors that follow the theme you chose for company documents. Save the document.

Part 3

You decide to purchase some reference books on grammar and punctuation. Using the Internet, search bookstores for books that provide information on grammar and punctuation and then choose three books. You know that the books will be purchased soon, so you decide to add the information in the writing manual document, telling readers what reference books are available. Include this information on a separate page at the end of the **WL2-C2-CS-NIManual.docx** document. Save, print, and then close the document.

Part 4

Nickell Industries does business in other countries, including Mexico. One of the executives in the Finance department has asked you to translate into Spanish some terms that will be used to develop an invoice. Create a document that translates the following terms from English to Spanish and also include in the document the steps for translating text. Your reason for doing this is that if the executive knows the steps, she can translate text at her own computer.

- city
- telephone
- invoice
- product
- description
- total

Format the document with the theme you chose for company documents and add any other enhancements to improve the appearance of the document. Save the completed document and name it **WL2-C2-CS-Translations**. Print and then close **WL2-C2-CS-Translations.docx**.

MICROSOFT® WORD

Chapter 3

Automating and Customizing Formatting

PERFORMANCE OBJECTIVES

Upon successful completion of Chapter 3, you will be able to:

- **Insert exceptions and add words to and delete words from the AutoCorrect dialog box**
- **Customize AutoFormat**
- **Use the AutoCorrect Options button**
- **Sort and insert building blocks**
- **Create, edit, modify, and delete building blocks**
- **Insert, update, and delete fields from Quick Parts**
- **Customize the Quick Access toolbar**
- **Customize the ribbon**

Tutorials

3.1 Customizing AutoCorrect and AutoFormatting
3.2 Inserting and Sorting Building Blocks
3.3 Saving Content as Building Blocks
3.4 Editing Building Block Properties
3.5 Inserting Custom Building Blocks
3.6 Modifying and Deleting Building Blocks
3.7 Inserting Document Properties
3.8 Inserting and Updating Fields from Quick Parts
3.9 Customizing the Quick Access Toolbar
3.10 Customizing the Ribbon

Microsoft Word offers a number of features to help you customize documents and streamline the formatting of documents. In this chapter, you will learn how to customize the AutoCorrect feature and use the AutoCorrect Options button. You will also learn how to build a document using building blocks; create, save, and edit your own building blocks; and customize the Quick Access toolbar and the ribbon. Model answers for this chapter's projects appear on the following pages.

Note: Before beginning computer projects, copy to your storage medium the WL2C3 subfolder from the WL2 folder on the CD that accompanies this textbook and then make WL2C3 the active folder.

Terra Travel Services

Family Adventure Vacations

Namibia and Victoria Falls Adventure

Terra Travel Services is partnering with Family Adventure Vacations® to provide adventurous and thrilling family vacations. Our first joint adventure is a holiday trip to Namibia. Namibia is one of the most fascinating holiday destinations in Africa and offers comfortable facilities, great food, cultural interaction, abundant wildlife, and a wide variety of activities to interest people of all ages.

During the 12-day trip, you and your family will travel across Namibia through national parks, enjoying the beautiful and exotic scenery and watching wildlife in natural habitats. You will cruise along the Kwando and Chobe rivers and spend time at the Okapuka Lodge located near Windhoek, the capital of Namibia.

If you or your family member is a college student, contact one of our college travel adventure consultants to learn more about the newest Student Travel package titled "STudent STyle" that offers a variety of student discounts, rebates, and free travel accessories for qualifying participants.

Through the sponsorship of Ameria Resorts, we are able to offer you a 15 percent discount for groups of twelve or more people.

For additional information on the Namibia adventure, as well as other exciting vacation specials, please visit our website at www.emcp.net/terratravel or visit www.emcp.net/famadv.

1050 Marietta Street ✧ Atlanta, GA 30315 ✧ 1-888-555-2288 ✧ www.emcp.net/terratravel

Project 1 Create a Travel Document Using AutoCorrect
WL2-C3-P1-TTSAfrica.docx

JANUARY 2, 2015

NORTHLAND SECURITY SYSTEMS

COMPUTER VIRUSES AND SECURITY RISKS

STUDENT NAME

Cover Page

Project 2 Build a Document with Predesigned and Custom Building Blocks
WL2-C3-P2-CompViruses.docx

CONTENTS

Page 1 of 4

CHAPTER 1: COMPUTER VIRUSES

One of the most familiar forms of risk to computer security is the computer virus. A computer virus is a program written by a hacker or cracker designed to perform some kind of trick upon an unsuspecting victim. The trick performed in some cases is mild, such as drawing an offensive image on the screen, or changing all of the characters in a document to another language. Sometimes the trick is much more severe, such as reformatting the hard drive and erasing all the data, or damaging the motherboard so that it cannot operate properly.

TYPES OF VIRUSES

Viruses can be categorized by their effect, which include nuisance, data-destructive, espionage, and hardware-destructive. A nuisance virus usually does no real damage, but is rather just an inconvenience. The most difficult part of a computer to replace is the data on the hard drive. The installed programs, the documents, databases, and saved emails form the heart of a personal computer. A data-destructive virus is designed to destroy this data. Some viruses are designed to create a backdoor into a system to bypass security. Called espionage viruses, they do no damage, but rather allow a hacker or cracker to enter the system later for the purpose of stealing data or spying on the work of the competitor. Very rarely, a virus is created that attempts to damage the hardware of the computer system itself. Called hardware-destructive viruses, these bits of programming can weaken or destroy chips, drives, and other components.

METHODS OF VIRUS OPERATION

Viruses can create effects that range from minor and annoying to highly destructive, and are operated and transmitted by a variety of methods. An email virus is normally transmitted as an attachment to a message sent over the Internet. Email viruses require the victim to click on the attachment and cause it to execute. Another common form of virus transmission is by a macro, a small subprogram that allows users to customize and automate certain functions. A macro virus is written specifically for one program, which then becomes infected when it opens a file with the virus stored in its macros. The boot sector of a compact disc or hard drive contains a variety of information, including how the disc is organized and whether it is capable of loading an operating system. When a disc is left in a drive and the computer reboots, the operating system automatically reads the boot sector to learn about that disc and to attempt to start any operating system on that disc. A boot sector virus is designed to alter the boot sector of a disc, so that whenever the operating system reads the boot sector, the computer will automatically become infected.

Other methods of virus infection include the Trojan horse virus, which hides inside another legitimate program or data file, and a stealth virus, which is designed to hide itself from detection software. Polymorphic viruses alter themselves to prevent antivirus software from detecting them by examining familiar patterns. Polymorphic viruses alter themselves randomly as they move from computer to computer, making detection more difficult. Multipartite viruses alter their form of attack. Their name derives from their ability to attack in several different ways. They may first infect the boot sector, and then later move on to become a Trojan horse type by infecting a disc file. These viruses are more sophisticated, and therefore more difficult to guard against. Another type of virus is the logic bomb, which generally sits quietly

Page 2 of 4

Model Answers

dormant waiting for a specific event or set of conditions to occur. A famous logic bomb was the widely publicized Michelangelo virus, which infected personal computers and caused them to display a message on the artist's birthday.

Page 3 of 4

CHAPTER 2: SECURITY RISKS

Although hackers, crackers, and viruses garner the most attention as security risks, companies face a variety of other dangers to their hardware and software systems. Principally, these risks involve types of system failure, employee theft, and the cracking of software for copying.

SYSTEMS FAILURE

A fundamental element in making sure that computer systems operate properly is protecting the electrical power that runs them. Power interruptions such as blackouts and brownouts have very adverse effects on computers. An inexpensive type of power strip called a surge protector can guard against power fluctuations and can also serve as an extension cord and splitter. A much more vigorous power protection system is an uninterruptible power supply (UPS), which provides a battery backup. Similar in nature to a power strip but much more bulky and a bit more expensive, a UPS provides not only steady spike-free power, but also keeps computers running during a blackout.

EMPLOYEE THEFT

Although accurate estimates are difficult to pinpoint, businesses certainly lose millions of dollars a year in stolen computer hardware and software. Often, in large organizations, such theft goes unnoticed or unreported. Someone takes a hard drive or a scanner home for legitimate use, then leaves the job some time later, and keeps the machine. Sometimes, employees take components to add to their home PC systems or a thief breaks into a business and hauls away computers. Such thefts cost far more than the price of the stolen computers because they also involve the cost of replacing the lost data, the cost of the time lost while the machines are gone, and the cost of installing new machines and training people to use them.

CRACKING SOFTWARE FOR COPYING

A common goal of hackers is to crack a software protection scheme. A crack is a method of circumventing a security scheme that prevents a user from copying a program. A common protection scheme for software is to require that the installation CD be resident in the drive whenever the program runs. Making copies of the CD with a burner, however, easily fools this protection scheme. Some game companies are taking the extra step of making duplication difficult by scrambling some of the data on the original CDs, which CD burners will automatically correct when copying. When the copied and corrected CD is used, the software checks for the scrambled track information. If the error is not found, the software will not run.

Page 4 of 4

FAMILY ADVENTURE VACATIONS

6553 Copper Avenue ◆ Albuquerque, NM 87107 ◆ 505-555-4910

January 2, 2015

Mrs. Jody Lancaster
Pacific Sky Cruise Lines
120 Montgomery Boulevard
Los Angeles, CA 97032

Dear Jody:

Your colorful brochures have made quite an impression on our clients, and consequently, we have given away our entire stock. Please send us an additional box of brochures as well as information and fact sheets about the various specialized cruises coming up.

Are you planning to offer the "Northern Lights" cruise next year? The cruise has been very popular with our clients, and I have had three inquiries in the past three weeks regarding the cruise. As soon as you know the dates of the cruise and stateroom prices, please let me know.

Sincerely,

Student Name
Travel Consultant

WL2-C3-P3-PSLtr.docx

Visit our website at www.emcp.net/worldwide to learn about our weekly vacation specials!

"Making your vacation dreams a reality"

Project 3 Create a Letter Document Using Custom Building Blocks WL2-C3-P3-PSLtr.docx

FAMILY ADVENTURE VACATIONS

6553 Copper Avenue ◆ Albuquerque, NM 87107 ◆ 505-555-4910

January 2, 2015

Mrs. Jody Lancaster
Pacific Sky Cruise Lines
120 Montgomery Boulevard
Los Angeles, CA 97032

Dear Jody:

I imagine you are extremely busy finalizing the preparations for the Pacific Sky Cruise Line's inaugural trip to the Alaska Inside Passage. The promotional literature you provided our company has been very effective in enticing our clients to sign up. This letter is a confirmation of the thirty staterooms that we have reserved for our clients for the inaugural cruise. We have reserved ten each of the following staterooms:

- Category H: Inside stateroom with two lower beds
- Category D: Deluxe ocean-view stateroom with window, sitting area, and two lower beds
- Category B: Superior deluxe ocean-view stateroom with window, sitting area, and two lower beds
- Category S: Superior deluxe suite with ocean view, private balcony, sitting area, and two lower beds

With only a few weeks to go before the cruise, I want to make sure our clients' bookings are finalized so they can enjoy the eight-day, seven-night cruise to the Alaska Inside Passage. Please confirm the stateroom reservations and send me a fax or email with the confirmation numbers.

Sincerely,

Student Name
Senior Travel Consultant

WL2-C3-P4-PSLtr.docx

"Making your vacation dreams a reality"

Project 4 Create a Letter Document with Modified Building Blocks WL2-C3-P4-PSLtr.docx

1/2/2015 2:39 PM

TESTING AGREEMENT

THIS AGREEMENT is made by and between Frontier Video Productions and ____________________ ("Licensee") having a principal place of business located at ________________________________.

In consideration of the mutual covenants and premises herein contained, the parties hereto agree as follows:

Frontier Video Productions grants to Licensee a non-exclusive, non-transferable license to use the Software on a single computer at Licensee's business location solely for beta testing and internal use until ______________, 20__, at which time the Software and all copies shall be returned to Frontier Video Productions.

In consideration for receiving a copy of the Software for testing, Licensee agrees to serve as a beta testing site for the Software and will notify Frontier Video Productions of all problems and ideas for enhancements which come to Licensee's attention during the period of this Agreement, and hereby assigns to Frontier Video Productions all rights, title and interest to such enhancements and all property rights therein including without limitation all patent, copyright, trade secret, mask work, trademark, moral right, or other intellectual property rights.

This Agreement shall be governed, construed, and enforced in accordance with the laws of the United States of America and of the State of California. Any notice required by this Agreement shall be given by prepaid, first class, certified mail, return receipt requested.

Frontier Video Productions: Licensee:

Name Name

First Draft
WL2-C3-P5-TestAgrmnt.docx
1/2/2015 2:39:00 PM

1/2/2015 3:17 PM

TESTING AGREEMENT

THIS AGREEMENT is made by and between Frontier Video Productions and ____________________ ("Licensee") having a principal place of business located at ________________________________.

In consideration of the mutual covenants and premises herein contained, the parties hereto agree as follows:

Frontier Video Productions grants to Licensee a non-exclusive, non-transferable license to use the Software on a single computer at Licensee's business location solely for beta testing and internal use until ______________, 20__, at which time the Software and all copies shall be returned to Frontier Video Productions.

In consideration for receiving a copy of the Software for testing, Licensee agrees to serve as a beta testing site for the Software and will notify Frontier Video Productions of all problems and ideas for enhancements which come to Licensee's attention during the period of this Agreement, and hereby assigns to Frontier Video Productions all rights, title and interest to such enhancements and all property rights therein including without limitation all patent, copyright, trade secret, mask work, trademark, moral right, or other intellectual property rights.

This Agreement shall be governed, construed, and enforced in accordance with the laws of the United States of America and of the State of California. Any notice required by this Agreement shall be given by prepaid, first class, certified mail, return receipt requested.

Frontier Video Productions: Licensee:

Name Name

First Draft
WL2-C3-P5-FVAgrmnt.docx
1/2/2015 3:17:00 PM

Project 5 Insert Document Properties and Fields in an Agreement Document WL2-C3-P5-TestAgrmnt.docx

WL2-C3-P5-FVPAgrmnt.docx

NATURAL INTERFACE APPLICATIONS

A major area of artificial intelligence has the goal of creating a more natural interface between human and machine. Currently, computer users are restricted in most instances to using a mouse and keyboard for input. For output, they must gaze at a fairly static, two-dimensional screen. Speakers are used for sound, and a printer for hard copy. The user interface consists of typing, pointing, and clicking. New speech recognition and natural-language technologies promise to change that soon.

SPEECH RECOGNITION

One of the most immediately applicable improvements comes in the area of speech recognition. Rather than typing information into the computer, users can direct it with voice commands. A computer that can take dictation and perform requested actions is a real step forward in convenience and potential. Speech recognition has developed rather slowly, mainly because the typical PC did not have the necessary speed and capacity until very recently.

NATURAL-LANGUAGE INTERFACE

Computers that are able to communicate using spoken English, Japanese, or any of the hundreds of other languages currently in use around the world, would certainly be helpful. In the not-so-distant future, computers will most likely be able to read, write, speak, and understand many human languages. Language translators already exist, and they are getting better all the time.

Programmers can look forward to a human-language computer interface. With better interfaces, programmers may be able to describe what they want using natural (human) languages, rather than writing programs in the highly restrictive and rather alien programming languages in use today. Natural-language interfaces are an area of artificial intelligence that is broader in scope than simple speech recognition. The goal is to have a machine that can read a set of news articles on any topic and understand what it has read. Ideally, it could then write its own report summarizing what it has learned.

VIRTUAL REALITY

Virtual reality (VR) describes the concept of creating a realistic world within the computer. Online games with thousands of interacting players already exist. In these games people can take on a persona and move about a virtual landscape, adventuring and chatting with other players. The quality of a virtual reality system is typically characterized in terms of its immersiveness, which measures how real the simulated world feels and how well it can

STUDENT NAME 1

make users accept the simulated world as their own and forget about reality. With each passing year, systems are able to provide increasing levels of immersion. Called by some the "ultimate in escapism," VR is becoming increasingly common—and increasingly realistic.

MENTAL INTERFACE

Although still in the experimental phase, a number of interfaces take things a bit further than VR, and they don't require users to click a mouse, speak a word, or even lift a finger. Mental interfaces use sensors mounted around the skull to read the alpha waves given off by our brains. Thinking of the color blue could be used to move the mouse cursor to the right, or thinking of the number seven could move it to the left. The computer measures brain activity and interprets it as a command, eliminating the need to physically manipulate a mouse to move the screen cursor. While this technology has obvious applications for assisting people with disabilities, military researchers are also using it to produce a superior form of interface for pilots.

STUDENT NAME 2

Project 6 Minimize the Ribbon and Customize the Quick Access Toolbar and Ribbon WL2-C3-P6-InterfaceApps.docx

Project 1 Create a Travel Document Using AutoCorrect 3 Parts

You will create several AutoCorrect entries, open a letterhead document, and then use the AutoCorrect entries to type text in the document.

Customizing AutoCorrect

The AutoCorrect feature in Word corrects certain text automatically as you type. Control what types of corrections are made with options at the AutoCorrect dialog box with the AutoCorrect tab selected, as shown in Figure 3.1.

Display this dialog box by clicking the FILE tab, clicking *Options*, clicking *Proofing*, clicking the AutoCorrect Options button, and then clicking the AutoCorrect tab. At the dialog box, turn AutoCorrect features on or off by inserting or removing check marks from the check boxes, specify AutoCorrect exceptions, replace frequently misspelled words with the correct spellings, add frequently used words, and specify keys to quickly insert the words in a document.

Specifying AutoCorrect Exceptions

The check box options at the AutoCorrect dialog box with the AutoCorrect tab selected identify the types of corrections made by AutoCorrect. Make exceptions to the corrections with options at the AutoCorrect Exceptions dialog box, shown in Figure 3.2 on the next page. Display this dialog box by clicking the Exceptions button at the AutoCorrect dialog box with the AutoCorrect tab selected.

Quick Steps

Display the AutoCorrect Exceptions Dialog Box

1. Click FILE tab.
2. Click *Options*.
3. Click *Proofing*.
4. Click AutoCorrect Options button.
5. Click AutoCorrect tab.
6. Click Exceptions button.

Figure 3.1 AutoCorrect Dialog Box with AutoCorrect Tab Selected

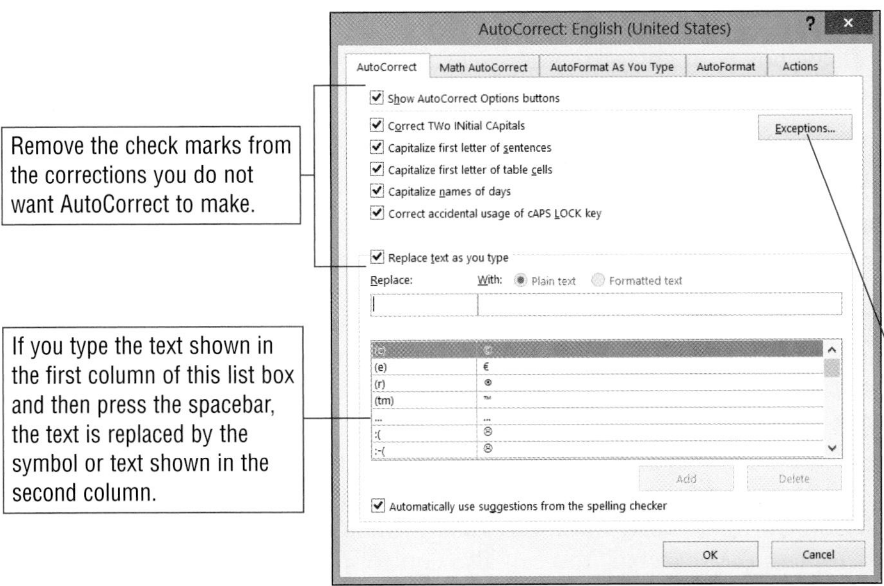

Click this button to display the AutoCorrect Exceptions dialog box.

Figure 3.2 AutoCorrect Exceptions Dialog Box

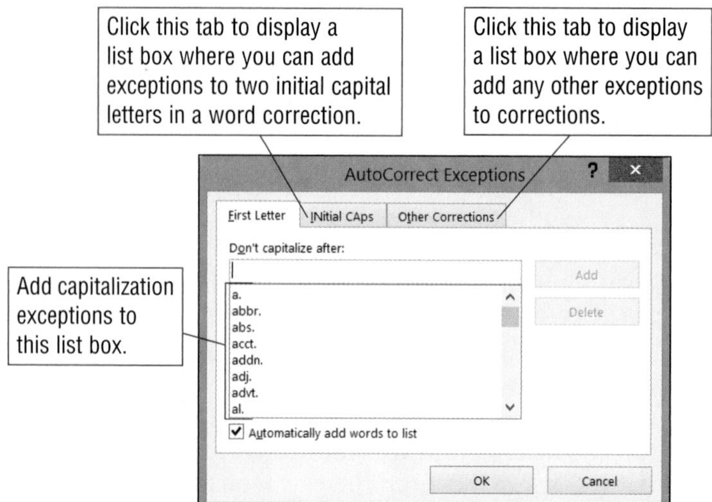
Click this tab to display a list box where you can add exceptions to two initial capital letters in a word correction.
Click this tab to display a list box where you can add any other exceptions to corrections.
Add capitalization exceptions to this list box.
AutoCorrect Exceptions
First Letter
INitial CAps
Other Corrections
Don't capitalize after:
Add
Delete
a.
abbr.
abs.
acct.
addn.
adj.
advt.
al.
Automatically add words to list
OK
Cancel

AutoCorrect usually capitalizes a word that comes after an abbreviation ending in a period, since a period usually ends a sentence. Exceptions to this general practice display in the AutoCorrect Exceptions dialog box with the First Letter tab selected. Many exceptions already display in the dialog box but you can add additional exceptions by typing each desired exception in the *Don't capitalize after* text box and then clicking the Add button.

By default, AutoCorrect corrects the use of two initial capital letters in a word. If you do not want AutoCorrect to correct the capitalizing of two initial capitals in a word, display the AutoCorrect Exceptions dialog box with the INitial CAps tab selected and then type the exception text in the *Don't correct* text box. At the AutoCorrect Exceptions dialog box with the Other Corrections tab selected, type text that you do not want corrected in the *Don't correct* text box. Delete exceptions from the dialog box with any of the tabs selected by clicking the desired text in the list box and then clicking the Delete button.

Adding Words to AutoCorrect

Quick Steps

Add a Word to AutoCorrect

1. Click FILE tab.
2. Click *Options.*
3. Click *Proofing.*
4. Click AutoCorrect Options button.
5. Click AutoCorrect tab.
6. Type misspelled or abbreviated word.
7. Press Tab.
8. Type correctly spelled or complete word.
9. Click Add button.
10. Click OK.

You can add words you commonly misspell and/or typographical errors you often make to AutoCorrect. For example, if you consistently type *relavent* instead of *relevant*, you can add *relavent* to AutoCorrect and tell it to correct it as *relevant*. The AutoCorrect dialog box also contains a few symbols you can insert in a document. For example, type *(c)* and AutoCorrect changes the text to ©. Type *(r)* and AutoCorrect changes the text to ®. The symbols display at the beginning of the AutoCorrect dialog box list box.

You can also add an abbreviation to AutoCorrect that, when typed, will insert an entire word (or words) in the document. For example, in Project 1a, you will add *fav* to AutoCorrect, which will insert *Family Adventure Vacations* when you type *fav* and then press the spacebar. You can also control the capitalization of the word (or words) inserted by controlling the capitalization of the abbreviation. For example, in Project 1a, you will add *Na* to AutoCorrect, which will insert *Namibia* when you type *Na* and *NAMIBIA* when you type *NA*.

Note that the AutoCorrect feature does not automatically correct text in hyperlinks. AutoCorrect is available only in Word, Outlook, and Visio.

Project 1a Adding Text and Specifying Exceptions to AutoCorrect

Part 1 of 3

1. At a blank document, click the FILE tab and then click *Options*.
2. At the Word Options dialog box, click *Proofing* in the left panel.
3. Click the AutoCorrect Options button in the *AutoCorrect options* section.
4. At the AutoCorrect dialog box with the AutoCorrect tab selected, add an exception to AutoCorrect by completing the following steps:
   a. Click the Exceptions button.
   b. At the AutoCorrect Exceptions dialog box, click the INitial CAps tab.
   c. Click in the *Don't correct* text box, type **STudent**, and then click the Add button.
   d. Click in the *Don't correct* text box, type **STyle**, and then click the Add button.
   e. Click the OK button.

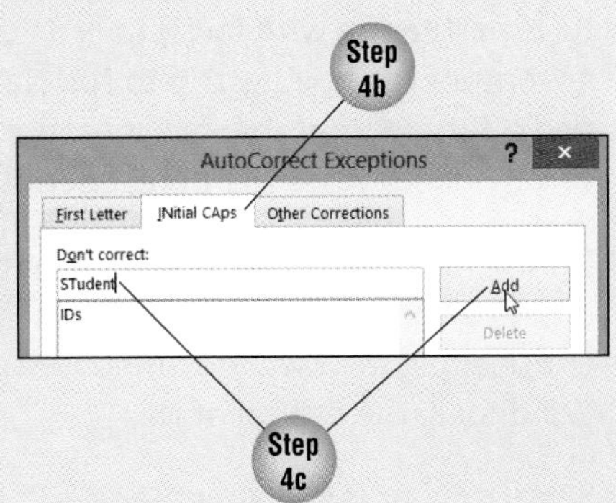

5. At the AutoCorrect dialog box with the AutoCorrect tab selected, click in the *Replace* text box and then type **fav**.
6. Press the Tab key (which moves the insertion point to the *With* text box) and then type **Family Adventure Vacations**.
7. Click the Add button. (This adds *fav* and *Family Adventure Vacations* to AutoCorrect and also selects *fav* in the *Replace* text box.)
8. Type **Na** in the *Replace* text box. (The text *fav* is automatically removed when you begin typing *Na*.)
9. Press the Tab key and then type **Namibia**.
10. Click the Add button.
11. With the insertion point positioned in the *Replace* text box, type **vf**.
12. Press the Tab key and then type **Victoria Falls**.
13. Click the Add button.
14. With the insertion point positioned in the *Replace* text box, type **tts**.
15. Press the Tab key and then type **Terra Travel Services**.
16. Click the Add button.
17. Click OK to close the AutoCorrect dialog box and then click OK to close the Word Options dialog box.
18. Open **TTSLtrhd.docx** and then save the document and name it **WL2-C3-P1-TTSAfrica**.
19. Type the text shown in Figure 3.3 on the next page. Type the text exactly as shown (including bolding and centering *fav* at the beginning of the document). AutoCorrect will correct words as you type.
20. Save **WL2-C3-P1-TTSAfrica.docx**.

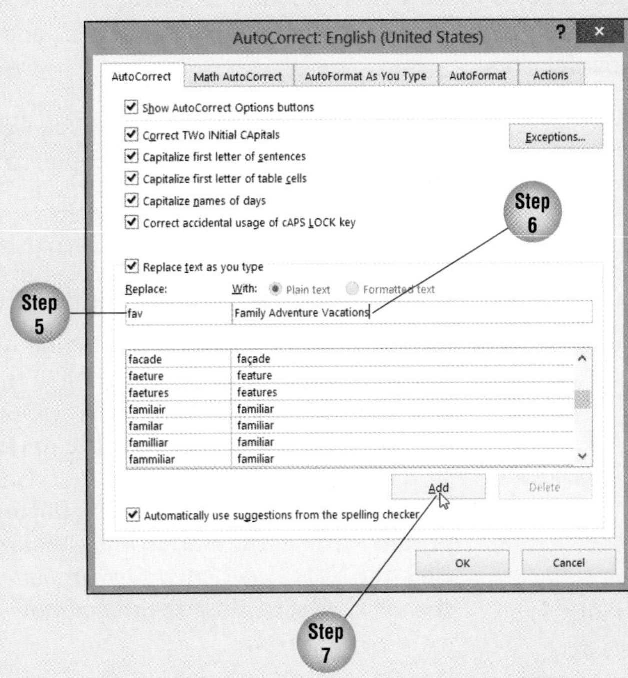

Figure 3.3 Project 1a

> **fav**
>
> Na and vf Adventure
>
> tts is partnering with fav(r) to provide adventurous and thrilling family vacations. Our first joint adventure is a holiday trip to Na. Na is one of the most fascinating holiday destinations in Africa and offers comfortable facilities, great food, cultural interaction, abundant wildlife, and a wide variety of activities to interest people of all ages.
>
> During the 12-day trip, you and your family will travel across Na through national parks, enjoying the beautiful and exotic scenery and watching wildlife in natural habitats. You will cruise along the Kwando and Chobe rivers and spend time at the Okapuka Lodge located near Windhoek, the capital of Na.
>
> If you or your family member is a college student, contact one of our college travel adventure consultants to learn more about the newest Student Travel package titled "STudent STyle" that offers a variety of student discounts, rebates, and free travel accessories for qualifying participants.
>
> tts and fav are offering a 15 percent discount if you sign up for this once-in-a-lifetime trip to Na. This exciting adventure is limited to twenty people, so don't wait to sign up.

Using the AutoCorrect Options Button

AutoCorrect Options

After AutoCorrect corrects a portion of text, hover the mouse pointer near the text and a small blue box displays below the corrected text. Move the mouse pointer to this blue box and the AutoCorrect Options button displays. Click this button to display a drop-down list with the options to change back to the original version, stop automatically correcting the specific text, and display the AutoCorrect dialog box. If the AutoCorrect Options button does not display, turn on the feature. To do this, display the AutoCorrect dialog box with the AutoCorrect tab selected, click the *Show AutoCorrect Options buttons* check box to insert a check mark, and then click OK to close the dialog box.

Project 1b **Using the AutoCorrect Options Button** **Part 2 of 3**

1. With **WL2-C3-P1-TTSAfrica.docx** open, select and then delete the last paragraph.
2. With the insertion point positioned on the blank line below the last paragraph of text (you may need to press the Enter key), type the following text.(AutoCorrect will automatically change *Ameria* to *America*, which you will change in the next step.) Through the sponsorship of Ameria Resorts, we are able to offer you a 15 percent discount for groups of twelve or more people.
3. Change the spelling of *America* back to *Ameria* by completing the following steps:
   a. Position the mouse pointer over *America* until a blue box displays below the word.
   b. Position the mouse pointer on the blue box until the AutoCorrect Options button displays.

c. Click the AutoCorrect Options button and then click the *Change back to "Ameria"* option.
4. Save and then print **WL2-C3-P1-TTSAfrica.docx**.

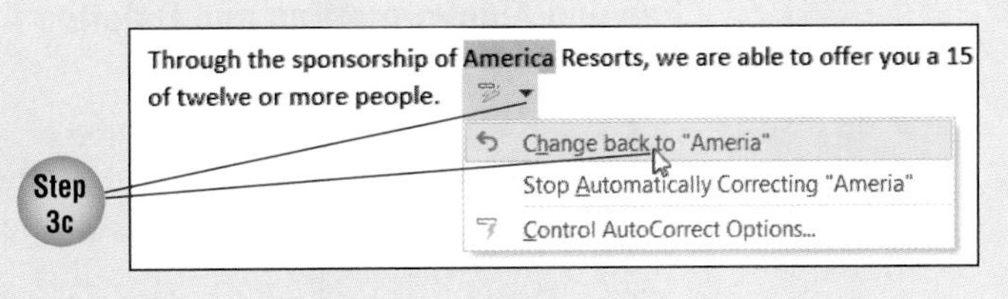

Customizing AutoFormatting

When you type text, Word provides options to automatically apply some formatting, such as changing a fraction to a fraction character (1/2 to ½), changing numbers to ordinals (1st to 1st), changing an Internet or network path to a hyperlink (www.emcp.net to www.emcp.net), and applying bullets or numbers to text. The AutoFormatting options display in the AutoCorrect dialog box with the AutoFormat As You Type tab selected, as shown in Figure 3.4. Display this dialog box by clicking the FILE tab and then clicking *Options*. At the Word Options dialog box, click *Proofing* in the left panel and then click the AutoCorrect Options button. At the AutoCorrect dialog box, click the AutoFormat As You Type tab. At the dialog box, remove the check marks from those options you want to turn off and insert check marks for those options you want Word to format automatically.

Deleting AutoCorrect Text

You can delete AutoCorrect text from the AutoCorrect dialog box. To do this, display the AutoCorrect dialog box with the AutoCorrect tab selected, click the desired word or words in the list box, and then click the Delete button.

Figure 3.4 AutoCorrect Dialog Box with the AutoFormat As You Type Tab Selected

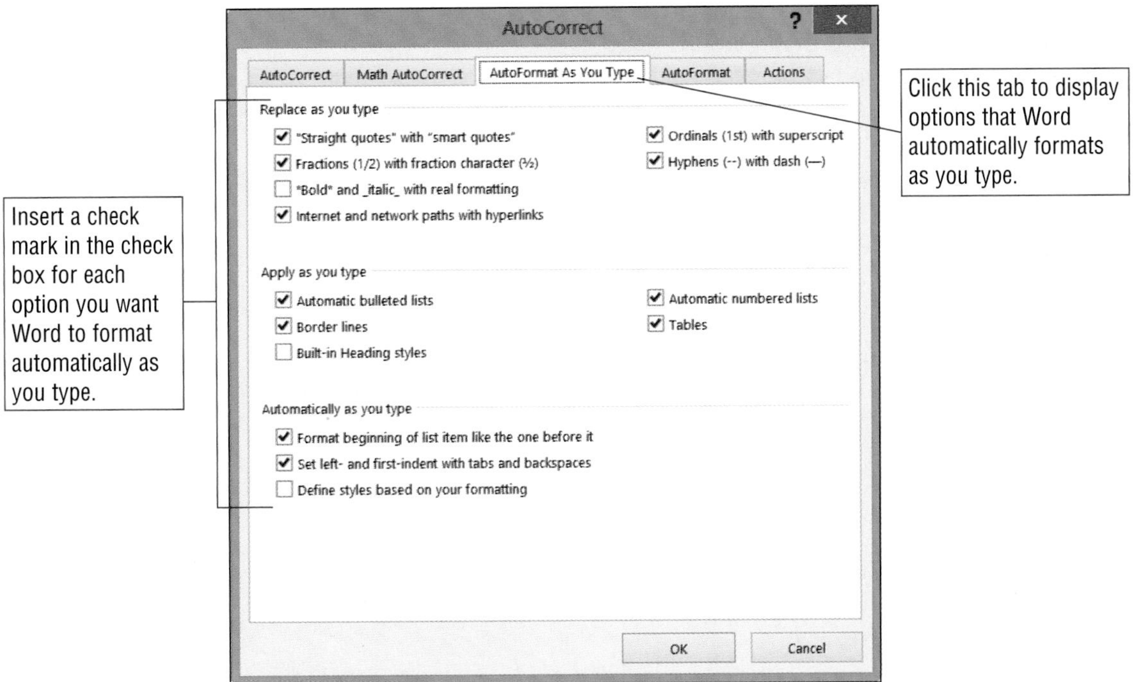

Project 1c Changing AutoFormatting and Deleting AutoCorrect Text

1. Make sure **WL2-C3-P1-TTSAfrica.docx** is open.
2. Suppose that you need to add a couple of web addresses to a document and you do not want the addresses automatically formatted as hyperlinks (since you are sending the document as hard copy rather than electronically). Turn off the AutoFormatting of web addresses by completing the following steps:
   a. Click the FILE tab and then click *Options*.
   b. At the Word Options dialog box, click *Proofing* in the left panel.
   c. Click the AutoCorrect Options button.
   d. At the AutoCorrect dialog box, click the AutoFormat As You Type tab.
   e. Click the *Internet and network paths with hyperlinks* check box to remove the check mark.
   f. Click OK to close the AutoCorrect dialog box.
   g. Click OK to close the Word Options dialog box.
3. Press Ctrl + End to move the insertion point to the end of the document, press the Enter key, and then type the text shown in Figure 3.5.
4. Turn on the AutoFormatting feature you turned off in Step 2 by completing Steps 2a through 2g (except in Step 2e, insert the check mark rather than remove it).
5. Delete *fav* from AutoCorrect by completing the following steps:
   a. Click the FILE tab and then click *Options*.
   b. At the Word Options dialog box, click *Proofing* in the left panel.
   c. Click the AutoCorrect Options button.
   d. At the AutoCorrect dialog box, click the AutoCorrect tab.
   e. Click in the *Replace* text box and then type fav. (This selects the entry in the list box.)
   f. Click the Delete button.
6. Complete steps similar to those in Step 5 to delete the *Na*, *tts*, and *vf* AutoCorrect entries.

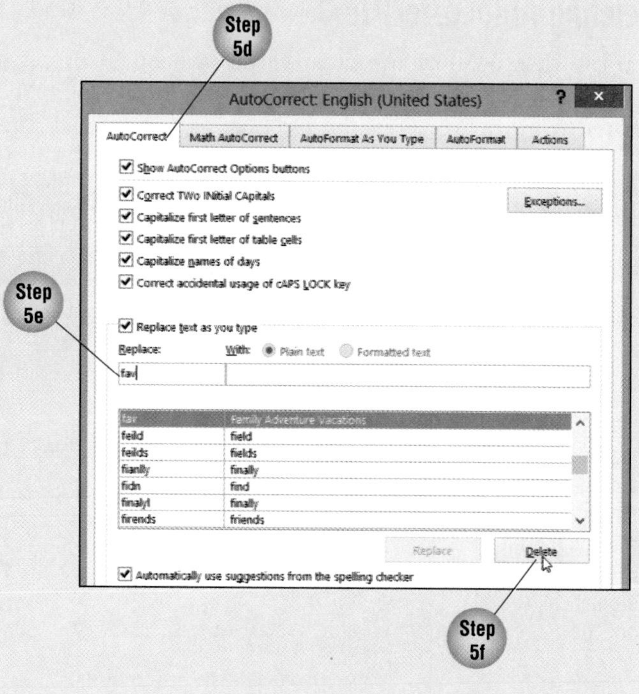

7. Delete the exceptions you added to the AutoCorrect Exceptions dialog box by completing the following steps:
   a. At the AutoCorrect dialog box with the AutoCorrect tab selected, click the Exceptions button.
   b. At the AutoCorrect Exceptions dialog box, if necessary, click the INitial CAps tab.
   c. Click *STudent* in the list box and then click the Delete button.
   d. Click *STyle* in the list box and then click the Delete button.
   e. Click OK to close the AutoCorrect Exceptions dialog box.
8. Click OK to close the AutoCorrect dialog box.
9. Click OK to close the Word Options dialog box.
10. Save, print, and then close **WL2-C3-P1-TTSAfrica.docx**.

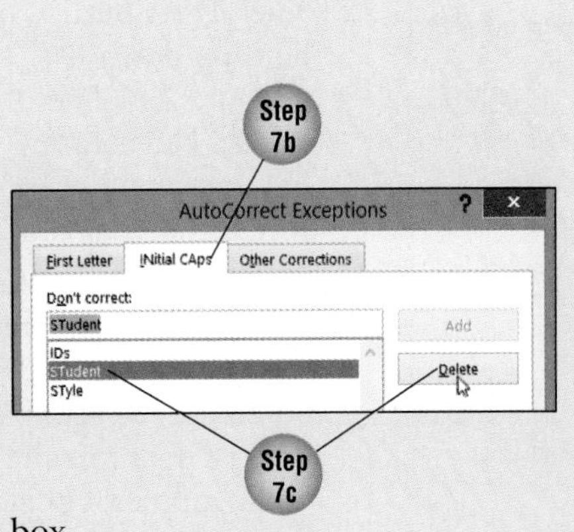

Figure 3.5 Project 1c

For additional information on the Na adventure, as well as other exciting vacation specials, please visit our website at www.emcp.net/terratravel or visit www.emcp.net/famadv.

Project 2 Build a Document with Predesigned and Custom Building Blocks — 1 Part

You will open a report document and then add elements to the document by inserting predesigned building blocks.

Inserting Quick Parts

Word includes a variety of tools for inserting data such as text, fields, objects, and other items to help build a document. To view some of the tools available, click the Quick Parts button in the Text group on the INSERT tab. Doing this displays a drop-down list of choices for inserting document properties, fields, and building blocks, as well as options for saving selected data to the AutoText gallery and Quick Part gallery.

Quick Parts

Inserting Building Blocks

Building blocks are tools for developing a document. Word provides a number of building blocks that you can insert into a document, or you can create your own.

Quick Steps
Insert a Building Block
1. Click INSERT tab.
2. Click Quick Parts button.
3. Click *Building Blocks Organizer* at drop-down list.
4. Click desired building block.
5. Click Insert button.
6. Click Close.

To insert a building block into a document, click the INSERT tab, click the Quick Parts button in the Text group, and then click *Building Blocks Organizer* at the drop-down list. This displays the Building Blocks Organizer dialog box, shown in Figure 3.6. The dialog box displays columns of information about the building blocks. The columns in the dialog box display the building block name, the gallery that contains the building block, the template in which the building block is stored, the behavior of the building block, and a brief description.

The Building Blocks Organizer dialog box is a central location for viewing all of the predesigned building blocks available in Word. You used some of the building blocks in previous chapters when you inserted a predesigned header or footer, cover page, page number, and watermark. Other galleries in the Building Blocks Organizer dialog box containing predesigned building blocks include bibliographies, equations, tables of contents, tables, and text boxes. The Building Blocks Organizer dialog box provides a convenient location for viewing and inserting building blocks.

Sorting Building Blocks

Quick Steps
Sort Building Blocks
1. Click INSERT tab.
2. Click Quick Parts button.
3. Click *Building Blocks Organizer* at drop-down list.
4. Click desired column heading.

When you open the Building Blocks Organizer dialog box, the building blocks display in the list box sorted by the *Gallery* column. Sort the building blocks by other columns by clicking the column headings. For example, to sort building blocks alphabetically by name, click the *Name* column heading.

Figure 3.6 Building Blocks Organizer Dialog Box

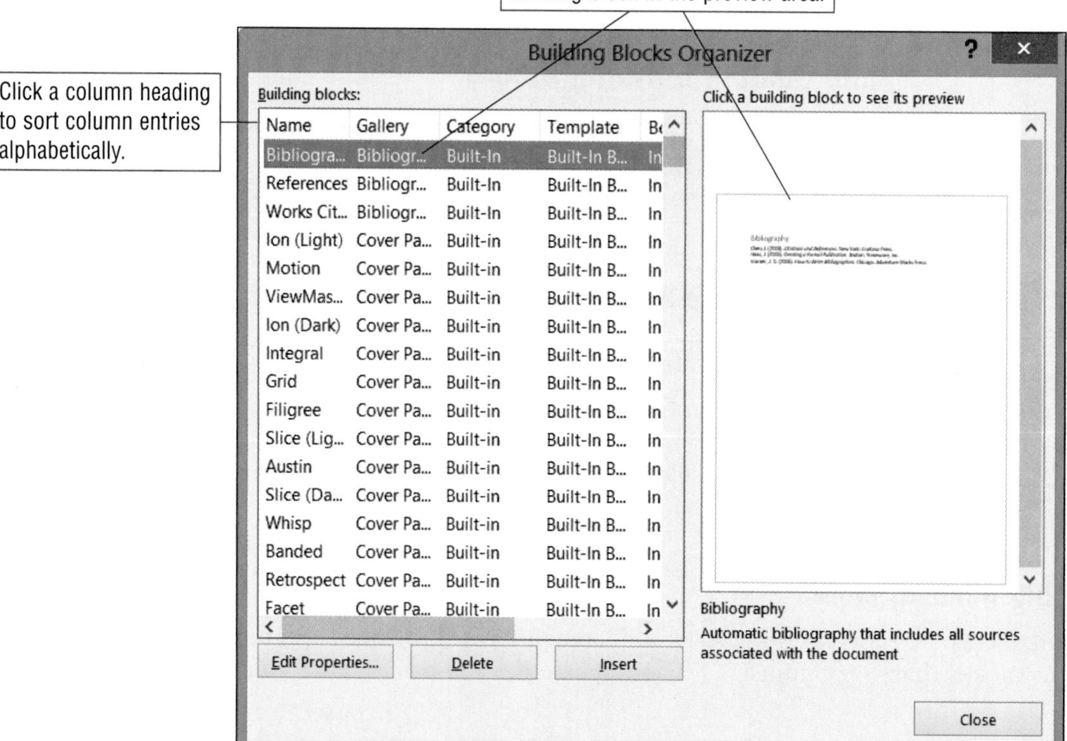

Project 2 Inserting Predesigned Building Blocks

Part 1 of 1

1. Open **CompViruses.docx** and then save the document and name it **WL2-C3-P2-CompViruses**.
2. Make the following changes to the document:
   a. Insert a continuous section break at the beginning of the first paragraph below the title *CHAPTER 1: COMPUTER VIRUSES*.
   b. Insert a section break that begins a new page at the beginning of the title *CHAPTER 2: SECURITY RISKS* located in the middle of the second page.
   c. Insert a continuous section break at the beginning of the first paragraph below the title *CHAPTER 2: SECURITY RISKS*.
   d. Change the line spacing to 1.0 for the entire document.
   e. Format the paragraphs in the section below the title *CHAPTER 1: COMPUTER VIRUSES* into two columns of equal width.
   f. Balance the columns where the text ends on the second page. ***Hint: Balance columns by inserting a continuous section break.***
   g. Format the paragraphs in the section below the second title *CHAPTER 2: SECURITY RISKS* into two columns of equal width.
   h. Balance the columns where the text ends on the page.
3. Sort the building blocks and then insert a table of contents building block by completing the following steps:
   a. Press Ctrl + Home, press Ctrl + Enter to insert a page break, and then press Ctrl + Home to move the insertion point back to the beginning of the document.
   b. Click the INSERT tab, click the Quick Parts button in the Text group, and then click *Building Blocks Organizer* at the drop-down list.
   c. At the Building Blocks Organizer dialog box, notice the arrangement of building blocks in the list box. (The building blocks are most likely organized alphabetically by the *Gallery* column.)
   d. Click the *Name* column heading. (This sorts the building blocks alphabetically by name. However, some blank building blocks may display at the beginning of the list box.)
   e. Scroll down the list box and then click *Automatic Table 1*. (You may see only a portion of the name. Click the name and the full name as well as a description display in the dialog box below the preview of the table of contents building block.)
   f. Click the Insert button that displays near the bottom of the dialog box. (This inserts a Contents page at the beginning of the document and uses the heading styles applied to the titles and headings in the document to create the table of contents.)
4. Insert a footer building block by completing the following steps:
   a. Click the Quick Parts button on the INSERT tab and then click *Building Blocks Organizer*.
   b. Scroll down the Building Blocks Organizer list box, click the *Sempahore* footer, and then click the Insert button.

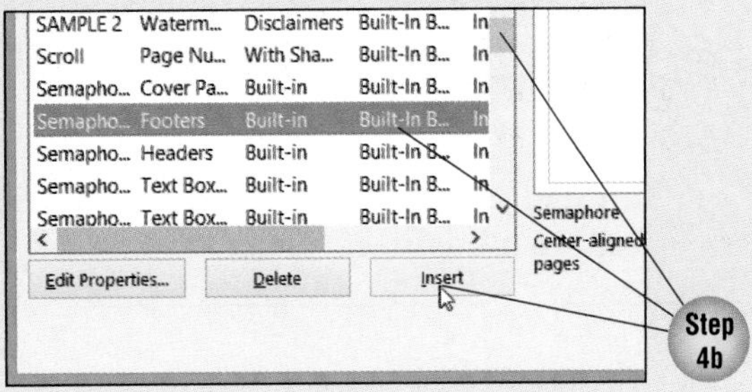

c. Decrease the *Footer from Bottom* measurement to 0.3 inch (located in the Position group on the HEADER & FOOTER TOOLS DESIGN tab).
d. Click the DESIGN tab, click the Theme Colors button, and then click *Red* at the drop-down list. (This changes the color of the footer text to Red.)
e. Double-click in the document.

5. Insert a cover page building block by completing the following steps:
a. Press Ctrl + Home to move the insertion point to the beginning of the document.
b. Click the INSERT tab, click the Quick Parts button, and then click *Building Blocks Organizer*.
c. Scroll down the Building Blocks Organizer list box, click the *Semaphore* cover page, and then click the Insert button.
d. Click the *[DATE]* placeholder and then type today's date.
e. Click the *[DOCUMENT TITLE]* placeholder and then type **Northland Security Systems**. (The text you type will be converted to all uppercase letters.)
f. Click the *[DOCUMENT SUBTITLE]* placeholder and then type **Computer Viruses and Security Risks**.
g. Select the name that displays above the [COMPANY NAME] placeholder and then type your first and last names.

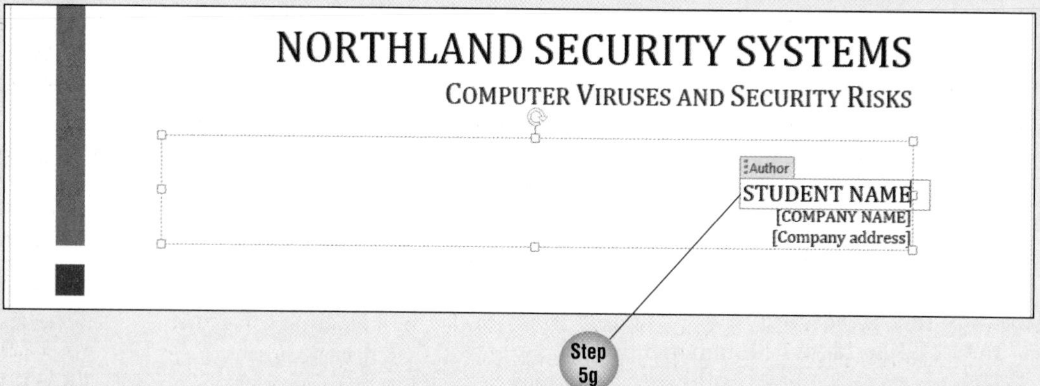

h. Select and then delete the [COMPANY NAME] placeholder.
i. Select and then delete the [Company address] placeholder.

6. Scroll through the document and look at each page in the document. The semaphore footer and cover page building blocks you inserted have similar formatting and are part of the *Semaphore* group. Using building blocks from the same group provides consistency in the document and gives it a polished and professional appearance.
7. Save, print, and then close **WL2-C3-P2-CompViruses.docx**.

Project 3 Create a Letter Document Using Custom Building Blocks — 3 Parts

You will create custom building blocks and then use those building blocks to prepare a business letter.

Saving Content as Building Blocks

If you find yourself typing and formatting the same data on a regular basis, consider saving the data as a ***building block***. Saving commonly created data as a building block saves you time and reduces errors that might occur each time you type data or apply formatting. You can save content as a building block in a specific gallery. For example, you can save a text box in the Text Box gallery, save content in the Header gallery, save content in the Footer gallery, and so on. To save content in a specific gallery, use the button for the desired gallery.

For example, to save a text box in the Text Box gallery, use the Text Box button. To do this, select the text box, click the INSERT tab, click the Text Box button, and then click the *Save Selection to Text Box Gallery* option at the drop-down gallery. At the Create New Building Block dialog box that displays, as shown in Figure 3.7, type a name for the text box building block, type a description if desired, and then click OK.

To save content in the Header gallery, select the content, click the INSERT tab, click the Header button, and then click the *Save Selection to Header Gallery* option at the drop-down gallery. This displays the Create New Building Block dialog box, as shown in Figure 3.7 (except *Headers* displays with the *Gallery* option box). Complete similar steps to save content to the Footer gallery and Cover Page gallery.

When you save data as a building block, it becomes available in the Building Blocks Organizer dialog box. If you save content as a building block in a specific gallery, the building block is available at both the Building Blocks Organizer dialog box and the gallery. For example, if you save a building block in the Footer gallery, the building block is available when you click the Footer button on the INSERT tab.

Content you save as a building block is saved in the Building Blocks.dotx template or Normal.dotm template. Saving a building block in either template makes it available each time you open Word. In a public environment such as a school, you may not be able to save data to a template. Before completing Project 3, check with your instructor to determine if you can save your building blocks. In Project 4b, you will be instructed to delete the building blocks you create.

Quick Steps

Save Content to a Text Box Gallery
1. Select content.
2. Click INSERT tab.
3. Click Text Box button.
4. Click *Save Selection to Text Box Gallery.*

Save Content to a Header Gallery
1. Select content.
2. Click INSERT tab.
3. Click Header button.
4. Click *Save Selection to Header Gallery.*

Save Content to a Footer Gallery
1. Select content.
2. Click INSERT tab.
3. Click Footer button.
4. Click *Save Selection to Footer Gallery.*

When selecting content to save as a building block, turn on the display of nonprinting characters by clicking the Show/Hide ¶ button in the Paragraph group on the HOME tab.

Figure 3.7 Create New Building Block Dialog Box

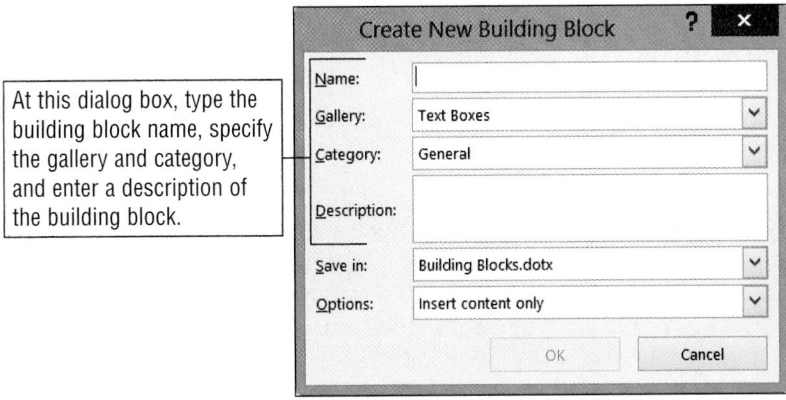

Quick Steps

Save Content to the AutoText Gallery
1. Select content.
2. Click INSERT tab.
3. Click Quick Parts button.
4. Point to *AutoText*.
5. Click *Save Selection to AutoText Gallery*.

Saving Content to the AutoText Gallery

You can save content as a building block in the AutoText gallery. The building block can easily be inserted into a document by clicking the INSERT tab, clicking the Quick Parts button, pointing to *AutoText*, and then clicking the desired AutoText building block at the side menu. To save content in the AutoText gallery, type and format the desired content and then select the content. Click the INSERT tab, click the Quick Parts button, point to *AutoText*, and then click the *Save Selection to AutoText Gallery* option at the side menu. You can also press Alt + F3 to display the dialog box. At the Create New Building Block dialog box, type a name for the building block, type a description if desired, and then click OK.

Quick Steps

Save Content to the Quick Part Gallery
1. Select content.
2. Click INSERT tab.
3. Click Quick Parts button.
4. Click *Save Selection to Quick Part Gallery*.

Saving Content to the Quick Part Gallery

Not only can you save content in the AutoText gallery, but you can also save selected content in the Quick Part gallery. To do this, select the desired content, click the INSERT tab, click the Quick Parts button, and then click the *Save Selection to Quick Part Gallery* option at the drop-down gallery. This displays the Create New Building Block dialog box with *Quick Parts* specified in the *Gallery* option box and *Building Blocks.dotx* specified in the *Save in* option box. Type a name for the building block, type a description if desired, and then click OK.

Project 3a **Saving Content to the Text Box, Footer, AutoText, and Quick Part Galleries** **Part 1 of 3**

1. Open **FAVContent.docx**.
2. Save the text box as a building block in the Text Box gallery by completing the following steps:
   a. Select the text box by clicking in the text box and then clicking the text box border.
   b. Click the INSERT tab, click the Text Box button, and then click *Save Selection to Text Box Gallery* at the drop-down list.
   c. At the Create New Building Block dialog box, type your last name followed by **FAVTextBox** and then click OK.

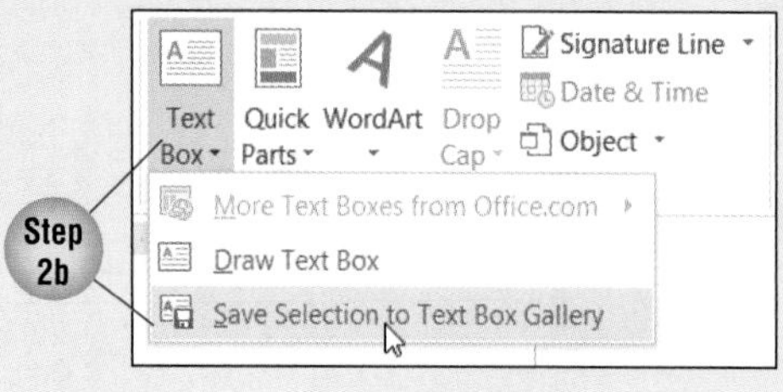

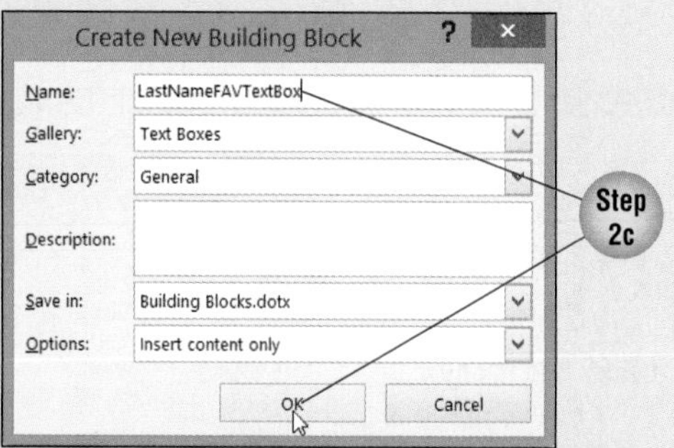

3. Save content as a building block in the Footer gallery by completing the following steps:
   a. Select the text *"Making your vacation dreams a reality"* located below the text box. (Make sure you select the paragraph mark at the end of the text. If necessary, click the Show/Hide ¶ button in the Paragraph group on the HOME tab to display the paragraph mark.)
   b. Click the Footer button in the Header & Footer group on the INSERT tab and then click *Save Selection to Footer Gallery* at the drop-down list.

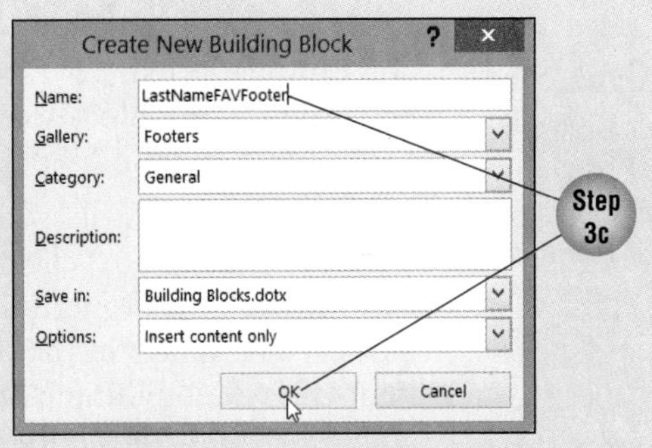

c. At the Create New Building Block dialog box, type your last name followed by **FAVFooter** and then click OK.

4. Save the company name *Pacific Sky Cruise Lines* and the address below it as a building block in the AutoText gallery by completing the following steps:
   a. Select the company name and address (the two lines below the company name). Make sure you include the paragraph mark at the end of the last line of the address.
   b. Click the Quick Parts button in the Text group on the INSERT tab, point to *AutoText*, and then click *Save Selection to AutoText Gallery* at the side menu.

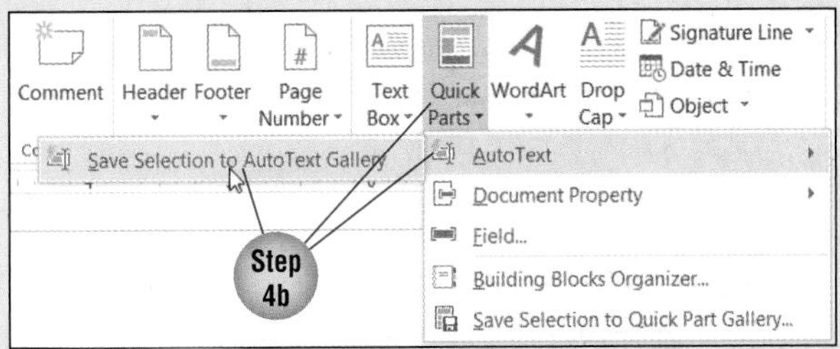

   c. At the Create New Building Block dialog box, type your last name and then type **PacificSky**.
   d. Click OK to close the dialog box.

5. Type your name and company title and then save the text as a building block in the AutoText gallery by completing the following steps:
   a. Move the insertion point to a blank line a double space below the Pacific Sky Cruise Lines address.
   b. Type your first and last names and then press the spacebar.
   c. Press the Down Arrow key to move the insertion point to the next line and then type **Travel Consultant**. (Do not press the Enter key.)
   d. Select your first and last names and the title *Travel Consultant*. (Include the paragraph mark at the end of the title.)
   e. Press Alt + F3.
   f. At the Create New Building Block dialog box, type your last name and then type **Title**.
   g. Click OK to close the dialog box.

6. Save the letterhead as a building block in the Quick Part gallery by completing the following steps:
   a. Select the letterhead text (the company name *FAMILY ADVENTURE VACATIONS*, the address below the name, and the paragraph mark at the end of the address and telephone number).
   b. Click the Quick Parts button in the Text group on the INSERT tab and then click *Save Selection to Quick Part Gallery* at the drop-down list.
   c. At the Create New Building Block dialog box, type your last name and then type **FAV**.
   d. Click OK to close the dialog box.

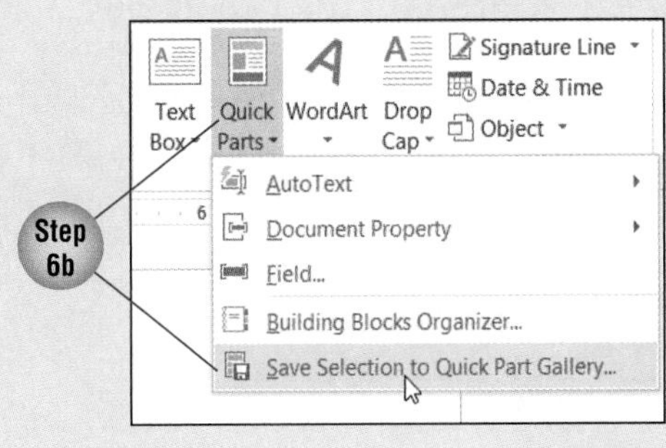

7. Close **FAVContent.docx** without saving it.

Editing Building Block Properties

Quick Steps

Edit a Building Block
1. Click INSERT tab.
2. Click Quick Parts button.
3. Click *Building Blocks Organizer.*
4. Click desired building block.
5. Click Edit Properties button.
6. Make desired changes.
7. Click OK.

OR
1. Click desired button.
2. Right-click custom building block.
3. Click *Edit Properties.*
4. Make desired changes.
5. Click OK.

You can make changes to the properties of a building block with options at the Modify Building Block dialog box. This dialog box contains the same options as the Create New Building Block dialog box.

Display the Modify Building Block dialog box by opening the Building Blocks Organizer dialog box, clicking the desired building block in the list box, and then clicking the Edit Properties button. You can also display this dialog box for a building block that displays in the drop-down gallery. To do this, click the Quick Parts button, right-click the building block that displays in the drop-down gallery, and then click *Edit Properties* at the shortcut menu. Make desired changes to the Modify Building Block dialog box and then click OK. At the message asking if you want to redefine the building block entry, click Yes.

You can also display this dialog box for a custom building block in a button drop-down gallery by clicking the button, right-clicking the custom building block, and then clicking the *Edit Properties* option at the shortcut menu. For example, to modify a custom text box building block, click the INSERT tab, click the Text Box button, and then scroll down the drop-down list to display the custom text box building block. Right-click the custom text box and then click *Edit Properties* at the shortcut menu.

Project 3b Editing Building Block Properties — Part 2 of 3

1. At a blank document, click the INSERT tab, click the Quick Parts button in the Text group, and then click *Building Blocks Organizer* at the drop-down list.
2. At the Building Blocks Organizer dialog box, click the *Gallery* column heading to sort the building blocks by gallery. (This displays the AutoText galleries at the beginning of the list.)
3. Scroll to the right in the list box and notice that the building block that displays with your last name followed by *PacificSky* does not contain a description. Edit the building block properties by completing the following steps:
   a. Click the building block in the AutoText gallery that begins with your last name followed by *PacificSky*. (The entire building block name does not display in the list box. To view the entire name, click the building block name in the *Building Blocks* list box and then look at the name that displays below the preview page at the right side of the dialog box.)
   b. Click the Edit Properties button located at the bottom of the dialog box.
   c. At the Modify Building Block dialog box, click in the *Name* text box and then type **Address** at the end of the name.
   d. Click in the *Description* text box and then type **Inserts the Pacific Sky name and address.**
   e. Click OK to close the dialog box.
   f. At the message asking if you want to redefine the building block entry, click Yes.
   g. Close the Building Blocks Organizer dialog box.

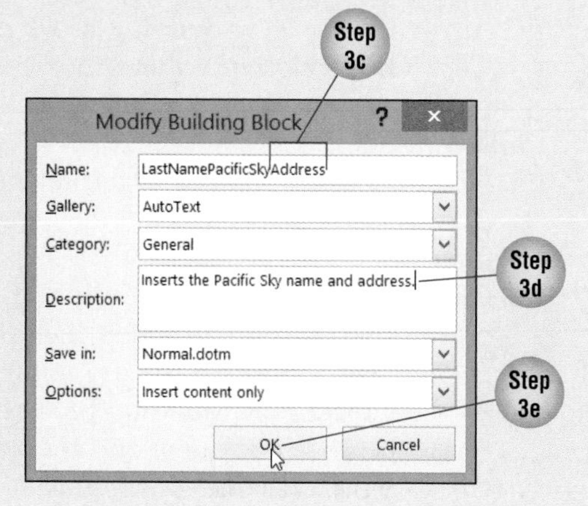

4. Edit the letterhead building block by completing the following steps:
   a. Click the Quick Parts button in the Text group on the INSERT tab, right-click the Family Adventure Vacations letterhead building block that begins with your last name, and then click *Edit Properties* at the shortcut menu.
   b. At the Modify Building Block dialog box, click in the *Name* text box and then type **Letterhead** at the end of the name.
   c. Click in the *Description* text box and then type **Inserts the Family Adventure Vacations letterhead including the company name and address.**
   d. Click OK to close the dialog box.
   e. At the message asking if you want to redefine the building block entry, click Yes.

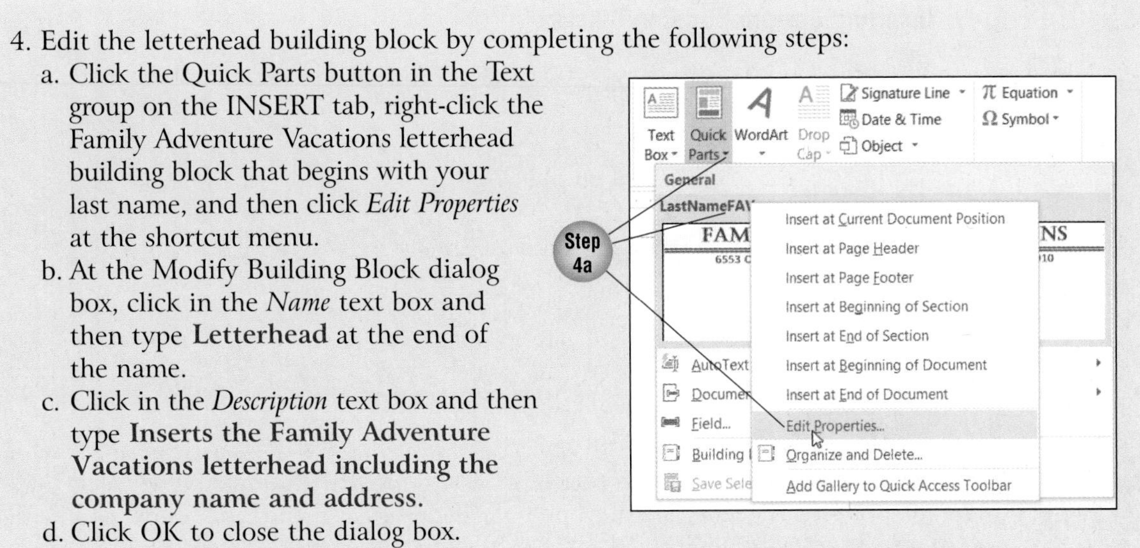

Inserting Custom Building Blocks

Any content that you save as a building block can be inserted in a document using the Building Blocks Organizer dialog box. Some content can also be inserted using specific drop-down galleries. For example, insert a custom text box building block by clicking the Text Box button on the INSERT tab and then clicking the desired text box at the drop-down gallery. Insert a custom header at the Header button drop-down gallery, a custom footer at the Footer button drop-down gallery, a custom cover page at the Cover Page button drop-down gallery, and so on.

You can use the button drop-down gallery to specify where you want custom building block content inserted in a document. To do this, display the button drop-down gallery, right-click the custom building block, and then click the desired location at the shortcut menu. For example, if you click the INSERT tab, click the Quick Parts button, and then right-click the *FAVLetterhead* building block (preceded by your last name), a shortcut menu displays, as shown in Figure 3.8.

Figure 3.8 Quick Parts Button Drop-down List Shortcut Menu

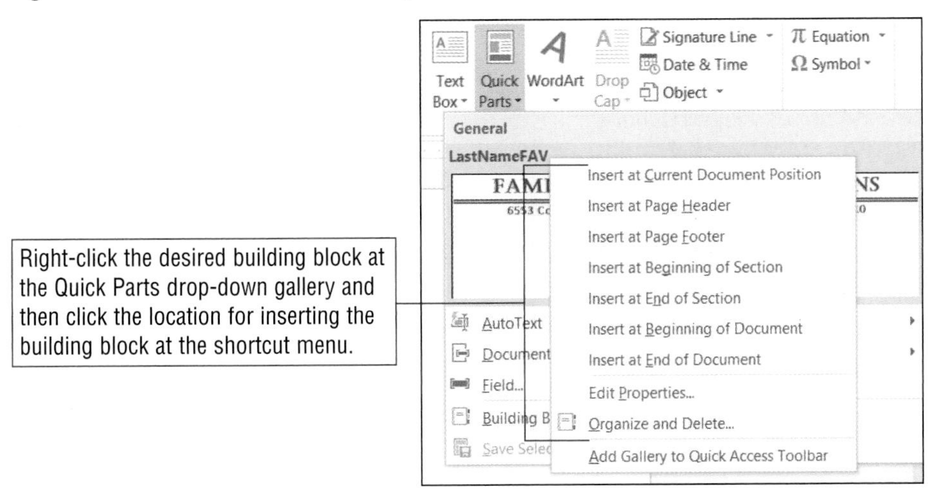

Project 3c Inserting Custom Building Blocks

1. At the blank document, click the *No Spacing* style thumbnail in the Styles group on the HOME tab and then change the font to Candara.
2. Insert the letterhead building block as a header by completing the following steps:
   a. Click the INSERT tab.
   b. Click the Quick Parts button, right-click the Family Adventure Vacations letterhead (preceded by your last name), and then click the *Insert at Page Header* option at the shortcut menu.
3. Press the Enter key twice, type the current date, and then press the Enter key five times.
4. Type **Mrs. Jody Lancaster** and then press the Enter key.
5. Insert the Pacific Sky Cruise Lines name and address building block by clicking the Quick Parts button, pointing to *AutoText*, and then clicking the Pacific Sky Address building block (preceded by your last name) at the side menu.

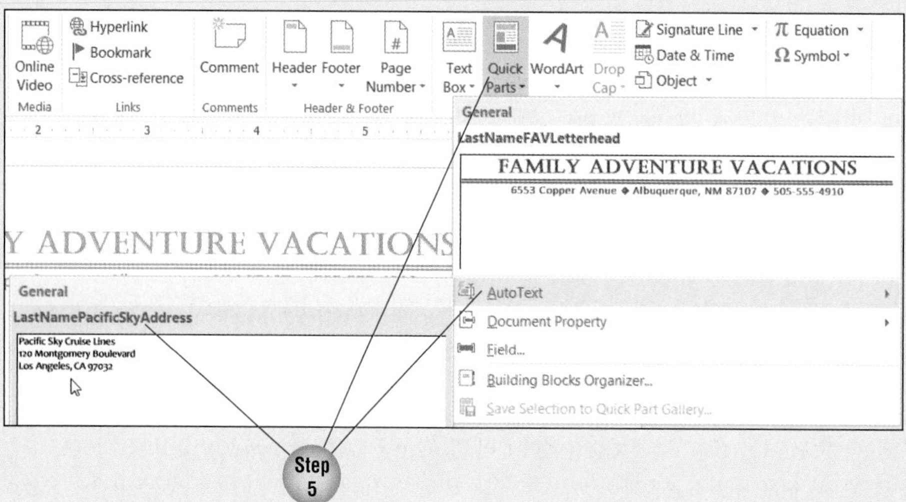

6. Press the Enter key once and then insert a letter document by completing the following steps:
   a. Click the Object button arrow in the Text group on the INSERT tab and then click *Text from File* at the drop-down list.
   b. At the Insert File dialog box, navigate to the WL2C3 folder on your storage medium and then double-click ***PacificSkyLetter01.docx***.
7. With the insertion point positioned a double space below the last paragraph of text in the body of the letter, type **Sincerely**, and then press the Enter key four times.
8. Insert your name and title building block by clicking the Quick Parts button, pointing to *AutoText*, and then clicking your name and title at the side menu.
9. Press the Enter key and then type **WL2-C3-P3-PSLtr.docx**.

10. Press the Enter key five times and then insert the custom text box you saved as a building block by completing the following steps:
    a. Click the Text Box button in the Text group on the INSERT tab.
    b. Scroll to the end of the drop-down gallery and then click your custom text box. (Your custom text box will display in the *General* section of the drop-down gallery.)
    c. Click in the document to deselect the text box. 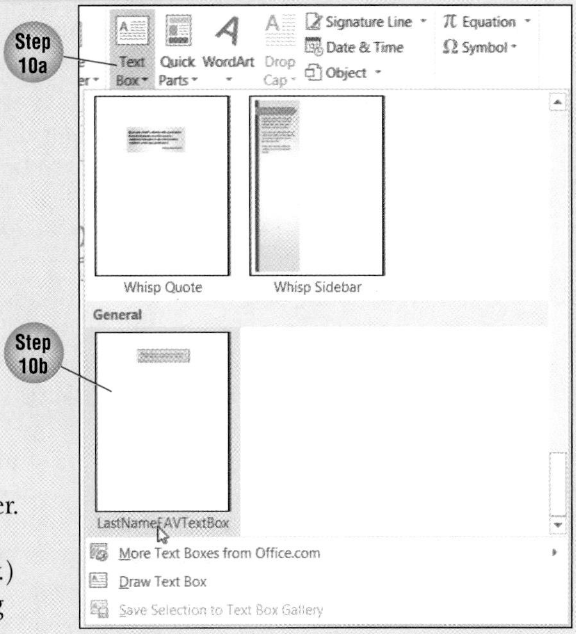
11. Insert the custom footer you created by completing the following steps:
    a. Click the INSERT tab.
    b. Click the Footer button in the Header & Footer group.
    c. Scroll to the end of the drop-down gallery and then click your custom footer. (Your custom footer will display in the *General* section of the drop-down gallery.)
    d. Close the footer pane by double-clicking in the document.
12. Save the completed letter and name it **WL2-C3-P3-PSLtr**.
13. Print and then close **WL2-C3-P3-PSLtr.docx**.

Step 10a

Step 10b

Project 4 Create a Letter Document with Modified Building Blocks — 2 Parts

You will modify your custom building blocks and use them to prepare a business letter. You will then delete your custom building blocks.

Modifying Custom Building Blocks

You can insert a building block in a document, make corrections or changes, and then save the building block with the same name or a different name. Save a building block with the same name when you want to update the building block to reflect any changes. Save the building block with a new name when you want to use an existing building block as the foundation for creating a new building block.

To save a modified building block with the same name, insert the building block into the document and then make the desired modifications. Select the building block data and then specify the gallery. At the Create New Building Block dialog box, type the original name and description and then click OK. At the message asking if you want to redefine the building block entry, click Yes.

Project 4a Modifying Building Blocks

1. As a travel consultant at Family Adventure Vacations, you have been given a promotion and are now a senior travel consultant. You decide to modify your name and title building block by completing the following steps:
   a. At a blank document, click the INSERT tab, click the Quick Parts button in the Text group, point to *AutoText*, and then click your name and title building block at the side menu.
   b. Edit your title so it displays as *Senior Travel Consultant*.
   c. Select your name and title, click the Quick Parts button, point to *AutoText*, and then click the *Save Selection to AutoText Gallery* option.
   d. At the Create New Building Block dialog box, type the original name (your last name followed by *Title*).
   e. Click OK.
   f. At the message asking if you want to redefine the building block entry, click Yes.
   g. With your name and title selected, press the Delete key to remove them from the document.

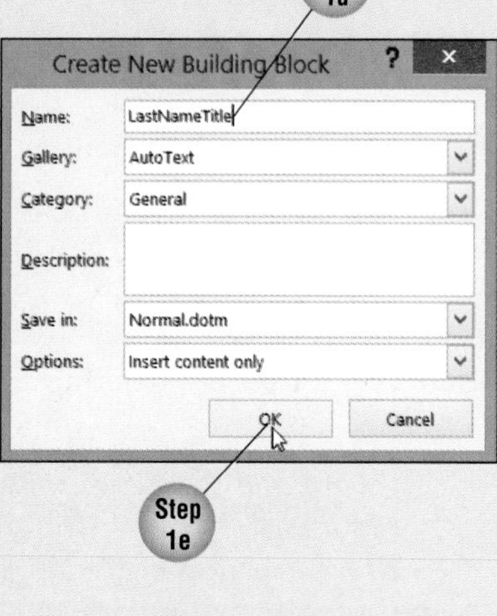

2. Since most of the correspondence you send to Pacific Sky Cruise Lines is addressed to Jody Lancaster, you decide to include her name at the beginning of the company name and address by completing the following steps:
   a. Click the INSERT tab, click the Quick Parts button, point to *AutoText*, and then click the Pacific Sky Cruise Lines name and address building block at the side menu.
   b. Type the name **Mrs. Jody Lancaster** above the name of the cruise line.
   c. Select the name, company name, and address.
   d. Click the Quick Parts button, point to *AutoText*, and then click the *Save Selection to AutoText Gallery* option.
   e. At the Create New Building Block dialog box, type the original name (your last name followed by *PacificSkyAddress*).
   f. Click OK.
   g. At the message asking if you want to redefine the building block entry, click Yes.

Step 2b
Mrs. Jody Lancaster
Pacific Sky Cruise Lines
120 Montgomery Boulevard
Los Angeles, CA 97032

3. Close the document without saving it.
4. Create a business letter by completing the following steps:
   a. Press Ctrl + N to display a blank document, click the *No Spacing* style in the Styles group on the HOME tab, and then change the font to Candara.
   b. At the blank document, insert the Family Adventure Vacations letterhead building block as a page header.
   c. Press the Enter key twice, type today's date, and then press the Enter key four times.
   d. Insert the building block that includes Jody Lancaster's name as well as the cruise line name and address.
   e. Press the Enter key and then insert the file named **PacificSkyLetter02.docx** located in the WL2C3 folder on your storage medium. ***Hint: Do this with the Object button in the Text group on the INSERT tab.***
   f. Type **Sincerely,** and then press the Enter key four times.

g. Insert the building block that contains your name and title.
h. Press the Enter key and then type WL2-C3-P4-PSLtr.docx.
i. Insert the footer building block you created.
j. Double-click in the document to make the document active.
5. Save the completed letter and name it **WL2-C3-P4-PSLtr**.
6. Print and then close **WL2-C3-P4-PSLtr.docx**.

Deleting Building Blocks

If you no longer use a building block you created, consider deleting it. To do this, display the Building Blocks Organizer dialog box, click the building block you want to delete, and then click the Delete button. At the message asking if you are sure you want to delete the selected building block, click Yes.

Another method for deleting a custom building block is to right-click the building block at the drop-down gallery and then click the *Organize and Delete* option at the shortcut menu. This displays the Building Blocks Organizer dialog box with the building block selected. Click the Delete button that displays at the bottom of the dialog box and then click Yes at the confirmation message box.

Quick Steps

Delete a Building Block
1. Display Building Blocks Organizer dialog box.
2. Click building block.
3. Click Delete button.
4. Click Yes.
5. Close dialog box.

OR

1. Display desired button drop-down gallery.
2. Right-click building block.
3. Click *Organize and Delete* option.
4. Click Delete button.
5. Click Yes.
6. Close dialog box.

Project 4b **Deleting Building Blocks** **Part 2 of 2**

1. At a blank document, delete the FAVLetterhead building block (preceded by your last name) by completing the following steps:
   a. Click the INSERT tab and then click the Quick Parts button in the Text group.
   b. Right-click the FAVLetterhead building block (preceded by your last name) and then click *Organize and Delete* at the shortcut menu.
   c. At the Building Blocks Organizer dialog box with the building block selected, click the Delete button.
   d. At the message that displays asking if you are sure you want to delete the selected building block, click Yes.
   e. Close the Building Blocks Organizer dialog box.

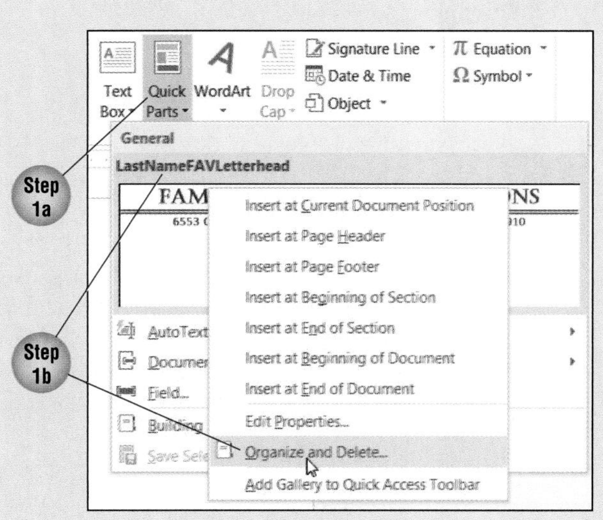

2. Delete the PacificSkyAddress building block (preceded by your last name) by completing the following steps:
   a. Click the Quick Parts button, point to *AutoText*, and then right-click the PacificSkyAddress building block (preceded by your last name).
   b. Click *Organize and Delete* at the shortcut menu.
   c. At the Building Blocks Organizer dialog box with the building block selected, click the Delete button.
   d. At the message asking if you are sure you want to delete the selected building block, click Yes.
   e. Close the Building Blocks Organizer dialog box.
3. Complete steps similar to those in Step 2 to delete the Title building block (preceded by your last name).
4. Delete the custom footer (located in the Footer gallery) by completing the following steps:
   a. Click the Footer button on the INSERT tab.
   b. Scroll down the drop-down gallery to display your custom footer.
   c. Right-click your footer and then click *Organize and Delete* at the shortcut menu.
   d. At the Building Blocks Organizer dialog box with the building block selected, click the Delete button.
   e. At the message asking if you are sure you want to delete the selected building block, click Yes.
   f. Close the Building Blocks Organizer dialog box.

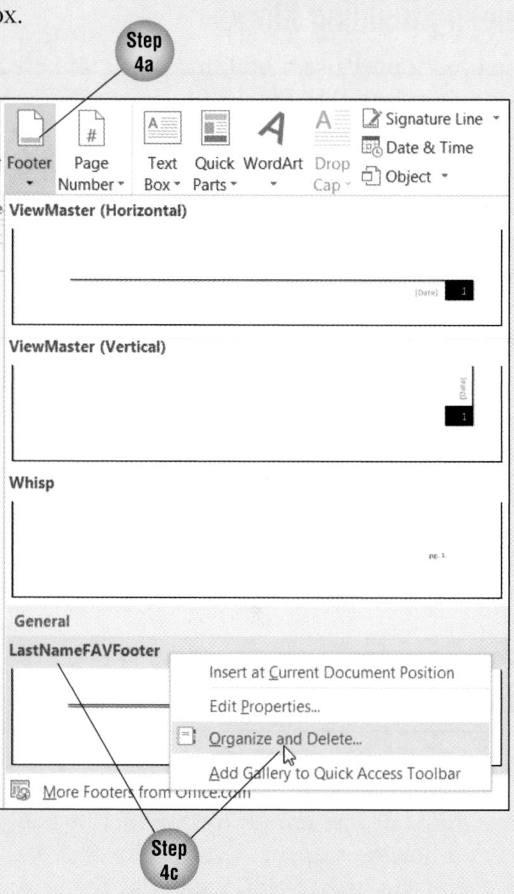

5. Delete the custom text box (located in the Text Box gallery) by completing the following steps:
   a. Click the Text Box button in the Text group on the INSERT tab.
   b. Scroll down the drop-down gallery to display your custom text box.
   c. Right-click your text box and then click *Organize and Delete* at the shortcut menu.
   d. At the Building Blocks Organizer dialog box with the building block selected, click the Delete button.
   e. At the message asking if you are sure you want to delete the selected building block, click Yes.
   f. Close the Building Blocks Organizer dialog box.
6. Close the document without saving it.

Project 5 Insert Document Properties and Fields in an Agreement Document

3 Parts

You will open a testing agreement document and then insert and update document properties and fields.

Inserting Document Properties

If you click the Quick Parts button on the INSERT tab and then point to *Document Property* at the drop-down list, a side menu displays with document property options. Click an option at this side menu and a document property placeholder is inserted in the document. Type the desired text in the placeholder.

If you insert a document property placeholder in multiple locations in a document, updating one of the placeholders will automatically update all occurrences of that placeholder in the document. For example, in Project 5a, you will insert a Company document property placeholder in six locations in a document. You will then change the content in the first occurrence of the placeholder and the remaining placeholders will update to reflect the change.

When you click the FILE tab, the Info backstage area displays containing information about the document. Document properties display at the right side of the Info backstage area and include information such as the document size, number of pages, title, and comments. Some of the document properties that you insert with the Quick Parts button will display at the Info backstage area.

Project 5a Inserting Document Property Placeholders

Part 1 of 3

1. Open **TestAgrmnt.docx** and then save the document and name it **WL2-C3-P5-TestAgrmnt**.
2. Select the first occurrence of *FP* in the document (located in the first line of text after the title) and then insert a document property placeholder by completing the following steps:
   a. Click the INSERT tab, click the Quick Parts button in the Text group, point to *Document Property*, and then click *Company* at the side menu.
   b. Type **Frontier Productions** in the Company placeholder.
   c. Press the Right Arrow key to move the insertion point outside the Company placeholder.

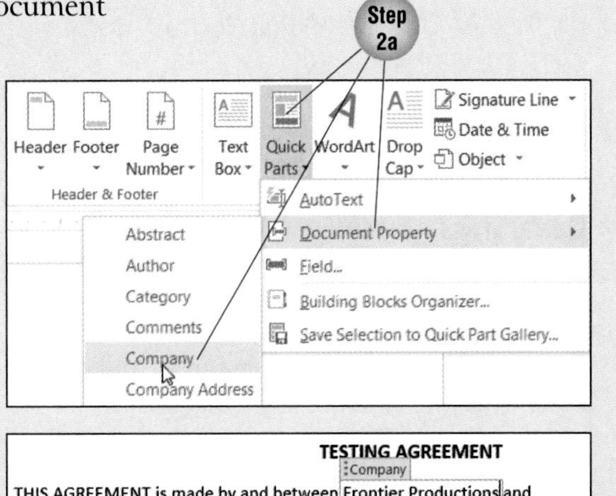

3. Select each remaining occurrence of *FP* in the document (it appears five more times) and insert the Company document property placeholder. (The company name, *Frontier Productions,* will automatically be inserted in the Company placeholder.)

4. Press Ctrl + End to move the insertion point to the end of the document and then insert a Comments document property placeholder by completing the following steps:
   a. Click the Quick Parts button, point to *Document Property*, and then click *Comments* at the side menu.
   b. Type **First Draft** in the Comments placeholder.
   c. Press the Right Arrow key.
   d. Press Shift + Enter.
5. Click the FILE tab, make sure the *Info* option is selected, and then notice that the comment you typed in the Comments document property placeholder displays at the right side of the backstage area. Click the Back button to display the document.

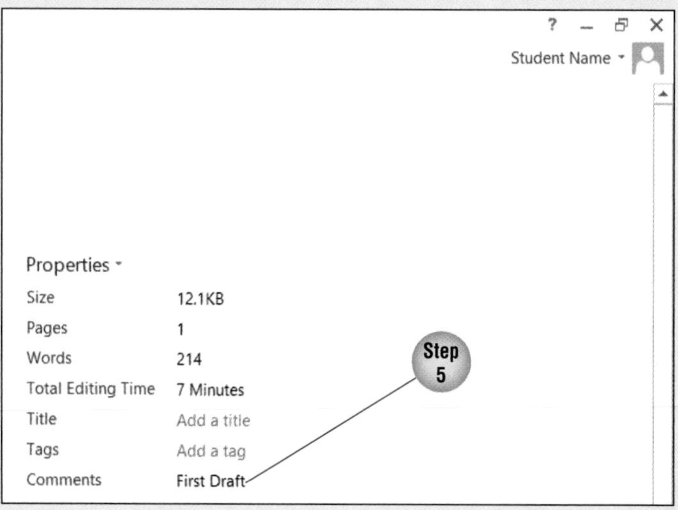

6. Save and then print **WL2-C3-P5-TestAgrmnt.docx**.
7. Click in the first occurrence of the company name *Frontier Productions* and then click the Company placeholder tab. (This selects the Company placeholder.)
8. Type **Frontier Video Productions**.
9. Press the Right Arrow key. (Notice that the other occurrences of the Company document property placeholder are automatically updated to reflect the new name.)
10. Save **WL2-C3-P5-TestAgrmnt.docx**.

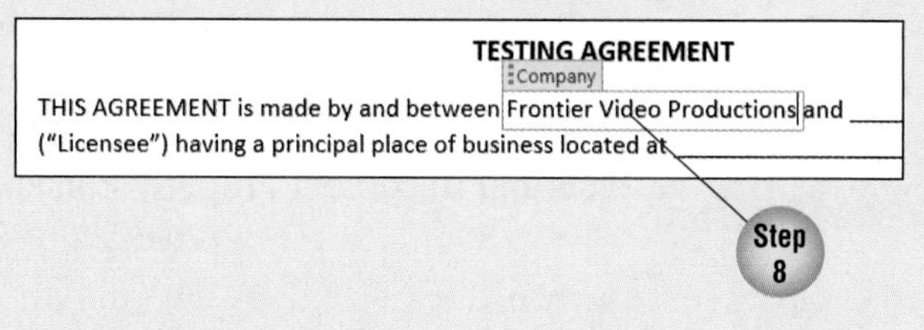

Inserting Fields

Quick Steps

Insert a Field

1. Click INSERT tab.
2. Click Quick Parts button.
3. Click *Field* at drop-down list.
4. Click desired field.
5. Click OK.

Fields are placeholders for data that varies and main documents that are merged with data source files. You have inserted fields in a main document, inserted the date and time field, inserted page numbering in a document, and so on. Word provides buttons for many of the types of fields that you may want to insert into a document as well as options at the Field dialog box, shown in Figure 3.9. This dialog box contains a list of all available fields. Just as the Building Blocks Organizer dialog box is a central location for building blocks, the Field dialog box is a central location for fields. To display the Field dialog box, click the INSERT tab, click the Quick Parts button in the Text group, and then click *Field* at the drop-down list. At the Field dialog box, click the desired field in the *Field names* list box and then click OK.

Figure 3.9 Field Dialog Box

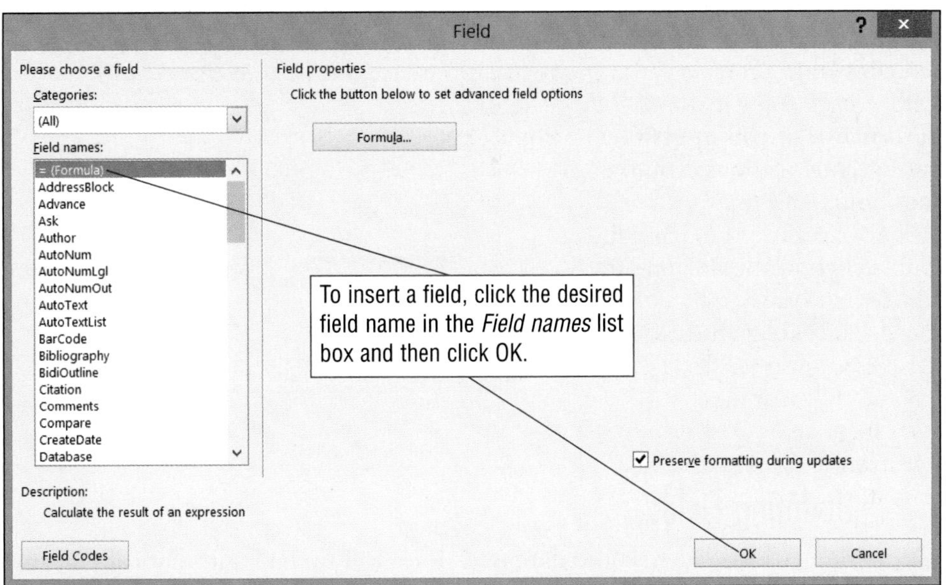

Project 5b Inserting Fields

Part 2 of 3

1. With **WL2-C3-P5-TestAgrmnt.docx** open, press Ctrl + End and then insert a field that inserts the current file name by completing the following steps:
   a. Click the INSERT tab, click the Quick Parts button in the Text group, and then click *Field* at the drop-down list.
   b. At the Field dialog box, scroll down the *Field names* list box and then double-click *FileName*. (This inserts the current file name in the document and closes the Field dialog box.)
2. Insert a field that provides the date the file is printed by completing the following steps:
   a. Press Shift + Enter.
   b. Click the Quick Parts button and then click *Field* at the drop-down list.
   c. At the Field dialog box, scroll down the *Field names* list box and then double-click *PrintDate*. (The date and time will display with zeros. The correct date and time will be filled in when you send the document to the printer.)
3. Insert a header and then insert a field in the header by completing the following steps:
   a. Click the Header button in the Header & Footer group and then click *Edit Header* at the drop-down list.
   b. In the header pane, press the Tab key twice. (This moves the insertion point to the right tab at the right margin.)
   c. Click the INSERT tab, click the Quick Parts button in the Text group, and then click *Field* at the drop-down list.

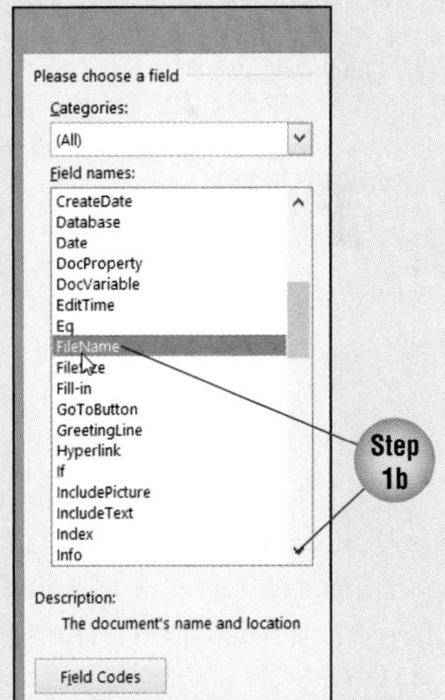

d. At the Field dialog box, scroll down the *Field names* list box and then click once on *Date*.
e. In the *Date formats* list box, click the format that will insert the date in figures followed by the time (hours and minutes).
f. Click OK to close the dialog box.
g. Double-click in the document.

4. Save and then print **WL2-C3-P5-TestAgrmnt.docx**.

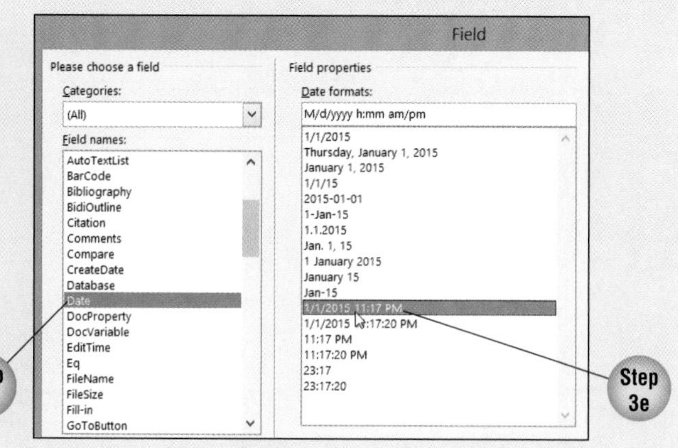

Updating Fields

Quick Steps

Update a Field
1. Click field.
2. Click Update tab.

OR
1. Click field.
2. Press F9.

OR
1. Right-click field.
2. Click *Update Field*.

Some fields, such as the date and time, will update automatically when you open the document. For example, open **WL2-C3-P5-TestAgrmnt.docx** and the time in the header is automatically updated. You can manually update a field by clicking the field and then clicking the Update tab (if possible; some fields do not have an Update tab), by clicking the field and then pressing F9, or by right-clicking the field and then clicking *Update Field* at the shortcut menu. You can also update all of the fields in a document (except headers, footers, and text boxes) by pressing Ctrl + A to select the document and then pressing F9.

Project 5c **Updating Fields** **Part 3 of 3**

1. With **WL2-C3-P5-TestAgrmnt.docx** open, update the time in the header by completing the following steps:
   a. Double-click the header.
   b. Click the date and time and then click the Update tab.
   c. Double-click in the document.
2. Save the document and name it **WL2-C3-P5-FVPAgrmnt**.
3. Press Ctrl + A to select the entire document and then press F9.
4. Save, print, and then close **WL2-C3-P5-FVPAgrmnt.docx**.

Project 6 Minimize the Ribbon and Customize the Quick Access Toolbar and Ribbon — 3 Parts

You will open a document and then minimize the ribbon, customize the Quick Access toolbar by adding and removing buttons, and customize the ribbon by inserting a new tab.

Displaying Ribbon Options

Control how much of the ribbon displays on the screen with the Ribbon Display Options button located in the upper right corner of the screen. Click this button and a drop-down list displays with options for hiding the ribbon, showing only the tabs, or showing tabs and commands. You can also turn off the display of the ribbon by clicking the Collapse the Ribbon button located above the vertical scroll bar or by pressing the keyboard shortcut Ctrl + F1. Redisplay the ribbon by double-clicking any tab or by pressing Ctrl + F1.

Ribbon Display Options

Collapse the Ribbon

Customizing the Quick Access Toolbar

The Quick Access toolbar contains buttons for some of the most commonly performed tasks. By default, the toolbar contains the Save, Undo, and Redo buttons. You can easily add or remove basic buttons to or from the Quick Access toolbar with options at the Customize Quick Access Toolbar drop-down list. Display this list by clicking the Customize Quick Access Toolbar button that displays at the right side of the toolbar. Insert a check mark before each button that you want displayed on the toolbar and remove the check mark from each button that you do not want to appear.

The Customize Quick Access Toolbar button drop-down list includes an option for moving the location of the Quick Access toolbar. By default, the Quick Access toolbar is positioned above the ribbon. To move the toolbar below the ribbon, click the *Show Below the Ribbon* option at the drop-down list.

You can add buttons or commands from a tab to the Quick Access toolbar. To do this, click the tab, right-click the desired button or command, and then click *Add to Quick Access Toolbar* at the shortcut menu.

Quick Steps

Customize the Quick Access Toolbar

1. Click Customize Quick Access Toolbar button.
2. Insert check mark before each desired button.
3. Remove check mark before each undesired button.

Customize Quick Access Toolbar

Project 6a **Changing Ribbon Options and Customizing the Quick Access Toolbar** **Part 1 of 3**

1. Open **InterfaceApps.docx** and then save the document and name it **WL2-C3-P6-InterfaceApps**.
2. Collapse the ribbon by clicking the Collapse the Ribbon button that displays above the vertical scroll bar.
3. Double-click a tab to redisplay the ribbon.
4. Hide the ribbon by clicking the Ribbon Display Options button in the upper right corner of the screen and then clicking *Auto-hide Ribbon* at the drop-down list.
5. Redisplay the ribbon by clicking the Ribbon Display Options button and then clicking *Show Tabs and Commands* at the drop-down list.
6. Add the New button to the Quick Access toolbar by clicking the Customize Quick Access Toolbar button that displays at the right of the toolbar and then clicking *New* at the drop-down list.
7. Add the Open button to the Quick Access toolbar by clicking the Customize Quick Access Toolbar button that displays at the right of the toolbar and then clicking *Open* at the drop-down list.
8. Click the New button on the Quick Access toolbar. (This displays a new blank document.)

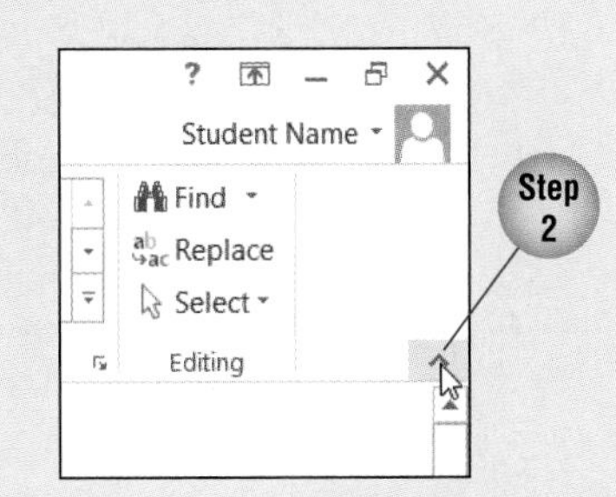

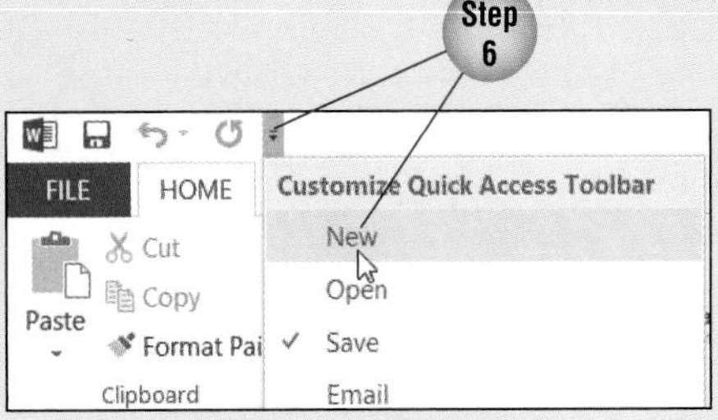

9. Close the document.
10. Click the Open button on the Quick Access toolbar to display the Open backstage area.
11. Press the Esc key to return to the document.
12. Move the Quick Access toolbar by clicking the Customize Quick Access Toolbar button and then clicking *Show Below the Ribbon* at the drop-down list.
13. Move the Quick Access toolbar back to the default position by clicking the Customize Quick Access Toolbar button and then clicking *Show Above the Ribbon* at the drop-down list.
14. Add the Margins and Themes buttons to the Quick Access toolbar by completing the following steps:
    a. Click the PAGE LAYOUT tab.
    b. Right-click the Margins button in the Page Setup group and then click *Add to Quick Access Toolbar* at the shortcut menu.
    c. Click the DESIGN tab.
    d. Right-click the Themes button in the Themes group and then click *Add to Quick Access Toolbar* at the shortcut menu.
15. Change the top margin by completing the following steps:
    a. Click the Margins button on the Quick Access toolbar and then click *Custom Margins* at the drop-down list.
    b. At the Page Setup dialog box, change the top margin to 1.5 inches and then click OK.
16. Change the theme by clicking the Themes button on the Quick Access toolbar and then clicking *View* at the drop-down list.
17. Create a screenshot of the Quick Access toolbar by completing the following steps:
    a. Click the New button on the Quick Access toolbar. (This displays a new blank document.)
    b. Click the INSERT tab, click the Screenshot button in the Illustrations group, and then click *Screen Clipping* at the drop-down list.
    c. In a few moments, the **WL2-C3-P6-InterfaceApps** document displays in a dimmed manner. Using the mouse, drag down and to the right from the upper left corner of the screen to capture the Quick Access toolbar and then release the mouse button.
    d. With the screenshot image inserted in the document, print the document and then close the document without saving it.
18. Save **WL2-C3-P6-InterfaceApps.docx**.

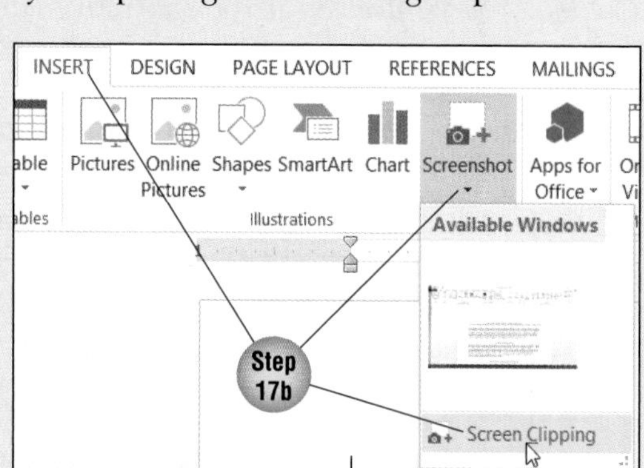

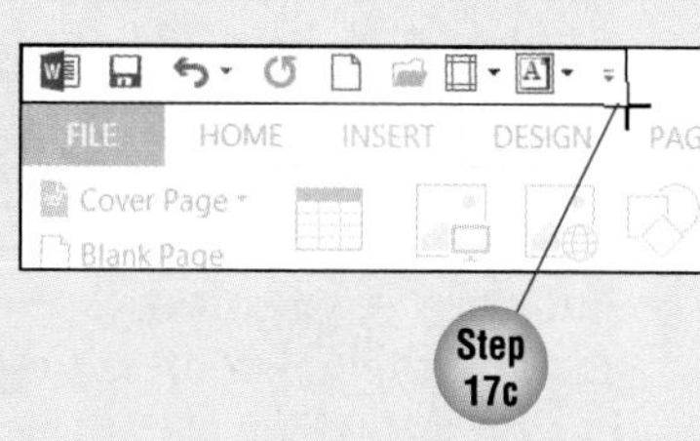

The Customize Quick Access Toolbar button drop-down list contains 11 of the most commonly used buttons. You can, however, insert many other buttons on the toolbar. To display the buttons available, click the Customize Quick Access Toolbar button and then click *More Commands* at the drop-down list. This displays the Word Options dialog box with *Quick Access Toolbar* selected in the left panel, as shown in Figure 3.10. Another method for displaying this dialog box is to click the FILE tab, click *Options*, and then click *Quick Access Toolbar* in the left panel of the Word Options dialog box.

To reset the Quick Access toolbar to the default (Save, Undo, and Redo buttons), click the Reset button that displays near the bottom of the dialog box. At the message asking if you are sure you want to restore the Quick Access toolbar shared between all documents to its default contents, click Yes.

You can customize the Quick Access toolbar for all documents or for a specific document. To customize the toolbar for the currently open document, display the Word Options dialog box with *Quick Access Toolbar* selected, click the down-pointing arrow at the right side of the *Customize Quick Access Toolbar* option, and then click the *For (document name)* option where the name of the currently open document displays.

Quick Steps

Add Buttons to the Quick Access Toolbar from the Word Options Dialog Box

1. Click Customize Quick Access Toolbar button.
2. Click *More Commands* at drop-down list.
3. Click desired command at left list box.
4. Click Add button.
5. Click OK.

Figure 3.10 Word Options Dialog Box with Quick Access Toolbar Selected

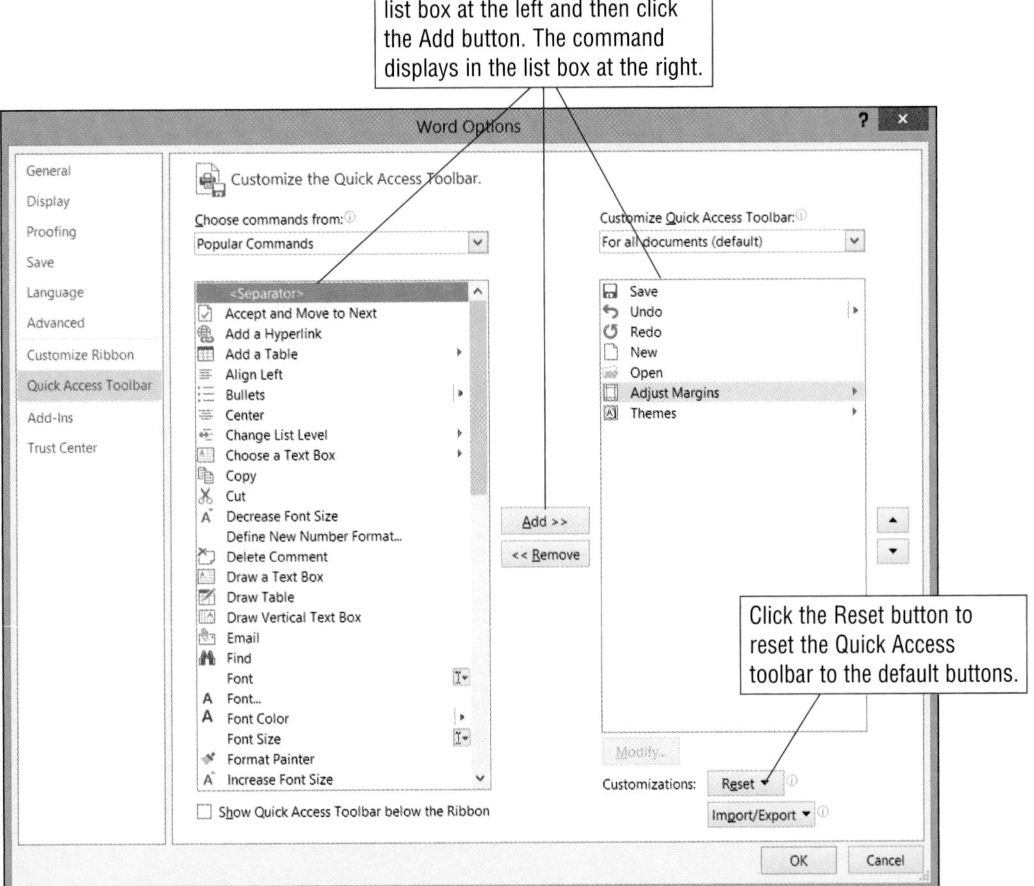

The *Choose commands from* option has a default setting of *Popular Commands*. At this setting, the list box below the option displays only a portion of all of the commands available to insert as a button on the Quick Access toolbar. To display all of the commands available, click the down-pointing arrow at the right side of the *Choose commands from* option box and then click *All Commands*. The drop-down list also contains options for specifying commands that are not currently available on the ribbon, as well as commands on the FILE tab and various other tabs.

To add a button, click the desired command in the list box at the left side of the commands list box and then click the Add button that displays between the two list boxes. Continue adding all of the desired buttons and then click OK to close the dialog box.

Project 6b Inserting and Removing Buttons from the Quick Access Toolbar — Part 2 of 3

1. With **WL2-C3-P6-InterfaceApps.docx** open, reset the Quick Access toolbar by completing the following steps:
   a. Click the Customize Quick Access Toolbar button that displays at the right of the Quick Access toolbar and then click *More Commands* at the drop-down list.
   b. At the Word Options dialog box, click the Reset button that displays near the bottom of the dialog box and then click *Reset only Quick Access Toolbar* at the drop-down list.
   c. At the message asking if you are sure you want to restore the Quick Access toolbar shared between all documents to its default contents, click Yes.
   d. Click OK to close the dialog box.

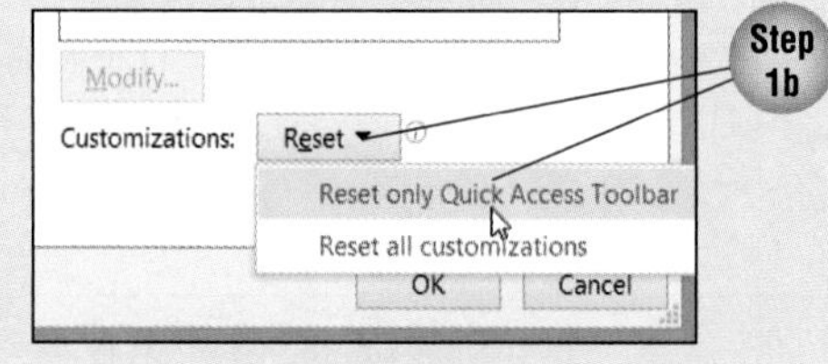

2. Insert buttons on the Quick Access toolbar for the currently open document by completing the following steps:
   a. Click the Customize Quick Access Toolbar button and then click *More Commands*.
   b. At the Word Options dialog box, click the down-pointing arrow at the right of the *Customize Quick Access Toolbar* option and then click *For WL2-C3-P6-InterfaceApps.docx* at the drop-down list.
   c. Click the down-pointing arrow at the right of the *Choose commands from* option box and then click *All Commands*.
   d. Scroll down the list box and then click the second *Close* command (the option preceded by a Close icon). (Commands are listed in alphabetical order.)
   e. Click the Add button that displays between the two list boxes.
   f. Scroll up the list box and then click *Add a Footer*.

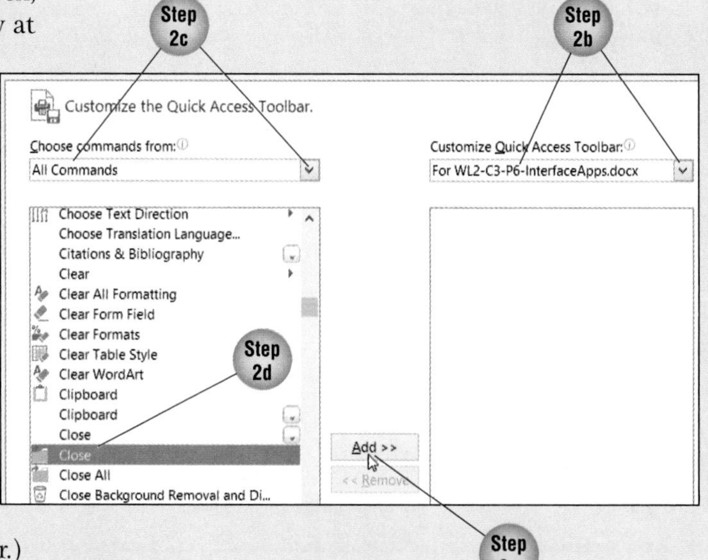

g. Click the Add button.
h. Click OK to close the dialog box.
i. Check the Quick Access toolbar and notice that the two buttons now display along with the default buttons.

3. Insert a footer by completing the following steps:
   a. Click the Footer button on the Quick Access toolbar.
   b. Click *Integral* at the drop-down list.
   c. Select the name that displays in the footer and then type your first and last names.
   d. Double-click in the document.
4. Save and then print **WL2-C3-P6-InterfaceApps.docx**.
5. Close the document by clicking the Close button on the Quick Access toolbar.

Customizing the Ribbon

In addition to customizing the Quick Access toolbar, you can customize the ribbon by creating a new tab and inserting groups with buttons on the new tab. To customize the ribbon, click the FILE tab and then click *Options*. At the Word Options dialog box, click *Customize Ribbon* in the left panel and the dialog box displays as shown in Figure 3.11.

Figure 3.11 Word Options Dialog Box with Customize Ribbon Selected

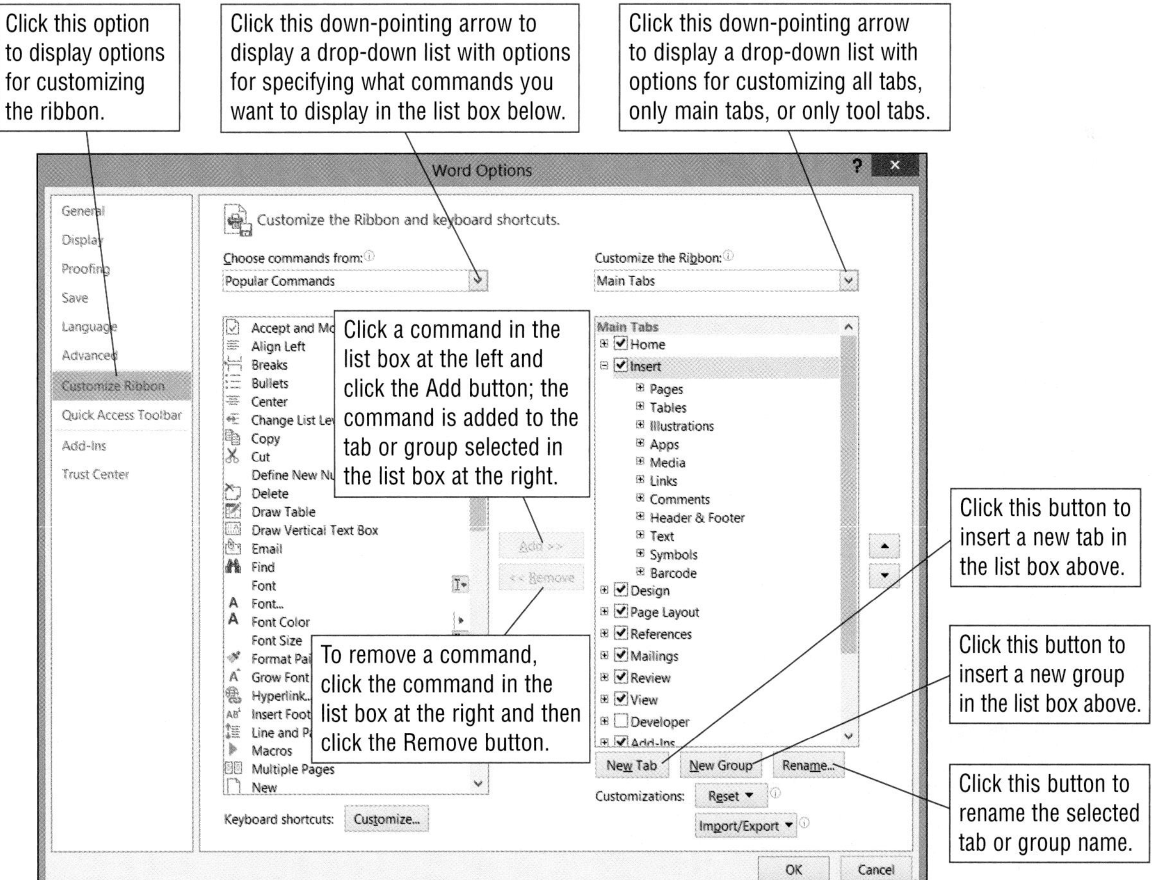
Click this option to display options for customizing the ribbon.
Click this down-pointing arrow to display a drop-down list with options for specifying what commands you want to display in the list box below.
Click this down-pointing arrow to display a drop-down list with options for customizing all tabs, only main tabs, or only tool tabs.
Word Options
Customize the Ribbon and keyboard shortcuts.
Choose commands from:
Popular Commands
Customize the Ribbon:
Main Tabs
Click a command in the list box at the left and click the Add button; the command is added to the tab or group selected in the list box at the right.
To remove a command, click the command in the list box at the right and then click the Remove button.
Click this button to insert a new tab in the list box above.
Click this button to insert a new group in the list box above.
Click this button to rename the selected tab or group name.

At the *Choose commands from* drop-down list, you can choose to display only popular commands, which is the default, or you can choose to display all commands, commands not on the ribbon, and all tabs or commands on the FILE tab, main tabs, tool tabs, and custom tabs and groups. The commands in the list box vary depending on the option you select at the *Choose commands from* option drop-down list. Click the down-pointing arrow at the right of the Customize the Ribbon option and a drop-down list displays with options for customizing all of the tabs, only the main tabs, or only tool tabs. By default, *Main Tabs* is selected.

Creating a New Tab

Add a command to an existing tab or create a new tab and then add commands in groups on the new tab. To create a new tab, click the tab name in the list box at the right side of the dialog box that you want to precede the new tab and then click the New Tab button that displays at the bottom of the list box. This inserts a new tab in the list box along with a new group below the new tab (see Figure 3.11). Move the new tab up or down in the list box by clicking the new tab and then clicking the Move Up or Move Down button. Both buttons display at the right of the list box.

Renaming a Tab and Group

Rename a tab by clicking the tab in the list box and then clicking the Rename button that displays below the list box at the right. At the Rename dialog box, type the desired name for the tab and then click OK. You can also display the Rename dialog box by right-clicking the tab name and then clicking *Rename* at the shortcut menu.

Complete similar steps to rename the group. When you click the group name and then click the Rename button (or right-click the group name and then click *Rename* at the shortcut menu), a Rename dialog box displays, containing a variety of symbols. Use the symbols to identify new buttons in the group, rather than the group name.

Adding Commands to a Tab Group

Add commands to a tab by clicking the group name on the tab, clicking the desired command in the list box at the left, and then clicking the Add button that displays between the two list boxes. Remove commands in a similar manner. Click the command you want to remove from the tab group and then click the Remove button that displays between the two list boxes.

Resetting the Ribbon

If you have customized the ribbon by adding tabs and groups, you can remove all of the customizations and return to the original ribbon by clicking the Reset button that displays below the list box at the right side of the dialog box. When you click the Reset button, a drop-down list displays with two options: *Reset only selected Ribbon tab* and *Reset all customizations*. If you click the *Reset all customizations* option, a message displays asking if you want to delete all ribbon and Quick Access toolbar customizations for this program. At this message, click Yes to reset all of the customizations to the ribbon.

Project 6c Customizing the Ribbon

Part 3 of 3

1. Open **WL2-C3-P6-InterfaceApps.docx** and then add a new tab and group by completing the following steps:
   a. Click the FILE tab and then click *Options*.
   b. At the Word Options dialog box, click *Customize Ribbon* in the left panel.
   c. Click *View* that displays in the list box at the right side of the dialog box. (Do not click the check box before *View*.)
   d. Click the New Tab button located below the list box. (This inserts a new tab below *View*.)

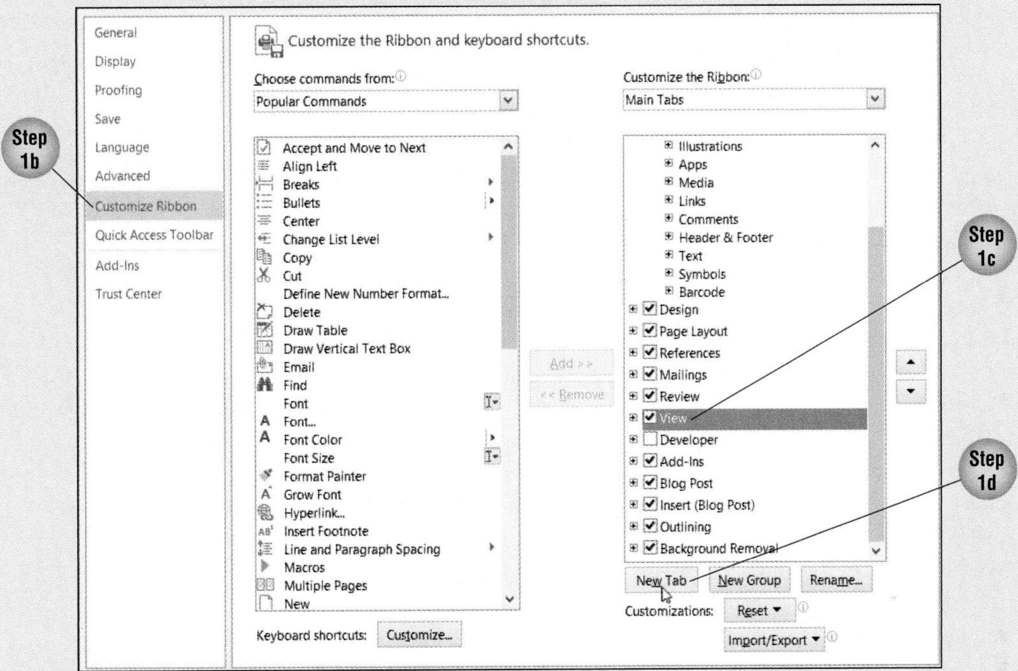

2. Rename the tab and group by completing the following steps:
   a. Click *New Tab (Custom)*. (Do not click the check box.)
   b. Click the Rename button that displays below the list box.
   c. At the Rename dialog box, type your initials and then click OK.
   d. Click *New Group (Custom)* that displays below your initials tab.
   e. Click the Rename button.
   f. At the Rename dialog box, type **IP Movement** and then click OK. (Use *IP* to stand for *insertion point*.)

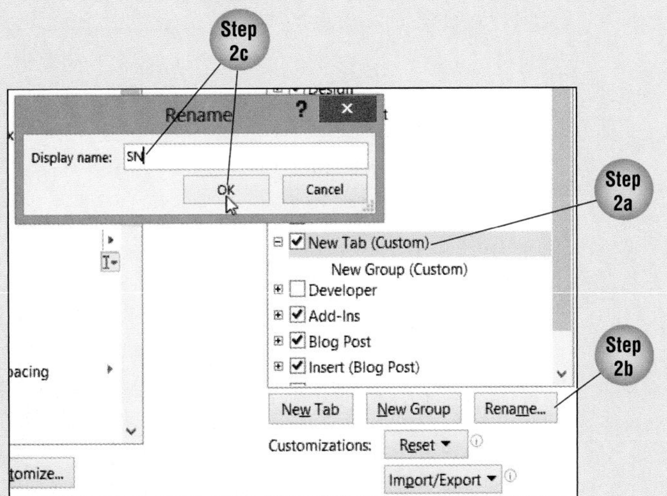

3. Add buttons to the IP Movement (Custom) group by completing the following steps:
   a. Click *IP Movement (Custom)* in the list box at the right side.
   b. Click the down-pointing arrow at the right of the *Choose commands from* option box and then click *Commands Not in the Ribbon* at the drop-down list.
   c. Scroll down the list box at the left side of the dialog box (the list displays alphabetically), click the *End of Document* command, and then click the Add button that displays between the two list boxes. (This inserts the command below the *IP Movement (Custom)* group name.) 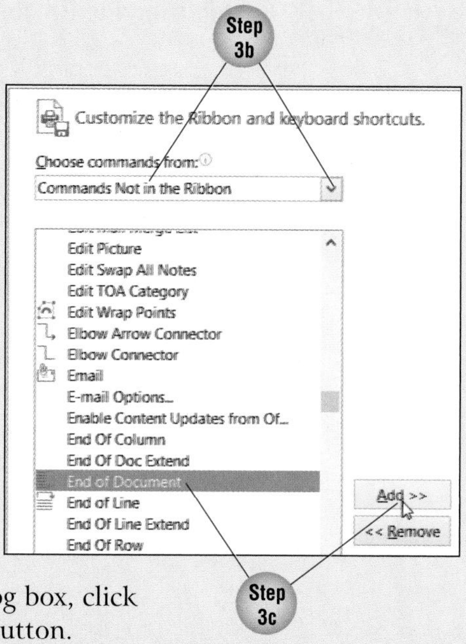
   d. With the *End of Line* command selected in the list box at the left side of the dialog box, click the Add button.
   e. Scroll down the list box at the left side of the dialog box, click the *Page Down* command, and then click the Add button.
   f. Click the *Page Up* command in the list box and then click the Add button.
   g. Scroll down the list box, click the *Start of Document* command, and then click the Add button.
   h. With the *Start of Line* command selected in the list box, click the Add button.
4. Click OK to close the Word Options dialog box.
5. Move the insertion point in the document by completing the following steps:
   a. Click the tab containing your initials.
   b. Click the End of Document button in the IP Movement group on the tab.
   c. Click the Start of Document button in the IP Movement group.
   d. Click the End of Line button.
   e. Click the Start of Line button. 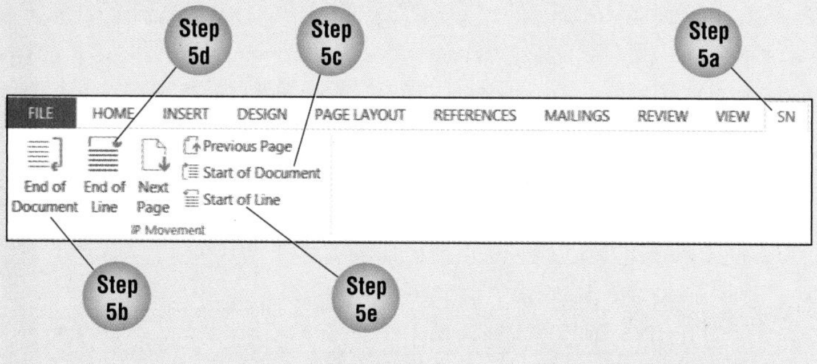
6. Create a screenshot of the ribbon with the tab containing your initials the active tab by completing the following steps:
   a. Make sure your tab is active and then press Ctrl + N to display a new blank document.
   b. Click the INSERT tab, click the Screenshot button in the Illustrations group, and then click *Screen Clipping* at the drop-down list.
   c. In a few moments, the **WL2-C3-P6-InterfaceApps.docx** document displays in a dimmed manner. Using the mouse, drag from the upper left corner of the screen down and to the right to capture the Quick Access toolbar and the buttons on the tab containing your initials, and then release the mouse button.
   d. With the screenshot image inserted in the document, print the document and then close the document without saving it.

7. Reset the Quick Access toolbar and ribbon by completing the following steps:
   a. Click the FILE tab and then click *Options*.
   b. At the Word Options dialog box, click *Customize Ribbon* in the left panel.
   c. Click the Reset button that displays below the list box at the right side of the dialog box and then click *Reset all customizations* at the drop-down list.

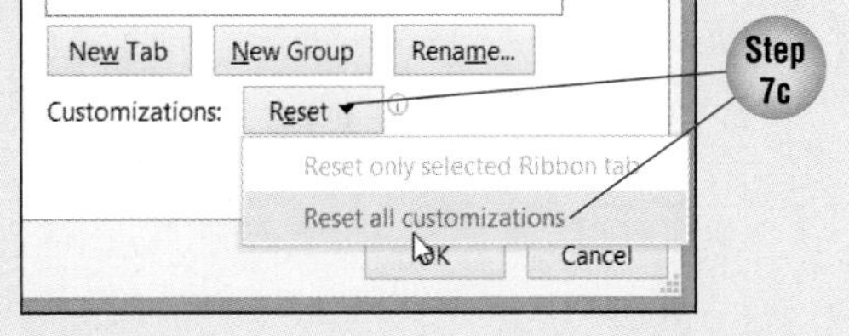

   d. At the message asking if you want to delete all ribbon and Quick Access toolbar customizations, click Yes.
   e. Click OK to close the Word Options dialog box. (The buttons you added to the Quick Access toolbar will display while this document is open.)
8. Save and then close **WL2-C3-P6-InterfaceApps.docx**.

Chapter Summary

- You can add words to AutoCorrect during a spelling check and at the AutoCorrect dialog box. Display the AutoCorrect dialog box by clicking the FILE tab, clicking *Options*, clicking *Proofing*, and then clicking the AutoCorrect Options button.
- Display the AutoCorrect Exceptions dialog box by clicking the Exceptions button at the AutoCorrect dialog box with the AutoCorrect tab selected. Specify AutoCorrect exceptions at this dialog box.
- Use the AutoCorrect Options button that displays when you hover the mouse over corrected text to change corrected text back to the original spelling, stop automatically correcting specific text, or display the AutoCorrect dialog box.
- When typing text, control what Word formats automatically with options at the AutoCorrect dialog box with the AutoFormat As You Type tab selected.
- Word provides a number of predesigned building blocks that you can use to help build a document.
- Insert building blocks at the Building Blocks Organizer dialog box. Display the dialog box by clicking the Quick Parts button on the INSERT tab and then clicking *Building Blocks Organizer* at the drop-down list. Sort building blocks in the dialog box by clicking the desired column heading.
- You can save content as building blocks to specific galleries, such as the Text Box, Header, Footer, and Cover Page galleries.
- Save content to the AutoText gallery by selecting the content, clicking the INSERT tab, clicking the Quick Parts button, pointing to *AutoText*, and then clicking the *Save Selection to AutoText Gallery* option.
- Save content to the Quick Part gallery by selecting the content, clicking the INSERT tab, clicking the Quick Parts button, and then clicking *Save Selection to Quick Part Gallery* at the drop-down gallery.

- Insert a building block at the Building Blocks Organizer dialog box by displaying the dialog box, clicking the desired building block in the *Building blocks* list box, and then clicking the Insert button.
- Insert a custom building block from a gallery using a button by clicking the specific button (such as the Text Box, Header, Footer, or Cover Page button), scrolling down the drop-down gallery, and then clicking the custom building block that displays near the end of the gallery.
- Insert a custom building block saved to the AutoText gallery by clicking the INSERT tab, clicking the Quick Parts button, pointing to *AutoText*, and then clicking the desired building block at the side menu.
- Insert a custom building block saved to the Quick Part gallery by clicking the INSERT tab, clicking the Quick Parts button, and then clicking the desired building block at the drop-down list.
- Edit a building block with options at the Modify Building Block dialog box. Display this dialog box by displaying the Building Blocks Organizer dialog box, clicking the desired building block, and then clicking the Edit Properties button.
- Delete a building block at the Building Blocks Organizer dialog box by clicking the building block, clicking the Delete button, and then clicking Yes at the confirmation question.
- Insert a document property placeholder by clicking the INSERT tab, clicking the Quick Parts button, pointing to *Document Property*, and then clicking the desired option at the side menu.
- Fields are placeholders for data and can be inserted with options at the Field dialog box, which is a central location for all of the fields provided by Word. Display the Field dialog box by clicking the Quick Parts button and then clicking *Field*.
- Some fields in a document update automatically when you open the document or you can manually update a field by clicking the field and then clicking the Update tab, pressing F9, or right-clicking the field and then clicking *Update Field*.
- Control how much of the ribbon displays with options from the Ribbon Display Options button drop-down list. Click the Collapse the Ribbon button or press Ctrl + F1 to collapse/display the ribbon.
- Customize the Quick Access toolbar with options from the Customize Quick Access Toolbar button drop-down list and options at the Word Options dialog box with the *Quick Access Toolbar* selected.
- Add a button or command to the Quick Access toolbar by right-clicking the desired button or command and then clicking *Add to Quick Access Toolbar* at the shortcut menu.
- With options at the Word Options dialog box with *Quick Access Toolbar* selected, you can reset the Quick Access toolbar and display all of the options and buttons available for adding to the Quick Access toolbar. You can customize the Quick Access toolbar for all documents or for a specific document.
- With options at the Word Options dialog box with *Customize Ribbon* selected, you can rename a tab or group, add a command tab to a new group, remove a command from a tab group, and reset the ribbon.

Commands Review

FEATURE	RIBBON TAB, GROUP/OPTION	BUTTON, OPTION	KEYBOARD SHORTCUT
AutoCorrect dialog box	FILE, *Options*	*Proofing*, AutoCorrect Options	
Building Blocks Organizer dialog box	INSERT, Text	, *Building Blocks Organizer*	
Create New Building Block dialog box	INSERT, Text	, *Save Selection to Quick Part Gallery*	Alt + F3
collapse/display ribbon			Ctrl + F1
Document Property side menu	INSERT, Text	, *Document Property*	
Field dialog box	INSERT, Text	, *Field*	
Ribbon Display Options button			
Word Options dialog box	FILE, *Options*		

Concepts Check

Test Your Knowledge

Completion: In the space provided at the right, indicate the correct term, symbol, or command.

1. This feature corrects certain words automatically as you type them. ________________
2. Use this button, which displays when you hover the mouse pointer over corrected text, to change corrected text back to the original spelling. ________________
3. The Quick Parts button is located on this tab. ________________
4. This dialog box is a central location where you can view all of the predesigned building blocks. ________________
5. To save a text box as a building block, select the text box, click the INSERT tab, click the Text Box button, and then click this option at the drop-down gallery. ________________
6. With the Quick Parts button, you can save a custom building block in the Quick Part gallery or this gallery. ________________
7. Delete a building block at this dialog box. ________________
8. Complete these steps to display the Field dialog box. ________________

9. Manually update a field by pressing this key on the keyboard. ____________

10. Collapse the ribbon by clicking the Collapse the Ribbon button or using this keyboard shortcut. ____________

11. Add or remove basic buttons to or from the Quick Access toolbar with options at this drop-down list. ____________

12. This is the default setting for the *Choose commands from* option at the Word Options dialog box with *Quick Access Toolbar* selected in the left panel. ____________

13. Add a new tab at the Word Options dialog box with this option selected in the left panel. ____________

Skills Check Assess Your Performance

Assessment

1 FORMAT A HEALTH PLAN DOCUMENT WITH AUTOCORRECT AND BUILDING BLOCKS

1. Open **KLHPlan.docx** and then save the document and name it **WL2-C3-A1-KLHPlan**.
2. Add the following text to AutoCorrect:
   a. Insert *kl* in the *Replace* text box and insert *Key Life Health Plan* in the *With* text box.
   b. Insert *m* in the *Replace* text box and insert *medical* in the *With* text box.
3. With the insertion point positioned at the beginning of the document, type the text shown in Figure 3.12.
4. Make the following changes to the document:
   a. Apply the Heading 1 style to the title *Key Life Health Plan*.
   b. Apply the Heading 2 style to the four headings in the document.
   c. Apply the Lines (Simple) style set.
   d. Apply the Frame theme.
5. Insert the Ion (Dark) header building block.
6. Insert the Ion (Dark) footer building block. Click the *[DOCUMENT TITLE]* placeholder and then type **key life health plan**. Select the name that displays at the right side of the footer and then type your first and last names.
7. Decrease the value in the *Footer from Bottom* measurement box to *0.3"*.
8. Double-click in the document.
9. Press Ctrl + End to move the insertion point to the end of the document, press the Enter key, and then insert the *FileName* field.
10. Press Shift + Enter and then insert the *PrintDate* field.
11. Save and then print **WL2-C3-A1-KLHPlan.docx**.
12. Delete the two entries you made at the AutoCorrect dialog box.
13. Close **WL2-C3-A1-KLHPlan.docx**.

Figure 3.12 Assessment 1

> kl
>
> **How the Plan Works**
>
> When you enroll in the kl, you and each eligible family member select a plan option. A kl option includes a main m clinic, any affiliated satellite clinics, and designated hospitals. Family members may choose different m plan options and can easily change options.
>
> Some m plan options do not require you to choose a primary care physician. This means a member may self-refer for specialty care within that m plan option. However, members are encouraged to establish an ongoing relationship with a primary care physician and develop a valuable partnership in the management of their m care.
>
> kl provides coverage for emergency m services outside the service area. If the m emergency is not life threatening, call your primary care physician to arrange for care before going to an emergency facility. If you have a life-threatening emergency, go directly to the nearest appropriate facility. Any follow-up care to emergency m services must be coordinated within your plan option.

Assessment 2

FORMAT A PROPERTY PROTECTION ISSUES REPORT

1. Open **PropProIssues.docx** and then save the document and name it **WL2-C3-A2-PropProIssues**.
2. Make the following changes to the document:
   a. Select the entire document and then change the spacing after paragraphs to 6 points.
   b. Press Ctrl + Home and then press Ctrl + Enter to insert a hard page break.
   c. Apply the Heading 1 style to the two titles (*PROPERTY PROTECTION ISSUES* and *REFERENCES*).
   d. Apply the Heading 2 style to the three headings in the document.
   e. Apply the Banded theme.
   f. Apply the Paper theme colors.
   g. Format the paragraphs of text below the title *REFERENCES* using a hanging indent.
   h. Indent the second paragraph in the *Fair Use* section 0.5 inch from the left and right margins.
3. Press Ctrl + Home to move the insertion point to the beginning of the document and then insert the Automatic Table 2 table of contents building block.
4. Make sure the Heading 1 style is applied to the title *TABLE OF CONTENTS*.
5. Insert the Banded header building block, click the [DOCUMENT TITLE] placeholder, and then type **property protection issues**.
6. Insert the Banded footer building block.
7. Double-click in the document.

8. Press Ctrl + Home and then insert the Banded cover page building block with the following specifications:
   a. Select the title *PROPERTY PROTECTION ISSUES* and then change the font size to 28 points.
   b. Select the name that displays near the bottom of the cover page above the [COMPANY NAME] placeholder and then type your first and last names.
   c. Click the *[COMPANY NAME]* placeholder and then type woodland legal services.
   d. Select and then delete the [Company address] placeholder.
9. Press Ctrl + End to move the insertion point to the end of the document, press the Enter key, and then insert a field that will insert the file name.
10. Press Shift + Enter and then insert a field that will insert the current date and time.
11. Save, print, and then close **WL2-C3-A2-PropProIssues.docx**.

Assessment 3

CREATE BUILDING BLOCKS AND PREPARE AN AGREEMENT

1. Open **WLSCSFooter.docx**.
2. Select the entire document, save the selected text in a custom building block in the Footer gallery, and name the building block with your initials followed by *WLSCSFooter*. ***Hint: Use the Footer button to save the content to the Footer gallery.***
3. Close **WLSCSFooter.docx**.
4. Open **WLSCSHeading.docx**.
5. Select the entire document, save the selected text in a custom building block in the Quick Part gallery, and name the building block with your initials followed by *WLSCSHeading*.
6. Close **WLSCSHeading.docx**.
7. At a blank document, type the text shown in Figure 3.13. (Make sure you apply bold formatting to *Fees*).
8. Select the entire document, save the selected text in a custom building block in the AutoText gallery, and name the building block with your initials followed by *WLSCSFeesPara*.
9. Close the document without saving it.
10. At a blank document, create an agreement with the following specifications:
    a. Insert the custom building block in the Quick Part gallery that is named with your initials followed by *WLSCSHeading*.

Figure 3.13 Assessment 3

Fees: My hourly rate is $350, billed in one-sixth (1/6th) of an hour increments. All time spent on work performed, including meetings, telephone calls, correspondences, and emails, will be billed at the hourly rate set forth in this paragraph. Additional expenses such as out-of-pocket expenses for postage, courier fees, photocopying charges, long distance telephone charges, and search fees, will be charged at the hourly rate set forth in this paragraph.

b. Insert the custom building block in the AutoText gallery that is named with your initials followed by *WLSCSFeesPara*.
c. Insert the file named **WLSRepAgrmnt.docx** located in the WL2C3 folder on your storage medium. ***Hint: Use the*** **Text from File** ***option from the Object button arrow drop-down list.***
d. Insert the footer custom building block that is named with your initials followed by *WLSCSFooter*. ***Hint: Do this with the Footer button.***

11. Save the completed agreement and name it **WL2-C3-A3-WLSRepAgrmnt**.
12. Print and then close **WL2-C3-A3-WLSRepAgrmnt.docx**.
13. Press Ctrl + N to open a blank document.
14. Click the INSERT tab, click the Quick Parts button, and then point to *AutoText*.
15. Press the Print Screen button on your keyboard and then click in the document.
16. At the blank document, click the Paste button.
17. Print the document and then close it without saving it.

Assessment 4

CREATE A CUSTOM TAB AND GROUP

1. At a blank screen, create a new tab with the following specifications:
   a. Insert the new tab after the *View* tab option in the list box at the Word Options dialog box with *Customize Ribbon* selected.
   b. Rename the tab *C3* followed by your initials.
   c. Rename the custom group below your new tab as *File Management*.
   d. Change the *Choose commands from* option to *File Tab*.
   e. From the list box at the left side of the dialog box, add the following commands to the File Management group on the new tab: *Close*, *Open*, *Quick Print*, *Save As*, and *Save As Other Format*.
   f. Change the *Choose commands from* option to *Popular Commands*.
   g. From the list box at the left side of the dialog box, add the *New* command.
   h. Click OK to close the Word Options dialog box.
2. At the blank screen, click your new tab (the one that begins with *C3* and is followed by your initials).
3. Click the Open button in the File Management group on your new tab.
4. At the Open backstage area, click ***WL2-C3-A3-WLSRepAgrmnt.docx*** that displays at the beginning of the Recent Documents list.
5. Use the Save As button in the File Management group on the new tab to save the document and name it **WL2-C3-A4-WLSRepAgrmnt**.
6. Save the document in the Word 97-2003 format by completing the following steps:
   a. Make sure the new tab is active.
   b. Click the Save As button arrow. (This is the second Save As button in the File Management group on your new tab.)
   c. Click *Word 97-2003 Document* at the drop-down list.
   d. At the Save As dialog box with *Word 97-2003 Document (*.doc)* selected in the *Save as type* option box, type **WL2-C3-A4-WLSRA-Word97-2003Format** and then press the Enter key.
   e. Close the document by clicking the Close button in the File Management group on the new tab.

7. Click the Open button on the new tab and then click ***WL2-C3-A4-WLSRepAgrmnt.docx*** in the Recent Documents list.
8. Send the document to the printer by clicking the Quick Print button on the new tab.
9. Close the document by clicking the Close button on the new tab.
10. Click the New Blank Document button on the new tab.
11. At the blank document, click the New Blank Document button on the new tab. (You now have two blank documents open.)
12. Click the INSERT tab, click the Screenshot button, and then click *Screen Clipping* at the drop-down list.
13. When the first blank document displays in a dimmed manner, use the mouse to select the Quick Access toolbar and ribbon, including the new tab with the File Management group buttons you created.
14. Print the document containing the screen clipping and then close the document without saving it.
15. Display the Word Options dialog box with *Customize Ribbon* selected and then reset the ribbon back to the default.

Assessment 5

INSERT AN EQUATION BUILDING BLOCK

1. The Building Blocks Organizer dialog box contains a number of predesigned equations that you can insert in a document. At a blank document, display the Building Blocks Organizer dialog box and then insert one of the predesigned equations.
2. Select the equation and then click the EQUATION TOOLS DESIGN tab. Notice the groups of commands available for editing an equation.
3. Type the steps you followed to insert the equation and type a list of the groups available on the EQUATION TOOLS DESIGN tab and then delete the equation.
4. Save the document and name it **WL2-C3-A5-Equations**. Print and then close the document.

Visual Benchmark Demonstrate Your Proficiency

CREATE AN AGREEMENT WITH BUILDING BLOCKS AND AUTOCORRECT TEXT

1. At a blank document, create the document shown in Figure 3.14 with the following specifications:
   a. Create AutoCorrect entries for *Woodland Legal Services* (use wls) and *Till-Harris Management* (use thm). Use these AutoCorrect entries when typing the text in Figure 3.14.
   b. Insert the WLSCSHeading building block (the one preceded by your initials) at the beginning of the document and insert the WLSCSFooter as a footer (the one preceded by your initials).
   c. Justify the six paragraphs of text in the document and then center-align the signature lines.
2. Save the completed document and name it **WL2-C3-VB-THMAgrmnt**.
3. Print and then close **WL2-C3-VB-THMAgrmnt.docx**.
4. Open a blank document, display the AutoCorrect dialog box, and then display the *thm* entry. Press the Alt + Print Screen button, close the dialog box, close the Word Options dialog box, and then click the Paste button at the blank document. (This inserts an image of the AutoCorrect dialog box. Alt + Print Screen makes a capture of the active dialog box.)
5. Press Ctrl + End and then press the Enter key.
6. Complete steps similar to those in Step 4 to make a screen capture of the AutoCorrect dialog box with the *wls* entry displayed and insert the screen capture image in the document (below the first screen capture image).
7. Make sure both images display on one page. Print and then close the document without saving it.
8. At a blank document, delete the *wls* and *thm* AutoCorrect entries and custom building blocks you created in Assessment 3.

Figure 3.14 Visual Benchmark

REPRESENTATION AGREEMENT

Carlos Sawyer, Attorney at Law

This agreement is made between Carlos Sawyer of Woodland Legal Services, hereafter referred to as "Woodland Legal Services" and Till-Harris Management for legal services to be provided by Woodland Legal Services.

Legal Representation: Woodland Legal Services will perform the legal services required by Till-Harris Management, keep Till-Harris Management informed of progress and developments, and respond promptly to Till-Harris Management's inquiries and communications.

Attorney's Fees and Costs: Till-Harris Management will pay Woodland Legal Services for attorney's fees for legal services provided under this agreement at the hourly rate of the individuals providing the services. Under this agreement,Till-Harris Management will pay all costs incurred by Woodland Legal Services for representation of Till-Harris Management. Costs will be advanced by Woodland Legal Services and then billed to Till-Harris Management unless the costs can be met from deposits.

Deposit for Fees: Till-Harris Management will pay to Woodland Legal Services an initial deposit of $5,000, to be received by Woodland Legal Services on or before November 1, 2015. Twenty percent of the deposit is nonrefundable and will be applied against attorney's fees. The refundable portion will be deposited by Woodland Legal Services in an interest-bearing trust account. Till-Harris Management authorizes Woodland Legal Services to withdraw the principal from the trust account to pay attorney's fees in excess of the nonrefundable portion.

Statement and Payments: Woodland Legal Services will send Till-Harris Management monthly statements indicating attorney's fees and costs incurred, amounts applied from deposits, and current balance owed. If no attorney's fees or costs are incurred for a particular month, the statement may be held and combined with that for the following month. Any balance will be paid in full within 30 days after the statement is mailed.

Effective Date of Agreement: The effective date of this agreement will be the date when it is executed by both parties.

Client: ______________________________ Date: _______________

Attorney: ___________________________ Date: _______________

7110 FIFTH STREET ◆ SUITE 200 ◆ OMAHA NE 68207 ◆ 402-555-7110

Case Study Apply Your Skills

Part 1

You have been hired as the office manager for Highland Construction Company. The address of the company is 9025 Palmer Park Boulevard, Colorado Springs, CO 80904, and the telephone number is (719) 555-4575. You are responsible for designing business documents that have a consistent visual style and formatting. You decide that your first task is to create a letterhead document. Create a letterhead for Highland Construction Company. Consider including the company name, address, and telephone number, along with a clip art image and/or any other elements to add visual interest to the letterhead. Save the completed letterhead document and name it **WL2-C3-CS-HCCLetterhead**. Using the text and elements in the letterhead document, create a building block and name it with your initials followed by *HCCLetterhead*. Save, print, and then close **WL2-C3-CS-HCCLetterhead.docx**. Create the following additional building blocks for your company. (Use your initials in the names of the building blocks; you decide on the names.)

- Create a building block footer that contains a border line (in a color matching the colors in the letterhead) and the company slogan:
  Building Dreams Since 1985
- Create the following complimentary close building block:

  Sincerely,

  Your Name
  Office Manager
- Create the following company name and address building block:

  Mr. Eric Rashad
  Roswell Industries
  1020 Wasatch Street
  Colorado Springs, CO 80902
- Create the following company name and address building block:

  Ms. Claudia Sanborn
  S & S Supplies
  537 Constitution Avenue
  Colorado Springs, CO 80911

Part 2

At a blank document, create a letter to Eric Rashad by inserting the company letterhead (the building block that begins with your initials followed by *HCCLetterhead*). Type today's date, press the Enter key twice, and then insert the Eric Rashad building block. Type an appropriate salutation (such as *Dear Mr. Rashad:*), insert the file named **HCCLetter.docx**, and then insert your complimentary close building block. Finally, insert the footer building block you created for the company. Check the letter and make modifcations to spacing as needed. Save the letter and name it **WL2-C3-CS-RashadLtr**. Print and then close the letter. Complete similar steps to create a letter to Claudia Sanborn. Save the completed letter and name it **WL2-C3-CS-SanbornLtr**. Print and then close the letter.

Part 3

At a blank document, insert the company letterhead building block you created in Part 1, type the title *Company Services*, and then insert a SmartArt graphic of your choosing that contains the following text:

Residential Construction
Commercial Construction
Design Consultation
Site Preparation

Apply a heading style to the *Company Services* title, insert the company footer building block, and then save the document and name it **WL2-C3-CS-CoServices**. Print and then close the document.

Part 4

Create an AutoCorrect entry that will replace *hcc* with *Highland Construction Company* and *bca* with *Building Construction Agreement*. Open **HCCAgrmnt.docx** and then type the text shown in Figure 3.15 at the beginning of the document. Apply or insert the following to the document:

- Insert at the end of the document a date printed field and a file name field.
- Insert your footer building block as a footer.
- Insert a cover page of your choosing.

Add or apply any other enhancements to improve the appearance of the document and then save the document and name it **WL2-C3-CS-HCCAgrmnt**. Print and then close the document.

Part 5

Make sure you are connected to the Internet and then display the New backstage area. Choose a business card template, download the template, and then create business cards for Highland Construction Company. Include your name and title (Office Manager) on the cards. Save the completed business cards document and name it **WL2-C3-CS-HCCBusCards**. Print and then close the document. Delete the building blocks you created and then delete the AutoCorrect entries *hcc* and *bca*.

Figure 3.15 Case Study, Part 4

bca

THIS bca made this ______day of ______________, 2015 by and between hcc and __________________, hereinafter referred to as "owner," for the considerations hereinafter named, hcc and owner agree as follows:

Financing Arrangements: The owner will obtain a construction loan to finance construction under this bca. If adequate financing has not been arranged within 30 days of the date of this bca, or the owner cannot provide evidence to hcc of other financial ability to pay the full amount, then hcc may treat this bca as null and void, and retain the down payment made on the execution of this bca.

MICROSOFT®
WORD

CHAPTER 4

Customizing Themes, Creating Macros, and Navigating in a Document

PERFORMANCE OBJECTIVES

Upon successful completion of Chapter 4, you will be able to:

- **Create custom theme colors, theme fonts, and theme effects**
- **Save a custom theme**
- **Apply, edit, and delete custom themes**
- **Reset to the template theme**
- **Apply styles and modify existing styles**
- **Record, run, and delete macros**
- **Assign a macro to a keyboard command**
- **Manage macro security**
- **Navigate in a document using the Navigation pane, thumbnails, bookmarks, hyperlinks, and cross-references**
- **Insert hyperlinks to a location in the same document, a different document, a file in another program, and an email address**

Tutorials

4.1 Creating Custom Theme Colors and Theme Fonts
4.2 Saving a Document Theme
4.3 Applying, Editing, and Deleting a Custom Theme
4.4 Applying and Modifying Styles
4.5 Recording and Running Macros
4.6 Inserting and Navigating with Bookmarks
4.7 Creating and Editing Hyperlinks
4.8 Inserting Hyperlinks to Other Locations
4.9 Creating a Cross-Reference

The Microsoft Office suite offers themes to provide you with consistent formatting and help you create documents with a professional and polished look. You can use the themes provided by Office or create your own custom themes. Word provides a number of predesigned styles, grouped into style sets, for applying consistent formatting to text in documents. Word also includes a time-saving feature called *macros* that automates the formatting of a document.

In this chapter, you will learn about customizing themes; how to modify an existing style; how to record and run macros; and how to insert hyperlinks, bookmarks, and cross-references to provide additional information for readers and to allow for more efficient navigation within a document. Model answers for this chapter's projects appear on the following pages.

Note: Before beginning the projects, copy to your storage medium the WL2C4 subfolder from the WL2 folder on the CD that accompanies this textbook and then make WL2C4 the active folder.

Model Answers

Northland Security Systems

Northland Security Systems Mission

We are a full-service computer information security management and consulting firm offering a comprehensive range of services to help businesses protect electronic data.

Security Services

Northland Security Systems is dedicated to helping businesses, private and public, protect vital company data through on-site consultation, product installation and training, and 24-hour telephone support services. We show you how computer systems can be compromised, and we walk you through the steps you can take to protect your company's computer system.

Security Software

We offer a range of security management software to protect your business against viruses, spyware, adware, intrusion, spam, and policy abuse.

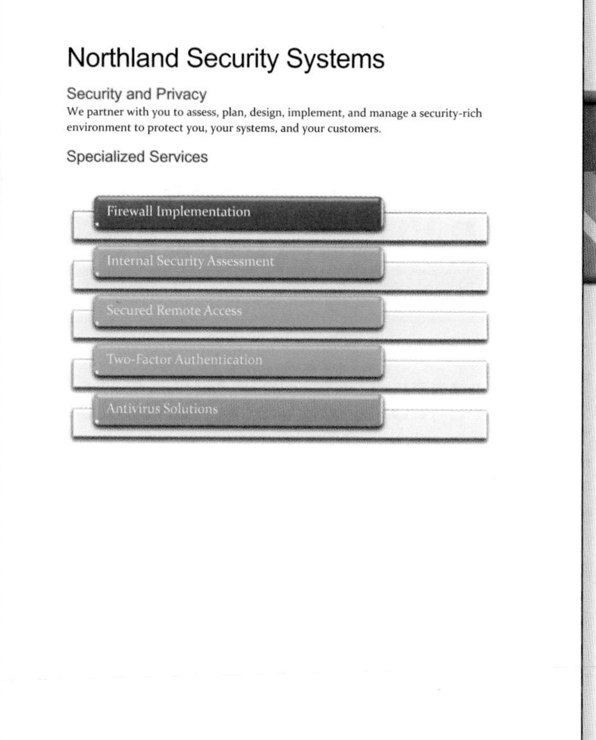

Northland Security Systems

Security and Privacy

We partner with you to assess, plan, design, implement, and manage a security-rich environment to protect you, your systems, and your customers.

Specialized Services

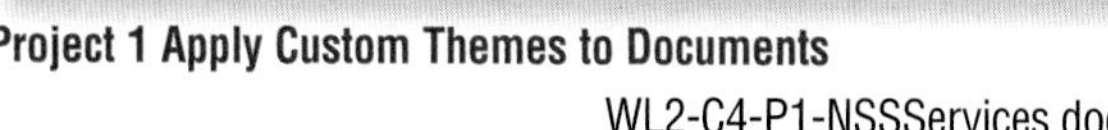

Project 1 Apply Custom Themes to Documents

WL2-C4-P1-NSSServices.docx

WL2-C4-P1-NSSSecurity.docx

"Travel is fatal to prejudice, bigotry and narrow-mindedness."
Mark Twain

African Study Adventure

The African Study Adventure program provide travelers with a unique opportunity to travel to African countries and make connections with local people, visit cultural institutions, and travel with knowledgeable tour guides who will provide insightful information about the countries, peoples, and customs.

Small Groups

The size of each group is limited so that African Study Adventure tour guides can deliver personal service and ensure that you feel comfortable in your surroundings. All tours are limited to a maximum of 25 participants.

Comprehensive Itineraries

Each program in the African Study Adventure program offers comprehensive sightseeing, exciting activities, and direct encounters with the people of the area you are visiting. Tour guides have developed a range of tours, each with its own principal theme and special highlights.

Custom Groups

For those who cannot fit African Study Adventure program scheduled departures into their calendars or who prefer to travel with their own friends and family, Bayside Travel has developed custom programs to suit your specific needs.

Accommodations and Meals

Accommodations will vary with the particular trip. However, Bayside Travel staff has selected accommodations with great care to make sure you will be as comfortable as local conditions allow and that you will enjoy the unique atmosphere of each destination. Most meals are included in the tour package.

Vacation Adventures

Hurry and book now for one of our special vacation packages. Book within the next two weeks and you will be eligible for our special discount savings as well as earn a complimentary $100 gift card you can use at any of the resorts in our vacation adventures.

Disneyland Adventure

- *Roundtrip air fare into Los Angeles, California*
- *Three-night hotel accommodations and hotel taxes*
- *Three-day Resort Ticket*
- *24-hour traveler assistance*

Florida Adventure

- *Roundtrip airfare to Orlando, Florida*
- *Seven-night hotel accommodations and hotel taxes*

Page 1

- *Four-day Resort Ticket*
- *Two-day Bonus Ticket*
- *Free transportation to some sites*

Cancun Adventure

- *Roundtrip airfare to Cancun, Mexico*
- *Five-night hotel accommodations and hotel taxes*
- *Free shuttle to and from the airport*
- *Two excursion tickets*

Book a complete air/hotel vacation package and SAVE on fall travel! Bookings must be made by October 14, 2015, for travel January 1 through June 30, 2016 (blackout dates apply). Take advantage of these fantastic savings!

Page 2

Project 2 Format a Travel Document with Styles

WL2-C4-P2-BTAdventures.docx

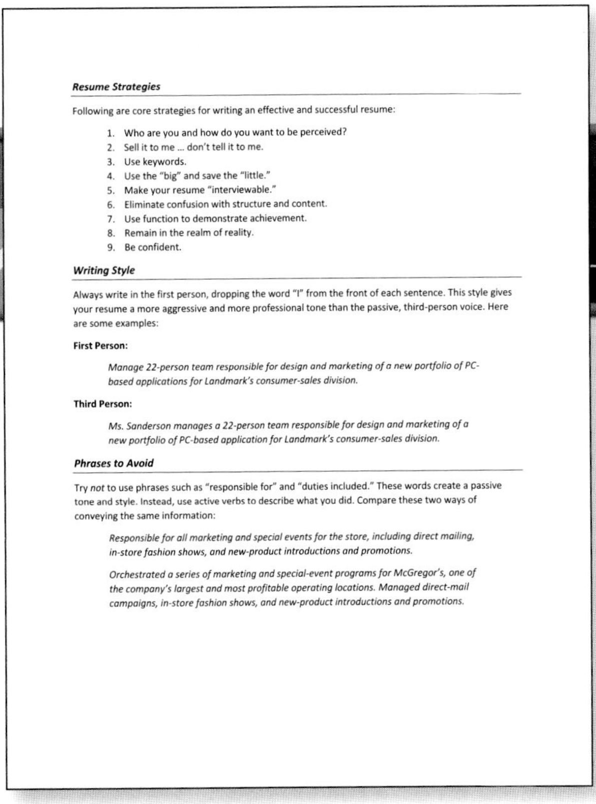

Resume Strategies

Following are core strategies for writing an effective and successful resume:

1. Who are you and how do you want to be perceived?
2. Sell it to me ... don't tell it to me.
3. Use keywords.
4. Use the "big" and save the "little."
5. Make your resume "interviewable."
6. Eliminate confusion with structure and content.
7. Use function to demonstrate achievement.
8. Remain in the realm of reality.
9. Be confident.

Writing Style

Always write in the first person, dropping the word "I" from the front of each sentence. This style gives your resume a more aggressive and more professional tone than the passive, third-person voice. Here are some examples:

First Person:

Manage 22-person team responsible for design and marketing of a new portfolio of PC-based applications for Landmark's consumer-sales division.

Third Person:

Ms. Sanderson manages a 22-person team responsible for design and marketing of a new portfolio of PC-based application for Landmark's consumer-sales division.

Phrases to Avoid

Try not to use phrases such as "responsible for" and "duties included." These words create a passive tone and style. Instead, use active verbs to describe what you did. Compare these two ways of conveying the same information:

Responsible for all marketing and special events for the store, including direct mailing, in-store fashion shows, and new-product introductions and promotions.

Orchestrated a series of marketing and special-event programs for McGregor's, one of the company's largest and most profitable operating locations. Managed direct-mail campaigns, in-store fashion shows, and new-product introductions and promotions.

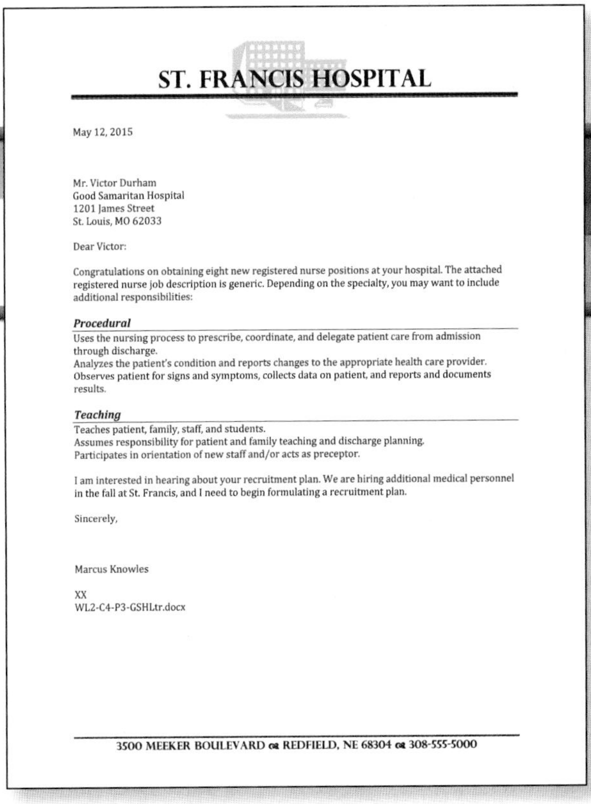

ST. FRANCIS HOSPITAL

May 12, 2015

Mr. Victor Durham
Good Samaritan Hospital
1201 James Street
St. Louis, MO 62033

Dear Victor:

Congratulations on obtaining eight new registered nurse positions at your hospital. The attached registered nurse job description is generic. Depending on the specialty, you may want to include additional responsibilities:

Procedural

Uses the nursing process to prescribe, coordinate, and delegate patient care from admission through discharge.
Analyzes the patient's condition and reports changes to the appropriate health care provider.
Observes patient for signs and symptoms, collects data on patient, and reports and documents results.

Teaching

Teaches patient, family, staff, and students.
Assumes responsibility for patient and family teaching and discharge planning.
Participates in orientation of new staff and/or acts as preceptor.

I am interested in hearing about your recruitment plan. We are hiring additional medical personnel in the fall at St. Francis, and I need to begin formulating a recruitment plan.

Sincerely,

Marcus Knowles

XX
WL2-C4-P3-GSHLtr.docx

3500 MEEKER BOULEVARD ◆ REDFIELD, NE 68304 ◆ 308-555-5000

Project 3 Record and Run Macros

WL2-C4-P3-WriteResumes.docx

WL2-C4-P3-GSHLtr.docx

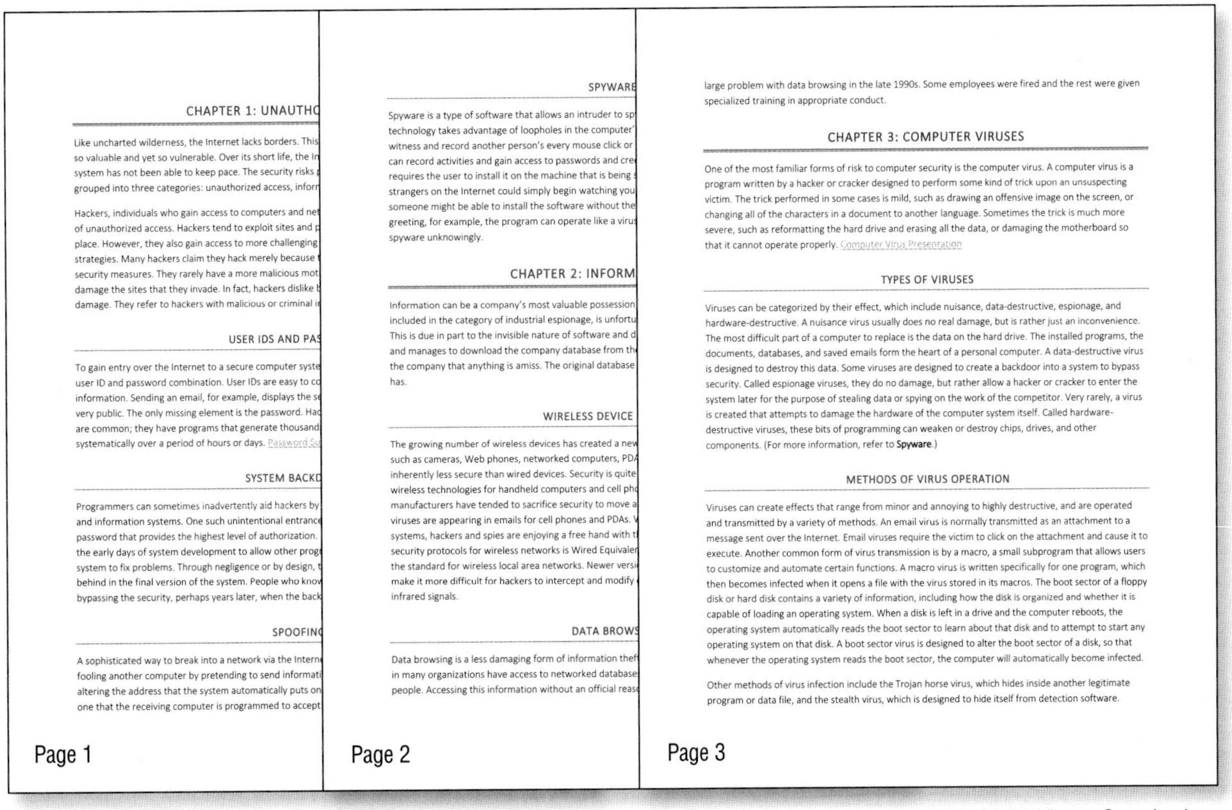

CHAPTER 1: UNAUTH

Like uncharted wilderness, the Internet lacks borders. This so valuable and yet so vulnerable. Over its short life, the In system has not been able to keep pace. The security risks grouped into three categories: unauthorized access, inform

Hackers, individuals who gain access to computers and net of unauthorized access. Hackers tend to exploit sites and p place. However, they also gain access to more challenging strategies. Many hackers claim they hack merely because security measures. They rarely have a more malicious mot damage the sites that they invade. In fact, hackers dislike b damage. They refer to hackers with malicious or criminal i

USER IDS AND PAS

To gain entry over the Internet to a secure computer syste user ID and password combination. User IDs are easy to c information. Sending an email, for example, displays the s very public. The only missing element is the password. Ha are common; they have programs that generate thousand systematically over a period of hours or days. Password Sa

SYSTEM BACKD

Programmers can sometimes inadvertently aid hackers by and information systems. One such unintentional entranc password that provides the highest level of authorization. the early days of system development to allow other prog system to fix problems. Through negligence or by design, t behind in the final version of the system. People who kno bypassing the security, perhaps years later, when the back

SPOOFIN

A sophisticated way to break into a network via the Intern fooling another computer by pretending to send informati altering the address that the system automatically puts on one that the receiving computer is programmed to accept

Page 1

SPYWARE

Spyware is a type of software that allows an intruder to sp technology takes advantage of loopholes in the computer' witness and record another person's every mouse click or can record activities and gain access to passwords and cre requires the user to install it on the machine that is being s strangers on the Internet could simply begin watching you someone might be able to install the software without the greeting, for example, the program can operate like a viru spyware unknowingly.

CHAPTER 2: INFORM

Information can be a company's most valuable possession included in the category of industrial espionage, is unfortu This is due in part to the invisible nature of software and d and manages to download the company database from th the company that anything is amiss. The original database has.

WIRELESS DEVICE

The growing number of wireless devices has created a new such as cameras, Web phones, networked computers, PDA inherently less secure than wired devices. Security is quite wireless technologies for handheld computers and cell ph manufacturers have tended to sacrifice security to move a viruses are appearing in emails for cell phones and PDAs. W systems, hackers and spies are enjoying a free hand with t security protocols for wireless networks is Wired Equivaler the standard for wireless local area networks. Newer versi make it more difficult for hackers to intercept and modify infrared signals.

DATA BROWS

Data browsing is a less damaging form of information thef in many organizations have access to networked database people. Accessing this information without an official reas

Page 2

large problem with data browsing in the late 1990s. Some employees were fired and the rest were given specialized training in appropriate conduct.

CHAPTER 3: COMPUTER VIRUSES

One of the most familiar forms of risk to computer security is the computer virus. A computer virus is a program written by a hacker or cracker designed to perform some kind of trick upon an unsuspecting victim. The trick performed in some cases is mild, such as drawing an offensive image on the screen, or changing all of the characters in a document to another language. Sometimes the trick is much more severe, such as reformatting the hard drive and erasing all the data, or damaging the motherboard so that it cannot operate properly. Computer Virus Presentation

TYPES OF VIRUSES

Viruses can be categorized by their effect, which include nuisance, data-destructive, espionage, and hardware-destructive. A nuisance virus usually does no real damage, but is rather just an inconvenience. The most difficult part of a computer to replace is the data on the hard drive. The installed programs, the documents, databases, and saved emails form the heart of a personal computer. A data-destructive virus is designed to destroy this data. Some viruses are designed to create a backdoor into a system to bypass security. Called espionage viruses, they do no damage, but rather allow a hacker or cracker to enter the system later for the purpose of stealing data or spying on the work of the competitor. Very rarely, a virus is created that attempts to damage the hardware of the computer system itself. Called hardware-destructive viruses, these bits of programming can weaken or destroy chips, drives, and other components. (For more information, refer to **Spyware**.)

METHODS OF VIRUS OPERATION

Viruses can create effects that range from minor and annoying to highly destructive, and are operated and transmitted by a variety of methods. An email virus is normally transmitted as an attachment to a message sent over the Internet. Email viruses require the victim to click on the attachment and cause it to execute. Another common form of virus transmission is by a macro, a small subprogram that allows users to customize and automate certain functions. A macro virus is written specifically for one program, which then becomes infected when it opens a file with the virus stored in its macros. The boot sector of a floppy disk or hard disk contains a variety of information, including how the disk is organized and whether it is capable of loading an operating system. When a disk is left in a drive and the computer reboots, the operating system automatically reads the boot sector to learn about that disk and to attempt to start any operating system on that disk. A boot sector virus is designed to alter the boot sector of a disk, so that whenever the operating system reads the boot sector, the computer will automatically become infected.

Other methods of virus infection include the Trojan horse virus, which hides inside another legitimate program or data file, and the stealth virus, which is designed to hide itself from detection software.

Page 3

Project 4 Navigate and Insert Hyperlinks in a Computer Viruses Report

WL2-C4-P4-VirusesSecurity.docx

Polymorphic viruses alter themselves to prevent antivirus software from detecting them by examining familiar patterns. Polymorphic viruses alter themselves randomly as they move from computer to computer, making detection more difficult. Multipartite viruses alter their form of attack. Their name derives from their ability to attack in several different ways. They may first infect the boot sector and then later move on to become a Trojan horse type by infecting a disk file. These viruses are more sophisticated, and therefore more difficult to guard against. Another type of virus is the logic bomb, which generally sits quietly dormant waiting for a specific event or set of conditions to occur. A famous logic bomb was the widely publicized Michelangelo virus, which infected personal computers and caused them to display a message on the artist's birthday.

CHAPTER 4: SECURITY RISKS

Although hackers, crackers, and viruses garner the most attention as security risks, a company faces a variety of other dangers to its hardware and software systems. Principally, these risks involve types of system failure, employee theft, and the cracking of software for copying. Click to view types of viruses

SYSTEMS FAILURE

A fundamental element in making sure that computer systems operate properly is protecting the electrical power that runs them. Power interruptions such as blackouts and brownouts have very adverse effects on computers. An inexpensive type of power strip called a surge protector can guard against power fluctuations and can also serve as an extension cord and splitter. A much more vigorous power protection system is an uninterruptible power supply (UPS), which provides a battery backup. Similar in nature to a power strip, but much more bulky and a bit more expensive, a UPS provides not only steady spike-free power, but also keeps computers running during a blackout.

EMPLOYEE THEFT

Although accurate estimates are difficult to pinpoint, businesses certainly lose millions of dollars a year in stolen computer hardware and software. Often, in large organizations, such theft goes unnoticed or unreported. Someone takes a hard drive or a scanner home for legitimate use, then leaves the job sometime later, and keeps the machine. Sometimes, employees take components to add to their home PC systems or a thief breaks into a business and hauls away computers. Such thefts cost far more than the price of the stolen computers because they also involve the cost of replacing the lost data, the cost of the time lost while the machines are gone, and the cost of installing new machines and training people to use them.

CRACKING SOFTWARE FOR COPYING

A common goal of hackers is to crack a software protection scheme. A crack is a method of circumventing a security scheme that prevents a user from copying a program. A common protection scheme for

Page 4

software is to require that the installation CD be resident in the drive whenever the program runs. Making copies of the CD with a burner, however, easily fools this protection scheme. Some game companies are taking the extra step of making duplication difficult by scrambling some of the data on the original CDs, which CD burners will automatically correct when copying. When the copied and corrected CD is used, the software checks for the scrambled track information. If the error is not found, the software will not run.

Hold down the Ctrl key and then click the logo shown below to display a list of training courses offered by Northland Security Systems

Click to send an email

Page 5

Model Answers

Project 1 Apply Custom Themes to Documents 5 Parts

You will create custom theme colors and theme fonts and then apply theme effects. You will save the changes as a custom theme, which you will apply to a company services document and a company security document.

Customizing Themes

A document you create in Word is based on the Normal.dotm template. This template provides your document with default layout, formatting, styles, and theme formatting. The default template provides a number of built-in or predesigned themes. You have used some of these built-in themes to apply colors, fonts, and effects to content in documents. The same built-in themes are available in Microsoft Word, Excel, Access, PowerPoint, and Outlook. Because the same themes are available across these applications, you can brand your business files—such as documents, workbooks, databases, and presentations—with a consistent and professional appearance.

HINT

Every document created in Word 2013 has a theme applied to it.

A ***theme*** is a combination of theme colors, theme fonts, and theme effects. Within a theme, you can change any of these three elements with the additional buttons in the Document Formatting group on the DESIGN tab. You can switch from the default theme (called *Office*) to one of the built-in themes or create your own custom theme. A theme you create will display in the *Custom* section of the Themes drop-down gallery. To create a custom theme, change the theme colors, theme fonts, and/or theme effects.

The Themes, Theme Colors, and Theme Fonts buttons in the Document Formatting group on the DESIGN tab display visual representations of the current theme. For example, the Themes button displays an uppercase and lowercase A with colored squares below it. If you change the theme colors, the changes are reflected in the small, colored squares on the Themes button and the four squares on the Theme Colors button. If you change the theme fonts, the letters on the Themes button and the Theme Fonts button reflect the change.

Themes

Theme Colors

Theme Fonts

Creating Custom Theme Colors

To create custom theme colors, click the DESIGN tab, click the Theme Colors button, and then click *Customize Colors* at the drop-down gallery. This displays the Create New Theme Colors dialog box, similar to the one shown in Figure 4.1. Theme colors contain four text and background colors, six accent colors, and two hyperlink colors, as shown in the *Themes colors* section of the dialog box. Change a color in the list box by clicking the color button at the right side of the color option and then clicking the desired color at the color palette.

After you have made all desired changes to colors, click in the *Name* text box, type a name for the custom theme colors, and then click the Save button. This saves the custom theme colors and also applies the color changes to the active document. Display the custom theme by clicking the Theme Colors button. Your custom theme will display toward the top of the drop-down gallery in the *Custom* section.

Quick Steps

Create Custom Theme Colors

1. Click DESIGN tab.
2. Click Theme Colors button.
3. Click *Customize Colors*.
4. Change to desired background, accent, and hyperlink colors.
5. Type name for custom theme colors.
6. Click Save button.

Figure 4.1 Create New Theme Colors Dialog Box

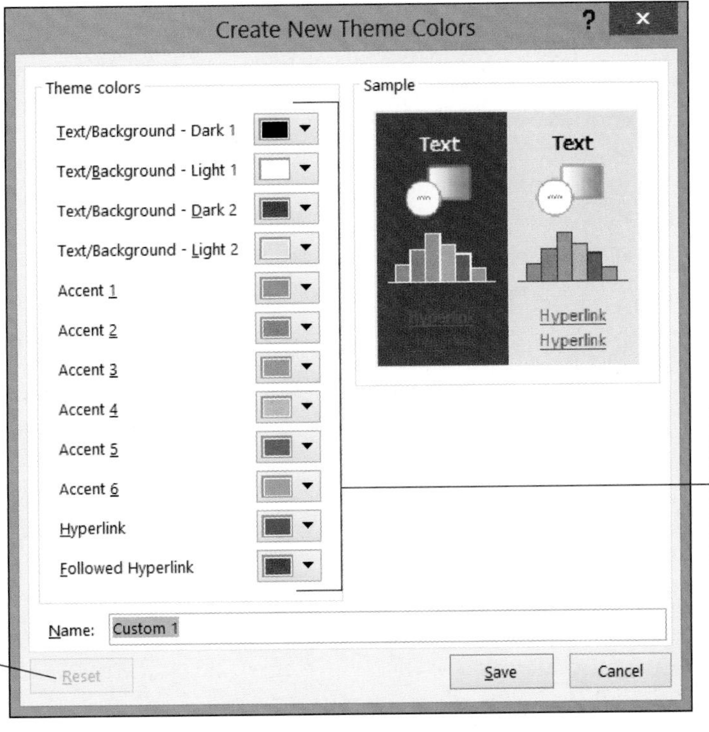

Change a theme color by clicking the color button and then clicking the desired color at the drop-down palette.

Click the Reset button to reset the colors back to the defult.

Resetting Custom Theme Colors

If you make changes to colors at the Create New Theme Colors dialog box and then decide you do not like the changes, click the Reset button in the lower left corner of the dialog box. Clicking this button resets the colors back to the default Office theme colors.

Project 1a **Creating Custom Theme Colors** **Part 1 of 5**

Note: If you are running Word 2013 on a computer connected to a network in a public environment, such as a school, you may need to complete all parts of Project 1 during the same session. Network system software may delete your custom themes when you exit Word. Check with your instructor.

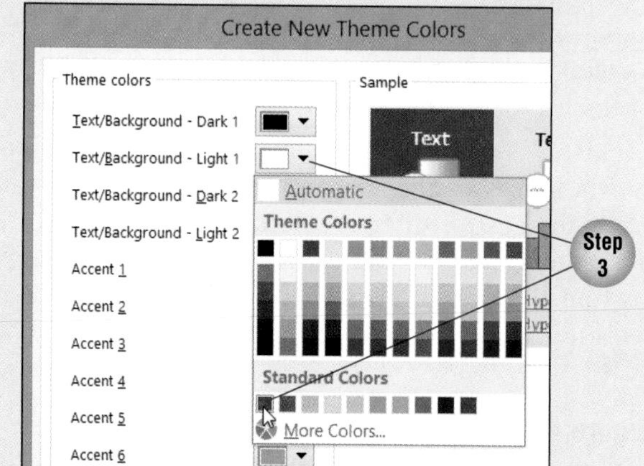

1. At a blank document, click the DESIGN tab.
2. Click the Theme Colors button in the Document Formatting group and then click *Customize Colors* at the drop-down gallery.
3. At the Create New Theme Colors dialog box, click the color button that displays to the right of the *Text/Background - Light 1* option and then click the *Dark Red* color in the color palette (first color in the *Standard Colors* section).
4. Click the color button that displays to the right of the *Accent 1* option and then click the *Yellow* color in the color palette (fourth color in the *Standard Colors* section).
5. You decide that you do not like the colors you have chosen, so you decide to start over. To do this, click the Reset button located in the lower left corner of the dialog box.
6. Click the color button that displays to the right of the *Text/Background - Dark 2* option and then click the *Blue* color in the color palette (eighth color in the *Standard Colors* section).
7. Change the color for the *Accent 1* option by completing the following steps:
   a. Click the color button that displays to the right of the *Accent 1* option.
   b. Click the *More Colors* option in the color palette.
   c. At the Colors dialog box, click the Standard tab.
   d. Click the *Dark Green* color, as shown at the right.
   e. Click OK to close the dialog box.
8. Save the custom colors by completing the following steps:
   a. Select the current text in the *Name* text box.
   b. Type your first and last names.
   c. Click the Save button.
9. Close the document without saving it.

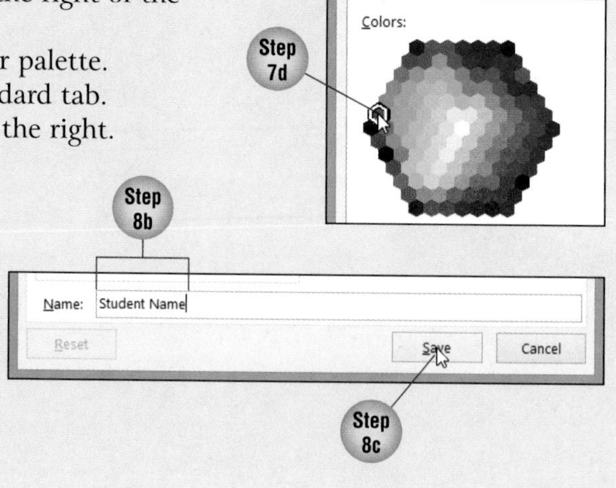

Creating Custom Fonts

To create a custom theme font, click the DESIGN tab, click the Theme Fonts button, and then click *Customize Fonts* at the drop-down gallery. This displays the Create New Theme Fonts dialog box. At this dialog box, choose a font for headings and a font for body text. Type a name for the custom fonts in the *Name* text box and then click the Save button.

Quick Steps

Create Custom Fonts
1. Click DESIGN tab.
2. Click Theme Fonts button.
3. Click *Customize Fonts.*
4. Choose fonts.
5. Type name for custom theme fonts.
6. Click Save button.

Project 1b **Creating Custom Theme Fonts** **Part 2 of 5**

1. At a blank document, click the DESIGN tab.
2. Click the Theme Fonts button in the Document Formatting group and then click the *Customize Fonts* option at the drop-down gallery.
3. At the Create New Theme Fonts dialog box, click the down-pointing arrow at the right side of the *Heading font* option box, scroll up the drop-down list, and then click *Arial.*
4. Click the down-pointing arrow at the right side of the *Body font* option box, scroll down the drop-down list, and then click *Cambria.*
5. Save the custom fonts by completing the following steps:
   a. Select the current text in the *Name* text box.
   b. Type your first and last names.
   c. Click the Save button.
6. Close the document without saving it.

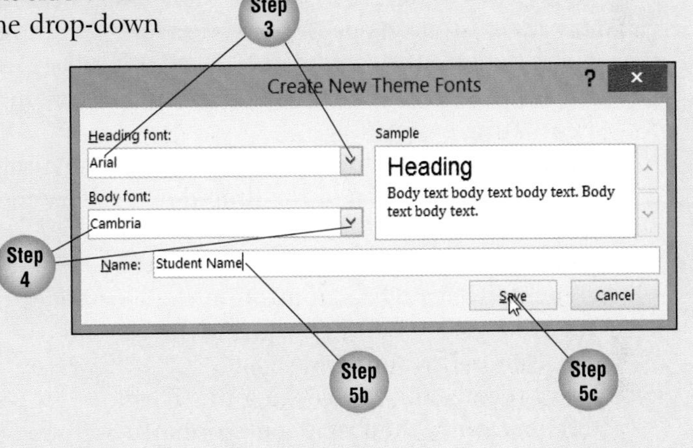

Applying Custom Theme Colors and Fonts

Apply to your document the custom theme colors you created by clicking the Theme Colors button in the Document Formatting group on the DESIGN tab and then clicking the custom theme colors option that displays near the top of the drop-down gallery in the *Custom* section. Complete similar steps to apply custom theme fonts.

Applying Theme Effects

The options in the Theme Effects button drop-down gallery apply sets of line and fill effects to graphics in a document. You cannot create your own theme effects but you can apply a theme effect and then save the formatting as your own document theme.

Quick Steps

Save a Document Theme
1. Click DESIGN tab.
2. Click Themes button.
3. Click *Save Current Theme.*
4. Type name for theme.
5. Click Save button.

Saving a Document Theme

Once you have customized theme colors and fonts and applied theme effects to a document, you can save them in a custom document theme. To do this, click the Themes button in the Document Formatting group on the DESIGN tab and then click *Save Current Theme* at the drop-down gallery. This displays the Save Current Theme dialog box, which has many of the same options as the Save As dialog box. Type a name for your custom document theme in the *File name* text box and then click the Save button.

Project 1c **Applying Theme Effects and Saving a Document Theme** **Part 3 of 5**

1. Open **NSSServices.docx** and then save the document and name it **WL2-C4-P1-NSSServices.**
2. Make the following changes to the document:
   a. Apply the Title style to the company name *Northland Security Systems.*
   b. Apply the Heading 1 style to the heading *Northland Security Systems Mission.*
   c. Apply the Heading 2 style to the remaining headings, *Security Services* and *Security Software.*
3. Apply the custom theme colors you saved by completing the following steps:
   a. Click the DESIGN tab.
   b. Click the Theme Colors button in the Document Formatting group.
   c. Click the theme colors option with your name that displays near the top of the drop-down gallery in the *Custom* group.

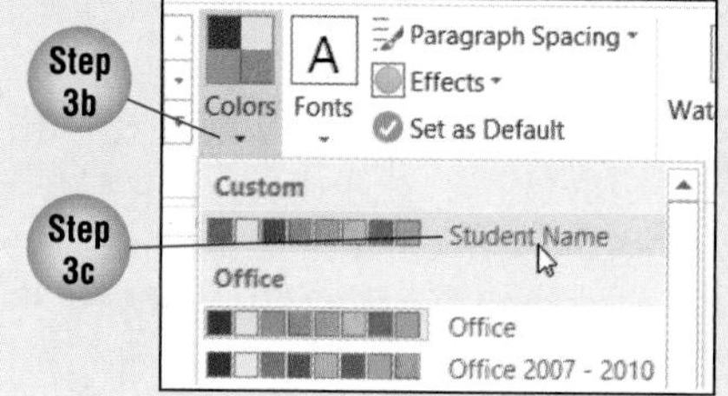

4. Apply the custom theme fonts you saved by clicking the Theme Fonts button in the Document Formatting group and then clicking the custom theme font with your name.
5. Apply a theme effect by clicking the Theme Effects button in the Document Formatting group and then clicking *Glossy* at the drop-down gallery.
6. Make the following changes to the SmartArt graphic:
   a. Click near the graphic to select it. (When the graphic is selected, a light gray border displays around it.)
   b. Click the SMARTART TOOLS DESIGN tab.
   c. Click the Change Colors button and then click *Colorful Range - Accent Colors 5 to 6* (the last color option in the *Colorful* section).
   d. Click the More button at the right side of the SmartArt Styles group and then click *Cartoon* in the *3-D* section (third column, first row in the *3-D* section).
   e. Click outside the SmartArt graphic to deselect it.

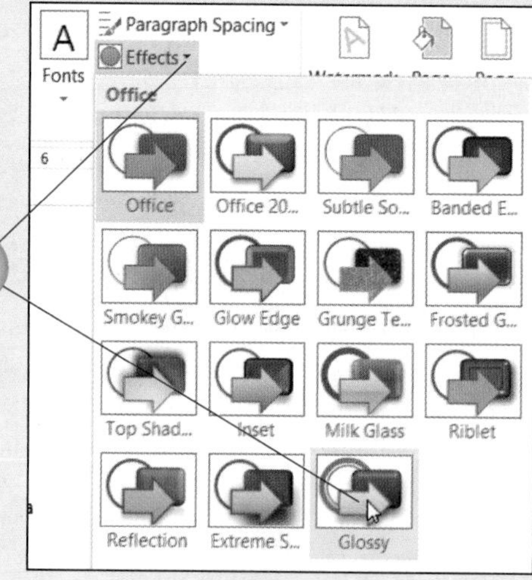

7. Save the custom theme colors and font, as well as the Glossy theme effect, as a custom document theme by completing the following steps:
   a. Click the DESIGN tab.
   b. Click the Themes button in the Document Formatting group.

c. Click the *Save Current Theme* option that displays at the bottom of the drop-down gallery.
d. At the Save Current Theme dialog box, type your first and last names in the *File name* text box and then click the Save button.

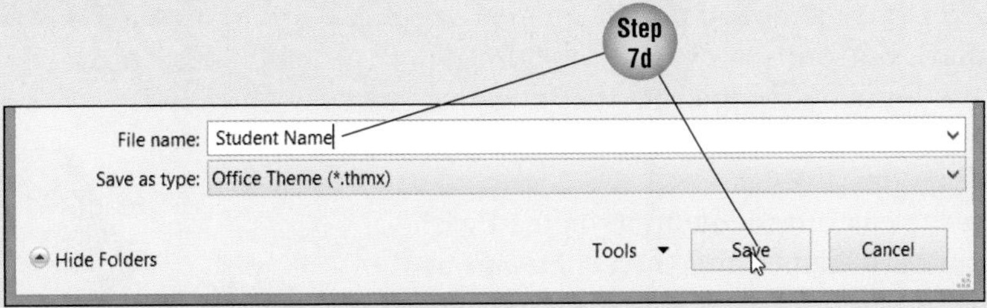

8. Save and then print **WL2-C4-P1-NSSServices.docx**.

Editing Custom Themes

Custom theme colors and theme fonts can be edited. To edit custom theme colors, click the DESIGN tab and then click the Theme Colors button in the Document Formatting group. At the drop-down gallery of custom and built-in theme colors, right-click your custom theme colors and then click *Edit* at the shortcut menu. This displays the Edit Theme Colors dialog box, which contains the same options as the Create New Theme Colors dialog box. Make the desired changes to the theme colors and then click the Save button.

To edit custom theme fonts, click the Theme Fonts button in the Document Formatting group on the DESIGN tab, right-click your custom theme fonts, and then click *Edit* at the shortcut menu. This displays the Edit Theme Fonts dialog box, which contains the same options as the Create New Theme Fonts dialog box. Make the desired changes to the theme fonts and then click the Save button.

Quick Steps

Edit Custom Theme Colors or Fonts
1. Click DESIGN tab.
2. Click Theme Colors button or Theme Fonts button.
3. Right-click desired custom theme colors or fonts.
4. Click *Edit*.
5. Make desired changes.
6. Click Save button.

Project 1d **Editing Custom Themes** **Part 4 of 5**

1. With **WL2-C4-P1-NSSServices.docx** open, edit the theme colors by completing the following steps:
   a. If necessary, click the DESIGN tab.
   b. Click the Theme Colors button.
   c. Right-click the custom theme colors named with your first and last names.
   d. Click *Edit* at the shortcut menu.
   e. At the Edit Theme Colors dialog box, click the color button that displays to the right of the *Text/Background - Dark 2* option.
   f. Click the *More Colors* option in the color palette.

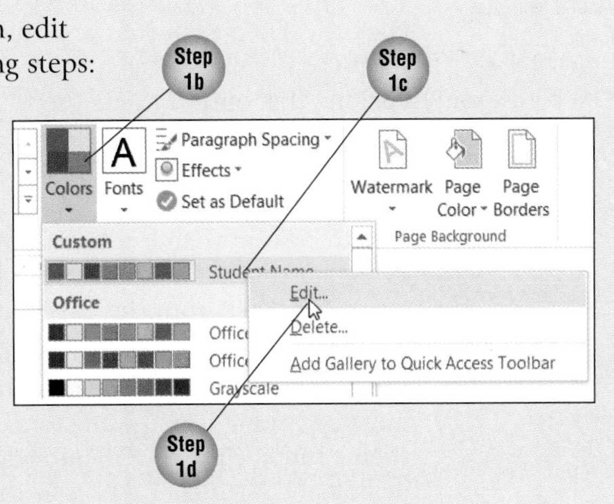

g. At the Colors dialog box, click the Standard tab.
h. Click the *Dark Green* color. (This is the same color you chose for *Accent 1* in Project 1a.)
i. Click OK to close the dialog box.
j. Click the Save button.

2. Edit the theme fonts by completing the following steps:
   a. Click the Theme Fonts button in the Document Formatting group.
   b. Right-click the custom theme fonts named with your first and last names and then click *Edit* at the shortcut menu.
   c. At the Edit Theme Fonts dialog box, click the down-pointing arrow at the right side of the *Body font* option box, scroll down the drop-down list, and then click *Constantia*.
   d. Click the Save button.

Step 1g

Colors
Standard
Custom
Colors:

Step 1h

3. Apply a different theme effect by clicking the Theme Effects button in the Document Formatting group and then clicking *Extreme Shadow* at the drop-down gallery. (This applies a shadow behind each shape.)
4. Save the changes to the custom theme by completing the following steps:
   a. Click the Themes button and then click *Save Current Theme* at the drop-down gallery.
   b. At the Save Current Theme dialog box, click the theme named with your first and last names in the content pane.
   c. Click the Save button.
   d. At the message telling you that the theme already exists and asking if you want to replace it, click Yes.
5. Save, print, and then close **WL2-C4-P1-NSSServices.docx**.

Resetting a Template Theme

Quick Steps

Reset a Template Theme
1. Click DESIGN tab.
2. Click Themes button.
3. Click *Reset to Theme from Template*.

Delete Custom Theme Colors or Fonts
1. Click DESIGN tab.
2. Click Theme Colors or Theme Fonts button.
3. Right-click desired custom theme.
4. Click *Delete*.
5. Click Yes.

If you apply a built-in theme other than the Office default theme or if you apply a custom theme, you can reset the theme back to the template default. To do this, click the Themes button and then click the *Reset to Theme from Template* at the drop-down gallery. If you are working in the default template provided by Word, clicking this option resets the theme to the Office default theme.

Deleting Custom Themes

Delete custom theme colors from the Theme Colors button drop-down gallery, delete custom theme fonts from the Theme Fonts drop-down gallery, and delete custom themes from the Save Current Theme dialog box.

To delete custom theme colors, click the Theme Colors button, right-click the theme you want to delete, and then click *Delete* at the shortcut menu. At the message asking if you want to delete the theme colors, click Yes. To delete custom theme fonts, click the Theme Fonts button, right-click the theme you want to delete, and then click *Delete* at the shortcut menu. At the message asking if you want to delete the theme fonts, click Yes.

Delete a custom theme (including custom colors, fonts, and effects) at the Themes button drop-down gallery or at the Save Current Theme dialog box. To delete a custom theme from the drop-down gallery, click the Themes button, right-click the custom theme, click *Delete* at the shortcut menu, and then click Yes at the message that displays. To delete a custom theme from the Save Current Theme dialog box, click the Themes button and then click *Save Current Theme* at the drop-down gallery. At the dialog box, click the custom theme document name, click the Organize button on the dialog box toolbar, and then click *Delete* at the drop-down list. If a message displays asking if you are sure you want to send the theme to the Recycle Bin, click Yes.

Quick Steps

Delete a Custom Theme
1. Click DESIGN tab.
2. Click Themes button.
3. Right-click custom theme.
4. Click *Delete*.
5. Click Yes.

Changing Default Settings

If you apply formatting to a document—such as a specific style set, theme, and paragraph spacing—and then decide that you want the formatting available for future documents, you can save the formatting as the default. To do this, click the Set as Default button in the Document Formatting group on the DESIGN tab. At the message box that displays asking if you want the current style set and theme as the default and telling you that the settings will be applied to new documents, click the Yes button.

Project 1e **Applying and Deleting Custom Themes** **Part 5 of 5**

1. Open **NSSSecurity.docx** and then save the document and name it **WL2-C4-P1-NSSSecurity**.
2. Apply the Title style to the company name and apply the Heading 1 style to the two headings in the document.
3. Apply your custom theme by completing the following steps:
   a. Click the DESIGN tab.
   b. Click the Themes button.
   c. Click the custom theme named with your first and last names that displays at the top of the drop-down gallery in the *Custom* section.
4. Save and then print **WL2-C4-P1-NSSSecurity.docx**.
5. Reset the theme to the Office default theme by clicking the Themes button and then clicking *Reset to Theme from Template* at the drop-down gallery.
6. Save and then close **WL2-C4-P1-NSSSecurity.docx**.
7. Press Ctrl + N to display a new blank document.
8. Delete the custom theme colors by completing the following steps:
   a. Click the DESIGN tab.
   b. Click the Theme Colors button in the Document Formatting group.
   c. Right-click the custom theme colors named with your first and last names.
   d. Click *Delete* at the shortcut menu.
   e. At the question asking if you want to delete the theme colors, click Yes.

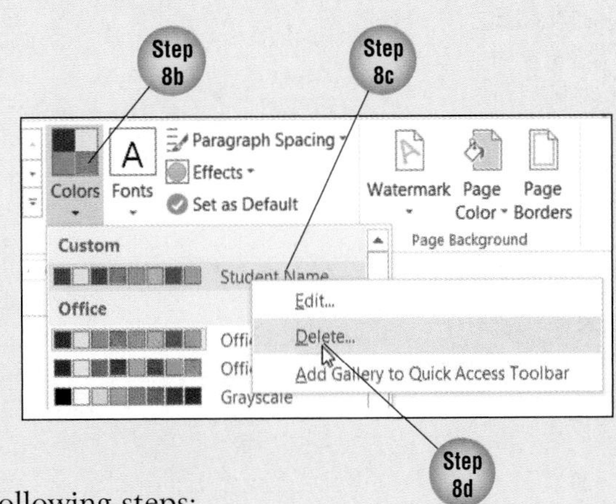

9. Complete steps similar to those in Step 8 to delete the custom theme fonts named with your first and last names.
10. Delete the custom theme by completing the following steps:
   a. Click the Themes button.
   b. Right-click the custom theme named with your first and last names.

c. Click Delete at the shortcut menu.
d. At the message asking if you want to delete the theme, click Yes.
11. Close the document without saving it.

Project 2 Format a Travel Document with Styles — 1 Part

You will open a First Choice Travel document, change the style set, and apply styles.

Formatting with Styles

A ***style*** is a set of formatting instructions that you can apply to text. Word provides a number of predesigned styles and groups those that apply similar formatting into style sets. While a theme changes the overall colors, fonts, and effects used in a document, a style set changes font and paragraph formatting for the entire document. Using the styles within a style set, you can apply formatting that gives your document a uniform and professional appearance.

Displaying Styles in a Style Set

The default style set is named *Word 2013,* and the styles in it are available in the Styles group on the HOME tab. Several styles display as ***thumbnails***, or miniature representations, in the Styles group. Generally, the visible style thumbnails include the Normal, No Spacing, Heading 1, Heading 2, Title, Subtitle, and Subtitle Emphasis styles. (Depending on your monitor and screen resolution, you may see more or fewer style thumbnails in the Styles group.) The styles change to reflect the style set that has been applied to the active document. Click the More button to the right of the style thumbnails in the Styles group and a drop-down gallery displays containing all of the styles available in the default style set. Hover your mouse pointer over a style in the drop-down gallery to see how the style will format text in your document.

You can also display the styles available in the style set by clicking either the down-pointing arrow or up-pointing arrow to the right of the style thumbnails. Clicking the down-pointing arrow scrolls down the style set, displaying the next styles. Clicking the up-pointing arrow scrolls up the set of styles.

Applying Styles

You can also display the Styles task pane by pressing Alt + Ctrl + Shift + S.

A variety of methods are available for applying styles to text in a document. Apply a style by clicking the style thumbnail in the Styles group on the HOME tab or by clicking the More button and then clicking the style at the drop-down gallery. The Styles task pane provides another method for applying a style. Display the Styles task pane, shown in Figure 4.2, by clicking the Styles group task pane launcher.

Figure 4.2 Styles Task Pane

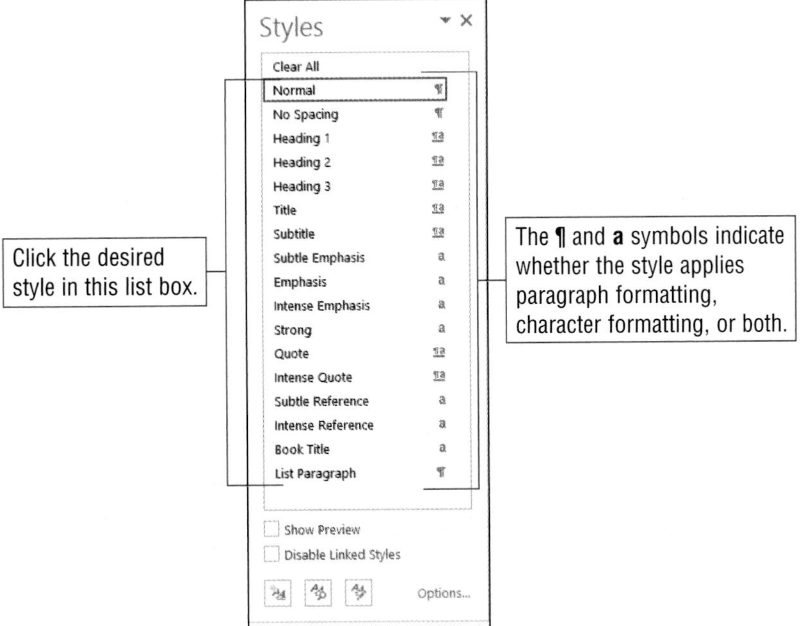

The styles in the currently selected style set display in the task pane followed by the paragraph symbol (¶), indicating that the style applies paragraph formatting, or the character symbol (**a**), indicating that the style applies character formatting. If both characters display to the right of a style, the style applies both paragraph and character formatting. In addition to displaying styles that apply formatting, the Styles task pane also displays a *Clear All* style that clears all formatting from the selected text.

If you hover the mouse pointer over a style in the Styles task pane, a ScreenTip displays with information about the formatting applied by the style. Apply a style in the Styles task pane by clicking the style. Close the Styles task pane by clicking the Close button located in the upper right corner of the task pane.

Quick Steps

Apply a Style

Click desired style in Styles group.

OR

1. Click More button in Styles group on HOME tab.
2. Click desired style.

OR

1. Display Styles task pane.
2. Click desired style in task pane.

Modifying a Style

If a predesigned style contains most, but not all, of the formatting you want applied to text in your document, consider modifying the style. For example, the Heading 1 style might apply most of the formatting you want for headings in your document, but you want to apply a different font or alignment. To edit a predesigned style, right-click the style in the Styles group or in the Styles task pane and then click *Modify* at the shortcut menu. This displays the Modify Styles dialog box, shown in Figure 4.3. Use options at this dialog box to make changes such as renaming the style, applying or changing formatting, and specifying whether you want the modified style available only in the current document or all new documents.

The *Formatting* section of the dialog box contains a number of buttons and options for applying formatting. Additional options are available by clicking the Format button in the lower left corner of the dialog box and then clicking an option at the drop-down list. For example, display the Font dialog box by clicking the Format button and then clicking Font at the drop-down list.

HINT

You can also apply styles at the Apply Styles window. Display this window with the keyboard shortcut Ctrl + Shift + S or by clicking the More button at the right side of the style thumbnails in the Styles group on the HOME tab and then clicking *Apply Styles* at the drop-down gallery.

Figure 4.3 Modify Styles Dialog Box

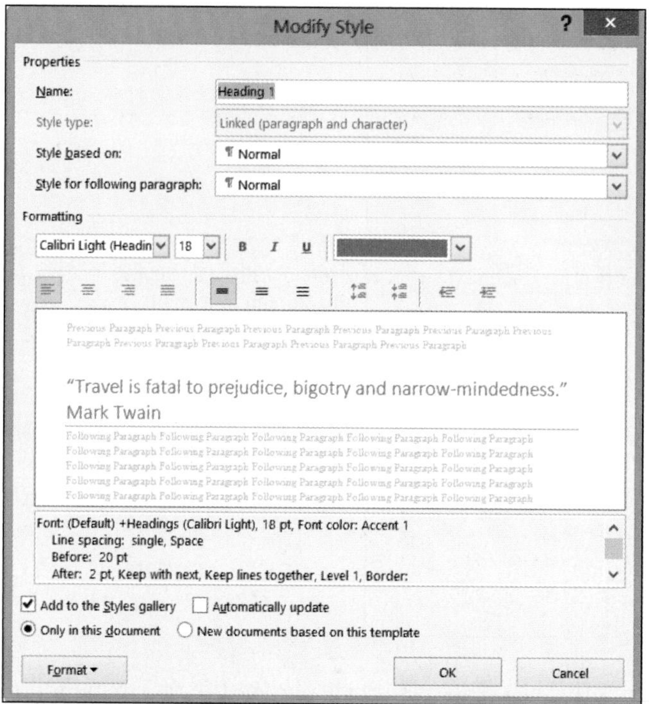

Project 2 Applying and Modifying Styles

Part 1 of 1

1. Open **BTAdventures.docx** and then save the document and name it **WL2-C4-P2-BTAdventures**.
2. Apply styles using the Styles task pane by completing the following steps:
   a. Move the insertion point to the end of the document and then select the last paragraph.
   b. With the HOME tab active, click the Styles group task pane launcher. (This displays the Styles task pane.)
   c. Click the *Subtle Reference* style in the Styles task pane. (Notice that the style is followed by the character symbol *a*, indicating that the style applies character formatting.)
   d. Select the bulleted text below the heading *Disneyland Adventure* and then click the *Subtle Emphasis* style in the Styles task pane.
   e. Apply the *Subtle Emphasis* style to the bulleted text below the *Florida Adventure* heading and the *Cancun Adventure* heading.
   f. Select the quote by Mark Twain that displays at the beginning of the document and then click *Quote* in the Styles task pane.
   g. After noticing the formatting of the quote, remove the formatting by making sure the text is selected and then clicking *Clear All* near the top of the Styles task pane.
   h. With the Mark Twain quote still selected, click the *Intense Quote* style in the Styles task pane.

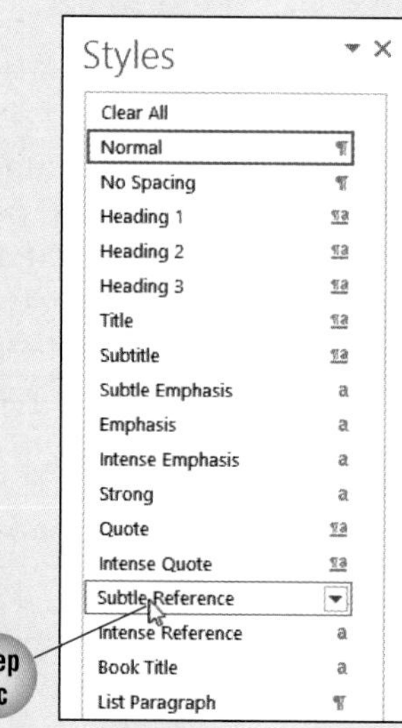

3. Modify the Heading 1 style by completing the following steps:
   a. Right-click the Heading 1 style in the Styles group.
   b. Click *Modify* at the shortcut menu.

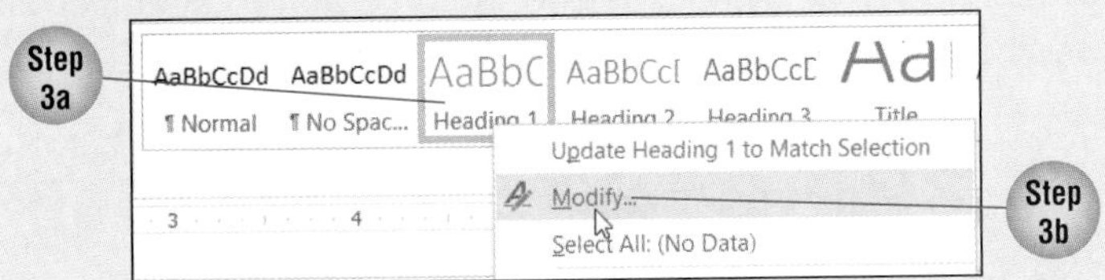

   c. At the Modify Styles dialog box, click the Bold button in the *Formatting* section.
   d. Click the Center button in the *Formatting* section.

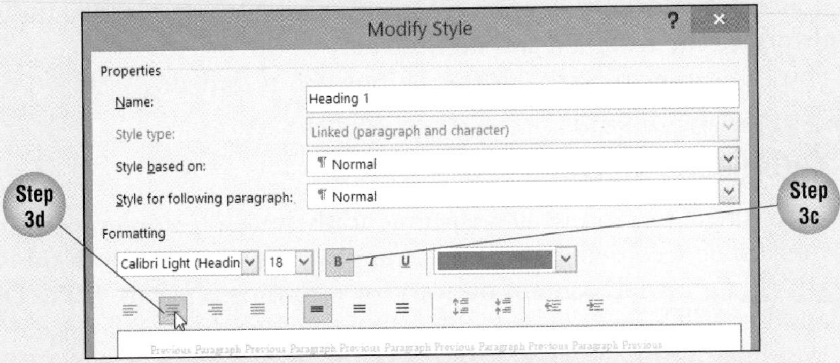

   e. Click OK to close the Modify Styles dialog box.
4. Modify the Heading 2 style by completing the following steps:
   a. Right-click the *Heading 2* style in the Styles task pane and then click *Modify* at the shortcut menu.
   b. At the Modify Styles dialog box, click the Format button in the lower left corner of the dialog box and then click *Font* at the drop-down list.
   c. At the Font dialog box, click the down-pointing arrow at the right side of the *Font color* option box and then click *Dark Red* (first option in the *Standard Colors* section).
   d. Click the *Small caps* check box to insert a check mark.
   e. Click OK to close the Font dialog box.
   f. Click the Format button in the dialog box and then click *Paragraph* at the drop-down list.
   g. At the Paragraph dialog box, click the up arrow in the *After* measurement box (this displays *6 pt* in the measurement box).
   h. Click OK to close the Paragraph dialog box and then click OK to close the Modify Styles dialog box.
5. Close the Styles task pane.
6. Save, print, and then close **WL2-C4-P2-BTAdventures.docx**.

Project 3 Record and Run Macros

5 Parts

You will record several macros, run the macros in a document, assign a macro to a keyboard command, delete a macro, and specify macro security settings.

Creating Macros

Macros are time-saving tools that automate the formatting of Word documents. The word *macro* was coined by computer programmers for a collection of commands used to make a large programming job easier and save time. Two basic steps are involved in working with macros: recording a macro and running a macro. When you record a macro, all of the keys pressed and dialog boxes displayed are recorded and become part of the macro. After a macro is recorded, you can run it to carry out the actions you recorded.

Recording a Macro

Quick Steps

Record a Macro

1. Click DEVELOPER tab.
2. Click Record Macro button.

OR

1. Click VIEW tab.
2. Click Macros button arrow.
3. Click *Record Macro.*
4. Make changes at Record Macro dialog box.
5. Click OK.
6. Complete macro steps.
7. Click Stop Recording button.

OR

7. Click macro icon on Status bar.

Recording a macro involves turning on the macro recorder, performing the steps to be recorded, and then turning off the recorder. Both the VIEW tab and DEVELOPER tab contain buttons for recording a macro. If the DEVELOPER tab does not appear on the ribbon, turn on the display of this tab by opening the Word Options dialog box with *Customize Ribbon* selected in the left panel, inserting a check mark in the *Developer* check box in the list box at the right, and then clicking OK to close the dialog box.

To record a macro, click the Record Macro button in the Code group on the DEVELOPER tab. You can also click the VIEW tab, click the Macros button arrow in the Macros group, and then click *Record Macro* at the drop-down list. This displays the Record Macro dialog box, shown in Figure 4.4. At the Record Macro dialog box, type a name for the macro in the *Macro name* text box. A macro name must begin with a letter and can contain only letters and numbers. Type a description for the macro in the *Description* text box located at the bottom of the dialog box. A macro description can contain a maximum of 255 characters and may include spaces.

Figure 4.4 Record Macro Dialog Box

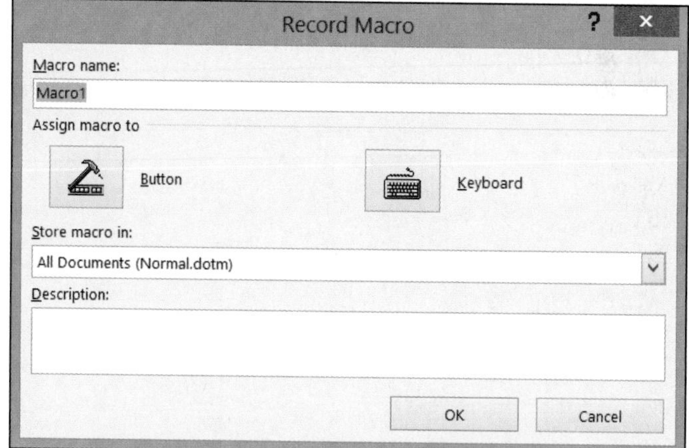

By default, Word stores macros in the Normal template. Macros stored in this template are available for any document based on the template. In a company or school setting, where computers may be networked, consider storing macros in personalized documents or templates. Specify the location for macros with the *Store macro in* option box at the Record Macro dialog box (refer to Figure 4.4).

After typing the macro name, specifying where the macro is to be stored, and typing a description of the macro, click OK to close the Record Macro dialog box. At the open document, a macro icon displays near the left side of the Status bar and the mouse displays with a cassette icon attached. In the document, perform the actions to be recorded. If you are selecting text as part of the macro, use the keyboard to select text because a macro cannot record selections made by the mouse. When all of the steps have been completed, click the Stop Recording button (previously the Record Macro button) located in the Code group on the DEVELOPER tab or click the macro icon that displays near the left side of the Status bar.

Stop Recording

When you record macros in Project 3a, you will be instructed to name the macros beginning with your initials. Recorded macros are stored in the Normal template document by default and display at the Macros dialog box. If the computer you are using is networked, macros recorded by other students will also display at the Macros dialog box. Naming macros with your initials will enable you to distinguish your macros from the macros of other users.

Project 3a Recording Macros

Part 1 of 5

1. Turn on the display of the DEVELOPER tab by completing the following steps. (Skip to Step 2 if the DEVELOPER tab is already visible.)
   a. Click the FILE tab and then click *Options*.
   b. At the Word Options dialog box, click *Customize Ribbon* in the left panel.
   c. In the list box at the right, click the *Developer* check box to insert a check mark.

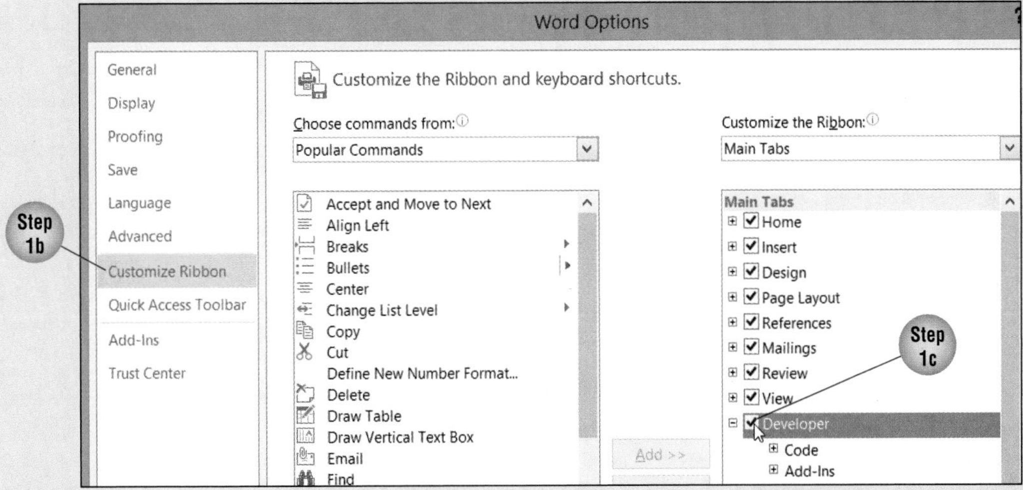

   d. Click OK to close the dialog box.

2. Record a macro that selects text, indents a paragraph of text, and then applies italic formatting by completing the following steps:
   a. Open **MacroText.docx** and then position the insertion point at the left margin of the paragraph that begins with *This is text to use for creating macros.*
   b. Click the DEVELOPER tab.
   c. Click the Record Macro button in the Code group on the DEVELOPER tab.

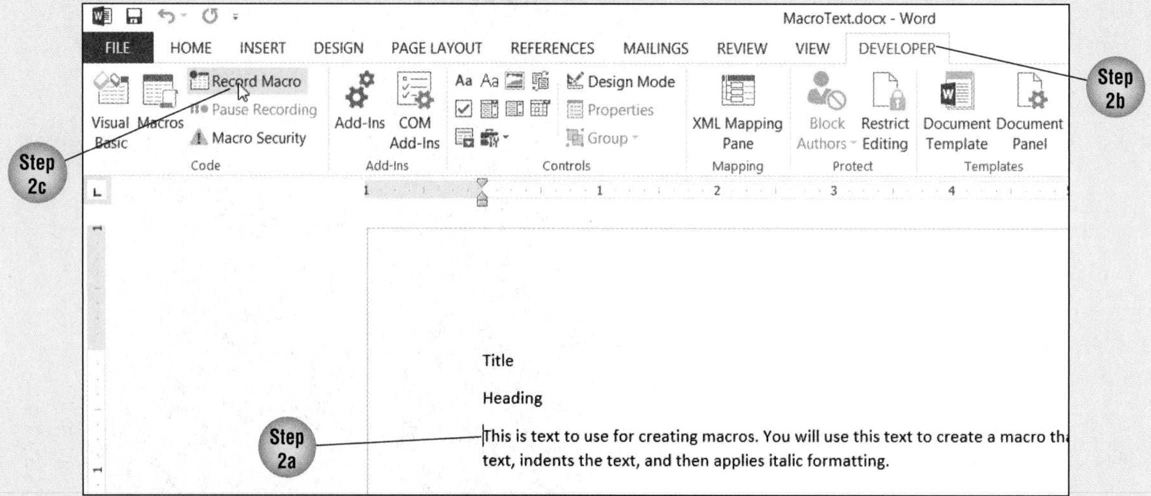

   d. At the Record Macro dialog box, type **XXXIndentItalics** in the *Macro name* text box. (Type your initials in place of the *XXX*.)
   e. Click inside the *Description* text box and then type **Select text, indent text, and apply italic formatting.** (If text displays in the *Description* text box, select the text first and then type the description.)
   f. Click OK.

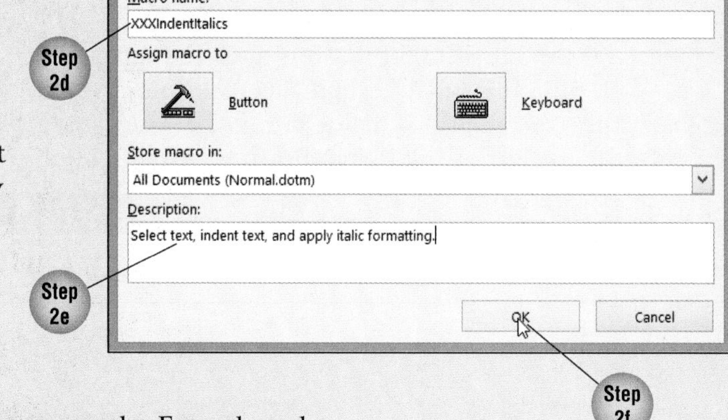

   g. At the document, press F8 to turn on the Extend mode.
   h. Hold down the Shift key and the Ctrl key and then press the Down Arrow key. (Shift + Ctrl + Down Arrow is the keyboard shortcut to select a paragraph.)
   i. Click the HOME tab.
   j. Click the Paragraph group dialog box launcher.
   k. At the Paragraph dialog box, click the up-pointing arrow in the *Left* measurement box until *0.5"* displays.
   l. Click the up-pointing arrow in the *Right* measurement until *0.5"* displays.
   m. Click OK.
   n. Press Ctrl + I to apply italic formatting.

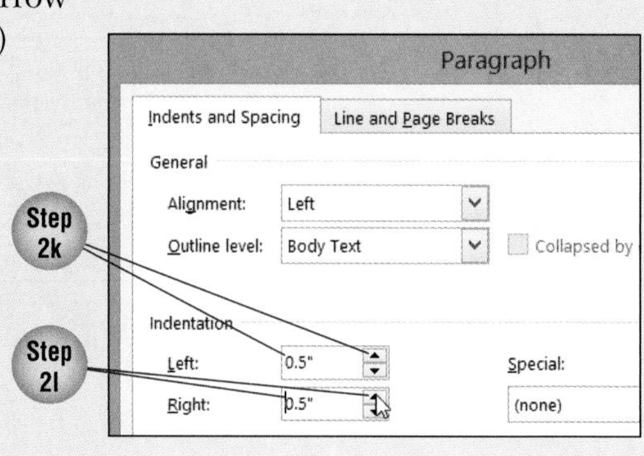

o. Press the Esc key and then press the Left Arrow key. (This deselects the text.)

p. Click the macro icon on the Status bar to turn off the macro recording.

3. Record a macro that applies formatting to a heading by completing the following steps:
   a. Move the insertion point to the beginning of the text *Heading*.
   b. Click the DEVELOPER tab and then click the Record Macro button in the Code group.
   c. At the Record Macro dialog box, type **XXXHeading** in the *Macro name* text box. (Type your initials in place of the *XXX*.)
   d. Click inside the *Description* text box and then type **Select text, change font size, turn on bold and italic, and insert bottom border line.** (If text displays in the *Description* text box, select the text first and then type the description.)
   e. Click OK.
   f. At the document, press F8 and then press the End key.
   g. Click the HOME tab.
   h. Click the Bold button in the Font group.
   i. Click the Italic button in the Font group.
   j. Click the Font Size button arrow in the Font group and then click *12* at the drop-down gallery.
   k. Click the Borders button arrow in the Paragraph group and then click *Bottom Border* at the drop-down list.
   l. Press the Home key. (This moves the insertion point back to the beginning of the heading and deselects the text.)
   m. Click the macro icon on the Status bar to turn off the macro recording.
4. Close the document without saving it.

Running a Macro

To run a recorded macro, click the Macros button in the Code group on the DEVELOPER tab or click the Macros button on the VIEW tab. This displays the Macros dialog box, shown in Figure 4.5. At this dialog box, double-click the desired macro in the list box or click the macro and then click the Run button.

Quick Steps

Run a Macro
1. Click DEVELOPER tab.
2. Click Macros button.
3. At Macros dialog box, double-click macro in list box.

OR
1. Click VIEW tab.
2. Click Macros button.
3. At Macros dialog box, double-click macro in list box.

Figure 4.5 Macros Dialog Box

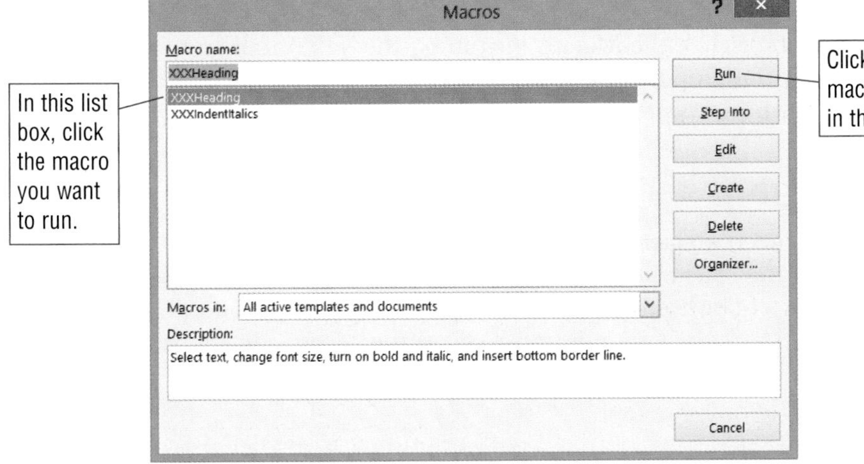

Project 3b Running Macros

1. Open **WriteResumes.docx** and save the document with the name **WL2-C4-P3-WriteResumes**.
2. With the insertion point positioned at the beginning of the heading *Resume Strategies*, run the XXXHeading macro by completing the following steps:
   a. Click the VIEW tab.
   b. Click the Macros button in the Macros group.
   c. At the Macros dialog box, click *XXXHeading* in the list box.
   d. Click the Run button.

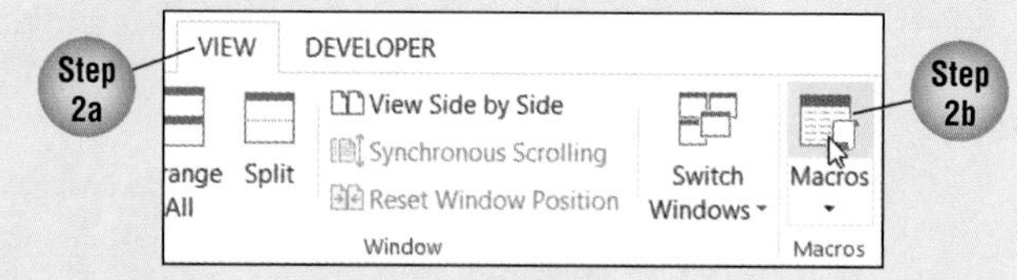

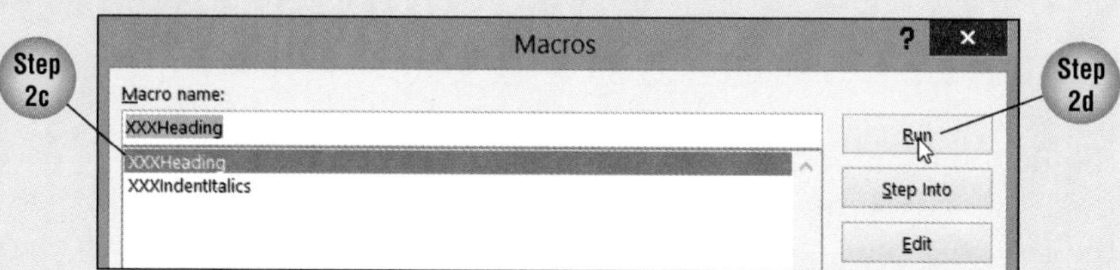

3. Complete steps similar to those in Steps 2a–2d to run the macro for the two other headings in the document: *Writing Style* and *Phrases to Avoid*.
4. Move the insertion point to the beginning of the paragraph below *First Person* and then complete the following steps to run the XXXIndentItalics macro:
   a. Click the DEVELOPER tab.
   b. Click the Macros button in the Code group.
   c. At the Macros dialog box, double-click *XXXIndentItalics* in the list box.
5. Complete steps similar to those in Step 4a–4c to run the XXXIndentItalics macro for the paragraph below *Third Person*, the paragraph that begins *Responsible for all marketing and special events*, and the paragraph that begins *Orchestrated a series of marketing and special-event programs*.
6. Save, print, and then close **WL2-C4-P3-WriteResumes.docx**.

Pausing and Resuming a Macro

Pause

When recording a macro, you can temporarily suspend the recording, perform actions that are not recorded, and then resume recording the macro. To pause the recording of a macro, click the Pause Recording button in the Code group on the DEVELOPER tab or click the Macros button on the VIEW tab and then click *Pause Recording* at the drop-down list. To resume recording the macro, click the Resume Recorder button (previously the Pause Recording button).

Deleting a Macro

If you no longer need a macro that you have recorded, you can delete it. To delete a macro, display the Macros dialog box, click the macro name in the list box, and then click the Delete button. At the message asking if you want to delete the macro, click Yes. Click the Close button to close the Macros dialog box.

Project 3c Deleting a Macro

Part 3 of 5

1. At a blank document, delete the XXXIndentItalics macro by completing the following steps:
   a. Click the DEVELOPER tab and then click the Macros button in the Code group.
   b. At the Macros dialog box, click *XXXIndentItalics* in the list box.
   c. Click the Delete button.

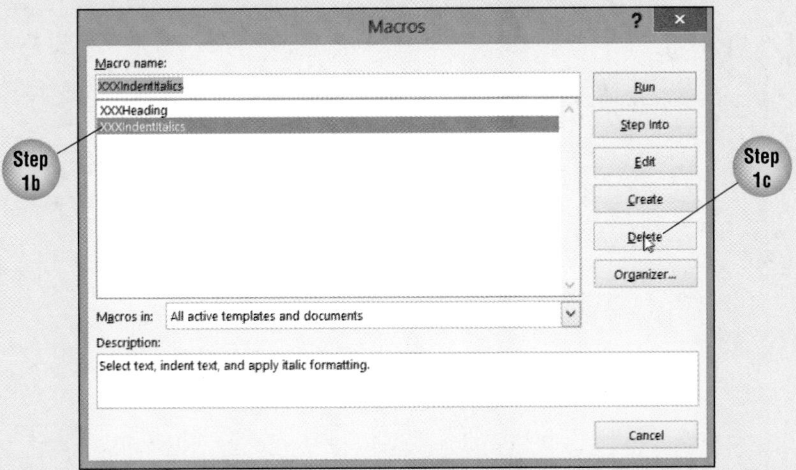

   d. At the message asking if you want to delete the macro, click Yes.
   e. Click the Close button to close the Macros dialog box.
2. Close the document without saving it.

Assigning a Macro to a Keyboard Command

Consider assigning macros that you use regularly to keyboard commands. To run a macro that has been assigned to a keyboard command, simply press the assigned keys. A macro can be assigned to a keyboard command with the following combinations:

Alt + letter
Ctrl + letter
Alt + Ctrl + letter
Alt + Shift + letter
Ctrl + Shift + letter
Alt + Ctrl + Shift + letter

Word already uses many combinations for Word functions. For example, pressing Alt + Ctrl + C inserts the copyright symbol.

Assign a macro to a keyboard command at the Customize Keyboard dialog box, as shown in Figure 4.6. Specify the keyboard command by pressing the desired keys, such as Alt + D. The keyboard command you enter displays in the *Press new shortcut key* text box. Word inserts the message *Currently assigned to:* below the *Current keys* list box. If the keyboard command is already assigned to a command, the command is listed after the *Currently assigned to:* message. If Word has not used the keyboard command, *[unassigned]* displays after the *Currently assigned to:* message. When assigning a keyboard command to a macro, make sure you use an unassigned keyboard command.

Figure 4.6 Customize Keyboard Dialog Box

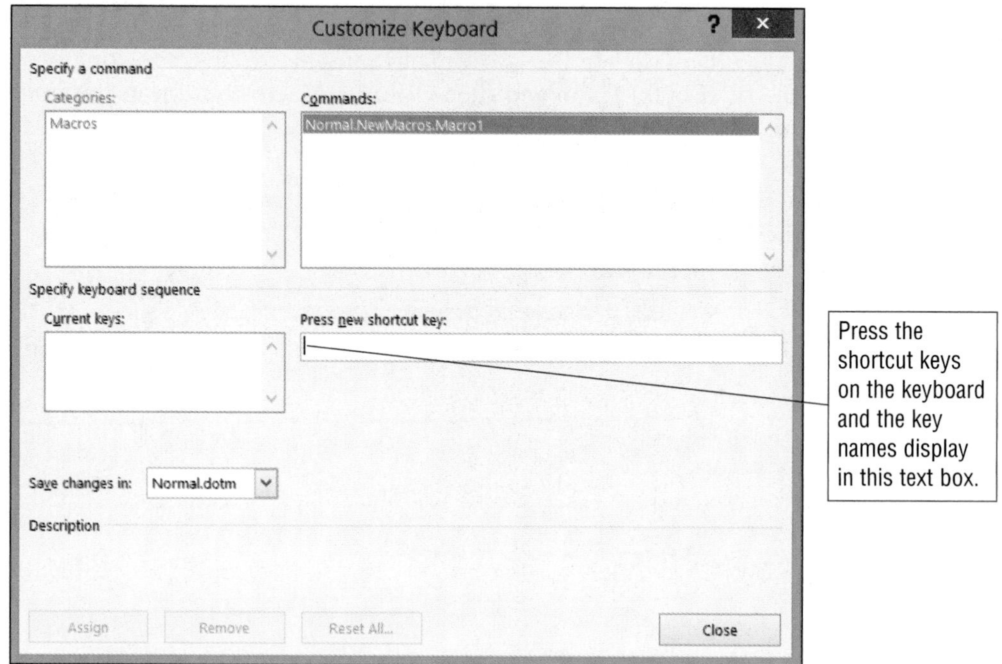

In Project 3d, you will record a macro and then assign it to a keyboard command. When you delete a macro, the keyboard command is no longer assigned to that action. This allows you to use the key combination again.

Project 3d Assigning a Macro to a Keyboard Command — Part 4 of 5

1. Record a macro named *XXXFont* that selects text and applies font formatting and assign it to the keyboard command Alt + Ctrl + A by completing the following steps:
   a. At a blank document, click the DEVELOPER tab and then click the Record Macro button in the Code group.
   b. At the Record Macro dialog box, type XXXFont in the *Macro name* text box. (Type your initials in place of *XXX*.).
   c. Click inside the *Description* text box and then type Select text and change the font and font color.
   d. Click the Keyboard button.

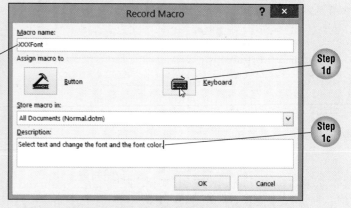

Record Macro
Macro name:
XXXFont
Assign macro to
Button
Keyboard
Store macro in:
All Documents (Normal.dotm)
Description:
Select text and change the font and the font color.
OK
Cancel
Step 1b
Step 1d
Step 1c

e. At the Customize Keyboard dialog box with the insertion point positioned in the *Press new shortcut key* text box, press Alt + Ctrl + A.
f. Check to make sure *[unassigned]* displays after *Currently assigned to:*.
g. Click the Assign button.
h. Click the Close button.
i. At the document, click the HOME tab.
j. Press Ctrl + A.
k. Click the Font group dialog box launcher.
l. At the Font dialog box, click *Cambria* in the *Font* list box and apply the Dark Blue font color (ninth color from left in the *Standard Colors* section).
m. Click OK to close the Font dialog box.
n. At the document, press the Down Arrow on the keyboard.
o. Click the macro icon on the Status bar to turn off the macro recording.

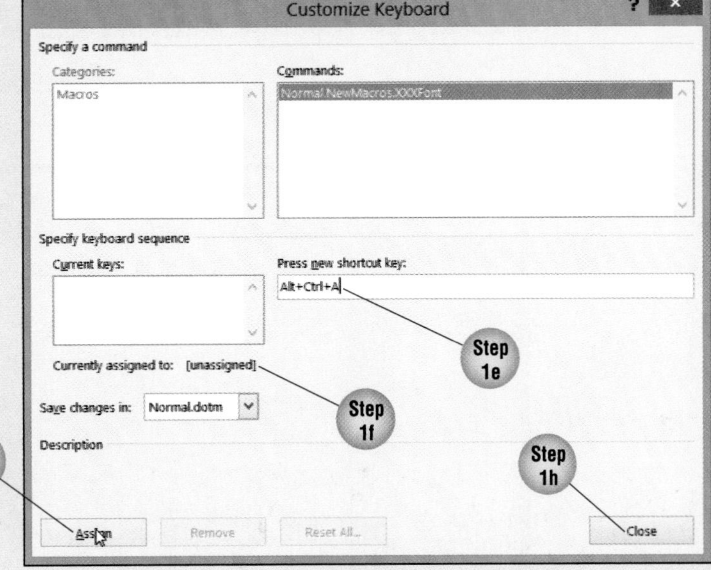

2. Close the document without saving it.
3. Open **GSHLtr.docx** and save the document with the name **WL2-C4-P3-GSHLtr**.
4. Run the XXXFont macro by pressing Alt + Ctrl + A.
5. Run the XXXHeading macro for the heading *Procedural* and the heading *Teaching*.
6. Save, print, and then close **WL2-C4-P3-GSHLtr.docx**.

Specifying Macro Security Settings

Some macros can create a potential security risk by introducing or spreading a virus to your computer or network. For this reason, Microsoft Word provides macro security settings for specifying what actions you want to perform with macros in a document. To display the macro security settings, click the DEVELOPER tab and then click the Macro Security button in the Code group. This displays the Trust Center with *Macro Settings* selected in the left panel, as shown in Figure 4.7.

Choose the first option, *Disable all macros without notification*, and all of the macros and security alerts are disabled. The second option, *Disable all macros with notification*, is the default setting. At this setting, a security alert appears if a macro is present and you can choose to enable the macro. If you choose the third option, *Disable all macros except digitally signed macros*, a digitally signed macro by a trusted publisher will automatically run, but you will still need to enable a digitally signed macro by a publisher that is not trusted. The last option, *Enable all macros (not recommended; potentially dangerous code can run)*, will allow all macros to run but, as the option implies, this is not recommended.

The changes that you make to the macro security settings in Word apply only to Word. The macro security settings are not changed in the other applications in the Office suite.

The Trust Center can also be opened by displaying the Word Options dialog box, clicking Trust Center in the left panel, and then clicking the Trust Center Settings button.

Figure 4.7 Trust Center

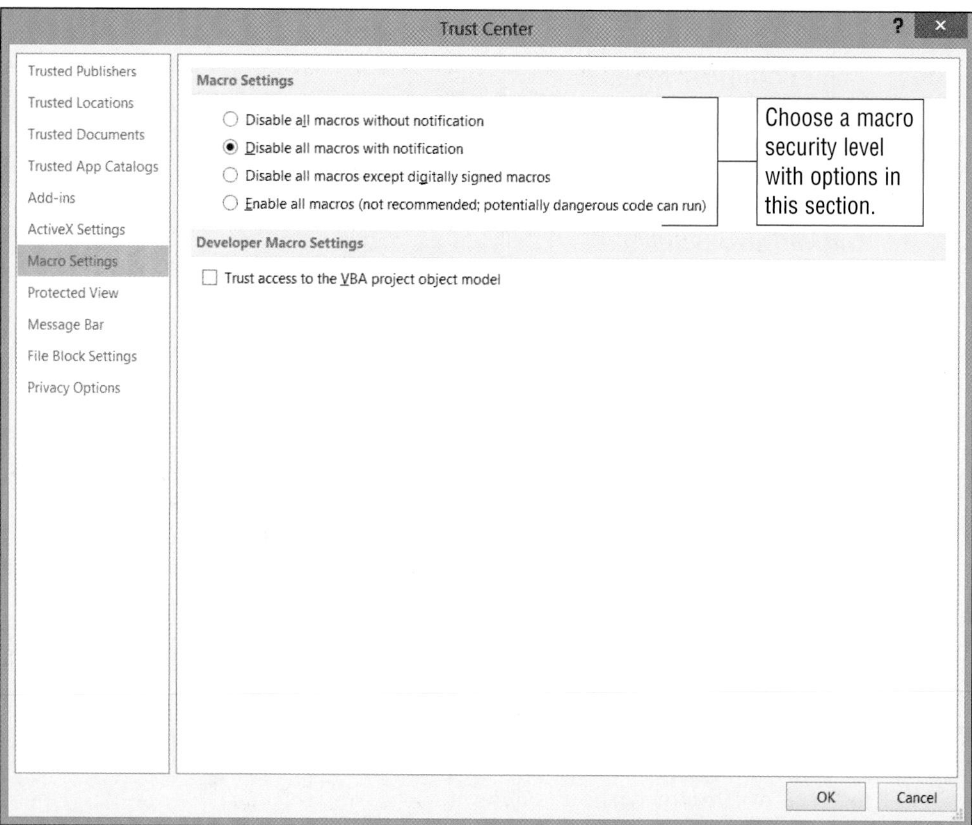

Saving a Macro-Enabled Document or Template

By default, the macros you create are saved in the Normal.dotm template. The .dotm extension identifies the template as ***macro-enabled***. A template or document must be macro-enabled for a macro to be saved in it. You can also save macros in a specific document or template to make them available when you open that document or template. To specify a location for saving a macro, display the Record Macro dialog box, click the down-pointing arrow at the right side of the *Store macro in* option box, and then click the desired document or template.

Save a document containing macros as a macro-enabled document. To do this, display the Save As dialog box and then change the *Save as type* option to *Word Macro-Enabled Document (*.docm)*. Save a template containing macros as a macro-enabled template by changing the *Save as type* option at the Save As dialog box to *Word Macro-Enabled Template (*.dotm)*.

Project 3e Changing Macro Security Settings and Saving a Macro-Enabled Template

Part 5 of 5

If you are using Microsoft Word in a public setting, such as a school, you may not be able to change macro security settings. If that is the case, skip to Step 4.

1. Open **Affidavit.docx**.
2. Change the macro security setting by completing the following steps:
   a. Click the DEVELOPER tab and then click the Macro Security button in the Code group.
   b. At the Trust Center, click *Disable all macros without notification*.
   c. Click OK.

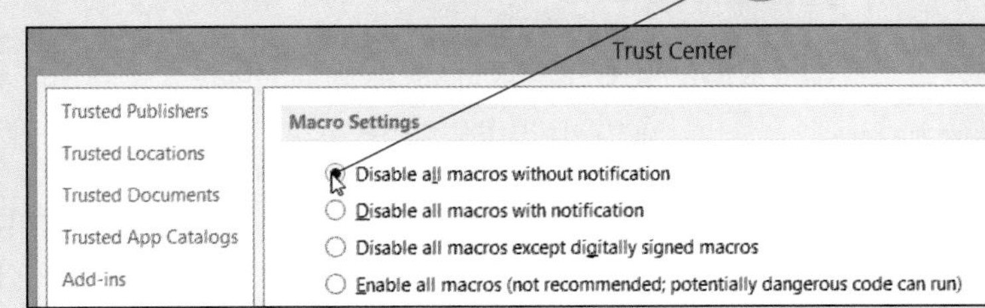

3. Change the macro security setting again by completing the following steps:
   a. Click the Macro Security button in the Code group.
   b. At the Trust Center, click *Disable all macros with notification*.
   c. Click OK.
4. Save the document as a macro-enabled template by completing the following steps:
   a. Press F12 to display the Save As dialog box.
   b. At the Save As dialog box, click the down-pointing arrow at the right side of the *Save as type* option box.
   c. Click *Word Macro-Enabled Template (*.dotm)* at the drop-down list.
   d. Select the text in the *File name* text box and then type **WL2-C4-P3-AffidavitTemplate**.
   e. Make sure the WL2C4 folder on your storage medium is the active folder.
   f. Click the Save button.

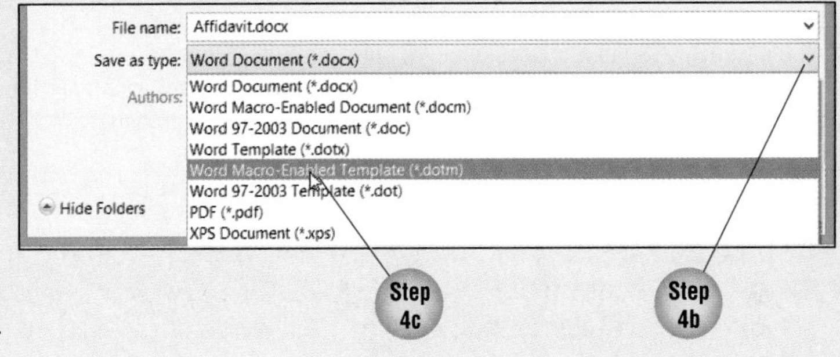

5. Close **WL2-C4-P3-AffidavitTemplate.dotm**.

Project 4 Navigate and Insert Hyperlinks in a Computer Viruses Report

5 Parts

You will open a report on computer viruses and computer security and insert and then navigate in the report with the Navigation pane, bookmarks, hyperlinks, and cross-references.

Navigating in a Document

Word includes a number of features for navigating in a document. In addition to the navigating features you have already learned, you can navigate using the Navigation pane and by inserting bookmarks, hyperlinks, and cross references.

Navigating Using the Navigation Pane

Quick Steps

Display the Navigation Pane

1. Click VIEW tab.
2. Click *Navigation Pane* check box.

To use the Navigation pane to navigate in a document, click the VIEW tab and then click the *Navigation Pane* check box in the Show group to insert a check mark. The Navigation pane displays at the left side of the screen, as shown in Figure 4.8, and includes a search text box and a pane with three tabs.

Click the first Navigation pane tab, HEADINGS, and titles and headings with certain styles applied display in the Navigation pane. Click a title or heading in the pane and the insertion point moves to that title or heading. Click the PAGES tab and a thumbnail of each page displays in the pane. Click a thumbnail to move the insertion point to that specific page. Click the RESULTS tab to browse the current search results in the document.

Close the Navigation pane by clicking the *Navigation Pane* check box in the Show group on the VIEW tab to remove the check mark. Another option is to click the Close button located in the upper right corner of the pane.

Figure 4.8 Navigation Pane

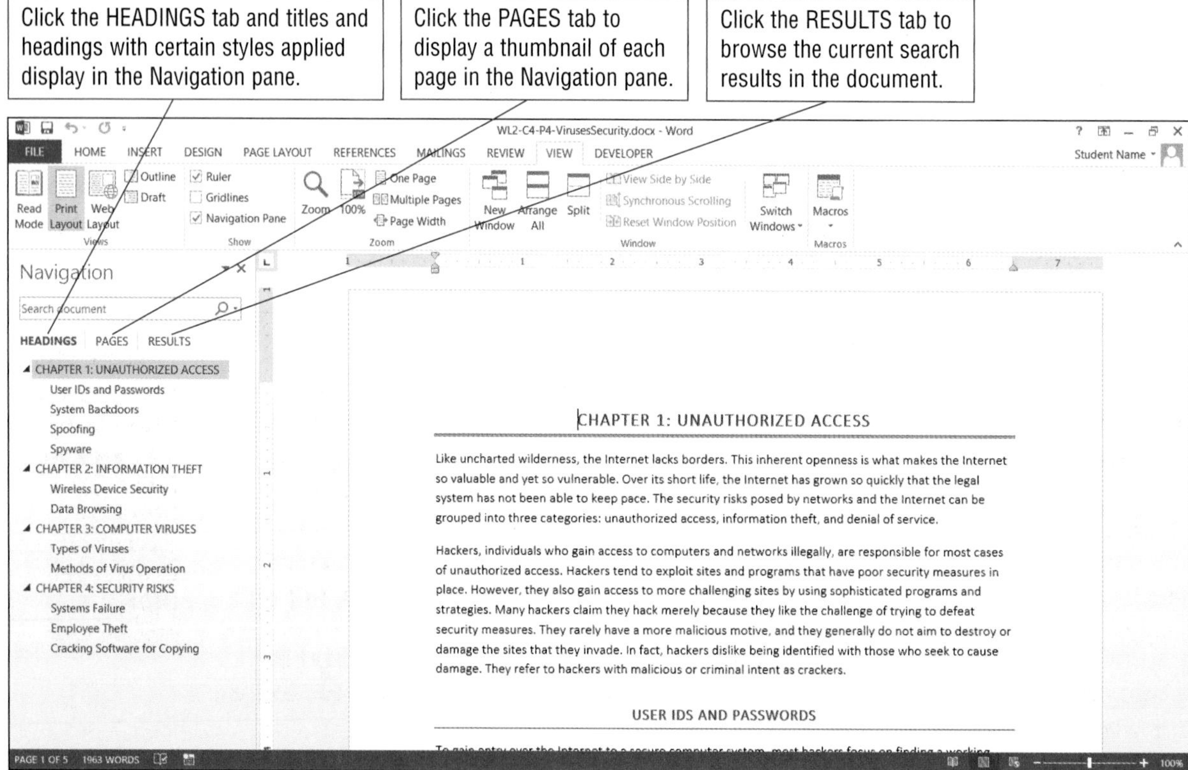

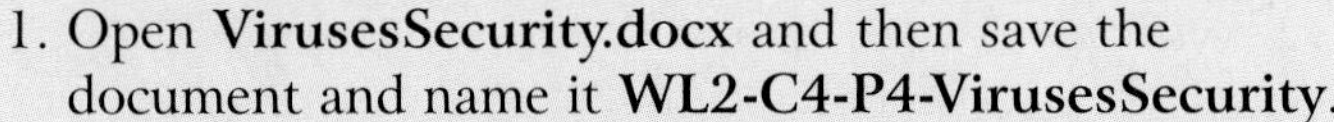

Project 4a Navigating Using the Navigation Pane

Part 1 of 5

1. Open **VirusesSecurity.docx** and then save the document and name it **WL2-C4-P4-VirusesSecurity**.
2. Since this document has heading styles applied, you can easily navigate in the document with the Navigation pane by completing the following steps:
   a. Click the VIEW tab.
   b. Click the *Navigation Pane* check box in the Show group to insert a check mark. (This displays the Navigation pane at the left side of the screen.)
   c. With the HEADINGS tab active, click the *CHAPTER 2: INFORMATION THEFT* heading in the Navigation pane.
   d. Click *CHAPTER 3: COMPUTER VIRUSES* in the Navigation pane.
   e. Click *Systems Failure* in the Navigation pane.
3. Navigate in the document using thumbnails by completing the following steps:
   a. Click the PAGES tab in the Navigation pane. (This displays page thumbnails in the pane.)
   b. Click the page 1 thumbnail in the Navigation pane. (You may need to scroll up the Navigation pane to display this thumbnail.)
   c. Click the page 3 thumbnail in the Navigation pane.
4. Close the Navigation pane by clicking the Close button in the upper right corner of the Navigation pane.
5. Save **WL2-C4-P4-VirusesSecurity.docx**.

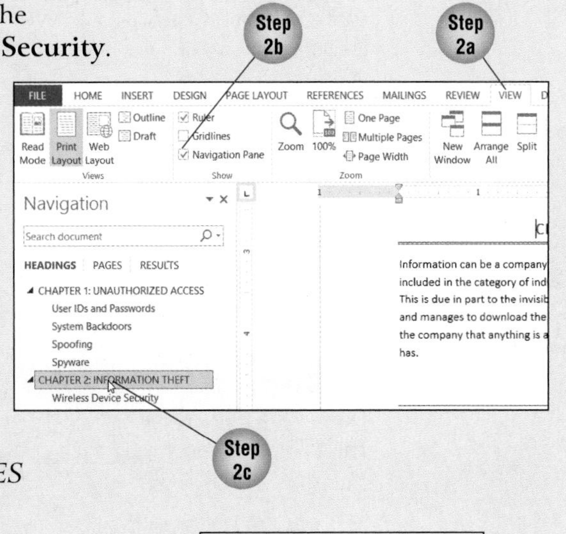

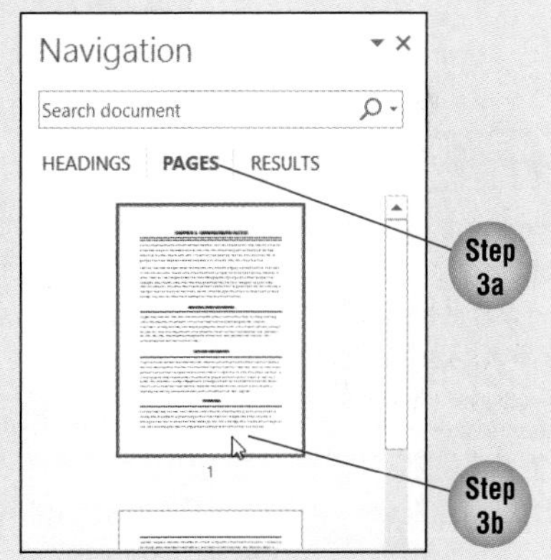

Inserting and Navigating with Bookmarks

When working in a long document, you may find it useful to mark a place in the document with a bookmark so you can quickly move the insertion point to the location. Create bookmarks for locations in a document at the Bookmark dialog box.

To create a bookmark, position the insertion point at the desired location, click the INSERT tab, and then click the Bookmark button in the Links group. This displays the Bookmark dialog box, as shown in Figure 4.9. Type a name for the bookmark in the *Bookmark name* text box and then click the Add button. Repeat these steps as many times as needed to insert the desired bookmarks. Give each bookmark a unique name. A bookmark name must begin with a letter and can contain numbers, but not spaces. Use the underscore character if you want to separate words in a bookmark name.

By default, the bookmarks you insert are not visible in the document. Turn on the display of bookmarks at the Word Options dialog box with *Advanced* selected. Display this dialog box by clicking the FILE tab and then clicking *Options*. At the Word Options dialog box, click the *Advanced* option in the left panel. Click the

Quick Steps

Insert a Bookmark
1. Position insertion point at desired location.
2. Click INSERT tab.
3. Click Bookmark button.
4. Type name for bookmark.
5. Click Add button.

Bookmark

Figure 4.9 Bookmark Dialog Box

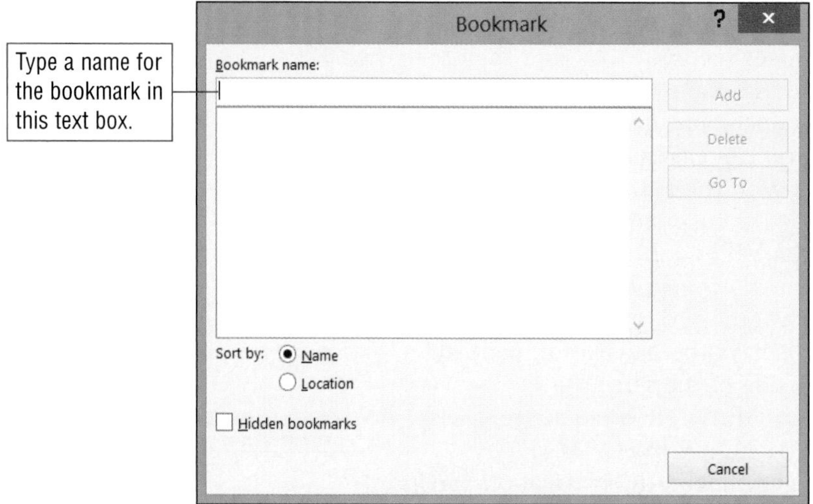

Show bookmarks check box in the *Show document content* section to insert a check mark. Complete similar steps to turn off the display of bookmarks. A bookmark displays in the document as an I-beam marker.

HINT

Bookmark brackets do not print.

You can also create a bookmark for selected text. To do this, first select the text and then complete the steps to create a bookmark. When you create a bookmark for selected text, a left bracket ([) indicates the beginning of the selected text and a right bracket (]) indicates the end of the selected text.

Quick Steps

Navigate with Bookmarks

1. Click INSERT tab.
2. Click Bookmark button.
3. Double-click desired bookmark name.

After you insert bookmarks in a document, you can move the insertion point to a specific bookmark. To do this, display the Bookmark dialog box and then double-click the bookmark name or click the bookmark name and then click the Go To button. When Word stops at the location of the bookmark, click the Close button to close the dialog box. If you move the insertion point to a bookmark created with selected text, Word moves the insertion point to the bookmark and selects the text. Delete bookmarks in the Bookmark dialog box by clicking the bookmark name in the list box and then clicking the Delete button.

Project 4b Inserting and Navigating with Bookmarks — Part 2 of 5

1. With **WL2-C4-P4-VirusesSecurity.docx** open, turn on the display of bookmarks by completing the following steps:
   a. Click the FILE tab and then click *Options*.
   b. At the Word Options dialog box, click *Advanced* in the left panel.
   c. Scroll down the dialog box and then click the *Show bookmarks* check box in the *Show document content* section to insert a check mark.
   d. Click OK to close the dialog box.
2. Insert a bookmark by completing the following steps:
   a. Move the insertion point to the beginning of the paragraph in the *TYPES OF VIRUSES* section (the paragraph that begins *Viruses can be categorized*).
   b. Click the INSERT tab.
   c. Click the Bookmark button in the Links group.

d. At the Bookmark dialog box, type **Viruses** in the *Bookmark name* text box.
e. Click the Add button.

3. Using steps similar to those in Steps 2a–2e, insert a bookmark named *Electrical* at the beginning of the paragraph in the *SYSTEMS FAILURE* section.
4. Navigate to the Viruses bookmark by completing the following steps:
   a. If necessary, click the INSERT tab.
   b. Click the Bookmark button in the Links group.
   c. At the Bookmark dialog box, click *Viruses* in the list box.
   d. Click the Go To button.
5. With the Bookmark dialog box open, delete the Electrical bookmark by clicking *Electrical* in the list box and then clicking the Delete button.
6. Click the Close button to close the Bookmark dialog box.
7. Save **WL2-C4-P4-VirusesSecurity.docx**.

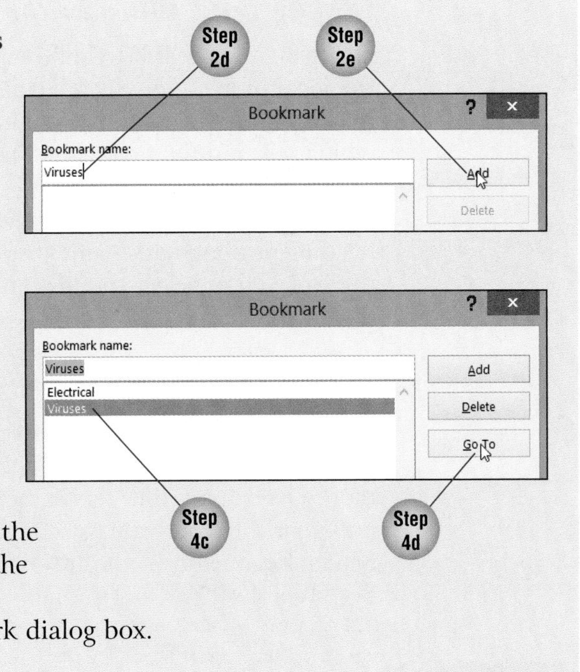

Inserting Hyperlinks

Hyperlinks can serve a number of purposes in a document. They can be used to navigate to a specific location in the document, to display a different document, to open a file in a different program, to create a new document, and to link to an email address.

Insert a hyperlink by clicking the Hyperlink button located in the Links group on the INSERT tab. This displays the Insert Hyperlink dialog box, as shown in Figure 4.10. You can also display the Insert Hyperlink dialog box by pressing Ctrl + K. At this dialog box, identify what you want to link to and the location of the link. Click the ScreenTip button to customize the hyperlink's ScreenTip.

Quick Steps

Insert a Hyperlink
1. Click INSERT tab.
2. Click Hyperlink button.
3. Make desired changes at Insert Hyperlink dialog box.
4. Click OK.

Hyperlink

Figure 4.10 Insert Hyperlink Dialog Box

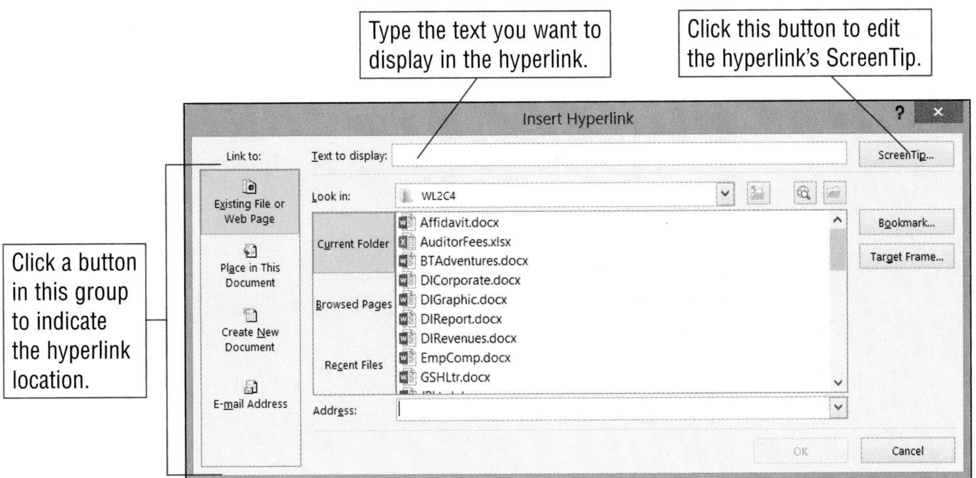

Linking to a Place in the Document

To create a hyperlink to another location in the document, you first need to mark the location by applying a heading style to the text or inserting a bookmark. To hyperlink to a heading or bookmark in a document, display the Insert Hyperlink dialog box and then click the Place in This Document button in the *Link to* section. This displays text with heading styles applied and bookmarks in the *Select a place in this document* list box. Click the desired heading style or bookmark name and the heading or bookmark name displays in the *Text to display* text box. Leave the text as displayed or select the text and then type the text you want to appear in the document.

Navigating Using Hyperlinks

Navigate to a hyperlink by hovering the mouse over the hyperlink text, holding down the Ctrl key, and then clicking the left mouse button. When you hover the mouse over hyperlink text, a ScreenTip displays with the name of the heading or bookmark. If you want specific information to display in the ScreenTip, click the ScreenTip button in the Insert Hyperlink dialog box, type the desired text in the Set Hyperlink ScreenTip dialog box, and then click OK.

Project 4c Inserting Hyperlinks — Part 3 of 5

1. With **WL2-C4-P4-VirusesSecurity.docx** open, insert a hyperlink to a bookmark in the document by completing the following steps:
   a. Position the insertion point at the immediate right of the period that ends the first paragraph of text in the *CHAPTER 4: SECURITY RISKS* section (located on page 4).
   b. Press the spacebar once.
   c. If necessary, click the INSERT tab.
   d. Click the Hyperlink button in the Links group.
   e. At the Insert Hyperlink dialog box, click the Place in This Document button in the *Link to* section.
   f. Scroll down the *Select a place in this document* list box and then click *Viruses,* which displays below *Bookmarks* in the list box.
   g. Select the text that displays in the *Text to display* text box and then type **Click to view types of viruses**.
   h. Click the ScreenTip button located in the upper right corner of the dialog box.
   i. At the Set Hyperlink ScreenTip dialog box, type **View types of viruses** and then click OK.
   j. Click OK to close the Insert Hyperlink dialog box.

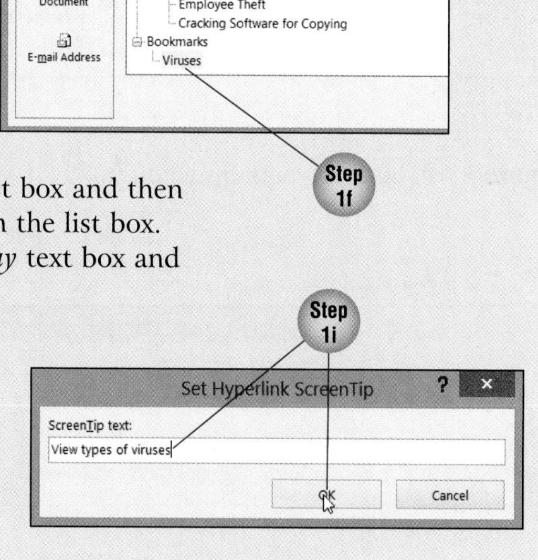

2. Navigate to the hyperlinked location by hovering the mouse over the Click to view types of viruses hyperlink, holding down the Ctrl key, and then clicking the left mouse button.
3. Insert a hyperlink to a heading in the document by completing the following steps:
   a. Press Ctrl + Home to move the insertion point to the beginning of the document.
   b. Move the insertion point to the immediate right of the period that ends the second paragraph in the document and then press the spacebar.
   c. Click the Hyperlink button on the INSERT tab.
   d. At the Insert Hyperlink dialog box with the Place in This Document button selected in the *Link to* section, click the *Methods of Virus Operation* heading in the *Select a place in this document* list box.
   e. Click OK to close the Insert Hyperlink dialog box.
4. Navigate to the hyperlinked heading by hovering the mouse over the Methods of Virus Operation hyperlink, holding down the Ctrl key, and then clicking the left mouse button.
5. Save **WL2-C4-P4-VirusesSecurity.docx**.

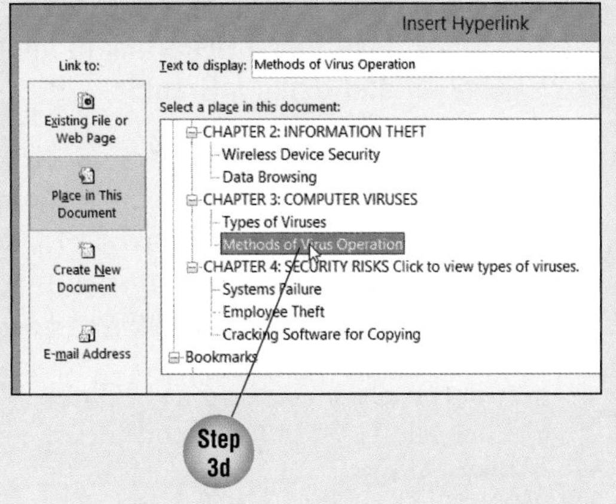

Linking to a File in Another Program

In some situations, you may want to provide information to your readers from a variety of sources, such as a Word document, Excel worksheet, or PowerPoint presentation. To link a Word document to a file in another application, display the Insert Hyperlink dialog box and then click the Existing File or Web Page button in the *Link to* section. Use the *Look in* option to navigate to the folder containing the desired file and then click the file name. Make other changes in the Insert Hyperlink dialog box as needed and then click OK.

Linking to a New Document

In addition to linking to an existing document, you can create a hyperlink to a new document. To do this, display the Insert Hyperlink dialog box and then click the Create New Document button in the *Link to* section. Type a name for the new document in the *Name of new document* text box and then specify if you want to edit the document now or later.

Linking Using a Graphic

You can insert a hyperlink to a file or website in a graphic such as a clip art image, picture, or text box. To hyperlink with a graphic, select the graphic, click the INSERT tab, and then click the Hyperlink button or right-click the graphic and then click *Hyperlink* at the shortcut menu. At the Insert Hyperlink dialog box, specify where you want to link to and the text you want to display in the hyperlink.

Linking to an Email Address

Insert a hyperlink to an email address at the Insert Hyperlink dialog box. To do this, click the E-Mail Address button in the *Link to* group, type the desired address in the *E-mail address* text box, and then type a subject for the email in the *Subject* text box. Click in the *Text to display* text box and then type the text you want to display in the document. To use this feature, the email address you use must be set up in Outlook.

Project 4d **Inserting a Hyperlink to Another Program, a New Document, and Using a Graphic** **Part 4 of 5**

1. The file **WL2-C4-P4-VirusesSecurity.docx** contains information used by Northland Security Systems. The company also has a PowerPoint presentation that contains similar information. Link the document with the presentation by completing the following steps:
   a. Move the insertion point to the immediate right of the period that ends the first paragraph in the *CHAPTER 3: COMPUTER VIRUSES* section and then press the spacebar.
   b. If necessary, click the INSERT tab.
   c. Click the Hyperlink button in the Links group.
   d. At the Insert Hyperlink dialog box, click the Existing File or Web Page button in the *Link to* section.
   e. Click the down-pointing arrow at the right side of the *Look in* list box and then navigate to the WL2C4 folder on your storage medium.
   f. Click ***NSSPres.pptx*** in the list box.
   g. Select the text in the *Text to display* text box and then type **Computer Virus Presentation**.
   h. Click OK to close the Insert Hyperlink dialog box.

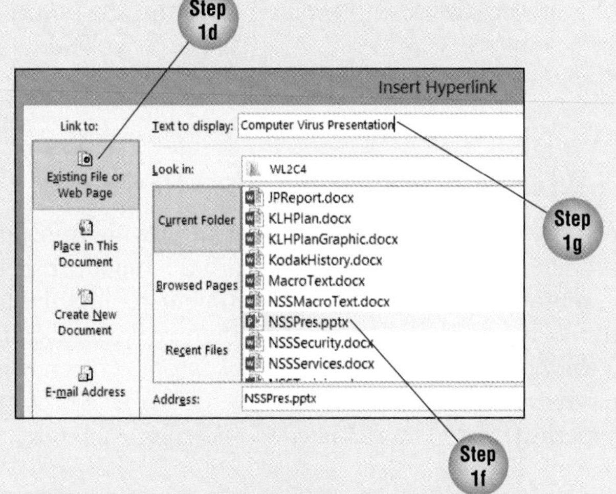

2. View the PowerPoint presentation by completing the following steps:
   a. Position the mouse pointer over the <u>Computer Virus Presentation</u> hyperlink, hold down the Ctrl key, and then click the left mouse button.
   b. At the PowerPoint presentation, click the Slide Show button in the view area on the Status bar.
   c. Click the left mouse button to advance each slide.
   d. Click the left mouse button at the black screen that displays the message *End of slide show, click to exit.*
   e. Close the presentation and PowerPoint by clicking the Close button (which contains an X) in the upper right corner of the screen.

Step 2b

3. Insert a hyperlink with a graphic by completing the following steps:
   a. Press Ctrl + End to move the insertion point to the end of the document.
   b. Click the compass image to select it.
   c. Click the Hyperlink button on the INSERT tab.

d. At the Insert Hyperlink dialog box, make sure the Existing File or Web Page button is selected in the *Link to* group.
e. Navigate to the WL2C4 folder on your storage medium and then double-click ***NSSTraining.docx***. (This selects the document name and closes the dialog box.)
f. Click outside the clip art image to deselect it.
4. Navigate to **NSSTraining.docx** by hovering the mouse pointer over the compass image, holding down the Ctrl key, and then clicking the left mouse button.
5. Close the document by clicking the File tab and then clicking the *Close* option.
6. Insert a hyperlink to a new document by completing the following steps:
a. Move the insertion point to the immediate right of the period that ends the paragraph in the *USER IDS AND PASSWORDS* section and then press the spacebar.
b. Click the Hyperlink button on the INSERT tab.
c. Click the Create New Document button in the *Link to* section.
d. In the *Name of new document* text box, type **PasswordSuggestions**.
e. Edit the text in the *Text to display* text box so it displays as *Password Suggestions*.
f. Make sure the *Edit the new document now* option is selected.
g. Click OK.
h. At the blank document, turn on bold formatting, type **Please type any suggestions you have for creating secure passwords:**, turn off bold formatting, and then press the Enter key.
i. Save and then close the document.

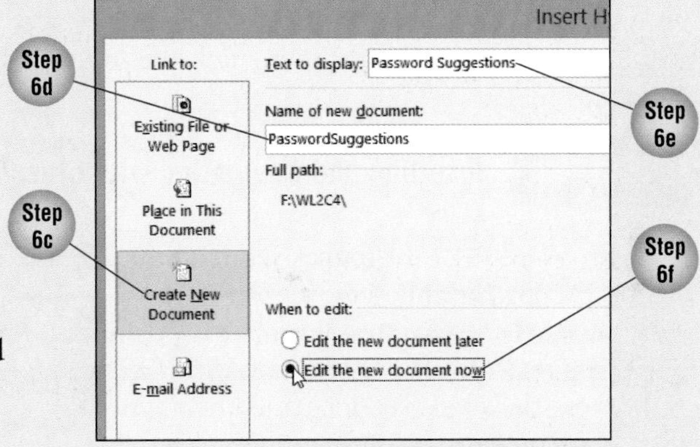

7. Press Ctrl + End to move the insertion point to the end of the document and then press the Enter key four times.
8. Insert a hyperlink to your email address or your instructor's email address by completing the following steps:
a. Click the Hyperlink button.
b. At the Insert Hyperlink dialog box, click the E-mail Address button in the *Link to* group.
c. Type your email address or your instructor's email address in the *E-mail address* text box.
d. Select the current text in the *Text to display* text box and then type **Click to send an email**.
e. Click OK to close the dialog box.
Optional: If you have Outlook set up, hold down the Ctrl key, click the Click to send an email hyperlink, and then send a message indicating that you have completed inserting hyperlinks in the WL2-C4-P4-VirusesSecurity.docx document.
9. Save **WL2-C4-P4-VirusesSecurity.docx**.

Creating a Cross-Reference

Quick Steps

Insert a Cross-Reference

1. Type introductory text.
2. Click INSERT tab.
3. Click Cross-reference button.
4. Identify reference type, where to refer, and specific text.
5. Click Insert.
6. Click Close.

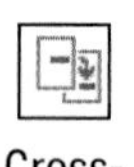

Cross-reference

A *cross-reference* in a Word document refers the reader to another location within the document. This feature is useful in a long document or a document containing related information. References to items such as headings, figures, and tables are also helpful to readers. For example, you can insert a cross-reference that refers readers to another location with more information about the topic, to a specific table, or to a specific page. Cross-references are inserted in a document as hyperlinks.

To insert a cross-reference, type introductory text, click the INSERT tab, and then click the Cross-reference button in the Links group. This displays the Cross-reference dialog box. At the Cross-reference dialog box, identify the reference type, where to refer, and the specific text.

The reference identified in the Cross-reference dialog box displays immediately after the introductory text. To move to the specified reference, hold down the Ctrl key, position the mouse pointer over the introductory text (the pointer turns into a hand), and then click the left mouse button.

Project 4e **Inserting and Navigating with Cross-References** **Part 5 of 5**

1. With **WL2-C4-P4-VirusesSecurity.docx** open, insert a cross-reference in the document by completing the following steps:
   a. Move the insertion point so it is positioned immediately right of the period that ends the paragraph in the *TYPES OF VIRUSES* section.
   b. Press the spacebar once and then type (For more information, refer to.
   c. Press the spacebar once.
   d. If necessary, click the INSERT tab.
   e. Click the Cross-reference button in the Links group.
   f. At the Cross-reference dialog box, click the down-pointing arrow at the right side of the *Reference type* option box and then click *Heading* at the drop-down list.
   g. Click *Spyware* in the *For which heading* list box.
   h. Click the Insert button.
   i. Click the Close button to close the dialog box.
   j. At the document, type a period followed by a right parenthesis.
2. Move to the reference text by holding down the Ctrl key, positioning the mouse pointer over *Spyware* until the pointer turns into a hand, and then clicking the left mouse button.

Step 1f

Cross-reference

Reference type: Heading

Insert reference to: Heading text

Insert as hyperlink

Include above/below

Separate numbers with

For which heading:

CHAPTER 1: UNAUTHORIZED ACCESS
User IDs and Passwords Password Suggestions
System Backdoors
Spoofing
Spyware
CHAPTER 2: INFORMATION THEFT
Wireless Device Security
Data Browsing
CHAPTER 3: COMPUTER VIRUSES Computer Virus Presentation
Types of Viruses (For more information, refer to
Methods of Virus Operation
CHAPTER 4: SECURITY RISKS Click to view types of viruses.

Insert Cancel

Step 1g

Step 1h

3. Save **WL2-C4-P4-VirusesSecurity.docx**.
4. Print the document.
5. Turn off the display of bookmarks by completing the following steps:
   a. Click the FILE tab and then click *Options*.
   b. At the Word Options dialog box, click *Advanced* in the left panel.
   c. Click the *Show bookmarks* check box in the *Show document content* section to remove the check mark.
   d. Click OK to close the dialog box.
6. Close **WL2-C4-P4-VirusesSecurity.docx**.

Chapter Summary

- Create custom theme colors with options at the Create New Theme Colors dialog box and create custom theme fonts with options at the Create New Theme Fonts dialog box.
- Click the Reset button in the Create New Theme Colors dialog box to reset colors back to the default Office theme colors.
- Create custom theme colors and custom theme fonts, apply a theme effect, and then save the changes in a custom theme. Save a custom theme at the Save Current Theme dialog box. Display this dialog box by clicking the Themes button in the Document Formatting group on the DESIGN tab and then clicking *Save Current Theme* at the drop-down gallery.
- Apply custom theme colors by clicking the Theme Colors button and then clicking the custom theme that displays near the top of the drop-down gallery. Complete similar steps to apply custom theme fonts and a custom theme.
- You can edit and delete custom themes. Delete a custom theme at the Themes button drop-down gallery or at the Save Current Theme dialog box.
- Click the *Reset to Theme from Template* option at the Themes button drop-down gallery to reset the theme to the template default.
- A *style* is a set of formatting instructions you can apply to text in a document. Word provides a number of predesigned styles grouped into style sets.
- Styles within a style set are available in the Styles group on the HOME tab.
- Apply a style by clicking the style thumbnail in the Styles group on the HOME tab, or clicking a style in the Styles task pane. Display the Styles task pane by clicking the Styles group task pane launcher.
- Modify a predesigned style with options at the Modify Styles dialog box. Display this dialog box by right-clicking the style in the Styles group or in the Styles task pane and then clicking *Modify* at the shortcut menu.
- Recording a macro involves turning on the macro recorder, performing the steps to be recorded, and then turning off the recorder.
- Run a macro by displaying the Macros dialog box and then double-clicking the desired macro name.
- Temporarily suspend the recording of a macro by clicking the Pause Recording button in the Code group on the DEVELOPER tab.

- Delete a macro by displaying the Macros dialog box, clicking the macro name to be deleted, and then clicking the Delete button.
- Assign a macro to a keyboard command at the Record Macro dialog box. To run a macro that has been assigned a keyboard command, press the keys assigned to the macro.
- Specify macro security settings at the Trust Center with *Macro Settings* selected in the left panel. Display the Trust Center by clicking the Macro Security button in the Code group on the DEVELOPER tab.
- Save a document as a macro-enabled document or a template as a macro-enabled template with the *Save as type* option at the Save As dialog box.
- Navigate in a document with the Navigation pane or by inserting bookmarks, hyperlinks, and cross-references.
- Insert bookmarks with options at the Bookmark dialog box.
- Insert hyperlinks in a document with options at the Insert Hyperlink dialog box. Insert a hyperlink to an existing file or web page, a location in the current document, a new document, or an email. You can also use a graphic to link to a file or website.
- Create a cross-reference with options at the Cross-reference dialog box.

Commands Review

FEATURE	RIBBON TAB, GROUP	BUTTON, OPTION	KEYBOARD SHORTCUT
Bookmark dialog box	INSERT, Links		
Create New Theme Colors dialog box	DESIGN, Document Formatting	, *Customize Colors*	
Create New Theme Fonts dialog box	DESIGN, Document Formatting	, *Customize Fonts*	
Cross-reference dialog box	INSERT, Links		
Insert Hyperlink dialog box	INSERT, Links		Ctrl + K
Macros dialog box	DEVELOPER, Code OR VIEW, Macros		Alt + F8
Record Macro dialog box	DEVELOPER, Code OR VIEW, Macros		
Save Current Theme dialog box	DESIGN, Document Formatting	, *Save Current Theme*	
Styles task pane	HOME, Styles		Alt + Ctrl + Shift + S
theme effects	DESIGN, Document Formatting		
Trust Center	DEVELOPER, Code		

Concepts Check Test Your Knowledge 

Completion: In the space provided at the right, indicate the correct term, symbol, or command.

1. The Themes button is located on this tab. ____________
2. Create custom theme colors at this dialog box. ____________
3. A theme that you save displays in this section in the Themes button drop-down gallery. ____________
4. If you hover the mouse pointer over a style in the Styles task pane, this displays with information about the formatting applied. ____________
5. This tab contains the Record Macro button in the Code group. ____________
6. A macro name must begin with a letter and can contain only letters and these. ____________
7. When macro recording is turned on, a macro icon displays on this. ____________
8. Delete a macro at this dialog box. ____________
9. Assign a macro to a keyboard command at this dialog box. ____________
10. The *Navigation Pane* check box is located in the Show group on this tab. ____________
11. The Bookmark button is located in this group on the INSERT tab. ____________
12. Turn on the display of bookmarks in a document with the *Show bookmarks* check box in this dialog box with *Advanced* selected. ____________
13. Navigate to a hyperlink by hovering the mouse over the hyperlink text, holding down this key, and then clicking the left mouse button. ____________
14. To link a Word document to a file in another application, click this button in the *Link to* group in the Insert Hyperlink dialog box. ____________
15. By default, cross-references are inserted in a document as this. ____________

Skills Check Assess Your Performance

Assessment 1

CREATE AND APPLY CUSTOM THEMES TO A MEDICAL PLANS DOCUMENT

1. At a blank document, create custom theme colors named with your initials that make the following color changes:
   a. Change the Accent 1 color to *Dark Red* (the first option in the *Standard Colors* section).
   b. Change the Accent 5 color to *Gold, Accent 4, Darker 50%* (eighth column, bottom row in the *Theme Colors* section).
2. Create custom theme fonts named with your initials that change the heading font to Corbel and the body font to Garamond.
3. Click the Theme Effects button and then click *Top Shadow* at the drop-down gallery (first column, third row).
4. Save the custom theme and name it with your initials. ***Hint: Do this with the* Save Current Theme *option at the* Themes *drop-down gallery.***
5. Close the document without saving the changes.
6. Open **KLHPlan.docx** and then save the document and name it **WL2-C4-A1-KLHPlan**.
7. Make the following changes to the document:
   a. Apply the Lines (Simple) style set.
   b. With the insertion point positioned at the beginning of the document, type the title Key Life Health Plan.
   c. Apply the Heading 1 style to the title.
   d. Apply the Heading 2 style to the three headings in the document.
8. Move the insertion point to the end of the document, press Ctrl + Enter to insert a page break, and then insert the document **KLHPlanGraphic.docx**. ***Hint: Do this with the Object button arrow on the INSERT tab.***
9. Apply the custom theme you created by clicking the DESIGN tab, clicking the Themes button, and then clicking the custom theme named with your initials.
10. Save, print, and then close **WL2-C4-A1-KLHPlan.docx**.
11. At a blank document, delete the custom theme colors named with your initials, the custom theme fonts named with your initials, and the custom theme named with your initials.

Assessment 2

RECORD AND RUN FORMATTING MACROS

1. Open **MacroText.docx** and then create a macro named *XXXTitle* (where *XXX* is your initials) with the following specifications:
   a. Position the insertion point at the beginning of the word *Title* and then turn on the macro recorder.
   b. Press the F8 key and then press the End key.
   c. Click the Center button and then click the Bold button.
   d. Change the font size to 14 points.

e. Click the Shading button arrow and then click *Blue, Accent 1, Lighter 40%* (fifth column, fourth row in the *Theme Colors* section).
f. Use the Borders button and insert a bottom border.
g. Turn off the macro recorder.

2. Create a macro named *XXXHd* (where *XXX* is your initials) with the following specifications:
   a. Position the insertion point at the beginning of the word *Heading* and then turn on the macro recorder.
   b. Press the F8 key and then press the End key.
   c. Click the Bold button and then click the Italic button.
   d. Change the font size to 12 points.
   e. Click the Shading button arrow and then click *Blue, Accent 1, Lighter 80%* (fifth column, second row in the *Theme Colors* section).
   f. Turn off the macro recorder.
3. Create a macro named *XXXDocFont* (where *XXX* is your initials) that selects the entire document and then changes the font to Cambria. Assign the macro the keyboard shortcut Alt + D.
4. Close **MacroText.docx** without saving it.
5. Open **WebReport.docx** and save the document with the name **WL2-C4-A2-WebReport**.
6. Press Alt + D to run the XXXDocFont macro.
7. Run the XXXTitle macro for the two titles in the document: *Navigating the Web* and *Searching the Web*.
8. Run the XXXHd macro for the four headings in the document: *IPs and URLs*, *Browsing Web Pages*, *Search Engines*, and *How Search Engines Work*.
9. Save, print, and then close **WL2-C4-A2-WebReport.docx**.
10. Delete the macros you created in this assessment: XXXDocFont, XXXTitle, and XXXHd.

Assessment 3

FORMAT AND NAVIGATE IN A CORPORATE REPORT DOCUMENT

1. Open **DIReport.docx** and then save the document and name it **WL2-C4-A3-DIReport**.
2. Move the insertion point to any character in the second paragraph in the document (the paragraph that begins *Assist the company's board of directors in fulfilling*), turn on the display of the Styles task pane, apply the *Intense Quote* style to the paragraph, and then turn off the display of the Styles task pane.
3. Apply the Lines (Distinctive) style set.
4. Turn on the display of bookmarks.
5. Move the insertion point to the end of the third paragraph in the document (the paragraph that begins *The audit committee selects*) and then insert a bookmark named *Audit*.
6. Move the insertion point to the end of the first paragraph in the *FEES TO INDEPENDENT AUDITOR* section, following the *(Excel worksheet)* text, and then insert a bookmark named *Audit_Fees*.
7. Move the insertion point to the end of the last paragraph of text in the document and then insert a bookmark named *Compensation*.
8. Navigate in the document using the bookmarks.
9. Move the insertion point to the end of the first paragraph in the *COMMITTEE RESPONSIBILITIES* section, press the spacebar, and then insert a hyperlink to the Audit_Fees bookmark.

10. Select the text *(Excel worksheet)* that displays at the end of the first paragraph in the *FEES TO INDEPENDENT AUDITOR* section and then insert a hyperlink to **AuditorFees.xlsx**, which is located in the WL2C4 folder on your storage medium.
11. Move the insertion point to the end of the document, click the clip art image, and then insert a hyperlink to the Word document named **DIGraphic.docx** located in the WL2C4 folder on your storage medium. At the Insert Hyperlink dialog box, create a ScreenTip with the text *Click to view a long-term incentives graphic.*
12. Hold down the Ctrl key and then click the *(Excel worksheet)* hyperlink and then print the Excel worksheet that displays by clicking the FILE tab, clicking the *Print* option, and then clicking the Print button in the Print backstage area.
13. Close the Excel program without saving the workbook.
14. Hold down the Ctrl key and then click the clip art to display the Word document containing the graphic. Print the graphic document and then close the document.
15. Save, print, and then close **WL2-C4-A3-DIReport.docx**.

Assessment

4 ASSIGN MACROS TO THE QUICK ACCESS TOOLBAR

1. In this chapter, you have learned how to record a macro and assign a keyboard shortcut to a macro. A macro can also be assigned to a button on the Quick Access toolbar. Using the Help feature, search for and then read the article *Create or run a macro*. Learn specifically how to assign a macro to a button.
2. Open **NSSMacroText.docx** and then use the document to create the following macros:
   a. Create a macro named *XXXNSSDocFormat* (where *XXX* is your initials) and assign it to a button (you determine the button icon) that selects the entire document (use Ctrl + A), applies the No Spacing style (click the *No Spacing* style in the Styles group), changes the line spacing to double (press Ctrl + 2), and changes the font to Constantia.
   b. Create a macro named *XXXNSSHeading* (where *XXX* is your initials) and assign it to a button (you determine the button icon) that selects a line of text (at the beginning of the line, press F8 and then press the End key), changes the font size to 12 points, turns on bold formatting, centers text, and then deselects the text.
3. Close **NSSMacroText.docx** without saving changes.
4. Open **EmpComp.docx** and save the document with the name **WL2-C4-A4-EmpComp**.
5. Click the button on the Quick Access toolbar to run the XXXNSSDocFormat macro.
6. Run the XXXNSSHeading macro (using the button on the Quick Access toolbar) for the title *COMPENSATION* and the five headings in the document.
7. Keep the heading, *Overtime*, with the paragraph of text that follows it.
8. Save, print, and then close **WL2-C4-A4-EmpComp.docx**.
9. Open a blank document and then open another blank document. Make a screenshot of the Quick Access toolbar. (Use the *Screen Clippings* option from the ScreenShot button drop-down list.) Print the document containing the screenshot and then close the document without saving it.

10. At the blank document, delete the macro buttons from the Quick Access toolbar and then delete the macros from the Macros dialog box.
11. Remove the DEVELOPER tab from the ribbon. (Do this by displaying the Word Options dialog box with *Customize Ribbon* selected in the left panel. Remove the check mark from the *Developer* check box, and then click OK to close the dialog box.)

Visual Benchmark Demonstrate Your Proficiency

INSERT SMARTART GRAPHICS IN A BUSINESS DOCUMENT

1. Open **DIRevenues.docx** and then save the document and name it **WL2-C4-VB-DIRevenues**.
2. Create the following custom theme colors named with your first and last names with the following changes:
   a. Change the Text/Background - Dark 2 color to *Orange, Accent 2, Darker 50%* (sixth column, last row in the *Theme Colors* section).
   b. Change the Accent 1 color to *Green, Accent 6, Darker 50%* (tenth column, last row in the *Theme Colors* section).
   c. Change the Accent 4 color to *Orange, Accent 2, Darker 50%*.
   d. Change the Accent 6 color to *Green, Accent 6, Darker 25%*.
3. Create the following custom theme fonts named with your first and last names with the following changes:
   a. Change the heading font to *Copperplate Gothic Bold*.
   b. Change the body font to *Constantia*.
4. Apply the Riblet theme effect.
5. Save the custom theme and name it *WL2C4* followed by your initials. ***Hint: Do this with the* Save Current Theme *option at the* Themes *drop-down gallery.***
6. Center the title and reposition the SmartArt graphic as shown in Figure 4.7.
7. Save, print, and then close **WL2-C4-VB-DIRevenues.docx**.
8. Open **DICorporate.docx** and then save the document and name it **WL2-C4-VB-DICorporate**.
9. Apply the WL2C4 (followed by your initials) custom theme to the document.
10. Center the title and reposition the SmartArt graphic as shown in Figure 4.8 on page 171.
11. Save, print, and then close **WL2-C4-VB-DICorporate.docx**.
12. At a blank document, use the Print Screen button to make a screen capture of the Theme Colors drop-down gallery (make sure your custom theme colors display), a screen capture of the Theme Fonts drop-down gallery (make sure your custom theme fonts display), and a screen capture of the Save Current Theme dialog box (make sure your custom themes are visible). Insert all three screen capture images on the same page. (You will need to size the images.)
13. Save the document and name it **WL2-C4-VB-ScreenImages**.
14. Print and then close **WL2-C4-VB-ScreenImages.docx**.
15. At a blank document, delete the custom color theme you created, as well as the custom font theme and the custom theme.

Figure 4.7 Visual Benchmark 1

Dearborn Industries

Revenues

We are evaluating markets for our current and future products. Prior to the fourth quarter of 2015, we recorded revenues as a result of development contracts with government entities focused on the design of flywheel technologies. We have produced and placed several development prototypes with potential customers and shipped preproduction units.

Research and Development

Our cost of research and development consists primarily of the cost of compensation and benefits for research and support staff, as well as materials and supplies used in the engineering design and development process. These costs decreased significantly during 2015 as we focused on reducing our expenditure rate by reducing product design and development activities.

Preferred Stock Dividends

Prior to our initial public offering of our common stock, we had various classes of preferred stock outstanding, each of which was entitled to receive dividends. We accrued dividend expenses monthly according to the requirements of each class of preferred stock.

Figure 4.8 Visual Benchmark 2

DEARBORN INDUSTRIES

CORPORATE VISION

Dearborn Industries will be the leading developer of clean and environmentally friendly products. Building on strong leadership, development, and resources, we will provide superior-quality products and services to our customers and consumers around the world.

CORPORATE VALUES

We value the environment in which we live, and we will work to produce and maintain energy-efficient and environmentally safe products and strive to reduce our carbon footprint on the environment.

CORPORATE LEADERSHIP

Dearborn Industries employees conduct business under the leadership of the chief executive officer, who is subject to the oversight and direction of the board of directors. Four vice presidents work with the chief executive officer to manage and direct business.

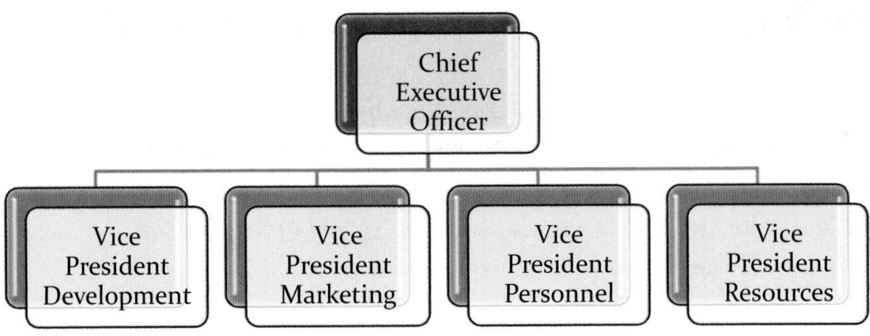

Case Study Apply Your Skills

Part 1

You work for Jackson Photography and want to create a new letterhead for the company. Open **JPLtrd.docx** and then customize the text and clip art to create an attractive and professional-looking letterhead. Save the completed letterhead with the same name (**JPLtrd.docx**). Create a building block with the letterhead.

Part 2

At a blank document, create and then save custom theme colors that match the letterhead you created in Part 1. Create and then save custom theme fonts that apply the Arial font to headings and the Constantia font to body text. Apply a custom theme effect of your choosing. Save the custom theme in the Save Current Theme dialog box and name it with your initials followed by *JP*.

Part 3

At a blank document, insert the company letterhead building block you created in Part 1, type the title **Photography Services**, and then insert a SmartArt graphic of your choosing that contains the following text:

- Wedding Photography
- Sports Portraits
- Senior Portraits
- Family Portraits
- Processing

Apply a heading style to the *Photography Services* title, apply the custom theme to the document, and then save the document and name it **WL2-C4-CS-JPServices**.

Part 4

Open **JPReport.docx** and then save the document and name it **WL2-C4-CS-JPReport**. Apply or insert the following in the document:

- Apply your custom theme.
- Apply the Intense Quote style to the quote at the beginning and the quote at the end of the document.
- Insert a footer of your choosing in the document.

Apply any other enhancements to improve the appearance of the document. Save **WL2-C4-CS-JPReport.docx**.

Part 5

With **WL2-C4-CS-JPReport.docx** open, insert at the end of the third paragraph in the *Photography* section a hyperlink that links to the document **KodakHistory.docx** located in the WL2C4 folder on your storage medium. Using the Internet, research and locate at least one company that sells digital cameras. At the end of the document, insert text that tells the reader to click the hyperlink text to link to that particular site on the Internet and then insert the hyperlink to the website you found. Save, print, and then close **WL2-C4-CS-JPReport.docx**.

MICROSOFT® WORD Performance Assessment

WL2U1

Note: Before beginning unit assessments, copy to your storage medium the WL2U1 subfolder from the WL2 folder on the CD that accompanies this textbook and then make WL2U1 the active folder.

Assessing Proficiency

In this unit, you have learned how to customize the spelling, grammar, and AutoCorrect features in a document; format documents with special features, such as customized bullets, numbering, headers, footers, and page numbering; automate formatting with macros; and apply and customize building blocks, themes, style sets, and styles.

Assessment 1 Format Stock Awards Document

1. Open **CMStocks.docx** and then save the document and name it **WL2-U1-A1-CMStocks**.
2. Apply the Title style to the title *Clearline Manufacturing*.
3. Apply the Heading 1 style to the headings *Stock Awards* and *Employee Stock Plan*.
4. Apply the Centered style set.
5. Select the bulleted paragraphs of text and then define a new picture bullet. At the Insert Pictures window, search for *blue globe with grid lines* and download the globe with blue grid lines and a black background.
6. Select the lines of text below the *Employee Stock Plan* heading and then apply a multilevel list (middle option in top row of the *List Library* section of the Multilevel List button drop-down gallery).
7. With the text still selected, define a new multilevel list that inserts capital letters followed by periods (A., B., C.) for level 2 and inserts arabic numbers followed by periods (1., 2., 3.) for level 3. (Make sure the new multilevel list applies to the selected text.)
8. Save, print, and then close **WL2-U1-A1-CMStocks.docx**.

Assessment 2 Format a Future of Computer Ethics Report

1. Open **FutureEthics.docx** and then save the document and name it **WL2-U1-A2-FutureEthics**.
2. Keep the heading *Self-Replicating Robots* (located at the bottom of the first page) together with the paragraph of text that follows it.
3. Keep the title *REFERENCES* (located at the bottom of the second page) together with the paragraph of text that follows it.
4. Insert the *FileName* and *PrintDate* fields at the end of the document (on separate lines).

5. Create an odd page footer that prints the document title *Future of Computer Ethics* at the left margin and the page number at the right margin. Also create an even page footer that prints the page number at the left margin and document title at the right margin.
6. Save, print, and then close **WL2-U1-A2-FutureEthics.docx**.

Assessment 3 Create and Format a Column Chart

1. At a blank document, use the data in Figure U1.1 to create a column chart with the following specifications:
   a. Choose the 3-D Clustered Column chart type.
   b. Apply the Layout 3 chart layout.
   c. Apply the Style 5 chart style.
   d. Change the chart title to *2015 Sales*.
   e. Insert a data table with legend keys.
   f. Select the chart area, apply the Subtle Effect - Green, Accent 6 shape style (last column, fourth row), and apply the Offset Bottom shadow shape effect (second column, first row in Outer section).
   g. Select the Second Half series and then apply the Dark Red shape fill.
   h. Change the chart height to 4 inches and chart width to 6.25 inches.
   i. Use the Position button in the Arrange group to position the chart in the middle of the page with square text wrapping.
2. Save the document with the name **WL2-U1-A3-SalesChart**.
3. Print **WL2-U1-A3-SalesChart.docx**.
4. With the chart selected, display the Excel worksheet and edit the data in the worksheet by changing the following:
   a. Change the amount in cell C2 from *$285,450* to *$302,500.*
   b. Change the amount in cell C4 from *$180,210* to *$190,150*.
5. Save, print, and then close **WL2-U1-A3-SalesChart.docx**.

Figure U1.1 Assessment 3

Salesperson	First Half	Second Half
Bratton	$235,500	$285,450
Daniels	$300,570	$250,700
Hughes	$170,200	$180,210
Marez	$358,520	$376,400

Assessment 4 Create and Format a Pie Chart

1. At a blank document, use the data in Figure U1.2 to create a pie chart with the following specifications:
   a. Apply the Layout 6 chart layout.
   b. Apply the Style 3 chart style.
   c. Change the chart title to *District Expenditures*.
   d. Move the legend to the left side of the chart.

e. Select the chart area, apply Gold, Accent 4, Lighter 80% shape fill (eighth column, second row in the *Theme Colors* section), and apply the Gray-50%, 11 pt glow, Accent color 3 glow shape effect (third column, third row in the *Glow Variations* section).
f. Select the legend and apply a Blue shape outline (eighth option in the *Standard Colors* section).
g. Apply the WordArt style Fill - Blue, Accent 1, Outline - Background 1, Hard Shadow - Accent 1 (third column, third row) to the chart title text.
h. Move the data labels to the inside ends of the pie pieces.
i. Select the legend and move it so it is centered between the left edge of the chart border and the pie.
j. Use the Position button in the Arrange group to center the chart at the top of the page.

2. Save the document with the name **WL2-U1-A4-ExpendChart**.
3. Print and then close **WL2-U1-A4-ExpendChart.docx**.

Figure U1.2 Assessment 4

	Percentage
Basic Education	42%
Special Needs	20%
Support Services	19%
Vocational	11%
Compensatory	8%

Assessment 5 Navigate in a Smoke Detector Report

1. Open **SmokeDetectors.docx** and then save the document and name it **WL2-U1-A5-SmokeDetectors**.
2. If necessary, turn on the display of bookmarks. (Do this at the Word Options dialog box with *Advanced* selected in the left panel.)
3. Move the insertion point to the end of the paragraph in the *Types of Smoke Detectors* section and then insert a bookmark named *Types*.
4. Move the insertion point to the end of the last paragraph in the *Safety Tips* section and then insert a bookmark named *Resources*.
5. Move the insertion point to the end of the first paragraph in the *Taking Care of Smoke Detectors* section (located at the bottom of the second page) and then insert a bookmark named *Maintenance*.
6. Navigate in the document using the bookmarks.
7. Select the text *(NFPA website)* that displays at the end of the first paragraph in the document and then insert a hyperlink to the website www.nfpa.org.
8. Hold down the Ctrl key and then click the *(NFPA website)* hyperlink. At the NFPA home page, navigate to web pages that interest you and then close your browser.
9. Move the insertion point to the end of the document and then create a hyperlink with the clip art image to the Word document named **SmokeDetectorFacts.docx**.

10. Click outside the clip art image to deselect it.
11. Hold down the Ctrl key and then click the clip art image. At the **SmokeDetectorFacts.docx** document, read the information, print the document, and then close the document.
12. Save, print, and then close **WL2-U1-A5-SmokeDetectors.docx**.

Assessment 6 Format a Computer Devices Report

1. Open **CompDevices.docx** and then save the document and name it **WL2-U1-A6-CompDevices**.
2. With the insertion point positioned at the beginning of the document, press Ctrl + Enter to insert a page break.
3. Apply the Heading 1 style to the two titles in the document: *COMPUTER INPUT DEVICES* and *COMPUTER OUTPUT DEVICES*.
4. Apply the Heading 2 style to the six headings in the document.
5. Apply the Minimalist style set.
6. Apply the Yellow Orange theme colors.
7. Apply the Corbel theme fonts.
8. Insert a section break that begins a new page at the beginning of the title *COMPUTER OUTPUT DEVICES* (located on the third page).
9. Create a footer for the first section in the document that prints *Computer Input Devices* at the left margin, the page number in the middle, and your first and last names at the right margin.
10. Edit the footer for the second section so it prints *Computer Output Devices* instead of *Computer Input Devices*. (Make sure you deactivate the *Link to Previous* feature.)
11. Move the insertion point to the beginning of the document and then insert the Slice (Dark) cover page. Type **COMPUTER DEVICES** as the document title and type **Computer Input and Output Devices** as the document subtitle.
12. Move the insertion point to the beginning of the second page (blank page) and then insert the Automatic Table 1 table of contents building block.
13. Save, print, and then close **WL2-U1-A6-CompDevices.docx**.

Assessment 7 Format a Building a Website Document

1. Open **BuildWebsite.docx** and then save the document and name it **WL2-U1-A7-BuildWebsite**.
2. Display the Word Options dialog box with *Proofing* selected in the left panel, insert a check mark in the *Show readability statistics* check box, change the *Writing Style* option to *Grammar & Style*, and then close the dialog box.
3. Complete a spelling and grammar checker on the document. Click the Ignore button when the grammar checker selects a sentence and displays the message *Passive Voice (consider revising)* in the Grammar task pane. After completing the spelling and grammar check, proofread the document and make any necessary changes not selected during the spelling and grammar check.
4. Format the document with the following:
    a. Apply the Title style to the title *Building a Website*; apply the Heading 1 style to the headings *Planning a Website, Choosing a Host,* and *Organizing the Site*; and apply the Heading 3 style to the subheadings *Free Web-Hosting Services, Free Hosting from ISPs,* and *Fee-Based Hosting Services*.
    b. Format the text (except the title) into two evenly spaced columns. Balance the end of the text on the second page.
    c. Apply the Shaded style set and then center the title.

d. Apply the Blue Warm theme colors and the Garamond theme fonts.
e. Insert the Ion (Dark) header building block.
f. Insert the Ion (Dark) footer building block. Type **BUILDING A WEBSITE** as the document title and type your first and last names at the right side of the footer.

5. Display the Word Options dialog box with *Proofing* selected in the left panel, remove the check mark from the *Show readability statistics* check box, change the *Writing Style* option to *Grammar Only*, and then close the dialog box.
6. Save, print, and then close **WL2-U1-A7-BuildWebsite.docx**.

Assessment 8 Format an Equipment Rental Agreement

1. At a blank document, create custom theme colors named with your initials that make the following color changes:
   a. Change the Text/Background - Dark 2 color to *Orange, Accent 2, Darker 50%* (sixth column, last row in the Theme Colors section).
   b. Change the Accent 1 color to *Green, Accent 6, Darker 25%* (tenth column, last row in the Theme Colors section).
2. Create custom theme fonts named with your initials that apply the Verdana font to headings and Cambria font to body text.
3. Save the custom theme and name it with your initials. (Do this with the *Save Current Theme* option at the Themes button drop-down gallery.)
4. Close the document without saving the changes.
5. Open **MRCForm.docx** and then save the document and name it **WL2-U1-A8-MRCForm**.
6. Search for all occurrences of *mrc* and replace them with *Meridian Rental Company*.
7. Add the following text to AutoCorrect:
   a. Insert *mrc* in the *Replace* text box and insert *Meridian Rental Company* in the *With* text box.
   b. Insert *erag* in the *Replace* text box and insert *Equipment Rental Agreement* in the *With* text box.
8. Move the insertion point to the blank line below the *Default* heading (located on the third page) and then type the text shown in Figure U1.3 on the next page. Use the Numbering feature to number the paragraphs with a lowercase letter followed by a right parenthesis. (If the AutoCorrect feature capitalizes the first word after the letter and right parenthesis, use the AutoCorrect options button to return the letter to lowercase.)
9. Apply the Title style to the title *Equipment Rental Agreement* and apply the Heading 1 style to the headings in the document: *Lease*, *Rent*, *Use and Operation of Equipment*, *Insurance*, *Risk of Loss*, *Maintenance*, *Return of Equipment*, *Warranties of Lessee*, *Default*, and *Further Assurances*.
10. Apply the Centered style set.
11. Apply your custom theme to the document.
12. Insert the Sample 1 watermark building block.
13. Insert the Banded footer building block.
14. Delete the two entries you made at the AutoCorrect dialog box.
15. Save, print, and then close **WL2-U1-A8-MRCForm.docx**.
16. At a blank document, delete the custom theme colors, custom theme fonts, and custom theme named with your initials.

Figure U1.3 Assessment 8

> Upon the occurrence of default, mrc may, without any further notice, exercise any one or more of the following remedies:
>
> a) terminate this erag as to any or all items of Equipment;
>
> b) cause Lessee at its expense to promptly return the Equipment to mrc in the condition set forth in this erag;
>
> c) use, hold, sell, lease, or otherwise dispose of the Equipment or any item of it on the premises of Lessee or any other location without affecting the obligations of Lessee as provided in this erag;
>
> d) proceed by appropriate action either at law or in equity to enforce performance by Lessee of the applicable covenants of this erag or to recover damages for the breach of them; or
>
> e) exercise any other rights accruing to mrc under any applicable law upon a default by Lessee.

Assessment 9 Create and Run Macros

1. Open a blank document and then create the following macros:
   a. Create a macro named *XXXAPMFormat* (use your initials in place of the *XXX*) that changes the top margin to 1.5 inches and then selects the entire document and changes the font to Candara.
   b. Create a macro named *XXXAPMSubtitle* with the keyboard command Alt + S that selects the line (press F8 and then press the End key), changes the font size to 12 points, turns on bold formatting, centers the text, and applies Blue, Accent 1, Lighter 80% paragraph shading (fifth column, second row in the Theme Colors section).
2. After recording the macros, close the document without saving it.
3. Open **Lease.docx** and then save the document and name it **WL2-U1-A9-Lease**.
4. Run the XXXAPMFormat macro.
5. Move the insertion point to the beginning of the heading *RENT* and then press Alt + S to run the XXXAPMSubtitle macro.
6. Run the XXXAPMSubtitle macro (using Alt + S) for the remaining headings: *DAMAGE DEPOSIT*, *USE OF PREMISES*, *CONDITION OF PREMISES*, *ALTERATIONS AND IMPROVEMENTS*, *NON-DELIVERY OF POSSESSION*, and *UTILITIES*.
7. Save, print, and then close **WL2-U1-A9-Lease.docx**.
8. Open **REAgrmnt.docx** and then save the document and name it **WL2-U1-A9-REAgrmnt**.
9. Run the XXXAPMFormat macro.
10. Run the XXXAPMSubtitle macro (using Alt + S) for each heading in the document: *Financing*, *New Financing*, *Closing Costs*, *Survey*, and *Attorney Fees*.
11. Save, print, and then close **WL2-U1-A9-REAgrmnt.docx**.
12. Delete the macros you created in this assessment: XXXAPMFormat and XXXAPMSubtitle.

Writing Activities

Activity 1 Create Building Blocks and Compose a Letter

You are the executive assistant to the director of the Human Resources department at Clearline Manufacturing. You are responsible for preparing employee documents, notices, reports, and forms. You decide to create building blocks to increase the efficiency of, and consistency in, department documents. Create the following:

- Create a letterhead for the company that includes the company name and any other enhancements to improve the appearance of the letterhead. Save the letterhead text as a building block.
- Create a building block footer that inserts the company address and telephone number. (You determine the address and telephone number.) Include a visual element to the footer, such as a border line.
- You send documents to the board of directors and so you decide to include the following names and addresses as building blocks:

  Mrs. Nancy Logan
  12301 132nd Avenue East
  Warminster, PA 18974

  Mr. Dion Jarvis
  567 Federal Street
  Philadelphia, PA 19093

  Dr. Austin Svoboda
  9823 South 112th Street
  Norristown, PA 18974

- Create a complimentary close building block that includes *Sincerely yours,* your name, and the title *Executive Assistant*.

Write the body of a letter to a member of the board of directors and include at least the following information:

- Explain that the Human Resources department director has created a new employee handbook and that it will be made available to all new employees. Also mention that the attorney for Clearline Manufacturing has reviewed the handbook document and approved its content.
- Open the **CMHandbook.docx** document and then use the headings to summarize the contents of the document in a paragraph in the letter. Explain in the letter that a draft of the handbook is enclosed with the letter.
- Include any additional information you feel the directors may want to know.

Save the body of the letter as a separate document. Using the building blocks you created, along with the letter document, create letters to Nancy Logan, Dion Jarvis, and Austin Svoboda. Save the letters individually and then print them.

Activity 2 Create a Custom Theme

Create a custom theme for formatting documents that includes the colors and/or fonts you chose for the Clearline Manufacturing letterhead. Open the document named **CMHandbook.docx** and then save the document and name it **WL2-U1-Act2-CMHandbook**. Apply at least the following formatting to the document:

- The footer building block you created as a footer in the document
- Table of contents building block
- Cover page building block
- Draft watermark building block
- Formatting to the title, headings, and subheadings
- Any additional formatting that improve the appearance and readability of the document

Select the text *(Click to display Longevity Schedule.)* that displays at the end of the first paragraph in the *Longevity Pay* section and insert a hyperlink to the Excel file named **CMPaySchedule.xlsx** located in the WL2U1 folder on your storage medium. After inserting the hyperlink, click the hyperlink and make sure the Clearline worksheet displays and then close Excel.

Save, print, and then close **WL2-U1-Act2-CMHandbook.docx**. Delete the custom themes you created and the building blocks you created in Activity 1.

Internet Research

Prepare Information on Printer Specifications

You are responsible for purchasing new color laser printers for the Human Resources department at Clearline Manufacturing. You need to research printers and then prepare a report about them to the director of the department. Using the Internet, search for at least two companies that produce color laser printers. Determine information such as printer make and model, printer performance, printer cost, and prices for printer cartridges. Using the information you find, prepare a report to the director, Deana Terril. Type at least one list in the report and then create and apply a customized bullet to the list. Insert a predesigned header or footer and create and apply a custom theme to the report document. Save the report document and name it **WL2-U1-Act3-Printers**. Print and then close **WL2-U1-Act3-Printers.docx**.

MICROSOFT®

WORD Level 2

Unit 2 ■ Editing and Formatting Documents

Inserting Special Features and References

5

PERFORMANCE OBJECTIVES

Upon successful completion of Chapter 5, you will be able to:

- **Sort text in paragraphs, columns, and tables**
- **Sort records in a data source file**
- **Select specific records in a data source file for merging**
- **Insert nonbreaking spaces**
- **Find and replace special characters**
- **Create and use specialized templates**
- **Create footnotes and endnotes**
- **Insert and modify sources and citations**
- **Insert, modify, and format source lists**

Tutorials

5.1 Sorting Text in Paragraphs, Columns, and Tables

5.2 Sorting Records in a Data Source File

5.3 Selecting Specific Records for Merging

5.4 Inserting Hyphens and Nonbreaking Characters

5.5 Finding and Replacing Special Characters

5.6 Creating and Using Templates

5.7 Creating Footnotes and Endnotes

5.8 Formatting the First Page of a Research Paper

5.9 Inserting and Modifying Sources and Citations

5.10 Inserting a Works Cited Page

In Word, you can sort text in paragraphs, columns, and tables, as well as sort records in a data source file. You can also select specific records in a data source file and merge them with a main document. Control the line breaks within text by inserting nonbreaking spaces and use the Find and Replace feature to search for special characters, such as nonprinting characters, in a document. Use the default template provided by Word to create a document or to create and use your own specialized template. When you prepare research papers and reports, citing information sources properly is important. In this chapter, you will learn to reference documents and acknowledge sources using footnotes, endnotes, citations, and bibliographies. Model answers for this chapter's projects appear on the following pages.

Note: Before beginning the projects, copy to your storage medium the WL2C5 subfolder from the WL2 folder on the CD that accompanies this textbook and then make WL2C5 the active folder.

Model Answers

Kelly Millerton, Chief Executive Officer

Chris Moreau, President

Danielle Roemer, President

Alexander Rohlman, President

Calvin Van Camp, Vice President

Amber Wahlstrom, Vice President

Eugene Whitman, Vice President

Employee	Department	Ext.
Millerton, Kelly	Administrative Services	102
Whitman, Eugene	Administrative Services	105
Langstrom, Jodie	Financial Services	421
Robertson, Jake	Financial Services	409
Holland, Bethany	Marketing	318
Iwami, Julia	Marketing	322

Salesperson	Sales, First Half	Sales, Second Half
Williams, Sylvia	$543,241	$651,438
Monroe, Nina	$623,598	$630,583
Gresham, Esther	$610,312	$593,412
Kaiser, Michael	$453,483	$510,382
Torres, Edward	$431,568	$486,340

Project 1 Sort Company Information

WL2-C5-P1-Sorting.docx

Mr. Martin Saunders
231 South 41st Street
P.O. Box 3321
Baltimore, MD 20156

Mrs. Darlene Fernandez
12115 South 42nd
#20-G
Baltimore, MD 20376

Mrs. Kaycee Stahl
450 Washington Ave.
Baltimore, MD 20376

Ms. Anita Grenwald
580 Capital Lane
#1002-B
Baltimore, MD 20384

Ms. Victoria Benoit
989 Graham Road
Rosedale, MD 20389

Mr. Steve Dutton
3490 East 145th
Apt. B
Baltimore, MD 20468

Ms. Amanda Perkins
9033 North Ridge Drive
Apt. #401
Baltimore, MD 20487

Mrs. Rebecca Bellamy
10291 East 212th Street
Towson, MD 21204

Mr. Brian Kaszycki
7613 33rd Street
Towson, MD 21204

Dr. Jillian Childers
5840 North 132nd
P.O. Box 9045
Rosedale, MD 21237

Mrs. Antonia Delaney
11220 East Madison
Rosedale, MD 21237

Mr. Gregory Hogan
622 First Street
Towson, MD 21252

WL2-C5-P2-Lbls01.docx

Mrs. Antonia Delaney
11220 East Madison
Rosedale, MD 21237

Mr. Gregory Hogan
622 First Street
Towson, MD 21252

Dr. Jillian Childers
5840 North 132nd
P.O. Box 9045
Rosedale, MD 21237

Mrs. Rebecca Bellamy
10291 East 212th Street
Towson, MD 21204

Mr. Brian Kaszycki
7613 33rd Street
Towson, MD 21204

WL2-C5-P2-Lbls02.docx

Mrs. Antonia Delaney
11220 East Madison
Rosedale, MD 21237

Mr. Gregory Hogan
622 First Street
Towson, MD 21252

Dr. Jillian Childers
5840 North 132nd
P.O. Box 9045
Rosedale, MD 21237

Mrs. Rebecca Bellamy
10291 East 212th Street
Towson, MD 21204

Ms. Victoria Benoit
989 Graham Road
Rosedale, MD 20389

Mr. Brian Kaszycki
7613 33rd Street
Towson, MD 21204

Project 2 Sort and Select Records in a Data Source File

WL2-C5-P2-Lbls03.docx

KEYBOARD SHORTCUTS

Microsoft Word includes a number of keyboard shortcuts you can use to access features and commands. The ScreenTip for some buttons displays the keyboard shortcut you can use to access the commands. For example, hover the mouse over the Font button and the ScreenTip displays Ctrl + Shift + F as the keyboard shortcut. Additional HOME tab Font group keyboard shortcut include Ctrl + B to bold text, Ctrl + I to italicize text, and Ctrl + U to underline text. You can also press Ctrl + Shift + + to turn on superscript and press Ctrl + = to turn on subscript.

Buttons in the Clipboard group include keyboard shortcuts. For example, to cut selected text press Ctrl + X, press Ctrl + C to copy selected text, and use the keyboard shortcut Ctrl + V to insert text. Ctrl + Shift + C is the keyboard command to turn on and off the Format Painter feature.

Project 3 Type a Keyboard Shortcut Document

WL2-C5-P3-Shortcuts.docx

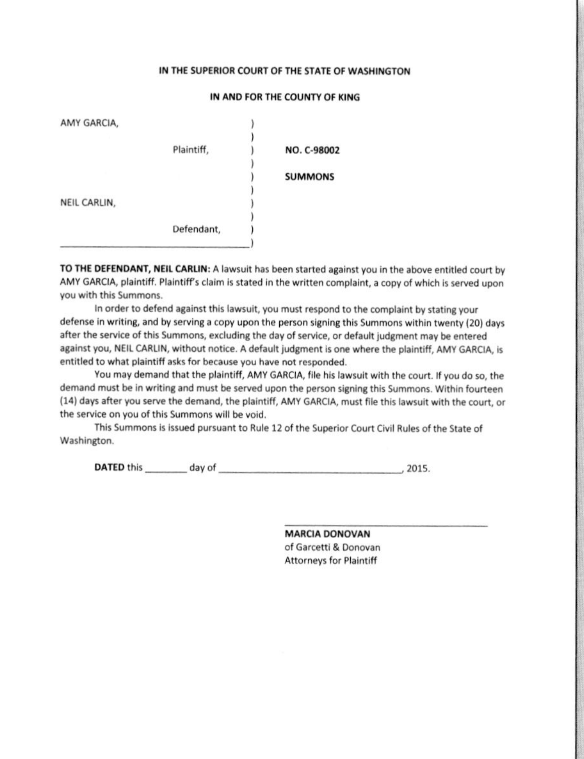

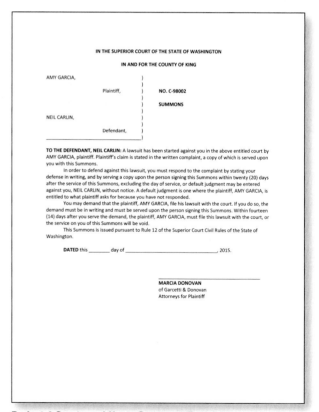

IN THE SUPERIOR COURT OF THE STATE OF WASHINGTON

IN AND FOR THE COUNTY OF KING

AMY GARCIA,)
Plaintiff,) **NO. C-98002**
) **SUMMONS**
NEIL CARLIN,)
Defendant,)

TO THE DEFENDANT, NEIL CARLIN: A lawsuit has been started against you in the above entitled court by AMY GARCIA, plaintiff. Plaintiff's claim is stated in the written complaint, a copy of which is served upon you with this Summons.

In order to defend against this lawsuit, you must respond to the complaint by stating your defense in writing, and by serving a copy upon the person signing this Summons within twenty (20) days after the service of this Summons, excluding the day of service, or default judgment may be entered against you, NEIL CARLIN, without notice. A default judgment is one where the plaintiff, AMY GARCIA, is entitled to what plaintiff asks for because you have not responded.

You may demand that the plaintiff, AMY GARCIA, file his lawsuit with the court. If you do so, the demand must be in writing and must be served upon the person signing this Summons. Within fourteen (14) days after you serve the demand, the plaintiff, AMY GARCIA, must file this lawsuit with the court, or the service on you of this Summons will be void.

This Summons is issued pursuant to Rule 12 of the Superior Court Civil Rules of the State of Washington.

DATED this _______ day of ______________________________, 2015.

MARCIA DONOVAN
of Garcetti & Donovan
Attorneys for Plaintiff

Project 4 Create and Use a Summons Template

WL2-C5-P4-Summons.docx

NATURAL INTERFACE APPLICATIONS

A major area of artificial intelligence has the goal of creating a more natural interface between human and machine. Currently, computer users are restricted in most instances to using a mouse and keyboard for input. For output, they must gaze at a fairly static, two-dimensional screen. Speakers are used for sound, and a printer for hard copy. The user interface consists of typing, pointing, and clicking. New speech recognition and natural-language technologies promise to change that soon.[1]

Speech Recognition

One of the most immediately applicable improvements comes in the area of speech recognition. Rather than typing information into the computer, users can direct it with voice commands. A computer that can take dictation and perform requested actions is a real step forward in convenience and potential. Speech recognition has developed rather slowly, mainly because the typical PC did not have the necessary speed and capacity until very recently.[2]

Natural-Language Interface

Computers that are able to communicate using spoken English, Japanese, or any of the hundreds of other languages currently in use around the world, would certainly be helpful. In the not-so-distant future, computers will most likely be able to read, write, speak, and understand many human languages. Language translators already exist, and they are getting better all the time.

[1] Kevin Novak, *Artificial Intelligence* (Chicago: Home Town Publishing, 2015), 45-51.
[2] Heather Everson and Nicolas Reyes, "Integrating Speech Recognition," *Design Technologies* (2014): 24-26.

Page 1

Programmers can look forward to a human-language computer interface. With better interfaces, programmers may be able to describe what they want using natural (human) languages, rather than writing programs in the highly restrictive and rather alien programming languages in use today. Natural-language interfaces are an area of artificial intelligence that is broader in scope than simple speech recognition. The goal is to have a machine that can read a set of news articles on any topic and understand what it has read. Ideally, it could then write its own report summarizing what it has learned.[3]

Virtual Reality

Virtual reality (VR) describes the concept of creating a realistic world within the computer. Online games with thousands of interacting players already exist. In these games people can take on a persona and move about a virtual landscape, adventuring and chatting with other players. The quality of a virtual reality system is typically characterized in terms of its immersiveness, which measures how real the simulated world feels and how well it can make users accept the simulated world as their own and forget about reality. With each passing year, systems are able to provide increasing levels of immersion. Called by some the "ultimate in escapism," VR is becoming increasingly common—and increasingly realistic.[4]

Mental Interface

Although still in the experimental phase, a number of interfaces take things a bit further than VR, and they don't require users to click a mouse, speak a word, or even lift a finger. Mental interfaces use sensors mounted around the skull to read the alpha waves

[3] James Glenovich, "Language Interfaces," *Corporate Computing* (2015): 8-12.
[4] William Curtis, *Virtual Reality Worlds* (San Francisco: Lilly Harris Publishers, 2013), 53-68.

Page 2

Project 5 Insert Footnotes and Endnotes in Reports

WL2-C5-P5-InterfaceApps.docx

given off by our brains. Thinking of the color blue could be used to move the mouse cursor to the right, or thinking of the number seven could move it to the left. The computer measures brain activity and interprets it as a command, eliminating the need to physically manipulate a mouse to move the screen cursor. While this technology has obvious applications for assisting people with disabilities, military researchers are also using it to produce a superior form of interface for pilots.[5]

[5] Marilyn Beal, "Challenges of Artificial Intelligence," *Interface Design* (2015): 10-18.

Page 3

FUTURE OF THE INTERNET

The Internet is having trouble keeping up with the rapid increase in users and the increased workload created by the popularity of bandwidth-intensive applications such as music and video files. The broadband connections needed to enjoy these new applications are not evenly distributed. Several ongoing projects promise to provide solutions for these problems in the future. Once these connectivity problems are dealt with, people around the world will be able to enjoy the new web services that are only a few short years away.[1]

Satellite Internet Connections

Many people living in remote or sparsely populated areas are not served by broadband Internet connections. Cable or optical fiber networks are very expensive to install and maintain, and ISPs are not interested in providing service to areas or individuals unless they think it will be profitable. One hope for people without broadband connections is provided by satellite TV networks. Remote ISPs connect to the satellite network using antennae attached to their servers. Data is relayed to and from ISP servers to satellites, which are in turn connected to an Internet backbone access point. While the connection speeds might not be as fast as those offered by regular land-based broadband access, they are faster than the service twisted-pair cable can offer and much better than no access at all.[2]

Second Internet

A remedy for the traffic clogging the information highway is **Internet2**, a revolutionary new type of Internet currently under development. When fully operational, Internet2 will enable large research universities in the United States to collaborate and share huge amounts of complex scientific information at amazing speeds. Led by over 170 universities working in partnership with industry and government, the Internet2 consortium is developing and deploying advanced network technologies and applications.

Internet2 is a testing ground for universities to work together and develop advanced Internet technologies such as telemedicine, digital libraries, and virtual laboratories. Internet2 universities will be connected to an ultrahigh-speed network called the Abilene backbone. Each university will use state-of-the-art equipment to take advantage of transfer speeds provided by the network.

Internet Services for a Fee

Industry observers predict that large portals such as AOL, MSN, and Yahoo! will soon determine effective structures and marketing strategies to get consumers to pay for Internet services. This new market, called bring-your-own-access (BYOA), will combine essential *content*, for example, news and weather, with *services*, such as search, directory, email, IM, and online shopping, into a new product with monthly access charges. But to entice current and potential customers into the BYOA market, ISP and telecom companies must offer improvements in the areas of security,

[1] Joshua Abrahamson, *Future Trends in Computing* (Los Angeles: Gleason Rutherford Publishing, 2014), 5-9.
[2] Aileen Clements, *Satellite Systems* (Boston: Robison Publishing House, 2015), 23-51.

Page 1

WL2-C5-P5-InternetFuture.docx

privacy, and ease of use. Additionally, they are expected to develop new ways to personalize content and add value to the current range of Internet services.[3]

Internet in 2030

Ray Kurzweil, a computer futurist, has looked ahead to the year 2030 and visualized a Web that offers no clear distinctions between real and simulated environments and people. Among the applications he sees as very possible are computerized displays in eyeglasses that could offer simultaneous translations of foreign language conversations, nanobots (microscopic robots) that would work with our brains to extend our mental capabilities, and sophisticated avatars (simulated on-screen persons) that people will interact with online. Technologies that allow people to project their feelings as well as their images and voices may usher in a period when people could "be" with another person even though they are physically hundreds or even thousands of miles apart.

[3] Jolene Campbell, "Fee-Based Internet Services," *Connections* (2014): 5-8.

Page 2

Last Name 1

Student Name

Instructor Name

Course Title

Current Date

Mobile Security

Computing is no longer just a sit-at-your-desk type of activity—it is mobile. Mobile is convenient, but it also brings its own security risks. Various settings and tools can help you keep your portable devices and the information stored on it safer (Suong).

When you bring your computer with you, you are carrying a big investment in both dollars and data, so protecting it from theft and damage is important. Corporations are struggling with protecting information technology assets as their workforces begin to carry smaller devices, which are prone to being left behind by mistake or stolen. Protecting mobile devices is important and several devices and procedures exist to physically secure a laptop computer.

Laptops have a cable device you can use to tie them to an airport chair or desk in a field office to deter potential thieves from stealing them. The determined thief with enough time can cut the cable and get away with the laptop, so it is only a slight deterrent. If you want stronger protection, consider a service that allows you to remotely delete data if your computer is stolen and uses GPS to track your laptop (Jackson).

Many newer laptops include fingerprint readers. Because fingerprints are unique to each individual, being able to authenticate yourself with your own set of prints to gain access to your computer is a popular security feature. If somebody without a fingerprint

Page 1

Project 6 Cite Sources in a Mobile Security Report

WL2-C5-P6-MobileSecurity.docx

Last Name 2

match tries to get into the computer data, the system locks up. If you travel with a laptop, activating password protection and creating a secure password is a good idea.

Stopping thieves is one concern when you are on the road, but stopping employees from making costly mistakes regarding company data is another area where companies must take precautions. Making sure that employees who take company laptops outside of the office are responsible for safe and secure storage offsite is vital to company security (Nakamura). Policies might require them to keep backups of data on physical storage media or to back up data to a company network.

If you travel and access the Internet using a public location, you have to be very careful not to expose private information (Jackson). Anything you send over a public network can be accessed by malicious hackers and cybercriminals. Limit your use of online accounts to times when it is essential. "Be especially on guard when accessing your bank accounts, investment accounts, and retail accounts that store your credit card for purchases, and avoid entering your social security number" (Miraldi 19).

Page 2

Last Name 3

Works Cited

Jackson, Gabriel. "Securing Laptops and Mobile Devices." *Future Computing Technologies* (2015): 8-10.

Miraldi, Georgia. *Evolving Technology*. Houston: Rio Grande Publishing, 2015.

Nakamura, Janet. "Computer Security." *Current Technology Times* VI (2015): 20-28.

Suong, Chay. *Securing and Managing Mobile Devices*. 20 April 2014. 5 January 2015. <www.emcp.net/publishing>.

Page 3

Project 1 Sort Company Information — 2 Parts

You will open a document containing information on company employees and then sort data in paragraphs, columns, and tables.

Sorting Text in Paragraphs

> **Quick Steps**
>
> **Sort Text in Paragraphs**
> 1. Click Sort button.
> 2. Make changes at Sort Text dialog box.
> 3. Click OK.
>
> **Display the Sort Options Dialog Box**
> 1. Click Sort button.
> 2. Click Options button.

Sort

Paragraphs of text in a document can be sorted alphanumerically, numerically, or chronologically. For example, you might want to sort a list of company employees to create an internal telephone directory or a list for a company-wide mailing. Sorting items in a Word document is also an effective way to organize a list of customers by zip code or by product purchased.

In an alphanumeric sort, punctuation marks or special symbols are sorted first, followed by numbers and then text. If you sort paragraphs alphanumerically or numerically, dates are treated as regular text. Also be aware that during a paragraph sort, blank lines in a document are moved to the beginning.

To sort text, select the text and then click the Sort button in the Paragraph group on the HOME tab. This displays the Sort Text dialog box containing sorting options. The *Sort by* option box has a default setting of *Paragraphs*. This default setting changes depending on the text in the document. For example, if you are sorting items within a table, the *Sort by* option box has a default setting of *Column 1*. The *Sort by* options will also vary depending on selections at the Sort Options dialog box, shown in Figure 5.1. To display this dialog box, click the Options button in the Sort Text dialog box. At the Sort Options dialog box, specify how fields are separated.

Figure 5.1 Sort Options Dialog Box

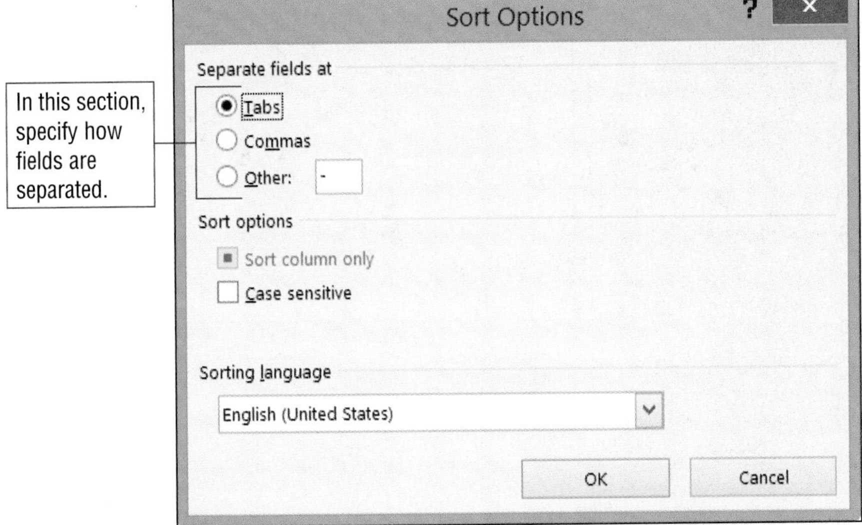

Quick Steps

Sort Text in Columns

1. Select specific text.
2. Click Sort button.
3. Click Options button.
4. Specify *Tabs* as separator.
5. Click OK.
6. Make changes at Sort Text dialog box.
7. Click OK.

When sorting on two fields, Word sorts the first field and then sorts the second field within the first.

Sorting Text in Columns

To sort text set in columns, the text must be separated with tabs. When sorting text in columns, Word considers the left margin *Field 1*, text typed at the first tab *Field 2*, and so on. When sorting text in columns, make sure the columns are separated from each other with only one tab, because Word recognizes each tab as a separate column. Thus, using more than one tab to separate columns may result in field numbers that correspond to empty columns.

Sorting on More Than One Field

When sorting text, you can sort on more than one field. For example, in Project 1a, Step 6, you will sort the department entries alphabetically and then sort the employee names alphabetically within the departments. To do this, specify the *Department* column in the *Sort by* option box and then specify the *Employee* column in the *Then by* option box. If a document contains columns with heading text, click the *Header row* option in the *My list has* section.

Project 1a **Sorting Text** **Part 1 of 2**

1. Open **Sorting.docx** and then save the document and name it **WL2-C5-P1-Sorting**.
2. Sort the text alphabetically by first name by completing the following steps:
   a. Select the seven lines of text at the beginning of the document.
   b. Click the Sort button in the Paragraph group on the HOME tab.
   c. At the Sort Text dialog box, click OK.
3. Sort the text by last name by completing the following steps:
   a. With the seven lines of text still selected, click the Sort button.
   b. At the Sort Text dialog box, click the Options button.
   c. At the Sort Options dialog box, click *Other* and then press the spacebar. (This indicates that the first and last names are separated by a space.)
   d. Click OK.
   e. At the Sort Text dialog box, click the down-pointing arrow at the right side of the *Sort by* option box and then click *Word 2* at the drop-down list.
   f. Click OK.

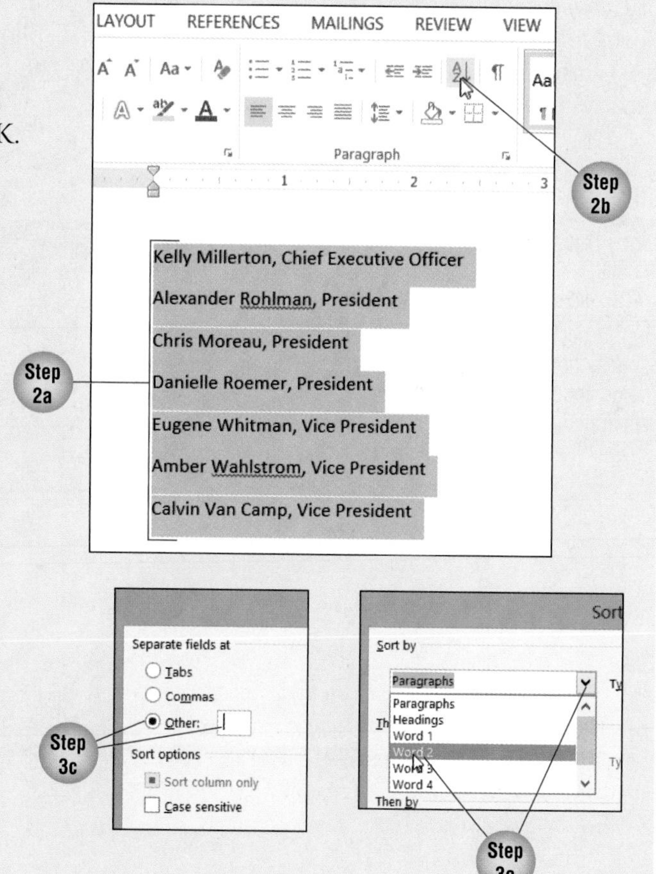

4. Sort text in columns by completing the following steps:
   a. Select the six lines of text set in columns below the headings *Employee*, *Department*, and *Ext*.
   b. Click the Sort button in the Paragraph group on the HOME tab.
   c. At the Sort Text dialog box, click the Options button.
   d. At the Sort Options dialog box, make sure the *Separate fields at* option is set to *Tabs* and then click OK to close the dialog box.

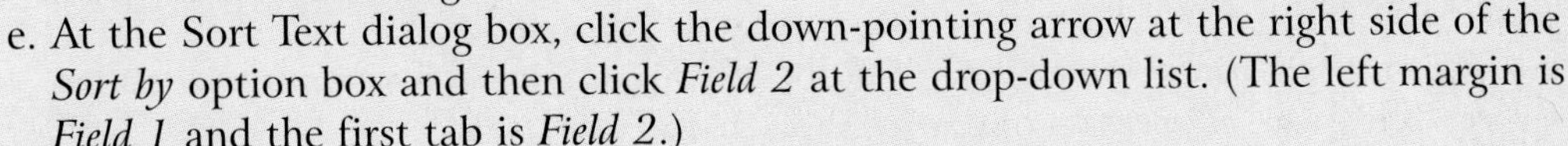

   e. At the Sort Text dialog box, click the down-pointing arrow at the right side of the *Sort by* option box and then click *Field 2* at the drop-down list. (The left margin is *Field 1* and the first tab is *Field 2*.)
   f. Click OK.
5. With the six lines of text still selected, sort the third column of text numerically by completing the following steps:
   a. Click the Sort button.
   b. Click the down-pointing arrow at the right side of the *Sort by* option box and then click *Field 4* at the drop-down list.
   c. Click OK.
6. Sort on two columns by completing the following steps:
   a. Select the seven lines of text set in columns, including the headings.
   b. Click the Sort button.
   c. At the Sort Text dialog box, click the *Header row* option in the *My list has* section of the dialog box.
   d. Click the down-pointing arrow at the right side of the *Sort by* option box and then click *Department*.
   e. Click the down-pointing arrow at the right side of the *Then by* option box and then click *Employee* at the drop-down list.
   f. Click OK.

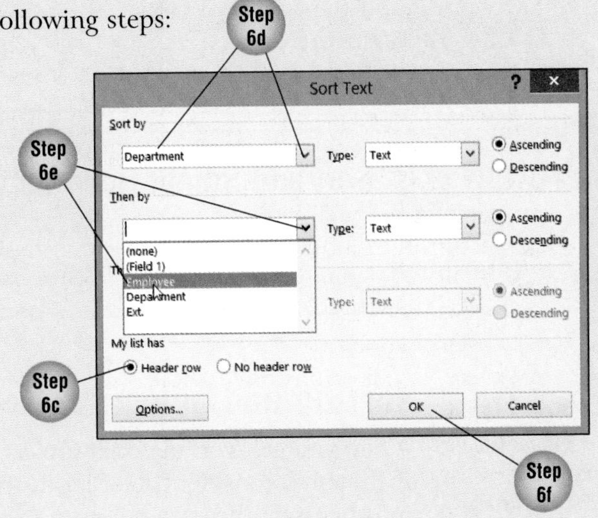

7. Save **WL2-C5-P1-Sorting.docx**.

Sorting Text in Tables

Sorting text in columns within tables is similar to sorting columns of text separated by tabs. If a table contains a header, you can tell Word not to include the header row when sorting by clicking the *Header row* option in the *My list has* section of the Sort dialog box. The Sort Text dialog box becomes the Sort dialog box when sorting a table. If you want to sort only specific cells in a table, select the cells and then complete the sort.

Quick Steps

Sort Text in a Table
1. Position insertion point in table.
2. Click Sort button.
3. Make changes at Sort dialog box.
4. Click OK.

Project 1b Sorting Text in a Table

Part 2 of 2

1. With **WL2-C5-P1-Sorting.docx** open, sort text in the first column in the table by completing the following steps:
   a. Position the insertion point in any cell in the table.
   b. Click the Sort button.
   c. At the Sort dialog box, make sure the *Header row* option is selected in the *My list has* section.
   d. Click the down-pointing arrow at the right side of the *Sort by* option box and then click *Sales, First Half* at the drop-down list.
   e. Click OK.
2. Sort the numbers in the third column in descending order by completing the following steps:
   a. Select all of the cells in the table except the cells in the first row.
   b. Click the Sort button.
   c. Click the down-pointing arrow at the right side of the *Sort by* option and then click *Column 3* at the drop-down list.
   d. Click *Descending*.
   e. Click OK.
3. Save, print, and then close **WL2-C5-P1-Sorting.docx**.

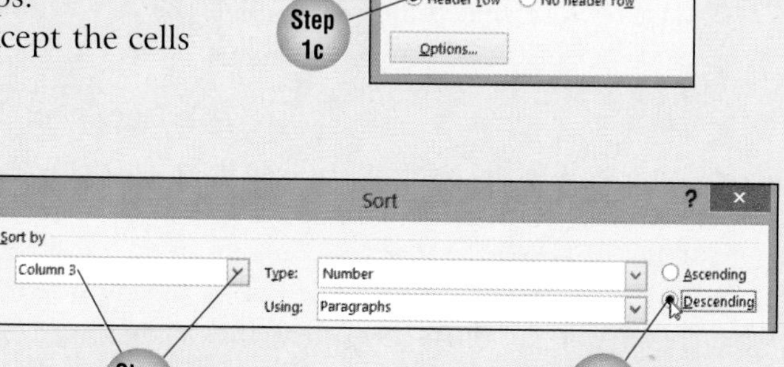

Project 2 Sort and Select Records in a Data Source File

3 Parts

You will sort data in a data source file, create labels and select specific records in a data source file, and then create labels.

Quick Steps

Sort Records in a Data Source

1. Click MAILINGS tab.
2. Click Select Recipients button.
3. Click *Use an Existing List.*
4. Double-click desired file.
5. Click Edit Recipient List button.
6. At Mail Merge Recipients dialog box, sort by specific field by clicking field column heading.
7. Click OK.

Sorting and Selecting Records in a Data Source

When you are working on a project that requires sorting data and merging documents, consider the order in which you want the merged documents printed and then sort the data before merging. To sort records in a data source, click the MAILINGS tab, click the Select Recipients button, and then click *Use an Existing List*. At the Select Data Source dialog box, navigate to the folder containing the data source file and then double-click the file. Click the Edit Recipient List button in the Start Mail Merge group on the MAILINGS tab and the Mail Merge Recipients dialog box displays, similar to the one shown in Figure 5.2.

Click the column heading to sort data in a specific column in ascending order. To perform additional sorts, click the down-pointing arrow at the right side of the column heading and then click the desired sort order. You can also click the Sort hyperlink located in the *Refine recipient list* section of the Mail Merge Recipients dialog box. Clicking this hyperlink displays the Filter and Sort dialog box with the Sort Records tab selected, as shown in Figure 5.3. The options at the dialog box are similar to the options available at the Sort Text (and Sort) dialog box.

Figure 5.2 Mail Merge Recipients Dialog Box

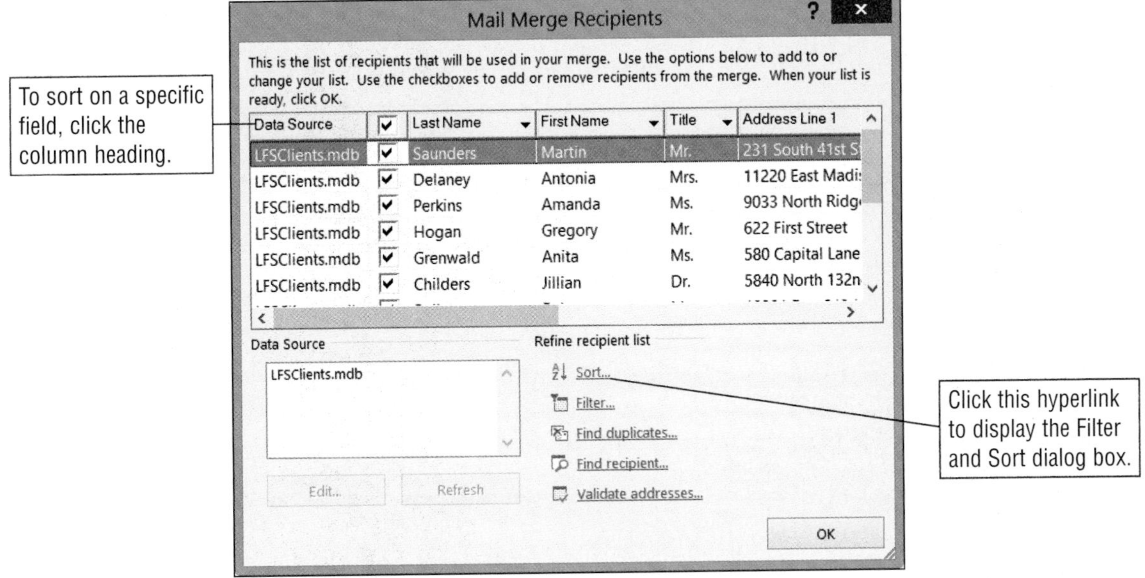

Figure 5.3 Filter and Sort Dialog Box with Sort Records Tab Selected

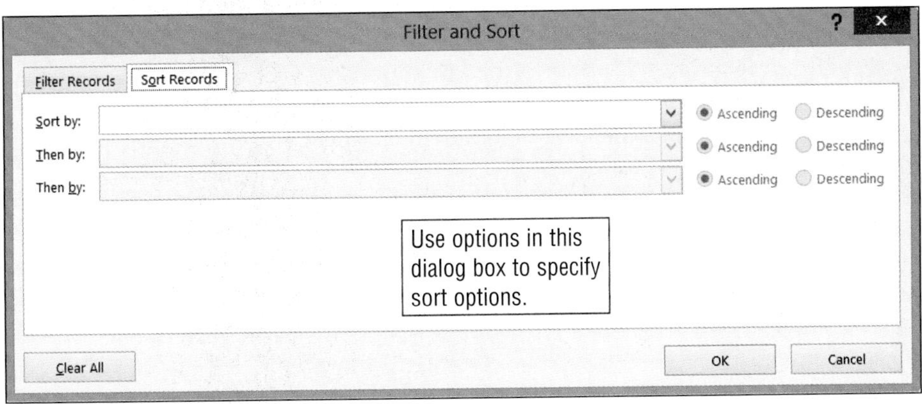

Project 2a Sorting Data in a Data Source

Part 1 of 3

1. At a blank document, click the MAILINGS tab, click the Start Mail Merge button in the Start Mail Merge group, and then click *Labels* at the drop-down list.

Step 1

2. At the Label Options dialog box, click the down-pointing arrow at the right side of the *Label vendors* option box and then click *Avery US Letter* at the drop-down list. Scroll down the *Product number* list box, click *5160 Easy Peel Address Labels*, and then click OK.

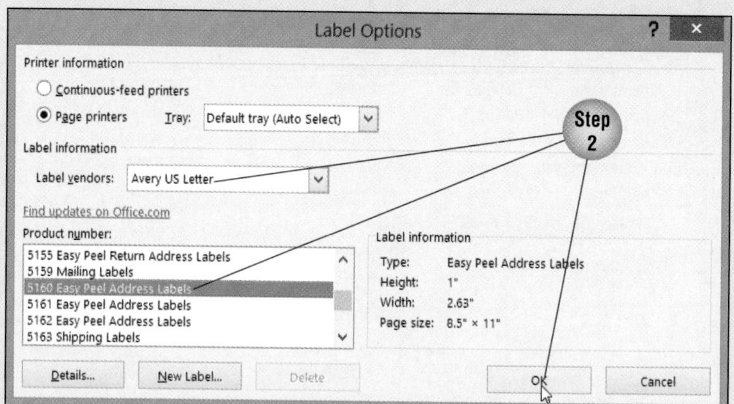

3. Click the Select Recipients button in the Start Mail Merge group and then click *Use an Existing List* at the drop-down list.
4. At the Select Data Source dialog box, navigate to the WL2C5 folder on your storage medium and then double-click the data source file named ***LFSClients.mdb***.
5. Click the Edit Recipient List button in the Start Mail Merge group on the MAILINGS tab.
6. At the Mail Merge Recipients dialog box, click the *Last Name* column heading. (This sorts the last names in ascending alphabetical order.)
7. Scroll to the right to display the *City* field and then click the *City* column heading.
8. Sort records by zip code and then by last name by completing the following steps:
   a. Click the Sort hyperlink located in the *Refine recipient list* section of the Mail Merge Recipients dialog box.
   b. At the Filter and Sort dialog box with the Sort Records tab selected, click the down-pointing arrow at the right side of the *Sort by* option box and then click *ZIP Code* at the drop-down list. (You will need to scroll down the list to display the *ZIP Code* field.)
   c. Make sure *Last Name* displays in the *Then by* option box.
   d. Click OK to close the Filter and Sort dialog box.
   e. Click OK to close the Mail Merge Recipients dialog box.

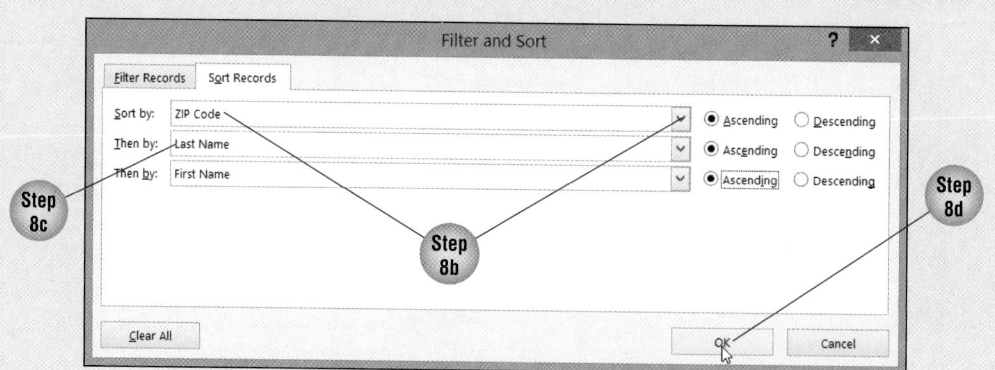

9. At the labels document, click the Address Block button in the Write & Insert Fields group.
10. At the Insert Address Block dialog box, click the OK button.
11. Click the Update Labels button in the Write & Insert Fields group.
12. Click the Finish & Merge button in the Finish group and then click *Edit Individual Documents* at the drop-down list.

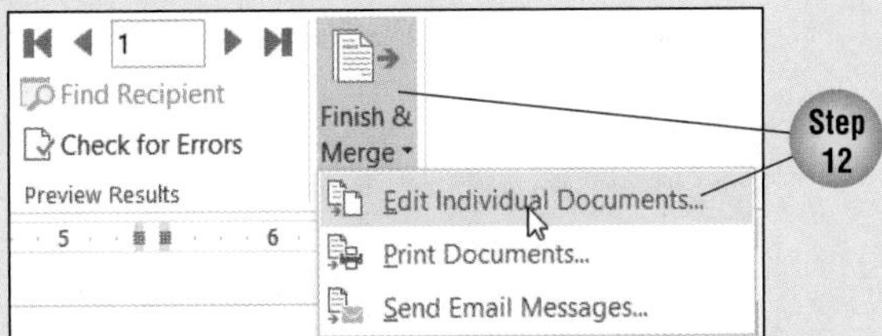

13. At the Merge to New Document dialog box, make sure *All* is selected and then click OK.
14. Press Ctrl + A to select the entire document and then click the *No Spacing* style thumbnail in the Styles group on the HOME tab.
15. Save the merged labels and name the document **WL2-C5-P2-Lbls01**.
16. Print and then close **WL2-C5-P2-Lbls01.docx**.
17. Close the labels main document without saving it.

If you have a data source file with numerous records, you may sometimes want to merge the main document with only specific records in the data source. For example, you may want to send a letter to customers who have a specific zip code or live in a particular city. One method for selecting specific records is to display the Mail Merge Recipients dialog box and then insert or remove check marks from specific records.

Including or excluding certain records from a merge is referred to as *filtering*.

Using check boxes to select specific records is useful in a data source containing a limited number of records, but it may not be practical in a data source containing many records. In a large data source, use options at the Filter and Sort dialog box with the Filter Records tab selected, as shown in Figure 5.4 on the next page. To display this dialog box, click the Filter hyperlink that displays in the *Refine recipient list* section of the Mail Merge Recipients dialog box.

When you select a field from the *Field* drop-down list, Word automatically inserts *Equal to* in the *Comparison* option box, but you can make other comparisons. Clicking the down-pointing arrow at the right of the *Comparison* option box causes a drop-down list to display with these additional options: *Not equal to*, *Less than*, *Greater than*, *Less than or equal*, *Greater than or equal*, *Is blank*, and *Is not blank*. Use one of these options to create a select equation.

Figure 5.4 Filter and Sort Dialog Box with Filter Records Tab Selected

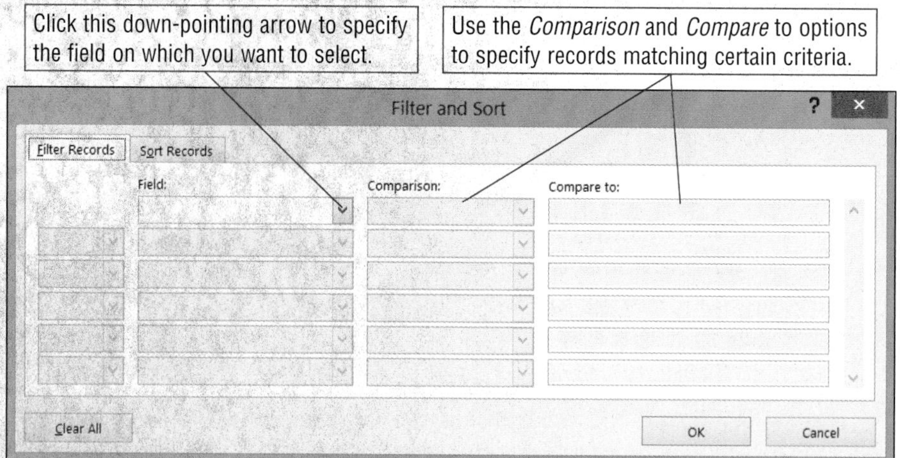

Project 2b Selecting Records

Part 2 of 3

1. At a blank document, click the MAILINGS tab, click the Start Mail Merge button in the Start Mail Merge group, and then click *Labels* at the drop-down list.
2. At the Label Options dialog box, make sure *Avery US Letter* displays in the *Label vendors* option box and *5160 Easy Peel Address Labels* displays in the *Product number* list box and then click OK.
3. Click the Select Recipients button in the Start Mail Merge group and then click *Use an Existing List* at the drop-down list.
4. At the Select Data Source dialog box, navigate to the WL2C5 folder on your storage medium and then double-click the data source file named ***LFSClients.mdb***.
5. Click the Edit Recipient List button.
6. At the Mail Merge Recipients dialog box, click the Filter hyperlink in the *Refine recipient list* section of the dialog box.
7. At the Filter and Sort dialog box with the Filter Records tab selected, click the down-pointing arrow at the right side of the *Field* option box and then click *ZIP Code* at the drop-down list. (You will need to scroll down the list to display *ZIP Code*. When *ZIP Code* is inserted in the *Field* option box, *Equal to* is inserted in the *Comparison* option box and the insertion point is positioned in the *Compare to* text box.)
8. Type 21000 in the *Compare to* text box.
9. Click the down-pointing arrow at the right side of the *Comparison* option box and then click *Greater than* at the drop-down list.

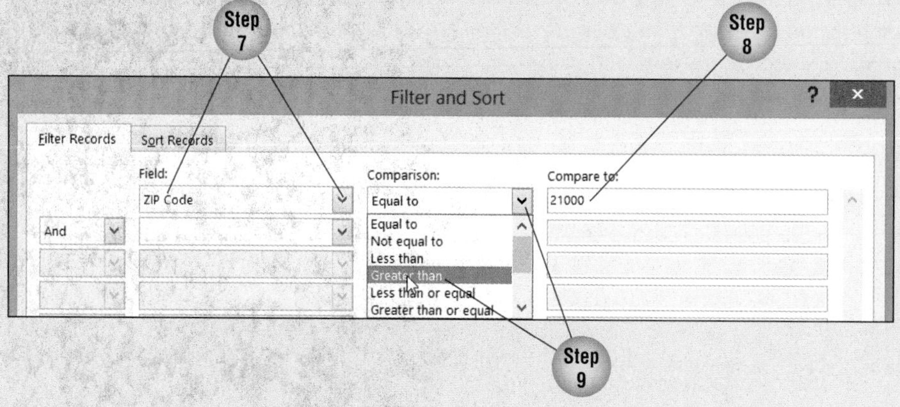

10. Click OK to close the Filter and Sort dialog box.
11. Click OK to close the Mail Merge Recipients dialog box.
12. At the labels document, click the Address Block button in the Write & Insert Fields group and then click OK at the Insert Address Block dialog box.
13. Click the Update Labels button in the Write & Insert Fields group.
14. Click the Finish & Merge button in the Finish group and then click *Edit Individual Documents* at the drop-down list.
15. At the Merge to New Document dialog box, make sure *All* is selected and then click OK.
16. Press Ctrl + A to select the entire document and then click the *No Spacing* style thumbnail in the Styles group on the HOME tab.
17. Save the merged labels and name the document **WL2-C5-P2-Lbls02**.
18. Print and then close **WL2-C5-P2-Lbls02.docx**.
19. Close the labels main document without saving it.

When a field is selected from the *Field* option box, Word automatically inserts *And* in the first box at the left side of the dialog box, but you can change this to *Or*, if necessary. With the *And* and *Or* options, you can specify more than one condition for selecting records. For example, in Project 2c, you will select all of the records of clients living in the cities of Rosedale or Towson. If the data source file contained another field, such as a specific financial plan for each customer, you could select all of the customers in a specific city that subscribe to a specific financial plan. In this situation, you would use the *And* option.

To clear the current options at the Filter and Sort dialog box with the Filter Records tab selected, click the Clear All button. This clears any text from text boxes and leaves the dialog box on the screen. Click the Cancel button if you want to close the Filter and Sort dialog box without specifying any records.

Project 2c Selecting Records with Specific Cities — Part 3 of 3

1. At a blank document, click the MAILINGS tab, click the Start Mail Merge button in the Start Mail Merge group, and then click *Labels* at the drop-down list.
2. At the Label Options dialog box, make sure *Avery US Letter* displays in the *Label vendors* option box and *5160 Easy Peel Address Labels* displays in the *Product number* list box and then click OK.
3. Click the Select Recipients button in the Start Mail Merge group and then click *Use an Existing List* at the drop-down list.
4. At the Select Data Source dialog box, navigate to the WL2C5 folder on your storage medium and then double-click the data source file named ***LFSClients.mdb***.
5. Click the Edit Recipient List button.
6. At the Mail Merge Recipients dialog box, click the Filter hyperlink in the *Refine recipient list* section of the dialog box.

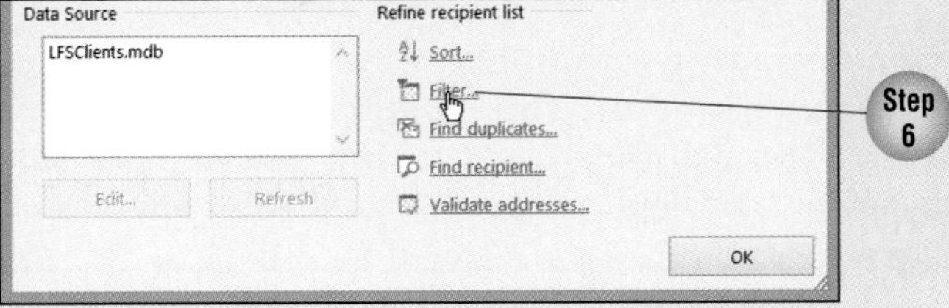

7. At the Filter and Sort dialog box with the Filter Records tab selected, click the down-pointing arrow at the right side of the *Field* option box and then click *City* at the drop-down list. (You will need to scroll down the list to display this field.)
8. Type **Rosedale** in the *Compare to* text box.
9. Click the down-pointing arrow to the right of the option box containing the word *And* (at the left side of the dialog box) and then click *Or* at the drop-down list.
10. Click the down-pointing arrow at the right side of the second *Field* option box and then click *City* at the drop-down list. (You will need to scroll down the list to display this field.)
11. With the insertion point positioned in the second *Compare to* text box (the one below the box containing *Rosedale*), type **Towson**.
12. Click OK to close the Filter and Sort dialog box.

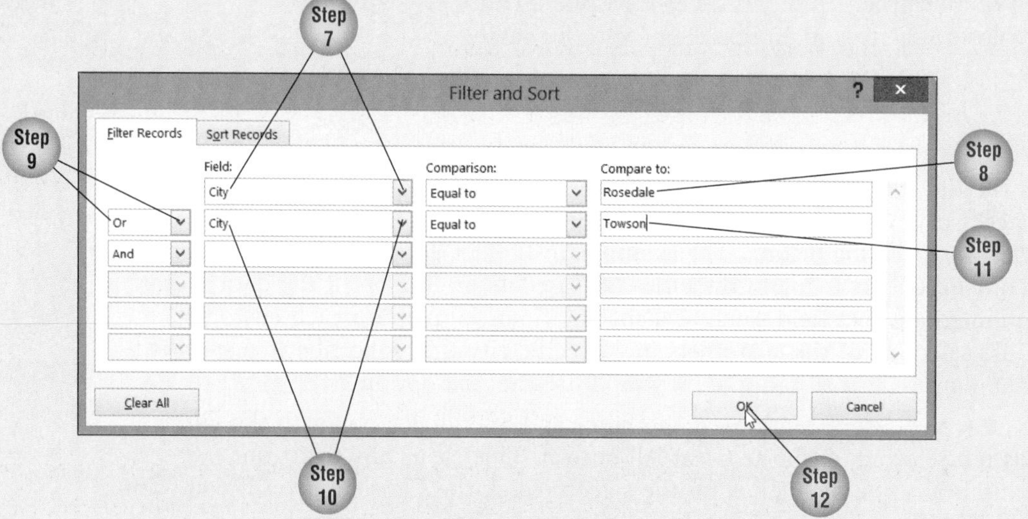

13. Click OK to close the Mail Merge Recipients dialog box.
14. At the labels document, click the Address Block button in the Write & Insert Fields group and then click OK at the Insert Address Block dialog box.
15. Click the Update Labels button in the Write & Insert Fields group.
16. Click the Finish & Merge button in the Finish group and then click *Edit Individual Documents* at the drop-down list.
17. At the Merge to New Document dialog box, make sure *All* is selected and then click OK.
18. Press Ctrl + A to select the entire document and then click the *No Spacing* style thumbnail in the Styles group on the HOME tab.
19. Save the merged labels and name the document **WL2-C5-P2-Lbls03**.
20. Print and then close **WL2-C5-P2-Lbls03.docx**.
21. Close the labels main document without saving it.

Project 3 Type a Keyboard Shortcut Document — 2 Parts

You will type a document with information on keyboard shortcuts and use nonbreaking spaces within the shortcuts to keep them from splitting between two lines of text. You will then use the Find and Replace feature to search for all nonbreaking spaces and replace them with regular spaces.

Inserting Nonbreaking Spaces

As you type text in a document, Word makes line-end decisions and automatically wraps text to each successive line. In some situations, words and phrases that should remain together are broken across two lines. To control where text is broken and wrapped to the next line, consider inserting ***nonbreaking spaces*** between words. Press Ctrl + Shift + spacebar to insert a nonbreaking space. With the display of nonprinting characters turned on, a normal space displays as a dot and a nonbreaking space displays as a degree (°) symbol.

You can insert a nonbreaking space at the Symbol dialog box with the (normal text) font selected.

Project 3a **Inserting Nonbreaking Spaces** **Part 1 of 2**

1. At a blank document, turn on the display of nonprinting characters by clicking the Show/Hide ¶ button in the Paragraph group on the HOME tab.
2. Type the text shown in Figure 5.5 and insert nonbreaking spaces in the keyboard shortcuts by pressing Ctrl + Shift + spacebar before and after each plus symbol.
3. Turn off the display of nonprinting characters. Bold and center the title as shown in the figure.
4. Save the document and name it **WL2-C5-P3-Shortcuts**.

Figure 5.5 Project 3a

KEYBOARD SHORTCUTS

Microsoft Word includes a number of keyboard shortcuts you can use to access features and commands. The ScreenTip for some buttons displays the keyboard shortcut you can use to access the command. For example, hover the mouse over the Font button and the ScreenTip displays Ctrl + Shift + F as the keyboard shortcut. Additional HOME tab Font group keyboard shortcuts include Ctrl + B to bold text, Ctrl + I to italicize text, and Ctrl + U to underline text. You can also press Ctrl + Shift + + to turn on superscript and press Ctrl + = to turn on subscript.

Buttons in the Clipboard group include keyboard shortcuts. For example, to cut selected text press Ctrl + X, press Ctrl + C to copy selected text, and use the keyboard shortcut Ctrl + V to insert text. Ctrl + Shift + C is the keyboard command to turn on and off the Format Painter feature.

Finding and Replacing Special Characters

You can use the Find feature to find special text and the Find and Replace feature to find specific text and replace it with other text. You can also use these features to find special formatting, characters, and nonprinting elements in a document. To display a list of special characters and nonprinting elements, display the Find and Replace dialog box with either the Find or Replace tab selected, expand the dialog box, and then click the Special button. This displays a pop-up list similar to the one shown in Figure 5.6 on the next page.

Quick Steps

Find and Replace a Special Character
1. Click Replace button.
2. Click More button.
3. Click Special button.
4. Click desired character.
5. Click in *Replace with* text box.
6. Click Special button.
7. Click desired character.
8. Click Replace All button.

Figure 5.6 Special Button Pop-up List

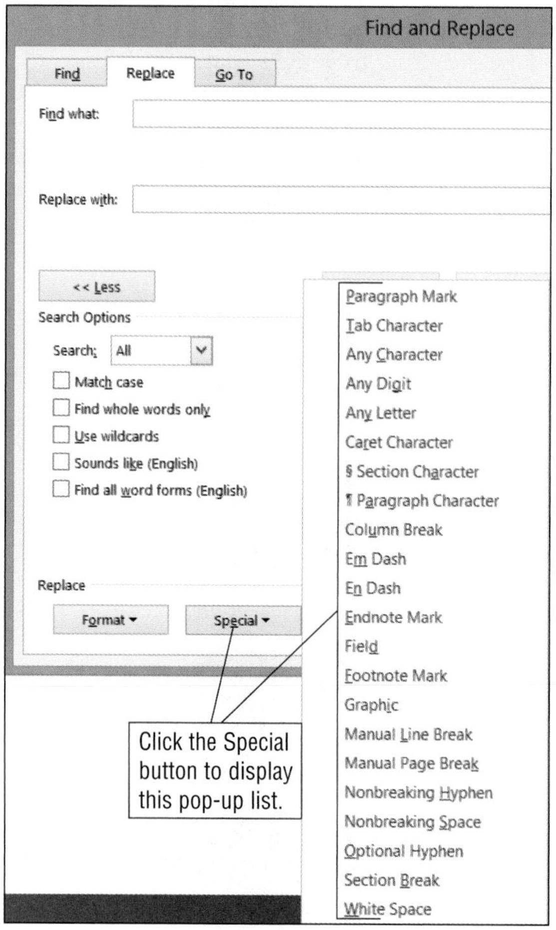

Press Ctrl + H to display the Find and Replace dialog box with the Replace tab selected.

If you are not sure about the name of the special character you want to find or are unclear about the names of the special characters in the Special button pop-up list, access Word's list of special characters to see the characters and their names. Click the Symbol button in the Symbols group on the INSERT tab and a short list of symbols displays. Click the *More Symbols* option at the drop-down list and the Symbol dialog box displays. Click the Special Characters tab to see a list of characters and their names. For example, some users may not know the difference between an em dash (—) and an en dash (–). The *Character* list box at the Symbol dialog box shows both types of dashes.

Project 3b Finding and Replacing Nonbreaking Spaces — Part 2 of 2

1. With **WL2-C5-P3-Shortcuts.docx** open, find all of the occurrences of nonbreaking spaces and replace them with regular spaces by completing the following steps:
   a. Click the Replace button in the Editing group on the HOME tab.
   b. At the Find and Replace dialog box with the Replace tab selected, click the More button.

c. With the insertion point positioned in the *Find what* text box, click the Special button that displays near the bottom of the dialog box.
d. At the pop-up list that displays, click *Nonbreaking Space*. (This inserts *^s* in the *Find what* text box.)
e. Click in the *Replace with* text box (making sure it does not contain any text) and then press the spacebar once. (This tells the Find and Replace feature to find a nonbreaking space and replace it with a regular space.)
f. Click the Replace All button.
g. At the message telling you that Word completed the search and made the replacements, click OK.
h. Click the Less button in the Find and Replace dialog box.

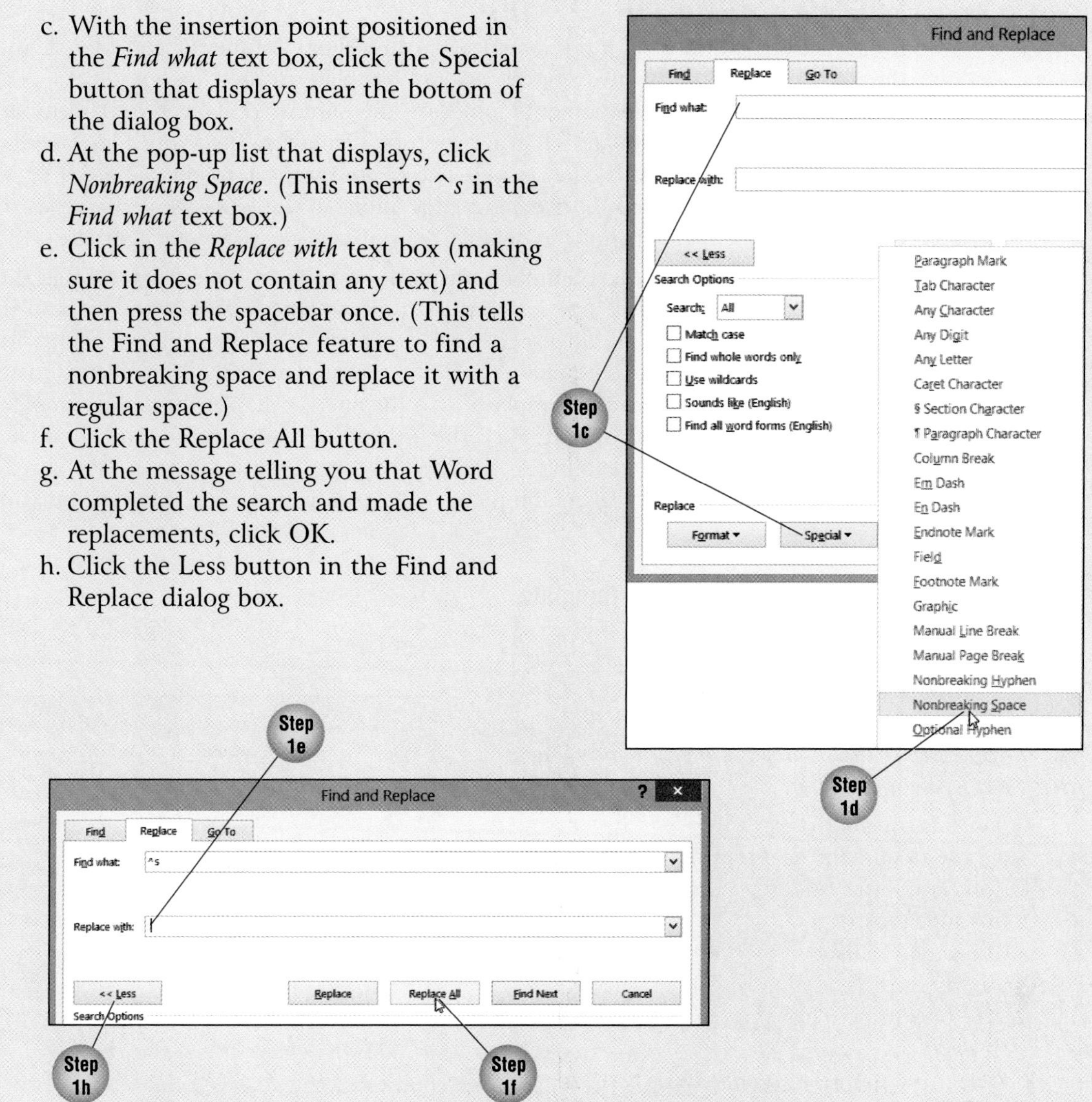

i. Click the Close button to close the Find and Replace dialog box.

2. Save, print, and then close **WL2-C5-P3-Shortcuts.docx**.

Project 4 Create and Use a Summons Template — 2 Parts

You will open a summons legal document, save it as a template, and then use it to create other summons documents.

Creating and Using Templates

If you use the contents of a document to create other documents, consider saving the document as a template. Save a personal template in the Custom Office Templates folder in the Documents folder on the hard drive. Check to determine the default personal template folder location by displaying the Word Options dialog box with *Save* selected in the left panel. The *Default personal templates location* option should display the Custom Office Templates folder in the Documents folder as the default location. If this is not the default location, check with your instructor.

Quick Steps

Create a Template

1. Display Save As dialog box.
2. Change *Save as type* to *Word Template (*.dotx)*.
3. Type template name in *File name* text box.
4. Click Save.

To save a document as a template, display the Save As dialog box, change the *Save as type* option to *Word Template (*.dotx)*, type a name for the template, and then press Enter. Word template documents are saved with the .dotx file extension. You can also save a template as a macro-enabled template with the .dotm file extension. Another method for saving a template is to display the Export backstage area, click the *Change File Type* option, click the *Template (*.dotx)* option, and then click the Save As button. At the Save As dialog box, type a name for your template, navigate to the Custom Office Templates folder, and then click the Save button.

Project 4a Saving a Document as a Template — Part 1 of 2

Before completing this project, check to make sure the default location for personal templates is the Custom Office Templates folder in the Documents folder on the hard drive. If this is not the default location, check with your instructor.

1. Open **Summons.docx**.
2. Save the document as a template in the Custom Office Templates folder by completing the following steps:
   a. Press the F12 key.
   b. At the Save As dialog box, click the *Save as type* option box and then click *Word Template (*.dotx)*.
   c. Select the name in the *File name* text box and then type your last name followed by *Summons*.
   d. Press Enter or click the Save button.
3. Close the summons template.

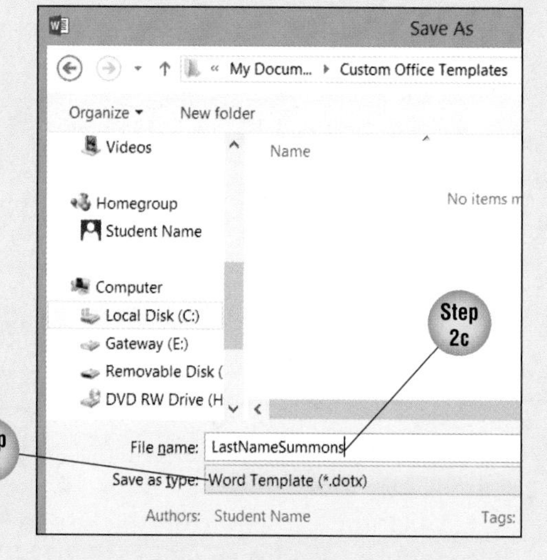

Quick Steps

Creating a Document with a Template

1. Click FILE tab.
2. Click *New* option.
3. Click *PERSONAL*.
4. Click template.

To create a document with a template you saved to the *Custom Office Templates* folder, click the FILE tab and then click the *New* option. At the New backstage area, click the *PERSONAL* option. This displays the templates available in the Custom Office Templates folder. Click the template you want to open and a document opens based on that template.

Project 4b Creating a Document Based on a Template — Part 2 of 2

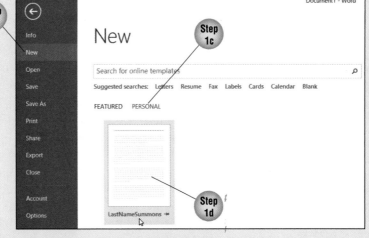

1. Open the summons template as a document by completing the following steps:
   a. Click the FILE tab.
   b. Click the *New* option.
   c. At the New backstage area, click the *PERSONAL* option.
   d. Click the summons template that is preceded by your last name.
2. With the summons document open, find and replace text as follows:
   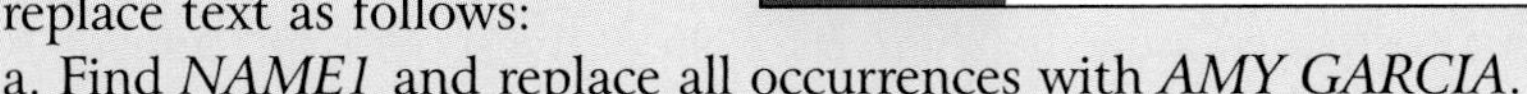
   a. Find *NAME1* and replace all occurrences with *AMY GARCIA*.
   b. Find *NAME2* and replace all occurrences with *NEIL CARLIN*.
   c. Find *NUMBER* and replace with *C-98002*.
3. Save the document in the WL2C5 folder on your storage medium and name it **WL2-C5-P4-Summons**.
4. Print and then close **WL2-C5-P4-Summons.docx**.
5. Delete the summons template from the hard drive by completing the following steps:
   a. Press Ctrl + F12 to display the Open dialog box.
   b. At the Open dialog box, click *Documents* in the Navigation pane.
   c. Double-click the *Custom Office Templates* folder in the Content pane.
   d. Click the summons template that begins with your last name.
   e. Click the Organize button and then click *Delete* at the drop-down list.
6. Close the Open dialog box.

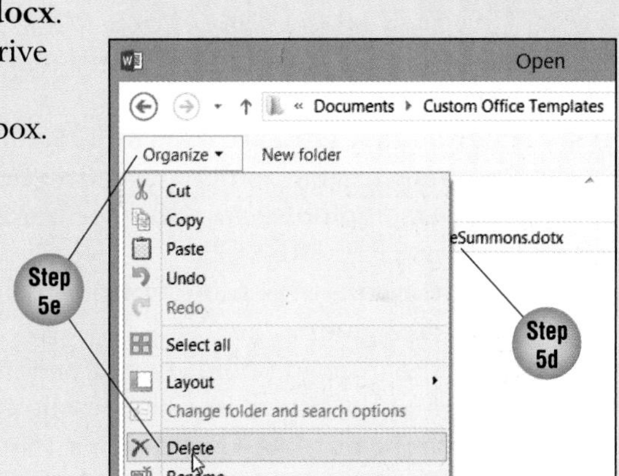

Project 5 Insert Footnotes and Endnotes in Reports — 3 Parts

You will open a report on artificial intelligence and then insert, format, and modify footnotes. You will also open a report on the future of the Internet and then insert endnotes.

Insert Footnote

Insert Endnote

Quick Steps

Insert a Footnote
1. Click REFERENCES tab.
2. Click Insert Footnote button.
3. Type footnote text.

Insert an Endnote
1. Click REFERENCES tab.
2. Click Insert Endnote button.
3. Type endnote text.

Ctrl + Alt + F is the keyboard shortcut to insert a footnote and Ctrl + Alt + D is the keyboard shortcut to insert an endnote.

Creating Footnotes and Endnotes

A research paper or report contains information from a variety of sources. To give credit to those sources, you can insert footnotes or endnotes in a document formatted in a specific reference style, such as Chicago style. (You will learn more about different reference styles in the next project.) A *footnote* is an explanatory note or source reference that is printed at the bottom of the page on which the corresponding information appears. An *endnote* is also an explanatory note or reference but it is printed at the end of the document.

Two steps are involved in creating a footnote or endnote. First, the note reference number is inserted in the document at the location where the corresponding information appears. The second step is to type the note entry text. Footnotes and endnotes are created in a similar manner.

To create a footnote, position the insertion point at the location the reference number is to appear, click the REFERENCES tab, and then click the Insert Footnote button in the Footnotes group. This inserts a number in the document along with a separator line at the bottom of the page and a superscript number below it. With the insertion point positioned immediately to the right of the superscript number, type the note entry text. Word automatically numbers footnotes with superscript arabic numbers and endnotes with superscript lowercase roman numerals.

Project 5a Creating Footnotes — Part 1 of 3

1. Open **InterfaceApps.docx** and then save the document and name it **WL2-C5-P5-InterfaceApps**.
2. Create the first footnote shown in Figure 5.7 by completing the following steps:
   a. Position the insertion point at the end of the first paragraph of text in the document.
   b. Click the REFERENCES tab.
   c. Click the Insert Footnote button in the Footnotes group.
   d. With the insertion point positioned at the bottom of the page immediately following the superscript number, type the first footnote shown in Figure 5.7.

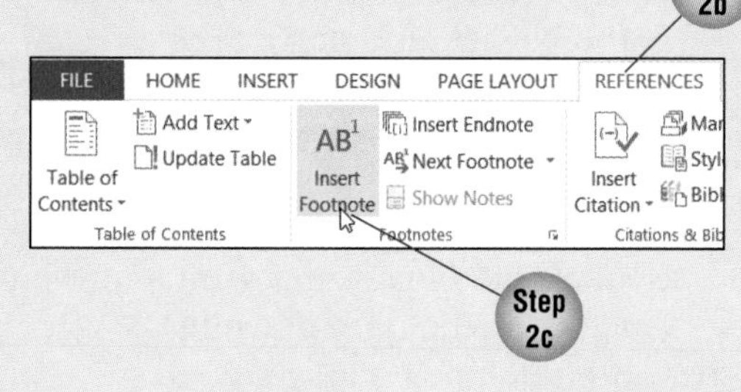

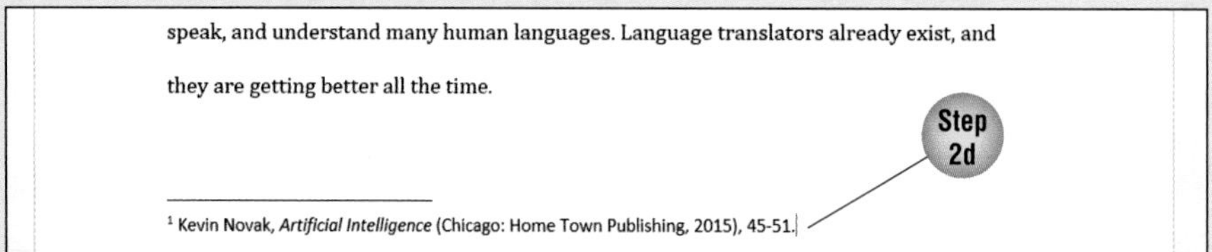

speak, and understand many human languages. Language translators already exist, and they are getting better all the time.

[1] Kevin Novak, *Artificial Intelligence* (Chicago: Home Town Publishing, 2015), 45-51.

3. Move the insertion point to the end of the paragraph in the *Speech Recognition* section, and using steps similar to those in Steps 2c and 2d, create the second footnote shown in Figure 5.7.
4. Move the insertion point to the end of the second paragraph in the *Natural-Language Interface* section and then create the third footnote shown in Figure 5.7.
5. Move the insertion point to the end of the paragraph in the *Virtual Reality* section and then create the fourth footnote shown in Figure 5.7.
6. Move the insertion point to the end of the last paragraph in the document and then create the fifth footnote shown in Figure 5.7.
7. Save, print, and then close **WL2-C5-P5-InterfaceApps.docx**.

Figure 5.7 Project 5a

Kevin Novak, *Artificial Intelligence* (Chicago: Home Town Publishing, 2015), 45-51.

Heather Everson and Nicolas Reyes, "Integrating Speech Recognition," *Design Technologies* (2014): 24-26.

James Glenovich, "Language Interfaces," *Corporate Computing* (2015): 8-12.

William Curtis, *Virtual Reality Worlds* (San Francisco: Lilly Harris Publishers, 2013), 53-68.

Marilyn Beal, "Challenges of Artificial Intelligence," *Interface Design* (2015): 10-18.

Printing Footnotes and Endnotes

When you print a document containing footnotes, Word automatically reduces the number of text lines on a page to create space for the number of lines in the footnotes and the separator line. If the page does not contain enough space, the footnote number and entry text are moved to the next page. Word separates the footnotes from the text with a 2-inch separator line that begins at the left margin. When endnotes are created in a document, Word prints all of the endnote references at the end of the document, separated from the text by a 2-inch line.

Project 5b Creating Endnotes — Part 2 of 3

1. Open **InternetFuture.docx** and then save the document and name it **WL2-C5-P5-InternetFuture**.
2. Create the first endnote shown in Figure 5.8 by completing the following steps:
   a. Position the insertion point at the end of the first paragraph of text in the document.
   b. Click the REFERENCES tab.
   c. Click the Insert Endnote button in the Footnotes group.
   d. Type the first endnote shown in Figure 5.8.
3. Move the insertion point to the end of the paragraph in the *Satellite Internet Connections* section and then complete steps similar to those in Steps 2c and 2d to create the second endnote shown in Figure 5.8.
4. Move the insertion point to the end of the second paragraph in the *Second Internet* section and then create the third endnote shown in Figure 5.8.
5. Move the insertion point to the end of the paragraph in the *Internet Services for a Fee* section and then create the fourth endnote shown in Figure 5.8.
6. Save **WL2-C5-P5-InternetFuture.docx**.

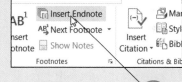

Figure 5.8 Project 5b

Joshua Abrahamson, *Future Trends in Computing* (Los Angeles: Gleason Rutherford Publishing, 2014), 8-12.

Aileen Clements, *Satellite Systems* (Boston: Robison Publishing House, 2015), 23-51.

Terry Ventrella, "Future of the Internet," *Computing Today* (2015): 29-33.

Jolene Campbell, "Fee-Based Internet Services," *Connections* (2014): 5-8.

Viewing and Editing Footnotes and Endnotes

Next Footnote

Show Notes

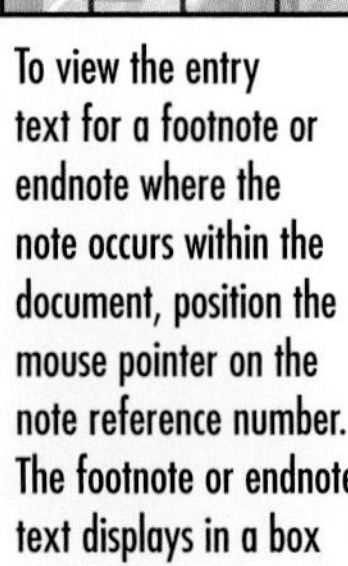

To view the entry text for a footnote or endnote where the note occurs within the document, position the mouse pointer on the note reference number. The footnote or endnote text displays in a box above the mark.

To view the footnotes in a document, click the Next Footnote button in the Footnotes group on the REFERENCES tab. This moves the insertion point to the location of the first footnote reference number following the location of the insertion point. To view the endnotes in a document, click the Next Footnote button arrow and then click *Next Endnote* at the drop-down list. With other options at the Next Footnote button drop-down list, you can view the previous footnote, next endnote, or previous endnote. You can move the insertion point to specific footnote text with the Show Notes button.

When you move, copy, or delete footnote or endnote reference numbers, all of the remaining footnotes or endnotes automatically renumber. To move a footnote or endnote, select the reference number and then click the Cut button in the Clipboard group on the HOME tab. Position the insertion point at the location you want the footnote or endnote inserted and then click the Paste button. To delete a footnote or endnote, select the reference number and then press the Delete key. This deletes the reference number as well as the footnote or endnote text.

Click the Footnotes group dialog box launcher and the Footnote and Endnote dialog box displays, as shown in Figure 5.9. At this dialog box, you can convert footnotes to endnotes and endnotes to footnotes; change the location of footnotes or endnotes; change the number formatting; start footnote or endnote numbering with a specific number, letter, and symbol; or change numbering within sections in a document.

Figure 5.9 Footnote and Endnote Dialog Box

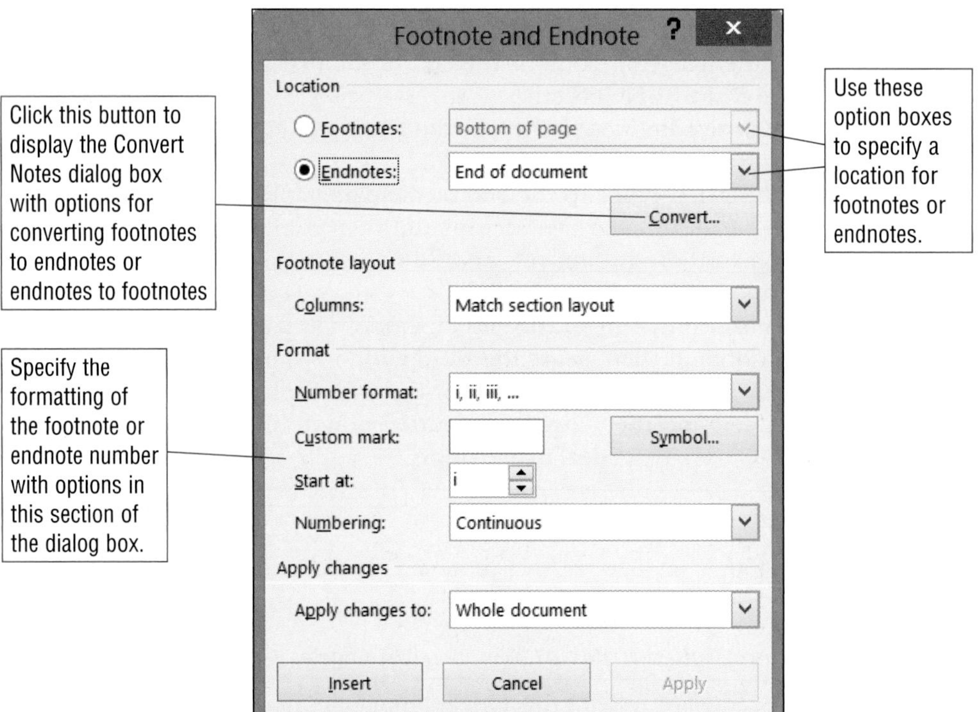

Project 5c Editing Endnotes, Converting Endnotes to Footnotes, and Editing Footnotes Part 3 of 3

1. With **WL2-C5-P5-InternetFuture.docx** open, edit the endnotes by completing the following steps:
   a. If necessary, click the REFERENCES tab.
   b. Click the Next Footnote button arrow and then click *Next Endnote* at the drop-down list.
   c. Click the Show Notes button to display the endnote text.
   d. Change the page numbers for the Joshua Abrahamson entry from *8-12* to *5-9*.
   e. Click the Show Notes button again to return to the reference number in the document.

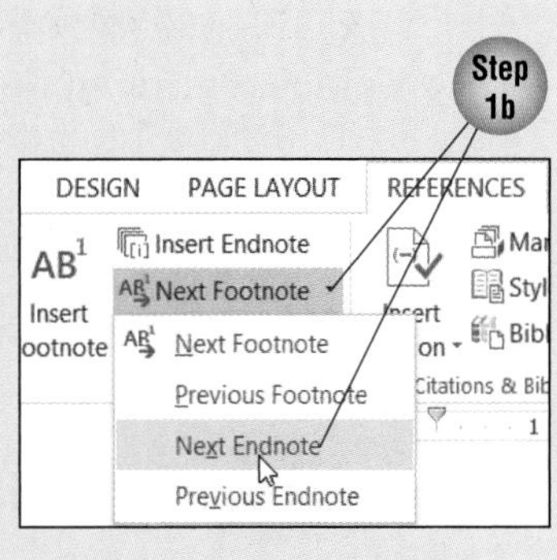

2. Press Ctrl + A to select the document (but not the endnote entry text) and then change the font to Constantia.
3. Change the fonts for the endnotes by completing the following steps:
   a. Press Ctrl + End to move the insertion point to the end of the document.
   b. Click on any endnote entry and then press Ctrl + A to select all of the endnote entries.
   c. Change the font to Constantia.
   d. Press Ctrl + Home.
4. Convert the endnotes to footnotes by completing the following steps:
   a. Click the REFERENCES tab and then click the Footnotes group dialog box launcher.
   b. At the Footnote and Endnote dialog box, click the Convert button.
   c. At the Convert Notes dialog box with the *Convert all endnotes to footnotes* option selected, click the OK button.
   d. Click the Close button to close the dialog box.
5. Change the footnote number format by completing the following steps:
   a. Click the Footnotes group dialog box launcher.
   b. Click the *Footnotes* option in the *Location* section of the dialog box.
   c. Click the down-pointing arrow at the right side of the *Footnotes* option and then click *Below text* at the drop-down list.
   d. Click the down-pointing arrow at the right side of the *Number format* option box and then click *a, b, c, ...* at the drop-down list.
   e. Change the starting number by clicking the up-pointing arrow at the right side of the *Start at* option until *d* displays in the option box.
   f. Click the Apply button and then scroll through the document and notice the renumbering of the footnotes.

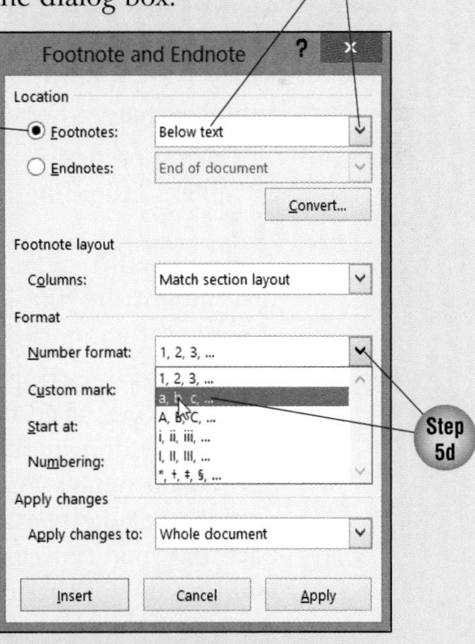

6. Change the footnote number format back to arabic numbers by completing the following steps:
   a. With the REFERENCES tab active, click the Footnotes group dialog box launcher.
   b. At the Footnote and Endnote dialog box, click the *Footnotes* option in the *Location* section.
   c. Click the down-pointing arrow at the right side of the *Number format* option box and then click *1, 2, 3, ...* at the drop-down list.
   d. Change the starting number back to 1 by clicking the down-pointing arrow at the right side of the *Start at* option until *1* displays in the option box.
   e. Click the Apply button.

7. Delete the third footnote by completing the following steps:
   a. Press Ctrl + Home.
   b. Make sure the REFERENCES tab is active and then click three times on the Next Footnote button in the Footnotes group.
   c. Select the third footnote reference number (superscript number) and then press the Delete key.
8. Save, print, and then close **WL2-C5-P5-InternetFuture.docx**.

Project 6 Cite Sources in a Mobile Security Report — 8 Parts

You will open a report on securing mobile devices, add information and insert source citations and a bibliography, and then modify and customize citation styles.

Creating Citations and Bibliographies

In addition to using footnotes and endnotes to credit sources in a research paper or manuscript, consider inserting in-text citations and a works cited page to identify sources of quotations, facts, theories, and other borrowed or summarized material. An in-text citation acknowledges that you are borrowing information from a source rather than plagiarizing (stealing) someone else's words or ideas.

Word provides three commonly used editorial styles for citing references in research papers and reports: the American Psychological Association (APA) reference style, which is generally used in the social sciences and research fields; the Modern Language Association (MLA) style, which is generally used in the humanities and English composition; and the *Chicago Manual of Style* (Chicago), which is used both in the humanities and social sciences and is considered more complex than either APA or MLA style.

If you prepare a research paper or report in APA or MLA style, format your document according to the following general guidelines: Use standard-sized paper (8.5 × 11 inches); set 1-inch top, bottom, left, and right margins; set text in a 12-point serif typeface (such as Cambria or Times New Roman); double-space text; indent the first line of each paragraph 0.5 inch; and insert page numbers in the upper right corners of pages.

When formatting a research paper or report according to MLA or APA standards, you need to follow certain guidelines for properly formatting the first page of the document. With MLA style, in the upper left corner of the first page, insert your name, your instructor's name, the course title, and the current date all double-spaced. Type the title of the document a double-space below the current date and then center the document title. Also, double-space between the title and first line of the text. Finally, insert a header in the upper right corner of the document that includes your last name followed by the current page number.

When using APA style, create a title page that is separate from the body of the document. On this page, include the title of your paper, your name, and your school's name, all double-spaced, centered, and located in the upper half of the page. Also, include a header with the text *Running Head:* followed by the title of your paper in uppercase letters at the left margin and the page number at the right margin.

Project 6a Formatting the First Page of a Research Paper Part 1 of 8

1. Open **MobileSecurity.docx** and then save the document and name it **WL2-C5-P6-MobileSecurity**.
2. Format the first page of the document by completing the following steps:
   a. Press Ctrl + A to select the entire document.
   b. Change the font to Cambria and the font size to 12 points.
   c. Change the line spacing to 2.0.
   d. Remove extra spacing after paragraphs by clicking the PAGE LAYOUT tab, clicking in the *After* text box in the *Spacing* section in the Paragraph group, typing **0**, and then pressing the Enter key.
   e. Press Ctrl + Home to position the insertion point at the beginning of the document, type your first and last names, and then press the Enter key.
   f. Type your instructor's name and then press the Enter key.
   g. Type the title of your course and then press the Enter key.
   h. Type the current date and then press the Enter key.
   i. Type the document title **Mobile Security** and then center the title.

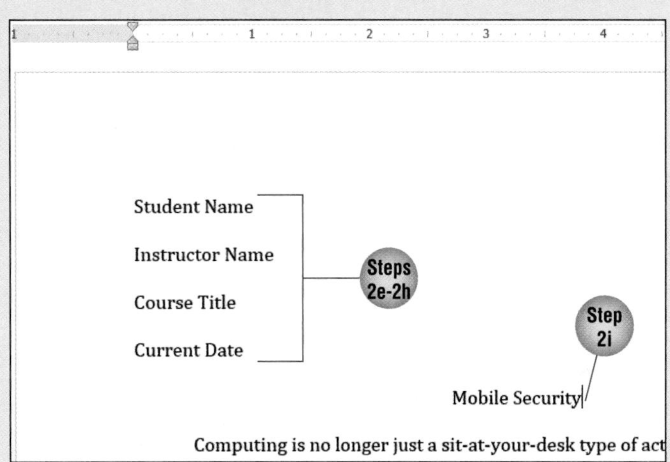

3. Insert a header in the document by completing the following steps:
   a. Click the INSERT tab.
   b. Click the Header button in the Header & Footer group and then click *Edit Header* at the drop-down list.
   c. Press the Tab key twice to move the insertion point to the right margin in the Header pane.
   d. Type your last name and then press the spacebar.
   e. Click the Page Number button in the Header & Footer group on the HEADER & FOOTER TOOLS DESIGN tab, point to *Current Position*, and then click the *Plain Number* option.

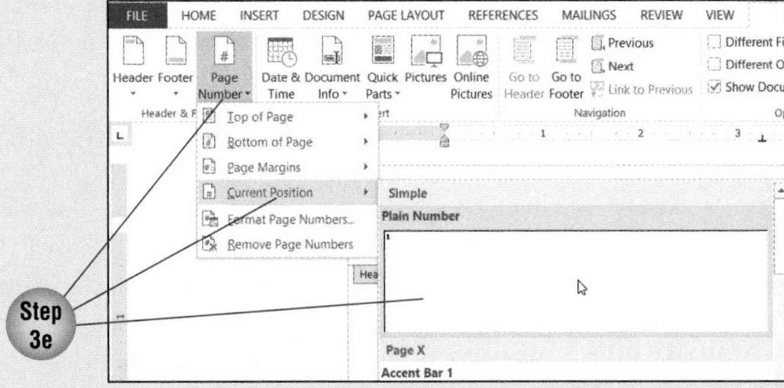

   f. Select the header text and change the font to 12-point Cambria.
   g. Double-click in the body of the document.
4. Save **WL2-C5-P6-MobileSecurity.docx**.

Inserting Source Citations

Quick Steps

Insert a New Citation
1. Click REFERENCES tab.
2. Click Insert Citation button.
3. Click *Add New Source* at drop-down list.
4. Type necessary source information.
5. Click OK.

Insert a Citation Placeholder
1. Click REFERENCES tab.
2. Click Insert Citation button.
3. Click *Add New Placeholder* at drop-down list.
4. Type citation name.
5. Click OK.

When you create an in-text source citation, Word requires you to enter information about the source in fields at the Create Source dialog box. To insert a citation in a document, click the REFERENCES tab, click the Insert Citation button in the Citations & Bibliography group, and then click *Add New Source* at the drop-down list. At the Create Source dialog box, as shown in Figure 5.10, select the type of reference you want to cite—such as a book, journal article, or report—and then type the bibliographic information in the required fields. If you want to include more information than required in the displayed fields, click the *Show All Bibliography Fields* check box to insert a check mark and then type the additional bibliographic details in the extra fields. After filling in the necessary source information, click OK. The citation is automatically inserted in the document at the location of the insertion point.

Inserting Citation Placeholders

If you want to insert the information for an in-text source citation later, insert a citation placeholder. To do this, click the Insert Citation button in the Citations & Bibliography group and then click *Add New Placeholder* at the drop-down list. At the Placeholder Name dialog box, type a name for the citation placeholder and then press Enter or click the OK button. Insert the citation text later at the Edit Source dialog box, which contains the same options as the Create Source dialog box.

Insert Citation

Figure 5.10 Create Source Dialog Box

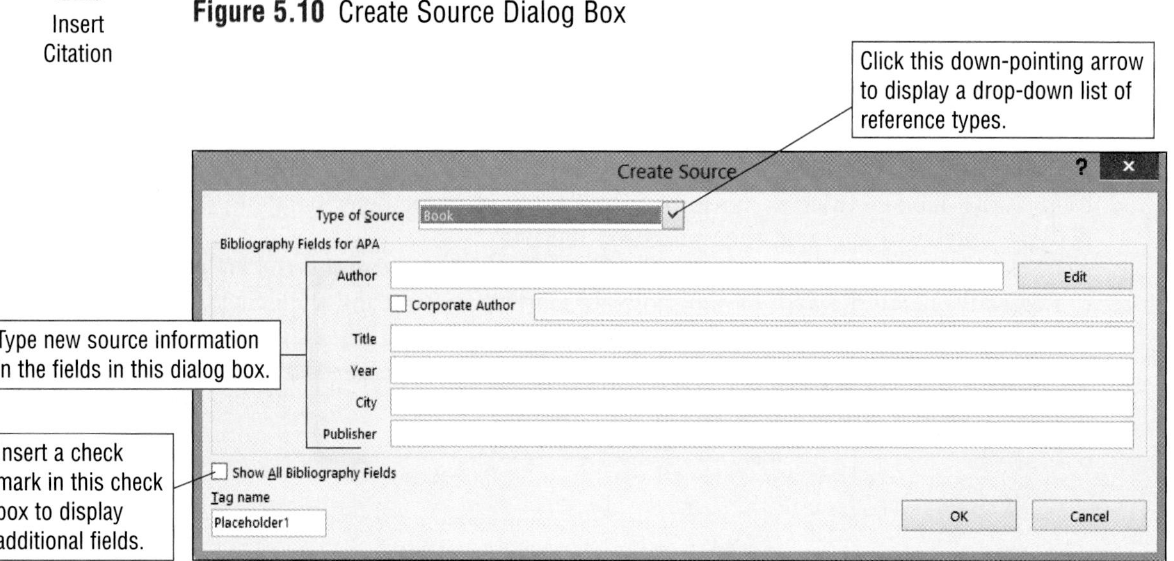

Project 6b **Inserting Sources and a Citation Placeholder** **Part 2 of 8**

1. With **WL2-C5-P6-MobileSecurity.docx** open, press Ctrl + End to move the insertion point to the end of the document and then type the text shown in Figure 5.11 on page 210 up to the first citation—the text *(Jefferson)*. To insert the citation, complete these steps:
   a. Press the spacebar once after typing the text *laptop*.

b. Click the REFERENCES tab.

c. Make sure the *Style* option box in the Citations & Bibliography group is set to *MLA*. If not, click the down-pointing arrow at the right of the *Style* option box and then click *MLA* at the drop-down list.

d. Click the Insert Citation button in the Citations & Bibliography group and then click *Add New Source* at the drop-down list.

e. At the Create Source dialog box, click the down-pointing arrow at the right of the *Type of Source* option box and then click *Journal Article* at the drop-down list.

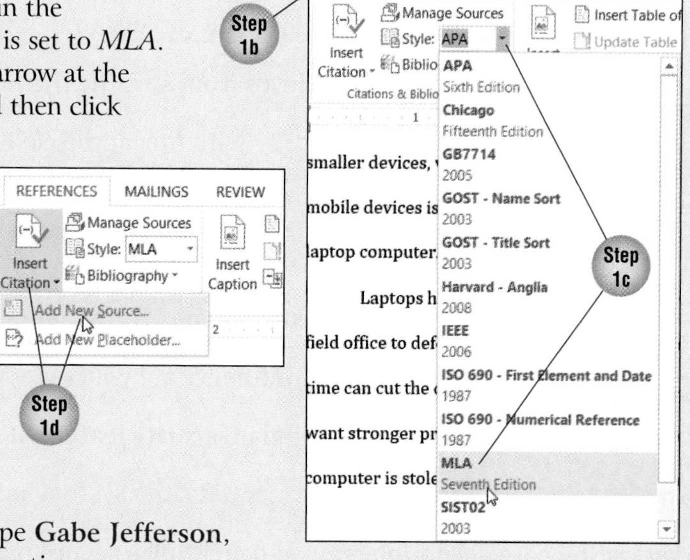

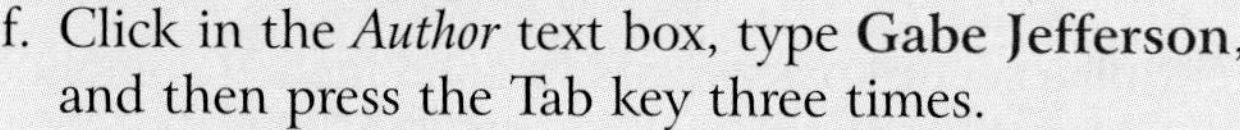

f. Click in the *Author* text box, type **Gabe Jefferson**, and then press the Tab key three times.

g. In the *Title* text box, type **Securing Laptops and Mobile Devices** and then press the Tab key.

h. In the *Journal Name* text box, type **Future Computing Technologies** and then press Tab.

i. In the *Year* text box, type **2015** and then press the Tab key.

j. Type **8-10** in the *Pages* text box.

k. Click OK.

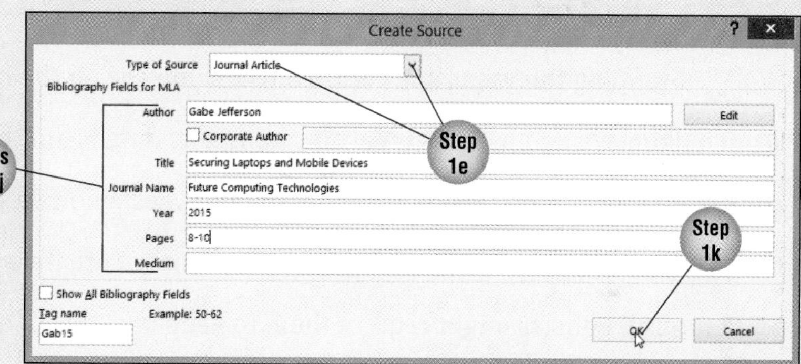

l. Type a period to end the sentence in the document.

2. Continue typing the text up to the next citation—the text *(Lopez)*—and insert the following source information for a book. (Click the down-pointing arrow at the right of the *Type of Source* option box and then click *Book* at the drop-down list.)

Author	**Rafael Lopez**
Title	**Technology World**
Year	**2015**
City	**Chicago**
Publisher	**Great Lakes Publishing House**

3. Continue typing the text up to the next citation—the text *(Nakamura)*—and then insert a citation placeholder by completing the following steps. (You will create the citation and fill in the source information in the next project.)
   a. Click the Insert Citation button in the Citations & Bibliography group.
   b. Click *Add New Placeholder* at the drop-down list.
   c. At the Placeholder Name dialog box, type **Nakamura** and then press Enter.
4. Type the remaining text shown in Figure 5.11.
5. Save **WL2-C5-P6-MobileSecurity.docx**.

Figure 5.11 Project 6b

Laptops have a cable device you can use to tie them to an airport chair or desk in a field office to deter potential thieves from stealing them. The determined thief with enough time can cut the cable and get away with the laptop, so it is only a slight deterrent. If you want stronger protection, consider a service that allows you to remotely delete data if your computer is stolen and uses GPS to track your laptop (Jefferson).

Many newer laptops include fingerprint readers. Because fingerprints are unique to each individual, being able to authenticate yourself with your own set of prints to gain access to your computer is a popular security feature. If somebody without a fingerprint match tries to get into the computer data, the system locks up. If you travel with a laptop, activating password protection and creating a secure password is a good idea. If somebody steals your laptop and cannot get past the password feature, he or she cannot immediately get at your valuable data (Lopez).

Stopping thieves is one concern when you are on the road, but stopping employees from making costly mistakes regarding company data is another area where companies must take precautions. Making sure that employees who take company laptops outside of the office are responsible for safe and secure storage offsite is vital to company security (Nakamura). Policies might require them to keep backups of data on physical storage media or to back up data to a company network.

Editing a Source

After inserting information about a source into a document, you may need to edit the source to correct errors or change data. One method for editing a source is to click the citation in the document, click the Citation Options arrow that displays at the right side of the selected citation, and then click *Edit Source* at the drop-down list. This displays the Edit Source dialog box, which contains the same options as the Create Source dialog box. Make the desired changes at this dialog box and then click OK.

Inserting a Citation with an Existing Source

Once you insert source information at the Create Source dialog box, Word automatically saves it. To insert a citation in a document for source information that has already been saved, click the Insert Citation button in the Citations & Bibliography group and then click the desired source at the drop-down list.

Quick Steps

Insert a Citation with an Existing Source
1. Click REFERENCES tab.
2. Click Insert Citation button.
3. Click desired source at drop-down list.

Project 6c **Edit an Existing Source and Inserting a Citation with an Existing Source** **Part 3 of 8**

1. With **WL2-C5-P6-MobileSecurity.docx** open, add the Nakamura source information by completing the following steps:
   a. Click the *Nakamura* citation in the document.
   b. Click the Citation Options arrow that displays at the right side of the selected citation.
   c. Click *Edit Source* at the drop-down list.
   d. At the Edit Source dialog box, click the *Type of Source* option box arrow and then click *Journal Article.*
   e. Type the following information in the specified text boxes:

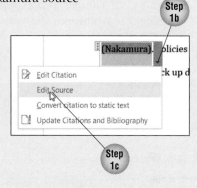

Author	**Janet Nakamura**
Title	**Computer Security**
Journal Name	**Current Technology Times**
Year	**2015**
Pages	**20-28**
Volume	**VI**

   (Display the *Volume* field by clicking the *Show All Bibliography Fields* check box and then scroll down the options list.)
   f. Click the OK button to close the Edit Source dialog box.
2. Press Ctrl + End to move the insertion point to the end of the document and then press the Enter key once. Type the text shown in Figure 5.12 up to the citation text *(Jefferson)* and then insert a citation from an existing source by completing the following steps:
   a. If necessary, click the REFERENCES tab.
   b. Click the Insert Citation button in the Citations & Bibliography group.
   c. Click the *Jefferson, Gabe* reference at the drop-down list.
   d. Type the remaining text in Figure 5.12.
3. Save **WL2-C5-P6-MobileSecurity.docx**.

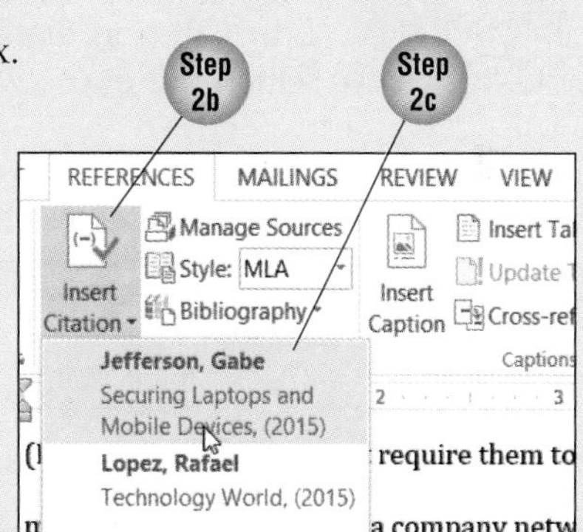

Figure 5.12 Project 6c

> If you travel and access the Internet using a public location, you have to be very careful not to expose private information (Jefferson). Anything you send over a public network can be accessed by malicious hackers and cybercriminals. Limit your use of online accounts to times when it is essential.

Managing Sources

Quick Steps

Manage Sources

1. Click REFERENCES tab.
2. Click Manage Sources button.
3. Edit, add, and/or delete sources.
4. Click Close.

Manage Sources

Click the Browse button in the Source Manager dialog box to select another master list.

All sources for the current document and sources created in previous documents display in the Source Manager dialog box, as shown in Figure 5.13. Display this dialog box by clicking the REFERENCES tab and then clicking the Manage Sources button in the Citations & Bibliography group. The *Master List* list box in the Source Manager dialog box displays all of the citations you have created in Word. The *Current List* list box displays all of the citations included in the currently open document.

Use options at the Source Manager dialog box to copy a source from the master list to the current list, delete a source, edit a source, and create a new source. To copy a source from the master list to the current list, click the desired source in the *Master List* list box and then click the Copy button that displays between the two list boxes. Click the Delete button to delete a source. Edit a source by clicking the source, clicking the Edit button, and then making changes at the Edit Source dialog box that displays. Click the New button to create a new source at the Create Source dialog box.

If the *Master List* list box contains a large number of sources, search for a specific source by typing keywords in the *Search* text box. As you type text, the list narrows to sources that match the text you are typing. When you are finished making changes at the Source Manager dialog box, click the Close button.

Inserting Page Numbers in a Citation

Quick Steps

Insert a Page Number in a Citation

1. Click citation to display placeholder.
2. Click Citation Options arrow.
3. Click *Edit Citation*.
4. Type page number(s).
5. Click OK.

If you include a direct quote from a source, be sure to include quotation marks around all of the text used from that source and insert in the citation the page number(s) of the quoted material. To insert specific page numbers into a citation, click the citation in the document to select the citation placeholder. Click the Citation Options arrow and then click *Edit Citation* at the drop-down list. At the Edit Citation dialog box, type in the page number or numbers of the source from which the quote was borrowed and then click OK.

Figure 5.13 Source Manager Dialog Box

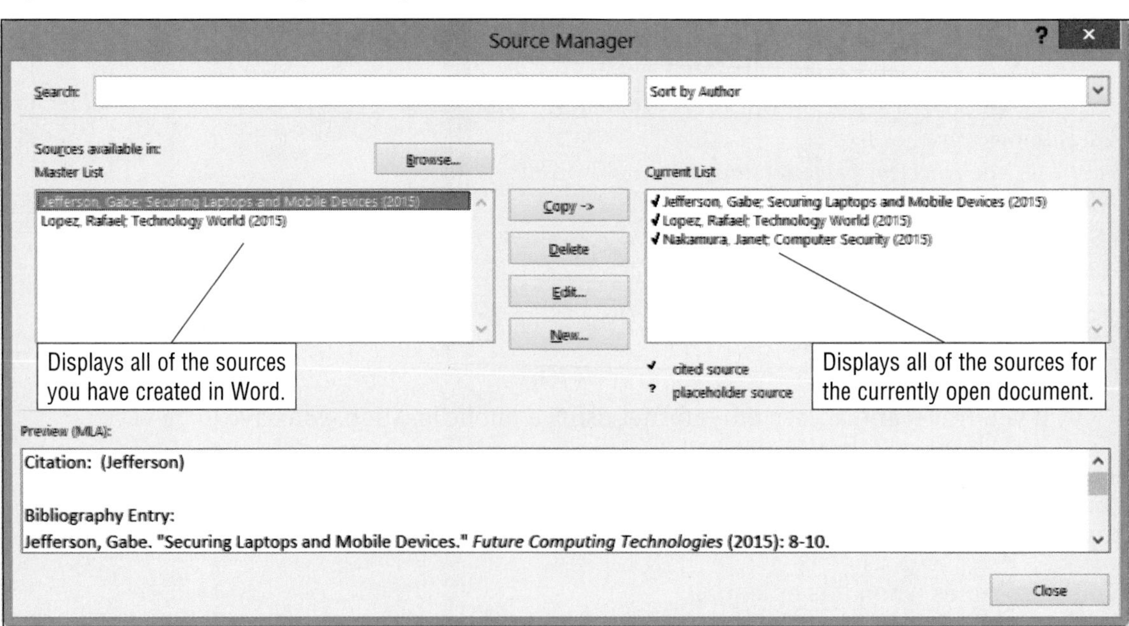

1. With **WL2-C5-P6-MobileSecurity.docx** open, edit a source by completing the following steps:
   a. If necessary, click the REFERENCES tab.
   b. Click the Manage Sources button in the Citations & Bibliography group.
   c. At the Source Manager dialog box, click the *Jefferson, Gabe* source entry in the *Master List* list box.
   d. Click the Edit button.
   e. At the Edit Source dialog box, delete the text in the *Author* text box and then type **Gabriel Jackson**.
   f. Click OK to close the Edit Source dialog box.
   g. At the message asking if you want to update both the master list and current list with the changes, click Yes.
   h. Click the Close button to close the Source Manager dialog box. (Notice that the last name changed in both of the Jefferson citations to reflect the edit.)

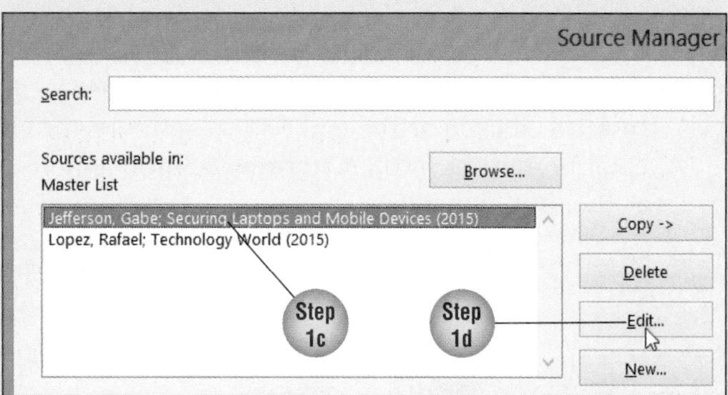

2. Delete a source by completing the following steps:
   a. Select and then delete the last sentence in the fourth paragraph in the document (the sentence beginning *If somebody steals your laptop*), including the citation.
   b. Click the Manage Sources button in the Citations & Bibliography group.
   c. At the Source Manager dialog box, click the *Lopez, Rafael* entry in the *Current List* list box. (This entry will not contain a check mark because you deleted the citation from the document.)
   d. Click the Delete button.
   e. Click the Close button to close the Source Manager dialog box.

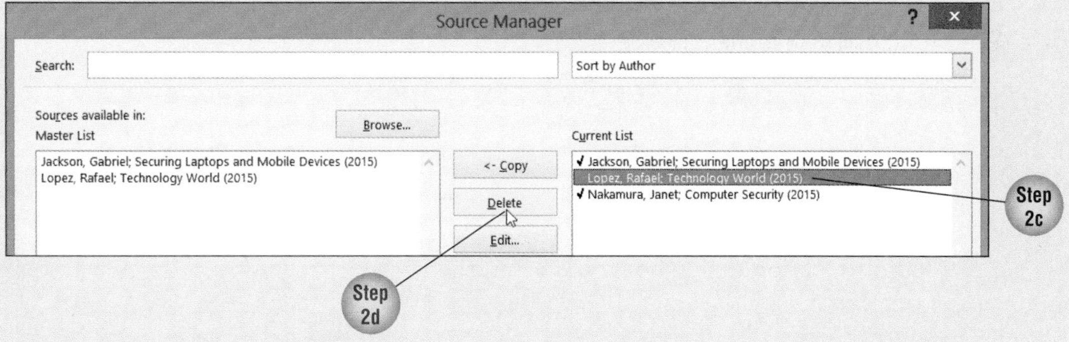

3. Create and insert a new source in the document by completing the following steps:
   a. Click the Manage Sources button in the Citations & Bibliography group.
   b. Click the New button in the Source Manager dialog box.
   c. Type the following book information in the Create Source dialog box. (Change the *Type of Source* option to *Book*.)

Author	**Georgia Miraldi**
Title	**Evolving Technology**
Year	**2015**
City	**Houston**
Publisher	**Rio Grande Publishing**

d. Click OK to close the Create Source dialog box.
e. Click the Close button to close the Source Manager dialog box.
f. Position the insertion point one space after the period that ends the last sentence in the document and then type this sentence: "**Be especially on guard when accessing your bank accounts, investment accounts, and retail accounts that store your credit card for purchases, and avoid entering your social security number**" (Press the spacebar once after typing the quotation mark that follows the word *number*.)
g. Insert a citation at the end of the sentence for Georgia Miraldi by clicking the Insert Citation button in the Citations & Bibliography group and then clicking *Miraldi, Georgia* at the drop-down list.

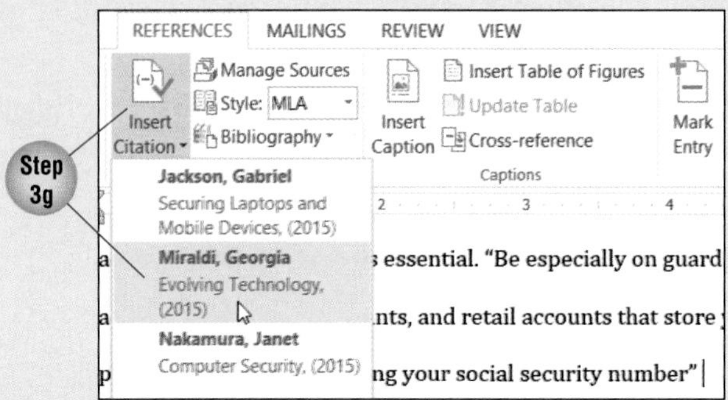

h. Type a period to end the sentence.

4. Because you inserted a direct quote from Georgia Miraldi, you will need to include the page number of the book in which you found the quote. Insert the page number within the citation by completing the following steps:
   a. Click the *Miraldi* citation in the document.
   b. Click the Citation Options arrow that displays at the right of the citation placeholder and then click *Edit Citation* at the drop-down list.

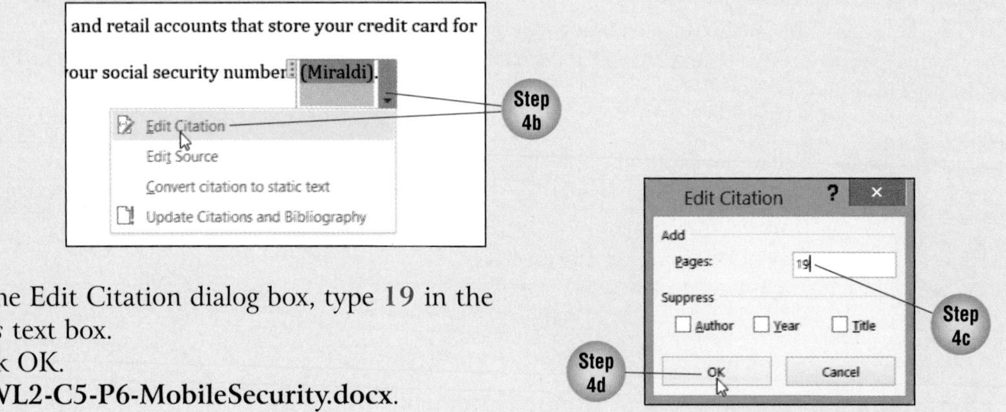

   c. At the Edit Citation dialog box, type 19 in the *Pages* text box.
   d. Click OK.
5. Save **WL2-C5-P6-MobileSecurity.docx**.

Inserting a Sources List

If you include citations in a report or research paper, you need to insert a sources list as a separate page at the end of the document. A sources list is an alphabetical list of the books, journal articles, reports, and other sources referenced in the report or paper. Depending on the reference style applied to a document, a sources list may be a bibliography, a references page, or a works cited page.

When you type source information for citations, Word automatically saves information from all of the fields and compiles a sources list, alphabetized by the authors' last names and/or the titles of the works. Insert a works cited page for a document formatted in MLA style, insert a references page for a document formatted in APA style, and insert a bibliography for a document formatted in Chicago style.

To insert a works cited page, move the insertion point to the end of the document and then insert a new page. Click the REFERENCES tab and make sure the *Style* option box is set to *MLA*. Click the Bibliography button in the Citations & Bibliography group and then click the desired works cited option. Complete similar steps to insert a bibliography in an APA-style document, except click the desired bibliography option.

Quick Steps

Insert a Sources List
1. Insert new page at end of document.
2. Click REFERENCES tab.
3. Click Bibliography button.
4. Click desired works cited, reference, or bibliography option.

Bibliography

Project 6e **Inserting a Works Cited Page** **Part 5 of 8**

1. With **WL2-C5-P6-MobileSecurity.docx** open, insert a works cited page at the end of the document by completing these steps:
   a. Press Ctrl + End to move the insertion point to the end of the document.
   b. Press Ctrl + Enter to insert a page break.
   c. If necessary, click the REFERENCES tab.
   d. Click the Bibliography button in the Citations & Bibliography group.
   e. Click the *Works Cited* option in the *Built-In* section of the drop-down list.
2. Save **WL2-C5-P6-MobileSecurity.docx**.

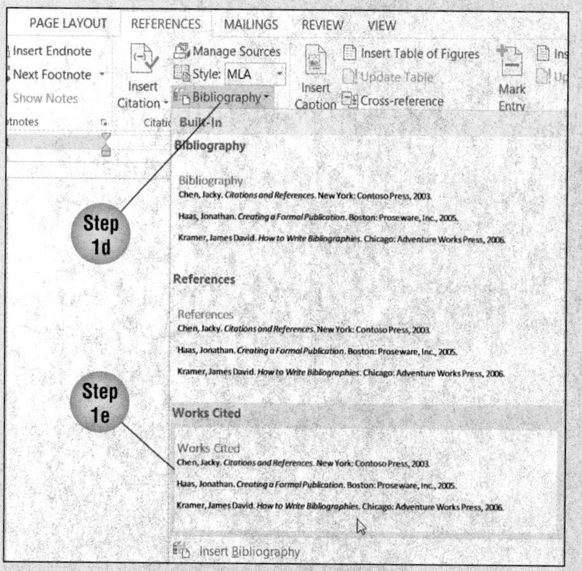

Modifying and Updating a Sources List

If you insert a new source at the Source Manager dialog box or modify an existing source, Word automatically inserts the source information in the sources list. If you insert a new citation that requires you to add a new source, Word will not automatically update the sources list. To update the sources list, click anywhere in list and then click the Update Citations and Bibliography tab.The updated sources list will reflect any changes made to the citations and source information in the document.

Quick Steps

Update a Sources List
1. Click anywhere in sources list.
2. Click Update Citations and Bibliography tab.

Project 6f Modifying and Updating a Works Cited Page

Part 6 of 8

1. With **WL2-C5-P6-MobileSecurity.docx** open, create a new source and citation by completing the following steps:
   a. Position the insertion point immediately left of the period that ends the last sentence in the first paragraph of the document (after the word *safer*).
   b. Press the spacebar once.
   c. If necessary, click the REFERENCES tab.
   d. Click the Insert Citation button in the Citations & Bibliography group and then click *Add New Source* at the drop-down list.
   e. At the Create Source dialog box, insert the following source information for a website. (Change the *Type of Source* option to *Web site* and click the *Show All Bibliography Fields* check box to display all fields.)

Author	**Chay Suong**
Name of Web Page	**Securing and Managing Mobile Devices**
Year	**2014**
Month	**April**
Day	**20**
Year Accessed	(type current year in numbers)
Month Accessed	(type current month in letters)
Day Accessed	(type current day in numbers)
URL	**www.emcp.net/publishing**

   f. Click OK to close the Create Source dialog box.
2. Update the works cited page to include the new source by completing the following steps:
   a. Press Ctrl + End to move the insertion point to the end of the document.
   b. Click anywhere in the works cited text.
   c. Click the Update Citations and Bibliography tab located above the heading Works Cited. (Notice that the updated works cited includes the Suong reference.)
3. Save **WL2-C5-P6-MobileSecurity.docx**.

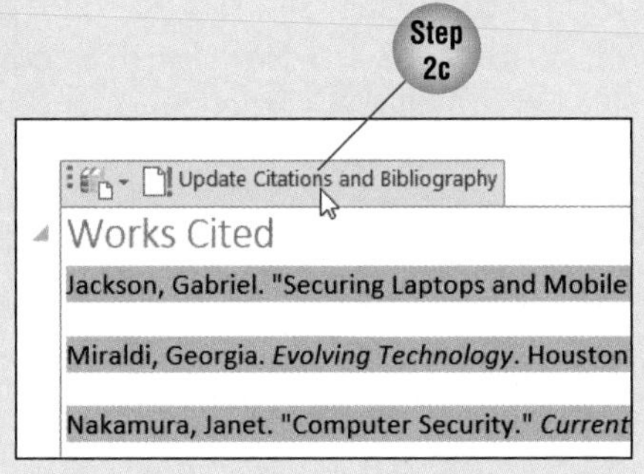

Formatting a Sources List

You may need to change formatting applied by Word to the sources list to meet the specific guidelines of MLA, APA, or Chicago reference style. For example, MLA and APA styles require the following formatting guidelines for sources list:

- Begin the sources list on a separate page after the last page of text in the report.
- Include the title *Works Cited*, *References*, or *Bibliography* at the top of the page and center it on the width of the page.
- Use the same font for the sources list as the font in the main document.
- Double-space between and within entries.
- Begin each entry at the left margin and format second and subsequent lines in each entry with a hanging indent.
- Alphabetize the entries.

The general formatting requirements for Chicago style are similar except that single spacing is applied within entries and double spacing is applied between entries.

Project 6g Formatting a Works Cited Page

Part 7 of 8

1. With **WL2-C5-P6-MobileSecurity.docx** open, make the following formatting changes to the works cited page:
   a. Select the *Works Cited* title and the entries below the title.
   b. Click the HOME tab and then click the *No Spacing* style thumbnail in the Styles group.
   c. With the text still selected, change the font to Cambria, the font size to 12 points, and the line spacing to 2.0.

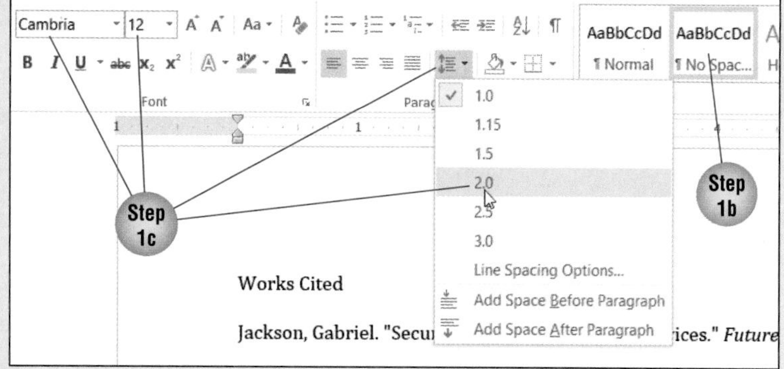

   d. Click anywhere in the title *Works Cited* and then click the Center button in the Paragraph group.
   e. Select only the works cited entries and then press Ctrl + T. (Doing this formats the entries with a hanging indent.)
2. Press Ctrl + Home to move the insertion point to the beginning of the document.
3. Save and then print **WL2-C5-P6-MobileSecurity.docx**.

Choosing a Citation Style

Different subjects and different instructors or professors may require different forms of citation or reference styles. You can change the citation or reference style before beginning a new document or while working in an existing document. To do this, click the REFERENCES tab, click the down-pointing arrow at the right of the *Style* option box, and then click the desired style at the drop-down list.

Quick Steps

Change the Citation Style

1. Click REFERENCES tab.
2. Click down-pointing arrow at right of *Style* option box.
3. Click desired style.

Project 6h Choosing a Citation Style

Part 8 of 8

1. With **WL2-C5-P6-MobileSecurity.docx** open, change the document and works cited page from MLA style to APA style by completing the following steps:
   a. With the insertion point positioned at the beginning of the document, click the REFERENCES tab.
   b. Click the down-pointing arrow at the right of the *Style* option box in the Citations & Bibliography group and then click *APA* at the drop-down list.

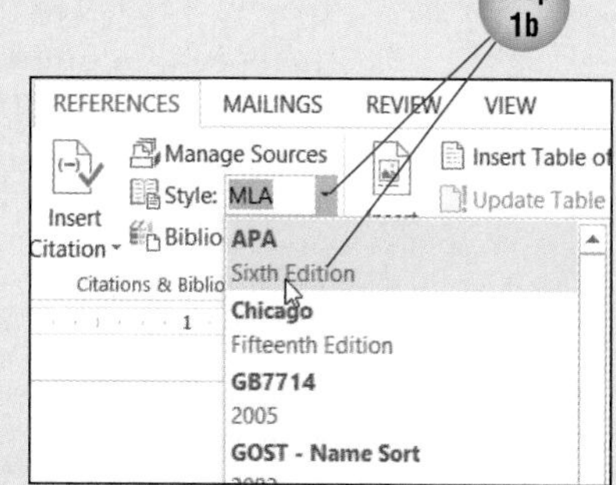

   c. Scroll to the last page in the document (notice the changes to the citations), change the title *Works Cited* to *References*, select the four references, change the font to 12-point Cambria, change the spacing after paragraphs to 0, and then change the line spacing to 2.0.
2. Save the document and then print only the references page.
3. Close **WL2-C5-P6-MobileSecurity.docx**.
4. Display a blank document, click the REFERENCES tab, change the style to *MLA*, and then close the document without saving it.

Chapter Summary

- You can sort text in paragraphs, columns, and tables and sort records in a data source file. You can also select specific records in a data source file for merging with a main document.
- Use the Sort button in the Paragraph group on the HOME tab to sort text in paragraphs, columns, and tables.
- When sorting text set in columns, Word considers the left margin *Field 1*, text typed at the first tab *Field 2*, and so on.
- Sort on more than one field with the *Sort by* and *Then by* options at the Sort dialog box.
- Use the *Header row* option in the *My list has* section in the Sort Text dialog box to sort all text in columns except the first row.
- Sort records in a data source file at the Mail Merge Recipients dialog box. Sort by clicking the column heading or with options at the Filter and Sort dialog box with the Sort Records tab selected.
- Select specific records in a data source file with options at the Filter and Sort dialog box with the Filter Records tab selected.
- When nonbreaking spaces are inserted between words, Word considers these words as one unit and will not divide them when breaking and wrapping text to the next line. Insert a nonbreaking space with the keyboard shortcut Ctrl + Shift + spacebar.
- Use the Find and Replace feature to find special formatting, characters, and nonprinting elements and then replace them with nothing or other special text.
- Save a document as a template by changing the *Save as type* option at the Save As dialog box to *Word Template (*.dotx)* or display the Export backstage area, click the *Change File Type* option, click the *Template (*.dotx)* option, and then click the Save As button. At the Save As dialog box, save the template in the Custom Office Templates folder.
- Word adds the file extension *.dotx* to a template.
- Open a template located in the Custom Office Templates folder by displaying the New backstage area, clicking the *PERSONAL* option, and then clicking the desired template.
- Footnotes and endnotes provide explanatory notes and source citations. Footnotes are inserted and printed at the bottom of pages and endnotes are printed at the end of the document.
- By default, footnotes are numbered with arabic numbers and endnotes are numbered with lowercase roman numerals.
- Move, copy, or delete a footnote/endnote reference number in a document and all of the other footnotes/endnotes automatically renumber.
- Delete a footnote or endnote by selecting the reference number and then pressing the Delete key.
- Consider using in-text citations to acknowledge sources in a paper. Commonly used citation and reference styles include American Psychological Association (APA), Modern Language Association (MLA), and *Chicago Manual of Style* (Chicago).

- Insert a citation using the Insert Citation button in the Citations & Bibliography group on the REFERENCES tab. Specify source information at the Create Source dialog box.
- Insert a citation placeholder in a document if you want to type the source information at a later time.
- Edit a source at the Edit Source dialog box. Display this dialog box by clicking the source citation in the document, clicking the Citation Options arrow, and then clicking *Edit Source* at the drop-down list. Another option is to display the Source Manage dialog box, click the source you want to edit, and then click the Edit button.
- Manage sources—such as copying, deleting, editing, and inserting a new source—with options at the Source Manager dialog box. Display this dialog box by clicking the Manage Sources button in the Citations and Bibliography group on the REFERENCES tab.
- Insert a sources list, such as a works cited page, references page, or bibliography at the end of the document on a separate page. To do so, use the Bibliography button in the Citations & Bibliography group on the REFERENCES tab.
- To update a sources list, click anywhere in list text and then click the Update Citations and Bibliography tab.
- Change the reference style with the *Style* option box in the Citations & Bibliography group on the REFERENCES tab.

Commands Review

FEATURE	RIBBON TAB, GROUP	BUTTON, OPTION	KEYBOARD SHORTCUT
bibliography	REFERENCES, Citations & Bibliography		
citation style	REFERENCES, Citations & Bibliography		
Create Source dialog box	REFERENCES, Citations & Bibliography		
Filter and Sort dialog box with Select Records tab selected	MAILINGS, Start Mail Merge	, Filter	
Filter and Sort dialog box with Sort Records tab selected	MAILINGS, Start Mail Merge	, Sort	
Find and Replace dialog box	HOME, Editing		Ctrl + H
endnote	REFERENCES, Footnotes		Alt + Ctrl + D
footnote	REFERENCES, Footnotes		Alt + Ctrl + F
nonbreaking space			Ctrl + Shift + spacebar
Sort Options dialog box	HOME, Paragraph	, *Options*	
Sort Text dialog box	HOME, Paragraph		
Source Manager dialog box	REFERENCES, Citations & Bibliography		

Concepts Check Test Your Knowledge 

Completion: In the space provided at the right, indicate the correct term, symbol, or command.

1. The Sort button is located in this group on the HOME tab. ____________
2. When sorting text in columns, Word considers the first tab this field number. ____________
3. Click this option at the Sort Text dialog box to tell Word not to include the column headings in the sort. ____________
4. Click the Filter hyperlink at this dialog box to display the Filter and Sort dialog box with the Filter Records tab selected. ____________
5. Use this keyboard shortcut to insert a nonbreaking space. ____________
6. Click this button at the expanded Find and Replace dialog box to display a pop-up list of special characters and nonprinting elements. ____________
7. Word saves template documents with this file extension. ____________
8. Click this option at the New backstage area to display templates saved in the Custom Office Templates folder. ____________
9. Word numbers footnotes with this type of number. ____________
10. Word numbers endnotes with this type of number. ____________
11. Three of the most popular reference styles are APA (American Psychological Association), Chicago (*Chicago Manual of Style*), and this. ____________
12. Click this tab to display the Citations & Bibliography group. ____________
13. Create a new source for a document with options at this dialog box. ____________
14. Click this button in the Citations & Bibliography group to display the Source Manager dialog box. ____________
15. To update a bibliography, click anywhere in the bibliography and then click this tab. ____________

Skills Check Assess Your Performance

Assessment 1

SORT TEXT AND CREATE KEYBOARD SHORTCUTS WITH NONBREAKING SPACES

1. Open **SFSSorting.docx** and then save the document and name it **WL2-C5-A1-SFSSorting**.
2. Select the nine lines of text below the *Executive Team* heading and then sort the text alphabetically by last name.
3. Sort the three columns of text below the title *New Employees* by date of hire in ascending order.
4. Sort the text in the *First Qtr.* column in the table numerically in descending order.
5. Press Ctrl + End to move the insertion point to the end of the document and then type the text shown in Figure 5.14. Insert nonbreaking spaces within all of the keyboard shortcuts.
6. Save, print, and then close **WL2-C5-A1-SFSSorting.docx**.

Figure 5.14 Assessment 1

Keyboard Shortcuts

Word includes keyboard shortcuts you can use for creating, viewing, and saving documents. Press Ctrl + N to display a new blank document or press Ctrl + F12 to open a document. Use the shortcut Ctrl + W to close the currently open document. Additional keyboard shortcuts include pressing Alt + Ctrl + S to split the document window and pressing Alt + Shift + C to remove the document window split.

Assessment 2

INSERT FOOTNOTES IN DESIGNING A NEWSLETTER REPORT

1. Open **DesignNwsltr.docx** and then save the document and name it **WL2-C5-A2-DesignNwsltr**.
2. Create the first footnote shown in Figure 5.15 at the end of the first paragraph in the *Applying Guidelines* section.
3. Create the second footnote shown in Figure 5.15 at the end of the third paragraph in the *Applying Guidelines* section.
4. Create the third footnote shown in Figure 5.15 at the end of the last paragraph in the *Applying Guidelines* section.
5. Create the fourth footnote shown in Figure 5.15 at the end of the only paragraph in the *Choosing Paper Size and Type* section.
6. Create the fifth footnote shown in Figure 5.15 at the end of the only paragraph in the *Choosing Paper Weight* section.
7. Save and then print **WL2-C5-A2-DesignNwsltr.docx**.
8. Select the entire document and then change the font to Constantia.
9. Select all of the footnotes and change the font to Constantia.

Figure 5.15 Assessment 2

James Habermann, "Designing a Newsletter," *Desktop Designs* (2015): 23-29.

Shirley Pilante, "Adding Pizzazz to Your Newsletter," *Desktop Publisher* (2014): 32-39.

Arlita Maddock, "Guidelines for a Better Newsletter," *Business Computing* (2015): 9-14.

Monica Alverso, "Paper Styles for Newsletters," *Design Technologies* (2014): 45-51.

Keith Sutton, "Choosing Paper Styles," *Design Techniques* (2015): 8-11.

10. Delete the third footnote.
11. Save, print, and then close **WL2-C5-A2-DesignNwsltr.docx**.

Assessment 3

INSERT SOURCES AND CITATIONS IN A PRIVACY RIGHTS REPORT

1. Open **PrivRights.docx** and then save the document and name it **WL2-C5-A3-PrivRights**.
2. Make sure that MLA style is selected in the Citations & Bibliography group on the REFERENCES tab.
3. Format the title page to meet MLA requirements with the following changes:
   a. Select the entire document, change the font to 12-point Cambria, change the line spacing to 2.0, and remove the extra spacing after paragraphs.
   b. Move the insertion point to the beginning of the document, type your name, press the Enter key, type your instructor's name, press the Enter key, type the title of your course, press the Enter key, type the current date, and then press the Enter key.
   c. Type the title **Privacy Rights** at the top of the page and centered on the width of the page.
   d. Insert a header that displays your last name and the page number at the right margin and change the font to 12-point Cambria.
4. Press Ctrl + End to move the insertion point to the end of the document and then type the text shown in Figure 5.16 up to the first citation—the text *(Hartley)*. Insert the source information for a journal article written by Kenneth Hartley using the following information:

Author	**Kenneth Hartley**
Title	**Privacy Laws**
Journal Name	**Business World**
Year	**2015**
Pages	**24-46**
Volume	**XII**

5. Continue typing the text up to the next citation—the text *(Ferraro)*—and insert the following source information for a book:

Author	**Ramona Ferraro**
Title	**Business Employee Rights**
Year	**2014**
City	**Tallahassee**
Publisher	**Everglades Publishing House**

Figure 5.16 Assessment 3

> An exception to the ability of companies to monitor their employees does exist. If the company has pledged to respect any aspect of employee privacy, it must keep that pledge. For example, if a business states that it will not monitor employee email or phone calls, by law, it must follow this stated policy (Hartley). However, no legal requirement exists mandating that companies notify their employees when and if monitoring takes place (Ferraro). Therefore, employees should assume they are always monitored and act accordingly.
>
> Privacy advocates are calling for this situation to change. "They acknowledge that employers have the right to ensure that their employees are doing their jobs, but they question the need to monitor employees without warning and without limit" (Aldrich 20). The American Civil Liberties Union has, in fact, proposed a Fair Electronic Monitoring Policy to prevent abuses of employee privacy.

6. Continue typing the text up to the next citations—the text *(Aldrich)*—and insert the following information for an article in a periodical:

Author	Kelly Aldrich
Title	What Rights Do Employees Have?
Periodical Title	Great Plains Times
Year	2015
Month	May
Day	6
Pages	18-22

7. Insert the page number in the Kelly Aldrich citation using the Edit Citation dialog box.
8. Type the remaining text shown in Figure 5.16.
9. Edit the Kenneth Hartley source title to read *Small Business Privacy Laws* in the *Master List* section of the Source Manager dialog box (update both the Master List and Current List).
10. Select and delete the last two sentences in the second paragraph and then delete the Ramona Ferraro source in the *Current List* section of the Source Manager dialog box.
11. Insert a works cited page on a separate page at the end of the document.

12. Create a new source in the document using the Source Manager dialog box and include the following source information for a website:

Author	**Harold Davidson**
Name of Web Page	**Small Business Policies and Procedures**
Year	**2014**
Month	**December**
Day	**12**
Year Accessed	**2015**
Month Accessed	**February**
Day Accessed	**23**
URL	**www.emcp.net/policies**

13. Insert a citation for Harold Davidson at the end of the last sentence in the first paragraph.
14. Update the works cited page.
15. Format the works cited page to meet MLA requirements with the following changes:
    a. Select the *Works Cited* heading and all of the entries and click the *No Spacing* style thumbnail.
    b. Change the font to 12-point Cambria and change the spacing to 2.0.
    c. Center the title *Works Cited*.
    d. Format the works cited entries with a hanging indent.
16. Save and then print **WL2-C5-A3-PrivRights.docx**.
17. Change the document and works cited page from MLA style to APA style. Make sure you change the title of the sources list to *References*, select the references in the list, and then change the spacing after paragraphs to 0, the line spacing to 2.0, and the font to 12-point Cambria.
18. Save, print page 2, and then close **WL2-C5-A3-PrivRights.docx**.

Visual Benchmark Demonstrate Your Proficiency

FORMAT A REPORT IN MLA STYLE

1. Open **SecurityDefenses.docx** and then save the document and name it **WL2-C5-VB-SecurityDefenses**.
2. Format the document so it displays as shown in Figure 5.17 with the following specifications:
    a. Change the document font to 12-point Cambria.
    b. Use the information from the works cited page when inserting citations into the document. The Hollingsworth citation is for a journal article, the Montoya citation is for a book, and the Gillespie citation is for a website.
    c. Format the works cited page to meet MLA requirements.
3. Save, print, and then close **WL2-C5-VB-SecurityDefenses.docx**.

Figure 5.17 Visual Benchmark

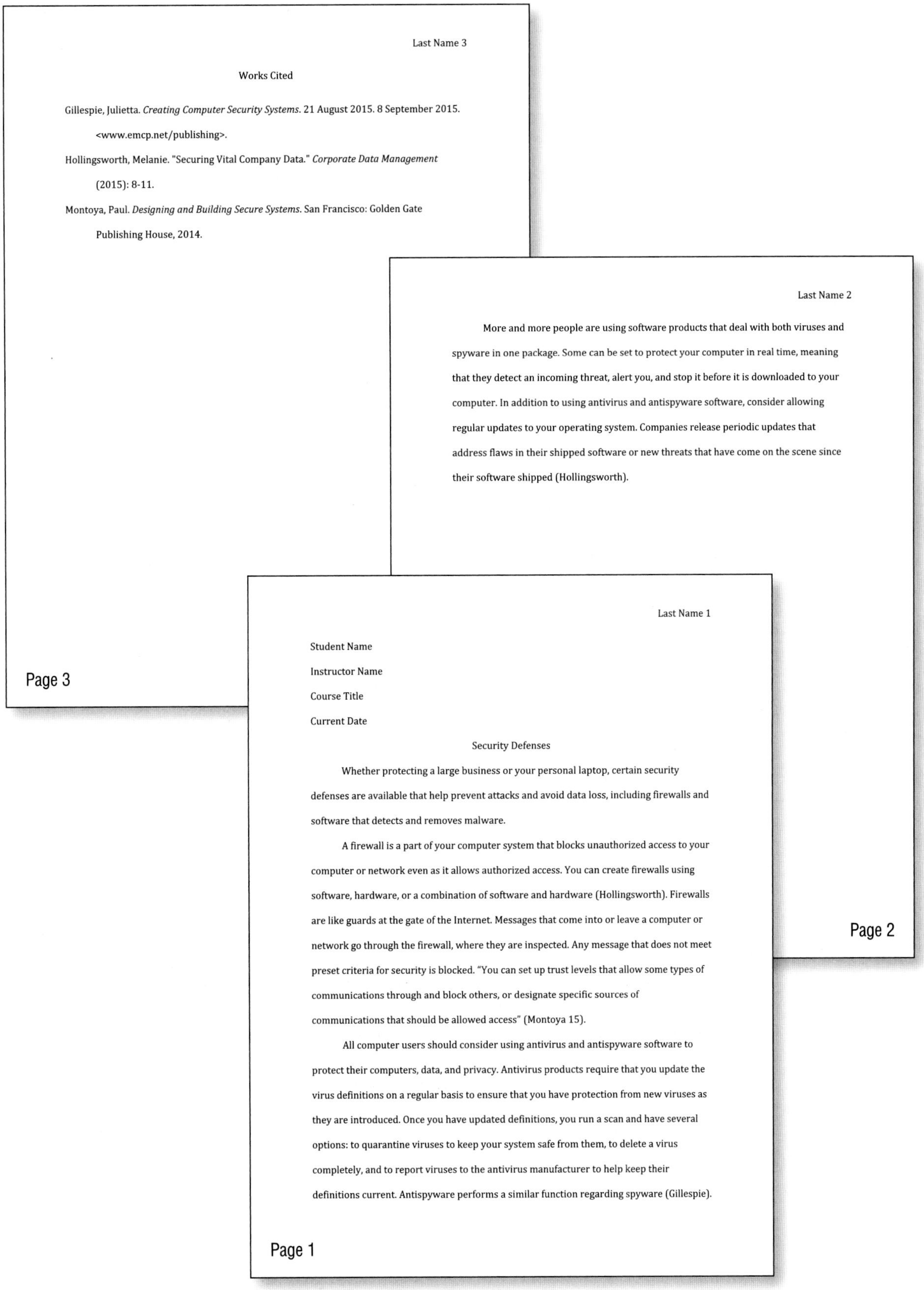

Last Name 3

Works Cited

Gillespie, Julietta. *Creating Computer Security Systems.* 21 August 2015. 8 September 2015. <www.emcp.net/publishing>.

Hollingsworth, Melanie. "Securing Vital Company Data." *Corporate Data Management* (2015): 8-11.

Montoya, Paul. *Designing and Building Secure Systems.* San Francisco: Golden Gate Publishing House, 2014.

Page 3

Last Name 2

More and more people are using software products that deal with both viruses and spyware in one package. Some can be set to protect your computer in real time, meaning that they detect an incoming threat, alert you, and stop it before it is downloaded to your computer. In addition to using antivirus and antispyware software, consider allowing regular updates to your operating system. Companies release periodic updates that address flaws in their shipped software or new threats that have come on the scene since their software shipped (Hollingsworth).

Page 2

Last Name 1

Student Name

Instructor Name

Course Title

Current Date

Security Defenses

Whether protecting a large business or your personal laptop, certain security defenses are available that help prevent attacks and avoid data loss, including firewalls and software that detects and removes malware.

A firewall is a part of your computer system that blocks unauthorized access to your computer or network even as it allows authorized access. You can create firewalls using software, hardware, or a combination of software and hardware (Hollingsworth). Firewalls are like guards at the gate of the Internet. Messages that come into or leave a computer or network go through the firewall, where they are inspected. Any message that does not meet preset criteria for security is blocked. "You can set up trust levels that allow some types of communications through and block others, or designate specific sources of communications that should be allowed access" (Montoya 15).

All computer users should consider using antivirus and antispyware software to protect their computers, data, and privacy. Antivirus products require that you update the virus definitions on a regular basis to ensure that you have protection from new viruses as they are introduced. Once you have updated definitions, you run a scan and have several options: to quarantine viruses to keep your system safe from them, to delete a virus completely, and to report viruses to the antivirus manufacturer to help keep their definitions current. Antispyware performs a similar function regarding spyware (Gillespie).

Page 1

Case Study Apply Your Skills

Part 1

You are the office manager for Lincoln Freelance Services and have been compiling information on keyboard shortcuts for an employee training manual. Using the Help feature, find information on keyboard shortcuts for finding, replacing, and browsing through text as well as keyboard shortcuts for creating works cited/references, footnotes, and endnotes. Type the information you find on the keyboard shortcuts in a Word document. Use nonbreaking spaces within all of the keyboard shortcuts. Provide a title for the document and insert any other formatting to improve the appearance of the document. Save the document and name it **WL2-C5-CS-Shortcuts**. Print and then close the document.

Part 2

Lincoln Freelance Services provides freelance employees for businesses in Baltimore and surrounding communities. A new industrial park has opened in Baltimore and you need to fill a number of temporary positions. You decide to send a letter to current clients living in Baltimore to let them know about the new industrial park and the temporary jobs that are available. Create a letter main document and include in the letter the information that a new industrial park is opening in a few months, the location of the park (you determine a location), and that Lincoln Freelance Services will be providing temporary employees for many of the technology jobs. Include a list of at least five technology jobs (find job titles on the Internet) for which you will be placing employees. Include any additional information in the letter that you feel is important. Merge the letter main document only with those clients in the **LFSClients.mdb** data source file who live in Baltimore. Save the merged letters and name the document **WL2-C5-CS-LFSLtrs**. Print and then close **WL2-C5-CS-LFSLtrs.docx**. Save the letter main document and name it **WL2-C5-CS-LFSMD** and then close the document.

Part 3

Your supervisor has given you a report on newsletter guidelines and asked you to reformat it using APA reference style. Open the **WL2-C5-A2-DesignNwsltr.docx** document and then save it and name it **WL2-C5-CS-DesignNwsltr**. Remove the title *CREATING NEWSLETTER LAYOUT* and add 6 points of space before the heading *Choosing Paper Size and Type*. Remove the footnotes and insert the information as in-text journal article citations and then add a references page on a separate page. Center the title *References* and then select the entire document and change the font to Cambria. Save **WL2-C5-CS-DesignNwsltr.docx**.

Part 4

Your supervisor has asked you to include some additional information on newsletter guidelines. Using the Internet, look for websites that provide information on desktop publishing and/or newsletter design. Include in the **WL2-C5-CS-DesignNwsltr.docx** report document at least one additional paragraph with information you found on the Internet and include a citation for each source from which you have borrowed information. Save, print, and then close the report.

MICROSOFT®

WORD

CHAPTER 6

Creating Specialized Tables and Indexes

PERFORMANCE OBJECTIVES

Upon successful completion of Chapter 6, you will be able to:

- **Create, insert, and update a table of contents**
- **Create, insert, and update a table of figures**
- **Create, insert, and update an index**

Tutorials

6.1 Inserting a Table of Contents

6.2 Customizing and Updating a Table of Contents

6.3 Assigning Levels to Table of Contents Entries

6.4 Inserting a Table of Figures

6.5 Creating and Customizing Captions

6.6 Marking Index Entries and Inserting an Index

6.7 Creating a Concordance File

6.8 Updating and Deleting an Index

A book, textbook, report, or manuscript often includes sections such as a table of contents, index, and table of figures. Creating these sections can be tedious when prepared manually. With Word, these sections can be created quickly and easily using automated functions. In this chapter, you will learn the steps to mark text for a table of contents, table of figures, and index and then insert the table or index. Model answers for this chapter's projects appear on the following pages.

Note: Before beginning the projects, copy to your storage medium the WL2C6 subfolder from the WL2 folder on the CD that accompanies this textbook and then make WL2C6 the active folder.

CONTENTS

i

Project 1 Create a Table of Contents for a Computer Interface Report WL2-C6-P1-AIReport.docx

TABLE OF CONTENTS

i

Project 2 Mark Text for and Insert a Table of Contents in a Company Handbook WL2-C6-P2-CompEval.docx

TABLE OF FIGURES

Page 1

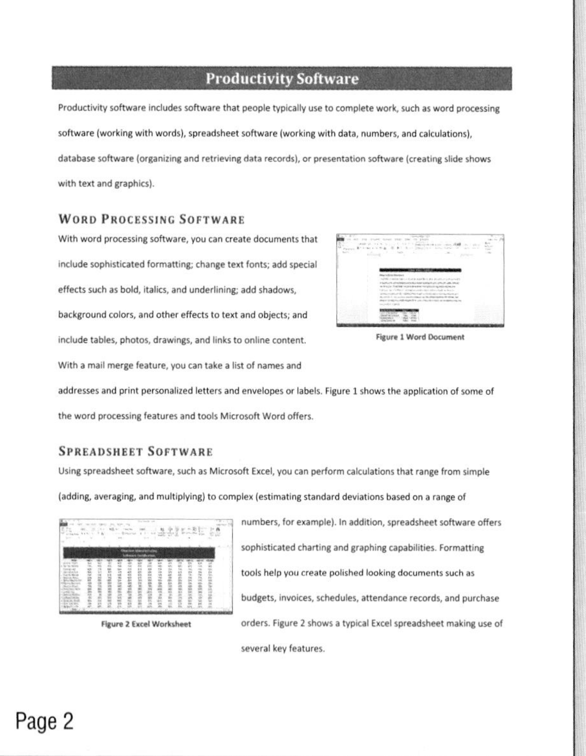

Productivity Software

Productivity software includes software that people typically use to complete work, such as word processing software (working with words), spreadsheet software (working with data, numbers, and calculations), database software (organizing and retrieving data records), or presentation software (creating slide shows with text and graphics).

WORD PROCESSING SOFTWARE

With word processing software, you can create documents that include sophisticated formatting; change text fonts; add special effects such as bold, italics, and underlining; add shadows, background colors, and other effects to text and objects; and include tables, photos, drawings, and links to online content. With a mail merge feature, you can take a list of names and addresses and print personalized letters and envelopes or labels. Figure 1 shows the application of some of the word processing features and tools Microsoft Word offers.

Figure 1 Word Document

SPREADSHEET SOFTWARE

Using spreadsheet software, such as Microsoft Excel, you can perform calculations that range from simple (adding, averaging, and multiplying) to complex (estimating standard deviations based on a range of numbers, for example). In addition, spreadsheet software offers sophisticated charting and graphing capabilities. Formatting tools help you create polished looking documents such as budgets, invoices, schedules, attendance records, and purchase orders. Figure 2 shows a typical Excel spreadsheet making use of several key features.

Figure 2 Excel Worksheet

Page 2

Project 3 Create a Table of Figures for a Technology Report and a Travel Document Project 3b, WL2-C6-P3-TechRpt.docx

Output Devices

To get information into a computer, a person uses an input device. To get information out, a person uses an output device. Some common output devices include monitors and printers.

Monitor

A monitor, or screen, is the most common output device used with a personal computer. The most common monitors use either a thin film transistor (TFT) active matrix liquid crystal display (LCD) or a plasma display. Plasma displays have a true level of color reproduction compared with LCDs. Emerging display technologies include surface-conduction electron-emitter displays (SED) and organic light emitting diodes (OLED).

Figure 3 Monitor

Printers

After monitors, printers are the most important output devices. The print quality produced by these devices is measured in dpi, or dots per inch. As with screen resolution, the greater the number of dots per inch, the better the quality. The earliest printers for personal computers were dot matrix printers that used perforated computer paper. These impact printers worked something like typewriters, transferring the image of a character by using pins to strike a ribbon.

Figure 4 Laser Printer

A laser printer uses a laser beam to create points of electrical charge on a cylindrical drum. Toner, composed of particles of ink with a negative electrical charge, sticks to the charged points on the positively charged drum. As the page moves past the drum, heat and pressure fuse the toner to the page. Inkjet printers use a print head that moves across the page that sprays a fine mist of ink when an electrical charge moves through the

Page 3

cartridge. An inkjet printer can use color cartridges and so provides affordable color printing suitable for home and small office use.

Developing Software

Through the years, some software products have become incredibly sophisticated as new features are added in each version. The *software development life cycle* (SDLC) has evolved over time. This procedure dictates the general flow of creating a new software product as shown in the figure below. The SDLC involves performing market research to ensure that a need or demand for the product exists; completing a business analysis to match the solution to the need; creating a plan for implementing the software, which involves creating a budget and schedule for the project; writing the software program; testing the software; deploying the software to the public, either by selling the product in a package or online; and performing maintenance and bug fixes to keep the product functioning optimally.

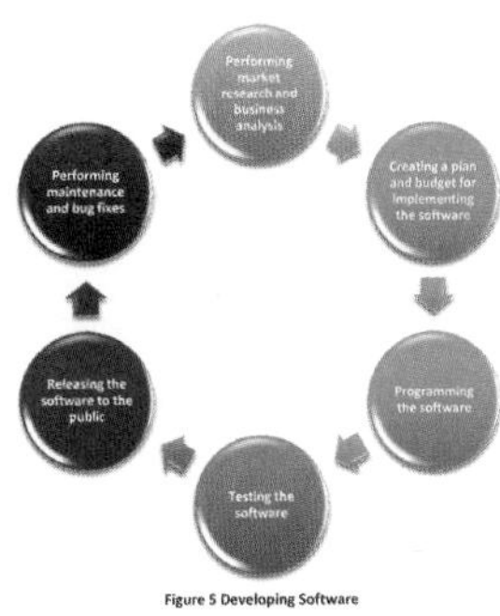

Figure 5 Developing Software

Page 4

TABLES

Page 1

TERRA TRAVEL SERVICES

Antarctic Zenith Adventures

Travel with our Antarctic experts, cruise on our state-of-the-art ships, and experience Antarctica in all of its grandeur. We use ice-rated expedition ships custom-designed for your comfort and safety. Each ship can carry up to 100 passengers and provides excellent viewing for watching whales, seabirds, and icebergs as well as facilities for educational presentations by our Antarctic experts. For our more adventurous clients, we offer additional activities such as snowshoeing, sea-kayaking, and camping on the Antarctic ice. Plan on a shore excursion where you can view penguin rookeries, seal colonies, and places of historical and scientific interest. To carry you to the Antarctic shore, we use inflatable boats that can carry 12 to 15 people. After a thrilling day on shore, we will take you back to the ship where you can enjoy a delicious meal prepared by our gourmet chefs. Our Antarctic travel experts are naturalists, historians, and adventurers committed to providing you with a fabulous Antarctic adventure.

Zenith Adventures	Length	Price
Antarctic Exploration	7 days	$4,399
Weddell Sea Adventure	10 days	$6,899
Falkland Islands	14 days	$7,699
Sailing Spectacular	14 days	$8,999

Adventure 1 Antarctic Zenith Adventures

Upcoming Adventures

Beginning next year, Zenith Adventures, together with Terra Travel Services, will offer volunteer vacation opportunities. Tentative volunteer adventures include building village and mountain paths, building homes, and helping the families of trail porters improve village facilities. Our volunteer adventures will provide you with an exciting vacation and a rewarding volunteer experience. The group size will be limited to a maximum of 15 and participants will be required to raise a minimum amount of money to contribute to the program and local charities. All charities have been carefully screened to ensure that funds are well-managed and distributed fairly. Look for more information in our next newsletter and consider a rewarding volunteer adventure.

Page 2

Project 3c, WL2-C6-P3-TTSAdventures.docx

Bicycling Adventure

A bicycle is the perfect form of transportation for a travel adventure. Sign up for one or our bicycle tours and travel at your own pace, interact with village residents, stay healthy and fit, and know that your adventure has a minimal effect on the environment. We offer bicycle tours ranging from a leisurely trip through the Loire Valley of France to a mountain-bike expedition in the Atlas Mountains in Morocco. Our Zenith Adventures bicycle guides provide you with historical and educational information about the region in which you are traveling. They also take care of luggage and transportation needs and maintain your bicycle. We are confident that we can provide the bicycle adventure of a lifetime!

Zenith Adventure	Length	Price
Loire Valley Tour	7 days	$1,999
Tuscan Village Tour	8 days	$2,499
Atlas Trek Extreme	9 days	$2,899
Great Wall of Chin	14 days	$3,299

Adventure 2 Tall-Ship Adventures

Page 3

INDEX

3

Project 4 Create an Index for a Desktop Publishing Report
WL2-C6-P4-DTP.docx

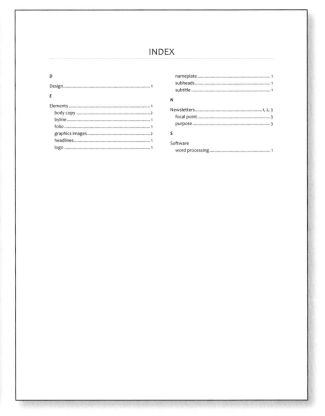

newsletters	Newsletters
Newsletters	Newsletters
Software	Software
Desktop publishing	Software: desktop publishing
word processing	Software: word processing
Printers	Printers
Laser	Printers: laser
Design	Design
Communication	Communication
Consistency	Design: consistency
Elements	Elements
Nameplate	Elements: nameplate
Logo	Elements: logo
Subtitle	Elements: subtitle
Folio	Elements: folio
Headlines	Elements: headlines
Subheads	Elements: subheads
Byline	Elements: byline
Body Copy	Elements: body copy
Graphics Images	Elements: graphics images
Audience	Newsletters: audience
Purpose	Newsletters: purpose
focal point	Newsletters: focal point

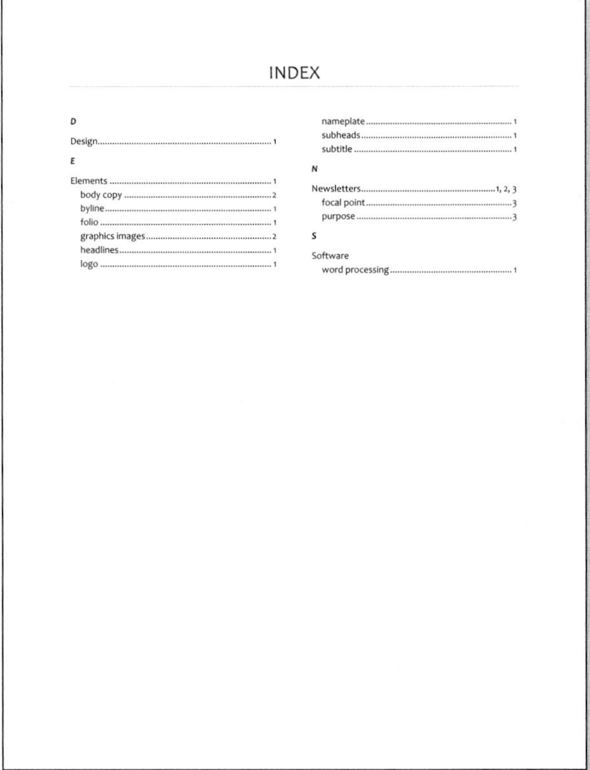

INDEX

Project 5 Create an Index with a Concordance File for a Newsletter WL2-C6-P5-CFile.docx

WL2-C6-P5-PlanNwsltr.docx

Project 1 Create a Table of Contents for a Computer Interface Report — 2 Parts

You will open a report on computer interfaces, mark text for a table of contents, and then insert the table of contents in the document. You will also make, customize, and update the table of contents.

Creating a Table of Contents

A ***table of contents*** appears at the beginning of a book, manuscript, or report and contains headings and subheadings with page numbers. In a previous chapter, you created a table of contents using the Quick Parts button in the Text group on the INSERT tab. You can also create a table of contents using the Table of Contents button in the Table of Contents group on the REFERENCES tab. Identify the text to be included in a table of contents by applying built-in heading styles or custom styles, assigning levels, or marking text.

You can use a table of contents to navigate quickly in a document and to get an overview of the topics it covers.

Applying Styles

To create a table of contents with built-in styles, open the document and then apply the desired styles. Word uses all text with the Heading 1 style applied for the first level of the table of contents, all text with the Heading 2 style applied for the second level, and so on. Apply built-in styles with options in the Styles group on the HOME tab.

If you apply heading styles to text in a document, you can easily insert a table of contents later.

Inserting a Table of Contents

After you have applied styles to the headings, insert the table of contents in the document. To do this, position the insertion point where you want the table of contents to appear, click the REFERENCES tab, click the Table of Contents button, and then click the desired option at the drop-down list.

Quick Steps

Insert a Table of Contents
1. Apply heading styles.
2. Click REFERENCES tab.
3. Click Table of Contents button.
4. Click desired option at drop-down list.

Number the Table of Contents Page
1. Click INSERT tab.
2. Click Page Number button.
3. Click *Format Page Numbers* at drop-down list.
4. Change number format to lowercase roman numerals at Page Number Format dialog box.
5. Click OK.

Table of Contents

Page Number

Numbering the Table of Contents Page

Generally, the pages containing the table of contents are numbered with lowercase roman numerals (*i, ii, iii*). Change the format of the page number to lowercase roman numerals at the Page Number Format dialog box, shown in Figure 6.1. Display this dialog box by clicking the INSERT tab, clicking the Page Number button in the Header & Footer group, and then clicking *Format Page Numbers* at the drop-down list.

The first page of text in the main document, which usually comes immediately after the table of contents, should begin with the arabic number 1. To make it possible to change from roman to arabic page numbers within the same document, separate the table of contents from the first page of the document with a section break that begins a new page.

Figure 6.1 Page Number Format Dialog Box

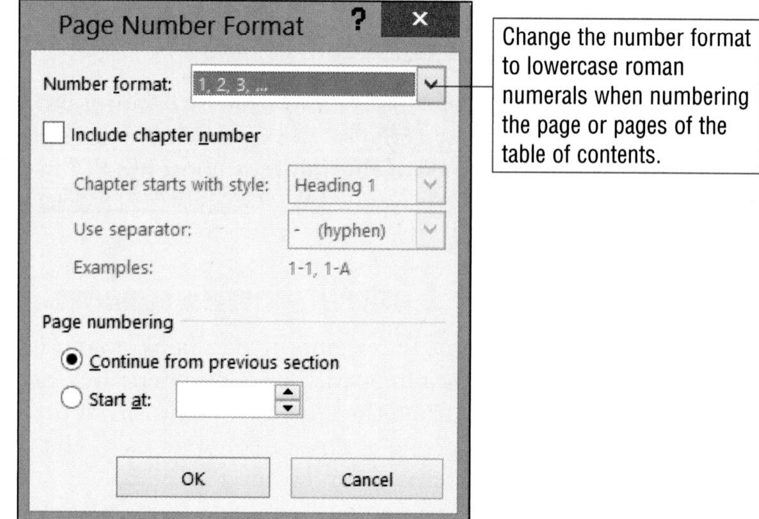

Navigating Using a Table of Contents

When you insert a table of contents into a document, you can use the headings it contains to navigate within the document. Table of contents headings are hyperlinks that are connected to the headings within the document.

To navigate in a document using table of contents headings, click in the table of contents to select it. Position the mouse pointer over the desired heading and a box will display with the path and file name as well as the text *Ctrl+Click to follow link*. Hold down the Ctrl key and click the left mouse button and the insertion point is positioned in the document at the location of the heading.

Project 1a Inserting a Table of Contents — Part 1 of 2

1. Open **AIReport.docx** and then save the document and name it **WL2-C6-P1-AIReport**. (This document contains headings with heading styles applied.)
2. Position the insertion point immediately left of the first *N* in *NATURAL INTERFACE APPLICATIONS* and then insert a section break by completing the following steps:
   a. Click the PAGE LAYOUT tab.
   b. Click the Breaks button in the Page Setup group.
   c. Click the *Next Page* option in the *Section Breaks* section.

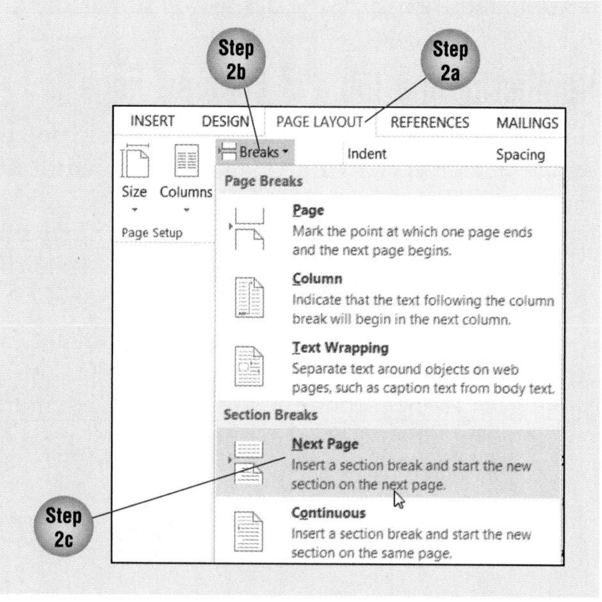

3. With the insertion point positioned below the section break, insert page numbers and change the beginning number to 1 by completing the following steps:
   a. Click the INSERT tab.
   b. Click the Page Number button in the Header & Footer group, point to *Bottom of Page*, and then click *Plain Number 2*.
   c. Click the Page Number button in the Header & Footer group on the HEADER & FOOTER TOOLS DESIGN tab and then click *Format Page Numbers* at the drop-down list.

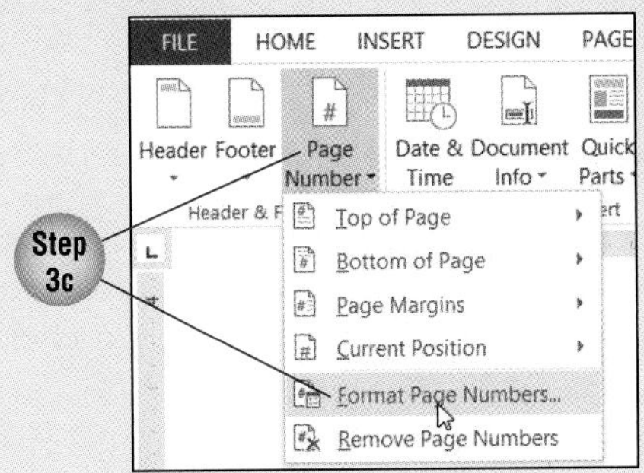

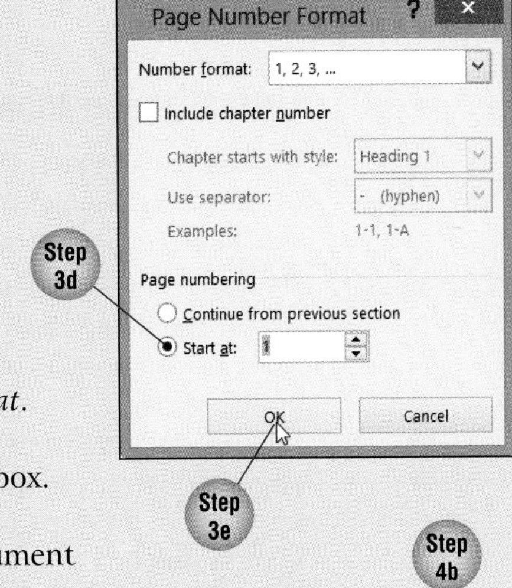

   d. At the Page Number Format dialog box, click *Start at*. (This inserts *1* in the *Start at* measurement box.)
   e. Click OK to close the Page Number Format dialog box.
   f. Double-click in the document to make it active.
4. Insert a table of contents at the beginning of the document by completing the following steps:
   a. Press Ctrl + Home to move the insertion point to the beginning of the document.
   b. Click the REFERENCES tab.
   c. Click the Table of Contents button in the Table of Contents group, and then click the *Automatic Table 1* option in the *Built-In* section of the drop-down list.

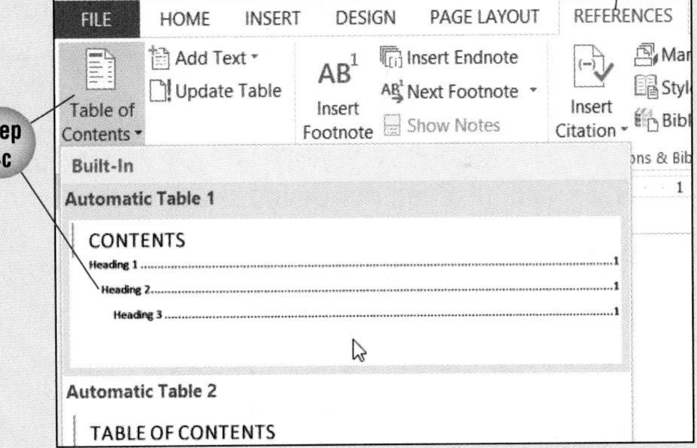

5. Insert page numbers in the table of contents page by completing the following steps:
   a. Scroll up the document and then click any character in the *CONTENTS* heading.
   b. Click the INSERT tab.
   c. Click the Page Number button in the Header & Footer group and then click *Format Page Numbers* at the drop-down list.
   d. At the Page Number Format dialog box, click the down-pointing arrow at the right side of the *Number format* option box and then click *i, ii, iii, …* at the drop-down list.
   e. Click OK to close the dialog box.

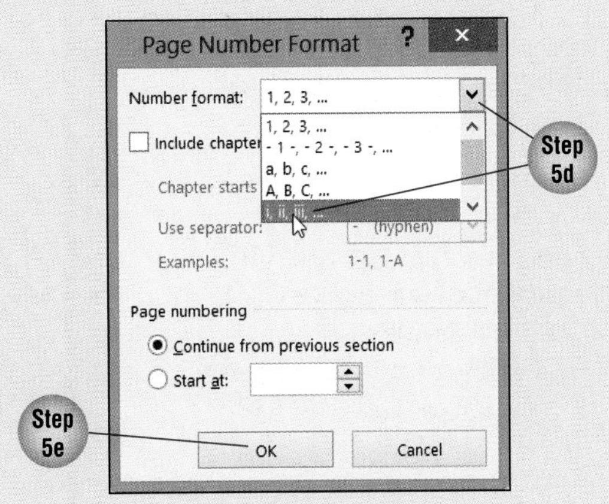

6. Navigate in the document using the table of contents by completing the following steps:
   a. Click on any character in the table of contents.
   b. Position the mouse pointer on the *Virtual Reality* heading, hold down the Ctrl key, click the left mouse button, and then release the Ctrl key. (This moves the insertion point to the beginning of the *Virtual Reality* heading in the document.)
   c. Press Ctrl + Home to move the insertion point to the beginning of the document.
7. Save **WL2-C6-P1-AIReport.docx** and then print only page 1 (the table of contents page).

Customizing a Table of Contents

Customize an existing table of contents in a document with options at the Table of Contents dialog box, as shown in Figure 6.2. Display this dialog box by clicking the Table of Contents button on the REFERENCES tab and then clicking *Custom Table of Contents* at the drop-down list.

At the Table of Contents dialog box, a sample table of contents displays in the *Print Preview* section. Change the table of contents format by clicking the down-pointing arrow at the right side of the *Formats* option box (located in the *General* section). At the drop-down list that displays, click the desired format. When you select a different format, that format displays in the *Print Preview* section. Page numbers in a table of contents will display after the text or aligned at the right margin, depending on what option is selected. You can also specify page number alignment with the *Right align page numbers* option. The number of levels that display depends on the number of heading levels specified in the document. Control the number of levels that display in a table of contents with the *Show levels* measurement box.

Figure 6.2 Table of Contents Dialog Box

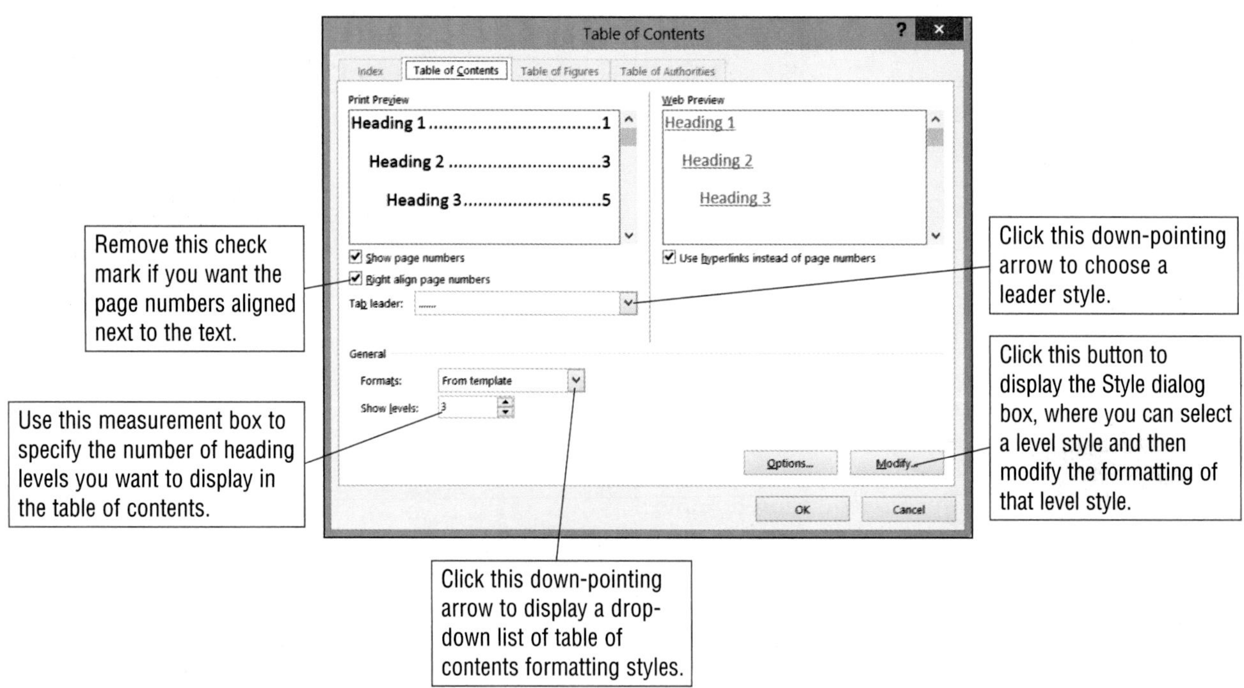
Table of Contents
Index
Table of Contents
Table of Figures
Table of Authorities
Print Preview
Heading 1 1
Heading 2 3
Heading 3 5
Web Preview
Heading 1
Heading 2
Heading 3
Show page numbers
Right align page numbers
Tab leader:
Use hyperlinks instead of page numbers
General
Formats:
From template
Show levels:
3
Options...
Modify...
OK
Cancel
Remove this check mark if you want the page numbers aligned next to the text.
Use this measurement box to specify the number of heading levels you want to display in the table of contents.
Click this down-pointing arrow to display a drop-down list of table of contents formatting styles.
Click this down-pointing arrow to choose a leader style.
Click this button to display the Style dialog box, where you can select a level style and then modify the formatting of that level style.

Tab leaders help guide readers' eyes from the table of contents heading to the page number. The default tab leader is a period. To choose a different leader, click the down-pointing arrow at the right side of the *Tab leader* option box and then click the desired leader character from the drop-down list.

Word automatically identifies headings in a table of contents as hyperlinks and inserts page numbers. You can use these hyperlinks to move the insertion point to a specific location in the document. If you are going to post your document to the Web, consider removing the page numbers since readers will only need to click the hyperlink to view a specific page. Remove page numbering by removing the check mark from the *Show page numbers* check box in the Table of Contents dialog box.

If you make changes to the options at the Table of Contents dialog box and then click OK, a message will display asking if you want to replace the selected table of contents. At this message, click Yes.

Updating a Table of Contents

If you add, delete, move, or edit headings or other text in a document after inserting a table of contents, you need to update the table of contents. To do this, click anywhere within the current table of contents and then click the Update Table button or press the F9 key (the Update Field key). At the Update Table of Contents dialog box, shown in Figure 6.3, click *Update page numbers only* if changes occur only to the page numbers or click *Update entire table* if changes were made to headings or subheadings within the table. Click OK or press Enter to close the dialog box.

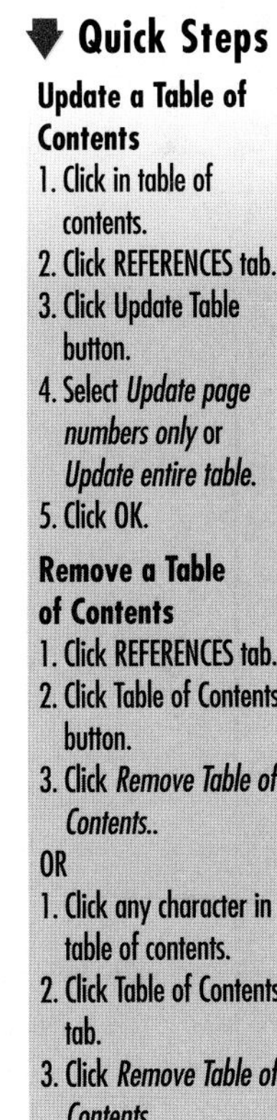

Quick Steps

Update a Table of Contents

1. Click in table of contents.
2. Click REFERENCES tab.
3. Click Update Table button.
4. Select *Update page numbers only* or *Update entire table*.
5. Click OK.

Remove a Table of Contents

1. Click REFERENCES tab.
2. Click Table of Contents button.
3. Click *Remove Table of Contents*..

OR

1. Click any character in table of contents.
2. Click Table of Contents tab.
3. Click *Remove Table of Contents*.

Update Table

Removing a Table of Contents

Remove a table of contents from a document by clicking the Table of Contents button on the REFERENCES tab and then clicking *Remove Table of Contents* at the drop-down list. Another way to remove a table of contents is to click any character in the table of contents, click the Table of Contents tab located in the upper left corner of the table of contents (immediately left of the Update Table tab), and then click *Remove Table of Contents* at the drop-down list.

Figure 6.3 Update Table of Contents Dialog Box

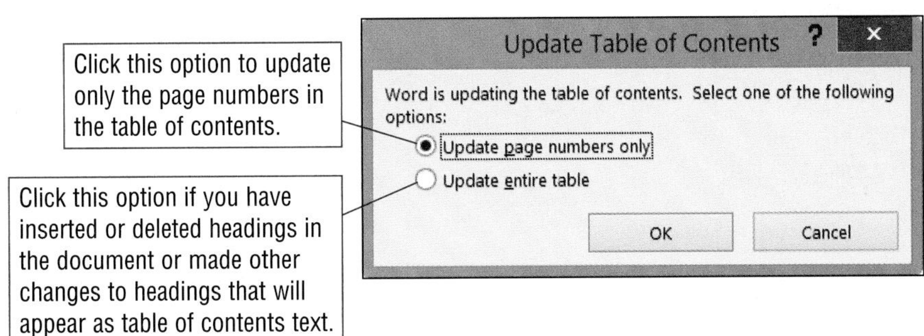
Click this option to update only the page numbers in the table of contents.
Click this option if you have inserted or deleted headings in the document or made other changes to headings that will appear as table of contents text.
Update Table of Contents
Word is updating the table of contents. Select one of the following options:
Update page numbers only
Update entire table
OK
Cancel

Project 1b Customizing and Updating the Table of Contents

Part 2 of 2

1. With **WL2-C6-P1-AIReport.docx** open and the insertion point positioned at the beginning of the document, apply a different formatting style to the table of contents by completing the following steps:
   a. Click the REFERENCES tab, click the Table of Contents button, and then click *Custom Table of Contents* at the drop-down list.
   b. At the Table of Contents dialog box with the Table of Contents tab selected, click the down-pointing arrow at the right of the *Formats* option box in the *General* section and then click *Formal* at the drop-down list.
   c. Click the down-pointing arrow at the right of the *Tab leader* option box and then click the solid line option (bottom option) at the drop-down list.
   d. Click once on the down-pointing arrow at the right side of the *Show levels* measurement box to change the number to *2*.
   e. Click OK to close the dialog box.
   f. At the message asking if you want to replace the selected table of contents, click Yes.
2. Use the table of contents to move the insertion point to the beginning of the *NAVIGATION* heading located at the bottom of page 3.
3. Press Ctrl + Enter to insert a page break.
4. Update the table of contents by completing the following steps:
   a. Press Ctrl + Home and then click on any character in the table of contents.
   b. Click the Update Table tab.
   c. At the Update Table of Contents dialog box, make sure *Update page numbers only* is selected and then click OK.

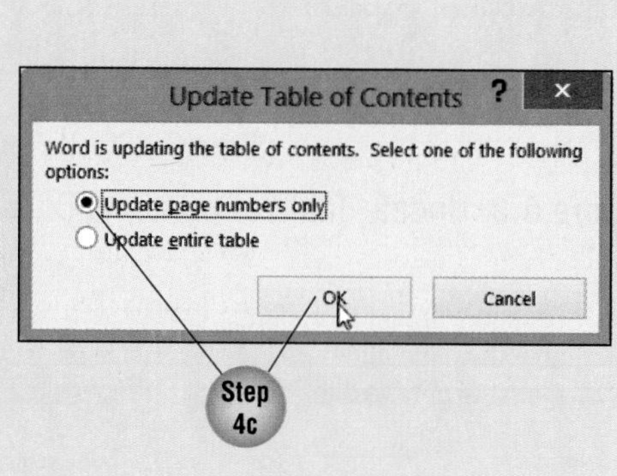

5. Save the document, print only the table of contents page, and then close **WL2-C6-P1-AIReport.docx**.

Project 2 Mark Text for and Insert a Table of Contents in a Company Handbook — 2 Parts

You will open a document that contains employee pay and evaluation information, mark text as table of contents fields, and then insert a table of contents in the document. You will also insert a file containing additional information on employee classifications and then update the table of contents.

Assigning Levels to Table of Contents Entries

Add Text

Another method for identifying text for the table of contents is to use the Add Text button in the Table of Contents group on the REFERENCES tab. Click this button and a drop-down list of level options displays. Click the desired level for the currently selected text. After specifying levels, insert the table of contents by clicking the Table of Contents button and then clicking the desired option at the drop-down list.

Marking Table of Contents Entries as Fields

Applying styles to text applies specific formatting. If you want to identify titles and/or headings for a table of contents but do not want heading style formatting applied, mark each title or heading as a field entry. To do this, select the text you want included in the table of contents and then press Alt + Shift + O. This displays the Mark Table of Contents Entry dialog box, shown in Figure 6.4.

In the dialog box, the text you selected in the document displays in the *Entry* text box. Specify the text level using the *Level* measurement box and then click the Mark button. This turns on the display of nonprinting symbols in the document and also inserts a field code immediately after the selected text.

For example, when you select the title in Project 2a, the following code is inserted immediately after the title: { TC "COMPENSATION" \f C \l "1" }. The Mark Table of Contents Entry dialog box also remains open. To mark the next entry for the table of contents, select the text and then click the Title bar of the Mark Table of Contents Entry dialog box. Specify the level and then click the Mark button. Continue in this manner until all of the table of contents entries have been marked.

If you mark table of contents entries as fields, you will need to activate the *Table entry fields* option when inserting the table of contents. To do this, display the Table of Contents dialog box and then click the Options button. At the Table of Contents Options dialog box, shown in Figure 6.5 on the next page, click the *Table entry fields* check box to insert a check mark and then click OK.

Figure 6.4 Mark Table of Contents Entry Dialog Box

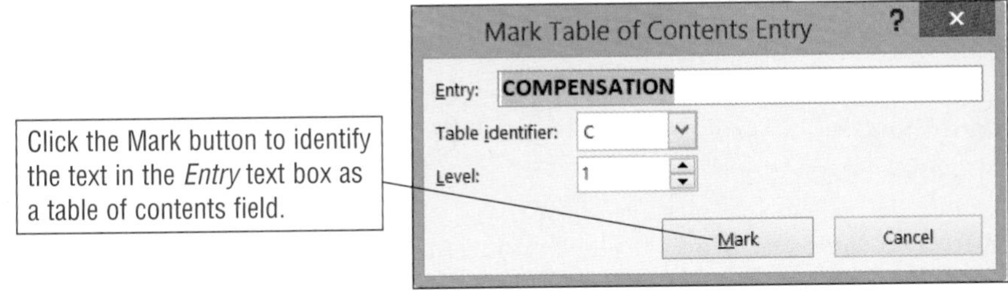
Click the Mark button to identify the text in the *Entry* text box as a table of contents field.
Mark Table of Contents Entry
Entry: COMPENSATION
Table identifier: C
Level: 1
Mark
Cancel

Figure 6.5 Table of Contents Options Dialog Box

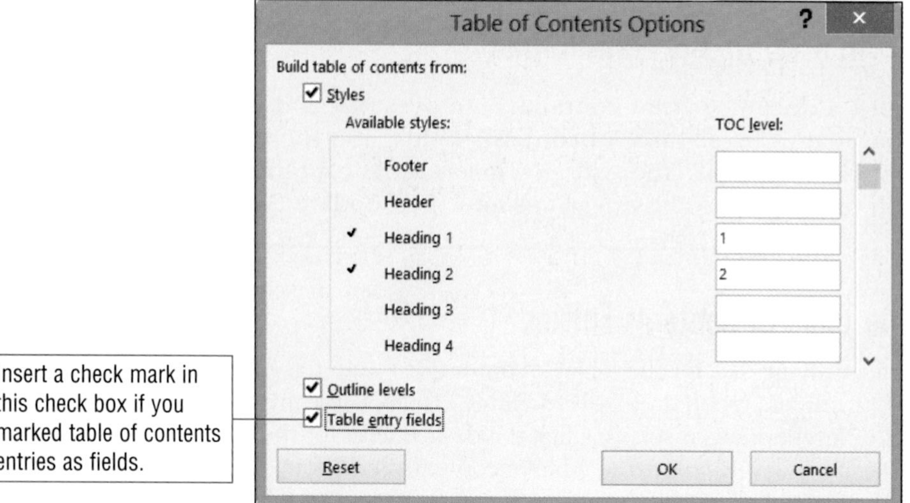

Project 2a Marking Headings as Fields

Part 1 of 2

1. Open **CompEval.docx** and then save the document and name it **WL2-C6-P2-CompEval.**
2. Position the insertion point immediately to the left of the *C* in *COMPENSATION* and then insert a section break that begins a new page.
3. Mark the titles and headings as fields for insertion in a table of contents by completing the following steps:
   a. Select the title *COMPENSATION.*
   b. Press Alt + Shift + O.
   c. At the Mark Table of Contents Entry dialog box, make sure the *Level* measurement box is set at *1* and then click the Mark button. (This turns on the display of nonprinting characters.)

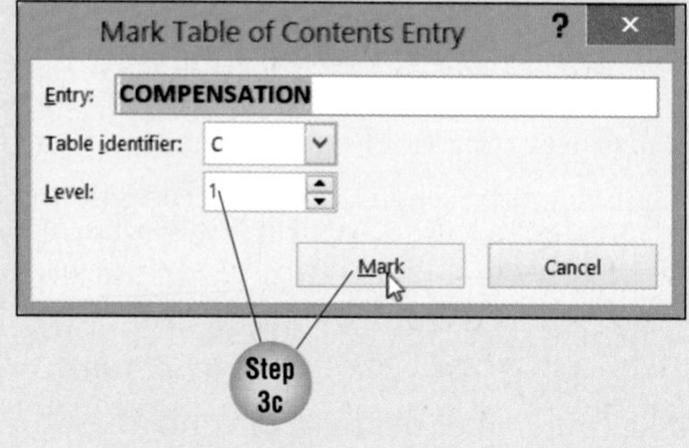

   d. Click in the document, scroll down, and then select the title *EVALUATION.*
   e. Click the dialog box Title bar and then click the Mark button.
   f. Click in the document, scroll up, and then select the heading *Rate of Pay*.
   g. Click the dialog box Title bar and then click the up-pointing arrow at the right of the *Level* measurement box in the Mark Table of Contents Entry dialog box until *2* displays.
   h. Click the Mark button.
   i. Mark the following headings as level 2:
      Direct Deposit Option
      Pay Progression
      Overtime
      Work Performance Standards
      Performance Evaluation
      Employment Records
   j. Click the Close button to close the Mark Table of Contents Entry dialog box.

4. Position the insertion point at the beginning of the title *COMPENSATION* and then insert page numbers at the bottom center of each page of the section and change the starting number to 1. ***Hint: Refer to Project 1a, Step 3.***
5. Double-click in the document.
6. Insert a table of contents at the beginning of the document by completing the following steps:
   a. Position the insertion point at the beginning of the document (on the new page).
   b. Type the title **TABLE OF CONTENTS** and then press the Enter key.
   c. Click the REFERENCES tab.
   d. Click the Table of Contents button and then click *Custom Table of Contents* at the drop-down list.
   e. At the Table of Contents dialog box, click the Options button.
   f. At the Table of Contents Options dialog box, click the *Table entry fields* check box to insert a check mark.
   g. Click OK to close the Table of Contents Options dialog box.
   h. Click OK to close the Table of Contents dialog box.
   i. Apply bold formatting and center the heading *TABLE OF CONTENTS*.
7. Insert a lowercase roman numeral page number on the table of contents page. ***Hint: Refer to Project 1a, Step 5.***
8. Click the Show/Hide ¶ button to turn off the display of nonprinting characters.
9. Save **WL2-C6-P2-CompEval.docx** and then print only page 1 (the table of contents page).

Table of Contents Options
Build table of contents from:
Styles
Available styles: TOC level:
Footer
Header
Heading 1 1
Heading 2 2
Heading 3 3
Heading 4
Outline levels
Table entry fields
Reset OK Cancel
Step 6f
Step 6g

If you insert additional information in a document, you can easily update the table of contents. To do this, insert the text and then mark the text with options at the Mark Table of Contents Entry dialog box. Click anywhere in the table of contents and then click the Update Table tab. At the Update Table of Contents dialog box, click the *Update entire table* option and then click OK.

Project 2b Updating the Entire Table of Contents Part 2 of 2

1. With **WL2-C6-P2-CompEval.docx** open, insert a file into the document by completing the following steps:
   a. Press Ctrl + End to move the insertion point to the end of the document.
   b. Press Ctrl + Enter to insert a page break.
   c. Click the INSERT tab.
   d. Click the Object button arrow in the Text group and then click *Text from File* at the drop-down list.
   e. At the Insert File dialog box, navigate to the WL2C6 folder on your storage medium and then double-click ***PosClassification.docx***.

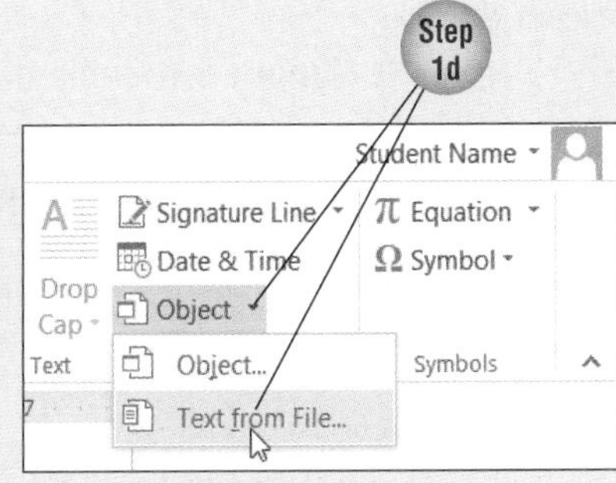

2. Select and then mark text for inclusion in the table of contents by completing the following steps:
   a. Select the title *POSITION CLASSIFICATION*.
   b. Press Alt + Shift + O.
   c. At the Mark Table of Contents Entry dialog box, make sure that *1* displays in the *Level* measurement box and then click the Mark button.
   d. Click the Close button to close the Mark Table of Contents Entry dialog box.
3. Update the table of contents by completing the following steps:
   a. Select the entire table of contents (excluding the title).
   b. Click the REFERENCES tab.
   c. Click the Update Table button in the Table of Contents group.
   d. At the Update Table of Contents dialog box, click the *Update entire table* option.
   e. Click OK.
4. Turn off the display of nonprinting characters.
5. Save the document, print only the table of contents page, and then close **WL2-C6-P2-CompEval.docx**.

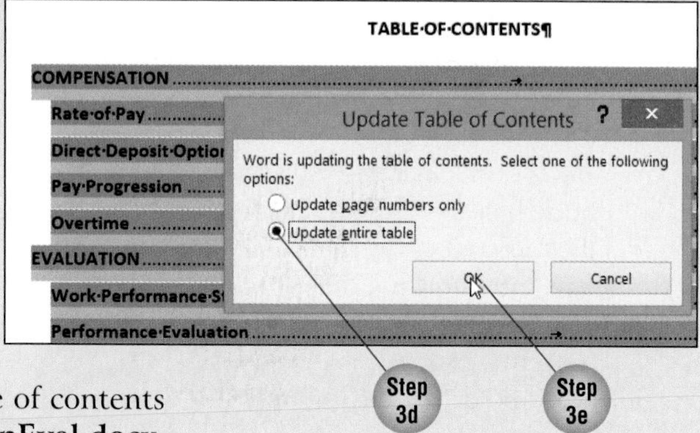

Project 3 Create a Table of Figures for a Technology Report and a Travel Document — 3 Parts

You will open a report containing information on software, output devices, and the software development cycle, as well as images and a SmartArt diagram; insert captions; and then create a table of figures. You will also create and customize captions and insert a table of figures for an adventure document.

Creating a Table of Figures

A table of figures includes a list of all figures, tables, and equations in the document.

A document that contains figures should include a ***table of figures*** so readers can quickly locate specific figures. Figure 6.6 shows an example of a table of figures. You can create a table of figures by marking figures or images with captions and then using the caption names to create the table.

Figure 6.6 Table of Figures

TABLE OF FIGURES

Creating Captions

A ***caption*** is text that describes an item such as an image, table, equation, or chart. A caption generally displays below the item. Create a caption by selecting the figure text or image, clicking the REFERENCES tab, and then clicking the Insert Caption button in the Captions group. This displays the Caption dialog box, shown in Figure 6.7. At the dialog box, *Figure 1* displays in the *Caption* text box and the insertion point is positioned after *Figure 1*. Type a name for the figure and then press the Enter key. Word inserts *Figure 1* followed by the caption you typed below the selected text or image. If the insertion point is positioned in a table when you display the Caption dialog box, *Table 1* displays in the *Caption* text box instead of *Figure 1*.

Quick Steps

Create a Caption

1. Select text or image.
2. Click REFERENCES tab.
3. Click Insert Caption button.
4. Type caption name.
5. Click OK.

Insert Caption

Inserting a Table of Figures

After you have marked figures or images with captions within a document, insert the table of figures. A table of figures generally displays at the beginning of the document, after the table of contents and on a separate page. To insert the table of figures, click the Insert Table of Figures button in the Captions group on the REFERENCES tab. At the Table of Figures dialog box, shown in Figure 6.8 on the next page, make any necessary changes and then click OK.

The options at the Table of Figures dialog box are similar to the options available at the Table of Contents dialog box. For example, you can choose a format for the table of figures from the *Formats* option box, change the alignment of the page numbers, or add leaders before page numbers.

Quick Steps

Insert a Table of Figures

1. Click REFERENCES tab.
2. Click Insert Table of Figures button.
3. Select desired format.
4. Click OK.

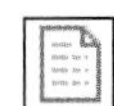

Insert Table of Figures

Figure 6.7 Caption Dialog Box

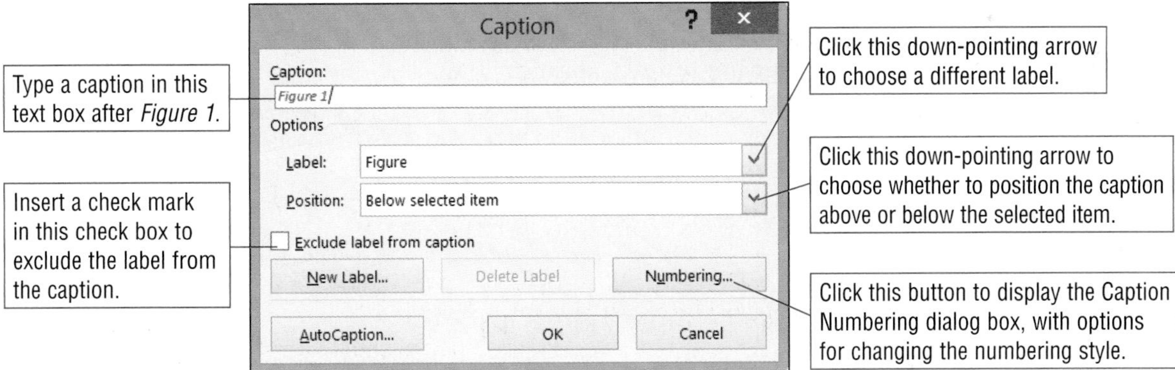
Caption
Caption:
Figure 1
Options
Label:
Figure
Position:
Below selected item
Exclude label from caption
New Label...
Delete Label
Numbering...
AutoCaption...
OK
Cancel
Type a caption in this text box after Figure 1.
Insert a check mark in this check box to exclude the label from the caption.
Click this down-pointing arrow to choose a different label.
Click this down-pointing arrow to choose whether to position the caption above or below the selected item.
Click this button to display the Caption Numbering dialog box, with options for changing the numbering style.

Figure 6.8 Table of Figures Dialog Box

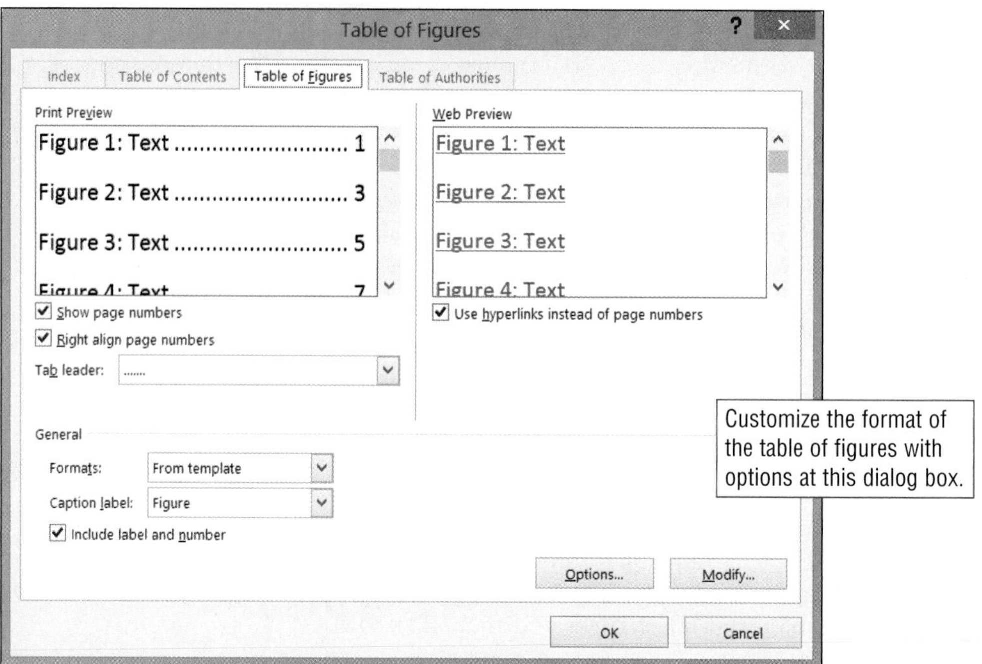

Project 3a Creating a List of Figures

Part 1 of 3

1. Open **TechRpt.docx** and then save the document and name it **WL2-C6-P3-TechRpt**.
2. Add the caption *Figure 1 Word Document* to an image by completing the following steps:
   a. Click the screen image that displays in the *Word Processing Software* section.
   b. Click the REFERENCES tab.
   c. Click the Insert Caption button in the Captions group.
   d. At the Caption dialog box with the insertion point positioned after *Figure 1* in the *Caption* text box, press the spacebar once and then type **Word Document**.
   e. Click OK or press Enter.

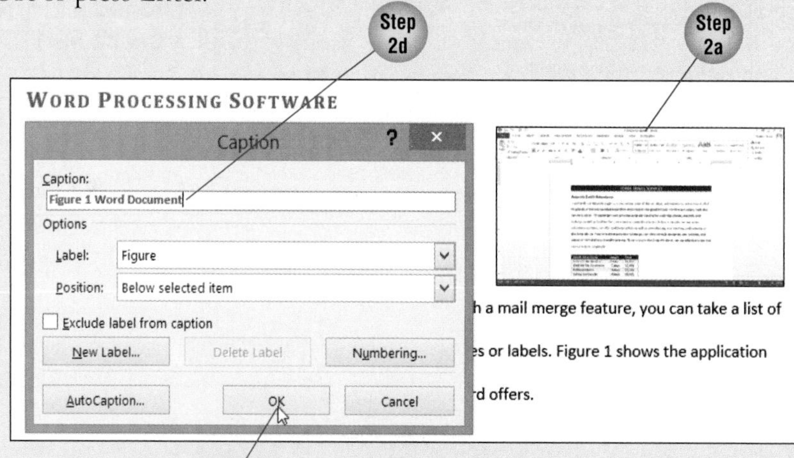

   f. Press Ctrl + E to center the caption in the text box.

3. Complete steps similar to those in Step 2 to create the caption *Figure 2 Excel Worksheet* for the image in the *Spreadsheet Software* section.
4. Complete steps similar to those in Step 2 to create the caption *Figure 3 Monitor* for the image in the *Monitor* section.
5. Complete steps similar to those in Step 2 to create the caption *Figure 4 Software Life Cycle* for the SmartArt graphic in the *Developing Software* section.
6. Insert a table of figures at the beginning of the document by completing the following steps:
   a. Press Ctrl + Home to move the insertion point to the beginning of the document.
   b. Press Ctrl + Enter to insert a page break.
   c. Press Ctrl + Home to move the insertion point back to the beginning of the document and then type **TABLE OF FIGURES** bolded and centered.
   d. Press the Enter key, turn off bold formatting, and then change the paragraph alignment back to left alignment.
   e. If necessary, click the REFERENCES tab.
   f. Click the Insert Table of Figures button in the Captions group.
   g. At the Table of Figures dialog box, click the down-pointing arrow at the right side of the *Formats* option box and then click *Formal* at the drop-down list.
   h. Click OK.
7. Save **WL2-C6-P3-TechRpt.docx.**

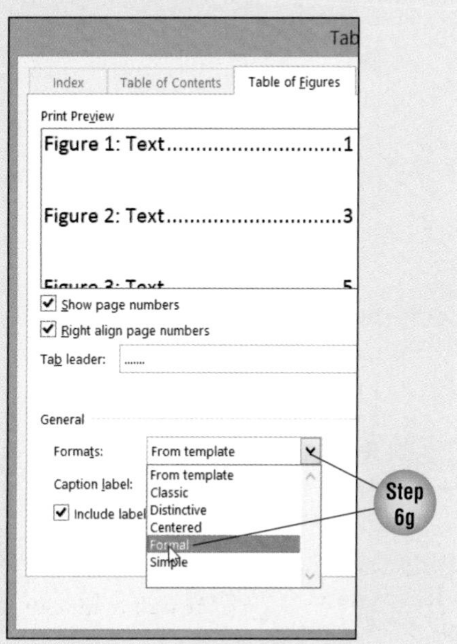

Updating or Deleting a Table of Figures

If you make changes to a document after inserting a table of figures, you can update the table of figures. To do this, click anywhere within the table of figures and then click the Update Table button in the Captions group on the REFERENCES tab or press the F9 key. At the Update Table of Figures dialog box, click *Update page numbers only* if the changes were made only to the page numbers or click *Update entire table* if changes were made to caption text. Click OK or press Enter to close the dialog box. To delete a table of figures, select the entire table using the mouse or keyboard and then press the Delete key.

Quick Steps

Update a Table of Figures
1. Click in table of figures.
2. Click REFERENCES tab.
3. Click Update Table button or press F9.
4. Click OK.

Delete a Table of Figures
1. Select entire table of figures.
2. Press Delete key.

Project 3b Updating the Table of Figures Part 2 of 3

1. With **WL2-C6-P3-TechRpt.docx** open, insert an image of a laser printer by completing the following steps:
   a. Move the insertion point to the beginning of the second paragraph of text in the *PRINTERS* section.
   b. Click the INSERT tab and then click the Pictures button in the Illustrations group.
   c. At the Insert Picture dialog box, navigate to the WL2C6 folder on your storage medium and then double-click the file named ***LaserPrinter.png***.
   d. Change the height of the clip art image to 1.5 inches.
   e. Change the text wrapping to *Square*.
2. Add the caption *Figure 4 Laser Printer* to the printer image and then center the caption.
3. Click on any character in the table of figures.
4. Press the F9 function key on your keyboard.
5. At the Update Table of Figures dialog box, click the *Update entire table* option and then click OK.
6. Save, print, and then close **WL2-C6-P3-TechRpt.docx**.
7. Close Word.

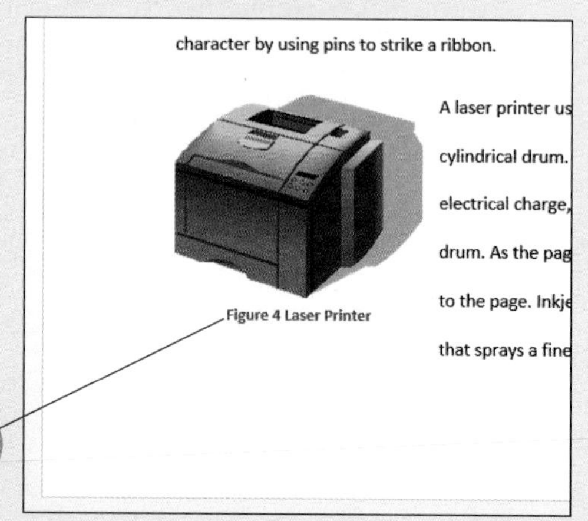
character by using pins to strike a ribbon.
A laser printer us
cylindrical drum.
electrical charge,
drum. As the pag
to the page. Inkje
that sprays a fine
Figure 4 Laser Printer
Step 2

Customizing Captions

The Caption dialog box contains a number of options for customizing captions. Click the down-pointing arrow at the right of the *Label* option to specify the caption label. The default is *Figure*, which you can change to *Equation* or *Table*. A caption, by default, is positioned below the selected item. With the *Position* option, you can change the position of the caption so it is above the selected item. A caption contains a label, such as *Figure*, *Table*, or *Equation*. If you want only a caption number and not a caption label, insert a check mark in the *Exclude label from caption* check box.

Click the New Label button and the Label dialog box displays. At this dialog box, type a custom label for the caption. Word automatically inserts an arabic number (*1, 2, 3,* and so on) after each caption label. If you want to change the caption numbering style, click the Numbering button. At the Caption Numbering dialog box that displays, click the down-pointing arrow at the right side of the *Format* option box and then click the desired numbering style at the drop-down list. For example, you can change caption numbering to uppercase or lowercase letters or roman numerals.

If you insert items such as tables in a document on a regular basis, you can specify that you want a caption inserted automatically with each item. To do this, click the AutoCaption button. At the AutoCaption dialog box, insert a check mark before the item, such as *Microsoft Word Table* in the *Add caption when inserting* list box, and then click OK. Each time you insert a table in a document, Word inserts a caption above the table.

Project 3c Creating and Customizing Captions and Inserting a Table of Figures Part 3 of 3

1. Open Word, open **TTSAdventures.docx**, and then save the document and name it **WL2-C6-P3-TTSAdventures**.
2. Insert a custom caption for the first table by completing the following steps:
   a. Click in any cell in the first table.
   b. Click the REFERENCES tab.
   c. Click the Insert Caption button.
   d. At the Caption dialog box, press the spacebar once and then type **Antarctic Zenith Adventures** in the *Caption* text box.
   e. Remove the label (*Table*) from the caption by clicking the *Exclude label from caption* check box to insert a check mark.
   f. Click the Numbering button.
   g. At the Caption Numbering dialog box, click the down-pointing arrow at the right side of the *Format* option box and then click the *A, B, C, …* option at the drop-down list.
   h. Click OK to close the Caption Numbering dialog box.
   i. At the Caption dialog box, click the down-pointing arrow at the right side of the *Position* option and then click *Below selected item* at the drop-down list.
   j. Click OK to close the Caption dialog box.

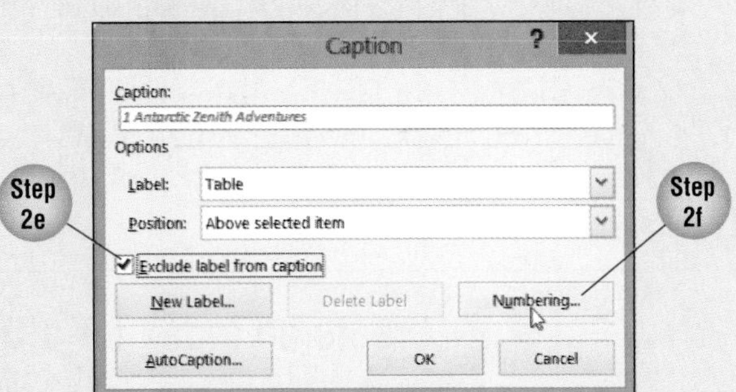

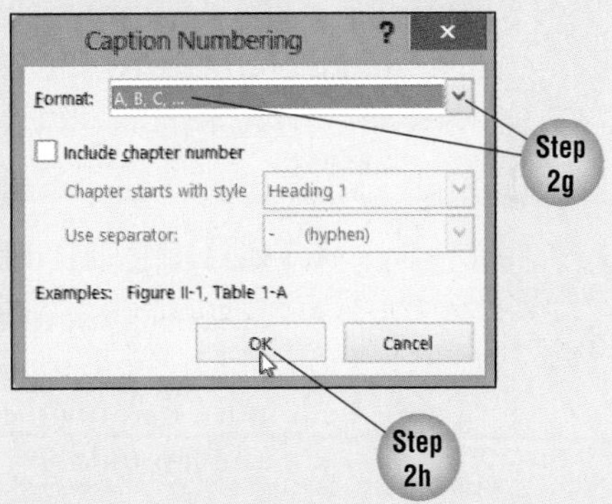

3. After looking at the caption, you decide to add a custom label and change the numbering. Do this by completing the following steps:
   a. Select the *A Antarctic Zenith Adventures* caption.
   b. Click the Insert Caption button in the Captions group on the REFERENCES tab.
   c. At the Caption dialog box, click the *Exclude label from caption* check box to remove the check mark.
   d. Click the New Label button.
   e. At the New Label dialog box, type **Adventure** and then click OK.
   f. Click OK to close the Caption dialog box.
4. Format the caption by completing the following steps:
   a. Select the *Adventure 1 Antarctic Zenith Adventures* caption.
   b. Click the HOME tab.
   c. Click the Font Color button arrow.
   d. Click the *Dark Blue* color (ninth color in the *Standard Colors* section).
   e. Click the Bold button.
5. Insert a custom caption for the second table by completing the following steps:
   a. Click in any cell in the second table.
   b. Click the REFERENCES tab and then click the Insert Caption button.
   c. At the Caption dialog box, press the spacebar and then type **Tall-Ship Adventures**.
   d. Make sure *Below selected item* displays in the *Position* option box and then click OK to close the Caption dialog box.
6. Select the *Adventure 2 Tall-Ship Adventures* caption, apply the Dark Blue font color, and apply bold formatting.

7. Insert a table of figures by completing the following steps:
   a. Press Ctrl + Home and then press Ctrl + Enter to insert a page break.
   b. Press Ctrl + Home to move the insertion point above the page break.
   c. Turn on bold formatting, type **TABLES**, turn off bold formatting, and then press the Enter key.
   d. Click the REFERENCES tab and then click the Insert Table of Figures button in the Captions group.
   e. At the Table of Figures dialog box, click OK.
8. Save, print, and then close **WL2-C6-P3-TSSAdventures.docx**.

Project 4 Create an Index for a Desktop Publishing Report — 2 Parts

You will open a report containing information on desktop publishing, mark specific text for an index, and then insert the index in the document. You will also make changes to the document and then update the index.

Creating an Index

An ***index*** is a list of topics contained in a publication that includes the page numbers on which those topics are discussed. Word lets you automate the process of creating an index in a manner similar to that used for creating a table of contents. When creating an index, you mark a word or words that you want included in the index.

Creating an index takes some thought and consideration. The author of the book, manuscript, or report must determine the main entries that will be included, as well as the subentries that will be added under main entries. An index may include such items as the main idea of a document, the main subject of a chapter or section, variations of a heading or subheading, and abbreviations. Figure 6.9 shows an example of an index.

Figure 6.9 Sample Index

INDEX

Marking Text for an Index

A selected word or words can be marked for inclusion in an index. Before marking words for an index, determine what main entries and subentries are to be included. Selected text is marked as an index entry at the Mark Index Entry dialog box.

To mark text for an index, select the word or words, click the REFERENCES tab, and then click the Mark Entry button in the Index group. You can also press Alt + Shift + X. At the Mark Index Entry dialog box, shown in Figure 6.10, the selected word or words appears in the *Main entry* text box. Make any necessary changes to the dialog box and then click the Mark button. (When you click the Mark button, Word automatically turns on the display of nonprinting symbols and displays the index field code.) Click the Close button to close the Mark Index Entry dialog box.

Quick Steps

Mark Text for an Index

1. Select text.
2. Click REFERENCES tab.
3. Click Mark Entry button.
4. Click Mark button.

Mark Entry

You can also mark text for an index using the keyboard shortcut Alt + Shift + X.

At the Mark Index Entry dialog box, the selected word or words displays in the *Main entry* text box. If the text is a main entry, leave it as displayed. If, however, the selected text is a subentry, type the main entry in the *Main entry* text box, click in the *Subentry* text box, and then type the selected text. For example, suppose a publication includes the terms *Page layout* and *Portrait.* The words *Page layout* are to be marked as a main entry for the index and *Portrait* is to be marked as a subentry below *Page layout*. To mark these words for an index, you would complete the following steps:

1. Select *Page layout*.
2. Click the REFERENCES tab and then click the Mark Entry button or press Alt + Shift + X.
3. At the Mark Index Entry dialog box, click the Mark button. (This turns on the display of nonprinting symbols.)
4. With the Mark Index Entry dialog box still displayed on the screen, click in the document to make the document active and then select *Portrait*.
5. Click the Mark Index Entry dialog box Title bar to make it active.
6. Select *Portrait* in the *Main entry* text box and then type Page layout.
7. Click in the *Subentry* text box and then type Portrait.
8. Click the Mark button.
9. Click the Close button.

Figure 6.10 Mark Index Entry Dialog Box

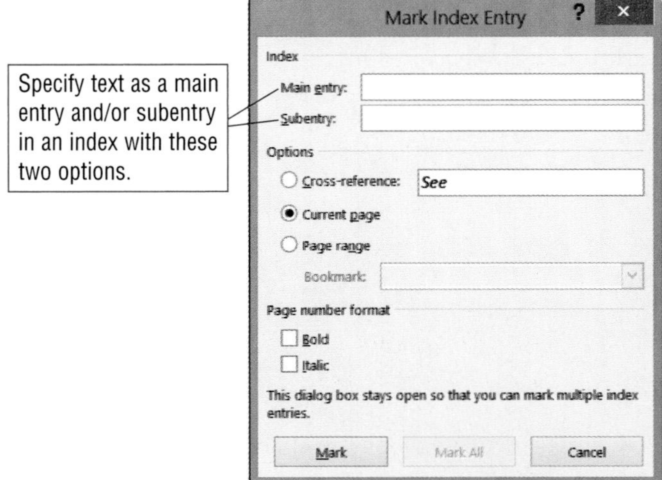

To include a third-level index entry, type the subentry text, type a colon, and then type the third-level entry text.

To delete an index entry, select the entire entry field, including the braces ({}), and then press the Delete key.

The main entry and subentry do not have to be the same as the selected text. You can select text for an index, type the text you want to display in the *Main entry* or *Subentry* text box, and then click the Mark button. At the Mark Index Entry dialog box, you can apply bold and/or italic formatting to the page numbers that will appear in the index. To apply formatting, click *Bold* and/or *Italic* to insert a check mark in the check box.

The *Options* section of the Mark Index Entry dialog box contains several options, with *Current page* the default. At this setting, the current page number will be listed in the index for the main entry and/or subentry. If you click *Cross-reference*, type the text you want to use as a cross-reference for the index entry in the *Cross-reference* text box. For example, you can mark the word *Serif* and cross reference it to *Typefaces*.

Click the Mark All button at the Mark Index Entry dialog box to mark all occurrences of the text in the document as index entries. Word marks only those entries whose uppercase and lowercase letters match the index entries.

Project 4a Marking Words for an Index

Part 1 of 2

1. Open **DTP.docx** and then save the document and name it **WL2-C6-P4-DTP**.
2. Insert a page number at the bottom center of each page.
3. In the first paragraph, mark the word *software* for the index as a main entry and mark *word processing* in as a subentry below *software* by completing the following steps:
   a. Select *software* (located in the second sentence of the first paragraph).
   b. Click the REFERENCES tab and then click the Mark Entry button in the Index group.
   c. At the Mark Index Entry dialog box, click the Mark All button. (This turns on the display of nonprinting symbols.)
   d. With the Mark Index Entry dialog box still displayed, click in the document to make the document active and then select *word processing* (located in the last sentence of the first paragraph). (You may want to drag the dialog box down the screen so more of the document text is visible.)
   e. Click the Title bar of the Mark Index Entry dialog box to make the dialog box active.
   f. Select *word processing* in the *Main entry* text box and then type **software**.
   g. Click in the *Subentry* text box and then type **word processing**.
   h. Click the Mark All button.

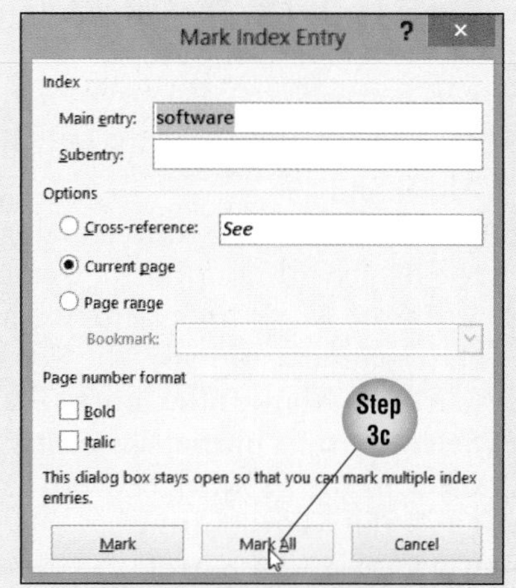

i. With the Mark Index Entry dialog box still displayed, complete steps similar to those in Steps 3d through 3h to select the first occurrence of each of the following words and then mark the word as a main entry or subentry for the index (click the Mark All button at the Mark Index Entry dialog box):
   1) In the first paragraph in the *Defining Desktop Publishing* section:
      spreadsheets = subentry (main entry = *software*)
      database = subentry (main entry = *software*)
   2) In the second paragraph in the *Defining Desktop Publishing* section:
      publishing = main entry
      desktop = subentry (main entry = *publishing*)
      printer = main entry
      laser = subentry (main entry = *printer*)
   3) In the third paragraph in the *Defining Desktop Publishing* section:
      design = main entry
   4) In the fourth paragraph in the *Defining Desktop Publishing* section:
      traditional = subentry (main entry = *publishing*)
   5) In the only paragraph in the *Initiating the Process* section:
      publication = main entry
      planning = subentry (main entry = *publication*)
      creating = subentry (main entry = *publication*)
      intended audience = subentry (main entry = *publication*)
      content = subentry (main entry = *publication*)
   6) In the third paragraph in the *Planning the Publication* section:
      message = main entry

j. Click Close to close the Mark Index Entry dialog box.

4. Turn off the display of nonprinting characters.
5. Save **WL2-C6-P4-DTP.docx**.

Inserting an Index

After you have marked all of the words that you want to include in an index as main entries or subentries, your next step is to insert the index. The index should appear at the end of a document, generally beginning on a separate page.

To insert the index, position the insertion point at the end of the document and then insert a page break. With the insertion point positioned below the page break, type *INDEX*, center it, apply bold formatting, and then press the Enter key. With the insertion point positioned at the left margin, click the REFERENCES tab and then click the Insert Index button in the Index group. At the Index dialog box, shown in Figure 6.11 on the next page, select the desired formatting and then click OK. Word inserts the index at the location of the insertion point with the formatting selected at the Index dialog box. Word also inserts section breaks above and below the index text.

Quick Steps

Insert an Index
1. Click REFERENCES tab.
2. Click Insert Index button.
3. Select desired format.
4. Click OK.

Insert Index

At the Index dialog box, specify how the index entries will appear. The *Print Preview* section shows how the index will display in the document. The *Columns* measurement box has a default setting of *2*. At this setting, the index will display in two columns. You can increase or decrease this number.

By default, page numbers are right-aligned in the index. If you do not want the numbers right-aligned, click the *Right align page numbers* check box to remove the check mark. The *Tab leader* option is dimmed for all formats except *Formal*. If you click

Figure 6.11 Index Dialog Box

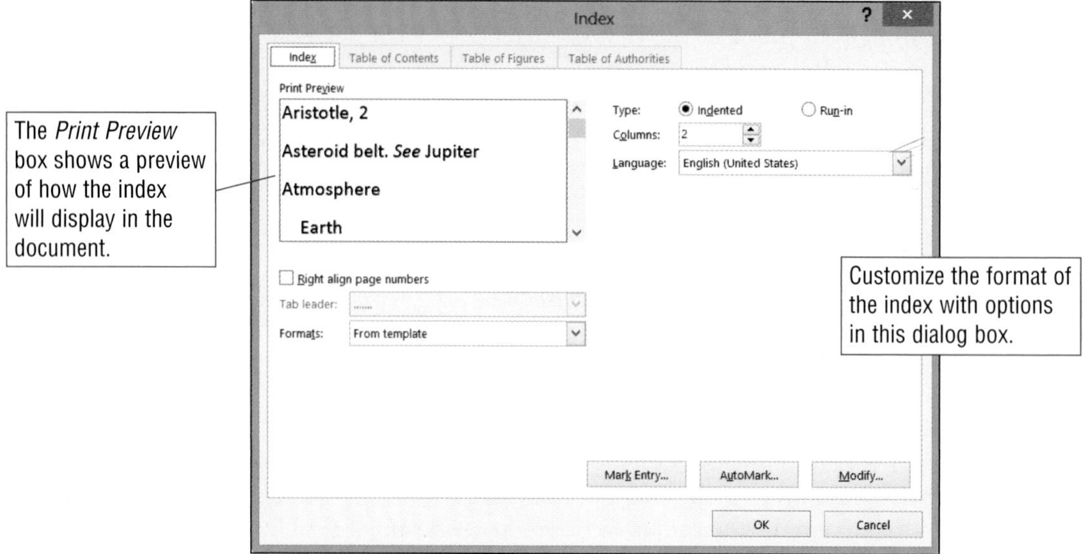

Formal in the *Formats* option box, the *Tab leader* option displays in black. The default tab leader character is a period. To change to a different character, click the down-pointing arrow at the right of the option box and then click the desired character.

In the *Type* section, the *Indented* option is selected by default. At this setting, subentries will appear indented below main entries. If you click *Run-in*, subentries will display on the same lines as main entries.

Click the down-pointing arrow at the right side of the *Formats* option box and a list of formatting choices displays. At this list, click the desired formatting and the *Print Preview* box displays how the index will appear in the document.

Project 4b Inserting an Index

Part 2 of 2

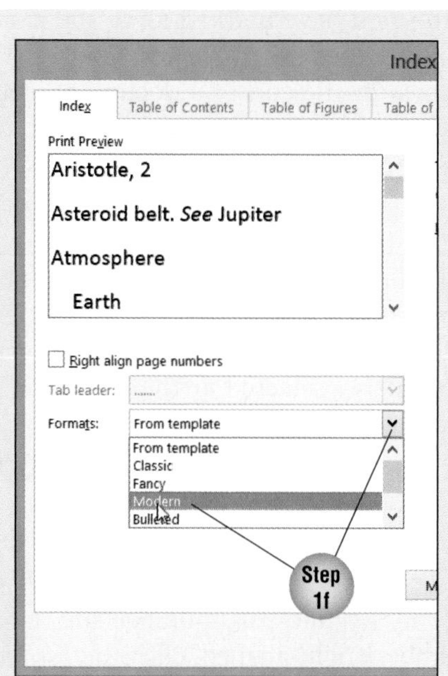

1. With **WL2-C6-P4-DTP.docx** open, insert the index into the document by completing the following steps:
   a. Press Ctrl + End to position the insertion point at the end of the document.
   b. Insert a page break.
   c. With the insertion point positioned below the page break, type INDEX and then press Enter.
   d. Click the REFERENCES tab.
   e. Click the Insert Index button in the Index group.
   f. At the Index dialog box, click the down-pointing arrow at the right side of the *Formats* option box and then click *Modern* at the drop-down list.
   g. Click OK to close the dialog box.
   h. Click in the title *INDEX*, apply the Heading 1 style, and then press Ctrl + E to center the title.
2. Save **WL2-C6-P4-DTP.docx** and then print the index page (the last page) of the document.
3. Close **WL2-C6-P4-DTP.docx**.

Project 5 Create an Index with a Concordance File for a Newsletter 3 Parts

You will create and then save a concordance file. You will then open a report containing information on designing newsletters and use the concordance file to create an index.

Creating a Concordance File

Another method for creating an index is to create a concordance file and use the information in the file to create the index. Creating a concordance file saves you from having to mark each reference in a document.

A ***concordance file*** is a regular Word document containing a two-column table with no text outside the table. In the first column of the table, you enter the words you want to include in the index. In the second column, you enter the main entry and subentry that should appear in the index. To create a subentry, type the main entry followed by a colon, a space, and then the subentry. Figure 6.12 shows an example of a completed concordance file.

In the concordance file shown in Figure 6.12, the text as it appears in the document is inserted in the first column (such as *World War I*, *Technology*, and *technology*). The second column contains the text as it should appear in the index,

Quick Steps

Create a Concordance File

1. Click INSERT tab.
2. Click Table button and drag to create table.
3. In first column, type words you want in index.
4. In second column, type main entry and subentry.
5. Save document.

Figure 6.12 Concordance File

World War I	World War I
Technology	Technology
technology	Technology
Teletypewriters	Technology: teletypewriters
motion pictures	Technology: motion pictures
Television	Technology: television
Radio Corporation of America	Radio Corporation of America
coaxial cable	Coaxial cable
Telephone	Technology: telephone
Communications Act of 1934	Communications Act of 1934
World War II	World War II
radar system	Technology: radar system
Computer	Computer
Atanasoff Berry Computer	Computer: Atanasoff Berry Computer
Korean War	Korean War
Columbia Broadcasting System	Columbia Broadcasting System
Cold War	Cold War
Vietnam	Vietnam
artificial satellite	Technology: artificial satellite
Communications Satellite Act of 1962	Communications Satellite Act of 1962

specifying whether each item is a main entry or subentry. For example, the text *motion pictures* in the concordance file will appear in the index as a subentry under the main entry *Technology*.

After you have created a concordance file, you can use it to quickly mark text for an index in a document. To do this, open the document containing the text you want marked for the index, display the Index dialog box with the Index tab selected, and then click the AutoMark button. At the Open Index AutoMark File dialog box, double-click the concordance file name in the list box. Word turns on the display of nonprinting symbols, searches the document for text that matches the text in the concordance file, and then marks it accordingly. After marking text for the index, insert the index in the document as described earlier.

As you create the concordance file in Project 5a, Word's AutoCorrect feature will automatically capitalize the first letter of the first word entered in each cell. In Figure 6.12, you can see that several of the first words in the first column do not begin with capital letters. Before beginning the project, consider turning off this AutoCorrect capitalization feature. To do this, click the FILE tab and then click *Options*. At the Word Options dialog box, click *Proofing* in the left panel of the dialog box and then click the AutoCorrect Options button. At the AutoCorrect dialog box with the AutoCorrect tab selected, click the *Capitalize first letter of table cells* check box to remove the check mark. Click OK to close the dialog box and then click OK to close the Word Options dialog box.

Project 5a Creating a Concordance File — Part 1 of 3

1. At a blank document, create the text shown in Figure 6.13 as a concordance file by completing the following steps:
   a. Click the INSERT tab.
   b. Click the Table button in the Tables group.
   c. Drag down and to the right until *2×1 Table* displays at the top of the grid and then click the left mouse button.
   d. Type the text in the cells as shown in Figure 6.13 on the next page. Press the Tab key to move to the next cell. (If you did not remove the check mark before the *Capitalize first letter of table cells* option at the AutoCorrect dialog box, the *n* in the first word in the first cell, *newsletters*, is automatically capitalized. Hover the mouse over the *N*, click the blue rectangle that displays below the *N*, and then click *Stop Auto-capitalizing First Letter of Table Cells*.)
2. Save the document and name it **WL2-C6-P5-CFile**.
3. Print and then close **WL2-C6-P5-CFile.docx**.

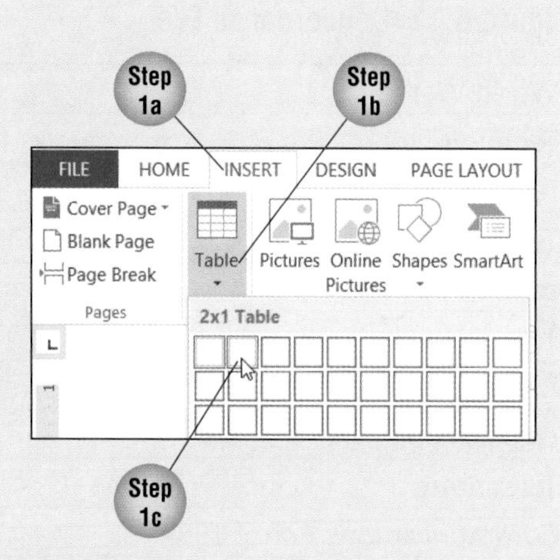

Figure 6.13 Project 5a

newsletters	Newsletters
Newsletters	Newsletters
Software	Software
Desktop publishing	Software: desktop publishing
word processing	Software: word processing
Printers	Printers
Laser	Printers: laser
Design	Design
Communication	Communication
Consistency	Design: consistency
Elements	Elements
Nameplate	Elements: nameplate
Logo	Elements: logo
Subtitle	Elements: subtitle
Folio	Elements: folio
Headlines	Elements: headlines
Subheads	Elements: subheads
Byline	Elements: byline
Body Copy	Elements: body copy
Graphics Images	Elements: graphics images
Audience	Newsletters: audience
Purpose	Newsletters: purpose
focal point	Newsletters: focal point

If you removed the check mark before the *Capitalize first letter of table cells* option at the AutoCorrect dialog box, you may need to turn this feature back on. To do this, click the FILE tab and then click *Options*. At the Word Options dialog box, click *Proofing* in the left panel of the dialog box and then click the AutoCorrect Options button. At the AutoCorrect dialog box with the AutoCorrect tab selected, click the *Capitalize first letter of table cells* check box to insert a check mark. Click OK to close the dialog box and then click OK to close the Word Options dialog box.

Project 5b Inserting an Index Using a Concordance File Part 2 of 3

1. Open **PlanNwsltr.docx** and then save the document and name it **WL2-C6-P5-PlanNwsltr**.
2. Mark text for the index using the concordance file by completing the following steps:
   a. Click the REFERENCES tab.
   b. Click the Insert Index button in the Index group.

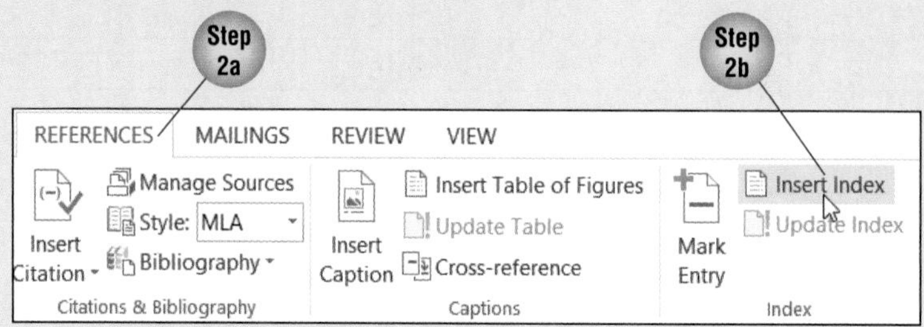

   c. At the Index dialog box, click the AutoMark button.
   d. At the Open Index AutoMark File dialog box, double-click ***WL2-C6-P5-CFile.docx*** in the Content pane. (This turns on the display of nonprinting symbols.)
3. Insert the index in the document by completing the following steps:
   a. Position the insertion point at the end of the document.
   b. Insert a page break.
   c. Type INDEX.
   d. Press the Enter key.
   e. Click the Insert Index button in the Index group.
   f. At the Index dialog box, click the down-pointing arrow at the right side of the *Formats* option box and then click *Formal* at the drop-down list.
   g. Click OK to close the dialog box.
4. Apply the Heading 1 style to the *INDEX* title and then center the title.
5. Turn off the display of nonprinting characters.
6. Save **WL2-C6-P5-PlanNwsltr.docx** and then print only the Index page.

Updating and Deleting an Index

Quick Steps

Update an Index
1. Click in index.
2. Click Update Index button or press F9.

Delete an Index
1. Select entire index.
2. Press Delete key.

Update Index

If you make changes to a document after inserting an index, update the index. To do this, click anywhere within the current index and then click the Update Index button in the Index group or press the F9 key. To delete an index, select the entire index using the mouse or the keyboard and then press the Delete key.

Project 5c Updating an Index

Part 3 of 3

1. With **WL2-C6-P5-PlanNwsltr.docx** open, insert a page break at the beginning of the title *PLANNING A NEWSLETTER*.
2. Update the index by clicking anywhere in the index, clicking the REFERENCES tab, and then clicking the Update Index button in the Index group.
3. Save **WL2-C6-P5-PlanNwsltr.docx** and then print only the index page.
4. Close **WL2-C6-P5-PlanNwsltr.docx**.

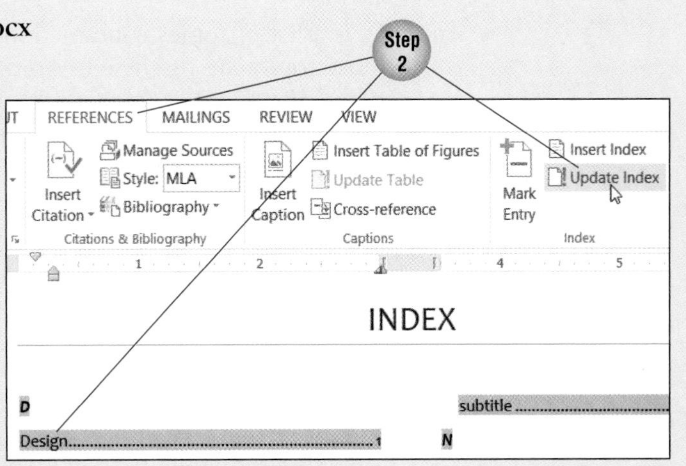

Chapter Summary

- Word provides options for automating the creation of a table of contents, table of figures, and index.
- Identify text to be included in a table of contents by applying a heading style, assigning a level, or marking text as a field entry.
- Mark text as a field entry at the Mark Table of Contents dialog box. Display this dialog box by pressing Alt + Shift + O.
- Creating a table of contents involves two steps: applying the appropriate styles to mark text that will be included and inserting the table of contents in the document.
- To insert the table of contents, position the insertion point where you want the table to appear, click the REFERENCES tab, click the Table of Contents button, and then click the desired option at the drop-down list.
- Generally the pages containing the table of contents are numbered with lowercase roman numerals.
- If you want the table of contents to print on a page separate from the document text, insert a section break that begins a new page between the table of contents and title of the document.
- If you make changes to a document after inserting a table of contents, update the table of contents by clicking anywhere in the table and then clicking the Update Table button on the REFERENCES tab or pressing the F9 key. Update a table of figures or index in a similar manner.
- Remove a table of contents by clicking the Table of Contents button on the REFERENCES tab and then clicking *Remove Table of Contents* at the drop-down list.
- Create a table of figures by marking specific text or images with captions and then using the caption names to create the table of figures. Mark captions at the Caption dialog box. Display this dialog box by clicking the Insert Caption button on the REFERENCES tab.

- Insert a table of figures in a document in a manner similar to that for inserting a table of contents. A table of figures generally displays at the beginning of the document, on a separate page after the table of contents.
- An index is a list of topics contained in a publication and the page numbers on which those topics are discussed. Word automates the process of creating an index in a manner similar to that for creating a table of contents.
- Mark text for an index at the Mark Index Entry dialog box. Display this dialog box by clicking the Mark Entry button on the REFERENCES tab or pressing Alt + Shift + X.
- After all of the necessary text has been marked as main entries and subentires for the index, insert the index, placing it on a separate page at the end of the document.
- Insert an index in a document by clicking the Insert Index button on the REFERENCES tab, making desired changes at the Index dialog box, and then clicking OK.
- Words that appear frequently in a document can be saved as a concordance file and used in creating an index. A concordance file is a regular document containing a two-column table. Using this table to create the index eliminates the need to mark each reference in a document.

Commands Review

FEATURE	RIBBON TAB, GROUP	BUTTON, OPTION	KEYBOARD SHORTCUT
Caption dialog box	REFERENCES, Captions		
Index dialog box	REFERENCES, Index		
Mark Index Entry dialog box	REFERENCES, Index		Alt + Shift + X
Mark Table of Contents Entry dialog box			Alt + Shift + O
Open Index AutoMark File dialog box	REFERENCES, Index	, AutoMark button	
Page Number Format dialog box	INSERT, Header & Footer	, *Format Page Numbers*	
Table of Contents dialog box	REFERENCES, Table of Contents	, *Custom Table of Contents*	
Table of Contents Options dialog box	REFERENCES, Table of Contents	, *Custom Table of Contents*, Options button	
Table of Figures dialog box	REFERENCES, Captions		
update table of contents	REFERENCES, Table of Contents		F9

Concepts Check Test Your Knowledge

Completion: In the space provided at the right, indicate the correct term, symbol, or command.

1. A table of contents generally appears in this location in a document. ________________
2. In a built-in table of contents, Word uses text with this heading style applied as the first level. ________________
3. The pages of a table of contents are generally numbered with this type of number. ________________
4. Use this keyboard shortcut to update a table of contents. ________________
5. Use this keyboard shortcut to display the Mark Table of Contents Entry dialog box. ________________
6. If you mark table of contents entries as fields, you will need to activate this option at the Table of Contents Options dialog box. ________________
7. Create a table of figures by marking figures or images with these. ________________
8. Use this keyboard shortcut to display the Mark Index Entry dialog box. ________________
9. An index generally appears at this location in the document. ________________
10. Create this type of file and then use it to save time when marking text for an index. ________________

Skills Check Assess Your Performance

Assessment 1

CREATE AND UPDATE A TABLE OF CONTENTS FOR A PHOTOGRAPHY REPORT

1. Open **PhotoRpt.docx** and then save the document and name it **WL2-C6-A1-PhotoRpt**.
2. Move the insertion point to the beginning of the heading *Photography* and then insert a section break that begins a new page.
3. With the insertion point positioned below the section break, insert page numbers at the bottom center of pages and change the beginning number to 1.
4. Press Ctrl + Home to move the insertion point to the beginning of the document (on the blank page) and then create a table of contents with the *Automatic Table 1* option at the Table of Contents button drop-down list.

5. Display the Table of Contents dialog box, change the *Formats* option box to *Distinctive* and make sure a *3* displays in the *Show levels* measurement box.
6. Change the page number format on the table of contents page to lowercase roman numerals.
7. Save the document and then print only the table of contents page.
8. Insert a page break at the beginning of the heading *Camera Basics*.
9. Update the table of contents.
10. Save the document and then print only the table of contents page.
11. Close **WL2-C6-A1-PhotoRpt.docx**.

Assessment 2

INSERT CAPTIONS AND A TABLE OF FIGURES IN A REPORT

1. Open **InputDevices.docx** and then save the document and name it **WL2-C6-A2-InputDevices**.
2. Insert a caption for each of the three images in the document that uses *Figure* as the label, numbers (1, 2, 3, and so on) as the figure numbers, and displays below the image and is centered. Use *Keyboard* for the first figure caption, *Mouse* for the second, and *Laptop* for the third figure caption.
3. Move the insertion point to the beginning of the title *Computer Input Devices* and then insert a section break that begins a new page.
4. Press Ctrl + Home, type **Table of Figures**, press the Enter key, and then insert a table of figures with the Formal format.
5. Apply the Heading 1 style to the title *Table of Figures*.
6. Move the insertion point to the title *Computer Input Devices* and then insert a page number at the bottom center of each page and change the starting number to 1.
7. Move the insertion point to the title *Table of Figures* and then change the page numbering style to lowercase roman numerals.
8. Insert a page break at the beginning of the *Mouse* heading.
9. Update the table of figures.
10. Save, print, and then close **WL2-C6-A2-InputDevices.docx**.

Assessment 3

CREATE AND UPDATE AN INDEX FOR A NEWSLETTER

1. At a blank document, create the text shown in Figure 6.14 on the next page as a concordance file and then save the document and name it **WL2-C6-A3-CFile**.
2. Print and then close **WL2-C6-A3-CFile.docx**.
3. Open **DesignNwsltr.docx** and then save the document and name it **WL2-C6-A3-DesignNwsltr**.
4. Make the following changes to the document:
   a. Mark text for an index using the concordance file **WL2-C6-A3-CFile.docx**.
   b. Move the insertion point to the end of the document, insert a page break, type INDEX, press Enter, and then insert the index with the Classic format.
   c. Apply the Heading 1 style to the index title.

5. Add a page number at the bottom center of each page.
6. Change the line spacing to 2.0 for the entire document.
7. Insert a page break at the beginning of the title *CREATING NEWSLETTER LAYOUT*.
8. Update the index. (The index returns to the default line spacing.)
9. Save the document and then print the index page only.
10. Close **WL2-C6-A3-DesignNwsltr.docx**.

Figure 6.14 Assessment 3

NEWSLETTER	Newsletter
newsletter	Newsletter
consistency	Newsletter: consistency
element	Elements
margins	Elements: margins
column layout	Elements: column layout
nameplate	Elements: nameplate
location	Elements: location
logos	Elements: logos
color	Elements: color
ruled lines	Elements: ruled lines
Focus	Elements: focus
balance	Elements: balance
graphics	Graphics
images	Images
photos	Photos
Headlines	Newsletter: headlines
subheads	Newsletter: subheads
White space	White space
directional flow	Newsletter: directional flow
paper	Paper
Size	Paper: size
type	Paper: type
weight	Paper: weight
stock	Paper: stock
margin size	Newsletter: margin size

Assessment 4

CUSTOMIZE AN INDEX

1. You can customize an index with options at the Index dialog box. At a blank document, display this dialog box by clicking the REFERENCES tab and then clicking the Insert Index button in the Index group. Look at the options offered at the dialog box and determine how to change leaders and number of columns. Close the blank document.
2. Open **WL2-C6-A3-DesignNwsltr.docx** and then save the document and name it **WL2-C6-A4-DesignNwsltr**.
3. Make the following changes to the index:
   a. Display the Index dialog box for the index.
   b. Change to a format that contains leaders.
   c. Change the leaders to hyphens (rather than periods).
   d. Specify three columns.
   e. Close the Index dialog box. When asked if you want to replace the selected index, click OK.
4. Save **WL2-C6-A4-DesignNwsltr.docx**.
5. Print only the index and then close the document.

Visual Benchmark Demonstrate Your Proficiency

CREATE A TABLE OF CONTENTS AND TABLE OF FIGURES

1. Open **Networks.docx** and then save the document and name it **WL2-C6-VB-Networks**.
2. Format the document so it appears as shown in Figure 6.15 on pages 261–262 with the following specifications:
   a. Insert the captions for the figures as shown (see the third page of Figure 6.15).
   b. Insert the table of contents as shown (see the first page of Figure 6.15) using the From template format with hyphen leaders.
   c. Insert the table of figures as shown (see the second page of Figure 6.15) using the *From template* format with dot leaders.
   d. Insert page numbers at the right margins as shown (see the second and fourth pages of Figure 6.15).
3. Save, print, and then close **WL2-C6-VB-Networks.docx**.

Figure 6.15 Visual Benchmark

TABLE OF CONTENTS

Page 1

FIGURES

ii

Page 2

continues

Figure 6.15 Visual Benchmark—*Continued*

COMMUNICATIONS SYSTEMS

A computer network is one kind of communications system. This system includes sending and receiving hardware, transmission and relay systems, common sets of standards so all the equipment can "talk" to each other, and communications software.

NETWORK COMMUNICATIONS

You use such a networked communications system whenever you send/receive IM or email messages, pay a bill online, shop at an Internet store, send a document to a shared printer at work or at home, or download a file.

The world of computer network communications systems is made up of:

- Transmission media upon which the data travels to/from its destination.
- A set of standards and network protocols (rules for how data is handled as it travels along a communications channel). Devices use these to send and receive data to and from each other.
- Hardware and software to connect to a communications pathway from the sending and receiving ends.

Figure 1 Wireless Network Base

The first step in understanding a co… transmission signals and transmissi…

TYPES OF SIGNALS

Two types of signals are used to tra… digital. An analog signal is formed b… voice is transmitted as an analog si… signal uses a discrete signal that is … 1, and low represents the digital bit…

Telephone lines carry your voice usi… rather, th… signals. If … phone lin… (modulat…

Figure 2 Computer Modem

Page 3

computer on the receiving end. The piece of hardware that sends and receives data from a transmission source such as your telephone line or cable television connection is a modem. The word modem comes from the combination of the words *mo*dulate and *dem*odulate.

Today, most new communications technologies simply use a digital signal, saving the trouble of converting transmissions. An example of this trend is the demise in 2009 of analog television transmissions as the industry switched to digital signals. Many people were sent scrambling to either buy a newer television set or buy a converter to convert digital transmissions back to analog to work with their older equipment. Newer computer networks, too, use a pure digital signal method of sending and receiving data over a network.

2

Page 4

Case Study Apply Your Skills

Part 1

You work in the Human Resources department at Brennan Distributors and are responsible for preparing an employee handbook. Open the **BDEmpHandbook.docx** document and then save the document and name it **WL2-C6-CS-BDEmpHandbook**. Apply the following specifications to the document:

- Insert page breaks before each centered title (except the first title, *Introduction*).
- Apply heading styles to the titles and headings.
- Change to a style set of your choosing.
- Apply a theme that makes the handbook easy to read.
- Insert a table of contents.
- Create a concordance file with a minimum of ten entries and then insert an index.
- Insert appropriate page numbering in the document.
- Insert a cover page.
- Add any other elements to improve the appearance of the document.

Save and then print **WL2-C6-CS-BDEmpHandbook.docx**.

Part 2

Open **NavigateWeb.docx** and then save the document and name it **WL2-C6-CS-NavigateWeb**. Apply the following specifications to the document:

- Move the insertion point to any cell in the first table in the document and then use the caption feature to create the caption *Table 1: Common Top-Level Domain Suffixes*.
- Move the insertion point to any cell in the second table and then create the caption *Table 2: Common Search Tools*.
- Move the insertion point to any cell in the third table and then create the caption *Table 3: Advanced Search Parameters*.
- Insert a table of contents.
- Insert a table of figures on the page following the table of contents.
- Insert appropriate page numbering in the document.
- Check the page breaks in the document. If a heading displays at the bottom of a page and the paragraph of text that follows displays at the top of the next page, format the heading so it stays with the paragraph of text that follows. ***Hint: Do this at the Paragraph dialog box with the Line and Page Breaks tab selected.***
- If necessary, update the entire table of contents and table of figures.

Save, print, and then close **WL2-C6-CS-NavigateWeb.docx**.

Part 3

Send an email to your instructor detailing the steps you followed to create table captions. Attach **WL2-C6-CS-NavigateWeb.docx** to the email.

MICROSOFT®

WORD

Working with Shared Documents

PERFORMANCE OBJECTIVES

Upon successful completion of Chapter 7, you will be able to:

- **Insert, edit, print, and delete comments**
- **Navigate between comments**
- **Distinguish comments from different users**
- **Track changes to a document**
- **Customize Track Changes**
- **Show markup**
- **Customize markup display**
- **Navigate to revisions**
- **Accept and reject revisions**
- **Compare documents**
- **Combine documents**
- **Show source documents**
- **Embed and link data between Excel and Word**

Tutorials

7.1 Inserting and Editing Comments
7.2 Inserting Comments in the Reviewing Pane; Distinguishing Comments from Other Users
7.3 Tracking Changes in a Document
7.4 Displaying Changes for Review and Showing Markup
7.5 Customizing Track Changes Options
7.6 Comparing Documents
7.7 Combining Documents
7.8 Embedding and Linking Objects

In a company environment, you may need to share and distribute documents to other employees or associates. You may be part of a *workgroup*, which is a networked collection of computers that share files, printers, and other resources. As a member of a workgroup, you can collaborate with other members and distribute documents for review and/or revision. In this chapter, you will perform workgroup activities such as inserting comments, tracking changes from multiple users, comparing documents, and combining documents from multiple users. Model answers for this chapter's projects appear on the following pages.

If a Word 2013 document (in the .docx format) is located on a server running Microsoft SharePoint Server, multiple users can edit the document concurrently. Concurrent editing allows a group of users to work on a document at the same time or a single user to work on the same document from different computers. If a document is not located on a server running SharePoint Server, Word 2013 supports only single-user editing. Projects and assessments in this chapter assume that the files you are editing are not located on a server running SharePoint Server.

Note: Before beginning the projects, copy to your storage medium the WL2C7 subfolder from the WL2 folder on the CD that accompanies this textbook and then make WL2C7 the active folder.

WL2-C7-P1-OMSNewEmps.docx

Main document changes and comments

Page 1: Commented	Student Name	1/6/2015 2:49:00 PM

Please include the total number of orientation hours.

Page 1: Commented	Taylor Stanton	1/6/2015 3:15:00 PM

Check with Barb on the total number of orientation hours.

Page 2: Commented	Student Name	1/6/2015 2:56:00 PM

Please include in this section the maximum probationary period, if any.

Page 2: Commented	Taylor Stanton	1/6/2015 3:11:00 PM

Provide additional information on performance evaluation documentation.

Header and footer changes

Text Box changes

Header and footer text box changes

Footnote changes

Endnote changes

Project 1 Insert Comments in a New Employees Document

WL2-C7-P1-OMSNewEmps.docx

BUILDING CONSTRUCTION AGREEMENT

THIS AGREEMENT made this ____________________ day of ______________________, 2015, by and between __________________, hereinafter referred to as "builder," and __________________, hereinafter referred to as "owner," the builder and the owner, for the considerations hereinafter named, agree as follows:

Construction Loan and Financing Arrangements: The owner either has or will obtain a construction loan to finance the work to be performed under this Agreement. If adequate financing has not been arranged within sixty (60) days of the date of this Agreement, or the owner cannot provide evidence to the builder of other financial ability to pay the full amount of the contract, then the builder at his option may treat this Agreement as null and void, and retain the down payment made on the execution of this Agreement.

Supervision of Work: Owner agrees that the direction and supervision of the working force including subcontractor, rests exclusively with the builder or his/her duly designated agent, and owner agrees not to issue any instructions to, or otherwise interfere with, same.

Start of Construction: The builder shall commence construction of the residence as soon as practical after signing of this Agreement and adequate financial arrangements satisfactory to the builder have been made.

Changes and Alterations: All changes in or departures from the plans and/or specifications shall be in writing. Where changes in or departures from plans and specifications requested in writing by owner will result in furnishing of additional labor and materials, the owner shall pay the builder for such extras at a price agreed upon in writing before commencement of said change. Where such change results in the omitting of any labor or materials, the builder shall allow the owner a credit therefore at a price agreed to in writing before commencement of said changes.

Possession of Residence: On final payment by owner and upon owner's request, builder will provide owner with affidavit stating that all labor, materials, and equipment used in the construction have been paid for or will be paid for in full by the builder unless otherwise noted. Builder shall not be required to give possession of the residence to the owner before final payment by owner. Final payment constitutes acceptance of the residence as being satisfactorily completed unless a separate escrow agreement is executed between the parties stipulating the unfinished items.

Exclusions: The owner is solely responsible for the purchase and installation of any septic tank or other individual subsurface sewage disposal system that may be required on the property.

Builder's Right to Terminate the Contract: Should the work be stopped by any public authority for a period of sixty (60) days or more, through no fault of the builder, or should the work be stopped through act or neglect of the owner for a period of seven days, or should the owner fail to pay the builder any payment within seven days after it is due, then the builder upon seven days written notice to the owner,

Page 1

may stop work or terminate the contract and recover from the owner payment for all work executed and any loss sustained and reasonable profit and damages.

The owner acknowledges that she/he has read and fully understands the provisions of this Agreement.

IN WITNESS WHEREOF, the builder and owner have hereunto set their hands this _____ day of ____________________, 20____.

______________________	______________________
BUILDER	OWNER

Page 2

Project 2 Track Changes in a Building Construction Agreement

WL2-C7-P2-Agreement.docx

COMMERCIAL LEASE AGREEMENT

This Commercial Lease Agreement ("Lease") is made by and between ____________________ ("Landlord") and ____________________ ("Tenant"). Landlord is the owner of land and improvements commonly known and numbered as ______________________________ and legally described as follows (the "Building"): ____ ____. Landlord makes available for lease a portion of the Building designated as ______________________________ (the "Leased Premises").

Landlord desires to lease the Leased Premises to Tenant, and Tenant desires to lease the Leased Premises from Landlord for the term at the rental, and upon the covenants, conditions, and provisions herein set forth.

THEREFORE, in consideration of the mutual promises herein contained, and other good and valuable consideration, it is agreed:

Term

A. Landlord hereby leases the Leased Premises to Tenant, and Tenant hereby leases the same from Landlord, for an "Initial Term" beginning ______________ and ending ______________. Landlord shall use his/her best efforts to give Tenant possession as nearly as possible at the beginning of the Lease term. If Landlord is unable to timely provide the Leased Premises, rent shall abate for the period of delay. Tenant shall make no other claim against Landlord for any such delay.

B. Tenant may renew the Lease for one extended term of ____________________. Tenant shall exercise such renewal option by giving written notice to Landlord not less than ninety (90) days prior to the expiration of the Initial Term. The renewal term shall be at the rental set forth below and otherwise upon the same covenants, conditions, and provisions as provided in this Lease.

Rental

A. Tenant shall pay to Landlord during the Initial Term rental of ____________________ per year, payable in installments of ____________________ per month. Each installment payment shall be due in advance on the first day of each calendar month during the lease term to Landlord at ______________________________ or at such other place designated by written notice from Landlord or Tenant. The rental payment amount for any partial calendar months included in the lease term shall be prorated on a daily basis. Tenant shall also pay to Landlord a "Security Deposit" in the amount of ____________________.

B. The rental for any renewal lease term, if created as permitted under this Lease, shall be ____________________ per year payable in installments of ____________________ per month.

Page 1

Use

Notwithstanding the forgoing, Tenant shall not use the Leased Premises for the purposes of storing, manufacturing, or selling any explosives, flammables, or other inherently dangerous substance, chemical, item, or device.

Repairs

During the Lease term, Tenant shall make, at Tenant's expense, all necessary repairs to the Leased Premises. Repairs shall include such items as routine repairs of floors, walls, ceilings, and other parts of the Leased Premises damaged or worn through normal occupancy, except for major mechanical systems or the roof, subject to the obligations of the parties otherwise set forth in this Lease.

Sublease and Assignment

Tenant shall have the right, without Landlord's consent, to assign this Lease to a corporation with which Tenant may merge or consolidate, to any subsidiary of Tenant, to any corporation under common control with Tenant, or to a purchaser of substantially all of Tenant's assets. Except as set forth above, Tenant shall not sublease all or any part of the Leased Premises, or assign this Lease in whole or in part without Landlord's consent, such consent not to be unreasonably withheld or delayed.

Property Taxes

Landlord shall pay all general real estate taxes and installments of special assessments coming due during the Lease term on the Leased Premises, and all personal property taxes with respect to Landlord's personal property, if any, on the Leased Premises. Tenant shall be responsible for paying all personal property taxes with respect to Tenant's personal property at the Leased Premises.

____

Landlord

____

Tenant

Page 2

Project 3 Compare Lease Agreement Documents

WL2-C7-P3-ComAgrmnt.docx

LEASE AGREEMENT

THIS LEASE AGREEMENT (hereinafter referred to as the "Agreement") is made and entered into this ____ day of ______________, 2015, by and between Lessor and Lessee.

Term

Lessor leases to Lessee and Lessee leases from Lessor the described Premises together with any and all appurtenances thereto, for a term of _____ year(s), such term beginning on ________________, and ending at midnight on ______________.

Damage Deposit

Upon the signing of this Agreement, Lessee shall deposit with Lessor the sum of ____________ DOLLARS ($_________) receipt of which is hereby acknowledged by Lessor, as security for any damage caused to the Premises during the leasing term. Such deposit shall be returned to Lessee, without interest ,upon the termination of this leasing Agreement.

Rent

The total rent for the term hereof is the sum of ______________ DOLLARS ($_________) less any reimbursements and payable on the ______ day of each month of the term. All such payments shall be made to Lessor at Lessor's address on or before the due date and without demand.

Use of Premises

The Premises shall be used and occupied by Lessee and Lessee's immediate family, exclusively, as a private, single-family dwelling, and no part of the Premises shall be used at any time during the term of this Agreement by Lessee for the purpose of carrying on any business, profession, or trade of any kind, or for any purpose other than as a private, single-family dwelling. Lessee shall not allow any other person, other than Lessee's immediate family or transient relatives and friends who are guests of Lessee, to use or occupy the Premises without first obtaining Lessor's written consent to such use.

Condition of Premises

Lessee stipulates, represents, and warrants that Lessee has examined the Premises, and that they are at the time of this Agreement in good order, repair, and in a safe, clean, and tenantable condition.

Alterations and Improvements

Lessee shall make no alterations to or improvements on the Premises without the prior written consent of Lessor. Any and all alterations, changes, and/or improvements built, constructed, or placed on the Premises by Lessee shall be and become the property of the Lessor and remain on the Premises at the expiration or earlier termination of this Agreement.

Page 1

Damage to Premises

In the event Premises are destroyed or rendered wholly unlivable by fire, storm, earthquake, or other casualty not caused by the negligence of Lessee, this Agreement shall terminate from such time except for the purpose of enforcing rights that may have accrued hereunder.

____

LESSEE

____

LESSOR

Page 2

Project 4 Combine Documents

WL2-C7-P4-CombinedLease.docx

Dearborn Industries

Revenues

Company revenues increased in 2015 as a result of development contracts with government entities focused on the design of flywheel technologies. Several development prototypes were produced and placed with potential customers and shipped and preproduction units have shipped. The increase in revenues is reflected in the following table:

Customer	1st Qtr	2nd Qtr	3rd Qtr	4th Qtr	Total
Lakeside Trucking	$ 69,450	$ 75,340	$ 88,224	$ 95,000	$ 328,014
Gresham Machines	25,210	28,340	33,400	43,199	130,149
Manchester County	30,219	28,590	34,264	40,891	133,964
Genesis Productions	35,290	51,390	59,334	72,190	218,204
Landower Company	12,168	19,355	25,209	262,188	318,920
Jewell Enterprises	24,329	21,809	33,490	49,764	129,392
Total	$ 196,666	$ 224,824	$ 273,921	$ 563,232	$ 1,258,643

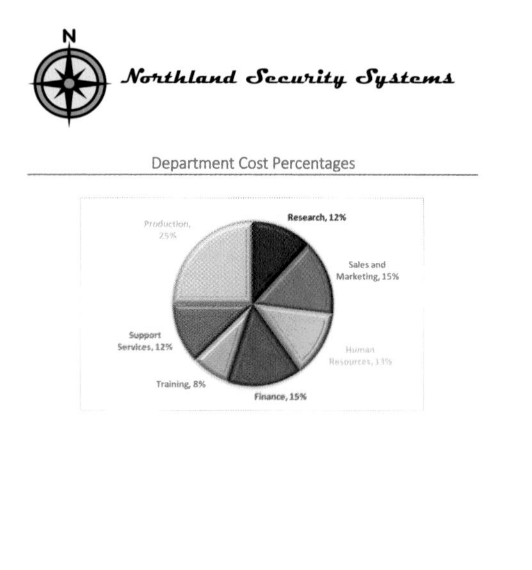

Project 5 Embed and Link Data between Excel and Word

WL2-C7-P5-DIRevs.docx

WL2-C7-P5-NSSCosts.docx

Project 1 Insert Comments in a New Employees Document — 4 Parts

You will open a report containing company information for new employees and then insert and edit comments from multiple users.

Inserting and Managing Comments

Quick Steps

Insert a Comment
1. Select text.
2. Click REVIEW tab.
3. Click New Comment button.
4. Type comment.

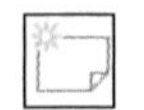

New Comment

HINT Use comments to add notes, suggestions, or explanations, and to communicate with members of your workgroup.

You can provide feedback on and suggest changes to a document that someone else has written by inserting comments into it. Similarly, you can obtain feedback on a document that you have written by distributing it electronically to others and having them insert their comments into it.

To insert a comment in a document, select the text or item on which you want to comment or position the insertion point at the end of the text, click the REVIEW tab, and then click the New Comment button in the Comments group. This displays a comment balloon at the right margin, as shown in Figure 7.1.

Depending on any previous settings applied, clicking the New Comment button may cause the Reviewing pane to display at the left side of the document, rather than the comment balloon. If this happens, click the Show Markup button in the Tracking group on the REVIEW tab, point to *Balloons*, and then click *Show Only Comments and Formatting in Balloons* at the side menu. Also, check to make sure the Display for Review button in the Tracking group is set to *Simple Markup*. If it is not, click the Display for Review button arrow and then click *Simple Markup* at the drop-down list.

Figure 7.1 Comment Balloon

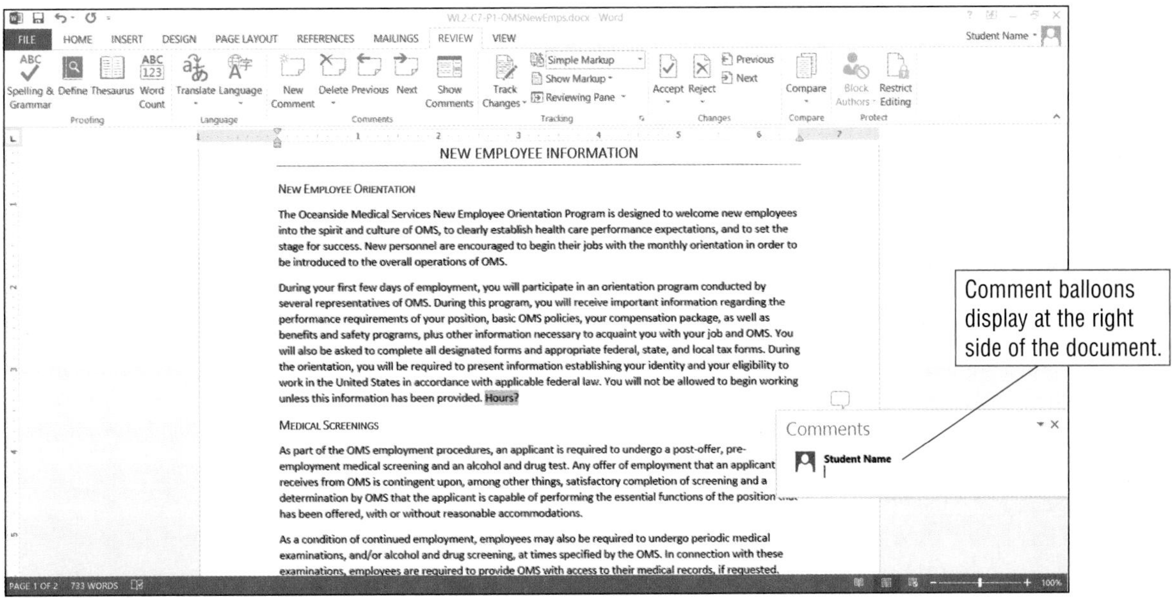

Project 1a Inserting Comments

Part 1 of 4

1. Open **OMSNewEmps.docx** and then save the document and name it **WL2-C7-P1-OMSNewEmps**.
2. Insert a comment by completing the following steps:
   a. Position the insertion point at the end of the second paragraph in the *NEW EMPLOYEE ORIENTATION* section.
   b. Press the spacebar once and then type **Hours?**.
   c. Select *Hours?*.
   d. Click the REVIEW tab.
   e. If the Show Comments button in the Comments group is active (displays with a blue background), click the button to deactivate it.
   f. Click the New Comment button in the Comments group.
   g. Type **Please include the total number of orientation hours.** in the comment balloon.

Step 2d

Step 2f

Steps 2b-2c

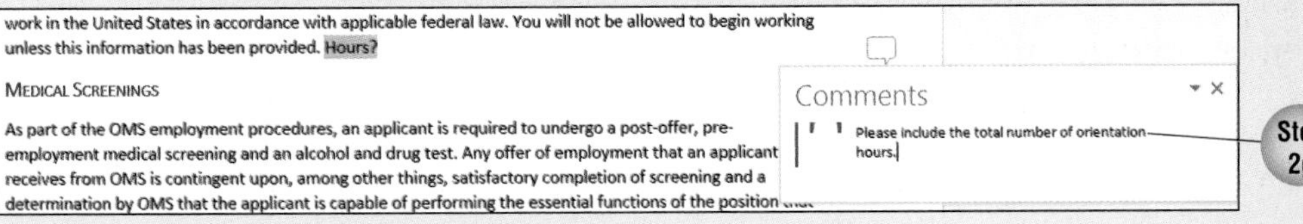

3. Insert another comment by completing the following steps:
   a. Move the insertion point to the end of the third (last) paragraph in the *MEDICAL SCREENINGS* section.
   b. Click the New Comment button in the Comments group.
   c. Type **Specify the locations where drug tests are administered.** in the comment balloon. (Since you did not have text selected when you clicked the New Comment button, Word selected the word immediately left of the insertion point).
   d. Click in the document to close the comment balloons.
4. Save **WL2-C7-P1-OMSNewEmps.docx**.

Inserting Comments in the Reviewing Pane

Quick Steps

Insert a Comment in the Reviewing Pane

1. Click REVIEW tab.
2. Click Reviewing Pane button.
3. Click New Comment button.
4. Type comment.

Reviewing Pane

If your computer has a sound card and microphone, you can record voice comments.

You may prefer to insert comments with the Reviewing pane displayed on the screen. The Reviewing pane displays inserted comments as well as changes recorded with the Track Changes feature. (You will learn about Track Changes later in this chapter.)

To display the Reviewing pane, click the Reviewing Pane button in the Tracking group on the REVIEW tab. The Reviewing pane usually displays at the left side of the screen, as shown in Figure 7.2. Click the New Comment button in the Comments group and a comment icon and balloon displays in the right margin and the reviewer's name followed by "Commented" displays in the Reviewing pane. Type your comment and the text displays in the comment balloon as well as the Reviewing pane. (The Reviewing pane might display along the bottom of the screen, rather than at the left side. To specify where you want the pane to display, click the Reviewing Pane button arrow in the Tracking group on the REVIEW tab and then click *Reviewing Pane Vertical* or *Reviewing Pane Horizontal*.)

A summary displays toward the top of the Reviewing pane and provides counts of the number of comments inserted and the types of changes that have been made to the document. After typing your comment in the Reviewing pane, close the pane by clicking the Reviewing Pane button in the Tracking group or by clicking the Close button (marked with an X) located in the upper right corner of the pane.

Figure 7.2 Vertical Reviewing Pane

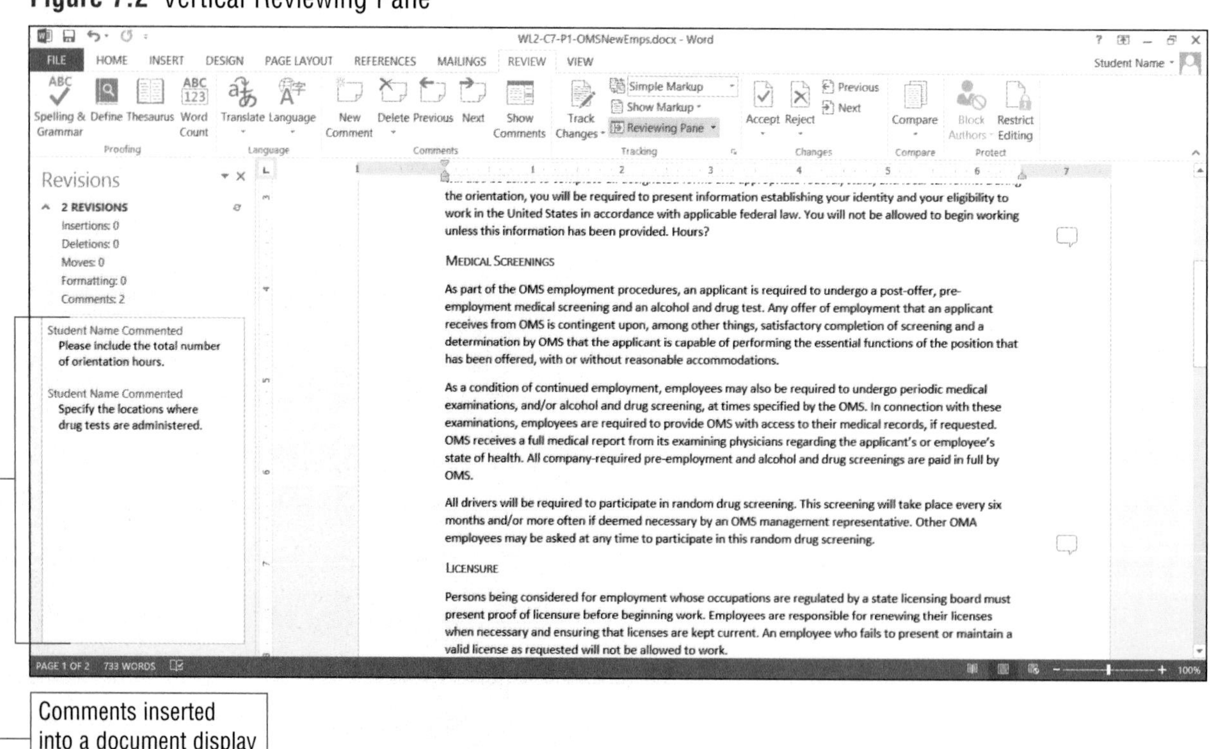

Comments inserted into a document display in this section of the Reviewing pane.

Project 1b Inserting a Comment in the Reviewing Pane Part 2 of 4

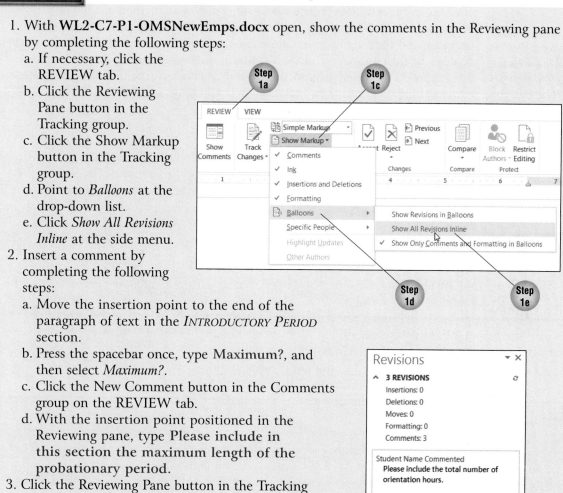

1. With **WL2-C7-P1-OMSNewEmps.docx** open, show the comments in the Reviewing pane by completing the following steps:
   a. If necessary, click the REVIEW tab.
   b. Click the Reviewing Pane button in the Tracking group.
   c. Click the Show Markup button in the Tracking group.
   d. Point to *Balloons* at the drop-down list.
   e. Click *Show All Revisions Inline* at the side menu.
2. Insert a comment by completing the following steps:
   a. Move the insertion point to the end of the paragraph of text in the *INTRODUCTORY PERIOD* section.
   b. Press the spacebar once, type **Maximum?**, and then select *Maximum?*.
   c. Click the New Comment button in the Comments group on the REVIEW tab.
   d. With the insertion point positioned in the Reviewing pane, type **Please include in this section the maximum length of the probationary period.**
3. Click the Reviewing Pane button in the Tracking group to turn off the display of the Reviewing pane.
4. Save **WL2-C7-P1-OMSNewEmps.docx**.

Navigating between Comments

When working in a long document with many comments, use the Previous and Next buttons in the Comments group on the REVIEW tab to move easily from comment to comment. Click the Next button to move the insertion point to the next comment or click the Previous button to move the insertion point to the preceding comment.

Previous

Next

Quick Steps

Edit a Comment
1. Click REVIEW tab.
2. Click Reviewing Pane button.
3. Click in desired comment in pane.
4. Make desired changes.

OR

1. Click REVIEW tab.
2. Turn on display of comment balloons.
3. Click in comment balloon.
4. Make desired changes.

Editing Comments

You can edit a comment in the Reviewing pane or in a comment balloon. To edit a comment in the Reviewing pane, click the Reviewing Pane button to turn on the pane and then click in the comment that you want to edit. Make the desired changes to the comment and then close the Reviewing pane. To edit a comment in a comment balloon, turn on the display of comment balloons, click in the comment balloon, and then make the desired changes.

Showing Comments

The Comments group on the REVIEW tab contains a Show Comments button. Click this button and comments display at the right side of the document. The Show Comments button is available only when the Display for Review button in the Tracking group is set to *Simple Markup*.

Project 1c Editing Comments — Part 3 of 4

1. With **WL2-C7-P1-OMSNewEmps.docx** open, navigate from one comment to another by completing the following steps:
   a. Press Ctrl + Home to move the insertion point to the beginning of the document.
   b. If necessary, click the REVIEW tab.
   c. Click the Next button in the Comments group. (This moves the insertion point to the first comment reference, opens the Reviewing pane, and inserts the insertion point in the pane.)
   d. Click the Next button to display the second comment.
   e. Click the Next button to display the third comment.
   f. Click the Previous button to display the second comment.
2. With the insertion point positioned in the Reviewing pane, edit the second comment to read: *Specify the locations within OMS where drug tests are administered as well as any off-site locations.*
3. Click the Reviewing Pane button to close the pane.
4. Edit a comment in a comment balloon by completing the following steps:
   a. Click the Show Markup button in the Tracking group, point to *Balloons*, and then click *Show Only Comments and Formatting in Balloons* at the side menu.
   b. Click the Show Comments button in the Comments group to display the balloons at the right side of the document.
   c. Display the paragraph of text in the *Introductory Period* section and then click in the comment balloon that displays at the right.
   d. Edit the comment so it displays as follows: *Please include in this section the maximum probationary period, if any.*

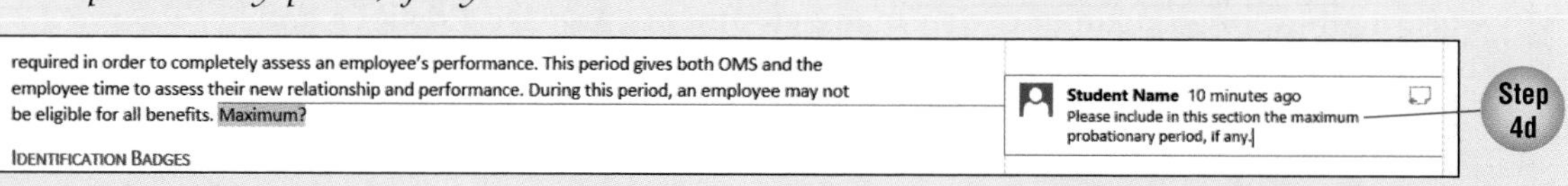

   e. Click in the document and then click the Show Comments button to turn off the display of comment balloons.
   f. Click the Show Markup button, point to *Balloons*, and then click *Show All Revisions Inline*.
5. Save **WL2-C7-P1-OMSNewEmps.docx**.

Distinguishing Comments from Different Users

More than one user can make comments in the same document. Word uses different colors to distinguish comments made by different users, generally displaying the first user's comments in red and the second user's comments in blue. (These colors may vary.)

You can change the user name and initials at the Word Options dialog box with *General* selected, as shown in Figure 7.3. To change the user name, select the name that displays in the *User name* text box and then type the desired name. Complete similar steps to change the user initials in the *Initials* text box. You may also need to insert a check mark in the *Always use these values regardless of sign in to Office.* check box.

Replying to Comments

When reviewing a document, you may want to reply to other people's comments. To reply to a comment, open the comment balloon, hover the mouse over the comment text, and then click the Reply button that displays to the right of the reviewer's name. Type the reply in the window that opens below the comment. You can also click in a comment and then click the New Comment button in the Comments group or right-click in a comment and then click *Reply to Comments* at the shortcut menu.

Printing Comments

To print a document with the comments, display the Print backstage area and then click the first gallery in the *Settings* category (which is the gallery containing the text *Print All Pages*). At the drop-down list, insert a check mark before the *Print Markup* option if you want to print the document with the comments. If you want to print the document without the comments, click *Print Markup* to remove the check mark. If you want to print only the comments and not the document, click *List of Markup* at the drop-down list. This prints the contents of the Reviewing pane, which may include comments, tracked changes, and changes to headers, footers, text boxes, footnotes, and endnotes.

Quick Steps

Change the User Name and Initials
1. Click FILE tab.
2. Click *Options.*
3. Type desired name in *User name* text box.
4. Type desired initials in *Initials* text box.
5. Click OK.

Reply to a Comment
1. Open comment balloon.
2. Hover mouse over comment text.
3. Click Reply button.
4. Type reply in reply window.

Print a Document with the Comments
1. Click FILE tab, *Print* option.
2. Click first gallery in *Settings* category.
3. If necessary, click *Print Markup* to insert check mark.
4. Click Print button.

Print Only the Comments
1. Click FILE tab, *Print* option.
2. Click first gallery in *Settings* category.
3. Click *List of Markup.*
4. Click Print button.

Figure 7.3 Word Options Dialog Box with *General* Selected

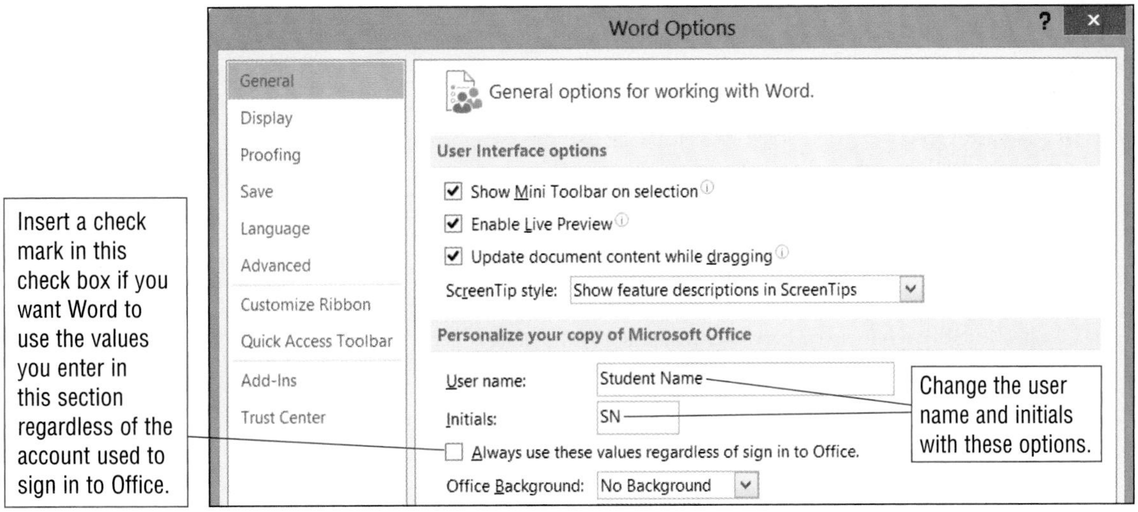

Deleting Comments

Quick Steps

Delete a Comment
1. Click REVIEW tab.
2. Click Next button until desired comment is selected.
3. Click Delete button.

Delete

Delete a comment by clicking the Next button in the Comments group on the REVIEW tab until the desired comment is selected and then clicking the Delete button in the Comments group. If you want to delete all of the comments in a document, click the Delete button arrow and then click *Delete All Comments in Document* at the drop-down list. A comment can also be dimmed in a document without being deleted. To dim a comment, right-click the comment and then click *Mark Comment Done* at the shortcut menu.

Project 1d **Changing User Information and Inserting and Deleting Comments** **Part 4 of 4**

1. With **WL2-C7-P1-OMSNewEmps.docx** open, change the user information by completing the following steps:
   a. Click the FILE tab.
   b. Click *Options*.
   c. At the Word Options dialog box, make sure *General* is selected in the left panel.
   d. Make a note of the current name and initials in the *Personalize your copy of Microsoft Office* section.
   e. Select the name displayed in the *User name* text box and then type **Taylor Stanton**.
   f. Select the initials displayed in the *Initials* text box and then type **TS**.
   g. Click the *Always use these values regardless of sign in to Office* check box to insert a check mark.
   h. Click OK to close the Word Options dialog box.

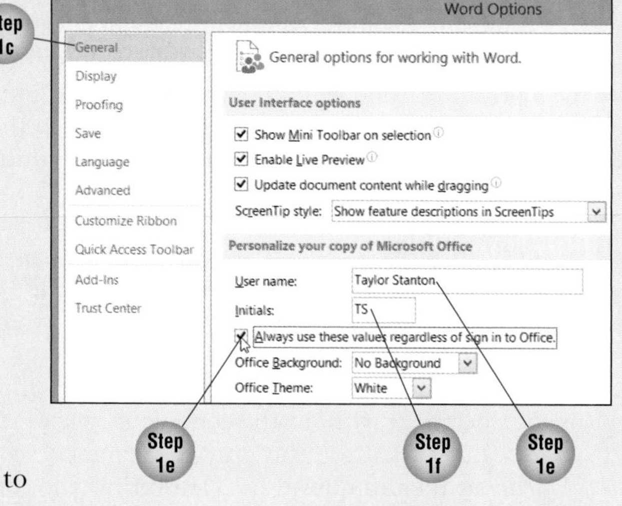

2. Insert a comment by completing the following steps:
   a. Move the insertion point to the end of the first paragraph of text in the PERFORMANCE REVIEW section.
   b. Click the New Comment button in the Comments group on the REVIEW tab.
   c. Type **Provide additional information on performance evaluation documentation.** in the Reviewing pane.
   d. Click the Reviewing Pane button to close the pane.

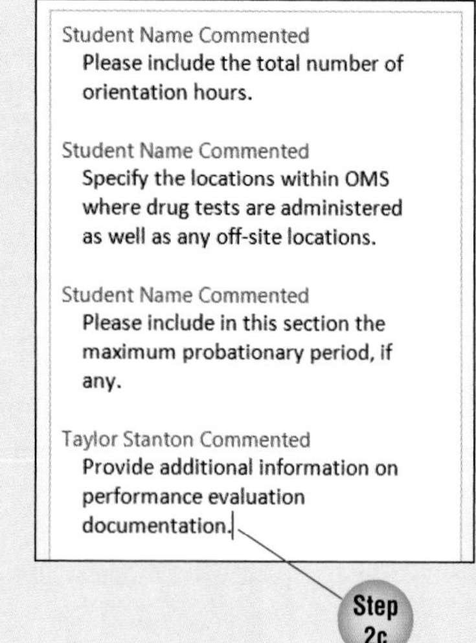

3. Respond to a comment by completing the following steps:
   a. Press Ctrl + Home to move the insertion point to the beginning of the document.
   b. Click the Show Markup button, point to *Balloons*, and then click *Show Only Comments and Formatting in Balloons* at the drop-down list.
   c. Click the Next button in the Comments group. (This opens the comment balloon for the first comment.)

d. Click the Reply button that displays to the right of the reviewer's name in the comment balloon.

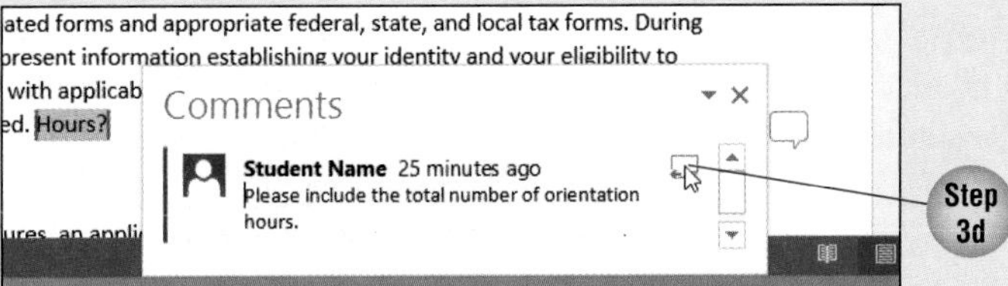

e. Type **Check with Barb on the total number of orientation hours.**

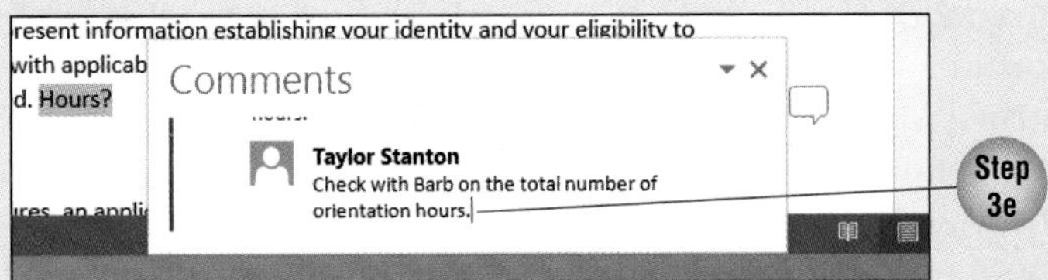

f. Click in the document to close the comment balloon.

4. Print only the information in the Reviewing pane by completing the following steps:
   a. Click the FILE tab and then click the *Print* option. (You can also display the Print backstage area by pressing Ctrl + P.)
   b. At the Print backstage area, click the first gallery in the *Settings* category and then click *List of Markup* in the *Document Info* section of the drop-down list.
   c. Click the Print button.

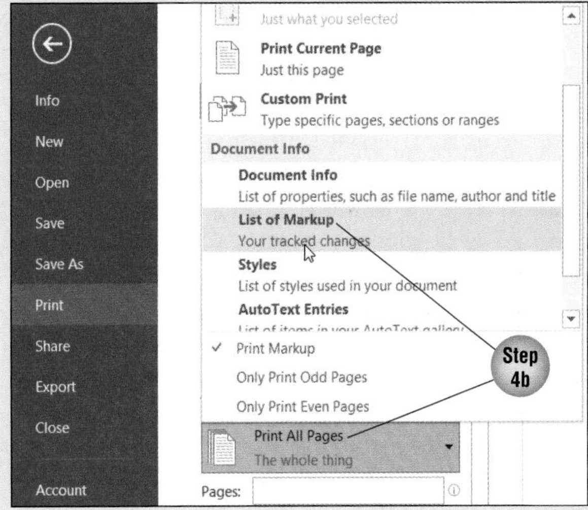

5. Delete a comment by completing the following steps:
   a. Press Ctrl + Home.
   b. If necessary, click the REVIEW tab.
   c. Click the Next button in the Comments group.
   d. Click the Next button again.
   e. Click the Next button again.
   f. Click the Delete button in the Comments group.

6. Print only the information in the Reviewing pane by completing Step 4.
7. Change the user information back to the default settings by completing the following steps:
   a. Click the FILE tab and then click *Options*.
   b. At the Word Options dialog box with *General* selected, select *Taylor Stanton* in the *User name* text box and then type the original name.
   c. Select the initials *TS* in the *Initials* text box and then type the original initials.
   d. Click the *Always use these values regardless of sign in to Office* check box to remove the check mark.
   e. Click OK to close the dialog box.
8. Save and then close **WL2-C7-P1-OMSNewEmps.docx**.

Project 2 Track Changes in a Building Construction Agreement 4 Parts

You will open a building construction agreement, turn on Track Changes, and then make changes to the document. You will also customize Track Changes and accept and reject changes.

Tracking Changes in a Document

Quick Steps
Turn on Track Changes
1. Click REVIEW tab.
2. Click Track Changes button.
OR
Press Ctrl + Shift + E.

Track Changes

Display for Review

Each of the four options at the Display for Review button drop-down list displays a document at various stages in the editing process.

If more than one person in a work group needs to review and edit a document, consider using the Track Changes feature in Word. When Track Changes is turned on, Word tracks each deletion, insertion, and formatting change made in a document. Turn on Track Changes by clicking the REVIEW tab and then clicking the Track Changes button in the Tracking group or by pressing the keyboard shortcut Ctrl + Shift + E. Turn off Track Changes by completing the same steps.

Displaying Changes for Review

The Display for Review button in the Tracking group on the REVIEW tab has a default setting of *Simple Markup*. At this setting, any changes you make to the document display in the document and Word inserts a vertical change line in the left margin next to the line of text in which the change was made. To see the changes, click the Display for Review button and then click the *All Markup* option.

With *All Markup* selected, all of the changes display in the document. For example, if you delete text, it stays in the document but displays in a different color with a line through it. You can also turn on the display of all markup by clicking one of the vertical change lines that display in at the left margin next to changes that have been made or by clicking a comment balloon.

If you have made tracked changes to a document, you can preview what the final document will look like with the changes applied by clicking the Display for Review button and then clicking *No Markup* at the drop-down list. This displays the document with the changes made but does not actually make the changes to the document. If you want to see the original document without any changes marked, click the Display for Review button and then click *Original* at the drop-down list.

Showing Markup

Show Markup

If the *Markup Area Highlight* option is active, the margin area where all of the balloons appear is highlighted.

With the display of all markup turned on, specify what tracking information displays in the body of the document with options at the Balloons side menu. To show all of the revisions in balloons in the right margin, click the Show Markup button, point to *Balloons*, and then click *Show Revisions in Balloons* at the side menu. Click *Show All Revisions Inline* to display all of the changes in the document with vertical change lines in the left margin next to the lines of text in which changes have been made. Click the *Show Only Comments and Formatting in Balloons* option at the side menu and insertions and deletions display in the text while comments and formatting changes display in balloons in the right margin.

Project 2a Tracking Changes in a Document Part 1 of 4

1. Open **Agreement.docx** and then save the document and name it **WL2-C7-P2-Agreement**.
2. Turn on Track Changes by clicking the REVIEW tab and then clicking the Track Changes button in the Tracking group.
3. Type the word **BUILDING** between the words *THIS* and *AGREEMENT* in the first paragraph of text in the document.

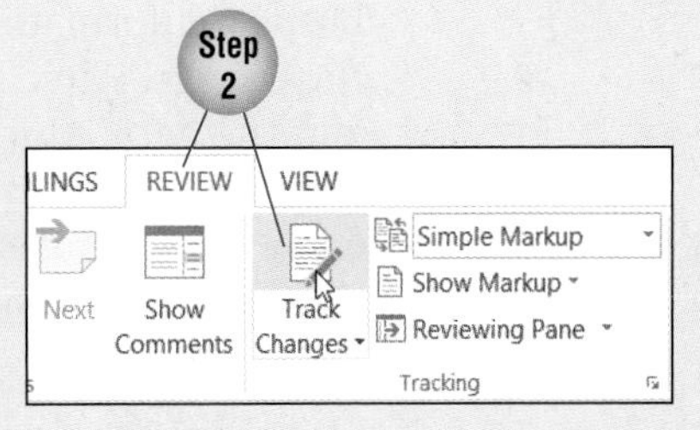

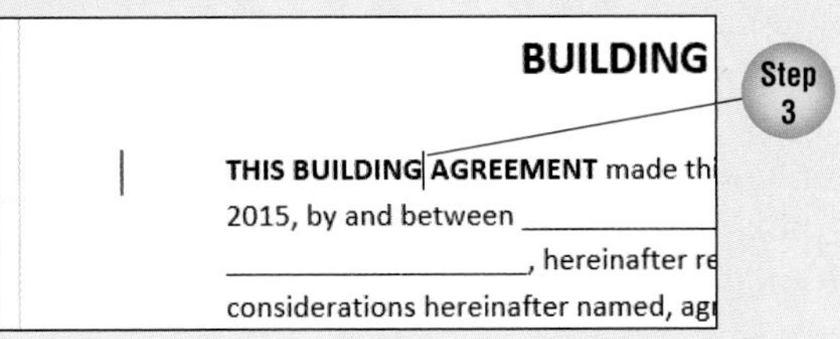

4. Show all markup by clicking the Display for Review button in the Tracking group on the REVIEW tab and then clicking *All Markup* at the drop-down list. (Notice that the text *BUILDING* is underlined and displays in red in the document.)
5. Select and then delete *thirty (30)* in the second paragraph. (The deleted text displays with a strikethrough in the document.)
6. Type sixty (60).

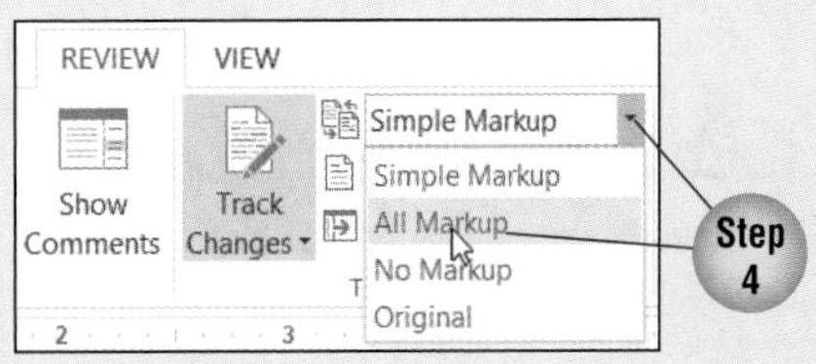

7. Move a paragraph of text by completing the following steps:
   a. Select the paragraph of text that begins *Supervision of Work*, including the blank line below the paragraph.
   b. Press Ctrl + X to cut the text. (The text stays in the document and displays in red with strikethroughs across it.)
   c. Position the insertion point immediately before the word *Start* (in the paragraph that begins *Start of Construction and Completion:*).
   d. Press Ctrl + V to paste the cut text in the new location. The inserted text displays in green with a double underline. Notice that the text in the original location changes to green with double-strikethrough characters.)
8. Turn off Track Changes by clicking the Track Changes button in the Tracking group.
9. Display revisions in balloons by clicking the Show Markup button, pointing to *Balloons*, and then clicking *Show Revisions in Balloons* at the side menu.
10. After looking at the revisions in balloons, click the Show Markup button, point to *Balloons*, and then click *Show All Revisions Inline* at the side menu.
11. Save **WL2-C7-P2-Agreement.docx**.

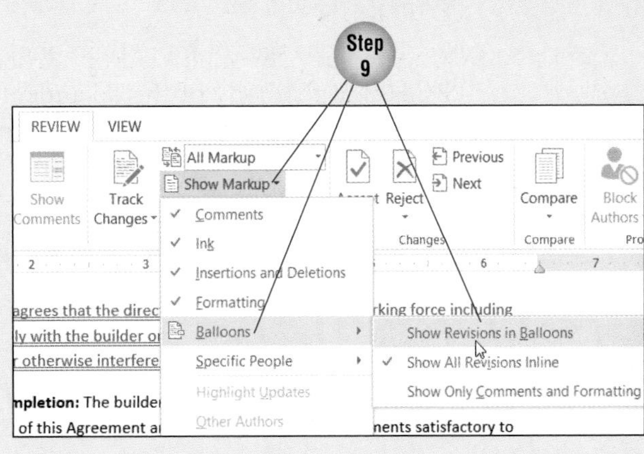

Displaying Information about Tracked Changes

Display information about a tracked change by hovering the mouse pointer over the change. After approximately one second, a box containing the author's name and the date, time, and type of change (for example, whether it was a deletion or insertion) displays above the change. You can also display information on tracked changes by displaying the Reviewing pane. Each change is listed separately in the Reviewing pane.

Changing User Information

Word uses a different color for each person (up to eight) who makes changes to a document. This color coding allows anyone looking at the document to identify which user made which changes. In the *Distinguishing Comments from Different Users* section earlier in this chapter, you learned how to change the user name and initials at the Word Options dialog box. In Project 2b, you will change the user name and initials and then make additional tracked changes.

Locking Track Changes

Quick Steps

Lock Track Changes
1. Click REVIEW tab.
2. Click Track Changes button arrow.
3. Click *Lock Tracking*.
4. Type password.
5. Press Tab.
6. Type password.
7. Click OK.

If you want to ensure that all changes to a document will be tracked, lock tracking so that it cannot be turned off. To do this, click the Track Changes button arrow and then click *Lock Tracking* at the drop-down list. At the Lock Tracking dialog box, type a password, press the Tab key, type the password again, and then click OK. Unlock tracking by clicking the Track Changes button arrow and then clicking *Lock Tracking*. At the Unlock Tracking dialog box, type the password and then click OK.

Customizing Markup Display

Customize which tracked changes display in a document with options at the Show Markup button drop-down list. If you want to show only one particular type of tracked change, remove the check marks before all of the options except the desired one. For example, if you want to view only formatting changes and not other types of changes, such as insertions and deletions, remove the check mark before each option except *Formatting*. In addition to the Show Markup button drop-down list, you can customize which tracked changes display with options at the Track Changes Options dialog box, shown in Figure 7.4. Display this dialog box by clicking the Tracking group dialog box launcher.

If the changes of more than one reviewer have been tracked in a document, you can choose to view only the changes of a particular reviewer. To do this, click the Show Markup button, point to *Specific People* at the drop-down list, then click the *All Reviewers* check box to remove the check mark. Click the Show Markup button, point to *Reviewers*, and then click the check box of the desired reviewer.

Figure 7.4 Track Changes Options Dialog Box

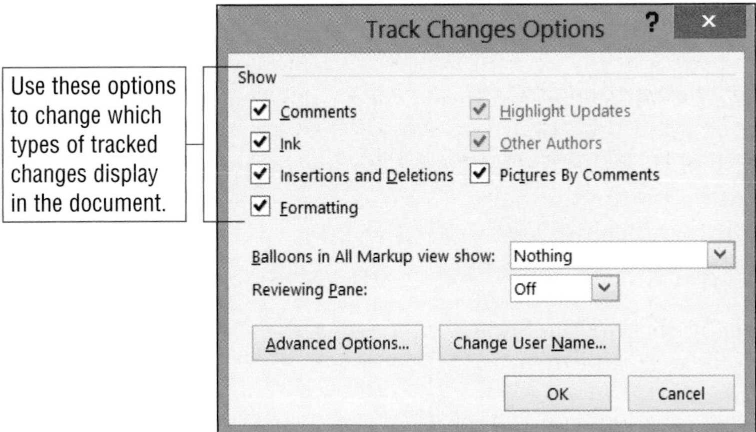

Project 2b Changing User Information and Tracking Changes

Part 2 of 4

1. With **WL2-C7-P2-Agreement.docx** open, change the user information by completing the following steps:
   a. Click the FILE tab and then click *Options*.
   b. At the Word Options dialog box with *General* selected, select the current name in the *User name* text box and then type **Julia Moore**.
   c. Select the initials in the *Initials* text box and then type **JM**.
   d. Click in the *Always use these values regardless of sign in to Office.* check box to insert a check mark.
   e. Click OK to close the dialog box.
2. Make additional changes to the contract and track the changes by completing the following steps:
   a. Click the Track Changes button on the REVIEW tab to turn on tracking.
   b. Select the title *BUILDING CONSTRUCTION AGREEMENT* and then change the font size to 14 points.
   c. Delete the text *at his option* (located in the second sentence in the second paragraph).
   d. Delete the text *and Completion* (which displays near the beginning of the fourth paragraph).

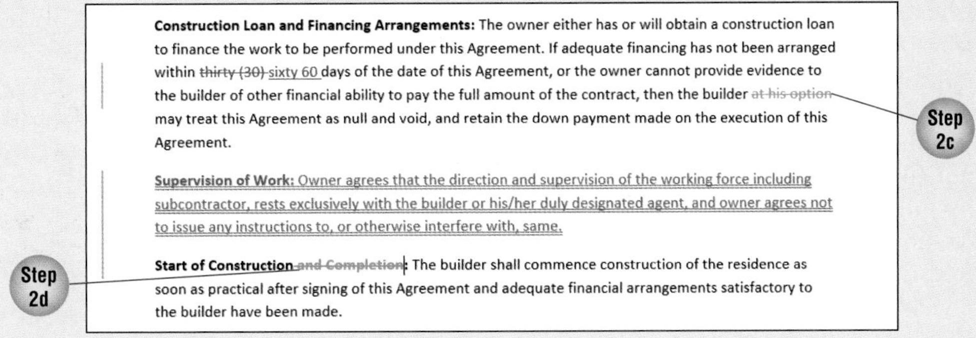

e. Delete *thirty (30)* in the paragraph that begins *Builder's Right to Terminate the Contract:* (located on the second page).
f. Type sixty (60).
g. Select the text *IN WITNESS WHEREOF* that displays near the bottom of the document and then turn on bold formatting.

3. Click the REVIEW tab and then click the Track Changes button to turn off tracking.
4. Click the Reviewing Pane button to turn on the display of the Reviewing pane and then use the vertical scroll bar at the right side of the Reviewing pane to review the changes.

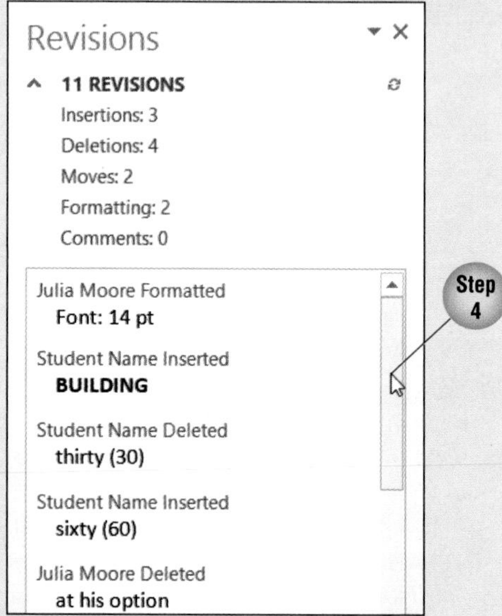

5. View the changes in balloons by clicking the Show Markup button, pointing to *Balloons*, and then clicking *Show Revisions in Balloons*.
6. Click the Reviewing Pane button to turn off the display of the pane.
7. Scroll through the document and view the changes in the balloons.
8. Click the Show Markup button, point to *Balloons*, and then click *Show All Revisions Inline* at the side menu.
9. Change the user information back to the information that displayed before you typed *Julia Moore* and the initials *JM* by completing the following steps:
   a. Click the FILE tab and then click *Options*.
   b. At the Word Options dialog box, select *Julia Moore* in the *User name* text box and then type the original name.
   c. Select the initials *JM* in the *Initials* text box and then type the original initials.
   d. Click in the *Always use these values regardless of sign in to Office.* check box to remove the check mark.
   e. Click OK to close the dialog box.
10. Display only those changes made by Julia Moore by completing the following steps:
   a. Click the Show Markup button in the Tracking group and then point to *Specific People*.
   b. Click *All Reviewers* at the side menu.
   c. Click the Show Markup button, point to *Specific People*, and then click *Julia Moore*.
   d. Scroll through the document and notice that only changes made by Julia Moore display in the document.
   e. Return the display to all of the reviewers by clicking the Show Markup button, pointing to *Specific People*, and then clicking *All Reviewers*.

11. Print the document with the markup by completing the following steps:
    a. Click the FILE tab and then click the *Print* option.
    b. At the Print backstage area, click the first gallery in the *Settings* category and then make sure a check mark displays before the *Print Markup* option. (If the *Print Markup* option is not preceded by a check mark, click the option.)
    c. Click the Print button.
12. Save **WL2-C7-P2-Agreement.docx**.

Customizing Track Changes Options

Default settings determine how tracked changes display in a document. For example, with all of the markup showing, inserted text displays in red with an underline below it and deleted text displays in red with strikethrough characters running through it. Moved text displays in the original location in green with double-strikethrough characters running through it and the text in the new location displays in green with double-underlining below the text.

Customize these options, along with others, at the Advanced Track Changes Options dialog box, shown in Figure 7.5. Use options at this dialog box to customize the display of markup text, moved text, table cell highlighting, formatting, and balloons. Display this dialog box by clicking the Tracking group dialog box launcher. At the Track Changes Options dialog box, click the Advanced Options button.

Figure 7.5 Advanced Track Changes Options Dialog Box

Change the display of markup with options in this section.

Advanced Track Changes Options

Insertions: Underline | Color: By author
Deletions: Strikethrough | Color: By author
Changed lines: Outside border
Comments: By author
Track moves
Moved from: Double strikethrough | Color: Green
Moved to: Double underline | Color: Green
Inserted cells: Light Blue | Merged cells: Light Yellow
Deleted cells: Pink | Split cells: Light Orange
Track formatting
Formatting: (none) | Color: By author
Preferred width: 3.7" | Measure in: Inches
Margin: Right
Show lines connecting to text
Paper orientation in printing: Preserve
OK | Cancel

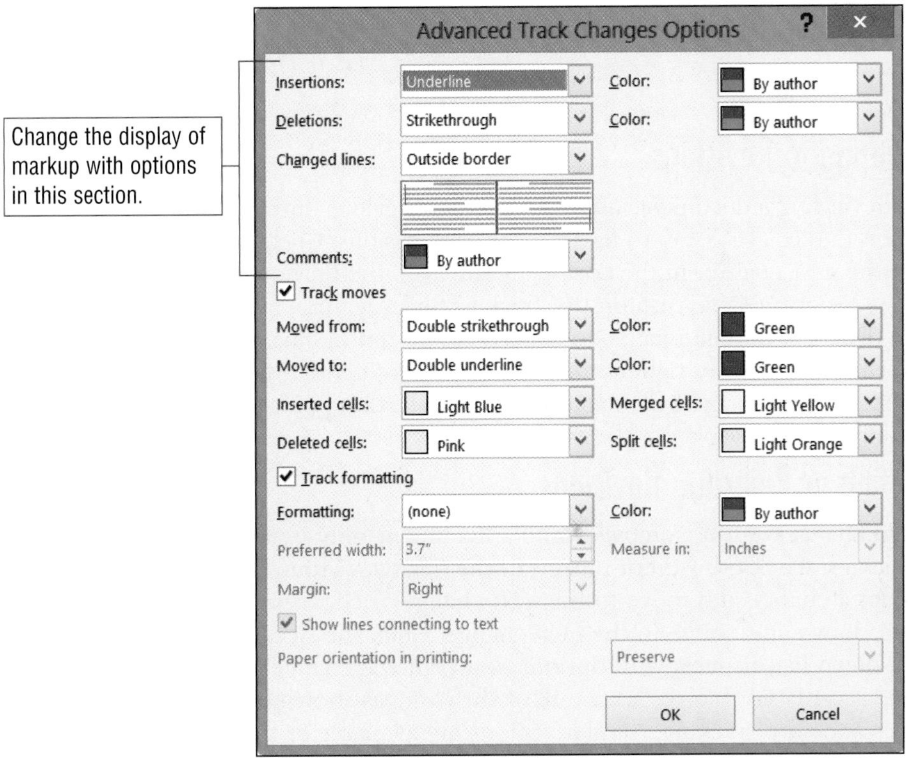

Project 2c **Customizing Track Changes Options** **Part 3 of 4**

1. With **WL2-C7-P2-Agreement.docx** open, customize the Track Changes options by completing the following steps:
   a. If necessary, click the REVIEW tab.
   b. Click the Tracking group dialog box launcher.
   c. Click the Advanced Options button at the Track Changes Options dialog box.
   d. At the Advanced Track Changes Options dialog box, click the down-pointing arrow at the right side of the *Insertions* option box and then click *Double underline* at the drop-down list.
   e. Click the down-pointing arrow at the right side of the *Insertions Color* option box and then click *Green* at the drop-down list. (You will need to scroll down the list to display this color.)
   f. Click the down-pointing arrow at the right side of the *Moved from Color* option box and then click *Dark Blue* at the drop-down list.
   g. Click the down-pointing arrow at the right side of the *Moved to Color* option box and then click *Violet* at the drop-down list. (You will need to scroll down the list to display this color.)
   h. Click OK to close the dialog box.
   i. Click OK to close the Track Changes Options dialog box.
2. Save **WL2-C7-P2-Agreement.docx**.

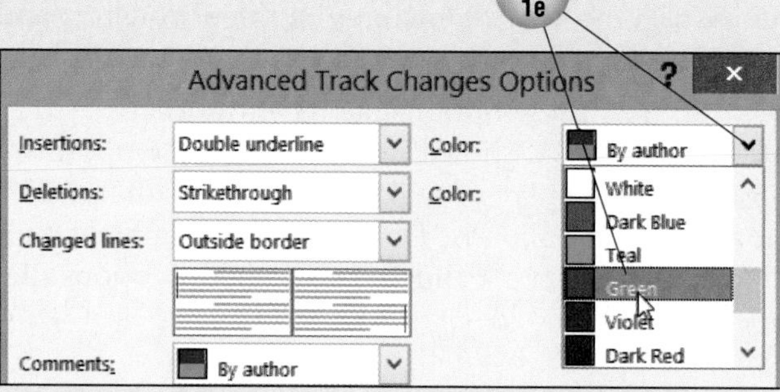

Navigating to Revisions

Next

Previous

When reviewing a document, use the Next and Previous buttons in the Changes group on the REVIEW tab to navigate among revisions. Click the Next button to review the next revision in the document and click the Previous button to review the previous revision. If you turn on the Track Changes feature, move text, and then turn on the display of revision balloons, a small Go button (a blue, right-pointing arrow) will display in the lower right corner of any balloon identifying moved text. Click the Go button in one of the balloons to move the insertion point to the other balloon.

Accepting or Rejecting Revisions

Accept

Reject

Tracked changes can be removed from a document only by accepting or rejecting the changes. Click the Accept button in the Changes group on the REVIEW tab to accept a change and move to the next change or click the Reject button to reject a change and move to the next change. Click the Accept button arrow and a drop-down list displays with options to accept the change and move to the next change, accept the change, accept all of the changes shown, and accept all of the changes and stop tracking. Similar options are available at the Reject button arrow drop-down list.

Project 2d Accepting or Rejecting Changes

Part 4 of 4

1. With **WL2-C7-P2-Agreement.docx** open, display all of the tracked changes *except* formatting changes by completing the following steps:
   a. Click the Show Markup button in the Tracking group and then click *Formatting* at the drop-down list. (This removes the check mark before the option.)
   b. Scroll through the document and notice that the vertical change line in the left margin next to the two formatting locations has been removed.
   c. Click the Show Markup button and then click *Formatting* at the drop-down list. (This inserts a check mark before the option.)
2. Navigate to review tracked changes by completing the following steps:
   a. Press Ctrl + Home to move the insertion point to the beginning of the document.
   b. Click the Next button in the Changes group to select the first change.
   c. Click the Next button again to select the second change.
   d. Click the Previous button to select the first change.
3. Navigate between the original and new locations of the moved text by completing the following steps:
   a. Press Ctrl + Home to move the insertion point to the beginning of the document.
   b. Click the Show Markup button, point to *Balloons*, and then click *Show Revisions in Balloons*.
   c. Click the Go button (a small, right-pointing arrow) that displays in the lower right corner of the Moved balloon. (This selects the text in the Moved up balloon.)
   d. Click the Go button in the lower right corner of the Moved up balloon. (This selects the text in the Moved balloon.)
   e. Click the Show Markup button, point to *Balloons*, and then click *Show All Revisions Inline*.

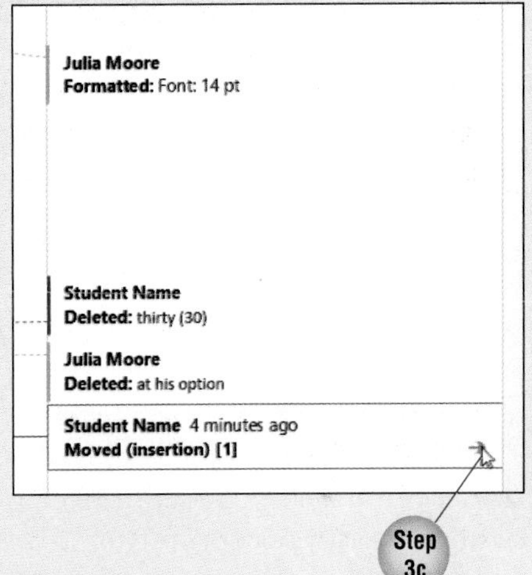

4. Press Ctrl + Home to move the insertion point to the beginning of the document.
5. Display and then accept only formatting changes by completing the following steps:
   a. Click the Tracking group dialog box launcher.
   b. At the Track Changes Options dialog box, click in the *Comments* check box to remove the check mark.
   c. Click the *Ink* check box to remove the check mark.
   d. Click the *Insertions and Deletions* check box to remove the check mark.
   e. Click OK to close the Track Changes Options dialog box.

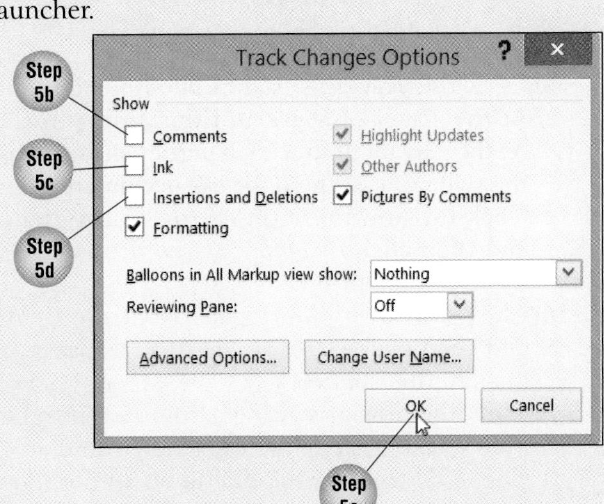

f. Click the Accept button arrow and then click *Accept All Changes Shown* at the drop-down list. (This accepts only the formatting changes in the document, because those are the only changes showing.)

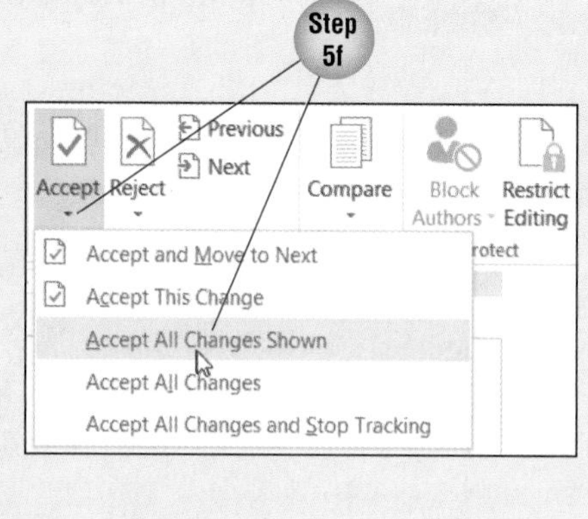

6. Redisplay all of the changes by completing the following steps:
   a. Click the Tracking group dialog box launcher.
   b. Click in the *Comments* check box to insert a check mark.
   c. Click in the *Ink* check box to insert a check mark.
   d. Click in the *Insertions and Deletions* check box to insert a check mark.
   e. Click OK to close the Track Changes Options dialog box.
7. Press Ctrl + Home to move the insertion point to the beginning of the document.
8. Reject the change inserting the word *BUILDING* by clicking the Next button in the Changes group and then clicking the Reject button. (This rejects the change and moves to the next revision in the document.)

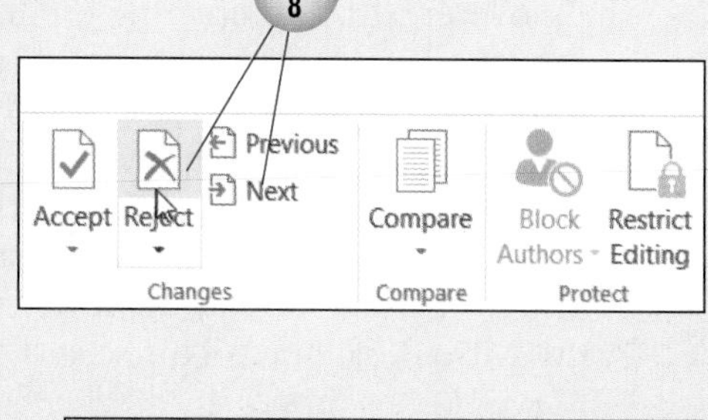

9. Click the Accept button to accept the change deleting *thirty (30)*.
10. Click the Accept button to accept the change inserting *sixty (60)*.
11. Click the Reject button to reject the change deleting the words *at his option*.
12. Accept all of the remaining changes by clicking the Accept button arrow and then clicking *Accept All Changes* at the drop-down list.

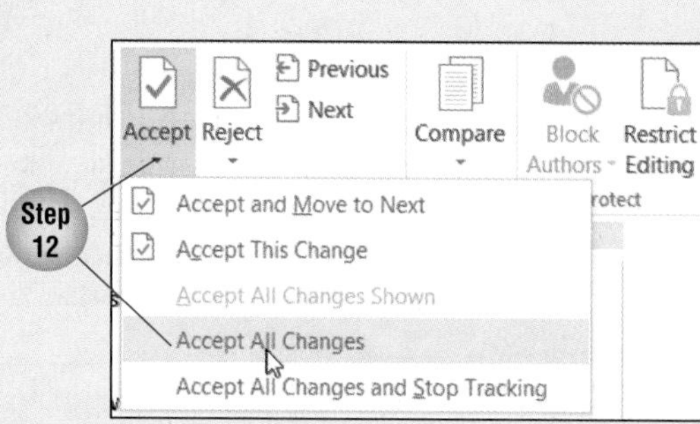

13. Return Track Changes options to the default settings by completing the following steps:
   a. If necessary, click the REVIEW tab.
   b. Click the Tracking group dialog box launcher.
   c. At the Track Changes Options dialog box, click the Advanced Options button.
   d. At the Advanced Track Changes Options dialog box, click the down-pointing arrow at the right side of the *Insertions* option and then click *Underline* at the drop-down list.
   e. Click the down-pointing arrow at the right side of the *Insertions Color* option box and then click *By author* at the drop-down list. (You will need to scroll up the list to display this option.)
   f. Click the down-pointing arrow at the right side of the *Moved from Color* option box and then click *Green* at the drop-down list. (You may need to scroll down the list to display this color.)
   g. Click the down-pointing arrow at the right side of the *Moved to Color* option box and then click *Green* at the drop-down list.
   h. Click OK to close the dialog box.
   i. Click OK to close the Track Changes Options dialog box.

14. Check to make sure all tracked changes are accepted or rejected by completing the following steps:
    a. Click the Reviewing Pane button in the Tracking group.
    b. Check the summary information that displays at the top of the Reviewing pane and make sure that zeros follow all of the options.
    c. Close the Reviewing pane.
15. Save, print, and then close **WL2-C7-P2-Agreement.docx**.

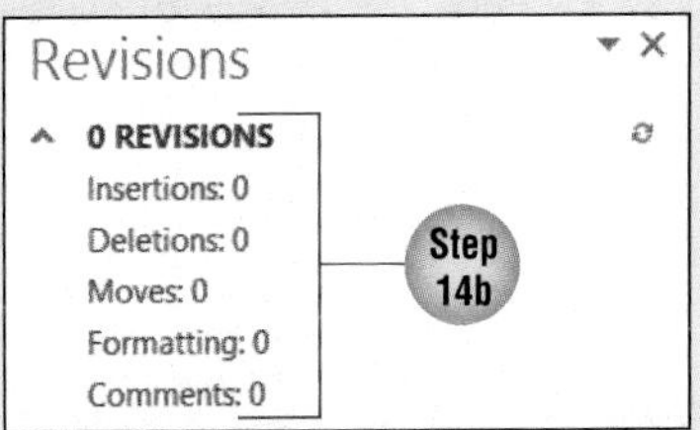

Project 3 Compare Lease Agreement Documents — 2 Parts

You will compare the contents of a lease agreement and an edited version of the lease agreement. You will then customize compare options and then compare the documents again.

Comparing Documents

Word contains a Compare feature that will compare two documents and display the differences as tracked changes in a third document. To use this feature, click the REVIEW tab, click the Compare button in the Compare group, and then click *Compare* at the drop-down list. This displays the Compare Documents dialog box, shown in Figure 7.6. At this dialog box, click the Browse for Original button. At the Open dialog box, navigate to the folder that contains the first of the two documents you want to compare and then double-click the document. Click the Browse for Revised button in the Compare Documents dialog box, navigate to the folder containing the second of the two documents you want to compare, and then double-click the document.

Quick Steps

Compare Documents
1. Click REVIEW tab.
2. Click Compare button.
3. Click *Compare* at drop-down list.
4. Click Browse for Original button.
5. Double-click desired document.
6. Click Browse for Revised button.
7. Double-click desired document.

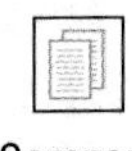

Compare

Word does not change the documents you are comparing.

Figure 7.6 Compare Documents Dialog Box

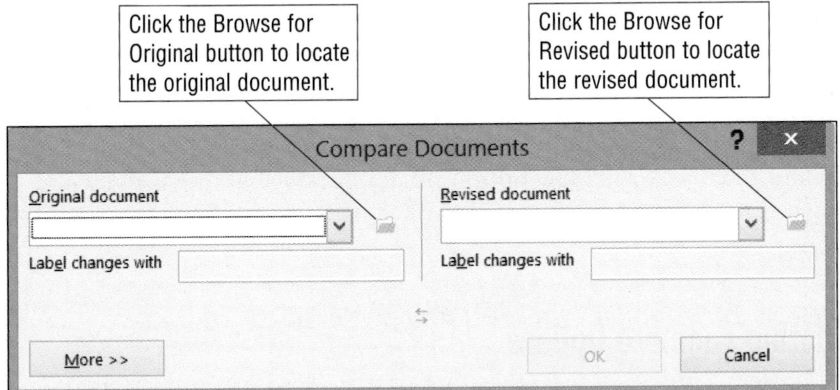

Viewing Compared Documents

When you click OK at the Compare Documents dialog box, the compared document displays with the changes tracked. Other windows may also display, depending on the option selected at the Show Source Documents side menu. Display this side menu by clicking the Compare button and then pointing to *Show Source Documents*. You may see just the compared document or you may see the compared document plus the Reviewing pane, original document, and/or revised document.

Project 3a **Comparing Documents** **Part 1 of 2**

1. Close any open documents.
2. Click the REVIEW tab.
3. Click the Compare button and then click *Compare* at the drop-down list.
4. At the Compare Documents dialog box, click the Browse for Original button.

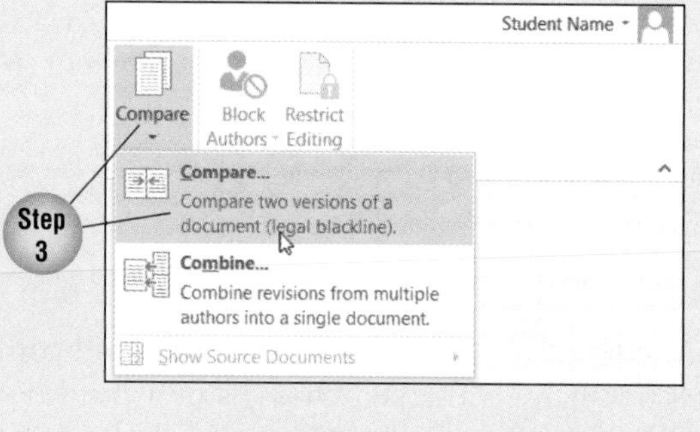

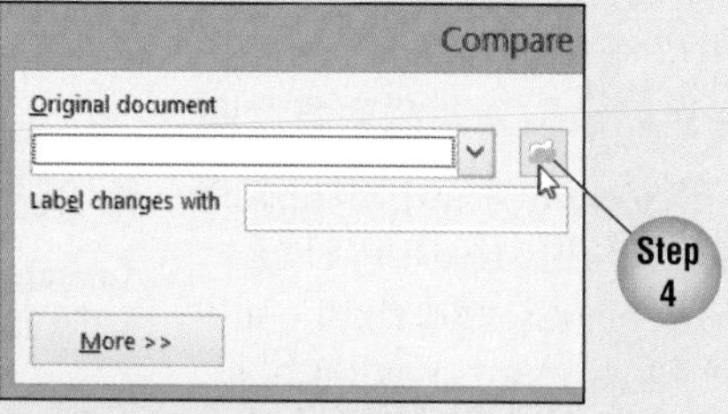

5. At the Open dialog box, navigate to the WL2C7 folder on your storage medium and then double-click ***ComAgrmnt.docx***.
6. At the Compare Documents dialog box, click the Browse for Revised button.
7. At the Open dialog box, double-click ***EditedComAgrmnt.docx***.
8. Click OK.
9. If the original and revised documents display along with the compared document, click the Compare button, point to *Show Source Documents* at the drop-down list, and then click *Hide Source Documents* at the side menu.
10. With the compared document active, print the document with markup.
11. Click the FILE tab and then click the *Close* option. At the message asking if you want to save changes, click the Don't Save button.

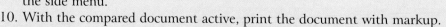

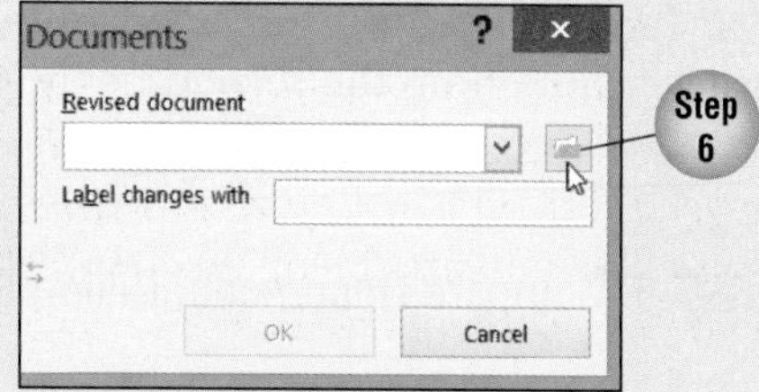

Customizing Compare Options

By default, Word compares the original document with the revised document and displays the differences as tracked changes in a third document. Change this default along with others by expanding the Compare Documents dialog box. Expand the dialog box by clicking the More button and additional options display, as shown in Figure 7.7.

Figure 7.7 Expanded Compare Documents Dialog Box

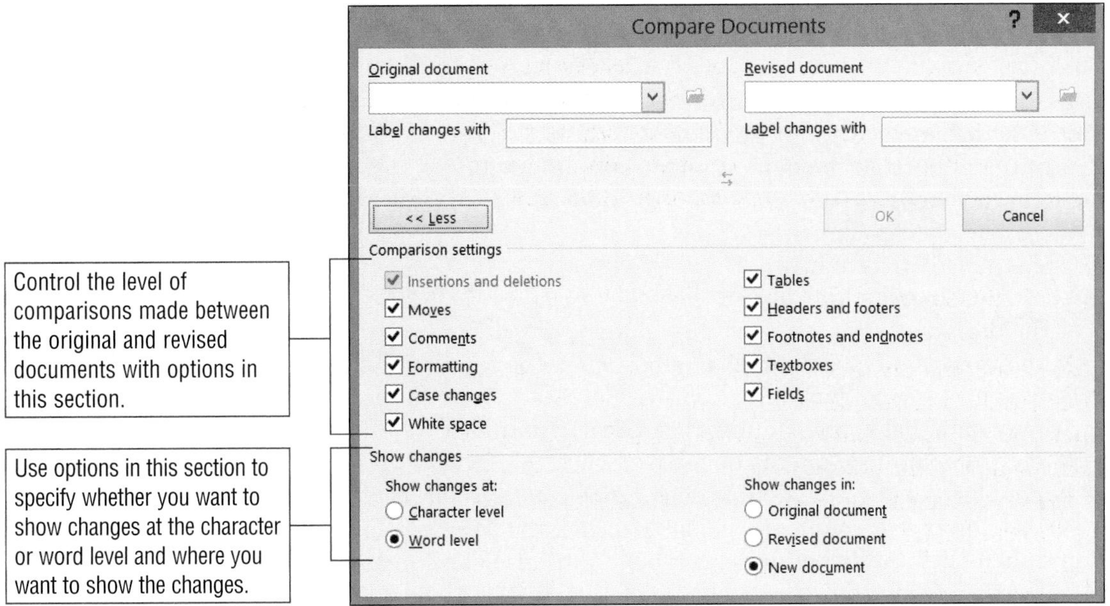

Control the level of comparison that Word makes between the original and revised documents with options in the *Comparison settings* section of the dialog box. The *Show changes at* option in the *Show changes* section of the dialog box has a default setting of *Word level*. At this setting, Word shows changes to whole words rather than individual characters within the word. For example, if you deleted the letters *ed* from the end of a word, Word would display the entire word as a change rather than just the *ed*. If you want to show changes by character, click the *Character level* option.

By default, Word displays differences between compared documents in a new document. With options in the *Show changes in* section, you can change this to *Original document* or *Revised document*. If you change options in the expanded Compare Documents dialog box, the selected options will be the defaults the next time you open the dialog box.

Project 3b Customizing Compare Options and Comparing Documents — Part 2 of 2

1. Close any open documents.
2. Click the REVIEW tab.
3. Click the Compare button and then click *Compare* at the drop-down list.
4. At the Compare Documents dialog box, click the Browse for Original button.
5. At the Open dialog box, navigate to the WL2C7 folder on your storage medium and then double-click ***ComAgrmnt.docx***.
6. At the Compare Documents dialog box, click the Browse for Revised button.
7. At the Open dialog box, double-click ***EditedComAgrmnt.docx***.
8. At the Compare Documents dialog box, click the More button. (Skip this step if the dialog box displays expanded and a Less button displays above the *Comparison settings* section.)

9. Click the *Moves* check box and then click the *Formatting* check box to remove the check marks.
10. Click OK.
11. Print the document with markup.
12. Close the document without saving it.
13. Return the options to the default settings by completing the following steps:
    a. Close any open documents.
    b. Click the REVIEW tab.
    c. Click the Compare button and then click *Compare* at the drop-down list.
    d. At the Compare Documents dialog box, click the Browse for Original button.
    e. At the Open dialog box, double-click ***ComAgrmnt.docx***.
    f. At the Compare Documents dialog box, click the Browse for Revised button.
    g. At the Open dialog box, double-click ***EditedComAgrmnt.docx***.
    h. At the Compare Documents dialog box, click the *Moves* check box to insert a check mark and then click the *Formatting* check box to insert a check mark.
    i. Click the Less button.
    j. Click OK.
14. At the new document, accept all of the changes.
15. Save the document and name it **WL2-C7-P3-ComAgrmnt**.
16. Print and then close the document.

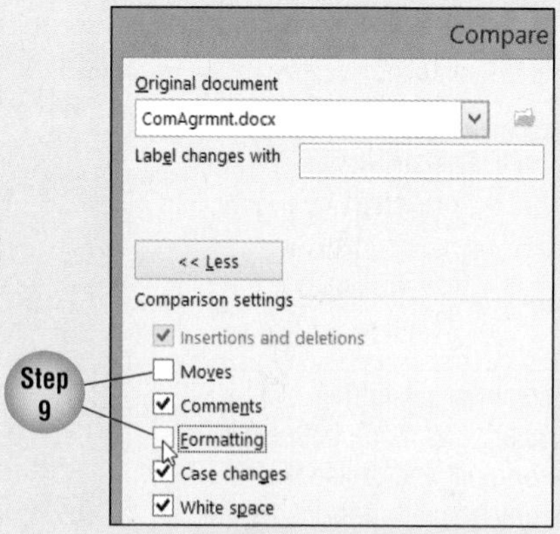

Compare
Original document
ComAgrmnt.docx
Label changes with
<< Less
Comparison settings
Insertions and deletions
Moves
Comments
Formatting
Case changes
White space
Step 9

Project 4 Combine Documents — 2 Parts

You will open a lease agreement document and then combine edited versions of the agreement with the original document.

Combining Documents

Quick Steps

Combine Multiple Versions of a Document
1. Click REVIEW tab.
2. Click Compare button.
3. Click *Combine* at drop-down list.
4. Click Browse for Original button.
5. Double-click desired document.
6. Click Browse for Revised button.
7. Double-click desired document.
8. Click OK.

If several people have made changes to a document, you can combine their changed versions with the original document. You can combine each person's changed document with the original until you have incorporated all of the changes into the original document. To do this, open the Combine Documents dialog box, shown in Figure 7.8 on the next page, by clicking the Compare button on the REVIEW tab and then clicking *Combine* at the drop-down list. The Combine Documents dialog box contains many of the same options as the Compare Documents dialog box.

To combine documents at the Combine Documents dialog box, click the Browse for Original button, navigate to the desired folder, and then double-click the original document. Click the Browse for Revised button, navigate to the desired folder, and then double-click one of the documents containing revisions. You can also click the down-pointing arrow at the right side of the *Original document* option box or the *Revised document* option box and a drop-down list displays with the most recently selected documents.

Figure 7.8 Combine Documents Dialog Box

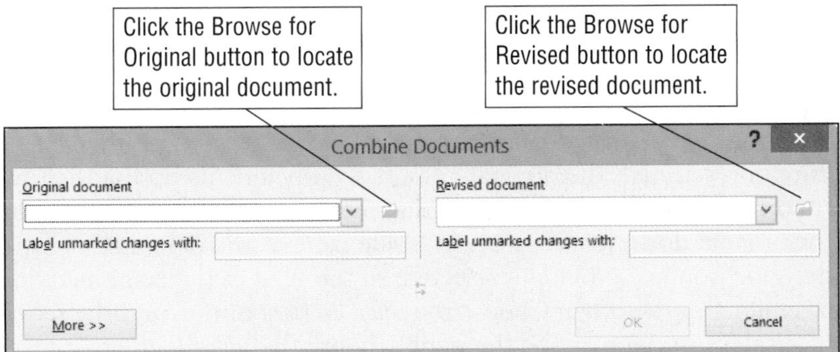

Combining and Merging Documents

Control how changes are combined with options in the expanded Combine Documents dialog box. This dialog box contains many of the same options as the expanded Compare Documents dialog box. By default, Word merges the changes in the revised document into the original document. Change this default setting with options in the *Show changes in* section. You can choose to merge changes into the revised document or a new document.

Project 4a Combining Documents

Part 1 of 2

1. Close all open documents.
2. Click the REVIEW tab.
3. Click the Compare button in the Compare group and then click *Combine* at the drop-down list.

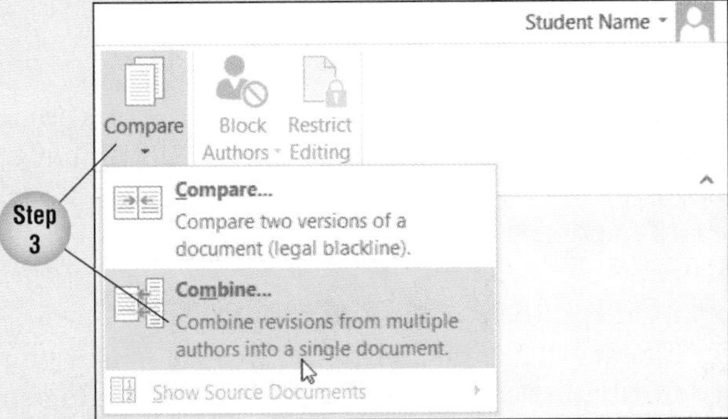

4. At the Combine Documents dialog box, click the More button to expand the dialog box.
5. Click the *Original document* option in the *Show changes in* section.
6. Click the Browse for Original button.
7. At the Open dialog box, navigate to the WL2C7 folder on your storage medium and then double-click ***OriginalLease.docx***.
8. At the Combine Documents dialog box, click the Browse for Revised button.
9. At the Open dialog box, double-click ***LeaseReviewer1.docx***.
10. Click OK.
11. Save the document and name it **WL2-C7-P4-CombinedLease**.

Showing Source Documents

Use options in the Show Source Documents side menu to specify which source documents to display. Display this side menu by clicking the Compare button and then pointing to *Show Source Documents*. Four options display at the side menu: *Hide Source Documents*, *Show Original*, *Show Revised*, and *Show Both*. With the *Hide Source Documents* option selected, the original and revised documents do not display on the screen; only the combined document displays. If you choose the *Show Original* option, the original document displays in a side pane at the right side of the document. Synchronous scrolling is selected, so scrolling in the combined document results in scrolling in the other. Choose the *Show Revised* option and the revised document displays in the panel at the right. Choose the *Show Both* option to display the original document in a panel at the right side of the screen and the revised document in a panel below the original document panel.

Project 4b **Combining and Showing Documents** **Part 2 of 2**

1. With **WL2-C7-P4-CombinedLease.docx** open, click the Compare button, point to *Show Source Documents*, and then click *Hide Source Documents* at the side menu if necessary. (This displays the original document with the combined document changes shown as tracked changes.)
2. Click the Compare button, point to *Show Source Documents*, and then click *Show Original* at the side menu. (This displays the original document at the right, the original document with tracked changes in the middle, and the Reviewing pane at the left side of the screen.)

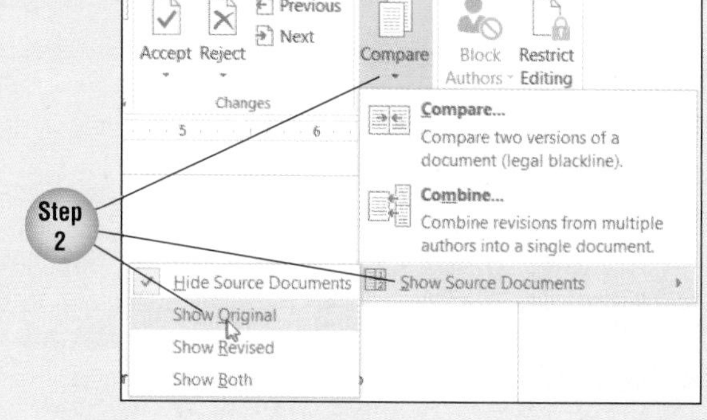

3. Click the Compare button, point to *Show Source Documents*, and then click *Show Revised*.
4. Click the Compare button, point to *Show Source Documents*, and then click *Show Both*. Scroll in the combined document and notice that the original document and revised document also scroll simultaneously.
5. Click the Compare button, point to *Show Source Documents*, and then click *Hide Source Documents*.
6. Close the Reviewing pane.
7. Click the Compare button and then click *Combine* at the drop-down list.
8. At the Combine Documents dialog box, click the Browse for Original button.
9. At the Open dialog box, double-click **WL2-C7-P4-CombinedLease.docx**.
10. At the Combine Documents dialog box, click the Browse for Revised button.
11. At the Open dialog box, double-click **LeaseReviewer2.docx**.
12. At the Combine Documents dialog box, click OK.
13. Save **WL2-C7-P4-CombinedLease.docx**.
14. Print the document with markup.
15. Accept all of the changes to the document. (Look through the document and notice that the *Rent* heading displays in blue. Select *Rent* and then change the font color to *Dark Red*.)
16. Keep the heading *Damage to Premises* together with the next paragraph.
17. Save, print, and then close **WL2-C7-P4-CombinedLease.docx**.

Project 5 Embed and Link Data between Excel and Word — 3 Parts

You will copy and embed Excel data into a Word document and then update the embedded data. You will also copy and link an Excel chart into a Word document and then update the data in the chart.

Embedding and Linking Objects

One of the reasons the Microsoft Office suite is used extensively in business is because it allows data from one program to be seamlessly integrated into another program. For example, a chart depicting sales projections created in Excel can easily be added to a corporate report prepared in Word.

Integration is the process of adding content from other sources to a file. Integrating content is different than simply copying and pasting it. While it makes sense to copy and paste objects from one application to another when the content is not likely to change, if the content is dynamic, the copy and paste method becomes problematic and inefficient. To illustrate this point, assume one of the outcomes from the presentation to the board of directors is a revision to the sales projections, which means that the chart originally created in Excel has to be updated to reflect the new projections. If the first version of the chart was copied and pasted into Word, it would need to be deleted and then the revised chart in Excel would need to be copied and pasted into the Word document again. Both Excel and Word would need to be opened and edited to reflect this change in projection. In this case, copying and pasting the chart would not be efficient.

To eliminate the inefficiency of the copy and paste method, you can integrate objects between programs. An ***object*** can be text in a document, data in a table, a chart, or picture, or any combination of data that you would like to share between programs. The program that was used to create the object is called the ***source*** and the program the object is linked or embedded to is called the ***destination***.

Embedding and linking are two methods you can use to integrate data. ***Embedding*** an object means that the object is stored independently in both the source and the destination programs. When you edit an embedded object in the destination program, the source program opens to help you make the changes, but the changes will not be reflected in the version of the object stored in the source program. If the object is changed in the source program, the changes will not be reflected in the version of the object stored in the destination program.

Linking inserts a code into the destination file that connects the destination to the name and location of the source object. The object itself is not stored within the destination file. When an object is linked, changes made to the content in the source program are automatically reflected in the destination program. Your decision to integrate data by embedding or linking will depend on whether the data is dynamic or static. If the data is dynamic, then linking the object is the most efficient method of integration.

Embedding Objects

An object that is embedded is stored in both the source and the destination programs. The content of the object can be edited in *either* the source or the destination; however, a change made in one will not be reflected in the other.

Quick Steps

Embed an Object

1. Open source and destination programs and files.
2. Click desired object in source program.
3. Click Copy button.
4. Click Taskbar button for destination program file.
5. Position insertion point where desired.
6. Click Paste button arrow.
7. Click *Paste Special*.
8. Click source file format in *As* list box.
9. Click OK.

The difference between copying and pasting and copying and embedding is that embedded objects can be edited with the source program's tabs and options.

Since embedded objects are edited within the source program, the source program must reside on the computer when the file is opened for editing. If you are preparing a Word document that will be edited on another computer, you may want to check before embedding any objects to verify that the other computer has the same programs.

To embed an object, open both programs and both files. In the source program, click the desired object and then click the Copy button in the Clipboard group on the HOME tab. Click the button on the Taskbar representing the destination program file and then position the insertion point at the location where you want the object embedded. Click the Paste button arrow in the Clipboard group and then click *Paste Special* at the drop-down list. At the Paste Special dialog box, click the source of the object in the *As* list box and then click OK.

Edit an embedded object by double-clicking the object. This displays the object with the source program tabs and options. Make any desired changes and then click outside the object to close the source program tabs and options.

Project 5a Embedding Excel Data in a Document — Part 1 of 3

1. Open **DIRevs.docx** and then save the document and name it **WL2-C7-P5-DIRevs**.
2. Start Excel and then open **DISales.xlsx**, located in the WL2C7 folder on your storage medium.
3. Select cells A2 through F9.
4. Click the Copy button in the Clipboard group on the HOME tab.
5. Click the Word button on the Taskbar.
6. Press Ctrl + End to move the insertion point to the end of the document.
7. Click the Paste button arrow and then click *Paste Special* at the drop-down list.
8. At the Paste Special dialog box, click *Microsoft Excel Worksheet Object* in the *As* list box and then click OK.
9. Save **WL2-C7-P5-DIRevs.docx**.
10. Click the Excel button on the Taskbar, close the workbook, and then close Excel.
11. With **WL2-C7-P5-DIRevs.docx** open, double-click in any cell in the Excel data. (This displays the Excel tabs and options for editing the data.)
12. Click in cell E3 (contains the amount *$89,231*), type **95000**, and then press Enter.
13. Click in cell F9 and then double-click the AutoSum button in the Editing group on the HOME tab. (This inserts the total *$1,258,643* in the cell.)
14. Click outside the Excel data to remove the Excel tabs and options.
15. Save, print, and then close **WL2-C7-P5-DIRevs.docx**.

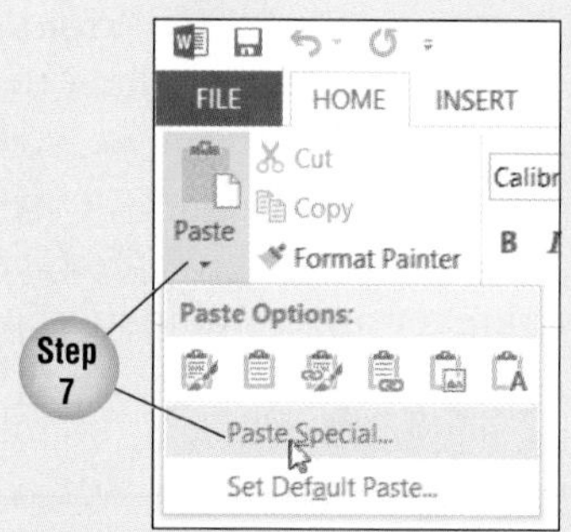

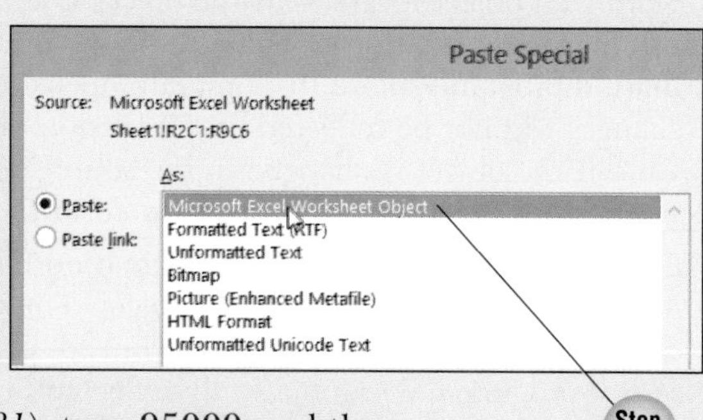

Linking Objects

If the content of the object that you will integrate between programs is likely to change, you can link the object from the source program to the destination program. Linking the object establishes a direct connection between the source and destination programs. The object is stored in the source program only, and the destination program contains a code that indicates the name and location of the source of the object. Whenever the document containing the link is opened, a message displays to indicate that the document contains links and asking if you want to update them.

To link an object, open both programs and program files. In the source program file, click the desired object and then click the Copy button in the Clipboard group on the HOME tab. Click the button on the Taskbar representing the destination program file and then position the insertion point in the desired location. Click the Paste button arrow in the Clipboard group on the HOME tab and then click *Paste Special* at the drop-down list. At the Paste Special dialog box, click the source program for the object in the *As* list box, click the *Paste link* option located at the left side of the *As* list box, and then click OK.

Quick Steps

Link an Object

1. Open source and destination programs and files.
2. Click desired object in source program.
3. Click Copy button.
4. Click Taskbar button for destination program file.
5. Position insertion point where desired.
6. Click Paste button arrow.
7. Click *Paste Special.*
8. Click source file format in *As* list box.
9. Click *Paste link* option.
10. Click OK.

Project 5b **Linking an Excel Chart to a Document** **Part 2 of 3**

1. Open **NSSCosts.docx** and then save the document and name it **WL2-C7-P5-NSSCosts**.
2. Open Excel and then open **NSSDept%.xlsx** located in the WL2C7 folder on your storage medium.
3. Save the workbook and name it **WL2-C7-P5-NSSDept%**.
4. Copy and link the chart to the Word document by completing the following steps:
   a. Click the chart to select it.
   b. Click the Copy button in the Clipboard group on the HOME tab.
   c. Click the Word button on the Taskbar.
   d. Press Ctrl + End to move the insertion point to the end of the document.
   e. Click the Paste button arrow and then click *Paste Special* at the drop-down list.
   f. At the Paste Special dialog box, click the *Paste link* option.
   g. Click *Microsoft Excel Chart Object* in the *As* list box.

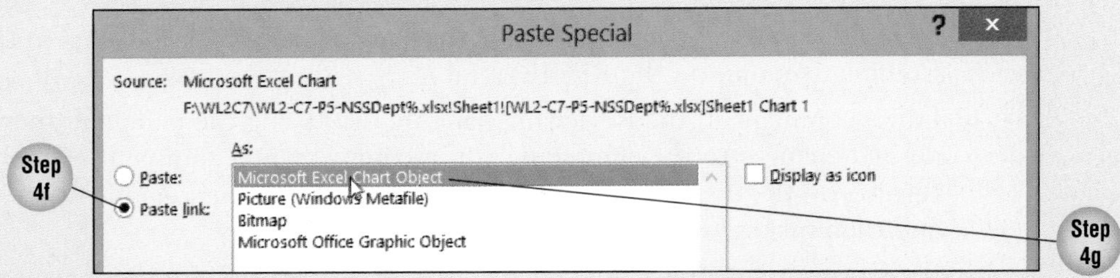

   h. Click OK.
5. Click the Excel button on the Taskbar, close **WL2-C7-P5-NSSDept%.xlsx**, and then close Excel.
6. With **WL2-C7-P5-NSSCosts.docx** open on the screen, save, print, and then close the document.

Editing a Linked Object

Edit linked objects in the source program in which they were created. Open the file containing the object, make the changes as required, and then save and close the file. If both the source and destination programs are open at the same time, the changed content is reflected immediately in both programs.

Project 5c **Linking an Excel Chart to a Document** **Part 3 of 3**

1. Open Excel and then open **WL2-C7-P5-NSSDept%.xlsx**.
2. Make the following changes to the data:
   a. In cell B4, change *18%* to *12%*.
   b. In cell B6, change 10% to *13%*.
   c. In cell B8, change 5% to 8%.
3. Click the Save button on the Quick Access toolbar to save the edited workbook.
4. Close **WL2-C7-P5-NSSDept%.xlsx** and then close Excel.
5. In Word, open **WL2-C7-P5-NSSCosts.docx**.
6. At the message telling you that the document contains links, click the Yes button. (Notice the changes to the chart data.)
7. Save, print, and then close **WL2-C7-P5-NSSCosts.docx**.

Chapter Summary

- Insert a comment in a document by clicking the New Comment button in the Comments group on the REVIEW tab. When you click the New Comment button, a comment balloon displays at the right margin. If any previous settings have been applied, the Reviewing pane, rather than a comment balloon, may display.
- Turn the display of the Reviewing pane on and off with the Reviewing Pane button in the Tracking group on the REVIEW tab.
- You can insert comments in the Reviewing pane. The summary section of the Reviewing pane provides a count of the number of comments inserted and a count of changes that have been made to the document.
- Navigate to review comments using the Previous and Next buttons in the Comments group on the REVIEW tab.
- Edit a comment in the Reviewing pane by displaying the pane and then making desired changes to the comment. Edit a comment in a comment balloon by turning on the display of balloons, clicking in the desired comment balloon, and then making the desired changes.
- If changes are made to a document by another person with different user information, the changes display in a different color. Change the user name and initials at the Word Options dialog box with *General* selected.
- Reply to a comment by clicking the Reply button that displays to the right of the reviewer's name in the comment balloon and then typing the reply.

- Print a document along with the inserted comments or choose to print only the comments and not the document.
- Delete a comment by clicking the Next button in the Comments group on the REVIEW tab until the desired comment is selected and then clicking the Delete button in the Comments group.
- Use the Track Changes feature when more than one person is reviewing a document and making changes to it. Turn on Tracked Changes by clicking the Track Changes button in the Tracking group on the REVIEW tab.
- Display information about tracked changes—such as the author's name, date and time, and type of change—by positioning the mouse pointer on a change. After approximately one second, a box displays with the information. You can also display information about tracked changes by displaying the Reviewing pane.
- Control how markup displays in a document with the Display for Review button in the Tracking group on the REVIEW tab. Control the markup that Word displays in a document with options at the Show Markup button drop-down list.
- Change Track Changes default settings with options at the Advanced Track Changes Options dialog box. Display this dialog box by clicking the Tracking group dialog box launcher and then clicking the Advanced Options button at the Track Changes Options dialog box.
- Move to the next change in a document by clicking the Next button in the Changes group on the REVIEW tab and move to the previous change by clicking the Previous button.
- Use the Accept and Reject buttons in the Changes group on the REVIEW tab to accept and reject changes made in a document.
- Use the Compare button in the Compare group on the REVIEW tab to compare two documents and display the differences between them as tracked changes in a third document.
- Customize options for comparing documents at the expanded Compare Documents dialog box. Click the More button to expand the dialog box.
- If several people review a document, you can combine their changed versions with the original document. Combine documents with options at the Combine Documents dialog box.
- Customize options for combining documents at the expanded Combine Documents dialog box. Click the More button to expand the dialog box.
- Specify which source documents to display by clicking the Compare button in the Compare group on the REVIEW tab, pointing to *Show Source Documents*, and then clicking the desired option at the side menu.
- An object created in one program in the Microsoft Office suite can be copied, linked, or embedded into another program in the suite. The program containing the original object is called the source program and the program in which it is inserted is called the destination program.
- An embedded object is stored in both the source and the destination programs. A linked object is stored in the source program only. Link an object if you want the contents in the destination program to reflect any changes made to the object stored in the source program.

Commands Review

FEATURE	RIBBON TAB, GROUP	BUTTON, OPTION	KEYBOARD SHORTCUT
accept changes	REVIEW, Changes		
Advanced Track Changes Options dialog box	REVIEW, Tracking	, *Advanced Options*	
balloons	REVIEW, Tracking	, *Balloons*	
Combine Documents dialog box	REVIEW, Compare	, *Combine*	
Compare Documents dialog box	REVIEW, Compare	, *Compare*	
delete comment	REVIEW, Comments		
display for review	REVIEW, Tracking		
new comment	REVIEW, Comments		
next comment	REVIEW, Comments		
next revision	REVIEW, Changes		
Paste Special dialog box	HOME, Clipboard	, *Paste Special*	
previous comment	REVIEW, Comments		
previous revision	REVIEW, Changes		
reject changes	REVIEW, Changes		
Reviewing pane	REVIEW, Tracking		
show markup	REVIEW, Tracking		
show source documents	REVIEW, Compare	, *Show Source Documents*	
Track Changes	REVIEW, Tracking		Ctrl + Shift + E
Track Changes Options dialog box	REVIEW, Tracking		

Concepts Check Test Your Knowledge 

Completion: In the space provided at the right, indicate the correct term, command, or number.

1. Insert a comment into a document by clicking this button in the Comments group on the REVIEW tab. ____________
2. Navigate to review comments by using these two buttons in the Comments group on the REVIEW tab. ____________
3. Change user information with options at this dialog box. ____________
4. If a document contains comments, print only the comments by displaying the Print backstage area, clicking the first gallery in the *Settings* category, clicking this option, and then clicking the Print button. ____________
5. Turn on the Track Changes feature by clicking the Track Changes button in this group on the REVIEW tab. ____________
6. Use this keyboard shortcut to turn on Track Changes. ____________
7. Show all markup in a document by clicking this button in the Tracking group on the REVIEW tab and then clicking *All Markup* at the drop-down list. ____________
8. Display information on tracked changes in this pane. ____________
9. With Track Changes turned on, text that has been moved displays in this color by default. ____________
10. Customize options for tracking changes at the Track Changes Options dialog box and this dialog box. ____________
11. Click the *Combine* option at the Compare button drop-down list and this dialog box displays. ____________
12. Specify which source document to display by clicking the Compare button, pointing to this option, and then clicking the desired option at the side menu. ____________
13. Do this to an object if you want the contents in the destination program to reflect any changes made to the object stored in the source program. ____________

Skills Check Assess Your Performance

Assessment 1

INSERT COMMENTS IN A WEB REPORT

1. Open **NavigateWeb.docx** and then save the document and name it **WL2-C7-A1-NavigateWeb**.
2. Delete the only comment in the document.
3. Position the insertion point at the end of the first paragraph in the *IPs and URLs* section and then insert a comment with the following text: *Please identify what the letters ICANN stand for.*
4. Position the insertion point at the end of the third paragraph in the *IPs and URLs* section and then insert a comment with the following text: *Insert a caption for the following table and the two other tables in the document.*
5. Position the insertion point at the end of the last paragraph in the document (above the table) and insert a comment with the following text: *Include in the following table additional examples of methods for narrowing a search.*
6. Save the document and then print only the comments.
7. Close **WL2-C7-A1-NavigateWeb.docx**.

Assessment 2

TRACK CHANGES IN A COMPUTER VIRUSES REPORT

1. Open **CompChapters.docx** and then save the document and name it **WL2-C7-A2-CompChapters**.
2. Turn on Track Changes and then make the following changes:
   a. Edit the first sentence in the document so it displays as follows: *The computer virus is one of the most familiar forms of risk to computer security.*
   b. Type **computer's** between *the* and *motherboard* in the last sentence in the first paragraph of the document.
   c. Delete the word *real* in the second sentence of the *Types of Viruses* section and then type **significant**.
   d. Select and then delete the last sentence in the *Methods of Virus Operation* section (which begins *A well-known example of the logic bomb was the*).
   e. Turn off Track Changes.
3. Display the Word Options dialog box with *General* selected and then change the user name to *Stacey Phillips* and the initials to *SP*. Insert a check mark in the *Always use these values regardless of sign in to Office.* check box.
4. Turn on Track Changes and then make the following changes:
   a. Delete the words *or cracker* located in the seventh sentence in the *Types of Viruses* section.
   b. Delete the word *garner* in the first sentence in the *CHAPTER 2: SECURITY RISKS* section and then type **generate**.
   c. Select and then move the *Employee Theft* section after the *Cracking Software for Copying* section.
   d. Turn off Track Changes.

5. Display the Word Options dialog box with *General* selected. Change the user name back to the original name and the initials back to the original initials. Also remove the check mark from the *Always use these values regardless of sign in to Office.* check box.
6. Print the document with the markup.
7. Accept all of the changes in the document *except* reject the change moving the *Employee Theft* section after the *Cracking Software for Copying* section.
8. Save, print, and then close **WL2-C7-A2-CompChapters.docx**.

Assessment 3

COMPARE ORIGINAL AND REVISED SECURITY STRATEGIES DOCUMENT

1. Compare **Security.docx** with **EditedSecurity.docx** and insert the changes into a new document. ***Hint: Choose* New document *at the expanded Compare Documents dialog box.***
2. Save the compared document and name it **WL2-C7-A3-Security.docx**.
3. Print only the list of markup (not the document).
4. Reject the changes made to the bulleted text and the last paragraph in the *Disaster Recovery Plan* section and accept all of the other changes.
5. Add a page number at the bottom center of each page.
6. Save the document, print only the document, and then close **WL2-C7-A3-Security.docx**.

Assessment

COMBINE ORIGINAL AND REVISED LEGAL DOCUMENTS

1. Open **LegalSummons.docx** and then save the document and name it **WL2-C7-A4-LegalSummons**.
2. Close **WL2-C7-A4-LegalSummons.docx**.
3. At a blank screen, combine **WL2-C7-A4-LegalSummons** (the original document) with **Review1-LegalSummons.docx** (the revised document) into the original document. ***Hint: Choose* Original document *at the Combine Documents expanded dialog box.***
4. Accept all of the changes to the document.
5. Save and then close **WL2-C7-A4-LegalSummons.docx**.
6. At a blank screen, combine **WL2-C7-A4-LegalSummons.docx** (the original document) with **Review2-LegalSummons.docx** (the revised document) into the original document.
7. Print only the list of markup.
8. Accept all of the changes to the document.
9. Save the document, print only the document, and then close **WL2-C7-A4-LegalSummons.docx**.

Assessment

LINKING AN EXCEL CHART WITH A WORD DOCUMENT

1. Open **WESales.docx** and then save it and name it **WL2-C7-A5-WESales**.
2. Open Excel and then open the workbook named **WESalesChart.xlsx**.
3. Save the Excel worksheet and name it **WL2-C7-A5-WESalesChart**.

4. Link the Excel chart to the end of **WL2-C7-A5-WESales.docx**. (Make sure you use the Paste Special dialog box.)
5. Save, print, and then close **WL2-C7-A5-WESales.docx**.
6. With Excel the active program, make the following changes to the data in the specified cells:
   a. Change the amount in cell F3 from *$500,750* to *$480,200*.
   b. Change the amount in cell E4 from *$410,479* to *$475,500*.
7. Save and close **WL2-C7-A5-WESalesChart.xlsx** and then close Excel.
8. Open **WL2-C7-A5-WESales.docx** and click Yes at the message asking if you want to update the document.
9. Save, print, and then close **WL2-C7-A5-WESales.docx**.

Assessment

6 TRACK CHANGES IN A TABLE

1. Open **SalesTable.docx** and then save the document and name it **WL2-C7-A6-SalesTable**.
2. You can track changes made to a table and customize the Track Changes options for a table. Display the Advanced Track Changes Options dialog box and then make the following changes:
   a. Change the color for inserted cells to *Light Purple*.
   b. Change the color for deleted cells to *Light Green*.
3. Turn on Track Changes and then make the following changes:
   a. Insert a new row at the beginning of the table.
   b. Merge the cells in the new row. (At the message saying the action will not be marked as a change, click OK.)
   c. Type **Clearline Manufacturing** in the merged cell.
   d. Delete the *Fanning, Andrew* row.
   e. Insert a new row below *Barnet, Jacqueline* and then type **Montano, Neil** in the first cell, **$530,678** in the second cell, and **$550,377** in the third cell.
   f. Turn off Track Changes.
4. Save and then print the document with markup.
5. Accept all of the changes.
6. Display the Advanced Track Changes Options dialog box and then return the inserted cells color back to *Light Blue* and the deleted cells color back to *Pink*.
7. Save, print, and then close **WL2-C7-A6-SalesTable.docx**.

Visual Benchmark Demonstrate Your Proficiency

TRACK CHANGES IN AN EMPLOYEE PERFORMANCE DOCUMENT

1. Open **NSSEmpPerf.docx** and then save the document and name it **WL2-C7-VB-NSSEmpPerf**.
2. Turn on Track Changes and then make the changes shown in Figure 7.8 on the next page. (Make the editing changes before you move the *Employment Records* section after the *Performance Evaluation* section.)
3. Turn off Track Changes and then print only the list of markup.

4. Accept all changes to the document.
5. Save the document, print only the document, and then close **WL2-C7-VB-NSSEmpPerf.docx**.
6. At a blank screen, combine **WL2-C7-VB-NSSEmpPerf.docx** (the original document) with **EditedNSSEmpPerf.docx** (the revised document) into the original document.
7. Accept all of the changes to the document.
8. Save, print, and then close **WL2-C7-VB-NSSEmpPerf.docx**.

Figure 7.8 Visual Benchmark

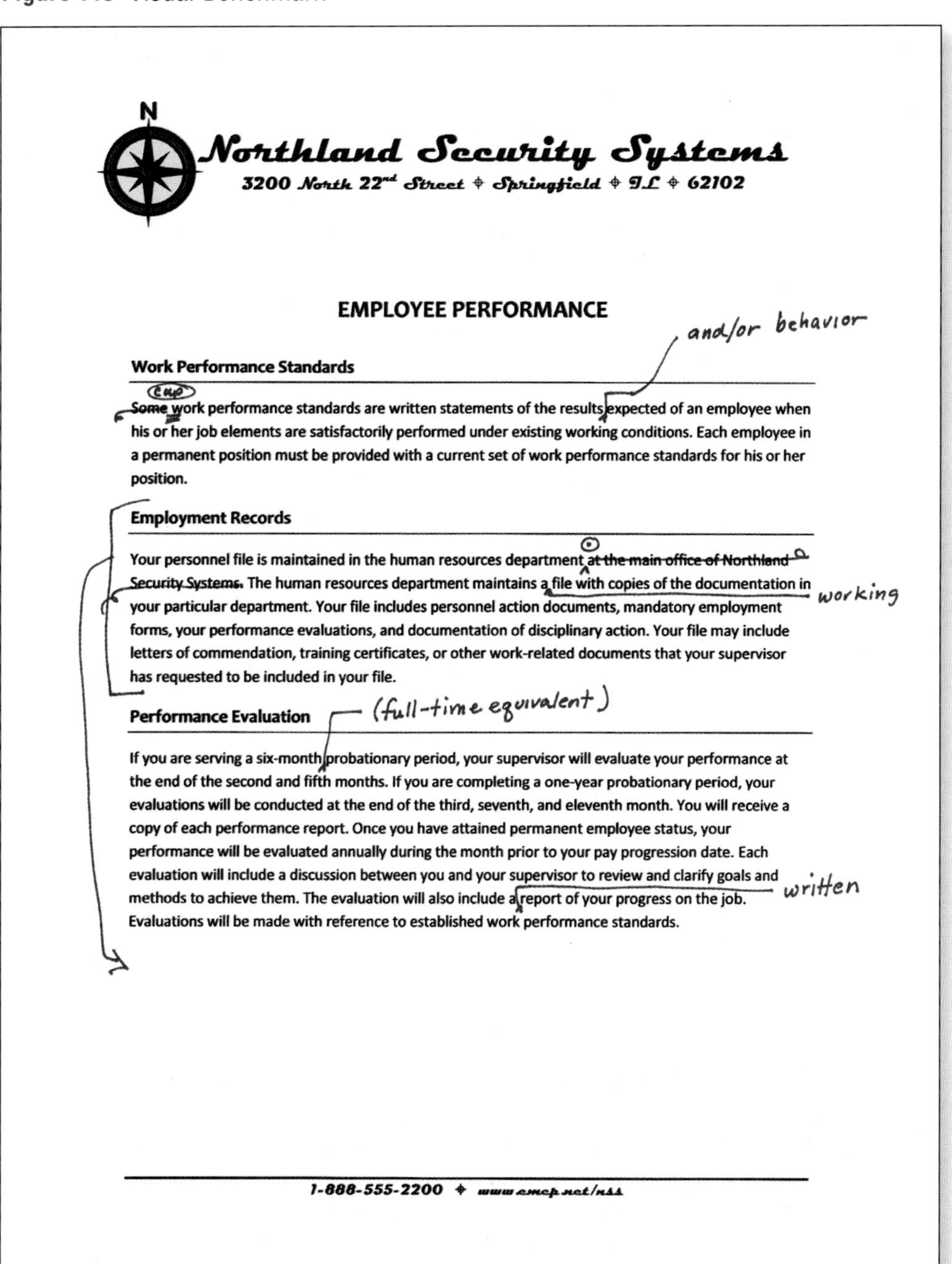

Northland Security Systems

3200 North 22nd Street ♦ Springfield ♦ IL ♦ 62102

EMPLOYEE PERFORMANCE

Work Performance Standards

Some work performance standards are written statements of the results expected of an employee when his or her job elements are satisfactorily performed under existing working conditions. Each employee in a permanent position must be provided with a current set of work performance standards for his or her position.

Employment Records

Your personnel file is maintained in the human resources department at the main office of Northland Security Systems. The human resources department maintains a file with copies of the documentation in your particular department. Your file includes personnel action documents, mandatory employment forms, your performance evaluations, and documentation of disciplinary action. Your file may include letters of commendation, training certificates, or other work-related documents that your supervisor has requested to be included in your file.

Performance Evaluation

If you are serving a six-month probationary period, your supervisor will evaluate your performance at the end of the second and fifth months. If you are completing a one-year probationary period, your evaluations will be conducted at the end of the third, seventh, and eleventh month. You will receive a copy of each performance report. Once you have attained permanent employee status, your performance will be evaluated annually during the month prior to your pay progression date. Each evaluation will include a discussion between you and your supervisor to review and clarify goals and methods to achieve them. The evaluation will also include a report of your progress on the job. Evaluations will be made with reference to established work performance standards.

1-888-555-2200 ♦ www.emcp.net/nss

Case Study Apply Your Skills

Part 1

You work in the training department at Hart International. Your department is responsible for preparing training material and training employees on how to use software applications within the company. Your supervisor, Nicole Sweeney, has asked you to help her prepare a Microsoft Word training manual. She has written a portion of the manual and has had another employee, Gina Singh, review the contents and make tracked changes. Ms. Sweeney has asked you to combine Gina's revised version with the original document. To do this, combine **HITraining.docx** with **HITrainingGS.docx**. Go through the original document with the tracked changes and accept and/or reject each revision. Not all of Gina's changes are correct, so check each one before accepting it. Save the combined document and name it **WL2-C7-CS-HITraining**.

Part 2

Ms. Sweeney has asked you to prepare training materials on how to check the spelling and grammar in a document and how to customize spelling and grammar options. Using the **WL2-C7-CS-HITraining.docx** document as a guideline, write information (including steps) on how to complete a spelling and grammar check in a document and how to change spelling and grammar options at the Word Options dialog box with *Proofing* selected. Include in the document a table that presents the names of the buttons available at the Spelling task pane and Grammar task pane and a brief description of what task each button completes. Save the completed document and name it **WL2-C7-CS-HISpelling**.

Part 3

If possible, send a copy of your document to one or two classmates and have them edit the document with Track Changes turned on. Combine their edited documents with your original **WL2-C7-CS-HISpelling** document. Save, print, and then close the document.

Part 4

Open **WL2-C7-CS-HITraining.docx**, move the insertion point to the end of the document, and then insert **WL2-C7-CS-HISpelling.docx**. Apply at least the following elements to the document:

- Heading styles
- Style set
- Theme
- Table style
- Table of contents
- Page numbering
- Cover page

Save, print, and then close the document.

MICROSOFT®

WORD

Protecting and Preparing Documents

PERFORMANCE OBJECTIVES

Upon successful completion of Chapter 8, you will be able to:

- **Restrict formatting and editing in a document and allow exceptions to restrictions**
- **Protect a document with a password**
- **Open a document in different views**
- **Modify document properties**
- **Inspect and encrypt a document**
- **Restrict permission to a document**
- **Mark a document as final**
- **Check a document for accessibility and compatibility issues**
- **Manage versions**

Tutorials

8.1 Restricting Formatting and Editing in a Document

8.2 Protecting a Document with a Password and Opening Documents in Different Views

8.3 Managing Document Properties

8.4 Restricting and Inspecting a Document

8.5 Checking the Accessibility and Compatibility of a Document

8.6 Managing Versions

In Chapter 7, you learned to perform workgroup activities such as inserting comments into a document, tracking changes made by other users, comparing documents, and combining documents from multiple users. In this chapter, you will learn how to protect the integrity of shared documents, limit the formatting or editing changes that other users can make, and prepare documents for distribution. Model answers for this chapter's projects appear on the following pages.

Note: Before beginning the projects, copy to your storage medium the WL2C8 subfolder from the WL2 folder on the CD that accompanies this textbook and then make WL2C8 the active folder.

TANDEM ENERGY CORPORATION

Overview

Tandem Energy Corporation is a development stage company that was incorporated on May 1, 2009. The corporation and its subsidiary (collectively referred to as the "Company") designs, develops, configures, and offers for sale power systems that provide highly reliable, high-quality, environmentally friendly power. The Company has segmented the potential markets for its products into two broad categories: high-energy, high-power, uninterruptible power system (UPS), and high-power distributed generation and utility power-grid energy storage system. We have available for sale several high-energy products that deliver a low level of power over a long period of time (typically measured in hours). These products are tailored to the telecommunications, cable systems, computer networks, and Internet markets.

We are developing a new high-energy product for potential applications in the renewable energy market for both photovoltaic and wind turbine uses. As part of exploring these markets, we have committed to invest $2 million in Clear Sun Energies and we have purchased the inverter electronics technology of Technology Pacific[SN1].

We have taken significant actions over the last eighteen months to reduce our expenditures for product development, infrastructure, and production readiness. Our headcount, development spending, and capital expenditures have been significantly reduced. We have continued the preliminary design and development of potential products for markets under consideration and with specific approval by the Company's board of directors.

Research and Development

We believe that our research and development efforts are essential to our ability to successfully design and deliver our products to our targeted customers, as well as to modify and improve them to reflect the evolution of markets and customer needs. Our research and development team has worked closely with potential customers to define product features and performance to address specific needs. Our research and development expenses, including engineering expenses, were approximately $8,250,000 in 2011, $15,525,000 in 2010, and $7,675,000 in 2009. We expect research and development expenses in 2011 to be lower than in 2012. As we determine market opportunities, we may need to make research and development expenditures in the future. As of December 31, 2011, we employed twenty-five engineers and technicians who were engaged in research and development.

Manufacturing

Historically, our manufacturing has consisted of the welding and assembly of our products. We have previously contracted out the manufacture of our high-energy flywheel components, using our design drawings and processes to facilitate more rapid growth by taking advantage of third-party installed manufacturing capacity. For a limited number of non-proprietary components, we generate performance specifications and obtain either standard or custom components.

Our facility is underutilized as a result of reductions in development work and customer orders for production. We are maintaining a limited manufacturing staff, many of whom are skilled in quality-control techniques. We expect to continue to utilize contract manufacturing and outside suppliers in the future based on our estimate of product demand from potential customers. The suppliers of the mechanical flywheel and the control electronics for our high-power UPS product are both single-source suppliers, and the

WL2-C8-P1-TECRpt.docx

Main document changes and comments

Page 1: Commented	Student Name	1/12/2015 11:34:00 AM

Include additional information on the impact of this purchase.

Header and footer changes

Text Box changes

Header and footer text box changes

Footnote changes

Endnote changes

Project 1 Restrict Formatting and Editing in a Company Report

WL2-C8-P1-TECRpt.docx

1

REAL ESTATE SALE AGREEMENT

The Buyer, BUYER, and Seller, SELLER, hereby agree that SELLER will sell and BUYER will buy the following property, with such improvements as are located thereon, and is described as follows: All that tract of land lying and being in Land Lot ____ of the __________ District, Section _______ of ______________ County, and being known as Address: ______________________________ City:____________ State: _________ Zip:_______, together with all light fixtures, electrical, mechanical, plumbing, air-conditioning, and any other systems or fixtures as are attached thereto; all plants, trees, and shrubbery now a part thereof, together with all the improvements thereon, and all appurtenances thereto, all being hereinafter collectively referred to as the "Property." The full legal description of said Property is the same as is recorded with the Clerk of the Superior Court of the County in which the Property is located and is made a part of this Agreement by reference.

SELLER will sell and BUYER will buy upon the following terms and conditions, as completed or marked. On any conflict of terms or conditions, that which is added will supersede that which is printed or marked. It is understood that the Property will be bought by Warranty Deed, with covenants, restrictions, and easements of record.

Financing: The balance due to SELLER will be evidenced by a negotiable Promissory Note of Borrower, secured by a Mortgage or Deed to Secure Debt on the Property and delivered by BUYER to SELLER dated the date of closing.

New financing: If BUYER does not obtain the required financing, the earnest money deposit shall be forfeited to SELLER as liquidated damages. BUYER will make application for financing within five days of the date of acceptance of the Agreement and in a timely manner furnish any and all credit, employment, financial, and other information required by the lender.

Closing costs: BUYER will pay all closing costs to include: Recording Fees, Intangibles Tax, Credit Reports, Funding Fees, Loan Origination Fee, Document Preparation Fee, Loan Insurance Premium, Title Insurance Policy, Attorney's Fees, Courier Fees, Overnight Fee, Appraisal Fee, Survey, Transfer Tax, Satisfaction and Recording Fees, Wood Destroying Organism Report, and any other costs associated with the funding or closing of this Agreement.

Prorations: All taxes, rentals, condominium or association fees, monthly mortgage insurance premiums, and interest on loans will be prorated as of the date of closing.

Title insurance: Within five (5) days of this Agreement SELLER will deliver to BUYER or closing attorney: Title insurance commitment for an owner's policy in the amount of the purchase price. Any expense of securing title, including but not limited to legal fees, discharge of liens, and recording fees will be paid by SELLER.

WL2-C8-P3-REAgrmnt.docx

2

Survey: Within ten (10) days of acceptance of this Agreement, BUYER or closing attorney, may, at BUYER's expense, obtain a new staked survey showing any improvements now existing thereon and certified to BUYER, lender, and the title insurer.

Default and attorney's fees: Should BUYER elect not to fulfill obligations under this Agreement, all earnest monies will be retained by SELLER as liquidated damages and fund settlement of any claim, whereupon BUYER and SELLER will be relieved of all obligations under this Agreement. If SELLER defaults under this agreement, the BUYER may seek specific performance in return of the earnest money deposit. In connection with any litigation arising out of this Agreement, the prevailing party shall be entitled to recover all costs including reasonable attorney's fees.

IN WITNESS WHEREOF, all of the parties hereto affix their hands and seals this _____ day of ____________________, 20______.

WL2-C8-P3-REAgrmnt.docx

Project 3 Prepare a Real Estate Agreement for Distribution

WL2-C8-P3-REAgrmnt.docx

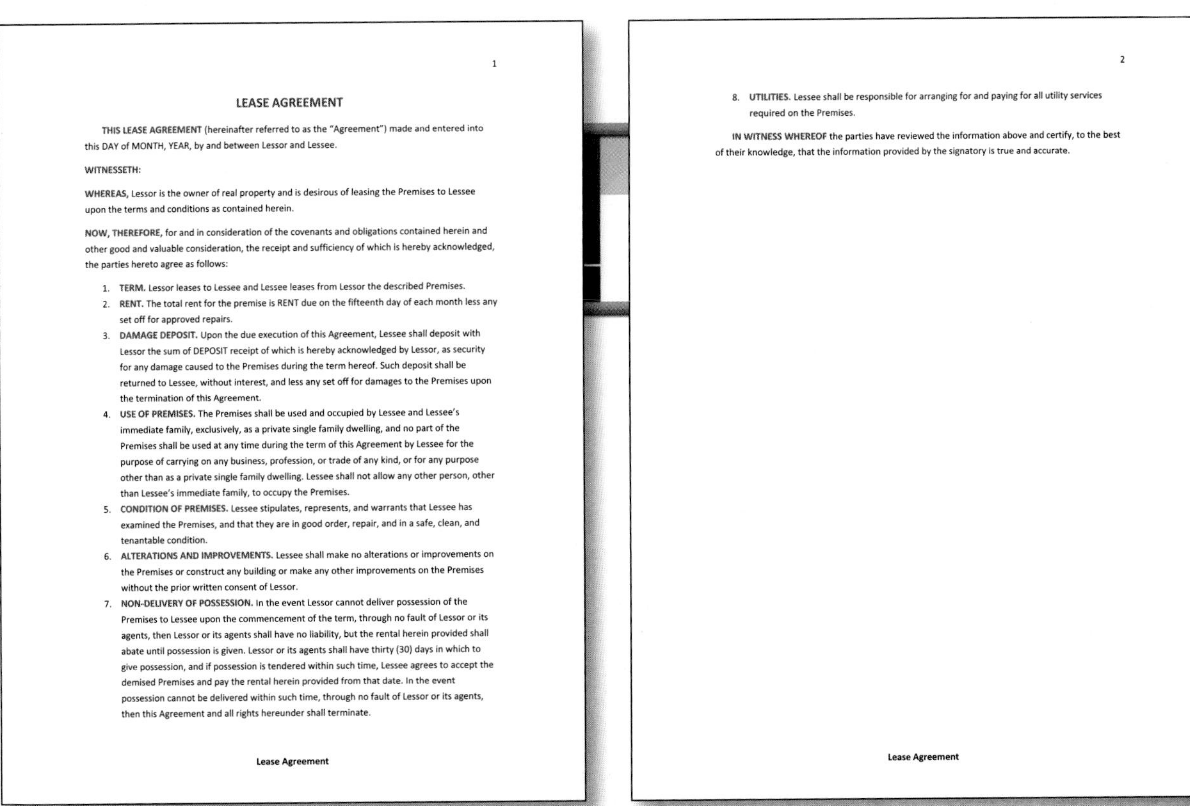
LEASE AGREEMENT

THIS LEASE AGREEMENT (hereinafter referred to as the "Agreement") made and entered into this DAY of MONTH, YEAR, by and between Lessor and Lessee.

WITNESSETH:

WHEREAS, Lessor is the owner of real property and is desirous of leasing the Premises to Lessee upon the terms and conditions as contained herein.

NOW, THEREFORE, for and in consideration of the covenants and obligations contained herein and other good and valuable consideration, the receipt and sufficiency of which is hereby acknowledged, the parties hereto agree as follows:

1. TERM. Lessor leases to Lessee and Lessee leases from Lessor the described Premises.
2. RENT. The total rent for the premise is RENT due on the fifteenth day of each month less any set off for approved repairs.
3. DAMAGE DEPOSIT. Upon the due execution of this Agreement, Lessee shall deposit with Lessor the sum of DEPOSIT receipt of which is hereby acknowledged by Lessor, as security for any damage caused to the Premises during the term hereof. Such deposit shall be returned to Lessee, without interest, and less any set off for damages to the Premises upon the termination of this Agreement.
4. USE OF PREMISES. The Premises shall be used and occupied by Lessee and Lessee's immediate family, exclusively, as a private single family dwelling, and no part of the Premises shall be used at any time during the term of this Agreement by Lessee for the purpose of carrying on any business, profession, or trade of any kind, or for any purpose other than as a private single family dwelling. Lessee shall not allow any other person, other than Lessee's immediate family, to occupy the Premises.
5. CONDITION OF PREMISES. Lessee stipulates, represents, and warrants that Lessee has examined the Premises, and that they are in good order, repair, and in a safe, clean, and tenantable condition.
6. ALTERATIONS AND IMPROVEMENTS. Lessee shall make no alterations or improvements on the Premises or construct any building or make any other improvements on the Premises without the prior written consent of Lessor.
7. NON-DELIVERY OF POSSESSION. In the event Lessor cannot deliver possession of the Premises to Lessee upon the commencement of the term, through no fault of Lessor or its agents, then Lessor or its agents shall have no liability, but the rental herein provided shall abate until possession is given. Lessor or its agents shall have thirty (30) days in which to give possession, and if possession is tendered within such time, Lessee agrees to accept the demised Premises and pay the rental herein provided from that date. In the event possession cannot be delivered within such time, through no fault of Lessor or its agents, then this Agreement and all rights hereunder shall terminate.

Lease Agreement

8. UTILITIES. Lessee shall be responsible for arranging for and paying for all utility services required on the Premises.

IN WITNESS WHEREOF the parties have reviewed the information above and certify, to the best of their knowledge, that the information provided by the signatory is true and accurate.

Lease Agreement

Project 4 Prepare and Inspect a Lease Agreement
WL2-C8-P4-Lease.docx

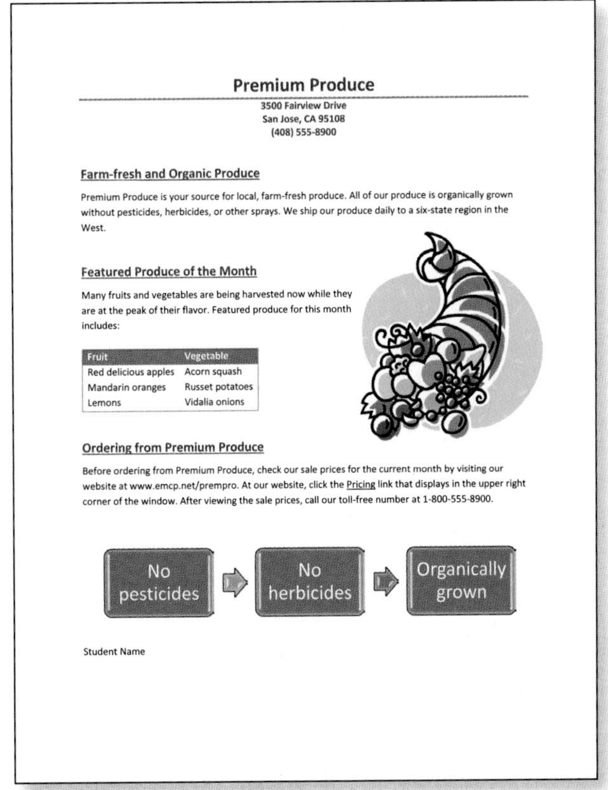
Premium Produce
3500 Fairview Drive
San Jose, CA 95108
(408) 555-8900

Farm-fresh and Organic Produce

Premium Produce is your source for local, farm-fresh produce. All of our produce is organically grown without pesticides, herbicides, or other sprays. We ship our produce daily to a six-state region in the West.

Featured Produce of the Month

Many fruits and vegetables are being harvested now while they are at the peak of their flavor. Featured produce for this month includes:

Fruit	Vegetable
Red delicious apples	Acorn squash
Mandarin oranges	Russet potatoes
Lemons	Vidalia onions

Ordering from Premium Produce

Before ordering from Premium Produce, check our sale prices for the current month by visiting our website at www.emcp.net/prempro. At our website, click the Pricing link that displays in the upper right corner of the window. After viewing the sale prices, call our toll-free number at 1-800-555-8900.

Student Name

Project 5 Check the Accessibility and Compatibility of a Produce Document
WL2-C8-P5-PremPro.docx

Project 1 Restrict Formatting and Editing in a Company Report

3 Parts

You will open a company report document, restrict formatting and editing in the document, insert a password, and allow exceptions to restrictions for specific users.

Protecting Documents

Within your organization, you may want to distribute copies of a document among members of a group. In some situations, you may want to protect your document and limit the changes that others can make to it. If you create a document containing sensitive, restricted, or private information, you should consider protecting it by saving it as a read-only document or securing it with a password.

With options at the Restrict Editing task pane, you can limit what formatting and editing users can perform on the text in a document. Limiting formatting and editing is especially useful in a workgroup environment, in which a number of people in an organization will review and edit the same document.

For example, suppose you are responsible for preparing the yearly corporate report for your company. This report contains information from a variety of departments, such as finance, human resources, and sales and marketing. You can prepare the report and then specify what portions of the document given individuals are allowed to edit. You might specify that a person in the finance department can edit only that portion of the report containing information on finances. Similarly, you might specify that someone in human resources can edit only data pertinent to the human resources department. By limiting others' options for editing, you can protect the integrity of the document.

Restrict Editing

To protect a document, display the Restrict Editing task pane, shown in Figure 8.1, by clicking the REVIEW tab and then clicking the Restrict Editing button in the Protect group. Use options in the *Formatting restrictions* section to

Figure 8.1 Restrict Editing Task Pane

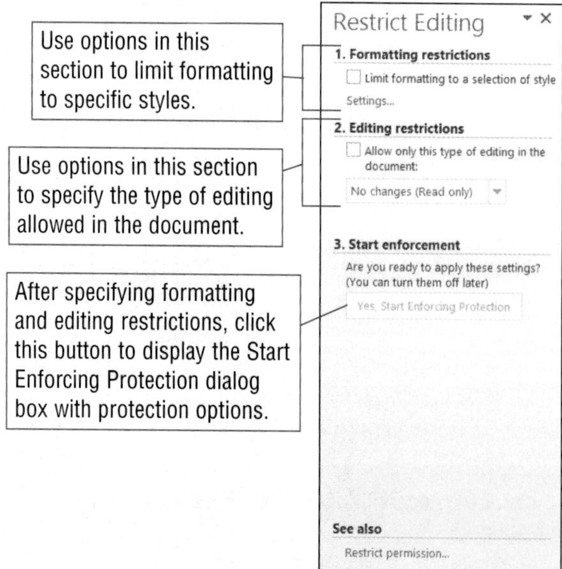

limit formatting to specific styles and use options in the *Editing restrictions* section to specify the type of editing allowed in the document.

The Protect group on the REVIEW tab contains a Block Authors button. This button is available only when a document is saved to a Microsoft SharePoint Foundation site that supports workspaces. If the button is active, select the portion of the document you want to block from editing and then click the Block Authors button. To unblock authors, click in the locked section of the document and then click the Block Authors button.

Restricting Formatting

With options in the *Formatting restrictions* section of the Restrict Editing task pane, you can lock specific styles used in a document, thus allowing the use of only those styles and prohibiting users from making other formatting changes. Click the Settings hyperlink in the *Formatting restrictions* section and the Formatting Restrictions dialog box displays, as shown in Figure 8.2.

Quick Steps

Display the Formatting Restrictions Dialog Box

1. Click REVIEW tab.
2. Click Restrict Editing button.
3. Click Settings hyperlink.

Insert a check mark in the *Limit formatting to a selection of styles* check box and the styles become available in the *Checked styles are currently allowed* list box. In this list box, insert check marks in the check boxes preceding the styles you want to allow and remove check marks from the check boxes preceding the styles you do not want to allow. Limit formatting to a minimum number of styles by clicking the Recommended Minimum button. This allows formatting with styles that Word uses for certain features, such as bulleted and numbered lists. Click the None button to remove all of the check marks and prevent all styles from being used in the document. Click the All button to insert check marks in all of the check boxes and allow all styles to be used in the document.

Use options in the *Formatting* section of the dialog box to allow or not allow AutoFormat to make changes in a document and to allow or not allow users to switch themes or style sets.

Figure 8.2 Formatting Restrictions Dialog Box

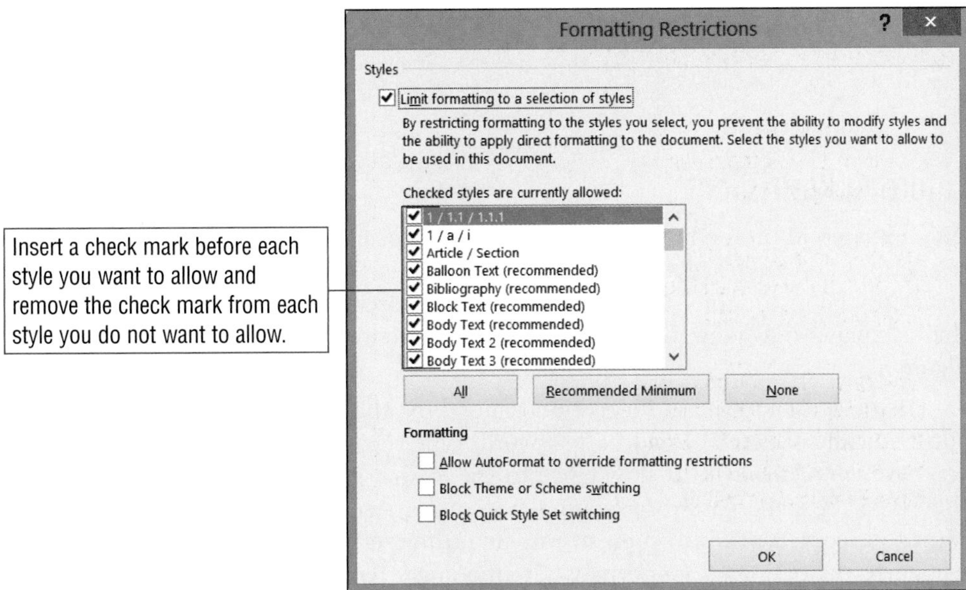

Project 1a Restricting Formatting of a Document

Part 1 of 3

1. Open **TECRpt.docx** and then save the document and name it **WL2-C8-P1-TECRpt**.
2. Restrict formatting to the Heading 1 and Heading 2 styles by completing the following steps:
   a. Click the REVIEW tab.
   b. Click the Restrict Editing button in the Protect group.

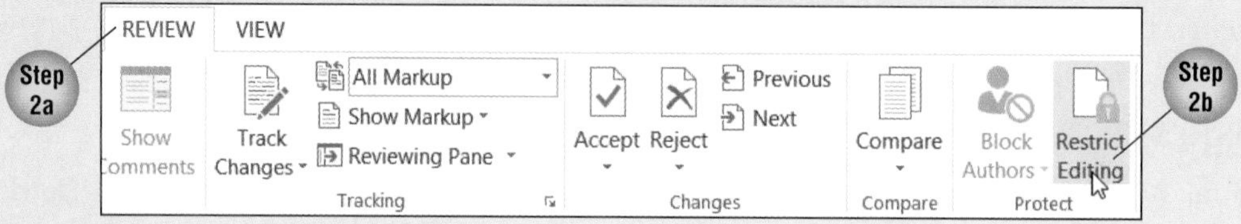

   c. At the Restrict Editing task pane, click the *Limit formatting to a selection of styles* check box to insert a check mark. (Skip this step if the check box already contains a check mark.)
   d. Click the Settings hyperlink.
   e. At the Formatting Restrictions dialog box, click the None button.
   f. Scroll down the list box and then click to insert check marks in the *Heading 1* check box and *Heading 2* check box.
   g. Click OK.
   h. At the message telling you that the document may contain direct formatting or styles that are not allowed and asking if you want to remove them, click Yes.
3. Save **WL2-C8-P1-TECRpt.docx**.

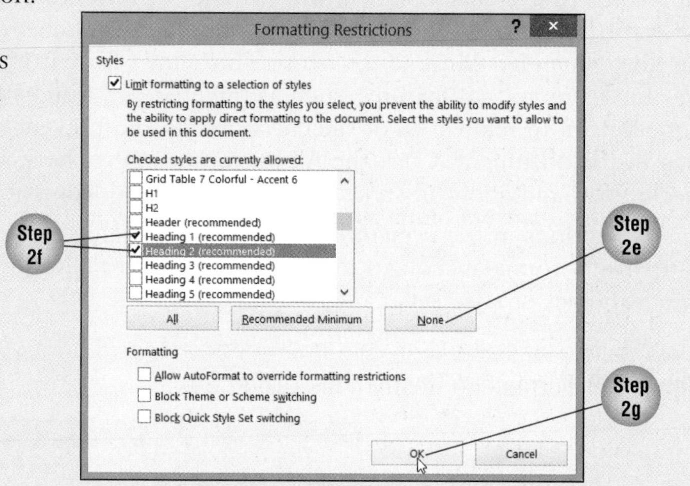

Quick Steps

Display the Start Enforcing Protection Dialog Box

1. Click REVIEW tab.
2. Click Restrict Editing button.
3. Specify formatting and/or editing options.
4. Click Yes, Start Enforcing Protection button.
5. Type password.
6. Press Tab key; type password again.
7. Click OK.

Enforcing Restrictions

The first step in protecting your document is to specify formatting and editing restrictions and any exceptions to those restrictions. The second step is to start enforcing the restrictions. Click the Yes, Start Enforcing Protection button in the task pane to display the Start Enforcing Protection dialog box, as shown in Figure 8.3.

At the Start Enforcing Protection dialog box, the *Password* option is automatically selected. To add a password, type the desired password in the *Enter new password (optional)* text box. Click in the *Reenter password to confirm* text box and then type the same password again. Choose the *User authentication* option if you want to use encryption to prevent any unauthorized changes. If Word does not recognize the password you type when opening a password-protected document, check to make sure Caps Lock is off and then try typing the password again.

Figure 8.3 Start Enforcing Protection Dialog Box

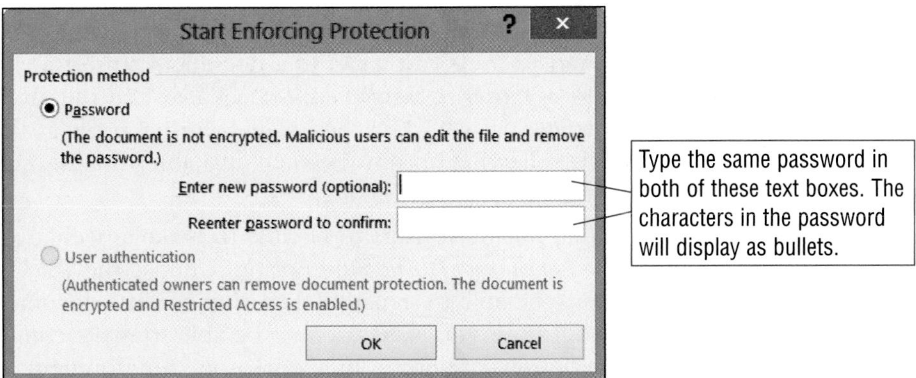

Type the same password in both of these text boxes. The characters in the password will display as bullets.

Project 1b Protecting a Document

Part 2 of 3

1. With **WL2-C8-P1-TECRpt.docx** open, click the Yes, Start Enforcing Protection button (located near the bottom of the task pane).
2. At the Start Enforcing Protection dialog box, type **formatting** in the *Enter new password (optional)* text box. (Bullets will display in the text box, rather than the letters you type.)
3. Press the Tab key (which moves the insertion point to the *Reenter password to confirm* text box) and then type **formatting**. (Bullets will display in the text box, rather than the letters you type.)
4. Click OK to close the dialog box.
5. Read the information in the task pane telling you that the document is protected and that you may format text only with certain styles. Click the Available styles hyperlink. (This displays the Styles task pane with only four styles in the list box: *Clear All*, *Normal*, *Heading 1*, and *Heading 2*.)

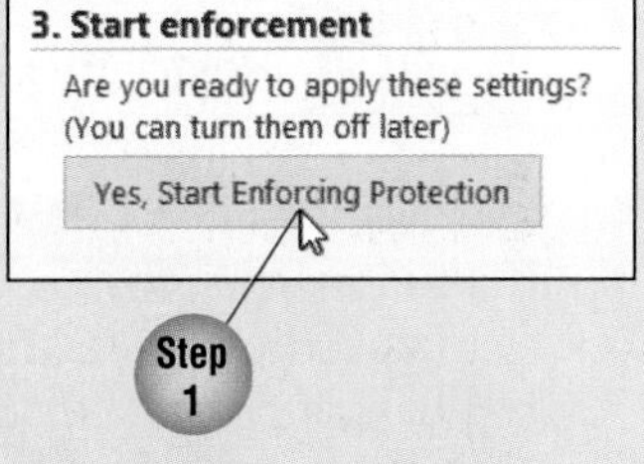

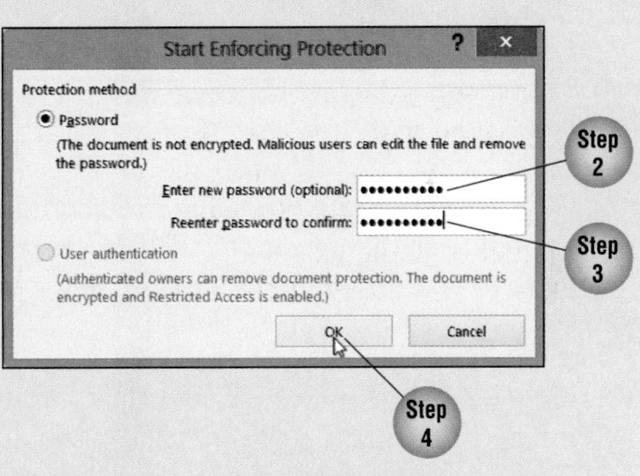

6. Apply the Heading 1 style to the title *TANDEM ENERGY CORPORATION* and apply the Heading 2 style to the following headings: *Overview*, *Research and Development*, *Manufacturing*, and *Sales and Marketing*.
7. Close the Styles task pane.
8. Apply the Lines (Simple) style set.
9. At the message indicating that some of the styles could not be updated, click OK.
10. Save the document.
11. Remove the password protection from the document by completing the following steps:
    a. Click the Stop Protection button located at the bottom of the task pane.
    b. At the Unprotect Document dialog box, type **formatting** in the Password text box.
    c. Click OK.
12. Save **WL2-C8-P1-TECRpt.docx**.

Restricting Editing

Use the *Editing restrictions* option at the Restrict Editing task pane to limit the types of changes users can make to a document. Insert a check mark in the *Allow only this type of editing in the document* check box and the drop-down list below the option becomes active. Click the down-pointing arrow at the right of the option box and the following options become available: *Tracked changes*, *Comments*, *Filling in forms*, and *No changes (Read only)*.

If you do not want users to be able to make any changes to a document, choose the *No changes (Read only)* option. Choose the *Tracked changes* option if you want users to be able to make tracked changes in a document and choose the *Comments* option if you want users to be able to make comments in a document. These two options are useful in a workgroup environment, in which a document is routed to various members of the group for review. Choose the *Filling in forms* option and users will be able to fill in the fields in a form but will not be able to make any other changes.

Project 1c **Restricting Editing of a Document** **Part 3 of 3**

1. With **WL2-C8-P1-TECRpt.docx** open, restrict editing only to comments by completing the following steps:
   a. Make sure the Restrict Editing task pane displays.
   b. Click the *Allow only this type of editing in the document* check box to insert a check mark.
   c. Click the down-pointing arrow at the right of the option box below *Allow only this type of editing in the document* and then click *Comments* at the drop-down list.
2. Click the Yes, Start Enforcing Protection button located near the bottom of the task pane.
3. At the Start Enforcing Protection dialog box, click OK. (Adding a password is optional.)
4. Read the information in the task pane telling you that the document is protected and that you may only insert comments.
5. Click each ribbon tab and notice the buttons and options that are dimmed and unavailable.
6. Insert a comment by completing the following steps:
   a. Move the insertion point immediately to the right of the period that ends the last sentence in the second paragraph of the *Overview* section.
   b. Click the REVIEW tab (if necessary), click the Show Markup button in the Tracking group, point to *Balloons*, and then click the *Show All Revisions Inline* option.
   c. Click the Reviewing Pane button to turn on the display of the Reviewing pane.
   d. Click the New Comment button in the Comments group on the REVIEW tab.

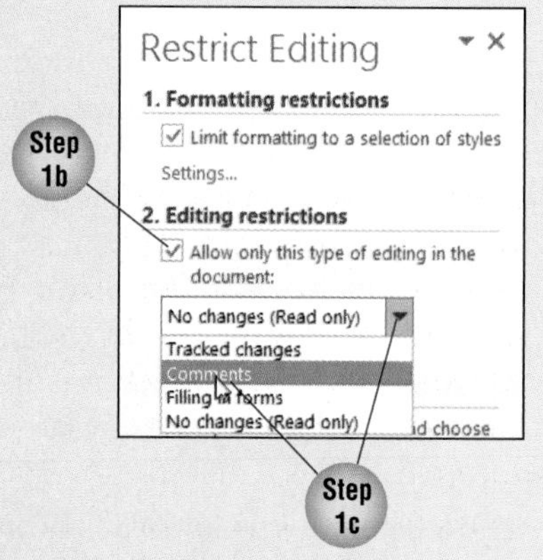

e. Type the following text in the Reviewing pane: **Include additional information on the impact of this purchase.**
f. Close the Reviewing pane.
g. Click the Stop Protection button located at the bottom of the Restrict Editing task pane.
h. Close the Restrict Editing task pane.

7. Save the document and then print only page 1.
8. Print only the comment. (To do this, display the Print backstage area, click the first gallery in the *Settings* category, click the *List of Markup* option, and then click the Print button.)
9. Close **WL2-C8-P1-TECRpt.docx**.

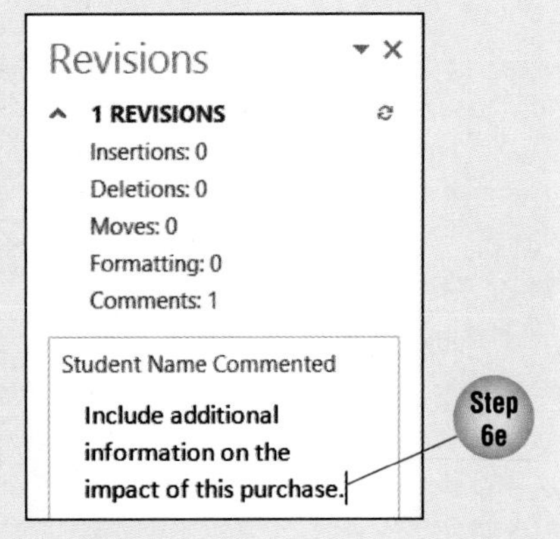

Project 2 Protect a Contract Document and Identify a Training Document as Read-Only — 2 Parts

You will open a contract document and then protect the document with a password. You will also open documents in different views.

Protecting a Document with a Password

In the previous section of this chapter, you learned how to protect a document with a password using options at the Start Enforcing Protection dialog box. You can also protect a document with a password using options at the General Options dialog box, shown in Figure 8.4 on the next page. To display this dialog box, press the F12 key to display the Save As dialog box, click the Tools button located near the bottom of the dialog box next to the Save button, and then click *General Options* at the drop-down list.

At the General Options dialog box, you can assign a password to open the document, modify the document, or both. To insert a password to open the document, click in the *Password to open* text box and then type the password. Passwords can contain up to 15 characters, should be 8 characters or more in length, and are case sensitive. Consider combining uppercase letters, lowercase letters, numbers, and/or symbols in your password to make it secure. Use the *Password to modify* option to create a password that a person must enter before he or she can make edits to the document.

At the General Options dialog box, insert a check mark in the *Read-only recommended* check box to save a document as a read-only document. If you open a document that is saved as a read-only document and then make changes to it, you have to save the document with a new name. Use this option if you do not want the contents of the original document changed.

Quick Steps

Add a Password to a Document

1. Press F12.
2. Click Tools button.
3. Click *General Options*.
4. Type password in *Password to modify* text box.
5. Press Enter.
6. Type same password again.
7. Press Enter.

A strong password contains a mix of uppercase and lowercase letters as well as numbers and symbols.

Figure 8.4 General Options Dialog Box

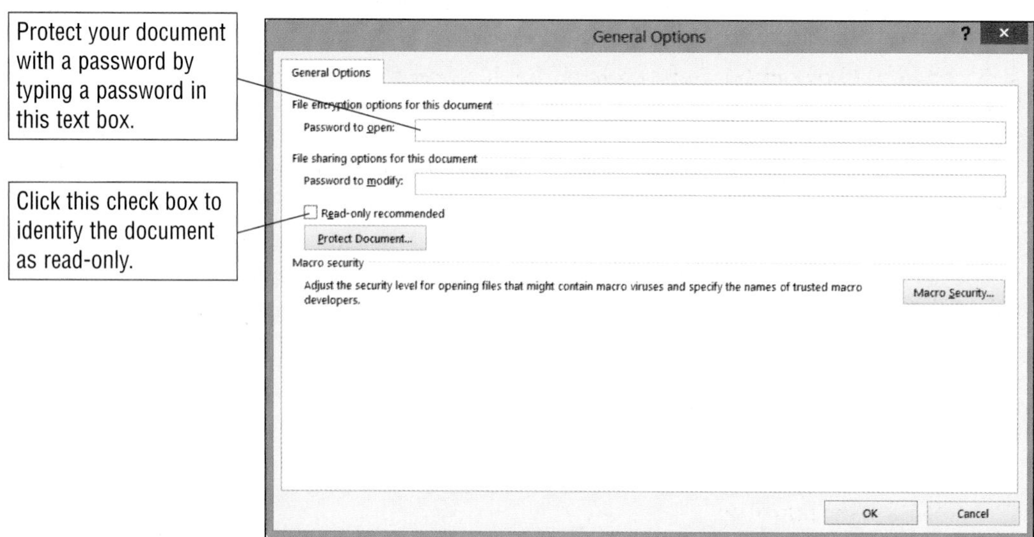

Project 2a Protecting a Document with a Password

Part 1 of 2

1. Open **TECContract.docx**.
2. Save the document and name it **WL2-C8-P2-TECContract**.
3. Save the document and protect it with a password by completing the following steps:
   a. Press F12 to display the Save As dialog box.
   b. Click the Tools button located near the bottom of the dialog box (next to the Save button) and then click *General Options* at the drop-down list.
   c. At the General Options dialog box, type your first name in the *Password to open* text box. (If your name is longer than 15 characters, abbreviate it. You will not see your name; Word inserts bullets in place of the letters.)
   d. After typing your name, press the Enter key.
   e. At the Confirm Password dialog box, type your name again in the Reenter password to open text box. (Be sure to type it exactly as you did in the *Password to open* text box, including uppercase or lowercase letters.) Press the Enter key.
   f. Click the Save button at the Save As dialog box.
4. Close **WL2-C8-P2-TECContract.docx**.
5. Open **WL2-C8-P2-TECContract.docx** and type your password when prompted in the *Enter password to open file* text box.
6. Close the document.

Step 3c

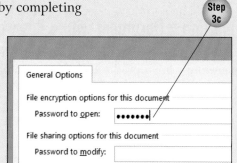

General Options
File encryption options for this document
Password to open: •••••••
File sharing options for this document
Password to modify:

Opening a Document in Different Views

Use the Open button in the Open dialog box to open a document in different views. At the Open dialog box, click the Open button arrow and a drop-down list of options displays. Click the *Open Read-Only* option and the document opens in Read Mode view and Read-Only mode. In Read-Only mode, you can make changes to the document but you cannot save the document with the same name. Exit Read Mode view and display the document in Print Layout view by pressing the Esc key on the keyboard.

Click the *Open as Copy* option and a copy of the document opens and the text *Copy (1)* displays at the beginning of the document name in the Title bar. Click the *Open in Protected View* option and the document opens with the text *(Protected View)* after the document name in the Title bar. A message bar displays above the document telling you that the file was opened in Protected view. To edit the document, click the Enable Editing button in the message bar. Open a document with the *Open and Repair* option and Word will open a new version of the document and attempt to repair any issues.

Quick Steps

Open a Document in Different Views

1. Display Open dialog box.
2. Click desired document name.
3. Click Open button arrow.
4. Click desired option at drop-down list.

Project 2b Opening a Document in Different Views

Part 2 of 2

1. Open **TECTraining.docx** and then save the document and name it **WL2-C8-P2-TECTraining.**
2. Close **WL2-C8-P2-TECTraining.docx.**
3. Open a document as a read-only document by completing the following steps:
   a. Press Ctrl + F12 to display the Open dialog box and then navigate to the WL2C8 folder on your storage medium.
   b. Click once on the document name ***WL2-C8-P2-TECTraining.docx.***
   c. Click the Open button arrow (located near the bottom right corner of the dialog box) and then click *Open Read-Only* at the drop-down list.
   d. The document opens in Read Mode view. Press the Esc key to exit Read Mode and display the document in Print Layout view. Notice that *[Read-Only]* displays after the name of the document in the Title bar.

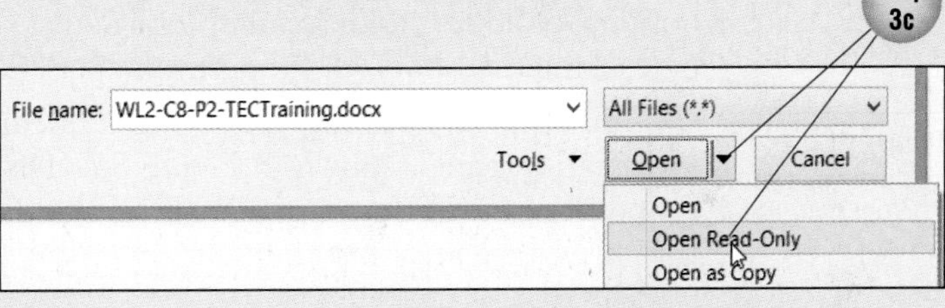

   e. Close the document.
4. Open a document in Protected view by completing the following steps:
   a. Press Ctrl + F12 to display the Open dialog box.
   b. Click once on the document name ***PremPro.docx.***
   c. Click the Open button arrow and then click *Open in Protected View* at the drop-down list.
   d. Press the Esc key to exit Read Mode view and display the document in Print Layout view. Notice the message bar that displays with information telling you that the file was opened in Protected view.
   e. Click each tab and notice that most of the formatting options are dimmed.
   f. Click in the document and then click the Enable Editing button in the message bar. This removes *(Protected View)* after the document name in the Title bar and makes available the options in the tabs.

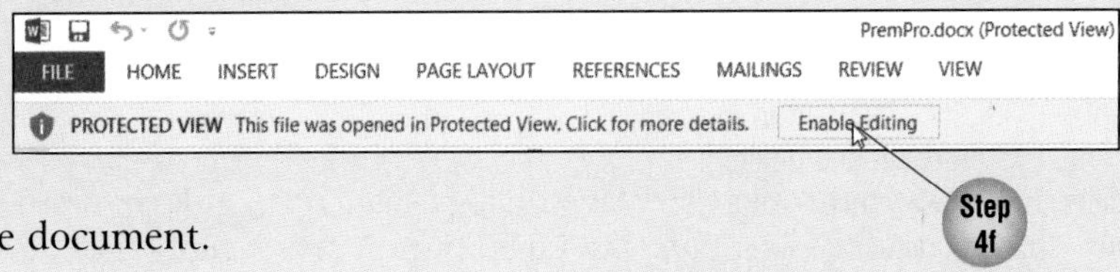

   g. Close the document.

Project 3 Prepare a Real Estate Agreement for Distribution 3 Parts

You will open a real estate agreement and then prepare it for distribution by inserting document properties, marking it as final, and encrypting it with a password.

Managing Document Properties

Quick Steps

Display Document Information Panel
1. Click FILE tab.
2. Click Properties button.
3. Click *Show Document Panel.*

Each document you create has properties associated with it, such as the type of document, the location in which it has been saved, and when it was created, modified, and accessed. You can view and modify document properties at the Info backstage area. You can also modify document properties at the document information panel. To display information about the open document, click the FILE tab. Document property information displays at the right side of the Info backstage area, as shown in Figure 8.5.

The document property information that displays in the Info backstage area includes the file size, number of pages and words, total editing time, and any tags or comments that have been added. Add or update a document property by hovering your mouse over the information that displays at the right of the property (a rectangular text box with a light blue border displays), clicking in the text box, and then typing the desired information. In the *Related Dates* section, dates display for when the document was created and when it was last modified and printed. The *Related People* section displays the name of the author of the document and provides options for adding additional author names. Display additional document properties by clicking the Show All Properties hyperlink.

Properties ▾

Properties

You also can add information to a document's properties at the document information panel, shown in Figure 8.6. Display this panel by clicking the Properties button that displays above the document property information in the Info backstage area and then clicking *Show Document Panel* at the drop-down list.

Figure 8.5 Info Backstage Area

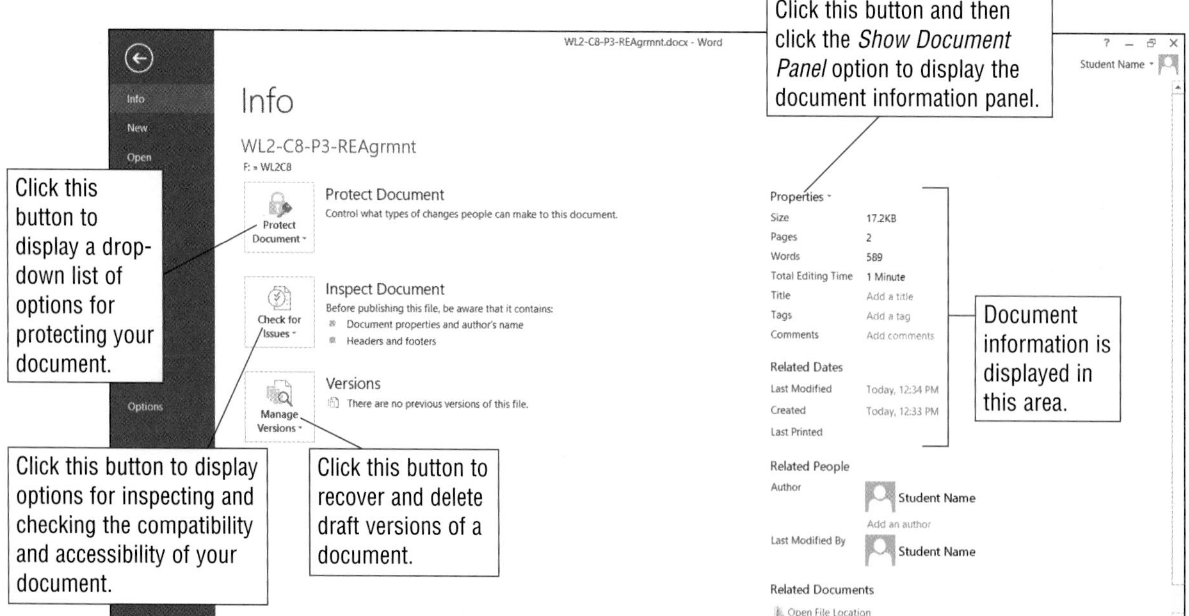

Figure 8.6 Document Information Panel

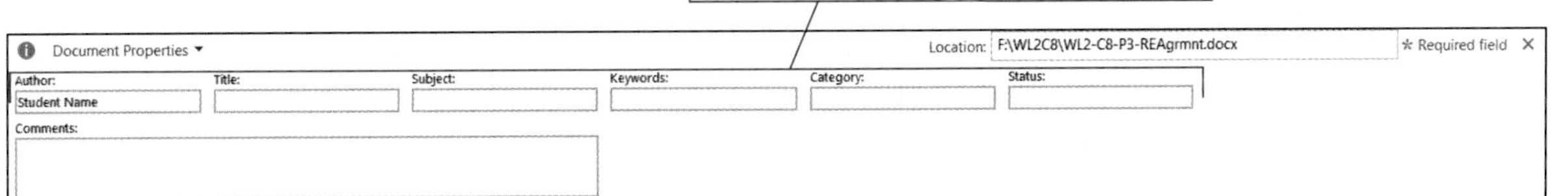

By typing specific information in each text box in the document information panel, you can describe a document. Inserting text in some of the text boxes can help you organize and identify your documents. For example, insert specific keywords contained in the document in the *Keywords* text box, and you can search for all documents containing those keywords. Text you type in the document information panel is saved with the document. Print the document properties for a document by displaying the Print backstage area, clicking the first gallery in the *Settings* category, clicking *Document Info* at the drop-down list, and then clicking the Print button.

In addition to inserting information about a document in the document information panel, you can insert specific information with options at the Properties dialog box, shown in Figure 8.7. The name of the dialog box reflects the currently open document. Display this dialog box by clicking the Document Properties button that displays in the upper left corner of the document information panel and then clicking *Advanced Properties* at the drop-down list. You can also display this dialog box by displaying the Info backstage area, clicking the Properties button, and then clicking *Advanced Properties* at the drop-down list. Another method for displaying the Properties dialog box is to display the Open dialog box, click the desired document, click the Organize button, and then click *Properties* at the drop-down list. You can also right-click on the desired file name and then click *Properties* at the shortcut menu.

Quick Steps

Display the Properties Dialog Box

1. Click FILE tab.
2. Click Properties button.
3. Click *Advanced Properties.*

Figure 8.7 Properties Dialog Box with General Tab Selected

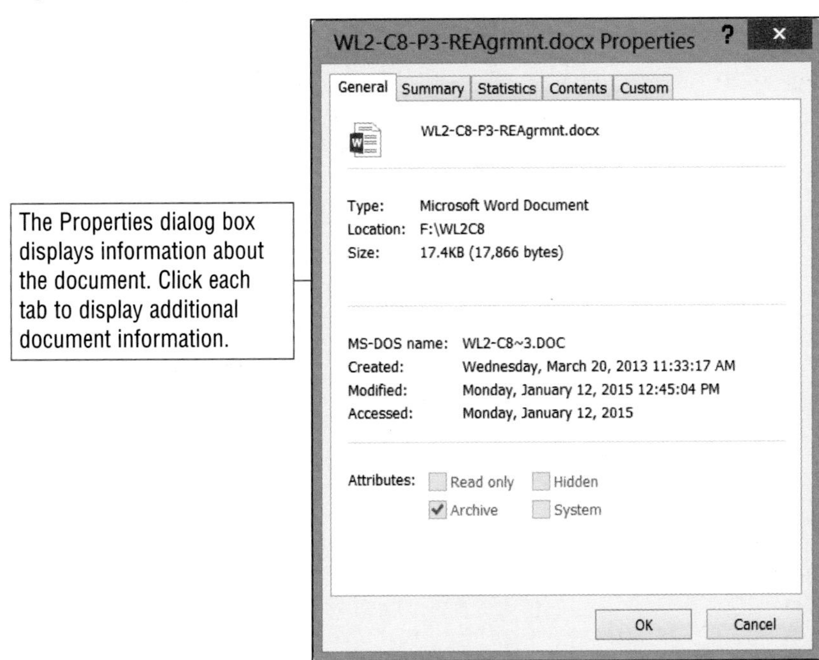

The Properties dialog box with the General tab selected displays information about the document type, size, and location. Click the Summary tab to view fields such as title, subject, author, company, category, keywords, and comments. Some fields may contain data and others may be blank. You can insert, edit, or delete text in the fields. With the Statistics tab selected, information displays such as the number of pages, paragraphs, lines, words, and characters and with the Contents tab active, the dialog box displays the document title.

Click the Custom tab to add custom properties to the document. For example, you can add a property that displays the date the document was completed, information on the department in which the document was created, and much more.

Project 3a Inserting Document Properties

Part 1 of 3

1. Open **REAgrmnt.docx** and then save the document and name it **WL2-C8-P3-REAgrmnt**.
2. Make the following changes to the document:
   a. Insert page numbers that print at the top of each page at the right margin.
   b. Insert the footer *WL2-C8-P3-REAgrmnt.docx* centered on each page.
3. Insert document properties by completing the following steps:
   a. Click the FILE tab. (Make sure the Info backstage area displays.)
   b. Hover your mouse over the text *Add a title* that displays at the right of the *Title* document property, click in the text box that displays, and then type **Real Estate Sale Agreement**.
   c. Display the document information panel by clicking the Properties button that displays above the document property information and then clicking *Show Document Panel* at the drop-down list.

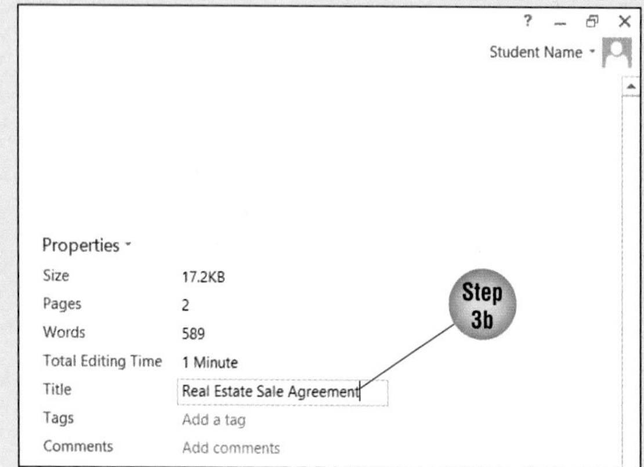

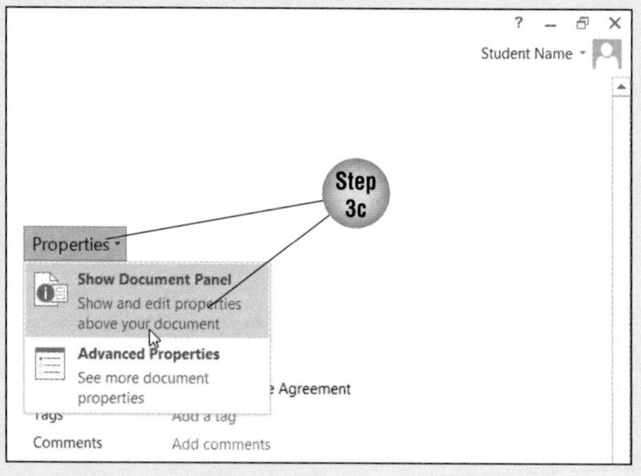

d. Select any text that appears in the *Author* text box and then type your first and last names.
e. Press the Tab key twice (which makes the *Subject* text box active) and then type **Real Estate Sale Agreement.**
f. Press the Tab key and then type the following words, separated by commas, in the *Keywords* text box: **real estate, agreement, contract, purchasing.**
g. Press the Tab key and then type **Agreement** in the *Category* text box.
h. Press the Tab key twice and then type the following text in the *Comments* text box: **This is a real estate sale agreement between two parties.**

4. Click the Close button that displays in the upper right corner of the document information panel.

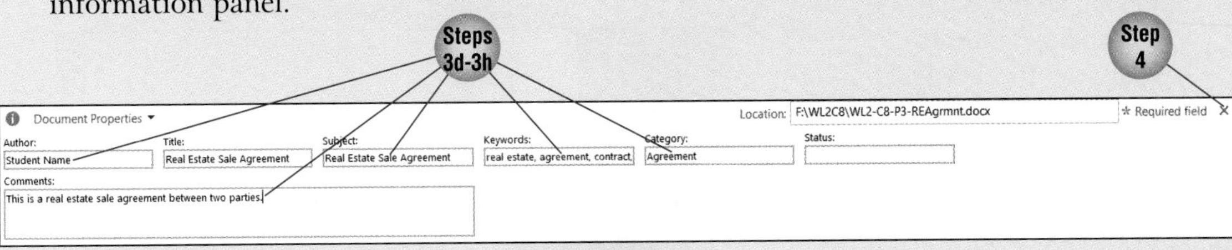

5. Save **WL2-C8-P3-REAgrmnt.docx** and then print only the document properties by completing the following steps:
   a. Click the FILE tab and then click the *Print* option.
   b. At the Print backstage area, click the first gallery in the *Settings* category and then click *Document Info* at the drop-down list.
   c. Click the Print button.
6. Save **WL2-C8-P3-REAgrmnt.docx**.

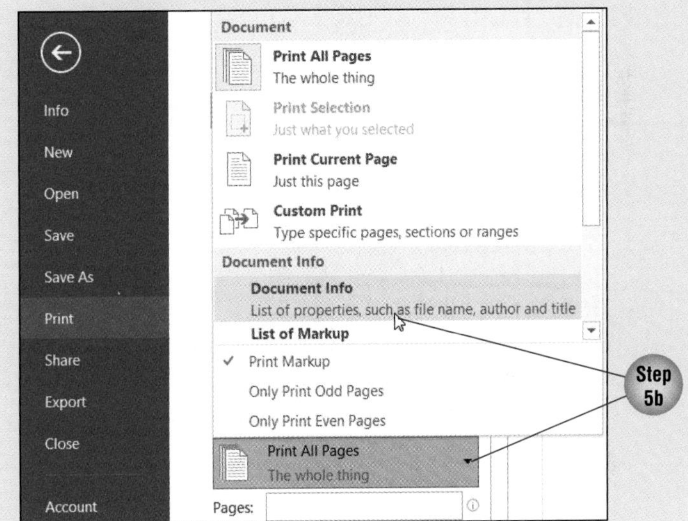

Restricting Documents

The middle panel in the Info backstage area contains buttons for protecting a document, checking for issues in a document, and managing versions of a document. Click the Protect Document button in the middle panel and a drop-down list displays with the following options: *Mark as Final*, *Encrypt with Password*, *Restrict Editing*, *Restrict Access*, and *Add a Digital Signature*.

Protect Document

Marking a Document as Final

Click the *Mark as Final* option to save the document as a read-only document. When you click this option, a message displays telling you that the document will be marked and then saved. At this message, click OK. This displays another message telling you that the document has been marked as final, which indicates that editing is complete and that this is the final version of the document. The message further indicates that when a document is marked as final, the status property is set to *Final*; typing, editing commands, and proofing marks are turned off; and the document can be identified by the Mark as Final icon, which displays toward the left side of the Status bar. At this message, click OK. After a document is marked as final, the message *This document has been marked as final to discourage editing.* displays to the right of the Protect Document button in the Info backstage area.

Project 3b Marking a Document as Final

Part 2 of 3

1. With **WL2-C8-P3-REAgrmnt.docx** open, mark the document as final by completing the following steps:
   a. Click the FILE tab.
   b. Click the Protect Document button at the Info backstage area and then click *Mark as Final* at the drop-down list.
   c. At the message telling you that the document will be marked and saved, click OK.
   d. At the next message that displays, click OK. Notice the message that displays to the right of the Protect Document button.
   e. Click the Back button to return to the document.
2. At the document, notice the message bar that displays near the top of the screen and then close the document.
3. Open **WL2-C8-P3-REAgrmnt.docx** and then click the Edit Anyway button on the yellow message bar.

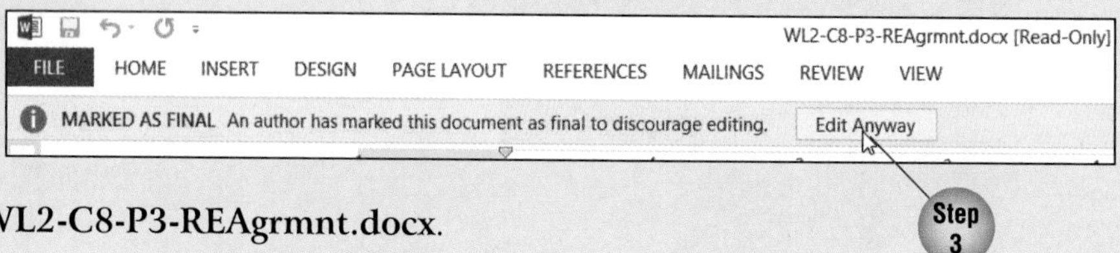

4. Save **WL2-C8-P3-REAgrmnt.docx**.

Encrypting a Document

Quick Steps

Encrypt a Document
1. Click FILE tab.
2. Click Protect Document button.
3. Click *Encrypt with Password.*
4. Type password and then press Enter.
5. Type password again and then press Enter.

Word provides a number of methods for protecting a document with a password. Previously in this chapter, you learned how to protect a document with a password using options at the Start Enforcing Protection dialog box and the General Options dialog box. In addition to these two methods, you can protect a document with a password by clicking the Protect Document button at the Info backstage area and then clicking the *Encrypt with Password* option at the drop-down list. At the Encrypt Document dialog box that displays, type your password in the text box (the text will display as bullets) and then press the Enter key or click OK. At the Confirm Password dialog box, type your password again (the text will display as bullets) and then press the Enter key or click OK. When you apply a password, the message *A password is required to open this document.* displays to the right of the Protect Document button.

Restricting Editing

Click the Protect Document button at the Info backstage area and then click the *Restrict Editing* option at the drop-down list and the document displays with the Restrict Editing task pane open. This is the same task pane you learned about previously in this chapter.

Adding a Digital Signature

Use the *Add a Digital Signature* option at the Protect Document button drop-down list to insert an invisible digital signature in a document. A *digital signature* is an electronic stamp that verifies a document's authenticity. Before adding a digital signature, you must obtain one. You can obtain a digital signature from a commercial certification authority.

Project 3c Encrypting a Document with a Password Part 3 of 3

1. With **WL2-C8-P3-REAgrmnt.docx** open, encrypt the document with a password by completing the following steps:
   a. Click the FILE tab, click the Protect Document button at the Info backstage area, and then click *Encrypt with Password* at the drop-down list.
   b. At the Encrypt Document dialog box, type your initials in uppercase letters in the Password text box. (The text will display as bullets.)
   c. Press the Enter key.
   d. At the Confirm Password dialog box, type your initials again in uppercase letters in the *Reenter password* text box (your text will display as bullets) and then press the Enter key.
2. Click the Back button to return to the document.
3. Save and then close the document.
4. Open **WL2-C8-P3-REAgrmnt.docx**. At the Password dialog box, type your initials in uppercase letters in the *Enter password to open file* text box and then press the Enter key.
5. Save, print, and then close **WL2-C8-P3-REAgrmnt.docx**.

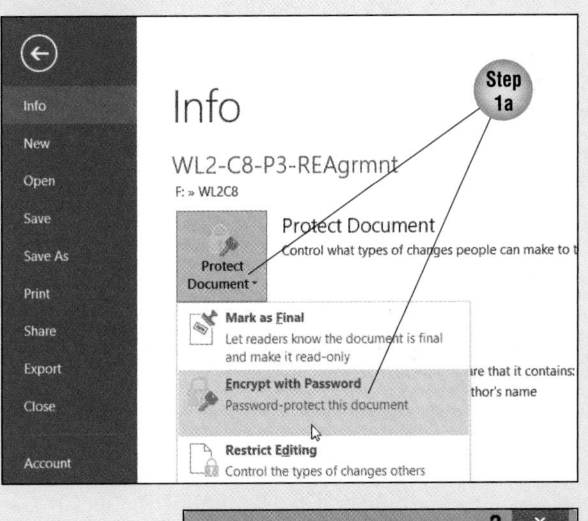

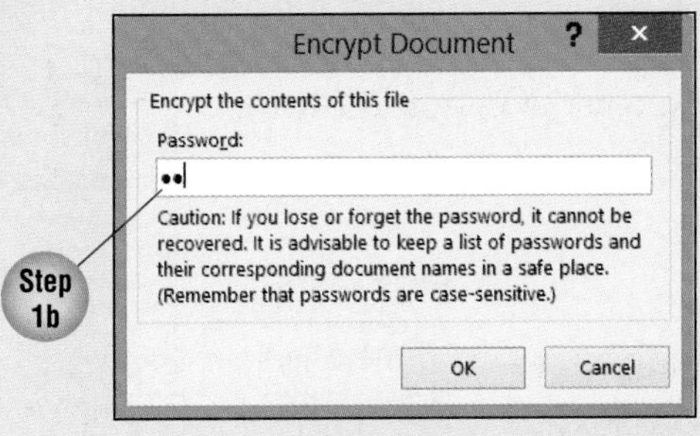

Project 4 Prepare and Inspect a Lease Agreement — 1 Part

You will open a lease agreement document, make tracked changes, hide text, and then inspect the document.

Inspecting Documents

Use options from the Check for Issues button drop-down list at the Info backstage area to inspect a document for personal and hidden data along with compatibility and accessibility issues. When you click the Check for Issues button, a drop-down list displays with the following options: *Inspect Document*, *Check Accessibility*, and *Check Compatibility*.

Using the Document Inspector

Check for Issues

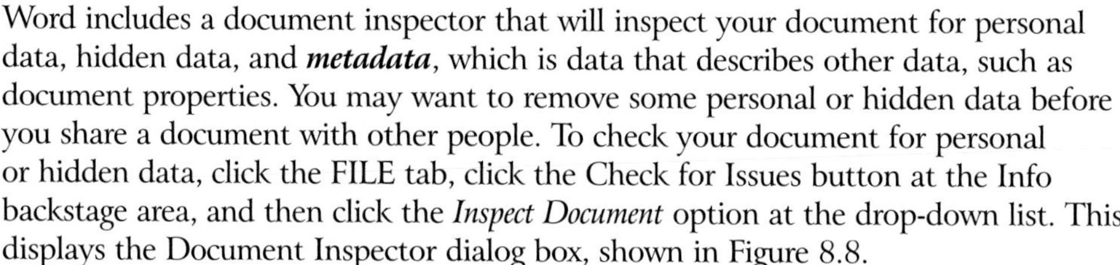

Word includes a document inspector that will inspect your document for personal data, hidden data, and ***metadata***, which is data that describes other data, such as document properties. You may want to remove some personal or hidden data before you share a document with other people. To check your document for personal or hidden data, click the FILE tab, click the Check for Issues button at the Info backstage area, and then click the *Inspect Document* option at the drop-down list. This displays the Document Inspector dialog box, shown in Figure 8.8.

By default, the document inspector checks all of the items listed in the dialog box. If you do not want the inspector to check a specific item in your document, remove the check mark preceding the item. For example, if you know your document has headers and footers that you do not need to check, click the *Headers, Footers, and Watermarks* check box to remove the check mark. To scan the document to identify information, click the Inspect button located near the bottom of the dialog box.

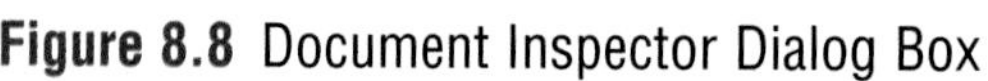

Figure 8.8 Document Inspector Dialog Box

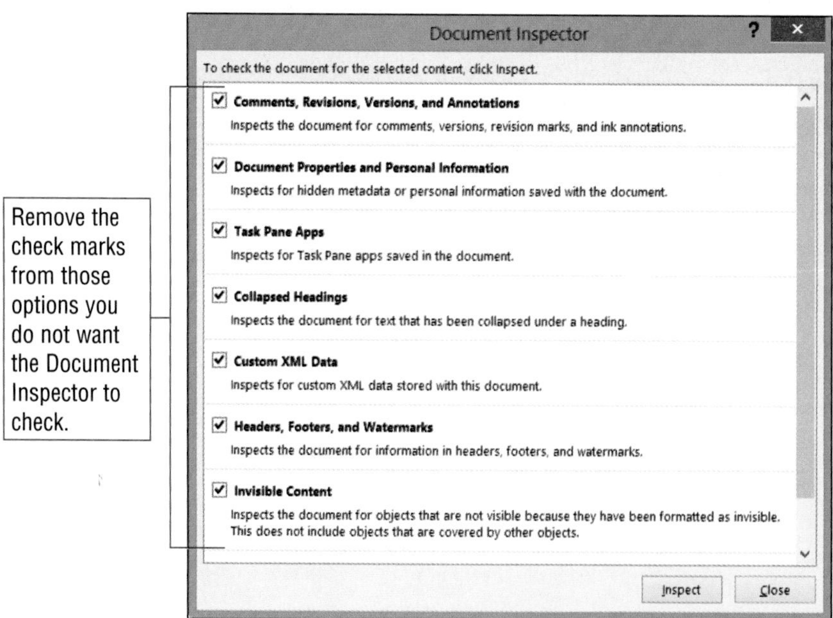

Remove the check marks from those options you do not want the Document Inspector to check.

When the inspection is complete, the results display in the dialog box. A check mark before an option indicates that the inspector did not find the specific items. If an exclamation point displays before an option, it means that the inspector found items and a list of the items displays. If you want to remove the found items, click the Remove All button that displays at the right of the desired option. Click the Reinspect button to ensure that the specific items were removed and then click the Close button.

Project 4 Inspecting a Document

Part 1 of 1

1. Open **Lease.docx** and then save the document and name it **WL2-C8-P4-Lease.docx**.
2. Make the following changes to the document:
   a. Turn on the Track Changes feature.
   b. Select the title *LEASE AGREEMENT* and then change the font size to 14 points.
   c. Delete the word *first* that displays in the second numbered paragraph (the *RENT* paragraph) and then type **fifteenth**.
   d. Move the insertion point to the beginning of the text *IN WITNESS WHEREOF* (located on page 2) and then press the Tab key.
   e. Turn off Track Changes.
3. Hide text by completing the following steps:
   a. Move the insertion point to the end of the first paragraph of text in the document (one space after the period at the end of the sentence).
   b. Type **The entire legal description of the property is required for this agreement to be valid.**
   c. Select the text you just typed.
   d. Click the HOME tab.
   e. Click the Font group dialog box launcher.
   f. At the Font dialog box, click the *Hidden* option in the *Effects* section.
   g. Click OK to close the dialog box.

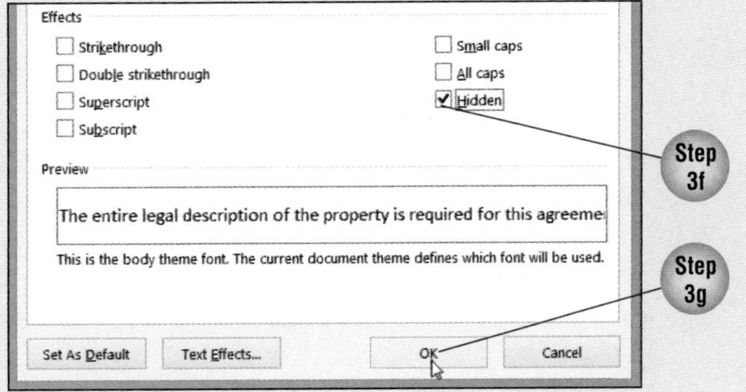

4. Click the Save button on the Quick Access toolbar.
5. Inspect the document by completing the following steps:
   a. Click the FILE tab.
   b. Click the Check for Issues button at the Info backstage area and then click *Inspect Document* at the drop-down list.

c. At the Document Inspector dialog box, tell the Document Inspector not to check the document for XML data by clicking the *Custom XML Data* check box to remove the check mark.

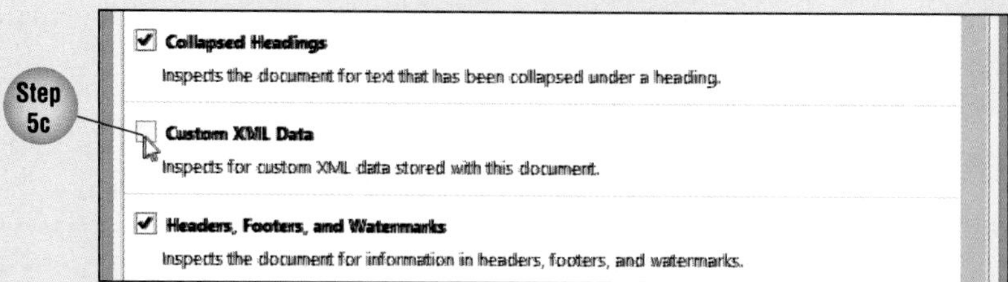

d. Click the Inspect button.

e. Read through the inspection results and then remove all of the hidden text by clicking the Remove All button that displays at the right side of the *Hidden Text* section. (Make sure that a message displays below *Hidden Text* indicating that the text was successfully removed.)

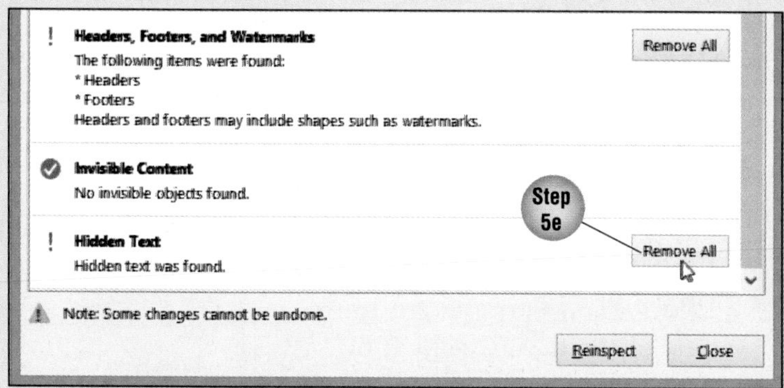

f. Click the Reinspect button.

g. To keep the header and footer text in the document, click the *Headers, Footers, and Watermarks* check box to remove the check mark.

h. Click the Inspect button.

i. Read through the inspection results and then remove all revisions by clicking the Remove All button that displays at the right side of the *Comments, Revisions, Versions, and Annotations* section.

j. Click the Reinspect button.

k. To leave the remaining items in the document, click the Close button.

6. Click the Back button to return to the document and then save the document.
7. Print and then close **WL2-C8-P4-Lease.docx**.

Project 5 Check the Accessibility and Compatibility of a Produce Document — 3 Parts

You will open a document containing information on produce, check for accessibility issues, and check the compatibility of elements with previous versions of Word. You will also manage unsaved versions of the document.

Checking the Accessibility of a Document

Word includes the accessibility checker feature, which checks a document for content that a person with disabilities, such as a visual impairment, might find difficult to read. Check the accessibility of a document by clicking the Check for Issues button at the Info backstage area and then clicking *Check Accessibility*. The accessibility checker examines the document for the most common accessibility problems in Word documents and groups them into three categories: errors (content that is unreadable to a person who is blind); warnings (content that is difficult to read); and tips (content that may or may not be difficult to read). The accessibility checker examines the document, closes the Info backstage area, and displays the Accessibility Checker task pane.

At the Accessibility Checker task pane, passages of text that are unreadable are grouped in the *ERRORS* section, passages with content that is difficult to read are grouped in the *WARNINGS* section, and passages with content that may or may not be difficult to read are grouped in the *TIPS* section. Select an issue in one of the sections, and an explanation of why this is an issue and how you can fix it displays at the bottom of the task pane.

Quick Steps

Check Accessibility
1. Click FILE tab.
2. Click Check for Issues button.
3. Click *Check Accessibility*.

Project 5a **Checking the Accessibility of a Document** **Part 1 of 3**

1. Open **PremPro.docx** and then save the document and name it **WL2-C8-P5-PremPro**.
2. Complete an accessibility check by completing the following steps:
   a. Click the FILE tab.
   b. At the Info backstage area, click the Check for Issues button and then click *Check Accessibility* at the drop-down list.
   c. Notice the Accessibility Checker task pane that displays at the right side of the screen. The task pane displays an *ERRORS* section and a *WARNINGS* section. Click *Picture 4* in the *ERRORS* section and then read the information that displays near the bottom of the task pane describing why you should fix the error and how to fix it.

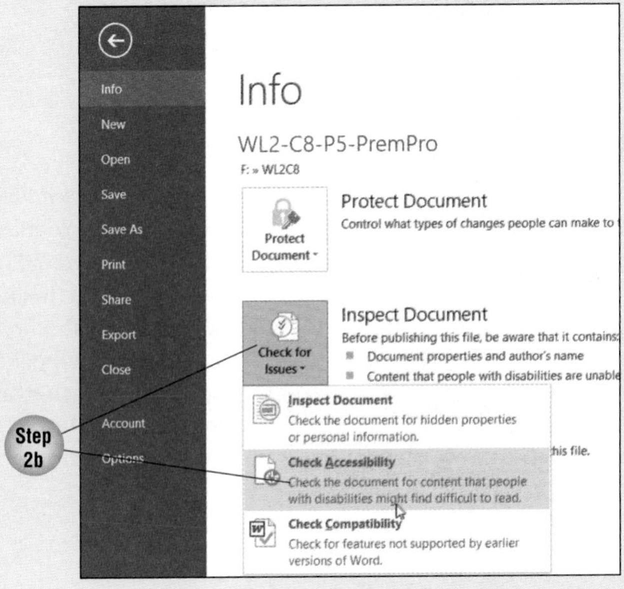

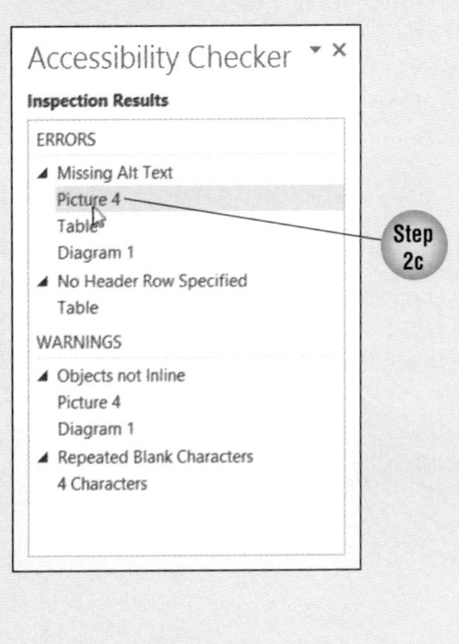

3. Add alternate text (which is a text-based representation of the clip art image) to the clip art by completing the following steps:
   a. Right-click on the clip art image in the document and then click *Format Picture* at the shortcut menu.
   b. At the Format Picture task pane, click the Layout & Properties icon and then click *ALT TEXT* to expand the options.
   c. Click in the *Title* text box, type **Cornucopia**, and then press the Tab key. (This selects the default text in the *Description* text box.)
   d. Type **Clip art image of a cornucopia of fruits and vegetables representing Premium Produce.**
   e. Click the Close button to close the task pane.

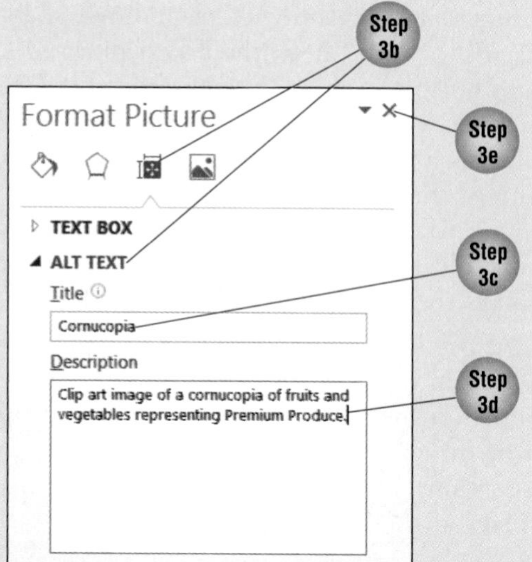

4. Click the first *Table* entry in the *ERRORS* section and then read the information that displays near the bottom of the task pane about creating alternate text for a table. Since the table contains text that is easily interpreted, you do not need to include alternate text.
5. Click the *Diagram 1* entry in the *ERRORS* section and then read the information about alternate text. Since this diagram contains text that is easily interpreted, you do not need to include alternate text.
6. Click *Picture 4* in the *WARNINGS* section and then read the information about objects that are not inline with text. You will not make the change suggested since the clip art would move to a different location on the page.
7. Click *Diagram 1* in the *WARNINGS* section and notice that it is the same information about objects that are not inline.
8. Close the Accessibility Checker task pane by clicking the Close button located in the upper right corner of the task pane.
9. Save **WL2-C8-P5-PremPro.docx**.

Checking the Compatibility of a Document

Quick Steps

Check Compatibility
1. Click FILE tab.
2. Click Check for Issues button.
3. Click *Check Compatibility*.
4. Click OK.

Use one of the Check for Issues button drop-down options, *Check Compatibility*, to check your document and identify elements that are not supported or will act differently in previous versions of Word from Word 97 through Word 2010. To run the compatibility checker, open the desired document, click the Check for Issues button at the Info backstage area, and then click *Check Compatibility* at the drop-down list. This displays the Microsoft Word Compatibility Checker dialog box, which displays a summary of the elements in the document that are not compatible with previous versions of Word. This box also indicates what will happen when the document is saved and then opened in a previous version.

Project 5b Checking the Compatibility of Elements in a Document

Part 2 of 3

1. With **WL2-C8-P5-PremPro.docx** open, check the compatibility of elements in the document by completing the following steps:
   a. Click the FILE tab, click the Check for Issues button at the Info backstage area, and then click *Check Compatibility* at the drop-down list.
   b. At the Microsoft Word Compatibility Checker dialog box, read the information that displays in the *Summary* text box.
   c. Click the Select versions to show button and then click *Word 97-2003* at the drop-down list. (This removes the check mark from the option.) Notice that the information about SmartArt graphics being converted to a static object disappears from the *Summary* text box. This is because Word 2007 and Word 2010 support SmartArt graphics.
   d. Click OK to close the dialog box.
2. Save the document in Word 2003 format by completing the following steps:
   a. Press F12 to display the Save As dialog box with WL2C8 the active folder.
   b. At the Save As dialog box, click the *Save as type* option box and then click *Word 97-2003 Document (*.doc)* at the drop-down list.
   c. Select the text in the *File name* text box and then type **WL2-C8-P5-PremPro-2003format**.
   d. Click the Save button.
   e. Click the Continue button at the Microsoft Word Compatibility Checker dialog box.
3. Close **WL2-C8-P5-PremPro-2003format.doc**.

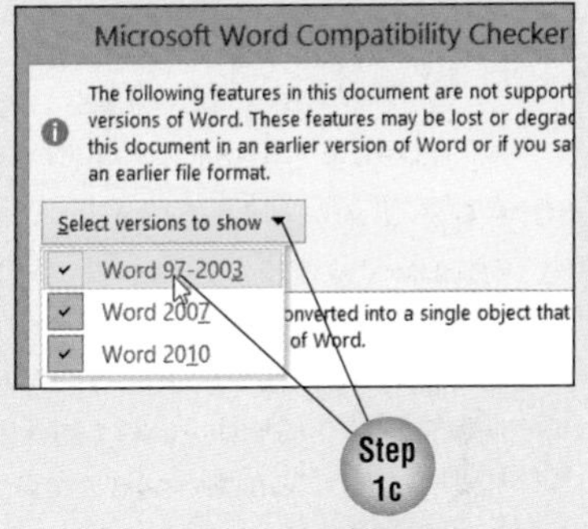

Managing Versions

While you are working in a document, Word automatically saves the document every 10 minutes. This automatic backup feature can be very helpful if you accidentally close your document without saving it or if the power to your computer is disrupted. As Word automatically saves backups of your currently open document, the saved versions are listed to the right of the Manage Versions button in the Info backstage area, as shown in Figure 8.9 on the next page. Each autosave document displays with *Today*, followed by the time and *(autosave)*. When you save and then close your document, the autosave backup documents are deleted.

Manage Versions

To open an autosave backup document, click the FILE tab and then click the backup document you want to open (backup documents display to the right of the Manage Versions button). The document opens as a read-only document and a

Figure 8.9 Autosave Documents in Info Tab Backstage View

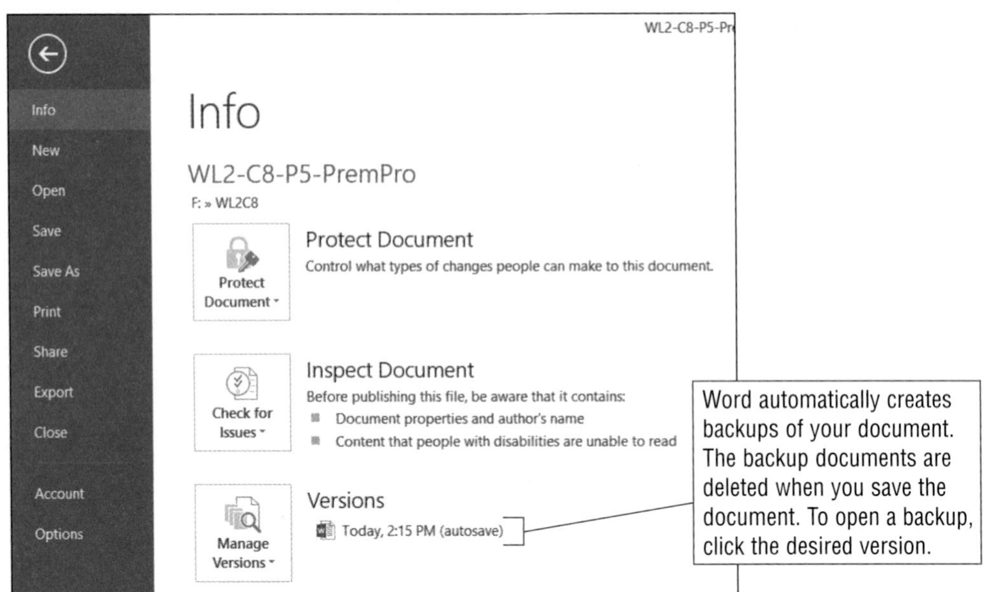

Quick Steps

Display the UnsavedFiles Folder
1. Click FILE tab.
2. Click Manage Versions button.
3. Click *Recover Unsaved Documents.*

OR
1. Click FILE tab.
2. Click *Open* option.
3. Click Recover Unsaved Documents button.

Delete a Backup File
1. Click FILE tab.
2. Right-click backup file.
3. Click *Delete This Version* at shortcut menu.

Delete All Unsaved Files
1. Click FILE tab.
2. Click Manage Versions button.
3. Click *Delete All Unsaved Documents.*
4. Click Yes.

Change the AutoRecover Time
1. Click FILE tab.
2. Click *Options.*
3. Click *Save.*
4. Type desired minutes in *Save AutoRecover information every* measurement box.
5. Click OK.

yellow message bar displays with a Compare button and Restore button. Click the Compare button and the autosave document is compared to the original document. You can review the comparison to decide which changes you want to accept and reject. Click the Restore button and a message displays indicating that you are about to overwrite the last saved version with the selected version. At this message, click OK.

When you save a document, the autosave backup documents are deleted. However, if you close a document without saving (after 10 minutes) or the power is disrupted, Word keeps the backup file in the UnsavedFiles folder on the hard drive. Access this folder by clicking the Manage Versions button at the Info backstage area and then clicking *Recover Unsaved Documents*. At the Open dialog box that displays, double-click the desired backup file that you want to open. You can also display the UnsavedFiles folder by clicking the FILE tab, clicking the *Open* option, and then clicking the Recover Unsaved Documents button that displays below the Recent Documents list. Files in the UnsavedFiles folder are kept for four days after the creation of the document. After that, they are automatically deleted.

Manage each backup file by right-clicking on it. At the shortcut menu that displays, click the *Open Version* option to open the backup file, click the *Delete This Version* option to delete the backup file, or click the *Compare with Current* option to compare the backup file with the currently open file. If you want to delete all of the unsaved files, open a blank document, click the FILE tab, click the Manage Versions button, and then click the *Delete All Unsaved Documents* option. At the message asking if you are sure you want to delete the unsaved documents, click Yes.

As mentioned previously, by default, Word automatically saves a backup of an unsaved document every 10 minutes. To change this default setting, click the FILE tab and then click *Options*. At the Word Options dialog box, click *Save* in the left panel. Notice that the *Save AutoRecover information every* measurement box is set at 10 minutes. To change this number, click the up-pointing arrow to the right of *10* to increase the number of minutes between autosaves or click the down-pointing arrow to decrease the number of minutes between autosaves.

Project 5c Opening an Autosave Document

Part 3 of 3

1. At a blank screen, decrease the autosave time by completing the following steps:
   a. Click the FILE tab and then click *Options*.
   b. At the Word Options dialog box, click *Save* in the left panel.
   c. Click the down-pointing arrow at the right of the *Save AutoRecover information every* measurement box until *1* displays.

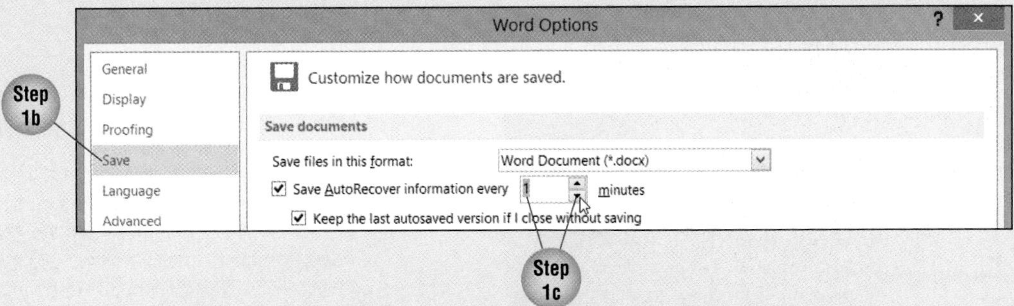

   d. Click OK to close the dialog box.
2. Open **WL2-C8-P5-PremPro.docx**.
3. Press Ctrl + End to move the insertion point to the end of the document and then type your first and last names.
4. Leave the document open for more than one minute without making any changes. After at least one minute has passed, click the FILE tab and then check to see if an autosave document displays to the right of the Manage Versions button. (If not, click the Back button to return to the document and wait a few more minutes.)
5. When an autosave document displays in the Info backstage area, click the Back button to return to the document.
6. Select the SmartArt graphic and then delete it.
7. Click the FILE tab and then click the autosave document that displays to the right of the Manage Versions button. If more than one autosave document displays, click the one at the bottom of the list. This opens the autosave document as read-only.

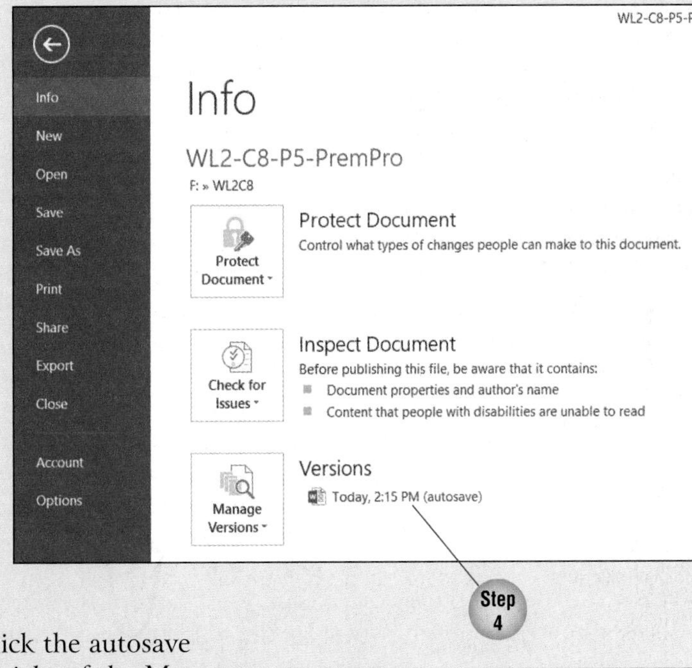

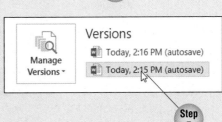

8. Restore the document to the autosave document by clicking the Restore button that displays in the yellow message bar.

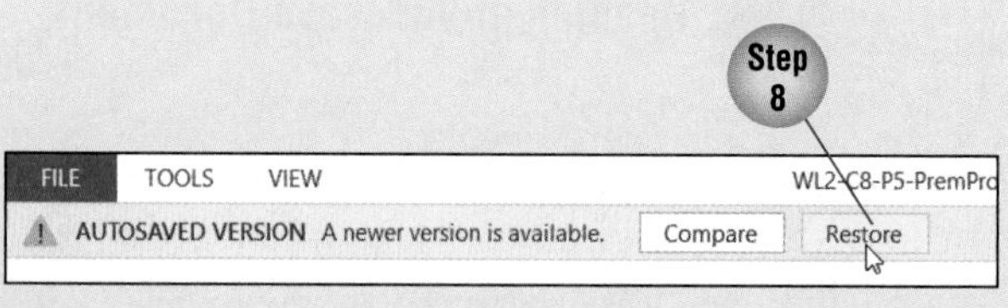

9. At the message that displays indicating that you are about to overwrite the last saved version with the selected version, click OK. (This saves the document with the SmartArt.)
10. Press the Esc key to display the document in Normal view.
11. Check to see what versions of previous documents Word has saved by completing the following steps:
    a. Click the FILE tab.
    b. Click the Manage Versions button and then click *Recover Unsaved Documents* at the drop-down list.
    c. At the Open dialog box, check the documents that display in the Content pane.
    d. Click the Cancel button to close the Open dialog box.

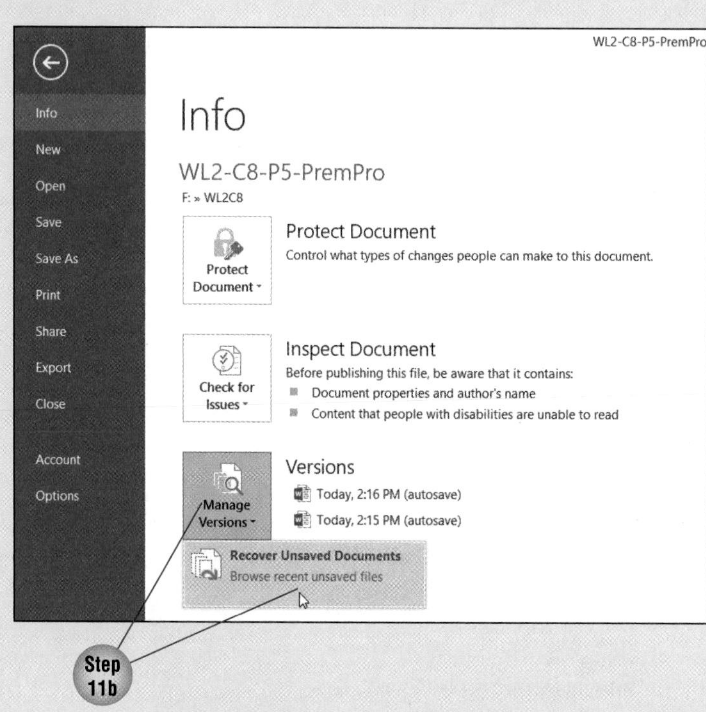

12. Delete a backup file by completing the following steps:
    a. Click the FILE tab.
    b. Right-click the first autosave backup file name that displays to the right of the Manage Versions button.
    c. Click *Delete This Version* at the shortcut menu.
    d. At the message that displays asking if you are sure you want to delete the selected version, click the Yes button.
13. Return the autosave time to 10 minutes by completing the following steps:
    a. At the Info backstage area, click *Options*.
    b. At the Word Options dialog box, click *Save* in the left panel.
    c. Click the up-pointing arrow at the right of the *Save AutoRecover information every* measurement box until *10* displays.
    d. Click OK to close the dialog box.
14. Save, print, and then close **WL2-C8-P5-PremPro.docx**.
15. Delete all of the unsaved backup files by completing the following steps:
    a. Press Ctrl + N to display a blank document.
    b. Click the FILE tab.
    c. Click the Manage Versions button and then click *Delete All Unsaved Documents*.
    d. At the message that displays, click Yes.
16. Click the Back button to return to the blank document.

Chapter Summary

- Restrict formatting and editing in a document and apply a password to it with options at the Restrict Editing task pane. Display this task pane by clicking the REVIEW tab and then clicking the Restrict Editing button in the Protect group.
- Restrict formatting by specifying styles that are allowed and not allowed in a document. Do this at the Formatting Restrictions dialog box. Display this dialog box by clicking the Settings hyperlink in the Restrict Editing task pane.
- To restrict editing in a document, insert a check mark in the *Allow only this type of editing in the document* check box at the Restrict Editing task pane, click the down-pointing arrow at the right of the option box, and then click the desired option.
- Enforce editing and formatting restrictions by clicking the Yes, Start Enforcing Protection button in the Restrict Editing task pane and make desired changes at the Start Enforcing Protection dialog box.
- Protect a document with a password using options at the Start Enforcing Protection dialog box or General Options dialog box.
- Open a document in different views with options at the Open button drop-down list in the Open dialog box.
- The Info backstage area displays information about document properties.
- Display the document information panel by clicking the Properties button at the Info backstage area and then clicking *Show Document Panel* at the drop-down list.
- You also can insert document information at the Properties dialog box. Display this dialog box by clicking the Properties button at the Info backstage area and then clicking *Advanced Properties* or by clicking the Document Properties button at the document information panel and then clicking *Advanced Properties*.
- When you mark a document as final, it is saved as a read-only document. Mark a document as final by clicking the Protect Document button at the Info backstage area and then clicking *Mark as Final* at the drop-down list. Typing, editing commands, and proofing marks are turned off when a document is marked as final.
- Protect a document with a password by clicking the Protect Document button at the Info backstage area and then clicking *Encrypt with Password*.
- Another method for displaying the Restrict Editing task pane is to click the Protect Document button at the Info backstage area and then click *Restrict Editing* at the drop-down list.
- Inspect a document for personal data, hidden data, and metadata with options at the Document Inspector dialog box. Display this dialog box by clicking the Check for Issues button at the Info backstage area and then clicking *Inspect Document* at the drop-down list.
- The accessibility checker checks a document for content that a person with disabilities might find difficult to read. Run the accessibility checker by clicking the Check for Issues button at the Info backstage area and then clicking *Check Accessibility* at the drop-down list.

- Run the compatibility checker to check your document and identify elements that are not supported or that will act differently in previous versions of Word. To determine the compatibility of the features in your document, click the Check for Issues button at the Info backstage area and then click *Check Compatibility* at the drop-down list.
- By default, Word automatically saves a backup of your unsaved document every 10 minutes. A list of backup documents displays to the right of the Manage Versions button at the Info backstage area. Click the document name to open the backup document.
- When you save a document, Word automatically deletes the backup documents. However, if you close a document without saving it or the power to your computer is disrupted, Word keeps a backup document in the UnsavedFiles folder on the hard drive. Display this folder by clicking the Manage Versions button at the Info backstage area and then clicking *Recover Unsaved Documents* at the drop-down list.
- Delete an autosave backup file by displaying the Info backstage area, right-clicking the desired autosave backup file, and then clicking *Delete This Version* at the shortcut menu.
- Delete all of the unsaved documents by displaying a blank document, clicking the FILE tab, clicking the Manage Versions button, and then clicking *Delete All Unsaved Documents*. At the message that displays, click Yes.
- You can change the 10-minute autosave default setting with the *Save AutoRecover information every* measurement at the Word Options dialog box with *Save* selected in the left panel.

Commands Review

FEATURE	RIBBON TAB, GROUP /OPTION	BUTTON, OPTION
accessibility checker	FILE, *Info*	[button], *Check Accessibility*
compatibility checker	FILE, *Info*	[button], *Check Compatibility*
document information panel	FILE, *Info*	Properties ▾, *Show Document Panel*
Document Inspector dialog box	FILE, *Info*	[button], *Inspect Document*
Encrypt Document dialog box	FILE, *Info*	[button], *Encrypt with Password*
Formatting Restrictions dialog box	REVIEW, Protect	[button], *Settings*
General Options dialog box	FILE, *Save As*	Tools, *General Options*
Properties dialog box	FILE, *Info*	Properties ▾, *Advanced Properties*
Restrict Editing task pane	REVIEW, Protect	[button]
UnsavedFiles folder	FILE, *Info*	[button], *Recover Unsaved Documents*

Concepts Check Test Your Knowledge 

Completion: In the space provided at the right, indicate the correct term, command, or number.

1. Limit what formatting users can perform on text in a document with options in this section of the Restrict Editing task pane. ________________
2. Limit what types of changes users can make to a document with options in this section of the Restrict Editing task pane. ________________
3. Click this button in the Restrict Editing task pane to display the Start Enforcing Protection dialog box. ________________
4. Protect a document with a password using options at the Start Enforcing Protection dialog box or using options at this dialog box. ________________
5. You can add or modify a document's properties at this panel. ________________
6. Display the Properties dialog box by clicking the Properties button at the Info backstage area and then clicking this option at the drop-down list. ________________
7. Use this feature to inspect your document for personal data, hidden data, and metadata. ________________
8. Use this feature to check a document for content that a person with disabilities might find difficult to read. ________________
9. Create alternate text for an image with *ALT TEXT* options at this task pane. ________________
10. Use this feature to check your document and identify elements that are not supported in previous versions of Word. ________________
11. Word keeps backup files in this folder on the hard drive. ________________

Skills Check Assess Your Performance

Assessment 1

RESTRICT FORMATTING AND EDITING OF A WRITING REPORT

1. Open **WritingProcess.docx** and then save the document and name it **WL2-C8-A1-WritingProcess**.
2. Display the Restrict Editing task pane and then restrict formatting to the Heading 2 and Heading 3 styles. (At the message asking if you want to remove formatting or styles that are not allowed, click No.)
3. Enforce the protection and include the password *writing*.
4. Click the Available styles hyperlink.
5. Apply the Heading 2 style to these two titles: *THE WRITING PROCESS* and *REFERENCES*.
6. Apply the Heading 3 style to the seven remaining headings in the document. (The Heading 3 style may not display until you apply the Heading 2 style to the first title.)
7. Close the Styles task pane and then close the Restrict Editing task pane.
8. Save the document and then print only page 1.
9. Close **WL2-C8-A1-WritingProcess.docx**.

Assessment 2

INSERT COMMENTS IN A SOFTWARE LIFE CYCLE DOCUMENT

1. Open **CommCycle.docx** and then save the document and name it **WL2-C8-A2-CommCycle**.
2. Display the Restrict Editing task pane, restrict editing to comments only, and then start enforcing the protection. (Do not include a password.)
3. Type the comment Create a SmartArt graphic that illustrates the software life cycle. at the end of the first paragraph in the document.
4. Type the comment Include the problem-solving steps. at the end of the paragraph in the *Design* section.
5. Type the comment Describe a typical beta testing cycle. at the end of the paragraph in the *Testing* section.
6. Print only the comments.
7. Close the Restrict Editing task pane.
8. Save and then close **WL2-C8-A2-CommCycle.docx**.

Assessment 3

INSERT DOCUMENT PROPERTIES, CHECK COMPATIBILITY, AND SAVE A PRESENTATION DOCUMENT IN A DIFFERENT FORMAT

1. Open **Presentation.docx** and then save the document and name it **WL2-C8-A3-Presentation**.
2. Make the following changes to the document:
   a. Apply the Heading 1 style to the title *Delivering a How-To Presentation*.
   b. Apply the Heading 2 style to the other three headings in the document.
   c. Change the style set to *Centered*.

d. Apply the View theme and apply the Green theme colors.
e. Change the color of the clip art image to *Green, Accent color 1 Light*.

3. Display the document information panel and then type the following in the specified text boxes:

Author	(Type your first and last names)
Title	**Delivering a How-To Presentation**
Subject	**Presentations**
Keywords	**presentation, how-to, delivering, topics**
Comments	**This document describes the three steps involved in developing a how-to presentation.**

4. Close the document information panel.
5. Save **WL2-C8-A3-Presentation.docx** and then print only the document properties.
6. Run the accessibility checker on the document and then create alternate text for the clip art image. Type the text **Presentation clip art image** for the title and type **Clip art image representing a person giving a presentation.** for the description. Close the accessibility checker.
7. Save and then print **WL2-C8-A3-Presentation.docx**.
8. Run the compatibility checker to determine what features are not supported by earlier versions of Word.
9. Save the document in the *Word 97-2003 Document (*.doc)* format and name it **WL2-C8-A3-Presentation-2003format**.
10. Save, print, and then close **WL2-C8-A3-Presentation-2003format.doc**.

Assessment 4

CREATE A DOCUMENT ON INSERTING AND REMOVING A SIGNATURE

1. The Text group on the INSERT tab contains a Signature Line button for inserting a signature in a document. Use Word's Help feature to learn about inserting and removing a signature by typing **add or remove a digital signature** at the Word Help window and then clicking the Add or remove a digital signature in Office files hyperlink. Read the information in the article and then prepare a Word document with the following information:
   - An appropriate title
   - How to create a signature line in Word
   - How to sign a signature line in Word
   - How to remove a signature from Word
   - How to add an invisible digital signature in Word
2. Apply formatting to enhance the apearance of the document.
3. Save the document and name it **WL2-C8-A4-Signature**.
4. Print and then close **WL2-C8-A4-Signature.docx**.

Visual Benchmark Demonstrate Your Proficiency

FORMAT A DOCUMENT, INSERT DOCUMENT PROPERTIES, CHECK COMPATIBILITY, AND SAVE A DOCUMENT IN A DIFFERENT FORMAT

1. Open **InfoSystem.docx** and then save the document and name it **WL2-C8-VB-InfoSystem**.
2. Format the document so it appears as shown in Figure 8.10 with the following specifications:
   a. Apply the Lines (Stylish) style set and then apply the Dividend theme.
   b. Insert the Integral footer and type your name as the author.
   c. Insert the SmartArt Continuous Cycle graphic and apply the Colorful - Accent Colors color and apply the Metallic Scene style.
   d. Recolor the clip art image as shown in the figure.
   e. Make any other changes needed so your document displays as shown in Figure 8.10.
3. Display the document information panel and then type the following in the specified text boxes:

Author	(Type your first and last names)
Title	**Developing an Information System**
Subject	**Software Development**
Keywords	**software, design, plan**
Category	**Software**
Status	**Draft**
Comments	**This document describes the four steps involved in developing an information system.**

4. Save the document and then print only the document properties.
5. Inspect the document and remove any hidden text.
6. Run the accessibility checker and then create alternate text for the clip art image.
7. Run the compatibility checker to determine what features are not supported by earlier versions of Word.
8. Save the document in the *Word 97-2003 Document (*.doc)* format and name it **WL2-C8-VB-InfoSystem-2003format**.
9. Save, print, and then close **WL2-C8-VB-InfoSystem-2003format.doc**.

Figure 8.10 Visual Benchmark

Developing an Information System

Identifying and assembling a team of employees with the required skills and expertise is a necessary first step in developing a new in-house information system. A management group may be involved in answering questions and providing information in the early planning phases of the project, but programmers and/or software engineers handle the design and implementation of any new system.

Programmers specialize in the development of new software, while software engineers are highly skilled professionals with programming and teamwork training. Their organized, professional application of the software development process is called software engineering.

Project Plan

The first step in the system development life cycle is planning. The planning step involves preparing a needs analysis and conducting feasibility studies. During this step, a company usually establishes a project team, and the team creates a project plan. The project plan includes an estimate of how long the project will take to complete, an outline of the steps involved, and a list of deliverables. Deliverables are documents, services, hardware, and software that must be finished and delivered by a certain time and date.

Project Team

Because of their large size, information systems require the creation of a project team. A project team usually includes a project manager, who acts as the team leader. Sometimes the project manager also functions as a systems analyst, responsible for completing the systems analysis and making design recommendations. Other project team members include software engineers and technicians. The software engineers deal with programming software, while technicians handle hardware issues. The comprehensive process software engineers initiate is called the system development life cycle (SDLC), a series of steps culminating in a completed information system.

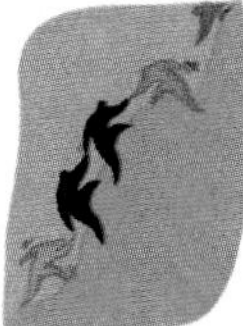

Designing the System

A project is ready to move into the design stage once the project team has approved the plan, including the budget. The design process begins with the writing of the documentation, which covers functional and design specifications. In most cases, the project team creates the functional specifications, describing what the system must be able to do.

Implementation

The project can move into the next phase, implementation, once the development team and the systems house develop the design specification and approve the plans. This step is where the actual work of putting the system together is completed, including creating a prototype and completing the programming. In most cases, implementing the new system is the longest, most difficult step in the process.

STUDENT NAM

Support Stage

A system goes into the support stage after it has been accepted and approved. A support contract normally allows users to contact the systems house for technical support, training, and sometimes on-site troubleshooting. Even if the system was designed in-house, the responsible department often operates as an independent entity—sometimes even charging the department acquiring the system. The support stage continues until a new information system is proposed and developed, usually years later. At that point, the existing system is retired and no longer used.

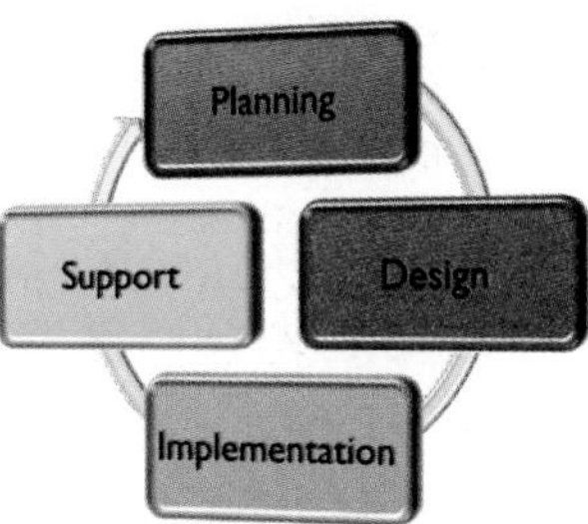

STUDENT NAME 2

Case Study Apply Your Skills

Part 1

You work in the Training department at Hart International. Your department is responsible for preparing training material and training employees on how to use software applications within the company. Your supervisor asked you to help her prepare a Microsoft Word training manual. She had already written a portion of the manual and had you add training information and then format the manual.

If you completed Part 1 of the Case Study for Chapter 7, you should have a document saved in your WL2C7 folder named **WL2-C7-CS-HITraining.docx**. Open **WL2-C7-CS-HITraining.docx** from the WL2C7 folder on your storage medium and then save the document in your WL2C8 folder and name it **WL2-C8-CS-HITraining**. Move the insertion point to the end of the document and then insert the document named **HIManual.docx** located in your WL2C8 folder. (Insert the file with the Object button in the Text group on the INSERT tab.)

If you do not have **WL2-C7-CS-HITraining.docx** in your WL2C7 folder, open **HIManual.docx** from your WL2C8 folder and then save the document and name it **WL2-C8-CS-HITraining.docx**.

Add information to the document on how to insert the following buttons on the Quick Access toolbar: Quick Print, Open, Close, Spelling & Grammar, and Thesaurus. Apply formatting to the document and then save the completed document.

Part 2

Your supervisor has decided that options on company computers should be modified and wants you to determine the steps for making the modifications and then include the steps in the training manual. Open the Word Options dialog box and then determine how to make the following modifications:

- Change the Office background to *Geometry* and the Office theme to *Light Gray*. (General)
- Change the grammar writing style to *Grammar & Style*. (Proofing)
- Change the minutes for saving AutoRecover information to 5 minutes. (Save)
- Change the number of documents that display in the Recent Documents list to 15. (Advanced) ***Hint: The option is located in the* Display *section of the dialog box. You will need to scroll down the dialog box to display this section.***

With **WL2-C8-CS-HITraining.docx** open, write the steps involved in making each customization listed above. If your document contains a table of contents, you will need to update the entire table. Save the document.

Part 3

Prepare the document for distribution by inspecting the document and then restricting editing to comments only. Save, print, and then close **WL2-C8-CS-HITraining.docx**.

MICROSOFT® WORD Performance Assessment

WL2U2

Note: Before beginning the unit assessments, copy to your storage medium the WL2U2 subfolder from the WL2 folder on the CD that accompanies this textbook and then make WL2U2 the active folder.

Assessing Proficiency

In this unit, you learned how to use features for citing sources in a document, such as footnotes, endnotes, in-text citations, and bibliographies; how to insert tables of contents, tables of figures, and indexes; and how to use features for sharing and distributing documents, such as inserting comments, tracking changes, comparing and combining documents, linking and embedding files between programs, and restricting access to documents.

Assessment 1 Sort Text

1. Open **SHSSort.docx** and then save the document and name it **WL2-U2-A01-SHSSort**.
2. Select the five clinic names, addresses, and telephone numbers below *SUMMIT HEALTH SERVICES* and then sort the text alphabetically in ascending order by clinic name.
3. Sort the three columns of text below *EXECUTIVE TEAM* by the extension number in ascending order.
4. Sort the text in the table in the *First Half Expenses* column numerically in descending order.
5. Save, print, and then close **WL2-U2-A01-SHSSort.docx**.

Assessment 2 Select Records and Create Mailing Labels

1. At a blank document, use the mail merge feature to create mailing labels with Avery US Letter, 5160 Easy Peel Address Labels and the **SHS.mdb** data source file (located in the WL2U2 folder). Before merging the data source file with the mailing labels document, sort the records alphabetically in ascending order by last name.
2. Merge the sorted data source file with the labels document.
3. Save the merged labels document and name it **WL2-U2-A02-Lbls1**.
4. Close the document and then close the labels main document without saving it.
5. Use the mail merge feature to create mailing labels using the **SHS.mdb** data source file (use the same label option as in Step 1). Select records from the data source file of clients living in the city of Greensboro and then merge those records with the labels document.

6. Save the merged labels document and name it **WL2-U2-A02-Lbls2**.
7. Close the document and then close the labels main document without saving it.

Assessment 3 Insert Footnotes in a Desktop Publishing Report

1. Open **DTP.docx** and then save the document and name it **WL2-U2-A03-DTP**.
2. Insert the first footnote shown in Figure U2.1 at the end of the second paragraph in the *Defining Desktop Publishing* section.
3. Insert the second footnote shown in Figure U2.1 at the end of the fourth paragraph in the *Defining Desktop Publishing* section.
4. Insert the third footnote shown in Figure U2.1 at the end of the second paragraph in the *Planning the Publication* section.
5. Insert the fourth footnote shown in Figure U2.1 at the end of the last paragraph in the document.
6. Keep the heading *Planning the Publication* together with the paragraph of text that follows it.
7. Save and then print **WL2-U2-A03-DTP.docx**.
8. Select the entire document and then change the font to Constantia.
9. Select all of the footnotes and then change the font to Constantia.
10. Delete the third footnote.
11. Save, print, and then close **WL2-U2-A03-DTP.docx**.

Figure U2.1 Assessment 3

Laurie Fellers, *Desktop Publishing Design* (Dallas: Cornwall & Lewis Publishing, 2015), 67-72.

Joel Moriarity, "The Desktop Publishing Approach," *Desktop Publishing* (2015): 3-6.

Chun Man Wong, *Desktop Publishing with Style* (Seattle: Monroe-Ackerman Publishing, 2014), 89-93.

Andrew Rushton, *Desktop Publishing Tips and Tricks* (Minneapolis: Aurora Publishing House, 2015), 103-106.

Assessment 4 Create Citations and Prepare a Works Cited Page for a Report

1. Open **DesignWebsite.docx** and then save the document and name it **WL2-U2-A04-DesignWebsite**.
2. Format the title page to meet MLA requirements with the following changes:
   a. Make sure the document's reference style is set to MLA.
   b. Select the entire document, change the font to 12-point Cambria, change the line spacing to 2.0, and remove the space after paragraphs.
   c. Move the insertion point to the beginning of the document, type your name, press the Enter key, type your instructor's name, press the Enter key, type the title of your course, press the Enter key, and then type the current date.
   d. Insert a header that displays your last name and the page number at the right margin and then change the font to 12-point Cambria.

3. Press Ctrl + End to move the insertion point to the end of the document and then type the text shown in Figure U2.2 (in MLA style) up to the first citation—the text (*Mercado*). Insert the source information from a journal article written by Claudia Mercado using the following information:

Author	**Claudia Mercado**
Title	**Connecting a Web Page**
Journal Name	**Connections**
Year	**2015**
Pages	**12-21**
Volume	**IV**

4. Continue typing the text up to the next citation—the text *(Holmes)*—and insert the following source information from a website:

Author	**Brent Holmes**
Name of Web Page	**Hosting Your Web Page**
Year	**2014**
Month	**September**
Day	**28**
Year Accessed	*(type current year)*
Month Accessed	*(type current month)*
Day Accessed	*(type current day)*
URL	**www.emcp.net/webhosting**

5. Continue typing the text up to the next citation—the text *(Vukovich)*—and insert the following information from a book:

Author	**Ivan Vukovich**
Title	**Computer Technology in the Business Environment**
Year	**2015**
City	**San Francisco**
Publisher	**Gold Coast Publishing**

6. Insert the page number in the citation by Ivan Vukovich using the Edit Citation dialog box.
7. Type the remaining text shown in Figure U2.2 on the next page.
8. Edit the Ivan Vukovich source by changing the last name to *Vulkovich* in the *Master List* section of the Source Manager dialog box. Click Yes at the message asking if you want to update the source in both the Master List and the Current List.
9. Create a new source in the document using the Source Manager dialog box and include the following source information for a journal article:

Author	**Sonia Jaquez**
Title	**Organizing a Web Page**
Journal Name	**Design Techniques**
Year	**2015**
Pages	**32-44**
Volume	**IX**

10. Type the following sentence at the end of the last paragraph in the document: **Browsers look for pages with these names first when a specific file at a website is requested, and index pages display by default if no other page is specified.**
11. Insert a citation for Sonia Jaquez at the end of the sentence you just typed.
12. Insert a citation for Claudia Mercado following the second sentence in the first paragraph of the document.
13. Insert a works cited page at the end of the document on a separate page.

Figure U2.2 Assessment 4

> One of the first tasks in website development is finding a good host for the site. Essentially, a web host lets you store a copy of your web pages on the hard drive of a powerful computer connected to the Internet with a fast connection that can handle thousands of users (Mercado). Hosting your own website is possible but is feasible only if you own an extra computer that can be dedicated to the role of a web server, have a high-speed Internet connection, and feel confident about handling the job of network security and routing (Holmes). Most people's situations do not fit those criteria. Fortunately, several free and fee-based web hosting services are available.
>
> As you plan a website, decide what types of content you will include and then think about how all of the pages should link together. Most websites consist of a home page that provides the starting point for users entering the site. "Like the top of a pyramid or the table of contents of a book, the home page leads to other web pages via hyperlinks" (Vukovich 26). Most home pages have the default name index.html (or sometimes index.htm).

14. Format the works cited page as follows to meet MLA requirements:
    a. Select the *Works Cited* title and all of the entries and then click the *No Spacing* style thumbnail.
    b. Change the font to 12-point Cambria and change the spacing to 2.0.
    c. Center the title *Works Cited*.
    d. Format the works cited entries with a hanging indent. ***Hint: Use Ctrl + T to create a hanging indent.***
15. Save and then print **WL2-U2-A04-DesignWebsite.docx**.
16. Change the document and works cited page from MLA style to APA style. Change the title *Works Cited* to *References* and apply 12-point Cambria font formatting to the references in the list.
17. Save, print page 3, and then close **WL2-U2-A04-DesignWebsite.docx**.

Assessment 5 Create an Index and Table of Contents for a Desktop Publishing Report

1. At a blank document, create the text shown in Figure U2.3 as a concordance file.
2. Save the document and name it **WL2-U2-A05-CF**.
3. Print and then close **WL2-U2-A05-CF.docx**.
4. Open **DTPDesign.docx** and then save the document and name it **WL2-U2-A05-DTPDesign**.
5. Make the following changes to the document:
   a. Apply the Heading 1 style to the title and apply the Heading 2 style to the two headings in the report.
   b. Apply the Minimalist style set.
   c. Mark text for an index using the concordance file **WL2-U2-A05-CF.docx**.
   d. Insert the index (choose the Formal format style) at the end of the document on a separate page.
   e. Apply the Heading 1 style to the title of the index.

Figure U2.3 Assessment 5

message	Message
publication	Publication
design	Design
flier	Flier
letterhead	Letterhead
newsletter	Newsletter
intent	Design: intent
audience	Design: audience
layout	Design: layout
thumbnail	Thumbnail
principles	Design: principles
Focus	Design: focus
focus	Design: focus
balance	Design: balance
proportion	Design: proportion
contrast	Design: contrast
directional flow	Design: directional flow
consistency	Design: consistency
color	Design: color
White space	White space
white space	White space
Legibility	Legibility
headline	Headline
subheads	Subheads

f. Insert a section break that begins a new page at the beginning of the title *DESKTOP PUBLISHING DESIGN*.
g. Move the insertion point to the beginning of the document and then insert the *Automatic Table 1* table of contents.
h. Number the table of contents page with a lowercase roman numeral at the bottom center of the page.
i. Number the other pages in the report with arabic numbers at the bottom center of the page and start the numbering with 1 on the page containing the report title.
j. Insert a page break at the beginning of the heading *Creating Focus*.

6. Update page numbers for the index and the table of contents.
7. Save, print, and then close **WL2-U2-A05-DTPDesign.docx**.

Assessment 6 Create Captions and Insert a Table of Figures in a Report

1. Open **SoftwareCareers.docx** and then save the document and name it **WL2-U2-A06-SoftwareCareers**.
2. Click in any cell in the first table and then insert the caption *Table 1 Software Development Careers* so it displays above the table. (Change the paragraph spacing after the caption to 3 points.)
3. Click in any cell in the second table and then insert the caption *Table 2 Application Development Careers*. (Change the paragraph spacing after the caption to 3 points.)
4. Move the insertion point to the beginning of the heading *SOFTWARE DEVELOPMENT CAREERS* and then insert a section break that begins a new page.
5. With the insertion point below the section break, insert a page number at the bottom center of each page and change the starting page number to 1.
6. Move the insertion point to the beginning of the document and then insert the *Automatic Table 1* table of contents.
7. Press Ctrl + Enter to insert a page break.
8. Type Tables, press the Enter key, and then insert a table of figures using the Formal format.
9. Apply the Heading 1 style to the title *Tables*.
10. Move the insertion point to the beginning of the document and then change the numbering format to lowercase roman numerals.
11. Update the entire table of contents.
12. Save, print, and then close **WL2-U2-A06-SoftwareCareers.docx**.

Assessment 7 Insert Comments and Track Changes in an Online Shopping Report

1. Open **OnlineShop.docx** and then save the document and name it **WL2-U2-A07-OnlineShop**.
2. Move the insertion point to end of the first paragraph in the report and then insert the comment Include the source where you found this definition.
3. Move the insertion point to the end of the paragraph in the *Online Shopping Venues* section and then insert the comment Include at least two of the most popular online shopping stores.
4. Click the Display for Review button arrow and then click *All Markup* at the drop-down list.

5. Turn on Track Changes and then make the following changes:
   a. Delete the comma and the words *and most are eliminating paper tickets altogether*, which display at the end of the last sentence in the second paragraph (do not delete the period that ends the sentence).
   b. Edit the heading *Advantages of Online Shopping* so it displays as *Online Shopping Advantages.*
   c. Bold the first sentence of each of the bulleted paragraphs on the first page.
   d. Turn off Track Changes.
6. Display the Word Options dialog box with *General* selected and then type **Trudy Holmquist** as the user name and TH as the user initials. (Make sure you insert a check mark in the *Always use these values regardless of sign in to Office.* check box.)
7. Turn on Track Changes and then make the following changes:
   a. Delete the words *the following* in the first paragraph in the *Online Shopping Advantages* section.
   b. Type the following bulleted text between the third and fourth bulleted paragraphs on the second page: **Keep thorough records of all transactions.**
   c. Turn off Track Changes.
8. Print the document with markup.
9. Display the Word Options dialog box with *General* selected and then change the user name back to the original name and the initials back to the original initials. (Remove the check mark from the *Always use these values regardless of sign in to Office.* check box.)
10. Accept all of the changes in the document *except* the change deleting the comma and the text *and most are eliminating paper tickets altogether*. (Leave the comments in the document.)
11. Save, print, and then close **WL2-U2-A07-OnlineShop.docx**.

Assessment 8 Combine Documents

1. Open **Software.docx** and then save the document and name it **WL2-U2-A08-Software**.
2. Close **WL2-U2-A08-Software.docx**.
3. At a blank screen, combine **WL2-U2-A08-Software.docx** (the original document) with **Software-AL.docx** (the revised document) into the original document.
4. Save **WL2-U2-A08-Software.docx**.
5. Print the document with markup.
6. Accept all of the changes to the document.
7. Make the following changes to the document:
   a. Apply the Basic (Stylish) style set.
   b. Apply the Wisp theme.
   c. Apply the Red theme colors.
   d. Insert the Austin footer.
8. Save, print, and then close **WL2-U2-A08-Software.docx**.

Assessment 9 Linking Excel Data with a Word Document

1. Open **NCUHomeLoans.docx** and then save the document and name it **WL2-U2-A09-NCUHomeLoans**.
2. Open Excel and then open **NCUMortgages.xlsx**.
3. Save the Excel workbook with Save As and name it **WL2-U2-A09-NCUMortgages**.

4. Select cells A2 through G14 and then link the cells to the **WL2-U2-A09-NCUHomeLoans** Word document as a Microsoft Excel Worksheet Object. (Use the Paste Special dialog box.)
5. Save, print, and then close **WL2-U2-A09-NCUHomeLoans.docx**.
6. With Excel the active program, make the following changes to the data:
   a. Click in cell A3, type 200000, and then press Enter.
   b. Position the mouse on the small green square (the fill handle) that displays in the lower right corner of cell A3 until the pointer displays as a black plus symbol. Hold down the left mouse button, drag down to cell A6, and then release the mouse button. (This inserts *$200,000* in the cells.)
7. Save and then close **WL2-U2-A09-NCUMortgages.xlsx**.
8. Open **WL2-U2-A09-NCUHomeLoans.docx** and click Yes at the message asking if you want to update the document.
9. Save, print, and then close **WL2-U2-A09-NCUHomeLoans.docx**.

Assessment 10 Restrict Formatting in a Report

1. Open **InterfaceApps.docx** and then save the document and name it **WL2-U2-A10-InterfaceApps**.
2. Display the Restrict Editing task pane and then restrict formatting to the Heading 1 and Heading 2 styles. (At the message that displays asking if you want to remove formatting or styles that are not allowed, click No.)
3. Enforce the protection and include the password *report*.
4. Click the Available styles hyperlink in the Restrict Editing task pane.
5. Apply the Heading 1 style to the title of the report and apply the Heading 2 style to the four headings in the report.
6. Close the Styles task pane.
7. Close the Restrict Editing task pane.
8. Save the document and then print only page 1.
9. Close **WL2-U2-A10-InterfaceApps.docx**.

Assessment 11 Insert Document Properties and Save a Document in a Previous Version of Word

1. Open **KLHPlan.docx** and then save the document and name it **WL2-U2-A11-KLHPlan**.
2. Make the following changes to the document:
   a. Apply the Heading 1 style to the three headings in the document: *Plan Highlights*, *Quality Assessment*, and *Provider Network*.
   b. Change the style set to Centered.
   c. Apply the Blue II theme colors.
3. Move the insertion point to the end of the document and then insert the document named **KLHPlanGraphic.docx**.
4. Display the document information panel and then type the following information in the specified text boxes:

Author	(Insert your first and last names.)
Title	Key Life Health Plan
Subject	Company Health Plan
Keywords	health, plan, network
Category	Health Plan
Comments	This document describes highlights of the Key Life Health Plan.

5. Close the document information panel.

6. Save the document and then print only the document properties.
7. Inspect the document and remove any hidden text.
8. Save and then print **WL2-U2-A11-KLHPlan.docx**.
9. Assume that the document will be read by a colleague with Word 2003 and run the compatibility checker to determine what features are not supported by earlier versions of Word.
10. Save the document in the *Word 97-2003 Document (*.doc)* format and name it **WL2-U2-A11-KLHPlan-2003format**.
11. Save, print, and then close **WL2-U2-A11-KLHPlan-2003format.doc**.

Writing Activities

The following writing activities give you the opportunity to practice your writing skills and demonstrate an understanding of some of the important Word features you have mastered in this unit.

Activity 1 Prepare an APA Guidelines Document

You work for a psychiatric medical facility and many of the psychiatrists and psychiatric nurses you work with submit papers to journals that require formatting in APA style. Your supervisor has asked you to prepare a document that describes the APA guidelines and then provides the steps on how to format a Word document in APA style. Find a website that provides information on APA style and include the hyperlink in your document. (Consider websites for writing labs at colleges and universities.) Apply formatting to enhance the appearance of the document. Save the document and name it **WL2-U2-Act1-APA**. Print and then close **WL2-U2-Act1-APA.docx**.

Activity 2 Create a Rental Form Template

You work in a real estate management company that manages rental houses. You decide to automate the standard rental form that is normally filled in by hand. Open **LeaseAgreement.docx** and then save the document and name it **WL2-U2-Act2-LeaseAgreement**. Look at the lease agreement document and determine how to automate it so it can be filled in using the Find and Replace feature in Word. Change the current *Lessor* and *Lessee* names to *LESSOR* and *LESSEE*. Save the document as a template named **LeaseForm** to the Custom Office Templates folder. Open the **LeaseForm.dotx** template (from the New backstage area) and then complete the following find and replaces. Use your judgment about which occurrences should be changed and which should not.

DAY	**24th**
MONTH	**February**
YEAR	**2015**
RENT	**$950**
DEPOSIT	**$500**
LESSOR	**Samantha Herrera**
LESSEE	**Daniel Miller**

Save the document and name it **WL2-U2-Act2-Lease1**. Use the **LeaseForm.dotx** template to create another rental document. You determine the text to replace with the standard text. Save the completed rental document and name it **WL2-U2-Act2-Lease2**.

Internet Research

Create a Job Search Report

Use a search engine to search for companies offering employment opportunities. Search for companies offering jobs in a field in which you are interested in working. Locate at least three websites that interest you and then create a report in Word that includes the following information about the sites:

- Site name, address, and URL
- A brief description of the site
- Employment opportunities available at the site

Create a hyperlink from your report to each site and include any additional information pertinent to the site. Apply formatting to enhance the document. Save the document and name it **WL2-U2-Act3-JobSearch**. Print and then close **WL2-U2-Act3-JobSearch.docx**.

Job Study

Format a Guidelines Report

As a staff member of a computer e-tailer, you are required to maintain cutting-edge technology skills, including being well versed in the use of new software programs such as those in the Office 2013 suite. Recently, your supervisor asked you to develop and distribute a set of strategies for reading technical and computer manuals that the staff will use as they learn new programs. Use the concepts and techniques you learned in this unit to edit the guidelines report as follows:

1. Open **Strategies.docx** and then save the document and name it **WL2-U2-JS-Strategies**.
2. Turn on Track Changes and then make the following changes:
   a. Change all occurrences of *computer manuals* to *technical and computer manuals*.
   b. Format the document with appropriate heading styles.
   c. Insert at least two comments about the content and/or formatting of the document.
   d. Print the list of markup.
   e. Accept all of the tracked changes.
3. Turn off Track Changes.
4. Insert a table of contents.
5. Number the pages in the document.
6. Create a cover page.
7. Save, print, and then close **WL2-U2-JS-Strategies.docx**.

Index

A

B

C

D

E

F

G

H

I

K

L

M

N

O

P

Q

R

S

T

U

V

W

Word 2013 Feature	Ribbon Tab, Group/Option	Button, Option	Keyboard Shortcut
AutoCorrect	FILE, *Options*	*Proofing*	
bibliography	REFERENCES, Citations & Bibliography		
bold text	HOME, Font	B	Ctrl + B
borders	HOME, Paragraph		
Building Blocks Organizer	INSERT, Text		
bullets	HOME, Paragraph		
center-align text	HOME, Paragraph		Ctrl + E
change case of text	HOME, Font	Aa	Shift + F3
chart	INSERT, Illustrations		
citation	REFERENCES, Citations & Bibliography		
clear all formatting	HOME, Font		
Clipboard task pane	HOME, Clipboard		
close document	FILE, *Close*		Ctrl + F4
close Word		×	Alt + F4
columns	PAGE LAYOUT, Page Setup		
copy text	HOME, Clipboard		Ctrl + C
cover page	INSERT, Pages		
cut text	HOME, Clipboard		Ctrl + X
Date and Time dialog box	INSERT, Text		
display nonprinting characters	HOME, Paragraph	¶	Ctrl + Shift + *
drop cap	INSERT, Text		
endnote	REFERENCES, Footnotes		Alt + Ctrl + D
envelopes	MAILINGS, Create		
Find and Replace dialog box	HOME, Editing		Ctrl +H
font	HOME, Font	Calibri (Body)	
font color	HOME, Font	A	
Font dialog box	HOME, Font		Ctrl + Shift + F
font size	HOME, Font	11	
footer	INSERT, Header & Footer		
footnote	REFERENCES, Footnotes	AB1	Alt + Ctrl + F
Format Painter	HOME, Clipboard		Ctrl + Shift + C Ctrl + Shift + V
header	INSERT, Header & Footer		
Help		?	F1
highlight text	HOME, Font		
hyperlink	INSERT, Links		Ctrl + K
hyphenate	PAGE LAYOUT, Page Setup		
insert comment	REVIEW, Comments		
Insert File dialog box	INSERT, Text	, *Text from File*	
Insert Picture dialog box	INSERT, Illustrations		
Insert Pictures window	INSERT, Illustrations		
italicize text	HOME, Font	*I*	Ctrl + I
justify text	HOME, Paragraph		Ctrl + J

Word 2013 Feature	Ribbon Tab, Group/Option	Button, Option	Keyboard Shortcut
labels	MAILINGS, Create		
left-align text	HOME, Paragraph		Ctrl + L
line spacing	HOME, Paragraph		Ctrl + 1 (single) Ctrl + 2 (double) Ctrl + 5 (1.5)
Mail Merge	MAILINGS, Start Mail Merge		
margins	PAGE LAYOUT, Page Setup		
multilevel list	HOME, Paragraph		
Navigation pane	VIEW, Show	*Navigation Pane*	Ctrl + F
new blank document	FILE, *New*	*Blank document*	Ctrl + N
New Line command			Shift + Enter
numbering	HOME, Paragraph		
Open backstage area	FILE, *Open*		Ctrl + O
orientation	PAGE LAYOUT, Page Setup		
page borders	DESIGN, Page Background		
page break	INSERT, Pages		Ctrl + Enter
page numbering	INSERT, Header & Footer		
page size	PAGE LAYOUT, Page Setup		
Paragraph dialog box	HOME, Paragraph		
paragraph spacing	DESIGN, Document Formatting		
paste text	HOME, Clipboard		Ctrl + V
Print backstage area	FILE, *Print*		Ctrl + P
redo an action			Ctrl + Y

Word 2013 Feature	Ribbon Tab, Group/Option	Button, Option	Keyboard Shortcut
repeat last action			F4 or Ctrl + Y
right-align text	HOME, Paragraph		Ctrl + R
save			Ctrl + S
Save As backstage area	FILE, *Save As*		F12
screenshot	INSERT, Illustrations		
shading	HOME, Paragraph		
shapes	INSERT, Illustrations		
SmartArt graphic	INSERT, Illustrations		
sort text	HOME, Paragraph		
spelling and grammar checker	REVIEW, Proofing		F7
Symbol dialog box	INSERT, Symbols	, *More Symbols*	
table	INSERT, Tables		
Tabs dialog box	HOME, Paragraph	, Tabs	
text box	INSERT, Text		
themes	DESIGN, Document Formatting		
thesaurus	REVIEW, Proofing		Shift + F7
Track Changes	REVIEW, Tracking		Ctrl + Shift + E
underline text	HOME, Font		Ctrl + U
undo an action			Ctrl + Z
watermark	PAGE LAYOUT, Page Background		
WordArt	INSERT, Text		